Excavations at Stonea

Cambridgeshire 1980–85

Excavations at Stonea
Cambridgeshire 1980–85

R. P. J. Jackson and T. W. Potter

with contributions by

F. Cameron, C. Carreras, C. Cartwright, A. Chadburn, J. Conheeney, P. Craddock, B. Dickinson,
I. Freestone, C. French, D. Gaimster, S. Greep, D. Hall, K. Hartley, S. Humphrey, S. James, C. Johns,
S. Keay, A. Legge, D. Mackreth, A. Middleton, S. Needham, S. Philpot, J. Price, M. Rhodes, V. Rigby, A. Russel,
D. Shotter, V. Smithson, S. Stallibrass, G. Varndell, M. van der Veen, L. Webster, M. Welch
and
A. Alderton, J. Ambers, N. Ashton, M. Bimson, A. Blackham, A. Bowman, T. Briscoe,
A. Challands, J. Cooper, J. Foster, D. Gilbertson, D. Gurney, I. Longworth, R. Switsur
and illustrations by
P. Compton, S. Crummy, P. Dean, K. Hughes, M. Moores

Published for the Trustees of the British Museum by
BRITISH MUSEUM PRESS

© 1996 The Trustees of the British Museum

First published in 1996 by British Museum Press
A division of The British Museum Company Ltd
46 Bloomsbury Street, London WC1B 3QQ

A catalogue record for this book is available from the British Library

ISBN 0–7141–1385–9

Designed by John Hawkins

Typeset in Ehrhardt by Wyvern Typesetting Ltd, Bristol
Printed and bound in Great Britain by Henry Ling Ltd,
The Dorset Press, Dorchester

For   Dr I. H. Longworth CBE, MA, PhD, FSA

Keeper of the Department of Prehistoric and
Romano-British Antiquities 1973–1995

vir bonus antiquitatum peritus

CONTENTS

PLATES

The plates are grouped together at the end of the volume, following page 749.

XXXIa Stonea Grange: Romano-British dog radius and ulna from context 1733, in well 1625. Both bones have been broken through the midshaft, and the proximal ulna has healed onto the distal radius. Scale 1 : 1.

XXXIb Stonea Grange: Romano-British dog femur from context 1756, in gully 23. This thigh bone was broken through the midshaft but never fully healed, leaving a false joint. Scale 1 : 1.

XXXIc Stonea Grange: Romano-British dog bones from context 1756, in gully 23. The broken femur has become shortened and has not fully healed. An infection has spread to the lower vertebrae of the spine and to both knee joints. Scale 1 : 4.

XXXII Stonea Grange: macrobotanical group from the sump, comprising moss, bracket fungus, (?)gall, acorn, acorn caps, hazel nut, cherry stones, hawthorn, thorn, briarthorn, puffballs and pine cones.

TEXT FIGURES

TABLES

ACKNOWLEDGEMENTS

Stonea was a large-scale 'volunteer' excavation, of a sort that is increasingly – and sadly – rare in Britain today. As such, it has incurred many debts, and it is most pleasurable to acknowledge as many as is practical. First and foremost, we would like to thank the Trustees of the British Museum, who financed the entire field project, and also bore the costs of many of the extramural specialists. Particular thanks are due to our former Director, Sir David Wilson, for his splendid support and leadership; to our present Director, Dr Robert Anderson, for his firm backing; and very especially to Dr Ian Longworth, Keeper of the Department of Prehistoric and Romano-British Antiquities. Dr Longworth's encouragement during the long process of fieldwork and post-excavation study has been unswerving, and his guidance consistently wise and incisive; we owe him an untold debt of gratitude, and have very great pleasure in dedicating this volume to him, in recognition of his distinguished Keepership.

As chance would have it, although Stonea was set up as a Roman project, it was to yield an archaeological record ranging from the Palaeolithic to post-medieval times. The result was that many of our colleagues in the Department of Prehistoric and Romano-British Antiquities, and also a number in the Department of Medieval and Later Antiquities, became involved in this publication; we are most grateful to them for their participation, which has lent an agreeable interdepartmental feel to the venture. We especially thank Catherine Johns who, her own sections apart, has played a more than significant role in the presentation and interpretation of the results.

Likewise, the staff of the Department of Scientific Research has made a very notable contribution to this report, through the study of a wide variety of material, and other analyses. This we gladly acknowledge, as we do the work of all our numerous extramural specialists. Collaborative projects of this sort are especially rewarding, and it was especially pleasant to underline this in a series of visits to the excavation, by non-curatorial members of staff of the British Museum, who themselves do so much behind the scenes. The idea of the then Deputy Director, Miss Maisie Webb, these aroused great interest, and we much enjoyed showing our colleagues something of our work and discoveries.

The land at Stonea Grange is owned by the Vauxhall and Associated Companies Pension Fund, managed by the Kleinwort, Benson Merchant Bank, and we are very grateful to them both for permission to excavate and for presenting the finds to the British Museum. We are also deeply indebted to the tenants, Hallsworth Farming Ltd, who did everything possible to smooth our way and who gave us a great deal of help in kind. Hallsworth's Regional Manager, Mr David Stacey, was as enthusiastic and interested in the project as ourselves, and contributed to the success of the excavation in countless ways: it is a particular pleasure to offer him our warmest thanks, and to his ever helpful manager at Stonea Grange, Mr Mark Grubb. Equally, we would like to thank the Cambridgeshire County Council, owners of Stonea Camp, and their tenant, Mr G. W. C. Cross, for permission to work at the site; Mr Cross aided that excavation in many ways, and we are most grateful to him for all his assistance.

As with any large-scale excavation, we were especially reliant upon our staff, and we were immensely fortunate in those who worked with us. Particular credit is due to Sarah Philpot, who was our principal supervisor, adding Stonea to a long list of sites in England, Italy and North Africa, where she has worked with me. Similarly, Fiona Cameron set up and ran the Finds Department with outstanding efficiency, and processed and recorded the coarse pottery with both speed and expertise. We are particularly grateful to them. As chance would have it, neither could be with us in the final season, but John Shepherd, a site assistant in the previous year, took over the role of senior supervisor in 1984, a task that he performed splendidly. So indeed did our other assistants, Robin Brunner–Ellis, Royston Clark, Matthew Edgeworth, Maria Fabrizi, Sandra Garside–Neville, Simon James, Michael Stone, Graham Watson and Jason Wood. Special thanks and credit are due to Kasia Gdaniec, who undertook the extremely onerous and demanding job of supervising the excavation of the 'wet-wood' deposits in the 'sump'. This involved extreme patience and care, under very trying conditions, and she and all those who worked on this feature deserve especial praise and thanks. Amongst them were many conservators from the British Museum. Conservation staff were part of the team from the first, but came into their own once the organic material started to appear. Particular thanks are due to Simon Dove, who was with us all five years, and was senior supervisor; to John Lee and Peter Winsor, senior conservators in the 'sump' excavation; and to all the others who worked so assiduously, namely Andrew Calver, Gaydre Carter, Robert Entwhistle, Penny Fisher, Ruth Goldstraw, Marilyn Hockey, Valerie Munday, Kirsty Norman, Allyson Rae, Fleur Shearman and Barbara Wills. We were indeed fortunate to have had such expertise to hand, and the Keeper, Dr Andrew Oddy, Hannah Lane and Sherif Omar deserve a great deal of gratitude for their organisational work in the British Museum.

We were likewise extremely fortunate in our team of volunteers. It was drawn from many parts of the world, so that one could often hear many different languages being spoken across the site, even Algerian Arabic! But from the very first year, there was always a large component from the local towns and villages, and especially from the sixth form of the Neale–Wade School at March. Our 'Neale–Waders' (of whom Caroline Wright worked with us every year, even after leaving school) were real Trojans, and deserve tremendous credit for all their hard work. Moreover, through the kindness of their Headmaster, Mr Norman Else, we were able to accommodate the team in Eastwood House, which is part of the Neale–Wade School. This was an excellent base, and we owe deep debts of gratitude to members of the staff, very especially Mr Peter Hewitt, the Deputy Head, and also Mr Peter Dawkins, Mrs Joyce Campbell and the ever helpful caretaker, Mr Jim Varden. We must also not omit our excellent cooks, Fred Butters, Kay Cubberley, Ian Eke, Francis McCabe, Mrs Oldfield and Kate Sandal, who carried out this vital task to splendid effect; nor the hospitality of Mrs Hubbard at The George, and David and Dee Reeves at The Griffin, where many of the staff, myself included, stayed.

On site we were particularly fortunate to have the services of Mr Erven Haupert, who did the machining every year. His skills became a matter of legend, and enormously facilitated our work. We are also indebted to Danny Andrews, who surveyed the machine-cut trenches; to the specialists who came to work on site, among them Adrian Challands, Paul Craddock, Charles French, David Gurney, Sue Stallibrass and Marijke van der Veen; and to our many visitors, who proffered wise counsel, notably the late (and greatly missed) Tony Gregory, Don Mackreth, Francis Pryor, Callum and Lindsay Rollo, Alison Taylor, Maisie Taylor and Philip Walker. We are especially grateful to David Hall, who has done so much to transform our knowledge of Fenland archeology, and who was a tower of strength throughout the project.

Our very warm thanks are also due to those who have been more than generous in sharing the results of their researches, particularly Chris Evans, Tim Malim and Bob Silvester. I would also like to thank Mr Bill Knowles, formerly the Coroner for the area, for much very valued support over more than three decades; and Professor Peter Salway for all his encouragement over a similar period. To my many debts to Peter Salway, from schoolboy days onwards, I must add his kindness in reading some of the manuscript, especially the chapter of conclusions. It is pleasing that so many of his early ideas are supported by the results of this excavation, the objectives of which were enormously sharpened by our long-standing debate over Fenland archaeology. Likewise, I recall with fondness all that the late Miss Joan Liversidge, my former teacher both as a schoolboy and as an undergraduate, did for me over the years: she visited many of my Fenland excavations, including Stonea, and would have been fascinated by what we report here.

Within my department, we have been fortunate to have the splendid support of a highly talented team of illustrators. Philip Compton and Robert Pengelly did much of the early work, but the main brunt has fallen upon Stephen Crummy, Phil Dean, Karen Hughes and Meredydd Moores. We thank them all most whole-heartedly, not least Stephen Crummy for his meticulous and thoughtful work on the plans, sections and reconstructions, where he has often made his own original contribution. We are also grateful to Noelle Derrett for mounting the figures. Equally, we are deeply indebted to Judith Cash, who has typed up virtually all of a huge and very complex manuscript with astounding good cheer and patience, together with some warmly appreciated assistance from Kate Down: the secretarial contribution is a truly major one, which we gladly acknowledge. Likewise, we thank Nina Shandloff and Susanna Friedman of British Museum Press, John Day and John Hawkins, for their immense joint effort in editing, designing and producing this book, a daunting task faced with good humour and enthusiasm, as is typical of the Press.

Finally, it gives me particular pleasure to underline my long-standing debt to my family, especially my late father, formerly Headmaster of the Neale–Wade School (previously March Grammar School); my late mother, a tireless supporter; my brother, with whom so much of my early Fenland work was carried out, and my sister; and now to my wife, Sandra, who has consistently aided these academic endeavours, however demanding. When my family moved to the town of March in 1950 we could not have known of the remarkable archaeological vistas that were to open up. This volume is in many senses the culmination of a youthful enthusiasm, nurtured with care and understanding, and now somewhat fulfilled by the results of the Stonea excavations. But my greatest debt in the current enterprise is to my co-director and co-author, Ralph Jackson. He cannot have realised the size of the commitment when he took on this task in 1980, and has indeed ended up with a far greater share of the burden. This he has done with commitment and distinction; I, and all who interest themselves in Fenland archaeology, owe him especial gratitude.

T. W. Potter

PREFACE

When the Department first put forward plans in 1980 to excavate sites in the Central Fenland, it did so with very clear aims. The Museum already held a certain amount of material from the region, but none was stratified and little had historical context. Organic artefacts too were few and far between. These were significant gaps that needed to be filled but from soundings made within the profession it was soon apparent that no other body was contemplating excavation in the region. If we were to recruit our collections we would perforce have to undertake the fieldwork ourselves. The choice of site was crucial, for any site collection would be of limited use if not accompanied by good evidence for date and environmental setting, while the campaign itself needed to be planned in such a way as to ensure a significant contribution was made to our understanding of the archaeology of the region. Given Dr Potter's intimate knowledge of the area around March it seemed natural for sites to be selected on the Fen 'island' of Stonea. Two in particular drew attention: Stonea Camp, a standing monument and candidate for being one of the retreats of the Iceni during the revolt of AD 47, and Stonea Grange where David Hall – surely the outstanding field-walker of his generation – had noted the unmistakeable presence of building stone, perhaps the site of a temple, more certainly something of very real significance in a Fenland setting. Initial plans were modest: three seasons, only two of which were to be directed to work at Stonea, each lasting perhaps four weeks.

What was to emerge in practice proved infinitely more rewarding and time consuming than any of us could have foreseen. For the excavations so brilliantly carried out by Dr Potter and Mr Jackson went on to reveal a truly remarkable sequence of settlement and use stretching over the better part of five millennia, offering en route important new insights into later Bronze and Iron Age resettlement. Stonea Grange proved not to be the temple complex presupposed but a Roman commercial centre of some importance introduced into the heartland of Iceni territory almost certainly by imperial decree. As Dr Potter has argued, the boldness of its conception was to be undermined not only by the hostility of the environment but by the incompetence of those detailed to execute the plan. The very stone building, metropolitan rather than rustic in aspect, and designed no doubt to symbolise imperial authority, had to be modified before it could be completed while the market centre itself was to prove unsustainable. Yet the excavators were able to demonstrate that despite the pressures of a rising water table and deteriorating climate, underlying commercial activity centred on the export of meat (lamb, presumably salted) continued beyond the phase when many of the standing buildings had been deliberately slighted. That compelling urge to continue and survive which underlies so much of Fenland history was already at work and the case for continuity of population through from late Roman into the early Anglo-Saxon period put forward here seems eminently plausible.

The excavations at Stonea detailed in this volume also have a more general importance: to underline the impact that research excavations can have in an area such as the Central Fens too often dismissed as too difficult and unrewarding, particularly if we consider that less than 3% of the Stonea 'island' has so far been examined. The quality of the evidence recovered is impressive but such a judgement must be tinged with sadness for the last 30 years or so have seen irreparable loss to the archaeological landscape. Indeed so much has gone that the exemplary survey work carried out by the Fenland Project team stands as much a record of what has been destroyed through inaction as what now survives to be salvaged in the future. In this area there is no alternative strategy to targeted research excavation and the longer that it is delayed the less evidence there will be for us to recover.

We are therefore particularly indebted to Dr Potter and Mr Jackson not only for the impressive and imaginative way that they responded to what proved to be such a major undertaking but for opening our eyes to the potential of the Central Fenland as a major untapped resource. To them and to the many specialists whose painstaking work has added many new insights and much detail to the overall picture presented here we owe a great debt of gratitude. Tribute too must surely be paid to our illustrators, past and present: Philip Compton, Stephen Crummy, Philip Dean, Karen Hughes, Simon James, Meredydd Moores and Robert Pengelly, who have laboured long and with great effort to bring this work to final completion. To all of these and to the many colleagues in my Department who have helped this remarkable project along over the intervening years, I offer my grateful thanks.

I. H. Longworth CBE, MA, PhD, FSA
Keeper, Department of Prehistoric
and Romano-British Antiquities
The British Museum

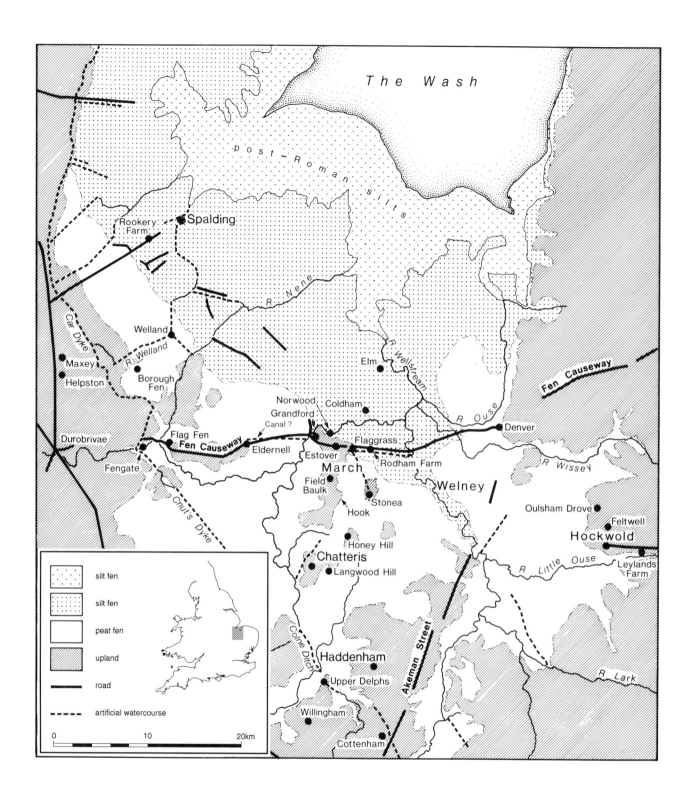

Fig. 1 The Roman Fens and the main sites referred to in the text.

1

INTRODUCTION

T. W. Potter

The revelation through aerial photography of the then remarkably preserved Roman landscape of the Cambridgeshire, Norfolk and Lincolnshire Fenland was one of the great archaeological discoveries of the 1930s. It was matched by the examination of the largely buried prehistoric landscapes beneath, where pollen analysis proved to be of crucial importance in defining environmental changes from Mesolithic times onwards. Co-ordinated by the Fenland Research Committee, set up in 1932, and led by illustrious scholars such as Sir Grahame Clark and Sir Harry Godwin, this was truly pioneering work. Although it built upon Fox's magisterial survey of the Cambridge region (1923), and earlier geological studies (Miller and Skertchly 1878), the investigations of the 1930s nevertheless created a new environmental and geological framework for the region.

Much less attention was paid, however, to the Romano-British landscape, despite the onset of deep ploughing. The way forward was seen as the production of maps on which the crop- and soil-marks were plotted; four were apparently prepared, although not published, the main hindrance being the sheer size of the task (Phillips 1951, 263). Little weight was placed upon excavation, apart from some limited trenching at Welney, and it is clear that this was regarded as an uncongenial exercise: 'villas, temples, forts etc. yes: but huts no', as Phillips (1970, vi) was later to write. Indeed, with the demise of the Fenland Research Committee in the post-war years, progress even with the maps faltered. Nevertheless, two important projects of field survey were initiated. One (with much encouragement from C. W. Phillips) was by Mrs Sylvia Hallam on the siltlands of Lincolnshire, and the other by Mr John Bromwich in southern Cambridgeshire. Published in 1970, these did much to keep the flame of Roman archaeology in the Fens alight, even though the Roman settlements and field systems were becoming increasingly eroded through ploughing, and ever more efficient drainage began to dry out the waterlogged archaeological deposits. The ubiquity of prehistoric 'bog-oaks', raised to the surface by deep ploughing, was a constant reminder of the way in which the past was being destroyed.

My own involvement with the region's archaeology began in July 1956, when the southern part of the well-known Romano-British settlement at Flaggrass, to the north-east of March (Frere and St Joseph 1983, Figs 131–2), was brought under the plough for the first time. The sheer bulk of finds that came to light, including huge quantities of pottery, remains truly memorable, and it paved the way for a programme of field-walking and, later, excavation in the area around the town of March, between 1958 and 1964. It was fortunate that this more or less coincided with the inception of the Royal Geographical Society project to examine the Roman Fenland, directed by Dr (now Professor) Peter Salway: this meant both that there was expert guidance to hand, and that a broader framework was being created in which to set our results. That most of the sites that we investigated were then under grass has always seemed important, for these have now without exception been deep-ploughed, and the late Roman levels (although not the bases of the larger features), destroyed. However small-scale and amateur that work was, it does at least constitute a record of evidence that is now in many respects irreplaceable.

The results of the field survey and, to a lesser extent, of the excavations were incorporated into the Royal Geographical Society Research Memoir, *The Fenland in Roman Times*, which appeared in 1970. Full publication of our excavations, which examined six sites, took longer; but by 1980, the task was done and something of a synthesis (Potter 1981) had been attempted. Broadly speaking, there was little to contradict Salway's conclusion (1970) that the Roman Fens were likely to have been farmed mainly by fairly impoverished tenants, engaged mainly in the raising of livestock and the production of salt, and that the main impetus for the development of the region came in the reign of Hadrian. In addition, one site to the east of Stonea Camp disclosed the remains of a Bronze Age barrow, with rich deposits of Neolithic date beneath.

By this time I had joined the British Museum, and had been asked to set up a research excavation, principally with the view to extending the collections in an area in which they were not well represented. Not unnaturally, the Fens seemed an obvious target. There were already some finds from the Coldham area in the Museum collections and there was a real prospect of finding well-preserved organic material, a goal that has come into increasing prominence in recent years. Moreover, it was an appropriate moment for further investigation of the Roman Fens. Since 1976, David Hall had been carrying out an intensive programme of field survey, funded by the Department of the Environment. This had yielded prodigious quantities of new information for all periods, and in so doing, compensated for the single-period emphasis of the Royal Geographical Society Memoir. At the same time, Francis Pryor's work in the Fengate and Maxey areas was yielding results of far-reaching significance for the development of that region from Neolithic to early Roman times, as demonstrated by excavation. Later, in 1981, Hall was to be joined by other field officers as part of a Fenland Survey Project, and Hodder and Evans began to investigate the prehistoric landscape in the vicinity of Haddenham. However, despite the vulnerability of the ever more deeply ploughed sites of the Roman period, virtually no excavation had taken place upon them (with the exception of some Fenedge sites) since the conclusion of our work at Grandford, near March, in 1964 (Potter and Potter 1982). The need for a carefully planned campaign of excavation seemed obvious, especially when a very strong case could also be made in terms of requirements for the Museum collections.

As it happened, in 1978 David Hall had located what seemed to be a most unusual Roman site to the south of Stonea Grange. This field had in the early 1960s already yielded prolific quantities of Roman pottery, but our survey had missed a concentration of Roman tile, ragstone and pottery, spread altogether over an area measuring some 50 m square, on a slight eminence. What made this discovery so extraordinary was that stone and tile occur very rarely on Fenland sites. Grandford, for example, yielded fewer than a dozen pieces of tile in five seasons of excavation, and we did not find a single fragment either on the other sites that we dug or in the course of the field survey. It was evident therefore that this material – if from a structure of Roman date – derived from a building that, in a Fenland context, was highly unusual and clearly merited investigation. Moreover, less than half a kilometre to the south lay Stonea Camp, a large enclosure with up to three lines of defences. The date of the Camp had been much discussed: the Iron Age was an obvious possibility, but the period of the Danelaw and that of the Civil War had also been canvassed. Excavation was confined to a small trench that we had cut into one of the ditches in 1959, but with inconclusive results, and the only firm chronological pointer was a small collection of samian of Claudio-Neronian date from the surface of the interior (Potter 1965). Nevertheless, the site was clearly one of outstanding potential in the context of Fenland archaeology, and its investigation a matter of urgency: for, by 1980, it had been so ravaged by modern agriculture that most of the banks and ditches had been ploughed away, as a glance at Pls I and II will show.

These two sites stood out as obvious targets in any research design for the region, and we decided to couple their investigation with samples from two other settlements, which would afford further comparative material. This meant that there would be great advantage in having two directors for the project, and I was exceptionally

fortunate that my colleague Ralph Jackson accepted my invitation to co-direct with me. Thenceforth, he took on the bulk of the organisation for each season, and also most of the day-to-day running of the excavation.

The first campaign, financed by the Trustees of the British Museum, took place in the late summer of 1980, with one team at Stonea Grange and another, led by Sarah Philpot, at Stonea Camp. At the Camp the work, while on a very restricted scale, nevertheless established something of the nature of the defences, and was subsequently followed up with geophysical and phosphate surveys of the interior. At the Grange, the foundations of an extremely curious stone building were partially uncovered and a late Hadrianic or early Antonine date for its construction demonstrated. However, it was clear that much more work would be necessary to elucidate its nature and purpose, and it was resolved to concentrate our full resources into its investigation in the following season. There was also the suspicion of a wing extending to the north, which showed up as a slight rise in the plough-soil and, in consequence, a much larger area was opened up in 1981. The stone building and other masonry structures attached to it were exposed in their entirety and, while the 'wing' proved to be illusory, timber constructions of both Roman and – very surprisingly – of Anglo-Saxon date did come to light. The complex was thus much larger and more complicated than we had hitherto realised, necessitating a considerable rethink of the research design. Plans to investigate the two other sites were therefore set aside, as was the idea of doing any further excavation at Stonea Camp. Instead, we opted to concentrate exclusively on the settlement at Stonea Grange.

It is worth commenting at this juncture that a carefully worked-out programme of post-excavation processing, together with a systematic strategy for environmental work, was already in operation. Environmental studies had always been envisaged as a vital aspect of the project and while in 1980 we relied solely upon the collecting of bulk samples, by 1981 an on-site wet-sieving programme (devised by Dr M. van der Veen) was under way. Close liaison with such specialists, including Dr S. Stallibrass, who had earlier reported on the Grandford animal bones, was obviously of key importance in a region with such sensitive ecological checks and balances. Indeed, the full potential of the site for environmental evidence soon became apparent. The deepest pits excavated in 1981 proved to be waterlogged, with well-preserved organic remains, and in 1982 part of what turned out to be an enormous sump was found. This feature (erroneously identified at first as the terminus of a canal) was filled with muds and peats which, below the water-table, conserved vast amounts of wood and all manner of other organic material. Altogether, three seasons were devoted to its excavation, a task that necessitated the application of a variety of special skills and techniques, many of which were evolved as the work proceeded. The sump became in effect an excavation within an excavation, with its own priorities and recording systems – and, in the end, many notable dividends both for the archeology of the site and for the environmental studies.

Planning the overall excavation strategy after the 1981 season was not, however, easy. Field-walking showed few significant trends in the distribution of finds, and the existing cover of aerial photographs proved exasperatingly unhelpful. Even the sump, which measured some 27 m in length and 10 m in width, did not register as a soil- or crop-mark on any of the quite extensive range of photographs. In 1982, therefore, we decided to focus attention on the area to the south and east of the stone building where ancillary features might lie. Close on 3000 m² were stripped, with most rewarding results. A boundary was found to separate the main stone complex from an area with fenced enclosures, containing timber structures and large numbers of pits and wells. In addition, part of a gravelled road was identified to the north, beside which was another Anglo-Saxon building. There was also one pit containing pottery and metalwork of Late Bronze Age type.

A 100 m length of the road was stripped in the following season, 1983, as well as large areas adjoining it. To the north, the dense Roman occupation debris petered out, but there were other Anglo-Saxon buildings, and a few features of very early Roman date that preceded the construction of the road. Beneath these was an estuarine silt, which sealed post-holes and a ring ditch of the Late Bronze Age. It was becoming possible, therefore, to begin to define the limits of the Roman settlement and to place it within a much broader chronological span.

At the same time, a programme of machine trenching was put in hand, so as to set the main area excavation within a wider context. A start had been made in 1982, when the former stackyard of the farm was trenched, to check whether some tesserae, which were presented to Wisbech Museum in 1855 and labelled 'from a Romano-British pavement in the Crew-Yard at Stonea Grange Farm' might have come from that area. As it happened, no features or deposits other than recent ones came to light; but the technique, that of using a JCB with a toothless bucket nearly 2 m wide, to cut the exploratory trenches, proved quick and efficient. Nearly 600 m were dug in 1983, demonstrating that occupation was very sparse to the west but continued a considerable distance to the east. Moreover, traces were recorded of what seemed to be two streets, running at right angles to the main road; a planned layout could now be discerned.

With some of the broad limits of the settlement defined, and with prodigious quantities of material to deal with from the excavated features, it was however becoming clear that it was time for the priorities to switch away from fieldwork to the preparation of the final report. Consequently, we decided to ask the Trustees of the British Museum to support one more, very large-scale, season. At the same time,

the farmer of the land, Mr David Stacey, very kindly offered to sow barley over the entire 73 ha (180 acres) of Stonea Grange so that, through the good offices of Mr Steven Upex, we might fly over the site the following year and attempt for ourselves to record some of the hitherto elusive crop-marks. In the event this optimism proved fully justified. Although parts of the crop had been laid flat by the bad spring weather, there was still some very significant new information to be gleaned. Immediately obvious was an avenue (Pl. IX) some 20 m across and delimited by ditches, aligned on the barrow excavated in 1961–2; it had all the appearances of being a Neolithic cursus, and conformed with none of the later alignments. Moreover, on the slightly higher ground to the north-east of the main excavation, there were indistinct traces of a circular enclosure, some 40 m in diameter, with what seemed to be a road heading towards it. The main street itself showed clearly, as did a probable barrow, some other Roman-period enclosures near the main site and the medieval field boundaries. It is unfortunate that we did not know at that stage of some recent Ministry of Agriculture aerial photographs, on which many of these new features also appeared, as well as a large ditch system, delimiting the east and south sides of the higher ground (Fig. 19, p. 62); but there was no doubting the usefulness of our new photographs, which greatly aided the planning of the 1984 season.

In this final season, therefore, we decided to strip over 4000 m² on the north-east side of the main excavation, while also concentrating a considerable amount of resources into concluding the work on the sump. The remaining part of the budget was invested in cutting very nearly 1000 m of trench which, when combined with those of 1983, were spread over an area of more than 8 ha. As a strategy, this worked well. Despite immensely damaging modern ploughing and pan-busting, the main site disclosed a pattern of blocks demarcated by regularly laid-out streets, each containing a wealth of evidence for occupation between the second and fourth centuries. The machine trenching extended the street pattern and established the eastern and southern limits of the main settlement. The cursus was investigated and, in the area to the north-east, a substantial site of the Late Bronze Age and the Iron Age was identified. Furthermore, the circular enclosure attested on the aerial photographs of this part of the Grange turned out to contain a small Romano-Celtic temple of unusual plan, probably preceded by an Iron Age sanctuary. Although the temple could only be partially investigated, it was a notable and unexpected discovery.

The sum result of these excavations, therefore, was to reveal a considerable part of a major Roman settlement, which was clearly a very important place within the Fenland region. Earlier still, in the Neolithic and Bronze Age, Stonea seems also to have enjoyed particular prominence, culminating in the construction of Stonea Camp in the later Iron Age, while the Anglo-Saxon buildings and, indeed, the post-medieval Grange attest a presence of no little interest. Coupled with this was a rich harvest of organic material, including some striking artefacts, and a wealth of environmental data. Indeed, the overall assemblage of finds is of very great size, quality and diversity, and forms a notable addition to the National Collections.

In addition, the British Museum has also acquired a large group of surface finds from Stonea Grange. These were discovered over a number of years by Mr D. Amps, using a metal detector, and were shown to us at the start of our investigation. The significance of the collection was immediately obvious, and it is here fully catalogued. Although not very precisely located, the objects derive in the main from the area examined by ourselves, and thus bear upon the interpretation of the site's role and history. Their importance in this respect is very considerable, and it is fair to say that, without the metal detector finds, we would be unable to advance some of the conclusions reached in this report. It is a clear illustration of the need for excavators and detectorists to work in harmony.

It is all the more unfortunate, therefore, to have to record that the excavations were raided by detectorists in the dead of night during the 1982, 1983 and 1984 seasons. We also know that many other objects, for some of which we have a rough listing, have also been looted from Stonea Grange and Stonea Camp over the past 20 years. It is almost impossible to prevent such activities, given the remote and unhabited nature of the farm at Stonea Grange, and there is conferred upon Mr Amps's responsibly collected finds still greater significance.

Likewise it is a pleasure to be able to report how in March 1982, Mr S. Hills of Field Baulk, March, discovered an important hoard of Icenian silver coins, while digging a hole for an apple tree, and immediately telephoned me. I was able to organise a small excavation, reported in pp. 45–8, and Amanda Chadburn has produced a full study (pp. 264–86) of what is the largest group of Icenian coins yet found.

We have included the Field Baulk discovery in this volume, since it has a not insignificant bearing upon the interpretation of the site at Stonea. Likewise, we have also prepared a short report (pp. 49–60) on Dr Simon James's excavation at Estover, on the north side of March, in 1985. This not only yielded important prehistoric material but, as at Field Baulk, evidence for activity around the time of the Roman conquest. Given that even in 1981 we envisaged Roman occupation beginning only in the Flavian period, and then on a very small scale, James's results are of some consequence. In combination, the investigations at Stonea, Field Baulk and Estover open new windows into the Claudio-Neronian landscape of the central Fens, and are properly part of this study.

The writing of this volume has taken longer than we would have liked, and it is unsatisfactory to note that one specialist, who was engaged to report upon the tile, has failed to do so, despite every encouragement. Other studies have been assembled at various points over the past seven years, but we have not generally sought updated versions of those who were so efficiently prompt. The problem is a familiar one in these days when an excavation can generate material for a plethora of specialists, most with numerous calls upon their time. Yet the importance of the results from Stonea, at any rate to our eyes, is such that we have tried to bring together studies of as much of the site's artefactual and environmental evidence as possible. Likewise, we have deemed it necessary to report in considerable detail on the excavations, mindful that the collections and their contexts will be a quarry for scholars for generations to come. Certainly, notwithstanding the bulk of this volume, we do not feel that the possibilities for research have been exhausted by it: much more, for example, could be done on the Roman pottery, as Dr Cameron makes clear. Similarly, we are well aware that further excavation would repay rich dividends; the complete strippage of the Romano-Celtic temple is but one obvious instance. But practicalities do intervene, and it seems better that we now have an investigation that is as fully reported as is possible.

Indeed, during the period of our post-excavation programme, much has been going on in the Fens. The Fenland Survey project has been the subject of a number of volumes, amongst them a general synthesis (Hall and Coles 1994), and more are to follow, including what will be a major study of the environmental and geological aspects (Waller, forthcoming). There have also been some very significant excavations in the last few years, not least at Stonea Camp (Malim 1992). We have done our best to take account of these, whilst recognising that our main task is to present the primary evidence, coupled with an interpretative sketch (Chapter 6). The latter is intended as a speculative exercise, which is unlikely to stand the test of time; the former is intended to be as definitive as we can make it, given the limitations of any archaeological enquiry, and the practicalities alluded to above.

Meanwhile, one awaits with fascination the developments in the investigation of the region. Phillips may have regarded some aspects of its study as dull; but we know from letters that he wrote to us, following the initial publication in 1982, that he thought Stonea to be a rather special place. And so it has proved to be: remarkable for its drab landscape, its extraordinary records of human settlement, some very unusual buildings and some exceptional finds, it is indeed precisely that. We trust that the pages which follow will provide a more than adequate justification for this claim.

2

EXCAVATIONS AT STONEA CAMP

S. J. Philpot and T. W. Potter

INTRODUCTION

T. W. Potter

The complex of earthworks known as Stonea Camp (or, locally, as 'The Stitches') has long been recognised as being of great potential in Fenland archaeology. Opinions as to the date of the Camp have, however, varied. Dyer compared the somewhat D-shaped plan of the inner enclosure with fortified sites of the Danelaw frontier, i.e. the ninth–tenth centuries AD, remarking that such earthworks on 'small islands surrounded by marsh or fenland...bear a superficial resemblance to the Viking town sites at Hedeby and Birka' (Dyer 1972, 254). With no artefacts to support the hypothesis, Dyer was necessarily tentative about his suggestion, and most other authors have favoured an Iron Age date for the earthworks.

East Anglia as a whole is in fact notable for its dearth of Iron Age 'hill-fort' type constructions. Whilst at their most dense in Essex (Morris and Buckley 1978) and southern Cambridgeshire (Evans 1991), there is just a single example in Suffolk (Martin 1988) and very few in Norfolk (Davies *et al* 1991). In the Fenland proper, the only other fortified enclosure, Stonea Camp apart, is at Borough Fen (French and Pryor 1993, 68ff), which has yielded pottery of the Middle Iron Age. There is a substantial enclosure, some 200 m in diameter, on the Fen edge at Belsar's Hill, near Willingham, Cambridgeshire, (Phillips 1948); but it is undated as is the enclosure at Narborough set some distance up the Nar valley, which drains into the north-east side of the Fens. However, a ring-work at Wardy Hill, near Coveney, has been shown from excavations in 1991–2 to have been occupied in the Late Iron Age by a small but well-to-do community (Evans 1992).

Indeed, until recently the Fens were thought to be largely devoid of any sort of Iron Age settlement (Salway 1970, 8–9 and Fig. 10), a picture that has been strikingly altered as a result of the Fenland Project survey. Many of the Fen 'islands' have now yielded substantial sherd scatters, and at the Upper Delphs, Haddenham, excavations have revealed a series of enclosures of Middle Iron Age date, extending over an area of 5 ha (Evans and Serjeantson 1988). Similarly, in south Lincolnshire, there have emerged numerous sites, again apparently in the main of the Middle Iron Age, and often associated with saltern debris (Lane 1988; Lane in

Hayes and Lane 1992, 218ff.). It is becoming clear, therefore, that the Fenland, a marginal but bounteous environment, was extensively exploited in this period, even though the social, economic and political mechanisms remain hardly understood.

Stonea Camp, while certainly not a monument of the Danelaw period (although this is a view recently reaffirmed: Richards 1991), has always seemed critical to our understanding of the region in pre-Roman times. It has often been associated with the hoard of silver Icenian coins recorded by Evans (1890, 586–7), but there is no direct evidence for this. Evans merely notes that it was 'a hoard of about thirty-eight coins found at Stonea, Cambs, and which was given me by Mr A. Peckover, FSA'.[1] This is the hoard discussed by Allen (1970), although he uses only the parish name (Wimblington); lists 50, not 38, coins; and observes that the original total was about 300. The hoard includes 'Ed', 'Symbols' and 'Aesu' issues which, on Allen's chronology, would take the concealment of the hoard well into the post-Conquest period, and quite possibly to the period of the Boudiccan revolt.

The first full description of Stonea Camp was prepared by C. W. Phillips for the Victoria County History, published in 1948.[2] At that time, almost the entire complex of earthworks was still fossilised under pasture (Pl. I), and the Stitches farmhouse (a magnificent building, probably of sixteenth–eighteenth century date, demolished in *c*.1973) remained intact. No surface finds were recovered, but an Iron Age date of construction was cautiously inferred, with two periods of rampart construction. The earlier was thought to consist of the outer circuit of ramparts, together with the curved sector of defences along the south-west side, thus giving a double line of protection on the part bordering Latches Farm. This inner curved bank and ditch was apparently succeeded by a double rampart placed within the enceinte, and protecting the interior along the north side. Phillips also drew attention to three 'earthern rings', marked on the Ordnance Survey map, but by 1948 no longer visible. These, he suggests, may have been older tumuli.

By 1959, when the present author first explored the site, the situation had changed. With the exception of some lengths of ditch and rampart, all of the monument had been brought under the plough (Pl. II); the south sector was given over to allotments, and the double ramparts and ditches that bordered Latches Fen had been more or less completely levelled. There was also a chicken run in the former quarry area.

The opportunity was taken at this time (October 1959) to cut a trench into the ditch of the innermost line of defences on the north side (Fig. 4). The full profile of the ditch was not revealed, but the top fill, some 0.80 m in depth, contained an abundance of post-medieval pottery and bone. Below that was a clayey deposit which yielded no finds. A clean reddish sand was located at a depth of 1.35 m, and was thought to mark the bottom of the ditch.

In 1959–61 the site was on several occasions examined for surface finds, and an adjacent Bronze Age barrow, overlying a Neolithic site, was partially excavated (Potter 1975–6). Others also explored Stonea Camp at or before this time, including Mr E. Standen of Whittlesey. Apart from a scatter of post-medieval pottery, presumably associated with Stitches Farm, the commonest finds were sherds in a distinctive orange-brown fabric, with a grey core. Some of this pottery is decorated, and a number of rims were preserved; the closest parallels lie in assemblages dating to the early Roman period, a conclusion supported by the finding of five pieces of samian, all of pre-Flavian date. Many of these sherds were, however, fairly abraded, especially the samian, although Mr Standen's sample (which was collected some time prior to 1961) included much larger, and much less worn material, as the published assemblage indicates (Potter 1965, Fig. 8, no. 6).

The sherds recovered between 1959 and 1961 were very thinly scattered over the inner part of the enclosures: none was found in the wide swathe between the outermost defences to the north and the double line of banks and ditches. The only slight concentration of pot sherds to be noted lay in the allotment area on the south side of the enclosure (Fig. 4), and included the small quantity of pre-Flavian samian noted above (Potter 1965, 29). The very worn nature of the sherds made it clear, however, that the deposits from which they derived had been long since disturbed by ploughing.

Thereafter matters rested, although a visit to the site in 1974 revealed a steady erosion through agricultural cultivation of the surviving earthworks. Consequently, when the present project was initiated in 1980, it seemed clear that some attempt should be made to place the chronology of the site upon a firmer footing. That the excavations were, in the end, limited to a single season was in no sense a comment upon the site's interest or potential. Further work has always seemed desirable, for the 1980 season did not, as it happened, advance our understanding of Stonea Camp as much as we had hoped. However, as the main excavation at Stonea Grange developed, it became evident that it was wiser to concentrate our resources there. Nevertheless, in February 1981, the interior of the site was examined with a resistivity meter, and phosphate samples were collected, while in 1983 the Ancient Monuments Laboratory carried out a magnetometer survey. None of these investigations yielded any very decisive results, and certainly did not provide any obvious targets for further excavation.

Much more recently, and since this report was prepared and published in summary form (Potter 1989b), the landowners (Cambridgeshire County Council) have finally taken matters in hand. In 1990, a programme was launched, under the direction of Mr T. Malim, to reinstate the ploughed-out ramparts, and turn the monument over to pasture. At the same time, a considerable number of sections were cut across the ditches, and other work is planned. We are grateful to Mr Malim for keeping us in touch with his important investigations, and something of the results (Malim 1992) are incorporated into the concluding discussion.

STONEA CAMP AND ITS TOPOGRAPHY

T. W. Potter   (Figs 2–7; Pls I–III)

The defences that comprise Stonea Camp lie at the south end of the 'island' of Stonea. They rest mainly upon boulder clays, although there are some gravels in the south-east corner. Taking the outermost line of defences as the perimeter, it can be seen from the contour survey that the central and north-east part of the enclosure lies on or just above the 3 m AOD contour, but to the south and west the ground slopes gradually down towards the fen. The defences along the south-west side in fact follow almost exactly the line of the 2 m contour, while those to the west run parallel to, and a short distance inside, the same contour.

As Gordon Fowler pointed out long ago (1934, 30), the south and west sides of the Camp were further protected by a maze of waterways. Two rivers, one rising at Hook (Wimblington) and the other towards Honey Hill, joined to the south of Stonea 'island', and then meandered north-eastwards before running into Darcey Lode. A third river headed southwards from the Flaggrass part of the 'island' of March, and down the west side of the 'island' of Stonea, where it was lost in fen between Wimblington and Stonea; there is also a further, more minor stream (Hall 1987, Fig. 23). Between the main river systems to the south-west of the 'island' of Stonea, were myriad small streams, creating what in antiquity must have been very marshy terrain, seamed with creeks. Given that these watercourses were active in the Late Iron Age–early Roman period, they must have provided an additional form of natural defence, and may explain why the double arc of secondary earthwork fortifications, referred to above, were constructed only on the 'island' side.

The earthworks cover a considerable area. The outermost line encloses some 9.1 ha (22.5 acres), with one possible

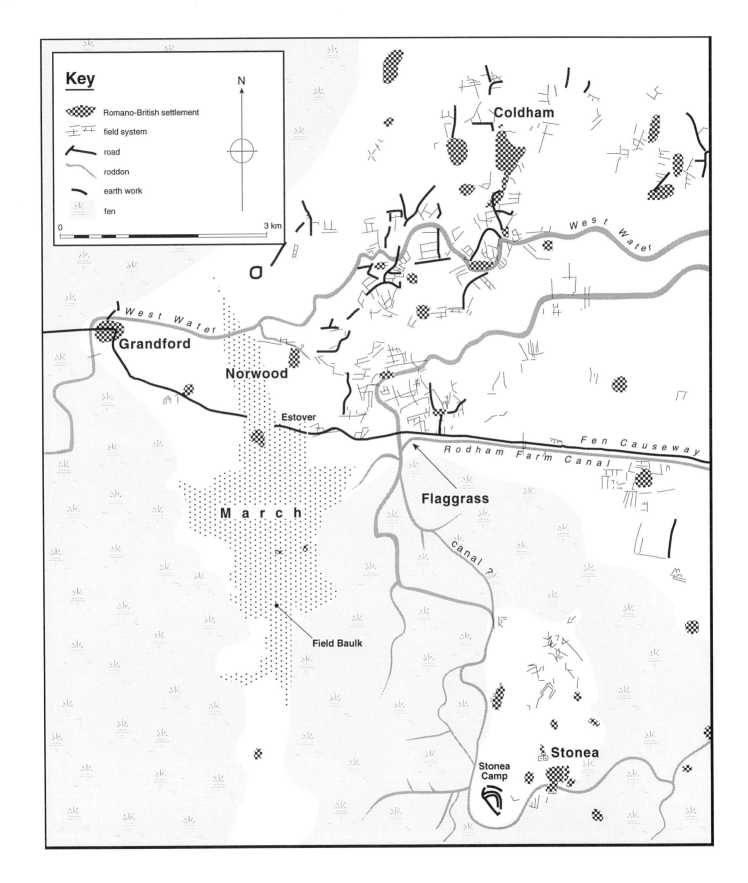

Fig. 2 Romano-British sites and crop-mark features in the vicinity of the town of March.

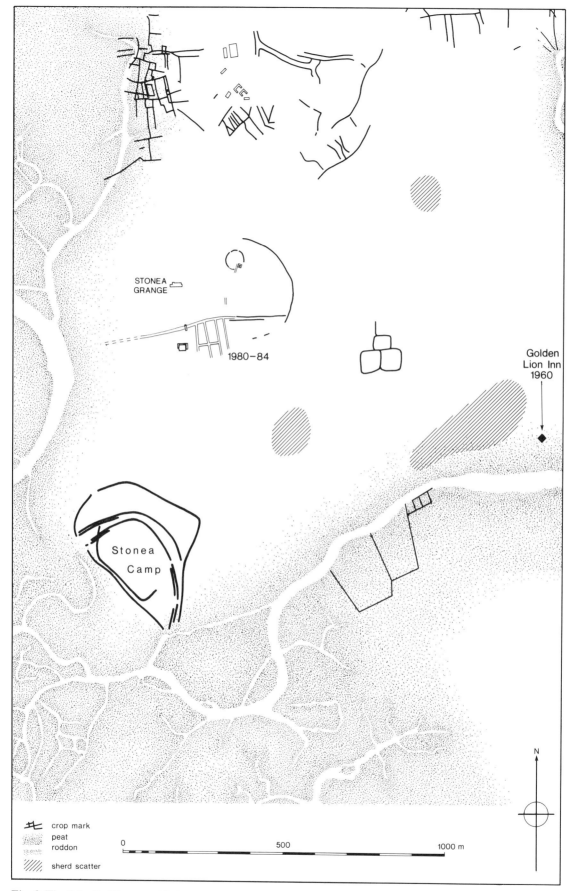

STONEA
GRANGE

1980–84

Golden
Lion Inn
1960

Stonea
Camp

N

⌇ crop mark

peat

roddon

sherd scatter

0   500   1000 m

Fig. 3 The 'island' of Stonea, with features that are likely to be of Romano-British date.

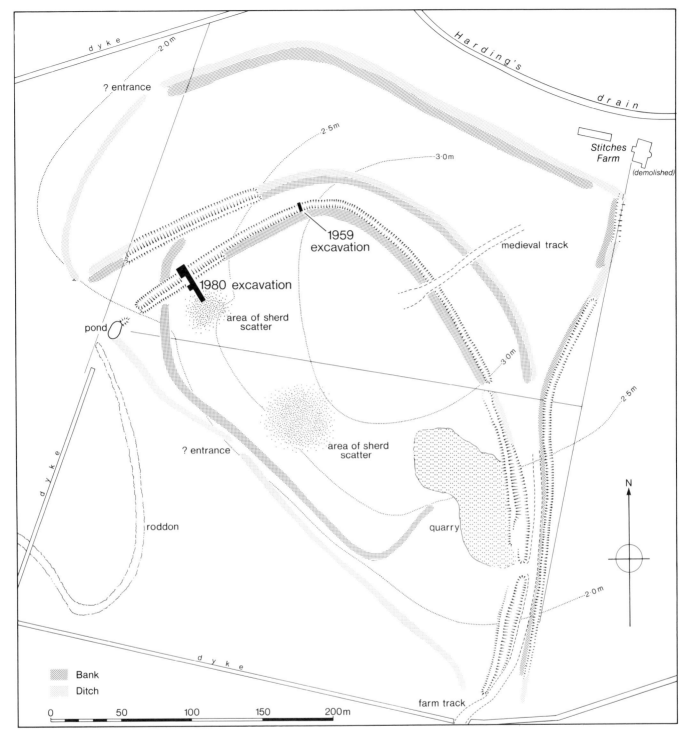

Fig. 4 Stonea Camp: plan.

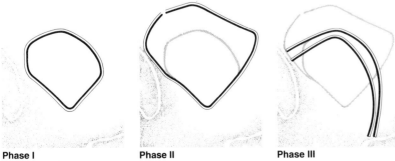

Phase I

Phase II

Phase III

Fig. 5 Stonea Camp: a possible phase sequence.

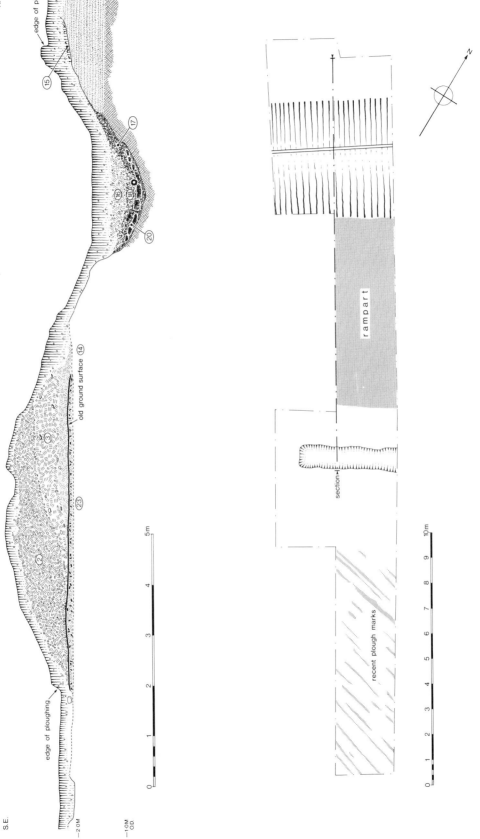

Fig. 6 Stonea Camp: section through the inner defences, 1980. For the location, see Fig. 4.

entrance to the north-west and another half way along the south-west side. Neither entrance has any sign of supplementary defences, however, and their identification is at best to be regarded as tentative. It is not impossible that there was an entrance in the north-east corner, close to where Stitches Farm was later to be built, a logical site given the nature of the topography of the 'island'; but, once again, certainty is ruled out, since there is a farm track that crosses through the ramparts at this point, heading down into the interior of the Camp.

We have already referred to Phillip's conclusion (1948) that the earthworks represent more than one phase of construction. This can be demonstrated at only one point, namely where the inner rampart of the double arc of defences overrides the bank in the south-west corner of the Camp. However, dictates of common sense suggest that the known pattern of earthworks represents a more complex

palimpsest, and it is worthwhile trying to unravel them. The sequence proposed in Fig. 5 is nothing more than educated guesswork, and other explanations are possible: but it does comprise what seems to be a feasible interpretation.[3]

It is reasonable to suppose that the two lines of bank and ditch that form the curved arc are coeval, and probably the latest episode of construction on the site. The deletion of the double arc leaves, however, an arrangement of ramparts which does not make a coherent pattern. In particular, there remains an inner semicircle on the south-west side which, on the basis of alignments alone, ought to form part of a complete enclosure. Whilst the matter is probably incapable of proof (principally due to the recent quarry in the south-east area of the Camp), it seems likely that the initial phase consisted of an enclosure with a single bank and ditch that incorporated both the 'semicircle' and part of the more northerly arc. This would give a rounded shape, except for a

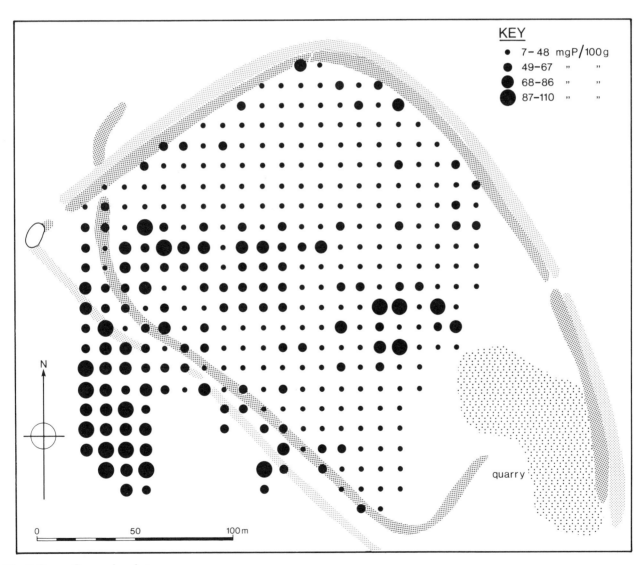

Fig. 7 Stonea Camp: phosphate survey.

fairly sharp angle in the south-east corner (Fig. 5, phase 1), and an internal area of some 4.3 ha (10.6 acres).

The putative second phase envisages the construction of the outermost line of earthworks along the west, north and north-east sides, thus enlarging the enclosed area to some 8 ha (20 acres). This also involved extending the south-east rampart of phase 1, and it is unfortunate that the junction between the ramparts of the two putative phases is obscured by the modern farm track. We might also suppose some remodelling of the defences bordering Latches Fen, to the south-west, where there are indications of more than one bank and ditch. The comparatively sharp angles of both the north-east and the south-east corners is here of interest; in combination with the long stretches of single bank and ditch, and the low-lying terrain, they recall the layout of some Late Iron Age *oppida* (Cunliffe 1975a, Fig. 5). The resemblances are rather generalised ones, but it is a point to bear in mind when considering the totality of evidence from the site, set out below. Evans (1991, 37) has also pointed out the general similarity of plan with the enclosure, dating to the first half of the first century AD, at Tattershall Thorpe, Lincolnshire (Chowne *et al* 1986), and with that at Burgh, Suffolk, an enclosure of the first centuries BC/AD (Martin 1988).

The notional third phase (Fig. 5) involved the construction of the double arc of bank and ditch, cutting across the interior of the phase 2 complex. This was a comparatively economical exercise, since the more northerly arc comprised an extension of the phase 1 rampart, with only the inner defences being a completely new construction.

To what extent the other earthworks remained in use at this time is not clear, but it is clear that the phase 3 ramparts and ditches were designed to make maximum defensive use of the rivers that flanked the south end of the 'island'. Indeed, these new earthworks (if correctly placed in sequence) present an altogether more formidable barrier than those of previous periods. This, as will be seen below, may indeed be a reflection of a somewhat different role in the final period of Stonea Camp.

THE EXCAVATION

Sarah Philpot with T. W. Potter

In 1980, the earthworks were well preserved at very few points, most notably along the eastern side of the Camp (where a farm track has helped to conserve them), and in the north-western sector of the two inner arcs. Field-walking identified a slightly denser scatter of sherds in the lee of the inner north-west arc, and consequently, it was this point that was selected for investigation.

The rampart along this stretch was heavily overgrown, but clearance of the bushes and vegetation revealed that it still stood to a height of just over 1m. Despite the insertion of concrete posts along the inner edge, the tail of the rampart had, however, been cut into by the plough, and there was recent disturbance on the top, brought about by earlier removal of the scrub, which harboured vermin.

The section through the rampart (Fig. 6; Pl. IVa) was of necessity narrow (2.5 m), and it must be considered a possibility that internal features, such as timber uprights, lay outside the excavated stretch. However, the results suggest that the bank, which was 7 m wide at the base, was here built up of three distinct dumps, without any revetting or strapping. The material used was local clays presumably quarried from the ditch, mixed with some roddon silts; this must have provided a comparatively stable base of the rampart, and is a technique that is entirely consistent with other defensive circuits constructed in south-east England in the Late Iron Age (Cunliffe 1978, 249). Beneath the rampart was a grey-brown horizon, containing some charcoal, but with no trace of a turf-line. This in turn sealed yellow roddon silts which derived from the extinct river to the west.[4] This is of particular interest, since it is a hint that slightly drier conditions may have begun to prevail here at the time the defences were built. However, no artefacts were found either in or beneath the rampart, and its period of construction remains, therefore, unestablished.

A section 5 m wide was excavated across the ditch (Fig. 6). It proved to be some 5 m in width, but only 2 m in depth below the present-day ground level. It had a U-shaped profile, and contained 1.2 m of deposits, which (as with the 1959 section) had been heavily disturbed in recent times, including the insertion of a land drain, probably in the 1930s. The bottom 0.30 m of deposit appeared, however, to be intact, although botanical work, described below, does suggest intrusions (possibly from rabbits which are ubiquitous on the site). Clearing of this primary deposit (Pl. IVb) showed that it consisted entirely of dark coloured peaty turves, with a roughly rectangular form, and some measurable sizes of 20×10 cm. It is a reasonable supposition that they represent part of a slighted rampart, most probably a top capping of the bank.

There was no silt whatsoever beneath the turves, and the only find was a single sherd in a grey-brown fabric of the sort that dominates the assemblages from the site. Either the ditch was cleaned immediately prior to the demolition of the rampart (and the cleaning deposits dispersed by ploughing) or it had been cut just prior to the deposition of the turves. That the latter possibility is the more likely is perhaps suggested by the shallow profile of the ditch, which has a somewhat unfinished appearance, and can have constituted only a modest obstacle by comparison with the fortifications of many *oppida* (and with other ditches at Stonea Camp: Malim 1992). Given the evidence of only a single small section, the inference must however remain highly speculative.

The rampart section was extended for a distance of 14 m into the interior of the enclosure, where surface indications were of a slightly denser scatter of sherds. The clay subsoil proved to be extremely shallow (Pl. IVa), and was heavily scarred with modern plough ruts, and no features were identified, with the exception of a very shallow trench, running parallel to the rampart; it contained no finds and its date is thus uncertain. Negative evidence of this sort is always difficult to interpret, but a combination of factors unite to indicate that occupation was probably not on a dense scale; that the quantity of surface sherds, even in the 1950s, has always been very small; that features have never shown up on the aerial photographs; and that neither geophysical survey nor phosphate analysis (Fig. 7) have indicated any areas of particular activity. This conclusion is supported by the results of more recent excavations (Malim 1992), and the evidence as it stands is for short-lived occupation. Only a comparatively rich collection of metal finds, collected by unauthorised detecting and said to be from the site of Stonea Camp, stands out in partial contradiction to this conclusion, and will be discussed below.

THE FINDS

No metal finds were recovered during the present excavations, but the site is known to be illegally examined by people with metal detectors. Through the good offices of the tenant, Mr Cross, one such collection was seized, and is reported on this page and p. 36. The objects, if genuinely from Stonea Camp, as seems very likely, form an important addition to our knowledge of the site's history. It should also be noted that during Mr Malim's campaigns of 1990–1, the site was extensively plundered by clandestine metal detectorists, clearly with profit. The late Mr T. Gregory told us in 1985 that he had heard of the following detectorised finds from the Camp: a hoard with gold coins of Cunobelin and silver issues of the Coritani (or Corieltauvi: Tomlin 1983); a second hoard with silver coins of the Iceni, as well as denarii; and a hoard of aes with Claudian issues. Individual coin finds were also numerous, especially of the Iceni, but also including potin coins and early denarii. Whilst using such reports is not without its difficulties, they clearly cannot be overlooked in evaluating the Camp's chronology and significance. They are further discussed by Chadburn (see pp. 264–86).

ROMAN COINS D. C. A. Shotter

Condition of coins: LW – little worn; MW – moderately worn; VW – very worn.

Gaius (1 coin)

1	AE As	*RIC* (Tiberius) 32	MW	*c.* AD 40

Claudius (2 contemporary imitations)

2	AE As	*RIC* 66		MW	*c.* AD 50–60
3	AE Dupondius	*RIC* 82		MW	*c.* AD 50–60

Hadrian (3 coins)

4	AE Dupondius	*RIC* 554	LW	AD 118
5	AE Sestertius		MW	AD 128–38
6	AE As		MW	AD 117–38

Antoninus Pius (1 coin)

7	AE As (M. Aurelius as Caesar)		VW	AD 144–61

Commodus (1 coin)

8	AE Sestertius		MW	AD 180–92

Gallienus (1 coin)

9	AE Radiate copy	*RIC* 167	LW	AD 259–68

Claudius II (1 coin; posthumous issue)

10	AE Radiate copy	*RIC* 259	MW	AD 270

Postumus (1 coin)

11	AE Radiate	*RIC* 66	LW	AD 260–8

Victorinus (1 coin)

12	AE Radiate copy	*RIC* 114	LW	AD 269–71

Tetricus I (1 coin)

13	AE Radiate copy		VW	AD 271–3

Tetricus II (1 coin)

14	AE Radiate copy		LW	AD 271–3
15–18	Illegible Radiates (4 coins)			

Allectus (1 coin)

19	AE Radiate	as *RIC* 55	LW	AD 292–6

Constantinian (3 coins)

20–22 Two probable GLORIA EXERCITVS issues (AD 330–41), and one imitation of the Fallen Horseman type of *c.* AD 350.

Valentinianic (1 coin)

23	AE GLORIA ROMANORVM type		LW	AD 364–75

Employing the period divisions adopted on p. 290, this gives the following distribution:

I	(–AD 41)	1	XII	(235–59)	–
II	(41–54)	2	XIII	(259–75)	10
III	(54–68)	–	XIV	(275–94)	1
IV	(69–96)	–	XV	(294–324)	–
V	(96–117)	–	XVI	(324–30)	–
VI	(117–38)	3	XVII	(330–46)	2
VII	(138–61)	1	XVIII	(346–64)	1
VIII	(161–80)	–	XIX	(364–78)	1
IX	(180–92)	1	XX	(378–88)	–
X	(192–222)	–	XXI	(388–)	–
XI	(222–35)	–			

Although this sample is too small for meaningful discussion, three points may be made. First, the presence of a coin of Gaius and of two Claudian copies provides *prima facie* numismatic evidence of a phase of Claudian/Neronian military occupation. Secondly, the absence of any other pre-Hadrianic issues (particularly Flavian and Trajanic) would appear to reflect the absence of major activity between the possible initial military phase and the major Hadrianic development of the area. Thirdly, although it would be dangerous to draw much from the distribution beyond the Hadrianic period, the picture from the third and fourth centuries appears to reflect that to be observed in other Fenland areas (Shotter 1981, 120ff.). It should also be noted that there is a small third-century AD hoard of 25 coins ranging from Gallienus to Tetricus II, now in Wisbech Museum, which is thought to come from Stonea Camp (Shotter 1981, 121).

BROOCHES AND OTHER BRONZES

The 13 brooches from the metal-detectorist collection are reported in detail elsewhere (Fig. 101, cat. nos 96–108: see p. 326) by Mr D. F. Mackreth. He concludes that the date range is from the period of the Conquest to c. AD 70/75 at the least, and that they are types that were passing out of use from c. AD 60. He also tentatively advances the thought that the high percentage of Aucissa and Hod Hill brooches indicates an 'unusual element in the occupation' [at the Camp], and that the high preponderance of Hod Hills would not be inconsistent with a military detachment having been there.

Two other bronze objects were also found and are described in the main catalogues: Jackson, Iron Age Metalwork, Fig. 89, no. 5 (see p. 263); Johns, Bracelets, Fig. 107, no. 15 (see pp. 336 and 338). One is a tankard handle of first century AD type, and the other a bracelet, datable to the second half of the first century AD. These dates are entirely compatible with the other finds certainly, or probably from the Camp.

SAMIAN WARE Catherine Johns

Other than the five pre-Flavian sherds reported previously (Potter 1965, 29), two new surface finds were made.

1 Small abraded Dr 27, South Gaulish. Not closely datable.
2 Dr 30, South Gaulish, Claudio-Neronian. Very thin, glossy, abraded surface. Vertical panel with part of hound set vertically (not, apparently, a Diana-and-hound type). Corner leaves with stems only surviving.

COARSE POTTERY Fiona Cameron (Fig. 8)

All but one of the 16 sherds are unstratified and many were collected during field-walking on the Camp, rather than in the course of the excavation. As might be expected of material from such a well-ploughed area, the pottery tends to be in small pieces and badly abraded. The poor condition of the sherds means that none of the surface finish or decoration has survived, and the fact that only the upper part of the rim remains in most cases, makes it difficult to draw parallels with any certainty. The fabric is very consistent – a gritty, dull orange or brownish ware with a dark grey core. A finer, darker fabric which characterises the smaller jars, as well as the only dish, is probably merely a variant of the standard one.

There are three main pottery assemblages of similar date in the general area which seem to provide valid comparisons for the types seen here: the Claudian site at Needham in Norfolk, dated AD 43–61 (Frere 1941); Longthorpe fortress, near Peterborough, dated AD 44–61 (Frere and St Joseph 1974, and now Dannell and Wild 1987); and the War Ditches Kilns, near Cambridge, thought to be first century (Hartley 1960). The report was prepared before the publication of the Fison Way, Thetford site (Gregory 1991). There are also certain similarities with the pottery from Period I at Coldham Clamp, probably AD 65–120 (Potter 1965).

The Stonea Camp material consists mainly of jars: storage jars, cooking pots and smaller jars, as well as a dish whose form is an imitation of Gallo-Belgic platters (not illustrated). The jars tend to belong to the tradition of necked jars, often with a raised cordon or groove marking the base of the neck, which seem to be typical of this period. Parallels for the storage jars can be seen at Needham (Frere 1941, Fig. 6, no. 39) and in the calcite-gritted wares at Longthorpe (Frere and St Joseph 1974, Fig. 55, nos 114 and 117 in particular). The only stratified sherd in the group, which is from the ditch, comes into this category. The cooking pots and larger jars can be compared with some from Needham (Frere 1941, Fig. 3, nos 12 and 13; Fig. 4, nos 14 and 16; Figs 6 and 7, nos 38–43) and again with the calcite-gritted jars from Longthorpe (Frere and St Joseph 1974, Fig. 54, nos 99 and 104). The smaller jars seem to be related to those at Coldham Clamp (Potter 1965, Fig. 2, nos C127 and C138), at the War Ditches (Hartley 1960, Fig. 1, nos 4–8) and some at Longthorpe (Frere and St Joseph 1974, Fig. 53, no. 80, for example) which are in the locally made coarse ware. The imitation Gallo-Belgic dish is similar to examples from Longthorpe (Frere and St Joseph 1974, Fig. 56, no. 141), from War Ditches (Hartley 1960, Fig. 1, no. 11 for example) and from Needham (Frere 1941, Fig. 6, no. 36).

The similarity between the range of vessels found here and those being produced at the War Ditches Kilns suggests that a similar type of kiln was supplying Stonea Camp. It was probably situated in the more immediate vicinity of March, producing pottery on a limited scale and for a fairly local market.

Note: In view of the unstratified nature of the collection, and the uniformity of fabric and forms, no detailed catalogue of the illustrated sherds has been provided.

HANDAXE Nick Ashton (Fig. 9)

The Stonea Camp handaxe (P1981, 5–3, 43) is made of flint from a gravel source as shown by the thin, worn cortex, while a remnant of a ventral surface and the plano-convex

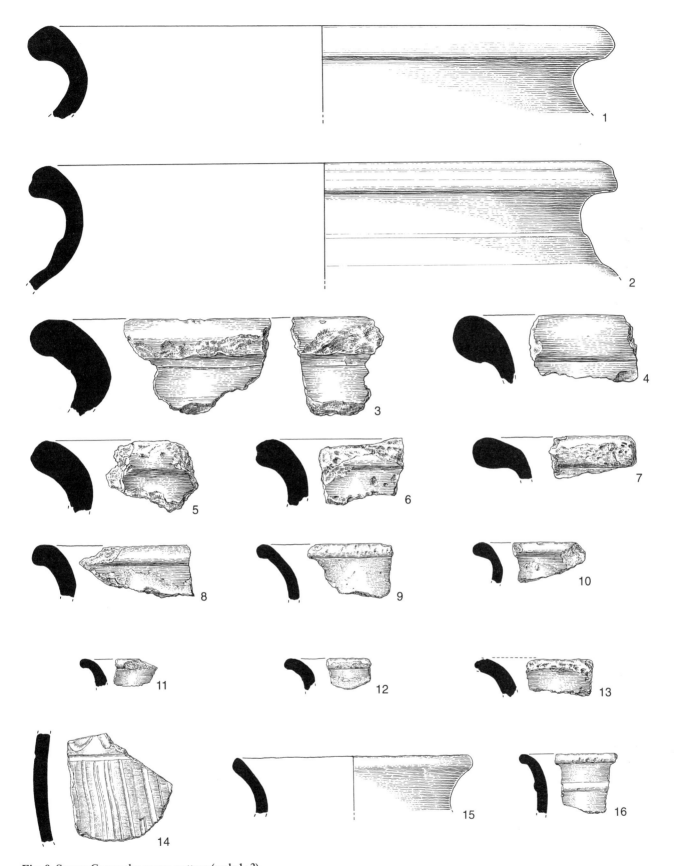

Fig. 8 Stonea Camp: the coarse pottery (scale 1:2).

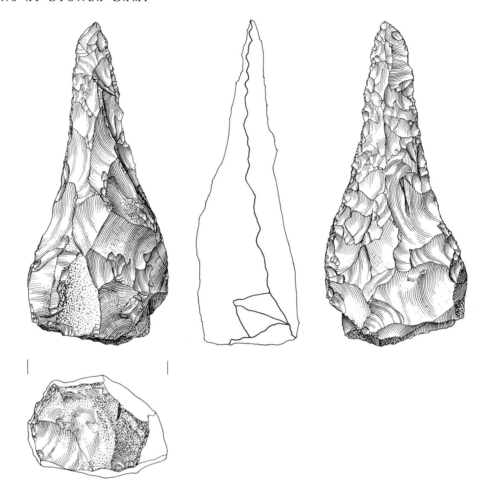

Fig. 9 Stonea Camp: the flint handaxe (scale 1 : 2).

cross-section indicate that a large, thick flake was used for the handaxe blank. The piece has been shaped by bifacial, soft-hammer flaking to form a pointed, tapering tip with slightly concave edges and a thick, flat butt. The butt is unworked other than one small removal and is partially cortical. Remnants of cortex have also been left on the convex face particularly towards the butt. The maximum dimensions are 172 × 75 × 55 mm with a weight of 542 g. The condition of the piece is moderately stained, unpatinated and slightly rolled.

Under Wymer's classification (1968, 59) the piece is a Ficron (type M), whereas under the Bordean typology (Bordes 1979, 69–70) it would be classified as a Micoquian handaxe (type 4). Although parallels might be found with other sites, it would be a fruitless task as such classifications give little indication of age. Equally, as the piece was found out of context, it could date from anytime between 500 000 and 150 000 years ago.

From Stonea Camp Surface Collection.

PALAEO-ECOLOGICAL STUDIES

A. M. Blackham, D. G. Gilbertson and M. van der Veen

INTRODUCTION

The investigations reported upon here concern bulk samples collected during the 1980 excavations. The stratigraphic details of the sampled deposits are shown in Fig. 6. Sample RZ (layer 23) represents fresh-water silts of Iron Age date; RP (layer 14) comes from a grey-brown humus layer developed upon the Iron Age silts. It is presumed to be an old ground surface. Samples RS and RW (layers 17 and 20) were obtained from deposits in the ditch, probably dating to the mid first century AD. Sample RS is a peaty silt, whereas RW below also includes peat turves. The area is underlain by till, and surrounded by roddon silts and fen peats.

This account describes the plant macrofossils, pollen and spores, and non-marine molluscs in the four samples. Unfortunately, our analyses have shown that two of the samples (i.e. RS and RW) are not entirely free from modern contaminants. In fact, some of the ditch deposits proved to be badly disturbed by the laying of a drainage pipe in the 1930s, and subsequent ditch clearance. The disturbance now appears to be of a larger extent than was realised during the field sampling. Consequently, we have adopted the following strategy: in the first place, we report on the biological materials found in the samples and discuss the ecological information that the samples provide. Secondly, we report on the evidence of contamination and assess its significance.

PLANT MACROFOSSILS

The peaty samples (RS and RW) were washed through a 1mm and 0.5mm sieve. The residues were examined for waterlogged plant remains. The clay-rich samples (RP and RZ) were processed using water-flotation into a 0.5mm sieve to extract carbonised plant remains. The results of the analysis are set out in Table 1.

The samples contained very few seeds and a number were in a poor state of preservation.

Table 1 Stonea Camp: plant macrofossils – number of seeds in each sample

Species	Sample code			
	RW	RS	RZ	RP
Ranunculus sp.	1	–	–	–
Rubus cf. *fruticosus* (cf. bramble)	17	–	–	–
Potentilla sp.	1	1	–	–
Urtica dioica (stinging nettle)	15	21	–	–
Umbelliferae indet.	6	1	–	–
Glechoma hederacea (ground ivy)	–	1	–	–
Mentha sp. (mint)	–	1	–	–
Solanum nigrum (black nightshade)	–	3	–	–
Galium aparine (goosegrass)	–	–	1	–
Sambucus nigra (elder)	2	1	–	–
Carex sp. (sedge)	2	–	–	–
Gramineae indet. (grasses)	11	1	–	–
Indeterminate	27	2	–	–
Totals	82	32	1	–

Both the low frequency of seeds and their poor state of preservation may be the result of induced oxidation and enhanced biological activity in the soil consequent upon its improvement by the installation of a field drain in the 1930s. Unfortunately, several of the sorted *Urtica* seeds and two of the Gramineae caryopses from samples RS and RW sprouted in the laboratory when exposed to light and oxygen. This also occurred in unsorted residues from the same samples.

Ecological notes

There are a number of taxa which may have been living within or close to a ditch environment: the sedges (*Carex* sp.), the grasses (Gramineae), the mint (*Mentha* sp.), and possibly some of the umbellifers (Umbelliferae), with the sedges and mint favouring damp conditions. The presence of disturbed ground is indicated by the elder (*Sambucus nigra*), the nettle (*Urtica dioica*) and the black nightshade (*Solanum nigrum*), with the first two favouring nitrogen-rich soils and often associated with the presence of people and animals. Evidence for nearby woodland, scrub or hedgerows comes from elder, bramble and ground ivy (*Glechoma hederacea*).

The poor preservation of some of the seeds prevented an identification down to species. This in its turn prevents a detailed description of their habitat. Goosegrass (*Galium aparine*), the only plant present in sample RZ, occurs in hedges, waste places and drained fen peat.

Discussion

Very few seeds were detected from the buried soil or Iron Age silts. This reflects the poor conditions of preservation in these oxygenated, biologically active environments.

The seed floras found in the ditch deposits RS and RW might be expected to collect in a wet ditch surrounded by a mixture of open and shrub-covered ground, with some evidence for the presence of people and/or grazing animals. This may have been the environment in the early Roman period. However, these same species might also have occurred in or around the ditch surface of the 1930s, when the field drains were installed. The fact that some of the most abundant taxa present germinated in the laboratory, inicates that modern contamination has almost certainly occurred. Unfortunately, we are unable to make a distinction between the ancient seeds and the modern ones.

POLLEN ANALYSIS

The samples were prepared using standard procedures, with the exception of long immersion in cold HF to remove the substantial quantities of quartz present. Pollen and spores were not abundant in any of the preparations. Five hundred grains were counted from samples RS and RW, whilst only 81 identifiable grains were recognised in RZ. Sample RP failed to yield identifiable pollen or spores. Five replicate preparations were performed on each sample, with the detail of the technique altered to try to improve pollen recovery, for example, no HF etc.; however, no further success was achieved. The pollen counts obtained are given in Table 2.

Basal ditch deposit with peat turves: sample RW

This layer included peat turves, presumably within a matrix of finer-grained, biogenic ditch deposits. The pollen assemblage therefore has to be treated as deriving from three sources: the vegetation of early Roman date from within and around the ditch; older pollen and spores introduced with the turves; and possible pollen and spores introduced in the 1930s during the construction and laying of drains.

Table 2 Stonea Camp: pollen count

	RW	%	RS	%	RZ	%
Trees						
Pinus	1	0.2	2	0.4	1	1.1
Betula	3	0.6				
Quercus	36	7.2	30	6.0		
Ulmus	2	0.4				
Alnus	7	1.4			1	1.1
Shrubs						
Salix	37	7.4	14	2.7		
Corylus/Myrica	34	6.8	23	4.6	3	3.7
Herbs						
Caryophyllaceae			3	0.6		
Chenopodiaceae			26	5.2		
Malvaceae	12	2.4	42	8.4	3	3.7
Filipendula	2	0.4	1	0.2		
Umbelliferae			12	2.4		
Rumex obtusifolia	1	0.2				
Urtica			10	2.0		
Lysmachia			2	0.4		
Calystegia			1	0.2		
Mentha type	1	0.2	2	0.4		
Plantago			7	1.4		
Compositae			19	3.8		
Cirsium	2	0.4	5	1.0		
Taraxacum	5	1.0	45	9.0	1	1.1
Cyperaceae	65	12.9	84	16.7	20	24.7
Gramineae	215	42.9	93	18.5	13	16.0
Cerealia	4	0.8				
Aquatic herbs						
Nuphar lutea	1	0.2				
Myriophyllum	9	1.8	3	0.6		
Potamogeton	13	2.6	8	1.6		
Typha latifolia	1	0.2	1	0.2		
Spores						
Filicales	40	7.9	64	12.8	39	48.1
Lycopodium			1	0.2		
Equisetum			2	0.4		
Pteridium			1	0.2		
Sphagnum	2	0.4	1	0.2		
Grains counted	501		502		81	

Unfortunately, it is not possible to separate these components by pollen analysis, only the *Sphagnum* spores being more strongly associated with the pollen and spore flora of peat turves. Consequently, the following details in the environmental reconstruction might relate to any of these pollen sources.

Ecological notes

There are a significant number of taxa which may have been living within or close to a ditch environment: some of the marsh ferns in the Filicales group; all the aquatic herbs – water lilies (*Nuphar*), water millfoil (*Myriophyllum*), pondweeds (*Potamogeton*), and reed-mace (*Typha*); some of the sedges (Cyperaceae) and the grasses (Gramineae); the mints (*Mentha*); possibly some of the umbellifers (Umbelliferae); fairly certainly the meadowsweet (*Filipendula*); and a fringe of wetland trees or shrubs: willows (*Salix*) and possibly alder (*Alnus*). It is quite possible that many of these pollen and spores may also have been derived from introduced peat turves.

There is evidence of arable cultivation: the cereal grains, together with a number of open ground herbs and weeds of cultivation, which might have been associated with arable or pasture nearby; the broad leaved dock (*Rumex obtusifolia*), the thistle (*Cirsium*), the dandelion (*Taraxacum*), grasses (Gramineae), and the mallows (Malvaceae).

The tree pollen indicate a dominance by oak (*Quercus*), with a small component of elm (*Ulmus*), hazel (*Corylus*), and perhaps birch (*Betula*) and pine (*Pinus*) growing in clearings or at the woodland edge. The alders (*Alnus*) may also with the oaks and willows have been occupying wetlands on the adjacent lowlands.

Ditch fill (sample RS): ecological notes

The environments represented by the pollen and spore flora of this sample are not dissimilar to those of sample RW from lower in the ditch. Wetland species or aquatics possibly growing in or near the ditch are still present in quantity, and additionally include spores of horsetails (*Equisetum*). The *Lycopodium* and *Sphagnum* spores may have been derived from nearby peaty ground, or possibly also from within the ditch. Indicators of open, cleared ground are present in greater numbers than in sample RW. The chenepods (Chenepodiaceae), and plantains (*Plantago*) are represented for the first time, and there is a significant increase in the quantity of dandelion (*Taraxacum*) pollen present. The nettle (*Urtica*) favours soils enriched in nitrogen and phosphorus, conditions that reflect the presence of animals and people. These cleared areas may also have been the habitat of bracken (*Pteridium*) which prefer better-drained, open ground. The abundance of mallow (Malvaceae) pollen is particularly interesting. It is associated with 'waste places' and is often spread by human activity. Most reliable records for mallows in the British Flandrian are from the Roman period (Godwin 1975). It has been found recently in similar context, and in similar quantities, in ditch deposits around the Roman fort at Scaftworth, South Yorkshire.

Wet shrubland or woodland is indicated by the presence of *Salix* pollen (willow). Oak is still the dominant tree. The absence of the few indications of birch, elm and alder, found in the lower sample RW, probably does not indicate any significant change in forest composition. The tree pollen frequencies are too low to justify such arguments.

If we believe the general integrity of the samples, then the overall picture is clear. A weed- and herb-filled ditch, often waterlogged, was surrounded by cleared land, some of which was cultivated. Significant numbers of mallows might have been introduced accidentally or possibly deliberately with the Roman occupation. Slightly further removed, oak was the dominant tree, with willows and alders favouring the many wetland habitats available.

Iron Age silts: sample RZ

The pollen flora of this layer is poor. It is dominated by taxa indicating wet, open marshland with the occasional alder or willow nearby. There are no indications of the nature of the surrounding woodland or of any agricultural activities. Further investigation is precluded by the very poor survival conditions which have prevailed since the deposition of the pollen.

Discussion

Unfortunately all of these observations and reconstructions must be tempered with the knowledge that some of the plant 'macrofossils' germinated on Petri dishes during examination. There are several possible explanations. First, the seeds might be of Roman age and had survived dormant in the soil since that time. This seems very unlikely indeed. Second, there is evidence that the layer may have been disturbed during the laying of a field drain in the 1930s. Seeds, pollen and spores may have been introduced on a wider scale by this activity than was realised during the field sampling. Third, samples may have been contaminated during the handling and study in the field. Finally, they might have been contaminated in the laboratory. We are confident of our own laboratory procedures, and consequently exclude the latter possibility. Although there is no proof, we believe the most likely time when the contamination occurred was the 1930s.

An optimistic view of the situation would be to regard all of the seeds of *Urtica* and Gramineae in the ditch deposits as contaminants, these being the taxa whose seeds germinated. However, it is also the case that the most abundant taxa represented by the seeds were also the taxa which germinated most frequently. Consequently, all of the conclusions based upon the macroplant remains must be treated with

extreme caution. If the contaminants were introduced with soil or surface sediments, then it is quite possible that substantial quantities of modern pollen have also been introduced into the original ditch deposits. Unfortunately, there is no method by which possible contaminant pollen can be distinguished from older pollen.

NON-MARINE MOLLUSCS

The samples were washed through a 0.5 mm mesh sieve. Very few species were found. The results are given in Table 3.

Table 3 Stonea Camp: non-marine molluscs – number in each sample

Species	Sample code			
	RW	RS	RZ	RP
Cochlicopa lubrica (Müller)	–	–	1	–
Vallonia pulchella (Müller)	–	1	–	–
Punctum pygmaeum (Draparnaud)	–	1	–	–
Aegopinella pura (Alder)	–	2	–	–
Derived gastropod	1	–	–	–

Ecological notes

Cochlicopa lubrica is very widespread throughout western Europe, ocurring in moderately damp places of all kinds, such as river banks, marshes, damp grassland or woods.

Vallonia pulchella occurs in open and damp habitats, e.g. damp grass pastures, marshes, and meadows, and favours calcareous situations. It is very widespread in western Europe.

Punctum pygmaeum is very widespread throughout Europe, favouring moist ground conditions with vegetation cover, for example marshes or leaf litter in woods.

Aegopinella pura favours moist ground conditions, typically leaf litter in deciduous woods; it is widespread throughout temperate Europe.

There is also one very abraded sinistral gastropod, possibly *Vertigo augustior* (Jeffreys). It is worn, affected by solution pitting, and has lost most of its teeth; only fragments of the last whorl are present. If it is *V. augustior*, it is certainly derived and affected by solution. *V. augustior* favours damp to wet marshy grassland and is very common in freshwater flood debris.

Discussion

The presence in the old land surface layer (RZ) of *Cochlicopa lubrica* indicates that relatively damp soil conditions prevailed before the period of bank construction. The taxa in the samples RS and RW suggests an open environment, probably moist, with grass and shrubby vegetation nearby. These species can be expected to have lived around ditches of all periods.

CONCLUSIONS

The fact that some of the plant macrofossils germinated in the laboratory during the analysis must indicate that the ditch deposits are contaminated with later material. The contamination probably took place in the 1930s when field drains were laid down. The drains not only caused contamination, but the subsequent drainage of the land also removed the preservation conditions, namely waterlogging, and caused deterioration of both seeds and pollen. Unfortunately, we cannot distinguish between the contaminant material and the old plant remains, and consequently we cannot reconstruct the palaeo-environment of the site with reasonable confidence (report submitted 1982).

PHOSPHATE SAMPLES

David Gurney

Phosphate samples were collected in February 1981 from most of the interior of the Camp, and the area beyond the south-west section of the defences. The results are shown in Fig. 7. Three main areas of enhancement are indicated: the transect outside the south-west defences; a band of slight enhancement across the west part of the middle of the Camp's interior; and the area close to the quarry (where, however, there were chicken runs in the 1950s, which may have introduced higher phosphate values).

The results as a whole indicate that phosphate levels are fairly low, and are not suggestive of very intensive occupation. Moreover, there is no very obvious correlation with areas of denser sherd scatters.

DISCUSSION

T. W. Potter

The very limited scope of our excavation renders it difficult to reach any very firm conclusions about the date and purpose of Stonea Camp. No stratified material was found in association with the rampart and we must consequently rely upon the surface finds, and the form of the earthworks themselves, in an appraisal of the site's date and function. However, Mr Malim's recent programme of work does add considerably to the picture, as will be seen.

The earthworks are most plausibly interpreted as the product of several phases of construction (Fig. 5). As proposed in 1989 (Potter 1989b), in a notional first phase, there

was an approximately circular enclosure, with a single bank and ditch and an internal area of about 4.3 ha. This was enlarged in a second phase by the construction of an additional rampart and ditch along the north and west sides, and also in the north-east corner, thus bringing the enclosed area up to some 8 ha; the layout bears some comparison with Late Iron Age *oppida*, especially in the use of long stretches of bank and ditch, as well as the sharply angled north-east and south-east corners. Indeed, the topography and archaeology fit well with Caesar's description of an *oppidum* as a place defended *silvis paludibusque munitum* and *cum silvas impeditas vallo atque fossa munierunt* (*BG* 5, 21). Finally, in a last phase, 3, the defences were radically modified by the construction of a double arc of ramparts and ditches, stretching from river to river, and so reducing the enclosed area to about 3.2 ha. This interpretation envisages some reuse of the phase 1 earthworks, for the more northerly bank and ditch, while the inner rampart and ditch were built *de novo*. The latter was the earthwork sectioned in the current programme of excavations, work which suggests that the bank was slighted very soon after it was constructed, and may indeed have never been properly completed.

It should be noted that the recent investigations (Malim 1992) do not wholly confirm this sequence. Previously undetected ditches were located, and the chances are that phases 1 and 2 should be reversed. However, there seems no doubt that the double D-shaped arc represent the latest phase of construction. The earlier ditches, by contrast, are rather deeper and, on the south-west sides, adjacent to the fen, contained roddon flood-silts overlying primary fills. The latter yielded little in the way of finds save for some wood (some of it worked) and human remains; these included a child's skull bearing cut marks from a sword or knife, and with a radiocarbon date of 2070±65 BP (OxA–3620). Botanical analysis showed that, unlike the largely cleared landscape of the period of the double arc of banks and ditches, the environs consisted of dense oak forest. Given the dearth of occupation debris in these contexts (even animal bone proved to be very scarce), it may be that Stonea Camp originated as an infrequently visited centre of a ritual nature, which perhaps came into being – if a single radiocarbon date is any guide – in the later second or first century BC.

It is perhaps not irrelevant that a Bronze Age barrow stood prominently outside the eastern earthworks (as it still did in 1960), and that Phillips (1948) describes three other barrow-like features within the Camp itself. One was investigated in 1992, and seems to have included a palisaded ring ditch probably of late Neolithic–Early Bronze Age date (Malim 1992, 32). The veneration of such monuments was certainly a feature of Roman times, with nearby examples at Haddenham (Evans and Hodder 1983–4; *Britannia* 15, 1984, 298), Stanwick (Neal 1989) and probably Great Wilbraham (*Archaeological Journal* 9, 1842, 229). The early activity at Stonea Camp could well belong in such a milieu.

The main period of activity belongs however to a quite short period between *c.* AD 40 and 60. It is almost entirely represented by surface finds, the pottery coming very largely, if not exclusively, from the area enclosed by the latest defences of phase 3. The total assemblage collected over the last 25 years is very small – probably a few hundred sherds at most – but the coarse ware is consistently of Claudio-Neronian type, as are the seven sherds of samian. One sherd of coarse ware also comes from the primary fill of the phase 3 ditch, excavated in 1980. To this evidence must be added a collection of metal finds, found with a detector. We do not know precisely where these objects were retrieved, beyond an assertion that they come from the area of Stonea Camp. However, many would fit satisfactorily with the pottery. The 13 brooches and the tankard handle and bracelet would all suit a Claudio-Neronian date, while the coins include an issue of Gaius (*c.* AD 40) and two of Claudius. The remaining coins include four second-century issues, nine of the third century and five of the fourth century, as well as an Elizabethan groat and a half-crown of William III.

One other find of later Roman coins is known from Stonea Camp, namely a small hoard comprising 25 issues ranging from Gallienus to Tetricus II; it is now in Wisbech Museum (Shotter 1981, 121). However, Roman pottery of the second to fourth centuries AD is conspicuously rare. The writer's notes made in 1960 record a Nene Valley colour-coated base and other 'Castor ware' in private collections, but his own surface finds from that time included no sherds of Roman pottery later than the beginning of the Flavian period. This in itself is remarkable in view of so much nearby Roman-period occupation, and the coins (if correctly provenanced) would seem to stand largely in chronological isolation.

However the coins are interpeted, it is the overall sparsity of finds that is so striking. This is matched by the evidence of both excavation, and of geophysical and phosphate surveys. All combine to suggest that occupation was on a minimal level. Interestingly, the work recently conducted at the enclosure (some 5 ha) at Arbury Camp, near Cambridge (Evans 1991), also revealed a dearth of internal features (and refuse except for pig bones and leather offcuts). It was provided with an imposing timber entranceway, but no other structures, or pits, were found. It is presumed to date to the Iron Age, although on somewhat lean evidence.

What then was the role of these sites? Evans (1991) has argued that Arbury may have been a place for occasional gatherings and exchange, its symbolic importance enhanced by its relatively elaborate architecture. The enigmatic site at Fison Way, Thetford, also in occupation in the Claudio-Neronian period, may be seen in a similar light (Gregory 1991). Stonea Camp, already perhaps marked out as a centre of ritual importance, may well have acquired such functions towards the time of the Roman conquest. As this volume shows, Stonea as a whole has yielded some signs that it was

emerging as a fairly high-status centre in the Late Iron Age–early Roman period, the evidence including Icenian coin hoards, several items of fine metalwork, and a sherd of a Dressel 1 amphora. The reported metal-detector finds would also support this view. Moreover, it is clear from the distribution of British coins that Stonea Camp lay on the western periphery of the Icenian 'sphere of influence' and close therefore to the territories of the Catuvellauni and the Coritani (or Corieltauvi). Tribal boundaries doubtless fluctuated considerably during the Late Iron Age, and there were probably never any very formally defined limits: but, on the evidence of the coinage, Stonea and the March area seems to have been largely an Icenian preserve (Chadburn, pp. 264–86), while the Nene Valley is generally regarded as the broad divide between the Catuvellauni and the Coritani (Todd 1973, 12–13; Whitwell 1982, 31). Given this distribution of tribal 'spheres of influence', Stonea could well be envisaged as an inland 'port of trade', thus explaining the finds of non-Icenian coinage from the area, where the Camp served as the focus for a combination of religious and commercial functions. *Oppida* generally may have fulfilled such roles in later Iron Age southern Britain (Bradley 1984, 151ff.), and the phenomenon was of course widespread within the Classical world (Macmullen 1970).

If so, its demise was abrupt and, as Frere (1967, 77) long ago pointed out, it could well have been the setting for the culminating battle of the Icenian revolt of AD 47–8. As described by Tacitus (*Annals* 12, 31), 'the surrounding tribes [*circumiectae nationes*] chose a battlefield at a place protected by a rustic earthwork, with an approach too narrow to give access to cavalry'. When the troops broke through 'the enemy, imprisoned by their own barrier, were overwhelmed', a description which is far from inconsistent with the topography of Stonea Camp, and its barrier of mires and fen to the south.

Such correlations between the archaeological and historical evidence are always hazardous. Indeed Rivet (1983) has assembled arguments which, if correct, would take the revolt of AD 47 out of Icenian territory altogether, and into that of the Dobunni. His suggestions, however, do not wholly convince: *circumiectae nationes* seems appropriate to the Fenland, and the fort at Saham Toney, Norfolk, founded on numismatic evidence *c.* AD 47, is surely a response to the uprising (Brown 1986). Moreover, there are some other, admittedly thin, indicators which support the historical interpretation. One is the apparent incompleteness of the latest phase of defences, with its shallow U-shaped ditch, and its slighted turf rampart, thrown down before any silt could accumulate. A second comprises the independent assessments of Mackreth (pp. 296–9) and Shotter (pp. 292–4) that the brooches and coins are not inconsistent with a Roman military presence. The third is the discovery by Malim (1992) of the complete skeleton of a man of 35–45, in the top of roddon silts filling the middle part of the westernmost ditch. It is suggested that the silts may derive from a deliberate breaching of the nearby river (although, since the phase 3 ramparts rest upon roddon silts, this seems unlikely). A radiocarbon date for the bones gave, remarkably, a result of AD 35 (1985 ± 55 BP: OxA-4064, *Archaeometry* 36, 1994, 364). The man seems to have been thrown into the ditch, without proper burial and, whilst not displaying any evidence of mortal wounds, could easily have been a casualty of battle. In addition, there have been persistent local reports, dating back to the 1950s and constantly reiterated (Malim 1992; Hall 1992), of other skeletons, brought to light by agricultural work, from around and in the ditches.

It is of course possible that the demise of Stonea Camp came in the wake of the Boudiccan revolt, which would certainly seem to provide the context for the burial of at least some of the Icenian coin hoards in the central Fens (Allen 1970; Chadburn, pp. 264–86). But, equally, it would be perverse to ignore the cumulative effect of a body of evidence which insistently points the finger at the setting of a military encounter sufficiently tumultuous for Tacitus to have noted it. Indeed, although the site was effectively abandoned by the Flavian period, if not before, the earthworks must have remained as conspicuous as they were until a few decades ago – an intriguing thought, since we might legitimately wonder whether this was to influence the thoughts of those who founded the Roman settlement at nearby Stonea Grange some 70–80 years later.

Notes

1 The hoard is not listed in the original edition (1864) of Evans' book, nor by Fowler, Rudsdale and Warby in *Proc. Camb. Archaeol. Soc.*, 43 (1950), 16–17, who examined the lists in the Peckover MS (which includes a note on 'British coins of copper and tin, found at March').

2 S. Inskip Ladds reports a visit to the site in 1928 (*Trans. Cambs. & Hunts. Archaeol. Soc.*, 4 (1930), 421), remarking that 'the defences . . . are still strong on the north and west but weak on the east and south. Within the enclosure there are signs of hut-circles and pits'. Work in 1992 revealed a ring ditch on one of these sites, with late Neolithic–Early Bronze Age material (Malim 1992).

3 Malim (1992) has now proposed a more complex sequence, based on his new excavations. Our phase 1 is his phase II, and our phase 2 his phase I.

4 In 1992 these silts were identified in Malim's trench XV, filling part of the outer ditch, and thus confirming a late date in the sequence for the phase 3 rampart.

3

THE FIELD BAULK (MARCH) ICENIAN COIN HOARD: ITS CONTEXT

T. W. Potter

On 7 March 1982, Mr S. Hills of Field Baulk Farm, March, was digging a pit on the north side of his farm so as to plant an apple tree. The pit, which after completion measured some 75 × 90 cm and was some 50 cm in depth, disclosed the broken remains of a pot and a total of 872 Iceni coins. The pot was encountered at a depth of some 40 cm and was clearly the container of the hoard since there were corrosion products from some coins inside the vessel.

Mr Hills' brother, Mr C. Hills, was in touch with me that evening, and I was able to visit the site the following day and to collect the coins and the pot. Subsequently, there was a certain amount of rain which disclosed further coins and Mr Hills and his brother enlarged the hole to the south and retrieved a number of other issues. Meanwhile, a team was organised to investigate the context of the hoard and, by use of metal detectors, to check for any other hoard in the vicinity. The work took place on 13 March 1982.[1]

THE HOARD AND ITS CONTEXT

(Fig. 10)

There was a deep accumulation of topsoil – in places more than 60 cm – containing sherds of recent date. We may assume that the field had already been disturbed by ploughing. The pot, described in detail below, had in fact lost its rim (although this could have taken place in antiquity) and had collapsed in upon itself; but the coins were by no means dispersed, being spread only a short distance from the container.

The precise form of the burial pit of the coins and their container could not be ascertained since it had already been removed by the finder. However, the excavation of a trench 2.40 × 3.00 m around the findspot did disclose some features (Fig. 10). The most prominent element was a small, curved ditch, some 45–60 cm wide and about 40 cm in depth, which ran through the excavated area. The ditch had been cut into the underlying yellow clay and was filled with silt. The few scraps of pot securely stratified in the fill were of Late Iron Age type. It seems likely that the pot and the coins were set into the side of the ditch, although this

cannot be proved. There was also a small depression on the east side of this ditch as well as a post-hole, which was certainly earlier than the coin hoard. Whether the ditch enclosed a building (like the ring ditches around the Cat's Water Iron Age buildings at Fengate, Peterborough: Pryor 1980), or whether it was a simple drainage gully, cannot be established from so small an excavation (cf. phosphate analysis, p. 47); but what is not in doubt is that there was occupation on the site in the Late Iron Age and early Roman periods, i.e. *c.* AD 40–60. The point is underlined by a scatter of Late Iron Age pottery throughout the topsoil, including wares closely similar to those from Stonea Camp. It would appear, therefore, that the coin hoard was buried *within* a settlement complex. The point is important since, hitherto, only Stonea Camp and Estover, March (James 1985–6; this volume, pp. 49–60) have yielded firm evidence for contemporary occupation in this part of the region. The main Roman development of the central Fenland did not begin until much later, particularly the period *c.*AD 60–90. At Grandford, for example, a site on the north-west corner of the March 'island', there was still marine flooding in the AD 60s, and the first buildings cannot be dated to before *c.* AD 90 (Potter and Potter 1982).

The coins themselves are discussed by Amanda Chadburn on pp. 264–86. She concludes that the hoard was buried at the time of the Boudiccan revolt, and provides an important discussion of its relationship with other hoards in the region, of Iron Age date.

THE VESSEL

Val Rigby   (Fig. 11)

Globular beaker in an orange sand-tempered ware with a grey core. The surface appears worn. There are incised lines decorating the body of the vessel. The pot is substantially complete but the rim has been lost in antiquity. The vessel form imitates in detail the beaker Camulodunum form 91 – a range of forms imported from north Gaul in the Claudio-Neronian period. Assuming that close copies had a very similar period of production to their prototypes, the dates for this type of vessel would lie between AD 50 and

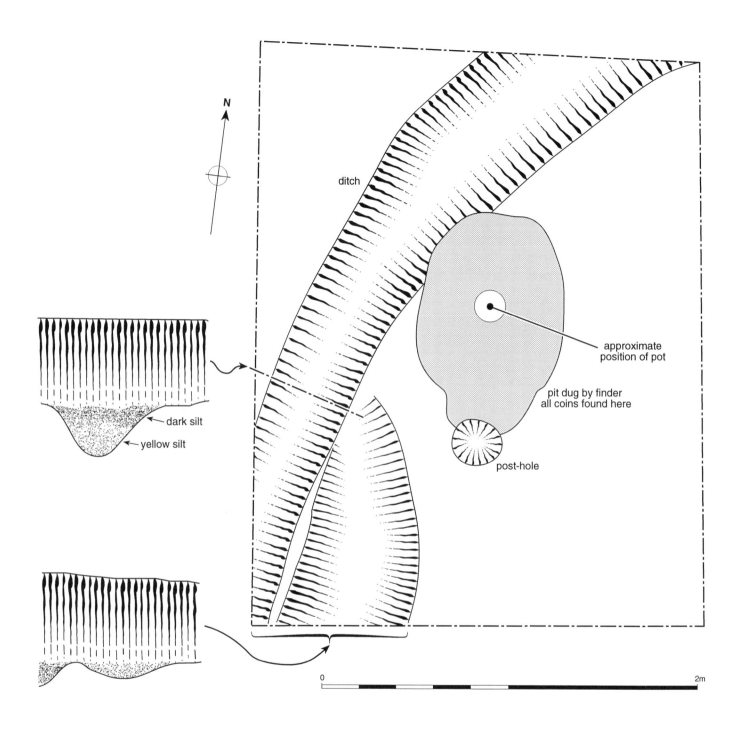

N

ditch

dark silt

yellow silt

approximate
position of pot

pit dug by finder
all coins found here

post-hole

0   2m

Fig. 10 Field Baulk, March: plan of the excavation of the site of the Icenian coin hoard, found in 1982.

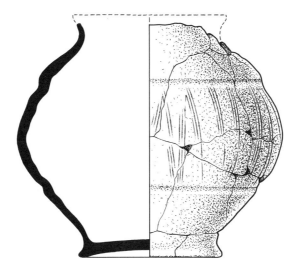

Fig. 11 Field Baulk, March: the vessel that contained the Icenian coin hoard (scale 1:2).

AD 70. However, the sand-tempered fabric is Roman in technique and belongs more happily to the Nero-Flavian period. The suggested date for the manufacture of this pot would be AD 60–70.

OTHER POTTERY

T. W. Potter

Ditch:

> 2 sherds of Late Iron Age pottery in a flint-tempered fabric

Topsoil:

> 10 sherds in Late Iron Age fabrics, including two in wares typical of those found at Stonea Camp.
>
> 8 sherds of sand-tempered dark grey ware, Roman
>
> 17 sherds of miscellaneous Roman wares
>
> 1 scrap of Nene Valley colour-coat
>
> 10 miscellaneous post-medieval sherds

South end of ploughed field immediately to the north of the orchard with the coin hoard:

> 2 sherds of Late Iron Age type
>
> miscellaneous Roman wares, including part of the base of a Nene Valley mortarium with dark grits and a sherd of Nene Valley colour-coat

FLINT

G. Varndell

A small collection of non-diagnostic struck flint was recovered.

Early Roman ditch:

> 4 small blades, 2 secondary and 2 tertiary
> 1 secondary flake

Surface:

> 5 struck flakes, 1 core remnant, 1 thick flake struck from a core
> 1 small notched flake

SOIL PHOSPHATE ANALYSIS

David Gurney

INTRODUCTION

Sampling for soil phosphate analysis was limited to a single column of five samples. Samples were air dried, sieved through a 1.4 mm mesh, and analysed using the colorimetric (molybdenum blue) method of Murphy and Riley (1962).

RESULTS

Sample	mg P/100 g
Topsoil (5–15 cm)	115
Topsoil (40–50 cm)	82
Ditch (50–60 cm)	88
Ditch (60–65 cm)	96
Ditch (65–70 cm)	110

CONCLUSIONS

In view of the limited nature of the excavation and the limited sampling strategy imposed by this, only tentative conclusions may be suggested. Phosphate values from the topsoil probably reflect the general 'background' level of the adjacent area, although whether this is an area of enhancement resulting from ancient occupation could only be established by a topsoil survey of a more extensive area. Results from a topsoil survey at Maxey (Gurney 1985b) suggest that values might be higher from an area of particularly intensive occupation.

Values for ditch samples would tend to support the view that large quantities of occupation debris were not being deposited in the ditch, and that occupation in the immediate vicinity of the excavated features was not intensive. The possibility that the ditch forms part of a house ring-gully cannot be confirmed or denied on the basis of the phosphate evidence. Again at Maxey, results from a ring-gully in an area of intensive activity in the Late Iron Age and early Roman period were consistently as high as 400 mg P/100 g, although similar ring-gullies on the same site gave results comparable to those discussed here.

The phosphate evidence from Field Baulk, March, most probably suggests that the ditch, whether part of a house ring-gully or not, forms part of a settlement, although in the immediate area of the excavation occupation was not particularly intensive.

Note

1   The team included members of the Norfolk Archaeological Unit, the Nene Valley Unit, the Welland Valley Project and the Institute of Archaeology, London. My thanks are due to Adrian Challands, Dave Crowther, Charlie French, Tony Frost, Tony Gregory, Sarah Philpot, Francis Pryor, Wendy Rix, Maisie Taylor and Jason Wood. We are also grateful to the landowners, Mr S. Hills and Mr C. Hills for permission to explore the site.

4

EXCAVATIONS AT ESTOVER, MARCH, 1985

S. T. James and T. W. Potter

The site at Estover lies on the north side of the March 'island', at a height of about 3.2 m AOD. It has long been known since a grass field, 3.93 ha in extent, conserved both the prominent remains of the Fen Causeway and a series of ditched enclosures. Although not as strongly etched upon the landscape as the earthworks which, before ploughing, once marked the settlements at Grandford and Flaggrass, the ditches at Estover appeared to relate to the Fen Causeway; a Romano-British date seemed likely. Although a section through the Causeway was cut in 1960 (Potter 1981, 116), the earthworks remained, however, unstudied in detail, even though they represented one of the few unploughed fields of the central Fenland.

The situation changed in 1985, when it was learnt that the field was to be developed as a housing estate. Archaeological investigation was clearly a priority and, at short notice, was organised by the Central Excavation Unit of English Heritage, under the direction of S. T. James (1985–6). Resources were such that only a relatively short season was possible and, with so large a field and so many features, excavation had necessarily to be fast and selective. It was in the main confined to machine-cut trenches, 1.8 m wide, some 275 m of which were cut. Selected ditch sections and features were then hand-excavated, while other fills were taken out by machine, to give access to the primary silts. In all, 14 trenches were excavated, and 5 of these were enlarged to create small 'area excavations', to check for the existence of buildings.

The location of the trenches was determined by a detailed survey of the earthworks (Fig. 12), which highlighted the crucial intersections. Immediately noteworthy was a ditched droveway, not previously recorded, which approached the Fen Causeway at an angle from the east. Many of the ditched enclosures shared its alignment, and a common date for these largely rectilinear features seemed likely. By contrast, the Fen Causeway deviated significantly from the general orientation, and only one enclosure (Fig. 13, E7) appeared to be approximately aligned with it. Immediately, therefore, there were targets for strategically sited trenches.

In the event, the results, while very partial, proved to be of particular interest, especially as they documented a period of landscape organisation that is coeval with the main period of activity at Stonea Camp and at the site of Field Baulk, March

(where the hoard of Icenian coins was found; see pp. 45–8). It is for this reason that this report is included here, where the significance of the results could be properly appreciated. It is, however, deliberately summary in form, for the site yielded few artefacts (e.g. only 390 sherds), and no real evidence for structures. Only crucial sections are therefore provided, and no detailed plans: these are available in the archive. Similarly, the artefacts are so fragmentary that very few merit illustration, a group of Beaker pottery, discussed by Longworth (pp. 56–8), apart. We would here especially acknowledge the help of Valery Rigby, on whose dating of the pottery we have wholly relied.

THE PHASES   (Fig. 14)

PREHISTORIC

A pit containing a relatively large group of Beaker pottery, an adjoining pit with flints of Bronze Age type (both in trench H), and an overall scatter of flintwork, attest early frequentation of the area. This is far from surprising. Neolithic and Bronze Age finds have quite commonly been found on the 'island' of March (Hall 1987, 39), and have also been identified in residual contexts at Grandford and Flaggrass (Wilson 1980), and at Field Baulk (pp. 45–8). Moreover, an excavation in 1962 at the playing fields 300 m to the south-east of the present excavations yielded small ditches, 0.90 m wide and 0.50 m deep, associated with pre-Roman pottery and flints (now lost). Whatever its nature, the signs are of quite dense settlement on some parts of the March 'island' in prehistoric times.

One enclosure, E3, may date to the Middle/Late Iron Age. It stands out for its almost circular plan, and excavation proved the ditch to be shallow. The north ditch yielded, however, a number of sherds of this general date (Val Rigby, personal communication), together with an assemblage of briquetage. This is somewhat surprising, given that the nearest watercourse is 300 m away (Hall 1987, Fig. 22); but the identification is plausible (Fig. 18). Iron Age salt-winning is now well attested in the Lincolnshire Fens (Lane 1988; Hayes and Lane 1992, 218f.), and is certainly to be expected in the central Fens of Cambridgeshire, although stratified evidence hitherto has been lacking.

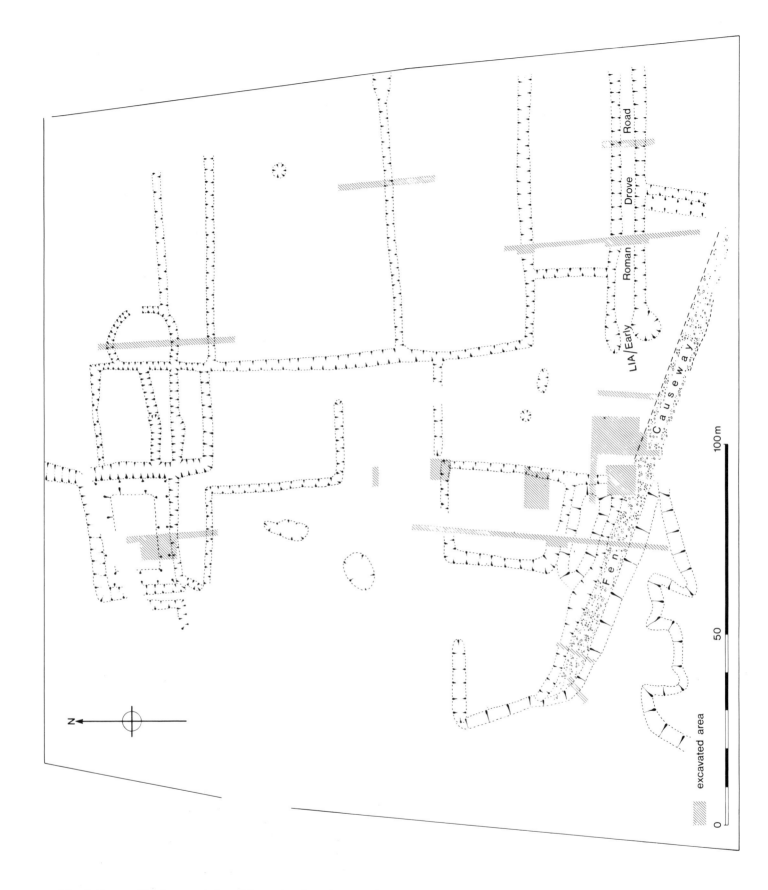

Fig. 12 Estover, March: general plan of the earthworks and excavated areas.

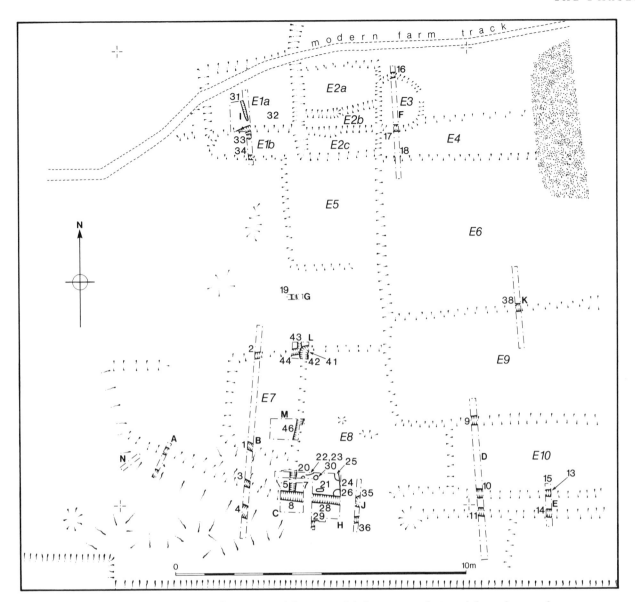

Fig. 13 Estover, March: plan, showing the trenches; excavated features and their group numbers; and the enclosure references.

LATE IRON AGE/EARLY ROMAN

The droveway, which was 4 m in width and had substantial ditches, in places 2 m wide and over 1 m deep (Fig. 15, 0154, 0156), undoubtedly belongs to this phase. The lower fills of the ditches yielded a relatively substantial quantity of pottery, closely paralleled by the forms and fabrics found at Stonea Camp. A Claudio-Neronian date is appropriate.

The south ditch of the droveway proved to continue beneath the Fen Causeway, thus firmly establishing the chronological sequence. The north ditch, on the other hand, appeared to butt. This may be explained by the fact that other ditches (none of them visible as earthworks) headed northwards, so that there may have been some sort

of junction at this point. It is, however, difficult to say much more about the site in this period, beyond the fact that limited trenching yielded no clear evidence for settlement nuclei and buildings. It probably makes sense to see these ditch-systems and droveways as vestiges of a phase of landscape organisation which, in the context of the Roman central Fenland, is surprisingly early.

THE FEN CAUSEWAY AND LATER ROMAN FILLS (Pls V–VI)

The ditches and *agger* survived as prominent earthworks although, at 5–6 m across, the road was less wide than at

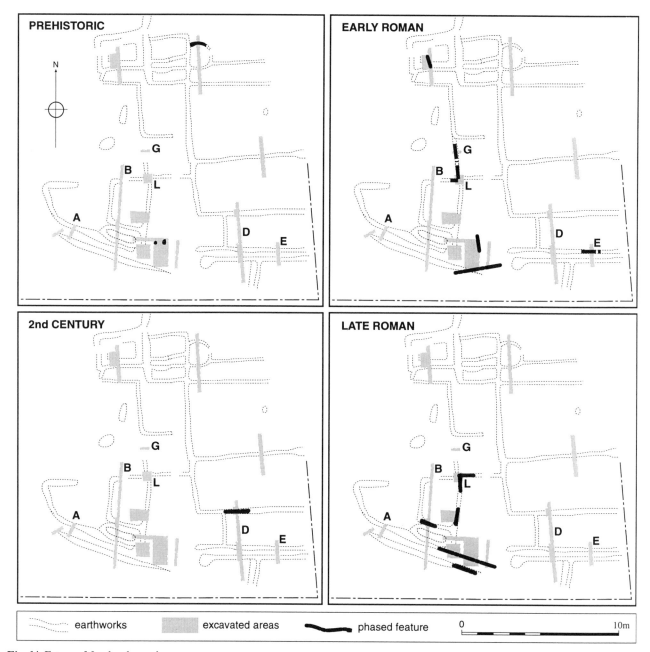

Fig. 14 Estover, March: phase plans.

Flaggrass (about 10 m: Potter 1981, 118), or Denver (about 8.84 m: Gurney 1986, 135). It had gravel metalling as is usual except at Flag Fen, where limestone was used, and was flanked by substantial ditches, 2–3 m wide and about 1 m in depth. As at Denver, the ditches showed evidence for a complex series of recuts, although these cannot be closely dated. However, there is second century AD pottery from the early fills, while third–fourth century AD pottery was found in the upper layers of the latest ditch cuts. There was also a noteworthy quantity of animal bone.

The date of the Fen Causeway has been much discussed. In origin, it is clearly an early feature, and Silvester (1991, 103f.) has now identified a primary 'northern' route, accompanied by a canal, in the Nordelph region of Norfolk. Later, the road was rebuilt along the south bank of the canal roddon. At Denver (Gurney 1986, 135), the evidence pointed to a construction in the first century for the primary road, quite possibly in the Neronian period, while the results from Fengate (Pryor 1980, 151–4) are also consistent with a first century AD date. At Estover, the Fen Causeway sealed a section of droveway ditch containing, as we have seen, a group of Claudio-Neronian pottery; this too sustains the idea of a first century AD origin for the road, and does not contradict the notion of an immediately post-Boudiccan date (Potter 1981, 131; 1989b, 158–9).

There was some evidence for localised patching of the gravel metalling, (cf. trench J, group 37, p. 55), but no indications of a major resurfacing, as was located at Fengate (Pryor 1980), and at Neatmoor Farm, Upwell (Fowler 1950). There is pottery of the third and fourth centuries AD from the fills of some of the ditches of the field system, showing that the site was frequented at this time; moreover, one would assume heavy traffic between the large settlements of Grandford and Flaggrass, both of which were densely occupied in the later Roman period. However, there is little evidence from the present excavation to show that there was any large-scale maintenance of the Fen Causeway in this sector.

SUMMARY OF THE EXCAVATED FEATURES BY TRENCH

(Fig. 13; Pls V–VII)

TRENCH A

This was dug to establish the position of the Fen Causeway, and its flanking ditches, in the south-west part of the site. The ditches were not excavated and there were no finds.

TRENCH B   (Fig. 15)

A long trench, north–south across enclosure E7 and the Fen Causeway.

1 South ditch (0073), enclosure E7: width 3 m, depth 0.8 m. Channel in bottom, silty fill. Seven Roman sherds, one a Nene Valley grey ware base; 9 sherds c. mid 1st century AD.

2 North ditch, enclosure E7: not excavated.

3 North ditch (0054), Fen Causeway: width 1.15 m, depth 1.0 m. Recut twice. Dark silt. No finds.

4 South ditch (0063), Fen Causeway: width 1.50 m, depth 1.0 m. Dark silt fill; ?deliberate. No finds, except for 51 animal bones.

TRENCH C

A trench intended to elucidate the relationship between the north ditch of the Fen Causeway, and the north–south ditch.

5 North–south ditch (0013); cuts ditch 0025; cut by north ditch of the Fen Causeway: width c. 1 m, depth 0.50 m. Dark grey-brown silt. Relationship with pit 0018 unclear. No finds, other than clay lumps, and 12 animal bones.

6 Short east–west ditch (0025); full dimensions not established. Dark brown fill. No finds.

7 Pit (0018): min. width 1.60 m, depth 1 m. Sandy, iron-stained fill, with daub. Cuts ditch 0025. One sherd of samian (not located); 5 sherds of pre-Roman pottery, including pieces of Early Bronze Age Urn or Food Vessel.

8 North ditch (0028), Fen Causeway: width c. 2 m, depth c. 0.80 m. Not fully excavated, but at least one recut. Cuts ditch 0013. Red-brown sandy silt. Upper fill: 3rd–4th century AD sherds; lower fill: two 2nd century AD sherds. The upper fill also yielded a large quantity of animal bones (130), and there were 23 animal bones in the lower fill.

TRENCH D

A long trench, north–south, across part of the enclosure E9, enclosure E10 and the droveway to the south.

9 South ditch (0107), enclosure E9: width 2.20 m, depth 1.30 m. V-shaped profile, possibly recut. Ten sherds in bottom silt; 1 Dr 31, Central Gaulish, Antonine, 9 coarse ware. Also 46 animal bones.

10 North droveway ditch: not excavated.

11 South droveway ditch (0113): width c. 1.50 m, depth c. 0.50 m. Several recuts. Dark fill. No finds.

12 Droveway: thin gravel metalling.

TRENCH E   (Fig. 15)

A trench across the droveway, which was 4 m in width.

13 North droveway ditch (0154): width 2 m, depth (below road surface): 1.10 m. Dark grey-brown fill. Recut. One sherd of c. mid 1st century AD.

14 South droveway ditch (0156): width 2.60 m, depth c. 1.0 m. Dark grey-brown fill. No finds.

15 To the north of the droveway, some (?)pits, not more fully identified. One Roman sherd.

TRENCH F

A north–south trench across enclosures E3 and E4.

16 North ditch (0173), enclosure E3: width 1.5 m, depth 0.35 m. Dark fill. The ditch contained 8 sherds in fabrics of Middle/Late Iron Age type, and some 12 lumps of briquetage. These include a bar with sides of 6 × 7 cm (Fig. 18, 10); the base of a (?)container; and various 'squeezed' pieces.

17 South ditch (0179), enclosure E3: width 1.0 m, depth 0.3 m. Dark grey-brown silt. One Roman sherd; 17 animal bones.

18 South ditch of enclosure E4: not located.

TRENCH G

A trench designed to see if the west ditch of enclosure E5 continued, which it proved to do.

19 Ditch (0203), north–south, dark silt fill: width 1.50 m, depth not recorded. One sherd of c. mid 1st century AD pottery, and 3 sherds of Late Iron Age type pottery, one possibly a piece of briquetage.

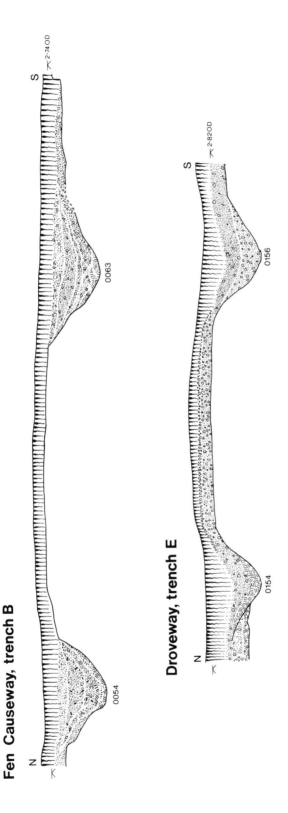

Fen Causeway, trench B

0054
0063

Droveway, trench E

0154
0156

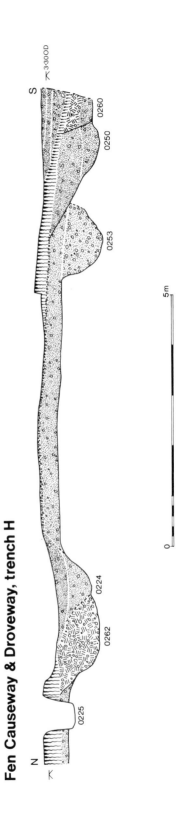

Fen Causeway & Droveway, trench H

0225
0262
0224
0253
0250
0260

0
5m

Fig. 15 Estover, March: sections. 0054, 0063 = groups 3, 4; 0154, 0156 = groups 13, 14; 0225 = group 21; 0224/0262 = group 27; 0253 = group 29; 0250 = group 28; 0260 = recent fill.

TRENCH H (Fig. 15)

A trench designed to investigate the relationship between the droveway and the Fen Causeway.

20 Ditch (0230), a continuation northwards of ditch 0013, in trench C: width 2.25 m, depth 0.80 m. No finds.

21 Grave (0225) in a rectangular pit, 3.55 × 0.50 m, depth 0.45 m, parallel with, and to the north of, the Fen Causeway. Adult inhumation. No finds. (?)Roman.

22 Rectangular pit (0235): width 0.60 m, depth 0.16 m. Burnt clay lining, 6 cm thick, and a black fill, with burnt bone. ?Cremation or (more probably) an oven. No other finds, except for 29 animal bones (almost all sheep).

23 Curved gully (0237): width 0.30 m, depth 0.10 m. Very dark grey fill. No finds.

24 Edge of ditch (0239), with silty fill. Cuts 0241 (below). Ten sherds in forms and fabrics typical of those from Stonea Camp; c. mid 1st century AD; 23 animal bones.

25 Part of one or more pits (0241): depth 0.80 m. Very dark silty fill. Contained flints of Bronze Age type (not located).

26 Pit (0242): not excavated.

27 North ditch (0224/0262), Fen Causeway. Recut once. Burial (0225) cuts earlier ditch. The earlier ditch contained a sherd of (?)2nd century AD date.

28 South ditch (0250), Fen Causeway. Cuts ditch 0253, which is probably a continuation of the droveway. The road metalling has been several times patched over the (?)droveway ditch. Six sherds, one early Roman, the others undiagnostic, but Roman; 20 animal bones.

29 Ditch (0253), probably the south ditch of the droveway. Contained a relatively large group of pottery (Fig. 18, 13–15), 33 sherds, with 5 rims. The forms and fabrics are very closely paralleled at Stonea Camp, and a date of c. AD 50 is indicated. One is a ripple-shouldered Late Iron Age jar (Val Rigby, personal communication). The ditch is cut by the Fen Causeway ditch, and sealed by the Fen Causeway itself.

30 Pit (0255): diameter 1.10 m, depth 0.50 m. Very dark grey-brown fill. Large pieces of Beaker pottery (Figs 16–17). Five animal bones (cow).

TRENCH I

A north-south trench across enclosures Ela and Elb.

31 Gully (0273). A linear gully was identified within the enclosures, running NW–SE: width 60 m; depth not established. One sherd of mid 1st century AD type in the top fill.

32 Ditch (0275) dividing enclosures Ela and Elb: width 1.75 m, depth 0.80 m. Dark grey silty fill. The lower fill yielded a Nene Valley cup rim, c. late 2nd–early 3rd century AD; the middle and upper fills contained 8 sherds of 2nd century AD date, including 1 Dr 18/31 or 31, Central Gaulish, Antonine. One jar sherd with two bands of wavy lines is c. mid 1st century AD.

33 Pits (0281, 0299, 0295), cut by ditch 0275. Dark fills, including tips of charcoal and white ash. Two scraps of ?briquetage.

34 Ditch (0279), south side of enclosure Elb. Largely cut away by a modern drain, and full dimensions not established.

TRENCH J

A north–south trench, excavated across the droveway, at the point where the Fen Causeway should intersect with it.

35 North ditch (0318) of droveway/Fen Causeway: not excavated. One mid 1st century AD sherd and 2 of the 2nd century AD from the top fill.

36 South ditch (0315) of droveway: width 1.60 m, depth 0.75 m. Sealed by metalling and make-up of the Fen Causeway. From the lower silt: large rim paralleled at Stonea Camp. c. mid 1st century AD. Middle layers: carinated jar, c. mid 1st century AD (not later than 1st century).

37 From the metalling of the Fen Causeway (0312): very worn piece of Central Gaulish samian, Antonine; 3 sherds of Nene Valley grey ware.

TRENCH K

A north–south trench cutting across the ditch dividing enclosures E6 and E9.

38 Ditch (0343) dividing the enclosures: width 2.10 m, depth 1.0 m. Cleaning channel at base; one probable recut. Dark grey silt fill. No finds.

39 Three possible post-holes were identified; none was excavated.

TRENCH L

A trench designed to examine the ditch intersections between enclosures E5, E7 and E8.

40 Gully, parallel with north–south ditch (0376): width 0.50 m, depth 0.25 m. Dark fill with some burnt clay. No finds. ?Fenceline.

41 Ditch (0367), east–west dividing enclosures E5 and E8: width 2.20 m, depth 1.0 m. It is cut through the fill of ditch 0369, and thus has a butt end. Well-defined stratigraphy, of grey and black layers, with 18 sherds, mainly of 3rd–4th century AD date, including one of the 4th century from the primary silt. There were also 48 animal bones, and a piece of *tegula* (a notable find in a region where tile is particularly rare, except at Stonea Grange).

42 Ditch (0369), north–south dividing enclosures E7 and E8: width 2.5 m, depth 1.10 m. Well-defined stratigraphy, with layers of grey, dark grey, brown and yellow silts. Comparatively rich in finds, with 43 sherds and 31 animal bones. Two large 2nd–3rd

century AD sherds in the primary fill; 3rd and 4th century AD sherds in middle and upper fill.

43 Ditch (0376), north–south, west side of enclosure E5: width 1.0 m, depth 0.50 m. Dark grey silt. No pottery, but a large dump of 79 animal bones, mainly cow and sheep. Same ditch as (0203) in trench G, which yielded Late Iron Age pottery.

44 Ditch (0378), east–west, north side of enclosure E7: width 1.0 m, depth 0.60 m. Dark grey silt. It is not impossible that this represents a continuation of ditch 0376. Three sherds, one perhaps early 1st century AD.

45 Gully (0380), parallel with ditch 0378: width 0.25 m, depth 0.15 m. Very dark grey fill. No finds. ?Fence-line.

TRENCH M

A trench designed to locate the north–south ditch dividing enclosures E7 and E8, and to sample some of the interior of enclosure E7, where, however, no features were found.

46 Ditch (0384), north–south: width 2.40 m, depth 0.90 m. Complex sequence of dark grey, brown and gravelly fills. Recut at least once. Two 3rd century AD grey ware sherds in ditch bottom (prior to recut); 6 4th century AD sherds in middle fill.

TRENCH N

A trench cut to confirm the line of the Fen Causeway.

THE FINDS (Figs 16–18)

As already noted, the site yielded few artefacts, and these merit little detailed treatment.

LATE NEOLITHIC AND BRONZE AGE POTTERY I. H. Longworth

Feature 0255, a pit in trench H (see 30, p. 55), produced a range of domestic Beaker wares together with fragments of burnt clay, probably loom weights. Many of the sherds are from vessels of some size (nos 2–6) likely to have been used for storage, but these are also accompanied by two sherds of typical Late Southern incised Beakers. Most of the elements of rusticated decoration can be matched at Hockwold Site 93 (Bamford 1982, Figs 1–11) including the use of widely spaced rows of light finger-pinching (*ibid*. Fig. 11, P93, 006), and on this site sherds of Late Southern incised Beakers are again present. Similar associations are recorded from Hockwold 'The Oaks' (*ibid*. Figs 19–26) and from Reffley Wood (*ibid*. Fig. 43).

Of particular interest is the large rim sherd no. 2. Though this could come from a Pot Beaker (Lehmann 1965, 1967), Gibson (1980) with the scheme of a zone of finger-pinching above horizontal finger-pinched ridges matched

on at least one of the Pot Beakers from the Netherlands–Doesburgerbuurt, Gelderland (Lehmann 1967, Fig. 5), internal decoration seems alien to this group. On balance, the sherd seems more likely to come from a large rusticated bowl, of still rare occurrence but known, for example, from Moordown, Bournemouth, Dorset (Calkin 1966, Fig. 5; Clarke 1970, no. 923).

Catalogue

Feature 0009 (residual; in north ditch of Fen Causeway)
Fragment of base, of well-fired, compact paste with shell and sparse grog inclusions, red externally, grey internally.

No decoration survives. Weathered. (Not illustrated.)

Feature 0015 (pit 0018; cf. 7, p. 53)
Early Bronze Age Urn or Food Vessel. Two joining wall sherds of poorly fired paste with grog and fine shell inclusions, patchy buff to pinkish buff externally, dark grey internally.

No decoration survives. (Not illustrated.)

Feature 0022 (pit 0018; cf. 7, p. 53)
Early Bronze Age Urn or Food Vessel. Three fragments of wall of poorly fired paste with medium to coarse grit inclusions, patchy grey-buff both faces with dark grey core.

No decoration survives. (Not illustrated.)

Feature 0101 (unstratified)
Wall sherd of well-fired, compact paste with trace of fine grit inclusion, buff externally, grey internally.

Early Bronze Age fabric. (Not illustrated.)

Feature 0223 (residual in north ditch of Fen Causeway; cf. 27, p. 55)
Probably Beaker. Wall sherd of well-fired, compact paste with fine grit inclusions, reddish buff externally, dark grey internally.

No decoration survives. Weathered. (Not illustrated.)

Feature 0255 (pit in trench H; cf. 30, p. 55; Figs 16–17)
1 Late Southern Beaker. Two sherds of well-fired paste with a little fine grit inclusion, pinkish buff externally, grey internally.

  Decoration: Part of an incised, lattice-filled ?hexagon pattern survives.

2 Pot Beaker or bowl. Diameter of mouth *c*. 32 cm. Rim sherd of coarse, well-fired paste with some coarse grit inclusions, light grey-buff externally, mid-grey internally. Extensive shrinkage cracks visible internally.

  Decoration: On the rim, finger-tip impressions. Internally, two rows of finger-pinching. Externally, two rows of coarse finger-pinching above horizontal ridges formed by further pinching leaving finger-nail impressions in the grooves.

3 Rusticated Beaker. Rim sherd of well-fired paste with sparse grit inclusions, pinkish buff both faces with grey core.

  Decoration: Rows of horizontal and diagonally placed finger-nail impressions.

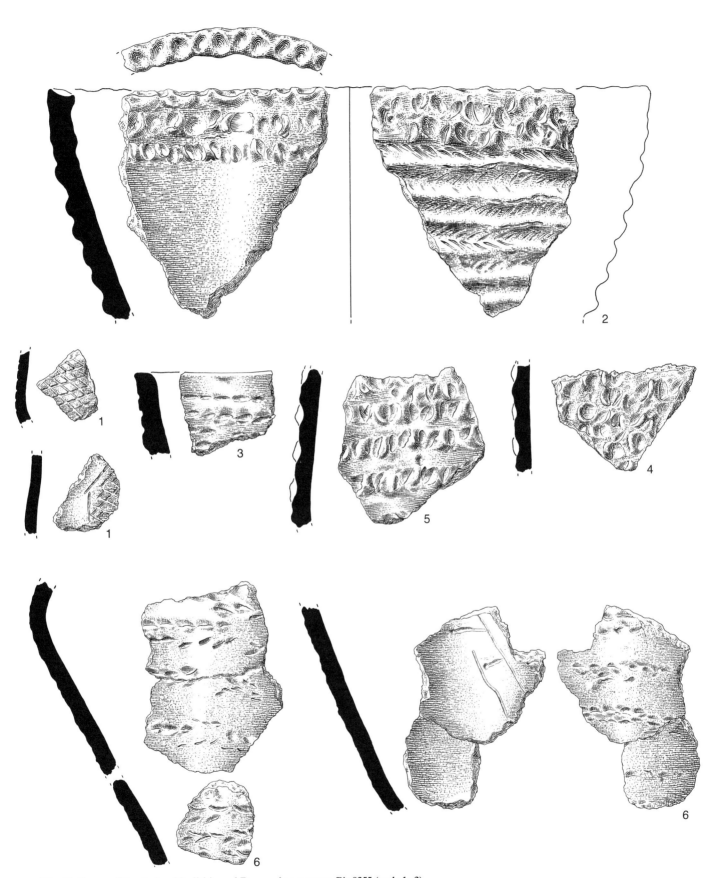

Fig. 16 Estover, March: late Neolithic and Bronze Age pottery. Pit 0255 (scale 1 : 2).

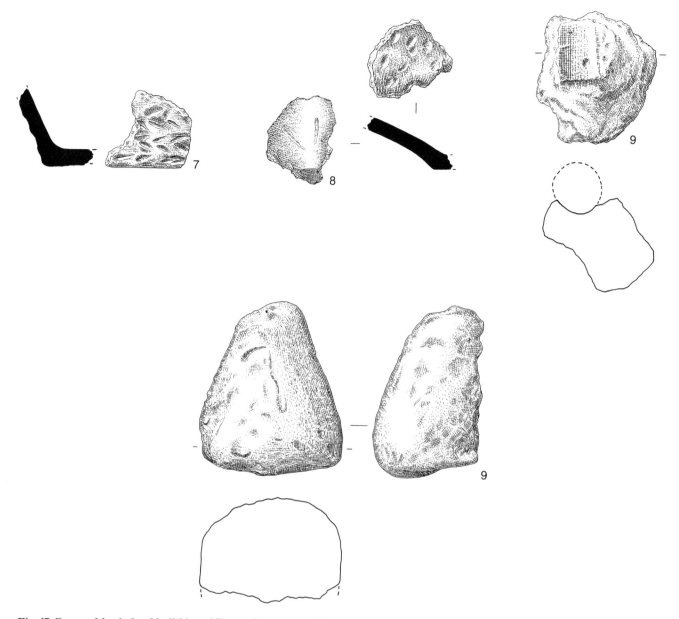

Fig. 17 Estover, March: late Neolithic and Bronze Age pottery (7, 8), and triangular clay weights (9). Pit 0255 (scale 1 : 2).

4 Rusticated Beaker. Two wall sherds of well-fired paste with grit and grog inclusions, reddish buff externally, dark grey internally.

Decoration: Deep finger-pinching.

5 Rusticated Beaker. Two wall sherds of well-fired paste with grog and sparse grit inclusions, possibly from same vessel as item 4 above. External surface, patchy buff to red buff; internally covered with encrustation. Core grey.

Decoration: Deep finger-pinching set out in rows.

6 Rusticated Beaker. Nine wall sherds of well-fired paste with grit and sparse grog inclusions, patchy buff to pinkish buff both faces, with light grey core. Internal surface shows tooling with a blunt instrument.

Decoration: Light finger-nail/finger-pinching to form roughly horizontal rows of widely spaced impressions. Some of the sherds are heavily weathered.

7 Rusticated Beaker. Base angle, paste similar to item 6 above, but more patchy grey internally.

Decoration: Finger-pinching set out in horizontal rows.

8 ?Rusticated bowl. Base angle, paste similar to item 6 above.

Decoration: internally, finger-tip impressions. Externally, shallow incised chevron.

9 Fragments of one or more triangular clay weights, one fragment retaining perforation.

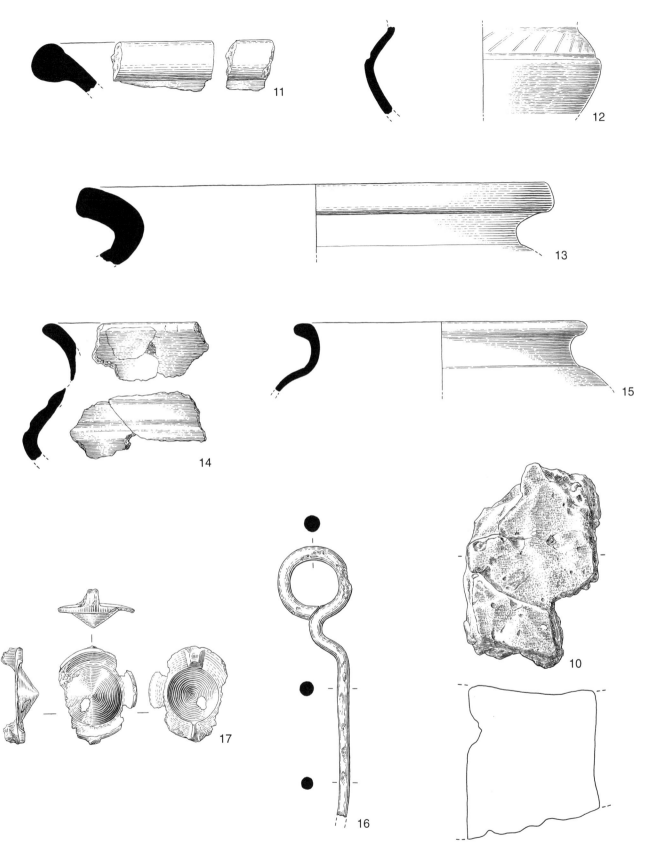

Fig. 18 Estover, March: Late Iron Age briquetage (10), Late Iron Age/early Roman pottery (11–15), Late Bronze Age/Early Iron Age pin (16) and Roman brooch (17) (scale 1:2 except 16–17 = 1:1).

IRON AGE–ROMAN POTTERY (Fig. 18)

Ditch (0173) (See 16, p. 53)
A ditch with Late Iron Age pottery, and briquetage.

10 Briquetage stand. Coarse fabric with numerous flint and pebble inclusions, fired buff on the external surfaces and red in the core.

Ditch (0315) of droveway (See 36, p. 55)
11 Rim of jar in gritty reddish fabric with grey core, wheelturned. Best paralleled at Stonea Camp, *c.* AD 40–60. Lower silt.

12 Carinated jar with diagonal lines on the carination. Gritty grey-brown surfaces, reddish core, flint temper. As Coldham, Period I (Neronian–Flavian: Potter 1965). Middle fill.

Ditch (0253) of droveway (See 29, p. 55)
13 Rim of jar in gritty reddish-brown fabric with grey core, wheel-turned. (See item 11 above.)

14 Ripple-shouldered jar in soft reddish-brown fabric with grey core. Cf. from Fison Way, Thetford, Gregory 1991, Fig. 143, 85 (Claudio-Neronian).

15 Hard, gritty, dark grey ware.

METAL FINDS (Fig. 18)

16 Ring-headed bronze pin, with swan's neck. Undecorated. Late Bronze Age/Early Iron Age. Unstratified.

17 Bronze plate-brooch with conical centre (Catherine Johns).

The brooch is a circular plate-brooch, 2.3 cm in diameter, with a raised conical centre surrounded by a flange which has a small upstanding rim. The object is extensively damaged. It has the remains of a simple hinge and catchplate, and there are no apparent traces of surface decoration.

Brooches of this type are of Middle Empire date, and according to Hattatt (1987, 185) are more common in Gaul than in Britain. His nos 1068–9, from 'South Dorset' and 'Kent' respectively are good parallels. There is surely also a connection with a common and more elaborate Romano-British type, the larger oval or less commonly circular plate-brooches gilded on the front and tinned on the reverse which are set with a conical glass gem.

Unstratified.

ANIMAL BONES Mark Beech

Preliminary analysis of the March animal bones revealed a total of 675 fragments. A very limited faunal range was represented. Cattle were by far the most commonly occurring species, followed (in decreasing numbers) by sheep/goat, dog, horse, pig and bird. Due to the sample size, and the presence of a limited range of species, only a preliminary analysis was deemed necessary.

Acknowledgements

We would like to thank all those who worked on the Estover excavation and post-excavation work, including Mark Beech, Louise Edwards, Nick Elsdon, John Fletcher, Lynn Gardiner, Jenny Hall, Martin Locock, Ian Mayes and Helen Smith; Varian Denham and John Hinchliffe for support during and after the excavation; Dr Ian Longworth, Catherine Johns and Val Rigby for looking at the pottery, and Steve Crummy for work on the publication drawings.

5

EXCAVATIONS AT STONEA GRANGE

Ralph Jackson

PART I THE EXCAVATIONS

SITE PHASES

0	Neolithic–Early Bronze Age
I	Late Bronze Age–Early Iron Age
Ia	Middle–Late Iron Age
II	Late Iron Age–Early Roman
III	Roman, *c.* AD 140–220
IV	Roman, *c.* AD 220–400
V	Early Anglo–Saxon, fifth–seventh century
Va	Middle–Late Anglo-Saxon, eighth–tenth century
VI	Medieval–Recent, mostly eighteenth–nineteenth century

RECORDING SYSTEM

The main site was located in the large field to the south of Stonea Grange Farm (TL 449937) (Fig. 19; Pl. Xa). As the principal farmyard buildings were inconveniently distant, the excavation recording grid was tied in to the large concrete-based glasshouse (which is marked on the 1979 Ordnance Survey 25 in map) and, in the absence of other durable landmarks, to the row of posts carrying a power line approximately north–south past the west side of the site. The survey of the machine-cut trenches was tied in both to the glasshouse and to the barn on the north side of the farmyard. A Temporary Bench Mark was established on one of the power-line posts and keyed in to the Bench Mark at the north-west corner of the barn (4.77 m AOD). The recording grid, based on a 5 or 10 m unit, was aligned approximately on the Cardinal Points. Sectional site plans were drawn at a scale of 1:50 with detailed plans at 1:10 or 1:20, and site masterplans at 1:100 and 1:200. Main sections were drawn at 1:20, smaller sections at 1:10. Each context on the main site was allotted a unique dual code comprising a unit number and a lettered code for the associated artefacts, e.g. 1820/DOH. The trench contexts were serially numbered and prefixed by their trench letter code, e.g. J4, 1. The contexts are listed on pp. 747–9.

On the main site, the Roman settlement comprised a number of plots demarcated by a street grid and drainage system. These plots have been adapted for recording purposes and are referred to throughout this report as 'blocks 1–11' (key, Fig. 45, p. 107).

MACHINE-CUT TRENCHES

(Figs 19–21)

When the extensive nature of the Roman site became apparent a strategy of area sampling by machine-cut trenches was adopted in order to supplement the results from the main excavation. The trenches were cut to a standard width of 1.8 m by use of a broad, toothless bucket of that size mounted on the back-actor of a JCB. Once the overburden had been machined off to the ploughsoil base, the exposed surface was hand-cleaned, following which features were planned and selected examples excavated. Although the limitations of this technique were appreciated it was considered, nevertheless, an economic and potentially fruitful method, especially where specific landscape features or hypotheses were to be tested. In the event the results in both 1983 and 1984 proved it to be a most worthwhile exercise.

The cutting of trenches B, C and D in 1983 were designed to establish the western extent of the Roman settlement. That the excavation edge lay close to the western limit of the settlement was implied by 1) the sparseness of ploughsoil finds; 2) the configuration of the local topography – a gentle downward slope away from the relatively elevated position of building R1; and 3) the fact that the wastewater drainage channels from the R1 building complex debouched into the area to the west of the excavation. As it transpired, the results from trenches B–D provided strong support for this view. Apart from the presence of a section of street 1 E/W at the north end of trench D, the trenches were devoid of features and finds other than a number of undated gullies. This paucity of remains is in marked contrast to the dense distribution of features and finds in the trenches to the east of the excavation, and it is evident that the built-up area of the settlement did not extend west of building R1.

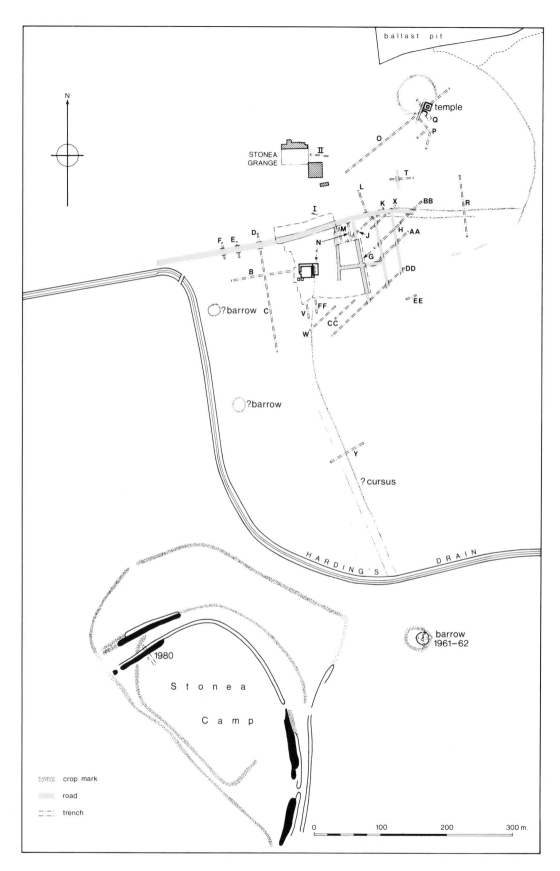

Fig. 19 Stonea: simplified plan of the main excavated areas at Stonea Grange and Stonea Camp.

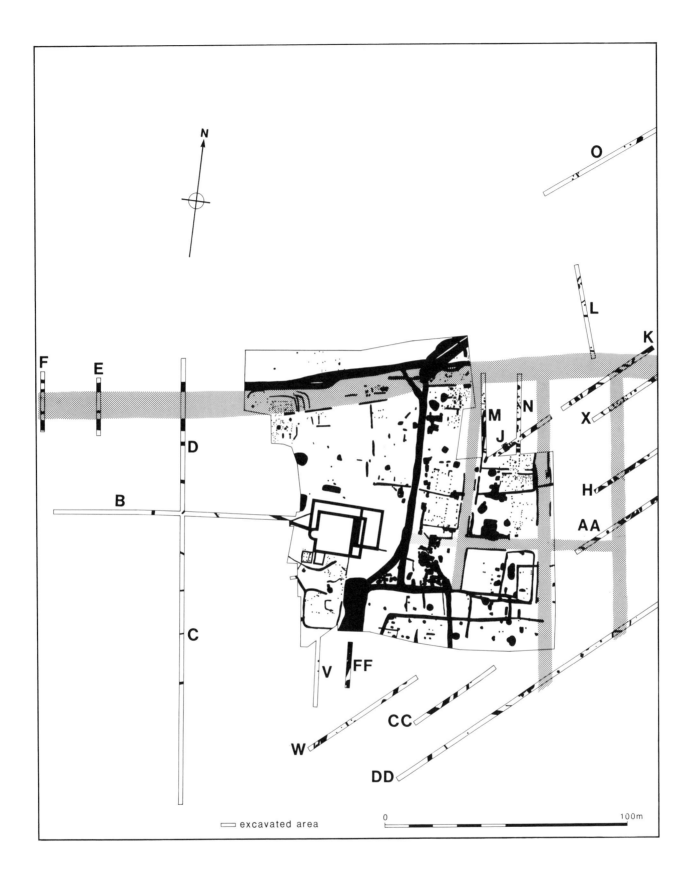

Fig. 20 Stonea Grange: simplified all-period plan of the main excavation and west trenches.

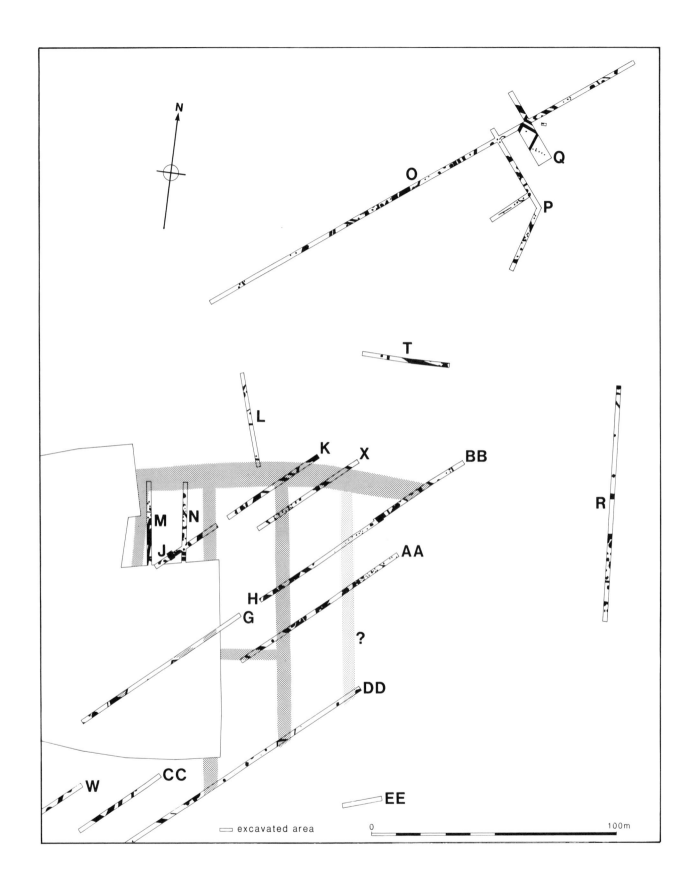

Fig. 21 Stonea Grange: simplified all-feature plan of the east trenches in relation to the main excavation.

One component that did continue to the west was street 1 E/W, as was ascertained by trenches D, E and F (see p. 74). Significantly, it was provided with flanking ditches to both north and south, whereas within the excavation area there was a north ditch only. The east butt of the south ditch must have lain between trench D and the west edge of the excavation, and that point probably marked the formal western limit of the settlement, beyond which the 'urban' role of street 1 E/W was replaced by that of a 'rural' road.

An interesting and salutary demonstration of both the successes and the potential pitfalls and distortions of machine trenching was provided by trench G. This trench, together with trenches H, J and K, was cut in 1983 in order to test the extent of the site to the east of the main excavation. In 1984 trench G was incorporated in the excavation area, and it was thus possible to discern how well the features located in the trench reflected their surrounding remains (cf. Figs 20–1). The data recovery proved to be good, with recognition of almost all the features subsequently disclosed on full excavation – streets, enclosure gullies and a well. However, fortuitously, the trench passed through one of the emptiest plots on the site – the west part of block 8 – and without the benefit of full excavation it would have been impossible to interpret correctly the context of the features, other than demonstrating the street grid. Thus, while the remains in trenches J, K, X, H, BB and AA signal, by their concentration, activity probably at least as intense as that in block 8 (trench G), the precise form of that activity cannot be confidently predicted. Nevertheless, they demonstrate that the settlement continued eastwards a considerable distance and that the street grid comprised at least one more east–west component and probably two further north–south components.

While trenches J, M and N disclosed a high density of features at the northern end of the settlement (block 10), trenches W, CC, DD and EE revealed a tailing off of activity beyond the south edge of the excavation. Though not as sparse as the evidence from trenches B–D it tended to confirm the indications in blocks 6 and 7 of a gradual shift from streets and houses to ditched enclosures, paddocks and fields.

Trenches V, W and FF were sited to define the form of the massive cut feature at the south-east of the excavation. They proved conclusively that it comprised a pair of huge pits or sumps and not the end of a waterway as had been postulated in 1983 (see pp. 87–94).

Trench Y was intended to clarify a pair of parallel ditches, extending perhaps 500 m to the south of the main site, which were identified on aerial photographs. The results were, unfortunately, inconclusive (see p. 68).

Equally inconclusive was the evidence from trench R which was located on the projected eastern route of street 1 E/W some 160 m east of the excavation. No certain metalling was found, though two parallel ditches (R10 and R24) were conceivably the flanking road drains.

The most spectacular results came from trenches O, P, Q and T, which were designed to locate and reveal a concentric-ringed cropmark feature observed during aerial survey, to sample an area to its west, and to test an apparent approach road to the south. The feature proved to be a temple complex (building R15), which is fully discussed later (pp. 214–21).

PHASE 0   (Figs 23, 26)

NEOLITHIC–EARLY BRONZE AGE

Early prehistoric activity in the vicinity of the excavations was already known from previous work. One of two round barrows to the south and south-west was sampled in 1961–2 (Potter 1976) and revealed Early Bronze Age burials in a tumulus sealing Neolithic occupation. A third round barrow, to the west of the excavation area (see Fig. 19) was discovered when the site was flown in 1984, but it was not excavated. In addition, the surface finds from Stonea Camp and Stonea Grange included a fine Ficron handaxe (Fig. 9) and a polished stone axehead (Fig. 80, no. 11, p. 244).

As it transpired, the excavation yielded very few finds and features of Neolithic and Early Bronze Age date. Although that suggests only small-scale activity, it is possible that some remains were obliterated by the intensity of Roman occupation on the site. The worked flints include leaf and triangular arrowheads, scrapers, piercer and knife (Fig. 80), while the ceramic component comprised single sherds from an Ebbsfleet style bowl and a Beaker (Fig. 81, p. 246). All these finds were in residual contexts. Just two features are regarded as belonging to this phase. One is part of a gully system of modest proportions; the other is a substantial ditch apparently of very considerable length, which, if correctly interpreted, may have been part of a cursus (Pls VIII–IX).

Gully 37   (Fig. 25)   Phase 0?

An indistinct shallow gully running approximately east–west from centre north of block 5, across street 1 N/S, to the south-west edge of block 9. There is a northward extension near the north-east corner of block 5. Neither the ends of the main east–west gully nor the north end of the extension was located. The west end was cut away by the pit complex 822 etc; the north end was cut away by the pit complex 1844 etc; and the east end was cut away by gully 31 and pit complex 1975 etc. A prehistoric date is probable given the composition of the fill, the lack of finds and the relationship with other features.

Main gully: width 0.8–1.1 m, length at least 16 m.

North extension: width c. 0.7 m, length at least 1.6 m.

Fill 1793 (DNE) Light grey, compact, sandy silt, with very few stones and some iron-pan staining.

Dating evidence No finds.

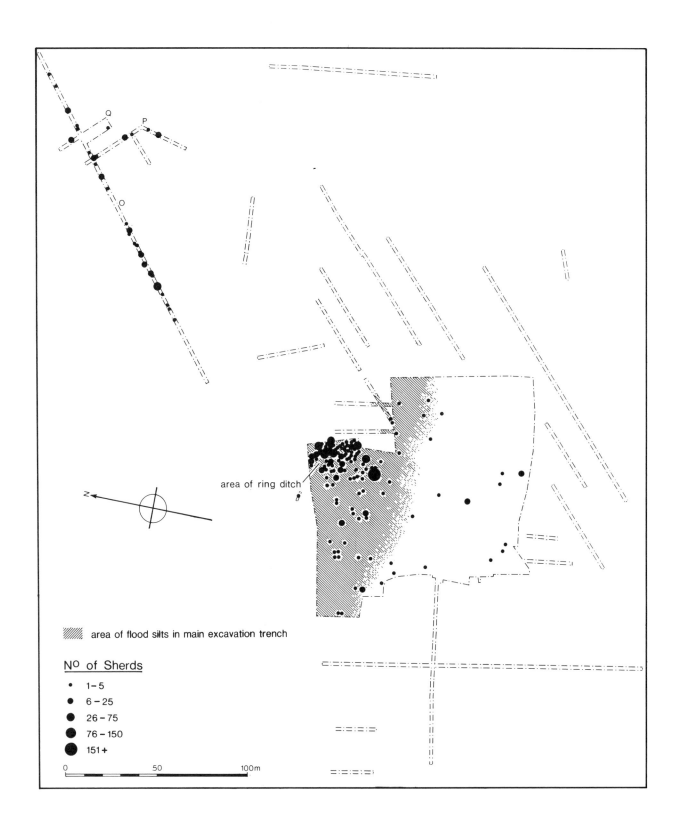

Fig. 22 Stonea Grange: distribution of Late Bronze Age and Iron Age pottery in relation to the extent of flood silts.

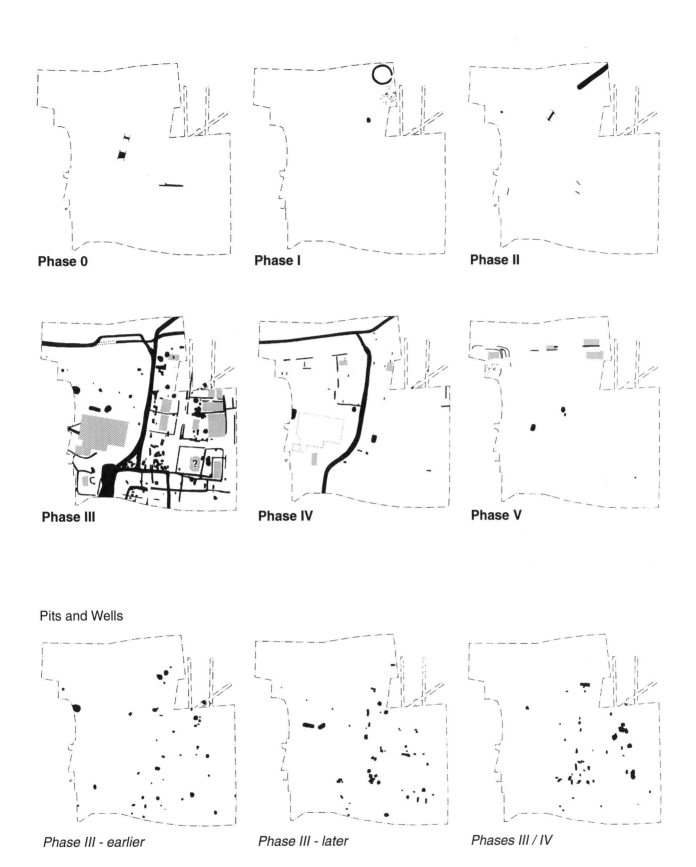

Phase 0

Phase I

Phase II

Phase III

Phase IV

Phase V

Pits and Wells

Phase III - earlier

Phase III - later

Phases III / IV

Fig. 23 Stonea Grange: phase plans.

Ditch 75 (Fig. 29a) Phase 0

A large ditch of broad U-shaped cross-section with a flat base. Initially identified from air photographs of the area to the south of the main site, ditch 75 was believed to be one of a pair of parallel ditches, possibly a cursus, with an approximate north–south alignment. Trench Y was cut 230 m south of the main excavation edge to locate and section this feature (Fig. 19). In the event, one ditch (the westernmost) proved to be illusory (or discontinuous) and no other feature was located with which ditch 75 could be shown to be contemporaneous. Part of the upper fill was cut by a modern drainage ditch (Y1, layers 1 and 2) with a ceramic pipe in the base. From the air photographs it appeared that the southern end of the double-ditched feature was sighted on the round barrow to the east of Stonea Camp (Potter 1976). The northern end appeared to swing eastwards and pass across the area of the main excavation, and it is possible that ditch 74 in block 1 (see pp. 146–7) is part of ditch 75.

Width 3.7 m, ?length *c.* 500 m, depth 1.02 m.

Fill Y1, layer 3. Orange and grey clay.

Dating evidence No finds.

PHASE I (Figs 23, 26)

LATE BRONZE AGE–EARLY IRON AGE

In 1982 and 1983 an area of later prehistoric occupation was located in the north-east corner of the excavation. The portion sampled included a dense but unintelligible scatter of post-holes, a ring-gully 13 m in diameter, a large pit or well, and an unurned cremation set in a small pit. Although subsequent activity, most notably the complex of Roman ditches, had severely damaged and truncated the prehistoric features and levels, sufficient remained, especially in the relatively undisturbed strip of land sealed beneath the main Roman east–west road (street 1 E/W), to discern a partial stratigraphic sequence: the features were cut into a thin layer of distinctive green-grey silt, perhaps representing a brief phase of alluviation, and were themselves sealed by the layer of grey silt which extended over the whole of the north part of the excavated site (Fig. 22).

Both the features and the grey silt above them yielded a sizeable assemblage of pottery as well as worked flint and stone and a few bronzes (Figs 81–7, pp. 246–58). Together with pottery and bronze artefacts from residual contexts and bronzes from the Stonea Grange Surface Collection they indicate a period of activity within, and probably throughout, the ninth–sixth century BC; while the form of the cremation and a ^{14}C determination of its charcoal component point to a date somewhat earlier than *c.* 1000 BC. Given that the remains of this phase of occupation were fragmentary and only partially sampled and that their main focus probably lay beyond the north-east corner of the excavated area, it is likely that further investigation would reveal an extensive settlement.

Post-holes

Fill Dark grey or green-grey silt with an occasional admixture of charcoal flecks or gravel.

a Within ring-gully

1345 (CPK) Sub-rectangular: 0.35 × 0.30 m. Contained LBA pottery.
1r382 (CQY) Rectangular: 0.18 × 0.15 m.
1383 (CQZ) Rectangular: 0.25 × 0.20 m.

b East and south of ring-gully

1199 (CIH) Rectangular: 0.25 × 0.20 m.
1103 (CEH) ?Sub-rectangular: *c.* 0.45 × 0.35 m. Contained LBA pottery.
1106 (CEL) Rectangular: 0.20 × 0.18 m. Contained LBA pottery.
1117 (CEX) Rectangular: 0.20 × 0.18 m.
1119 (CEZ) Rectangular: 0.25 × 0.20 m. Contained LBA pottery.
1435 (CTD) Sub-rectangular: 0.22 × 0.22 m.
1436 (CTE) Sub-rectangular: 0.20 × 0.15 m.
1434 (CTC) Sub-rectangular: 0.25 × 0.20 m.
1433 (CTB) Sub-rectangular: 0.25 × 0.20 m. Contained LBA pottery.
1325 (COO) Sub-rectangular: 0.20 × 0.20 m.
1320 (COI) Sub-rectangular: 0.35 × 0.25 m.
1278 (CMP) Sub-rectangular: 0.18 × 0.15 m.
1310 (CNY) Round: 0.15 m.
1439 (CTH) Ovoid: 0.27 × 0.25 m.
1324 (CON) Square: 0.15 m.
1319 (COH) Round: 0.15 m.
1318 (COG) Round: 0.13 m.
1323 (COM) Square: 0.15 m.
1185 (CHS) Round: 0.20 m.
1308 (CNW) Square: 0.30 m. Contained LBA pottery.
1317 (COF) Double post-hole. i) Round: 0.17 m. ii) Round: 0.10 m.
1316 (COE) Ovoid: 0.35 × 0.25 m.
1315 (COD) Ovoid: 0.40 × 0.32 m. Contained LBA pottery.
1309 (CNX) Double post-hole. i) Square: 0.33 m. ii) Square: 0.22 m.
1275 (CMM) Sub-rectangular: 0.30 × 0.28 m.
1381 (CQX) Ovoid: 0.50 × 0.45 m.
1368 (CQI) Ovoid: 0.48 × 0.38 m. Contained LBA pottery.
1369 (CQK) Square: 0.20 m. Contained LBA pottery.
1359 (CPZ) Square: 0.28 m. Contained LBA pottery.
1380 (CQW) Sub-rectangular: 0.33 × 0.25 m. Contained LBA pottery.
1370 (CQL) Round: 0.24 m.
1327 (COQ) Square: 0.23 m.
1431 (CSZ) Round: 0.20 m.
1394 (CRL) Round: 0.20 m. Contained LBA pottery.
1393 (CRK) Round: 0.18 m.
1392 (CRI) Round: 0.21 m. Contained LBA pottery.
1391 (CRH) Round: 0.28 m.
1398 (CRP) Round: 0.19 m.

Pit 920 (BIX) E23.1, N53.6 (Fig. 29b; Fig. 50, p. 150) Phase I

A large, deep, sub-rectangular pit or well, cut by the Roman pits 966 and 990.

Width 2.45 m, length 2.7 m (excavation incomplete: original length *c.* 3.7 m), depth 0.95 m (possibly deeper: actual base not definitely found)

Fill

920 (BIX) Grey silty clay with green inclusions, small pebbles and flecks of tile and charcoal.

928 (BKF) Grey silt with iron-pan staining and charcoal flecks.

957 (BLL) Mixed yellow-orange silts with flecks of charcoal.

981 (BML) Dark grey silty loam with flecks of charcoal.

Dating evidence

920 (BIX) Post Deverel–Rimbury sherds; NVCC types 20/21, 3.2.; NVGW types 47, 27; NVSC type 65; buff ware cf. types 63, 57. Date: 3rd century.

928 (BKF) Post Deverel–Rimbury sherds. 9th–6th century BC.

957 (BLL) Post Deverel–Rimbury sherds. 9th–6th century BC.

981 (BML) Post Deverel–Rimbury sherds. 9th–6th century BC.

Small finds

920 Copper-alloy object (SF 385)

957 Copper-alloy ring-like object, Needham cat. no. 9 (SF 418).

The sequence is:

1 928/957/981, prehistoric pit fill, 9th–6th century BC.

2 920, Roman fill in sinkage/slump of prehistoric fill, 3rd century AD.

3 966, 990, Roman pits cutting edge of prehistoric pit, later 2nd/3rd century AD.

Pit 927 (BKE) E22.9, N45.8 (Fig. 50) ?Phase I/II

A small irregularly-shaped pit, at the south edge of block 2. Width 0.5 m, length *c.* 1.0 m, depth *c.* 0.2 m.

Fill (BKE) Dark grey silt with patches of yellow clay, with small pebbles and flecks of charcoal.

Dating evidence No datable material. Probably Phase I/II

Pit 1909 (DSA)/1968 (DVM) See p. 202

Gully 1 (Figs 25, 30b, 49) Phase I

A narrow, shallow penannular gully at the east end of block 11. One butt remains, but the second, together with most of the south-west and north-east sections, has been cut away by later ditches. The enclosed circular space is likewise almost completely obliterated by later features, and post-hole 1345 and, perhaps, post-holes 1382 and 1383, are likely to be the sole survivors of a contemporaneous structure in the interior.

Width 0.9–1.0 m. Diameter: int. 11.0 m; ext. 13.0 m. Depth 0.3–0.45 m.

Fill

Cut 1 1140 (CFW) Light grey silt with pebbles.

Cut 2 1303 (CNQ) Dark grey silt with pebbles, small stones and charcoal flecks.
1321 (COK) Grey silt with pebbles.

Cut 3 1104 (CEI) As cut 2, 1303.
1125 (CFF) Dark grey/black silt with clods of yellow clay and pebbles. [The north butt]

Cut 4 1348 (CPN) Mixed grey-green silts. A cleaning spit above 1384.
1384 (CRA) As cut 2, 1303.

Cut 5 1095 (CDZ) Dark grey silt. A cleaning spit above 1374.
1374 (CQP) Light grey-green silt.

Cut 6 1329 (COS) Grey silt with much gravel. A cleaning spit above 1139.
1139 (CFV) Light grey silt with pebbles.

Dating evidence Post Deverel–Rimbury pottery.

Small finds

1374 Flint scraper, Varndell cat. no. 4 (SF 604).

1384 Rubbing stone, Varndell cat. no. 12 (SF 645).

Pit 1360 (CQA): the Bronze Age cremation
Stuart Needham

One feature within the Late Bronze Age post-hole complex at the north-east corner of the main site (Fig. 49, p. 111) contained a human cremation, but no accompanying artefacts. The feature, 1360/CQA, was a small, circular, vertical-sided pit 0.55 m in diameter, with a lightly hollowed base. It was cut into the same green-grey silt surface as the post-hole complex and was sealed by the dark grey silt layer 1122. Its top was eroded and the maximum surviving depth was 0.15 m. The basal 3 cm was filled with a grey-brown silt, but above that was a deposit of black silt with an approximately 75% component of charcoal and cremated bone. The charcoal was submitted for radiocarbon dating and yielded a measurement of 2910 ± 90 bp (BM-2445). On calibration this gives a date range of *c.* 1280–900 cal BC at one sigma (68% probability) or *c.* 1400–870 cal BC at two sigma (95% probability). The charcoal therefore dates to the later Middle Bronze Age or the early part of the Late Bronze Age, with a higher probability attached to the former. It would seem most likely that this is an isolated burial within the Deverel–Rimbury/Ardleigh tradition, pre-*circa* 1100 cal BC. A good proportion of burials in that tradition are unaccompanied cremations, lacking even an urn container (Erith and Longworth 1960; Ellison 1980). This feature would appear to predate the early first millennium BC settlement activity nearby (see p. 68) although it was associated with the same buried land surface.

The cremated bone Janice Conheeney

Cranial	55.1 g
Upper limb	21.3 g
Lower limb	16.6 g
Torso	1.8 g
Unidentified	24.7 g
Total weight	119.5 g

Fragment size: 3 mm min. to 34 mm max.

Although some fragments are blackish and 'charcoally', indicating that they were not fully oxidised, most are of similar range – patchy blue, white and black – suggesting they were all burnt under similar conditions. There is nothing to suggest the remains are those of more than one individual, and the size, especially the cranial thickness, implies an adult. The average weight of a complete, cremated adult is about 3000 g according to McKinley (1989). The present cremation, at only 119.5 g falls far short of that figure. Furthermore, McKinley states that the cranium should make up about 18.2% of the total weight of the cremated remains, whereas the cranial fragments of the present cremation comprise over 46% of the total weight. Although selection may have occurred at burial, a more probable explanation is that the greater part of the cremation was lost through post-depositional disturbance: like the post-holes cut into the same land surface the upper part of the cremation burial pit was evidently truncated.

PHASE Ia

MIDDLE–LATE IRON AGE

One of the most remarkable objects in the Stonea Grange Surface Collection is a small bronze attachment in the form of a duck (Fig. 89, no. 1, p. 263). It was one of the first pieces to be shown to the writers by the finder in September 1980, and it signalled the possibility of Middle Iron Age activity in the general area of the excavation, for its form and style of decoration suggested a date perhaps as early as the late fourth/early third century BC. In the event, it was not until the final (1984) season of excavation that traces of occupation of this period were encountered, not on the main site, but in trenches O, P and Q.

These trenches were designed to locate and elucidate the circular ditched enclosure observed during aerial survey and to test the intervening area between the enclosure and the main site. The enclosure proved to be that of a Romano-Celtic temple, but excepting that complex (building R15: see pp. 214–21) Roman features were virtually absent, and the mass of features – pits, ditches, gullies and post-holes – were associated with plain and decorated handmade pottery of Middle–Late Iron Age date, as well as a small quantity of Late Bronze Age/Early Iron Age wares (see Fig. 86, nos 51–5, p. 253 and Fig. 88 nos 1 and 4, p. 261). Lack of time and resources prevented anything more than the sampling of a few pits and gullies, but the heavy concentration of features suggests that trenches O, P and Q transected a major focus of Iron Age activity which may have been the direct descendant of the LBA/EIA settlement some 150 m to the south-west.

The features as located were all truncated, comprising only their base and lower sides, and their fill was hardly differentiated from the grey-black silt – in places nearly a metre thick – which sealed them. This silt is ill-understood geomorphologically but may be a product of alluviation (see French, pp. 222–3). It sealed and/or contained the features; incorporated a similar range of Middle–Late Iron Age pottery, as well as a few early Roman finds; and was cut by (or possibly sealed) the wooden building which preceded the Phase III temple (building R15) (see Fig. 74, unit Q23, 1, p. 216). If, as seems likely, the wooden predecessor to building R15 was also of religious character, then a settlement of some importance is implied. Certainly, other finds in the Surface Collection indicate a degree of prosperity. Most notable are two terrets and a fine strap union (Fig. 89, nos 2–4, p. 263), which are broadly contemporary with the ceramic assemblage. Conclusive evidence is lacking, but continuity of settlement at Stonea Grange between the Late Bronze Age and the Roman period seems probable.

Pit O9   Phase Ia

A large, shallow, rectangular pit in trench O, aligned approximately north–south. Its north-west corner and south side lay outside the trench edges.

Width 2.1 m, length at least 3.5 m, depth 0.25 m.

Fill O9, 1. Dark grey-brown peaty silt.

Dating evidence Four sherds pre-Roman pottery.

Pit O33   Phase Ia

A sub-circular pit in trench O.

Diameter 1.3 m, depth *c*. 0.3 m.

Fill O33, 1. Grey silt with gravel and flecks of burnt earth.

Dating evidence Twenty-five sherds pre-Roman pottery.

Pit O36   Phase Ia

A sub-rectangular pit in trench O, aligned approximately north–south. Its south side lay outside the trench edge. Unexcavated.

Width 1.1 m, length at least 1.3 m.

Fill O36, 1. Grey silt with gravel.

Dating evidence Three sherds pre-Roman pottery.

Pit O72   Phase Ia

A shallow sub-rectangular pit in trench O, aligned approximately NW–SE, to the east of the temple complex. Its south-east side lay outside the trench edge.

Width 2.6 m, length at least 1.35 m, depth 0.2 m.

Fill O72, 1. Grey silt with gravel, patches of burnt earth, and a large quantity of light grey ashy material.

Dating evidence Two sherds pre-Roman pottery.

Gully 79

A very shallow gully, aligned approximately north–south in trench O, sealed by amorphous black silts. Lies parallel to gully 80.

Width 1.1 m, length unknown, depth 0.12 m.

Fill O11, layer 1. Brown-black silt with gravel.

Dating evidence One sherd LBA/EIA pottery.

Gully 80

A shallow gully aligned approximately north–south in trench O, sealed by amorphous black silts. Lies parallel to gully 79.

Width 1.2 m, length unknown, depth 0.25 m.

Fill O12, layer 1. Brown-black silt with gravel.

Dating evidence Thirty-six sherds coarse ware, mainly pre-Roman; NVCC. NVGW. Date: AD 125 or later.

Gully 81

A shallow gully, aligned approximately east–west, in trench O, sealed by amorphous black silts. Lies parallel to gully 82. It is possible that gully 81 is part of gully 80 and that gully 82 is part of gully 79.

Width 0.9 m, length unknown, depth 0.12 m.

Fill O14, layer 1. Grey-black silt with gravel.

Dating evidence Nine sherds LBA/IA pottery.

Gully 82

A shallow gully, aligned approximately east–west, in trench O, sealed by amorphous black silts. Lies parallel to gully 81. Possibly the same as gully 79.

Width 0.7 m, length unknown, depth 0.18 m.

Fill O15, layer 1. Grey silt with gravel.

Dating evidence None.

PHASE II (Figs 23, 26)

LATE IRON AGE–EARLY ROMAN

Immediately prior to the Phase III development the main site appears to have been virtually uninhabited. However, there is a little evidence for activity, if not occupation. In the north-east corner of block 1 a ditch or large pit was revealed late in the 1983 excavation. It had been levelled first in Phase III, with a layer of redeposited clay (unit 1421), and then again in Phase IV, when its subsided fill was sealed with a capping of clay and stones (unit 1400). Neither the ends nor the base of the feature was reached, but the lowest layer to be excavated (unit 1422) yielded a pottery assemblage of first century AD date (Rigby, pp. 260–2). The very small quantity of late second century AD pottery within unit 1422 was doubtless incorporated just before or at the time of the initial levelling of the part-filled feature, when the site was being prepared for construction of the R1 complex.

Less closely dated, but probably contemporary, were ditch 2 and hearth 422. The former, a large ditch at the north-east corner of the site with a south-west butt some 18 m inside the excavation, comprised a broad, flat-bottomed ditch with virtually no datable finds. The fill of its secondary phase, a V-sectioned recut, incorporated very small amounts of second–third century AD pottery and glass; but the relationships with adjacent features indicate that the primary ditch, at least, was cut in Phase II.

Similarly lacking in finds was hearth 422, a small clay-lined structure in the north-west corner of block 1. Probably for smelting or smithing, it had been destroyed before being sealed by the grey-brown silt layer 364. Despite its fire-reddened wall bases and ashy fill no industrial waste remained to identify its function. Finally, parts of two small gullies (38, 39) and a possible beam slot (92/431), the latter sealed by part of the Phase III building R1, appear to have belonged to Phase II.

In addition to the pottery from ditch 69, pit 520 and silt layer 268 (Fig. 88, nos 5–8, p. 261), a number of finds from the excavations and from the Surface Collection support the evidence for first century AD activity. These include Iron Age and early Roman coins (Chadburn cat. nos 1–61; Shotter cat. nos 1–2, Table 14 and pp. 294–6), several brooches (Mackreth cat. nos 1–7) and a few sherds of South Gaulish samian (Johns cat. nos 1–4). Such activity, though its exact nature is uncertain, is likely to relate to contemporaneous use of, and occupation around, Stonea Camp and, perhaps, to the structure(s) which preceded the Phase III temple (building R15).

?Beam slot 92 (DZ)/431 (WT) (Fig. 58, p. 120) Phase II

A narrow, vertical-sided slot cut into the grey silt natural (unit 86) beneath the small hypocausted room of building R1. It ran approximately north–south and was partially sealed by two *pila* bases, while its north end continued beneath the redeposited 'platform clay' of building R1. The south end was not traced.

Width 0.27 m, length at least 4.6 m.

Fill Yellow clayey silt with charcoal flecks.

Dating evidence No finds.

Hearth 422 (WJ)
N56.65, W30.85 (Fig. 48, p. 110) Phase II(?)

A small pear-shaped hearth, probably a metal-working furnace, near the north-west corner of the site. Only the base survived, the upper part having been truncated and sealed by about 0.25 m of the grey-brown silt layer 364, which incorporates pottery of fourth century AD date. The broader end preserved the base of a fire-reddened clay lining some 2–3 cm thick. The floor of the narrower end, evidently the flue/access, sloped up to its tapered terminal.

Max. width 0.45 m, length 0.85 m, surviving depth 0.13 m.

Fill Grey-black ashy silt.

Dating evidence No finds.

Ditch 69 (Figs 25, 46, 50) Phase II

A wide ditch (or, more probably, a large pit), sectioned but not bottomed, in the north-east corner of block 1.

Width 6.2 m, length unknown, depth unknown.

Fill
1400 (CRR) Yellow clay with stones and tile.
1421 (CSO) Mixture redeposited natural clay.
1422 (CSP) Grey silt with charcoal flecks and shell fragments.

Dating evidence
Layer 1400: NVCC type 25/26. Date: mid/late 3rd century AD.
Layer 1422: 1st century AD wares; NVGW; grey wares. Date: 1st century AD with a small quantity of intrusive late 2nd century.

Layers 1400 and 1421, and possibly part of 1422, are backfill/levelling/sealing layers. Layer 1422 and the layers (unexcavated) beneath are thus of earlier date, almost certainly associated with the 1st century pottery.

Ditch 2 (Figs 25–6, 29–30, 49) Phase II(?)

A broad, deep ditch in the north-east corner of the site. It is aligned SW–NE and forms a butt at its south-west end. The primary ditch is steep-sided with a flat base; in its secondary phase it is of V-section with a rectangular basal slot. It cuts gully 1, and is cut by ditches 3, 6, 12, 13 and 14.

Width: primary c. 3.8 m; secondary c. 3.6 m. Length at least 18 m.
Depth: primary 1.25 m; secondary 1.10 m.

Fill
Cut 1 [Butt]
    1136 (CFR) Grey-green silt with pebbles = 1366 (CQG)
    1371 (CQM) Fine grey silt.
    1388 (CRE) Redeposited natural clay and gravels.
Cut 2 1137 (CFS) As cut 1, 1136.
Cut 3 [Secondary phase]
    1080 (CDI) Green-brown silt with large stones and pebbles.
    1101 (CEF) Grey silt.
    [Primary phase]
    1127 (CFH) Dark grey silt with much gravel.
    1126 (CFG) As cut 1, 1388.
    1189 (CHX) Grey silt and pebbles.
Cut 4 [Secondary phase]
    1296 (CNI) Light brown pebbly silt.
    1336 (CPA) Grey silt [a spit, part of 1343]
    1343 (CPH) Grey silt
    1350 (CPP) Grey/green silt.
    1353 (CPS) Dark grey silt with many oyster shells.
    [Primary phase]
    1272 (CMI) Grey silt with much gravel and pebbles.
    1326 (COP) As cut 1, 1388.

Dating evidence Later prehistoric pottery in units 1136, 1137, 1296, 1336, 1350, 1353. Very small quantities of second–third century Roman pottery – 10 g and less – in 1137, 1080, 1296, 1353, 1272, 1326 are probably contamination.

Small finds
1350 Glass vessel fragment, Price cat. no 11 (SF 598).
1353 Glass vessel fragment, Price cat. no 11 (SF 597).

Gully 38 See p. 176

Gully 39 See p. 176

PHASES III–IV (Fig. 23)

III: c. AD 140–220
IV: c. AD 220–400

During the main Roman period of occupation the excavated part of the Stonea Grange site comprised two distinct zones: an approximately north–south site division, most enduringly preserved as ditch 9, separated a west sector (block 1) from an east sector (blocks 2–10) (Fig. 24). In addition, both these sectors were separated from an apparently blank north zone (block 11) by street 1 E/W.

In the earlier part of the main period (Phase III) almost the entire west sector was occupied by the extraordinary R1 stone building complex and its grounds. Concurrent with the erection and functioning of that building was the establishment of the street grid and the construction and occupation of timber buildings in the east sector (blocks 2–10). Occupation of the two sectors differed both in character and longevity, and while the grandiose official complex ceased to function early in the third century AD, the unpretentious domestic settlement to its east saw no break in activity at that time, though there was a gradual reduction in size and indications of a slackening of (or release from) central control. Thus, while Phases III and IV may be clearly differentiated on some parts of the site, notably on block 1, their distinction elsewhere is less precise, especially in those locations where occupation was relatively intense and sustained (e.g. block 9). There, as the pit groups revealed (Figs 56–7, pp. 118–19), Phase III shaded almost imperceptibly into Phase IV.

Change, though gradual, there certainly was, however, and the scattered rural appearance of the Phase IV settlement contrasts with the organised gridded 'proto-urban' layout of Phase III. Streets were encroached upon, drainage channels re-routed piecemeal and clay ovens located with scant regard for earlier plots and boundaries, while wooden houses with attached paddocks were built in the north-east quadrant of block 1 and in block 2, and an apparently more impressive building constructed over part of the levelled remains of the R1 building complex. Had it not been for recent agricultural damage the fourth century remains may have been more extensive. At all events, while proof is lacking either way, it is possible that there was no hiatus between the end of Phase IV occupation and the establishment of the Phase V Anglo-Saxon village.

THE STREET SYSTEM (Fig. 24)

The streets were very poorly preserved, and while their general alignment and dimensions were usually apparent it

Fig. 24 Stonea Grange: simplified all-period plan of the main excavation, showing street and block numeration.

was seldom possible to make precise measurements. Metalling rarely survived and streetside drains/ditches were neither invariably provided nor continuous. Nevertheless, the general lack of features within the street areas, the occasional survival of gravel metalling and the frequent presence of streetside gullies or plot boundary lines revealed a more or less regular gridded layout of streets.

For ease of reference the streets have been given a code which combines a serial number with their (approximate) alignment. Thus, those identified with certainty are: street 1 E/W, street 2 E/W, street 1 N/S and street 2 N/S.

Owing to the severe plough damage to the streets, dating evidence was minimal, and no closely-dated material was found beneath the very few surviving areas of metalling. The streets were evidently contemporary with the Phase III settlement and were probably laid out at the very start of that phase. But they equally clearly continued in use in Phase IV and beyond and must have been repaired and resurfaced on a number of occasions, events, however, for which no evidence remained.

In Phase V it was the slight but significant eminence of the surface of street 1 E/W together, presumably, with its good drainage, that caused it to be chosen as the site for a line of Anglo-Saxon houses. There, the orange gravel metalling, whether Phase III or Phase IV, was best preserved. Just one other stretch remained, on street 2 N/S where it passed to the east of block 9. Even in these cases the gravel was rarely more than one layer deep, and elsewhere the surface had gone entirely. On street 1 N/S in particular, ploughing had scoured away part of the underlying ground surface (see Pl. XVa). Nowhere was found any evidence for flanking sidewalks or colonnaded walkways.

Street 1 E/W   (Figs 46, 48–9, pp. 108–11)

The main street, perhaps broadly to be equated with the *decumanus maximus* of more formal Roman towns, is street 1 E/W. This ran across the north of the site for a distance of 95 m within the area of excavation. Its presence in the machine-cut trenches F, E, D, M, N, L, K, X and BB demonstrates that it continued at least 85 m beyond the west edge of the excavation and at least 120 m beyond the east edge, giving a total confirmed minimum length of 300 m, and aerial photographs (Pl. VIII) appear to show it continuing at least another 160 m to the east. It is highly probable that it continued as a road much further in both directions. To the west it would presumably have linked Stonea with the 'island' of March; to the east it probably connected with various settlements on the Stonea 'island'.

The line of street 1 E/W, in contrast to that of the other streets, is by no means straight, a feature probably explicable in terms of its dual role as both a 'rural' road and an 'urban' street. Reading from west to east, the first change to its

approximate east–west alignment occurs at a point almost immediately north of the main stone building complex R1, where it turns several degrees to the north. This point probably corresponded to the western edge of the settlement, for trenches B–D revealed virtually no activity to the west of the main area of excavation. The next change occurs north of the junction between blocks 1 and 2 where street 1 E/W turns back a few degrees to the south. This was a major junction separating two very different zones of the settlement. Finally, a further slight turn to the south occurs at a point some 10 m to the east of the junction with street 3 N/S. The overall impression is of a long-range road adapted to the planning requirements of the settlement, which suggests that, in its final form at least, the east–west road that incorporated street 1 E/W postdated the foundation of the Phase III settlement.

As befitted the main thoroughfare, street 1 E/W was broad – about 10 m wide, though in places it was reduced to about 7.5 m. On its south side within the main excavation area was a discontinuous gully which, though it would not have conducted water away, would have acted as a catchwater draining both the street and its margins. However, this feature appears to have been added only in Phase IV, until which time the south side was devoid of any drainage system. On the north side in the earlier part of Phase III there appears to have been a small continuous ditch (ditch 3). In common with other drainage features, however, this was replaced in the later part of Phase III by a much more substantial ditch (ditch 4), part of the main site drainage system. Ditch 4 took a rather sinuous route, kinking north near the centre of block 1 before turning south-east to pass beneath the line of the street (via ditch 5) and connect with ditch 9. Subsequently, in Phase IV, this ditch was modified and, via ditch 10, ran solely east–west, the connection with ditch 9 being blocked. Interestingly, this ditch line was maintained down to recent times when the Phase VI ditch 12 was cut along its route.

Curiously, there appears to have been no development of the street frontage on the north of street 1 E/W, where no Roman features other than the roadside ditches were found in block 11. Whether or not development there was planned, the second century settlement as it materialised was situated predominantly, if not exclusively, to the south of street 1 E/W.

Street 1 N/S   (Figs 51–2, 55–7, pp. 113–19)

This street was laid off to the south of street 1 E/W and is the most westerly of the north–south streets. Its line forms the junction between two Roman planning grids: to the west the common alignment of buildings R6 and R7, blocks 1–5 and ditch 9 conforms to that of the building complex R1; to the east the orientation of streets 2–3 N/S and the blocks to their east is several degrees different. Blocks 8–10, which lie between streets 1 and 2 N/S accommodate this difference by means of their trapezoidal plan. In addition, because street 1 N/S adopted the line of the grid to its west its junction with street 1 E/W is not set at a right angle.

Street 1 N/S was traced for a total distance of 82 m, of which almost two-thirds lay within the area of excavation. At the point where it passes the junction between blocks 3 and 4, the street appears to deviate slightly from its otherwise straight line. However, this was probably a later adjustment (later Phase III or Phase IV) rather than an original feature. Sixty-one metres south of the junction with street 1 E/W, street 1 N/S intersects with street 2 E/W. By the later part of Phase III the south terminal of the street lay some 22 m beyond this crossroads, immediately north of block 7, where gully 15 (cut 3) blocked its route (see Fig. 55, p. 117). Prior to that it is probable that it continued further south, for the primary fence-line along the west and south sides of block 5, which preceded ditches 9 and 8, did not impinge on the street, but stopped immediately to its west (see Fig. 27, Phase IIIa). This implies that, as originally planned, street 1 N/S continued southward through block 7 and beyond the excavation edge. Its course was not discerned, however, in trench CC, where a number of (later) ditches lay in its path. The apparent shrinkage of street 1 N/S in the later part of Phase III may be part of a general contraction of the settlement at that time, and the loose arrangement of blocks 6–7 probably reflects the adaptation to other uses of plots where building, if intended, never took place on anything other than the smallest scale.

Almost no metalling of street 1 N/S survived: there was a thin patchy scattering of gravel on the stretch east of block 3, but south of that point the metalling was entirely absent and the surface had been deeply scarred by recent agricultural (pan-busting) activity (see Pl. XVa). The street was identifiable, therefore, solely as a reserved zone, devoid of features, between streetside gullies and plot boundaries. Its width was most readily ascertained in the stretch flanked by block 9 and blocks 3–4, where it measured between 3.7 and 4.1 m.

Discontinuous catchwater gullies were provided on each side of the street serving, as elsewhere, to drain both the street and its flanking plots. On the west gullies 35 and 36 were cut where the street passed blocks 3 and 4. Similarly, on the east, gully 18 lay at the interface of the street and block 8. Further north, however, the situation was slightly less clearcut. A parallel series of gullies – gullies 30 and 31 – extended along the west side of blocks 9 and 10. The dating evidence was insufficiently precise to determine whether one gully replaced another or whether they were contemporaneous. The latter seems probable and may have been a response to increasingly wet conditions.

Equally uncertain is the date at which gully 29 was cut across the line of street 1 N/S (unit 1995), presumably in

the form of a recessed box drain, to join gully 35, though it would appear to have been contemporary with the similar breaching of street 2 N/S by gully 34, the east extension of gully 29. Surface indications (uninvestigated) suggested that a number of other features, probably an eastward extension of the pit complex at the south-east corner of block 3, were cut across street 1 N/S at this point. The implication is that the street had by then gone out of use, at least as a thoroughfare.

Street 2 N/S (Figs 54–7, pp. 116–19)

This street was laid off at a right angle south from street 1 E/W, about 25 m east of street 1 N/S (road centre to road centre). It forms the east access to blocks 10, 9, 8 and 7 and was traced for a minimum length of 120 m. Sixty-two metres south of the junction with street 1 E/W it intersects with street 2 E/W. Its south end was not identified: from the south of block 8 its route is unproven, there being neither metalling nor streetside gullies to confirm the negative evidence of lack of features along the course of its projected line. Nevertheless, it seems probable that as originally laid out the street continued beyond the southern side of trench DD.

The metalling on the stretch adjacent to block 9 was better preserved than that anywhere else on the minor streets. This may have been entirely fortuitous, but as block 9 was the most intensively occupied region of the site it is possible that these two things are connected. Certainly, the internal arrangement of block 9 (see Fig. 68, p. 156) would suggest that street 2 N/S rather than street 1 N/S constituted the major access to the plots within the block. As elsewhere, the metalling was orange-brown gravel in the range 0.5–2.0 cm. The street width, most readily measured along the stretch adjacent to block 9, was about 4.9 m with variations from 4.5 to 5.2 m.

Discontinuous streetside gullies were provided on both sides of the street, though slightly more extensively on the west side, as far south as the end of block 8. Beyond that they were entirely absent. As was the case with street 1 N/S, there was a pairing of gullies in several places with, apparently, separate gullies provided for the drainage of the street and for the buildings in adjacent blocks. Thus, on the west side, the streetside gully 24 was 'shadowed' by gully 18 of block 8 and by gully 29 in the north sector of block 9. On the east side the streetside gully 27 is overlapped by gully 28 opposite the northern sector of block 9.

In the area excavated, street 2 N/S was cut by very few features, all of them linear. At the south end, adjacent to block 7, the enigmatic and irregular gully 16 ran eastwards from ditch 15 (which it antedates) onto the street, where it petered out before reaching the other side. It yielded insufficient finds for close dating, but it may belong to the later part of

Phase III when street 2 N/S, like street 1 N/S, may have contracted northwards and the south part was neglected or turned over to an alternative use. Further north, adjacent to block 8, gully 26, apparently an eastward extension of gully 17, probably crossed the line of the street in the form of a recessed box-drain. Still further north, adjacent to block 9, the unexcavated gully 73 crossed the street opposite the southern arm of gully 29, with which an association is probable though incapable of proof. Immediately to its north gully 34, on a slightly more oblique line, also cut the line of the street and linked with gully 29. As with unit 1995 of gully 29, which cut the line of street 1 N/S, it is probable that gully 34 was a minor adaptation to the drainage in the latter part of Phase III.

Street 2 E/W　(Figs 55–6, pp. 117–18)

This street lies about 61 m south of street 1 E/W, with which it is approximately parallel, and is the only other known east–west aligned street of the settlement. It ran for a minimum distance of some 61 m, connecting with streets 1, 2 and 3 N/S, and may have extended further both to the west and the east. It conforms to the eastern of the two Roman grids and, therefore, while its intersection with streets 2 and 3 N/S is at right angles that with street 1 N/S is not.

Virtually no metalling survived, but its width could be measured with a good degree of accuracy between the street-side gullies 18 and 31 of blocks 8 and 9, where it was 4.1 m.

Gully 31 did not extend the full length of the southern side of block 9 but terminated about 13 m short of the south-east corner. This point coincides roughly with the end of the nearby pit complex and the south-west corner of building R13, and it is possible that this represents the access to building R13 from street 2 E/W. Further west the street may have become of less importance for the series of pits on the south margin of block 9 was allowed to encroach on the north side of the street, reducing its width in that region to about 3.2 m.

It is virtually certain that, as originally planned and laid out, street 2 E/W continued westwards beyond its intersection with street 1 N/S. A projection of its line reveals five significant features along its route. 1) The most southerly component of the linear pit cluster on the west side of block 4 coincides with the north side of the projected street. 2) The small pit cluster at the south-east corner of block 4, while it lies south of gully 36, also keeps to the north of the projected street. 3) The only pits which impinge on the projected route are those in the discrete complex 741/760/830/822. The character and fill of these pits would suggest they were cut late in Phase III, or more probably in Phase IV, at a time when the street had passed out of use. 4) At the point where ditch 9 cuts across the projected route of the

street, the ditch is reduced in width from about 3 m to about 1.8 m. As there is no other obvious reason for this narrowing it is possible that it was to permit the bridging of the ditch by traffic along the street. 5) Although the street is aligned differently from the stone building complex R1, its projected line coincides precisely with the apse at the west end of the building, implying that an approach from the east, along street 2 E/W, existed (or was planned) at some stage in Phase III, and presumably before the secondary construction phase of the building.

To the east of street 2 N/S the predicted route of street 2 E/W lay almost entirely outside the area of excavation (Figs 19–21). However its presence was detected with reasonable certainty near the south-west end of trench AA, where a patch of gravel metalling survived between two gullies set about 4.5 m apart. The point of intersection with street 3 N/S was unexcavated as also the projected route between streets 3 and 4 N/S which must, therefore, remain uncertain.

Street 3 N/S　(Figs 19–21, pp. 62–4)

This street was laid off at a right angle south from street 1 E/W, about 30 m east of street 2 N/S (road centre to road centre). Traces of its gravel metalling were found in trenches X, H, AA and DD giving a probable minimum length of about 100 m. Its width appears to have corresponded to that of streets 1 and 2 N/S.

Street 4 N/S　(Figs 19, 21)

A rather tenuous identification: while the remains of the gravel metalling are tolerably clear at the north-east end of trench DD, the route northwards was traced with difficulty in trenches AA and H. If the line of the street is correctly interpreted it lies about 27 m east of street 3 N/S (road centre to road centre).

DRAINAGE AND SITE DIVISIONS
(Figs 25–8)

Although the Roman settlement, sited on the edge of a gravel and clay 'island', occupied a relatively elevated and well-drained position by comparison with the adjacent peat fen, standing water and occasional inundation were evidently constant problems which are reflected in the extensive and complex network of gullies and ditches. The precise relationship, sequence, date and function of individual components are not always apparent, but the overall picture is clear enough: the gridded plan of the initial Phase III settlement gradually lost its rigidity as the practicalities of drainage

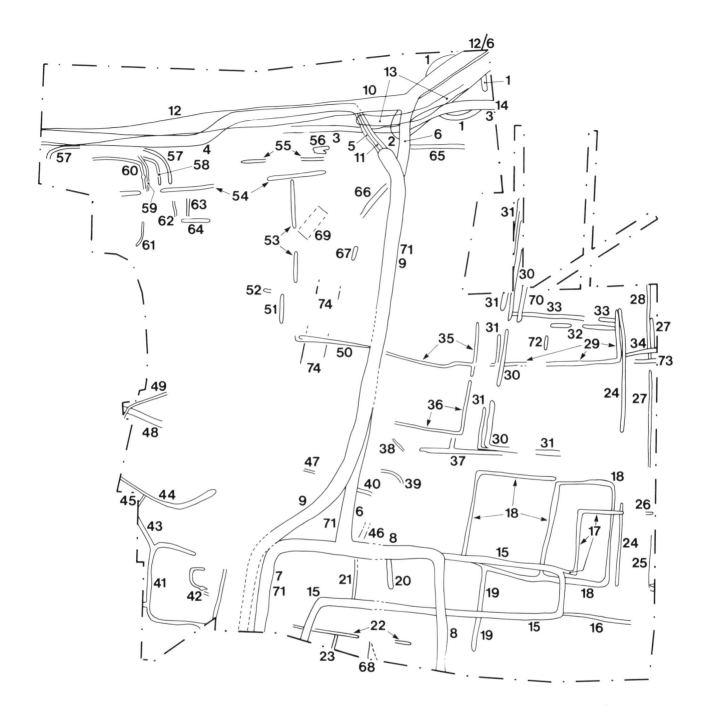

Fig. 25 Stonea Grange: key plan of drainage features in the main excavation, showing ditch and gully numeration.

Phase 0

Phase I

Phase II

Phase III(a-e)

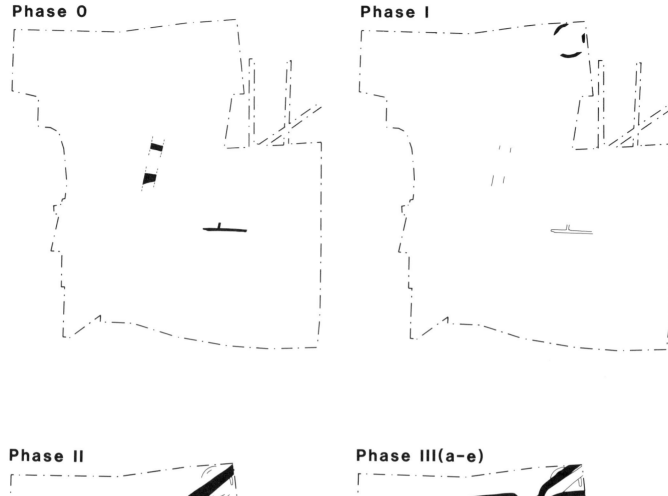

Fig. 26 Stonea Grange: drainage phase plans 0–III.

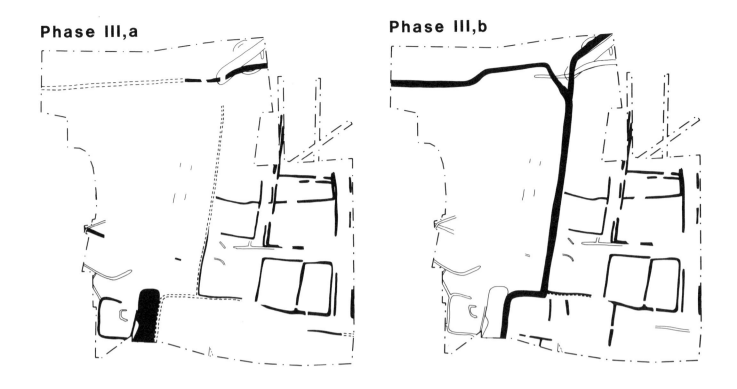

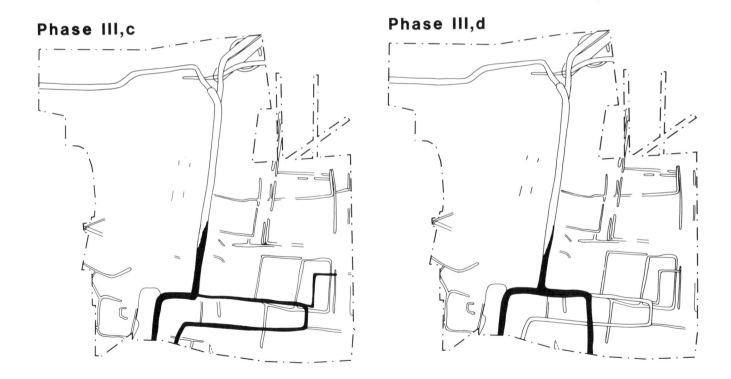

Fig. 27 Stonea Grange: drainage phase plans IIIa–IIId.

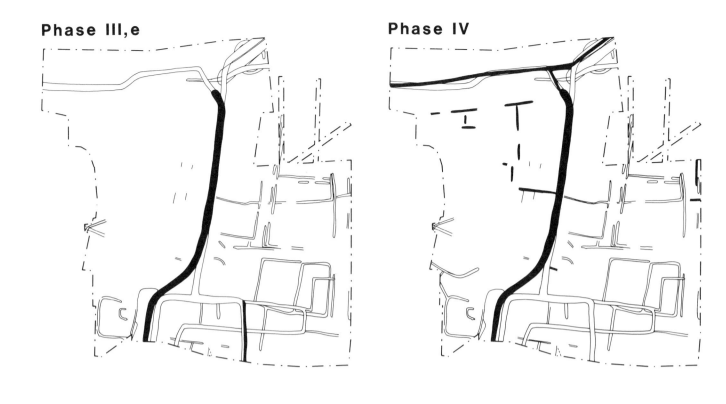

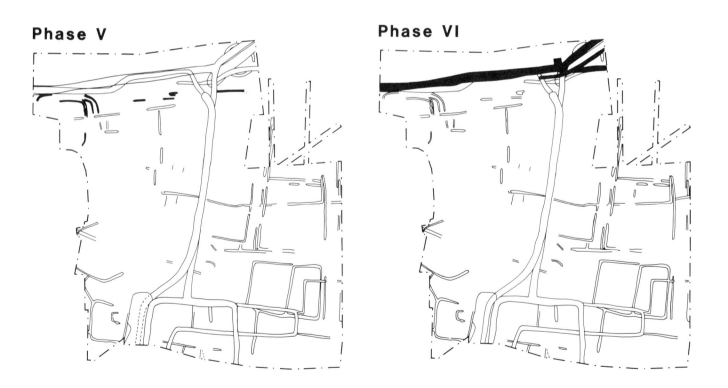

Fig. 28 Stonea Grange: drainage phase plans IIIe–VI.

imposed less regular but more natural routes on gullies, drains and ditches. Although some integration is apparent much of this adaptation was piecemeal, and in some cases defies an exact chronological concordance from one part of the site to another.

At the earliest stage (Fig. 27, Phase IIIa) there seems to have been little appreciation of the need for anything more than localised and small-capacity drainage features. Although a ditch of modest proportions (ditch 3) was provided on the north side of street 1 E/W, the other streets appear to have lacked drains completely. Instead, discontinuous narrow gullies were cut along the sides of the blocks demarcated by the street grid. They appear to have been inserted as the building plots within the blocks were developed (blocks 1b, 3, 4, 8 and 9). They were presumably intended to collect, hold and filter away ground-water. By positioning them at the interface of streets and blocks they provided a drainage facility for streets and buildings alike, though in some places the presence of a second gully running in parallel suggests that a single gully proved inadequate for the task.

Both at the edge of and within blocks the gullies clearly functioned as, or conformed to, private property boundaries and official site divisions, and in blocks 8 and 9, especially, the sequence of gullies complements other evidence for the form of, and changes to, plot divisions. There is a little evidence that some of the gullies were preceded by fence-lines or initially functioned as fence-slots, while others appear to have run adjacent to fences (see e.g. Fig. 55, north-west corner block 8, p. 117). The main site division was a linear boundary on a north–south axis, which separated block 1 and the R1 building complex from blocks 2–10. In its initial form it, too, comprised a wooden fence, the footing trench for which had been destroyed in most places by subsequent changes, but was partially preserved in the stretch adjacent to block 5. There it was found to contain a palimpsest of post impressions in its base, attesting to relative longevity of the boundary or frequent replacement of the posts. Exactly the same sequence was observed on the north side of ditch 8, and, a little more tenuously, on the east side of ditch 7. It may be assumed, therefore, that the whole of the ditch 6, 7, 8 system was preceded by a stout fence.

The appearance of the earliest Phase III settlement will thus have been of buildings within fenced or partially fenced compounds, which were laid out according to a regular grid of streets. Progressively, drainage features were inserted, starting with narrow gullies which were generally sited on or adjacent to existing boundary lines. Although usually self-contained catch-waters, some of these gully systems were later integrated with larger drainage features. Thus, gully 17 in block 8 fed into ditch 15, which itself was a south-east branch of ditch 6; and, once ditch 6 was dug, gullies 35 and 36 (blocks 3 and 4) probably drained into it from the east. Gully 35 also appears to have been linked with gully

29 and gully 34 via channels passing beneath streets 1 and 2 N/S. This long and slightly sinuous drain thus took water westwards from blocks 3/4, 9 and beyond, to empty into the main north–south drainage feature, ditch 6.

The cutting of ditch 6/7 (Fig. 27, Phase IIIb) from the north-east to the south-west corners of the site was evidently a co-ordinated response to the need for large-scale drainage. Probably at the same time the main east–west drainage route was improved by the provision on the north side of street 1 E/W of another substantial ditch, ditch 4. This replaced or extended ditch 3 and, at its east end, connected with ditch 6 via ditch 5, a large culvert cut obliquely beneath street 1 E/W. The resulting Y-shaped axis formed by ditches 4, 5 and 6 comprised the main site drainage feature of Phases III–IV and remained so up to recent times.

To this stage also probably belong a number of modifications to blocks 6 and 7. A reserved space on the north sides of these blocks had probably been planned as an east–west street. Indeed, gully 16 at the east end may have been intended as a drain for its south side. However, if a metalled surface was ever laid, none of it survived and the street was clearly abandoned by the time the north–south ditch 20 and gullies 19 and 21 were cut. The cutting of gully 19, which intersected with the south branch of gully 18, may have been an attempt to drain away southwards the water which collected in the block 8 gully system. Alternatively, with gullies 21–23 it may have been part of a separate catch-water system dividing up plots in blocks 6 and 7.

Subsequently (Fig. 27, Phase IIIc), gully 19 and the south branch of gully 18 (the block 8 gully system) were superseded by the rather curious ditch 15, an east extension of ditch 6 at its south end. With ditch 7 it enclosed an elongated L-shaped zone on the west of block 6 and the north of blocks 6 and 7. An additional drainage unit, gully 17, linked up with the north-east corner of ditch 15. Its reverse Z-shape defined and drained a rectangular plot in the east part of block 8 containing building R8.

The next stage (Fig. 27, Phase IIId) involved the cutting of a still more substantial ditch (ditch 8), as the south-east branch of the now bifurcated ditch 6. Ditch 15, though partially replaced, may have continued to function as an east branch of ditch 8. The clear impression is of a need for increasingly large and extensive drainage features, whether as a consequence of changed climatic conditions or, more probably, an increase in the volume of water consumption and waste generation.

One more major change occurred (Fig. 28, Phase IIIe) before the end of Phase III: the connection between the main east–west and north–south drainage routes (ditches 4 and 6) was blocked by the back-filling with gravel of the partially silted ditch 5. Ditch 6 was then recut on a changed line. This new, more substantial ditch (ditch 9) had a butted terminal at the south side of street 1 E/W, adopted the same line as ditch 6 along the west side of blocks 2–4, but then turned

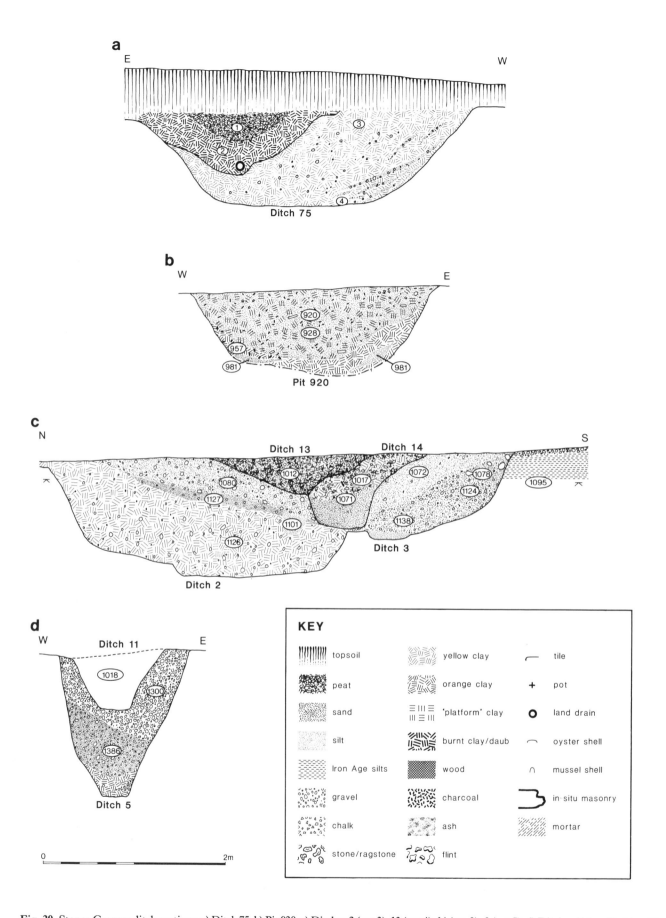

Fig. 29 Stonea Grange: ditch sections. a) Ditch 75. b) Pit 920. c) Ditches 2 (cut 3), 13 (cut 4), 14 (cut 3), 3 (cut 5). d) Ditches 11 (cut 2), 5 (cut 2).

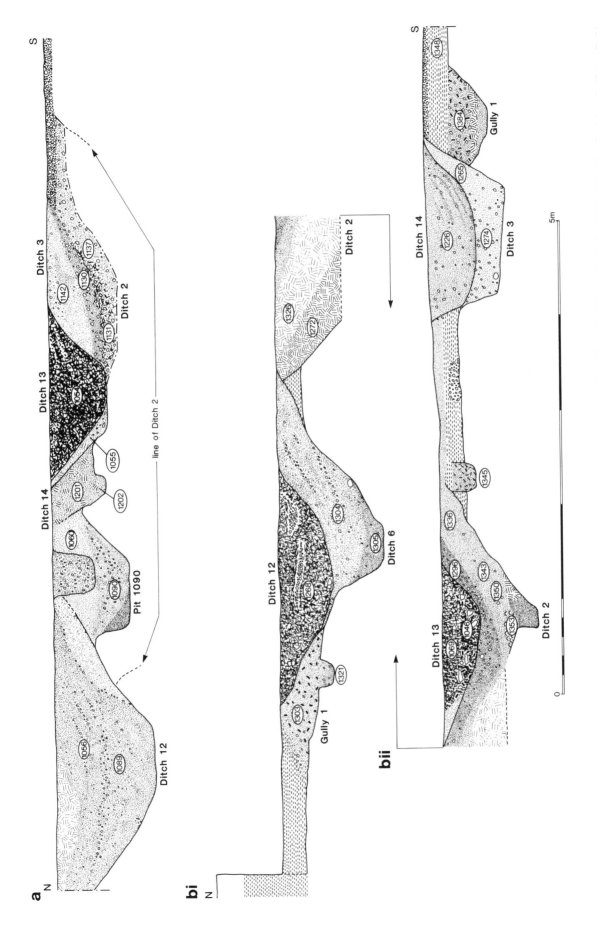

Fig. 30 Stonea Grange: ditch sections. a) Ditch 12 (cut 12), pit 1090, ditches 14 (cut 2), 13 (cut 3), 3 (cut 4), 2 (cut 2). b) Gully 1 (cut 2), ditches 12 (cut 13), 6 (cut 1), 2 (cut 4), 13 (cut 5), 14 (cut 4), 3 (cut 6), Gully 1 (cut 4). For key, see Fig. 29.

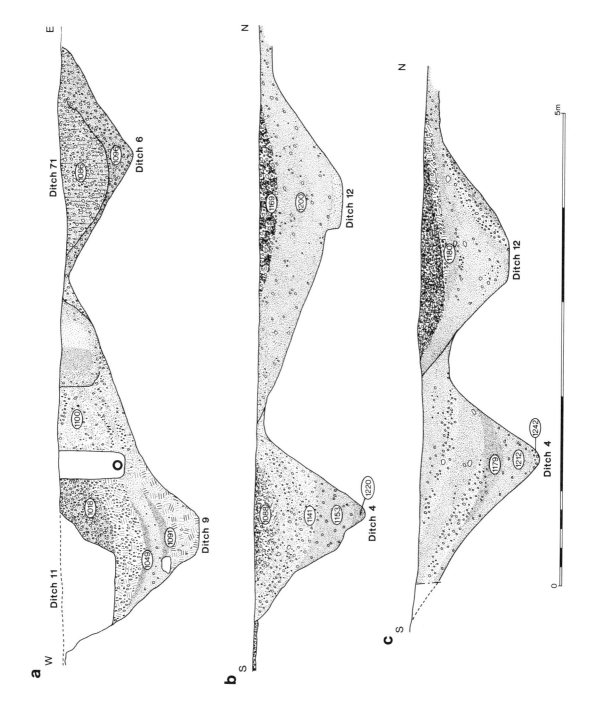

Fig. 31 Stonea Grange: ditch sections. a) Ditches 11 (cut 2), 9 (cut 1b), 71 (cut 11), 6 (cut 4). b) Ditches 4 (cut 4), 12 (cut 4). c) Ditches 4 (cut 3), 12 (cut 3). For key, see Fig. 29.

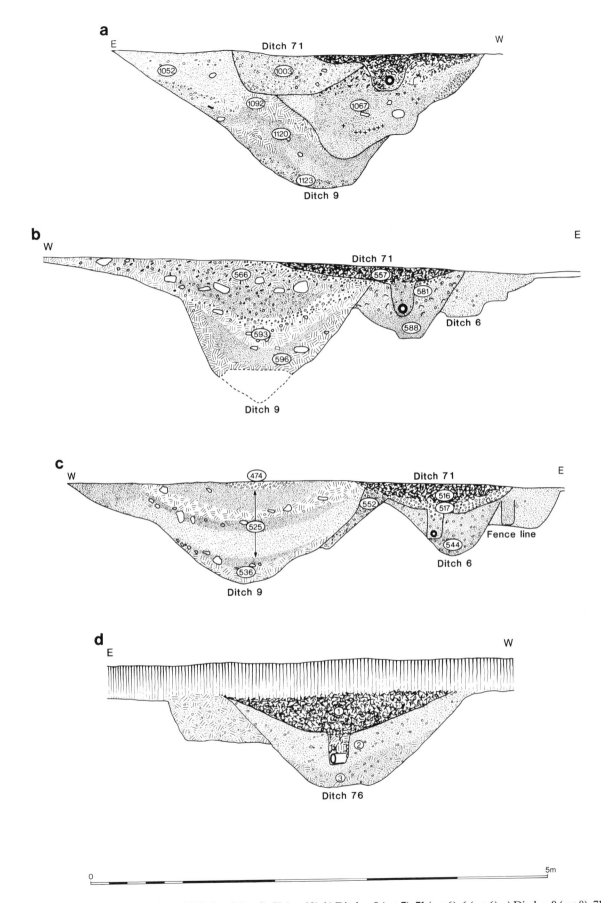

Fig. 32 Stonea Grange: ditch sections. a) Ditches 9 (cut 2), 71 (cut 10). b) Ditches 9 (cut 7), 71 (cut 6), 6 (cut 6). c) Ditches 9 (cut 8), 71 (cut 5), 6 (cut 7), and fence-line. d) Ditch 76. For key, see Fig. 29.

south-westward in an ellipse across the south-east corner of block 1. This was a more natural line for drainage than the previous right angle formed by ditches 6 and 7. At the south end it appears to have terminated in the south sump just beyond the excavation edge.

In this reorganisation ditch 8, formerly the south-east branch of ditch 6, became isolated from the main north–south drainage, and it is probably to this stage that the

recutting of the east branch of ditch 8 belongs. The recut would have continued to drain away southwards, via ditch 15, the water emanating from the south part of street 2 N/S and from the block 8 gully system. At the north end of the site, ditch 4 continued to drain westwards the water from street 1 E/W, and the drainage of the north-east part of the site was linked to ditch 9 by the remaining part of ditch 6.

Table 4 Stonea Grange: gully and ditch concordance to site phase and block number

Table 4 continued

Gully/ditch number	Site phase	Block number
Gully 1	I	11
Ditch 2	II(?)	11
Ditch 3	III	11
Ditch 4	III	11
Ditch 5	III	11
Ditch 6	III	1
Ditch 7	III	1
Ditch 8	III	6
Ditch 9	III and IV	1
Ditch 10	IV(?)	11
Ditch 11	IV(?)	11
Ditch 12	VI	11
Ditch 13	VI	11
Ditch 14	VI	11
Ditch 15	III	6, 7, 8
Gully 16	III	7
Gully 17	III	8
Gully 18	III	8
Gully 19	III	7
Ditch 20	III	6
Gully 21	III	6
Gully 22	III	6
Gully 23	III	6
Gully 24	III	8, 9
Gully 25	III	8
Gully 26	III	8
Gully 27	III	9
Gully 28	III/IV	9
Gully 29	III	9
Gully 30	III	9
Gully 31	III	9
Gully 32	III	9
Gully 33	III	9
Gully 34	III	9
Gully 35	III	3
Gully 36	III	4
Gully 37	0?	5
Gully 38	II?	5
Gully 39	?	5
Gully 40	IV	5
Gully 41	III	1b
Gully 42	III	1b
Gully 43	III	1a
Gully 44	III	1a

Gully/ditch number	Site phase	Block number
Gully 45	III	1a
Gully 46	III	5
Gully 47	III	1
Gully 48	III	1
Gully 49	III	1
Gully 50	IV	1
Gully 51	IV	1
Gully 52	IV?	1
Gully 53	IV/V	1
Gully 54	IV	1
Gully 55	V	11
Gully 56	V	11
Gully 57	V	11
Gully 58	V	11
Gully 59	V	11
Gully 60	V	11
Gully 61	V	1
Gully 62	V	1
Gully 63	IV?	1
Gully 64	IV	1
Gully 65	V	2
Gully 66	IV	1
Gully 67	III?	1
Ditch 68	III	6
Ditch 69	II?	1
Gully 70	III	9
Ditch 71	VI	1
Gully 72	?	9
Gully 73	IV?	9
Ditch 74	?0–IV	1
Ditch 75	0	Trench Y
Ditch 76	III?	Trench W
Gully 77	III	Trench N
Gully 78	III	Trench N
Gully 79	?	Trench O
Gully 80	?	Trench O
Gully 81	?	Trench O
Gully 82	?	Trench O
Ditch 83	II–III	Trench O
Ditch 84	IV	Trench O, Q
Ditch 85	II/III	Trench P
Ditch 86	III?	Trench R
Ditch 87	III?	Trench R

Ditch 9 had a long life, and there was evidence of recutting in several places along its route, most notably at the north. The latest of the recuts (excepting the insertion of modern field drains) belongs to Phase IV, but the ditch remained open in Phase V. Within Phase IV (Fig. 28) adaptations were also made to the main east–west drainage to the north of street 1 E/W. Ditch 4 had become heavily silted, and its rather eccentric route was abandoned in favour of a more direct line. Additionally, its eastern end, which had been blocked with the closure of ditch 5, was now reopened and linked to the north-east branch of ditch 6 by a newly-cut spur, ditch 10. To this phase, also, probably belonged the cutting of ditch 11. This drain-like feature, inserted in the top of the backfilled ditch 5, reunited the east–west and north–south drainage routes, ditches 4 and 9.

Although the character of the settlement had changed by Phase IV, the main site divisions of the earlier phase were maintained by street 1 E/W and ditch 9. Thus, when a new series of gullies was cut in block 1, its components were intimately related to those two boundaries: the discontinuous gully 54 lay along the south flank of street 1 E/W, while the related gullies 50–53, together with the east end of gully 54, enclosed a large rectangular plot of land backing on to ditch 9. The function of these gullies is uncertain. Gully 54 may well have been a roadside drain but, with the other gullies, it probably also served to demarcate stock enclosures, building compounds or, perhaps, both, in a sparsely-populated farming community. There is little evidence for the 'planning control' of the Phase III settlement: not only was the reserved area of block 1 impinged upon, but a gully (gully 73) was cut across street 2 N/S midway along block 9, implying that it had become little-used as a street south of that point.

The discovery of Anglo-Saxon pottery in the upper levels of ditch 9 (cut 3, unit 765), ditch 71 (cuts 5, 8 and 9) and ditch 4 (cut 2, unit 1163; cut 5, unit 1216) as well as in the top of several pits and wells (wells 135, 171/558, 730, J4; pits 170, 711, 774, 860) implies continuity of settlement, rather than a hiatus, through Phases IV and V, an impression which gains support from the sheep bones (Stallibrass, pp. 587–612), from the early dating of the pottery, and from the metal finds. Continuity is also implied by the occurrence of Anglo-Saxon sherds in gullies 35 and 53. That in gully 53, from the north section, is probably to be associated with the recutting observed in the south section. If the Phase IV gully 50/53/54 system enclosed a plot connected with building R4, it is tempting to link the recutting and the Anglo-Saxon pottery with the nearby Phase V building S2 and see that building as the successor to building R4 and its associated enclosure. The same sequence can be applied to an adjacent plot in block 2/3, where building S3 and S4 could be seen as the successor to building R5, and where Anglo-Saxon pottery was found in gully 35 (cut 2, unit 754).

THE SUMP
(Figs 33–6; Fig. 53, p. 115; Pls IX, XVI)

In 1982 a huge cut feature was located at the south end of the site, adjacent to and east of block 1b. Of sub-rectangular shape, and aligned approximately on the Roman site grid, it began 7.5 m south of the east end of building R1 and ran within the excavation area for a distance of 17 m. It continued beyond the excavation edge where it was traced as a stubble crop-mark for at least a further 10 m. It was quadranted but was found to be so deep and extensive that excavation of the south-east quadrant was soon discontinued and, after establishing something of the nature of the feature and its fill in the north-west quadrant, work there was halted, too.

At that stage it was evident that the feature was of considerable depth and that it contained in its lower levels large quantities of well-preserved waterlogged Roman organic material, including leather and wooden artefacts. While the function of the feature was not obvious, its contents were clearly of importance. However, their extraction, while desirable, posed considerable problems: the feature was at least 20 m long, 9–10 m wide and over 3 m deep; its sides were steeply sloping, both at east and west and at the north terminal; and the waterlogged remains were very densely packed and vulnerable. Thus, it was necessary to contrive a means of access and to develop modes of extraction and recording which avoided the application of any pressure to the deposit. In addition, the moisture level of the excavated surface had to be maintained and ultraviolet rays excluded, if the organic material was not to deteriorate. While certain techniques developed on other wetland excavations were adapted, few were directly applicable to the character of the feature, and it was necessary to devise a new system of excavation and recording. The result was a judicious compromise between the ideal and the practical, and the northern half of the feature was completely excavated in 1983 and 1984.

Sinkage and compaction of the Roman deposits meant that the feature remained as a deep hollow up to recent times, and the upper layers (units 451/514, 464/518, 462, 523, 484, A4) contained field drains and other debris of post-medieval date. These were removed mechanically, using a 2 m wide bucket on the back-actor of a JCB positioned on the edge of the feature. After hand-cleaning of the machined surface in the northern part of the exposed deposits, a datum line was established and two adjacent square settings of four vertical scaffold poles were driven into the deposit. With a minimum of potential damage these provided the substructure for two raised, rectangular, scaffold–plank platforms, the height of which was adjustable. In this way it was possible both to establish and to maintain the optimum vertical distance between the platforms and the excavated surface as removal of the deposit proceeded (Pl. XVIa).

Two shelters were then constructed from alloy scaffolding and heavy-duty pva translucent sheeting. The use of these

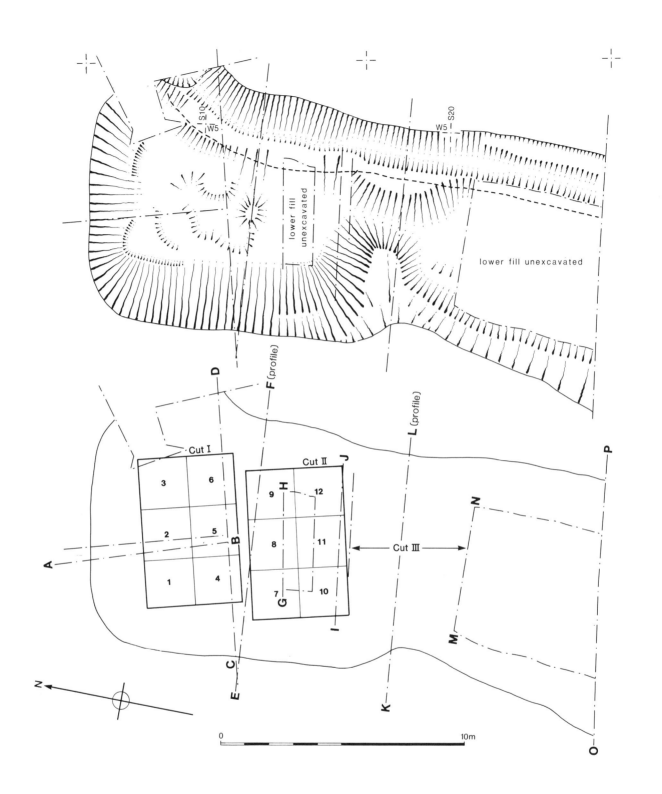

Fig. 33 Stonea Grange: the sump, plan and key.

materials and a careful design ensured sufficient stability, headroom, weather protection and illumination without loss of manoeuvrability. To simplify the recording process, their basal area – 6 × 4 m – was made to correspond to the 2 × 3 grid of 2 m squares selected as the basic spatial recording unit (cut I, grid–squares 1–6; cut II, grid–squares 7–12). As the main Roman waterlogged deposit in the northern part of the feature covered an approximately rectangular area only a little in excess of 8 × 5 m, the two shelters and their associated grids encompassed effectively the whole of the deposit (Fig. 33).

To reveal and disengage the waterlogged wood and other organics from their peat matrix, wooden spatulas (lollysticks) and hand spray-bottles were used in place of trowels, but where the matrix was compact and unyielding or clayey the implements were used in conjunction. Numbers were allocated and plastic tags pinned to the wooden and other objects as they were found. To start with, complete layers, lenses or spits were removed from the entire deposit (cuts I and II) and the artefacts and debitage spread was planned prior to the lifting and conservation. However, it soon became necessary for the excavation of cuts I and II to proceed independently in order to avoid the deterioration of wood by prolonged exposure. In fact, it had already become apparent that the deposit was a random accumulation of debris, with no in situ structure, so there was no necessity to reveal it entire at every level.

A pump mounted part way down the west side of the feature was activated intermittently to drain away excess water, while pressurised water spray bottles were in constant use to maintain the moisture content of the exposed wood. When excavation was not in progress the surface was covered with sheets of thin polyurethane foam saturated in water. In these ways, damage and deterioration, though not entirely eliminated, were kept to a minimum.

The waterlogged deposit was not only extremely arduous to excavate but was also difficult, almost to the point of opacity, to interpret. Few clear layer interfaces or lines of cut were discernible, even in section, and there was considerable variation in the composition and configuration of layers laterally over quite short distances. Post-depositional changes in the water-table, with consequent desiccation and shrinkage of the upper layers and compaction of the lower layers, were no doubt partly the cause, but it must also reflect the nature of the deposit.

The sequence began early in Phase III with the excavation to a maximum depth of just 0.4 m AOD, of a large, rectangular, steep-sided pit or trench. The configuration of the contours at the base of the feature is suggestive of a revetted, vertical-sided tank, about 8 × 5 m. However, neither timber cladding nor posts were found in the waterlogged debris, nor was there any evidence for a planked floor, indeed the base was very irregular. If a timber lining is postulated, therefore, it is necessary to envisage its entire removal. The alternative and more probable interpretation is to regard the angled upper margins not as an erosion cone but as an integral part

of the original feature, a steep-sided subrectangular trench, about 13 × 9.5 m and 3.2 m deep. Whichever, if either, of these interpretations is correct, a second similar, if not identical, feature was dug immediately to the south. After ascertaining its overall form and sampling its north end in 1983–4 its main lower waterlogged fill was left intact (Pl. XVIb).

Prior to the 1983 excavation the theory was formulated that these connected features comprised the terminal of a waterway – a canal or lode – which had been used to transport building materials to the site at the start of Phase III, in particular the large quantity of stone, lime and tile required for building R1. Aerial photographs hinted at a linear feature in approximately the correct position and, in the autumn of 1983, a resistivity survey seemed to confirm the presence of a broad canal-like feature running southwards at least a further 70 m from the edge of the excavation. The hypothesis was tested in 1984, when a number of trenches were cut by machine across the projected route. The end of the second pit was located in trench FF, but the feature was completely absent from trenches V and W. The canal theory was therefore disproved, unequivocally, and the original function of the pair of pits remains a mystery.

Although large quantities of tile were used in the construction of building R1, there is no evidence for the manufacture of tiles (or pottery) on the site, so it seems most unlikely that they were dug as clay pits, especially as they were in such close proximity to the R1 building complex. Another possibility is that they were dug as relieving tanks to divert and hold displaced ground-water at the stage when the foundations of building R1 were being put in. Certainly the considerable depth and volume of the footings combined with the high water-table could have posed a problem of this kind. However, it is not clear why, in that case, the pits remained open after the construction work was completed. Their intimate relationship with the main north–south ditch system implies a connection with drainage, and, intentionally or not, they must have taken on the function of sump/soakaway when ditch 7 and, later, ditch 9 were cut through them.

By that stage they had become partially-filled with organic debris in matrices of peat and clay. This included a considerable amount of worked and unworked wood, and botanical remains (Cartwright, pp. 552–83; van der Veen, pp. 613–39). Several pieces of bracket fungus and numerous puffballs, together with pieces of wormed wood, provide a vivid impression of the decaying character of the assemblage (Pl. XXXII). The worked wood was largely debitage, with numerous chippings and offcuts, but it also included artefacts, most notably writing tablets (Fig. 204, p. 545; Pl. XXIX), and a complete wooden spade (Fig. 205, p. 546; Pl. XXX) as well as a large plank or floorboard. Leather offcuts and several shoes were also incorporated in the deposit (Rhodes, pp. 540–4), including a well-worn pair which may have belonged to an artisan. It is tempting to link them with the spade which, with its iron blade encrusted with a

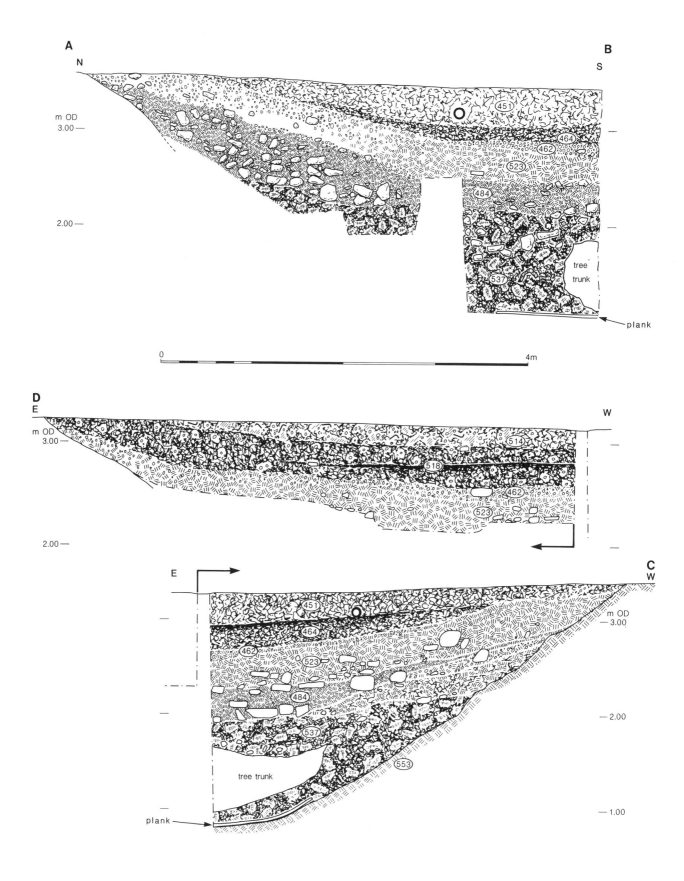

Fig. 34 Stonea Grange: the sump, sections A–D. For key, see Fig. 29.

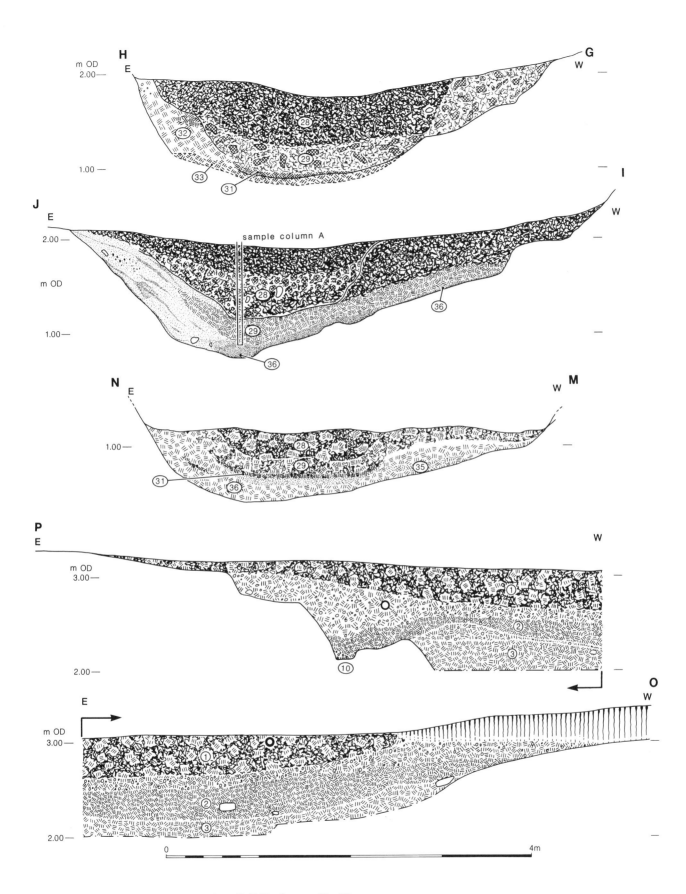

Fig. 35 Stonea Grange: the sump, sections G–P. For key, see Fig. 29.

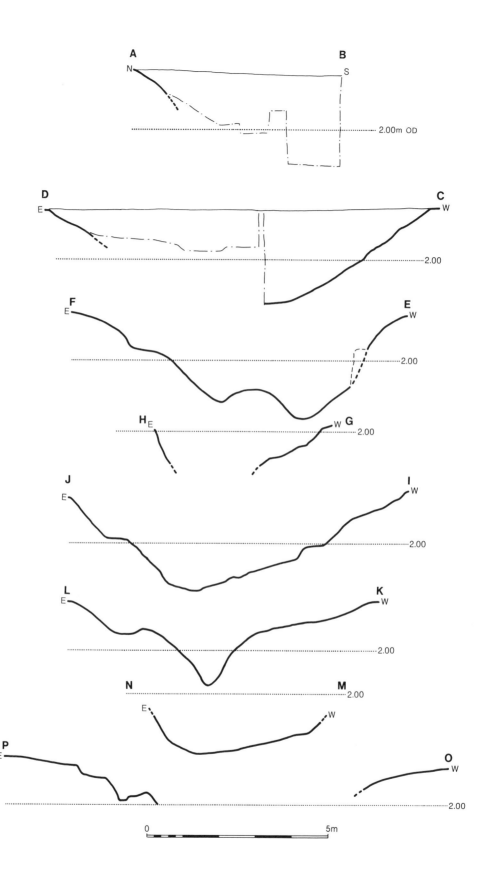

Fig. 36 Stonea Grange: the sump, profiles A–P.

mortar-like concretion (Middleton, pp. 524–5), may have been discarded at the construction phase of building R1. Leaving aside the question of its original function, the north pit appears to have become a receptacle for rubbish, initially, perhaps, for the detritus of construction work, later, for the debris and by-products of craft activities as well as for more general refuse. That it was also used at some stage as a source of water is implied by the presence of wooden and metal parts from buckets and barrels (Jackson, pp. 364, 550–2). However, it must have become entirely choked by the time ditch 7 was routed down its east side. As elsewhere, the ditch was probably preceded by a fenced boundary line, for the ledge on its east side, though without continuous post settings, is perhaps the remains of a footing trench. Linear post-hole arrangements on the west, (A19–A25) and east (A5–A9) sides of the sumps may have comprised an enclosure fence, a sensible precaution, perhaps, for such deep and steep-sided features (Figs 33, 53).

The truncated form of ditch 7 as seen in the southernmost section (Fig. 35, O–P, 10) may be due to compaction of the peaty deposits of the sumps through which it passed. The east side of ditch 7, which was cut through undisturbed gravelly clay, was clearly visible but the west side could be traced only near its base. The upper margin, cut through the peaty sump fill was not readily distinguishable. Still more obscure was the route of ditch 9 which, like ditch 7, entered the north sump at its north-east corner but then took a more central line through the feature. Its sides and base were cut entirely within the peaty deposit and could not be clearly distinguished. Only where it was cut through the previously undisturbed clay baulk which separated the two sumps was its profile seen again. There its base was at a much lower level (1.0 m AOD) than elsewhere along its route. As it was observed neither in the south section of the south sump nor in the trenches cut to the south of the excavation (trenches FF, V and W), it may be assumed that it debouched into, and ended within, the south sump. Although its sides were not visible in the north sump, its route was disclosed both by, in places, a grey clayey fill, and by the distribution of finds. The ditch had been especially prolific in complete and semi-complete pots, and a similar profusion was found in the north sump: two pots (SF 1983A, 4; 1984A, 21) were found in the base of the ditch as it passed from one sump to another (cut III), while the remainder (SF 1983A, 2, 6, 8, 9; 1984A, 16, 23, 27, 36) were all found in grid squares 3, 6 and 9, which lie on the natural projected route of ditch 9 between the north-east corner and cut III (see Fig. 33). This distribution is in marked contrast to that of the other grid squares, which yielded almost exclusively organic artefacts, and no complete or semi-complete pots.

The subsequent history of the sump–ditch complex is one of gradual silting throughout Phases III–V. Stabilisation, though still as a distinct negative feature, seems to have occurred with the formation of layer 484/A4. This contained Roman and Anglo-Saxon pottery and heavy concentrations of stone rubble, including a number of interesting architectural components (e.g. Pl. XXIIb) which probably derived from building R1. A little post-medieval disturbance in layer 484/A4 preceded the levelling-up of the feature (by stages) and the insertion of field drains.

At an early stage in the excavation of the sump, before a dated ceramic assemblage had been amassed, a bundle of willow sticks (ST 82, W38) from layers 537/553, one of several withy bundles from the deposit, was sampled for a ^{14}C determination. The sample (BM-2157R) yielded a result of 2170 ± 110 BP (*Radiocarbon* 32(1), 1990, 70).

Data

Unit number		Site phase	Coarse pottery date
451	Fine brown peaty silty soil, upper layer, NW quadrant, N sump	VI	–
462	Mixed light sand and clay with gravel, below 464	VI	–
464	Fine yellow/brown peaty loam, below 451	VI	–
484	Black clay with some preserved organics and much building debris, below 462	IV/V	Anglo-Saxon
514	As 451, upper layer SE quadrant, N sump	VI	–
518	As 464, below 514	VI	–
523	Grey clay with rubble, below 518	?IV/V	Late 2nd cent AD
537	Black peat with much organics, below 484, as A, 26	III/IV	–
553	Grey-blue clay on sides of N sump, below 537	III	?3rd cent AD
A, 1	As 451, upper layer, S sump	VI	–
A, 2	Dark-grey clayey soil, below A, 1	?	–
A, 3	Light grey clay, below A, 2	?	–
A, 4	Rubbly grey clay, N sump, as 484	IV/V	–
A, 5–A, 9	Post-holes to E of sumps	?III/IV	–
A, 10–A, 11	Grey clay, primary fill of ditch 7	III	Later 2nd cent AD
A, 19–A, 25	Post-holes to W of sumps	?III/IV	–
A, 26	Brown waterlogged peat, below A, 4 as 537	III/IV	3rd–4th cent AD
A, 27	Grey clay on SW edge of N sump, below A, 4	IV?	–
A, 28	Grey-black waterlogged clay, below A, 26, as 553	III	Late 2nd–3rd cent AD
A, 29	Dark grey-green clay, highly organic, below A, 28	III	Late 2nd–early 3rd cent AD

Data (*continued*)

Unit number		Site phase	Coarse pottery date
A, 29A	Clayey light-brown peat, between A, 28 and A, 29 in cut I	III	–
A, 31	Thin layer of oily, silty, grey-black clay, below A, 29	III	Mid 2nd cent AD on
A, 32	Black peaty clay and gravel, below A, 31, in cuts I and II	III	Late 2nd–3rd cent AD
A, 33	Silty grey gravel with a mass of charred wood, below A, 31, in cut III	III	Late 2nd–early 3rd cent AD
A, 34	Grey silty slump, W side of cut III, probably antecedes A, 33	III	–
A, 35	Brown sandy clay and clay slump, W side of cut II, probably antecedes A, 32	III	Late 2nd–3rd cent AD
A, 36	Primary silty grey clay, above natural	III	?

Matrix

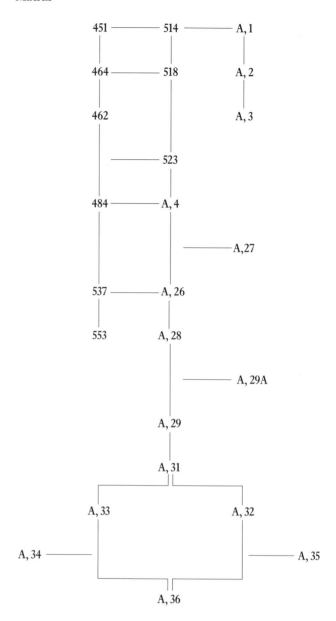

WELLS AND PITS   (Figs 37–42; Pl. XVb)

In Phase III the disposal of rubbish appears to have been organised with some care. The clear impression is that pits were seldom haphazardly placed. They tend to occupy particular zones within the site. Most regular are the linear clusters along the boundaries of blocks and buildings. Also prominent are the rather more amorphous foci adjacent to and between buildings in blocks 2–4 and 8–9. Most striking of all are the concentrations of pits dug in the 'vacant' plots, blocks 5 and 5a.

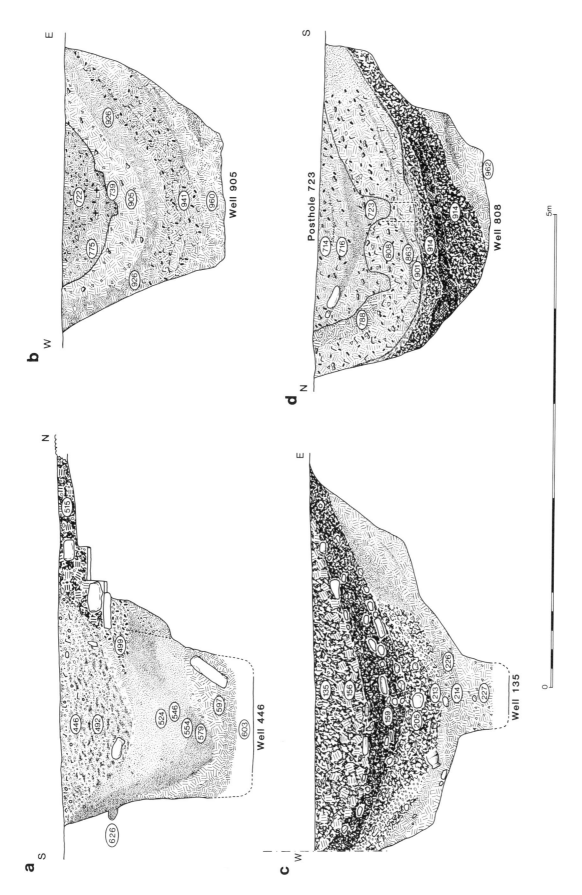

Fig. 37 Stonea Grange: well sections. a) Well 446. b) Well 905. c) Well 135. d) Well 808 and post-hole 723. For key, see Fig. 29.

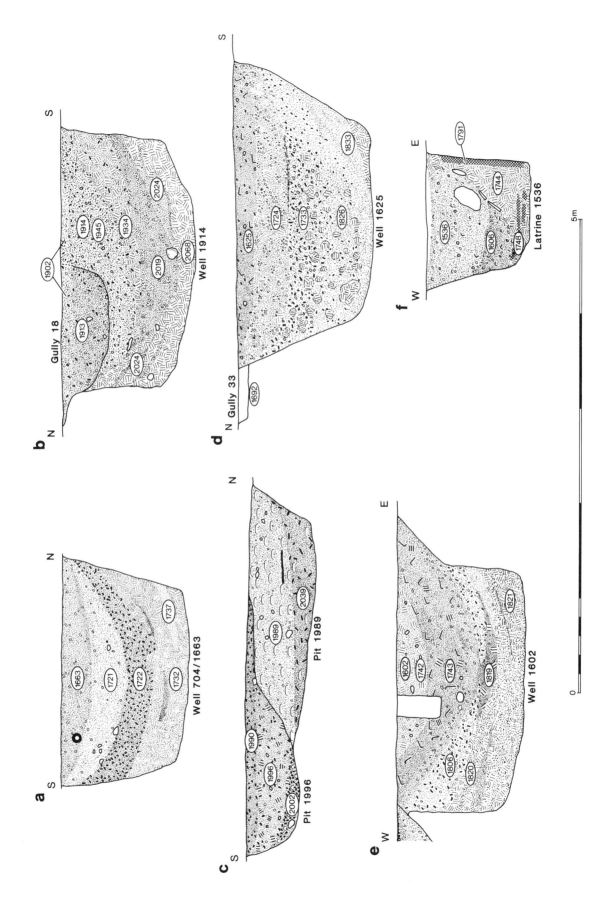

Fig. 38 Stonea Grange: well, pit and latrine sections. a)Well 704/1663. b) Well 1914 and gully 18 (cut 11). c) Pits 1989, 1996. d) Well 1625 and gully 33 (cut 2). e) Well 1602. f) Latrine 1536. For key, see Fig. 29.

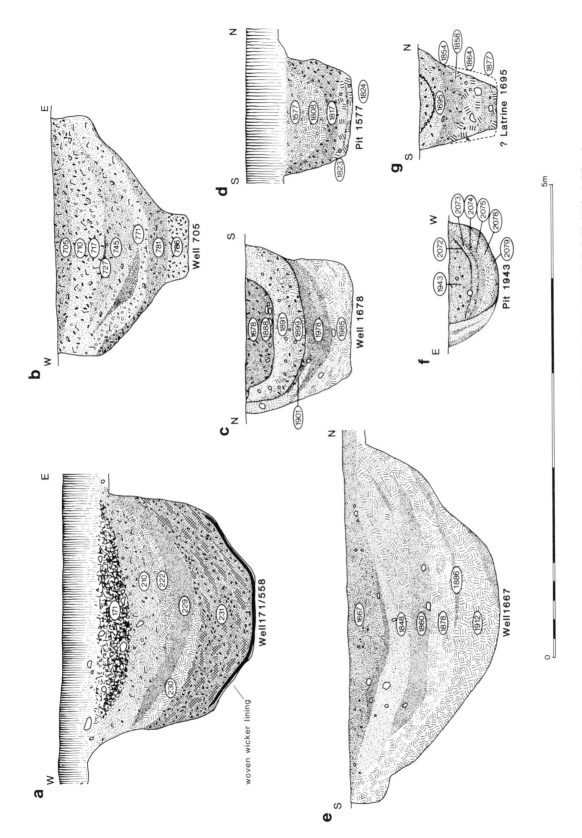

Fig. 39 Stonea Grange: well, pit and latrine sections. a) Well 171/558. b) Well 705. c) Well 1678. d) Pit 1577. e) Well 1667. f) Pit 1943. g) (?)Latrine 1695. For key, see Fig. 29.

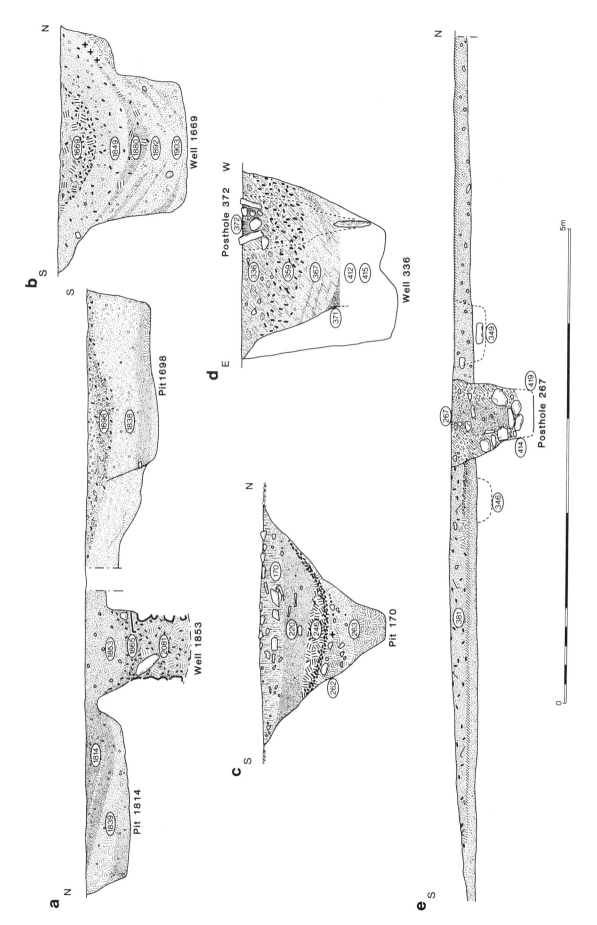

Fig. 40 Stonea Grange: Well, pit and post-hole sections. a) Pit 1814, well 1853, pit 1698. b) Well 1669. c) Pit 170. d) Well 336 and post-hole 372. e) Low rubbly mound 381 etc., and post-hole 267. For key, see Fig. 29.

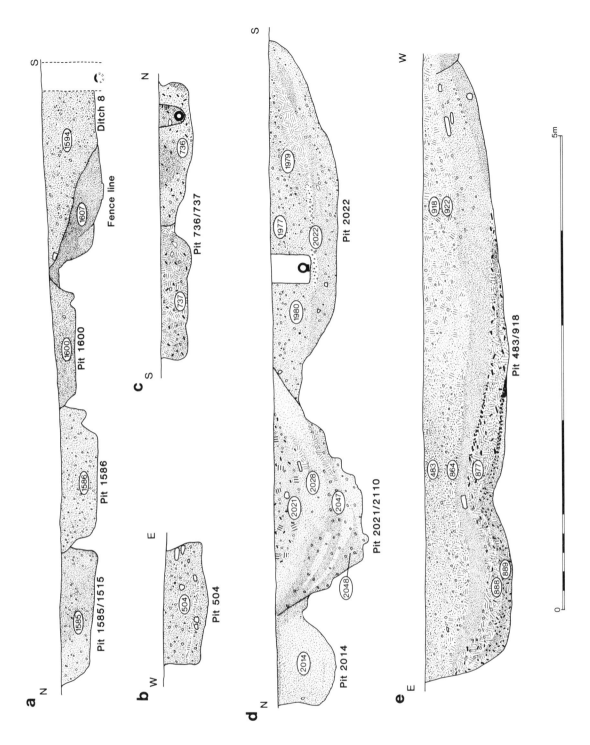

Fig. 41 Stonea Grange: pit sections. a) Pits 1585/1515, 1586, 1600, fence line, and ditch 8 (cut 4). b) Pit 504. c) Pit 736/737. d) Pits 2014, 2021/2110, 2022. e) Pit 483/918. For key, see Fig. 29.

Linear clusters

The most distinctive linear clustering was in blocks 3 and 4 (Fig. 51, p. 113). Occupation there appears to have been less intense in the later part of Phase III and in Phase IV, so the earlier Phase III pit alignments remained relatively undisturbed by the later Roman features.

The pits, mainly rectangular, were disposed along the strip of ground between the west side of the post-hole buildings, and the west boundary line of the blocks. At the south of block 4 the pit sequence cut the fence-line and continued a short distance into block 5. The coarse pottery from the two pits which were excavated – pits 701(i) and (ii) – gave dates which suggested they were cut and filled after the pits to their north. Such sequential evidence is in agreement with their breaching of the fence-line. The final pit, pit 701(i), terminates at a point which coincides with the projected north edge of street 2 E/W. It is noteworthy that the northernmost pit (pit 874) of the main pit cluster in block 5 also occupies a position respecting the projected southern side of street 2 E/W.

At the north of block 3 a similar sequence occurred to that at the south of block 4. The three-unit pit 860, with a coarse pottery date of early third century or later, was cut into the upper fill of well 944. The linear clustering in block 9 was not quite as regular or extensive as that of blocks 3 and 4 but was still very marked in one region near the centre of the south side (Fig. 56, p. 118). There, a series of shallow rectangular pits (pits 1960, 1972/1976, 1973, 1974 and 1975), of almost tank-like appearance, was cut along and through the fence-line and encroached somewhat onto the north side of street 2 E/W. Too little survived of their upper stratigraphy to determine whether they were a line of contemporary pits or a sequence with only one operative at any time.

It seems likely that the pit complex near the centre of block 9 (Figs 56–7) also began as one or more linear clusters, there being both an east–west axis related to gully 29, and a north–south axis which respects the west side of a region of post-holes marked by gully 72.

Corner sites

Another favoured zone for pit construction was at the corner of plots (Figs 45–57, pp. 107–19) as, for example, the north-east corner of block 2 (pit 1184); the south-west corner of block 9 (pits 1994 and 1909); the north-west and north-east corners of block 3 (well 944 and pit 1663); the north-east corner of block 4 (pit 1836); the south-east corner of block 8 (pits 2129 and 2103), and the north-east corner of block 5 (pit 2045).

Like the linear clusters, the siting of these pits was probably determined by the position of buildings, fenced/ditched boundaries, and streets. There is nothing in their fill, finds, or morphology that suggests they shared a common function other than that (at least ultimately) of rubbish disposal. Indeed, one at least was probably a well (well 944, north-west corner of block 3).

Amorphous clusters

Elsewhere pits were in dense or diffuse amorphous clusters or were individually sited. The density may be presumed to be proportionate to the degree and duration of activity on different parts of the site. Thus, block 9 (Figs 56–7), with several (and successive) buildings, has a high density of pits, while block 8 (Fig. 55), with less evidence for buildings, has fewer pits. However, rubbish generated within particular blocks was not necessarily (or, perhaps, even usually) disposed of close at hand. Household refuse may have been taken away from the site, some to be spread on fields as compost. Furthermore, block 5 (Fig. 52), with no trace of a building, was clearly a 'vacant plot', which became a focus for rubbish disposal. Whether the rubbish came from the wooden buildings in blocks 2–4 and 6–9 or from the stone buildings in block 1 is not demonstrable: though the presence of the main north–south boundary would tend to suggest the former, the dearth of pits clearly associated with the buildings in block 1 might indicate the latter. Whichever the case, it was clearly essential that the pits were dug on land outside block 1. It is only with the rerouting of the boundary (in the form of ditch 9) across the south-east corner of block 1 that pits were cut into that part of the block, because it was then isolated from block 1 and became effectively an extension of block 5. The pits in block 5a should, therefore, either be contemporary with or postdate those in block 5. Unfortunately, the coarse pottery dating is not sufficiently precise to discern a difference.

Morphology

As usual on Roman sites, the pits were cut in a variety of shapes and sizes. Some were clearly positioned with care and were cut with an equal precision. Others show less evidence for organisation and are less regular in shape. Commonest are rectangular or sub-rectangular pits, especially in the linear clusters where the available space seems to have determined shape, size and care with siting. Circular and ovoid pits are less common: most are large, deep and isolated and were either certainly or probably wells. The proportion of amorphous pits is greater in the less highly organised zones of rubbish disposal, as, for example, in block 5.

Function

With few exceptions it was impossible to determine the function of individual pits. Even identifying wells proved difficult, especially as the ancient water-table lay close to the surface (as it does today) with the result that well shafts

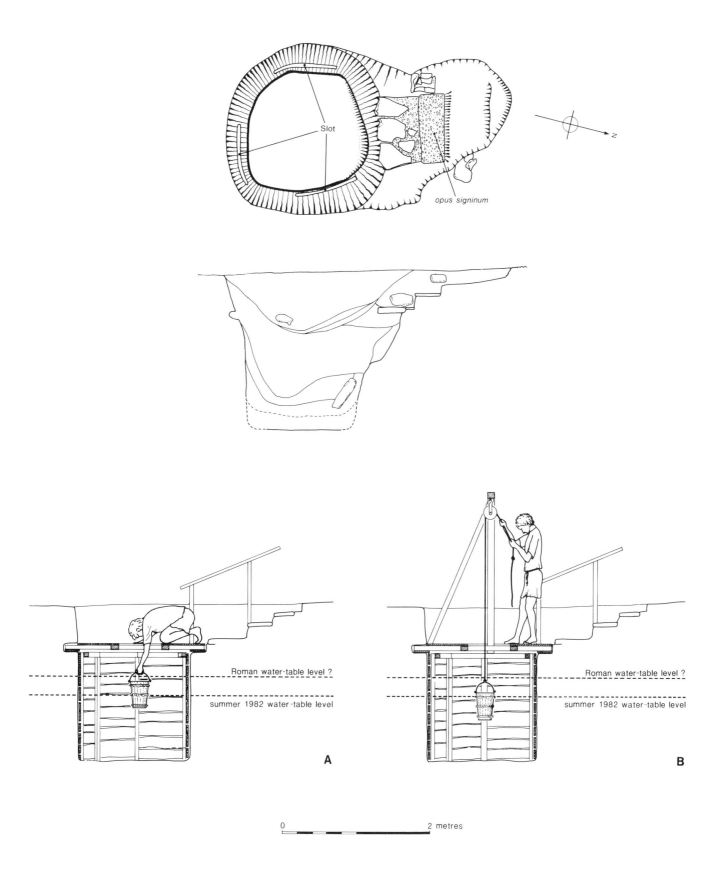

Fig. 42 Stonea Grange: well 446, block 1b. Plan, simplified section, and two possible modes of use. For section details, see Fig. 37a.

were not sunk very deep: a maximum of 2.2 m below the excavated surface. The base of most pits identified as wells lay within the range 1.1–1.8 m AOD, while the range for those pits not assumed to be wells was 2.2–3.2 m AOD. However, the distinction was made less clear by a number of large pits whose depth overlapped with that of the shallowest putative wells.

Wells

Pits identified as certain or probable wells: 135; 171/558; 336; 446; 704/1663; 705; 730; 808; 905; 944; 1602; 1625; 1667; 1669; 1678; 1834; 1836; 1853; 1885; 1914; 2020; G4; J4.

Well 1853 was the only one which retained a stone lining (Figs 40a, 55). The shaft was square, measuring 0.5 × 0.45 m internally. Elsewhere on the site, the wells appear to have had a timber lining (e.g. well 446) or a wicker lining (well 171/558), although it is possible that a stone lining was removed from well 135 and, perhaps, from others, too.

Well 446 (Figs 37a, 42, 47) was of particular interest as its upper margins were better preserved than most, and the Roman ground surface could be identified with some certainty. Three steps, with limestone treads set in *opus signinum* cement, descended from the north to give access to the well. At the level of the lowest step, three horizontal slots were cut into the wall of the well-pit – one opposite and one either side of the steps. It is suggested that these slots accommodated the ends of planks which formed a decking above the timber-lined well. In combination with the relatively high water-table this arrangement may have been designed to obviate the need for the usual well-head pulley system, though two alternative possible modes of use have been illustrated in Fig. 42. The stone-packed post-hole to the west of the second step probably held one of a pair of posts supporting a hand rail, the second post being mortised into the decking/lining timbers. The waterlogged basal silts preserved fragments of the timber lining and also a twisted withy binding from a wooden bucket (Fig. 208, no. 10, p. 551).

Well 336 (Figs 40d, 48), with four symmetrically-disposed post-holes around the lip of the pit, is the only other example with possible remains of a wooden well-head structure. However, the small hollow projecting from the side of well 944 (Fig. 51), well 1667 (Figs 39e, 56) and well 1914 (Figs 38b, 54) may originally have accommodated steps affording similar access to that provided for well 446.

The lower part of the lining of the Phase IV well 171/558 (Figs 39a, 51) was preserved in situ by waterlogging. It comprised a woven wicker revetment around the side and base of the sub-circular pit and, as such, was more closely related to the wooden-lined pit of well 446 than the stone-lined square shaft of well 1853 or the circular shaft of well J4 (Fig. 57). It was the only surviving example of the technique, which may, therefore, have been used only in Phase IV.

Latrines

Pits identified as probable or possible latrines: 1535; 1536; 1542; 1563; 1638; 1184; 1695; 1909; 2103.

The proportions and character of these pits gave rise to the suggestion that they were latrines. However, scientific analysis of soil samples from the sediments provided no confirming evidence of such use. (Note, however, the faunal and floral evidence from pits 1535 and 1536 – Stallibrass, p. 610; van der Veen, pp. 612, 630–6). The pits have a number of features in common. All are relatively deep rectangular pits with vertical sides which, in at least three cases (pits 1535, 1536, 1563), had a wooden lining. The best preserved of these, pit 1536, had decayed in situ planking almost up to the excavated surface on its south and east sides, as well as decayed collapsed lining at various levels in the lower fill (Fig. 38f). Of the more probable latrine pits, four were located in block 6 (Fig. 53, 1535, 1536, 1542, 1563) and one in block 9 (Fig. 57, 1638). The three most convincing examples, 1535, 1536 and 1563, form a tightly-knit group in the south-west quadrant of block 6, set in an L-shaped formation and aligned on a common axis. If, indeed, they were latrines these wood-lined tanks may have functioned as recesses for removable buckets. Otherwise they would have required periodic emptying, the resulting night earth probably being spread on the fields as manure. There is no evidence for any cover building, but a light superstructure could have been mortised into the framework, of the timber lining. The dating evidence for all three points to the third century AD for their disuse but is insufficiently precise to discern whether one succeeded another or whether they were all in contemporary use. The fill of 1536 is dated to the early third century AD, so its period of use (and, by implication, that of 1535 and 1563) almost certainly fell within Phase III. It is not clear why four putative latrines were provided in block 6, where no certain building was identified. However, the absence of a building may be significant: latrines might be deliberately sited on the periphery of habitation areas in order to reduce the level of offensive smells near houses. [It is possible that some of the pits sited on the corners of blocks were also latrines (pits 1184, 1695, 1909, 2103). Most are rectangular and of similar dimensions to those above.] On the other hand, such niceties were seldom observed at e.g. Pompeii; and one of the Stonea examples (Fig. 57, pit 1638) is not only adjacent to several buildings in block 9, but is also immediately next to well 1625

Characteristic fills

A number of pits contained especially characteristic fills signifying particular, though seldom precisely identifiable, events or processes.

'Flood' silts

Given that the site is low-lying and that a number of extensive regional flooding episodes are attested, more localised flooding might be predicted. The deposition of a thin lens of fine silt into excavated features following prolonged and heavy rainstorms on various occasions during the course of excavations corresponded well to the fine silt lenses encountered in a number of the ancient pit fills. However, three pits contained especially thick layers of a fine mottled pink and grey silt (block 9, pit 2087, unit 2087; block 7, pit 1943, units 2073 and 2075 (Fig. 39f); and block 7, pit 2106, units 2107, 2125, and 2127). If, indeed, these layers truly represent flooding, there is no way of establishing how localised or widespread that flooding was. However, the fact that two blocks were affected and that the pits in block 7 had a sequence of two and three apparent flood deposits might be taken as a possible indication of increasingly wet conditions in the later part of Phase III.

Burnt clay/daub deposits

Heavy concentrations of daub and unburnt clay were found in three pits, either side of street 2 E/W (Fig. 56) – pit 2061 on the north side of block 8; pits 1962 and 1695 (Fig. 39g), two adjacent pits, opposite pit 2061, on the south side of block 9. Additionally, in the adjacent south-east corner of block 9, as in the north-east corner of block 9, there were disturbed spreads of similar burnt debris. The close proximity of building R13 to these pits and spreads suggests that the burnt/ unburnt clay units were destruction/dereliction debris from that building. The huge concentration of small finds in pit 1695 might be interpreted as part of the same clearance episode; while a lens of wall-plaster in the fill of the nearby well 1678 (Fig. 39c) could also be viewed in this light.

Clay sealing layers

Caps or sealing layers of clean clay were identified in three pits. In block 6, pit 1577 (Figs 39d, 53) was used for the burial of ?industrial debris, comprising a sequence of layers of ash, burnt clay and charcoal, and was then capped with a layer of yellow clay and gravel. In block 2, wells 808 and 905 (Figs 37b, d; 50) accumulated a deep deposit of organic debris which, in the late third or fourth century, was sealed with a thick layer of yellow clay. Subsequent sinkage required a levelling of their surface when posts of building S3 were sited above them.

Density of finds

The very variable density of finds in pits also implies differing usage of groups and zones of pits. Thus, the pits in blocks 3, 4, 5 and 5a yielded very few small finds and correspondingly little coarse pottery, while the few pits in block 1 and the concentrations in blocks 2 and 9 contained significantly greater quantities of both categories of material. The paucity of finds in the pits of blocks 3 and 4 is perhaps to be explained in terms of relatively short duration of occupation of buildings R6 and R7. In blocks 5 and 5a, on the other hand, it may be that a different type of rubbish was being buried – perhaps not general household debris but rather smelly kitchen refuse that might be more appropriately dumped in an area free of buildings. The comparative 'richness' of the rubbish in the pits of blocks 1 and 9 probably reflects respectively the relative prosperity and longevity of occupation in those areas.

OVENS   (Figs 43–4; Pl. XVIII)

The remains of ten surface-built ovens or kilns were found. All were of similar size and form, and all except one (oven 9) were located in the northern part of the site. They were generally rather superficial structures recessed only slightly into the ground. In consequence, all had suffered from recent agricultural damage, and a few had been virtually obliterated. Nevertheless, sufficient of their structure remained to allow the identification of two related types:

Type 1: boat- or bottle-shaped, ovens 2, 3, 6, 8 and, probably, ovens 4 and 9.

Type 2: figure-of-eight or dumbell-shaped, ovens 1, 5, 10 and, probably, oven 7.

Structure

The majority of both types of oven had a length measurement within the range 1.8–2.05 m and a width in the range 0.55–0.7 m. All were orientated approximately north–south except ovens 4 and 9, which had an approximate east–west alignment. Of those aligned north–south all had flues at the south where identification of that feature was possible (ovens 1, 2, 5, 6, 7, 10 and, probably, oven 8). This was presumably designed to take best advantage of a prevailing southwesterly wind.

The overall structure and layout, common to all, comprised the oven chamber, the flue, and the stoke-hole, with an area of firing debris and rake-out material. The stokeholes were generally very poorly defined as they seldom penetrated far below the surface. Additionally, the quantity of surviving rake-out debris was often negligible, presumably having been either cleared away during the functioning of the ovens or more gradually dispersed subsequently. However, in some cases (e.g. oven 6) there was an extensive deposit of ashy debris surrounding the flue area.

The flue was also generally poorly preserved, especially on the type 1 ovens. Only in the case of oven 5 and, to a

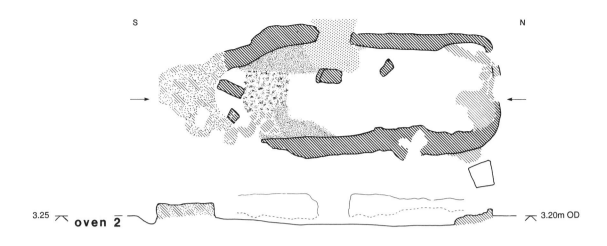

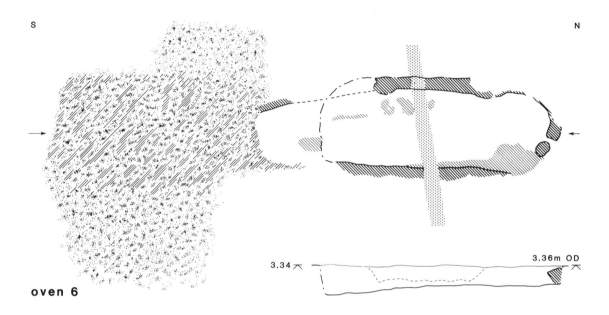

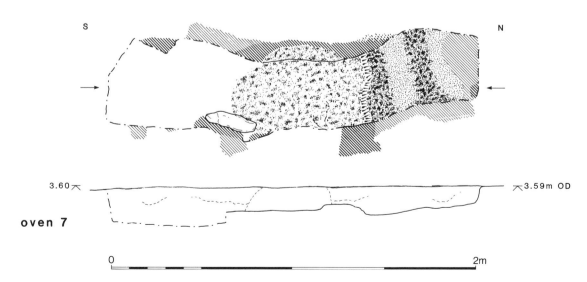

Fig. 43 Stonea Grange: ovens 2, 6 and 7. Plan and profile.

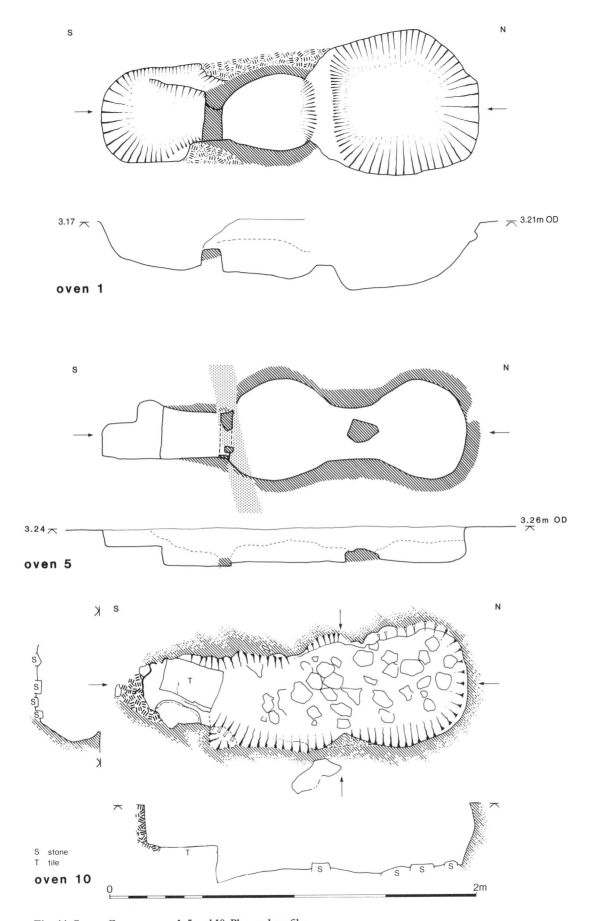

S   N

3.17   3.21m OD

oven 1

S   N

3.26m OD

3.24

oven 5

S   N

S   stone
T   tile

oven 10

0   2m

Fig. 44 Stonea Grange: ovens 1, 5 and 10. Plan and profile.

lesser extent, ovens 1 and 10, was its form apparent – a small rectangular clay-walled adjunct to the oven chamber, joined to it by means of a low basal plinth of fired clay. The flue of oven 10 was floored with a single sub-rectangular tile.

The chamber of both types had a clay-walled superstructure which was about 0.05–0.12 m thick at ground level. In the case of type 1 the superstructure was presumably semi-cylindrical or hull-shaped, while in type 2 ovens it appears to have comprised two connected domes. The maximum surviving above-ground height of the chamber wall in type 1 ovens was 0.12 m (oven 2), while oven 10, with a floor-to-surface measurement of 0.32 m had the best-preserved chamber of the type 2 ovens, and incorporated the springing of the domes. Fragments of collapsed superstructure were found in the chamber fill of several ovens, but never in large enough pieces to clarify their form.

In only a single case was there any surviving evidence for internal structure: oven 5 preserved in situ a fired clay pedestal base at the central constriction which divided its figure-of-eight chamber into two domed units. Had the second unit of the chamber of oven 1 not been quarried away, it is likely that the same feature would have been encountered there. The fill of the ovens included fragments of the collapsed clay superstructure, pieces of burnt tile and stone, pockets and lenses of ash, sand and charcoal, and areas and lumps of fire-heated clay, mainly red, but shading through orange and yellow to buff. Ash, charcoal and other burnt remains were concentrated in the region of the flue.

Function

It was initially supposed that these structures were pottery kilns. However, on excavation, they were found to contain no pottery vessels, and they failed to produce either a single piece of kiln furniture or any pottery wasters. Nor were there any waster sherds from the site as a whole. In addition, the discoloration of the clay – yellow, and red rather than purple – together with the possibility that part of the superstructure comprised yellow rather than red clay (see oven 10, N10, 2, p. 211) appears to indicate a relatively low operating temperature.

To test an alternative hypothesis, that they were ovens for the malting of grain or something similar, the contents of ovens 1, 2, 5, 6, 7 and 10 were sampled for plant remains. However, the results proved negative. Their function therefore remains indeterminate, though a purely domestic role should not be discounted.

Date

A very small quantity of pottery, mostly residual, was found in ovens 1–3, 5, and 7–10, but there were virtually no other finds and no usefully-stratified, closely-dated artefacts. This paucity of finds not only hindered the identification of func-tion but also prevented any internal dating of the ovens. However, external factors indicated a period of usage in Phase IV. Such mundane structures as ovens 1–3 would certainly not be expected during Phase III in the open space to the north of the stone building complex R1. More conclusively, a post-hole of the Phase III building R6 was sealed by the chamber floor of oven 5, while ovens 8 and 9 were constructed within the wall areas of respectively buildings R5 and R8. Presumably, those buildings were then either derelict or completely levelled. Finally, fragments of oven superstructure, probably derived from oven 6, 7 or 8, were found in well 905, layer 868, dated third or fourth century AD; and oven 7 was cut by post-hole 718/719 of Anglo-Saxon building S3.

The lack of precise dating evidence also prevented an assessment of the life-span or contemporaneity of the ovens. However, the close grouping of ovens 1 and 2, ovens 6, 7 and 8, and perhaps oven 3 and 4 is suggestive of replacement. Furthermore, the first two groups include ovens of both types, which may also imply a chronological sequence, though it may, alternatively, suggest functional diversity.

Location

Ovens 1–4, Block 1; Oven 5, Block 3; Ovens 6–8, Block 2; Oven 9, Block 8; Oven 10, Block 10.

BLOCK 1   (Figs 45–6)

A large sub-rectangular plot, about 90 × 64 m, on the west side of the site, bounded on the east by ditch 9, on the north by street 1 E/W, and on the west by the excavation edge. On the south are blocks 1a and 1b.

Structures Buildings R1 and R4.

Wells 135, 171/558, 336

Pits 132, 170, 270, 272, 277, 295, 323, 327, 349, 363, 424, 505, 511, 512, 513, 520, 528, 539, 543, 545, 587, 600, 997, 1020.

Ovens 1–4.

Ditches and gullies 6, 7, 9, 44, 45, 47–54, 63, 64, 66, 67, 74.

Sumps See pp. 87–94.

BUILDING R1
(Figs 58–66; Pls X–XIII, XVII, XXII)

This large rectangular stone building complex was constructed on a slight natural eminence about 50 m south of street 1 E/W. Its orientation is almost precisely that of the cardinal points. The overall dimensions, including ancillary rooms and later additions, are 29.5 × 25.7 m. Two main structural phases were defined. Both belong to Phase III and have been labelled Phase III and Phase IIIa accordingly.

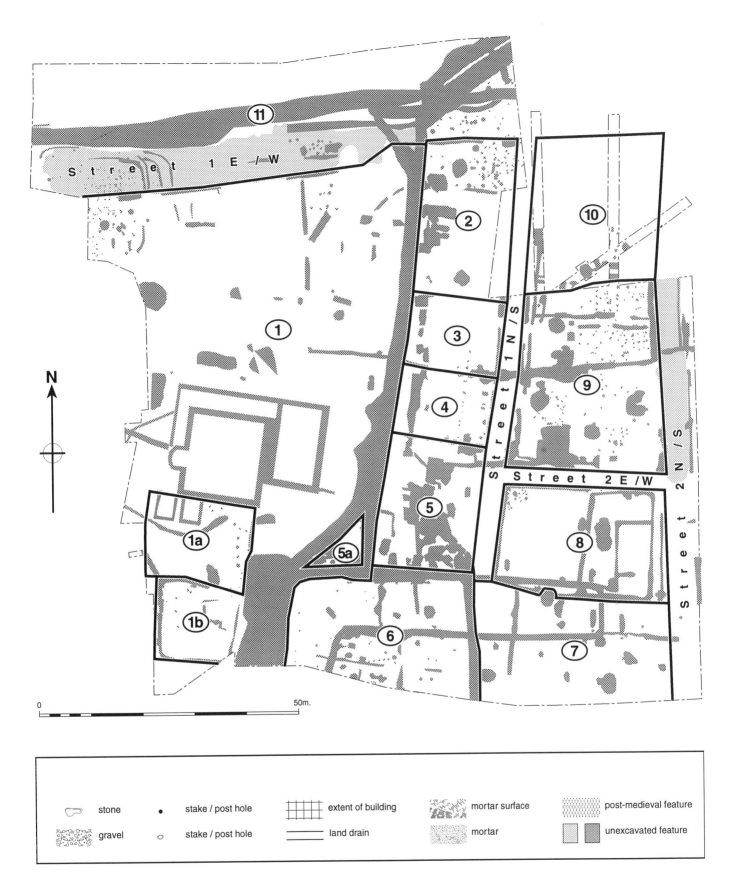

Fig. 45 Stonea Grange: keys to the block plans.

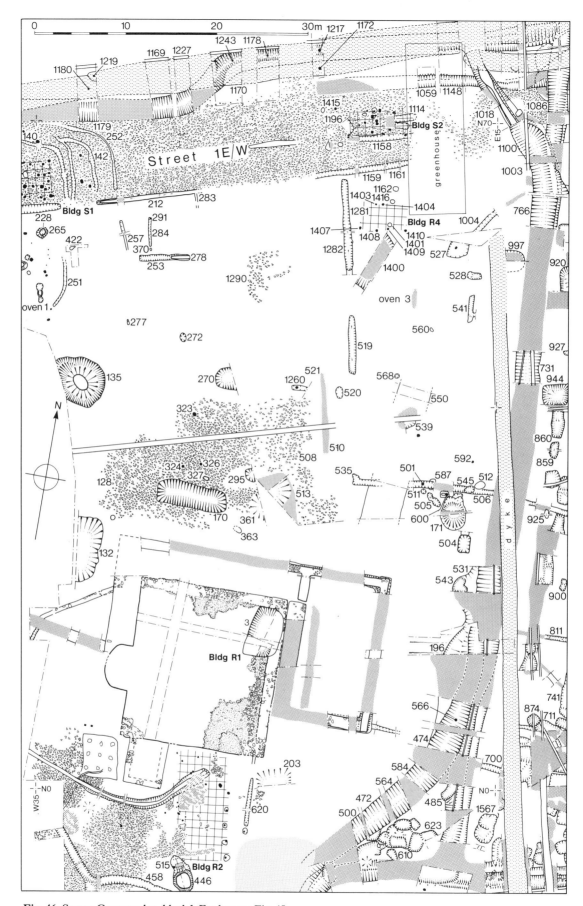

Fig. 46 Stonea Grange: plan, block 1. For key, see Fig. 45.

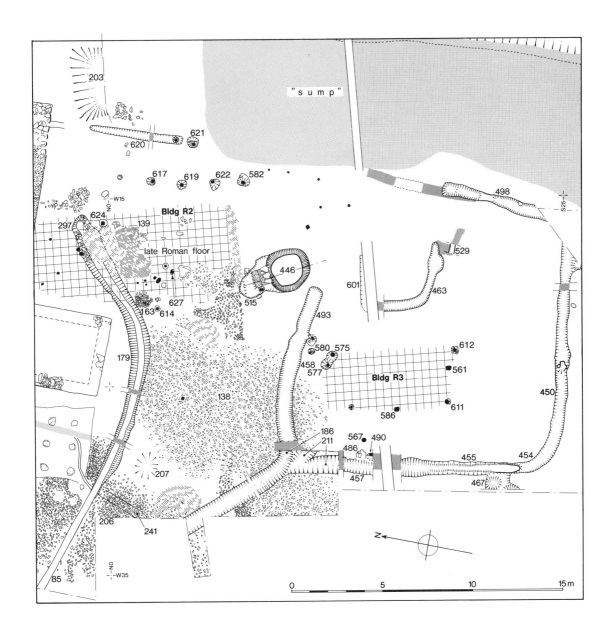

Fig. 47 Stonea Grange: plan, blocks 1a and 1b. For key, see Fig. 45.

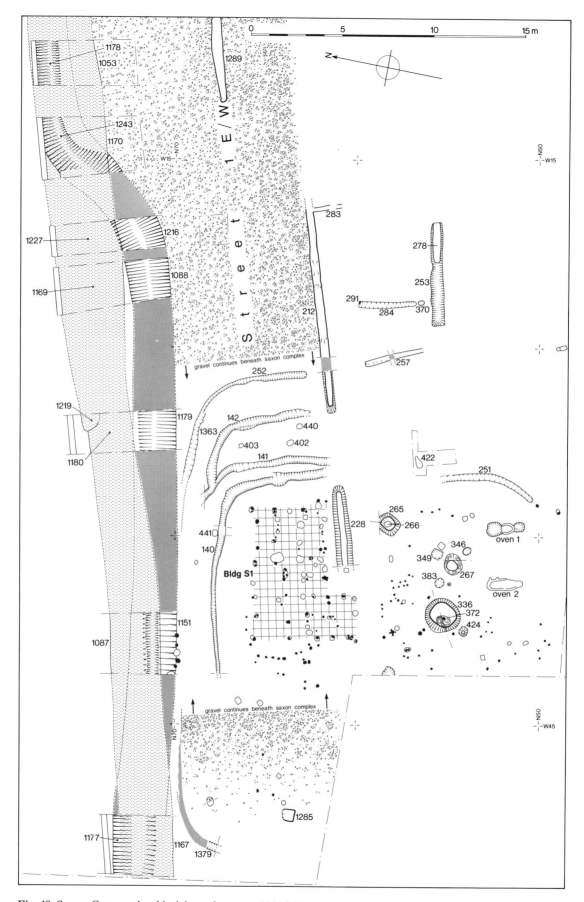

Fig. 48 Stonea Grange: plan, block 1, north-west and block 11, west. For key, see Fig. 45.

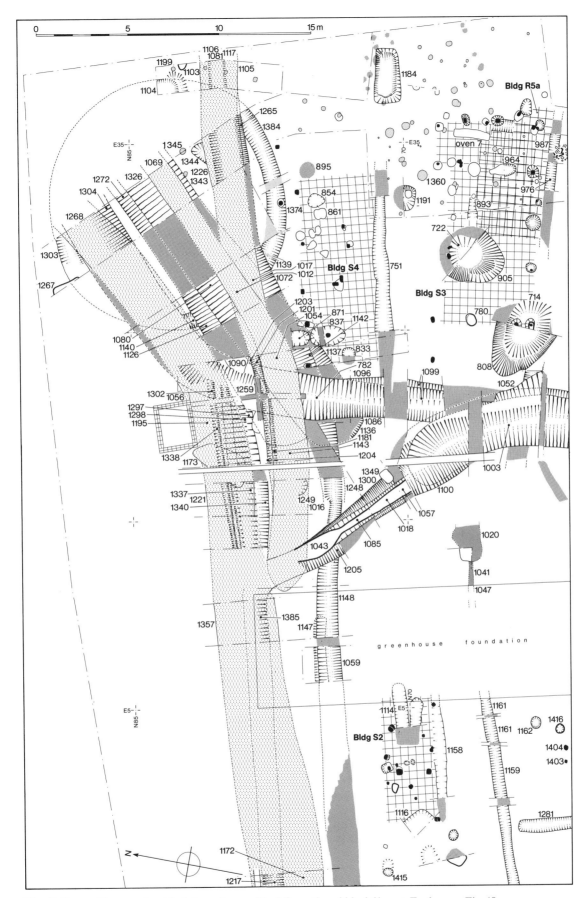

Fig. 49 Stonea Grange: plan, block 1, north-east, block 2, north and block 11, east. For key, see Fig. 45.

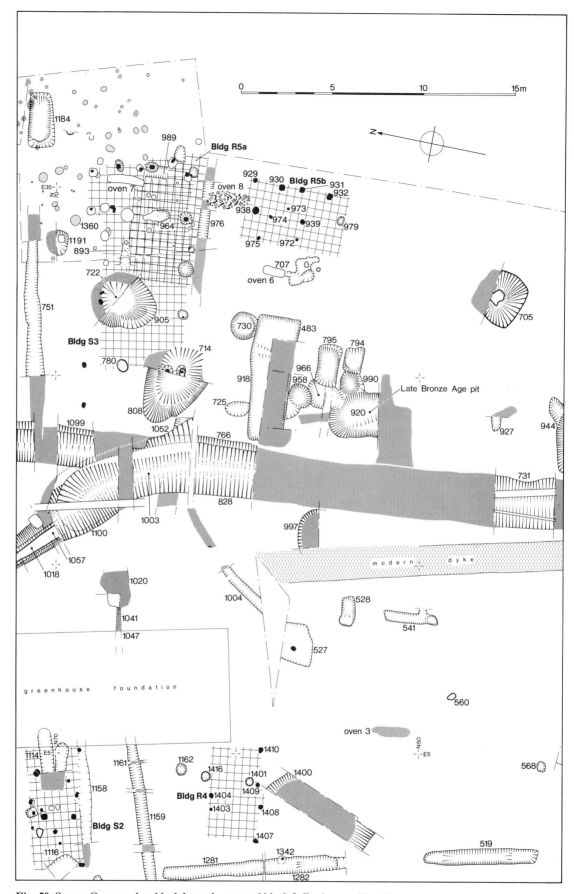

Fig. 50 Stonea Grange: plan, block 1, north-east and block 2. For key, see Fig. 45.

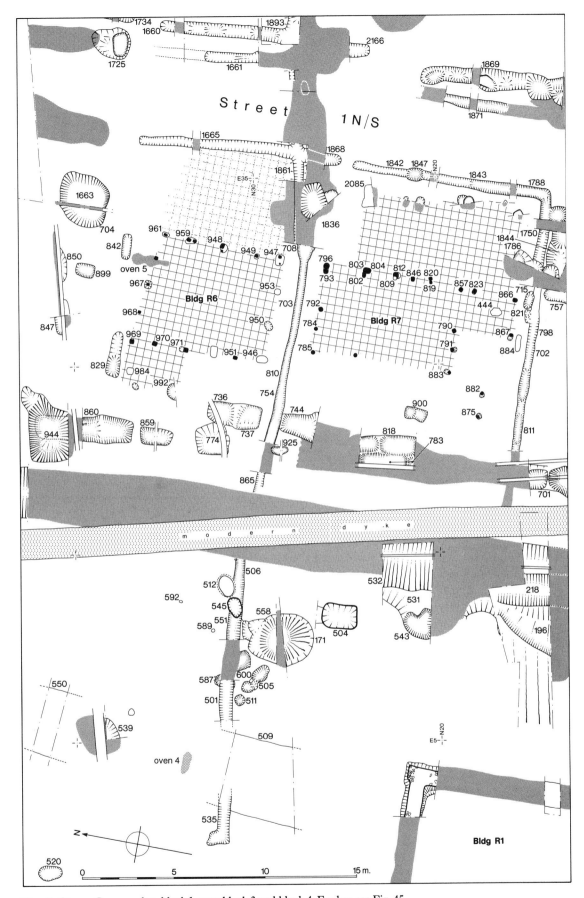

Fig. 51 Stonea Grange: plan, block 1, east, block 3 and block 4. For key, see Fig. 45.

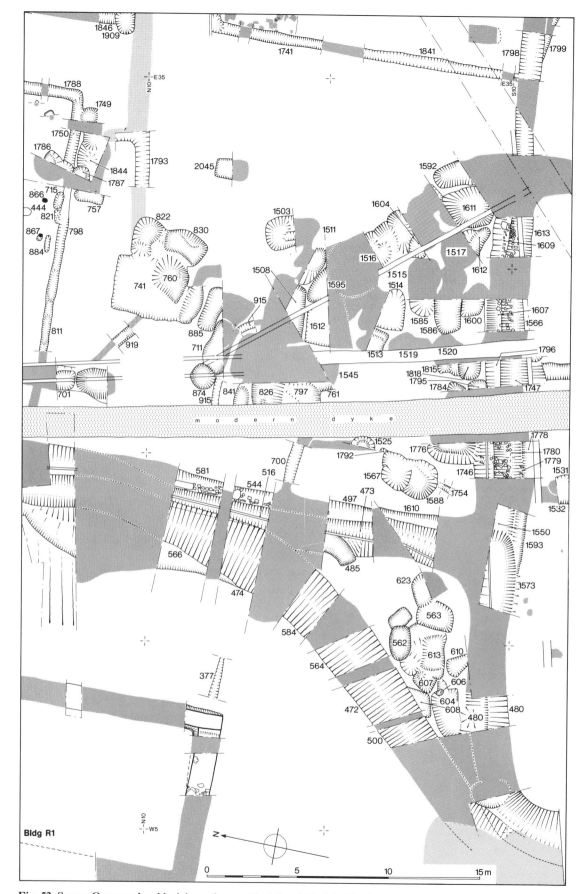

Fig. 52 Stonea Grange: plan, block 1, south-east, block 5 and block 5a. For key, see Fig. 45.

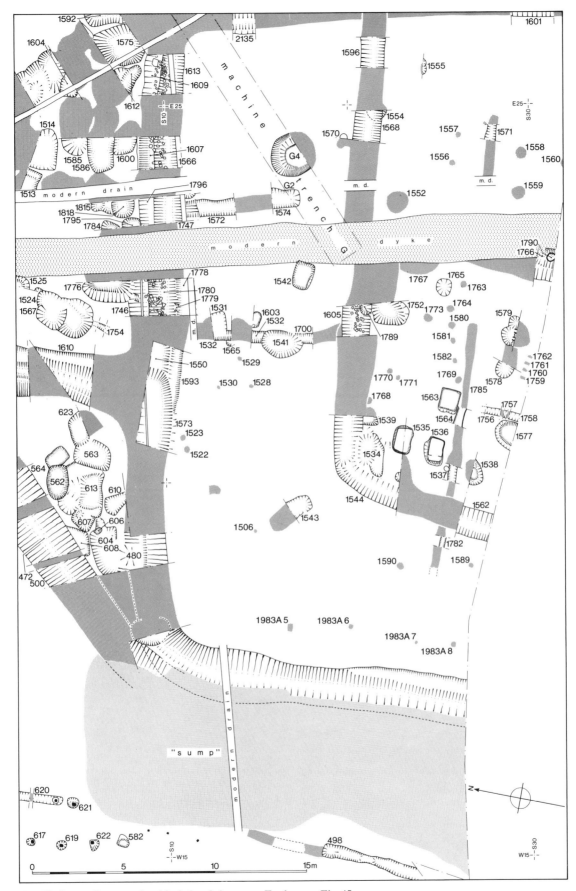

Fig. 53 Stonea Grange: plan, block 6 and the sump. For key, see Fig. 45.

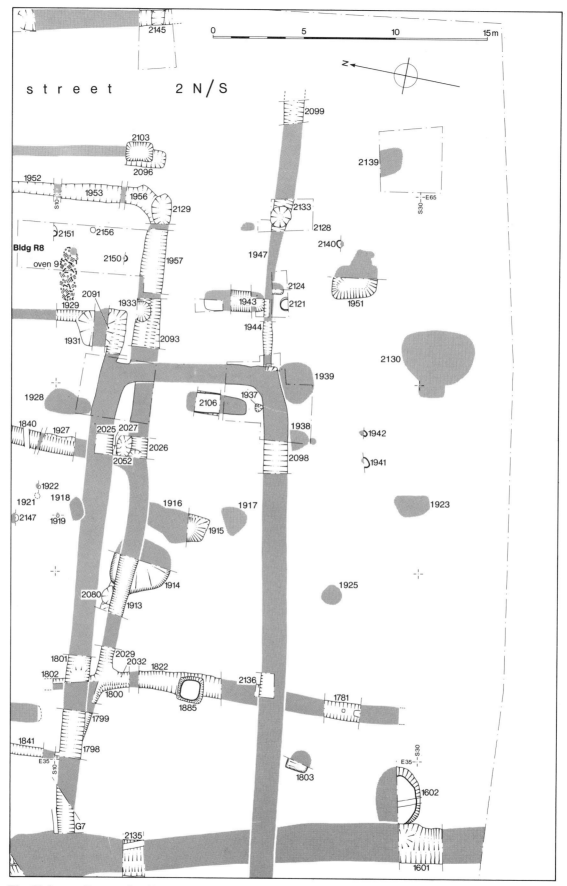

Fig. 54 Stonea Grange: plan, block 7. For key, see Fig. 45.

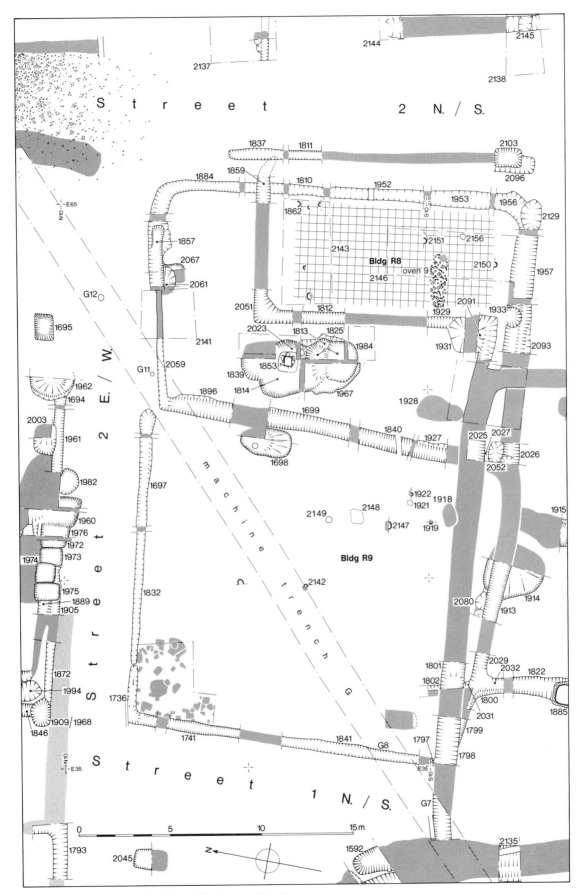

Fig. 55 Stonea Grange: plan, block 8. For key, see Fig. 45.

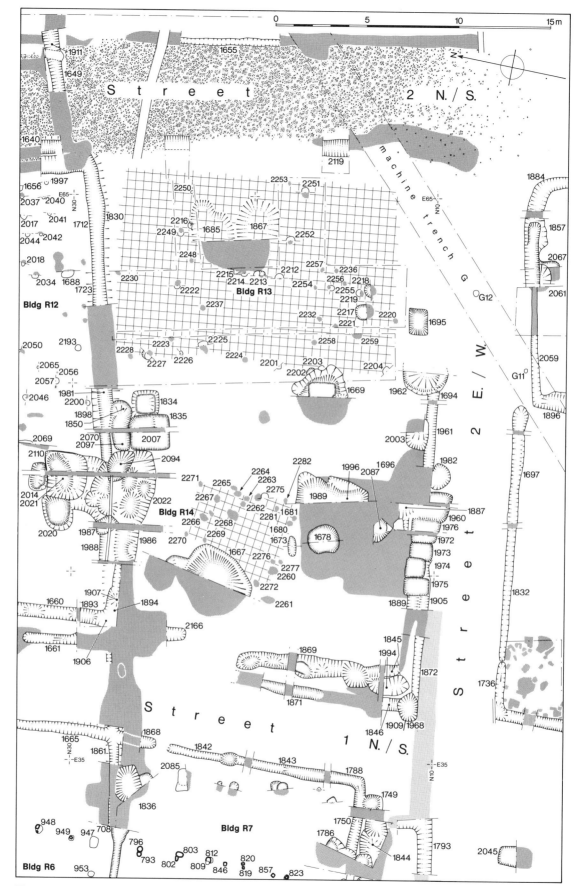

Fig. 56 Stonea Grange: plan, block 9, south. For key, see Fig. 45.

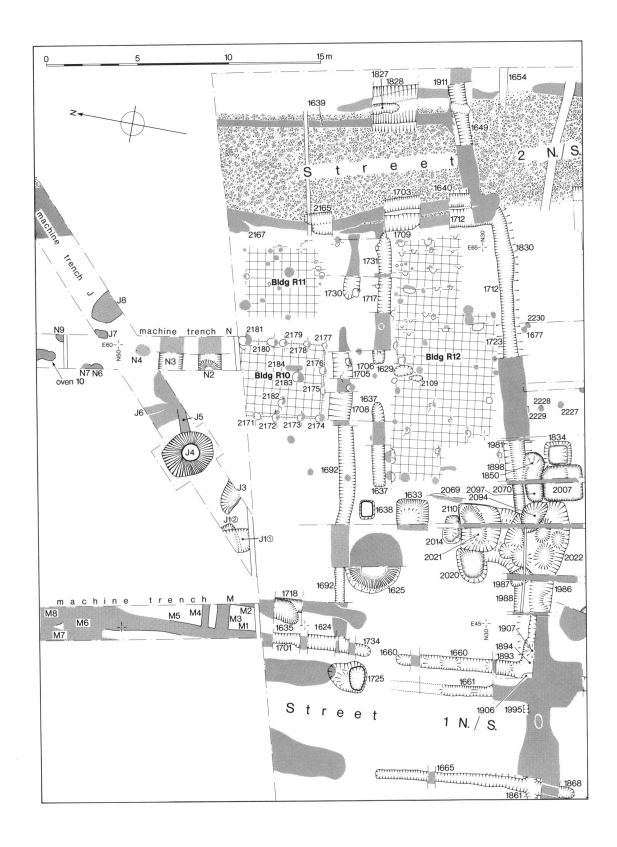

Fig. 57 Stonea Grange: plan, block 9, north and block 10, south. For key, see Fig. 45.

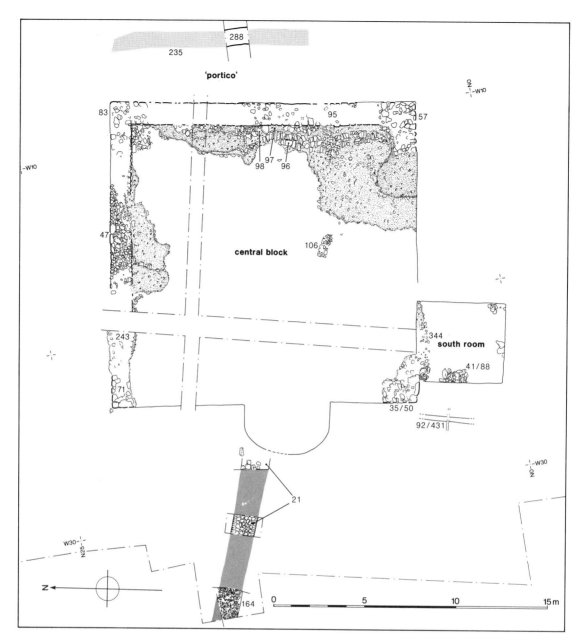

Fig. 58 Stonea Grange: plan, building R1, Phase III. For key, see Fig. 45.

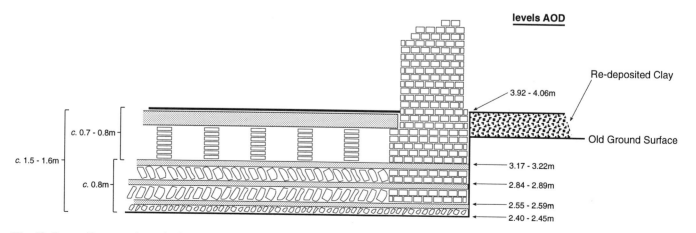

Fig. 59 Stonea Grange: schematic drawing of the foundations and substructure of the central block of building R1.

1 Description

Phase III

THE CENTRAL BLOCK
(Figs 58–9, 61d–63; Pls Xb–XI, XVII)

This was the heart of the building and comprised an almost square unit (16.0–16.25 m by 16.8–16.9 m) with an asymmetrically-placed apsidal projection (4.7 × 2.7 m) at the west. The Roman surveying/construction was not completely accurate, and in addition to the slightly different lengths of the east and west walls and the north and south walls, both the east wall and the west wall bowed slightly inwards.

Excavation of the central block began in 1980 and was completed in 1981. It was divided into four unequal quadrants by a single cross-baulk, which was left unexcavated as a record of the stratigraphy. Later Roman robbing of the building for stone was found to be very extensive. The footings of the west and south walls were entirely removed, excepting only the corners, and the greater part of the internal foundation was similarly totally quarried away. However, the north and east wall footings preserved their length intact, with a maximum height mid-way along the north side of about 1.4 m (3.81 m AOD, and 0.2 m below the Roman ground level); and three areas of the internal foundation, at the north and east sides and at the south-east corner, were sufficiently well preserved to elucidate the construction technique. This was most unusual and extremely lavish in its use of stone (see Fig. 59; Pl. XI).

A huge box trench, corresponding in size to the maximum external dimensions of the building, was dug about 1.0 m below the old ground surface into the boulder clay (2.4–2.45 m AOD). The resulting spoil was spread around the exterior to raise the surrounding ground level (see Fig. 61d, p. 126; Pl. XVII). The remains of this 'platform' measured up to 0.5 m in height (about 3.92–4.06 m AOD). The base of the trench was then covered with a pitched layer of irregular limestone blocks, about 0.1–0.15 m deep, which was capped with a layer of lime mortar about 0.05–0.1 m thick (2.55–2.59 m AOD). The next stage involved the construction around the sides of the trench of the first two courses of a wall footing 1.15–1.2 m thick. This had a mortared rubble core and a facing of limestone blocks.

A second pitched layer of irregular limestone blocks, about 0.2 m deep, was then laid across the entire area between the wall footings, and a capping layer of lime mortar, some 0.1 m deep, was spread across both the pitched layer and wall footings alike. On the resulting level surface (2.84–2.89 m AOD) two more courses of the wall footings were constructed, and a third pitched stone layer, about 0.2 m deep, was laid in the interior. A third and final overall layer of lime mortar, about 0.1 m deep was spread (3.17–3.22 m AOD), and the wall footings alone were constructed from that point upwards.

This 'raft' foundation of the central block was thus some 0.8 m thick and filled the lower part of the box trench. The upper part, at least 0.7 m deep, almost certainly accommodated a hypocaust, with the *pilae* stacks standing on the third mortar layer and supporting a floor at, or around, the new artificially raised, ground level. Stone robbing had destroyed virtually the whole of the interior leaving no in situ remains of the hypocaust. However, its existence may be adduced from the provision of a recessed cavity of appropriate height, from the identification of a *praefurnium* (see The South Room, p. 124), and from the presence of iron T-clamps and large quantities of box flue-tiles in the dereliction/destruction debris in and around building R1.

Data: SW quadrant

Unit number		Site phase	Coarse pottery date
27	Robbing debris/levelling, above 52	IV	Late 2nd/ early 3rd cent AD
35	Wall footing, SW corner, same as 50	III	–
36	Silt in robbing void under 35, same as 233	IV	–
45	Robbing debris	IV	–
50	Wall footing, SW corner, same as 35	III	–
52	Robbing debris, below 27	IV	–
54	Robbing debris, below 52	IV	–
62	Clay slump after robbing of wall footing, W wall, S of apse	IV	–
67	Lowest pitched stone foundation, remnant, below 45	III	–
80	Clay natural, below 67	–	–
120	Robbing debris	IV	AD 125 on
233	Robbing void under 35, same as 36	IV	–

Matrix

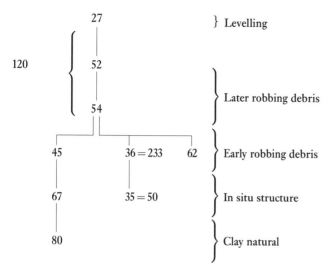

Data: NW quadrant

Unit number		Site phase	Coarse pottery date
65	Robbing debris, above and adjacent to 71, cf. 136, 151, 154	IV	–
71	Wall footing, NW corner, adjacent to 243	III	–
107	Soil in robbing void below 71	IV	–
118	Robbing debris cf. 27 (SW quadrant)	IV	–
136	Robbing debris/levelling	IV	4th cent AD
151	Robbing debris, below 154	IV	4th cent AD
153	Robbing debris, below 136	IV	–
154	Robbing debris, below 153	IV	–
160	Robbing debris, below 151	IV	–
174	Robbing debris, below 160	IV	?Late 2nd cent AD
176	Robbing debris, below 174	IV	–
243	N wall footing, E of 71	III	–

Matrix

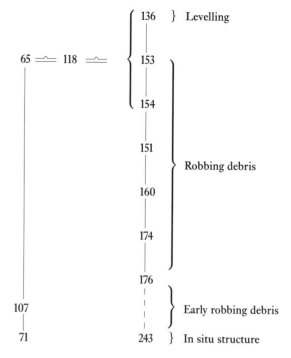

Small finds

65 Copper-alloy ear scoop, Jackson cat. no. 55 (SF 25); iron T-clamps, Jackson cat. nos 63–4 (SF 20, 23 and 30).
151 Lead sheet fragments, Jackson cat. no. 29 (SF 78).
243 Icenian silver coin, Chadburn cat. no. 60 (SF 120).

Data: NE quadrant

Unit number		Site phase	Coarse pottery date
12	Robbing hollow in top of 47	IV/V	–
14	Upper robbing debris/levelling, above 15	IV	–
15	Upper robbing debris, below 14	IV	?3rd cent AD
16	Upper robbing debris, below 15	IV	–
47	Wall footing, N side, centre	III	–
78	Robbing debris, above 105	IV	–
79	Robbing debris, E of 78	IV	Late 3rd–4th cent AD
83	Wall footing, NE corner	III	–
105	Robbing debris, below 78, adjacent to 83	IV	–
133	Sub-floor foundation, NE and SE quadrants	III	AD 125 on
136	Robbing debris/levelling	IV	4th cent AD
177	Robbing debris	IV	–
182	Robbing debris, below 185	IV	–
185	Robbing debris, below 177	IV	4th cent AD
195	Robbing debris, patches, against N wall footing	IV	–

Data: NE quadrant *(continued)*

Unit number		Site phase	Coarse pottery date
204	Robbing debris, below 182	IV	–
3	Pit, top layer	V	
13	Pit, layer, below 3	V	Residual
31	Pit, layer, same as 13	V	3rd cent AD
221	Pit, layer, same as 13	V	

Matrix

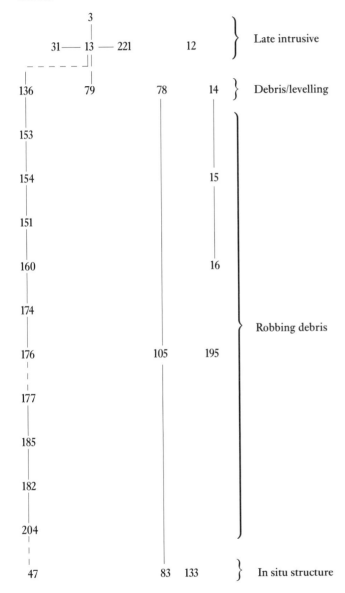

Small finds

182 Coin, Shotter cat. no. 23, As, VW, AD 117–38 (SF 83).

185 Bone pin, Greep cat. no. 15 (SF 198).

3 Coin, Shotter cat. no. 57, AE copy, MW AD 350+ (SF 3); lead sheet fragment (SF 4).

Data: SE quadrant

Unit number		Site phase	Coarse pottery date
32	Upper robbing debris, S side	IV	4th cent AD
33	Upper robbing debris, SE corner	IV	Early/mid 3rd cent AD
37	Robbing debris, below 38	IV	Late 3rd–4th cent AD
38	Robbing debris, below 32	IV	–
55	Robbing debris, several layers, bulked	IV	4th cent AD
56	Robbing debris, several layers, bulked	IV	4th cent AD
57	Wall footing, SE corner	III	–
64	Robbing debris, E side, several layers, bulked	IV	3rd or 4th cent AD
68	Robbing debris, below 33	IV	–
76	Robbing debris, below 37	IV	4th cent AD
77	Early robbing debris, below 76	IV	4th cent AD
81	Clay natural, below 55	–	–
82	Clay natural, below 77	–	–
95	Wall footing, E side	III	–
96	Lowest pitched stone foundation below 97	III	–
97	Lowest mortar foundation layer, below 98	III	–
98	Second pitched stone foundation, below 64	III	–
106	Lowest pitched stone foundation remains, below 56	III	–
119	Robbing debris, SE corner	IV	–
133	Lowest pitched stone foundation remains in NE and SE quadrants	III	AD 125 on
215	Robbing debris, above 216	IV	4th cent AD
216	Robbing debris, above 225	IV	–
225	Robbing/footing debris of S wall footing, W of 57	IV	–

Matrix

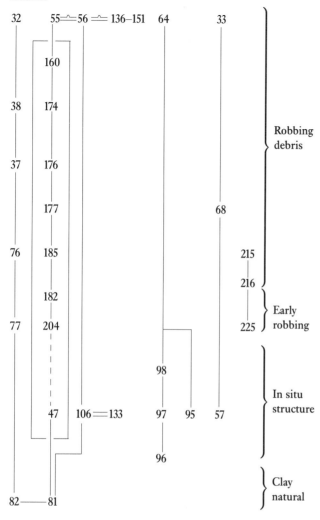

Small finds
32 Mortarium stamp, Hartley cat. no. 13.
55 Fused lump of lead, Jackson cat. no. 36 (SF 17).
56 Bone pin fragment (SF 16).
68 Brooch, Mackreth cat. no. 5, Colchester Derivative, mid 1st century AD, (SF 19).
82 Iron T-clamp, Jackson cat. no. 65 (SF 32).

THE SOUTH ROOM
(Figs 58, 61a–b; Pl. XIIb).

This rectangular room was attached to the south side of the central block 1.1 m to the east of the south-west corner. It measured externally 4.85 × 4.25 m with the long axis orientated east–west. It was recessed 0.6–0.65 m below the surface of the raised 'platform' clay, which was dug from the foundation trench of the central block and spread around its margins. The room had suffered even more comprehensive stone-robbing than the central block, presumably because its walls were slighter and more readily removed. Only a few

fragments of the pitched limestone footings remained in situ, most notably on the north and west sides. Their width appears to have been about 0.6 m. At the centre of the north side, flanked by the mortared wall footings, was a 1 m wide deposit of yellow, green and red burnt clay with burnt stone, tile and ash. No associated structural or architectural component survived, but it is suggested that this was the remains of furnace debris in the flue of the *praefurnium* which served the hypocaust of the central block. The floor level, 3.28 m AOD, corresponds almost exactly to that of the surface of the uppermost mortar layer of the 'raft' foundation of the central block (3.17–3.22 m AOD).

Data

Unit number		Site phase	Coarse pottery date
26	Robbing/dereliction debris	IV/V	Late 3rd cent and Saxon
41	Footings, W wall	III	–
42	Robbing/dereliction debris	IV/V	AD 125 on
43	Robbing/dereliction debris, burnt	IV/V	–
88	Footings, W wall	III	–
122	Robbing/dereliction debris, S side	IV/V	AD 125 on
344	Footings, N wall	III	–

Matrix

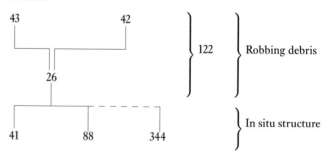

Small finds 122 Lead offcuts, Jackson cat. nos 17 and 22 (SF 39 and 61).

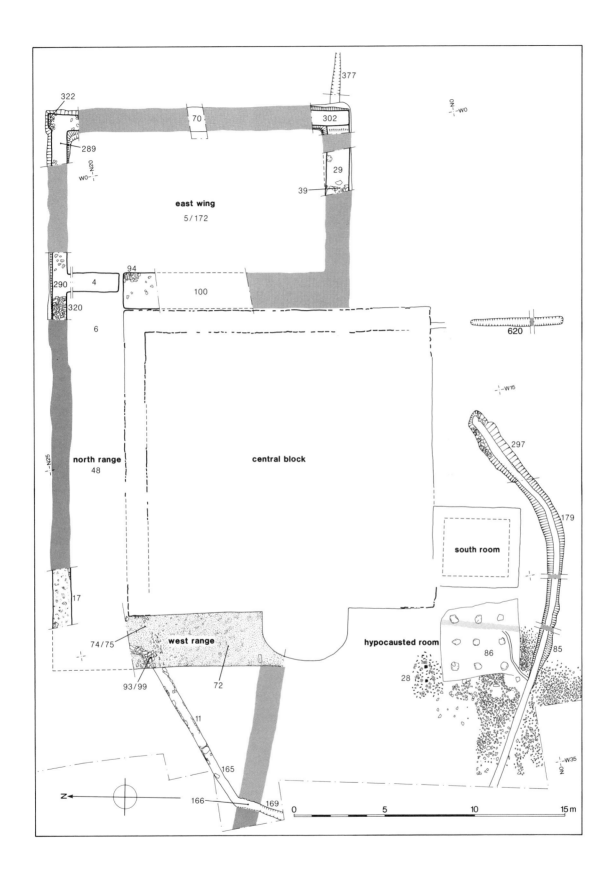

Fig. 60 Stonea Grange: plan, building R1, Phase IIIa. For key, see Fig. 45.

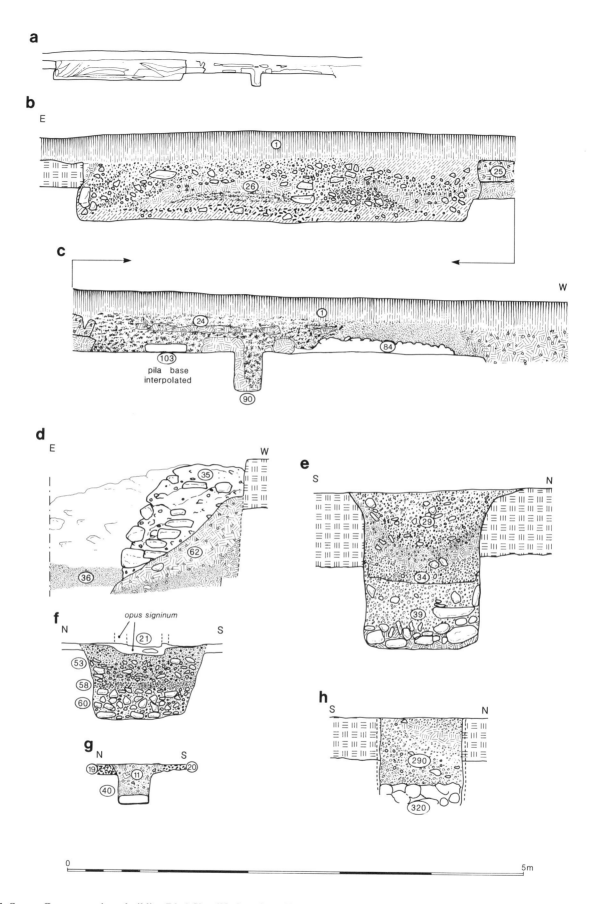

Fig. 61 Stonea Grange: sections, building R1. a) Simplified version of b) and c). b) South room, south side. c) Small hypocausted room, south side. d) Central block, south-west quadrant, combined section and view of wall footing. e) East wing, south side, wall footing. f) Drain (gully 48). g) Drain (gully 49). h) North range, east end, wall footing. For key, see Fig. 29, p. 82.

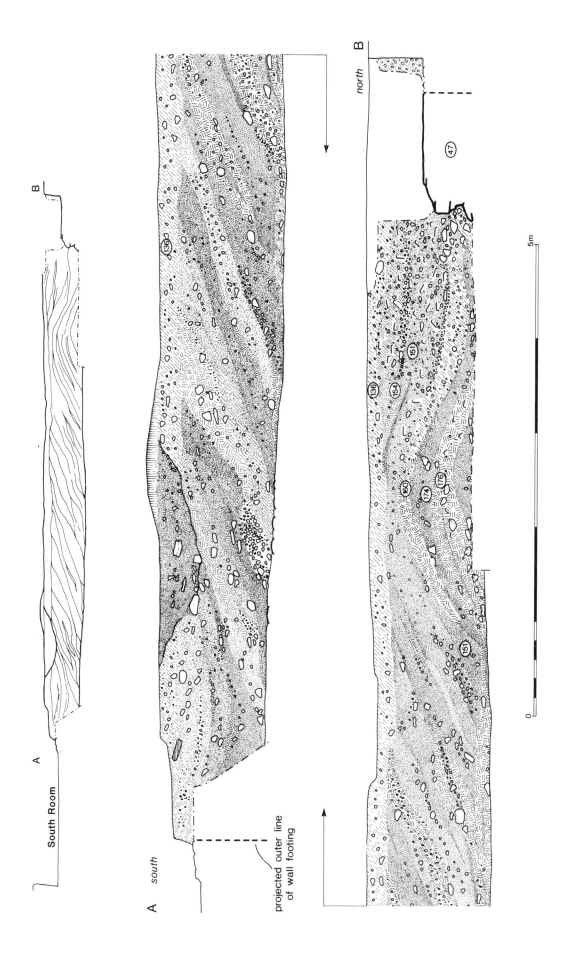

B

A

South Room

A

B

A *south*

projected outer line
of wall footing

north

B

136

151

136

154

160

174

176

47

151

0   5m

Fig. 62 Stonea Grange: north–south section and simplified version, central block, building R1. For location, see Fig. 58; for key, see Fig. 29, p. 82.

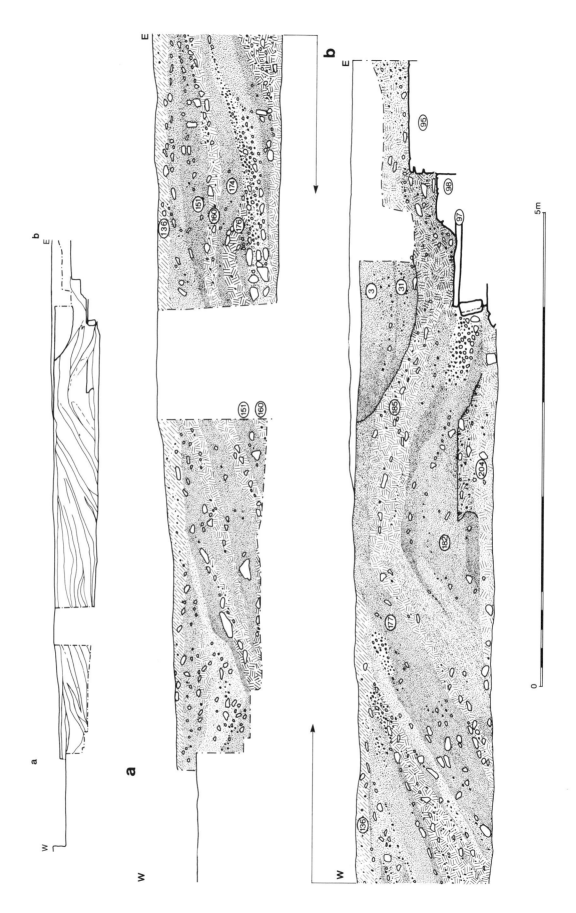

Fig. 63 Stonea Grange: east–west section and simplified version, central block, building R1. For location, see Fig. 58; for key, Fig. 29, p. 82.

THE 'PORTICO'
(Fig. 58)

This was a very indefinite linear feature which lay parallel to, and about 3 m east of, the east wall of the central block. Despite intensive and sensitive surface trowelling its north and south ends could not be ascertained, and its edges remained ill-defined. It was at least 10 m long, and about 0.8–0.9 m wide. Excavation of part of the central sector did not clarify the feature. It produced no finds and was only some 0.25 m deep. An association with the central block seems inescapable in view of the shared orientation and proximity. However, it seems too ephemeral to have taken the footing for a portico as was at first suggested (Potter and Whitehouse 1982, 218), and it is more likely to have been an unused foundation trench or a feature connected in some way with the laying-out or construction of the central block or the Phase IIIa east wing.

Data

Unit number	Site phase	Coarse pottery date
235/288 Shallow silt-filled ?wall trench	?III	–

DRAINAGE
(Figs 25, 58, 61f; Pl. XIIa)

A substantial drainage feature, gully 48, extended for a distance of at least 18 m from the north side of the apse of the central block on a line slightly north of due west. There was no obvious explanation for its deviation from the orientation of the building, though its course may have been determined by its ultimate destination. In any case, as a subterranean feature, there was no need for it to conform to surface structures. Its junction with the apse had been cut away by stone robbers (unit 44) who had removed the whole of the apse wall and the first 40 cm of the stone-packed fill of the drain. The drain comprised two parts: the upper component (unit 21), perhaps a secondary feature, was a box-drain made of *opus signinum* slabs. Only the base and the decayed stub of the two flanking walls survived; the lower component was a broad, deep, near vertical-sided trench with a flat base. It was filled with two layers of limestone chips, divided by a thin layer of gravel, all heavily iron-panned, and appears to have functioned as a soakaway drain. The base of the trench was covered with small to medium-sized limestone slabs. It continued beyond the west excavation edge and was located again in trench B. It was cut by the stone-lined drain (gully 49).

Width i) box drain: internal 0.45 m, external 0.65 m; ii) soakaway: 1.3 m. Length at least 18 m. Depth, soakaway: 0.8 m.

Fill

Cuts 1 and 2	21 (AX)	Red-brown sandy silt within *opus signinum* box-drain.
	53 (CG)	Loosely-packed angular limestone chippings, heavily iron-panned
	58 (CM)	Thin compact layer of angular brown gravel in a fine gritty matrix, heavily iron-panned.
	60 (CP)	Loosely-packed angular limestone chippings, slightly larger and a little less iron-panned than those of 53, resting on a layer of limestone slabs.

Cut 3 164 (HC) As cuts 1–2.

Cut 4 B1 Limestone chips and gravel in mixed orange and brown sand. [Unexcavated.]

Dating evidence Nothing datable.

Phase IIIa

THE EAST WING
(Figs 60, 61e; Pl. XIIIa)

A large rectangular unit (16.4 × 9.6 m) built on to the east side of the central block. Its length matches that of the east wall of the central block, but it is offset 4 m to the north. In contrast to the unusual foundation of the central block, its footings were set in narrow trenches along the wall lines. Later Roman robbing of the stone was very comprehensive, and in only a few places did the last vestige of the footings survive. They consisted of irregular blocks and slabs of limestone, carefully pitched in the clay natural and bedded in a loose, ginger-coloured sandy matrix. Scientific analysis of samples of this matrix (see pp. 524–5) detected very little lime, and it was concluded that the material was probably a clay and gravel aggregate rather than a lime mortar. The relative looseness of this aggregate explains why the footings were even more completely robbed-out than the mortared foundations of the central block.

Nevertheless, enough of the footings survived to demonstrate that they varied somewhat, in both width and depth. The north and east sides were 0.85 m wide and 2.8–3.0 m AOD at their lowest point. The south side was 1.3 m wide and its east end, 3.02 m AOD at its base. However, 3.8 m west of the south-east corner the footing was cut 0.4 m lower (2.63 m AOD). The north end of the west side, that part which projected north of the central block, was 0.95 m wide and 3.0 m AOD at its base. The remainder of the west side was 1.9 m wide, for no gap was left between the new footing trench and the east side of the central block, and the intervening space was incorporated into a broad foundation 3.01 m AOD at its base. These variations are probably attributable to constructional and/or architectural requirements, actual or perceived, for they cannot be explained in terms of changes in subsoil or ground level.

No divisions were detected in the interior, which measured 14.2 × 7.6 m. However, as surface erosion had reduced the remains to sub-floor level any evidence for partitioning above that point would have been completely erased. The room was not hypocausted.

Data

Unit number		Site phase	Coarse pottery date
4	Robbing debris in footing trench W side, N end	IV	4th cent AD
8	Robbing debris in footing trench, N side	IV	–
29	Robbing debris in footing trench, S side, E end	IV	Later 2nd/3rd cent AD
34	Robbing debris in footing trench, S side, E end, below 29	IV	AD 125 on
39	Footing remains, S side, E end, below 34	IIIa	–
64	Robbing debris in footing trench, W side, centre	IV	3rd or 4th cent AD
70	Robbing debris in footing trench, E side, centre	IV	–
94	Footing remains, W side, N end, below 4	IIIa	–
100	Robbing debris in footing trench, W side, centre	IV	–
101	Clay natural, W side, centre, below 100	–	–
289	Robbing debris in footing trench, NE corner	IV	AD 125 on
290	Robbing debris in footing trench NW corner	IV	3rd cent AD
299	Robbing debris in footing trench, NE corner, below 289	IV	AD 125 on
302	Robbing debris in footing trench, SE corner	IV	4th cent AD
320	Footing remains, NW corner, below 290	IIIa	–
322	Footing debris, NE corner, below 299	IIIa	–
5	Interior, sub-floor natural clay surface, W side	IIIa	–
172	Interior, sub-floor natural clay surface, E side	IIIa	?3rd cent AD

Small finds

29 Copper-alloy finger ring, Johns cat. no. 4 (SF 12); bone needle, Greep cat. no. 48, (SF 14).
70 Iron knife, Jackson cat. no. 18 (SF 21).
172 Samian stamp, Dickinson cat. no. 36 (SF 109).

THE NORTH RANGE
(Figs 60, 61h)

This long rectangular unit, abutting the north wall of the central block, was created by extending westwards by some 20 m the north wall of the east wing. The internal dimensions were 19 × 3 m. The foundation trench was sampled at the east and west ends. It measured 0.9–1.0 m wide, and its base was 2.91–3.0 m AOD. The footings, better preserved at the east than the west, were identical to those of the east wing – pitched limestone rubble embedded in the natural clay and set in a ginger-coloured sandy gravel matrix. Later Roman stone-robbing of both the long walls, together with recent agricultural damage, had destroyed most of the interior surface, but a small area of the pinkish mortar floor foundation survived in situ. No internal divisions were found.

Data

Unit number		Site phase	Coarse pottery date
6	Robbed floor footing, E end	IV	–
17	Robbed footing, N wall, W end	IV	–
48	Mortar floor remains, centre S	IIIa	–
49	Clay surface, below 48	IIIa	–
73	Clay surface, below robbed floor, W end	IIIa	–
290	Robbing debris in footing trench, N wall, E end	IV	3rd cent AD
320	Footing remains, N wall, E end, below 290	IIIa	–

Matrix

	NW corner	N side	NE corner	E side	SE corner	S side	W side corner	W side north
Robbing {	290	8	289	70	302	29	64	4
			299			34		79
Footings {	320		322			39	100	94
Natural {							101	

Matrix

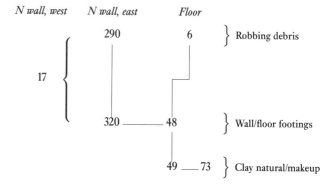

THE WEST RANGE
(Fig. 60)

This narrow rectangular unit, about 11.5 × 2.8 m, was contrived by linking the west end of the north range to the north side of the apse of the central block. The foundations appear to have been laid in the same way as those of the west wall of the east wing – in the sector flanking the west wall of the central block the footing trench spanned the entire gap. Its base was 3.04 m AOD. A small area of the footing survived. It comprised pitched limestone rubble in a ginger-coloured gravelly matrix. The north-west corner was not excavated but it was probably similar to the north-west corner of the east wing.

Data

Unit number		Site phase	Coarse pottery date
18	Robbing debris, upper, N end	IV	AD 125 on
44	Robbing debris, upper, S end	IV	3rd cent AD
51	Robbing debris, below 44	IV	–
61	Robbed wall footing, S end	IV	–
72	Robbing debris/footing of floor and wall, below 44	IV	–
74	Robbing debris, floor, below 18	IV	–
75	Robbing debris, below 18	IV	–
89	Robbing debris, wall and floor, below 18	IV	3rd cent AD
93	Pitched stone footing, N end	IIIa	–
99	Robbed stone footing, S of 93	IV	–
102	Natural clay, below 61	–	–

Matrix

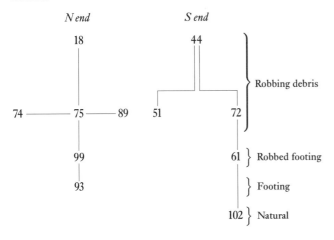

THE SMALL HYPOCAUSTED ROOM
(Figs 60, 61c; Pl. XIIb)

A rectangular structure outside the south-west corner of the central block. It is of similar size, adjacent to, and west of, the south room. No walls were located, but a regular grid of nine limestone *pila* bases (unit 103) lay within a distorted rectangular area, about 4.5 × 3.8 m, recessed about 0.15–0.4 m into the platform clay and natural clay. The orientation of the *pila* bases, and, by implication, that of the walls, was the same as that of the wall footings of the other component structures of building R1.

Outside the south and west walls of the room were preserved the partial and truncated remains of a cobbled surface of limestone chips (units 84 and 240). A two-post setting within an area of reddened clay, stone, and charcoal (unit 28) outside the north-west corner is the remains of a furnace structure which, from the reddening of the proximal (north-west) *pila* base, is confirmed as the heat source for the small hypocausted room. A layer of dark grey ash (unit 24), 0.3–0.5 m deep, which extended across the whole room and sealed the *pilae* bases, is the destruction deposit. It incorporated thick lenses of fine grey ashy clay and large quantities of burnt daub, tile and mortar, structural debris which implies that the building was of timber and daub with a tiled roof. Beneath was a thin layer of silt (unit 63) lying on the clay ground surface (units 86 and 362). A small trench (units 92 and 431), perhaps a beam-slot, cut into the clay, was sealed by the north-east *pila* base. Given the aberrant orientation and the fact that it was observed to continue northwards beneath the 'platform' clay which was redeposited when the central block of building R1 was constructed, it evidently belongs to Phase II.

The use of water within the room is indicated by a narrow, sinuous slot, with a burnt silt and charcoal fill, which connects the south-east corner of the room with gully 45. Its dimensions and its angular 'segmented' form are suggestive of a pipeline of lead or of connecting wooden pipes.

Data

Unit number		Site phase	Coarse pottery date
24	Destruction deposit, above 63	IV	Early 3rd cent AD
28	Furnace, structure and debris	IIIa	Late 2nd/early 3rd cent AD
63	Secondary silt, above 86	IIIa	Early 3rd cent AD
86	Primary silt on clay ground surface, same as 362	IIIa	Late 2nd cent AD
90	Post-hole or part of beam-slot 92	II	–
92	Beam-slot, same as 431	II	–
103	*Pilae* bases	IIIa	–
362	Clay ground surface, same as 86	IIIa	–
431	Beam-slot, same as 92	II	–

Matrix

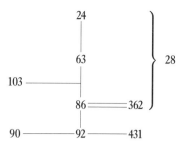

Small finds

24 Samian stamp, Dickinson cat. no. 119 (SF 15); bone pin, Greep cat. no. 23 (SF 33); lead offcuts, Jackson cat. nos 120 and 20 (SF 28 and 35); whetstone, Jackson cat. no. 34; stone tessera, Jackson cat. no. 54.

28 Carnelian intaglio, Johns cat. no. 2, probably 2nd century AD (SF 11)

63 Iron object and hobnails, Jackson cat. no. 42 (SF 31 and 18).

362 Sandstone disc, Jackson cat. no. 47 (SF 223).

DRAINAGE

Gully 49 (Fig. 25, p. 77; Figs 60, 61g)

A stone-lined box-drain which runs obliquely – approximately south-west – from the middle of the west range. It cuts unit 164 of gully 48 (which it probably replaced) at which point it turns southwards (SSW) in order to reduce to a minimum the effort involved in cutting through the packed stone fill of gully 48, and continues beyond the west excavation edge.

Its fall, NE–SW, over the 12 m exposed length, is 0.5 m. It was heavily robbed of its stone lining: all the capping stones, all except two of the basal slabs, and most of the wall stones had been removed.

Width: internal 0.25–0.35 m; external 0.4–0.5 m. Length at least 12 m. Depth 0.45 m.

Fill

Cut 1 11 (AL) Red-brown gravelly silt with iron-pan staining. Secondary fill
40 (BS) Blue-grey silty clay with iron-pan staining. Basal silt.

Cut 2 165 (HD) Red-brown silty clay with a few pebbles and iron-pan staining. Secondary fill.
250 (LW) Green-grey silty clay. Basal silt.

Cut 3 166 (HE) Red-brown silty clay with sparse rubble. Secondary fill.
258 (ME) Dark brown-grey silt with brick and tile fragments.

Cut 4 169 (HH) Dark brown silt with iron-pan staining.
274 (MX) As 169.
276 (MZ) As 169.

Dating evidence

Upper layers: Gritty buff type 74; NVCC? type 4. Date: ?3rd century AD.

Cut 1, layer 40: NVCC type 4. Date: mid/late 3rd century AD.

Cut 3, layer 258: Gritty buff type 69. Date: late 2nd century AD.

Small finds 258 Window glass, (SF 152).

Gully 47 (Figs 25, 60)

A small, rather irregular, tapering gully, probably a drain, which runs in an easterly direction from the south-east corner of the east wing. The east end was not located, but it appears likely that it debouched into ditch 6 or ditch 9. Gully 47 is cut through the mortar surface/spread (unit 378) which appears to have been contemporary with the construction and/or occupation of the R1 building complex.

Width 0.25–0.5 m, length at least 3.0 m, depth 0.35 m.

Fill 377 (TJ) Yellow-brown sandy rubbly fill.

Dating evidence Nothing datable.

Gully 45 (Fig. 25; Fig. 47, p. 109)

A small, steep-sided gully, probably a formerly wood-lined box-drain, which runs SSE from the south-west corner of the small hypocausted room. The 'shadow' of a former pipeline was detected within the hypocausted room. Its junction with gully 45 was cut away by gully 44. Gully 45 was sealed by the cobble surface 206.

Width 0.45 m (pipeline 0.1 m), length at least 3 m (pipeline 3 m), depth 0.1 m.

Fill 241 (LL) Stony grey silt.

Dating evidence NVSC flagon cf. type 52; NVGW imitation samian. Date: late 2nd/early 3rd century AD.

Gully 44 (Figs 25, 60)

A U-sectioned gully, with near-vertical sides, a lightly rounded base, and badly eroded upper margins. Almost certainly a drain (perhaps originally a wood-lined box-drain), it begins near the south-east corner of the central block and runs westwards, curving round the south room and the small hypocausted room. It cuts the small drain, gully 45, and continues beyond the west excavation edge. Its fall, east–west, over the 22 m exposed length, is 0.3 m. At its east end it is sealed by the pink mortar floor (unit 139) of building R2.

Width 0.3–0.5 m (1.15 m including erosion), length at least 22 m, depth 0.05–0.4 m.

Fill

Cut 1 297 (NX) Mixed light and dark brown silt with charcoal flecks.

Cut 2 179 (HT) Dark brown/black clayey silt.
208 (KA) Brown silt.
209 (KB) Yellow sandy silt.
219 (KM) Dark brown loose silt.
217 (KK) Light brown silt. Slump.

Cut 3 85 (DR) Brown silt.

Dating evidence (Fig. 163, nos 103–12, p. 460)

Upper layers: (85, 179, 297) NVCC types 2, 20/21; Flagon cf. type 52; NVGW type ?29; gritty buff type 69. Date: 3rd century AD.

Cut 2, layer 208: NVCC type 2.8; NVGW type 27; buff ware type 74. Date: later 2nd century AD.

Small finds

297 Lead object, Jackson cat. no. 2 (SF 209); copper-alloy rosette stud, Jackson cat. no. 66 (SF 217).

179 Copper-alloy snake bracelet, Johns cat. no. 4 (SF 86); iron object, Jackson cat. no. 51 (SF 96); marble gaming counter, Jackson cat. no. 45, (SF 164); lead sheet fragment, Jackson cat. no. 34 (SF 165); samian stamp, Dickinson cat. no. 106 (SF 235)

208 NVCC barbotine-figured sherd, Johns cat. no. 3 (SF 108).

209 Lead offcut, Jackson cat. no. 14 (SF 170); bone needle fragment, Greep cat. no. 39 (SF 173); bone hairpin, Greep cat. no. 14 (SF 176).

2 Discussion

The environs

Building R1 was planned, laid out and constructed with considerable care. Its precise position was determined by a localised rise in the clay subsoil. The choice of this slight elevation gave added prominence to a building which seems to have been designed to impress. In accordance with the apparent importance attached to the visual impact the building was erected on an extensive plot of land. The spacious surroundings prevented other structures and activities from impinging upon, or detracting from the view of the building. In particular, a large open tract was reserved to the north. It measured about 35–45 m north–south and at least 60 m east–west. There were very few Phase III cut features in this area, just two wells (135 and 336) and a few pits, and those probably belonged to the latter part of the phase. A hard-standing of limestone chippings survived at the southern end adjacent to the building (Fig. 46, p. 108; Pl. XIIIb), where plough damage was less severe, and it seems probable that this surface originally extended over the whole area. The pottery retrieved from and beneath this cobbling included a sherd of 'London ware' c. AD 120–80. Outside the south-east corner of the east wing limestone chippings were surfaced with a layer of mortar, a surface that was traced almost to the lip of ditch 9, and it is conceivable that the chippings north of the building were similarly surfaced or perhaps formed the foundation for a stone-paved piazza. Further traces of the mortar surface were found to south and east of the building (units 376, 378, 445, 449, 452, 453, 460 and 461).

Bounding this space on the north and giving access to it was street 1 E/W and it seems probable that this provided the main approach to the building. Travelling from the west along this road there would have been an unimpeded view of the building from a considerable distance away, and it must have been a striking landmark in an otherwise unremittingly flat rural landscape. No evidence was found of any formal entrance to the piazza from the street and, as no roadside ditch or drain was provided on the south side of street 1 E/W within the settlement area, there were no ditch cause-ways as existed elsewhere on the site (e.g. blocks 3, 4, 9) to

indicate the point or points of access. It is possible, indeed, that the whole frontage was used.

Consistent with the apparent desire to set building R1 in splendid isolation was the provision on the east of not only an extension of the piazza but also a clearly marked boundary. This began as a fence-line, over 75 m long, and orientated with building R1, but was replaced by a sequence of progressively larger ditches (ditches 6 and 9, with recuts) on the same line. These ditches, silted-up but still surviving as a linear depression, remained a landscape feature up to recent times when a ditch (ditch 71) and field drain were inserted in them and a modern dyke cut along a similar route. The Roman boundary was evidently intended to prevent the settlement to the east from encroaching upon the R1 building complex. It appears to have served that function very successfully if the distribution of pits is taken as an indicator. The few pits to the west of the boundary belong to later phases, and the sole encroachment, at the south-east (block 5a) occurred only when the boundary ditch was rerouted across the corner to adopt a less angular line better suited to drainage.

A number of features seem to indicate an access, perhaps the main entrance, to building R1 at the east, however short-lived that access may have been. The first is an aspect of the street system. As argued elsewhere (p. 76) it seems virtually certain that street 2 E/W, as both planned and initially laid out, extended westwards between blocks 4 and 5. The axis of this street and the line of sight of those who approached from the east coincides exactly with the focus of building R1, its off-centre apse. The width of the apse also corresponds to that of the street.

Between the street and the apse lay the east boundary line. Although the remains of the original boundary fence had been cut away in this region, the ditch which replaced it was reduced markedly in width at the precise point where the projected street met it. Such a reduction might well have occurred in order to facilitate a bridged crossing. No certain evidence, in the form of post-holes, was found, but a shallow, hollowed area on the western lip of the ditch appears to have been associated. It is suggested, therefore, that an east access to building R1 was provided at the outset, and that the entrance to the original building was in the east wall of the central block, opposite the apse. Furthermore, an east entrance (whether or not it was the main entrance) may have been maintained after the Phase IIIa additions, for ditch 9 belonged to that period, and its width reduction implies continuity of access.

The unencumbered expanses of the north and east zones of block 1 contrast strikingly with the areas to the south and west. More modest in scale, these appear to have been designated as service zones at the back of the building. Thus they accommodated drains and furnaces, and the limestone and gravel metalling at the south-west may have combined the roles of hard-standing and approach road for carted

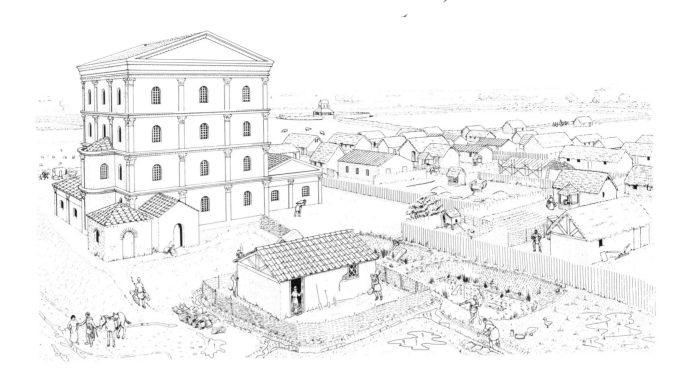

Fig. 64 Stonea Grange: imaginative reconstruction of the Phase III settlement, looking north-east. (*By Simon James*)

Fig. 65 Stonea Grange: imaginative reconstruction of the Phase III settlement, looking south-east. (*By Stephen Crummy*)

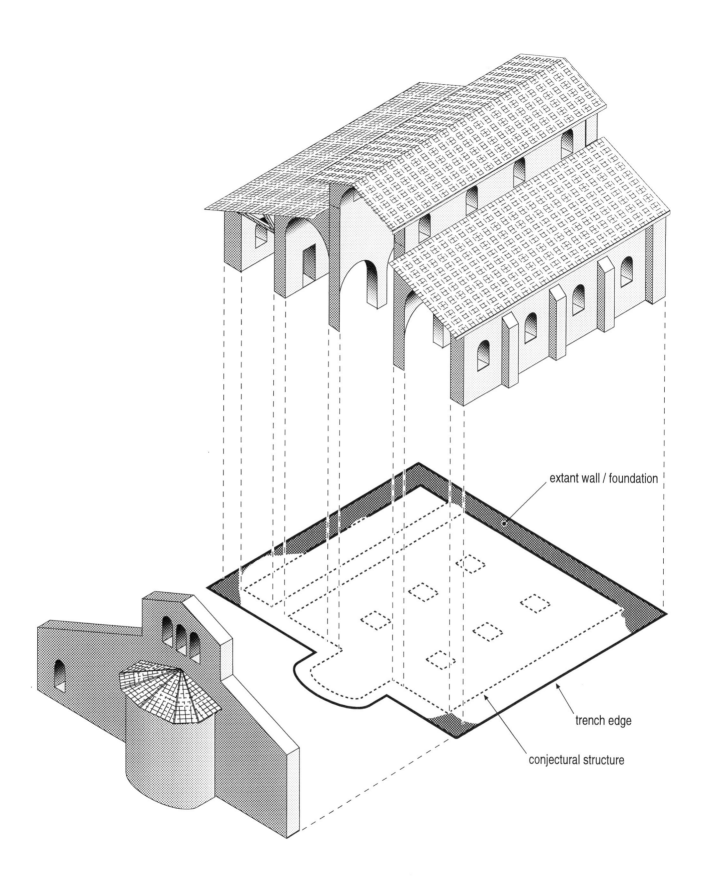

extant wall / foundation

trench edge

conjectural structure

Fig. 66 Stonea Grange: schematic reconstruction of building R1. (*By Stephen Crummy*)

materials and provisions. The proximity of timber building R3 in block 1b and the adjacent sump, which are more of the character of the settlement in blocks 2–10, also imply a lack of concern with the southern facade of building R1 and its approach.

Materials

No part of building R1 survived above the level of wall footings. However, large quantities of building debris, albeit mainly in small fragments, were preserved in 1) the dereliction/destruction deposits which filled the robbed-out foundation trench of the central block, 2) the robbed-out wall trenches of the Phase IIIa additions, and 3) the sump and other deep features in and around block 1. The range of materials and the quality of construction can therefore be ascertained, even if the architectural details and decorative schemes are impossible to determine.

The walls had a mortared rubble core and were faced with coursed blocks of limestone. It is probable that they had tile string-courses, while fragments of tufa blocks and voussoirs (Pl. XXIIb) were probably used in arched apertures such as door and window embrasures and as vaulting components. Tiles from a variety of clay sources, some local, covered the roof and were used in quantity in the hypocaust system as box flue-tiles, suspended floor tiles and *pila* bricks (Figs 185–8, pp. 503–7). Flooring included *opus signinum* cement of varying grain size and thickness, some of it finely polished. Sparse finds of individual stone and brick tesserae attest to the existence of mosaic floors, and coarse cubes of tile and limestone were found on other parts of the site, too (Pl. XXI). The internal wall faces were coated with painted plaster, most of which had been reduced to the tiniest fragments when it was hacked down by the later Roman stone robbers (Figs 181–4, pp. 495–500). It was rarely possible to discern even the simplest designs, but at least one piece appears to have been painted in imitation of cipollino marble (Fig. 181, no. 10, p. 495). Pellets of Egyptian Blue from various contexts may have been part of the stock of paint pigments used in the decoration of building R1, though other uses are possible (see Bimson and Jackson, pp. 501–2).

While the windows were almost certainly provided with wooden shutters, a vast quantity of broken window glass, including a semi-complete pane (Pl. XXVIa), demonstrates that many, if not all, were also glazed. Lead sheet fragments and semi-coalesced masses had probably been used for waterproofing in various parts of the building. One large flanged fragment (Fig. 121, no. 6, p. 371) may have been part of the inlet/outlet of a tank or bath. No lead piping was found, but its former existence in the small hypocausted room (p. 131) and elsewhere in the complex seems probable. It would have been one of the first and easiest targets for those collecting materials for re-use after the demise of the

building. The copper-alloy lion-head terminal in the surface collection (Fig. 113, no. 104, p. 352), which appears to have been a fountain jet, would presumably have been mounted at the end of a lead pipeline.

Roman planning and mensuration (Fig. 67)

From an early stage in the excavations it became apparent that building R1 and the west sector of the Phase III settlement were laid out according to a grid orientated almost exactly on the cardinal points. Furthermore, repeating units of measurement – 50 Roman feet and 100 Roman feet (using the conversion 1 Roman foot = 11.65 in = 29.57 cm) –were clearly discernible both in the R1 building complex and in the plots to its south and east. Neither the measurements nor the orientations were absolutely precise, and there was no slavish following of a grid. However, as the fixed points of the Roman surveyor/planner would have been above-ground features, none of which now survive, it is hardly surprising to find that the evidence from cut features and building foundations tends to be occasionally anomalous and a little less than precise. The central block of building R1, for example, was clearly planned as a unit 50 Roman feet (RF) square. The fact that it is not an exact square of that size may be explained both by invoking slight leeway/error in its construction and/or by the assumed provision from ground level upwards of an offset to the exterior of the walls.

The picture is similar to the south of building R1. There the 50 RF square persisted in the form of blocks 1a and 1b, though later adjustment of the ditched boundary of block 1b introduced a degree of distortion and imprecision. To the east the building plots in blocks 3 and 4 were also evidently planned as 50 RF squares, while two further such units, possibly combined as a double-size unit 100 × 50 RF, may be postulated within block 2.

The 100 RF unit occurs again elsewhere: 1) in the length of the north wall of the Phase IIIa additions to building R1; 2) in the distance from the east end of that wall to the east end of block 4; and 3) in the width of the south boundary of block 9 and the north boundary of block 8. Another less certain repeating unit is 15 RF, which corresponds to the width of streets 1 N/S and 2 E/W and may have been the intended width of the other minor streets. The same unit of measurement can be discerned in the ancillary rooms at the south-west of building R1 which together occupy a space of about 15 × 30 RF, and in the north range of the building which is 15 RF wide. The west range was 10 RF wide. Compelling, too, is the fact that the thickness of the wall footings of the central block of building R1, 1.15–1.2 m, is precisely 4 RF (1.18 m).

For some reason, not now apparent, a second grid, orientated a few degrees counter-clockwise of that in the west sector, was employed in the layout of the east part of the settlement. Street 2 N/S, laid off at a right angle from the

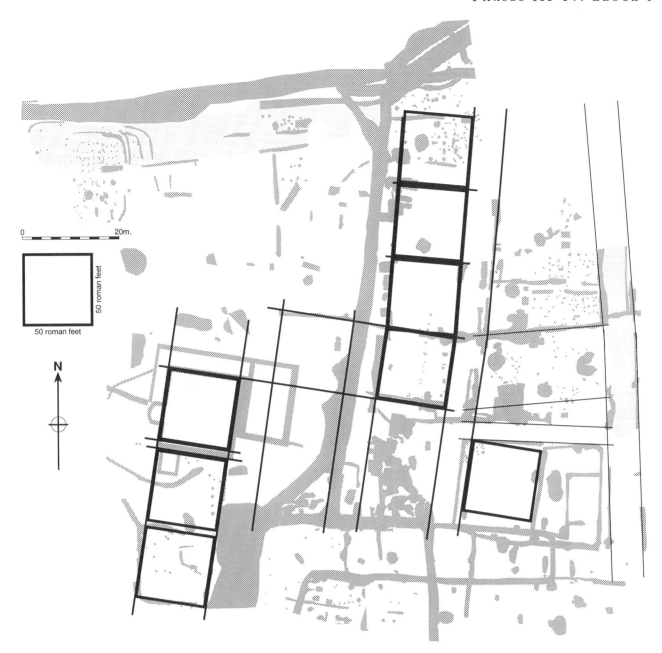

Fig. 67 Stonea Grange: evidence for a planned layout based on two grids and a repeating unit of 50 RF square.

main east–west thoroughfare street 1 E/W, and streets 3 and 4 N/S, together with the intervening blocks, conform to this grid, as does building R10 and, presumably, the other buildings in block 9. Blocks 8, 9 and 10 were at the interface of the two grids and were accommodated to them. Accordingly, they are of trapezoidal shape, and the building plots within them display a similar irregularity. However, the use of the 100 RF unit on the south boundary of block 9 and the north boundary of block 8, and the correspondence in size of the building plot at the south-east corner of block 8 to a unit of 50 × 30 RF imply a degree of standardisation in planning similar to that on the west part of the site.

The implication of this planned layout and use of standard units of measurement is of central control rather than organic growth. The Phase III settlement was laid out as an entity, and it was only later in the phase, with the demise of building R1, that streets and boundaries began to be encroached upon and re-aligned. Then the impression is of central authority giving way to private enterprise and to individual rather than corporate initiative. The regular planning and standardisation of measurement raise the possibility of military involvement in the setting out and construction of the settlement, in particular the R1 building complex. However, no further evidence than a few items of second–third century AD military equipment was found (Pl. XXVb), and the question must remain open.

Dating

After it was abandoned, building R1 was so rapidly, heavily and systematically quarried for its building stone and other re-usable materials that very few contexts of the construction period remained undisturbed. Of those that did survive intact the majority yielded either no finds at all or insufficient to permit close dating. Thus, context 133, remains of the lowest pitched stone foundation in the north-east and south-east quadrants of the central block, produced a little coarse pottery, but enough only to indicate a date of AD 125 or later. Interesting, but of little dating value, was the Iceni silver coin (Chadburn cat. no. 60) embedded in the mortared wall footing at the west end of the north side of the central block. In view of the discovery of several coin hoards around the site (Chadburn, pp. 264–86), it is possible that this coin was part of one such hoard disturbed by the Roman foundation diggers, who unwittingly incorporated it in the building.

One part of the building was spared the depradations of the stone robbers. The walls of the small hypocausted room appear to have been constructed of timber and daub, not insubstantial materials, but ones with very limited scope for re-use, and therefore of little interest to scavengers. At some time after it went out of use, the room was burnt down. It was not possible to determine whether this was the result of a deliberate act or an accident. Whatever the case, the thick deposit of burnt debris contained a good assemblage of finds which dated the destruction. Furthermore, it sealed beneath it two layers of silt on the hypocaust floor, both of which also yielded datable assemblages of coarse pottery (Figs 172–3, pp. 472–3).

The sequence revealed was

Unit number		Coarse pottery date
86/362	Primary silt on ground surface	Later 2nd cent AD
63	Secondary silt, above 86/362	Early 3rd cent AD
24	Destruction deposit, above 63	Early 3rd cent AD

In addition, the external deposit (unit 28) which comprised the hypocaust furnace structure and debris, though not as firmly sealed as the interior silting, gave a coarse pottery date of late second/early third century AD, which corresponds well with that established for the interior stratigraphy.

It seems improbable that debris, other than wood ash, would have been able to penetrate the sub-floor space or that it would have been allowed to accumulate there during the period of usage of the hypocaust. The small quantity of pottery (about 300 g) from the primary silt (unit 86), which

rested directly upon the ground surface, should therefore be regarded as rubbish belonging to the earliest stage of neglect of the hypocaust. Such neglect need not necessarily indicate disuse. However, the fact that joining halves of a stone disc were found in layer 86 and layer 24 (Fig. 193, no. 47, p. 523) suggests there was no long interval between their deposition. Certainly, the secondary silt (unit 63), which incorporated much more pottery (about 4300 g), and other debris must represent the point of abandonment of the original functions of the room.

While, therefore, the evidence of the stratigraphy within the hypocaust is instructive as to the demise of the room, it sheds little direct light on its date of construction, other than to indicate that it took place before the later second century AD. For the date of construction of this room and the rest of the R1 building complex, it is necessary to examine the wider dating evidence from the site as whole.

The intimate relationship between building R1 and the street/plot grid leaves little room for doubt that they were integral parts of a single scheme and that they were, to all intents and purposes, contemporaneous. The evidence of orientation and the use of regular units of measurement is compelling. Additionally, excepting a very few traces of prehistoric and first century AD activity, block 1, in which building R1 was sited, was essentially virgin land. No Phase III features are known to have preceded building R1, and it can be regarded as *a* if not *the* primary structure of the phase. For that reason it is valid to date the construction of R1 with reference to the earliest Phase III finds from the site. The various groups of datable finds yielded slightly differing results, but, taking the consensus, a foundation date of *c*. AD 130–50 is indicated. The coins and glass perhaps argue for the earlier part of the bracket while the samian and coarse pottery tend to point towards the latter part. At all events an early Antonine beginning is assured, and it is possible that the initiative was late Hadrianic.

Disuse, abandonment and dereliction

Towards the end of the first quarter or early in the second quarter of the third century AD, building R1 went out of use. There are a number of indications – including the pattern of coin loss (Fig. 92, p. 295) and the chronology of the glassware – that the building and its functions had already been in decline for some years, and the structure may already have been 'mothballed' or in disrepair. There is no evidence for re-use of the building, but its fabric is likely to have been dismantled and quarried for re-usable materials, systematically or opportunistically, as soon as, if not before, it had been formally relinquished. The fixtures and fittings and more easily removeable architectural components will have been first to go, soon to be followed by the facing stones and flooring materials. There may then have been a hiatus, with a period of dereliction, before the wall cores and footings and, finally, the massive 'raft' foundation of the central block, were laboriously broken up and carried away for re-use.

So thorough was the recycling/scavenging process that in most parts of the building by the later third century AD nothing more remained than heaps of sorted debris consisting of small limestone and brick rubble, with occasional larger masonry fragments in a variety of soil matrices (see Figs 62–3; Pl. XVII). There appears to have been a further hiatus or period of stabilisation, when the plot was abandoned, and the quarried remains, especially in the deep foundation trench of the central block, were frequently or semi-permanently subject to localised flooding, as evidenced by the molluscan assemblage (see French, p. 651).

Ultimately, in the fourth century AD, the derelict plot was returned to use by the backfilling and levelling of the destroyed foundations and the construction above of a mortared stone building. Sadly, this was virtually completely destroyed, with only faint traces of north–south aligned walling (unit 2, and possibly 9) at the north, and even those parts which survived had been severely scarred by pan-busting, subsoiling and other recent agricultural activity. These last vestiges comprised the robbed core of a wall footing about 1.0–1.2 m wide, traced for a distance of some 8 m, composed of limestone rubble and tile fragments in a white mortar matrix. The discovery of two iron T-clamps (Jackson cat. nos 61–2) hard up against the west side of the wall (unit 2) might be taken as evidence that the building had a hypocausted heating system, though they could alternatively have been residual finds from building R1. Further south, but probably part of the same building, a small expanse of good quality pink mortar flooring remained in situ (unit 139, building R2). Additionally, the cutting of pit 3 may have been associated with this building, though its final fill probably belongs to Phase V.

DATED DERELICTION/ROBBING CONTEXTS

Small hypocausted room

Final use/destruction   Phase IIIa

86/362 Later 2nd century AD
   63 Early 3rd century AD
   24 Early 3rd century AD

South room

Dereliction/robbing debris   Phase IV

26 Late 3rd century AD

East wing and north and west ranges

Main robbing debris   Phase IV

 29 Later 2nd/3rd century AD
 44 3rd century AD

 89 3rd century AD
290 3rd century AD
 64 3rd or 4th century AD
 79 Late 3rd/4th century AD
  4 4th century AD
302 4th century AD

Central block

Early robbing debris   Phase IV

77 4th century AD

Main robbing/dereliction debris   Phase IV

 32 4th century AD ⎫
 55 4th century AD ⎪
 56 4th century AD ⎬ SE quadrant
 64 4th century AD ⎪
 76 4th century AD ⎪
215 4th century AD ⎭
185 4th century AD   NE quadrant
151 4th century AD   NE and NW quadrants

Levelling debris   Phase IV

136 4th century AD

Intrusive   Phases IV–V

Pit 3 4th century AD

BUILDING R4   (Figs 46, 50, pp. 108, 112)

The remains of this structure in the north-east corner of block 1 were revealed in 1983. In this area of the site there was virtually no stratigraphy and in most places the modern ploughsoil lay directly above the grey-green silts which sealed prehistoric features. Roman negative features cut these silts, but in every case their upper part was truncated. Entirely lost to erosion, too, were Roman floors and ground level, excepting only the last remnant of the base of the gravel metalling of street 1 E/W. Additional surface depletion and destruction had occurred when the concrete foundation of the glasshouse was put in (and when it was demolished), and by the contemporaneous or near contemporaneous insertion of a number of large rectangular post-holes to the west of the glasshouse (see p. 240).

The vestigial remains of building R4 comprised, therefore, a scatter of truncated post-holes in the west angle formed by the junction of gullies 53 and 54. Although they were clearly an associated group, united by their dimensions, shape and fill, they defied attempts, both in the field and subsequently, to fit them into a coherent framework of wall-lines. However, an incomplete rectangular structure at least 5 × 3 m is possible, based on a south wall incorporating posts 1407–10 and a north wall comprising posts 1403, 1404 and, perhaps, 1416, but lacking posts at the north-west and north-east, the latter probably a victim of the glasshouse construction.

The post-holes yielded nothing closely datable, indeed virtually no finds at all, though fragments of roof tile and daub from post-hole 1401 may signify the form of the super-structure. As, too, neither the internal flooring nor the external ground surface survived, the building yielded no directly associated material to provide evidence of date or function.

Ten small holes dug by illicit metal-detector users in the area to the west and south of building R4 probably represent ten copper-alloy objects or coins, implying a concentration of ancient activity in the immediate vicinity of the building. In addition, there are a number of pointers towards a Phase IV date for the building. First, its location in the angle of the Phase IV gullies 53 and 54 is unlikely to be coincidental and suggests a relationship between contemporaneous features. Second, the clay and rubble capping (unit 1400) which seals the slumped primary levelling layer (unit 1421) in pit/ditch 69 contains pottery and other debris of mid/late third century AD date. As this large feature lies immediately adjacent to the south side of building R4, the latter is unlikely to have been constructed prior to the levelling. Third, the proximity of oven 3 and the midden deposit (unit 527) with its asso-ciated drain/gully (gully 66), all of which belong to Phase IV, are perhaps best interpreted as ancillary components of a homestead centred on building R4.

If these assumptions are correct, building R4 would have stood within a sub-rectangular enclosure, in part, perhaps, for stock, _c._ 33 × _c._ 18 m, bounded by gullies 50, 51, 53, 54 and ditch 9. Contemporaneous features within that enclo-sure, other than those already mentioned, include a second oven (oven 4) in the south-west corner, and a large pit (pit 997), probably a well, in the north-east corner. The latter was only partially excavated, but its upper fill, which con-tained pottery of the later third century AD, was similar to the distinctive clay capping of pit/ditch 69. Such an arrange-ment – a post-built house within a sub-rectangular enclo-sure containing also ovens, pits and wells – may also have existed on the east side of ditch 9 (blocks 2 and 3), where a phase of building 5 was, perhaps, the counterpart to build-ing R4, neighbouring plots, maybe, in a village-based farm-ing community.

Data

Post-holes

1401 (CRS) Squarish, 0.45 × 0.50 m and 0.31 m deep. Brown soil with clay, burnt clay and charcoal flecks. No post-pipe discerned.

1403 (CRV) Square, 0.15 × 0.15 m and 0.20 m deep. Dark brown soil with charcoal flecks. Post-pipe only.

1404 (CRW) Ovoid, 0.25 × 0.30 m and 0.11 m deep. Brown soil.

1407 (CRZ) Ovoid, 0.25 × 0.30 m and 0.15 m deep. Grey-brown pebbly silt with small fragments of limestone pack-ing. Indications of a post-pipe _c._ 0.10 m in width.

1408 (CSA) Ovoid, 0.20 × 0.25 m and 0.13 m deep. Brown-grey silt with small fragments of limestone packing. Indica-tions of a post-pipe _c._ 0.10 m in width.

1409 (CSB) Square, 0.20 × 0.20 m and 0.10 m deep. Light brown silt with small fragments of limestone packing.

1410 (CSC) Ovoid, unexcavated. 0.25 × 0.25 m. Fill as 1409.

1416 (CSI) Ovoid, 0.50 × 0.55 m and 0.29 m deep. Yellow clay packing with near-central post-pipe filled with grey-green silt. Width of post-pipe 0.10 m.

Midden 527 (ADO) E11, N57

A shallow sub-rectangular depression, near the north-east corner of block 1, densely packed with oyster shells.

Width 2 m, length at least 1.5 m.

Fill Oyster shells (_c._ 50%–75%) in a brown-grey clayey soil matrix, with fragments of window glass, daub, floor and roof tiles.

Dating evidence NVCC type 25/26, 20/21. Horningsea. Date: 3rd century AD.

Small finds Coin, Shotter cat. no. 35, dupondius, MW, AD 152–3 (or 155–6) (SF 335).

WELLS AND PITS (Fig. 46, p. 108)

Pit 1020 (CAW) E14.0, N66.7

A sub-rectangular shallow pit at the north-east corner of block 1. Cuts unit 1041 of gully 54, and therefore belongs to Phase IV or later. Width 1.3 m, length _c._ 2.5 m.

Fill Dark grey-brown soil with charcoal and oyster shell.

Dating evidence NVCC; ?NV mortarium. Date: AD 125 or later.

Small finds Coin, Shotter cat. no. 2, Claudius copy Minerva As (SF 467).

Pit 997 (BNC) E16.9, N55.5

An ovoid pit or well near the north-east corner of block 1. Lies just west of ditch 9. West side truncated by modern dyke. Only the north-east quadrant of this pit was excavated and it was not bot-tomed.

Width _c._ 2.25 m, length at least 2.0 m.

Fill Dark grey silty clay with lumps of gritty yellow clay and flecks of tile and charcoal.

Dating evidence – upper layer only
NVCC type 20/21; Horningsea; buff ware type 69/70; shell-gritted type 102, jar with parallel at Chesterton of later 3rd/4th century AD. Date: ?later 3rd century AD.

Small finds Glass vessel rim, Price cat. no. 37 (SF 394); a coin, Shotter cat. no. 16, dupondius, VW, AD 99–100 (SF 293), was found in topsoil/cleaning above this pit.

Pit 528 (ADP)   E12.6, N53.9   Phase III/IV

A small narrow sub-rectangular ?pit, near the north-east corner of block 1.

Width 0.75 m, length 1.6 m, depth 0.27 m.

Fill Black-brown peaty soil with a few pebbles and flecks of mortar and charcoal.

Dating evidence NVGW types 29, 45.3; Horningsea. Date: 3rd century AD.

Well 336 (QP)   W39.15, N55.25   (Fig. 40d, p. 98)   Phase III

A large sub-rectangular pit near the north-west corner of block 1. The lower 50 cm, uneroded, is vertical-sided. Four post-holes, symmetrically disposed around the pit may have supported a wooden well-head structure. The late Anglo-Saxon post-pit 372, complete with its waterlogged post base, cuts the fill of well 336.

Width: pit 1.8 m, shaft 1.15 m. Length: pit 1.9 m, shaft 1.35 m. Depth 1.65 m.

Fill

336 (QP)	Dark grey silt with small pieces of ragstone and lumps and flecks of mortar.
359 (SP)	Grey, charcoal-rich, silts with some gravel and mortar flecks.
367 (SY)	Light grey silt with burning, charcoal and mortar flecks.
371 (TC)	Black waterlogged sludge.
412 (VY)	Mixed grey/black clay with charcoal flecks.
415 (WB)	Yellow sand with occasional lumps of yellow/blue clay. Slumping onto west side of well base.

Dating evidence (Fig. 159, p. 454)
Upper layers: a version of NVCC type 9 with late 3rd century AD parallel at Chesterton; NVCC type 8.2, sherd of NVCC jar or Castor box. Date: late 3rd–4th century AD.
Fill: NVSC type 65; NVGW types 47, 28, 27; NVCC type 2. Date: late 2nd–3rd century AD.
Lower layers: fragment, undatable.

Small finds

336	Iron knife, Jackson cat. no. 24 (SF 206); enamelled disc brooch, Mackreth cat. no. 19 (SF 213); copper-alloy ligula, Jackson cat. no. 52 (SF 216).
359	Bone point, Greep cat. no. 61 (SF 234).
367	Pottery counter rough-out, Jackson cat. no. 5 (SF 237).

Pit 349 (SD)   W35.9, N55.6   Phase III, later

A small shallow sub-rectangular pit or post-hole near the north-west corner of block 1.

Width 0.5 m, length 0.55 m, depth 0.1 m.

Fill Loose brown soil with mortar flecks.

Dating evidence Horningsea. Date: early 3rd century AD or later.

Pit 424 (WL)   W40.0, N54.1

A small shallow sub-circular pit, near the north-west corner of block 1, and adjacent to well 336.

Diameter *c.* 0.45 m, depth 0.15 m.

Fill Dark charcoal-rich silt with heavily burnt clay at base.

Dating evidence Nothing datable.

Well 135 (FW)   W30.15, N42.45   (Fig. 37c)   Phase III(?)

A very large steep-sided ovoid pit in the north-west quadrant of block 1. At the base of the large weathering cone is the lower part of an ovoid vertical-sided well shaft. The west lip of the erosion cone lay outside the area of excavation.

Width: erosion cone 4.8 m; shaft 1.2 m. Length: erosion cone 6.2 m; shaft 1.9 m. Depth 2.2 m.

Fill

135 (FW)	Very dark peaty-soil with sparse gravel and bone. Large quantities of building rubble – tile and *opus signinum* fragments.
156 (GT)	Dark fill, peaty and clayey. Less building rubble than 135; more bone.
159 (GX)	Dark peat-textured deposit. Darker, and with greater quantities of rubble than 156. Large tile frags.
158 (GW)	Grey, iron-stained clay.
205 (JX)	Brown, pebble-free peat.
213 (KF)	Grey-brown peaty soil, high organic content.
214 (KG)	Grey clay.
226 (KV)	Brown-yellow clay, thick lens within 214.
227 (KW)	Green-grey clay.

Dating evidence
Top layers: Anglo-Saxon and residual Roman.
Fill: NVCC types 4 and 21. NVGW type 29. Date: 3rd century AD, later part.
Lowest layers: fragments of NVGW and Horningsea.

Small finds

135	Copper-alloy twisted wire ?handle fragment, Jackson cat. no. 76 (SF 44); bone point, Greep cat. no. 58 (SF 50); bone comb, Greep cat. no. 77 (SF 52); iron object, Jackson cat. no. 76 (SF 53); brooch, Mackreth cat. no. 6 (SF 54); stone gaming counter, Jackson cat. no. 46 (SF 58); pottery base marked with 'X', Potter cat. no. 16 (SF 162); copper-alloy tweezers, Jackson cat. no. 57 (SF 174).
156	Copper-alloy pin fragment, Jackson cat. no. 9 (SF 57); glass vessel fragment, Price cat. no. 36 (SF 77); iron ox-goad, Jackson cat. no. 7 (SF 181); lead object, Jackson cat. no. 37 (SF 73).
159	Glass vessel, rim fragment, Price cat. no. 21 (SF 123).
205	Bone gaming counter, Greep cat. no. 52 (SF 193).
213	Lead object, Jackson cat. no. 6 (SF 107).

The sequence is:
1 Period of last usage of well, unit 227, later 2nd/early 3rd century AD.
2 Period of disuse of well, accumulation of debris in clay fills, units 226, 214, 259, 158, 3rd century AD.
3 Period of stabilisation, formation of first peaty fills, units 213, 205, 3rd–4th century AD.
4 Formation of second peaty fills, units 159, 156, 135, 4th–7th century AD.

Pit 277 (NA)   W24.95, N48.8

A small ovoid ?pit in the north-west quadrant of block 1.

Width 0.25 m, length 0.60 m, depth 0.2 m.

Fill Dark grey silt with much charcoal.

Dating evidence Nothing datable.

Pit 272 (MV)   W19.05, N47.2   ?Phase III, later

A small oval pit in the north-west quadrant of block 1.

Width 0.65 m, length 0.9 m, depth 0.28 m.

Fill Grey-green silt.

Dating evidence NVCC type 3.2; grey ware flanged bowl. Date: ?early 3rd century AD.

Pit 270 (MS)   W14.3, N42.9   Phase III/IV

An ovoid pit north of centre, block 1. Part-sectioned only.

Width 2.3 m, length at least 2.3 m, depth 0.93 m.

Fill
270 (MS)   Dark grey-brown loamy soil, with large quantities of small ragstone and tile fragments.
293 (NS)   Grey silt with sparse ragstone fragments.
343 (QX)   Grey-green clay with white flecks.

Dating evidence NVGW type 45.3; shell-gritted 101; Horningsea. Date: ?3rd century AD.

Pit 323 (QA)   W17.85, N39.15

A small circular ?pit near the centre of block 1. Sealed by cobble/rubble spread 128.

Diameter 0.4 m, depth 0.15 m.

Fill Grey-brown silt with patches of yellow silt.

Dating evidence Nothing datable.

Pit 520 (ADG)   W1.95, N41.5   Phase III, later

A small very shallow sub-oval pit in the north-east quadrant of block 1.

Width 0.8 m, length 1.3 m, depth c. 0.2 m.

Fill Blue-grey clay with tile fragments.

Dating evidence NVCC type 3.2. Date: late 2nd/early 3rd century AD.

(?)Pit 539 (AEB)   E5.15, N38.8   Phase III

A very shallow sub-oval pit, or sinkage into ditch 74, in the north-east quadrant of block 1, bisected by a modern land drain. One quadrant only excavated.

Width c. 2.0 m, length c. 2.5 m, depth c. 0.15 m.

Fill Black silt with burnt clay.

Dating evidence NVCC type 2; NVGW type 27. Date: mid/late 2nd century AD.

Well 171(HK)/558 (AEW)

E10.4, N28.65   (Fig. 39a, p. 97)   Phases IV and V

A large steep-sided sub-circular pit, centre east side, block 1. First half (171) excavated 1981; second half (558) excavated 1982. Waterlogging preserved part of a woven wicker lining in situ.

Width 2.9 m, length 3.6 m, depth 1.9 m.

Fill
171 (HK)   Dark brown/black peaty soil. [Contained articulated skeleton of pig.]
210 (KC)   Dark grey/brown silty clay.
222 (KQ)   Mixed yellow and grey clay with sandy and silty lenses.
229 (KY)   Dark grey silty clay with grits. [Contained a ?dog skull.]
230 (KZ)   Yellow/green silty clay with white flecks.
231 (LA)   Dark grey/green silty clay with preserved wicker lining around edge.
[558 (AEW) = 171, 210.   583 (AFX) = 222, 229, 230.   605 (AGV) = 231]

Dating evidence
Upper layers: NVCC types 20/21, 2.6, 7.2; NVGW types 28, cf. 3.2; Horningsea. Date: 3rd century AD.
Fill: NVCC types 20/21, 25/26, 3.2, 7, 18; NVGW types 45, 28, 29, 28.2. Date: late 3rd/4th century AD. *Anglo-Saxon sherds in 171, 558 and 583.*

Small finds
171   Iron object, Jackson cat. no. 8 (SF 97).
231   Copper-alloy tweezers, Jackson cat. no. 56 (SF 117).
558   Bone pin fragment, Greep cat. no. 3. (SF 368).
605   Lead sheet fragment, Jackson cat. no. 33 (SF 404).

The sequence appears to be:
1 Cutting of pit/well; placement of wicker lining, late 3rd/4th century AD.
2 Accumulation of primary fill, 231/605, late 3rd/4th century AD.
3 Accumulation of secondary fill, 230, 229, 222/583, 210, 171/558, 5th–7th century AD.

Pit 512 (ACY)   E13.8, N31.75   Phase IV

A small ovoid pit, part of the cluster around well 171, centre east side block 1. Cuts unit 506 of gully 50.

Width 1.0 m, length 1.3 m, depth 0.4 m.

Fill Dark grey silt with much charcoal.

Dating evidence NVCC type cf. 8. Date: ?2nd or 4th century AD.

Pit 545 (AEH)   E12.2, N31.3   Phase IV

A small ovoid pit, part of the cluster around well 171, centre east side block 1. Cuts unit 506 of gully 50.

Width 0.8 m, length 1.15 m, depth 0.5 m.

Fill dark grey silt with much charcoal.

Dating evidence Grey ware jar with parallel at Chesterton of 4th century AD; shell-gritted jar with parallel at Chesterton of late 3rd/4th century AD. Date: late 3rd/4th century AD.

Pit 587 (AGB)   E8.25, N32.15   ?Phase III/IV

A small ovoid pit, part of the cluster around well 171, centre east side block 1. Bisected by unit 501 of gully 50.

Width *c.* 0.65 m, length *c.* 1.15 m, depth 0.15 m.

Fill Black soil

Dating evidence NVCC; NVGW; Horningsea. Date: ?late 2nd/3rd century AD.

Pit 511 (ACX)   E7.2, N31.1   Probably Phase IV

A small square pit, part of the cluster around well 171, centre east side block 1.

Width/length 0.6 m, depth 0.25 m.

Fill Black soil with much charcoal and burnt clay (superficial), above orange silt with occasional tile.

Dating evidence No datable material.

Pit 505 (ACQ)   E8.3, N30.2   Probably Phase IV

Two small shallow conjoined pits, part of the cluster around well 171, centre east side block 1.

Dimensions i)   Width 0.7 m, length 1.0 m, depth 0.3 m.
　　　　　 ii)   Width 0.6 m, length 0.6 m, depth 0.15 m.

Fill Dark grey silt with occasional pebbles and ragstone fragments, flecked with charcoal and burnt clay.

Dating evidence NVCC type 3.2; gritty buff ware type 69/70; Horningsea. Date: late 2nd/early 3rd century AD [probably residual].

Pit 600 (AGP)   E9.35, N30.8   Phase III, later

A small sub-rectangular pit, part of the cluster around well 171, centre east side block 1.

Width 0.7 m, length 0.95 m, depth 0.25 m.

Fill Black soil with daub and charcoal flecks.

Dating evidence NVGW type 27; Horningsea. Date: early 3rd century AD.

Pit 543 (AEF)   E11.1, N21.1   Phase III/IV

An irregular heart-shaped pit, possibly two intercutting pits with an undifferentiated fill; centre of east side block 1, near the west lip of ditch 6 (unit 581). Part-sectioned only.

Width *c.* 1.8 m, length 1.9 m, depth 0.35 m.

Fill Brown/black peaty silt with pebbles, occasional ragstone fragments and mortar flecks.

Dating evidence NVGW type 47, Horningsea. Date: ?3rd century AD.

Pit 513 (ACZ)/361 (SR)   W9.5, N30.6   Phase III, later

A large ovoid pit near the centre of block 1. Cuts unit 508 of the ragstone and pebble 'cobbling' north of building R1. Part-excavated only, in 1981 and 1982.

Width *c.* 2.7 m, length *c.* 5.2 m, depth *c.* 0.4 m.

Fill Brown peaty silt with occasional pebbles and ragstone fragments.

Dating evidence London-type ware; NVCC type 3.2; NGVW type 45. Date: late 2nd/early 3rd century AD.

Pit 363 (ST)   W12.75, N27.0

A small ovoid pit, south of centre block 1.

Width 0.5 m, length 0.9 m.

Fill Loose brown sandy soil with much ragstone.

Dating evidence NVGW type 27. Date: AD 125 or later.

Pit 295 (NV)   W11.0, N32.9

A very shallow ?ovoid pit near the centre of block 1. Cuts unit 128 of the ragstone and pebble 'cobbling' north of building R1. Part-sectioned only.

Width 1.45 m, length at least 0.9 m, depth 0.1 m.

Fill Grey-black loamy soil with much gravel, small ragstone fragments and flecks of tile and mortar.

Dating evidence No datable material.

Pit 327 (QE)   W16.5, N32.4

A small shallow sub-rectangular pit, west of centre block 1. Sealed by 'cobbling' north of building R1.

Fill Loose grey-brown soil with occasional pebbles and frequent flecks and patches of yellow mortar.

Dating evidence NVGW. Date: AD 125 on.

Pit 170 (HJ)   W17.95, N30.65   (Fig. 40c, p. 98)   Phase III, later

A long rectangular pit with V-shaped cross-section, just to the north of building R1 and on the same alignment. Possibly originally two pits recut as one. Cuts unit 128 of the 'cobbled' surface. Excavated in three sections.

Width 2.6 m, length 7.6 m, depth 1.42 m.

Fill

Section (i)

170 (HJ)   Black soil with large quantities of tile and rubble debris.
220 (KN)   Black silty clay with large quantity of daub, charcoal, tile fragments, lumps of yellow mortar and a few pebbles.
246 (LR)   Large quantities of daub, burnt clay and charcoal in brown silty clay.
262 (MJ)   Grey-green sandy clay with some rubble and tile fragments below a thin charcoal-rich layer.
263 (MK)   Heavy yellow clay with some sand, white flecks and ragstone rubble.

Section (ii)

254 (MA)   As unit 170, section (i) above.
285 (NJ)   As unit 246, section (i) above.
287 (NL)   As unit 262, section (i) above.
311 (PM)   Loose brown soil with charcoal and mortar flecks and occasional small fragments of tile and ragstone.

Section (iii)

255 (MB) As unit 170, section (i) above.

271 (MT) As unit 262, section (i) above.

311 (PM) See section (ii) above.

Matrix

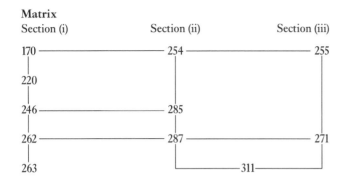

Section (i)   Section (ii)   Section (iii)

Dating evidence   (Fig. 162, nos 69–79, p. 458)

Top layer: NVCC types 18, 20/21; NVGW type 45.3; mortarium cf. Verulamium no. 1098 (AD 270–90); BB type flanged bowl cf. Gillam no. 44 (mid/late 3rd century AD); shell-gritted types 87, 98. Date: 3rd/4th century AD.

Second layer: NVCC type ?18; NVGW type 29; Horningsea; ?Oxbridge ware dog-dish; pedestal base cf. Jesus Lane. Date: 3rd/4th century AD.

Third layer: NVCC types 25/26, 2.3, 3.2; NVGW types 29, 45, 46; buff ware type 74. Date: ?3rd century AD.

Fourth layer: NVCC types 20/21 or 18, 2.4; NVGW type 27. Date: 3rd/4th century AD.

Lower layers: NVGW type 45; buff ware type 74; Horningsea. Date: early 3rd century AD.

Small finds

170 Coin, Shotter cat. no. 55, AE, LW, AD 323–4 (SF 66); samian stamp, Dickinson cat. no. 79 (SF 76); lead sheet fragment, Jackson cat. no. 32 (SF 91); bone needle fragment, Greep cat. no. 50 (SF 100); whetstone, Jackson cat. no. 38 (SF 232).

254 Samian stamps, Dickinson cat. nos 16, 44 (SF 168 and 185); bone needle fragment (SF 177).

220 Bone needles, (SF 111 and 114); glass vessel handle fragment, Price cat. no. 63 (SF 112); copper-alloy object, Jackson cat. no. 92 (SF 113).

287 Coin, Shotter cat. no. 30, dupondius, MW, AD 153–54 (SF 183); mortarium stamp, Hartley cat. no. 6 (SF 189).

Pit 132 (FS)   W30.5, N25.4   Phase IV(?)

A large sub-rectangular pit, just beyond the north-west corner of building R1. Most of the pit, including the base, lay outside the area of excavation. The pit contained a large chunk of a tufa-turned arch, presumably part of a window embrasure from building R1.

Width at least 2.75 m, length 6.9 m, depth at least 1.05 m.

Fill

131 (FR) Cleaning above pit

132 (FS) Light grey soil with much gravel and some stone rubble and tile fragments.

190 (JF) Yellow clay with gravel and occasional rubble.

191 (JG) Black gravelly silt with tile fragments.

192 (JH) Dark grey silty clay with large quantities of ragstone rubble, yellow mortar, tile and gravel.

193 (JJ) Thin band of dark grey silt with gravel.

194 (JK) Yellow-grey silt. [Water-table reached.]

Pit not bottomed.

Dating evidence

Cleaning: NVCC type 20/21; buff ware type 74; Horningsea. Date: 3rd century AD.

Fill: NVGW types 46/48, 45.3. Date: late 2nd/early 3rd century AD [presumably residual – see Small finds below].

Small finds

131 Iron key, Jackson cat. no. 47.

132 Iron objects, Jackson cat. nos 49 and 68 (SF 80 and 88).

190 Copper-alloy scabbard slide, Jackson cat. no. 65 (SF 94).

192 Tile with graffito, Potter cat. no. 1 (SF 101); bone needle, Greep cat. no. 50 (SF 100).

194 Coin, Shotter cat. no. 56, AE, AD 330–5 (SF 102).

OVENS   (Figs 43–4, 46, 48, pp. 104–10)

Oven 1   W34.5, N51.85   (Fig. 44)   Phase IV

Type 2. Length 2.05 m, width 0.65 m, depth 0.42 m.

North–south orientation, with flue at south.

Only the basal part of one unit of the chamber remained relatively undisturbed, together with the base wall of the aperture which connected the flue with the chamber.

264 (ML) Fill, upper. Patches of burnt clay, with flecks of white mortar and small pebbles.

321 (PY) Fill, lower. Burnt red and yellow clay mixed with brown and yellow silts.

Finds

264 (ML) Coarse pottery, late 3rd century AD.

321 (PY) Coarse pottery, late 2nd century AD; lead strip, Jackson cat. no. 25 (SF 195).

Oven 2   W37.5, N51.85   (Fig. 43)   Phase IV

Type 1. Length 1.9 m, width 0.7 m, depth 0.05 m.

North–south orientation, with flue at south.

The wall still stood to a height of 0.12 m but was partially plough-damaged.

325 (QC) Fill, upper. Burnt orange and red clay mixed with dark grey silt.

358 (SN) Fill, lower. Burnt red and orange clay mixed with grey silt. In the flue region, soft white ash flanked by pockets of grey silt flecked and stained with burnt clay.

Finds

325 (QC) Coarse pottery, 3rd or 4th century AD. Antonine samian.

358 (SN) Coarse pottery, AD 125 or later.

Oven 3   E6.2, N51.5   Phase IV

Type 1. Length 2.05 m, width 0.55 m.

North–south orientation, flue position uncertain.

A badly damaged example with no in situ structure remaining.

559 (AEX) Superficial debris. Mixed burnt red clay and black ashy soil.

Finds Coarse pottery, AD 125 on.

Oven 4   E3.4, N34.1   Phase IV

Type 1(?). Length 1.4 m+, width 0.6 m.

East–west orientation, flue position uncertain, though probably at west.

A badly damaged example, both ends truncated. Beyond the west end was an area of grey ash, probably the stoke-hole.

573 (AFM) A mass of burnt red clay, disturbed at east and west and mixed with ash.

Finds None.

DITCHES AND GULLIES   (Figs 25–32, 46, 48–52)

Gully 63   Phase IV(?)

A small, narrow, steep-sided gully, aligned approximately north–south in the north-west corner of block 1. It appears to be complete and lies between gullies 54 and 64 with which it was probably associated. Each end terminates in a post-hole (291 and 370).

Width 0.25–0.35 m, length 3.5 m, depth 0.10–0.15 m.

Fill 284 (NH) Dark grey silt.

Dating evidence NVGW. Date: AD 125 or later.

Gully 54   Phase IV

A discontinuous steep-sided gully aligned approximately east–west along the north side of block 1. Its line is that of the south side of street 1 E/W and it probably served as a roadside drain. The squared cross-section beneath an erosion 'cone', particularly pronounced in cut 5, is indicative of a wood-lined culvert: the carbonised wood in cut 5, unit 212 is almost certainly the remains of such a lining.

Width 0.3–0.9 m, length at least 51 m, depth 0.25–0.95 m.

Fill
Cut 1   1041 (CBS) Grey-green silt.
Cut 2   1047 (CBZ) As cut 1, 1041
Cut 3   1161 (CGS) Grey-green silt with a little gravel.
Cut 4   1159 (CGQ) As cut 1, 1041.
Cut 5   202 (JT) Brown silt with iron-pan staining.
        212 (KE) Dark, charcoal-rich, iron-pan stained silt, with small fragments of burnt wood.
        283 (NG) A short, narrow rather superficial gully, possibly a southern extension of 202.
Cut 6   228 (KX) As cut 5, 202.

Dating evidence (Fig. 162, nos 80–92, p. 458)
NVCC types 4, 7.2, ?20/21; NVGW types 45, cf. 39, 29; NV mortarium type 66: shell-gritted type 90. Date: mid/late 3rd century AD.

Small finds
212 Iron knife, Jackson cat. no. 25 (SF 147); iron hipposandal fragment, Jackson cat. no. 5 (SF 157).
228 Coin, Shotter cat. no. 33, sestertius, VW, AD 138–61 (SF 231).

Gully 64   Phase IV

A comparatively short trench, of U-shaped cross-section, aligned approximately east–west, in the north-west corner of block 1. The deeper section at the east end (cut 2) is almost certainly an inserted grave.

Width 0.7 m, length 5.5 m, depth 0.32 m.

Fill
Cut 1   253 (LZ) Dark grey charcoal-rich silt.
        256 (MC) Charcoal with a little dark grey silt.
Cut 2   278 (NB) Grey silt, with charcoal-stained shadow around edges; remains of decayed wooden coffin(?)
        298 (NY) Dark grey-brown silt, heavily charcoal-stained.

Dating evidence
Upper layer: NVCC cf. type 6.
Lower layer: NVCC cf. type 6.
Date: late 3rd–4th century AD.

Small finds
253 Iron object, Jackson cat. no. 50 (SF 129); silver and gilt brooch, Mackreth cat. no. 17, *c.* AD 200–50 (SF 134 and 144); coin, Shotter cat. no. 32, dupondius, AD 138–61 (SF 221).
256 Mortarium stamp, Hartley cat. no. 12 (SF 149).
278 Copper-alloy finger ring, Johns cat. no. 3, probably 2nd–3rd century AD (SF 169).

Gully 53   Phases IV and V(?)

A discontinuous gully, of broad U-shaped cross-section, aligned approximately north–south, in the north-east quadrant of block 1. The north section (unit 1281) butts up against gully 54 (unit 1159), and the cross-section of both gullies in this region is so similar that they were almost certainly contemporaneous. With gullies 50, 51 and ditch 9 they define a roughly rectangular enclosure. A recut was clearly visible in cut 2; and a sherd of Anglo-Saxon pottery in cut 3 may well be associated with that recutting.

Width 0.65–0.8 m. Length: cut 1 6.25 m; cuts 2 and 3 9.7 m. Overall length 20.7 m. Depth: primary 0.3–0.35 m; recut 0.2 m.

Fill
Cut 1   519 (ADF) Grey gravelly silt.
Cut 2   1282 (CMT) Grey silt (recut); mixed grey silt and yellow clay below (primary). These were not differentiated on excavation.
Cut 3   1281 (CMS) Dark grey silt.

Dating evidence (Fig. 163, nos 93–102, p. 460)
NVCC types 4, 20/21; NVGW types 45, 47, 7.2; grey ware jars cf. types 28, 39; NV mortarium type 66; Horningsea. Date: late 3rd to 4th century AD.
From unit 1281: Anglo-Saxon pottery, bowl, rim sherd, Fabric 8, Ill. Cat. no. 18. [Note: this sherd probably from recut.]

Small finds

519   Perforated oyster shell, Cartwright cat. no. 1 (SF 427).

1282 Bone pin fragment (SF 567); glass vessel fragment, Price cat. no. 64q (SF 605); whetstone, Jackson cat. no. 42 (SF 631).

Gully 51   Phase IV

A narrow gully of shallow irregular form, in the north-east quadrant of block 1. Although offset to the west it is on the same alignment (approximately north–south) as gully 53 and 'fills' the gap between gullies 53 and 50. It presumably belonged to the same phase of activity, though it is much less substantial.

Width 0.6–0.8 m, length *c*. 6 m, depth 0.05 m.

Fill

Cut 1   510 (ACW) Grey gravelly silt with ragstone fragments.

Cut 2   521 (ADH) Pebbly grey silt with ragstone fragments.

Dating evidence ?Horningsea. Date: early 3rd century AD or later.

Gully 50   Phase IV

A narrow gully, aligned approximately east–west, with steeply-sloping sides and a flat base, in the north-east quadrant of block 1. Its west end butts on the line of gully 53, and gully 50 appears to be the southern component of the enclosure complex ditch 9, gullies 54/53/51/50. Evidence of recutting was most noticeable at the west end. The character of gully 50 was not dissimilar to that of gullies 35 and 29, and it is possible that all three gullies were at one stage connected, or that they reflect a long-standing boundary. Gully 50 cuts ditch 74 and pit 587. Pits 512 and 545 cut gully 50.

Width 0.5–0.75 m, length 15.5 m, depth 0.23 m.

Fill

Cut 1   506 (ACR) Grey-brown gravelly silt.

Cut 2   551 (AEO) Grey silt with ragstone fragments and flecks of mortar and burnt clay.

Cut 3   501 (ACM)/470 (ABE) Grey-black clayey silt with gravel, tile and ragstone fragments and mortar flecks.

Cut 4   535 (ADX) Mixed grey/brown/yellow silts with gravel and ragstone fragments.

Dating evidence NVCC types 4, 20/21, 3.2; NVGW types 48, 28, 47, 45.3; gritty buff type 69; Horningsea; Date: 3rd century AD.

Small finds 506 Glass vessel fragment, Price cat. no. 12a (SF 409).

Gully 52   Phase IV(?)

A small, narrow, steep-sided gully, aligned approximately east–west, in the north-east quadrant of block 1. It has a butt at the west but its east end was not located, and its relationship, if any, with gullies 51 and 53, was not established.

Width 0.45–0.5 m, length at least 1.8 m, depth 0.15 m.

Fill 1260 (CLW) Dark brown/grey silt with pebbles and occasional lumps of ragstone.

Dating evidence NVGW. Date: AD 125 or later.

Gully 66   Phase IV

A curving gully, of rather irregular cross-section, in the north-east corner of block 1. Some discontinuity and variation in depth caused by machine disturbance. The north-east end appears to have debouched into ditch 9, while the south-west end, though not located, may well have issued from the midden deposit 527. The likelihood is, therefore, that gully 66 was a drain or leet for the drainage of waste matter, and the post-hole scatter to the west is suggestive of a building in this region.

Width 0.45–0.55 m, length at least 7 m, depth 0.06–0.23 m.

Fill

Cut 1   1004 (CAE) Dark brown/black silt, with charcoal, clay and shell flecks.

Cut 2   1013 (CAO) As cut 1, 1004.
        1068 (CCW) Light grey silt with gravel, sealed by clay slump.

Cut 3   1175 (CHH) Grey-green silt.

Cut 4   1174 (CHG) Black peaty silt with charcoal, mortar and burnt clay flecks.

Dating evidence Sparse: buff ware type 74; ?Horningsea. Date: late 2nd/early 3rd century AD.

Gully 67   Phase III?

A short, narrow, steep-sided slot in the north-east corner of block 1.

Width 0.55 m, length 3.0 m, depth 0.25 m.

Fill 541 (AED) Dark grey silt with mortar flecks.

Dating evidence NVCC type 6.2; NVGW type 27. Date: mid/late 2nd century AD.

Small finds Samian stamp, Dickinson cat. no. 1 (SF 338).

Function unclear, though as likely structural or 'industrial' as drainage.

Ditch 74   Phases ?0–IV

A broad ditch, not easily defined, on the east side of block 1. Its existence was signified by the dark, secondary fill of sinkage into the primary silts. The uppermost secondary fill dates to the later Roman period; the primary ditch had no datable material in the lower fill and may be pre-Roman. Its dimensions and profile (as far as it could be ascertained) are similar to those of ditch 75 (trench Y), and the two may be part of the same ditch.

Fill

Cut 1   509 (ACV) Black peaty silt with gravel, small grits, and flecks of mortar and charcoal.
        555 (AES) Mixed brown/orange silt.
        534 (ADW) Grey/brown gravelly silt.
        570 (AFI) Yellow silt with large amounts of ragstone fragments.
        602 (AGR) Mixed grey silt and clay.

Cut 2   550 (AEN) Mixed grey silt with small pebbles and tile fragments.
        569 (AFH) Yellow-orange silt.
        571 (AFK) Grey silt.
        615 (AHF) Mixed grey/orange silts and grey clay.

Dating evidence

Cut 1   509: NVCC types 20/21,11; shell-gritted jar with 4th century AD parallel at Chesterton. Date: late 3rd/4th century AD.

555/534/570: NVCC types 19, 20/21, 9, ?18; shell-gritted jar with late 3rd/4th century AD parallel at Chesterton. Date: late 3rd/4th century AD.

602: NVCC type 2. Date: late 2nd/early 3rd century AD.

Cut 2   550: NVCC type 25/26. Date: late 3rd/4th century AD.

Small finds

509   Coin, Shotter cat. no. 26, sestertius, VW, AD 125–38 (SF 305); samian stamp, Dickinson cat. no. 84 (SF 310); iron key, Jackson cat. no. 45 (SF 328); graffito on samian base, Potter cat. no. 15 (SF 329); copper-alloy needle, Jackson cat. no. 38 (SF 331).

534   Glass bead, Price cat. no. 74 (SF 337).

Ditch 6   (Figs 25, 30b, 31a, 32b–c, pp. 77, 83–5)   Phase III

A V-sectioned ditch with gently sloping sides and, in places, a basal cleaning slot. Its line is approximately north–south down the east side of block 1. As the successor to a fence-line, it runs along the 'boundary' between block 1 and blocks 2–6. At the north end it crosses the line of street 1 E/W into block 11 and veers north-east. In the central region ditch 6 is entirely or mostly cut away by the succeeding ditch 9. Towards the south, where ditch 9 takes a different line, ditch 6 re-emerges and bifurcates west and east to form respectively, ditches 7 and 8, which mark the edges of block 6. At both north and south ditch 6 continues (at the south as ditches 7 and 8) outside the area of excavation. Where not cut away by ditch 9, ditch 6 is truncated or contaminated by the post-medieval ditches 12, 14 and 71; is cut by pit 485 (in cut 8, unit 489); and cuts gully 1 and ditches 2–3.

Width 2.4 m, length at least 110 m (excluding ditches 7 and 8), depth 0.8–1.2 m.

Fill

Cut 1   1304 (CNR) Brown-grey silt with pebbles and a few stones.
1305 (CNS) Grey silt with sparse pebbles.

Cut 2   1259 (CLV) Grey-green gravelly clay.
1301 (CNO) As cut 1, 1305.

Cut 3   1202 (CIL) Grey-green gravelly silt.
1222 (CKG)/835 (BFK) Grey silt with pebbles and stones.

Cut 4   1096 (CEA) Brown silt with abundant gravel

Cut 5   1099 (CED) Dark brown peat with gravel.

Cut 6   581 (AFV) Light brown/yellow gravelly silt, with a few stones and tile fragments. [Post-medieval contamination.]
588 (AGC) Dark brown pebbly silt.

Cut 7   544 (AEG) Brown gravelly silt.

Cut 8   489 (ABZ) Brown silty clay with gravel.

Cut 9   1610 (DEO) Reddish brown peaty soil. [Post-medieval contamination.]

Dating evidence

Cut 1   NVGW. Date: AD 125 or later.

Cut 2   No datable material.

Cut 3   No datable material.

Cut 4   NVCC type 3.2. Date: late 2nd/early 3rd century AD.

Cut 5   Missing.

Cuts 6–9   Date: late 2nd/early 3rd century AD.

Ditch 7   Phase III

A V-sectioned ditch with gently sloping sides and a basal cleaning slot. Ditch 7 is the west arm of the bifurcated ditch 6. It demarcates the north and west sides of block 6; cuts the east side of the sump; is cut/truncated/contaminated by ditch 71; and continues beyond the southern limit of the main excavation. Ditch 76, located in trenches W and FF, may be the southern continuation.

Width c. 2.5 m, length at least 31 m, depth 1.05 m.

Fill

Cut 1   1533 (DBI) Reddish peat and grey-brown with much gravel. [Post-medieval contamination.]
1573 (DDA) Grey-brown silt with much gravel.

Cut 2   491 (ACB) Brown clayey silt with a little gravel.

Cut 3   A10 Grey clay.

Cut 4   A11 As cut 3.

Dating evidence

1533   Mortarium cf. Gillam 253; Horningsea. Date: late 2nd/early 3rd century AD.

Rest   Buff ware type 69; Horningsea. Date: late 2nd/early 3rd century AD.

Small finds

1533   Copper-alloy hairpin, Jackson cat. no. 4 (SF 627); copper-alloy pin/ligula, Jackson cat. no. 26 (SF 701).

1573   Glass vessel handle fragment, Price cat. no. 63h (SF 710).

Ditch 9   (Figs 25, 31a, 32a–c)   Phases III and IV

A large V-sectioned ditch with slightly flattened/rounded base. It supersedes ditch 6, following the latter's north–south alignment, but at the north end it veers to the north-west while its south end veers south-west before turning south again. It was the most prominent drainage feature of the boundary line between block 1 and blocks 2–6. Ditch 6 maintained the angularity of the earliest fenced boundary line, but ditch 9 adopted a more curving line better suited to drainage. Thus, the right angle formed by ditches 6 and 7 was 'by-passed' by ditch 9, isolating a small block of land (block 5a), which, like the adjacent block 5, was used for rubbish disposal. Originally ditch 9 appears to have been united with ditch 4 via ditch 5. Subsequently ditch 5 was backfilled and at this stage ditch 9 butted at the south side of street 1 E/W. In a later modification, ditches 9 and 4 appear to have been re-united via ditch 11, probably a wood-lined culvert running beneath the metalling of the road surface. There is evidence of recutting, especially at the north end. Opposite the north end of block 5 a distinct narrowing of the ditch coincides with the projected line of street 2 E/W, and it is likely that ditch 9 was bridged there.

Width 2.4–3.7 m, length at least 105 m, depth 1.35–1.6 m.

Fill

Cut 1a   937 (BKP) Dark grey silty clay with small pebbles, flecks of tile and charcoal and iron-pan staining.
978 (BMH) Dark grey clay with stone and flint fragments.
945 (BKY) Grey/brown gravelly silt.
993 (BMY) Orange-brown gritty sand.
954 (BLH) Grey gravelly silt with charcoal flecks and iron-pan concentration.

963 (BLR) Grey-green/brown gravelly silt with a few stones, fragments of charcoal and flecks of tile and chalk.

998 (BND) Dark grey-brown silty clay with iron-pan staining.

Cut 1b   1100 (CEE) Grey-green silt with gravel.

1049 (CCB) Grey-green clayey silt.

1091 (CDV) Dark grey and orange clay.

Cut 2   1067 (CCV) Dark grey-green silt.

1073 (CDB) Dark grey-brown peaty silt.

1077 (CDF) As 1073.

1074 (CDC) Yellow-brown sandy silt with pebbles.

1084 (CDN) Yellow clay. Slump.

1079 (CDH) Greenish-grey pebbly silt.

1052 (CCE) Grey-green silt.

1058 (CCL) Mixed grey-black clay

1092 (CDW) Mixed yellow/grey clay. Slump.

1120 (CFA) Grey silty clay.

1123 (CFD) Dark grey silt.

Cut 3   765 (BCM) Dark brown clay with flecks of tile and mortar.

828 (BFC) Dark brown silty clay with small pebbles and flecks of tile and mortar. ?Recut.

766 (BCN) Grey gritty silty peat with small stones and flecks of tile and mortar.

801 (BDZ) Dark grey/brown gritty sandy clay with many pebbles and flecks of tile and charcoal.

890 (BHQ) Light grey/yellow gritty silt.

909 (BIL) Dark brown gritty silty clay with flecks of tile and charcoal.

913 (BIP) Grey/brown gravel mixed with orange silt.

924 (BKB) Grey/brown gravelly silt with pebbles, iron-pan concentrations and flecks of chalk.

933 (BKL) Grey silt with hard concentrations of green/yellow iron-pan deposit.

926 (BKO) Dark grey silt with much stone, tile fragments and flecks of charcoal, chalk and mortar.

952 (BLF) Grey/yellow silty gravel with charcoal flecks.

Cut 4   767 (BCO) Dark grey/brown clay with flecks of tile, mortar and charcoal.

907 (BII) Dark grey gritty clay with flecks of tile and chalk.

886 (BHM) Dark grey gritty silty clay with pebbles and tile flecks.

912 (BIO) Mixed yellow clay/grey silt with pebbles and flecks of tile and chalk.

908 (BIK) Green-grey clay with heavy iron-pan staining.

Cut 5   531 (ADS) Black loamy soil with large quantity of ragstone rubble.

532 (ADT) Homogeneous brown peaty silt.

542 (AEE) Dark grey/black clay with some small ragstone fragments.

556 (AET) Light grey clay.

Cut 6   218 (KL) Light grey-green silty clay with many pebbles and iron-pan staining.

223 (KR) Grey-green silty clay with many small pebbles and fragments of tile, mortar and *opus signinum*.

232 (LB) Yellow silty clay with many tile fragments.

242 (LM) Mixed green/yellow clay and silt with gravel, tile fragments, and flecks of charcoal and mortar.

248 (LT) Green-grey silty clay with large tile fragments and flecks of mortar.

Cut 7   566 (AFE) Black silty clay with much ragstone rubble and pebbles and flecks of charcoal and mortar.

593 (AGH) Green-grey silt with much gravel and pink mortar fragments

596 (AGL) Grey-green silt with gravel.

Cut 8   474 (ABI) Gravely grey silt with much ragstone rubble and mortar fragments.

525 (ADM) Mixed black/brown peat and clay with gravel and ragstone fragments.

536 (ADY) Mixed yellow/grey/green silts and clays with a little gravel and charcoal flecks.

552 (AEP) Grey/brown gravel.

Cut 9   584 (AFY) Brown/black soil with much ragstone rubble and pebbles.

595 (AGK) Grey/green silt and clay with pebbles and ragstone fragments.

599 (AGO) Mixed light orange/grey silt.

Cut 10   564 (AFC) Dark grey/black clay and silt with much ragstone rubble.

572 (AFL) Grey/black clay with flecks of charcoal and mortar and iron-pan staining.

574 (AFN) Dark black gritty clay with gravel and ragstone fragments and flecks of mortar.

578 (AFR) Yellow/grey silt.

Cut 11   472 (ABG) Grey/black soil with gravel and large quantity of ragstone rubble and tile.

487 (ABX) Grey gravelly silt and clay with many ragstone and mortar fragments and iron-pan staining.

494 (ACE) Mixed black clay and grey silt with ragstone and mortar fragments and iron-pan staining.

507 (ACS) Grey/green clay and silt.

565 (AFD) Orange/grey silt and clay.

585 (AFZ) As 565.

Cut 12   500 (ACL) As cut 11, 472.

Dating evidence (Figs 164–70, pp. 461–9; Pl. XXVIIIa)
Lower fill: all cuts, late 2nd/early 3rd century AD.
Main fill: all cuts, 3rd/4th century AD.

Cut 1   Upper layers (937, 978): NVCC types 28, 28.2; Horningsea. Date: 3rd century AD.
Lower layers (993, 954, 963, 998, 1100, 1091): NVGW type 45; gritty buff type 69; Horningsea. Date: late 2nd/early 3rd century AD.

Cut 2   NVCC types 1, 4, 3, 25/26, 21; NVGW types 45, 45.3, 47, 39, 28; buff ware type 74, Central Gaulish beaker; Horningsea. Date: 3rd century AD.
Lower layer (1123): NVGW type 41.2; Horningsea. Date: late 2nd/early 3rd century AD.

Cut 3   Upper layers (765, 766, 828): NVCC types 20/21, 4, 8; NVGW types 39, 37, 29; grey ware flanged bowl; Horningsea. Date: late 3rd/early 4th century AD.
Lower layers (890, 909, 913): NVCC types 3.2, 19; NVSC type 66 (mortarium); Central Gaulish beaker. Date: late 2nd/early 3rd century AD.

Cut 4   Upper layers (767, 907, 886, 912): NVCC types 20/21, 4, 2.7; Horningsea. shell-gritted jars with parallels at Chesterton. Date: late 3rd/4th century AD.
Lower layer (908): NVCC type 2; NVGW type 27; buff ware type 74; Horningsea. Date: late 2nd/early 3rd century AD.

Cut 5   Upper layer (542): NVCC types 20, 3, 4: NVGW types 45, 47; buff ware type 74; Horningsea. Date: 3rd century AD.
Lower layer (556): NVCC types 2.5, 3.2; NVGW types 28, 45; Horningsea. Date: early 3rd century AD.

Cut 6   NVCC types 20, 7; NVGW type 28.2; Horningsea. Date: 3rd century AD.

Cut 7   Upper layers (566, 593): NVCC types 8, 20/21; NVGW types 37, 29, 47; Horningsea. Date: 3rd century AD.
Lower layer (596): NVCC type 40; NVGW type 45; Horningsea. Date: early 3rd century AD.

Cut 8   Upper layer (525): NVCC types 20/21, 4; NVGW types 45, 45.3, 46, 31, 28.2, 47; Horningsea. Date: 3rd century AD.
Lower layers (536, 552): NVCC type 2; NVGW type 45; NVSC types 51/52, 57; buff ware type 69; Horningsea type 107/8. Date: late 2nd/early 3rd century AD.

Cut 9   NVCC types 20, 25/26, 11.2; NVGW types 45.3, 28; Horningsea. Date: late 3rd/early 4th century AD.

Cut 10   Upper layers (564, 572, 574): NVCC types 20/21, 6.2, 20, 2.9; NVGW type 45.3; Horningsea. Date: 3rd century AD.
Bottom layer (578) NVCC type 2; NVGW type 27; NVSC types 51/52, 57. Date: late 2nd/early 3rd century AD.

Cut 11   NVCC types ?7, 2.4, 20/21; NVGW types 45, 48, 50; Horningsea. Date: 3rd century AD.

Cut 12   NVCC type 20/21; Horningsea. Date: 3rd century AD.

Small finds

937   Samian stamp, Dickinson cat. no. 53 (SF 384).

954   Glass vessel, Price cat. no. 64a (SF 441); milling stone fragment, Jackson cat. no. 2; rubbing stone, Jackson cat. no. 31 (SF 437).

1067 Copper-alloy finger ring, Johns cat. no. 6 (SF 465); iron object, Jackson cat. no. 55 (SF 469); window glass fragment (SF 471); copper-alloy scoop probe, Jackson cat. no. 44 (SF 473).

1077 Iron hobnails, Jackson cat. no. 43 (SF 514).

1058 Copper-alloy pin/ligula fragment, Jackson cat. no. 12 (SF 479).

909   Bone needle (SF 356).

913   Copper-alloy needle, Jackson cat. no. 36 (SF 359).

936   Stone object, Jackson cat. no. 24 (SF 434).

542   Samian stamp, Dickinson cat. no. 66 (SF 339); coarse-ware stamped bowl, Rigby cat. no. 1.

556   Samian stamp, Dickinson cat. no. 92 (SF 420).

223   Copper-alloy seal box lid, Jackson cat. no. 74 (SF 116).

248   Samian stamp, Dickinson cat. no. 26 (SF 124); samian stamp, Dickinson cat. no. 91 (SF 145).

593   Samian stamp, Dickinson cat. no. 73 (SF 417).

596   NVCC barbotine-figured beaker, Johns cat. no. 12.

525   Iron object, Jackson cat. no. 73 (SF 332).

536   Glass vessel fragments, Price cat. nos 4–5 (SF 334a and 334b).

595   Samian stamp, Dickinson cat. no. 115 (SF 371).

599   Samian stamps, Dickinson cat. nos 35, 12, 17 (SF 373–375); glass vessel fragment, Price cat. no. 8 (SF 419b).

564   Glass vessel fragment, Price cat. no. 55a (SF 406).

574   Bone pin, Greep cat. no. 4 (SF 366); NVCC barbotine-figured beaker, Johns cat. no. 5; sharpening stone, Jackson cat. no. 25 (SF 433).

578   Glass vessel fragment. Price cat. no. 6 (SF 407).

487   Copper-alloy ligula, Jackson cat. no. 47 (SF 267).

494   Glass vessel, rim fragment, Price cat. no. 8 (SF 294); milling stone fragment, Jackson cat. no. 12.

585   Lead object, Jackson cat. no. 18 (SF 369).

500   Iron knife, Jackson cat. no. 22a (SF 308).

BLOCK 1a   (Figs 46–7, pp. 108–9)

A rectangular plot, about 21 × 15 m, to the south of building R1, block 1.

Structures Building R2, and two ancillary rooms of building R1.

Well 446.

Gullies 43–5.

BUILDING R2   (Fig. 47, p. 109)

The vestigial remains of this building were found in 1981–2, immediately south of building R1, in the east half of block 1a. This was the highest point of the main site and, accordingly, the remains had suffered severe plough damage. The main surviving component was a mortar floor (unit 139), but a scatter of post-holes to the north and a stone setting to the west (unit 163) were probably parts of the same structure. The post-holes formed no coherent plan and it seems probable that the building was walled by means of a superficial structure or one that had only very shallow footings like, for example, that of the small hypocausted room of building R1. It seems probable, too, that the traces of walling further north, above the levelled debris of building R1 (p. 139), were also parts of building R2.

Such tantalising fragments suggest a building of some pretension, with, at least in part, stone walls, glazed windows, a hypocaust and mortar floors. Whatever may have been the form of the building it evidently stood long enough for floor 139 to be replaced more than once for there were at least two successive and distinctive surfaces, each a little over 2 cm thick, the lower a pink *opus signinum* type mortar, the upper a yellow sandy mortar with a hard grey calcareous surface. Beneath the lower surface was a third layer of decayed yellow sandy mortar (unit 286), either a third surface or, more probably, the degraded foundation of the upper surfaces. A short distance to the south-west, and probably contemporary with 139/286, if not part of the same floor, was a small patch of pink-white mortar flooring, while below 139 on its west side were the remains of an earlier floor (unit 549) comprising fragments of tile and large pot sherds set in white mortar.

Excepting an iron stylus (p. 364, no. 33) no occupation debris remained on the upper surface of 139 which lay at the base of the ploughsoil and had been deeply scored by plough and pan-buster. However, a *terminus post quem* is provided by gully 44, the east end of which was sealed by the degraded floor foundation, unit 286. The coarse pottery date for the upper fill of gully 44 is third century AD, and it seems improbable that floor 139 was laid prior to the beginning of the fourth century or the very end of the third century AD. While this date may be applied to one phase of building R2 it probably does not signify its beginning, for a build-up of occupation debris throughout the third century, around and stratigraphically below 139, may well have derived from an earlier phase despite the absence of confirmatory structural evidence.

In fact, this part of the site preserved one of the longer stratigraphical sequences at Stonea, albeit localised and not securely associated with coherent structural remains. Adjacent to, and south of, floor 139/286 was a burnt deposit (units 236, 247), probably to be identified as debris from the destruction/dereliction of building R2, for the lower unit (247) appeared to encroach upon the edge of 139. Beneath 139/286, was a dark soil horizon (unit 328/461), which incorporated the flooring fragment 549, and which was presumably occupation debris associated with an earlier phase of building R2. A third century AD date is indicated by the finds. Beneath this layer was a roughly rectangular spread of 'platform' clay (unit 503) which may have been laid in order to prepare and level the site prior to the construction of building R2. The modest finds assemblage points to the end of Phase III providing a likely context for structural change.

Sealed beneath 503 was a spread of black ashy soil (unit 598), probably part of the same general layer as unit 178 further west. The concentration of burnt debris and the presence of large numbers of nails suggests that this may have been a destruction/dereliction deposit associated with the end of Phase III, and the date of the finds assemblage from the layer – late second/early third century AD – accords well with that interpretation. Layer 598/178 sealed 138/459, parts of the gravel-metalled area outside the southern rooms of building R1, a Phase III exterior surface/hardstanding incorporating pottery of later second century AD date. It also sealed 609, another layer of redeposited 'platform' clay with an admixture of grey ashy silt, dated by the coarse pottery to the late second century. 609 was cut by a number of post-holes – 614, 627, 624 – and had a possible floor surface made of tile fragments and large pot sherds. It sealed layer 618, a yellow-orange sandy spread, and the gully and post-holes which cut that layer – 620, 617, 619, 621. Although these units contained no closely datable finds, they evidently date to the earlier part of Phase III. The gully (620) probably marked or coincided with the east edge of the plot, and the line of post-holes 617, 619, 622, 582, was clearly associated with post-hole 621 and, perhaps, the gully. However, it was not possible to identify the form of the structure of which they were a part. The interface of the contemporary units 618 and 628, both of which lay above undisturbed natural, coincided with the post-hole line strengthening the impression of the line as a structural divide.

The evidence thus appears to indicate two structural phases within Phase III followed by a further two in Phase

IV. Although direct evidence for the form of the structures is lacking, a number of features appear to define the potential extent and limits of the ground plan: to the east the block boundary marked by gully/slot 620 and the west side of the sump; to the north (in Phase III) the south wall of building R1; to the west the line marked by the east wall of building R1 south room and the east edge of the gravel hard-standing 138; and to the south a line shared by the small gully/slot 502, the southernmost extent of the superimposed layers 628, 609, 598, 503 and 461, and the north side of the access steps to well 446.

While the whole of this rectangular area, about 11.5 × 9.5 m, was available in Phase IV, the Phase III structure was further restricted by the presence of gully 44. The drainage function of this feature is apparent but its precise role cannot be determined. Its capacity was fairly considerable, and although a connection with building R1, rather than with any predecessor to R2, seems probable, it is singular that its terminal is several metres short of building R1. Rather enigmatic, too, is well 446. Its elaborate access steps clearly indicate an approach from the north, though whether it was associated with the structure(s) which preceded building R2 or, more probably, with building R1, cannot now be demonstrated. At all events, it was a Phase III water source and was already choked with rubbish when building R2 was constructed.

Data

117 (FB)/23 (AZ)   Grey ashy spread south and west of the small hypocausted room of building R1. Above 178.

Phases III–V.

Dating evidence   NVCC types 2.6, 20/21; NVGW type 47; NVSC cf. type 68; gritty buff type 73/74. Date: later 3rd century AD; Anglo-Saxon.

Small finds   Mortarium stamp, Hartley cat. no. 4 (SF 55); two bone pins, Greep cat. nos 12 (SF 56) and 21 (SF 34); two coins, Shotter cat. nos 29 (SF 22) and 38 (SF 6); glass vessel fragments, Price cat. no. 64 (SF 13); iron objects, Jackson cat. nos 53 (SF 24) and 66 (SF 29).

138 (FZ)/459 (AAS)   Metalled surface/hard-standing, south of building R1. At least three superimposed layers of compact orange gravel, the surface of the uppermost destroyed. Sealed by 178.

Phase III.

Dating evidence   NVCC type 2.5; grey ware cf. NVCC type 45; gritty buff type 69/70. Date: later 2nd century AD.

139 (GA)   Heavily-burnt mortar floor, c. 5 cm thick, comprising two layers: the lower, a pinkish mortar; the upper, a yellow sandy mortar with a hard grey calcareous surface. Above 286.

Phase IV.

Dating evidence   Nothing datable.

Small finds   Iron stylus, Jackson cat. no. 33 (SF 196).

163(HB) Plinth or floor fragment, west of 139, and probably contemporary, comprising a sub-circular setting of closely-packed stones with a flat surface on which are remains of burnt yellow-orange mortar.

Phase IV.

Dating evidence NVCC types 2.5, 25/26; NVGW type 41.2. Date: late 2nd/3rd century AD.

Small finds Lead offcut and fused lumps, Jackson cat. nos 19 (SF 202), 43, 46 and 47 (SF 203, 205, 204).

178(HS) Loose, thin, black soil spread over 138. Sealed by 117/23.

Phase III, later.

Dating evidence NVCC type 25/26; buff types 69/70, 73/74; NVGW type 47; Horningsea. Date: early 3rd century AD.

236(LF) Spread of burnt red and yellow sandy clay south of 139. Incorporates large irregular cobbles. Part of general burnt spread. Seals 247.

Phase IV.

Dating evidence NVCC type 2.5. Date: late 2nd/3rd century AD.

Small finds Fused lead lump, Jackson cat. no. 42 (SF 135).

247 (LS) Loose black ashy spread with burnt daub and much charcoal. Encroaches on to fragmentary south side of 139. Sealed by 236.

Phase IV.

Dating evidence NVCC types 2, 25/26; NVGW type 46/48; Horningsea. Date: early 3rd century AD.

Small finds Copper-alloy vessel handle, Jackson cat. no. 77 (SF 212); lead scrap and fused lumps, Jackson cat. nos 7–8 and 38–9 (SF nos 133, 125, 126).

286(NK) Damaged and degraded foundation of mortar floor 139, comprising decayed yellow sandy mortar with occasional small *opus signinum* fragments. Below 139, slumped into the upper fill of gully 44, east end, cuts 1 and 2, sealing units 297 and 179.

Phase IV.

Dating evidence NVGW type 47; NVCC type 4.2; Horningsea. Date: 3rd century AD.

Small finds Coin, Shotter cat. no. 43, dupondius, AD 145–61 (SF 179); copper-alloy pin/ligula, Jackson cat. no. 21 (SF 178).

328(QF)/461(AAV) Loose black soil spread with ashy and heavily burnt patches, much charcoal and flecks of white mortar. Parts sealed by 139, 286 and 460. Seals 502, 503 and 138/459.

Phase IV.

Dating evidence NVCC types 2, 2.5, 20/21; NVGW types 41.2, 45 and imitation samian; gritty buff type 69/70; Horningsea. Date: early 3rd century AD or later.

Small finds Copper-alloy pin, Jackson cat. no. 8 (SF 326); mortarium stamp, Hartley cat. no. 3 (SF 295); lead offcut and fused lumps, Jackson cat. nos 21 and 44 (SF 422 and 300); tile with graffito, Potter cat. no. 3 (SF 416).

460(AAT) Small irregular patch of pink/white mortar surface, south-west of 139. Above 328/461.

Phase IV.

Dating evidence Nothing datable.

502(ACN) A very shallow, narrow, sinuous gully running east–west immediately north of well 446. Its fill, a black-brown ashy soil, is probably part of the 328/461 spread. Cuts 503 and marks its south edge.

Phase IV.

Dating evidence NVGW type 49. Date: 3rd century AD.

503(ACO) A roughly rectangular area of slumped or redeposited 'platform' clay, incorporating burnt red flecks, to the south and west of 139. Below 549 and 461. Cut by 503. Seals 598.

Phase IV.

Dating evidence BB2-type pie-dish; NVGW type 34. Date: late 2nd/3rd century AD.

549(AEM) A small floor fragment composed of tile and pot sherds set in white mortar. Stratified between 139 and 503. Presumably part of a floor of building R2 earlier than 139.

Phase IV.

Dating evidence None.

598(AGN) A very irregular and patchy spread of black ashy soil with gravel, incorporating many iron nails. Probably a destruction/dereliction layer, and probably part of the same general layer as 178. Above 138/459 and 609. Sealed by 503.

Phase III/IV.

Dating evidence NVCC type 3.2; NVGW type 45/45.3; gritty buff types 69/70, 73/74. Date: late 2nd/early 3rd century AD.

Small finds Glass vessel fragment, (SF 377); bone weaving plate, Greep cat. no. 62 (SF 378); samian stamp, Dickinson cat. no. 86 (SF 380); mortarium stamp, Hartley cat. no. 7 (SF 396); whetstone, Jackson cat. no. 41 (SF 438).

609(AGZ) Slumped or redeposited 'platform' clay mixed with grey ashy silt with a possible made-surface of large sherds and tile fragments. Below 598. Above 618.

Phase III.

Dating evidence NVCC type 2.4; NVGW type 45. Date: late 2nd century AD.

Small finds Glass vessel fragment, Price cat. no. 64c (SF 398).

618(AHI) Yellow/orange sandy spread with brown patches, in area of post-holes and gully/slot 620, north-west of the sump. Below 609. Seals undisturbed natural. Cut by post-holes 617, 619 etc. and, on its east side, by gully/slot 620.

Phase III.

Dating evidence Nothing datable.

628 (AHT) Mixed grey ash and green-grey silt spread to the west of 618. Seals undisturbed natural. Cut by post-holes 614 and 627.

Phase III.

Dating evidence AD 125 on.

Post-holes

614 (AHE) Sub-rectangular, 0.30 × 0.30 m and 0.36 m deep. Grey silt, with limestone packing in upper part. Incorporates a central square post-pipe, 0.18 × 0.17 m. Cuts 609 and 628.

627 (AHS) Sub-rectangular, 0.30 × 0.20 m and 0.14 m deep. Brown/grey silt. Incorporates a central square post-pipe, 0.18 × 0.18 m. Cuts 609 and 628.

624 (AHP) Squarish, 0.45 × 0.40 m and 0.30 m deep. Grey ash with lumps of yellow 'platform' clay. Incorporates a central square post-pipe 0.18 × 0.18 m. The post-hole yielded a small amount of coarse pottery, dated ?late 2nd/3rd century AD, and a glass vessel fragment (SF 442). Cuts 609. Sealed by 503.

582 (AFW) Sub-triangular, 0.65 × 0.65 m and 0.53 m deep. Dark grey/black silt with lumps of yellow 'platform' clay. Post-pipe probably on west side. Yielded coarse pottery of late 2nd–early 3rd century AD date.

622 (AHN) Sub-triangular, 0.60 × 0.55 m. Brown and yellow sand with limestone fragments. Incorporates a rectangular post-pipe, 0.17 × 0.15 m, at the north-east. Cuts 618.

619 (AHK) Ovoid, 0.55 × 0.50 m and 0.40 m deep. Grey-brown sandy silt with occasional pebbles and charcoal, and pink mortar flecks. Incorporates a central rectangular post-pipe, 0.18 × 0.15 m. Cuts 618. Sealed by 609.

617 (AHH) Sub-rectangular 0.50 × 0.40 m. Fill as 619. Incorporates a rectangular post-pipe, 0.18 × 0.18 m, at the south. Cuts 618. Sealed by 609.

621 (AHM) Ovoid, 0.65 × 0.60 m. Brown/yellow sandy silt with limestone packing around a rectangular post-pipe, 0.18 × 0.18 m, at the south-west. Cuts 618. Sealed by 609.

620 (AHL) Gully or construction slot, length 5.15 m, width 0.45 m, with a post-hole in the south end – ovoid, 0.35 × 0.30 m, with a central rectangular post-pipe 0.15 × 0.15 m. Dark grey/black silt with charcoal, burnt clay and limestone fragments. Coarse pottery date ?3rd century AD. Cuts 618. Sealed by 609.

Matrix

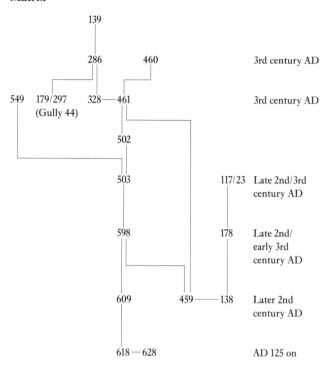

WELL

Well 446 (AAE)

W18.9, S9.75 (Figs 37a, 42, pp. 95, 101) Phase III

A deep, steep-sided, polygonal pit, on the south side of block 1a. An irregular projection at the north-west side incorporates access steps (unit 515).

Width 2.3 m, length 2.35 m, depth 2.13 m.
Lower, uneroded, shaft 1.6 × 1.6 m.

Fill

443 (AAB) Black soil with small pebbles, mortar lumps, charcoal and other burnt material. Disturbed uppermost layer of pit fill.

446 (AAE) Fine black ashy silt with occasional stones and gravel, tile fragments and mortar flecks.

492 (ACC) Loose black ashy silt with charcoal and some stone. Lower part of 446.

499 (ACK) Tips of white, brown and grey ash, with charcoal flecks and lumps.

515 (ADB) Black peaty soil with gravel and burnt clay. [Debris over access steps. Equivalent, stratigraphically, to 499/524/546.]

524 (ADL) Black soil with tips of grey/white ash [water seepage at this level].

546 (AEI) Mixed dark peaty soil, ash, and charcoal tips. Preserved organics.

554 (AER) Grey clay with lenses of ash and black, charcoal-rich soil.

579 (AFS) Dark grey/black clay with patches of orange/yellow clay, flecked with charcoal.

597 (AGM) Mixed grey and yellow clay probably slump. Traces of wooden lining.

603 (AGS) As 597, lower part.

626 (AHR) Timber slot in well side opposite steps.

Dating evidence (Fig. 160, nos 23–34, p. 455)

Upper layer: Oxford mortarium, Young type WC 7; NVGW types 45.3, 47. Date: mid 3rd century AD at the earliest.

Fill: NVCC types 8, 2, 2.7; NVGW type 45; NVSC types 57, 62/63. Date: late 2nd–3rd century AD.

Small finds

443 Coin, Shotter cat. no. 10, dupondius, VW, AD 81–96 (SF 242).

446 Tiny fragments silver sheet (SF 247); brooch, Mackreth cat. no. 21, penannular, probably 1st–2nd century AD (SF 252); lead sheet fragments, Jackson cat. no. 35 (SF 264).

554 Mortarium stamp, Hartley cat. no. 14 (SF 370); milling stone fragment, Jackson cat. no. 4.

603 Twisted withy ?bucket-binding, Jackson cat. no. 10 (SF 381).

626 Lead offcut, Jackson cat. no. 12.

GULLIES

Gully 44   (Figs 25, 60, pp. 77, 125)   Phase III

A U-sectioned gully, with near-vertical sides, a lightly rounded base, and badly eroded upper margins. Almost certainly a drain (perhaps originally a wood-lined box-drain), it begins near the south-east corner of building R1 and runs westwards, curving around the (?)furnace room and the small hypocausted room to the south of building R1. It cuts the small drain, gully 45, and continues beyond the west excavation edge. Its fall, east–west, over the 22 m exposed length, is 0.3 m. At its east end it is sealed by the mortar floor (139) of building R2. Further west it is sealed by layer 178.

Width 0.3–0.5 m (1.15 m including erosion); length at least 22 m; depth 0.05–0.4 m.

Fill

Cut 1 297 (NX) Mixed light and dark brown silt with charcoal flecks.

Cut 2 179 (HT) Dark brown/black clayey silt.
   208 (KA) Brown silt.
   209 (KB) Yellow sandy silt.
   219 (KM) Dark brown loose silt.
   217 (KK) Light brown silt. Slump.

Cut 3 85 (DR) Brown silt.

Dating evidence (Fig. 163, nos 103–12, p. 460)

Upper layers (85, 179, 297): NVCC types 2, 20/21; flagon cf. type 52; NVGW type ?29; gritty buff type 69. Date: 3rd century AD.

Cut 2, layer 208: NVCC type 2.8; NVGW type 27; buff ware type 74. Date: later 2nd century AD.

Cut 2, layer 209: NVCC type 2.8 (joins layer 208); flagon cf. type 52; buff ware types 69, 74; mica-dusted dog-dish. Date: late 2nd century AD

Cut 2, layers 217 and 219: NVCC type 2.8; buff ware types 69, 74. Date: late 2nd century AD.

Small finds

297 Lead object, Jackson cat. no. 2 (SF 209); copper-alloy rosette stud, Jackson cat. no. 66 (SF 217).

179 Copper-alloy snake bracelet, Johns cat. no. 4 (SF 86); iron object, Jackson cat. no. 51 (SF 96); marble gaming counter, Jackson cat. no. 45 (SF 164); lead sheet fragment, Jackson cat. no. 34 (SF 165); samian stamp, Dickinson cat. no. 106 (SF 235).

208 NVCC barbotine-figured sherd, Johns cat. no. 3 (SF 108).

209 Lead strip, Jackson cat. no. 14 (SF 170); bone needle fragment, Greep cat. no. 39 (SF 173); bone hairpin, Greep cat. no. 14 (SF 176).

Gully 45   Phase III

A small steep-sided gully, probably a formerly wood-lined box drain which runs SSE from the south-west corner of the small hypocausted room at the south of building R1. The 'shadow' of a former pipeline was detected within the hypocausted room. Unexcavated, it was very narrow with a burnt silt and charcoal fill. Its sinuous 'segmented' form suggests a series of connecting wooden pipes rather than the slot for a lead pipe. The junction between the pipeline and gully 45 was cut away by gully 44. Gully 45 was sealed by the cobble surface 206.

Width 0.45 m (pipeline 0.1 m), length at least 3 m (pipeline 3 m), depth 0.1 m.

Fill 241 (LL) Stony grey silt.

Dating evidence NVSC flagon cf. type 52; NVGW imitation samian. Date: late 2nd/early 3rd century AD.

Gully 43   Phase III

A wide, shallow, U-sectioned gully with rather irregular base, running north-west from the north-west corner of the gully system, gully 41. Cuts gravel surface 138.

Width 1 m, length at least 7 m, depth 0.3 m.

Fill 186 (JB) Loose brown/black soil with gravel and small pebbles.

Dating evidence NVCC ?type 20/21. Date: 3rd century AD.

BLOCK 1b   (Fig. 47)

A quadrilateral plot, about 16 × 16 m, south of block 1a, bounded by gully 41.

Structures Building R3.

Pit 467.

Gullies 41–2.

BUILDING R3   (Fig. 47, p. 109)

The remains of this timber building, located in the west half of block 1b, were excavated in 1982. They comprise a somewhat meagre scattering of post-holes, enough to attest the existence of a rectangular building but insufficient to determine a coherent plan or overall dimensions. An angle at the south-west, though not necessarily the building's south-west

corner, is indicated, with 611 as the corner post, two additional posts on the south side – 561 and 612 – and two
further posts on the west side – 586 and unnumbered. The
right angle formed by these two lines of post-holes is orientated on building R1 and the Phase III west grid, as is the
enclosure gully of block 1b. The block, like 1a to its north, is
based on a unit of 50 Roman feet square, its boundary
marked by gully 41, the east branch of which is aligned on
the east wall of the central block of building R1.

Midway along the north side of block 1b is a thin and localised spread of dark soil (unit 469) probably the remnant of a
once more extensive deposit of Phase III occupation debris
generated by the users of building R3. Its modest finds
assemblage is of late second century AD date, as is that of
the gravel surface (unit 459) to its west, the southernmost
surviving part of the metalled surface 138. Both 469 and 459
seal a thin cobbling of ragstone chips pressed into the grey-
green silt subsoil (units 466, 468), vestiges of the primary
Phase III surface which yielded too few finds to provide a
precise date. There were virtually no finds, either, from the
post-holes of building R3, though post-hole 567 contained a
NVCC beaker sherd of late second century type. Although
there is little stratigraphy directly related to building R3,
therefore, and little datable material from its post-holes, it
is evident that the building was a Phase III structure.

The surviving portion measures at least 5.5 × 3.5 m with a
probable extension of uncertain plan at the north-west
(post-holes 486, 490, 567). It is possible that it was originally
a rectangular structure occupying the entire west zone of the
block – about 12 × 6 m – perhaps even with an extension
into the south-east corner. The absence of post-holes along
the south side may be a consequence of differential erosion,
as the surface of the yellow and grey-green silt subsoil drops
away southwards quite markedly in this region, and some of
the surviving post-holes on the north are quite shallow (e.g.
561, 586). The presence of the contemporaneous but enigmatic U-shaped gully 42 in the north-east quadrant of
block 1b limits the potential extent of the building in that
direction. In fact, the discontinuation of the north branch
of gully 41 implies that access to the block was at the north-
east. There, too, just outside the block, was a water source,
well 446, the position of which presumably dictated the elliptical southward-curving course of the north branch of gully
41. The secondary nature of the north branch is also demonstrated at the north-west corner where it cuts the west
branch and, as part of gully 43, channelled away water to
the north-west. It is possible, therefore, that blocks 1a and
1b were originally a single plot measuring 100 × 50 Roman
feet and that their subdivision into two equal units occurred
part way through Phase III. If the occupants of building R3
were permitted to draw water from well 446 they were evidently not the prime users, for after the division it lay in
block 1a and its stepped access was designed to serve those
approaching from the north.

In its lack of a well and rubbish pits within the block,
building R3 differs from buildings R6 and R7 in the two
other 50 RF blocks, 3 and 4. A different function is probable, and the proximity to building R1 might suggest that
R3 was an ancillary structure of that complex rather than a
separate dwelling. However, rubbish disposal may have been
confined to areas outside the block and this is perhaps
implied by the presence of a pit cluster immediately outside
the south-west corner of gully 41. The excavated component,
pit 467, yielded a late second century AD coarse pottery
assemblage.

Data

Post-holes

SOUTH

612 (AHC)   Rectangular, 0.40 × 0.40 m and 0.31 m deep. Mixed
brown-grey silt with dense limestone packing around
a central rectangular post-pipe, 0.15 × 0.15 m.

561 (AEZ)   Rectangular, post-pipe only, 0.30 × 0.25 m and 0.11 m
deep. Grey silt.

611 (AHB)   Sub-rectangular, 0.45 × 0.40 m and 0.31 m deep. Mixed
grey/brown silt with charcoal flecks, sparse pebbles,
and limestone packing around a central post-pipe
c. 0.25 m in diameter.

WEST

586 (AGA)   Base of post-pipe only, rectangular, 0.25 × 0.20 m and
0.04 m deep. Grey silt.

Unnumbered   Sub-rectangular, 0.35 × 0.30 m. Limestone packing
around a central rectangular post-pipe, 0.15 × 0.10 m.

567 (AFF)   Post-pipe only, ovoid, 0.25 × 0.20 m and 0.22 m deep.
Grey/green silt. Contained a late 2nd century NVCC
beaker sherd.

486 (ABW)   Rectangular, 0.50 × 0.45 m. Loose black soil with limestone packing. Post-pipe not located.

490 (ACA)   Ovoid, apparently post-pipe only, c. 0.35 m in diameter
and 0.40 m deep. Grey-brown silt with some gravel.

NORTH

575 (AFO)   Ovoid, 0.55 × 0.50 m. Dark grey silt with flecks of charcoal, tile and mortar and limestone packing around an
eastern circular post-pipe, 0.25 m in diameter.

577 (AFQ)   Ovoid, 0.60 × 0.55 m. Dark grey silt with flecks of charcoal, tile and mortar and limestone packing around a
west post-pipe c. 0.15 m square. Perhaps a replacement
for 575.

580 (AFT)   Sub-rectangular, 0.35 × 0.30 m and 0.27 m deep. Grey/
brown silt with patchy yellow clay and limestone packing around a post-pipe c. 0.15 m square.

Unnumbered   Sub-rectangular, 0.60 × 0.40 m. Post-pipe not certainly located.

Pit 467 (ABB) W30.3, S20.95 Phase III

A small ovoid pit, part of an intercutting cluster at the west edge of the excavation area. Relationship with unit 454 of gully 41 unclear.

Width 0.7 m, length *c.* 1.0 m, depth 0.3 m.

Fill Light grey silty clay with iron-pan staining.

Dating evidence Coarse pottery: late 2nd century AD.

GULLIES

Gully 41 Phase III

A shallow gully, of very irregular cross-section, which encloses an approximately square plot about 14 × 14 m. The north branch is incomplete and deviates from its line to respect well 446. It cuts the west branch and joins gully 44. The irregular cross-section of the gully system is probably due to partial recutting, e.g. on the west side. Gully 41 cuts the gravel surface 138. The east branch appears to coincide with a boundary system laid off from the south-east corner of building R1 (see slot 620 and associated post-holes, pp. 150–2).

Width 0.4–1.0 m. Length: N 9.5 m; W 15 m; S 14 m; E *c.* 2 m. Depth 0.15–0.35 m.

Fill

Cut 1 498 (ACI) Grey silt with a little gravel.
Cut 2 450 (AAI) Grey/brown silty clay with a few stones and charcoal flecks.
       456 (AAP) Mixed light grey silt and clay with sparse pebbles.
Cut 3 454 (AAN) Mixed grey/brown silt and clay with sparse charcoal flecks.
Cut 4 455 (AAO) Mixed grey/brown silt and clay with gravel.
Cut 5 457 (AAQ) Dark grey/brown silt with much gravel.
Cut 6 211 (KD) Brown-grey silt with gravel.
Cut 7 458 (AAR) Black silty soil with gravel.
Cut 8 493 (ACD) Mixed grey and yellow silt with gravel.

Dating evidence
East branch: no datable material.
South branch: NVGW. Date: AD 125 or later.
West branch: NVCC types 2.8, 3.2, 2.4; NVGW type 45; Horningsea type 107/8; NVSC type 57; gritty buff type 74. Date: late 2nd/early 3rd century AD.
North branch: NVCC, NVGW. Date: AD 125 or later.

Small finds
450 Lead object, Jackson cat. no. 41 (SF 265).
455 Glass vessel fragments, Price cat. nos 70 and 6a (SF 344 and 419a).
457 Samian stamp, Dickinson cat. no. 60 (SF 257).

Gully 42 Phase III

A small U-shaped gully within the enclosure defined by gully 41.

Width 0.45–0.6 m. Length: N 3.0 m; W 3.5 m; S 3.5 m. Depth 0.23 m.

Fill
Cut 1 601 (AGQ) Dark brown silt.
Cut 2 463 (AAX) Grey-brown silt with much gravel.
Cut 3 529 (ADQ) Grey silt.

Dating evidence NVCC types 2.8, 40; NVGW type 47; NVSC type 57; Gritty buff type 74; flagon cf. type 51; Horningsea. Date: late 2nd/early 3rd century AD.

Small finds 463 Copper-alloy pin fragment, Jackson cat. no. 16 (SF 365).

BLOCKS 2–9: SPATIAL ORGANISATION
(Fig. 68)

The relationship between pits, wells, buildings and boundaries revealed in part the varied usage of different zones of the site. Thus, in block 5 there was no evidence for buildings but a great concentration of pits. It seems probable that no building was ever constructed on the plot which, in time, was relegated to the status of a rubbish disposal area. In block 7, which also yielded virtually no evidence of buildings, the pits and wells were much less numerous and were rather randomly scattered across the block, although some were clearly related to the line of ditches or gullies. In block 6, too, traces of buildings were very vestigial and no coherent plan emerged, but the patterning of pits was different again. The north-west and south-east quadrants were virtually free of pits, while concentrations, which included a well and four probable latrines, were located centre south and in the north-east quadrant. It is possible that the pit concentrations and apparently empty reserved areas represent 'yards' and buildings respectively.

Much better evidence for this relationship survives in blocks 3, 4 and 9 and, to a lesser extent, in blocks 2 and 8. In blocks 3 and 4, because of the low density of Phase III occupation and the virtual absence of later features, the spatial organisation is tolerably clear. The plot sizes were obviously carefully determined – both measure *c.* 13.3 × *c.* 19.3 m and were aligned on the axis of building R1, ditch 9, and street 1 N/S. Each contains a rectangular earth-bound post-built structure of similar but not identical plan – buildings R6 and R7. They were constructed end-to-end either side of the plot division marked by gully 35. Access to both buildings was at the east, from street 1 N/S, as disclosed by the interruption to the boundary gullies – gullies 35 and 36 – at their north-east corners. Household debris was disposed of in an organised fashion in a sequence of sub-rectangular pits which were cut in the 'dead ground' or yard area between the west boundary line of the plot and the west side of the buildings. Water was drawn from wells in the north-west and north-east corners of block 3 and in the north-east corner of block 4 (wells 944, 1663, 1836). Although occupation appears to have been neither intensive nor very long-lived it was clearly of some duration. For both building R6 and R7 display pairing of post-holes (e.g. R6: 959, 948; R7: 796/793, 803/802/804, 812/809, 820/819), implying in situ replacement of old timbers. In addition, a number of back-filled pits were subsequently cut by other pits; some pits

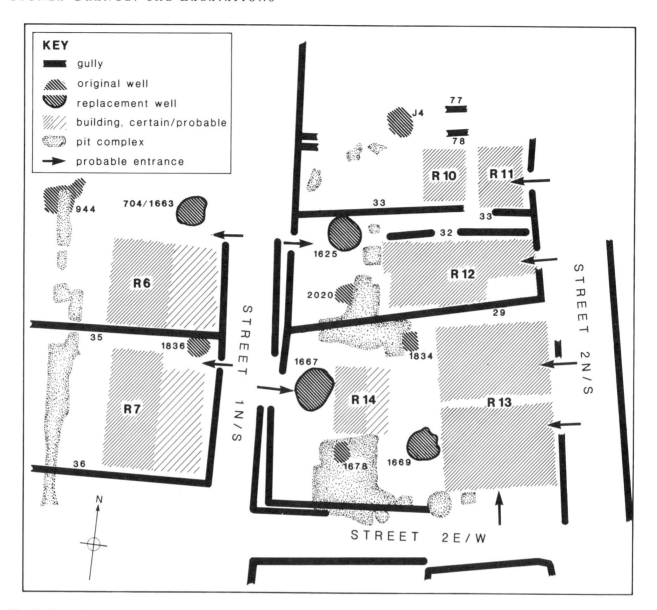

Fig. 68 Stonea Grange: schematic plan of blocks 3, 4 and 9 in Phase III, showing spatial organisation within blocks.

cut the boundary gullies; and well 1663 appears to have been a replacement for well 944 when the latter went out of use.

In the neighbouring block 2 a similar arrangement seems to have prevailed though it is less clearly discernible. In part, this is because the boundaries of the plot are less apparent: there is no enclosing gully and the frontage on to street 1 N/S lay outside the area of excavation. In part, too, it is due to both earlier and later activity on the plot which rendered the Phase III remains less readily intelligible. But it is also due to the character of the localised subsoil, a mixed silt, in which post-holes in particular were revealed only under optimum ground and weather conditions, and then only with the greatest difficulty.

However, a number of shared aspects with blocks 3 and 4 can be identified: the plot of block 2 is exactly double the unit size of blocks 3 or 4; the vestigial remains of building R5 are on the same alignment as R6 and R7, while its east side appears to be recessed the same distance from the frontage of street 1 N/S; the dimensions of the area from which pits were excluded corresponds almost precisely to that in blocks 3 and 4 combined; the single major pit concentration is situated in the same west boundary linear zone as those of blocks 3 and 4; and wells were provided at north and south of the block. Access to the block could have been at the north from street 1 E/W (where there is sufficient space for an entrance between pits 1184 and 1191) and/or at the east from street 1 N/S.

The plots in block 9 display the same spatial organisation as those in blocks 2–4, though there are some differences, attributable in part to the irregular shape of the block, but mainly to the intensity of occupation. The block is divided into three zones, arguably three plots, by a number of east–west gullies. The largest plot lies at the south of the block, between street 2 E/W and gully 29; the second plot occupies the area between gully 29 and gullies 32/33; and the third plot is bounded by gullies 32/33 and gullies 77/78. The dimensions of each are different, but they display a similar patterning of features. At the east end of each is a wood post-built structure or structures; at the west end is a 'yard' area in which are wells and clusters of rubbish pits. In both of the south plots the pit clusters show a high degree of care in their siting, but in time the later pits encroached on both the gullies and on street 2 E/W. A possible sequence of wells (as in block 3) can also be discerned: in the south plot wells 1669 and 1667 appear to have replaced wells 1678 and 1834 respectively when the latter went out of use and became incorporated in the expanding pit clusters. In the centre plot the same sequence appears to have occurred, with the abandonment/re-use of well 2020 and its replacement by well 1625. Only one well (J4) was located in the north plot, but part of its area lay outside the excavation. If the configuration of the enclosing gullies can be taken as a guide, access to the plots seems originally to have been from the west and south. Thus, causewayed entrances, such as those in blocks 3 and 4, were provided at the west of the south and central plots while the gullies continued unbroken on their east side, implying that access to buildings R12 and R14 in those two plots, as originally planned, was from the west via street 1 N/S. Equally, the termination of gully 31 some 12–13 m short of the south-east corner of block 9 implies a south access via street 2 E/W to building R13 in the south plot. However, while the latter entrance may have continued in use, those on the west side may have been replaced by an east access from street 2 N/S. There was no positive evidence in the form of causeway provision across the gullies (though the gullies were silted up at an early stage anyway), but the 'upstaging', if not complete blocking, of the west entrances by the secondary wells 1667 and 1625, together with the slight evidence for relative neglect of street 1 N/S (p. 75) in contrast to the apparent relative longevity of street 2 N/S (p. 75), all combine to make later access from the east to all three plots a probability.

Block 8, also of irregular trapezoidal shape, was subdivided like block 9. Its division into two plots seems to have been an early if not a primary planning feature. The west unit, a rhombus of about 20 × 17 m, was aligned on the axis of building R1, ditch 9 and street 1 N/S. It is enclosed by gully 18, which is unbroken except for a gap of less than 1 m at its north-east corner. The interior was virtually blank, the cut features comprising only three pits and a scatter of post-holes. The contrast with block 9, even with the east plot of

block 8, is very marked, and the lack of wells and rubbish pits may be telling. However, block 5, with its concentration of rubbish pits, lies immediately opposite, and it may always have served as the rubbish disposal area for the occupants of the west plot of block 8, amongst others. Additionally, the presence of wells to the south (wells 1914 and 1885, block 7) and to the east (well 1853, east plot block 8) may have rendered superfluous a well in the west plot. While the lack of wells and pits can be explained in this way, the paucity of observed structural remains is probably attributable to poor preservation rather than indicating a real absence. Like street 1 N/S, the west plot of block 8 had suffered particularly badly from the gouging and scouring of recent agricultural activity. Consequently the original surface was eroded away and cut features were heavily truncated. In addition, the remaining surface of the clay subsoil was deeply furrowed and ridged, making recognition of the less obvious features extremely difficult. That there was a post-hole building (R9) seems virtually certain, but its plan and dimensions were irretrievable. An intensive surface investigation of the north-west corner revealed a fence-line running along the inner lip of gully 18 and a thick scatter of other probable post-holes.

Rather fuller and more convincing evidence survived in the east plot of block 8. Also enclosed by gully 18, this was a slightly smaller (about 20 × 12–14 m) but equally irregular unit. Its organisation, however, was much closer in appearance to that of the plots in block 9. The structural component, building R8, a rectangular post-hole building, was situated in the south-east quadrant, a unit of about 13 × 6 m, and was enclosed by, on the north and west, gully 17, and on the south and east, gully 18. The strip of ground to the west contained a well (1853) outside the north-west corner of gully 17, which, after its disuse as a well, became the centre of an area of rubbish disposal. Further rubbish pits were cut to the north and south, several into the fill of the silted gully 18. It is possible that pit 1698, just inside the west plot, 'belonged' to the east plot. Access to the east plot may have been at the north via street 2 E/W, for gully 18 was extremely narrow in this region and may have been a covered box-drain there.

BLOCK 2 (Figs 49–50, pp. 111–12)

A rectangular plot, about 29 × 18 m, bounded on the north by street 1 E/W, on the west by ditch 9, and on the east by street 1 N/S. To the south is block 3.

Structures Building R5.

Hearth 964.

Wells 705, 730, 808, 905.

Pits 483/918, 725, 794, 795, 958, 966, 990, 1184, 1191.

Ovens 6–8.

BUILDING R5   (Fig. 50)

The poorly-preserved structural remains found at the north end of block 2 in 1982 and partially re-examined in 1983 comprised a scatter of post-holes (building R5b) and an incomplete arrangement of beam slots (building R5a) cut into the mixed grey-green silts which sealed prehistoric features. Modern plough damage in the relatively soft silts had resulted in the loss of the Anglo-Saxon and Roman ground surfaces and the truncation of the upper part of cut features. The shallow beam slots, for example, had been completely erased in some places. In addition, the nature of the silts rendered it extremely difficult to discern cut features whose fill, in many cases, differed little from the surrounding soil, and whose edges were seldom distinct. Thus, although there is no doubt that at least one building stood in the region its structural elements proved frustratingly elusive despite an intensive search.

The surviving identifiable post-holes of building R5b, an evidently incomplete but fairly discrete group some 12 m south of the frontage on to street 1 E/W, did not resolve themselves into a coherent ground plan. Although they occupied a slightly distorted rectangular area about 5 × 3 m, this is unlikely to have been the full extent of the building. There was only one regular alignment – post-holes 929 to 932 – while the position of some post-holes and the variation in their fill, shape and size, is suggestive of more than one period of construction.

Immediately to the north of the post-hole scatter were the vestigial remains of three narrow gullies or beam slots and traces of a fourth (building R5a). Despite the lack of any confirmed corner or junction, it appeared that they would originally have formed a rectangular unit 6.6 × 4.7 m enclosing the probable hearth 964, with a further unit extending eastwards. Significantly, the orientation is consistent with that of the post-hole row 929–32, and both conform to the Roman Phase III grid. It is possible, therefore, that the remains are those of a single Phase III building combining both earth-fast post (R5b) and sill beam (R5a) construction, or that they are the remains of two adjacent Phase III buildings. Furthermore, it appears that one phase of the post-hole structure belongs to the Phase IV settlement. In the absence of good stratigraphic evidence or of any datable finds from the post-holes, certainty is lacking, but there are a number of relevant indicators. The most direct evidence came from building R5a: the east beam slot was cut by posts of the east wall of Anglo-Saxon building S3; the north-east corner was impinged upon by oven 7; and the south slot was sealed by the north end of oven 8, both ovens of Phase IV date.

A Phase III date for building R5a gains support from its modest finds assemblage – a later second century AD samian stamp and coarse pottery of the later second and early/mid third century. Third/fourth century sherds from the east slot date the disuse of the structure, when the beam slots of the dismantled building were levelled up with a capping of yellow clay. This levelling episode was observed elsewhere on the site (e.g. building R4, block 1) and appears to have been a feature of Phase IV. In the immediate vicinity of building R5, for example, the disused and partially silted wells 905 and 808 were both sealed with clay in the third–fourth century. Such levelling implies occupation which is endorsed by the presence of three ovens (ovens 6–8). Since these ovens are disposed around the post-hole scatter without encroaching upon it (in contrast to their relationship with building R5a), it seems probable that building R5b was contemporary, in at least one phase, with the ovens. Thus, just as in block 1 in Phase IV building R4 appears to have been associated with oven 3 (and perhaps oven 4) and pit 997, there seems to have been a similar relationship in block 2 in Phase IV between building R5b and ovens 6–8. Also probably related to the Phase IV component of building R5 were the pit cluster to its west and the disused wells 705, 730, 808 and 905, all of which were used for the disposal of rubbish in the third and fourth centuries.

Like building R4, too, building R5b may have been set within a large sub-rectangular enclosure, c. 35 × c. 18 m, though the boundaries – ditch 9 on the west, street 1 E/W on the north, street 1 N/S on the east, and gully 35 on the south – cannot be proven. At all events there was no joint occupancy of the area with building R6 at the south – a post-hole of its north wall was sealed by oven 5 demonstrating that that building was out of use (and probably levelled) by Phase IV.

Reference has already been made to the fact that building R5a probably continued eastwards originally. The east end of the south slot extended beyond the point of intersection with the east slot and was traced to the edge of the excavated area. Further components of building R5b, too, may have lain beyond the east excavation edge, for a space of over 4 m separated post row 929–32 from the east side of block 2 (street 1 N/S). Furthermore, while pit 1184 occupied the north-east angle of the block, the blank area to its south has the appearance of a reserved space for a building. Certainly, it seems probable that full advantage would have been taken of the corner site, although it has to be admitted that few of the buildings at Stonea were built right up to the street frontages.

As in blocks 3, 4 and 9 wells and rubbish pits were confined to the periphery of the block, most notably on the west, which tends to support the notion of further structural components of building R5 in the 'blank' area to its east. Of the wells, 808 and 730 were probably functional as water sources in the earlier part of Phase III while well 905, which encroached further into the plot, was perhaps a replacement of the later part of Phase III, though the dating evidence is insufficiently precise for certainty. Well 705, set in isolation some distance to the south-east of the main pit group, is either another replacement functioning in the later part of Phase III, or, perhaps, a Phase IV feature contemporary with the ovens and part of building R5. Certainly it is to Phase IV that its use as a receptacle for rubbish is to be dated.

To summarise, the palimpsest of post-holes and the reworking of the silt subsoil at the north of block 2 rendered it at best difficult to unravel the sequence of structures and activity there. They attest concentrated and prolonged occupation from the Late Bronze Age onwards, and it is the one area of the site within the excavation where structural continuity from Phase III to Phase V was demonstrated. Just as Anglo-Saxon building S2 looks to have been the successor to the Phase IV building R4, so it is possible to regard Anglo-Saxon building S3 as the counterpart to the Phase IV building R5b, the latter conceivably a replacement or modified version of a Phase III structure.

Data

Building R5a

BEAM SLOTS

South side 976 (BMF), 987 (BMR), 1331 (COV)
Unit 987 sealed by the north end of oven 8.

Width 0.6 m, length at least 6.5 m, depth 0.2 m.

Dark brown silt with a capping of patchy yellow clay.

Dating evidence
976 Gritty buff type 73/74; NVGW type 27. Date: later 2nd century AD.
987 NVCC type 26; Horningsea. Date: early/mid 3rd century AD.

Small finds 976 Bone hairpin, Greep cat. no. 19 (SF 391).

East side 989 (BMT)
Unit 989 cut by post-hole 805/988 of Anglo-Saxon building S2.

Width 0.65 m. Length: excavated 1.2 m; original probably 4.5 m.

Fill As south side.

Dating evidence NVCC type 20/21? Date: 3rd/4th century AD.

Small finds Bone object, Greep cat. no. 69a (SF 393).

North side 893 (BHT)
Severely eroded. Finds included patterned daub fragments.

Width 0.6 m, length at least 2.5 m.

Fill Brown silt with patchy yellow clay.

Dating evidence Coarse pottery, AD 125 on.

Small finds Samian stamp, Dickinson cat. no. 39 (SF 354) (Macrianus, *c.* AD 150–80).

(?)HEARTH 964 (BLS)/1334 (COY)   E33.5, N64.5

A small bottle-shaped pit south-west of oven 7, within building R5a.

Width 0.6 m, length 1.1 m, depth 0.3 m.

Fill
964 (BLS)/1334 (COY) Mixed grey-brown silt and dark grey ash with charcoal and daub and a red burnt clay 'halo'.
965 (BLT) A thin lens of charcoal on the base of the pit.

Dating evidence 1334 ?3rd century AD coarse pottery.

Building R5b

POST-HOLES

851 (BGB) Ovoid, 0.30 × 0.25 m. Light grey/yellow pebbly silt.
929 (BKG) Squarish, 0.25 × 0.25 m. Grey/black pebbly loam mixed with yellow sand.
930 (BKH) Square, 0.30 × 0.30 m. Fill as 929.
931 (BKI) Square, 0.30 × 0.30 m. Fill as 929.
932 (BKK) Squarish, 0.30 × 0.30 m. Fill as 929.
938 (BKQ) Ovoid, 0.40 × 0.35 m. Dark grey silty clay with stones mixed with orange/yellow silt.
939 (BKR) Round, 0.25 m diameter. Light grey silt mixed with sandy clay.
940 (BKS) Round, 0.20 m diameter. Grey silt with charcoal and tile flecks.
972 (BMB) Square, 0.15 × 0.15 m. Dark brown clayey loam. Post-pipe only.
973 (BMC) Square, 0.15 × 0.15 m. Orange/brown gravelly clay. Post-pipe only.
974 (BMD) Rectangular, 0.20 × 0.15 m. Orange/brown silty clay. Post-pipe only.
975 (BME) Rectangular, 0.20 × 0.15 m. Fill as 972. Post-pipe only.
979 (BMI) Ovoid, 0.50 × 0.30 m. Fill as 940.

WELLS AND PITS

Pit 1191 (CHZ)   E32.0, N70.0   Phase III

Sub-rectangular pit, south of street 1 E/W, between Anglo-Saxon buildings 3 and 4; LBA post-hole in base.

Width 1.15 m, length 1.35 m, depth 0.17 m.

Fill Green-grey silty earth with pebbles and stones

Dating evidence NVSC type 57; NVCC; NVGW. Later 2nd century AD.

Pit 1184 (CHR)   E38.5, N70.8   Phase III, later

Rectangular pit, south of street 1 E/W, on its frontage, and aligned on its axis.

Width 0.95 m, length 2.90 m, depth 0.90 m.

Fill
1184 (CHR) = 996 (BNB) Dark grey-green silty earth with pebbles and clay patches, and large ragstone rubble near the base of the layer.
1193 (CIB) Dark black sooty silty earth, with charcoal flecks.

Dating evidence
996/1184 NVGW type 45
1193 NVCC type 3.2; NVGW type 46; NVSC type 57; shell-gritted type 105/106. Date: early 3rd century AD.

Small finds

1184　Copper-alloy object, Jackson cat. no. 80 (SF 486); copper-alloy needle, Jackson cat. no. 37 (SF 488); glass vessel, base fragment (SF 494); pottery counter, Jackson cat. no. 4 (SF 495); milling stone fragment, Jackson cat. no. 14 (SF 559).

1193　Coarse grey ware stamp fragment, Rigby cat. no. 5 (SF 489); glass vessel, base fragment, Price cat. no. 69 (SF 490); milling stone fragment, Jackson cat. no. 15 (SF 556).

Well 905 (BIG)　E29.5, N66.3　(Fig. 37b, p. 95)　Phase III

Sub-oval well, south of street 1 E/W; beneath Anglo-Saxon building 3.

Width 2.9 m, length 3.6 m, depth 1.8 m.

Fill

868 (BGS)　Red tile and daub in brown silty earth – oven debris.

905 (BIG)　Yellow-brown clay with fragments of flint and chalk – clay seal.

926 (BKD)　Dark grey silt mixed with yellow clay.

941 (BKT)　Grey silty clay with charcoal flecks, tile fragments and lenses of orange-yellow sand.

960 (BLO)　Mixture of orange sand and clays and grey silty clay.

Dating evidence

868/905　NVCC type 20; NVGW type 45; shell-gritted type 102 and jar with parallel at Chesterton of late 3rd/4th century AD; Horningsea. Date: 3rd/4th century AD.

926/941/960　NVCC type 2.6; NVSC type 5; shell-gritted type 102 and jars with parallels at Chesterton of late 3rd/4th century AD; Horningsea. Date: late 3rd century AD.

Small finds

868　Samian stamp, Dickinson cat. no. 89 (SF 352).

926　Glass vessel rim fragment, Price cat. no. 22 (SF 360).

941　Triangular clay loom-weight (SF 435).

The sequence is:

1　Period of well usage, basal silts 960, AD 125 on.

2　Period of well disuse and rubbish disposal: primary, 941, late 2nd century AD; secondary, 926, 3rd century AD.

3　Sealing of filled pit, 905, late 3rd–4th century AD.

4　Oven structural debris, 868, 3rd/4th century AD.

5　Digging of Anglo-Saxon post-holes and filling of sinkage, 'cone', 739, 799, 897, 878, 775, 722, 813, 814, 5th–8th century AD.

?Well 808 (BEG)　E24.5, N63.5　(Fig. 37d, p. 95)　Phase III

Sub-oval pit, south of street 1 E/W; beneath the south-west corner of Anglo-Saxon building 3.

Width 3.4 m, length 4.9 m, depth 1.9 m.

Fill

772 (BCT)　Patchy yellow clay with brown sand and small pebbles and flecks of tile, tufa and mortar – clay seal.

788 (BDL)　Soft light brown sandy clay with iron – clay seal.

808 (BEG)　Patchy yellow clay with brown silts, lumps of chalk and flint, and flecks of charcoal, tile, mortar, iron pan – clay seal.

863 (BGN)　A thin lens of grey-black silty clay with patches of yellow clay and flecks of charcoal and tile.

901 (BIC)　Yellow clay with patches of light grey clay and flecks of mortar and tile – clay seal.

917 (BIT)　Light grey silty gravelly clay with patches of mottled yellow-orange clay and flecks of charcoal, tile and iron pan.

914 (BIQ)　Heavy grey-black clay with flecks of charcoal, traces of waterlogged wood and peaty/leafy deposits.

962 (BLQ)　Sticky light grey clay with blue streaks.

Dating evidence

772/788/808/863/901　NVCC types 4, 2, 25/26; NVGW type 27; NVSC types 57, 59; buff ware type 69/70; Horningsea. Date: 3rd century AD.

917/914/962　NVCC type 2.6; 20/21; NVGW types 29, 45.

Small finds

772　Bone scoop probe, Greep cat. no. 64 (SF 317); bone needle, Greep cat. no. 51 (SF 321).

788　Lead object, Jackson cat. no. 1 (SF 323).

914　Glass vessel, rim fragment, Price cat. no. 62 (SF 382).

The sequence is:

1　Period of well usage, basal silts 962.

2　Period of well disuse and rubbish disposal, 914, 917, late 2nd–3rd century AD.

3　Sealing of filled pit, 901, 863, 808, 788, 772, late 3rd–4th century AD.

4　Digging of Anglo-Saxon post-holes and filling of sinkage 'cone', 724, 723, 716, 763, 750, 714, 5th–8th century AD.

Pit 725 (BAV)　E23.25, N60.0　Phase IV

Small shallow oval pit, near the south-west corner of Anglo-Saxon building 3.

Width 0.8 m, length 1.3 m, depth 0.25 m.

Fill

725 (BAV)　Grey silty clay with iron panning, charcoal flecks and small stones.

729 (BAZ)　Light grey silt with orange clay patches, iron panning and charcoal flecks.

Dating evidence

725　?NVCC bowl with parallel at Chesterton of early 4th century AD.

729　Two sherds LBA pottery, probably residual.

Well 730 (BBA)　E28.0, N59.5　Phase III

Circular well south of Anglo-Saxon building 3.

Diameter 1.5 m, depth 1.1 m.

Fill

730 (BBA)　Dark grey silty clay with patches of yellow clay, a few small pebbles, and flecks of mortar, tile, charcoal, chalk and iron panning.

738 (BBI)　Grey-brown sandy earth with patches of yellow clay, a few stones, and flecks of mortar, tile and charcoal.

748 (BBT) Patchy yellow/orange clay.
749 (BBV) Grey/yellow clay with patches of mottled brown silt and flecks of mortar, tile, charcoal and iron-panning.
762 (BCI) Grey silt with patches of gritty yellow clay and flecks of charcoal, mortar and iron-panning.
817 (BEQ) Patchy fawn/lilac silt with flecks of tile and charcoal.
843 (BFS) Orange/yellow clay with patches of grey silt, lumps of chalk and flecks of tile and charcoal.

Dating evidence
Upper layers: NVCC types 20/21, 25/26, 18. Date: later 3rd century AD.
Fill: shell-gritted jars with parallels at Chesterton of late 3rd/4th century AD. Horningsea. Date: 3rd/4th century AD.
Lower layers: NVCC type 2; NVGW type 45; mortarium cf. Verulamium Fig. 130 no. 1042 mid/late 2nd century AD. Horningsea. Date: late 2nd/3rd century AD.

Small finds 730 Two holes were dug in this layer by illicit metal-detector users.

Pit 483 (ABS)/918 (BIV)

E21.6, N58.3 to E28.2, N57.4   (Fig. 41e, p. 99)   Phase III/IV

A long rectangular pit, aligned east–west, possibly dug as two units, but with a uniform fill in all but the final layer. The relationship with well 730 was uncertain.

Width 2.0–2.4 m, length 6.7 m, depth 0.95 m.

Fill
483 (ABS) Black sandy silt, with a few small stones and flecks of tile, mortar and flint.
918 (BIV) Light grey silty clay with gritty yellow clay, heavy iron-pan flecking and a few stones and pebbles.
864 (BGO) As 483 but with clay.
922 (BIZ) As 918; a lower spit, with ragstone and tile.
877 (BHC) Green-yellow silty clay with patches of gritty yellow clay, large lumps of charcoal and flint fragments.
881 (BHG) Dark grey/brown silty clay with lumps of yellow clay, small pebbles and flecks of charcoal.
888 (BHO) Patchy green-yellow silt with gravel and flecks of charcoal, tile and mortar.
889 (BHP) Dark grey-black peaty silty clay with much charcoal and flecks of tile and mortar.
892 (BHS) Compact black silty clay with patches of gritty yellow clay, waterlogged wood, many snail shells and flecks of mortar, tile and charcoal.
911 (BIN) Patchy yellow clay with dark grey silts and flecks of charcoal, tile and chalk.
921 (BIY) Orange/grey clay with brownish silts and pebbles.

Dating evidence (Figs 160–1, pp. 455, 457)
Upper layers: shell-gritted cf. type 98, in addition to 3rd century AD material.
Fill: NVCC types 20/21, 4, 9, 25/26, 3.2; NVGW types 29, 45, 49, 37, 39. Date: mid/late 3rd century AD.

Small finds
483 Coin, Shotter cat. no. 6, dupondius, VW, AD 69–79 (SF 259); copper-alloy ring, Jackson cat. no. 89 (SF 350).
864 Samian stamp, Dickinson cat. no. 22 (SF 421).
877 Samian stamp, Dickinson cat. no. 76 (SF 355).

889 Copper-alloy object, Jackson cat. no. 31 (SF 383); bone hairpin, Greep cat. no. 35 (SF 387); samian stamp, Dickinson cat. no. 7 (SF 443).
892 Graffiti on amphora, Keay and Carreras cat. no. 22; Potter cat. no. 8 (SF 440).
911 Bone disc, Greep cat. no. 54a (SF 357).
918 Glass vessel fragment, Price cat. no. 59o.

Pit 958 (BLM)   E24.0, N56.6   Phase III/IV

An ovoid pit, adjacent to pit 483/918, cutting pit 966.

Width 1.2 m, length 1.4 m, depth 0.46 m.

Fill
956 (BLK) Dark grey-brown silty loam with small patches of gritty yellow clay, small pebbles, chips of flint and tile and flecks of charcoal and iron-pan staining.
958 (BLM) Yellow/grey silty clay with patches of gritty yellow clay and flecks of tile, mortar, charcoal and iron-pan staining.

Dating evidence NVCC type 20/21; NVGW type 47. Date: 3rd century AD or later.

Pit 966 (BLV)   E24.1, N55.2   Phase III, later

A sub-triangular pit which cuts the north side of pit 920 and is cut by pits 958 and 795.

Width 0.95 m, length 2.1 m, depth 1.25 m.

Fill
956 (BLK) See pit 958, fill.
958 (BLM) See pit 958, fill.
966 (BLV) Dark grey gritty clay with patches of gritty yellow sandy clay and chips of ragstone.

Dating evidence
Upper layer: NVCC type 20/21; NVGW type 47. Date: 3rd century AD.
Lower layer: NVCC type 2.6. Date: late 2nd/3rd century AD.

Pit 795 (BDS)   E25.6, N55.0   Phase III, later

A rectangular pit, aligned east–west, cutting pit 966.

Width 1.2 m, length 2.2 m, depth 1.5 m.

Fill
795 (BDS) Grey-brown silty clay with flecks of charcoal, tile and iron-pan staining.
815 (BEO) Light grey sandy clay with flecks of charcoal, tile and iron-pan staining.
825 (BEZ) Very dark grey silty clay with patches of gritty yellow clay and flecks of tile and charcoal.

Dating evidence
Upper layers: NVCC type 20/21; Horningsea; shell-gritted type 103/4; jars with parallels at Chesterton of later 3rd/4th century AD. Date: late 3rd/4th century AD.
Lower layer: NVCC type 2.6. Date: late 2nd/3rd century AD.

Small finds 795 Decorated copper-alloy strip, Jackson cat. no. 94 (SF 322); enamelled plate brooch, Mackreth cat. no. 18, probably 2nd or early 3rd century AD (SF 324).

Pit 794 (BDR)   E25.9, N53.7   Phase III, later

A rectangular pit, aligned east–west, adjacent to pits 795 and 990.

Width 1.0 m, length 1.3 m, depth 0.55 m.

Fill
794 (BDR)   Same as 795 in pit 795, above.
824 (BEY)   Same as 815 in pit 795, above.
840 (BFP)   Dark grey-brown silty clay with patches of gritty yellow clay, a few pebbles, and flecks of charcoal, tile and mortar.

Dating evidence
Upper layer: Oxford ware; Horningsea; shell-gritted type cf. 102; jars with parallels at Chesterton of 4th century AD. Date: late 3rd/4th century AD.
Lower layers: NVCC barbotine-figured beaker, Johns cat. no. 13. NVGW ?jar sherd. Date: ?late 2nd/3rd century AD.

Pit 990 (BMV)   E24.7, N53.8   Phase III/IV

A sub-rectangular pit, adjacent to pit 794, and cutting pit 920.

Width 1.05 m, length 1.2 m, depth *c.* 0.4 m.

Fill Dark grey-brown silty clay, with flecks of tile, mortar, charcoal and iron-pan staining.

Dating evidence NVCC type 20/21; NVSC type 65. Date: 3rd century AD.

Well 705 (AZZ)

E29.3, N45.6   (Fig. 39b, p. 97)   Phase III, later

A large, deep rectangular pit at the south edge of block 2.

Width 2.6 m, length 2.8 m, depth 1.5 m.

Fill
705 (AZZ)   Dark grey sandy clay with patches of burnt clay, *c.* 10% stones, and flecks of tile, flint, charcoal and iron-pan staining. (A spit of 0.2 m depth.)
710 (BAE)   As 705 (a spit of 0.2 m depth).
717 (BAM)   As 705 (a spit of 0.2 m depth).
727 (BAX)   As 705, but with patches of yellow clay, heavier iron-panning, and a greater concentration of stones (a spit of 0.2 m depth).
745 (BBQ)   As 727, but with traces of a wicker lining (a spit of 0.2 m depth).
771 (BCS)   As 727, but with very few stones (a spit of 0.2 m depth).
781 (BDD)   As 771, but mixed with natural grey silts and orange clay, and with stones; waterlogged.
786 (BDI)   Dark grey clay with many charcoal flecks; waterlogged.

Dating evidence NVCC types 20/21, 4, 18, bowl cf. *NV Guide* no. 82: NVGW types 45.3, 29; shell-gritted jar with parallel at Chesterton of 4th century AD. Horningsea; mortarium cf. Young M21 (Oxford). Date: 3rd/4th century AD.

Small finds
705   Copper-alloy vessel handle fragment?, Jackson cat. no. 82 (SF 272); coin, Shotter cat. no. 15, dupondius, MW, AD 103–11 (SF 274); coin, Shotter cat. no. 7, denarius, MW, AD 74 (SF 278); copper-alloy beads, Jackson cat. nos 63–4 (SF 279, SF 280).

710   Copper-alloy spoon handle, Jackson cat. no. 84 (SF 281); bone hairpin, Greep cat. no. 30 (SF 285); samian stamp, Dickinson cat. no. 114 (SF 290); pipeclay figurine fragment, Johns cat. no. 1; limestone tessera, Jackson cat. no. 53.
717   Bone hairpin, Greep cat. no. 34 (SF 306).
727   Bone ligula, Greep cat. no. 63 (SF 312)
745   Samian stamps, Dickinson cat. nos 87 and 99 (SF 314 and 340).

The sequence is:
1   Cutting and usage of well shaft, probably 2nd century AD.
2   786, silting of shaft, 3rd century AD.
3   781, 771, 745, 727, 717, 710, 705, period of disuse as well, formation of erosion cone and filling of erosion cone, late 3rd/4th century AD.

OVENS

Oven 6   E30.6, N57.8   (Fig. 43, p. 104)   Phase IV

Type 1. Length, *c.* 1.65 m, width 0.55 m, depth 0.16 m.

North–south orientation, with flue at south.

Agricultural damage had badly affected the chamber wall and had destroyed most of the southern end of the oven, including the flue. However, a very extensive spread of stoke-hole debris survived beyond the flue.

816 (BEP)   Stoke-hole rake-out debris. Grey ashy soil extending 1.1 m south of the oven flue, flanked by smaller areas of mixed light grey ash and silt.
827 (BFB)   Flue area, fill. Burnt red and yellow clay patches with charcoal and pockets of brown silty sand. Like the flue of oven 2, the filling debris preserved the line of the flue channel into the chamber.
707 (BAB)   Chamber, upper fill. Grey-brown ashy sandy soil with yellow clay and burnt red clay lumps.
806 (BEE)   Chamber, lower fill. Burnt red clay superstructure fragments in a matrix of brown silt. Rests on oven floor of discoloured fire-hardened sandy silt.

Finds Animal bone.

Oven 7   E35.4, N66.2   (Fig. 43)   Phase IV

Type 2 (?). Length 2.05 m, width 0.65 m, depth 0.15 m.

North–south orientation, with flue at south.

The superstructure and even the base of the walls is very poorly-preserved, rendering uncertain the identification of the oven type. The poor preservation is not just a result of recent agricultural damage: the oven lay within the walls of Anglo-Saxon building S3 and was cut by a post-hole of that building (718/719). Already by Phase V, therefore, it must have been dismantled and levelled. Those processes, together with a certain amount of disturbance during the occupation of the building, will have been responsible for the disappearance of the superstructure and the distortion of the wall-lines.

923 (BKA)   Stoke-hole, with rake-out debris. Ashy grey-brown silt with charcoal, pebbles, and lumps of ragstone.
753 (BBZ)   Flue. Grey-brown sand with patches of yellow clay, grey silt and charcoal.

709 (BAD) Chamber, surface debris. Brown sandy soil, with burnt clay lumps, ash and charcoal.

740 (BBL) Chamber, upper fill. Brown silty sand with many flecks of tile.

768 (BCP) Chamber, collapsed superstructure. Burnt red clay wall fragments with patches of brown silt, ragstone blocks, and a shattered millstone fragment of Niedermendig lava.

787 (BDK) Chamber, lower fill. Grey-brown silty sand with small pebbles. Rests on oven floor of hard white ash, compacted black ash, and baked red clay with a whitened surface.

Finds

923 (BKA) Coarse pottery, ?3rd century AD.

753 (BBZ) Coarse pottery, AD 125 on.

768 (BCP) Coarse pottery, AD 125 on.

Oven 8   E34.5, N60.6   Phase IV

Type 1. Length *c.* 2.6 m, width *c.* 0.9 m.

North–south orientation, with flue probably at the south.

Virtually destroyed. A surface spread of burnt red clay debris, with no in situ structure.

977 (BMG) Burnt red clay, patchy yellow clay, tile and chalk in grey-brown silty loam.

Finds Coarse pottery, late 2nd century AD.

DITCHES AND GULLIES

Ditch 9, cuts 1–4   See pp. 147–9

Gully 35, cuts 1–7   See pp. 167–8

BLOCK 3   (Fig. 51, p. 113)

A rectangular plot, about 18 × 13.25 m, south of block 2, bounded on the west by ditch 9, on the south by gully 35, and on the east by gully 35 and street 1 N/S.

Structures Building R6.

Wells 704/1663, 944.

Pits 736/737, 774, 829, 842, 850, 859, 860, 899.

Oven 5.

Gully 35.

BUILDING R6   (Figs 51, 68–9)

This rectangular timber building, excavated in 1982, was located a little to the south of centre in block 3. Its dimensions were at least 7 × 5.8 m and, together with its ancillary components – wells and pits – it occupied the entire block. Its construction incorporated earth-fast squared posts a little unevenly spaced about 1.3–1.7 m apart. Unlike block 2, with its reworked mixed grey and grey-green silts,

block 3 lay within a subsoil zone of mixed orange sand and yellow clay. The patchy nature of the subsoil posed some problems in identification, but in general it disclosed post-holes more readily than the silts. In consequence, a tolerably complete ground plan was recovered, and it was possible in many cases to define both post-pipe and post-pit. Nevertheless, it is evident that several post-holes and other structural elements eluded discovery. Neither internal floors nor external ground surface survived, and accompanying their destruction would have been the evidence for partitions and extensions. It is hard to believe, for example, that the apparently 'empty' space along the east side of the block was not, in reality, occupied by a part of the structure. The combination of severe plough damage and especially arid conditions in the excavation season of 1984 prevented a proper examination of this blank area, but a limited investigation in that year of the equivalent zone of block 4 demonstrated the presence there of a scattering of features, including post-holes, and it seems probable that a similar density of features would have been located in block 3. The one other area of block 3 which was reserved by the careful linear disposition of pits and wells is a unit of about 4.5 × 3.5 m at the north-west of building R6, and the presence there of three post-holes hints at a rectangular extension to the main building.

Building R6, like building R1 and the west sector of the Phase III settlement, was aligned on a grid orientated almost exactly on the cardinal points. Its south (?gable-) end lay back-to-back with the north end of building R7; and gully 35, which marked the boundary of the block, ran between. Although the north edge of block 3 was not marked by a gully the organisation of features in that region leaves little room for doubt that building R6, like building R7, occupied a plot measuring 50 Roman feet square (see pp. 136, 168). Both blocks had a frontage on to street 1 N/S which, in the case of block 3, was the sole direct access (see Fig. 51, p. 113). Hardly surprisingly, therefore, rubbish pits were relegated to the peripheral zones along the north and west sides, where they would not impede access nor be visible from the front of the building.

The density of pits is not great, but the character of several (multi-unit form with a uniform fill) suggests that they may have been regularly emptied for composting fields. At all events, a chronological sequence, revealed by the pits in the north-west corner, indicates that building R6 was occupied throughout most, if not all, of Phase III: well 944 ceased functioning as a water source and was filled with debris, dated by its coarse pottery assemblage to the late second/ early third century AD, before being cut by part of pit 860, the primary fill of which was dated early third century AD or later. The disuse of well 944 probably coincided with the cutting of well 704/1663, which probably continued in use as a source of water until the end of Phase III. Its lower layers contained a mid/later third century coarse pottery

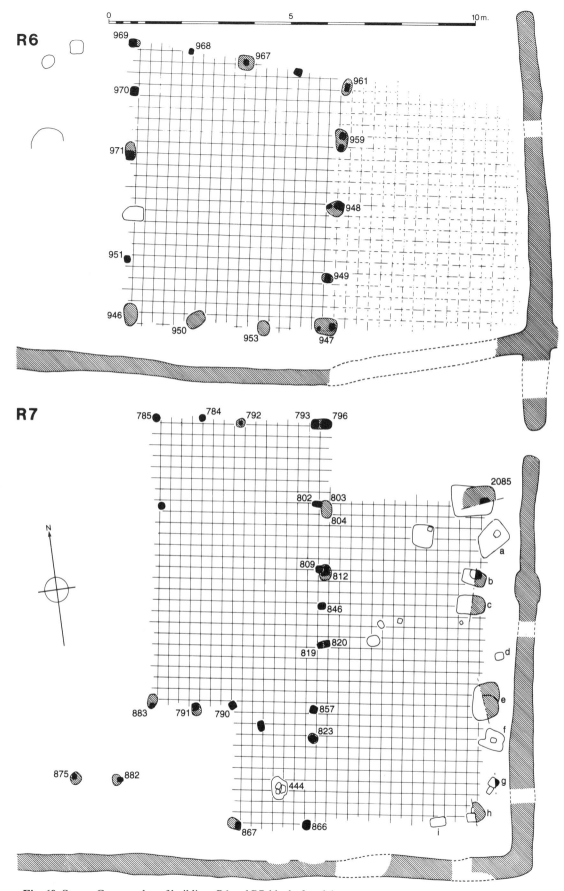

Fig. 69 Stonea Grange: plan of buildings R6 and R7, blocks 3 and 4.

assemblage, while the upper section was filled in the late third/early fourth century AD. Building R6 itself yielded no direct evidence for the longevity of its period of use, though the duplication of posts in several post-holes of the east wall-line implies partial replacement if not rebuilding. Finds from the post-holes were restricted to a few sherds of coarse pottery, an illegible broken copper-alloy coin from post-hole 947 at the south-east corner, and a stamp of the samian potter Vosecunnus (c. AD 140–70) from post-hole 959 of the east wall.

The absence of floors and the irregular spacing of the posts of building R6 rendered it impossible to determine the point of entry to the building. All that can be safely said is that with a main access to street 1 N/S at the north-east of the block (where gully 35 stops short of the corner leaving a 'causeway' of some 4 m), the entrance is likely to have been in the north or east side, and if the former, the location of pits 829 and 842 would point to a central doorway between posts 967 and 968. If the entrance were originally in the north side, then the position chosen for the replacement well 704/1663, which restricted the direct route from street 1 N/S to the north side of the building, may imply a change of entrance at that time to the east side or to the east end of the north side.

The dating evidence from building R6 and its associated gully, wells and pits, sparse though it is, points to a single period of use in Phase III. This is confirmed by oven 5, which straddled the north wall-line and sealed a post-hole of that wall beneath its floor: when oven 5 was constructed building R6 must have been long since disused. There is no evidence of any nearby Phase IV structure, but the upper fills of the disused well 704/1663 and of pits 860 and 774 were presumably associated with the period of usage of the oven.

Data

Post-holes

NORTH SIDE

969 (BLY)   Rectangular, 0.35 × 0.20 m. Dark grey/brown silt with charcoal, daub and burnt clay fragments. Incorporates, on the west side, a square post-pipe, 0.20 × 0.20 m.

968 (BLX)   Square, post-pipe only, 0.15 × 0.15 m. Fill as 969.

967 (BLW)   Rectangular, 0.45 × 0.40 m. Light grey silt with iron-pan staining. Incorporates a central square post-pipe, 0.15 × 0.15 m.

Unnumbered   Rectangular, post-pipe only, 0.20 × 0.15 m. Sealed beneath floor of oven 5. Unexcavated.

961 (BLP)   rectangular, 0.40 × 0.25 m. Fill as 967. Incorporates a central rectangular post-pipe, 0.20 × 0.15 m.

EAST SIDE

959 (BLN)   Sub-rectangular, 0.55 × 0.35 m. Fill as 967. Incorporates two square post-pipes, one at the north,

0.18 × 0.18 m, and one at the south, 0.15 × 0.15 m. The post-hole yielded a single find – a samian stamp, Dickinson cat. no. 96, Vosecunnus, c. AD 140–70 (SF 389).

948 (BLB)   Ovoid, 0.50 × 0.40 m. Dark grey silt with orange sandy flecks. Incorporates two rectangular post-pipes, one at the east, 0.25 × 0.20 m, and one at the west, 0.15 × 0.10 m.

949 (BLC)   Ovoid, 0.30 × 0.25 m. Fill as 948. Incorporates a central post-pipe, 0.20 × 0.15 m.

SOUTH SIDE

947 (BLA)   Sub-rectangular, 0.65 × 0.45 m. Fill as 967. Incorporates a square, stone-packed post-pipe, 0.15 × 0.15 m, at the east, and a clay-packed ?stake-hole, 0.08 × 0.08 m, at the west. The post-hole yielded a single find – an illegible copper-alloy coin, Shotter cat. no. 61 (SF 386).

953 (BLG)   Squarish, 0.30 × 0.30 m. Fill as 967. Partial stone-packing, but no post-pipe identified.

950 (BLD)   Sub-rectangular, 0.50 × 0.40 m. Fill as 967. No post-pipe identified.

946 (BKZ)   Sub-rectangular, 0.60 × 0.40 m. Fill as 967. No post-pipe identified.

WEST SIDE

951 (BLE)   Square, post-pipe only, 0.20 × 0.20 m. Fill as 967.

Unnumbered   Rectangular, 0.60 × 0.40 m. An uncertain and incompletely excavated post-pit.

971 (BMA)   Rectangular, 0.55 × 0.25 m. Grey/brown clayey silt with chalk flecks. Incorporates a square post-pipe, 0.25 × 0.25 m, at the south.

970 (BLZ)   Square, post-pipe only, 0.25 × 0.25 m. Fill as 969, but with light grey silt capping.

NORTH-WEST PROJECTION

984 (BMO)   Square, 0.35 × 0.35 m. Light grey silt. An uncertain and incompletely excavated post-hole.

Unnumbered   Ovoid, 0.40 × 0.30 m.

991 (BMW)/992 (BMX), Large sub-circular post-pit (992), c. 0.90 × 0.90 m. Grey/brown silt with small pebbles. Incorporates a square post-pipe (991) c. 0.25 × 0.25 m, at the north. Dark grey/brown silt.

WELLS AND PITS

Well 944 (BKX)   E21.4, N40.8   Phase III

A large rectangular pit with an irregular projection at one corner. North-west corner of block 3. Cut by pit 860.

Width 2.5 m, length 2.8 m.

Fill

944 (BKX)   Mixed yellow/orange clay, dark grey silts and rubble, with flecks of tile, mortar, charcoal etc.

943 (BKW) Grey silty clay with sandy patches and large rocks.

Dating evidence NVCC type 1. Date: late 2nd/early 3rd century AD.

It was not clear whether the corner projection was a constructional feature or a means of access to the well; its fill was as 944.

Pit 860 (BGK)   E21.5, N36.8 to E21.8, N42.1   Phase III, later

A long rectangular pit, aligned north–south, along west side of block 3; probably cut in three units, but with a uniform fill. Cuts well 944.

Width 1.3–1.5 m, length 5.3 m, depth 0.75 m.

Fill
860 (BGK) Dark grey silty clay
876 (BHB) Light grey/orange sandy clay with patches of yellow clay and flecks of tile, mortar, chalk and iron-pan staining. There was a concentration of large rocks against the north-east edge.
904 (BIF) Orange/grey clay with flecks of chalk and fragments of ragstone.

Dating evidence
Upper layers: NVCC type 20/21; Horningsea type 107/8; shell-gritted ware with parallels at Chesterton of 3rd/4th century AD. Date: 3rd/4th century AD. There is also a possible Saxon sherd.
Lower layer: NVGW; Horningsea. Date: early 3rd century AD or later.

Small finds
860 [A hole was dug in this layer by illicit metal-detector users.] Pellet of Egyptian Blue, Bimson cat. no. 1 (SF 410).
876 Bone needle, Greep cat. no. 49 (SF 405).

The upper layers (860, 876) appeared to be a recut pit into 904.

Pit 859 (BGI)   E21.25, N35.5   Phase III/IV

A shallow rectangular pit, aligned north–south along west side of block 3, the central unit of the pit line 860–859–774.

Width 1.4 m, length 1.8 m, depth 0.16 m.

Fill Dark grey-brown silty clay with occasional pebbles and patches of orange/yellow clay.

Dating evidence NVGW type 45; Horningsea. Date: 3rd century AD.

Pit 774 (BCW)   E21.2, N32.5   Phase III/IV

A sub-rectangular pit, aligned north–south, at the south-west corner of block 3.

Width 1.65 m, length 1.85 m, depth 0.4 m.

Fill
774 (BCW) Dark grey sandy clay with small and medium fragments of ragstone and flint, and flecks of tile, mortar, charcoal and iron-pan staining.
807 (BEF) Grey silty clay with heavy iron-pan staining and flecks of chalk.

Dating evidence
Upper layer: NVCC type 20/21; NVGW type 45. Date: 3rd/4th century AD; also intrusive Anglo-Saxon pottery.
Lower layer: no datable material.

Pit 736 (BBG)/737 (BBH)

E22.35, N31.25   (Fig. 41c, p. 99)   Phase III, later
A rectangular pit, aligned north–south, near the south-west corner of block 3. Like pit 860, it was cut as more than one unit – 736, 737 – but has a uniform fill.

Width 1.2–1.4 m, length 2.95 m, depth 0.35 m.

Fill
732 (BBC) Grey silty clay with patches of yellow clay, flecks of tile, charcoal and chalk, and heavy iron-pan staining.
736 (BBG) As 732
737 (BBH) As 732

Dating evidence
Upper layer (732) NVCC; NVGW; Horningsea. Date: early 3rd century AD or later.
736 NVCC; NVGW. Date: AD 125 or later.
737 NVGW flanged bowl; buff ware type 74. Date: late 2nd/3rd century AD.

Pit 829 (BFD)   E25.6, N37.75   Phase III

A narrow, shallow rectangular pit, aligned east–west, outside the north-west corner of building R6, block 3.

Width 0.6–0.75 m, length 2.4 m.

Fill Dark grey silty clay with patches of yellow clay, flecks of tile and charcoal, and fragments of flint.

Dating evidence NVGW type 45. Date: late 2nd/early 3rd century AD.

Pit 847 (BFX)   E27.7, N40.65

A shallow rectangular pit, aligned east–west, at the north side of block 3; badly damaged by a modern field drain.

Width 0.85 m, length 1.9 m.

Fill Dark brown earth with patches of yellow clay, pebbles and flecks of tile and charcoal.

Dating evidence No datable material.

Pit 850 (BGA)   E30.45, N40.65

A shallow, narrow oval pit, aligned east–west, at the north side of block 3; the north side was cut away by a modern field drain.

Width c. 0.65 m, length 1.8 m.

Fill Grey/brown loam with patches of yellow/grey clay, occasional pebbles and flecks of tile.

Dating evidence No datable material.

Pit 899 (BIA) E30.15, N39.35 Phase III, later

A small rectangular pit, north of building R6, block 3.

Width 0.7 m, length 1.05 m, depth 0.45 m.

Fill

899 (BIA) Grey-brown clay, with patches of yellow clay, flecks of tile and chalk and iron-pan staining.

902 (BID) Dark grey silty sand with small pebbles and flecks of mortar.

903 (BIE) Light grey silty clay, with patches of yellow silt and flecks of charcoal, tile and mortar.

Dating evidence NVGW type 45; Horningsea. Date: early 3rd century AD or later.

Pit 842 (BFR) E31.35, N37.1 Probably Phase III

A shallow narrow rectangular pit, aligned with pit 829 E/W, to the north of the north-east corner of building R6, block 3.

Width 0.5 m, length 1.35 m.

Fill Light grey/brown silty clay with flecks of tile, flint and iron-pan staining.

Dating evidence NVGW sherd. Date: AD 125 onwards.

(?)Well 704 (AZY)/1663 (DGT)
E33.8, N39.6 (Fig. 38a, p. 96) Phase III, later

A large sub-rectangular steep-sided pit in the north-east corner of block 3. Excavated in two, unequal, parts in 1982 (704) and 1984 (1663).

Width 2.7 m, length 2.8 m, depth 1.43 m.

Fill

704 (AZY)/1663 (DGT) Grey/black sandy clay with small fragments of flint and burnt stone and flecks of tile and charcoal.

713 (BAH)/1721 (DKE) Grey/brown silt with patches of yellow clay, a few stones and flecks of tile, charcoal and iron-pan staining.

728 (BAY)/734 (BBE)/1722 (DKF) Grey silts with patches of orange/yellow clay, much charcoal and flecks of tile and mortar.

1732 (DKQ) Brown/grey silts mixed with yellow clay. Waterlogged.

1737 (DKW) Pale grey silt lens within 1732.

Dating evidence

Upper layers and main fill (704/1663, 713/1721, 728/734/1722): NVCC types 9, 20/21, beaker with parallel at Chesterton of late 3rd/4th century AD; NVGW type 45; NVSC type 57; Horningsea. Date: late 3rd/early 4th century AD.

Lower fill (1732, 1737): NVCC types 4, 2.4, 2.5, 20/21; NV mortarium; Horningsea. Date: mid/late 3rd century AD.

Small finds

704 Whetstone, Jackson cat. no. 36 (SF 275)

1663 Glass vessel fragment, Price cat. no. 3 (SF 662).

1722 Coin, Shotter cat. no. 19, dupondius, MW, AD 103–17 (SF 801); glass vessel fragment, Price cat. no. 64e (SF 671).

The sequence is:
1 Period of well usage, Phase III
2 Beginning of well disuse, basal silts 1732, mid 3rd century AD.
3 Period of well disuse and rubbish disposal, later 3rd–4th century AD.

OVEN

Oven 5 E30.6, N35.9 (Fig. 44, p. 105; Pl. XVIII) Phase IV

Type 2. Length 2.05, width 0.65 m, depth 0.19 m.

Internal measurements
Stoke-hole: length 0.32 m; width i) 0.19 m, ii) 0.31 m; depth 0.09 m.
Flue: length 0.31 m; width 0.25 m; depth 0.2 m.
Chamber: total length 1.27 m; chamber units diameter *c.* 0.5 m; depth 0.18 m.

North–south orientation, with flue at south.

The best-preserved ground plan of all the ovens. A small L-shaped recess at the south was the remnant of the stoke-hole. A step down of 0.1 m led to the rectangular flue, which had fire-reddened clay walls. A low base-wall of fired clay at the north of the flue was all that survived of the aperture connecting the flue to the oven chamber (this region had suffered recent damage by agricultural equipment). The figure-of-eight shape of the base wall of the double-domed superstructure was well preserved, though little depth remained. The chamber floor was at about the same level as the flue. In the central linking zone between the two domed units was an irregularly-shaped fired clay pedestal base or plinth. The floor of the south unit of the chamber sealed a post-hole of the north wall of building R6.

733 (BBD) Stoke-hole, and flue, upper fill. Patches of charcoal mixed with grey ash and light grey silt.

735 (BBF) Flue, lower fill. Burnt red and yellow clay mixed with charcoal.

706 (BAA) Chamber, surface debris. Patchy orange/grey silty clay, with flecks of tile, mortar, and charcoal and some stone.

712 (BAG) Chamber, upper fill. Patchy yellow clay with grey silt, pockets of charcoal, and flecks of tile, mortar and chalk.

755 (BCB) Chamber, collapsed superstructure. Burnt red clay walling fragments with patches of yellow clay.

756 (BCC) Chamber, lower fill. Charcoal and brown silt with many fragments of tile and burnt stone. Rests on oven floor of discoloured yellow sandy clay, with blackened, fire-hardened areas.

Finds 706 (BAA) Coarse pottery, late 2nd century AD.

GULLY

Gully 35 Phase III

A narrow gully with steep sides and flat bottom. It defines the south and east sides of block 3. The profile of the east branch is broader and shallower than that of the south branch, but this is probably a result of the severe modern plough erosion in that area. The east branch has a butted north terminal. Its south end meets gully 36. The west end of the south branch meets ditch 5. Due to modern damage the relationship between the two could not be established. The small pit 925 (block 4) clips the south side of the south branch.

Width 0.3–0.55 m. Length: south branch 18.6 m (originally *c*. 19.0 m); east branch 9.1 m. Depth: south branch 0.26–0.35 m; east branch 0.1 m.

Fill

Cut 1   865 (BGP) Light grey-brown silt with flecks of chalk and flint and iron-pan staining.

Cut 2   754 (BCA) Grey-brown sandy clay with much charcoal and flecks of mortar, tile and flint.

Cut 3   810 (BEI) Light grey-brown sandy silt with flecks of charcoal, mortar and flint.
872 (BGX) Orange-yellow clay with flecks of charcoal and chalk and a few pebbles.

Cut 4   703 (AZX) Light grey sandy clay with stones and flecks of tile, charcoal and iron-pan staining.

Cut 5   708 (BAC) As cut 4.

Cut 6   1855 (DPT) Grey-brown sandy silt with a little clay, some gravel and stone [A sealing layer in the pit/gully cluster at the south-east corner of block 3.]
1861 (DQA) Dark grey sandy silt with some clay and gravel.

Cut 7   1665 (DGW) Dark grey silt with some gravel.

Dating evidence

East branch: NVCC type 20/21; Horningsea type 107/8. Date: 3rd century AD.
South branch, layer 810: NVCC type 20/21. Date: 3rd century AD.
Layer 1855: NVGW types 27, 28; buff ware type 59. Date: late 2nd century AD.
Rest: NVCC types 2.8, 20/21, 25/26; NVGW types 47, 28; buff ware cf. type 59; mortarium cf. Grandford no. 97. Date: 3rd century AD.

Small finds 1665 Samian stamp, Dickinson cat. no. 110 (SF 807).

BLOCK 4   (Fig. 51, p. 113)

A rectangular plot, about 18 × 13.25 m, south of block 3, bounded on the west by ditch 9, on the south by gully 36, and on the east by gully 36 and street 1 N/S.

Structures Building R7.

Hearth 444.

Well 1836.

Pits 744, 783, 818, 900, 925, 1786, 1847.

Gully 36.

BUILDING R7   (Fig 51, p. 113; Figs 68–9)

This building, a rectangular timber structure excavated in 1982 and 1984, is the counterpart to building R6 in block 3, though its ground-plan appears to have differed in a number of respects. Like R6, its walls were supported by earth-fast squared posts, rather irregularly spaced. The subsoil in block 4 was similar to that in block 3, a dissected

natural comprising white-flecked yellow clay interspersed with occasional patches of light grey silt and pockets of orange silty sand filling hollows and gullies. This patchy nature rendered it difficult sometimes to differentiate post-holes from natural features on surface indications alone. The situation was aggravated on the east by very severe surface irregularity caused by modern ploughing. Careful trowelling of the surface in 1984 revealed a considerable number of features. Although there was insufficient time to excavate all, several were confirmed as post-holes of the east frontage of building R7.

Building R7, like its counterpart in block 3, was orientated according to the main Phase III grid, and it occupied the entire east section of its block, which was laid out as a unit of 50 Roman feet square. The building measures about 10.8 × 9.2 m overall and appears to have been indented at its north-east corner. The indentation very probably accommodated the entrance as it corresponds to the position of the access causeway to the block, across gully 36, from street 1 N/S. Theoretically, building R7 could also have been approached from the south, where it had a frontage on to the west end of street 2 E/W. However, that part of the street appears to have been short-lived (see p. 76) and, in conjunction with the fact that no causeway was provided across the south branch of gully 36, it may be assumed that the east access was the principal if not the sole means of entry. Unfortunately, the incomplete nature of the building's ground-plan does not permit identification of the exact location of the doorway, which may have been via the east end of the north wall or the north end of the central wall.

In view of the absence of floors and the demonstrable incompleteness of the ground-plan, especially on the west side, certainty is lacking, but the surviving post-holes may be interpreted as the remains of two large rectangular rooms 8.5 × 4.5 and 7.5 × 4.5 m (probably divided by internal partitions), offset north and south along a shared wall-line, with a third small room at the south-west. The latter room, 3 × 2 m, contains hearth 444, the only indicator of function in any part of the building. The same combination of one small and two large rectangular rooms is postulated for building R6, although the evidence there is even more tenuous.

The central wall-line, like that of building R6, shows evidence of post-replacement in its central and north sector, and the apparent proliferation of post-holes along the east side hints at replacement there, too. None of the post-holes yielded any closely datable artefacts, but the finds assemblage from the associated rubbish pits along the west edge of the block and from well 1836 in the north-east corner is directly comparable to that from the pits and wells in block 3 and attests a single phase of occupation of building R7 in Phase III. Although the pit cluster is slightly greater than that in block 3, the spatial organisation of well and pits is exactly the same. The careful linear pit arrangement down the west side was even more pronounced than that in block

3. It appears that a primary row was succeeded by a secondary row immediately to its east, when the former had exhausted the available space to north and south. Subsequently two pits (701(i) and (ii)), breached gully 36 and encroached onto the west end of street 2 E/W. At the north, however, the boundary line between blocks 3 and 4 continued to be respected, and pit 744 in the secondary row terminated at the very lip of gully 35.

The pits in the main body of the linear cluster, together with the adjacent pits 900 and 925, contained coarse pottery of the late second/early third century AD, while those pits at the north and south extremities (701 and 744) yielded coarse pottery of third century AD date. Well 1836 was strategically placed at the north-east of the block, just to the north of the causewayed entrance, in the angle formed by the junction of gullies 35 and 36. Its period of use as a water source was followed by one of rubbish disposal, dated by the coarse pottery to the late second/third century AD. No certain Phase IV feature was located in block 4, and it may be assumed that at the end of Phase III building R7 was abandoned and its surrounding plot deserted.

Data

Post-holes

WEST SIDE

833 (BHI) Ovoid, 0.40 × 0.25 m. Grey silt with iron-pan staining and tile and charcoal flecks. Incorporates a square post-pipe, *c*. 0.15 × 0.15 m at the south.

856 (BGF) Post-pipe only, circular, 0.20 × 0.20 m. Fill as 785.

785 (BDH) Post-pipe only, circular, 0.20 × 0.20 m. Light grey sandy silt with patches of orange clay and flecks of tile.

NORTH SIDE

784 (BDG) Post-pipe only, circular, 0.20 × 0.20 m. Light grey sandy silt with tiny pebbles.

792 (BDP) Circular, 0.25 × 0.25 m. Grey silt with iron-pan staining. Incorporates a square post-pipe, *c*. 0.10 × 0.10 m, centrally.

793 (BDQ) Post-pipe only, sub-rectangular, 0.25 × 0.25 m. Fill as 792. Adjacent to 796.

796 (BDT) Post-pipe only, sub-rectangular, 0.30 × 0.25 m. Fill as 792. Adjacent to 793.

CENTRE

802 (BEA) Ovoid, 0.25 × 0.15 m, probably post-pipe only. Dark grey silt with charcoal flecks and a few stones. Cuts 803/804.

803 (BEB)/804 (BEC) Sub-rectangular, 0.45 × 0.30 m, though possibly two intercutting post-pipes. Fill as 792, with packing stones. Cut by 802.

809 (BEH) Post-pipe only, square, 0.18 × 0.18 m. Grey-brown silt with flecks of charcoal and small stones. Cuts 812.

812 (BEL) Rectangular, 0.40 × 0.30 m. Fill as 809. Incorporates a square post-pipe, 0.25 × 0.25 m, at the north. Cut by 809.

846 (BFW) Rectangular, 0.25 × 0.20 m, probably post-pipe only. Light grey silty clay with iron-pan staining.

819 (BES) Post-pipe only, square, 0.15 × 0.15 m. Orange/grey silt with iron-pan staining. Adjacent to 820.

820 (BET) Post-pipe only, square, 0.15 × 0.15 m. Fill as 819. Adjacent to 819.

857 (BGG) Post-pipe only, rectangular, 0.25 × 0.20 m. Orange-grey clay with flint fragments.

823 (BEX) Sub-rectangular, 0.30 × 0.25 m. Light grey silt with iron-pan staining. Incorporates a rectangular post-pipe, 0.22 × 0.18 m, centrally.

EAST SIDE

2085 (EAI) Sub-rectangular, 1.10 × 0.80 m, depth 0.65 m. Yellow clay with white flecks, and flint packing stone. Incorporates a rectangular post-pipe, 0.22 × 0.18 m, at the east, with orange sand and gravel fill.

Unnumbered *a* Sub-rectangular, 0.80 × 0.65 m, unexcavated. Fill as 2085. Incorporates a rectangular post-pipe, 0.20 × 0.17 m, east of centre, with yellow gravel fill.

Unnumbered *b* Rectangular, 0.65 × 0.35 m, depth 0.10 m. Brown clay. Incorporates an ovoid post-pipe, 0.25 × 0.20 m, centrally, with grey silt fill.

Unnumbered *c* Rectangular, 0.75 × 0.50 m, depth 0.20 m. Pale cream silt.

Unnumbered *d* Post-pipe only, rectangular, 0.25 × 0.20 m, unexcavated.

Unnumbered *e* Two intercutting sub-rectangular post-pits, 0.70 × 0.60 m, depth 0.60 m, brown clay with gravel, cuts 0.70 × 0.60 m, depth 0.30 m, yellow clay with white flecks.

Unnumbered *f* Squarish, 0.50 × 0.50 m, unexcavated. Brown clay with gravel. Incorporates a rectangular post-pipe, 0.15 × 0.15 m, centrally.

Unnumbered *g* Two intercutting post-pipes, square, 0.25 × 0.25 m, depth 0.10 m, pale grey silt; rectangular, 0.20 × 0.12 m, unexcavated, brown clay.

Unnumbered *h* Sub-rectangular, 0.50 × 0.35 m, depth 0.40 m. Brown clay. Cut by square post-pipe, 0.25 × 0.25 m, brown clay fill, at the west.

SOUTH SIDE

Unnumbered *i* Rectangular, 0.45 × 0.25 m, unexcavated. Brown clay with gravel.

866 (BGQ) Sub-rectangular, 0.30 × 0.23 m. Grey silt with iron-pan staining. Probably post-pipe only.

867 (BGR) Ovoid, 0.45 × 0.25 m. Fill as 866. Incorporates a square post-pipe, 0.18 × 0.18 m at the south-east.

790 (BDN) Post-pipe only, square, 0.20 × 0.20 m. Fill as 866.

791 (BDO) Sub-rectangular, 0.35 × 0.25 m. Fill as 866. Incorporates a square post-pipe, 0.20 × 0.20 m, at the north.

SOUTH-WEST ?EXTENSION

882 (BHH) Ovoid, 0.30 × 0.25 m. Fill as 866. Incorporates a rectangular post-pipe, 0.18 × 0.12 m, at the east.

875 (BHA) Squarish, 0.30 × 0.30 m. Light grey/orange silt with iron-pan staining. Incorporates a square post-pipe, 0.15 × 0.15 m, at the north.

Hearth 444 (AAC) E27.7, N16.8

A shallow ovoid recess within the south-west post-setting of building R7. It incorporated a fire-reddened and blackened hearth stone heat-shattered into three pieces.

Width 0.45 m, length 0.60 m, depth 0.12 m.

Fill Grey/brown silty clay with mortar flecks and much charcoal.

Dating evidence Gritty buff jar. Horningsea. Date: late 2nd–early 3rd century AD.

WELL AND PITS

Well 1836 (DOZ) 33.75, N26.75 Phase III

A sub-rectangular pit; part of an otherwise unexcavated pit cluster at the north-east corner of block 4.

Width 1.5 m, length 1.8 m, depth 1.3 m.

Fill
1740 (DKZ) Grey-brown silts with gravel and stone.
1836 (DOZ) Dark grey-green silts with gravel and stone and flecks of tile and charcoal
1851 (DPP) Grey/orange silts with gravel, burnt patches and large limestone lumps.
1856 (DPV) Dark grey-brown silts with stones and tile and charcoal flecks.
1971 (DVP) Unrecorded.

Dating evidence NVCC types 2.6, 8, 12; NVGW type 27; Horningsea type 107/8; buff ware types 69/70, 74. Date: late 2nd/3rd century AD.

Small finds
1740 Samian stamp, Dickinson cat. no. 26a (SF 677).
1836 Bone hairpin, Greep cat. no. 17 (SF 881); mortarium stamp, Hartley cat. no. 10 (SF 675).
1851 Copper-alloy ligula, Jackson cat. no. 53 (SF 848).
1971 Quern fragment (SF 930).

The sequence is:
1740   Upper fill.
1836/1851/1856 Middle fill.
1971   Lower fill.

Pit 744 (BBP) E21.8, N27.8 Phase III/IV

A sub-rectangular shallow pit, aligned north–south, along the west side of block 4.

Width 0.9–1.2 m, length 1.9 m, depth 0.52 m.

Fill Grey/brown sandy silt (sandier towards base) with patches of yellow clay, heavy iron-pan staining, a few stones and flecks of mortar.

Dating evidence NVCC type 20; NVGW type 37. Date: 3rd century AD.

Pit 925 (BKC) E20.5, N28.8 Phase III, later

A small oval pit, aligned north–south at the north-west corner of block 4; cuts unit 754 of gully 35.

Width 0.45 m, length 0.9 m, depth 0.2 m.

Fill Dark grey/brown silty clay with patches of orange/yellow sandy clay and flecks of tile and chalk.

Dating evidence NVGW type 28.2; NVCC. Date: late 2nd/3rd century AD.

Pit 818 (BER) E20.75, N24.4 to E20.5, N21.4 Phase III, later

Two adjacent shallow rectangular units of a linear pit complex, aligned north–south, along the west side of block 4.

Width: i) 0.9 m; ii) 1.1 m. Length: i) 1.05 m; ii) 1.95 m. Depth 0.72 m.

Fill
818 (BER) Red/brown peaty silty clay with small pebbles and heavy iron-pan staining.
858 (BGH) Patchy orange clay with grey silts and tile and ragstone fragments.
916 (BIS) Orange sandy clay slump, with dark grey silts, pebbles and tile flecks.

Dating evidence NVCC type 3; NVSC type 65; Horningsea. Date: late 2nd/3rd century AD.

Pit 783 (BDF) E20.0, N24.5 to E19.85, N21.5 Phase III, later

Two adjacent rectangular units of a linear pit complex, aligned north–south, running parallel to pit complex 818/744 etc. along the west side of block 4.

Width 0.6 m (west side cut away by modern land drain); length 2.55 m, depth 0.54 m.

Fill Dark grey sandy clay with flecks of flint and iron-pan staining.

Dating evidence NVCC Hunt Cup, cornice rim cf. 142; NVGW dish and bead rim cf. 84. Date: late 2nd/3rd century AD.

Pit 900 (BIB) E22.4, N21.3 Phase III

A sub-rectangular double unit pit, aligned north–south, immediately to the west of building R7, block 4.

Width 0.65 m, length 1.25 m, depth 0.31 m.

Fill Light grey-brown silty clay with iron-pan staining.

Dating evidence NVCC type 3. Date: late 2nd/early 3rd century AD.

Pit 1786 (DMX) E30.25, N14.8 Phase III, later

An irregular double unit pit, immediately outside the south-east corner of building R7, block 4; cuts unit 1750 of gully 36 (cut 5); is cut by pit 1787 (block 5).

Width 1.1 m (half-sectioned only), length 1.75 m, depth 0.58 m.

Fill

1786 (DMX) Grey sandy silt with iron-pan staining, some gravel and small stones, and tile and charcoal flecks.

1809 (DNW) Yellow and grey silt.

Dating evidence NVCC cf. type 8, 2, 2.8. Date: late 2nd/3rd century AD.

Small finds 1786 NVCC barbotine figured sherd, Johns cat. no. 4 (SF 798).

Pit 1847 (DPL)   E35.15, N21.05

A small oval pit, on the east side of block 4, in the base of unit 1842 of gully 36 (cut 9); relationship not established.

Width 0.7 m, length 0.9 m.

Fill Dark grey silt, with gravel and redeposited natural.

Dating evidence No finds.

GULLY

Gully 36   Phase III

A narrow gully with steep sides and flat bottom. It defines the south and east sides of block 4. Like gully 35 (block 3), the butted north end of the east branch provides access to the block via the north-east corner. The west end of the south branch was cut away by the modern dyke. Pit cluster 1786, 1749 cuts the gully near the south-east corner, while clear surface indications demonstrate that the linear pit cluster cuts the west end of the south branch. A short extension beyond the butted north end of the east branch links gully 36 to the corner of gully 35.

Width 0.4–0.55 m. Length: south branch 17.0 m (originally *c.* 19.0 m); east branch 13.8 m. Depth 0.15–0.21 m.

Fill

Cut 1   811 (BEK) Grey/brown sandy silt with flecks of tile and charcoal and some stones.

Cut 2   702 (AZW) Grey/brown sandy clay with flecks of mortar, tile, charcoal and flint.

Cut 3   798 (BDW) Grey/brown sandy silt with flecks of tile and charcoal and some pebbles.

Cut 4   715 (BAK) Grey/brown silty clay with flecks of tile and charcoal, heavy iron-pan staining and some stones.

Cut 5   1750 (DLK) Light grey sandy silt with flecks of tile and charcoal, a little gravel, and iron-pan staining.

Cut 6   1788 (DMZ) Grey sandy silt with flecks of tile and charcoal, a little gravel, and iron-pan staining.

Cut 7   1843 (DPG) Dark grey silt with gravel and iron-pan staining.

Cut 8   1847 (DPL) Dark grey silt with gravel and redeposited natural. [Possibly a small pit.]

Cut 9   1842 (DPF) Grey silt with fine-gravel.

Cut 10 1868 (DQH) Grey-brown sandy silt.

Dating evidence
East branch: NVCC types 9, ?20/21; NVSC type 57; Horningsea. Date: 3rd century AD.
South branch: NVCC types 20/21, 25/26, 4; NVGW type 45.3. Date: 3rd century AD.

Small finds

702   Bone object, Greep cat. no. 71a.
1843 Samian stamp, Dickinson cat. no. 50 (SF 1181).
1842 Samian stamp, Dickinson cat. no. 5 (SF 836).

BLOCK 5   (Fig. 52, p. 114)

A rectangular plot, about 24 × 19 m, south of block 4, bounded on the west by ditch 9, on the south by ditch 8, and on the east by street 1 N/S.

Structures None.

Pits 701, 711, 741, 757, 760, 761, 797, 822, 826, 830, 841, 874, 885, 1503, 1508, 1511–14, 1516, 1519, 1525, 1567, 1585, 1586, 1588, 1592, 1595, 1600, 1604, 1611, 1612, 1749, 1776, 1784, 1787, 1795, 1815, 1818, 1844, 2045.

Gullies 38–40, 46.

PITS

Pit 1749 (DLI)   E32.9, N13.25   Phase III, later

A rectangular pit; part of a cluster in the north-east corner of block 5; cuts unit 1788 of gully 36 (cut 6).

Width 0.75 m, length 1.2 m, depth 0.48 m.

Fill

1749 (DLI)   Grey silt with some sand and gravel and iron-pan staining.

1794 (DNF)   Light grey silt with orange sand and a few small stones and iron-pan staining.

Dating evidence NVCC types 2.6, 25/26; grey beaker cf. type 39. Date: early/mid 3rd century AD.

Pit 1844 (DPH)   E30.5, N13.15   Phase III, later

An oval pit; part of a cluster in the north-east corner of block 5; respects unit 1750 of gully 36 (cut 5); cut by pit 1787.

Width *c.* 1.3 m, length at least 2.1 m.

Fill Light grey sandy silt with few stones and some iron-pan staining.

Dating evidence Fragments of NVCC and Horningsea. Date: early 3rd century AD or later.

Pit 1787 (DMY)   E29.7, N13.7   Phase III/IV

A rectangular pit; part of a cluster in the north-east corner of block 5; cuts pits 1844, 1786.

Width *c.* 1.0 m, length at least 1.3 m (half-sectioned only), depth 0.7 m.

Fill Dark grey-brown silt with a little gravel and some larger stones.

Dating evidence NVCC type 20/21; NVGW type 47; large grey ware beaker cf. type 39. Date: 3rd century AD.

Pit 757 (BCD)   E28.65, N13.3

A shallow sub-rectangular pit, only part-sectioned; part of a pit cluster in the north-east corner of block 5; respects unit 798 of gully 36.

Width at least 0.55 m (only part-sectioned), length 1.65 m, depth 0.12 m.

Fill Grey/brown silty sand with iron-pan staining and flecks of tile and charcoal.

Dating evidence Nothing datable.

Pit 701 (AZV)   E18.9, N15.0 to E18.5, N12.2   Phase III/IV

Parts of two abutting pits with uniform fill, one sub-rectangular, one ovoid; the southern two units in the linear pit complex which runs along the west side of blocks 3 and 4.

Width: i) *c*.1.0 m; ii) *c*.1.6 m. Length: i) at least 1.0 m; ii) *c*.2.2 m. Depth 0.75 m.

Fill Dark grey/brown silty clay with patches of yellow clay and iron-pan staining, particularly in lower fill, a few stones, fragments of flint and flecks of tile.

Dating evidence NVCC type 4; Horningsea. Date: 3rd century AD.

Small finds Samian stamp, Dickinson cat. no. 30 (SF 268).

Pit 2045 (DYR)   E30.1, N5.3

An isolated rectangular pit, aligned north–south, near the east side of block 5.

Width 1.1 m, length 1.85 m.

Fill Light grey-brown silts with some gravel and iron-pan staining.

Dating evidence No datable finds.

Pit 741 (BBM)   E24.45, N9.4   Phase IV

An extensive, shallow, sub-rectangular hollow, near the north side of block 5, which incorporates pits 760, 822 and 830. Its fill forms the top layer of those pits.

Width 5.0 m, length 5.3 m, depth *c*. 0.1–0.3 m.

Fill Light grey/brown silt with heavy iron-pan staining and a few small pebbles.

Dating evidence NVCC type 21. Date: 3rd/4th century AD.

Pit 760 (BCG)   E24.35, N8.8   Phase III, later

A sub-rectangular pit within the pit/hollow 741.

Width 1.8 m, length 2.05 m, depth 0.48 m.

Fill
741 (BBM) See pit 741 above.
760 (BCG) Grey/brown silty sand with flecks of chalk and iron-pan staining.

Dating evidence
741 3rd/4th century AD.

760 NVGW type 46; Horningsea. Date: 3rd century AD, possibly early.

Pit 822 (BEW)   E26.5, N10.15   Phase III

A sub-rectangular, double-unit pit within the pit/hollow 741.

Width 1.15–1.45 m, length 2.1 m.

Fill
741 (BBM) See pit 741 above.
822 (BEW) Light brown/grey silty clay with pebbles, flecks of tile and iron-pan staining.

Dating evidence
741 3rd/4th century AD.
822 NVGW type 45. Date: late 2nd/early 3rd century AD.

Pit 830 (BFE)   E26.1, N7.95   Phase III, later

A curved rectangular pit within the pit/hollow 741.

Width 1.3 m, length 2.4 m.

Fill
741 (BBM) See pit 741 above
830 (BFE) Light grey/brown silt with collapsed orange sandy clay edges, flecks of charcoal and iron-pan staining.

Dating evidence
741 3rd/4th century AD.
830 NVCC type 3.2; Horningsea. Date: late 2nd/3rd century AD.

Small finds 830 Glass bead, Price cat. no. 76 (SF 349).

Pit 874 (BGZ)   E19.1, N6.9   Probably Phase III/IV

A rectangular pit, part of the cluster west of centre in block 5; cuts pit 711.

Width 1.2 m, length 1.35 m, depth 0.42 m.

Fill Light brown peaty earth with small pebbles and iron-pan staining.

Dating evidence NVCC. Date: AD 125 or later.

Pit 711 (BAF)   E20.65, N6.0   Phase III/IV

A sub-rectangular pit, aligned east–west, part of the cluster west of centre in block 5; cut by pit 874; contaminated by modern field drain.

Width 1.0–1.3 m, length 3.0 m, depth 0.42 m.

Fill Light brown sandy silt with small pebbles, chips of flint, flecks of tile and iron-pan staining.

Dating evidence Horningsea. Date: 3rd century AD or later. A sherd of Anglo-Saxon pottery (Russell, Fabric 3, jar rim sherd, Fig. 240, no. 3, p. 655) is intrusive, either through Anglo-Saxon activity or the cutting of the modern field drain.

Pit 885 (BHL)   E22.65, N6.4   Phase III/IV

A sub-rectangular pit, aligned east–west, part of the cluster west of centre in block 5; similar and adjacent to pit 711.

Width 0.9–1.1 m, length 2.95 m, depth 0.5 m.

Fill

885 (BHL) Light grey/brown sandy earth with a few patches of orange/yellow gritty clay and flecks of tile and charcoal.

910 (BIM) patchy orange clay with grey/brown silts, small pebbles, flecks of chalk and iron-pan staining.

Dating evidence NVGW type 45.3. Date: 3rd century AD.

Small finds 885 Samian stamp, Dickinson cat. no. 76 (SF 355).

Pit 841 (BFQ)   E18.05, N4.75   Phase III/IV?

An ovoid pit, aligned east–west, part of the cluster west of centre in block 5; west end truncated by modern dyke.

Width 0.85 m, length at least 1.0 m.

Fill

742 (BBN) Brown peaty earth with patches of orange clay and iron-pan staining.

769 (BCQ) Light grey clay with heavy iron-pan staining.

841 (BFQ) Light grey/brown earth with pebbles, flecks of chalk and iron-pan staining.

Dating evidence

742, 769 3rd/4th century AD.

841 Nothing datable.

Small finds 769 Samian stamp, Dickinson cat. no. 18 (SF 429).

Pit 826 (BFA)   E18.25, N3.35   Phase III/IV

An apparently rectangular pit, only the central part of which was excavated, aligned east–west; part of the cluster west of centre in block 5; west end truncated by modern dyke.

Width 1.7 m, length at least 1.1 m, depth 0.8 m.

Fill

742 (BBN) See pit 841 above.

769 (BCQ) See pit 841 above.

797 (BDV) Dark grey clay with patches of orange clay, chalk and charcoal flecks, flint fragments and iron-pan staining.

826 (BFA) Orange/yellow gritty sand.

831 (BFF) Dark grey silt with patches of orange clay, small pebbles and iron-pan staining.

Dating evidence

742 3rd/4th century AD.

769, 797 3rd century AD.

826, 831 Nothing datable.

Small finds 769 Samian stamp, Dickinson cat. no. 18 (SF 429).

Pit 797 (BDV)   E18.3, N1.45   Phase III/IV

An apparently ovoid pit, aligned east–west, part of the cluster west of centre in block 5; west end truncated by modern dyke. Its lower fill (797) extended into pit 826.

Width 1.9 m, length at least 1.0 m, depth 0.55 m.

Fill Dark grey clay with patches of orange clay, chalk and charcoal flecks, flint fragments and iron-pan staining.

Dating evidence NVCC type 20; NVGW type 45; NVSC mortarium type 102; shell-gritted types 88/91 and 102. Date: 3rd century AD.

Pit 761 (BCH)/1545 (DBW)   E19.2, N0.0   Phase IV

An apparently rectangular pit, probably aligned east–west, part of the cluster west of centre in block 5; cut by pit 797. Only the west side of the pit fell within the 1982 excavation area; part of the central section was identified in 1984 (pit 1545) but was not excavated; the east side had been truncated by a modern field drain.

Width at least 1.1 m, length at least 1.4 m (max. 2.0 m), depth 0.55 m.

Fill

742 (BBN) See pit 841 above.

761 (BCH) Grey/brown sandy clay with patches of yellow clay and flecks of charcoal, tile and chalk.

Dating evidence

742 3rd/4th century AD.

761 NVCC type 20/21; NVGW type 28. Date: 3rd/4th century AD.

Pit 1508 (DAH)   E22.7, N2.3   Phase III(?)

A large, shallow rectangular pit, aligned east–west, part of the cluster west of centre in block 5. Cuts unit 915 of gully 39. Only a half-section of the east part, which lay within the 1984 excavation area, was excavated.

Width 2.0–2.4 m, length at least 3.2 m.

Fill Brown silts with much gravel.

Dating evidence Mid 2nd century AD onwards.

Pit 1512 (DAM)   E21.85, S0.05   Phase III, later

A large shallow trapezoidal pit/hollow, similar and adjacent to pit 1508; part of the cluster west of centre in block 5. Its fill also seals pit 1595.

Width 1.8–c. 2.4 m, length c. 2.1–2.6 m.

Fill Grey-brown silts with much gravel.

Dating evidence NVGW type 29. Date: early 3rd century AD or later.

Pit 1595 (DDY)   E23.8, N0.15   Phase III/IV

A sub-rectangular pit, part of the linear cluster in the south–east quadrant of block 5. Only part-sectioned.

Width at least 1.9 m, length at least 1.2 m.

Fill

1512 (DAM) See pit 1512 above.

1595 (DDY) Grey-brown silt with much gravel.

1599 (DEC) Yellow-brown clay with tile flecks.

Dating evidence

1512 Early 3rd century AD or later.

1595, 1599 NVGW, NVCC and Horningsea but difficult to date. ?3rd century AD.

Pit 1511 (DAL) E25.1, N0.9

An ovoid pit, or possibly two intercutting pits, part of the linear cluster in the south-east quadrant of block 5.

Width *c.* 0.8–1.0 m, length 2.4 m.

Fill Light grey-brown silt with much gravel.

Dating evidence NVGW. AD 125 onwards.

Pit 1503 (DAC) E26.9, N2.1 Phase III/IV(?)

A shallow sub-rectangular pit, on the periphery of the linear cluster in the south-east quadrant of block 5. Half-sectioned.

Width 1.7 m, length 3.0 m, depth 0.28 m.

Fill
1503 (DAC) Brown silt with much gravel and charcoal flecks.
1576 (DDD) Brown-grey silt with much gravel.

Dating evidence
1503 Sherd of NVGW which may be from a 3rd century AD vessel.
1576 Nothing datable.

Small finds 1503 Coin, Shotter cat. no. 27, sestertius, VW, AD 117–38 (SF 623); brooch fragment, Mackreth cat. no. 11 (SF 624).

Pit 1516 (DAQ) E26.1, S3.0 Phase III, later

An irregular oval pit, or several intercutting pits; part of the linear cluster in the south-east quadrant of block 5. The fill also seals pit 1604.

Width at least 2.0 m, length at least 1.6 m.

Fill Reddish-brown peat.

Dating evidence NVCC type 2.5; Horningsea. Date: early 3rd century AD onwards.

Pit 1604 (DEH) E26.0, S4.8 Phase III

A sub-rectangular pit; part of the linear cluster in the south-east quadrant of block 5. Part-sectioned only. Sealed by the fill of pit 1516.

Width 0.95 m, length at least 1.2 m.

Fill
1516 (DAQ) See pit 1516 above.
1604 (DEH) Grey brown silts with gravel.

Dating evidence
1516 Early 3rd century AD onwards.
1604 NVGW fragment. Date: AD 125 or later.

Pit 1592 (DDV) E29.9, S6.8 Phase III/IV

A sub-rectangular pit at the south end of the linear cluster in the south-east quadrant of block 5. Part-sectioned only.

Width 1.1–1.5 m, length at least 2.1 m, depth 0.67 m.

Fill
1521 (DAW)/1575 (DDC) Reddish-brown peaty earth.
1592 (DDV) Brown silt with a little gravel.

Dating evidence
1521/1575 NVCC type 25/26; NVGW type 39 (with applied scales). Date: 3rd century AD.
1592 Nothing datable.

Small finds 1592 Glass vessel fragment, Price cat. no. 63e (SF 715).

Pit 1611 (DEP) E28.15, S7.6 Phase III, later

A sub-rectangular pit, possibly two intercutting pits, at the south end of the linear cluster in the south-east quadrant of block 5.

Width 1.7–2.2 m, length 3.0 m, depth 0.6 m.

Fill
1521 (DAW)/1575 (DDC) See pit 1592 above.
1611 (DEP) Mixed grey silts with some gravel and a few stone fragments.

Dating evidence
1521/1575 3rd century AD (see pit 1592 above).
1611 NVCC type cf. 5 (overslip barbotine). Date: early/mid 3rd century AD.

Small finds 1611 Glass fragment, Price cat. no. 64w (SF 779).

Pit 1612 (DEQ)/1517 (DAR) E26.1, S7.3 Phase III/IV

A sub-rectangular pit with a projection at its south-east corner; part of the cluster along the south side of block 5. Part-sectioned only.

Width *c.* 1.8 m, length *c.* 3.0 m, depth 0.47 m.

Fill
1521 (DAW)/1575 (DDC) See pit 1592 above.
1612 (DEQ) Grey-green silts with some gravel.

Dating evidence
1521/1575 3rd century AD (see pit 1592 above).
1612 NVGW type 28; Horningsea. Date: 3rd century AD.

Pit 1600 (DED) E23.35, S7.9 (Fig. 41a, p. 99) Phase III, later

A shallow rhomboidal pit, aligned east–west; part of the cluster along the south side of block 5. Part-sectioned only. Cuts pit 1586. There was slight evidence for a timber lining along its south side.

Width 1.2 m, length *c.* 1.8 m, depth 0.3 m.

Fill
1518 (DAS) Dark grey silts with much gravel.
1600 (DED) Grey-brown silt.

Dating evidence NVCC type 2.5; ?Horningsea. Date: later 2nd/3rd century AD.

Pit 1586 (DDO) E23.35, S6.55 (Fig. 41a, p. 99) Phase III, later

A large shallow rectangular pit, aligned east–west; part of the cluster along the south side of block 5. Half-sectioned only. Cuts pit 1585/1515. Cut by pit 1600. It appears to have been of triple-unit form. A possible timber lining was detected on the south side.

Width 1.5 m, length at least 1.4 m (probably originally *c.* 3.5 m), depth 0.45 m.

Fill
1518 (DAS)   See pit 1600 above.
1586 (DDO)   Brown-grey silt with much gravel.

Dating evidence NVGW. Date: AD 125 or later.

Pit 1585 (DDN)/1515 (DAP)
E24.0, S5.1   (Fig. 41a)   Phase III, later

A large shallow rectangular pit, aligned east–west; part of the cluster along the south side of block 5. Part-sectioned only. Cut by pit 1586. A possible timber lining was detected on the south side.

Width *c.* 1.5–1.8 m, length *c.* 3.0 m, depth 0.4 m.

Fill
1518 (DAS)   See pit 1600 above.
1585 (DDN)   Brown-grey silts with lumps of redeposited clay natural, much gravel and stones.

Dating evidence ?Horningsea; NVGW; NVCC; shell-gritted. Date: ?late 2nd/3rd century AD.

Pit 1514 (DAO)   E22.8, S3.0   Phase III, later

A shallow sub-rectangular pit/hollow; part of the cluster along the south side of block 5. Part-sectioned only.

Width *c.* 2.1 m, length *c.* 2.3 m, depth 0.15 m.

Fill Grey-brown silt with much gravel.

Dating evidence
Castor box lid with parallel at Chesterton of late 2nd/early 3rd century; Horningsea. Date: early 3rd century AD or later.

Pit 1513 (DAN)   E21.1, S2.3   Phase III/IV

A rhomboid pit; part of the cluster along the south side of block 5. West end truncated by modern field drain; remainder part-sectioned only.

Width at least 1.3 m, length *c.* 1.3–1.5 m, depth 0.4 m.

Fill Grey-brown silts with clay tip-lines and much gravel.

Dating evidence NVCC types 3.2 and 25/26. Date: mid/late 3rd century AD.

Pit 1519 (DAT)   E21.0, S4.35

Large unexcavated pit, part of the cluster along the south side of block 5. Surface indications suggest a 'double unit' pit or two inter-cutting pits. The west side is truncated by a modern field drain.

Width at least 0.6–1.0 m, length 2.4 m.

Fill Grey-brown mixed silts with much gravel.

Pit 1815 (DOC)/1520 (DAV)   E20.4, S6.5   Phase III/IV

A sub-rectangular pit, aligned east–west, part of the cluster along the south side of block 5. It is bisected by a modern field drain.

The west part (1815) was excavated; the east part (1520) unexcavated. 1815 was cut by pit 1818.

Width (1815) 1.15 m; (1520) *c.* 1.5 m. Length *c.* 2.0 m.

Fill
1775 (DML)   Reddish peat with grey-brown silts and gravel.
1815 (DOC)   Grey-brown silt with much gravel.

Dating evidence
1775 (General layer sealing pits 1815, 1818, 1784, 1795 and ditch units 1747 and 1796): Horningsea type 107/8; NVCC type 3 or 4. Date: 3rd century AD.
1815   Nothing datable.

Pit 1818 (DOF)   E20.0, S7.75   Probably Phase III/IV

A sub-rectangular pit, aligned east–west, part of the cluster along the south side of block 5. Its east side is truncated by a modern field drain. Cuts pit 1815, and therefore Phase III/IV, or later.

Width 1.2 m, length at least 0.9 m (probably originally *c.* 1.9 m).

Fill
1775 (DML)   See pit 1815/1520 above.
1818 (DOF)   Grey-brown silts with some gravel.

Dating evidence
1775   3rd century AD (see pit 1815/1520 above).
1818   NVCC; NVGW. Date: AD 125 or later.

Pit 1784 (DMV)   E18.65, S7.1   Phase III

A sub-rectangular pit, apparently aligned approximately east–west, part of the cluster along the south side of block 5. Its west side is truncated by the modern dyke.

Width 1.0 m, length at least 1.0 m.

Fill
1775 (DML)   See pit 1815/1520 above.
1784 (DMV)   Grey-brown silts with stones, flecks of tile and iron-pan staining.

Dating evidence
1775   3rd century AD (see pit 1815/1520 above)
1784   Horningsea type 107/8; NVCC type 3 or 4; NVGW. Date: late 2nd/early 3rd century AD.

Pit 1795 (DNG)   E18.65, S8.2   Phase III/IV

A rectangular pit, apparently aligned east–west, part of the cluster along the south side of block 5. Its west side is truncated by the modern dyke.

Width 1.05 m, length at least 0.9 m.

Fill
1775 (DML)   See pit 1815/1520 above.
1795 (DNG)   Grey-brown silts with many small stones and iron-pan staining.

Dating evidence
1775   3rd century AD (see pit 1815/1520 above).
1795   Fragments of NVCC and NVGW. Date: AD 125 or later.

Pit 1776 (DMM)   E15.7, S7.1   Phase III/IV

A large sub-rectangular pit, aligned north–south, part of the cluster in the south-west corner of block 5. Only part-sectioned; the east side is cut by the modern dyke.

Width at least 1.8 m, length 2.9 m.

Fill
1751 (DLL)   Brown peaty silt with a few stones and gravel.
1776 (DMM)   Brown sandy silt with some gravel and chalk fragments.

Dating evidence
1751 (General layer sealing pit 1776 and ditch layers 1746, 1780, 1779, 1778): NVCC type 20/21; Horningsea; grey beaker cf. type 39. Date: 3rd century AD.
1776 NVCC; NVGW. Date: AD 125 or later.

Small finds
1751   Bone pin fragment (SF 670).
1776   Glass vessel, handle fragment, Price cat. no. 55 (SF 789).

Pit 1588 (DDQ)   E13.75, S5.0   Phase III/IV

A rhomboid pit, part of the cluster in the south-west corner of block 5. Cut by pit 1567; sealed by layer 1524.

Width *c.* 1.9 m, length 2.1 m, depth 0.83 m.

Fill
1524 (DAZ)   Dark grey/black silt with much gravel and fragments of chalk and tile.
1549 (DCA)   Dark grey/black silt with much charcoal, burnt clay fragments and gravel.
1588 (DDQ)   Yellow-grey silt and gravel.

Dating evidence
Top layers: NVCC types 5, 9, 20/21. Date: 3rd century AD.
Fill: NVCC cf. type 25/26. Castor box lid. Date: probably 3rd century AD.

Small finds
1524   Bone pin/stylus. (SF 732).
1549   Bone needle, Greep cat. no. 42 (SF 706); bone needle (SF 707).

Pit 1567 (DCT)   E14.1, S3.8   Phase III/IV

A rhomboid pit, part of the cluster in the south-west corner of block 5. Cuts pit 1588; and, like 1588, sealed by layer 1524.

Width 1.8 m, length 1.8 m, depth 0.64 m.

Fill
1524 (DAZ)   See pit 1588 above.
1549 (DCA)   See pit 1588 above.
1567 (DCT)   Dark grey/black silt, with large quantities of charcoal and burnt clay/daub fragments.
1587 (DDP)   Greyish silt with much gravel.

Dating evidence   Fill: NVCC types 5, 9, 2.5, 2.6, 20/21, cf. types 17 or 14 buff ware types 74, 69/70. Date: mid 3rd century AD or later. All layers contain 3rd century material.

Small finds
1524, 1549   See pit 1588 above.
1567   Iron handle staple, Jackson cat. no. 31 (SF 734).
1587   Iron T-clamp, Jackson cat. no. 67 (SF 712).

Pit 1525 (DBA)   E15.5, S1.9   Phase III/IV

A small sub-circular pit, part of the cluster in the south-west corner of block 5; part-sectioned only.

Width 1.3 m, length at least 0.6 m, depth 0.52 m.

Fill   Grey-brown silt with much gravel, tile fragments and mortar flecks.

Dating evidence   NVCC types 2.3 and 4; NVGW type 29. Date: mid 3rd century AD.

GULLIES

Gully 38   Phase II?

A narrow V-sectioned gully in the north-west quadrant of block 5. Only one section was excavated, and both ends are truncated: at the south-east by the pit cluster 741 etc.; at the north-west by a modern field drain, and ?by pit 701.

Width 0.58 m, length at least 3.8 m, depth 0.30–0.35 m.

Fill   919 (BIW) Soft pale grey silt with iron-pan staining.

Dating evidence   No finds.

Gully 39

A narrow curved gully north-west of centre, block 5. Cut by pit 711. The west end was truncated by the modern dyke. The south end was cut away by pit 1508.

Width 0.37–0.49 m, length at least 5.35 m, depth 0.12–0.21 m.

Fill   915 (BIR) Light grey silty clay with iron-pan staining, flecks of tile and small pebbles.

Dating evidence   Horningsea. Date: early 3rd century AD or later.

Gully 40   Phase IV

A narrow steep-sided east–west gully with a flat bottom, south of centre, west side block 5. Its west end meets ditch 6, but the relationship was not established. The east end was truncated by the modern dyke.

Width 0.45–0.6 m, length at least 3.6 m, depth 0.3 m.

Fill   700 (AZT) Hard, pale grey clay with iron-pan staining and flecks of tile, mortar and flint.

Dating evidence   NVCC type 20/21; Horningsea; ?Oxford ware. Date: late 3rd/early 4th century AD.

Gully 46   Phase III

A small narrow gully with steep sides, in the south-west quadrant of block 5. Cut by unit 1524 of pits 1567/1588.

Width 0.25 m, length at least 4.4 m, depth 0.15 m.

Fill

Cut 1   1754 (DLO) Grey silt with some gravel and large proportion of burnt clay and charcoal.

1755 (DLP) Brown-orange sandy silt with gravel and iron-pan staining.

Cut 2   1792 (DND) Grey sandy silt with a few small stones, flecks of tile and iron-pan staining. The north butt.

Dating evidence NVCC type 2.6. Horningsea. Date: 3rd century AD.

BLOCK 5a   (Fig. 52, p. 114)

A small triangular plot, in the south-east corner of block 1 (of which it was originally a part), bounded on the north-west by ditch 9, on the east by ditch 6, and on the south by ditch 7.

Structures None.

Pits 485, 562, 563, 604, 606–8, 610, 613, 623.

PITS

Pit 485 (ABV)   E10.1, S0.6   Phase III

A curved rectangular pit, perhaps an outlier from the cluster to its south-west. Relationship with unit 489 of ditch 6 uncertain, but seemingly cuts it. Both are sealed by unit 473.

Width 1.1 m, length at least 2.0 m, depth 0.78 m.

Fill Brown silty clay with gravel, charcoal flecks and iron-pan staining.

Dating evidence NVCC type 2.4; NVGW type 45; buff ware type 74. Date: late 2nd/early 3rd century AD.

Pit 623 (AHO)   E7.9, S5.4   Phase III/IV

A rhomboid pit, part of the cluster in block 5a; cuts pit 563; half-sectioned only.

Width 1.7 m, length *c.* 1.9 m.

Fill Brown/yellow mixed sandy soil with pebbles and ragstone fragments.

Dating evidence NVCC type 2; NVGW type 45; ?Horningsea. Date: late 2nd/early 3rd century AD.

Pit 563 (AFB)   E6.45, S5.9   Phase III/IV

A sub-rectangular pit, part of the cluster in block 5a; cut by pit 623.

Width 1.5 m, length 2.1 m.

Fill Medium brown silty soil.

Dating evidence NVCC types 20/21, 25/26; Horningsea. Date: 3rd century AD.

Small finds Silver coin, Icenian, Chadburn cat. no. 61 (SF 397).

Pit 562 (AFA)   E5.3, S4.0   Phase III/IV

Two intercutting pits with a uniform, indistinguishable fill; the larger pit ovoid, the smaller rectangular; part of the cluster in block 5a. Bases very irregular.

Width: i) 1.2 m; ii) 0.9 m. Length i) 1.9 m; ii) 1.3 m.

Fill Brown peaty soil with gravel and ragstone fragments.

Dating evidence NVCC type 20/21: Horningsea. Date: 3rd century AD or later.

Pit 613 (AHD)   E4.5, S5.85   Phase IV

A sub-rectangular pit within an amorphous hollow, part of the cluster in block 5a. Cuts pit 607.

Width 1.3 m, length 1.95 m, depth 0.35 m.

Fill Mixed grey silts with occasional pebbles and patches of orange sand.

Dating evidence NVCC type cf. 8 but 4th century AD type: Horningsea; NVGW Date: ?4th century.

Pit 607 (AGX)   E3.0, S5.35   Phase III, later

A rhomboid pit, part of the cluster in block 5a. Cut by pit 613.

Width 1.2 m, length at least 1.1 m, depth 0.3 m.

Fill Brown peaty soil with gravel.

Dating evidence NVCC type 2.3; NVGW type 27. Date: late 2nd/early 3rd century AD.

Pit 610 (AHA)   E3.75, S7.1   Phase III, later

A shallow pear-shaped pit with an irregular base, part of the cluster in block 5a.

Width 0.55–1.0 m, length 1.4 m.

Fill Mixed brown sands and silts with pebbles and occasional ragstone fragments.

Dating evidence NVCC; NVGW. Date: AD 125 or later.

Pit 608 (AGY)   E1.75, S5.05   Phase III, later

A sub-rectangular pit, part of the cluster in block 5a. Cut by ditch 9 (unit 472).

Width 1.2 m, length at least 1.3 m.

Fill Black clayey soil with occasional pebbles, ragstone fragments and charcoal flecks.

Dating evidence Nothing datable.

Pit 606 (AGW)   E2.35, S6.2   Phase III, later

A tiny oval pit within, and cut by, pit 604; part of the cluster in block 5a.

Width 0.3 m, length 0.45 m.

Fill Grey silt with occasional pebbles and charcoal flecks.

Dating evidence Nothing datable.

Pit 604 (AGT)   E1.3, S6.6   Phase III, later

A sub-rectangular pit, part of the cluster in block 5a; cuts pit 606.

Width 1.5 m, length 2.5 m, depth 0.52 m.

Fill Mixed brown-yellow silts, very gravelly.

Dating evidence NVCC type 2; grey ware dish cf. NVGW type 46/48. Date: late 2nd/3rd century AD.

BLOCK 6   (Fig. 53, p.115)

A quadrilateral plot about 36 × 22.5 m, south of blocks 5 and 5a, bounded on the west by ditch 7, on the north by ditches 7 and 8, on the east by ditch 8, and on the south by the excavation edge.

Structures Short alignments and scatters of post-holes; no coherent plan.

Post-holes 1983A, 5–8; 1589, 1590; 1759–62; 1763, 1764, 1580–2, 1769; 1773; 1770, 1771, 1768; 1556, 1557; 1528–30; 1522, 1523; 1506.

Hearth 1578.

Well G4.

(?)Latrines   1535, 1536, 1542, 1563.

Pits 1534, 1538–41, 1543, 1552, 1554, 1555, 1558–60, 1577, 1579, 1591, 1752, 1765, 1767, 1789.

Ditches and gullies 8, 15, 20–3, 68.

HEARTH

Hearth 1578 (DDF)   E11.0, S28.7   Phase III

A sub-rectangular shallow pit with gently-sloping sides/base, south of centre, block 6. Adjacent to pit 1579 and seemingly associated, though the precise relationship was unclear. Part-sectioned only.

Width 0.95 m, length 2.2 m, depth 0.2 m.

Fill Red burnt clay, chalk and gravel, with an area of yellower clay and more stones in the upper centre.

WELL, (?)LATRINES AND PITS

Well G4   E22.3, S17.1   Phase III

A near-circular well, in the north-east quadrant of block 6. Although it fell within the 1984 excavation area, the well was located and excavated in trench G in 1983.

Diameter of well pit 2.4–2.5 m, depth 2.15 m.

Fill G4
1 Black silty soil with charcoal and burnt clay flecks.
2 Gravel in ashy/mortar matrix.
3 Orange gravel.
4 Dark grey silt with pebbles and tile frags.
5 Hard, compact redeposited natural clay.

6 Clean grey silts.
7 Red silts with yellow/cream bands; very fine and smooth.
8 Grey clay.
9 Dark grey silts with many pebbles and gravel.

Dating evidence
1   NVCC types 25/26, 7.2. Date: late 3rd/4th century AD.
2, 3   Nothing datable.
4   NVCC types 12, 25/26; NVGW type 45; gritty buff types 69, 74; Horningsea. Date: early 3rd century AD.
5, 6, 7   Nothing datable.
8, 9   Gritty buff types 69, 74; Horningsea. Date: early 3rd century AD.

Small finds
1 Glass vessel fragment (SF 487); pottery counter, Jackson cat. no. 7 (SF551).
4 Bone hairpin, Greep cat. no. 16 (SF 496); bone hairpin, Greep cat. no. 24 (SF 493); bone needle, Greep cat. no. 38 (SF 499); samian stamps, Dickinson cat. nos 23 and 45 (SF 526 and 522); iron flesh-fork, Jackson cat. no. 27 (SF 497).
8 Wooden tankard stave, Jackson cat. no. 8 (SF 548); glass vessel fragments, Price cat. no. 58 (SF 539).

The sequence is:
1 Cutting and usage of well shaft, 2nd century AD.
2 Layers 9 and 8, primary silting, period of final use/earliest disuse of well, early 3rd century AD.
3 Layers 7 and 6, main silting, period of disuse of well, early to mid 3rd century AD.
4 Layers 5 and 4, infilling/sealing of disused well pit, mid 3rd century AD.
5 layers 3, 2, 1, successive filling/debris accumulation in subsidence hollow, later 3rd/early 4th century AD.

Pit 1555 (DCG)   E27.0, S24.2   Phase III

A small ovoid pit in the south-east quadrant of block 6.

Width c. 0.4 m, length 0.8 m.

Fill Dark grey/black silt with charcoal flecks.

Dating evidence NVSC type 57. Date: late 2nd century AD.

Pit 1554 (DCF)   E24.6, S21.6   Phase III

An ovoid pit in the east part of block 6; cut by ditch 15 (cut 11, unit 1568).

Width/length c. 1.1–1.2 m.

Fill Dark grey silt with gravel and charcoal flecks.

Dating evidence NVCC type 20/21?; NVGW type 27. Date: 2nd/3rd century AD.

Pit 1552 (DCD)   E19.8, S7.25

An almost circular pit in the south-east quadrant of block 6. Unexcavated.

Diameter c. 1.2 m.

Fill Light grey gravelly silt.

Pit 1558 (DCK)   E22.4, S29.4

A circular pit in the south-east quadrant of block 6. Unexcavated. Diameter 0.6 m.

Fill Dark grey fine silt with charcoal flecks.

Pit 1559 (DCL)   E20.3, S29.45

An ovoid pit in the south-east quadrant of block 6. Unexcavated. Width 0.65 m, length 0.75 m.

Fill Fine grey silt with occasional gravel.

Pit 1560 (DCM)   E21.8, S32.1

An ovoid (?)pit in the south-east quadrant of block 6. Unexcavated, and partially outside the area of excavation. Width 0.6 m, length at least 0.4 m.

Fill Dark grey silt with some gravel.

Pit 1542 (DBS)   E15.9, S17.55   Phase III/IV

A rectangular pit, ?latrine pit, aligned east–west, in the north-east quadrant of block 6.

Width 1.1 m, length 1.5 m, depth 0.72 m.

Fill
1542 (DBS) Dark grey silt with fine gravel.
1551 (DCC) Dark grey silt with gravel, shell and tile fragments.

Dating evidence NVCC types 4, 2.5; NVGW types 85, 45, 39 (with scroll decoration); Horningsea. Date: mid 3rd century AD.

Small finds
1542 Indeterminate copper-alloy plate fragment (SF 702).
1551 Coin, Shotter cat. no. 18, denarius, MW, AD 103–11 (SF 703).

Pit 1541 (DBR)   E12.4, S16.3   Phase III

An ovoid pit, aligned approximately north–south, north of centre, block 6; cuts gully 21 (units 1532, 1700).

Width 1.4 m, length 2.25 m, depth 0.7 m.

Fill
1541 (DBR)   Dark grey/black silt with some gravel and heavy charcoal flecking.
1584 (DDM)   Grey-brown sandy silt with few stones and flecks of tile and charcoal.
1598 (DEB)   Mixed orange/grey silts.

Dating evidence
Top layers: NVCC types 20/21, 8; NVGW type 45; Horningsea type 107/8/10; gritty buff type 74. Date: 3rd century AD.
Bottom layer: gritty buff type 69. Date: later 2nd century AD.

Small finds 1541 Stamped grey ware sherd, Rigby cat. no. 3 (SF 705); glass vessel, base fragment, Price cat. no. 67 (SF 746).

Pit 1591 (DDT)   E1.6, S11.7

A small ovoid pit, in the north-west quadrant of block 6. Unexcavated. South edge truncated by modern field drain.

Width 0.8 m, length c. 1.3 m.

Fill Dark grey silt.

Pit 1543 (DBT)   E3.4, S16.8   Phase III, later

A very shallow rectangular ?pit/slot in the north-west quadrant of block 6; half-sectioned.

Width 1.0 m, length 2.6 m, depth 0.17 m.

Fill Grey silt with some stones, gravel and tile flecks.

Dating evidence Horningsea. Date: early 3rd century AD onwards.

Pit 1767 (DMC)   E16.35, S23.9

An ?ovoid pit, in the south-east quadrant of block 6, its east side truncated by the modern dyke. Unexcavated.

Width at least 0.7 m, length c. 2.3 m.

Fill Grey-brown silt with some gravel, and tile flecks.

Pit 1765 (DMA)   E15.3, S25.3

An almost circular shallow pit, in the south-east quadrant of block 6. Possibly a hearth.

Diameter 0.8–0.9 m, depth 0.12 m.

Fill Grey-brown silt with some gravel and much burnt clay.

Dating evidence Nothing datable.

Pit 1752 (DLM)   E13.9, S22.25   Probably Phase III

A sub-rectangular pit, near the centre of block 6. Its relationship with pit 1789, adjacent to the north, and to ditch 15 (cut 12, unit 1605) was unclear; but it seems probable that pit 1789, which was cut by ditch 15 (unit 1605), was part of, or near contemporary with, pit 1752.

Width at least 1.2 m (east side unexcavated), length 2.1 m, depth 0.65 m.

Fill
1752 (DLM) Grey-brown silt with gravel and iron-pan staining.
1783 (DMT) Grey silt with some clay, orange sand, a few stones and heavier iron-pan staining than 1752.

Dating evidence NVCC; NVGW. Date: AD 125 or later.

Pit 1789 (DNA)   E14.85, S20.95   Probably Phase III

A small ovoid pit, possibly part of pit 1752, near the centre of block 6. Cut by ditch 15 (cut 12, unit 1605), and therefore probably Phase III.

Width 0.6 m, length at least 0.55 m (east part unexcavated), depth 0.65 m.

Fill Grey-brown silt with some gravel, and flecks of tile and charcoal.

Dating evidence Grey ware only; body sherds. Nothing datable.

Pit 1540 (DBQ)   E11.45, S23.0

A sub-triangular pit, near the centre of block 6. Unexcavated.

Width *c.* 1.0 m, length *c.* 1.5 m.

Fill Dark grey silt mixed with gravel, stone and burnt clay patches.

Pit 1579 (DDG)   E12.85, S29.2   Phase III

An ovoid 'double-unit' pit or hearth, south of centre block 6. Part-sectioned only. Adjacent to hearth 1578, and seemingly associated with it.

Width at least 0.8 m, length at least 1.6 m, depth 0.28–0.43 m.

Fill Dark grey silt with some gravel, large limestone fragments and much burnt clay and charcoal.

Dating evidence NVCC type 2. Date: mid 2nd/early 3rd century AD.

Pit 1539 (DBP)   E8.4, S21.0   Phase III, later

A rhomboid pit, in the south-west quadrant of block 6; cut by ditch 15 (cut 13, unit 1544). Half-sectioned only.

Width *c.* 0.9 m, length *c.* 1.1 m, depth 0.4 m.

Fill Dark grey silt with much gravel.

Dating evidence Horningsea. Date: early 3rd century AD onwards.

Pit 1534 (DBK)   E6.45, S21.1   Phase III

Two intercutting ovoid pits, with a uniform indistinguishable fill, in the south-west quadrant of block 6. They lie at the inside angle of ditch 15 (cut 13, unit 1544). The relationship with the ditch was unclear, but it is probable that the ditch cut the pits.

Width: i) *c.* 1.1 m; ii) *c.* 1.4 m; Length: i) *c.* 2.0 m; ii) *c.* 1.9 m.

Fill Grey-brown silt with some gravel and flecks of tile.

Dating evidence NVCC type 8: gritty buff ware type 67/70. Date: late 2nd century AD.

Latrine pit 1563 (DCP)   E9.3, S25.5   Phase III/IV

A precisely cut rectangular pit, in the south-west quadrant of block 6, with near-vertical sides, aligned east–west. It is adjacent to the ?fence slot/gully (gully 22) and is clearly related to (?)latrine pits 1535 and 1536. At the top of the fill was the partial skeleton of a human infant (Fig. 229, p. 584).

Width 1.05 m, length 1.15 m, depth 0.65 m.

Fill Dark grey silt with some pebbles and stones.

Dating evidence NVCC type 20/21; NVGW types 28, 49/50; Horningsea. Date: 3rd century AD.

Small finds Lead scrap, Jackson cat. no. 9 (SF 914).

Latrine pit 1535 (DBL)   E7.2, S22.95   Phase III/IV

A rectangular, near-vertical sided pit, aligned east–west, one of a group of three related rectangular pits, in the south-west quadrant of block 6.

Width 0.9 m, length 1.45 m, depth 0.87 m.

Fill

1535 (DBL)   Grey-brown silt with gravel, tile flecks and limestone fragments.

1924 (DSQ)   Light grey-green silt with wood staining and fragments of mineralised wood.

Dating evidence

1535   NVCC types 20/21, 2.5; grey ware cf. type 39. Date: 3rd century AD.

1924   Nothing datable.

Small finds 1535 Iron hipposandal fragment, Jackson cat. no. 4 (SF 711); copper-alloy ligula, Jackson cat. no. 48 (SF 713, 714).

In the lower part of the pit remains of a wooden lining were discerned. The fill of the few centimetres gap between the lining and the pit edge was given the number 1924. For faunal evidence of faecal material in 1535, see Stallibrass, p. 610.

Latrine pit 1536 (DBM)

E6.6, S24.7   (Fig. 38f, p. 96)   Phase III, later

A precisely cut, rectangular, near-vertical sided pit, aligned east–west, one of a group of three related rectangular pits in the south-west quadrant of block 6.

Width 0.9 m, length 1.1–1.4 m, depth 1.15 m.

Fill

1536 (DBM)   Grey-brown silt with gravel and flecks of tile.

1791 (DNC)   Green-grey gravelly silt with a few wood fragments.

1816 (DOD)   Light grey silt.

1606 (DEK)   Grey-brown silt with gravel and flecks of tile.

1744 (DLD)   Yellow clay with grey silty patches and stones.

1748 (DLH)   Dark grey sandy silt with dark brown woodstains and some small stones.

Dating evidence NVCC types 2.7, 2.5; shell-gritted cf. type 90; Horningsea. Date: early 3rd century AD.

Small finds

1536   Coin, Shotter cat. no. 1, denarius, MW, 32–31 BC (SF 828); copper-alloy bracelet fragment. Johns cat. no. 3 (SF 829).

1606   Coin, Shotter cat. no. 44, as, MW, AD 161–80 (SF 776).

The wooden lining was better-preserved in this pit than in pits 1535 or 1563. In situ decayed planking was located on the southern and eastern sides almost as high as the excavated surface; while decayed collapsed lining was found at various levels in the lower fill. Plant remains (including fig seeds) from 1536, 1816 and 1606 are probably of faecal origin – see van der Veen, pp. 612, 630–6.

Pit 1538 (DBO)   E5.45, S26.8   Phase III

A sub-rectangular pit, aligned approximately east–west, in the south-west quadrant of block 6. Part-sectioned only.

Width *c.* 1.0 m, length *c.* 1.3 m, depth 0.45 m.

Fill

1538 (DBO)   Grey-brown silt with gravel and flecks of tile and charcoal.

1774 (DMK)   Grey silty sand with some small gravel and iron-pan staining.

Dating evidence Little datable material; gritty buff type 74. Date: probably later 2nd century AD.

Pit 1577 (DDE)

E7.5, S28.8   (Fig. 39d, p. 97)   Phase III, later

An (?)ovoid pit in the south-west quadrant of block 6. Its south part lay outside the excavation area.

Width 1.5 m, length at least 1.1 m, depth 0.78 m.

Fill

1577 (DDE)	Grey silt with gravel and flecks of tile, chalk, and iron-pan staining.
1808 (DNV)	Yellow clay with gravel and burnt earth.
1817 (DOE)	Dark grey-brown silt with much charcoal.
1823 (DOL)	Orange/red burnt clay mixed with grey silt.
1824 (DOM)	Silver-grey ashy silt.

Dating evidence NVCC types 2.5, 2.7, 20/21, 2.3; NVGW types 27, 28; buff ware types 69, 74. Date: ?late 2nd or 3rd century AD.

Small finds
1577 Copper-alloy hairpin, Jackson cat. no. 3 (SF 796).
1817 Graffiti on samian vessel, Potter cat. no. 9 (SF 674); bone peg, Greep cat. no. 66 (SF 683).

The sequence is:
1 Period of ?industrial usage of pit, main fill, 1824, 1823, 1817. Late 2nd/early 3rd century AD.
2 Disuse of pit and 'capping' with clay seal, 1808. Early 3rd century AD.
3 Debris accumulation in hollow caused by subsidence of pit fill, 1577. 3rd century AD.

DITCHES AND GULLIES

Ditch 8   (Figs 25, 41a, pp. 77, 99)   Phase III

A south-east extension of ditch 6 (block 1) which forms part of the north and east sides of block 6. It is broad and flat-bottomed and is relatively late in the fence/ditch sequence. On the north side it partially cut away an earlier fence-line (units 1746, 1796, 1607, 1609), and on the east side it was recut eastwards. The north part also removed/replaced the west part of the north branch of ditch 15 (a short section survives at the west end – units 1593 and 1778 on the south edge of ditch 8 in cuts 1 and 2); and its east part cut the south branch of ditch 15. The relationship between ditches 6, 7 and 8 at their junction was not completely clear, but they are likely to have been contemporaneous or very nearly so. Ditch 8 also cuts the north end of ditch 20 and, probably, the north end of gully 21. There are few relationships with pits, but the recut east branch of ditch 8 cuts the west edge of pit 1602.

Width 1.2–1.4 m. Length: north branch 19 m; east branch 23 m. Depth 0.52–0.62 m.

Fill

Cut 1 1550 (DCB) Grey-brown silt with much gravel.
Cut 2 1780 (DMQ) Grey-brown silt with some gravel and stones and iron-pan staining.
Cut 3 1775 (DML) Reddish peat with grey-brown silt and gravel.
        1747 (DLG) Brown silt with gravel and iron-pan staining.

Cut 4 1566 (DCS) Reddish-brown peat.
        1594 (DDX) Grey-brown silt with much gravel and some stone.
Cut 5 1613 (DER) Brown gritty silt with gravel.
Cut 6 2135 (ECL) Grey-brown silt with some gravel.
Cut 7 1601 (DEE) Red-brown peat.
        1615 (DET) Grey-brown silt with sparse gravel.

Dating evidence NVCC types 3, ?20/21; NVGW ?type 50; NVSC types 57, ?68; buff ware type 74; Horningsea. Date: 3rd century AD.

Small finds
1594 Copper-alloy strap end, Jackson cat. no. 72 (SF 721).
1613 Glass vessel fragment, Price cat. no. 7 (SF 720).
1601 Iron hinge, Jackson cat. no. 52 (SF 722).

Ditch 15   [See also blocks 7 and 8]   Phase III

A comparatively shallow flat-bottomed ditch with gently sloping sides. With ditch 7 it enclosed a narrow L-shaped area in blocks 6 and 7 and encroached on to the south side of block 8. It postdates the system of fence-lines/gullies but antedates ditch 8. It cuts pits 1534, 1539, 1789, 1752, 1554, 1938 and 1939.

Width 1.1–1.55 m, depth 0.33–0.5 m.

Fill

Cut 1   1593 (DDW) Dark grey silt and clay with much gravel and tile and charcoal flecks.
Cut 2   1778 (DMO) Grey-brown silty sand with some gravel and stone.
Cuts 3–7 See block 8.
Cuts 8–9 See block 7.
Cut 10 1596 (DDZ) Grey-brown silt with much gravel.
Cut 11 1568 (DCV) Reddish-brown peaty silt. Cuts pit 1554.
Cut 12 1605 (DEI) Brown peaty silt with some gravel.
        1753 (DLN) Brown-grey sandy silt with gravel, stones and iron-pan staining. Cuts pits 1789, 1752.
Cut 13 1544 (DBV) Grey-brown silt with much gravel. Cuts pits 1539, 1534.
Cut 14 1562 (DCO) Grey-brown silt with much gravel.

Dating evidence (Ditch 15, all cuts)
NVCC types ?20/21, 9, 2.6; NVGW type 44; buff ware type 69; Horningsea. Date: early/mid 3rd century AD.

Small finds 1544 Copper-alloy tack/pin, Jackson cat. no. 85 (SF 704); copper-alloy pin/ligula fragment, Jackson cat. no. 30 (SF 709).

Ditch 20   Phase III

A small steep-sided trench with a flat bottom, running approximately north–south, in the north-east quadrant of block 6. Its north end is truncated by ditch 8 (cut 3, unit 1747). To the south it butts short of ditch 15.

Width 0.9–1.0 m, length 6.25 m, depth 0.4 m.

Fill

Cut 1 1572 (DCZ) Grey-brown silt with much gravel.
Cut 2 1574 (DDB) Grey-brown silt with much gravel and tile flecks. The south butt.

Dating evidence NVCC; NVGW; Horningsea. Date: early 3rd century AD.

Gully 21   Phase III

A small V-sectioned gully, aligned approximately north–south, north of centre block 6. It is cut by pit 1541, hearth 1531, ditch 15 (cut 12, unit 1605) and probably by ditch 8 (a modern field drain had destroyed the intersection).

Width 0.7 m, length at least 7.85 m, depth 0.45 m.

Fill
Cut 1 1532 (DBH) Dark grey-black silt with much gravel and flecks of charcoal and burnt clay.
Cut 2 1700 (DIH) Grey sandy silt with gravel and iron-pan staining.

Dating evidence NVCC types 19, 2.5, ?20/21, 2.3; NVGW type 45; NVSC type 57; buff ware type 74; flagon cf. Gillam no. 9. Date: early 3rd century AD.

Small finds
1532 Glass vessel fragments, Price cat. nos 59d and 59e (SF 628 and 630).
1700 Iron hobnailed shoe, Jackson cat. no. 36 (SF 775).

Gully 22   Phase III

A small, shallow, flat-bottomed gully, of rather variable cross-section, which runs approximately east–west within the south part of block 6. Its character is similar to that of gullies 35, 36 etc., and, like them, it is discontinuous, with an entrance 'causeway'. Gully 23 is presumably integral, but the junction was not excavated. The pits in this region respect the line of gullies 22, 23, but gully 22 is cut by ditch 15, and its east component has its west end truncated by a modern field drain.

Width 0.3–0.6 m, length at least 24 m, depth 0.07–0.2 m.

Fill
Cut 1 1782 (DMS) Grey-brown sandy silt with a little gravel.
Cut 2 1537 (DBN) Grey-brown silt with a little gravel.
Cut 3 1564 (DCQ) Dark grey silt.
Cut 4 1785 (DMW) Grey-brown sandy silt with a little gravel. Unexcavated.
Cut 5 1571 (DCY) Dark grey silt with a little gravel and tile flecks.

Dating evidence East: NVCC, NVGW, ?Horningsea. Date: early 3rd century AD or later.

Gully 23   Phase III

As gully 22, a small, shallow flat-bottomed gully, running approximately north–south from gully 22 to the south edge of the excavation. Pit 1577 is adjacent but neither impinges on the other.

Width 0.35–0.42 m, length at least 1.9 m.

Fill
Cut 1 1756 (DLQ) Grey-green clayey silt with iron-pan staining and a little gravel.

Cut 2 1757 (DLR) Grey-green clayey silt with iron-pan staining, a little gravel, and charcoal flecks.
Cut 3 1758 (DLS) Grey sandy silt with iron-pan staining and charcoal flecks.

Dating evidence NVCC type 2.5; buff ware type 69; Horningsea. Date: late 2nd/early 3rd century AD.

Ditch 68   Phase III

An approximately north–south aligned ditch, most of which has been cut away by the modern dyke or lies outside the area of excavation. It is probable that its north end linked in to the south branch of ditch 15, but the junction is obliterated by the modern dyke.

Width c. 1.7 m, length unknown.

Fill
1766 (DMB) Dark grey-brown sandy silt with a little gravel and flecks of tile and charcoal.
1745 (DLE) Grey-brown silt with orange sand, flecks of tile, and iron-pan staining.

Dating evidence
1766 NVCC types 2.7, 20/21. Date: 3rd century AD.
1745 NVCC type 2; grey ware jar cf. type 28. Date: late 2nd/early 3rd century AD.

Small finds
1766 Glass vessel fragment (SF 792).
1745 Bone hairpin, Greep cat. no. 8 (SF 794).

BLOCK 7   (Fig. 54, p. 116)

A quadrilateral plot, about 37 × 23 m, east of block 6, bounded on the west by ditch 8, on the north by gully 18, on the east by street 2 N/S, and on the south by the excavation edge.

Structures None found. Isolated post-holes: 1941, 1942, 2140.

Wells 1602, 1885, 1914.

Pits 1803, 1915–17, 1923, 1925, 1937–9, 1943, 1951, 2080, 2106, 2121, 2124, 2130, 2139.

Ditches and gullies 15, 16, 19.

WELLS AND PITS

(?)Well 1602 (DEF)
E33.1, S28.95   (Fig. 38e, p. 96)   Phase III, later

An oval, vertical-sided pit, aligned approximately east–west, at the west side of block 7. Final fill clipped by unit 1601 of ditch 8 (cut 7); possibly a well, though no sign of a shaft or lining was found. 1602, 1742, 1743 cut by modern field drain.

Width 2.4 m, length 3.0 m, depth 1.42 m.

Fill

1602 (DEF)	Grey-brown silt with tile fragments and much gravel.
1742 (DLB)	Grey/orange sandy silt with tile flecks and a few small stones.
1743 (DLC)	Dark grey silt with abundant burnt clay/tile fragments and occasional stones and chalk.
1806 (DNS)	Light grey silt with gravel and flecks of charcoal and burnt clay.
1819 (DOG)	Dark grey silt with abundant burnt clay fragments and occasional stones.
1820 (DOH)	Light grey/orange sandy silt with distinctive 'banded' appearance.
1821 (DOI)	As 1820.

Dating evidence

Upper layers: NVCC type 2.7, earlier type of Castor box lid, beaker cf. type 172; buff ware type 74. Date: later 2nd/3rd century AD. Lower layer: ?Horningsea jar. Date: ?3rd century AD.

Small finds 1743 Glass fragment, Price cat. nos. 64r (SF 799).

Pit 1803 (DNP)   E34.9, S23.5   Phase III/IV

A small rectangular pit, aligned north–south, near the west side of block 7.

Width *c*. 1.0 m, length 1.2 m, depth 0.55 m.

Fill Dark grey silt, with some gravel and flecks of burnt clay.

Dating evidence Mid–late 3rd century AD.

Small finds Glass vessel fragments, Price cat. nos. 49, 62d and 64aq (SF 813, 814).

Well 1885 (DRA)   E38.75, S17.55   Phase III

A square, vertical-sided pit near the north-west corner of block 7. Unit 1950, localised around the sides, may be a decayed wooden lining. Worked and unworked wood and bark fragments, found in unit 1954 near the waterlogged base, may also have been part of the lining. The relationship with unit 1822 of gully 19 (cut 5) was unclear, though it was thought that 1885 cut 1822.

Width 1.4 m, length 1.4 m, depth 1.7 m.

Fill

1885 (DRA)	Black ashy fill with much charcoal.
1926 (DSS)	Brown-grey sandy silt with some gravel.
1949 (DTR)	Brown sand and gravel.
1950 (DTS)	Fine pale grey silt.
1954 (DTX)	Waterlogged black silt.
2001 (DWW)	Waterlogged peaty silt.

Dating evidence

Upper layer: NVCC type 33; NVGW types 34, 49/50; Horningsea type 107/8; large grey ware beaker cf. type 39. Date: 3rd century AD. Fill: NVCC types 2.6, 3; NVGW types 59, 29; buff ware types 59, 55; Horningsea. Date: 3rd century AD. Bottom layer: NVGW type 27. Date: later 2nd century AD.

Small finds

1885 Glass vessel fragment, Price cat. no. 59n (SF 896); iron ox-goad, knife, and ?chisel, Jackson cat. nos 6, 23 and 12 (SF 883, 892, 906).

1926 Iron objects, Jackson cat. nos 22 and 71 (SF 928, 927); bone pin fragment (SF 924).

Pit 2080 (EAD)   E43.8, S13.0   Phase III, later

A small ovoid pit, apparently cut by unit 1913 of gully 18 (cut 11). The pit is adjacent to ?well 1914, and although the relationship is unclear, it is possible that pit 2080 is the remains of an access point to the well, similar to that of well 446.

Width *c*. 0.8 m, length 1.05 m.

Fill Dark grey sandy silt with some charcoal.

Dating evidence NVCC type 2.6. Date: late 2nd/3rd century AD.

?Well 1914 (DSF)   E45.4, S14.7   (Fig. 38b, p. 96)   Phase III

A large ovoid pit with vertical sides near the north side of block 7; cut by unit 1913 of gully 18 (cut 11). Like well 944 (block 3) and well 1667 (block 9) there is a projection which links the pit to the adjacent small pit 2080. These features may represent the remains of an access point.

Width *c*. 2.7 m, length 3.2 m, depth 1.5 m.

Fill

1902 (DRS)	Grey silt with gravel.
1914 (DSF)	Grey-brown silt with some gravel and localised heavy iron-pan staining.
1945 (DTN)	Mixed grey and orange silts, with a little gravel and sand and some tile and charcoal flecking.
1934 (DTB)	Dark grey silt with some gravel and pieces of charcoal and tile.
2019 (DXP)	Grey silt mixed with orange-brown sand, with a little gravel and some sandy concretions. Lower level waterlogged.
2024 (DXV)	Light grey fine sandy silt with orange sand. Waterlogged.
2068 (DZQ)	Orange-brown sandy silt. Waterlogged.

Dating evidence

Trowelling above pit (unit 1902): NVCC types 20, 3.2; NVGW cf. type 61; Horningsea. Date: 3rd century AD.
Fill: NVCC types 2.5, 2.6, 25/26, 33, 20/21, 8, 2; NVGW types 27, 45.3, 45, 47, 49/50; buff ware types 55, 74, 53; Horningsea. Date: 3rd century AD.
Bottom layer: buff ware type 74. Date: late 2nd century AD.

Small finds

1902 Glass vessel fragment, Price cat. no. 64n (SF 915).

1914 Copper-alloy rings (SF 939); copper-alloy pin fragment (SF 946); copper-alloy scoop probe, Jackson cat. no. 45 (SF 947).

1945 Copper-alloy ligula, Jackson cat. no. 50 (SF 1029).

1934 Glass fragment (SF 1009); iron hobnailed shoe, Jackson cat. no. 35 (SF 681).

Pit 1915 (DSG)   E47.35, S17.3   Phase III, later

A rhomboid pit, part of the group 1915/1916/1917, near the north side of block 7. Relationship with pit 1916 not established.

Width 1.5 m, length *c*. 2.4 m, depth 0.74 m.

Fill

1915 (DSG)	Grey-brown silt with gravel and heavy iron-pan staining in parts.

1946 (DTO) Light grey sandy silt mixed with orange sand, a few stones and a little charcoal.
1955 (DTY) Grey sandy silt.
1948 (DTQ) Dark grey silt, with charcoal, burnt clay, occasional lumps of flint and limestone and a few small stones.
1958 (DVB) Mixed light grey and orange sandy silts with a little gravel.

Dating evidence NVCC types 2.5, 8; NVGW type 37; buff ware type 74; Horningsea type 107/8. Date: early 3rd century AD.

Small finds
1946 Glass fragment (SF 1003); enamelled plate brooch, Mackreth cat. no. 20 (SF 948).
1948 Graffito on NVCC sherd, Potter cat. no. 14 (SF 1164).

Pit 1916 (DSH)   E47.9, S15.5

A rhomboid pit, part of the group 1915/1916/1917, near the north side of block 7. Unexcavated. Cut by gully 18. Relationship with pit 1915 not established.

Width 1.4 m, length at least 1.1 m.

Fill Light grey-brown silt with gravel, tile fragments and heavy iron-pan staining.

Pit 1917 (DSI)   E47.8, S19.9

A D-shaped pit, part of the group 1915/1916/1917, near the north side of block 7. Unexcavated.

Width 1.3 m, length 1.6 m.

Fill Grey-brown silt with gravel, tile fragments and some iron-pan staining.

Pit 1925 (DSR)   E43.85, S25.25

A small sub-circular pit, west of centre block 7. Unexcavated.
Diameter c. 1.1 m.

Fill Grey-brown silt with some gravel.

Pit 1923 (DSP)   E48.6, S29.7

A sub-rectangular pit, south of centre block 7. Unexcavated.
Width 1.1 m, length 1.9 m.

Fill Light grey silt with some gravel and much iron-pan staining.

Small finds A hole was dug into this feature by an illicit metal detector user.

Pit 1938 (DTF)   E52.1, S23.3

An ovoid pit east of centre block 7, cut by ditch 15. Unexcavated.
Width 1.1 m, length at least 0.95 m.
Fill Grey-brown silt with some gravel and iron-pan staining.

Pit 1939 (DTG)   E55.1, S23.3

A sub-circular pit, east of centre block 7, cut by ditch 15. Unexcavated.

Diameter c. 2.2 m.

Fill Light grey sandy silt with some gravel and iron-pan staining.

Pit 1937 (DTE)   E53.75, S21.2

A small sub-triangular pit, east of centre block 7; clips edge of ditch 15, and therefore belongs to Phase III or later.

Width 0.4 m, length 0.45 m.

Fill Grey-brown silt with gravel and much crushed tile/burnt clay fragments.

Dating evidence Nothing datable.

Small finds Glass, two fragments (SF 1098).

Pit 2106 (EBF)   E53.9, S18.75   Phase III, later

A narrow rectangular, vertical-sided pit, aligned north–south in the north-east quadrant of block 7. It is nearly identical to the nearby pit 1943.

Width 1.1 m, length 3.3 m, depth 0.58 m.

Fill
2106 (EBF) Brown sandy silt with some gravel and burnt clay fragments.
2107 (EBG) Mottled pinkish silt ('flood silt') with burnt material on surface.
2123 (EBY) Brown sandy silt with abundant burnt clay and daub.
2125 (ECA) Pinkish-grey fine silt ('flood silt').
2126 (ECB) Orange sand, gravel and brown silt with burnt material and blackish silt in the lower part. Localised layer/dump concentrated on the west side of the pit.
2127 (ECC) Mottled pinkish 'flood silt', cf. 2107 above. ?Rotted wood stains in top.
2131 (ECG) Light grey and orange mixed sandy silts, with occasional dark grey patches.
2134 (ECK) Dark grey silt with some burnt material, including burnt daub.

Dating evidence NVGW type 46; NVCC. Date: ?late 2nd/3rd century AD.

Small finds
2131 Glass vessel fragment, Price cat. no. 57 (SF 1111).

Pit 1943 (DTL)
E59.35, S19.9   (Fig. 39f, p. 97)   Phase III, later

A narrow, rectangular, steep-sided pit, aligned north–south, in the north-east quadrant of block 7. Its dimensions, fill and alignment are virtually identical to the nearby pit 2106. Its south edge is clipped by unit 1944 of gully 16 (cut 1).

Width 1.1 m, length 3.45 m, depth 0.56 m.

Fill
1943 (DTL) Grey-brown silt with much gravel, some burnt clay fragments and iron-pan staining.
2072 (DZV) Grey silt, containing ash and burnt clay.

2073 (DZW) Mottled orange-pink sandy silt ('flood silt').
2074 (DZX) Dark grey sandy silt.
2075 (DZY) Light grey sandy silt.
2078 (EAB) Mottled pink sandy silt ('flood silt'), cf. 2073 above.
2079 (EAC) Light grey sandy silt with occasional small stones.

Dating evidence No datable material except Horningsea in top layer, i.e. 3rd century AD.

Small finds
2074 Copper-alloy binding, Jackson cat. no. 73 (SF 1088).

Pit 2124 (EBZ)   E60.1, S22.25

A small sub-rectangular pit, in the north-east quadrant of block 7. Apparently cuts unit 1947 of gully 16 (cut 2). Incompletely excavated.

Width 0.65 m, length at least 0.65 m, depth at least 0.08 m.

Fill Brown sandy silt with a little gravel and some flecks of charcoal.

Dating evidence No datable material.

Pit 2121 (EBW)   E59.25, S22.75   Phase III/IV

A small round or oval pit, in the north-east quadrant of block 7, adjacent to pits 2124 and 1943.

Width 0.7 m, length at least 0.45 m, depth 0.55 m.
Fill
2121 (EBW) Brown sandy silt with some gravel and a few flecks of burnt clay.
2122 (EBX) Light grey sandy silt.

Dating evidence NVCC types 20/21, 25/26, 7; Horningsea. Date: 3rd century AD.

Pit 1951 (DTT)   E60.45, S26.5   Phase III

A sub-rectangular pit, aligned north–south, near the east side of block 7.

Width c. 1.7 m, length 2.4 m, depth 0.58 m.
Fill
1951 (DTT) Dark grey silt with much gravel and occasional fragments of burnt clay.
1959 (DVC) Light grey and orange sandy silts.
2008 (DXD) Grey-brown silt mixed with orange sand; with some charcoal.

Dating evidence NVCC type 2; NVGW type 45, jar with parallel at Chesterton of late 2nd century AD. Date: late 2nd century AD.

Pit 2130 (ECF)   E56.5, S31.0

A large oval pit, with a rectangular projection on its west side, in the south-east quadrant of block 7. Unexcavated. Possibly a well, or a pit cluster.

Width 2.9 m, length 4.0 m.

Fill Mixed gravelly silt.

Pit 2139 (ECP)   E66.7, S28.0

A rhomboid pit, on the east side of block 7. Unexcavated.

Width 1.2 m, length at least 1.4 m.

Fill Dark grey-brown silt with some gravel.

Dating evidence [Material from surface trowelling over pit] coarse pottery: nothing datable.

Small finds Coin, Shotter cat. no. 21, As, MW, AD 98–99 (SF 1114).

DITCHES AND GULLIES

Ditch 15   [See also blocks 6 and 8]   Phase III

A comparatively shallow flat-bottomed ditch with gently sloping sides. See ditch 15, block 6 (p. 181) for relationships etc.

Width 1.1–1.55 m, depth 0.33–0.5 m.
Fill
Cut 8 2098 (EAX) Grey-brown silt with some gravel.
Cut 9 2136 (ECM) As cut 8.

Dating evidence (Ditch 15, all cuts).
NVCC types ?20/21, 9, 2.6; NVGW type 44; buff ware type 69; Horningsea. Date: early/mid 3rd century AD.

Gully 16   Phase III

An approximately east–west aligned gully of irregular width and profile: it narrows markedly in its western part, the end of which is cut by the south-west corner of ditch 15. The end of the east part could not be traced, but it ran across the line of street 2 N/S, which, if ever it continued south of this point, may have gone out of use at this time. Gully 16 clipped the edge of pit 1943. Its relationship with the small pit 2124 was unclear.

Width 0.45–1.10 m, length at least 14.25 m, depth 0.3–0.4 m
Fill
Cut 1 1944 (DTM) Brown-grey silt with much gravel and iron-pan staining.
Cut 2 1947 (DTP) As cut 1.
Cut 3 2133 (ECI) Grey-brown silt with gravel.
Cut 4 2099 (EAY) As cut 3.

Dating evidence NVCC; NVGW. Date: AD 125 or later.

Gully 19   Phase III

A shallow gully, with flat bottom and gently sloping sides, in the west part of block 7. It is aligned approximately north–south and intersects with the south part of gully 18. Gully 19 projects north of this intersection, but its north terminal was not located. At the south a possible butt was identified. Gully 19 was cut by the north and south parts of ditch 15 and by pit 1885.

Width 0.6–1.1 m, length at least 19.5 m, depth 0.28 m.
Fill
Cut 1 1802 (DNO) Dark grey silt with gravel.
Cut 2 2031 (DYC) As cut 1.

Cut 3 1800 (DNM) Grey-black silt with tile flecks and shell.

Cut 4 2032 (DYD) As cut 1.

Cut 5 1822 (DOK) Black sandy silt with flecks of tile, charcoal, daub and shell.

Cut 6 2136 (ECM) Grey-brown silt with gravel.

Cut 7 1781 (DMR) Grey-brown silt with gravel and tile flecks.

Cut 8 CC 2, layer 1. Grey-brown silt with a little stone and charcoal flecks.

Dating evidence NVCC types 3.2, 25/26, 1, 20/21, 4, 8, 3.3; NVGW types 31, 39, 44; mortarium cf. Gillam no. 279. Date: mid 3rd century AD.

Small finds

2031 Glass vessel fragment, Price cat. no. 64z (SF 1078); iron ring, Jackson cat. no. 78 (SF 1080).

1800 Glass vessel fragment, Price cat. no. 6b (SF 839).

2032 Glass vessel fragment, Price cat. no. 59k (SF 1084); samian stamp, Dickinson cat. no. 62 (SF 1085).

1822 Coin, Shotter cat. no. 49, denarius, AD 198–212 (SF 840); NVCC barbotine-figured sherd, Johns cat. no. 1 (SF 854); iron object, Jackson cat. no. 74 (SF 870); samian stamp, Dickinson cat. no. 122 (SF 1180); bone hairpin, Greep cat. no. 9 (SF 673); pottery counter, Jackson cat. no. 8 (SF 1162); samian vessel, Johns cat. no. 38 (SF 672).

BLOCK 8   (Fig. 55, p. 117)

A quadrilateral plot, about 33 × 21 m, north of block 7, bounded on the west by street 1 N/S, on the north by street 2 E/W, on the east by street 2 N/S, and on the south by gully 18.

Structures Buildings R8 and R9.

Well 1853.

Pits 1698, 1814, 1825, 1918, 1928, 1931/2091, 1967, 1984, 2023, 2052, 2061, 2067, 2103, 2129, 2145.

Oven 9.

Ditches and gullies 15, 17, 18, 24 (south), 25, 26.

BUILDING R8   (Fig. 55)

The sparse remains of this structure were found in 1984 in the east sector of block 8. The reworked mixed silt and gravel subsoil did not readily disclose features, and in an attempt to trace and define the structural components a spit of about 10 cm was removed in two rectangular areas within the building area enclosed by the drip-gully – gully 17. Despite this reduction of the ground surface only a handful of shallow post-holes was located, and it seems probable that earth-fast posts did not comprise the main frame of the building. However, in combination with the position of the drip-gully the located post-holes seem to indicate a rectangular structure about 11 × 5 m, its wall-lines inset from the gully by about 0.3–0.8 m.

The gully has the appearance of a secondary feature, an impression reinforced by the fact that it cuts the east branch of the block 8 enclosure gully 18. However, while it was probably an afterthought or modification, its finds assemblage places it within Phase III and it is but one of several changes that were made during that phase of occupation. Another change can be discerned in the organisation of rubbish disposal and water provision. Initially a well was provided (well 1853) just to the west of the north-west corner of the building, and rubbish seems to have been carried off-site, possibly buried in pits to the south, in block 7, where street and buildings, if ever planned, were never constructed.

Certainly, the proximity of, especially, pits 1943, 2106 and 1951 and the early date of their fill tends to link them with building R8. Subsequently, however, well 1853 ceased to function as a water source and became the centre of an area of rubbish disposal immediately outside the building (pits 1814/2023/1825/1984/1967). Later still, perhaps, but still within Phase III, additional rubbish pits were dug at various points around the perimeter of the plot – pits 2052, 1931/ 2091, 2129 and 2103 at the south and pits 2061 and 2067 at the north. The siting of the well and pits points to an entrance to building R8 from either the north or east, and the narrowing of the north branch of gully 18 opposite the building also implies access to the block from street 2 E/W on the north.

The sequence of features apparently associated with the building indicates a comparatively prolonged usage within Phase III. At the end of that phase, however, if not before, the building either went out of use or was radically altered, for the Phase IV oven 9 was constructed across its southern end. Although there was a little fourth century AD material in the top of pits 1698 and 1967 (and Anglo-Saxon debris in pit 1933) there is no evidence for a building on the site of R8 in Phase IV or V.

Data

Post-holes

NORTH

Unnumbered Circular, 0.35 m diameter.

Unnumbered Circular, 0.20 m diameter.

1862 (DQB) Ovoid, 0.40 × 0.30 m and 0.07 m deep. Grey and yellow sandy silt.

Unnumbered Circular, 0.18 m diameter.

Unnumbered Circular, 0.25 m diameter.

SOUTH

2151 (EDC) Circular, 0.60 m diameter. Brown sandy silt with small stones. Incorporates a post-pipe, 0.30 m diameter, at the west.

2156 (EDH) Squarish 0.30 × 0.30 m. Brown gravelly silt.

2150 (EDB) Circular, 0.30 m diameter. Fill as 2156.

BUILDING R9   (Fig. 55, p. 117)

A very few traces of an earth-fast post-built structure were found in the west sector of block 8 in 1984. That they are the remnant of a once extensive Phase III building or building complex seems probable in view of the large size of the plot and the fact that it had been kept clear of non-structural features – the restriction of rubbish pits to just three examples placed near the edges of the plot is striking. However, the severe agricultural disturbance, at its most extreme in the western half of the plot (see Pl. XVa), had erased or rendered virtually irretrievable, the features in that area, and it proved impossible in the time available to define the outer limits, or even to prove the existence, of the building(s) which, at the maximum, could have occupied the entire plot, about 15 × 16 m. An irregular concentration of post-holes (1919, 1921, 1922, 2147–9) was identified in the south-east quadrant of the plot, while intensive surface investigation, under optimum weather and soil conditions, of an area in the north-west corner revealed an abundance of features, most of which appeared to be post-holes. Most readily interpreted was a fence-line set against the inner lip of gully 18 with rectangular posts at intervals of about 0.7–1.0 m. In addition, there were scatters of post-holes deeper into the plot which conceivably belonged to a timber building.

Assuming there was at least one Phase III building in the west sector of block 8, any rubbish emanating from it must have been disposed of outside the block, perhaps carted away as compost for fields or buried to the south or west in pits in blocks 6 or 5. For, apart from pit 1698, there are no pits within the plot. Water could have been drawn from well 1853 to the east and/or from wells 1914 and 1885 to the south. Pit 1698 yielded a pottery assemblage dated to the third or fourth century AD, but there is no other evidence for use of the plot after the end of Phase III.

In terms of the potential extent of the Phase III settlement, it is interesting to note the apparently blank nature of the west plot of block 8 were one to have only the evidence disclosed in 1983 in machine-cut trench G (cf. Figs 20 and 21, pp. 63–4): it is quite probable that similar 'blank' areas revealed most notably in trenches G, H and X (Fig. 21) also represent zones occupied by buildings and therefore free from ditches and conglomerations of pits.

Data

Post-holes

1919 (DSL) Post-pipe only, ovoid, 0.35 × 0.20 m. Grey-brown gravelly silt with iron-pan staining.

1921 (DSN) Post-pipe only, ovoid, 0.35 × 0.25 m. Fill as 1919. Unexcavated.

1922 (DSO) Post-pipe only, ovoid, 0.35 × 0.20 m. Fill as 1919.

2147 (ECY) Rectangular, 0.60 × 0.50 m. Grey gravelly silt with (?packing) stones.

2148 (ECZ) Rhomboid, 0.75 × 0.65 m. Grey gravelly silt. Unexcavated.

2149 (EDA) ?Post-pipe only, ovoid, 0.40 × 0.35 m. Fill as 2148. Unexcavated.

2142 (ECS) ?Post-pipe only, ovoid, 0.35 × 0.25 m. Grey silt with abundant charcoal in upper fill.

Unnumbered Sub-rectangular, c. 0.50 × 0.30 m.

WELL AND PITS

Pit 2067 (DZP)   E61.3, N3.75   Phase III, later

A sub-rectangular pit near the north-east corner of block 8. Cut by pit 2061 and unit 1857 of gully 18 (cut 20).

Width 1.05 m, length at least 1.2 m.

Fill Grey-brown silt with some gravel and burnt clay flecks.

Dating evidence ?NVCC type 20/21; NVGW. Date: ?3rd century AD.

Pit 2061 (DZI)   E60.9, N4.4   Phase III, later

An oval, steep-sided pit near the north-east corner of block 8. Cuts pit 2067. Cut by unit 1857 of gully 18 (cut 20).

Width 1.25 m, length 1.5 m, depth 0.82 m.

Fill
2061 (DZI) Grey-brown silt.
2062 (DZK) Mixed grey-brown silt and yellow clay.
2066 (DZO) Burnt clay, daub and tile fragments with a little brown silt.
2077 (EAA) Mixed grey-brown silt and orange sand.
2086 (EAK) Grey sandy silt.

Dating evidence NVGW type 48; NVCC; ?Horningsea. Date: ?early 3rd century AD. Coin (SF 1093, see below), found with a decayed wood fragment in the primary silt.

Small finds 2086 Coin, Shotter cat. no. 9, As, VW, AD 69–79 (SF 1093).

Pit 2103 (EBC)   E67.25, S14.5   Phase III/IV

A shallow, rectangular pit aligned north–south at the south-east corner of block 8. Cuts unit 2096 of gully 24 (cut 3).

Width 1.05 m, length 1.5 m.

Fill Brown-grey silt with some gravel.

Dating evidence NVCC type 20/21. Date: ?3rd century AD.

Pit 2129 (ECE)   E64.3, S15.85   Phase III, later

A shallow, ovoid pit, aligned east–west, at the south-east corner of block 8. Cuts unit 1956 of gully 18 (cut 15).

Width 1.1 m, length 1.65 m.

Fill Dark grey silt with some gravel.

Dating evidence NVCC types 8, 3. Date: late 2nd/3rd century AD.

Small finds Glass fragment. (SF 1110).

Pit 1931 (DSY)/2091 (EAP)   E57.95, S12.35   Phase III, later

A shallow rhomboid pit in the south-east quadrant of block 8. Cuts unit 1929 of gully 17 (cut 4).

Width 1.9 m, length 2.1 m, depth 0.32 m.

Fill Grey-brown silt with some gravel, and flecks of tile, and burnt clay.

Dating evidence NVCC types 2.5, 2, 8; NVGW type 45; Horningsea. Date: early 3rd century AD.

Small finds 1931 Iron knife, Jackson cat. no. 17 (SF 1062).

Pit 1928 (DSV)   E53.95, S10.5   Phase III, later

An amorphous pit or pit complex, south of centre, block 8. Unexcavated.

Width c. 1.3 m, length 2.6 m.

Fill Grey-brown silt with some gravel and crushed tile.

Pit 2052 (DYZ)   E51.65, S13.75   Phase III, later

An oval pit, centre of south side block 8. Cuts units 2026 and 2027 of gully 18 (cuts 12 and 26).

Width 0.85 m, length at least 1.10 m, depth 0.6 m.

Fill
2052 (DYZ) Grey-brown silt with some gravel and burnt clay flecks.
2053 (DZA) Light grey sandy silt with some orange-staining and a few small stones.

Dating evidence NVCC type 8; buff ware type 74. Date: late 2nd/3rd century AD.

Small finds 2052 Lead fragment, Jackson cat. no. 49 (SF 1165).

Pit 1918 (DSK)   E48.3, S11.2

A rhomboid pit, centre south block 8. Unexcavated.

Width 1.3 m, length 1.7 m.

Fill Dark grey silt with a little gravel and charcoal.

Pit 1698 (DIF)   E52.35, S1.05   (Fig. 40a, p. 98)   Phase III/IV

An ovoid pit, aligned north–south, north of centre block 8. Adjacent to unit 1699 of gully 18 (cut 23).

Width 1.5 m, length 2.8 m, depth 0.54 m.

Fill
1698 (DIF) Grey-brown silt with some gravel, sand and charcoal flecks.
1838 (DPB) Mixed yellow/grey/brown silts with some gravel.

Dating evidence NVCC type 20/21. Date: 3rd or 4th century AD.

Small finds 1698 Iron object, Jackson cat. no. 69 (SF 858); rivetted samian sherd (SF 875); copper-alloy pin/ligula fragment, Jackson cat. no. 20 (SF 878).

Well 1853 (DPR)   E56.5, S2.3   (Fig. 40a)   Phase III

A square, stone-lined well, north-east of centre, block 8. Cut and sealed by the pit complex 1814/2023/1825/1984/1967. *Not bottomed.*

Width: int. 0.45 m; ext. c. 1.05 m. Length: int. 0.5 m; ext. 1.1 m. Depth 1.2 m.

Fill
1853 (DPR) Grey-brown silt with a few stones.
1865 (DQE) Grey silt with much charcoal and other burnt material.
2081 (EAE) Grey clayey silt with charcoal flecks and lumps. *Shaft not bottomed.*

Dating evidence NVCC types 20/21, 25/26, 2.6, 2.5, 8; Horningsea type 107/8; NVSC type 51/52; buff ware type 74. Date: 3rd century AD.

Pit 1814 (DOB)   E55.8, S1.6   (Fig. 40a)   Phase III/IV

Not a separate pit, but parts of several intercutting pits, the north-west quadrant of the pit complex east of centre, block 8. Pit 2023 comprises the remaining parts of the 1814 units. The pit complex postdates well 1853.

Width: i) 2.0 m; ii) 2.50 m. Length i) at least 2.0 m; ii) 3.0 m. Depth 0.5 m.

Fill
1814 (DOB) Dark grey-brown silt and gravel. (Same as unit 1813 of pit 1825.)
1839 (DPC) Banded light-grey and yellow silts with iron-pan staining and some gravel. (Same as unit 1825 of pit 1825.)
1852 (DPQ) Dark grey silt with abundant charcoal lumps and flecks, other burnt material and some gravel. (Seals well 1853.)
1866 (DQF) Grey-brown silt with small gravel.

Dating evidence Horningsea; NVCC types 20/21, 25/26, 3, 3.2; NVGW type 27. Date: 3rd century AD.

Small finds
1814 Samian stamps, Dickinson cat. nos 40 and 94 (SF 666 and 812).
1852 Mortarium stamp, Hartley cat. no. 15 (SF 676).
1866 Graffito on London-type bowl, Potter cat. no. 17 (SF 678).

Pit 2023 (DXT)   E57.35, S1.4   Phase III/IV

Not a separate pit, but parts of several intercutting pits, the north-east quadrant of the pit complex east of centre, block 8. For the remaining parts see pit 1814, above. Postdates well 1853.

Dimensions as pit 1814.

Fill
2023 (DXT) Grey-brown silt with some gravel.
2082 (EAF) Light grey-brown silt with sparse gravel.

Dating evidence NVCC type 25/26; buff ware type 74; Horningsea. Date: early/mid 3rd century AD.

Small finds 2023 Glass vessel fragment, Price cat. no. 12e (SF 1068).

Pit 1825 (DON) E57.4, S4.2 Phase III/IV

Not a separate pit, but parts of several intercutting pits, the south-east quadrant of the pit complex east of centre, block 8. For the remaining parts see pits 1967 and 1984 below.

Dimensions as pit 1967.

Fill
1813 (DOA) Grey-brown silt with gravel (same as unit 1814 of pit 1814).
1825 (DON) Light grey sandy silt with occasional gravel and iron-pan staining (same as unit 1839 of pit 1814 and unit 2000 of pit 1984).

Dating evidence Horningsea type 107/8; NVCC types 20/21, 25/26, 2.6; NVGW type 27; buff ware type 74. Date: 3rd century AD.

Small finds 1825 Semi-complete samian Dr 37, Johns cat. no. 5 (SF 691).

Pit 1984 (DWD) E57.3, S6.0 Phase III/IV

Not a separate pit, but part of the south-east quadrant of the pit complex east of centre, block 8. For the remaining parts see pits 1825 and 1967.

Dimensions as pit 1967.

Fill
1983 (DWC) Dark grey silt with pebbles.
1984 (DWD) Dark grey silt with burnt clay and charcoal flecks.
2000 (DWV) Mixed grey and orange silt (same as unit 1825 of pit 1825 and unit 1839 of pit 1814).

Dating evidence NVCC type 2.5; NVGW type 45; Horningsea. Date: early 3rd century AD.

Small finds
1983 Samian stamp, Dickinson cat. no. 8 (SF 1002).
1984 Bone pin fragment (SF 944); Egyptian Blue fragment, Bimson cat. no. 9 (SF 945).

Pit 1967 (DVL) E55.5, S4.75 Phase III/IV

Not a separate pit, but parts of several intercutting pits, the south-west quadrant of the pit complex east of centre block 8. For the remaining parts see pits 1825 and 1984 above.

Width: i) c. 1.1 m; ii) 1.7 m. Length: i) c. 2.4 m; ii) 2.2 m. Depth: i) 0.6 m; ii) 0.8 m.

Fill Dark grey silt with gravel and some redeposited natural.

Dating evidence Late 3rd–early 4th century AD.

Small finds Coin, Shotter. cat. no. 28, dupondius, VW, AD 117–38 (SF 938).

Pit 2145 (ECW) E74.35, S15.55 Phase III

A small ovoid ?pit, east of street 2 N/S, beyond the south-east corner of block 8. Cut by unit 2138 of gully 25 (cut 1).

Width 0.75 m, length at least 1.0 m.

Fill Brown gravelly silt with flecks of charcoal and burnt clay.

Dating evidence NVCC; NVGW. Date: AD 125 or later.

OVEN

Oven 9 E60.8, S10.6 Phase IV

Type 1(?). Length c. 2.8 m, width c. 0.9 m.

East–west orientation, flue position uncertain.

Virtually destroyed. A surface scatter of burnt red clay debris, with no in situ structure.

1930 (DSX) A heavy concentration of burnt red clay mixed with yellow clay and gravel.

Finds Coarse pottery, mid 2nd century AD on. Antonine samian.

DITCHES AND GULLIES

Ditch 15 [See also blocks 6 and 7] Phase III

A comparatively shallow flat-bottomed ditch with gently sloping sides. See ditch 15, block 6 (p. 181) for relationships etc.

Width 1.1–1.55 m, depth 0.33–0.5 m.

Fill
Cut 3 G7, layer 1 Grey-brown silt.
    G6, layer 1 As G7, 1.
Cut 4 1798 (DNK) Brown peaty silt with some gravel.
Cut 5 1801 (DNN) As cut 4.
Cut 6 1920 (DSM) Grey-brown silt with some gravel and iron-pan staining (unexcavated).
Cut 7 2025 (DXW) Grey-brown silt with some gravel and iron-pan staining.

Dating evidence (Ditch 15, all cuts)
NVCC types ?20/21.9, 2.6; NVGW types 44; buff ware type 69; Horningsea. Date: early/mid 3rd century AD.

Small finds
G7, layer 1 Copper-alloy pin fragment, Jackson cat. no. 14 (SF 552).
1801 Bone pin (SF 815).
2025 Copper-alloy object (SF 1069); glass fragment (SF 1074).

Gully 17 Phase III

A shallow, round-bottomed gully which partially encloses a rectangular area in the south-east corner of block 8. It cuts gully 18 and is cut by pit 1931/2091. It joins ditch 15, but the relationship was not established. It appeared to form a butt at, or a little beyond, gully 24, but, again, the relationship could not be established.

Width 0.6–0.8 m, depth 0.1–0.15 m.

Fill
Cut 1 1859 (DPY) Brown silt with small stones and tile fragments.
Cut 2 2051 (DYY) Grey-brown silt with some gravel.
Cut 3 1812 (DNZ) Dark grey-brown silt with gravel.
Cut 4 1929 (DSW) Grey-brown silt with gravel, a few stones and tile fragments.

Dating evidence NVCC ?type 20/21; buff ware type 69; Horningsea type 107/8. Date: 3rd century AD.

Small finds 1859 Glass vessel fragment (SF 865).

Gully 18   Phase III

A gully system enclosing and subdividing block 8. The gullies vary somewhat in dimensions and profile. The south branch may have been recut, while the north–south aligned central branch which divides the block into two unequal parts, may have been an addition. Unit 1857 (cut 20) cuts pits 2061 and 2067; unit 1913 (cut 11) cuts well 1914 and pit 2080; units 2029 and 2030 (cuts 9–10) intersect with gully 19; units 1797 and 1799 (cuts 7–8), and 2027 (cut 26) are cut by ditch 15; unit 1810 (cut 18) is cut by gully 17; and units 2026/2027 (cuts 12 and 26), 2093 (cut 13) and 1956 (cut 15) are cut by pits 2052, 1933 and 2129 respectively.

Width 0.45–1.2 m, depth 0.06–0.55 m.

Fill
Cut 1   1697 (DIE) Grey-brown silt with gravel and small stones.
Cut 2   1832 (DOV) As cut 1.
Cut 3   1736 (DKV) Grey silt with gravel.
Cut 4   1741 (DLA) Light grey sandy silt with a few small stones and much iron-pan staining.
Cut 5   1841 (DPE) Dark grey silt with charcoal flecks.
Cut 6   G8, layer 1 Dark grey silt with pebbles.
Cut 7   1797 (DNI) Dark grey silt with gravel and tile fragments.
Cut 8   1799 (DNL) Dark grey/black silt with burnt earth and gravel.
Cut 9   2030 (DYB) Black silt with charcoal flecks and many tile fragments.
Cut 10   2029 (DYA) Dark grey-brown silt, blackish in places, with gravel.
Cut 11   1913 (DSE) Grey-brown sandy silt with some gravel and pieces of charcoal.
Cut 12   2026 (DXX) Grey silt with patches of heavy iron-pan staining.
Cut 13   2093 (EAR) Grey silt.
         2108 (EBH) Yellow-brown silt with some gravel.
Cut 14   1957 (DVA) Dark grey and brown silts with gravel and some iron-pan staining.
Cut 15   1956 (DTZ) Dark grey silt with brown silt and gravel.
Cut 16   1953 (DTW) As cut 15.
Cut 17   1952 (DTV) As cut 15.
Cut 18   1810 (DNX) Dark grey-brown silt with gravel.
Cut 19   1884 (DQZ) As cut 18.
Cut 20   1857 (DPW) Brown-black sandy silt with charcoal, a few small stones, and flecks of tile.
Cut 21   2059 (DZG) Grey-brown silt with some gravel and a little charcoal.
Cut 22   1896 (DRM) As cut 21.
Cut 23   1699 (DIG) Dark grey silt with gravel.
Cut 24   1840 (DPD) Dark grey silt with gravel and charcoal flecks.
Cut 25   1927 (DST) As cut 24.
Cut 26   2027 (DXY) Grey-brown silt with some stones.

Dating evidence NVCC types 4, 3, 40, 20/21, 25/26, 3.2, 9; NVGW types 45, 45.3, 39, 47, 29, 37; Horningsea type 107/8; buff ware type 74. Date: 3rd century AD.

Small finds
1841 Samian stamp, Dickinson cat. no. 15 (SF 1152).
G8, layer 1 Glass vessel fragment, Price cat. no. 64p (SF 498); pottery counter, Jackson cat. no. 3 (SF 523); bone point, Greep cat. no. 56 (SF 565).

1799 Bone pin (SF 852).
2029 Glass vessel fragment, Price cat. no. 65 (SF 1072); pottery counter, Jackson cat. no. 6 (SF 692); stone counter Jackson cat. no. 46a (SF 696).
2026 Iron hobnails, Jackson cat. no. 41 (SF 1087).
2093 Glass vessel fragment, Price cat. no. 48 (SF 1094).
2108 Mortarium stamp, Hartley cat. no. 9 (SF 1095).
1956 Glass vessel fragments, Price cat. nos 17 and 68 (SF 1057 and 1046).
1953 Coin, Shotter cat. no. 50, denarius (fragment), AD 193–218 (SF 1028); glass vessel fragment, Price cat. no. 35 (SF 1056).
1810 Bone pin (SF 822).
1857 Pottery gaming counter, Jackson cat. no. 2 (SF 857); glass vessel fragments, Price cat. nos 6c and 55k (SF 861, 863, 882, 888); lead object, Jackson cat. no. 23 (SF 1086).
1896 Glass vessel fragment, Price cat. no. 64o (SF 899); bone pin fragment (SF 932).
1699 Glass vessel fragment, Price cat. no. 55g (SF 816).
1927 Crucible fragment (SF 1163), see p. 359; NVCC barbotine-figured sherd, Johns cat. no. 8; pottery counter, Jackson cat. no. 9 (SF 699).

Gully 24: south branch

[See also block 9, p. 207]   Phase III

A narrow streetside gully, with steep sides and flat bottom. It is aligned approximately north–south at the interface of block 8 and street 2 N/S. Both north and south butts were identified. Pit 2103 cuts the south end.

Width 0.47–0.95 m, length 16.85 m, depth 0.25 m.

Fill
Cut 1   1837 (DPA) Dark grey silt with gravel.
Cut 2   1811 (DNY) Grey-brown silt with gravel.
Cut 3   2096 (EAV) Black silt with gravel and burnt clay.

Dating evidence [See also gully 24: north branch, block 9, p. 207] NVCC types 2.5, 25/26; NVGW type 46; buff ware types 69, 74; Horningsea type 107/8. Date: early 3rd century AD.

Small finds 1811 Coin, Shotter cat. no. 42, dupondius, AD 141 + (SF 823); samian stamp, Dickinson cat. no. 31 (SF 825); graffito on samian vessel, Potter cat. no. 11 (SF 826).

Gully 25

[See also gully 27, block 9, p. 209]   Phase III

A shallow, ill-defined, streetside gully, aligned approximately north–south on the east side of street 2 N/S opposite block 8. For the north branch, see gully 27, block 9 (p. 209). Cuts pit 2145. There is a possible butt or turn at the north end.

Width c. 0.85 m, length at least 8.5 m.

Fill
Cut 1   2138 (ECO) Dark grey-brown silt with gravel.
Cut 2   2144 (ECV) Mixed grey-brown silt with gravel.

Dating evidence (combined with gully 27)
NVCC types 3, 1.2, 2.3, 2.5; NVGW types 45, 46, 27; buff ware types 59, 74. Date: late 2nd/early 3rd century AD.
Small finds 2138 Samian stamp, Dickinson cat. no. 90 (SF 1115).

Gully 26 Phase III

A short section of a narrow gully aligned approximately east–west on the east side of street 2 N/S opposite block 8. The dimensions, position and alignment suggest it may have been part of the gully 17 system of block 8.

Width 0.4 m, length at least 1.6 m.

Fill 2137 (ECN) Grey-brown silt.

Dating evidence None.

BLOCK 9 (Figs 56–7, pp. 118–19)

A trapezoidal plot, about 34 × 30 m, north of block 8, bounded on the west by street 1 N/S, on the south by street 2 E/W, on the east by street 2 N/S and on the north by the excavation edge.

Structures Buildings R10–R14.

Wells 1625, 1667, 1669, 1678, 1834, 2020.

?Latrine 1638.

Pits 1633, 1635, 1695, 1725, 1835/2007, 1850, 1887, 1906, 1907, 1909/1968, 1960, 1962, 1972/1976, 1973–5, 1982, 1986, 1987, 1989, 1994, 1996 2003, 2014, 2020, 2021/2110, 2022, 2087, 2094.

Gullies 24 (north), 27–34, 70, 72, 73.

BUILDING R10
(Figs 57, 68, pp. 119, 156; Figs 70–1; Pl. XIV)

This earth-fast post-built structure, excavated in 1984, was the best preserved wooden building on the site. Situated at the north end of block 9, it was orientated on the block's east boundary, a few degrees anti-clockwise of the Cardinal Points. Although most of the north side lay just outside the excavation edge its line and form may be restored with near-certainty on the strength of evidence from the south end of trench N. Thus restored (Fig. 70), the building measures 4.5 × 4.0 m, with five posts on each of the longer sides (east and west) and four posts on the shorter sides. The spacing of post-holes was not completely regular, but their dimensions, fill and character were consistent. They had been cut into the mixed green-grey silt subsoil to a depth of between 0.33 and 0.60 m and packed with a mixture of the silt, orange clay and pebbles. Their original depth may have been a little greater as no remains of the internal floor were found. However, the sealing of the post-holes with a clay layer (unit 2005), which was deposited when the building went out of use and its site had been levelled, had protected them from subsequent destructive processes.

In the absence of any evidence for a mosaic, stone or mortar surface, it may be assumed that the building had a floor of wooden boards, other organic materials or beaten earth, and that it was only marginally higher than the preserved level. Some corroboration for a boarded floor is provided by the infant burials found adjacent to three of the posts (2173, 2177, 2178: Pl. XIVb; Fig. 71 and Fig. 229, p. 584; Conheeney cat. nos 1–3). The semi-flexed skeletons were revealed at the same level as the post-holes (Pl. XIVb), laid upon, and only slightly impressed into the green-grey silt 2033. Despite careful investigation no feature edges were defined, and it is possible that the bodies were not inserted in cut features but were placed directly upon the ground surface beneath a suspended board floor. That they were interred during the period of use of the building is implied by their position. For, although each of the three is in close association with a post-hole, they are all precisely set just within the wall-line (Fig. 71). This suggests burial from inside the building during occupation rather than some form of ritual foundation deposit at the construction stage. They may represent domestic tragedies of a single family over a relatively short span of time, for they share a number of common traits. All were neonates; all were semi-flexed, perhaps bound and/or wrapped in a shroud or cloth; and all seem to have been placed on their right side facing east. The absence of the skull in two cases is intriguing, but a post-depositional cause cannot be entirely ruled out.

A post-pipe was found in most of the post-holes and none contained more, which indicates a single structural phase. The width of the post-pipes varied from 0.10 to 0.18 m, but the majority were 0.15 m. Most had a darker fill than the surrounding packing material, but 2174, 2175 and 2181 had a fill of yellow clay similar to that of the sealing layer 2005. The implication of post withdrawal, perhaps for reuse of the timber, gains support from the inverted cone observed at the top of post-holes 2174 and 2181. Certainly the building was very stoutly constructed, and posts measuring 0.15 m across may well have been reusable.

Neither the spacing of posts nor external or internal features revealed the building's entrance, and the incomplete investigation of the area to the north renders it impossible to predict the position with certainty. It is equally impossible to determine the main approach to the building. However, given the proximity of buildings R11 and R12 to the east and south, a main access from the west, via street 1 N/S, seems most likely, though a northerly route cannot be ruled out.

Inside the building there was no evidence for divisions, and just three contemporary features were found, towards the south end. None provided conclusive evidence of function. Two had the appearance of post-holes, but on excavation proved to be extremely shallow and yielded no trace of a post pipe. The ashy fill of one (2183) and the interleaved fill of the other (2182) raises the possibility that they were hearth bases, originally presumably stone-lined. The third feature was not excavated.

The buildings in block 9 appear to have occupied discrete plots, the edges of which are now defined only by gullies but which may originally also have been fenced. The gullies

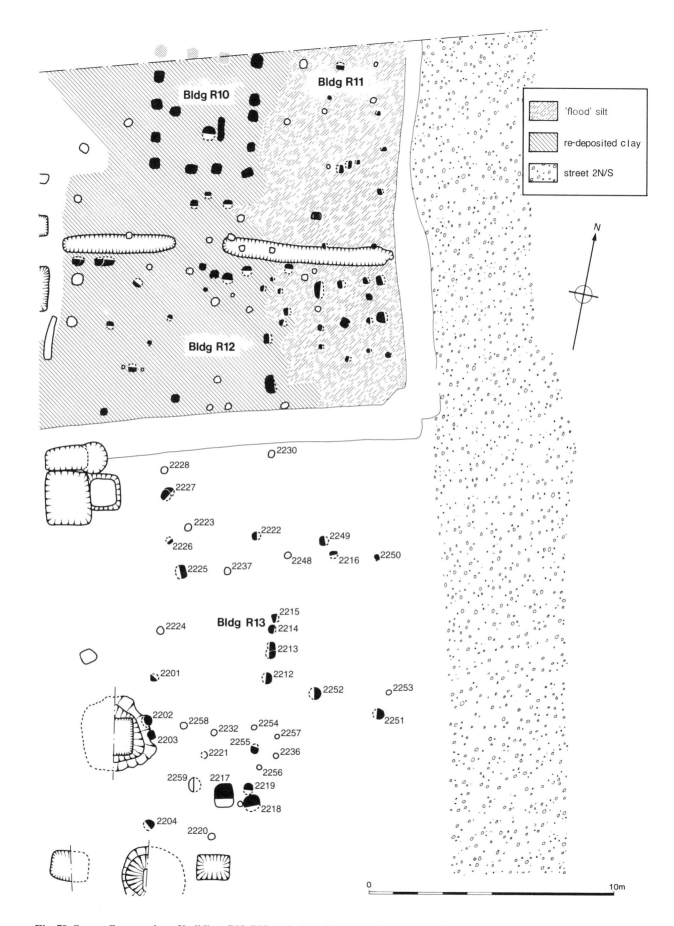

Bldg R10

Bldg R11

Bldg R12

N

2230

2228

2227

2223

2222

2249

2226

2248

2216

2250

2225

2237

2224

Bldg R13

2215

2214

2213

2201

2212

2252

2253

2251

2202

2258

2232

2254

2203

2255

2257

2221

2236

2259

2256

2217

2219

2218

2204

2220

0   10m

Fig. 70 Stonea Grange: plan of buildings R10–R13, and selected features, block 9, east side.

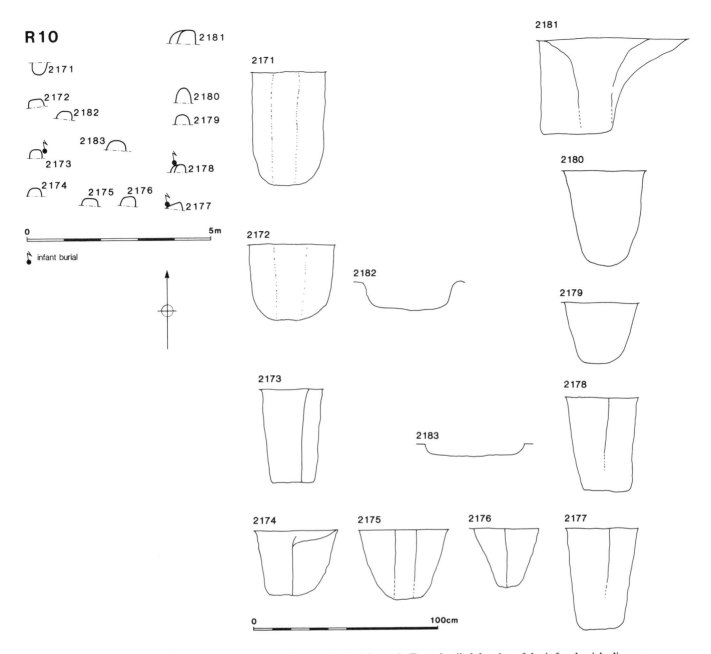

Fig. 71 Stonea Grange: plan and post-hole profiles of building R10, block 9, north. For a detailed drawing of the infant burial adjacent to post-hole 2173, see Fig. 229, p. 584.

undoubtedly served a dual role as plot dividers and as catchwaters. The fairly rapid silting of these comparatively slight gullies and the longevity of their use would have necessitated occasional clearing or recutting, either of the complete gully or of localised stretches, processes reflected in their irregular sides and profile. Gully 33, the northernmost of the three main east–west gullies, separates the plots containing buildings R10 and R12. Its importance as a boundary marker is underlined by the fact that it continued in use after building R10 had been abandoned. An association with building R10 could not be demonstrated unequivocally but seems probable in view of the fact that the north edge of the gully is more heavily eroded along the building's south

frontage than elsewhere on its route. Immediately beyond the south-east corner of the building it is interrupted by a causeway, about 1.5–2 m wide, which may have been an access point for building R11 or R10, or for both. Significantly, the eroded part of gully 33 in front of building R10 lies opposite a causeway across the drip gully (gully 32) on the north side of building R12. The causeway is off-centre, implying that its site was chosen specifically to provide a link between buildings R10 and R12.

While the south edge of the plot containing building R10 is marked by gully 33 and its west and east sides are delimited by the streetside gullies 30 and 24, the line of the north edge is uncertain. However, it is probable that well J4 lay within the plot and was the building's water source. The apparently open space to the west of building R10 and the thin scatter of rubbish pits (N2, J3, J1, 1635) tend to support other indications that building R10 was not occupied for a very long period and that it was certainly abandoned by the end of Phase III, if not before.

None of the post-holes nor the infant burials incorporated any datable finds. However, the modest finds assemblage from the clay sealing layer 2005, coarse pottery and samian, gave a date of early third century AD, while the occupation debris above 2005 (unit 1715) was dated to the mid third–fourth century AD. Thus, the sequence appears to have been: 1) Construction of building R10; occupation; insertion of infant burials. Phase III. 2) Desertion/dereliction/destruction/dismantling of building R10; levelling/sealing of site with redeposited clay layer. End Phase III/start Phase IV. 3) Occupation debris, but no structure. Phase IV.

Data

Post-holes

WEST SIDE

2171 (EDY) Sub-rectangular, 0.45 × 0.40 m, and 0.60 m deep. Grey-green silt mixed with orange clay, pebbles and crushed tile flecks. Traces of a central post-pipe, c. 0.15 m width/diameter.

2172 (EDZ) Sub-rectangular, 0.45 × 0.45 m, and 0.40 m deep. Fill as 2171. Traces of a central post-pipe, c. 0.15 m width/diameter.

2173 (EFA) Sub-rectangular, 0.40 × 0.35 m, and 0.50 m deep. Fill as 2171. Incorporates a post-pipe, c. 0.10 m width/diameter, against the west side.

Immediately adjacent to the north-east corner was an infant burial, north–south aligned, placed on its right side, semi-flexed, head to south, facing east (Fig. 229, p. 584; Conheeney cat. no. 1).

SOUTH SIDE

2174 (EEB) Sub-rectangular, 0.40 × 0.40 m, and 0.35 m deep. Fill as 2171. Incorporates a post-pipe, c. 0.15 m width/diameter, against the east side.

2175 (EEC) Sub-rectangular, 0.45 × 0.40 m, and 0.38 m deep. Fill as 2171. Incorporates a central post-pipe, c. 0.12 m width/diameter.

2176 (EED) Sub-rectangular, 0.40 × 0.40 m, and 0.33 m deep. Fill as 2171. Incorporates a post-pipe, c. 0.15 m width/diameter, against the west side.

2177 (EEE) Sub-rectangular, 0.45 × 0.40 m, and 0.55 m deep. Fill as 2171. Incorporates a post-pipe, c. 0.15 m width/diameter, against the west side.

Immediately adjacent to the north-west corner was an infant burial, north–south aligned, semi-flexed, head to south (Conheeney cat. no. 3). After lifting the bones the area was trowelled but no feature edges were found.

EAST SIDE

2178 (EEF) Sub-rectangular, 0.40 × 0.40 m, and 0.50 m deep. Fill as 2171. Incorporates a post-pipe, c. 0.15 m width/diameter, against the west side.

Immediately adjacent to the north-west corner was an infant burial, north–south aligned, placed on its right side, semi-flexed, head to south, facing east (Pl. XIVb; Conheeney cat. no. 2). After lifting the skeleton in a soil block the area was trowelled. No feature edges were revealed, but about 5 cm below the level of the skeleton the grey silts were found to lie upon a distinct, firm iron-panned surface, perhaps to be equated with the LBA/EIA turf-line. Finds were restricted to a few animal bones and an undiagnostic copper-alloy binding, Jackson cat. no. 93 (SF 1161).

2179 (EEG) Sub-rectangular, 0.40 × 0.40 m, and 0.33 m deep. Fill as 2171.

2180 (EEH) Sub-rectangular, 0.50 × 0.40 m, and 0.51 m deep. Fill as 2171.

NORTH SIDE

2181 (EEI) Sub-rectangular, 0.50 × 0.45 m, and 0.51 m deep. Fill as 2171. Incorporates a post-pipe, c. 0.18 m Width/diameter, against the west side; and a milling stone fragment, Jackson cat. no. 7 (SF 1133).

INTERIOR

2182 (EEK) Sub-rectangular, 0.45 × 0.30 m, and 0.16 m deep. Dark grey silt interleaved with yellow clay lenses. The shallowness of this feature and the character of its fill suggests it probably was not a post-hole.

2183 (EEL) Sub-rectangular, 0.50 × 0.50 m, and 0.07 m deep. Dark grey silt with ash. The extreme shallowness of this feature and the character of its fill suggest it probably was not a post-hole.

2184 (EEM) Sub-rectangular, 0.95 × 0.25 m. Unexcavated. Fill as 2171. Like 2182 and 2183 it is improbable that this feature was a post-hole.

Matrix

Coarse pottery date			Site phase
N/A	1597	Topsoil	N/A
mid 3rd–4th cent	1715	Occupation layer	IV+
early 3rd cent	2005	Redeposited clay	III/IV
Building R10	2033	Disturbed green-grey silt on old ground surface	III

BUILDING R11 (Figs 57, 68, 70, pp. 119, 156, 192)

This structure, excavated in 1984, comprised a scatter of post-holes in the north-east corner of block 9. They occupied a rectangular plot defined on the west and south by buildings R10 and R12 and on the east by street 2 N/S. Although the post-holes could not be resolved into a coherent plan there seems little doubt that they were the remains of a small building, and a right angle formed by post-holes 2186, 1675, 2240, 2241 and 2092 was probably its north-east corner. If so, its dimensions are likely to have been similar to those of the adjacent building R10, about 5 × 4 m, on which the right angle is aligned. Like building R10 its south side is flanked by gully 33, and the causeway across that gully, outside the south-west corner of building R11, probably provided access to the two buildings. However, the main entrance to building R11 was probably on its east side, where a causeway across gullies 24 and 29 provided direct access to and from street 2 N/S.

No certain associated wells or pits were found, as the only available area of any size for such features lay beyond the north edge of the main excavation. However, the unexcavated pit J8, revealed in trench J, just 6 m to the north, may have belonged to building R11.

The post-holes of building R11 were cut into the mixed green-grey silt natural. Post-hole 1675 alone yielded finds, coarse pottery of the late second to early third century AD. Above was a spread of dark green-grey silt with a broken surface of tile, chalk and limestone fragments (2162/2170), perhaps the disturbed floor foundation. The coarse pottery was of late second to third century AD date. This, in turn, was sealed by a layer of pale yellow/pink silt, 2118, a 'flood' deposit, either laid as the result of a single inundation or, progressively, as wash from street 2 N/S. The same deposit was also found in the east part of building R12 and at the south of block 9, to the south-west of building R13, where it sealed the partially-filled pit 2007. The coarse pottery assemblage from 2118 was of ?late third to early fourth century AD. As the deposit extended across the interior, the building was evidently out of use by that stage. However, the posts, or their bases, were still standing, as the silt surrounded but did not seal the post-holes. Subsequently a mixed grey silt layer (1711/1715), with pottery of mid third or fourth century date, was deposited, by which time some of the posts were entirely gone and their post-holes sealed, while others which were not sealed (1675, 1631, 1620, 1621, 1726–9, 2095) must still have held the stub of their post. Thus, the site of building R11, like that of R10, was covered with a scattering of Phase IV debris but was devoid of evidence of any contemporaneous structure. Oven 10 lay some 11 m to the north-west.

In summary, the structural sequence of building R11, as far as it can be deduced from the surviving stratigraphy, is similar to that of R10:

1 Construction of building R11. Gravel path 2168 laid between R10 and R11. Floor foundation/occupation debris 2162/2170. Phase III.

2 Desertion/dereliction/dismantling. Deposition of 'flood' silt 2118. Phase III/IV.

3 Occupation debris/refuse 1711/1715, but no structure. Phase IV.

Data

1711 (DIT)/1715 (DIY)

Mixed grey silt spread over building R11. Dereliction/occupation debris. Above 2118.

Phase IV.

Dating evidence Coarse pottery, mid 3rd or 4th century AD.

2118 (EBS)

'Flood' deposit of pale yellow/pink silt. Above 2162.

Phase III/IV

Dating evidence Coarse pottery, ?late 3rd–early 4th century AD.

2162 (EDO)/2170 (EDX)

Dark green-grey silt (disturbed natural), incorporating a broken surface of tile, chalk and limestone fragments. Above green-grey silt natural.

Phase III.

Dating evidence Coarse pottery, late 2nd–3rd century AD; Antonine samian.

2168 (EDV)

Spread of orange gravel, stone and flint pebbles, between buildings R10 and R11. Its east edge sealed by the western limits of 2162 and 2118.

Phase III.

Dating evidence Antonine samian.

Post-holes

2186 (EEO)   Circular, 0.3 m diameter, and 0.14 m deep. Dark grey silt with a little gravel.

1675 (DHG)   Circular, 0.3 m diameter, and 0.11 m deep. Dark grey silt. The post-hole yielded a small amount of coarse pottery of late 2nd–early 3rd century AD date.

2240 (EGV)   Unexcavated, circular, 0.2 m diameter. Fill as 2186.

2241 (EGW)   Unexcavated, circular, 0.25 m diameter. Fill as 2186.

1631 (DFL)   Circular, 0.2 m diameter, and 0.14 m deep. Fill as 2186.

2242 (EGX)   Unexcavated, circular, 0.25 m diameter. Fill as 2186.

2239 (EGT)   Unexcavated, circular, 0.2 m diameter. Fill as 2186.

1621 (DFA)   Unexcavated, circular, c. 0.5 m diameter. Fill as 2186.

1620 (DEZ)   Unexcavated, circular, 0.3 m diameter. Fill as 2186.

2092 (EAQ)   Circular, 0.2 m diameter, and 0.19 m deep. Fill as 2186.

1726 (DKK)   Circular, 0.15 m diameter, and 0.1 m deep. Dark grey-brown silt.

1727 (DKL)   Circular, 0.2 m diameter. Dark brown silt.

1728 (DKM)   Circular, 0.3 m diameter. Fill as 1727.

1729 (DKN)   Circular, 0.3 m diameter. Fill as 1727.

2095 (EAT)   Circular, 0.25 m diameter and 0.22 m deep. Fill as 2186.

BUILDING R12   (Figs 57, 68, 70, pp. 119, 156, 192)

This was an extensive post-hole complex in the central region of block 9. It occupied the eastern two-thirds of a sub-rectangular plot defined by gullies 33 and 29 to the north and south and streets 1 N/S and 2 N/S to the west and east. Although its precise plan is uncertain it seems to have comprised two rectangular units orientated approximately east–west, a west unit about 8 × 6 m and an east unit about 4 × 3 m. It was not possible to ascertain whether these were parts of a single building or two separate structures, although the relationship with the 'drip gully' (gully 32), which ran the full length of the north side of the two units, does imply a single structure. If the east unit was not a separate and later structure, it at least appears to have outlived the west unit. For the post-holes of the latter were sealed by the layer of redeposited clay (unit 2005) (see Fig. 70, p. 192) which also sealed building R10 to its north; while the posts of the east unit were still standing when the layer of 'flood' silt (unit 2118, which also engulfed building R11) was deposited; and, although no direct relationship could be established between the two layers, such evidence as there is points to their broad contemporaneity.

The east unit is a rather curious structure: despite its modest size it has a dense concentration of post-holes arranged loosely on a 5 × 3 grid. Such an arrangement recalls the substructure of Roman timber granaries and, although the dimensions are too small to make a valid comparison it is, nevertheless, possible that this was a storage area for which a considerable floor loading was envisaged. No trace of doorway or floor was found.

The floor level was also absent from the west unit, and although its four corner posts were identifiable (2063, 2233, 2280, 2200) the spacing of posts along the wall-lines was insufficiently regular to permit the certain identification of doorways. However, the proliferation of posts midway along the north side is suggestive of post replacement at an entrance. It also coincides with a 2 m wide causeway in the 'drip-gully' (gully 32), which would have connected the entrance to the narrow strip of land (?footpath) between gullies 32 and 33. This would have provided access to and from street 2 N/S to the east and street 1 N/S to the west (where a causeway of about 1.5 m was provided in the streetside gullies 30 and 31), though the latter access was soon effectively blocked by the digging of pit 1638 and well 1625. Another possible entrance was at the north-west where posts 2064, 2192 and 2046 appear to have comprised a small projecting porch. However this entrance, too, was rendered difficult of access by the insertion of pit 1663. Thus, in the later part of Phase III it is likely that the main approach to building R12 was from the east, via street 2 N/S; and the constriction of gully 29 centrally opposite the east end of the plot is also in accord with an east entrance.

Building R12 yielded very few finds: Antonine samian and a glass vessel fragment from post-holes 2210 and 2046 of the west unit; and Antonine samian and a very small quantity of coarse pottery of mid second–third century AD date from post-holes 1998, 1656, 2041 and 2034 of the east unit. However, the west unit is securely dated to Phase III, both by the third century AD redeposited clay layer 2005 which sealed its post-holes and by its relationship to the wells and pits on the west side of the plot. These respected the west end of the building and clearly belonged to it. Furthermore, the relationship between the pits and the dating of their earliest fill demonstrates a sequence of use. Thus the primary Phase III water source was well 2020, 4 m west of the south-west corner of R12, but when this was abandoned and given over to the dumping of refuse towards the end of the phase it appears to have been replaced by well 1625, 3 m beyond the north-west corner of the building. The rubbish pits were also quite systematically organised. First cut and filled were pits 2014, 1633 and 1638, a linear arrangement clear of both the building and its well. Next, rubbish was dumped in the abandoned well 2020. Subsequently pit 2021/2110 was cut, by which time rubbish pits probably belonging to building R13 and/or R14 in the neighbouring plot had encroached on to and obliterated the plot division, gully 29. Finally, well 1625, which may have continued in use as a water source after the end of Phase III, perhaps for the east unit of the building, was filled with rubbish in the third/fourth century AD.

Data

Post-holes

WEST UNIT: NORTH SIDE

2243 (EGY)   Circular, c. 0.25 m diameter. Unexcavated. Orange clay with crushed tile flecks mixed with grey-green silt.

2190 (EES)   Ovoid, c. 0.35 × 0.25 m. Unexcavated. Fill as 2243.

2114 (EBO)   Sub-rectangular, 0.35 × 0.25 m, and 0.2 m deep. Dark grey silt.

2211 (EFP)   Circular, 0.35 m diameter, and 0.17 m deep. Fill as 2243.

2210 (EFO)   Circular, 0.45 m diameter, and 0.17 m deep. Fill as 2243. Contained Antonine samian.

2207 (EFL)   Ovoid, 0.35 × 0.25 m, and 0.33 m deep. Fill as 2243. Incorporates a central post-pipe c. 0.15 m square, with dark grey silt fill.

WEST UNIT: EAST SIDE

2233 (EGN)   Ovoid, 0.35 × 0.3 m, and 0.3 m deep. Fill as 2243. Incorporates a central post-pipe c. 0.15 m square, with dark grey silt fill.

2246 (EHB)   Two overlapping circular post-holes, both c. 0.6 m diameter. Unexcavated. Fill as 2243.

2280 (EIM)   Ovoid, 0.35 × 0.25 m. Unexcavated. Fill as 2243.

WEST UNIT: SOUTH SIDE

2195 (EEY)   Circular, *c.* 0.25 m diameter. Unexcavated. Fill as 2243.

2194 (EEX)   Circular, *c.* 0.25 m diameter. Unexcavated. Fill as 2243.

2193 (EEW)   Sub-rectangular, 0.35 × 0.35 m. Fill as 2243.

WEST UNIT: WEST SIDE

2200 (EFD)   Sub-rectangular, 0.3 × 0.3 m, and 0.36 m deep. Fill as 2243.

2046 (DYS)   Sub-rectangular, 0.3 × 0.3 m, and 0.33 m deep. Fill as 2243 but with much charcoal. Contained a glass vessel fragment, Price cat. no. 64u (SF 1077).

2063 (DZL)   Sub-rectangular, 0.8 × 0.5 m, and 0.15 m deep. Fill as 2243. Incorporates a post-pipe *c.* 0.2 m square and 0.43 m deep at the west side, with a dark grey silt fill.

WEST UNIT: WEST 'PORCH'

2064 (DZM)   Sub-rectangular, 0.5 × 0.5 m, and 0.15 m deep. Fill as 2243. Incorporates a post-pipe *c.* 0.2 m square and 0.23 m deep at the west side, with a grey-brown silt fill.

2192 (EEV)   Ovoid, *c.* 0.5 × 0.45 m. Unexcavated. Fill as 2243.

2206 (EFK)   Sub-circular, *c.* 0.45 m diameter. Unexcavated. Dark grey silt with gravel.

WEST UNIT: INTERIOR

2058 (DZF)   Ovoid, 0.35 × 0.25 m, and 0.15 m deep. Fill as 2243.

2057 (DZE)   Sub-circular, 0.3 m diameter, and 0.13 m deep. Fill as 2243.

2065 (DZN)   Circular, 0.18 m diameter, and 0.09 m deep. Dark grey silt with gravel.

2050 (DYX)   Ovoid, 0.3 × 0.2 m, and 0.1 m deep. Dark grey silt with gravel.

2109 (EBI)/2111 (EBL)   Ovoid, 0.6 × 0.3 m, and 0.22 m deep. Dark grey silt mixed with clay. Incorporates a post-pipe 0.15 m diameter and 0.25 m deep at the north side, with a dark grey silt and gravel fill.

2196 (EEZ)   Circular, *c.* 0.35 m diameter. Unexcavated. Fill as 2243 but with much charcoal.

2244 (EGZ)   Circular, *c.* 0.15 m diameter. Unexcavated. Dark grey silt with gravel.

2245 (EHA)   Circular, *c.* 0.3 m diameter. Unexcavated. Fill as 2243.

2278 (EIK)   Circular, *c.* 0.25 m diameter. Unexcavated. Fill as 2243.

EAST UNIT

1998 (DWS)   Sub-rectangular, 0.45 × 0.4 m, and 0.24 m deep. Dark grey silt. Contained Antonine samian.

1656 (DGM)   Sub-rectangular, 0.45 × 0.4 m, and 0.31 m deep. Dark grey silt with tile and limestone packing. Contained sparse coarse pottery of mid 2nd century AD on.

1997 (DWR)   Ovoid, 0.3 × 0.25 m, and 0.2 m deep. Dark grey silt with fine gravel.

Unnumbered   Sub-rectangular, 0.3 × 0.25 m.

2036 (DYH)   Sub-rectangular, 0.25 × 0.25 m, and 0.18 m deep. Dark grey silt.

2037 (DYI)   Sub-rectangular, 0.3 × 0.25 m, and 0.2 m deep. Dark grey silt.

2040 (DYM)   Sub-rectangular, 0.2 × 0.2 m, and 0.2 m deep. Light grey-brown silt with a little gravel.

2016 (DXM)   Three circular stake-holes, all *c.* 0.15 m diameter and 0.25 m deep. Dark grey silt.

2084 (EAH)   Circular stake hole, 0.1 m diameter and 0.15 m deep. Dark grey silt.

2043 (DYP)   Sub-rectangular, 0.3 × 0.25 m, and 0.26 m deep. Light grey-green silt.

2017 (DXN)   Sub-rectangular, 0.4 × 0.3 m, and 0.22 m deep. Dark grey silt.

2041 (DYN)   Sub-rectangular, 0.2 × 0.2 m, and 0.17 m deep. Light grey-brown silt with a little gravel. Contained Antonine samian and coarse pottery of late 2nd–3rd century AD date.

2235 (EGP)   Ovoid, *c.* 0.2 × 0.2 m. Unexcavated.

2015 (DXL)   Ovoid, 0.7 × 0.4 m, and 0.24 m deep. Dark grey silt.

2279 (EIL)   Ovoid, *c.* 0.3 × 0.25 m. Unexcavated.

2044 (DYQ)   Ovoid, 0.25 × 0.25 m, and 0.12 m deep. Dark grey silt.

2042 (DYO)   Ovoid, 0.25 × 0.18 m, and 0.16 m deep. Light grey-green silt.

2234 (EGO)   Circular, *c.* 0.3 m diameter. Unexcavated.

2035 (DYG)   Ovoid, 0.3 × 0.3 m, and 0.25 m deep. Dark grey silt with a large lump of burnt daub at the top. Contained sparse coarse pottery of mid 2nd century AD on.

2018 (DXO)   Ovoid, 0.3 × 0.25 m, and 0.16 m deep. Dark grey silt with fine gravel.

2060 (DZH)   Circular, 0.25 m diameter, and 0.24 m deep. Dark grey-brown silt with a patch of burnt daub at the top.

2083 (EAG)   Ovoid, 0.2 × 0.15 m, and 0.14 m deep. Dark grey silt mixed with yellow clay.

2049 (DYW)   Sub-rectangular, 0.25 × 0.25 m, and 0.24 m deep. Dark grey silt mixed with yellow clay. Contained iron object, Jackson cat. no. 72 (SF 1079).

2034 (DYF)   Sub-rectangular, 0.35 × 0.25 m, and 0.19 m deep. Dark grey silt with gravel. Contained sparse coarse pottery of mid-late 2nd century AD date.

BUILDING R13   (Figs 56, 68, 70, pp. 118, 156, 192)

This post-hole complex, one of the largest on the site, extended over the entire south-east quadrant of block 9. The building (or buildings) thus occupied the east part of the southernmost and largest plot of the block. At the south and east the building fronted on to street 2 E/W and 2 N/S respectively, and at the north it was bounded by building R12 and the flanking plot-divider gully 29. On the west was an open courtyard occupied by wells, clusters of pits and building R14.

Like the other buildings in block 9 the post-holes of building R13 were cut into the mixed green-grey silt subsoil, but, unlike building R10, there was no sealing layer of redeposited clay. Although the relatively dark fill of the pits could be discerned, the subtler and less extensive post-hole fills, though present, proved elusive in the upper, more disturbed, part of the silt. No trace of flooring or the floor level remained, and the post-holes were ultimately located only after the removal of a spit about 10–15 cm thick. It is important to note, therefore, that the post-holes were revealed at sub-floor level, and at least 10–15 cm has to be added to their depth measurement. Unfortunately, pressure of time prevented removal of the spit from the entire area of building R13, and although the west half was laid bare the eastern half, whose central region had, in any case, been subject to later disturbance, could only be sampled in two zones. Thus, while the overall layout was determined, most of the detail of the groundplan could not be ascertained.

The building, which may have comprised more than one unit, covered a rectangular area of c.15.5 × c.9.5 m, and its alignment corresponds to that of building R10. Despite the general incoherence of the post-hole scatter two substantial parallel alignments were defined, one of which formed the west wall and the other, apparently, a central axial wall, about 4.7 m to the east. The projected course of the east wall, 4.7 m further east, coincides with the line of the easternmost located post-holes, 2250, 2253 and 2251. Internal subdivisions are indicated by several shorter east–west post alignments, e.g. 2223, 2222, 2249; 2248, 2216, 2250; and 2203, 2258, 2232, 2254, 2257. No direct evidence for doorways survived, but the termination of the enclosure gully at the south-west corner of building R13 implies that access to the building, perhaps the main entrance, was on the south side, via street 2 E/W. Alternatively, or additionally, the building may have been entered from the east via street 2 N/S, where the streetside gully 24 was breached by at least one causeway. Clearly there would have been a doorway (or doorways) on the west opening on to the courtyard, and access to/from street 1 N/S was provided by the causeway across gullies 30 and 31. However, the presence of building R14 and well 1667 effectively upstaged that entrance and, if building R14 was independent of building R13, then the west access may have served only, or principally, the former.

The wells and pits in the south plot are, with only a few outliers, concentrated in two groups within the courtyard to the west of building R13, one group disposed along the west sector of the north plot division, the other occupying a similar position on the south boundary but extending further into the courtyard. Both groups show signs of careful organisation. That at the north closely reflects the pit arrangement in the adjoining plot, in particular the combination and intimate association of well 1834, pit 1835/2007 and pit(s) 1850 and 2097, which is mirrored by that of well 2020 and pits 2021/2110 and 2014. In both these groups the well is marginally cut by the adjacent large square pit, which itself is carefully integrated with the smaller, sub-rectangular pit(s) to its north. The similarity is striking and suggests an identical range of functions which, excepting the provision of water, are unfortunately indeterminate. Broadly contemporary with these ordered groups are the adjacent diffuse areas of recut and intercutting pits which encroach on to gully 29 from both north and south. Their amorphous appearance and irregular edges could have resulted from the repeated emptying of their contents, perhaps for composting fields, i.e. they may have functioned as negative compost heaps.

The chronology of building R13's north pit group is compact, with no component certainly postdating Phase III. Despite the difficulty in dating within that phase the coarse pottery does suggest a sequence similar to that of the pit group in the adjacent plot: 1) Cutting and usage of well 1834, pit 1850 and pit 1835/2007. Later second/early third century AD. 2) Well 1834 disused; filled with refuse. Cutting and usage of pit 2097. Last refuse dumped in pit complex 2022. Cutting and usage of pits 2094 and 1987. Third century AD. When well 1834 went out of use it was probably replaced by well 1669 or, less likely, by well 1667.

The south pit group was less completely investigated. Surface indications of rectangular grouping, and a well (1678) of similar proportions to well 1834, might be taken to imply a similar combination to the north group. However, there are differences, most notably the linear arrangement of five rectangular pits – 1960, 1972/1976, 1973, 1974 and 1975 – which obliterates gullies 30 and 31 and encroaches on to street 2 E/W. No certain relationship could be established between these pits, so that it is not known whether they were all contemporaneous or whether they were cut and used in sequence. Nor is their function apparent. Excepting 1960, all are shallow, share the same sealing layer and upper fill – units 1873 and 1904 – and have a sterile basal fill of fine grey silt. They may have been cut as recesses for the base of tanks, though there is no direct evidence to confirm this. Coarse pottery in the upper fill dates their disuse to the third century AD, while their construction postdates the cutting of gullies 30 and 31. They belong, therefore, to the latter part of Phase III. Of the pits to their north only a few were sampled. They yielded finds of late second–third century AD date. Pit 2087 is of particular interest as its lower fill (late second/early third century AD) was sealed by a layer of the 'flood' silt encountered also in the north-east quadrant of block 9 (unit 2118; see buildings R11 and R12, p. 194 and p. 196).

Three outliers of the south pit group were more intimately associated with building R13: well 1669, hard up against the south end of the west wall, was probably cut in the latter part of Phase III as a replacement for well 1678 or well 1834 or both. Coarse pottery in the fill dates its disuse to the mid/late third century AD. The large ovoid pit 1962, also possibly a well, lay immediately outside the south-west corner and straddles the east terminal of gully 30. Adjacent to its east was the small, rectangular, shaft-like pit 1695, probably a latrine pit. Whatever its original function it was particularly remarkable for the density of small finds, especially in the upper fill. Samian stamps, iron and bone artefacts and glass vessel fragments were numerous. Large quantities of burnt clay in the lower fill may be remains of a structure destroyed by fire. If so, the finds incorporated in the upper fill (which includes much charcoal) may be part of the associated debris subsequently cleared out in a tidying-up operation, though none shows evidence of burning. The coarse pottery date for the fill is late second/early third century AD, while the samian stamps all fall within the bracket c. AD 150–80.

Although pit 1695 was exceptional, the total number of small finds from the pits of the south plot of block 9 far exceeded that from any other part of the site implying relatively intense and sustained occupation of building R13 throughout, and possibly beyond, Phase III. The prosperity of the occupants is attested by the samian pottery and glassware, but their status is unknown. A clue to their identity, perhaps, is provided by the iron buckle from a second–third century AD military belt, found near the bottom of well 1678; but there are no other associated items to supplement it. Finds from the pit clusters also give a tantalising glimpse of the superstructure of building R13. Several pits included in their fill fragments of burnt daub (e.g. pits 2087, 1989) and painted plaster (e.g. well 1678), while most of the Egyptian Blue pellets (see p. 501) came from pits in this plot (pits 1989, 1996, 1972/1976, 1834 and well 1667).

Data

Post-holes

WEST SIDE

2204 (EFH)   Sub-rectangular, 0.4×0.35 m, and 0.2 m deep. Dark grey silt with a little gravel.

2203 (EFG)   Rectangular, 0.3×0.25 m, and 0.39 m deep. Fill as 2204.

2202 (EFF)   Rectangular, $0.5 \times c. 0.4$ m, and 0.11 m deep. Fill as 2204.

2201 (EFE)   Rectangular, 0.3×0.25 m, and 0.32 m deep. Dark grey silt sealed with orange clay.

2224 (EGD)   Circular, 0.3 m diameter. Unexcavated.

2226 (EGF)   Sub-rectangular, 0.35×0.25 m. Coarse redeposited orange clay and gravel natural.

2227 (EGG)   Rectangular, 0.55×0.4 m, and 0.1 m deep. Fill as 2226. Incorporates a post-pipe at the south, c. 0.35 m square and 0.27 m deep.

2228 (EGH)   Circular, 0.3 m diameter. Unexcavated. Fill as 2226.

NORTH SIDE

2230 (EGK)   Ovoid, 0.35×0.3 m. Unexcavated.

EAST SIDE

2250 (EHF)   Sub-rectangular, 0.25×0.17 m, and 0.19 m deep. Fill as 2204.

2253 (EHI)   Circular, 0.2 m diameter. Unexcavated. Fill as 2204.

2251 (EHG)   Ovoid, 0.5×0.4, and 0.42 m deep. Grey-green silt mixed with orange clay, pebbles and crushed tile flecks (same fill as the post-holes of building R10).

SOUTH SIDE

2220 (EFZ)   Circular, 0.3 m diameter. Unexcavated. Fill as 2204.

CENTRE ROW

2218 (EFX)   Ovoid, 0.65×0.55 m, and 0.18 m deep. Fill as 2204.

2219 (EFY)   Ovoid, 0.4×0.35 m, and 0.16 m deep. Fill as 2251.

2256 (EHM)   Circular, 0.2 m diameter. Unexcavated. Fill as 2204.

2255 (EHL)   Ovoid, 0.35×0.3 m, and 0.17 m deep. Fill as 2204.

2254 (EHK)   Circular, 0.2 m diameter. Unexcavated. Fill as 2204.

2212 (EFQ)   Ovoid, 0.5×0.4 m, and 0.3 m deep. Fill as 2251.

2213 (EFR)   Rectangular, 0.65×0.45 m, and 0.1 m deep. Fill as 2204. Incorporates a rectangular post-pipe at the north, 0.35×0.3 m, and 0.25 m deep.

2214 (EFS)   Ovoid, 0.35×0.3 m, and 0.1 m deep. Fill as 2204.

2215 (EFT)   Sub-rectangular, 0.3×0.25 m, and 0.37 m deep. Fill as 2204.

2248 (EHD)   Sub-circular, 0.25 m diameter. Unexcavated. Fill as 2204.

INTERIOR

2223 (EGC)   Sub-circular, 0.3 m diameter. Unexcavated. Fill as 2226.

2222 (EGB)   Circular, 0.35 m diameter, and 0.32 m deep. Fill as 2204.

2249 (EHE)   Circular, 0.35 diameter, and 0.24 m deep. Fill as 2204. Contained coarse pottery of late 2nd–3rd century AD date.

2216 (EFV)   Sub-rectangular, 0.3×0.25 m, and 0.27 m deep. Fill as 2204.

2225 (EGE)   Sub-rectangular, $0.5 \times c. 0.35$ m, and 0.4 m deep. Fill as 2226.

2237 (EGR)   Circular, 0.3 m diameter. Unexcavated. Fill as 2204.

2252 (EHH)   Ovoid, 0.5×0.4 m, and 0.39 m deep. Fill as 2204.

2258 (EHO)   Circular, 0.3 m diameter. Unexcavated. Fill as 2251.

2232 (EGM)   Circular, 0.3 m diameter. Unexcavated. Fill as 2204.

2257 (EHN)   Circular, 0.2 m diameter. Unexcavated. Fill as 2251.

2221 (EGA)   Circular, 0.3 m diameter. Unexcavated. Fill as 2204.

2236 (EGQ)   Circular, 0.2 m diameter. Unexcavated. Fill as 2204.

2259 (EHP)   Ovoid, 0.55×0.5 m. Unexcavated. Fill as 2204.

2217 (EFW)/2231 (EGL) Rectangular, 1.0×0.8 m, and 0.43 m deep. Probably a small pit rather than a post-hole. Lower fill (2231) dark grey silt with stone and tile fragments. Upper fill (2217) pale yellow/pink silt, a 'flood' deposit, as unit 2118 in buildings R11 and R12.

BUILDING R14   (Figs 56, 68, pp. 118, 156)

The post-holes of this structure, in the west part of the south plot of block 9, were revealed in the closing stages of the final season of excavation. There was insufficient time to excavate them and the building therefore remains ill-understood. What is apparent is its close relationship with well 1667. It may, indeed, have been a subsidiary structure (?out-building) of building R13, a small well-side building with one open side fronting on to the well. Certainly, while the post-holes enclose a roughly rectangular area *c*. 5.5 × *c*. 3.5–4.0 m, there was no post-line on the west (well) side. The positioning of both well and building, monopolising the west courtyard of building R13 and hindering if not blocking the west entrance to the plot, implies that both are secondary features, probably constructed late in Phase III and possibly continuing in use in Phase IV. In fact, well 1667 (alone among the pits of the plot) includes late third/fourth century AD coarse pottery in its lower fill.

The fill of the post-holes is quite consistent, comprising either dark grey silt or an orange/yellow gravelly clay, similar to that of the east post-holes of buildings R6 and R7. However, this merely reflects the underlying subsoil into which they were cut. Although the post-holes of building R14 were unexcavated, a short gully, 1673, immediately outside the south wall-line, yielded coarse pottery of probable third century AD date. As the gully flanked a space, between post-holes 1680 and 2276, rather larger than that between the remaining post-holes, it is possible that 1673 was a drip gully outside a doorway. No trace of flooring or floor level was found.

Data

Post-holes

NORTH SIDE

2270 (EIB)   Circular, 0.25 m diameter. Dark grey silt with a little gravel. Unexcavated.
2269 (EIA)   Circular, 0.25 m diameter. Fill as 2270. Unexcavated.
2266 (EHX)   Two, ovoid: i) 0.55 × 0.35 m; ii) 0.35 × 0.2 m. Orange/yellow clay with gravel. Unexcavated.
2267 (EHY)   Ovoid, 0.45 × 0.3 m. Fill as 2266. Unexcavated.

EAST SIDE

2271 (EIC)   Ovoid, 0.3 × 0.25 m. Fill as 2270. Unexcavated.
2265 (EHW)   Rectangular, 0.4 × 0.2 m. Fill as 2266. Unexcavated.
2264 (EHV)   Sub-rectangular, 0.4 × 0.25 m. Fill as 2266. Unexcavated.
2263 (EHT)   Sub-rectangular, 0.3 × 0.3 m. Fill as 2266. Unexcavated.
2262 (EHS)   Sub-rectangular, 0.3 × 0.3 m. Fill as 2266. Unexcavated.
2275 (EIG)   Circular, 0.4 m diameter. Fill as 2266. Unexcavated.
2282 (EIO)   Ovoid, 0.35 × 0.2 m. Fill as 2266. Unexcavated.

SOUTH SIDE

2281 (EIN)   Ovoid, 0.35 × 0.2 m. Fill as 2270. Unexcavated.
1681 (DHN)   Ovoid, 0.3 × 0.25 m. Fill as 2270. Unexcavated.
1680 (DHM)   Ovoid, 0.3 × 0.25 m. Fill as 2270. Unexcavated.
2276 (EIH)   Ovoid, 0.3 × 0.25 m. Fill as 2266. Unexcavated.
2277 (EII)   Ovoid, 0.25 × 0.2 m. Fill as 2266. Unexcavated.
2260 (EHQ)   Ovoid, 0.55 × 0.4 m. Fill as 2266. Unexcavated.

INTERIOR

2268 (EHZ)   Sub-rectangular, 0.7 × 0.45 m. Fill as 2266. Incorporates a post-pipe, ovoid, 0.25 × 0.2 m. Dark grey silt. Unexcavated.

EXTERIOR

2272 (EID)   Ovoid, 0.4 × 0.3 m. Fill as 2270. Unexcavated.
2261 (EHR)   Ovoid, 0.8 × 0.4 m. Fill as 2266. Unexcavated.

Gully

1673 (DHE)   A short, shallow U-sectioned gully, perhaps a drip-gully for the ?threshold in the south wall between post-holes 2276 and 1680. Length 1.05 m, width 0.5 m, depth 0.12 m. Fill as 2266. Contained ?3rd century AD coarse pottery.

WELLS, ?LATRINE AND PITS

Well 1669 (DHA)

E54.4, N16.15   (Fig. 40b, p. 98)   Phase III/IV

An ovoid pit in the south-east quadrant of block 9. The irregular oval shape is the erosion cone above a smaller, rectangular, vertical-sided pit. Half sectioned only.

Erosion cone: width 3.0 m, length *c*. 3.2 m.

Pit: width at least 0.85 m, length 1.55 m, depth 1.42 m.

Fill
1669 (DHA)   Dark grey/black silt and ash with large quantities of charcoal, daub and burnt clay.
1849 (DPN)   Dark grey-green silt with charcoal flecks.
1880 (DQV)   Light grey silt with a few small stones, charcoal and burnt clay flecks.
1892 (DRH)   Grey and orange mixed silt with occasional stones and a little sand.
1903 (DRT)   Waterlogged orange silts mixed with sand.

Dating evidence   NVCC type 20/21 (throughout pit), 4, 2.5, 2.7, Castor box lid; NVGW types 27, 45; buff ware type 69/70; Horningsea throughout pit. Date: mid/late 3rd century AD.

Small finds
1669   Two glass vessel fragments, Price cat. nos. 25 and 55e (SF 833); copper-alloy ring, Jackson cat. no. 90 (SF 834); bone pin, Greep cat. no. 33 (SF 838).
1849   Glass fragment (SF 843); copper-alloy pin, Jackson cat. no. 29 (SF 872); samian stamp, Dickinson cat. no. 52 (SF 867); bone object, Greep cat. no. 68a.
1880   Samian stamp, Dickinson cat. no. 24 (SF 1171).

1903 Samian stamp, Dickinson cat. no. 29 (SF 908); graffito on NVCC beaker, Potter cat. no. 12 (SF 884).

Pit 1695 (DIC)

E58.5, N11.0   (Fig. 39g, p. 97)   Phase III, later

A small rectangular pit, with steep sides, on the frontage of street 2 E/W, on the south side of block 9. Possibly a latrine pit. At the top of the fill was the partial skeleton of a human infant (Conheeney cat. no. 6).

Width 1.05 m, length 1.4 m, depth 0.9 m.

Fill

1695 (DIC)   Dark grey silt with some stones and charcoal and patches of yellow sand.

1854 (DPS)   Black sandy silt with some charcoal and a few pebbles.

1858 (DPX)   Grey-brown sandy silt with some gravel.

1864 (DQD)   Brown silt with some gravel and large quantities of burnt clay.

1877 (DQR)   Brown-grey silt with clay, orange sand and gravel, and some burnt clay, increasing towards the base.

Dating evidence

Top layer: NVCC 20/21. Date: 3rd/4th century AD.
Fill: NVCC type 1, 2.4; NVGW types 45, 47. Date: later 2nd/3rd century AD.

Small finds

1695   Samian stamps, Dickinson cat. nos 10, 13, 42 and 61 (SF 1015, 1014, 1005 and 1020); glass vessel fragments, Price cat. nos 51, 64j and 64al (SF 1010, 1016 and 841); iron objects, Jackson cat. no. 58 (SF 1021); two bone needles, Greep cat. nos 45–6 (SF 842 and 1017); bone handle, Greep cat. no. 70 (SF 835).

1854   Glass vessel fragments, Price cat. nos 59b, 59g, 61, 64m, 64v, 64x and 64an (SF 1033–6, 690 and 850); bone needle, Greep cat. no. 47 (SF 1030).

1858   Copper-alloy pin fragments, Jackson cat. no. 22 (SF 1037); glass vessel fragment, Price cat. no. 59a (SF 682).

1877   Brooch, Mackreth cat. no. 4, Colchester Derivative, mid 1st century AD (SF 1052); samian stamps, Dickinson cat. nos 27 and 41 (SF 1051 and 1049); iron hobnailed shoe, Jackson cat. no. 39 (SF 1050).

Pit 1962 (DVF)

E55.8, N10.6   Phase III

An ovoid pit on the south side of block 9, projecting into street 2 E/W. Half-sectioned only.

Width at least 1.2 m, length 2.45 m, depth 1.18 m.

Fill

1962 (DVF)   Grey silt with much redeposited natural clay, yellow silt, and some gravel.

2009 (DXE)   Yellow clay and silt mixed with burnt daub and some gravel.

2010 (DXF)   Grey silt with flecks of charcoal and burnt clay.

Dating evidence   NVCC type cf. 2.5 (indented), 25/26; buff ware type 74. Date: late 2nd/early 3rd century AD.

Small finds

1962   Glass vessel fragment, Price cat. no. 63a (SF 1055).

2010   Burnt window glass fragment (SF 1064).

Pit 2003 (DWY)

E52.6, N10.95   Phase III, later

A rectangular pit on the south edge of block 9. Cuts unit 1961 of gully 31 (cut 8).

Width 1.2 m, length 1.6 m.

Fill

2003 (DWY)   Dark grey silt with gravel and iron-pan staining.

2004 (DWZ)   Dark grey silt with charcoal flecks.

Dating evidence   NVCC type 2.4; NVSC types 59, 62/63; grey ware vessel cf. type 27; Horningsea. Date: late 2nd/3rd century AD.

Small finds   2003 Copper-alloy pinhead, Jackson cat. no. 7 (SF 1043); NVCC barbotine-figured sherd, Johns cat. no. 7 (SF 1048); glass vessel fragment, Price cat. no. 641 (SF 1047).

Pit 1982 (DWB)

E50.25, N9.75   Phase III/IV

A shallow irregular oval pit on the south edge of block 9. Encroaches on street 2 E/W. Cuts unit 1961 of gully 31 (cut 8).

Width 1.05 m, length 1.35 m, depth 0.3 m.

Fill

1982 (DWB)   Dark grey silt with gravel.

2012 (DXH)   Grey-green silt with fine gravel.

2013 (DXI)   Yellow/brown/grey soft silts.

Dating evidence

Top layer: NVCC type 2.7. Date: late 2nd/3rd century AD.
Fill: NVCC type 7, 20/21. Date: ?3rd century AD or later.

Small finds   1982 Copper-alloy needle fragment, Jackson cat. no. 43 (SF 1038).

Pit 1960 (DVD)

E48.65, N10.1   Phase III, later

A rhomboid pit on the south edge of block 9, part of the linear cluster 1960, 1972/1976, 1973, 1974, 1975. Encroaches on street 2 E/W. Entirely cuts away gully 31 in this area. Cuts pit 1887. Relationship with pit 1972/1976 uncertain.

Width 1.6 m, length 1.9 m, depth 0.65 m.

Fill

1875 (DQP)   Dark grey/black/brown silts.

1881 (DQW)   Dark grey-brown silt with occasional limestone lumps and some crushed tile.

1908 (DRZ)   Dark grey-brown silt with some gravel and charcoal flecks.

1960 (DVD)   Dark grey/black silt with much charcoal and burnt clay flecks.

1966 (DVK)   Yellow/grey/brown mixed silts and gravel. [Units 1875, 1881, and 1908 are sealing spreads; units 1960 and 1966 are the filling layers of the pit.]

Dating evidence   NVCC types 2.7, beaker cf. type 40, 7; Horningsea; NVSC type 61; buff ware types 57/59, 74; grey ware beaker cf. type 39. Date: late 2nd/3rd century AD.

Small finds   1960 Copper-alloy ?handle, Jackson cat. no. 79 (SF 918); glass vessel fragment, Price cat. no. 16 (SF 919); iron hobnailed shoe, Jackson cat. no. 32 (SF 920).

Pit 1972 (DVQ)/1976 (DVV)
E47.35, N10.5   Phase III, later

A shallow rhomboid pit on the south edge of block 9, part of the linear cluster 1960, 1972/1976, 1973, 1974, 1975. Encroaches on street 2 E/W. Entirely cuts away gully 31 in this area. Relationship with pits 1960 and 1973 uncertain.

Width c. 1.4 m, length 1.6 m, depth 0.42 m.

Fill

1873 (DQN)/1874 (DQO) Dark grey sandy silt with gravel and flecks of burnt clay.
1904 (DRV) Dark grey silt with some gravel and much iron-pan staining.
1972 (DVQ)/1976 (DVV) Fine grey silt with iron-pan staining.

Dating evidence
Top layer: NVCC type 2.3; NVGW type 45, 46; buff ware type 69/70. Date: late 2nd/3rd century AD.
Fill: NVCC type 20/21; NVGW type 45; NVSC type 52; Horningsea type 107/8. Date: 3rd century AD.
Bottom layer: no datable material.

Small finds 1904 Two fragments of Egyptian Blue, Bimson cat. nos 3–4 (SF 907 and 922).

Pit 1973 (DVR)   E46.3, N10.7   Phase III, later

A shallow rectangular pit on the south edge of block 9, part of the linear cluster 1960, 1972/1976, 1973, 1974, 1975. Entirely cuts away gully 31 in this area. Cut by pit 1974. Relationship with pit 1972/1976 uncertain.

Width 1.0 m, length 1.3 m, depth 0.4 m.

Fill

1873 (DQN)/1874 (DQO) Dark grey sandy silt with gravel and flecks of burnt clay.
1904 (DRV) Dark grey silt with some gravel and much iron-pan staining.
1973 (DVR) Fine grey silt with iron-pan staining.

Dating evidence
Top layers: NVCC type 2.3; NVGW types 45, 46; buff ware type 69/70. Date: late 2nd/3rd century AD.
Fill: NVCC type 20/21; NVGW type 45; NVSC type 52; Horningsea type 107/8. Date: 3rd century AD.

Small finds 1904 See pit 1972/1976, above.

Pit 1974 (DVS)   E45.4, N11.0   Phase III, later

A shallow rectangular pit on the southern edge of block 9, part of the linear cluster 1960, 1972/1976, 1973, 1974, 1975. Entirely cuts away gully 30 in this area. Cuts northern part of gully 31. Cuts pit 1973. Relationship with pit 1975 uncertain.

Width 1.1 m, length 1.1 m, depth 0.45 m.

Fill

1873 (DQN)/1874 (DQO) Dark grey sandy silt with gravel and flecks of burnt clay.
1904 (DRV) Dark grey silt with some gravel and much iron-pan staining.
1974 (DVS) Fine grey silt with iron-pan staining.

Dating evidence
Top layers: NVCC type 2.3; NVGW types 45, 46; buff ware type 69/70.
Fill: NVCC type 20/21; NVGW type 45; NVSC type 52; Horningsea type 107/8. Date: 3rd century AD.
Bottom layer: no datable material.

Small finds 1904 See pit 1972/1976, above.

Pit 1975 (DVT)   E44.45, N10.95   Phase III, later

A shallow rectangular pit on the south edge of block 9, part of the linear cluster 1960, 1972/1976, 1973, 1974, 1975. Entirely cuts away gully 30 in this area, and most of gully 31. Relationship with pit 1974 uncertain.

Width 1.0 m, length 1.4 m, depth 0.5 m.

Fill

1873 (DQN)/1874 (DQO) Dark grey sandy silt with gravel and flecks of burnt clay.
1904 (DRV) Dark grey silt with some gravel and much iron-pan staining.
1975 (DVT) Fine grey silt with iron-pan staining.

Dating evidence
Top layer: NVCC type 2.3; NVGW types 45, 46; buff ware type 69/70. Date: late 2nd/3rd century AD.
Fill: NVCC type 20/21; NVGW type 45; NVSC type 52; Horningsea type 107/8. Date: 3rd century AD.
Bottom layer: no datable material.

Small finds 1904 See pit 1972/1976, above.

Pit 1994 (DWO)   E39.05, N12.35   Phase III/IV

A shallow elliptical pit inside the south-west angle of block 9. Respects gully 31. Clips the west edge of gully 30.

Width 0.95 m, length c. 2.1 m, depth 0.4 m.

Fill

1845 (DPI)   Grey silt with fine gravel and iron-pan staining.
1994 (DWO) Dark grey silt with charcoal flecks.

Dating evidence NVCC type 33; NVGW type 49/50; Horningsea. Date: 3rd century AD.

Small finds 1845 Coin, Shotter cat. no. 45, dupondius, MW, AD 161–80 (SF 846); bone pin, Greep cat. no. 13 (SF 855).

Pit 1909 (DSA)/1968 (DVM)   E37.95, N11.3   Phase III

An irregular ovoid pit, at the south-west corner of block 9. The pit comprises two distinct parts: i) an upper, Roman period, pit (units 1909, 1910) cut into ii) a lower, prehistoric, pit (units 1968, 1969). Pit 1909/1910 cuts away the corner of gully 31 (cut 5, unit 1846), and encroaches on street 1 N/S.

Width 1.05 m, length 1.5 m, depth 0.65 m.

Fill

i 1909 (DSA) Fine grey silt with some gravel.
   1910 (DSB) Dark grey silt with some gravel and many charcoal flecks.
ii 1968 (DVM) Light grey silt with fine charcoal flecks.
   1969 (DVN) Dark grey silt with much charcoal.

Dating evidence

i NVCC types 2.4, 3, 3.3 and early Castor box type. Date: late 2nd/ early 3rd century AD.

ii Early to Middle Bronze Age.

?Well 1678 (DHK)

E46.85, N16.05   (Fig. 39c, p. 97)   Phase III, later

An irregular oval, steep-sided pit, within the cluster near the centre of the south side of block 9.

Width 1.45 m, length 1.7 m, depth 1.2 m.

Fill

1678 (DHK) Dark grey-black silt with much gravel and charcoal flecks.

1879 (DQT) Mixed black silt and orange sand, with some gravel, iron-pan staining and occasional tile flecks.

1888 (DRD) Dark grey-black silt with some gravel and charcoal flecks.

1891 (DRG) Mixed brown and grey silt with some iron-pan staining and a few small stones.

1899 (DRP) Dark grey silt with some sand, some redeposited yellow silty clay, gravel and charcoal flecks.

1901 (DRR) Dark grey silt with a little sand, some small stones and charcoal flecks.

1978 (DVX) Dark grey silt sealed below a lens of wall plaster.

1985 (DWE) Mixed grey silt, slumped orange silt and redeposited natural clay and silt.

Dating evidence

Upper layers: NVCC type 3; NVSC with painted decoration. Date: late 2nd/3rd century AD.

Fill: NVCC types 20/21, 2.7, 26. Date: 3rd century AD or later.

Lower layer: NVCC type 2; NVSC type 59. Date: late 2nd/3rd century AD.

Small finds

1879 Two glass fragments (SF 874).

1899 Glass vessel fragments, Price cat. nos 44 and 591 (SF 1073 and 689).

1901 Glass vessel fragment, Price cat. no. 551 (SF 923).

1978 Iron military buckle, Jackson cat. no. 1 (SF 693); glass vessel rim fragment, Price cat. no. 38 (SF 1082).

Pit 2087 (EAL)   E47.55, N12.95   Phase III, later

A pit of uncertain shape (only part-sectioned) within the cluster near the centre of the south side of block 9.

Width at least 0.85 m, length at least 1.4 m, depth 0.65 m.

Fill

1882 (DQX) Grey-brown silt [sealing layer, cf. pit 1887 below].

2087 (EAL) Pale pink fine silt mottled with grey and iron-pan staining. ?Flood silt. cf. units 2073 and 2078 in pit 1943 (block 7, pp. 184–5).

2169 (EDW) Dark grey silt with burnt daub, redeposited clay, much chalk and shell and some stone.

Dating evidence Horningsea type 107/8; NVCC; NVGW. Date: early 3rd century AD or later.

Pit 1887 (DRC)   E48.6, N11.55   Phase III

A pit of uncertain shape (only part-sectioned) within the cluster near the centre of the south side of block 9.

Width at least 0.8 m, length at least 1.0 m, depth 0.5 m.

Fill

1882 (DQX) Grey-brown silt [sealing layer, cf. pit 2087 above].

1887 (DRC) Dark grey/black silt with much charcoal and some fine gravel.

1895 (DRL) Mixed grey silt and orange sand with some gravel.

Dating evidence Buff ware type 74; NVGW Date: late 2nd century AD.

The sequence is:

1 Silting of pit (unit 1895).

2 Area covered with fine pale yellow-pink silt c. 10 cm thick, seemingly a water-lain 'flood' silt.

3 Unit 1887 fills recut pit.

4 Unit 1882 fills and seals the tops of several pits in the area.

Pit 1989 (DWI)   E49.25, N16.75   (Fig. 38c, p. 96)   Phase III

A sub-rectangular pit within the cluster near the centre of the south side of block 9. Half-sectioned only. Cut by pit 1996, but sealed by the same two units (1963, 1990).

Width at least 1.6 m, length at least 1.7 m, depth 0.8 m.

Fill

1963 (DVG) Dark grey/black silt with much charcoal and burnt clay/daub.

1990 (DWK) Dark grey-green gritty silt with charcoal flecks.

1989 (DWI) Dark grey silt with some gravel and large quantity of mussel shells.

2039 (DYL) Dark grey silt, with large charcoal flecks and some shell, sealed beneath a sterile redeposited clay/silt layer separating it from 1989.

Dating evidence

Top layer: NVCC types, 12, 3; NVGW type 28.2 Date: late 2nd century AD.

Fill: buff ware type 69/70, 74, 52. Date: late 2nd century AD.

Small finds

1963 Glass vessel fragment, Price cat. no. 54 (SF 940); iron object, Jackson cat. no. 57 (SF 936).

1990 Glass fragments (SF 942 and 949).

1989 Pellet of Egyptian Blue, Bimson cat. no. 2 (SF 1022); glass fragment (SF 1041).

Pit 1996 (DWQ)

E49.1, N14.8   (Fig. 38c, p. 96)   Phase III/IV

A sub-rectangular pit within the cluster near the centre of the south side of block 9. Half-sectioned only. Cuts pit 1989, but sealed by the same two units (1963, 1990).

Width at least 1.25 m, length at least 2.2 m, depth 0.6 m.

Fill

1963 (DVG) See pit 1989 above.

1990 (DWK) See pit 1989 above.

1996 (DWQ) Mixed dark grey/green/brown silts with fine charcoal and burnt clay flecks.

2002 (DWX) Dark grey/black silt with much charcoal, some gravel and oyster shell.

Dating evidence

Top layer: NVCC types 12, 3; NVGW type 28.2. Date: 3rd century AD.

Fill: NVCC type 2.7, 20/21. Date: 3rd century AD.

Small finds

1963, 1990 See pit 1989 above.

1996 Samian stamp, Dickinson cat. no. 47 (SF 1008); fragment of Egyptian Blue, Bimson cat. no. 7 (SF 1007).

2002 Glass vessel fragments, Price cat. nos 28 and 55d (SF 1039 and 1040).

?Well 1667 (DGY)

E44.6, N22.1   (Fig. 39e, p. 97)   Phase III/IV

A large sub-rectangular pit, in the south-west quadrant of block 9. Half-sectioned only. There is a shallow projection at the north edge, similar to that of well 944, block 3.

Width c. 3.4 m, length 3.9 m (5.0 m including projection), depth 1.75 m.

Fill

1667 (DGY) Dark grey gritty silt with much building debris.

1848 (DPM) Dark grey-brown silt with much gravel and stone.

1860 (DPZ) Light grey clayey silt with some small gravel and sand, crushed shell and flecks of burnt clay.

1878 (DQS) Yellow-grey clayey silt with some gravel.

1886 (DRB) Dark grey silt with much charcoal.

1912 (DSD) Dark grey/black clay, rich in organic material. No stone or gravel.

Dating evidence NVCC types 3, 2.4, 20/21, 24; NVGW 45.3, 27; Horningsea. Date: late 3rd/4th century AD.

Small finds

1848 Glass bead, Price cat. no. 72 (SF 866).

1878 Samian stamp, Dickinson cat. no. 117 (SF 1182).

If this pit was originally a well, its sides must have suffered considerable erosion before the resulting 'cone' was filled with rubbish. The shallow projection may have afforded access in a form similar to that of well 446, block 1a.

Well 1834 (DOX)   E53.9, N25.9   Phase III, later

A regular rectangular pit with vertical sides which are eroded only in the top 25 cm. Part of the pit cluster west of centre, block 9. West edge clipped by pit 1835/2007.

Width c. 1.4 m, length 1.5 m, depth 1.16 m.

Fill

1668 (DGZ) Dark grey/black silt with much gravel, charcoal flecks and shell. [An amorphous layer which seals pits 1834, 1835/2007, and 1850.]

1834 (DOX) Dark grey silt with some gravel and charcoal and burnt clay flecks.

1863 (DQC) Green-grey sandy silt with some iron-pan staining and charcoal flecks.

1890 (DRF) Dark grey silt with much charcoal and burnt clay flecks.

1897 (DRN) Dark grey silt with charcoal flecks, divided from 1890 by a slump of natural and a lens of charcoal.

Dating evidence NVCC types 2.6, 20/21, 4.2, 2.5, 8; buff ware types 74, 69/70; NVGW types 45, 29, 39; Horningsea throughout pit. Date: 3rd century AD.

Small finds

1668 Glass vessel fragments, Price cat. nos 13, 44a–44c, and 46 (SF 821, 664, 804, 805, 809 and 818); coin, Shotter cat. no. 8, denarius, VW, AD 69–79 (SF 810); copper-alloy pin fragment, Jackson cat. no. 17 (SF 817); bone needle, Greep cat. no. 41 (SF 824).

1834 Glass vessel fragments, Price cat. no. 55h (SF 831, 849 and 862).

1863 Fragment of Egyptian Blue, Bimson cat. no. 5 (SF 885); NVCC barbotine-figured sherd, Johns cat. no. 15.

1897 Copper-alloy needle, Jackson cat. no. 41 (SF 910); NVCC barbotine-figured beaker, Johns cat. no. 11.

Pit 1850 (DPO)   E53.5, N27.25   Phase III, later

An ovoid pit, part of the pit cluster west of centre, block 9. Apparently cut by pit 2097. Relationship with unit 1981 of gully 29 (cut 6) uncertain.

Width 1.2 m, length c. 1.2 m, depth 0.6 m.

Fill

1668 (DGZ) See pit 1834, above.

1850 (DPO) Dark grey silt with fine gravel, stone, and charcoal flecks.

Dating evidence

Upper layer: NVCC types 2.6, 20/21, 4; NVGW types 29, 39, 45. Date: 3rd century AD.

Fill: NVCC types 2.7, 3; buff ware type 69/70; large grey ware beaker cf. type 39. Date: later 2nd/3rd century AD.

Small finds

1668 See pit 1834, above.

1850 Glass vessel fragment (SF 868); millingstone fragment, Jackson cat. no. 9 (SF 891).

Pit 2097 (EAW)   E52.4, N27.25   Phase III/IV

A narrow rectangular pit, part of the pit cluster west of centre, block 9. Apparently cuts pit 1850. Relationship with pit 2007 uncertain.

Width 0.95 m, length 1.9 m.

Fill

2071 (DZT) Black silt with some gravel and flecks of charcoal and burnt clay.

2097 (EAW) Dark grey silt with some small stones and flecks of charcoal and burnt clay.

Dating evidence

Top layer: NVCC types 12, 20/21, 25/26. Date: 3rd century AD.

Fill: NVCC types 20/21, 25/26; NVGW type 39, 45. Date: 3rd century AD.

Pit 1835 (DOY)/2007 (DXC)   E52.5, N25.75   Phase III/IV

A shallow, regular rectangular pit, part of the pit cluster west of centre, block 9. Excavated in two parts (1835, 2007) with an intervening baulk. It is carefully integrated with pits 1834, 1850 and 2097 and all may have been contemporaneous, or nearly so.

Width 1.9 m, length 2.2 m, depth 0.55 m.

Fill
1668 (DGZ)   See pit 1834, p. 204.
1835 (DOY)/2007 (DXC)   Dark grey/black silt with ash, gravel, much charcoal and burnt clay flecks.
1876 (DQQ)/2116 (EBQ)   Dark grey sandy silt mixed with yellow and orange clay, with some stones and burnt daub.

Dating evidence
Pit 1835
Upper layers: NVCC types 20/21, 2.6, 4; NVGW types 29, 39, 45. Date: 3rd century AD.
Lower layers: NVCC types 2.3, 2.6; NVSC type 55. Date early 3rd century AD.

Pit 2007
Cleaning: NVGW type 45; NVCC type 20. Date: 3rd century AD.
Fill: NVCC types 20/21, 25/26; buff ware types 55, 57, 69/70. Date: 3rd century AD.

Small finds
1668   See pit 1834, p. 204.
1835   Late La Tène brooch, Mackreth cat. no. 14 (SF 832); glass vessel fragment, Price cat. no. 14 (SF 837); samian stamp, Dickinson cat. no. 112 (SF 880).

Pit 2094 (EAS)   E50.7, N27.45   Phase III/IV

An irregular rhomboid pit; cuts the intercutting pit complex 2022 within the cluster west of centre, block 9.

Width 1.2 m, length 1.7 m.

Fill
2071 (DZT)   Black silt with some gravel, charcoal and flecks of burnt clay.
2094 (EAS)   Grey-green slightly chalky silt with some gravel.

Dating evidence
Top layer: NVCC types 20/21, 25/26, 12. Date: 3rd century AD.
Fill: NVCC types 2, 25; NVGW types 45, 47; buff ware types 69/70, 74; Horningsea type 107/8. Date: 3rd century AD.

Small finds   2094 Glass vessel fragment, Price cat. no. 64y (SF 1124).

Pit 2022 (DXS)   E49.3, N27.2   (Fig. 41d, p. 99)   Phase III/IV

A complex of intercutting pits within the cluster west of centre, block 9. Only pits 2094 and 1987 were identifiable as discrete pits cutting the complex.

Width *c.* 3.5 m, length *c.* 4.0 m.

Fill
1965 (DVI)   Dark grey/black silt with gravel, stone and some charcoal flecks.
1977 (DVW)   Dark grey silt with gravel.

1979 (DVY)/1980 (DVZ)   Dark grey/black silt.
2022 (DXS)   Grey silt with gravel and redeposited natural clay.

Dating evidence
Upper layers: NVCC ?type 20/21, 2, 8; NVGW types 45.3, 39; NVSC 55; buff ware types 59, 69/70; Horningsea. Date: 3rd century AD.
Fill: NVCC type 20/21, 2.5; Horningsea type 107/8. Date: 3rd century AD.

Small finds
1979   Glass fragment (SF 1024); potter's stamp on grey-ware base, Rigby cat. no. 2 (SF 1031); iron knife, Jackson cat. no. 21 (SF 1054); samian stamp, Dickinson cat. no. 48 (SF 1059); lead lump, Jackson cat. no. 40 (SF 695).
1980   Samian stamp, Dickinson cat. no. 75 (SF 943); iron ?punch, Jackson cat. no. 14 (SF 1011).
2022   Iron hobnailed shoe, Jackson cat. no. 40 (SF 1081).

Pit 1986 (DWF)   E46.4, N26.95

A ?sub-rectangular pit, part of the cluster west of centre, block 9; possibly a westward extension of pit complex 2022.

Width *c.* 1.25 m, length at least 2.0 m.

Fill
1964 (DVH)   Dark grey silt with gravel.
1986 (DWF)   Dark grey silt with a little gravel.

Dating evidence   Nothing datable.

Small finds
1964   Bone needle, Greep cat. no. 51a.
1986   Bone pin fragment (SF 1000).

Pit 1987 (DWG)   E47.5, N28.0   Phase III/IV

A small rhomboid pit; cuts the intercutting pit complex 2022 within the cluster west of centre, block 9.

Width 0.85 m, length 1.3 m.

Fill
1964 (DVH)   Dark grey silt with gravel.
1987 (DWG)   Dark grey silt with redeposited clay.

Dating evidence   Nothing datable.

Well 2020 (DXQ)   E48.25, N30.65   Phase III

An ovoid, steep-sided pit; part of the cluster west of centre, block 9. The erosion cone extends only 10–20 cm below the top edge. Clipped by pit 2021.

Width 1.2 m, length 2.0 m, depth 1.4 m.

Fill
1965 (DVI)   Dark grey/black silt with gravel, some stone and charcoal flecks.
1977 (DVW)   Dark grey silt with gravel.
1980 (DVZ)   Dark grey/black silt.
2006 (DXB)   Dark grey/black silt with some gravel and charcoal and burnt clay flecks.
2020 (DXQ)   Dark grey/black silt with gravel and charcoal and burnt clay flecks, and a lens of ash/charcoal.

2088 (EAM)   Red burnt clay.

2089 (EAN)   Black peaty silt with charcoal.

2090 (EAO)   Mixed black and grey silt with a little sand and gravel.

2102 (EBB)   Mixed grey and yellow sandy silt.

Dating evidence
Top layer: NVGW type 45.3; buff ware types 69/70, 73.
Upper fill (1977–2006): NVCC types 1.2, 3.2, 3/4, 4, 7, 8, 20–24, 25/26; NVGW type ?44; NVSC type 55; buff ware types 69/70, 73/74.
Lower fill (2020–2102): NVCC types 20–24, 25/26; NVGW types 45, 49/50; NVSC type ?68. Date: late 2nd–3rd century AD.

Small finds
1980   See pit 2022 above.
2006   Samian stamp, Dickinson cat. no. 57 (SF 1058).
2020   Iron object, Jackson cat. no. 60 (SF 1066); limestone tessera, Jackson cat. no. 52 (SF 1075).

Pit 2021 (DXR)/2110 (EBK)
E50.1, N30.3   (Fig. 41d, p. 99)   Phase III/IV

A large sub-rectangular pit, part of the cluster west of centre, block 9. Cuts pit 2022 and clips edge of pit 2020. Excavated in two parts with an intervening baulk.

Width 2.35 m, length 2.5 m, depth 1.05 m.

Fill
1965 (DVI)   See pit 2020 above.
1977 (DVW)   See pit 2020 above.
1980 (DVZ)   See pit 2020 above.
2006 (DXB)   See pit 2020 above.
2021 (DXR)/2110 (EBK)   Dark grey-black silt with gravel, charcoal and burnt clay flecks.
2028 (DXZ)/2117 (EBR)   Mixed grey/brown silts beneath a sterile layer of redeposited natural clay.
2047 (DYT)/2161 (EDN)   Light grey-green silt with some yellow clay, iron-pan staining and gravel.
2048 (DYV)/2163 (EDP)/2164 (EDQ)   Mixed grey sandy silt with orange sand, gravel, and some burnt material.

Dating evidence
Upper layers: NVCC types 20/21, 2, 8; NVGW types 45.3, beaker cf. type 39; NVSC type 55; buff ware type 59, 69/70; Horningsea. Date: 3rd century AD.
Fill: Horningsea throughout including type 107/8; NVCC types 20/21, 25/26, 3, 3.2, 7, 8, 2.6, 2.5; NVGW types 44, 45. Date: 3rd century AD.

Small finds
1980   See pit 2022 above.
2006   See pit 2020 above.
2110   Samian stamp, Dickinson cat. no. 11 (SF 1151).
2028   Samian stamp, Dickinson cat. no. 97 (SF 1071); coin, Shotter cat. no. 20, dupondius, VW, AD 103–17 (SF 1076); iron finger-ring, Johns cat. no. 1, 1st–2nd century AD (SF 1070).
2163   Samian stamp, Dickinson cat. no. 98 (SF 1126).

Pit 2014 (DXK)   E50.0, N31.85   (Fig. 41d, p. 99)   Phase III

A sub-rectangular pit, adjacent to pit 2021/2110, part of the cluster west of centre, block 9. Sealed by the redeposited clay layer 2005.

Width 1.0 m, length 1.45 m, depth 0.65 m.

Fill   Grey-green silt with some gravel.

Dating evidence   NVSC 51/52; buff ware type 74. Date: later 2nd century AD.

Small finds   Brooch, Mackreth cat. no. 1, Colchester, mid-1st century AD (SF 1127).

This pit cuts no other pits or linear features and is sealed by the layer 2005. It is likely to have been one of the earliest pits in block 9 and was probably dug for the disposal of refuse from the wooden building (R12) to its east.

Pit 1633 (DFN)   E50.8, N34.0   Phase III

A rectangular pit, in the north-west quadrant of block 9. Part-sectioned only.

Width 1.75 m, length *c*. 2.0 m.

Fill
1633 (DFN)   Dark grey silt with much gravel and some charcoal flecks.
2011 (DXG)   Dark grey silt with much gravel and some charcoal and burnt clay flecks.

Dating evidence   NVCC type 3; buff ware type 69/70, 74; NV mortarium. Date: late 2nd century AD.

Small finds   2011 Glass vessel fragment, Price cat. no. 15 (SF 1089).

Pit 1638 (DFS)   E51.15, N36.5   Phase III

A small, regular rectangular pit (?latrine) in the north-west quadrant of block 9. Its vertical sides have only a slight erosion cone in the top 20–30 cm. In form and dimensions similar to ?latrine pits 1535, 1536, 1542 and 1563.

Width 0.85 m, length 1.0 m, depth 1.08 m.

Fill
1638 (DFS)   Dark grey silt with much charcoal.
1738 (DKX)   Mixed yellow, green and grey-brown silts with clods of apparently redeposited natural.
1739 (DKY)   Dark grey silt with gravel and some charcoal flecks.

Dating evidence   NVCC types 2, 3; NVGW types, 27, 28; buff ware type 74; NVSC type 68. Date: late 2nd–early 3rd century AD.

Small finds
1638   Bone pin, Greep cat. no. 9a (SF 806).
1739   Bone pin fragment, Greep cat. no. 27 (SF 886).

Positioning, form and dimensions suggest this is a latrine.

Well 1625 (DFE)
E48.2, N36.25   (Fig. 38d, p. 96)   Phase III

A large, circular, steep-sided pit in the north-west quadrant of block 9. Half-sectioned only. Adjacent to, but not cutting, unit 1692 of gully 33 (cut 2).

Diameter 3.1 m, depth 1.6 m.

Fill
1625 (DFE)   Dark grey silt with some stone fragments, crushed tile and charcoal flecks.

1724 (DKH) Mixture of grey-green silt and fine gravel with some clods of redeposited natural yellow clay and gravel.

1733 (DKR) Grey silt with much charcoal, some crushed tile and gravel, mixed with many lumps of redeposited natural yellow clay and silt.

1826 (DOO) Dark grey silt with much clay, some charcoal flecks and burnt clay.

1833 (DOW) Grey silt with much clay.

Dating evidence Sherds of NVCC 20/21 in all layers. Date: 3rd/4th century AD.

Fill (may be residual) NVCC types 3, 2, 6; NVSC types 52, 55; buff ware types 69/70, 74. Date: late 2nd/early 3rd century.

Pit 1635 (DFP) E45.85, N41.15 Phase III

An irregular rhomboid pit at the north-west corner of block 9. Part-sectioned only. Cuts units 1716, 1718 of gully 70.

Width 1.1 m, length *c*. 2.2 m (at least 1.3 m), depth 0.5 m.

Fill

1635 (DFP) Dark grey silt with gravel, much charcoal and some crushed tile.

1719 (DKC) Grey silt with sparse gravel and a little charcoal.

Dating evidence NVCC type 3.2; NVGW type 45; buff ware type 69/70. Date: late 2nd/early 3rd century AD.

In form, dimensions and fill, very similar to pit J3, block 10.

Pit 1725 (DKI) E42.2, N37.6 Phase III/IV

An irregular ovoid pit at the north-west corner of block 9. Cuts gully 31 in an unexcavated section north of cut 3 (unit 1661). Encroaches on street 1 N/S.

Width 1.7 m, length 2.1 m, depth 0.87 m.

Fill Dark grey silt with much gravel.

Dating evidence NVCC type 2.6, 3, 4; NV mortarium type 68; Horningsea type 107/8. Date: mid/late 3rd century AD.

Small finds Bone needle, Greep cat. no. 40 (SF 803); bone pin, Greep cat. no. 28 (SF 917).

Pit 1906 (DRX) E42.1, 27.6 Phase III, later

A small pit, of uncertain form, centre west side, block 9. Part-excavated only. Sealed by layer 1883; apparently cuts unit 1894 of gully 29 (cut 2).

Width at least 0.5 m, length at least 0.9 m.

Fill

1883 (DQY) Dark grey silt with much gravel.

1906 (DRX) Dark grey-green silt with some gravel and a few charcoal flecks.

Dating evidence Nothing datable. [1883: late 2nd/early 3rd century AD.]

Small finds 1883 Glass vessel fragment, Price cat. no. 55f (SF 1001).

Pit 1907 (DRY) E43.5, N27.55 Phase III, later

A small ovoid pit, centre west side block 9. Part-sectioned only. Sealed by layer 1883; cuts unit 1894 of gully 29 (cut 2).

Width at least 0.7 m, length 1.45 m.

Fill

1883 (DQY) See pit 1906 above.

1907 (DRY) Mixed grey silt with orange sand, some clay and gravel, and iron-pan staining.

Dating evidence Late 2nd/early 3rd century AD.

Small finds 1883 See pit 1906 above.

GULLIES

Gully 24: north branch

[See also block 8, p. 190] Phase III

A streetside gully, with sloping sides and flat bottom. It is aligned approximately north–south at the interface of block 9 and street 2 N/S. Neither end was proven, and the gully appears to have been discontinuous. It was located in block 10 (feature J9). The relationship with gully 29 could not be established.

Width 0.6–0.9 m, depth 0.2–0.25 m.

Fill

Cut 1 2167 (EDT) Dark grey silt with much gravel.

Cut 2 2165 (EDR) As cut 1.

Cut 3 1703 (DIL) As cut 1.

Cut 4 1640 (DFV) As cut 1.

Cut 5 2115 (EBP) As cut 1.

 2119 (EBT) As cut 1, with much iron-pan staining.

Cut 6 G13, layer 1. Mixed brown gravelly silt.

Dating evidence [See also gully 24: south branch, p. 190] NVCC types 2.6, 20/21; grey beaker cf. type 39. Date: 3rd century AD.

Small finds

2165 Glass vessel fragment, Price cat. no. 12f (SF 1130).

2115 Glass vessel fragment, Price cat. no. 64ae (SF 1121).

Gully 30 Phase III

A discontinuous enclosure gully, with sloping sides and a flat or gently rounded bottom. It is aligned approximately north–south along the west edge of blocks 9 and 10, and east–west along the south edge of block 9, immediately inside the streetside gully 31. Two causeways between butted terminals on the west side provide access to the north and south units of block 9. Each of these causeways lies approximately opposite the causeways leading into blocks 3 and 4. Unit 1845 (cut 11) is cut by pit 1994 and unit 1889 (cut 12) is cut by pit 1975. East of this point gully 30 is entirely cut away by a pit complex. It does not appear east of this complex and may have terminated there or merged with the streetside gully 31.

Width 0.5–1.2 m. Length: E–W at least 4.6 m; N–S *c*. 46 m. Depth 0.15–0.4 m. Width of causeways: north 1.05 m; south 3.05 m.

Fill

Cut 1 M5, layer 1. Dark grey-brown silt with gravel. [Unexcavated.]

Cut 2 M1, layer 1. Dark grey silt with gravel. [Unexcavated.]

Cut 3   1701 (DII) Mixed grey silts with much crushed tile and charcoal flecks.

Cut 4   1734 (DKS) Dark grey silt with gravel.

Cut 5   1660 (DGQ) As cut 4.

Cut 6   1883 (DQY) As cut 4.

1893 (DRI) Dark grey silt with gravel and charcoal flecks.

Cut 7   2166 (EDS) As cut 4.

Cut 8   1869 (DQI) Grey-brown sandy silt with gravel and charcoal flecks.

1870 (DQK) Light grey clayey silt with gravel.

Cut 9   1991 (DWL) As cut 4.

1992 (DWM) As cut 4.

Cut 10   1991 (DWL) As cut 4.

1993 (DWN) Mixed grey, brown and yellow silts.

Cut 11   1845 (DPI) Grey silt with fine gravel and iron-pan staining.

Cut 12   1889 (DRE) As cut 4.

Dating evidence

West branch

Cut 3   NVCC type 4. Date: mid/late 3rd century AD.

Cut 4   NVCC type 25/26; NVGW type 47; buff ware type 74. Date: 3rd century AD.

Cut 5   NVCC types 3.2, 20/21; Horningsea. Date: 3rd century AD.

Cut 6   NVCC type 7/8. Date: early 3rd century AD.

Cut 7   NVCC type ?20/21; NVGW type 45; buff ware type 69. Date: 3rd century AD.

Cut 8   NVCC types 2.7. 25/26; buff ware type 57; Horningsea. Date: early 3rd century AD.

Cut 9   NVGW type 44. Date: late 2nd/early 3rd century AD.

Cut 10   NVGW. Date: AD 125 or later.

South branch

Cut 12   NVCC type 2. Date: late 2nd century AD.

Small finds

1701   Colander sherd (SF 1158).

1734   Samian stamp, Dickinson cat. no. 51 (SF 811).

1883   Glass vessel fragment, Price cat. no. 55f (SF 1001).

2166   Samian stamp, Dickinson cat. no. 108 (SF 1177).

1845   Coin, Shotter cat. no. 45, dupondius, MW, AD 161–80 (SF 846); bone pin, Greep cat. no. 13 (SF 855).

Gully 31   Phase III

A narrow streetside gully with steep sides and a flat bottom. It is aligned approximately north–south along the west edge of blocks 9 and 10 and east–west along the south edge of block 9, immediately outside the enclosure gully 30, and marking the limits of street 1 N/S and street 2 E/W. Its 'shadowing' of gully 30 extends to the provision of causeways in the same positions. Unit 1846 (cut 5) is cut by pit 1909; unit 1905 (cut 7) is cut by pit 1975; unit 1961 (cut 8) is cut by pits 1982 and 2003; and unit 1694 (cut 9) is cut by pit 1962. At this point gully 31 appears to have terminated.

Width 0.4–0.6 m. Length: E–W *c.* 17.5 m; N–S *c.* 51 m. Depth *c.* 0.35 m.

Fill

Cut 1   M9, layer 1. Dark grey silt with gravel. [Unexcavated.]

Cut 2   M7, layer 1. Dark grey silt with gravel and mortar flecks. [Unexcavated.]

Cut 3   1661 (DGR) Dark grey silt with gravel.

Cut 4   1871 (DQL) Mixed grey silt and orange sand with gravel and stones.

Cut 5   1846 (DPK) Grey silt with gravel and iron-pan staining.

Cut 6   1872 (DQM) Grey-brown silt with gravel and iron-pan staining.

Cut 7   1905 (DRW) Grey silt with burnt clay flecks.

Cut 8   1961 (DVE) As cut 3.

Cut 9   1694 (DIB) Dark grey silt with charcoal flecks and crushed tile fragments.

Dating evidence

West branch NVCC type 2; NVGW. Date: late 2nd century AD.

South branch NVCC type 20/21; NVGW types 28, 29. Date: late 2nd/3rd century AD.

Small finds

1905   Glass vessel fragments, Price cat. no. 55c (SF 861).

1961   Samian stamp, Dickinson cat. no. 109 (SF 1178); glass vessel fragments. Price cat. no. 59f (SF 929); iron knife, Jackson cat. no. 22 (SF 928).

Gully 29   Phase III

An L-shaped enclosure gully of rather variable width, depth and profile. Its south branch is aligned approximately east–west and divides block 9 into two slightly unequal parts. Its east branch follows, and lies just within, the north part of gully 24, at the interface of block 9 and street 2 N/S. The south branch lies opposite the south branch of the block 3 enclosure gully (gully 35). It shows evidence of recutting, and the primary gully, identified at the east end as unit 1830 (cut 8, cut by 1712), appears to have joined gully 35 across the line of street 1 N/S. At the east end, unit 1712 of gully 29 turns northwards at the point where it meets the streetside gully 24. However unit 1830, the primary gully, continues its rather sinuous route across the line of street 2 N/S to join gully 34. Units 1988 (cut 3) and 2070 (cut 4) are cut by the pit complex pits 1987, 2071 etc.

Width 0.55–1.35 m. Length: south branch at least 27 m; east branch *c.* 11 m. Depth 0.1–0.15 m.

Fill

Cut 1   1995 (DWP) Mixed grey and yellow silts.

Cut 2   1894 (DRK) Dark grey silt with gravel and charcoal flecks.

Cut 3   1988 (DWH) Mixed grey, brown and yellow silts with gravel.

Cut 4   2070 (DZS) Light grey silt with clay and gravel.

Cut 5   1898 (DRO) Dark grey-brown silt with iron-pan staining.

Cut 6   1981 (DWA) Dark grey silt with gravel.

Cut 7   1713 (DIW) Trowelling over 1723.

1723 (DKG) As cut 2.

Cut 8   1712 (DIV) As cut 2.

1830 (DOS) Grey-green silt with gravel.

Cut 9   1712 (DIV) As cut 2.

Cut 10   1709 (DIR) As cut 2.

Cut 11   2165 (EDR) As cut 6.

Cut 12   2167 (EDT) As cut 6.

Dating evidence

NVCC types 4, 20, 40; NVGW types 45, 45.3, 39, 47; Horningsea type 107/8. Date: 3rd century AD.

Primary gully (cut 8, unit 1830): NVCC type 3; NVSC type 65. Date: late 2nd/early 3rd century

Small finds

1894 Milling stone fragments, Jackson cat. no. 10 (SF 912).

1898 Iron object, Jackson cat. no. 28 (SF 902).

1981 Glass vessel fragments, Price cat. no. 18 (SF 1060).

1712 Glass vessel fragment, Price cat. no. 63c (SF 793).

1709 Coin, Shotter cat. no. 51, denarius, LW, AD 226 (SF 780); coin, Shotter cat. no. 48, denarius, MW, AD 193–8 (SF 782).

2165 Glass vessel fragment, Price cat. no. 12f (SF 1130).

Gully 34   Phase III

A rather irregular east–west gully which cuts across the line of street 2 N/S and links with gully 29. To the east of street 2 N/S it passed outside the area of excavation. The poor preservation of the street surface prevented the establishment of the precise relationship between gully and street.

Width 0.65–0.9 m, length at least 7 m.

Fill

Cut 1 1649 (DGE) Dark grey silt with dense gravel.

Cut 2 1911 (DSC) As cut 1.

Dating evidence NVCC types 3.2, 3.3; NVGW type 44; buff ware type 74; Horningsea type 107/8. Date: late 2nd/early 3rd century AD.

Small finds

1649 Iron object (SF 1013); samian stamp, Dickinson cat. no. 120 (SF 1027).

1911 Bone (?)gaming piece, Greep cat. no. 65 (SF 935); iron binding, Jackson cat. no. 59 (SF 934).

Gully 33   Phase III

A very shallow gully, with gently sloping sides aligned approximately east–west across the north part of block 9. The west end terminates at gully 30 and appears (from surface indications) to have been cut by gully 70. The east end terminates at gully 29. There is a 'causeway' beyond the south–east corner of building R10, and in front of that building the north edge of gully 33 is more markedly eroded than elsewhere.

Width 0.5–1.2 m, length 21.4 m, depth 0.1–0.18 m.

Fill

Cut 1 1624 (DFD) Dark grey-green silt. [Unexcavated.]

Cut 2 1692 (DHZ) Dark grey silt with stone and tile fragments and flecks of charcoal.

Cut 3 1708 (DIQ) Dark grey silt with much gravel.

Cut 4 1705 (DIN) Dark grey silt with gravel, charcoal flecks and tile fragments.

Cut 5 1730 (DKO) Mixed dark grey silt and yellow clay with gravel, stone and daub.

Dating evidence NVCC types 2, 2.4; NVGW type 45. Date: late 2nd/early 3rd century AD.

Small finds

1708 Whetstone, Jackson cat.no. 40 (SF 1125).

1705 Glass fragment (SF 773).

1730 Copper-alloy needle, Jackson cat. no. 40 (SF 941).

Gully 32   Phase III

A shallow gully, with gently sloping sides aligned approximately east–west across the north part of block 9, just to the south of gully 33. It is clearly associated with building R12 to its south. It terminates at the west just before the pit complex, while at the east it butts up against gully 29. There is a causeway 2 m wide slightly to the west of centre.

Width 0.65–0.7 m, length 13.5 m, depth 0.14–0.20 m.

Fill

Cut 1 1637 (DFR) Dark grey silt with gravel and charcoal flecks.

Cut 2 1706 (DIO) As cut 1.

Cut 3 1717 (DKA)/1636 (DFQ) Dark grey/black sooty silt with gravel, much charcoal and some crushed tile.

Cut 4 1731 (DKP) As cut 3.

Dating evidence NVCC types 3, 3.2, 25/26, 2; NVGW types 45, 44, 28; NVSC types 57, 65; buff ware type 74; Horningsea. Date: early 3rd century AD.

Small finds

1637 Samian stamp, Dickinson cat. no. 59 (SF 894); glass fragment (SF 904).

1717 Iron ?latch lifter, Jackson cat. no. 48 (SF 791); bone pin fragment (SF 802).

1731 Iron ?spearhead, Jackson cat. no. 2 (SF 820).

Gully 70   Phase III

A steep-sided gully with flat bottom aligned approximately north–south in the north-west corner of block 9. From surface indications it seems to cut or join gully 33, though the apparent terminal expansion may be an intercutting pit. Further north, gully 70 is cut by pit 1635.

Width 0.65 m, length at least 6.5 m, depth 0.25 m.

Fill

Cut 1 1718 (DKB)/1716 (DIZ) Grey silt with a little gravel and few stones.

Cut 2 M2, layer 1. Dark grey silt with gravel and flecks of tile and charcoal. [Unexcavated.]

Dating evidence NVGW type ?45.3. Date: 3rd century AD.

Gully 72

A short slender gully or slot, aligned approximately north–south, on the east edge of the pit complex near the centre of block 9. Possibly a constructional feature rather than a gully, though its position and alignment appear to relate it to the interrupted east–west gully (32).

Width 0.3 m, length 1.8 m.

Fill 2069 (DZR) Grey silt with burnt clay and stone fragments.

Dating evidence Nothing datable.

Gully 27   [See also gully 25, block 8, p. 190]   Phase III

A narrow discontinuous streetside gully, recut and rather ill-defined in its north part, aligned approximately north–south on the east side of street 2 N/S opposite block 9. For the south branch, see gully 25, block 8.

Width 0.35–0.5 m, length *c*. 30 m.

Fill
Cut 1   1655 (DGL) Dark grey silt with gravel.
Cut 2   1827 (DOP)/1650 (DGF) Light grey ashy soil. [Recut section.]
        1828 (DOQ) Dark grey-green silt and gravel.
Cut 3   J11, layer 1 Grey-brown gravelly silt. [Unexcavated.]

Dating evidence (Combined with gully 25) NVCC types 3, 1.2, 2.3, 2.5; NVGW types 45, 46, 27; buff ware types 59, 74. Date: late 2nd/early 3rd century AD.

Small finds 1655 Bone object, Greep cat. no. 72 (SF 844).

Gully 28   Phase III/IV

A narrow streetside gully, aligned approximately north–south on the east side of street 2 N/S opposite the north part of block 9. It is on the same alignment as gully 27, but is offset a little to the west so that its south butt, which terminates at gully 34, overlaps with the north end of gully 27. It also encroaches a little on to the east side of street 2 N/S.

Width 0.3–0.6 m, length at least 13.7 m.

Fill 1639 (DFT) Dark grey silt with much gravel.

Dating evidence Nothing datable.

Gully 73   Phase IV?

A narrow gully, aligned approximately east–west, which crosses the line of street 2 N/S opposite the south arm of gully 29. In this respect it resembles gully 26 (block 8).

Width *c*. 0.4 m, length at least 4.3 m.

Fill 1654 (DGK) Dark grey silt with gravel. [Unexcavated.]

Dating evidence None.

BLOCK 10   (Fig. 57, p. 119)

A rectangular plot, about 29 × 25 m, north of block 9, bounded on the west by street 1 N/S, on the north by street 1 E/W, and on the east by street 2 N/S. The block was sampled only, in 1983 and 1984, by trenches J, M and N.

Structures None found.

Well J4.

Pits J1,1, J1,2, J3, J8, M6/M7/M8, M11, N2, 4, N12/N13, N14, N27.

Oven 10.

Gullies 77, 78.

The density of features within trenches M, N and J indicates an intensity of occupation similar to, or greater than, that revealed in block 9. This is hardly more than might have been predicted for a plot with a frontage on the main street

(1 E/W), though the adjacent block 2 preserved less structural evidence for Phase III activity than was anticipated.

WELL AND PITS

Pit J1   E49.6, N43.65   Phase IV

Two intercutting sub-rectangular pits, near the south-west corner of block 10. J1, 1 cuts J1, 2.

Width: 1) 1.25 m; 2) at least 0.6 m. Length: 1) at least 1.5 m; 2) *c*. 1.6 m. Depth: 1) 0.3 m; 2) 0.65 m.

Fill
J1,1 Dark grey-green silt with charcoal flecks, pebbles and occasional ragstone fragments.
J1,2 Mixed grey silt and yellow clay with patches of charcoal and burnt clay.

Dating evidence NVCC types 18, 20/21, 2.9, 11.2. Date: late 3rd/early 4th century AD.

Small finds
J1,1 Glass vessel fragments, Price cat. nos 47 and 63d (SF 577 and 578); iron chisel, Jackson cat. no. 11 (SF 590); NVCC barbotine-figured beaker, Johns cat. no. 6; graffito on samian vessel, Potter cat. no. 10 (SF 569).
J1,2 Glass vessel fragment, Price cat. no. 19 (SF 594); iron hobnailed shoe, Jackson cat. no. 37 (SF 595).

Pit J3   E51.85, N44.0   Phase III/IV

An irregular rhomboid pit near the south-west corner of block 10. Part-sectioned only.

Width 1.0 m, length at least 1.7 m, depth 0.93 m.

Fill Dark black-grey silt with a few pebbles and small stones, and flecks of charcoal and burnt clay.

Dating evidence NVCC types 4, 20/21; NVGW types 45.3, 45.4; Horningsea. Date: 3rd century AD.

Small finds Glass fragment (SF 602).

In form, dimensions and fill very similar to pit 1635, block 9.

Well J4   E54.25, N46.25   Phase III

A large ovoid pit with central circular shaft, in the south-west quadrant of block 10.

Width 2.3 m, length 2.8 m, diameter of shaft 0.9 m, depth 1.7 m.

Fill
J4,1 Black silt with charcoal and burnt clay flecks, and some pebbles and stones.
J4,2 Dark grey silt with charcoal flecks.
J4,3 Mixed grey silt with yellow clay lumps with much charcoal flecking.
J4,4 Part of J4,7.
J4,5 Grey silt and clay.
J4,6 Grey clay with charcoal flecking and burnt clay patches.
J4,7 and 4 Dark grey peaty silt with small gravel and charcoal.

Dating evidence (Fig. 170, nos 240–8, p. 469)
Upper layers (1–5): NVCC types 7.2, 20/21, 18; NVGW type 39;

NVSC type 55; Horningsea; buff ware type 74. Date: late 3rd/early 4th century AD.

Lower layers (6 & 7): NVCC types 7.2; NVGW type 30; buff ware types 69, 74; grey ware jar cf. type 34; Horningsea. Date: early 3rd century AD.

Small finds

J4, topsoil Bone pin fragment (SF 599).

J4,1 Glass vessel fragments, Price cat. nos 12, 12h, 26, 33 and 62b (SF 533–535 and 576); NVCC barbotine-figured sherds, Johns cat. nos 2 and 9; copper-alloy pin, Jackson cat. no. 11 (SF 542); NVGW pierced base, Jackson cat. no. 13 (SF 544); milling stone fragment, Jackson cat. no. 8 (SF 639).

J4,2 Glass vessel fragment, Price cat. no. 55b (SF 601); samian stamp, Dickinson cat. no. 43 (SF 587); lead object, Jackson cat. no. 24 (SF 581).

J4,3 Copper-alloy wire hook, Jackson cat. no. 83 (SF 585).

J4,5 Bone needle, Greep cat. no. 44 (SF 591); bone needle, Greep cat. no. 10 (SF 592); copper-alloy hairpin, Jackson cat. no. 5 (SF 603).

J4,4 (=7) Glass vessel fragment, Price cat. no. 59p (SF 611).

Pit J8 E62.0, N50.7

A sub-rectangular pit, in the south-east quadrant of block 10. Unexcavated. Only partly within the excavated area.

Width 1.4 m, length at least 1.6 m.

Fill Light grey-brown silt with stones.

Pits M6, M7, M8 E45.3, N53.5

A ?pit cluster in the south-west quadrant of block 10. Unexcavated.

Dimensions at least 6 m × 1.8 m.

Fill Dark grey silt with gravel, some stone, and flecks of charcoal, tile and mortar.

Pit M11 E45.6, N59.85

A ?sub-rectangular pit, centre west side block 10. Only the west side lies within trench M. Unexcavated.

Width 3.0 m, length at least 1.25 m.

Fill Dark grey silt with gravel, charcoal and burnt clay flecks, oyster shell and bone fragments.

Pit N2,4 E58.7, N45.1 Phase III

An ovoid pit in the south-east quadrant of block 10. Only partly within trench N. Cut by gully 78.

Width at least 0.6 m, length 1.25 m, depth 0.65 m.

Fill N2, 4 Grey silt.

Dating evidence Gully 78: 3rd century AD. Pit N2,4: ?late 2nd century AD.

Pits N12, N13, N14 E59.7, N57.8

A ?pit cluster, east of centre, block 10. Unexcavated.

Fill Grey-brown silt with gravel and patches of burnt clay.

Pit N27 E59.7, N70.2

A sub-circular pit, east of centre, north side block 10. Lies just to the south of street 1 E/W.

Diameter *c*. 2.3 m.

Fill Grey-green silt with patches of yellow silt.

OVEN

Oven 10 E59.5, N54.3 (Fig. 44, p. 105) Phase IV

Type 2. Length 2.0 m, width 0.7 m, depth 0.32 m.

North–south orientation, with flue at south.

A relatively well-preserved example which appeared to owe its survival to the fact that it was recessed more deeply into the ground than the other ovens. This preserved both the lower wall section and a thick deposit of collapsed superstructure.

N10,1 Upper fill: dark grey-brown silt with gravel.

N10,2 Upper fill: collapsed upper superstructure?. Yellow-brown clay.

N10,3 Lower fill: collapsed superstructure. Thick deposit of burnt red clay fragments.

N10,4 Burnt red clay oven lining, in situ. The springing of the vault of the twin-domed superstructure is preserved on the east side.

N10,5 Oven floor: flint nodules embedded in greenish-yellow clay comprised the floor of the chamber, while a single sub-rectangular tile floored the flue.

Finds N10,1 Coarse pottery, mid 2nd century AD on.

GULLIES

Gully 77 Phase III

A broad shallow gully, aligned approximately east–west on the south side of block 10. It lies, seemingly, parallel to gully 78 and, in their relationship to building R10, block 9, this pair of gullies may correspond to gullies 32 and 33. Gully 77 would appear not to run beyond J6 and certainly not beyond well J4.

Width 1.3 m, length unknown, depth 0.15 m.

Fill N3, layer 1 Grey-brown silt with gravel and flecks of tile and charcoal.

Dating evidence NVCC type 2.5. Date: late 2nd/early 3rd century AD.

Gully 78 Phase III

A broad shallow gully aligned approximately east–west on the south side of block 10, parallel to gully 77. It cuts a layer of redeposited clay (N2, layer 3 – cf. unit 2005, immediately to the south, which sealed the post-holes of building R10, block 9), which itself seals pit N2, layer 4.

Width 1.25 m, length unknown, depth *c.* 0.15 m.

Fill

N2, layer 1   Grey-brown silt, with tile and mortar flecks and much burnt clay.

N2, layer 2   Dark brown-grey silt with gravel and flecks of charcoal and burnt clay.

Dating evidence NVCC types 1, 2.6, 4, 20/21. NVGW. NVSC. Date: 3rd century AD.

Small finds N2,2 Bone hairpin, Greep cat. no. 7 (SF 770); bone gaming-counter, Greep cat. no. 54 (SF 1099).

BLOCK 11   (Figs 46, 48–9, pp. 108–11)

A narrow, sub-rectangular area, about 94 × 8.5 m, north of blocks 1 and 2, bounded on the south by street 1 E/W and on all other sides by the excavation edge.

Structures None found.

Pits 871, 1090, 1249.

Ditches 3–5, 10, 11.

PITS

Pit 871 (BGW)   E 24.5, N 75.5   Phase IV

Small shallow sub-rectangular pit in street 1 E/W.

Width 0.85 m, length at least 1.0 m.

Fill Brown silt and gravel.

Dating evidence NVCC flagon. 4th century AD.

Pit 1090 (CDT)   E 23.0, N 79.5 (Fig. 30a, p. 83)   Phase IV

?Oval pit, north of street 1 E/W; only part-excavated, and truncated by unit 1089 of post-medieval ditch 12 (cut 12).

Width/length at least 1.2 × 1.0 m; depth 0.83 m.

Fill Grey-green sandy earth with pebbles.

Dating evidence NVCC type 20/21. 3rd/4th century AD.

Pit 1249 (CLK)   E 16.85, N 75.9

An ovoid pit, towards the east end of block 11. Truncated by unit 1016 of ditch 13.

Width at least 0.7 m, length at least 0.8 m.

Fill Grey/orange silt.

Dating evidence One shell-gritted sherd.

DITCHES

Ditch 3   (Figs 25, 29c, 30a–b, 49, pp. 77, 82–3, 111)   Phase III

A sinuous ditch, aligned approximately east–west, at the east end of block 11. The west end was not ascertained, while the east section

continues beyond the limit of excavation. The cross-section is rather irregular and it is possible that more than one ditch is involved [cuts 1–3 and cuts 4–7]. Ditch 3 cuts gully 1 and ditch 2 and is cut by ditches 5, 6, 13 and 14.

Width 1.1–1.9 m, length at least 35 m, depth 0.7–0.9 m.

Fill

Cut 1   1059 (CCM)   Grey-green silt below yellow clay.
         1147 (CGD)   Yellow-green silt.
Cut 2   1148 (CGE)   Fine grey silty clay.
Cut 3   1248 (CLI)   Grey silt with gravel.
Cut 4   1142 (CFY)   As cut 1, 1147.
         1130 (CFL)   Reddish-brown gravelly silt.
         1131 (CFM)   Dark grey peaty soil with pebbles.
Cut 5   1072 (CDA)   Greenish-grey silt.
         1078 (CDG)   Greenish-brown silt with some large stones.
         1124 (CFE)   Brown pebbly silt.
         1138 (CFT)   Grey-green silt.
Cut 6   1265 (CMB)   Greenish-grey silt.
         1274 (CML)   Brown silt with much gravel and pebbles.
Cut 7   1081 (CDK)   Grey-brown silt.

Dating evidence

Cut 1   No datable material.
Cut 2   NVCC; Horningsea. Date: early 3rd century AD.
Cut 3   Horningsea. Date: early 3rd century AD.
Cut 4   No datable material.
Cut 5   NVCC types 20/21, 3; NVGW types 47, 39; gritty buff types 57, 69. Date: 3rd century AD.
Cut 6   NVCC types 20, 4, 7.2; NVGW types 45, 29, 28.2; buff ware type 74; Horningsea. Date: 3rd century AD.
Cut 7   NVCC type ?4. Date: 3rd century AD.

Small finds

1072 Bone pin, Greep cat. no. 5 (SF 476) [joins SF 466 from unit 1012 of ditch 13, which cuts ditch 3 via ditch 14]; samian stamp, Dickinson cat. no. 85 (SF 484); glass vessel fragment, Price cat. no. 10 (SF 477).

1265 'Hod Hill' brooch fragment, Mackreth cat. no. 16a (SF 531).

1274 Iron ladle, Jackson cat. no. 26 (SF 547); rubbing stone, Jackson cat. no. 32 (SF 568).

Ditch 4   (Figs 25, 31b–c, 48–9, pp. 77, 84, 110–11)   Phase III

A broad, deep, V-sectioned ditch with basal slot, which flanks the north side of street 1 E/W in block 11. The west end continues beyond the limit of excavation, and was located again in trenches D, E and F. [D9, E2, F8, all unexcavated.] Near the centre of block 11 the ditch kinks northwards, and its east end appears to turn south-east to link with ditch 6 or ditch 9 via ditch 5. Ditch 4 is cut by ditch 12.

Width 2.2–2.8 m. Length at least 65 m within main excavation; at least 150 m including trenches. Depth 1.2–1.6 m.

Fill

Cut 1   1177 (CHK)   Fine brown peaty silt.
         1215 (CIZ)   Fine grey silt.
         1208 (CIR)   Orange/grey sandy silt. Slump.
         1209 (CIS)   Grey/red clayey silt. Slump.

1218 (CKC) Grey silt with a little gravel.

1210 (CIT) Orange/grey sandy silt with a few pebbles.

1339 (CPD) Fine grey silt. Waterlogged.

Cut 2 1151 (CGH) Mixed grey silts with blackish sandy peat and a few pebbles.

1160 (CGR) Orange/grey sandy silt with gravel and with large ragstone debris.

1163 (CGV) Fine orange silt with a little gravel. Slump.

Cut 3 1179 (CHM) Black-brown silt with many pebbles.

1212 (CIW) Dark red-brown silt with a little gravel.

1242 (CLC) Mixed fine grey and orange silts.

Cut 4 1088 (CDR) Brown gravely peat.

1141 (CFX) Brown/yellow silt with much gravel.

1153 (CGK) Dark grey silt.

1220 (CKE) Grey/yellow silty clay with a little gravel and pebbles. Waterlogged.

Cut 5 1216 (CKA) Red-stained grey silt with much gravel and pebbles.

1241 (CLB) Red-stained (iron-pan) light grey gravelly silt.

1244 (CLE) Dark grey charcoal-rich silt. Waterlogged.

1246 (CLG) Fine grey silt with a little gravel and pebbles. Waterlogged.

Cut 6 1243 (CLD) Grey-green sandy silt with a few pebbles and larger stones.

1291 (CND) Grey clay.

1245 (CLF) Grey-brown pebbly silt, with occasional lumps of yellow clay. Waterlogged.

Cut 7 1156 (CGN) Mixed grey silt and brown peat.

1171 (CHD) Grey silt with small grits and flecked with shell. Waterlogged.

1178 (CHL) Orange sand. Slump.

Cut 8 1217 (CKB) Compact dark grey-black clay with cluster of oyster shells.

Cut 9 1405 (CRX) Yellow clay. Slump.

1385 (CRB) Dark grey-brown silt with many pebbles.

1417 (CSK) Mixed silt and gravel.

Dating evidence

Cut 1 NVCC, NVGW. Date: AD 125 or later.

Cut 2 NVGW types 42, 58; Horningsea. Date: early 3rd century AD.

Cut 3 NVCC types 2. 5, 3; Date: late 2nd century AD.

Cut 4 NVCC type 3. 2; gritty buff type 74; Horningsea. Date: early 3rd century AD.

Cut 5 Upper layer (1216): NVCC type 4. Date: mid/late 3rd century AD.

Rest: NVCC type 2; buff ware type 69. Date: late 2nd century AD.

Cut 6 NVCC type 4; NVGW types 46, 47, Date: mid 3rd century AD.

Cut 7 Grey jar cf. type 27. Date: late 2nd century AD.

Cut 8 NVCC type 3; NVGW type 44; NVSC type 69. Date: late 2nd/early 3rd century AD.

Cut 9 NVCC types 20/21, ?18. Date: 3rd or 4th century AD.

Small finds

1177 Rubbing stone, Jackson cat. no. 30 (SF 554).

1220 Glass vessel fragment, Price cat. no. 60a (SF 528).

1216 Glass bead, Price cat. no. 73 (SF 492).

Ditch 5 (Figs 25, 29d, 49, pp. 77, 82, 111) Phase III

A steep-sided ditch of V-section with a slight basal slot. It linked the east–west aligned roadside ditch 4 with the north–south aligned 'boundary' ditch 9 by crossing the line of street 1 E/W. Before becoming fully silted, ditch 5 was backfilled with gravel identical to that of the metalled surface of street 1 E/W. As a consequence ditch 9 formed a north butt at the south side of the road, while ditch 4 was extended eastwards via ditch 10 to link with ditch 6. In a subsequent reorganisation of the drainage system ditches 4 and 9 were reunited by the cutting of ditch 11 through the upper fill of ditch 5.

Width 1.4–1.8 m, length 9.5 m, depth 1.6 m.

Fill

Cut 1 1205 (CIO) Gravel in a yellow-green sandy matrix. Backfill.

1224 (CKI) Grey silt with gravel.

Cut 2 1300 CNN) Orange gravel. Backfill.

1386 (CRC) Grey silt with much gravel and pebbles. Waterlogged.

Dating evidence

Cut 1 1205 NVCC type 3; NVGW type 28; Horningsea. Date: early 3rd century AD.

Cut 2 1386 NVCC; NVGW. Date: AD 125 or later.

Ditch 11 (Figs 25, 29d, 31a, 49, pp. 77, 82, 84, 111) Phase IV(?)

A narrow ditch with near-vertical sides and a flat base cut into the upper fill of ditch 5. Its cross-section is suggestive of a wood-lined box drain, though no trace of wood remained.

Width 0.8/0.9 m, length 7.5 m, depth 0.7 m.

Fill

Cut 1 1057 (CCK) Gravel in light grey silt matrix.

Cut 2 1018 (CAT) As cut 1, 1057.

Cut 3 1085 (CDO) Gravel in brown silt matrix.

Cut 4 1043 (CBV) As cut 3, 1085.

Dating evidence NVCC type 3; NVGW. Date: mid/late 3rd century AD.

Small finds 1085 Stone roof tile fragment, Jackson cat. no. 55 (SF 481); samian stamp, Dickinson cat. no. 100 (SF 512).

Ditch 10 (Figs 25, 49, pp. 77, 111) Phase IV(?)

A broad V-sectioned ditch at the east end of block 11, which appeared to be the east extension of ditch 4. It was largely truncated and cut away by later ditches (ditches 12 and 13), and its east end could not be located. Very little undisturbed fill remained intact.

Width c. 2.8 m (by projection), length at least 9.0 m.

Fill

Cut 1 1337 (CPB) Grey-brown silt with pebbles and large ragstone lumps.

1340 (CPE) Grey clayey silt with a few pebbles.

Cut 2 1297 (CNK) Black clayey silt with gravel and much large ragstone debris.

1338 (CPC) Mixed yellow/grey silty clay.

Dating evidence NVGW. Date: AD 125 or later.

BUILDING R15: THE TEMPLE
(Fig. 19, p. 62; Figs 72–5)

1 Description

On 4 July 1984 the Grange site, planted with barley, was overflown in the early evening sunlight. One of several cropmarks observed and photographed was an approximately circular ditched enclosure, some 50–60 m in diameter, located near to the ballast pits *c*. 200 m north-east of the main excavation area. A linear feature leading to the circular crop-mark from the direction of the main site was also discerned on aerial photographs. In order to investigate these features, which appeared to be associated with the main Roman complex, a number of trenches (trenches O, P, Q, T) were cut by machine during the 1984 season of excavation.

The linear feature was confirmed as a street in trenches T and P. Like the other streets of the Phase III settlement it had a gravel metalling. In trench T(T10) its alignment was approximately north–south, its orange gravel metalling, about 4.5 m wide, preserved a slight camber, and on its west there was a roadside gully (T8). In trench P the alignment was several degrees further north–east signifying a gradual or abrupt change of angle somewhere along the intervening route. The gravel metalling (P2, P15, P16), though rather disturbed, appeared to preserve a slight camber and survived to a width of *c*. 3 m (Fig. 73).

Due to the imprecision in plotting an oblique aerial photograph and to the narrow confines of the machine-cut trenches it proved impossible to identify unequivocally the circular feature. However, sections of a ditch (ditch 83) were revealed approximately on the line of its predicted course at the south-west (O49) and at the north-east (O86). That it was a temenos ditch seems very probable, given the character of the sequence of structures found within it (Fig. 19, p. 62; Fig. 72).

The earliest structural remains comprised a row of five post-holes (Q26–Q30), about 25 cm in diameter and about 1.3 m apart, aligned a few degrees clockwise of east–west (Figs 73–4). They were located in the base of a narrow sondage taken down to subsoil through the subsequent make up (layers Q23; Q5). It is probable that the row continued beyond the limits of excavation, both to the east and to the west, and also that north–south components would have been located had there been sufficient time and resources to reduce the whole area to subsoil level. Only the very base of the post-holes survived, (about 2–3 cm) filled with grey-green silt, and they yielded no datable finds.

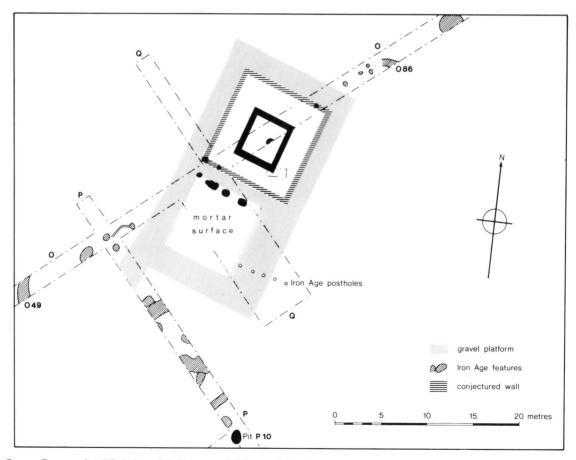

Fig. 72 Stonea Grange: simplified plan of the Romano-Celtic temple (building R15) and the adjacent features in trenches O, P and Q.

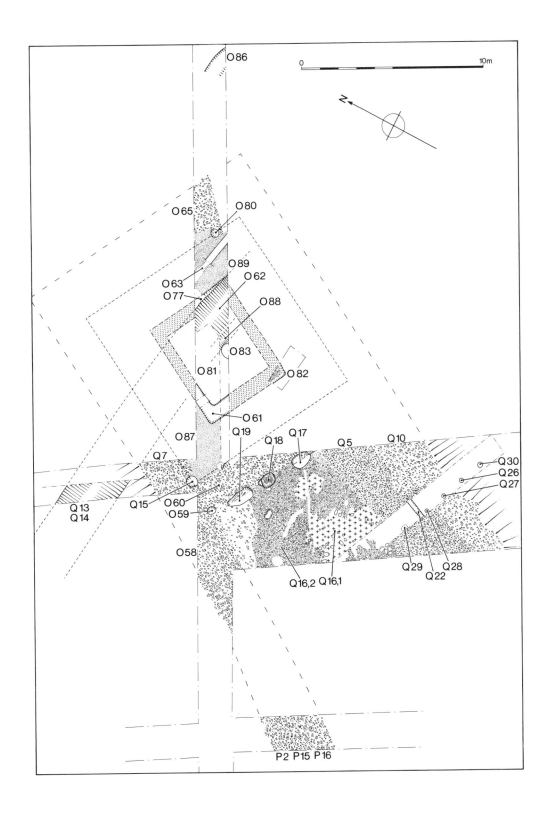

Fig. 73 Stonea Grange: plan of the temple (building R15). For key, see Fig. 45, p. 107.

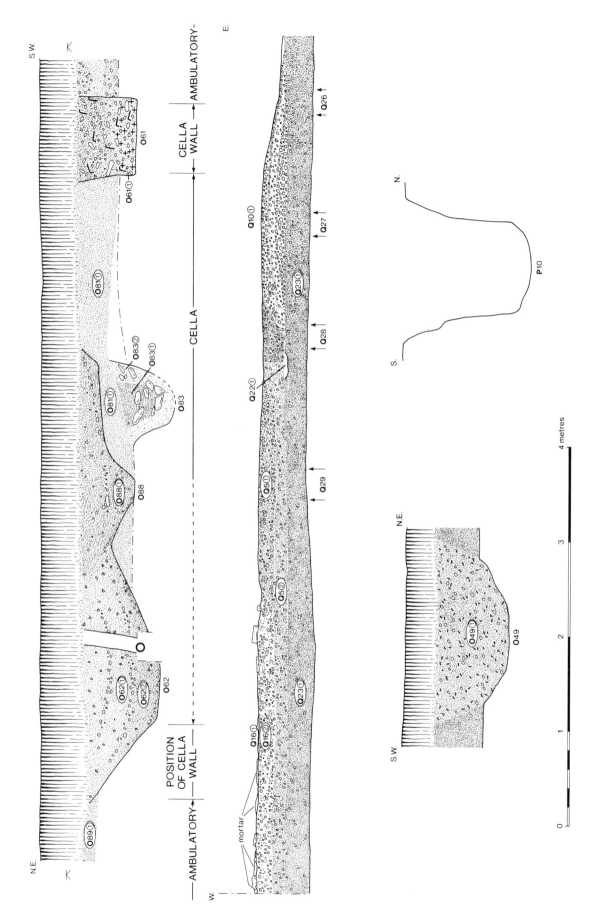

Fig. 74 Stonea Grange: sections, of the temple (building R15) and associated features (ditch 83, cut 1, and pit P10). For key, see Fig. 29, p. 82.

The post-holes were detected on removal of layer Q23 which either sealed them or through which they were cut: like other units of the black silt that sealed truncated cut features containing Iron Age pottery, Q23 did not disclose any features within it (Fig 74). The finds from Q23 were dominated by pottery of Middle/Late Iron Age date but also included two sherds from a Dr 27 samian cup of Flavian date and a copper-alloy brooch fragment (brooch no. 21a, p. 306). A period of build-up in Phase II, spanning several centuries up to the first century AD, seems likely.

Cut into the upper part of Q23 was a narrow, shallow slot of rectangular cross-section, about 27 cm wide and 3 cm deep (Q22), probably the seating for a sill beam (Figs 73–4). A short section only was exposed, but interestingly, although it was set at a right angle to the earliest post alignment, it retained the same orientation, implying a continuity of structures. Unfortunately it contained no datable finds.

The slot lay beneath a layer of gravel (Q5), part of an apparently rectangular hardstanding or platform (4.25–4.35 m AOD) connected to the similarly metalled surface of the approach road P2/P16, and on the same alignment (Figs 73–4). The dimensions of this hardstanding were approximately 27 m by 16 m, divided into two roughly equal parts, a south-east and a north-west unit. The south-east unit, which incorporated pottery of late second–third century AD date in its make-up, sealed the sequence of structures just described. It was itself sealed and partially cut by a mortar surface (Q16,1) and its sand and gravel foundations (Q16,2). Although badly fragmented and scored by modern agricultural equipment, sufficient of the mortar surface remained to suggest an original rectangular shape, about 7 m by at least 8 m (4.34 m AOD), and set a little to the west of centre of the gravel standing (though this asymmetry may be a result of more severe erosion of the south-east side). The coarse pottery gave a probable early third century AD date, and the other finds included a copper-alloy ligula (no. 46, p. 342) and two objects looted by illicit metal detectorists.

Along the north edge was a row of four post-holes, the three easternmost (Q17–Q19) having more substantial post pits than that on the north-west (O59). There seems little doubt that the row would have continued to the south-east beyond the edge of excavation (Figs 73, 75). No post-holes were found along the west and east edges of Q16, and the south edge lay outside the area of excavation. Although a very shallow linear hollowing along the east edge was originally thought of as a possible foundation line, it was very tenuous, was not observed on the west and was in marked contrast to the substantial nature of the north post-line. There is, thus, no direct evidence for walls around the mortar surface Q16, which is rather to be regarded as an open area than a roofed building. The post-holes on the north side would appear, therefore, to relate to the structure within the north-west unit of the gravel standing.

This rectangular structure (building R15) was aligned about 20° clockwise of the cardinal points, its longer axis approximating to NNE–SSW. (For ease of description in the following account, however, components of the structure are referred to by their closest major compass point – north side, south-west corner etc.) The inner component was a rectangular room measuring externally 5.6 × 5.0 m with stone walls 0.5–0.6 m wide at sub-ground level, set in a foundation trench 0.6–0.8 m wide. The measurements of both wall and footing trench are approximate in places due to the comprehensive stone robbing that had occurred. Trench O, designed to test the circular crop mark feature, diagonally bisected, almost exactly, building R15 (Figs 72–3). The robbed-out south-west corner footing of the central room (O61) was the first part of the complex to be identified, soon to be followed by the less well preserved north-east corner (O77). Trenches P and Q were cut to broaden the area of excavation, while a small trench was positioned to locate the south-east corner of the room (O82) and establish its width.

The floor makeup of the central room (O81) comprised a layer of light grey, stone-free silt, some 30 cm thick (Fig. 74), containing late second–third century AD pottery and residual Iron Age sherds. Over half the floor area was cut away by ditch 84 (unit O62). The sole surviving feature within the room was a small pit (O83) which was set almost centrally and was sealed beneath the floor makeup (Figs 73–4). Only part of the pit lay within the excavated area, but enough to indicate that it was of circular or ovoid shape, about 85 cm wide and about 70 cm deep. The primary fill, possibly packing for a post, consisted of limestone rubble in a yellow silt matrix. The secondary fill, perhaps a post pipe, comprised grey-brown silt. Neither the form of the pit nor its contents permitted a certain identification of its function, and the sparse finds, which included Roman and pre-Roman sherds, were insufficient to provide a close date.

To judge from the rubble debris remaining in the robbed footing trenches, the walls of the central room were made of limestone from the same source as that used to construct building R1. At the south-west corner the footing trench O61 measured 90 cm wide (80 cm at the base) and 65 cm deep (below the base of modern ploughsoil; 3.65 m AOD) and was filled with grey-brown silt, much gravel and small fragments of tile and limestone, with a mortary matrix in the lower part (Fig. 74). At the north the footing trench O77 was almost entirely cut away by ditch 84 (unit O62) but a partial section was preserved in the excavation edge (Fig. 73). Its profile was identical to that of O61 and its base was 75 cm below that of the modern ploughsoil. It contained limestone debris, in a greater concentration than O61, in a yellow mortar and gravel matrix. No datable finds were discovered in any of the sampled sections of the footing trench.

Outside the wall trenches of the central room was a zone of stone-free grey-brown silt about 2.5 m wide and about 15–30 cm thick, sampled at the south-west (O87) and north-east (O89) (Fig. 74). It yielded no datable finds, but its character was very similar to the floor make-up of the central room, with which it was, presumably, contemporary. At the south-west it was observed to cut the gravel hard-standing O60. Both at the north-east and south-west, post-holes were discerned at the interface of the gravel and silt surfaces, and they appear to mark a timber wall-line enclosing the central room in an almost square area with sides about 10.5–11 m. (Fig. 73). At the north-east, post-hole O80, 40 cm in diameter and 20 cm deep, was filled with orange-grey gravelly silt. At the south-west, post-hole Q15, 45 cm in diameter and 15 cm deep, had a fill of greyish silt with gravel. About 1.75 m to its east was another post-hole of similar dimensions and fill. No more post-holes along the silt–gravel interface were located, but, assuming a standard spacing of about 1.75 m, no others would have fallen within the excavated area.

Fig. 75 Stonea Grange: schematic plan of the temple (building R15). The light tone shows restored features.

At this interval the sides would have accommodated seven evenly-spaced posts (Fig. 75). However, the south side, evidently the main frontage, was treated differently. There, the line of post-holes already referred to (p. 217, O59 and Q17–Q19) formed a second wall-line approximately 1.75 m to the south. O59 was a near-circular post-hole about 50 cm in diameter and at least 30 cm, deep, filled with dark grey-brown silt. Q17–Q19 were sub-rectangular or ovoid post-holes 1–1.5 m in length and 48–60 cm deep, filled with dark grey-brown silt and limestone packing. Q19 had two post-pipes, and all three were associated with smaller post-holes on the same line implying post-replacement. Q17 contained second–third century AD coarse wares and Q18 Antonine samian. The two westernmost post-holes, O59 and Q19, were paired with the two to their north, and it seems probable that the two walls shared a common layout. Thus, the greater spacing between Q19 and Q18 – about 2.5 m – was presumably adopted, too, by the posts to its north. In this way there would have been an approximately axial entrance through both wall-lines, with three posts on either side (Figs 73, 75).

2 Discussion

Although poorly preserved and only partially sampled, the remains of building R15 and its associated features are clearly those of a Romano-Celtic temple within a precinct. The dimensions and general layout – a rectangular cella within a square ambulatory – are in conformity with other examples.

The walls of the modest-sized rectangular cella (5.6 × 5.0 m) were either of stone or a combination of stone and timber. Too little remained to indicate either the appearance of the elevation or the treatment of the walls. No facings survived and it is possible that the masonry component was mortared rubble, perhaps with rendered surfaces, but, as revealed by building R1, stone-robbing is likely to have been very thorough, and inscribed slabs and faced blocks, the choicest pieces, will have been quickly and scrupulously collected as soon as the building went out of use. Similarly, there are sufficient tile fragments to indicate that the roof may have been tiled but insufficient to prove that it was.

As at a number of other temples there is a pit within the cella, though it is devoid of any finds bearing on its function or date. The ambulatory, about 2.5 m wide, had timber walls 10.5–11 m in length. The entrance was on the south side via a timber portico, about 2.5 m wide, which ran the full width of the building. South of this was a forecourt area surfaced with mortar, originally, perhaps, covered with paving, though a scatter of finds on the mortar surface tends to suggest otherwise. The whole complex was constructed on a prepared rectangular gravel emplacement or hard-standing, about 27 × 16 m, at the south-west corner of which the approach road terminated.

The temenos ditch, if correctly identified, appears to have enclosed a roughly circular area somewhat over 50 m in diameter, with the temple positioned off-centre to the north. The size of the temenos is, therefore, modest and the shape unusual, though neither feature is without parallel, while the apparently eccentric positioning of the temple within its enclosure is a common feature of Romano-Celtic temples. Like building R1 the temple occupies a slightly elevated position, the surface of the forecourt (4.34 m AOD) being about a metre higher than the general level of the main site. However, the determining factor in its choice of site was probably the existence of an earlier temple or shrine, of which the post-holes sealed beneath the forecourt are likely to have been a part.

The date of the earlier structure is lacking in precision: it produced no datable finds and, though identified beneath the silt layer Q23, which yielded Flavian samian and Middle/Late Iron Age pottery, was not unequivocally earlier than that layer. For the main structural phase the dating evidence, though still limited, is more plentiful. It is also consistent and provides a coherent sequence. The precinct hard-standing sealed units of the black silt including Q23 and O79 which both contained sherds of Flavian samian, a significant component in view of the extreme rarity of Flavian samian on the main site (see p. 409). The hard-standing itself incorporated coarse-ware sherds of late second–third century AD date, as did the cella floor make-up, while the portico post-holes Q17 and Q18 contained Antonine samian and late second–mid third century AD coarse wares; the temenos ditch O49 yielded Antonine samian and second century AD coarse wares; the approach road P15 incorporated in its metalling sherds of Hadrianic and Hadrianic/Antonine samian and late second century AD coarse wares; and the early fill of pit P10 (layer 2) contained late second century AD sherds. These features were all broadly contemporaneous and suggest a date of construction and period of usage of the temple complex of mid second–early third century AD.

Final use contexts yielding datable material were restricted to the forecourt floor (Q16) and debris upon it (Q11) and, almost certainly, the uppermost fill of pit P10 (layer 1). The early third century AD date which is indicated by the coarse-ware and samian assemblages from those deposits echoes the sequence for building R1 on the main site. No datable finds were retrieved from the admittedly limited excavations of the debris filling the robbed cella wall footings, but the fill of ditch 84, unit O62, which cut the robber-trench, incorporated pottery of third century AD date which tends to confirm an early third century disuse of the building.

Within the temenos beyond the limits of the hardstanding no feature could be demonstrated to belong unequivocally to the temple complex (e.g. ditch 85). However, pit P10, by its proximity and character, was almost certainly associated with the temple or an attendant building. Its form (Fig. 74),

a deep, near-vertical-sided shaft (base 2.45 m AOD) was different from that of most other pits on the main site, while its fill and finds assemblage also differed to that of other pits. The pit top was not located until the amorphous black silt layer had been removed, but the true mouth almost certainly lay somewhat higher within that layer.

The primary fill, P10,2, which occupied the basal 40 cm, was unexceptional. The finds comprised a modest coarse pottery assemblage of late second century AD date together with a few fragments of window and vessel glass. In contrast, the upper fill (P10,1), about 1 m deep, yielded an astonishing range of finds. Most prominent was a large group of complete and semi-complete samian vessels (see Pl. XXI and no. 13; and p. 421ff. nos 3, 37, 55, 58, 65, 67, 77, 81, 93, 95) which, projecting from the upper layer, first disclosed the ill-defined pit top. They comprise, mainly, vessels with little or moderate wear which would still have been serviceable at the time of deposition, and they were evidently discarded as a single act rather than over a prolonged period. The manufacture date falls consistently within the later second century AD, pointing to a date of deposition in the early third century which is in accord with the coarse pottery assemblage (p. 470, nos 249–71). This includes amphorae, jars, bowls, dishes, flagons and some fine colour-coated beakers. Completing the ceramic assemblage are fragments of a pipeclay figurine depicting a horse (p. 486, no. 2). As terracotta figurines were primarily religious objects, and the horse type was often associated with the goddess Epona, it may be inferred that the figurine derived from a building within the temple complex if not from the temple itself. The remainder of the finds consisted of iron objects (pp. 362 and 368, nos 13 and 56), fragments of window and vessel glass, a bone point (p. 532, no. 55), animal bones, oyster and mussel shells, fragments of daub and floor tile and a quantity of tesserae (p. 523, no. 51). The latter, coarse limestone cubes, imply the presence nearby of a mosaic, probably either a plain tesselated floor or a more ornate mosaic with coarse border (e.g. Hinks 1933, 116-17, Fig. 130, two panels from a fourth century villa mosaic at Abbots Ann, Hants).

The P10 assemblage is, thus, striking but a little enigmatic. Its dating parallels that of the main structural phase of the temple complex, with a period of usage in the later second and early third century AD and a final deposition of early third century date. The latter event mirrors the 'closure' deposit in ditch 9 on the main site, which accompanied the demise of building R1 and signalled the ending of Phase III. If, as seems probable, this involved the withdrawal of an official administration from Stonea then the similarity between the two closure deposits may be more than a coincidence. The apparent disuse of the temple at the same time certainly suggests a direct connection, and it may be that the person or personnel involved in the running of the temple belonged to the outgoing official corp. In view of the temple closure it is perhaps not too fanciful to imagine that the P10,1 pit group comprised a selection of sacred objects chosen for ritual burial – cult objects and vessels and a token part of the structure, tesserae from the temple floor – similar to the votives and temple clearance groups in pits or *bothroi* in other parts of the ancient world.

In addition to the excavated finds a number of objects in the Stonea Grange Surface Collection which have votive connotations may have derived from the temple complex. It is regrettable, therefore, that the metal detectorist did not localise the provenance of his finds within the Stonea Grange Farm area. The two copper-alloy model axes (p. 350, nos 101, 102) are a common votive type, while the copper-alloy cockerel finial (p. 350, no. 100) paralleled at the Uley temple site, might suggest the worship of Mercury. That the cult was not monotheistic, however, is implied by the pipeclay equine figurine from pit P10 which hints at Epona, as too, perhaps, does the head of a small copper-alloy animal figurine (p. 350, no. 99), and by several objects relating to Minerva. These include three certain and two probable copper-alloy busts of the goddess (p. 350, nos 95–8, and Wisbech Museum: C. M. Johns in Potter 1981, 101–4, Fig. 10,2), as well as a tiny gold votive plaque inscribed with a dedication to Minerva (C. M. Johns and M. W. C. Hassall in Potter 1981, 101–4, Fig. 10, 1–2).

Data

1 Phases II and II/III

	Coarse pottery date
Post-line Q26–Q30	–
Silt makeup Q23	Middle/Late Iron Age pottery; Flavian samian
?Sill beam slot Q22	–
Ditch 85 P5	Late 2nd–3rd cent

2 Phases III and III/IV

Cella: wall, SW corner O61	–
wall, N side O77	–
wall, SE corner O82	–
floor, make-up O81	Late 2nd–3rd cent; Iron Age pottery
central pit/post-hole O83	Roman and pre-Roman sherds
Ambulatory: wall posts, SW corner Q15; no number	–
wall posts, NE corner O80	–
floor, SW corner O87	–
floor, NE corner O89	–
Portico: wall-posts O59: Q17–Q19	Late 2nd–mid 3rd cent; Antonine samian
Forecourt: debris Q11	Mid 2nd cent on; Antonine samian
flooring Q16	?Early 3rd cent
Precinct: hard-standing W Q7	–
hard-standing SW O57; O58; O60	–
hard-standing S Q5	–
hard-standing SE Q10	Late 2nd–3rd cent
hard-standing N O65	
Approach road: P2; P15; P16; T10	?Late 2nd cent; Hadrianic and Hadrianic/Antonine samian

Temenos: ditch 83, SW O49	2nd cent and pre-Roman; Antonine samian
ditch NE O86	–
?votive pit/shaft P10	Late 2nd–3rd cent

3 Phase IV

Cella: robbed footings O61; O77; O82	–
Ditch 84: O62; O88; Q13; Q14	3rd cent
Gully/footing trench: O63	–

Ditch 85   Phase II/III

A broad U-sectioned ditch, aligned approximately SW–NE, immediately east of the temple approach road in trench P.

Width 1.35 m, length unknown, depth 0.45 m.

Fill P5, layer 1 Dark grey-brown silt with patches of burning and tile fragments.

Dating evidence
Upper fill: NVCC types 2.5; NVGW type 45. Date: late 2nd–3rd century AD.
Lower fill: nothing datable.

Ditch 83   (Figs 72, 74)   Phases II–III

Putative 'temenos ditch' (the curving ditch seen on aerial photographs), a lightly-curved, broad U-sectioned ditch in trench O, sectioned either side of the temple complex. Cuts ?ditch O50, 1 and the 'buried soil'.

Width 1.25–1.5 m, diameter (from APs) *c.* 50–60 m, depth *c.* 0.75 m.

Fill
Cut 1 O49, layer 1 Dark grey silt with gravel and flecks of charcoal and burnt clay.
Cut 2 O86, layer 1 Grey-brown silt with gravel.

Dating evidence Seventeen pre-Roman sherds; NVGW. Date: mid 2nd century AD on.

Pit P10   (Figs 72, 74)   Phase III

A deep ovoid pit, lying to the east of the temple complex, but probably just within the temenos ditch (ditch 83). The pit top was ill-defined and was located by the large quantity of pottery in the upper fill, but it soon resolved itself into an ovoid, near-vertical-sided shaft.

Width 1.1 m, length 1.4 m, depth 1.4 m.

Fill
P10,1 Dark grey-brown silt with gravel.
P10,2 Dark grey clay

Dating evidence (Figs 170–1, pp. 469-71) NVCC types 2.7, 5; NGVW types 29, 42; NVSC types 62/63, 52; buff ware types 69, 74; Horningsea. Date: early 3rd century AD.

Small finds
P10,1 Pipeclay figurine fragments, Johns cat. no. 2 (SF 1157); samian stamps, Dickinson cat. nos 3, 37, 55, 58, 65, 67, 77, 81, 93, 95 (SF 753 and 758–66); 15 limestone tesserae, Jackson cat. no. 51 (SF 1105); bone point, Greep cat. no. 55 (SF 756); iron objects, Jackson cat. nos 13 and 56 (SF 768 and 752); glass vessel fragment (SF 754): bronze-stained bone fragment (SF 755).
P10,2 Flint flake (SF 767); glass vessel fragment (SF 1100).

Ditch 84 (Figs 73–4) Phase IV

A wide U-sectioned ditch with a flat base, aligned approximately east–west, in trenches O and Q. Cuts the cella wall (O77,1, and O61,1) of the temple.

Width *c*. 2.5–3.0 m, length unknown, depth *c*. 0.8–1.1 m.

Fill

Cut 1 O62, layer 1 Grey-brown silt with gravel and stone.
        O62, layer 2 Dark grey silt with gravel.
Cut 2 Q13, layer 1 As cut 1, O62, 2.
        Q13, layer 2 Dark grey-brown silt with gravel.
        Q14, layer 1 As cut 1, O62, 2.
Cut 3 O88, layer 1 As cut 1, O62, 1.

Dating evidence

Cut 1 O62, 1. NVGW type 47. Date: 3rd century AD.
Cut 2 All layers. 98 sherds pre-Roman. Undatable Roman sherds.
Cut 3 Nothing datable.

Small finds O62,1 Bone point. Greep cat. no. 57 (SF 1103).

Matrix

```
        O62                        3rd cent
         |
       O61; O77
          └─ Q11
               |
              Q16          P10,1    Early 3rd
               |                    cent
P15—O87; O89—O81—Q10—Q17—Q19; P10,2  Late 2nd
         etc.      O59             – early
                                    3rd cent
O49; O86       O83       Q22
 |                        |
 |              O79—Q23             1st–early
 |                 |                2nd cent
 |                 |
 |              Q26—Q30
```

MICROMORPHOLOGY OF THE BURIED SOIL IN TRENCH P   Charles French

Introduction

A layer of buried soil, approximately 20 cm thick, was found preserved beneath about 80 cm of silt alluvium in trench P, 22 m south-west of the centre of the temple (building R15). The profile has developed on sand and gravel deposits of the March Gravels, which form the fen 'islands' of Stonea and adjacent March.

Three contiguous samples were taken for micromorphological analysis (after Bullock *et al* 1981; 1985) through the buried soil, at a point just to the north of the intersection of trenches P and O. Undisturbed buried soil contexts were not found elsewhere on the site due to the intensity of archaeological occupation, modern ploughing and thin overlying deposits.

Numerous sherds of local wheel-made coarse pottery of earlier Roman date were found throughout the buried soil. This suggests that the overlying silt was deposited at some time later than the Roman occupation of the Stonea Grange site.

This buried soil will be described in sequence from top to bottom, samples 1, 2 and 3 respectively.

Descriptions

Sample 1: c. 1–6 cm

Structure Weakly developed sub-angular blocky; intrapedal crumb/granular, 60/40, unaccomodated, random/clustered. **Porosity** 30%; mainly intrapedal channels (50%), fine (50 μm), to medium (200 μm), short to elongate (1–9 mm), moderately serrate; and vughs (50%), sub-round to irregular, smooth to weakly serrate, 50–200 μm; random. **Mineral components** Limit 50 μm; coarse/fine ratio: 60/40. *Coarse fraction* Very fine (10%), fine (25%) and medium (25%), sub-rounded to sub-angular quartz, moderately well sorted. *Fine fraction* Mainly silt (35%) with some clay (5%); reddish brown (PPL), yellowish brown (RL); very slightly speckled. **Organic components** About 25% organic matter; mainly amorphous organic matter in the fine fabric and abundant fine flecks of charcoal, 25–100 μm, throughout groundmass, with a few plant tissues, 50–100 μm. *Groundmass* Undifferentiated b-fabric; porphyric; low birefringence, weakly speckled. *Pedofeatures*: *Excrements* Many pellets (*c*. 50–100 μm) in channels, containing organic matter and fine flecks of charcoal, brown. *Crystalline* Few aggregates of calcitic crystals, 25–50 μm. *Fabric* Zones (*c*. 100–300 μm) within fine fabric of calcitic crystals, very fine sand and numerous fine flecks of charcoal. *Amorphous* Few (<2%) rounded sesquioxide nodules, 50–100 μm; amorphous sesquioxidic impregnation of some of fine fabric; few rounded clay with organic matter aggregates, 50–100 μm, in the fine fabric.

Sample 2: c. 8–14 cm

Structure Similar to sample 1. **Porosity** 40%; mainly intrapedal channels (40%), fine (50 μm) to medium (200 μm), short to elongate (0.5–8 mm), moderately serrate; and vughs (60%), sub-round to irregular, smooth to weakly serrate, 50–200 μm; random. **Mineral components** Limit 50 um; coarse/fine ratio: 70/30. *Coarse fraction* Very fine (10%), fine (30%) and medium (30%), sub-rounded to sub-angular quartz, moderately well sorted. *Fine fraction* (a) Mainly silt (20%) with some clay (10%); golden brown (PPL), yellowish brown (RL); very slightly speckled; (b) abundant calcitic crystals with very fine sand and silt; golden brown with greyish white speckles (PPL), light yellowish grey brown (RL); speckled; up to 70% of groundmass. **Organic components** In fine fabric (a) 20% amorphous organic matter and abundant fine flecks of charcoal, 50–200 μm; in fine fabric (b) many fine flecks of charcoal, 25–50 μm; few large fragments of charcoal, 1–3 mm; occasional plant tissue fragment. *Groundmass* (a) Undifferentiated b-fabric; porphyric; low to moderate birefringence; weakly speckled. *Pedofeatures*: *Excrements* abundant pellets (*c*. 50–100 μm) in channels and void space, containing organic matter and fine flecks of charcoal. *Crystalline* Abundant aggregates of and dis-aggregated calcitic crystals with fine flecks of charcoal (fine fabric (b)). *Textural* Few (<2%) non-laminated, dusty coatings of grains and fine fabric (a). *Fabric* See fine fraction (b) and crystalline pedofeatures (above). *Amorphous* Some (<5%) sesquioxide nodules, 50–100 μm; fine fabric (a) has some amorphous sesquioxide impregnation; some (<5%) rolled clay with organic matter aggregates, 50–100 μm, in fine fabric (a).

Sample 3: c. 14-20 cm

Structure Similar to samples 1 and 2. **Porosity** 30–45%; mainly intrapedal channels (50%), fine (50 μm) to medium (300 μm), short to elongate (0.5–14 mm), smooth to weakly serrate; and vughs (50%), sub-round to irregular, smooth to weakly serrate, 50–300 μm; random. **Mineral components** Limit 50 μm; coarse/fine fraction: 60/40. *Coarse fraction* Very fine (15%), fine (30%) and medium (15%), sub-angular to sub-rounded quartz, moderately well sorted. *Fine fraction* (a) and (b) similar to sample 2 (above). **Organic components** Similar to sample 2 (above). *Groundmass* Similar to sample 2 (above). *Pedofeatures*: *excrements* Abundant pellets (c. 50–100 μm) in channels and void spaces, containing organic matter and fine flecks of charcoal. *Crystalline* Abundant aggregates and dis-aggregated calcitic crystals with fine flecks of charcoal (in fine fabric (b)). *Textural* Few (<2%) non-laminated, dusty/dirty coatings of grains and fine fabric (a). *Fabric* See fine fraction (b) and crystalline pedofeatures (above). *Amorphous* Few (<1%) sesquioxide nodules, 50–100 μm; fine fabric (a) has some amorphous sesquioxide impregnation; some (2–5%) rolled clay with organic matter aggregates, 50–100 μm, in fine fabric (a); one fragment of bone, 2 × 5 mm; occasional phytoliths; few large fragments (1–5 cm) of pottery (observed in the field).

Interpretation

Thin section analysis of sample 1 suggests that this is upper A horizon material. It has a high organic matter content and is subject to intense biological activity as indicated by the abundant excrements of the soil fauna. The small amounts of wood ash, indicated by the small aggregates of calcitic crystals intermixed with amorphous organic matter and fine charcoal, are suggestive of some soil disturbance due to human occupation.

Thin section analysis of samples 2 and 3 indicate that the lower two-thirds of the buried soil is in fact midden material. The sample 1 material is possibly acting as a more mineral soil layer above the midden material. It is just possible that a thin layer of 'fresh, clean' soil was deliberately thrown over the midden accumulation.

In the field, large (up to 5 cm across) fragments of pottery were common. In thin section, there were large quantities of wood ash, both aggregated and disaggregated, with abundant very fine charcoal, occasional coarse fragments of charcoal, much amorphous organic matter, occasional fragments of bone and a few phytoliths. There is no doubt that this heterogeneous mixture of anthropogenically derived materials is indicative of midden material (R. Macphail, personal communication). Similar accumulations of midden material

have been observed in thin section from the Late Bronze Age site of Potterne, Wiltshire (Macphail, in preparation).

The intense biological activity in this midden material is indicated by the abundant excrements of the soil fauna. The large amounts of very fine charcoal as well as coarser charcoal fragments suggest that the agencies of incorporation and homogenisation were active both during and after the coarse material had been worked into the soil. The potentially high potash – or potassium (K) – content of the wood ash may have made the midden an unsuitable habitat for earthworms. Mites and enchytraeids may have been common amongst the soil mixing fauna. The presence of a few grass phytoliths in the midden material may possibly indicate some grass burning, or perhaps old thatch or 'chaff-type' material being incorporated in the midden.

Throughout samples 2 and 3 there is a minor but consistent presence of dusty, impure clay coatings. Their presence plus the large amounts of fine charcoal in the fine fabric are suggestive of some reworking of the soil, most probably due to human disturbance. The clay coatings also suggest that this midden material may have been occasionally influenced by freshwater flooding and the consequent deposition of fines (silt and clay).

All three samples contain some rolled fragments of clay in the fine fabric. They are suggestive of 'old' alluvium that has been well worked into the soil by the soil fauna. The sesquioxide impregnation of only some of the fine fabric also suggests that there has been slight gleying and some seasonal waterlogging, but it has not been very wet.

Conclusions

1 The buried soil is a disturbed A/B horizon profile developed on the sand and gravel subsoil of the March Gravels which form Stonea 'island'. The profile is preserved because of a considerable thickness of overlying silt alluvium.

2 The lower two-thirds of the buried soil was in fact largely composed of midden material. The incorporation and deposition of anthropogenic materials both into and on the soil formed a shallow midden deposit. As this midden was discovered in a test trench away from the main area of the Stonea Grange excavations, its exact relationship to the surrounding archaeology is unclear. It may be a dump of domestic refuse from the extensive Romano-British settlement, or it may possibly have had a functional relationship with possible activities being performed at the adjacent Romano-British temple site (building R15), about 5–10 m to the north-east.

3 There is only minor evidence of some pre-Roman alluvial influence of the soil of even the higher parts of the 'island'. Although the deposition of alluvium cannot be dated precisely at this site, it may have been associated with the

same event that deposited alluvial silts in the lower, north-eastern part of the excavated area, which seals Late Bronze Age features and through which Roman features were dug.

4 There is no direct evidence on site for the deposition of alluvial silts during the early/middle third century AD, such as occurred at other fen margin sites such as Fengate (Pryor 1980), Hockwold cum Wilton and Earith (Salway 1967; Churchill 1970). Nevertheless, the molluscan evidence from Stonea Grange (French, pp. 639–54) gives indications that the site was becoming increasingly damp and wet in the later second and early third centuries AD.

5 The overlying silt alluvium probably began to accumulate in late Saxon/early medieval times. As the water-table in the fen generally rose during these periods, peat began to encroach on many areas of higher ground. Peat growth made a considerable obstacle to freshwater movement, both on local and regional scales. The alluvial silt was probably deposited in the 'channel' created between two areas of 'higher' ground: Stonea 'island' to the north-west, and the upstanding silt/peat fen to the south-east. This type of sedimentary feature has been commonly observed by D. N. Hall (1987). Also, during this period the River Nene was deliberately diverted through the centre of March 'island' from its previous course, and the natural drainage of the adjacent fen was being rearranged (Hall 1987). This may well have had a local effect on the drainage pattern on the south-eastern edge of Stonea 'island'.

Acknowledgements

I would like to thank Dr R. I. Macphail of the Department of Human Environment, Institute of Archaeology, London.

PHASE V: THE ANGLO-SAXON SETTLEMENT

(Figs 48–9, pp. 110–11; Figs 76–9; Pls XIX–XX)

Within the period AD 400–650 a linear settlement comprising at least four buildings grew up along the line of the main Roman road (street 1 E/W).

BUILDING S1   (Figs 48, 76–7; Pl. XIXa)

This structure, excavated in 1981, lies north-west of the main Roman building complex (R1) on the gravel surface of street 1 E/W. It is aligned east–west, but this was an inevitable consequence of its location on the road and need signify nothing more than the choice of a solid, well-drained, slightly elevated site. Buildings S2 and S4, subject to the same constraint on the road further east, were similarly orientated.

While the overall lines of a rectangular building measuring some 7 × 4 m are tolerably clear, the exact plan is not. The multiplicity of post-holes, many of which show evidence of post replacements, demonstrate that there were at least two building phases. Unfortunately, the brown gravelly fill of the post-holes was very uniform and permitted no phase differentiation. From a comparison of post-hole depths various arrangements can be postulated (Welch, p. 234), though none with certainty, and the precise layout and building sequence remain perplexingly ill-understood. An arc of stake-holes in close proximity to the building, runs around its west end and north-west corner. Its relationship to the building indicates contemporaneity, but the function is not apparent. Further west, a thin irregular scatter of post-holes cut through the road probably belongs to this phase too. Two of these 'post-holes' (1257, 1258) are particularly intriguing for they contained a mass of iron nails.

Less certainty attaches to the date of the post-holes located to the south of building S1. Though some at least are likely to be Anglo-Saxon, their position, just off the road, leaves open the possibility that they belong to one of the Roman phases, especially as well 336 (Phase III) and ovens 1 and 2 (Phase IV) lie adjacent. Indeed four post-settings around the perimeter of well 336 would appear to have supported a timber well-head structure. Apart from these and several short alignments, the post-holes showed no semblance of order. Their identification, in any case, was made extremely difficult by the homogeneity of the mixed silty soil in this region.

Building S1 stood in some kind of compound, delineated by a series of gullies (gullies 57–62), which enclosed an apparently sub-rectangular area. None of the gullies was traced in its entirety: at best only the very base survived and in many places every vestige had been removed. Although this is partly the result of recent agricultural activity, it seems probable that the gullies were never of any great depth. As with the post-holes it was considerably more difficult to identify the gullies once they had run off the orange gravel metalling of the road. Despite a careful search on the east side no certain southern continuation of gullies 58 and 59 was found, and, taken together with the discontinuity of gullies 60/61 and 57/62, a break for an entrance at the centre of the east side seems certain. The south butt of gully 61 probably marks a second entrance at the south-east. The south side and much of the west side lay beyond the area of excavation. The north-west corner was located but, in common with other features in that area, including the road surface, it had been severely eroded by ploughing.

Like the post-holes of building S1, the configuration of the gullies indicates at least two phases of activity. Although the relationship between gullies 58 and 59 at their intersection could not be established beyond doubt, 58 appeared to be an extension of 59 and, with 57, must represent a modification, probably an enlargement, of the enclosed area.

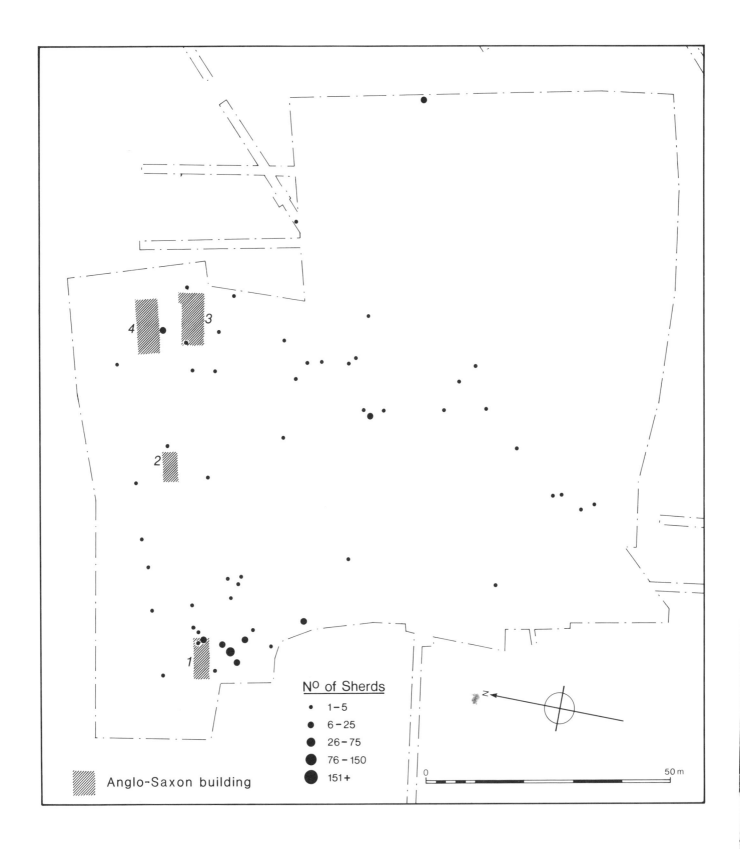

Fig. 76 Stonea Grange: distribution of Anglo-Saxon pottery and buildings (S1–S4).

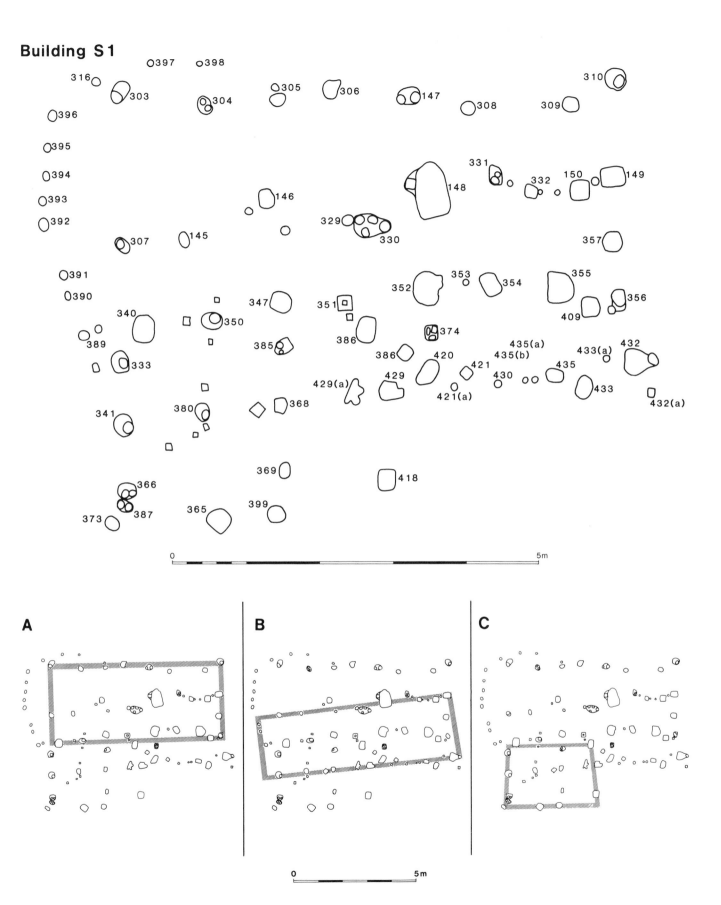

Fig. 77 Stonea Grange: plan of Anglo-Saxon building S1, with interpretative plans showing a scheme for the possible succession of structures (A–C).

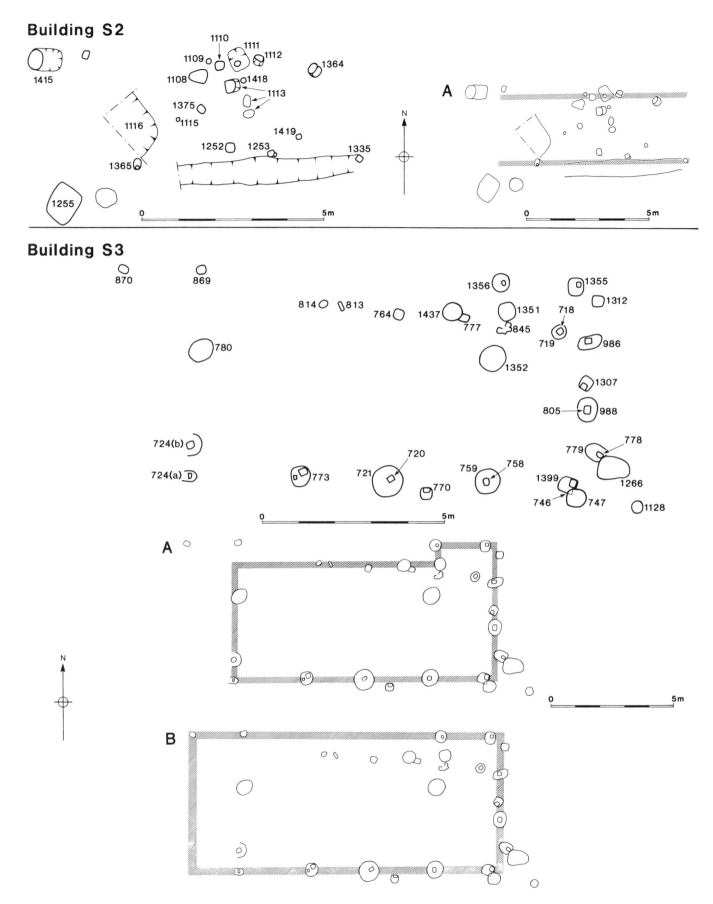

Fig. 78 Stonea Grange: plan of Anglo-Saxon buildings S2 and S3, with interpretative plans showing possible wall-lines, and, for S3, two alternative possible arrangements.

Building S4

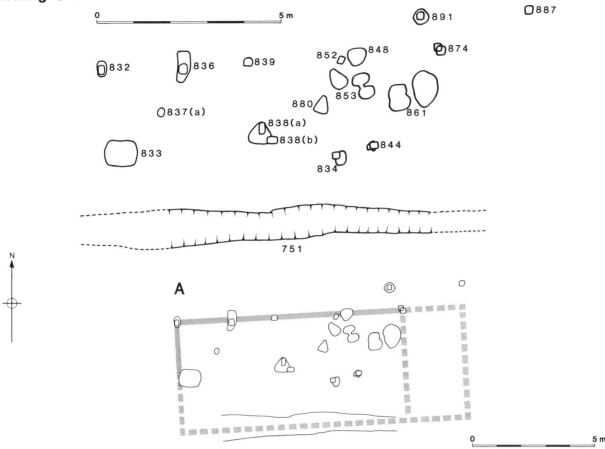

Fig. 79 Stonea Grange: plan of Anglo-Saxon building S4, with an interpretative plan showing a possible arrangement.

With so little of their structure surviving, the function of the gullies could not be established with certainty. The fill of 57–60 was a loose brown gravel and that of 61–2 a soft grey silt. Probably they were slots for anchoring a light wicker fence, but on a low-lying site like Stonea, and at a time when the region was relatively wet, a use as drainage slots cannot be discounted. In support of the first suggestion is the line of post-holes found on the south lip of the road (ditch 4, cut 2, unit 1151). Although gully 57 had disappeared at this point, these posts are on its projected line and presumably survived because they sank into the edge of the relatively soft ditch fill. Post-holes were not found on the lip of ditch 4, in any other of its excavated sections.

Building S1 occupied only the north-east quarter of the area enclosed by the gullies. The remaining space was presumably a yard area with, perhaps, a number of small wooden structures. Other than the post-holes already mentioned no further cut features of this phase were located

within the enclosure. However a spread of occupation debris (units 137, 279, 381) some 0.20 m deep at its thickest (Fig. 40e, p. 98), extended across most of the south-east quarter and through the east entrance. The presence of small pebbles at the base of this spread in the region of the entrance may be the remains of a cobbled surface, while traces of a thin mortary floor beneath the spread in the south-east quarter may represent the original yard surface. The spread extended almost to the centre of building S1, sealing the post-holes of its southern side. However there seems little doubt that it was contemporary with the building and that it originally covered a more restricted area. Probably it was a midden deposit that became dispersed by subsequent natural and human agencies, notably by the late Anglo-Saxon builders of post-hole structure 265/267/372 (see p. 233) and by recent agricultural activity. The latter has destroyed the surface of the north-west quarter and removed any deposits that once existed above the north side of building S1.

Data

Post-holes

E/W row 1		Width/ diameter (m)	Depth (m)	Comments/dating
310	pipe *a*	0.19	0.31	
	pipe *b*	0.10	0.15	Angled stake
309	pit(?)	0.25	0.13	
308	pipe	0.18	0.21	
147	pipe *a*	0.14	0.25	
	pipe *b*	0.11	0.31	
306	pipe	0.20	0.11	
305	pipe *a*	0.14	0.25	
	pipe *b*	0.11	0.19	
304	pipe *a*	0.09 +	0.44	
	pipe *b*	0.09 +	0.48	
303	pit	0.32	0.40	
	pipe	0.17	0.40	

E/W row 2				
149	pipe *a*	0.18	0.36	
	pipe *b*	0.13	0.37	
	stake	0.08	0.15	
150	pit(?)	0.31	0.35	Anglo-Saxon pottery
332	pipe	0.19	0.33	Poss. replacement
	stake(?)	0.05	0.07	
331	stake	0.08	0.21	
	pipe *a*	0.15	0.30	Poss. replacement
	pipe *b*	0.06	0.21	
148	pit	0.68 × 0.48	0.29	
	pipe	0.17	0.28	
330	pipe *a*	0.15	0.16	
	pipe *b*	0.14	0.33	
	pipe *c*	0.14	0.24	
	pipe *d*	0.14	0.24	
329	pipe	0.14	0.29	Poss. replacement
146	pipe	0.21	0.31	
145	pipe	0.13	0.20	
307	pipe	0.13	0.17	
	?pit/pipe *b*?	0.11 +	0.14	

E/W row 2/3				
357	pipe	0.27	0.32	

E/W row 3				
356	pipe *a*	0.17	0.26	
	pipe *b*	0.09	0.25	
409	pit(?)	0.30	Unrecorded	
355	pit	0.40	0.31	
354	pit(?)	0.33	0.35	Poss. 2 pipes
353	stake(?)	0.10	Unrecorded	
352	pit	0.40	0.30	
	pipe	0.18	0.31	
351	pit	0.25	0.36	
	pipe	0.12	0.36	
347	pit	0.32	0.32	
	pipe	0.14	0.36	
350	pit	0.30	0.15	
	pipe	0.19	0.33	
340	pit	0.50	0.16	
(= 144)	pipe(?)	0.25	0.21	

E/W row 3/4		Width/ diameter (m)	Depth (m)	Comments/dating
374	pipe *a*	0.18	0.26	
	pipe *b*	0.06	0.20	
386	pit	0.40	0.29	
385	pipe *a*	0.14	0.28	
	pipe *b*	0.08	0.27	
333	pit	0.30	0.20	
	pipe	0.14	0.20	

E/W row 4				
432	pit	0.33	0.15	
432a	pipe	0.11	0.14	
433a	pipe	0.09	0.15	
433	pit(?)	0.31	0.20 +	Not bottomed
435	pipe(?)	0.25	0.19	
435a	pipe	0.14	0.18	
435b	pipe	0.09	0.10	
430	pipe	0.18	0.30	Slightly angled
421	pipe	0.14	0.24	Angled
421a	pipe	0.13	0.18	
420	pit	0.42	0.29	
429	pit	0.32	0.29	
429a	pit	0.25	0.24	
368	pipe	0.18	0.25	
380	pipe	0.15	0.20	Anglo-Saxon pottery
341	pit	0.34	0.33	
(= 143)	pipe	0.15	0.33	

E/W row 4/5				
418	pit	0.47	0.23	
	pipe	0.18	0.23	
369	pipe	0.18	0.23	
366	pit?	0.20	0.14	
	pipe	0.08	0.24	
387	pipe	0.12	0.23	

E/W row 5				
399	pit(?)	0.28	0.23	
365	pit	0.41	0.25	
373	pipe	0.23	0.31	

N/S stake arc			
398	0.05	0.07	
397	0.06	0.10	
316	0.08	0.18	
		(0.42)	
396	0.10	0.23	
395	0.08	0.13	
394	0.10	0.21	
393	0.09	0.16	
392	0.12	0.24	
391	0.08	0.16	
390b	0.09	0.09	
389	0.14	0.26	
388	0.08	0.13	

POST-HOLES WITHIN/BETWEEN ENCLOSURE GULLIES, OF UNCERTAIN STRUCTURAL SIGNIFICANCE OR DATE

	Width/diameter (m)	Depth (m)	Comments/dating
440 pit(?)	0.27	0.25	
402 pit	0.40	0.26	
403 pit(?)	0.27	0.23	
441 pipe	0.25	0.40	
1414 pipe	0.22	0.15	
1292	0.40	0.09	
1293	0.40	0.20	
1257	0.33 × 0.43	0.20	Mass of iron nails at base
1258	0.33	0.20	Mass of iron nails at base
1411 pipe (= 1254)	0.18	0.15	
1412 pipe	0.15	0.19	
1413 pipe	0.15	0.18	

ENCLOSURE GULLIES (GULLIES 57–62)
(Figs 25, 48, pp. 77, 110)

Gully 57   Phase V

Outermost enclosure gully of building S1, cut into the surface of street 1 E/W, at the west end of block 11. It has a shallow U-shaped cross-section. A line of post-holes on the south lip of ditch 4 may have been cut within the line of gully 57, all trace of which had disappeared at this point. The west side is also completely truncated except for the north-west corner. On the east side gully 57 butts. Gully 62 may be the southern continuation.

Width 0.2–0.4 m, length E–W 25 m, depth 0.15–0.2 m.

Fill

Cut 1 252 (LY) Loose brown gravelly silt.
Cut 2 1363 (CQD) Grey gravelly silt.
Cut 3 1379 (CQV) As cut 1, 252.

Dating evidence Early Anglo-Saxon pottery in unit 252. AD 400–650.

Post-holes probably within gully 57

		Width/diameter (m)	Depth (m)
1149	post-pipe	0.20	0.16
115	post-pipe	0.16	0.14
1152a	post-pit	0.25 × 0.35	Unrecorded
1157	post-pipe	0.21	0.32
1157A	post-pipe	0.20	0.21

Gully 58   Phase V

An elliptical, shallow U-shaped, flat-bottomed gully at the north-east corner of the building S1 enclosure. It butts at the south. Its west end cuts gully 59, of which it seems to be an extension.

Width 0.35–0.55 m, length N–S 6 m, depth 0.15 m.

Fill 142 (GD) Loose brown gravelly silt.

Dating evidence Nothing datable.

Gully 59   Phase V

Enclosure gully, shallow U-sectioned, of building S1. East side and north-east corner only survive, both ends incomplete. Cut by gully 58.

Width 0.3–0.45 m, length N–S 7 m, depth 0.15 m.

Fill 141 (GC) Loose brown gravelly fill.

Dating evidence Nothing datable.

Gully 60   Phase V

Innermost enclosure gully, shallow, U-sectioned, flat-bottomed, of building S1. A substantial part of both east and north sides survives. Their alignment is very close to that of gully 57. Both the south and west ends are incomplete. Gully 61 may be the southern extension of the east side of gully 60. There is a gap of c 0.8–1.7 m between gully 60 and the north and east walls of building S1. The function of the 'expansion' of gully 60, opposite the east end of the building is unknown.

Width 0.15–0.6 m. Length: E–W 10 m; N–S 6.5 m. Depth 0.1 m.

Fill 140 (GB) Loose brown gravelly silt. Beyond expansion, grey silt.

Dating evidence Nothing datable.

Gully 61   Phase V

A small, narrow, elliptical U-sectioned gully, in the north-west corner of block 1. It is incomplete at its north end but the south end forms a butt. The date, form, position and alignment of the gully suggest it is part of the enclosure gully complex of building S1, probably an extension of the innermost gully 60.

Width 0.25–0.35 m, length 5 m, depth 0.1 m.

Fill 251 (LX) Grey silt.

Dating evidence Early Anglo-Saxon pottery, AD 400–650.

Gully 62   Phase V

A small narrow steep-sided gully in the north-west corner of block 1. The south end is incomplete; the north end butts opposite the butt of the outermost enclosure gully (57) of building S1. If gully 62 is an extension of gully 57, an 'entrance' of 3.2 m would be provided to the enclosure. However, the alignment of gully 62 does not assist this explanation.

Width 0.2–0.3 m, length 3.25 m, depth 0.25 m.

Fill 257 (MD) Dark silt.

Dating evidence Early Anglo-Saxon pottery, AD 400–650.

Small finds Glass vessel fragment, Price cat. no. 52 (SF 132).

Occupation debris   (Fig. 40e, p. 98)

Main deposit, 279, 381, grey-green silty spread with burnt areas, charcoal and tile.
Dispersed edges, 137, grey silty gravel.

Dating evidence 137 Early Anglo-Saxon pottery, AD 400–650. (Drawn sherds: Fig. 240, nos 7, 14, 15, 22, p. 655)

Small finds

137 Bronze coin, Shotter cat. no. 54, radiate, *c.* AD 270 (SF 130); bone pin, Greep cat. no. 1 (SF 154).

279 Bone pins, Greep cat. nos. 11 and 26 (SF 167 and 182); bronze coin, Shotter cat. no. 34, dupondius, AD 140–4 (SF 240); bronze bracelet fragment, Johns cat. no. 5 (SF 180).

BUILDING S2   (Fig. 49, p. 111; Figs 76, 78)

Excavated in 1983, this structure lies some 30 m east of building S1. Like the latter it is located on the gravel surface of street 1 E/W and, insofar as it is possible to tell, it, too, has an approximate east–west alignment. It appears to have been rectangular, measuring perhaps as much as 9×3 m, but the ground plan defies full comprehension. Two wall-lines may be postulated, on the north and south sides, but their post-holes are irregular in arrangement, character and spacing. Within them lie several shallow scoops and gullies and a scatter of post-holes. These features are all very super-ficial – none has a depth greater than 0.36 m, and most are considerably shallower – and the post-holes of the east end of the building may have been obliterated during the con-struction of the concrete-based glasshouse or in its removal immediately prior to excavation.

The relationship between this building and the east–west running gully 55 is uncertain. Both were dug into the street surface, and in its alignment, position, fill and rather superfi-cial nature gully 55 resembles the features of building S2. How-ever, it is unclear whether it had a structural function or whether it was for drainage. Post-hole 1253 lies on its north edge, while posthole 1335 was cut through the fill of its east end.

A similar linear feature (gully 65) comprises a more defi-nite component of building S4. A recutting of the north–south gully 53 may belong to this phase, for a sherd of Anglo-Saxon pottery (bowl rim, fabric 8, Fig. 240, no. 18, p. 655) was found in its north end. If so it is possible that the block of land bounded on its west, south and east sides by gullies 50, 53 and ditch 9, and on its north side by street 1 E/W, was an enclosure belonging to building S2 (see p. 86 for further details).

Data

Post-holes

North side	Width/diameter (m)	Depth (m)	Comments/dating
1415 post-hole	0.50×0.55	0.15	
Unnumbered pipe	0.25	Not recorded	
1109 pipe, or stake	0.16	0.36	
1110 post-hole	0.25	–	Not excavated
1111 pit	0.45×0.60	0.12	Anglo-Saxon
pipe	0.18	Not recorded	pottery
1112 pit	0.35	0.19	
pipe	0.25	0.19	
1364 pit	0.30×0.35	0.20	
pipe	0.25	0.20	

Interior	Width/diameter (m)	Depth (m)	Comments/dating
Unnumbered	1.10×2.00	*c.* 0.05	Shallow scoop
1116	*c.* 1.80×2.50	*c.* 0.10	Shallow scoop
1115*a*	*c.* 1.25×1.25	0.04	Shallow scoop
b	0.12	Not recorded	Stake-hole
1375 pipe	0.20	0.29	Sealed by 1115
1108 post-hole	0.37×0.50	0.23	
1113*a*	1.00×1.40	Not recorded	V. shallow scoop
b pit	0.30×0.40	Not recorded	
pipe	0.25×0.30	Not recorded	
c ?post-hole	0.20×0.30	Not recorded	V. shallow
d ?post-hole	0.20×0.30	Not recorded	V. shallow
1418 pipe, or stake	0.17	0.28	

South side	Width/diameter (m)	Depth (m)	Comments/dating
1158	*c.* 6.00×0.70	0.03	Shallow gully cf. gully 55
1365 post-hole	0.30	0.25	
1252 post-hole	0.30	0.21	
1253 post-hole	0.25	0.17	
1419 post-hole	0.12	0.26	
1335 post-hole	0.22	0.28	

South: exterior	Width/diameter (m)	Depth (m)	Comments/dating
1255	0.80×1.00	*c.* 0.05	
Unnumbered	0.50	Not recorded	Small hollow

GULLIES   (Fig. 25, p. 77)

Gully 55   Phase V

A narrow, very shallow gully, aligned approximately E/W, cut into the surface of street 1 E/W. It is adjacent to and immediately to the south of building S2, with which it was undoubtedly asso-ciated. A probable butt was discerned at the west end of unit 1289. All trace of the east end of unit 1158 had been obliterated by the base of the modern greenhouse. There may have been a 'causeway' between units 1158 and 1289, but this was not suscep-tible of proof.

Width 0.4–0.7 m, length at least 17 m, depth 0.03 m.

Fill
Cut 1 1158 (CGP) Grey-brown pebbly silt.
Cut 2 1289 (CNB) Grey gravelly silt.

Dating evidence Nothing datable

Gully 56   Phase V

A pair of conjoined short, irregular, very shallow gullies within building S2 on street 1 E/W.

Width 0.7 m, length a) *c.* 3.5 m. b) *c.* 2.6 m. Depth 0.05 m.

Fill 1114 (CET) Dark gravelly silt with stones.

Dating evidence Anglo-Saxon pottery, stamped sherd, fabric 7, Fig. 240, no. 23, p. 655.

BUILDING S3 (Fig. 49, p. 111; Figs 76, 78; Pl. XIXb)

This building, excavated in 1982 and 1983, lies 20 m east of building S2, on the north side of block 2. Unlike the other three Anglo-Saxon buildings, which were sited on the metalled surface of street 1 E/W, building S3 was constructed on the grey silts just to the south of the road and building S4. Its orientation, a few degrees north of due east, corresponds exactly to that of building S1 and closely to that of building S4.

Although details of the ground plan are imperfectly understood, the overall structure was rectangular, post-built, measuring perhaps 10.5 × 4.5 m. The post-holes, cut into mixed grey silts, were located with some difficulty. Even under optimum conditions of light and moisture, it was occasionally impossible to trace both the post-pipe and its post-pit, especially on the west and north sides. This may account for the apparent absence of posts in one or two places. There is some evidence for post replacement (post-holes 773, 1399 and 746/747, 1266 and 778/779) though not on the same scale as building S1. The majority of posts were fairly substantial, about 0.18–0.20 m square and 0.18–0.36 m deep, though a few were shallower, especially on the north side. Unlike buildings S1, S2 and S4 which, because of their position on the main Roman street were virtually devoid of relationships with Roman features other than the road surface itself, several of the posts of building S3 were cut through earlier features, notably two Phase III wells (905 and 808) and a Phase IV oven (7). The softness of the fill of 808 probably accounts for the greater thickness (0.24 m) and extreme depth (over 1.24 m) of post 724(a) which was positioned near its centre.

Anglo-Saxon pottery found in a recut section of gully 35 (cut 2, unit 754) may indicate an enclosure attached to the south side of building S3 of the same form and size (about 23.5 × 13 m) as that postulated for building S2 and sharing with it as a common boundary ditch 9 (see also p. 86).

Data

Post-holes

East side		Width/diameter (m)	Depth (m)	Comments/dating
986	pit	0.47 × 0.55	0.17	
	pipe	0.18	0.26	
1307	pit	0.35	0.35	
	pipe	0.20	0.35	
988	pit	0.55 × 0.65	0.15	
805	pipe	0.20	0.15	
779	pit	0.55 × 0.60	0.18	
778	pipe	0.18	0.18	

Additional features outside SE corner

1266	0.65 × 0.85	0.63	Small pit, not post-hole
1128	0.33	0.33	

South side		Width/diameter (m)	Depth (m)	Comments/dating
1399	pit	0.40 × 0.45	0.30	
	pipe	0.20	0.30	
746	pit	0.50	0.25	
747	pipe	0.15	0.30	
759	pit	0.65	0.26	
758	pipe	0.18	0.36	
770	pit	0.32	0.10	
	pipe	0.12	0.14	
721	pit	0.84	0.36	
720	pipe	0.20	0.36	
773	pit	0.55	0.24	
	pipe *a*	0.10	0.28	
	pipe *b*	0.20	0.24	

West side		Width/diameter (m)	Depth (m)	Comments/dating
724	(a) pit	0.45 × 0.55 +	0.57	Cut into Roman pit (808) subsided. Post not bottomed
	pipe	0.24	1.24 +	
724	(b) pit	0.55	Not recorded	Cut into Roman pit (808)
	pipe	0.20	Not recorded	
780		0.55 × 0.70	0.34	

North side		Width/diameter (m)	Depth (m)	Comments/dating
814	pipe	0.20	0.22	Cut into side of Roman pit (905)
813	pipe	0.20	0.11	Cut into side of Roman pit (905)
764	pit(?)	0.30	0.11	
1437	pit	0.45 × 0.55	0.34	
777 (= 1438)	pipe	0.20	0.20	
1351	pit	0.45 × 0.50	0.14	
	pipe	0.20	0.14	Seen in section only
845	pipe	0.20	0.18	Three possible replacements observed
719	pit	0.40	Not recorded	Cut into Roman oven 7
718	pipe	0.20	Not recorded	

Interior		Width/diameter (m)	Depth (m)	Comments/dating
722	pit or post-hole	1.8 × 1.6	0.60	Cut into top of Roman pit (905); comprises units 722, 775, 878, 897, 739, 799
1352	pit	0.74	0.29	
	pipe?	0.18	0.26	

Additional posts outside NW corner

870	pipe	0.25	0.28
869	pipe	0.25	0.31

Additional posts outside NE corner

1356	pit	0.45 × 0.50	0.21
	pipe	0.20(?)	0.21?
1355	pit	0.45 × 0.50	0.18
	pipe	0.20(?)	0.18?
1312	pit(?)	0.35	0.17

BUILDING S4 (Fig. 49, p.111; Figs 76, 79)

The traces of this structure, which lies just 4 m north of building S3, on the gravelled surface of street 1 E/W, were excavated in 1982 and 1983, but were not immediately recognised as the remains of an Anglo-Saxon building. Although the alignment is evidently closely similar to that of buildings S1–3 the dimensions are very uncertain. A rectangular structure about 9.5 × 4.5 m may be postulated, though neither the east nor west end was clearly identified. Only the north side was preserved as a coherent line of post-holes, with posts about 0.20–0.25 m square. Parallel to this line and 4.5 m south of it lay gully 65, a shallow, flat-bottomed feature which contained early Anglo-Saxon pottery. Originally regarded as a drainage gully this feature assumed greater significance once the north line of posts had been interpreted as a wall-line of an Anglo-Saxon building. An alternative interpretation of the gully as a beam slot was then considered. There is little evidence to be mustered in support of either theory: the ends were indistinct but seemed to coincide approximately with the limits of the north line of post-holes; while the fill, a mixed brown silt, provides no clear guidance as to use. Whether a footing itself for the south wall of the building or a drainage gully which had destroyed the remains of a south row of post-holes, its upper levels had been eroded by subsequent activity and a maximum depth of 0.12 m was all that survived.

Inside the building was an irregular scatter of cut features, both post-holes and small shallow hollows of uncertain purpose. Despite the paucity of dating evidence – only one hollow (unit 854) contained Anglo-Saxon pottery – their concentration within the building implies that they were more probably contemporary with its occupation than with earlier or later phases of activity.

Data

Post-holes

North side		Width/ diameter (m)	Depth (m)	Comments/dating
832	pit	0.40	Not recorded	
	pipe	0.25	Not recorded	
836	pit	0.35 × 0.85	Not recorded	
	pipe	0.30	Not recorded	
839	pipe	0.25	Not recorded	
852	pipe	0.24	Not recorded	
848	pit(?)	0.45 × 0.50	Not recorded	Shallow, c. 0.10 m
894	pipe	0.25	Not recorded	

Interior				
833	pit(?)	0.70 × 0.90	Not recorded	Prob. not post-hole; shallow, c. 0.10 m
837		1.10 × 1.95	0.09	Shallow pit, not post-hole
837	(a) pipe	0.25	Not excavated	Unexcavated pipe in shallow pit (837)
838	pit (?)	0.60 × 0.70	Not recorded	Shallow c. 0.10 m

North side		Width/ diameter (m)	Depth (m)	Comments/dating
	pipe a	0.30	Not recorded	
	pipe b	0.25	Not recorded	
880	pit?	0.40 × 0.45	Not recorded	Shallow c. 0.10 m
853		0.40 × 0.60	Not recorded	Shallow c. 0.10 m
861a		0.30 × 0.45	Not recorded	Two conjoined
b		0.30 × 0.45	Not recorded	post-holes; shallow c. 0.10 m
854		0.45 × 0.70	Not recorded	Shallow pit or hole. Early Anglo-Saxon pottery c. 0.10 m
834	pipe	0.30	Not recorded	
844	pipe	0.25	Not recorded	Shallow, c. 0.10 m

South side				
751		c. 10.65 × 0.95	0.12	?Beam slot or gully. Early Anglo-Saxon pottery

North and NE exterior				
871		0.85 × 1.06	0.20	Small pit
891	pipe	0.24	Not recorded	
887	pipe	0.25	Not recorded	
896		0.40 × 0.45	Not recorded	

Other features

Sherds of Anglo-Saxon pottery were found widely, if thinly scattered across the site, in surface spreads and in the top of earlier cut features (Fig. 76). In a few cases, either the quantity of sherds or their depth within the feature suggested the feature had been cut or recut in Phase V, though the evidence was seldom unequivocal, as, for example, the possible Phase V recutting of the Phase IV enclosure gully systems to the south of buildings S2 and S4. However, a characteristic and recurrent feature of several of the pits which contained Anglo-Saxon pottery was the presence of the complete or semi-complete articulated skeleton of an animal: a pig carcase in pit 1933 (Pl. XX, pit 3 and well 171/558 (unit 171); and a dog in pit 504. The significance, if any, of this form of deposition is unclear, but it did not occur in Phases III–IV and may be safely attributed to the Anglo-Saxon phase of settlement. Pits 3, 504 and 1933 were cut *de novo*, but in well 171/558 the Anglo-Saxon assemblage occupied the upper part of what was probably a disused Phase IV well.

Pit 3 (AC) W10.0, N16.7 (Figs 46, 63, pp.108, 128) Phase V

A large sub-rectangular pit cut into the rubble debris infill of the north east corner of the derelict R1 building.

Width 2.95 m, length 5.3 m, depth 0.95 m.

Fill
3 (AC) Loose brown gravelly soil with much comminuted tile. [Contained articulated skeleton of pig(?).]
13 (AN)/221 (KP) Brown soil with much comminuted tile, gravel, and larger rubble fragments.

31 (BH) Dark brown soil with gravel and large proportion of ragstone and mortar fragments.

Dating evidence NVGW types 45.3?, 29?, 46. Date: ?3rd century
AD [residual – see Small finds below].

Small finds 3 Coin, Shotter cat no. 57, AE copy, MW AD 350 +
(SF 3); lead sheet, Jackson cat. no. 27 (SF 4).

Pit 504 (ACP) E11.6, N25.6 (Figs 41b, p.99) Phase V

A rectangular pit, part of the cluster around well 171, centre east
side block 1.

Width 1.35 m, length 2.0 m, depth 0.5 m.

Fill Brown peaty silt with occasional gravel and small ragstone
fragments. [Contained articulated skeleton of dog.]

Dating evidence NVCC type 2.6; NVGW imitation samian; Horningsea. Date: early 3rd century AD [probably residual]; Anglo-
Saxon pottery, one small sherd.

Pit 1933 (DTA) E58.9, S14.65 Phase V

An ovoid pit near the south-east corner of block 8. Cuts unit 2093
of gully 18 (cut 3). The articulated skeleton of a pig was found in the
upper fill (Pl. XX).

Width 1.05 m, length at least 0.8 m, depth 0.32 m.

Fill Grey-brown silt with much gravel and a little iron-pan staining.

Dating evidence ?3rd century AD. Anglo-Saxon sherd.

Small finds Copper-alloy pin fragments (SF 1096); glass vessel
fragment, Price cat. no. 64ad (SF 1097).

Well 171 (HK)/558 (AEW) E10.4, N28.65 Phases IV and V

See Phase III/IV, block 1, p.142.

PHASE Va: LATE/POST ANGLO-SAXON STRUCTURE (Figs 40, 48, pp.98, 110)

During the 1980 season a low mound was observed in
ploughsoil some 35 m north-west of the excavation. From
the presence of tile and mortar fragments it seemed possible
that it marked the site of another Roman masonry building,
perhaps a wing of the main R1 complex. Consequently, in
1981, the mound was incorporated into the excavation area.
It soon became apparent, however, that it was of a rather different character to the mound which had signalled the presence of the stone building, R1.

The upper layer (units 127, 184, 199, 201), which covered a
roughly circular area some 8–9 m in diameter, was composed
of grey-green silty clay with tile fragments, rubble and
decayed white mortar (Fig. 40e, p.98). Within this area were
a number of localised mortar spreads and patches of mortary
rubble. On excavation three of the patches proved to be large
stone-packed post-holes (units 265, 267, 372). These had been
dug through the 'mound' make-up (units 137, 279, 381) but

were contemporary with the upper layer, for the mortar component of the post-packing was the same as the superficial
spreads of decayed white mortar.

Unfortunately, no further structural elements could be
located and the form and the function of the building
remain enigmatic. However, it appears to have been a substantial post-built structure set on a prepared platform with
made floor. The source of the mortar and rubble, at least, was
evident – it derived from the derelict third/fourth century
AD stone building which had been erected on the levelled
debris of the R1 building complex.

Post-holes (Fig. 40d–e, p.98)

265 Rectangular, 1.24×1.00 m, 1.06 m deep.
    Steeply sloping sides at top, vertical in lower half. A central
    grey stain (266), 0.35×0.30 m within the white mortary upper
    fill was thought to be a timber 'ghost' but could not be differen-
    tiated beyond a depth of 0.07 m. A further stain, not quite syn-
    chronous, was seen in the section continuing to a depth of
    $c.$ 0.45 m below the surface of the pit.

267 Oval, 1.10×0.97 m, 0.89 m deep. (Fig. 40e)
    Steep sides. Upper fill mortary. Loose dark soil in post-pipe,
    $c.$ 0.20–0.30 m wide and $c.$ 0.62 m deep. Packed with large
    stones in lower region.

372 Oval, $c.$ 0.80×0.60 m, 1.43 m deep. (Fig. 40d)
    Identified in partly excavated surface of 127 as localised mor-
    tary spread. Sides of pit unclear in layers of well 336. Upper
    region stone-packed. End of post or stake (length 0.397 m)
    found at base.

'Mound' (Fig. 40e)

After the topsoil had been machined, the cleaned surface
was quadranted.

	Upper layer (Phase Va)	Lower layer (Phase V)
NW quadrant	127	137
SW quadrant	184	279
SE quadrant	199	381
NE quadrant	201	137

Dating

Finds and stratigraphy point to a probable ninth–tenth
century AD date: the mound sealed the south side of the
Anglo-Saxon building S1, and early Anglo-Saxon pottery
was incorporated in its make-up; a mid to late Saxon
bronze pin (Webster cat. no. 1) was found in layer 127 adjacent to post-hole 267, and a ninth century AD strap-end
from the Stonea Grange Surface Collection (Webster cat.
no. 2) may relate to the same area and period of activity;
finally, and most fortunately, the waterlogged base of the
post surviving in post-hole 372 yielded a ^{14}C date of
1005 ± 40 BP, calibrated to AD 955–1045 (University of Cambridge, Sub-Department of Quaternary Research).

Small finds

127 Bronze pin, Webster cat. no. 1 (SF 75); iron objects, Jackson cat. nos. 34 and 54 (SF 74 and 82); bone pin-beater, Greep cat. no. 75 (SF 103); pierced pottery counter, Jackson cat. no. 11 (SF 79); pottery face mask (flagon handle), p. 491, no. 16 (SF 45).

184 Bronze globular-headed pin, Jackson cat. no. 1 (SF 89).

199 Iron decorative pin, Jackson cat. no. 32 (SF 139); bone pin, Greep cat. no. 2 (SF 137); samian stamp, Dickinson cat. no. 105 (SF 155).

201 Pottery spindle whorl, p. 488, no. 15 (SF 95).

[For small finds from the lower layer (units 137, 279, 381), see building S1, p. 230.]

THE EARLY ANGLO-SAXON TIMBER BUILDINGS: DISCUSSION

Martin G. Welch

There is no doubt that the Stonea excavation recovered traces of four rectangular timber buildings of post-Roman date, which probably represent an Anglo-Saxon settlement on the site. Unfortunately, the post-holes, which once contained the earthfast planks or posts, did not preserve impressions of those timbers to assist their interpretation as buildings. Such impressions have been recorded from sites on chalkland at Cowdery's Down, Hampshire, and on gravels at Heslerton, North Yorkshire, Thirlings and Yeavering, Northumberland. (James *et al* 1984, 190; Powlesland *et al* 1986, 167. Fig. 72). Their absence is not in itself unusual, but coupled with the inevitable problems on a multi-period site of separating out post-holes and other similar features of different phases and allowing that sometimes substantial numbers of the post-holes have been removed by subsequent features or disturbances, it is not easy to reconstruct these buildings convincingly.

A recent study of early Anglo-Saxon timber buildings of the type generally labelled in the archaeological literature as halls has identified a building tradition based on a double-square module, though there are a range of variants on this module (James *et al* 1984, 186–90, Fig. 4). The doorways are normally located at the centre of a long wall, commonly in pairs but it is possible to have an additional door in one of the short walls. Internal divisions do occur, usually of a partitioned area at one end of the building. Annexes are also restricted to a narrow extension attached to one or both walls of the main rectangle, with normally just an internal entrance, which rules out their functioning as porches. In the following reconstructions the plans are interpreted wherever possible as simple rectangular modules and the presence of double-square proportions noted. No credence is given to side porches or other extensions off the long walls, though they cannot be entirely ruled out. The relative depths of the recorded post-holes are utilised in an attempt to distinguish one building phase from another and to identify

doorways, external raking timbers and other major earthfast structural timbers.

BUILDING 1   (Fig. 77, p. 225)

This complex of post-holes must represent a succession of buildings dug into the Roman roadway, but it is a succession which is difficult to disentangle. Orientated east–west there are four roughly parallel full-length lines of post-holes and two such shorter lines. On the north side of the complex an east–west rectangle (A) approximately 7×3 m, a double-square with a gap for doorways, can be proposed from post-holes more than 30 cm deep. Slightly to the south a second east–west rectangle (B), perhaps 7.5×3 m, an extended double-square, might be postulated on the basis of post-holes more than 10 cm deep. A shorter building (C) in the south-east corner might have had dimensions of either 3×2.5 m or 3 m square. This by no means exhausts the range of possibilities, of course. For example, the north wall of building 1B conceivably might incorporate post-holes 308 and 309, which are aligned east–west only slightly to the south of the north wall of building 1A, though this would give us a very wide structure. None of the three buildings postulated here incorporates the series of small post-holes at the west end (389–96), which should probably be interpreted as two separate straight alignments (389–90 and 391–6 respectively) of fence posts related to the series of ditches, again dug into the roadway, which enclose these buildings, two of which contain Anglo-Saxon pottery in their fills, as do post-holes 382 and 150 within the building complex. Inevitably other sets of post-holes have also been ignored in this interpretation. On the other hand, the postulated building 1A does at least have potential door openings set midway along its long walls: nos 147 and 306 on the north side and 351 and 352 on the south side, though neither is particularly convincing.

BUILDING 2   (Fig. 78, p. 226)

The rather limited pattern of post-holes which represents this building imply a small and narrow east–west rectangular structure, again dug into the Roman road surface some 32 m to the east of building 1. It is truncated by the modern greenhouse, however, and its dimensions can only be guessed. A minimum length of 6 m and a minimum width of 1.5 m are suggested here. This leaves a rather random pattern of possible internal post-holes whose functions are difficult to explain.

BUILDING 3   (Fig. 78)

A simple rectangular building aligned east–west can be postulated here, with the east end well defined. The west wall is more problematic. Should it incorporate post-hole 780, which contained handmade pottery sherds, or should it be offset from 870 ? If the former (A) its dimensions would be 10×5 m, a double-square. In the latter case (B) it would be 12.5×5 m. It may seem tempting to see a small porch extension at the north-east corner, but the alternative that two post-holes (1355 and 1356) might represent external raking timbers and may be matched by two others (869 and 870) at the north-west corner, cannot be ignored. Unfortunately, no convincing doorways can be postulated from the surviving post-holes. Finally, it should be noted that it is difficult to find any function for the large post-hole 1352 within this scheme, despite the fact that it contained handmade pottery sherds.

BUILDING 4   (Fig. 79, p. 227)

Effectively only the north wall of this postulated east–west rectangular structure is marked by post-holes with 887 and 891 perhaps representing external raking timbers, suggesting a building around 11 m long. On the other hand, if 894 represents the north-east corner and 832 is at the north-west corner, that gives a length of 9 m. It is assumed that gully 751 has removed the post-holes of the south wall, implying a width of 5 m. Whichever length is accepted, this is close to a double-square plan. The absence of post-holes for the east and west walls can be put down to erosion.

THE ARCHAEOLOGICAL AND HISTORICAL SETTING OF THE ANGLO-SAXON SETTLEMENT

Martin G. Welch

The excavation of post-holes from rectangular ground-level buildings associated with early Anglo-Saxon artefacts at Stonea represents the first such settlement to be archaeologically investigated in the Fenlands. This occupation of a gravel 'island' site is matched by records of past discoveries of early Anglo-Saxon burials on other similar Fenland 'islands'. No such burials have been reported from March as yet, but what may well be cropmarks indicating a handful of Anglo-Saxon sunken-featured buildings at Whittlesey have been identified from air photographs. This probable settlement site has been scheduled as an ancient monument; while seven inhumations forming part of a cemetery were discovered at another site in the same parish in 1838, one of which was associated with a fifth-century Anglian shoulder-bossed pot (Hall 1987, 59, Fig. 41: sites 22 and 23; Myres 1977, Fig. 220, no. 405).

Part of a further cemetery was found in a gravel quarry at Eye in 1908 and a secondary female burial was recovered from a Bronze Age barrow at another site there in 1984

(Hall 1987, 32, 36, Fig. 15: site 3 and Fig. 17: site 16). Burials from yet another cemetery were uncovered at Chatteris in 1757 (Stukeley 1766; Evison 1982, 47, 61, Pl. VIIb), while a single cremation bossed urn at Somersham, dug up in 1736 and presented to St John's College, Cambridge, belongs to the fifth century AD (Meaney 1964, 107; Myres 1977, Fig. 179.2366). Four burial sites have been located on the Isle of Ely: at Little Downham (1928 and 1933); Ely Fields Farm (1947); the High Barns estate on the north side of Ely (1959); and on high ground between Sutton and Earith (c.1938) (Meaney 1964, 64 and 70). There is material from Coldham (Potter 1981, 94f.), but the reported discovery in 1858 of two T-headed brooches in the foundations of the Corn Exchange at Wisbech (Meaney 1964, 71) provides rather less satisfactory evidence for a potential Anglo-Saxon inhumation burial there, as does a string of amber beads reported as from Manea Fen (Meaney 1964, 68).

In Norfolk, evidence for early Anglo-Saxon burials was revealed in two parishes of the Nar Valley. The first was discovered through quarrying in 1890 at Tottenhill (Silvester 1988, 135, Fig. 104: site TTH A1) and the other at Wormegay (Silvester 1988, 146–7, Fig. 109: site WGY A5). Two possible pottery sherds of this period were also found near the church at Wormegay and near Wormegay Road there. On the other hand, finds of early Anglo-Saxon sherds in the Marshland parishes of Norfolk are extremely rare (Silvester 1988; 156–8, Fig. 113). Indeed, the 40 sherds from the top of the silted ridge of the Aylmer Hall canal, in the centre of Tilney St Lawrence, provide an important *terminus ante quem* evidence for the silting of this waterway. This stands in isolation, however, and it is still unclear whether this debris was associated with a temporary settlement here or whether some other explanation should be sought (Silvester 1988, 60, 156, Fig. 43: site TYL 19). Pottery sherds as indication of occupation across the Norfolk fens only become widespread in the period of Ipswich Ware, which defines the middle Saxon period here, beginning around the middle of the seventh century (Silvester 1988, 158–60, 172, Figs 113 and 123).

Of course, the majority of recorded early Anglo-Saxon burial sites in the present-day counties of Norfolk, Cambridgeshire, Northamptonshire and Lincolnshire are located away from the Fens. On the other hand, there are also many found ringing the edges of the Fens and overlooking the Fenland and its 'islands' (e.g. Ordnance Survey 1966; Clough and Green 1973, map 3; Davies and Vierck 1974, Figs 5, 7 and 8; Stafford 1985, Fig. 30).

Publication of surveys of Fenland parishes have now appeared for just five parishes (Borough Fen, Eye, March, Thorney and Whittlesey) in Cambridgeshire (Hall 1987) and the Norfolk parishes (Silvester 1988) discussed above. The appearance in print of the survey of a block of parishes in south Lincolnshire is awaited with anticipation, following the recent release of preliminary results (Hayes 1988).[1] This has revealed a pattern of settlement shift, which resulted from the formation of peat, usually on top of marine sediments in Lincolnshire, turning the landscape into true fen and making that land uninhabitable. Long-term shift from south to north and west to east can be demonstrated from the Iron Age through the Roman period to the early and middle Anglo-Saxon periods (Hayes 1988, Figs 1–3). Unfortunately, the handmade pottery sherds which indicate the presence of Anglo-Saxon settlement here have not proved particularly easy to date and it is not always possible to differentiate between early and middle period occupation.

Nevertheless two important conclusions have been drawn form the survey of south Lincolnshire parishes. The first is that the discontinuity present between the Roman and the earliest Anglo-Saxon settlements is too abrupt and too universal to be explained as simply a response to environmental change. A real break in settlement patterns is indicated here. Second, two distinct clusters of early Anglo-Saxon sites have been identified and these have been tentatively associated with two of the peoples listed in an Anglo-Saxon document known as the *Tribal Hidage*. The *Bilmiga* are seen as occupying the west cluster and the *Spalda* the east one near Spalding.

The interpretation of the *Tribal Hidage* and the associated place-name evidence certainly do pose considerable problems. Everything about the *Tribal Hidage* is controversial. The text, as it survives, is in Old English in one eleventh-century manuscript and in Latin in a series of other manuscripts (Davies and Vierck 1974, 288–92; Dumville 1989a). It is certainly very corrupt, with the names of some peoples reduced by successive scribal errors to nonsense, e.g. the *Noxgaga* and *Ohtgaga*.

Dispute also exists as to who might have commissioned it and when. Most scholars have viewed it as a Mercian document. As Elmet in present-day West Yorkshire is listed, the seventh-century reigns of Wulfhere (657–74) and Æthelred (674–704) and in particular the two decades between 670 and 690 provide the most believable context from this point of view (Davies and Vierck 1974, 227). Professor N. Brooks takes a contrary position, for he does not believe that a tribute or tax list would begin with the hidage or land tax assessment of the kingdom that is levying the tribute. He prefers to see it as a Northumbrian document of the reign of Oswald (634–42), Oswiu (642–70) or Ecgfrith (670–85). All three kings enjoyed brief periods of dominance south of the Humber, with Oswald dying in battle outside his own kingdom and his successors playing a leading role in 655–8 and *c*. 674–8 (Brooks 1989, 159, 167–8).

The seventh century was a period of rapid political change, which saw the creation of a kingdom for the Middle Angles in the east Midlands, including most of the smaller peoples listed in the *Tribal Hidage* (Dumville 1989b). It was first ruled by Peada, son of the great Mercian king Penda, who died only two years after his father in 657. This century

also witnessed East Anglian expansion westwards into the Midlands, further squeezing the small 'tribes' listed in the *Tribal Hidage*. These peoples had become mere pawns in the bigger game being played by the East Anglian, Mercian and Northumbrian superpowers. The fact that they are still listed as if independent provinces or small kingdoms perhaps indicates that, at the time the hidage document was composed, no final decision had been taken as to their fate. These small provinces have been of great interest to historians, as they have often been seen, rightly or wrongly, as representing the scale of the territories or building blocks, whose earlier amalgamation provided the basis for the larger kingdoms emerging into the historical record during the seventh century. Perhaps the process had been delayed in the east Midlands, giving us a view of the sub-groups which still existed within other kingdoms. A simpler alternative is that a detailed Middle Anglian survey formed a major element of the *Tribal Hidage*, which is perhaps a composite document derived from several such hidage surveys (Kirby 1991, 9).

Few of the peoples listed in the *Tribal Hidage* were also mentioned by name in the early eighth-century *Historia Ecclesiastica* of the Venerable Bede. The *Gyrwe* or 'fen-people' have been particularly fortunate in this respect. Most of the *Tribal Hidage* folk have been identified and located instead on the basis of place-name evidence. The problem is that even where a place-name which appears to contain the name of a people has been correctly associated with that folk, it seems that place-names incorporating a tribal name were more commonly given to locations on or near the boundaries of that people. After all, that was where there was a real need to differentiate the land one people held from territory owned by their neighbours. For example, the proximity of Sonning to Reading in Berkshire is an indication that the boundary between the lands of the *Rædingas* and the *Sonningas* or *Sunningas* ran between these two places. But of course this does not do much to help us to define the full extent of the territories of these two peoples, though fortunately charter evidence exists for the province of the *Sonningas* (Davies and Vierck 1974, 240; Gelling 1988, 66). It is very difficult then to identify the central area of a tribal province from just one or two place-names, or, as in some cases, from no more than a river name. Even when this evidence is combined with the possibility of clues provided by the order in which peoples are listed and the relative size of their hidage in the *Tribal Hidage* document, the task of mapping their territories remains a difficult one.

Our earliest reliable written source for this region is Bede's *Historia Ecclesiastica*, though it was compiled far away from the Fens in a Northumbrian monastery on the basis of correspondence with churchmen elsewhere in England. Bede's occasional references to events and individuals outside of his own kingdom are invaluable, but often prove difficult to interpret. Thus he records the marriage of

Tondberht, a prince of the South *Gyrwe* to Æthelthryth daughter of Anna, King of the East Angles, but when Tondberht died shortly afterwards, she was married off *c.*660 to Ecgfrith, King of the Northumbrians (*HE* IV, 19; Kirby 1991, 103 and 111 n.99). He also mentions that Felix was succeeded as bishop of the East Anglians by his Gyrwean deacon Thomas (*HE* III, 20), reinforcing the picture of close relations between the East Anglians and the *Gyrwe*. We are further informed that the monastery of *Medeshamstede* (later to be renamed Peterborough) lay in the province of the *Gyrwe*. (*HE* IV, 6) and that Oundle to the west of Peterborough takes its name from a separate province of *Inundulam* (*HE* V, 19). Finally, we learn that Ely, where the Æthelthryth, formerly married to Tondberht and Ecgfrith, subsequently served as abbess, was a province of the East Anglian kingdom, valued at about 600 families, which is Bede's translation into Latin of the English hides (*HE* IV, 19). A hide was a taxable land unit, whose area varied according to the productivity of the soil, but which was notionally sufficient to support a single family, according to Bede.

The *Gyrwe* are also listed in the *Tribal Hidage* as the North and South *Gyrwa*, valued together at 1200 hides. If Æthelthryth had not married the Northumbrian Ecgfrith, we would certainly know much less about the *Gyrwe/Gyrwa*. Bede would have less reason to describe her prior relationship with Tondberht, her virginity, or her subsequent career as a nun at Coldingham and finally as abbess at Ely. As it is, it is difficult to know how much credence should be given to the claim in a much later source, the *Liber Eliensis*, that Æthelthryth received Ely as her dower from Tondberht.

Was Ely then the central 'island' for the southern half of the *Gyrwe* or fen-people's territory and Peterborough its mainland equivalent for the northern half? This would make the *Gyrwe* the principal occupants of the fenland 'islands', which seems reasonable enough in view of their name. There is nothing in the written sources, however, to compel us to locate the *Gyrwe* in the Isle of Ely (Davies and Vierck 1974, 231 and 234) and the late Professor Dorothy Whitelock was just one of a number of leading scholars who have expressed scepticism of any such claim. Her reasons include Bede's identification of Ely as an East Anglian province and his statement that the opportunity to return to her homeland was Æthelthryth's reason for becoming abbess there (*HE* IV, 19). Whitelock coupled these points to her belief that the peoples listed in the *Tribal Hidage* after the *Gyrwa* imply that their territory did not come as far south as Ely (Whitelock 1972, 7; see also Hart 1971, 142–3; Davies and Vierck 1974, 282–3; Warner 1988, 17–21).

Against such a view, there need be no discrepancy between the listing of a supposedly independent small province in the *Tribal Hidage* and its annexation by a larger kingdom at some date within the same century. As we have seen, the date of the *Tribal Hidage* depends on such factors as whether it is a Mercian or a Northumbrian document. While it is

likely to reflect a seventh-century situation, we cannot attribute a secure date range for its composition. Indeed, as already mentioned, Dr Kirby has recently pointed out that it might well represent a composite of several hidage lists (Kirby 1991, 9–12). In any case, Bede does not bother to tell us precisely when Ely came under East Anglian control. Tondberht's unconsummated and therefore perhaps purely symbolic marriage surely reflects the need to obey an overlord East Anglian king. The only alternative was presumably Mercian control of his province. It would seem likely that Tondberht's death, presumably before *c.*660, might mark the point in time that Ely became a province of the East Anglian kingdom. Like Dr Barbara Yorke (1990, 11, 63–5, 70, 108 and 161), I can see no problem in equating Ely with the territory of the South *Gyrwe*.

Then there is a tradition recorded in *The Resting-Places of the English Saints*, apparently first compiled in the late tenth century, which places Crowland some ten miles (16 km) north of Peterborough *'on middan Gyruwan fenne'* (Birch 1892, 88). There is also a tenth century reference to the *'Gyruwan fen'* on the east boundary of an estate at Conington, some 10 miles (16 km) south of Peterborough. This occurs in a single-sheet copy of a land diploma or charter of 957 (Sawyer 1968, 220: S.649). Peterborough and Crowland presumably belonged then to the North *Gyrwe*, whose territory was apparently limited by Bede's 'province of Oundle' immediately to the west of Peterborough. With at least part of the fen of the *Gyrwe* located to the east of Conington towards Ramsey, the *Gyrwe* seem likely to have occupied a number of the fenland 'islands' to the south and east of Peterborough. If their territory extended as far as the Isle of Ely, then the occupants of Stonea can certainly be attributed to one of the two divisions of the *Gyrwe*. Even if Ely was never occupied by the South *Gyrwe*, there seems to be a reasonable possibility that the *Gyrwe* might have occupied March and Stonea.

Alternatives must also be canvassed, in view of Whitelock's objections. We should first look at the peoples listed immediately before and after the *Gyrwe*. The kingdom of Lindsey and Hatfield Chase in South Yorkshire precede mention of the south *Gyrwa*, who surprisingly enough are listed before their northern branch. So there is an immediate geographical leap from Lindsey and a territory immediately west of it to the Fens south of Peterborough. The *Gyrwa* are followed by the East and then West *Wixna* (with 300 and 600 hides respectively), the *Spalda* (600 hides), the *Wigesta* (900 hides), the *Herefinna* (1200 hides) and the *Sweord ora* (300 hides).

The *Wixna* have often been identified with the *Wissa*, a people named in the eighth-century *Life of Guthlac* by Felix (Colgrave 1956, 169 and 195), who have been located in the Fens by the names of the River Wissey in Norfolk and the town of Wisbech in Cambridgeshire (Hart 1971, 143–4). This would place them to the east of the *Gyrwa*. On the other hand, Professor Wendy Davies once favoured a rather bizarre alternative location in Middlesex, by linking the *Wixna* to the place-names of Uxbridge, Waxlow and Uxendon (Davies and Vierck 1974, 231–2 and 234).

Next there are the *Spalda*, who could be associated with Spalding in Lincolnshire, though Professor Davies preferred to identify them with Spaldwick (formerly in Huntingdonshire) to the south-west of the *Gyrwa* (Davies and Vierck 1974, 232 and 234). On the other hand, a good case has been made recently to identify the *Spalda* with the eastern group of sites identified from pottery scatters in south Lincolnshire, immediately to the west of the town of Spalding (Hayes 1988, Fig. 3). The *Wigesta* cannot be satisfactorily located, other than to note the probability from their position in the list that they were a Middle Anglian people, perhaps to be located in Cambridgeshire (Davies and Vierck 1974, 232 and 236). Then the *Herefinna* might be the *Hyrstingas*, who gave their name to Hurstingstone, formerly in Huntingdonshire, to the south of the *Gyrwa* (Davies and Vierck 1974, 232) and the *Sweord ora* seem to have given their name to Sword Point overlooking Whittlesey Mere, again formerly in Huntingdonshire, between the *Hyrstingas* and the *Gyrwa* (Davies and Vierck 1974, 232).

A second grouping of Middle Anglian peoples appears rather later in the list with the *Bilmiga* coming first, next the *Widerigga* and finally the East and West *Willa*, all rated at 600 hides. The *Bilmiga* may now be seen as including the settlements represented by pottery scatters to the west of the *Spalda* group in south Lincolnshire (Hayes 1988, Fig. 3), an identification supported by the place-names of Horbling, Billingborough and Billingley (Davies and Vierck 1974, 233–6). Then the *Widerigga* can be linked to Wittering and Werrington in Northamptonshire, only a short distance to the north and west of Peterborough (Davies and Vierck 1974, 233) and the *Willa* to the Old Well Stream in the Fens to the east of the *Gyrwa* (Davies and Vierck 1974, 234–6).

Comparisons of published maps (e.g. Davies and Vierck 1974, Fig. 3; Courtney, 1981, Fig. 6.1; Hart 1971, map on p. 157; Hill 1981, 76–7, map 136) show approximate locations for all these provinces, which simply reveal how little agreement exists between those who have examined the evidence of the *Tribal Hidage*. Courtney is the only one to place the *Gyrwe* or *Gyrwa* between Crowland and Ely. It should be obvious by now, however, that certainty over precise locations and boundaries of the Middle Anglian peoples of the Fens will continue to elude us, unless the type of fieldwork results obtained in south Lincolnshire can be matched throughout the region.

To conclude, while it is possible that the occupants of the settlements at Stonea might have belonged to the *Wissa*, the *Willa* or *Sweorda*, it would seem rather more likely that they were in fact members of Bede's *Gyrwe*. Whichever is the case, during the seventh century the inhabitants of Stonea, in common with their neighbours on the Fen islands, must have lost much of their former independence, despite the relative isolation of their island. Their loyalty to a local tribal king such as Tondberht, who held the status of *princeps* in Bede's terminology, was being threatened by the demands of an overlord or his appointee, whether Mercian or East Anglian, or even on occasion Northumbrian. Providing they met the exactions of those great kings in terms of livestock tribute, food rents, military or labour services, they would generally be left in peace. Presumably they had lost long ago the freedom of action, which, in all probability, they had possessed in the fifth and sixth centuries.

Finally, though the *Gyrwe* may have nominally consisted of 1200 families or hides, such round numbers should never be read literally. Until one or more of the early Anglo-Saxon settlement sites or cemeteries is systematically excavated on the islands of the Fens, estimates of the size of population can be no more than shots in the dark. Isolated farmsteads or small hamlets of around three farm units, comparable to that excavated at West Stow by the River Lark, which flows into the Fens (West 1985; Welch 1985) may have existed there. Their Anglian population may well have consisted of a mixture of ethnic Germanic migrants from north-west Germany and southern Scandinavia with members of the native British population. Yet until some of their cemeteries are excavated and analysed to modern standards further comment along these lines is really superfluous.

Note

1 Since this discussion was prepared, three more volumes (including south-west Lincolnshire) have appeared: Silvester 1991; Hayes and Lane 1992; and Hall 1992.

DOCUMENTARY EVIDENCE FOR THE MEDIEVAL PERIOD

David Hall

After the Anglo-Saxon occupation, the focus of activity moved to Doddington, which became the successor to Stonea as a local administration centre, probably because the Stonea 'island' proved difficult to access as fenland conditions became wetter.

Stonea belonged to Doddington manor, which was one of the more important possessions of Ely monastery and bishopric. Doddington was, until about 1700, the chief settlement lying at the south end of the long fen 'island', on which are also the settlements of Wimblington in the middle and March towards the north. Stonea is a separate small 'island' located east of Doddington. The name, meaning 'stone island', may be a recognition of the large quantity of Roman building stone that was probably visible as ruins in the late Saxon period. Benwick, lying on a roddon of the

Nene was also a dependency, bringing the total area of the medieval parish to 15 200 ha (37 800 acres).

The Ely estate at Doddington was accumulated by several purchases before the Conquest (Pugh 1953, 110), Doddington and Wimblington both being mentioned in *c*.975 (Reaney 1943, 251, 265), and meaning respectively 'Dudda's farm' and 'Wimbel's' or 'Wynnbeald's farm'. A little detail is recorded in the *Liber Eliensis*, an early twelfth century record of the estates of Ely compiled from tenth and eleventh century sources. Wine, son of Osmund, sold 60 acres (24 ha) in Doddington and Wimblington with 1000 eel rent, and Thurcytil granted Weremere. 'Staneie' and its marsh were granted with a rent of 2000 eels from a fishery, and March was purchased from Oswi (Blake 1962, 96–7, 139, 423).

In the Domesday Survey of 1086, the Abbot of Ely possessed at Doddington 5 hides and 8 ploughlands. In demesne were 2.5 hides and 3 ploughlands, the other 5 ploughlands being held by 24 villans. One hide belonged to 8 freemen; there were 8 cottagers, meadow, wood for 250 pigs, and fisheries rented for 27 150 eels. March was an outlier of the manor with 12 villans each having 12 acres of arable (Rumble 1981, 5–45).

On the foundation of the See in 1109, when Ely was elevated to a bishopric, Doddington became one of the bishop's main residences. There are surveys of Doddington manor which illustrate the type of economy and land-use at the time. The first two, taken in 1222 and 1251 (British Library, Cotton Tib. B ii (1222); Cambridge University Library, EDR G/3/27 (1251)), afford the most detail and show that Stonea had no permanent dwellings in the Middle Ages, being described as a cow pasture. However, the fishery, also mentioned, may well have had a temporarily used site of the type identified around Whittlesey Mere (Hall 1992, 30–2).

The arable land belonging to the demesne farm of Doddington amounted to 267.5 acres in 1222 (f.97d), dispersed in blocks of about 20–50 acres:

Stanhihoue	23.5 acres
Tenstirhoue	18
Hoo	20
Northfenhoue	52
Hyrsthoue	24.5
Fenegedeshoue	29
Allehoue	40 with meadow
Byriwong	19
Akermanesland	27.5

The names are those of the various 'hills' (*houe* equals 'hoo') or peninsulas of the main 'island'. The first name of 'stanhihoue' probably refers to a peninsula opposite Stonea 'island' rather than Stonea itself. *Hoo* is identified as How Moor.

The 1251 survey lists a similar demesne amounting to 246.5 acres having 1.25 acres of new assart, called *stokynshou* added to it. More land had been brought into cultivation at

estwode (Eastwood), *bretchoue*, *bothoue* and *suthhythehoue*, bringing the 1251 arable to 330.25 acres. It was possible to plough this land with three ploughs, each having 8 oxen. Since 1222 the manor had acquired the Little Park, 70 acres, and the Great Park, 80 acres, and there was a new windmill.

The fisheries of 1222 and 1251, identifiable as the River Nene, were described as lying at 'Westmor with appurtenances and medefens, to akermannespoles, to Duditunefrith, leading from Wymeliton to Wyssbeche being 6 leagues.' There was the right to have 5 fishing boats, worth a rent of 25 shillings per annum if let out, one each in *weremere*, *sudmere*, half of *weremere math*, half *ewer* and al *herting*, for a rent of 2500 eels. More fisheries at Eggenwere, Utwere, Fernegey, Ascenwer, Estfen, Herdelade, Sretwere, Strode, Estewere, Sulbig were, Littlewere and Nuewere were also rented out.

Belonging to the manor, in 1222, was the cow pasture of *stonheye* (Stonea), able to feed 40 cows and 2 bulls. Another cow pasture at *westheye* (Westry) was capable of feeding 20 cows and 1 bull, and *dereford* (Dartford) cow pasture supported 40 cows and 2 bulls.

Wimblington, March and Marchford are mentioned as settlements distinct from Doddington in 1251. 'March' was the area with arable fields in the St Wendreda's Church area. Formerly the 'island' south of the Nene was covered with strip fields of the Midland ridge and furrow type, and the linear banks left at the field (furlong) boundaries are visible in modern arable. Many of these strips are marked on a map of Doddington and March dated *c*.1630, and were once the arable lands described in the 1222 demesne.

In 1251 'Marchford' had only cottages and paddocks with no arable land. These properties and their closes are still identifiable on the modern map, and more easily on a Tithe Map of 1840 (CUL EDR Doddington Tithe Apportionment), as a series of closes lying either side of the Nene. Benwick also consisted of a few cottages without arable, precariously situated on the levees of the Nene.

Service owed by the whole vill of March was to cut, turn, load and cart 22.5 acres of meadow at hethelod, sidehal, stretacre, blech, wesreyedale (Westry), newenesdale, nededol, avenho and next to hithedol (Hythe House).

All the tenants are named in both surveys and included Alan the Merchant, Robert de Marsh, Cecily de Hachwode (Hatchwood) and Geoffrey Knit (of Knights End). Many of them had access to the fishery of Bradenhee (Bradney), such as 24 'nights' for 2000 eels and rent 3s 3d (1221, f.98). Details of work service are listed, that included f.100 day-works in the arable, ploughing and harrowing, hoeing, mowing, loading, with carriage to Upwell, and rents for collecting wood.

Among the many place-names mentioned in 1222 (f.99d) are stanimere, erdelode fen, stittelbech (Stiches), *estiworth* (Estover), Mercheforde (March Bridge). Other identified place names are Ranson Moor, *revensho* in 1227, and near to it is Copalder *kekaldre* in 1244 meaning a 'hollow alder'. Beezling Fen to the south-west was *bilsinge* in the thirteenth century (Reaney 1943, 252–3), and Latches Fen was *lechewer*. Benwick was *Beymwich* in 1222.

By 1493 the manor house was leased and in the late sixteenth century Ely had to relinquish some of its estates, Doddington being granted to the lessee Sir John Peyton in 1602. The manor continued with the Peyton family until the end of the nineteenth century. Various other small manors existed in the thirteenth and fourteenth centuries, the details being given by Pugh (1953, 110–6). The site of the grange and palace was at the present Manor Farm.

A grange at Stonea (presumably Stonea Grange Farm destroyed in *c.*1960) is first mentioned in 1600 as part of Bishop Heyton's alienations (BL Add MS 5847 p. 89).

PHASE VI

In five seasons of excavation only a single piece of medieval pottery was found – a sherd from a Saintonge jug of thirteenth–fourteenth century date, an intrusive find in the Phase III gully 29 (block 9, cut 6, unit 1981). If any medieval building existed on the site, its refuse was clearly disposed of elsewhere. The Stonea Grange Surface Collection, too, includes only a meagre selection of finds of late medieval date – an ampulla fragment, a gilded mount and two cast bronze feet from a cauldron and a skillet or ewer (Gaimster, p. 663) – and the finder did not record the exact location of any of these finds.

In fact, from the documentary evidence it would appear that the site was largely uninhabited in the Middle Ages (Hall, pp. 238–9). The grange, first mentioned in 1600, is probably to be equated with the Stonea Grange farmhouse which, until its demolition in *c.*1960 (Hall 1992, 72), dominated the farmyard. Its site, some 30 m north of the excavation area, is now partially sealed by a large grain-drying barn and the concrete hardstanding of the farmyard.

An early seventeenth century date accords well with the finds assemblage from the Phase VI features and from topsoil on the site, as well as with the metal finds from the Stonea Grange Surface Collection. These incorporate a modest range and quantity of sixteenth–seventeenth century material, but the majority is of eighteenth–nineteenth century date. The Phase VI features are concentrated along the north edge of the excavated area and comprise mainly ditches and pits disposed along the boundary between farmyard and fields. Thus, ditch 12 may have combined the roles of a drainage channel and a ha-ha, though it soon became used as a receptacle for refuse. It appears to have been dug in the later seventeenth century, and its lower fill (levels 5, 4 and 3) accumulated in the late seventeenth–mid eighteenth century. Its north edge was cut by the construction trench of a rectangular brick-lined cess pit (external dimensions 2.5 × 2.1 m) which, though unexcavated, may be dated by its

brickwork to the eighteenth century (G. Soffe, personal communication).

Broadly contemporary with the cess pit were ditch 14 and pit 1267, the latter, like the cess pit, situated on the north lip of ditch 12, some 7–8 m further north-east. Too small a section of the pit was excavated to determine its function, though rubbish disposal seems likely. The main fill of ditch 12 (level 2) was of mid eighteenth–early nineteenth century date, while the upper fill (level 1) spans the nineteenth century. Cut into the upper fill, and also of nineteenth century date was pit 1173, situated immediately to the south-west of the brick cess pit and perhaps sharing the same or a similar function. Approximately contemporaneous was ditch 13, the west edge of which abutted the north-east corner of the greenhouse. In 1983 the greenhouse was dismantled and its concrete base demolished prior to excavation of that part of the site. Parallel to and about 1 m outside its east and west wall-lines was found a row of rectangular post-holes, five on each side, each measuring about 0.70 × 0.45 m and set about 2.5 m apart:

East row, from south: 1007, 1006, 1042, 1015, 1014
West row, from south: unnumbered, 1162, unnumbered × 3

These post-holes enclosed a space of about 12 × 8 m and were symmetrically disposed, so that the double-size spacing (5 m) between posts 1042 and 1015 on the east was matched by that between the opposing pair on the west. The fact that the rows stopped some 5 m short of the north end of the greenhouse suggests they were not a fence-line surrounding the greenhouse. Their size, too, suggests that they held something more substantial than fence posts, and they may be the remains of a small barn or stable. The structure was evidently associated with ditch 13, which abutted its north-west corner, and with the north–south dyke, which abutted its south-east corner. A nineteenth century date is thus indicated and is supported by the finds from the postholes.

The greenhouse evidently replaced this structure in the late nineteenth or early twentieth century but was longer and slightly narrower (its concrete base measured 18 × 6 m) and was not necessarily intended to serve the same function.

Ditch 12

(Figs 25, 28, 30a–b, 31b–c, 46, 48, 49, pp. 77, 80, 83–4, 108–11)
Phase VI

A broad ditch, aligned approximately east–west, to the north of street 1 E/W. Near the east end of block 11, immediately beyond the brick-lined cesspit, it veers to the north-east. Its cross-section is broad V-shaped with a rounded base and sides varying in steepness in different places. It cuts all other ditches in its path (gully 1 and ditches 6, 10, 4) but is cut by pit 1173 and by the construction trench of the brick-lined cesspit. To the west of the main excavation it was located in trench D (D8, unexcavated).

Width 2.5–3.5 m. Length within main excavation 95 m; including trench D, at least 120 m. Depth 0.6–1.1 m.

Fill

Cut 1 1167 (CGZ) Brown peaty silt with many pebbles and gravel.

Cut 2 1087 (CDQ) As cut 1, 1167.
1145 (CGB) Fine brown peaty silt with iron-pan staining and gravel.
1150 (CGG) As cut 1, 1167.
1164 (CGW) Gravel in orange/grey silty matrix. Slump.

Cut 3 1180 (CHN) As cut 1, 1167.

Cut 4 1169 (CHB) As cut 1, 1167.
1200 (CII) As cut 2, 1145.

Cut 5 1227 (CKM) As cut 1, 1167.
1264 (CMA) Dark grey silt with pebbles.
1251 (CLM) Grey-green silty clay.
1256 (CLR) Fine grey-green silt with iron-pan staining.

Cut 6 1170 (CHC) Grey-black silty clay with pebbles.
1213 (CIX) Brown peaty silt with a few pebbles and gravel.
1214 (CIY) Grey-brown clayey silt.

Cut 7 1053 (CCF) Dark brown silt.
1098 (CEC) Brown peaty silt.

Cut 8 1172 (CHE) Grey silt with pebbles and iron-pan staining.
1165 (CGX) As 1172.

Cut 9 1357 (CPY) As cut 7, 1053.
1373 (CQO) As cut 5, 1251.

Cut 10 1196 (CIE) Dark grey silt with pebbles, stones and brick fragments.
1221 (CKF) Dark grey silt with a few pebbles.
1269 (CMF) Dark grey silt with many pebbles.

Cut 11 1195 (CID) Grey silty clay with many pebbles.
1299 (CNM) Brown peaty silt.

Cut 12 1056 (CCI) Compact brown silt.
1089 (CDS) Brown silt.
1097 (CEB) Grey clayey silt with charcoal flecks and occasional pebbles.
1302 (CNP) Grey silt.

Cut 13 1268 (CME) Dark brown peaty silt.

Dating evidence Post-medieval pottery, glass, brick/tile, clay pipes.

Small finds

1087 Stone rubber, Jackson cat. no. 27 (SF 501); iron object (SF 502); bone knife handle, Smithson cat. no. 3 (SF 506); bone sledge runner, Smithson cat. no. 2 (SF 517).

1145 Bone sledge runner, Smithson cat. no. 1 (SF 524).

1227 Brass button, Gaimster cat. no.8 (SF 560).

1251 Lead object, Jackson cat. no. 50 (SF 532).

1098 Copper-alloy disc washer (SF 483).

1172 Copper-alloy ferrule/binding (SF 520).

1373 Copper-alloy pin/needle (SF 572).

The stratigraphic sequence, from top to bottom, is:

Level 1 Cut 6 unit 1170; cut 10, unit 1196; cut 11, unit 1173.

Level 2 Cut 1, unit 1167; cut 2, unit 1087; cut 3, unit 1180; cut 4, unit 1169; cut 5, unit 1227; cut 6, unit 1213; cut 7, unit 1053; cut 8, unit 1165, unit 1172; cut 9, unit 1357; cut 10, unit 1221; cut 11, unit 1195, unit 1299; cut 12, unit 1056; cut 13, unit 1268.

Level 3 Cut 2, unit 1145; cut 4, unit 1200; cut 5, unit 1264; cut 7, unit 1098; cut 12, unit 1089.

Level 4 Cut 2, unit 1150; cut 5, unit 1251; cut 6, unit 1214; cut 9, unit 1373; cut 10, unit 1269; cut 12, unit 1097, unit 1302.

Level 5 Cut 2, unit 1164.

Ditch 13

(Figs 25, 28, 29c, 30a–b, 49, pp. 77, 80, 82–3, 111) Phase VI

A medium-sized ditch at the east end of block 11. It has a broad V-section with gently sloping sides and a rounded base, and is of rather irregular width and depth. It terminates at the north-east corner of the greenhouse, and at a point opposite the brick-lined cesspit it veers north-east from its approximate east–west alignment. Its north-east end lay beyond the area of excavation. Ditch 13 cuts ditches 5, 11, 2, 6, 14.

Width 1.2–1.9 m, length within excavation 31 m, depth 0.4–0.75 m.

Fill

Cut 1 1016 (CAR) Light brown peaty silt.
1051 (CCD) Dark brown silty clay with pebbles.
1182 (CHP) Greenish-brown silt with pebbles.

Cut 2 1143 (CFZ) Brown peaty silt.
1146 (CGC) Brown peaty silt mixed with grey-green silt, pebbles and occasional lumps of yellow clay.
1204 (CIN) Brown peat.
1132 (CFN) Dark grey silt with gravel and pebbles.
1133 (CFO) Grey silt with pebbles.
1134 (CFP) Gravel.
1135 (CFQ) Lens of burnt clay and silt.

Cut 3 1054 (CCG) Dark brown peaty silt.
1055 (CCH) Light brown silt with gravel.
1203 (CIM) Redeposited yellow clay.

Cut 4 1012 (CAN) Brown pebbly silt.

Cut 5 1069 (CCX) Brown peaty silt.
1046 (CBY) Dark brown/black peaty silt with gravel, mortar and charcoal flecks.

Dating evidence Post-medieval pottery, glass, clay pipes etc.

Small finds 1012 Coin, Shotter cat. no. 41, sestertius, LW, AD 141 + (SF 463); bone pin, Greep cat. no. 5 (SF 466) [Joins SF 476 from unit 1072 of ditch 3.]

The stratigraphic sequence, from top to bottom, is:

Level 1 Cut 1, unit 1016; cut 2, unit 1143, unit 1204; cut 3, unit 1054; cut 4, unit 1012; cut 5, unit 1069.

Level 2 Cut 1, unit 1051; cut 2, unit 1146; cut 3, unit 1055, unit 1203; cut 5, unit 1046.

Level 3 Cut 1, unit 1182; cut 2, unit 1132.

Level 4 Cut 2, unit 1133.

Level 5 Cut 2, unit 1134, unit 1135.

Ditch 14 (Figs 25, 28, 29c, 30a–b, 49) Phase VI

A medium-sized ditch, aligned approximately east–west, at the east end of block 11. It has a broad, rounded V-shaped cross-section. To the south of the brick-lined cesspit it kinks slightly southward before resuming its east–west line. No west butt was located. The east end runs beyond the limit of excavation. Ditch 14 is cut by ditch 13, but it cuts gully 1 and ditches 2 and 3.

Width 1.8–2.1 m, length at least 24 m, depth 0.4–0.8 m.

Fill

Cut 1   1181 (CHO) Dark grey silt with pebbles.

Cut 2   1201 (CIK) Grey-green clayey silt.
1176 (CHI) Same as 1201.
1202 (CIL) Grey-green silt with gravel.

Cut 3   1017 (CAS) Mixed brown silt and gravel with clay patches and some peat.
1071 (CCZ) Dark grey silt.

Cut 4   1226 (CKL) Dark grey silt with pebbles.

Cut 5   1105 (CEK) Brown sandy silt with pebbles.
879 (BHE) Same as 1105.

Dating evidence   Post-medieval pottery, glass etc.

Small finds   1226 Bone object, Greep cat. no. 71 (SF 529); coin, Shotter cat. no. 39, sestertius, MW, AD 151–61 (SF 530); stone block, Jackson cat. no. 49 (SF 570).

The stratigraphic sequence, from top to bottom, is:

Level 1   Cut 2, unit 1201, unit 1176; cut 3, unit 1017; cut 4, unit 1226; cut 5, unit 1105, unit 879.

Level 2   Cut 1, unit 1181; cut 2, unit 1202; cut 3, unit 1071.

Ditch 71   (Figs 25, 31a, 32a–c, pp. 77, 84–5)   Phase VI

A broad, shallow, irregular U-sectioned ditch with gently sloping sides, cut into the upper fill of ditches 6, 9 and 7. In most places, ditch 71 seals or incorporates a nineteenth/twentieth century field drain (clay pipe), in a narrow slot.

Width 1.6–3.0 m, length at least 127 m, depth 0.35–0.65 m.

Fill

Cut 1   480 (ABP) Fine brown peaty silt.
488 (ABY) Brown silty soil with iron-panning.

Cut 2   1533 (DBI) Reddish peat and grey-brown silt with much gravel.

Cut 3   1610 (DEO) Reddish brown peaty soil.

Cut 4   473 (ABH) Light brown peaty silt.
496 (ACG) Light brown silty clay.

Cut 5   516 (ADC) Brown peaty silt.
517 (ADD) Brown peaty silt with much gravel.

Cut 6   557 (AEV) Brown peaty soil.

Cut 7   196 (JM) Dark grey/black peaty silt.

Cut 8   731 (BBB) Red/brown peaty silt with patches of charcoal, tile flecks and small stones.
752 (BBY) Dark brown clay with charcoal patches and flecks of tile and mortar.

Cut 9   726 (BAW) Brown peaty silt with small stones and tile flecks.

Cut 10   1003 (CAD) Brown peaty soil.

Cut 11   1086 (CDP) Brown peaty soil with much gravel.

Cut 12   782 (BDF) Light grey/brown gravelly silt.

Dating evidence   Post-medieval finds in most units.

Small finds
480   Milling stone fragment, Jackson cat. no. 1.
752   Mortarium stamp, Hartley cat. no. 16 (SF 432).
726   Iron axe-butt, Jackson cat. no. 9 (SF 343).
1003   Rubbing stone, Jackson cat. no. 28 (SF 525).

Pit 1267 (CMD)   E27.5, N88.5   (Fig. 49, p. 111)   Phase VI

?Rectangular pit, north of street 1 E/W, one edge only excavated; overlies unit 1303 of the LBA ring ditch (gully 1).

Width/length 1.6 m.

Fill   Dark, peaty earth

Dating evidence   Post-medieval glass, pottery and brick.

Pit 1173 (CHF)   E18.0, N80.0   (Fig. 49)   Phase VI

A large rhomboid pit towards the east end of block 11. Cuts units 1338 and 1195 of, respectively, ditches 10 and 12. Also cuts the construction trench of the brick-lined cesspit.

Width 1.6 m, length 3.4 m.

Fill   Loose brown soil with much building debris.

Dating evidence   Post-medieval pottery and glass.

Pit 1285 (CMX)   W49.8, N63.6   (Fig. 48, p. 110)   Phase VI

A rectangular pit cut into the surface of street 1 E/W some 10 m west of building S1. An irregular scatter of post-holes nearby is probably associated.

Width 0.65 m, length 0.75 m.

Fill   Grey/brown gravel and silt with limestone fragments.

Dating evidence   Post-medieval pottery, brick and tile.

Pit 1344 (CPI)   E34.50, N81.0   (Fig. 49)   Phase VI?

?Rectangular pit, north of street 1 E/W, cut by unit 1226 of post-medieval ditch 14.

Width/length at least 1.7 × 0.9 m, depth 0.26 m.

Fill   Pebbly grey silty earth.

It produced no finds but is probably of post-medieval date.

PREHISTORIC FLINT AND STONE

Gill Varndell   (Fig. 80)

All but two pieces of flint are from contaminated or late contexts which in many cases contain other residual material. A side-scraper (no. 4) and an unretouched flake (n) both come from gully 1, the Late Bronze Age ring gully, which also yielded a rubbing stone (no. 12).

1 ST 84 DEA, SF 750   Leaf arrowhead with flat retouch over the whole of one surface and part of the other. Brown flint. Neolithic.

Length 35 mm, width 20 mm, thickness 4 mm.

From topsoil/cleaning (unit 1597), block 8, west of pit 1698.

2 ST 84 DEA, SF 937   Triangular arrowhead with flat retouch over both surfaces. Hinge fracture at one corner. Brown flint. According to Green (1980, 142) these belong to the early-mid second millennium BC; known associations are Beaker.

Length 32 mm, width 25 mm, thickness 5 mm.

From topsoil/cleaning (unit 1597), blocks 8, 9, and east 3 and 4.

3 ST 84 DEA, SF 745   Half of a well-executed thumbnail scraper; broken edge utilised. Chocolate-coloured flint. Probably Beaker.

Length 26 mm, width 14 mm, thickness 5 mm.

From topsoil/cleaning (unit 1597), block 9, near pit 2003.

4 ST 83 CQP, SF 604   Side-scraper: scraper edge formed by invasive and subsequently steep retouch. Mottled grey flint. Later Neolithic–Bronze Age.

Length 39 mm, width 35 mm, thickness 9 mm.

From LBA ring gully (gully 1), cut 5, unit 1374. Phase I.

5 ST 81 PP   Broken piercer with some edge-retouch distally: bulb has been removed. Chocolate-coloured flint. Mesolithic–early Neolithic.

Length 44 mm, width 12 mm, thickness 13 mm.

From metalled surface (unit 313) north of building R1. 2nd–3rd century AD. Phase III.

6 ST 82 AAQ   (*Unillus.*)   Knife, near-oval, with pressure flaking on dorsal surface only. Blunting retouch half-way down one edge. Chocolate-coloured flint. Probably Early Bronze Age.

Length 39 mm, width 24 mm, thickness 9 mm.

From gully 41, cut 5, unit 457. Phase III.

7 ST 84 DEH   (*Unillus.*)   Endscraper on irregular flake: steep retouch on distal edge. Grey-yellow mottled flint. Middle/Late Bronze Age.

Length 43 mm, width 37 mm, thickness 10 mm.

From pit 1604, unit 1604. Phase III.

8 ST 84 ECT   (*Unillus.*)   Broken blade from prepared core, otherwise unretouched. Chocolate-coloured flint. On technological grounds could date from Upper Palaeolithic–early Neolithic.

Length 22 mm, width 23 mm, thickness 7 mm.

From trowelling layer (unit 2143), east gully 17, block 8. Unphased.

Miscellaneous retouched pieces   (*Unillus.*)

Recorded from the following contexts:

a   ST 82 ABQ   Topsoil (unit 481), N.E. area.

b   ST 83 CPN   Spit (unit 1348) above LBA ring gully (gully 1). Phase I.

Utilised flakes   (*Unillus.*)

c   ST 82 BCQ   Pit 797, unit 769. Phase III.

d   ST 82 BGM   Silt layer (unit 862) beneath street 1 E/W (unit 982). Phase I–III.

e   ST 83 CIS   Ditch 4, cut 1, unit 1209. Phase III.

Unretouched flakes   (*Unillus.*)

f   ST 80 AA   Topsoil (unit 1) in region of building R1. (Two pieces.)

g   ST 81 QC   Oven 2, unit 325. Phase IV.

h   ST 82 ABQ   Context as (a) above.

i   ST 82 BBA   Upper layer (unit 730) in pit 730 (residual with prehistoric pottery). Phase III.

j   ST 82 BCT   Pit 808, unit 722 (residual). Phase III.

k   ST 82 BGD   Post-hole 853. Unphased.

l   ST 82 BGM   Context as (d) above. (Two pieces.)

m   ST 83 CAA   Topsoil (unit 1000), block 11, east and block 2, north. (One blade.)

n   ST 83 CEI   Upper layer (unit 1104) in butt of LBA ring gully (gully 1, cut 3). Phase I.

o   ST 83 CFR   Upper layer (unit 1136) in butt of ditch 2 (cut 1), with prehistoric pottery. Phase II/III.

p   ST 83 CFS   Ditch 2, cut 2, unit 1137, with prehistoric pottery. Phase II/III.

q   ST 83 CGQ   Gully 54, cut 4, unit 1159 (residual). Phase III.

r   ST 83 CMY   Post-hole 1286. Unphased. (One blade.)

s   ST 83 CPN   Context as (b) above. (Three pieces.)

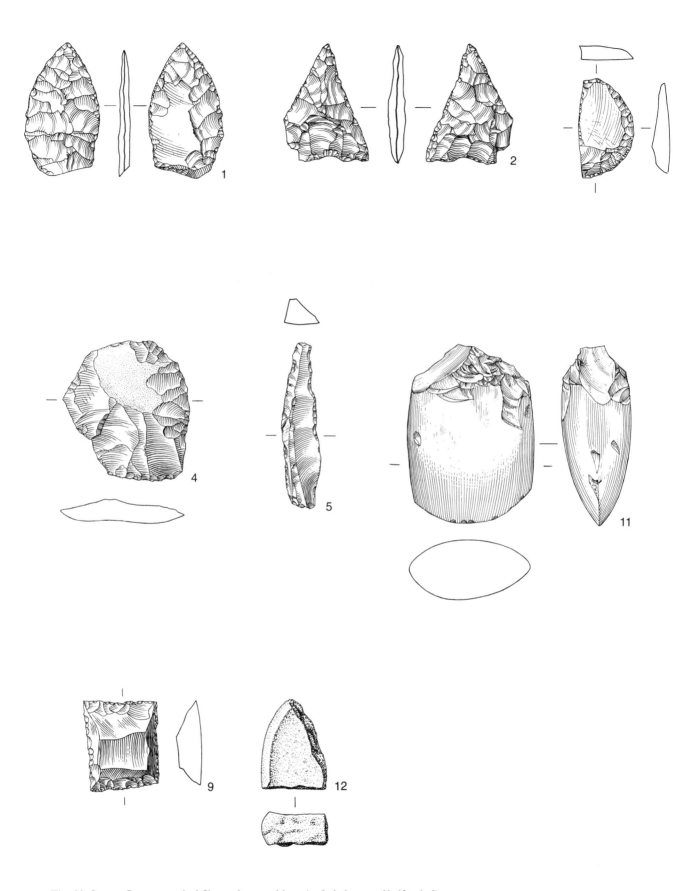

Fig. 80 Stonea Grange: worked flint and stone objects (scale 1 : 1 except 11–12 = 1 : 2).

t ST 83 CPS   Ditch 2, cut 4, unit 1353, with prehistoric pottery. Phase II/III.

u ST 83 H8,3   Layer in ditch/pit (residual). Phase IV.

v ST 84 DAB   Topsoil (unit 1502) blocks 7 and 8.

w ST 84 DMY   Fill of pit 1787 (residual). Phase III/IV.

x ST 84 P10, 2, SF 767   Lower layer of 'votive' pit P10. Phase III.

Modern flint

9 ST 81 FQ, SF 41   Gunflint. A complete example on brown flint.

Length 24 mm, width 20 mm, thickness 7 mm.

From street 1 E/W, denuded surface at west (unit 130). Phase III onwards.

10 ST 83 CPN   (*Unillus.*) ?Unfinished gunflint, spoiled during manufacture. Brown flint.

Context as (b) and (s) above.

Stone

11 P1982, 6–2, 178   Polished stone axe, broken. Distinctly curved edge with marked junction to faceted sides. Thick profile. Butt end missing: broken surface has battered appearance as if reused. Grey-green, fine grained rock of Group VI type (but sources outside the north-west are possible).

Length 91 mm, width 68 mm, thickness 36 mm.

Stonea Grange Surface Collection.

12 ST 83 CRA, SF 645   ?Rubbing stone. Small fragment of an ovoid pebble of fine micaceous sandstone. One face appears to have been deliberately made; the other appears to have been produced through breakage (ancient) along the bedding plane. The remains of the convex circumference is smooth through use-wear. Function unknown.

Length 49 mm.

From gully 1, cut 4, unit 1384, basal layer of LBA ring gully.

NEOLITHIC POTTERY

I. H. Longworth   (Fig. 81)

1 ST 83 CPD   Rim sherd from Ebbsfleet style bowl of well fired paste tempered with large quantity of angular crushed burnt flint, reddish brown externally, greyish brown internally with light grey core.

Decoration   On the external rim bevel short diagonal whipped cord lines. On the internal surface, remains of whipped cord vertical chevron.

Residual, in the basal fill (unit 1339) of the Phase III ditch 4, cut 1, at the extreme north-west corner of the site.

2 ST 82 ACI   Wall sherd of ?Beaker, well-fired sandy paste, light brown with grey core.

Decoration   Remains of herringbone pattern in ?technique very weathered.

Residual, in the fill (unit 498) of the Phase III gully 41, cut 1, east side of block 1b, south-west of the site.

[For (1), compare *inter alia* S. Piggott (1962) *The West Kennet Long Barrow Excavations 1955–56*, Fig. 11, Pl.]

POST DEVEREL–RIMBURY POTTERY

Stuart Needham   (Figs 81–6)

The material considered here is necessarily selective, given a complex site with many periods represented and much rede-position. The core of the report is based on the few undisturbed or minimally disturbed contexts which yielded good quantities of identifiable later prehistoric pottery and where the diagnostic material was Post Deverel–Rimbury (PDR). From these contexts all featured pottery considered to be informative has been catalogued and illustrated. To this has been added diagnostic sherds from insecurely dated or later contexts. Material considered to belong to the second half of the first millennium BC is not treated here.

The PDR assemblage is not considered large enough to merit attempting a fabric classification. It will suffice to summarise the range. Fabrics of catalogue sherds are individually described below. As usual in PDR assemblages crushed burnt flint is the dominant temper; its density and grade of grit size largely defines quality of ware.

Flint is occasionally sparse, more normally light, moderate or dense. The finer wares, burnished bowls, are characterised more by a finer grade of flint, whereas large grits tend to be associated with coarseware jars. A good proportion of the wares contain some sand, generally fine, and occasionally this is the predominant or sole temper. There appears to be no direct/or inverse correlation between presence of sand and character of flint inclusions. Shell is exceptionally present as a minor inclusion (54), but in two catalogued sherds (nos 51 and 53) it is dense and the sole or main temper. Vessels 26, 28, 50 and perhaps 20 include grog in their mixtures, while nos 10, 22 and 46 have small black inclusions as well as more standard agents. Some vessels also have many voids indicative of eroded organic temper (nos 4, 43, 44). Petrography has not been attempted, but would be necessary to identify some of the more infrequent inclusions.

CATALOGUE

The material is arranged by context groups, followed by miscellaneous contexts (for which the contexts are given in individual entries).

Qualitative descriptions for temper:

temper size: fine, small, medium, large
temper density: sparse, light, moderate, dense.

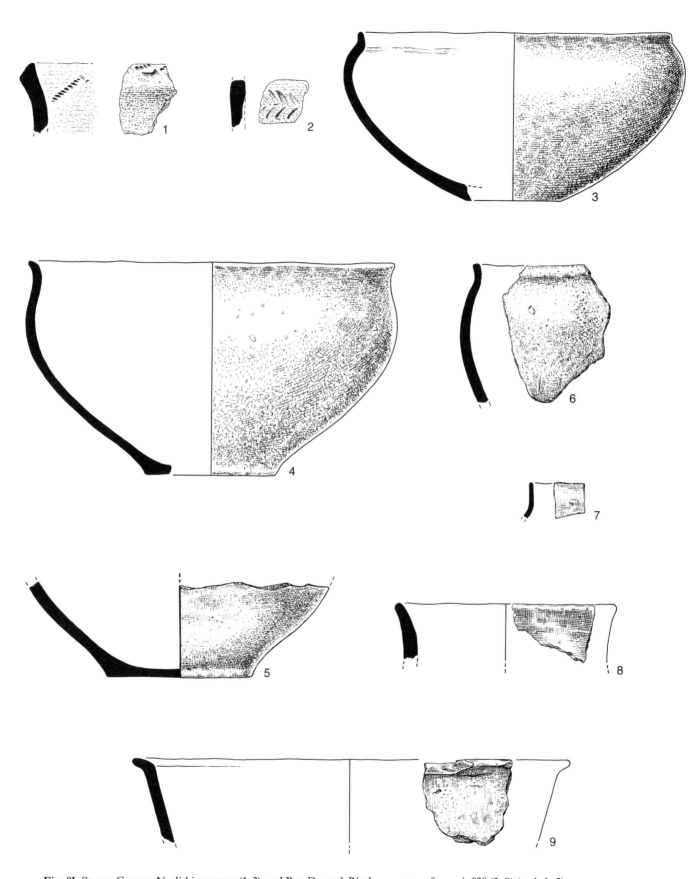

Fig. 81 Stonea Grange: Neolithic pottery (1–2), and Post Deverel–Rimbury pottery from pit 920 (3–9) (scale 1 : 2).

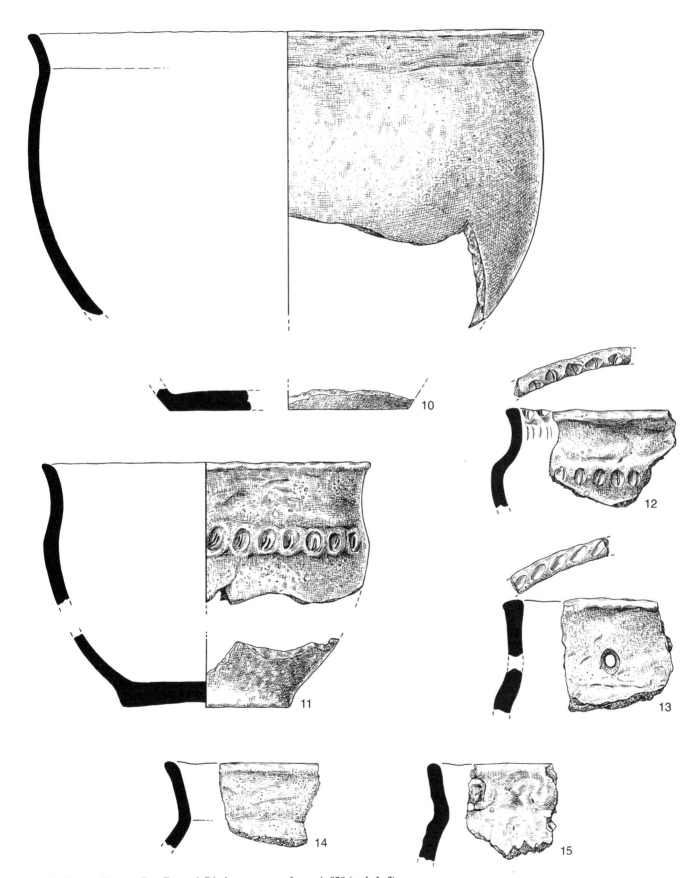

Fig. 82 Stonea Grange: Post Deverel–Rimbury pottery, from pit 920 (scale 1 : 2).

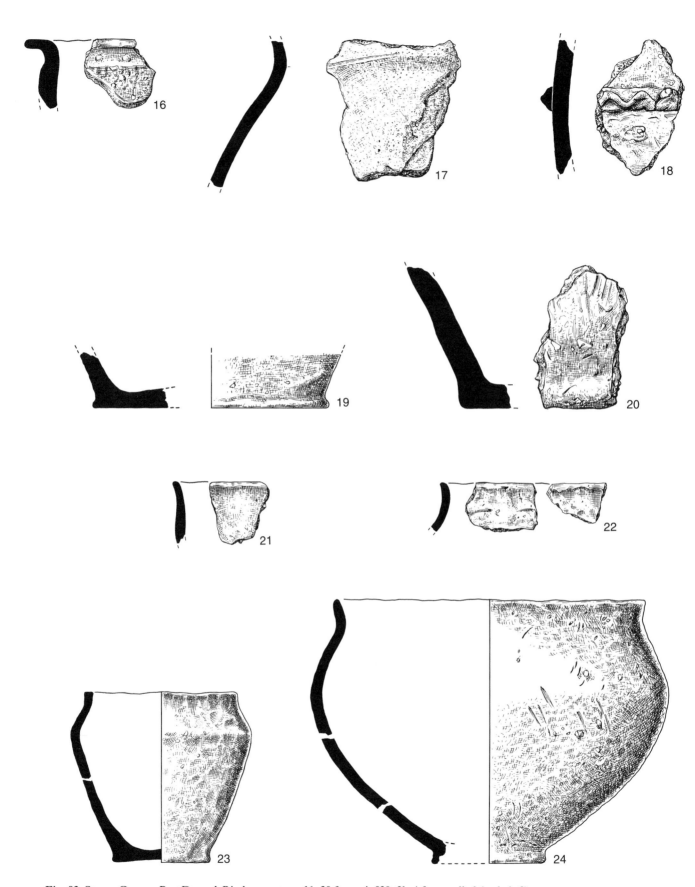

Fig. 83 Stonea Grange: Post Deverel–Rimbury pottery, 16–20 from pit 920, 21–4 from gully 1 (scale 1 : 2).

a) Pit 920 (Figs 81–3)

This pit yielded some 163 sherds from the three excavated layers (920/BIX, 928/BKF, 957/BLL). The base was waterlogged, whilst the upper layer (920/BIX) had some 'intrusive' Roman sherds. The material is presented as one group since no significant form or fabric distinctions were noted. In one case (no. 4) joining sherds came from two of the layers.

3 About one-third of a bowl with strong bulbous body and short upright neck, dark reddish brown fabric, smoothly finished on the exterior with traces of burnish; grittier on the interior due to erosion. Moderate quantity of small crushed burnt grits and some sand. Thickness 5.5 mm ST 82 BKF

4 Almost half of a round-bodied bowl with slightly out-turned lip giving smooth asymmetric S profile; rim flattened in parts; slightly emphasised base angle. Base portion 5 might belong. Burnished dark brown exterior, light grey (?eroded) interior, pinkish along rim. Sand and moderate small flint, plus numerous vesicles – perhaps eroded organic filler. Thickness 5 mm. ST 82 BIX and BKF

5 Base portion of a bowl with flat base and neat foot angle; bowed and well flared lower wall of regular thickness. Could have belonged to no. 4. Pale grey/reddish, with moderate small flint and sand filler. Thickness 5.5 mm. ST 82 BKF

6 Sherd from a deep round-bodied bowl with small upright neck. Pale orange-red with sand and fairly dense fine flint; surfaces seem eroded. Thickness 5.5 mm. ST 82 BKF

7 Small rim sherd from fineware bowl or small jar. Light grey sandy ware. Thickness 3 mm. ST 82 BIX

8 Simple rim with gently concave neck. Rust brown surfaces on a black core; moderate amounts of medium flint grit, plus sand. Thickness 8 mm. ST 82 BKF

9 Two joining sherds with near cylindrical neck and strongly out-turned rim defined by an internal bevel. Grey surface, eroding to exposed reddish core; fairly profuse fine to medium flint, plus sand; surfaces in part smooth, possible light burnish originally. Thickness 6 mm. ST 82 BIX

10 Large deep bowl with weak-angled neck and internal bevel; rim flattened in places; detached belonging base has simple, neat angle and swollen centre. Dark grey ripple-burnished surfaces overlying grey core. 'Silty' fabric with copious black inclusions and light small-flint gritting. Thickness 6 mm. ST 82 BKF

11 Portion of jar with moderate carination carrying fingertipped row; gentle hollow neck and flattened rim with possible (eroded) remnants of cabling; detached belonging base with slight hollowing above simple angle. Sandy with moderate grits up to large size of flint and ?other rocks. Rust brown and grey weathered surfaces over dark grey core. Thickness 7 mm. ST 82 BKF

12 Sherd of jar with pronounced shoulder and externally thickened rim. Fingertipped rows on shoulder and inner lip of rim. Light fingernail impressions on interior below rim. Dark to reddish-brown surfaces on grey core; rather uneven; sand and moderate medium flint filler. Thickness 6 mm. ST 82 BKF

13 Probable jar rim with rounded neck angle and beginning of weak shoulder. Thickened rim top carries neat fingertipped cabling; neck hour-glass perforated after firing. Light burnish in places; exterior very dark brown, interior grey-brown, core grey; fairly dense small grit and some sand. Thickness 8 mm. ST 82 BKF

14 Rim with light external beading, near cylindrical neck and neat bevel-defined angle to body. Grey throughout (?refired); traces of smooth surface inside, but most eroded – probably a well finished vessel; densely gritted with small flint. Thickness 6 mm. ST 82 BIX

15 Probable jar rim with moderate neck angle (not crisp) and flattish rim; very uneven faces, but some grass-wiping apparent. Brown to dark brown surfaces on black core. 'Silty' with moderate amounts of large flint grit. Thickness 8 mm. ST 82 BLL

16 Rim sherd with strongly out-turned flange and weak rounded shoulder immediately beneath. Refired fabric, pale grey and brick red: moderate medium flint grits and sand. Thickness 9 mm. ST 82 BIX

17 Neck sherd, probably from a large jar or deep bowl (cf. 10); light internal bevel. Grey to buff fabric; dense fine and small flint, plus sand. Thickness 8 mm. ST 82 BKF

18 Convex walled body sherd carrying cordon finger-impressed in 'pie-crust' manner. Orange-brown fabric; fairly dense medium flint and some sand. Thickness 8.5 mm. ST 82 BKF

19 Portion of flat base with pinched out foot and uneven walls. Dark grey-brown fabric; moderate medium flint and some sand. Thickness 7 mm. ST 82 BIX

20 Flat base and thick wall with simple foot angle; some rough scoring on exterior. Pale brown exterior, grey interior and core, 'silty' fabric with fairly dense large flint grits and ?some grog. Thickness 12 mm. ST 82 BKF

b) Ring gully (Gully 1) (Figs 83–4)

Stretches of a curving ditch, much dissected by later features, can nevertheless be reconstructed as a ring gully, probably penannular. Its fill appeared in plan after the late pre-Roman silt was removed (see (c) below). A total of 188 sherds were recovered from the gully fill, the great majority being of small size.

21 Rim of small bowl with vestigial carination, giving very slack S profile; not particularly smooth surfaces. Dark grey fabric; moderate medium flint grits. Thickness 5 mm. ST 83 CFV

22 Two non-joining sherds of hollow-necked rim in a thin but uneven ware, probably from a bowl. Orange-red fabric; sand, many tiny black inclusions, lightly gritted with small flint and some iron-rich pellets. Thickness 4.5 mm. ST 83 CEI

23 Non-joining portions (five sherds) from a small shouldered jar; the shoulder is not strong and is ill-defined, the neck slightly hollow and the rim top flattened; the foot is erratically pinched out; uneven surfaces. Dark grey and reddish brown fabric. Sand and fairly dense flints, mainly medium sized, but one exception 10 mm across. Thickness 5.5 mm. ST 83 CEI and CRA

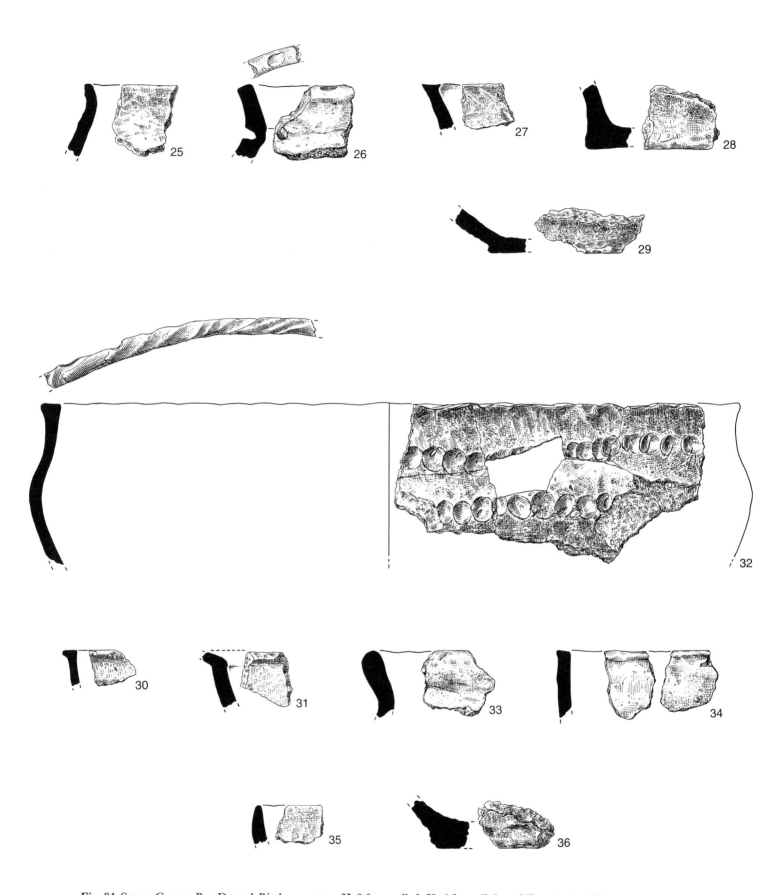

Fig. 84 Stonea Grange: Post Deverel–Rimbury pottery, 25–9 from gully 1, 30–6 from silt layer 862 etc. (scale 1 : 2).

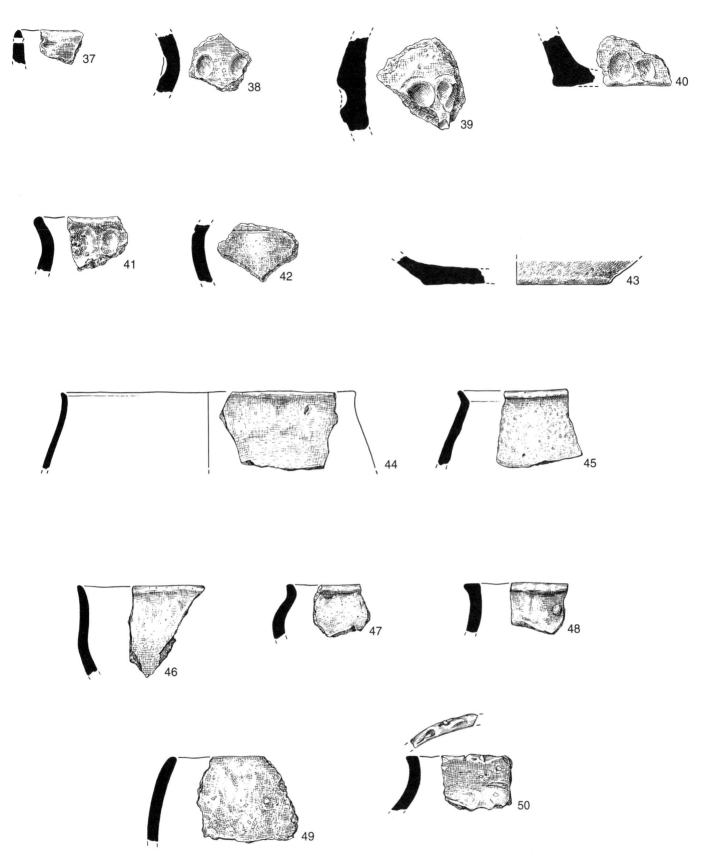

Fig. 85 Stonea Grange: Post Deverel–Rimbury pottery, 37–40 from silt layer 862 etc., 41–3 from post-hole 1345 (within gully 1), 44–50 from miscellaneous contexts (scale 1 : 2).

24 Portions of slack S profile vessel (six sherds) with simple rim; tiny fragment of foot suggests rough 'plinth' for base. Surfaces left rough with occasional scoremarks. Grey-brown exterior, dark grey core, black interior with remnants of charred food residue; moderate medium flint, plus some sand. Thickness 6.5 mm. ST 83 CRA

25 Rim slightly out-turned and top flattened. Grey fabric; uneven surfaces; moderate medium flint. Thickness 6.5 mm. ST 83 CRA

26 Probable jar rim with weakly angled neck and internal bevel; one finger impression survives on flattened rim top; deep pits at intervals in neck. Dark grey-brown surfaces on grey core; moderate medium flint gritting, coarse sand and a little grog. Thickness 10 mm. ST 83 CPN

27 Sherd with well flattened rim giving rise to pronounced internal lip. Grey-brown surfaces on grey core; sand and light small flint. Thickness 7 mm. ST 83 CFV

28 Base sherd with slightly pulled out foot. Pale orange-brown exterior, brown interior, grey core; light small flint, sand and a little grog. Thickness 9 mm. ST 83 CRA

29 Base sherd with small foot beneath splayed wall. Brown exterior, grey interior and core; moderate large flint filler. Thickness 8 mm. ST 83 CFV

c) Silt layer (862 *et al*)   (Figs 84–5)

Sondages into the silt layer north of and sealed beneath street 1 E/W at points adjacent to the ring gully (group (b) above). This unit contained mainly late prehistoric pottery (some 75+ sherds) probably deriving from occupation deposits associated with the nearby ring gully building. There was also a little Roman pottery thought to have been introduced by natural agencies.

30 Rim sherd with flattened top and pronounced external lip; probably from a bowl. Dark grey fabric with smooth, ?lightly burnished exterior; light small flint and a little sand. Thickness 4.5 mm. ST 82 BGM

31 Sherd with strongly out-turned rim and internal lipped bevel; the rim edge is chipped away. Grey-brown to red-brown surfaces on grey core; well-finished even and smooth surfaces; moderate fine flint, sand and occasional iron-rich pellets. Thickness 8.5 mm. ST 82 BGM

32 Portion of carinated jar or large bowl; rim curvature suggests a large diameter, assuming no gross distortion of this hard fabric; slightly thickened rim top carries finger-moulded cabling; row of fingertip impressions on carination, and second in neck. Rusty-brown to dark grey-brown surfaces on grey core; surfaces partially smoothed by grass-wiping; moderate medium flint (occasional large grits), plus sand. Thickness 6.5 mm. ST 82 BGM

33 Thickened rim with S profile giving slight hollowing inside and bulbous exterior. Grey-brown fabric; no smoothing; fairly dense large flint, plus some sand. Thickness 9 mm. ST 82 BGM

34 Two non-joining sherds with flattened rim and irregular external lipping; upper body near straight. Grey-brown exterior, dark grey interior and core. Moderate-light small flint gritting. Thickness 7 mm. ST 82 BGM

35 Simple thinned rim. Grey-brown surfaces on grey core; moderate medium flint and sand. Thickness 8 mm. ST 82 BGM

36 Base sherd with simple foot angle. Brown and dark grey fabric; fairly dense large flint, plus sand. Thickness 8 mm. ST 82 BGM

37 Simple rim with narrow perforation through wall just below. Grey fabric; sand and light small flint. Thickness 5.5 mm. ST 83 CRF

38 Body sherd with weakly angled neck defined by internal bevel; row of fingertip impressions sited in neck. Grey-brown surfaces on grey core; sand and moderate small flint. Thickness 8.5 mm. ST 83 CRG

39 Body sherd with weak shoulder/carination carrying fingertipped row. Orange-brown exterior, core grey, interior eroded; light medium flint, plus sand. Thickness 14 mm. ST 83 CRF

40 Base sherd with small pinched out foot. Light grey-brown surfaces on dark grey core; moderate medium flint and sand. Thickness 10 mm. ST 83 CRF

d) Post-hole 1345 within gully 1   (Fig. 85)

41 Simple rim above slightly hollow neck. Grey-brown fabric; sand and light medium flint. Thickness 6.5 mm. ST 83 CPK

42 Body sherd with a horizontal groove above rounded ?belly. Grey-brown surfaces on grey core; even and possibly originally burnished surfaces; moderate fine flint and sand. Thickness 7 mm. ST 83 CPK

43 Sherd with flat base and simple angle to well splayed lower wall. Buff exterior, dark grey interior, grey core; moderate medium-large flint, some sand and voids, perhaps from burnt out chaff/seeds. Thickness 7 mm. ST 83 CPK

e) Miscellaneous contexts   (Figs 85–6)

Various contexts in the excavated areas and the machine-cut trenches which are either of later date, or yielded only isolated diagnostic sherds.

44 In-sloped and slightly concave neck from a closed vessel; rim with internal bevel; probably broken at carination. Red-brown burnished 'slip' on exterior, rest light grey; moderate fine flint, plus sand and tiny voids. Thickness 3.5 mm. ST 82 ABQ. Topsoil, blocks 2–4

45 Sharply everted rim with neat internal bevel above in-sloping upper body. Light pinkish-brown and light grey fabric; exterior smooth, interior undulates; sand and sparse fine flint. Thickness 5 mm. ST 83 CME

Residual in post-medieval ditch 12 (cut 13, unit 1268), on north side of gully 1.

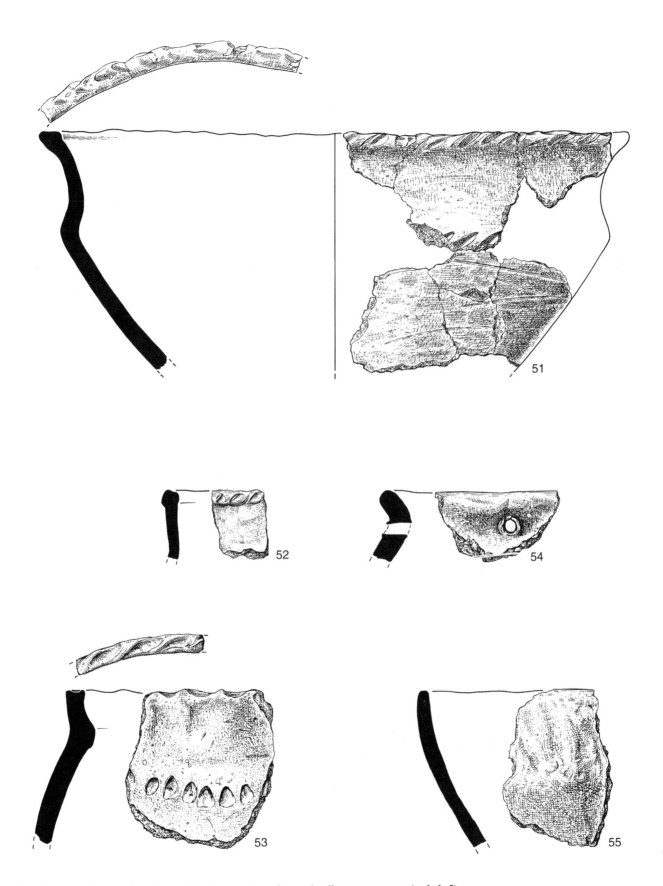

Fig. 86 Stonea Grange: Post Deverel–Rimbury pottery, from miscellaneous contexts (scale 1:2).

46 Simple rim, gently hollowed neck and weakly defined carination. Brown to grey fabric; surfaces with traces of burnish, but
slight undulations; sand, light small flint and small black inclusions. Thickness 6 mm. ST 82 BEP

Residual in stokehole/rake-out debris of Roman oven 6 (unit
816).

47 Sherd of small bowl or cup with bulbous body and short, near
upright neck. Grey-brown exterior, rest dark grey; moderate
fine flint, plus sand. Thickness 5 mm. ST 83 CEH. Post-hole
1103

48 Flat-topped, externally thickened rim above slightly hollow
neck. Grey-brown exterior, rest grey; moderate small-flint,
and sand. Thickness 5.5 mm. ST 83 CGA. Unit 1144, post-medieval context near ring gully

49 Rim of convex-walled vessel, probably a tub. Black-brown
fabric; dense medium flint. Thickness 6.5 mm. ST 83 CMR.
Unit 1280, spread near ring gully

50 Flattened rim carrying irregular stab marks above concave
neck. Dark grey-brown fabric; light medium flint and a little
grog; traces of grass-wiping. Thickness 6.5 mm. ST 82 BAZ.
Unit 729 in Roman pit 725

51 Portion of a large carinated bowl with externally thickened, flat-
topped rim; slight beading internally; diagonally slashed decoration on outer lip of rim and carination; wall thickness fairly regular – traces of tool facets but no real burnish. Light brown
exterior, rest dark grey; fairly dense shell (?fossil) gritting, some
having eroded out, and a little sand. Thickness 8 mm. ST 84 O17.
Machine-cut trench O, ?post-hole O17

52 Flattened rim with finger-impressed decoration on outer lip
giving cabled effect; neat but slight internal beading. Grey-
brown surfaces on grey core; sand and sparse fine flint. Thickness 7 mm. ST 84 O14. Machine-cut trench O, ditch layer O14

53 Sherd of slack profile jar with out-turned rim and internal hollowing, perhaps for lid-seat; deeply impressed 'pie-crust' decoration on rim top; decoration on vestigial shoulder has been
carried out with a bullet-ended instrument applied flat to the
pot surface, then the tip rocked in furthest – the result is a *kerbschnitt*-like motif. Grey exterior, pale grey interior, black core;
fairly dense medium-sized shell (?fossil), plus occasional flint
grits. Thickness 9 mm. ST 84 P21(1). Machine-cut trench P,
from surface layer of unexcavated ?pit

54 Thick out-turned rim, neck perforated prior to firing. Grey-
brown surfaces, grey cores; dense large flint, plus some sand
and shell. Thickness 10.5 mm. ST 84 O26. Machine-cut trench
O, from surface layer of unexcavated ?pit

55 Sherd from convex-walled vessel, rim top flattened; rather
uneven exterior, grass-wiped interior. Light grey-brown exterior, grey interior and core; light medium flint. Thickness
8 mm. ST 84. Machine-cut trench O unstratified

DISCUSSION

It would be unwise to attempt to place the Stonea assemblage
of Post Deverel–Rimbury ware (PDR) too closely. There are

only three useable context groups to consider – pit group 920
(sherds 3–20), penannular ring gully (21–9) and an adjacent
silt layer (30–40) – the latter of which had probably suffered
a little disturbance allowing a minor admixture of Roman
finds. Even the largest group (920) is not extensive. The
more isolated feature sherds from a range of contemporary
and later contexts are of limited value. The very fragmentary
survival of pre-Roman contexts at Stonea leaves little by way
of stratigraphic or spatial basis for assessing the extent or
duration of activity. All judgement on such issues therefore
hangs on the limited ceramic groups.

The PDR ceramic tradition was defined by Barrett (1980).
He outlined a major development from 'plainware' to 'decorated wares' during the early half of the first millennium BC
which has become well established. Unfortunately this has
probably led to an overdependence on the presence/absence
of decoration as a criterion for placing assemblages where
stratigraphy or independent dating evidence is lacking (cf.
Knight 1984, 68–9). This distinction is undoubtedly a simplification and glosses over local and functional variation. More
attention needs to be paid to associations of particular morphological and decorative traits, as well as to establishing
regional sequences (cf. Barrett in Thomas *et al* 1986, 187).

So far, however, East Anglia, the Fens and the East Midlands have not been very forthcoming in yielding useful
early first millennium BC pottery assemblages. In Norfolk,
Lawson (1980b) was hard-pressed to find much at all to fill
the vacuum between Deverel–Rimbury/Ardleigh wares and
transitional LBA/EIA wares (e.g. West Harling) although the
small assemblage from Witton OS 171 (Lawson 1983, 42–3)
now seems best placed within this bracket. It is possible
that there are some PDR elements amongst the miscellany
of later prehistoric pottery recovered at Grimes Graves, but
there are no useful stratified groups (Rigby 1988). Knight's
study of the Nene and Ouse basins reveals little evidence
for pottery groups belonging to the first quarter of the first
millennium BC (Knight 1984). Even the extensive excavations around Fengate during the 1970s and 1980s have produced only sporadic stratified groups to add to the earlier
Fengate pit groups (Hawkes and Fell 1945), particularly now
that the Flag Fen Platform pottery is seen to have more in
common with Deverel–Rimbury traditions (Anderson and
Barrett 1992). Three of the Fengate contexts have provided a
single radiocarbon determination each. These, however,
cover a fair span in calendar years and led Pryor to envisage
a rather static ceramic tradition over a period of a few centuries (his group 1: 1984, 143–53). However, in areas where more
plentiful evidence exists, there are indications that ceramic
assemblages were actually being rapidly adapted during the
Late Bronze Age to meet changing social circumstances;
this begs the question as to whether the Fens and East
Anglia differ only in the poor record currently extant.

A recently published site at Barham, Suffolk, includes
some small, but useful PDR and Darmsden–Linton pottery

groups in association with a round house and other structural evidence (Martin 1993, 23–40). The largest group of plainware PDR is associated with an oven set in a shallow pit (pit 1), a group that suggests a date around the eleventh–ninth centuries BC. A radiocarbon date of 2640 ± 70 BP (HAR-3610) is unfortunately based on a mixture of charcoal from two pits.

Martin suggests that pit 1 contains a sherd of Darmsden type pottery (*ibid.*, 38, no. 19), but this small sherd offers little diagnostic and could readily be accepted as a fine burnished ware of the early ('plain') PDR. Furthermore, whilst accepting Martin's reservations about the relationship between West Harling and Darmsden style groups, the present writer finds it difficult to accept true Darmsden forms (as opposed to fine-ware carinated bowls generally) as starting in the ninth century BC. This seems rather too early, even if conventional wisdom (fifth–third centuries BC) is too conservative.

On this basis, part of the complex of post-holes lying 15 m from the oven at Barham should be later since several post-holes contain Darmsden ware. However, the relevant post-holes could be viewed as belonging to one or more structures overlapping and distinct from the round house. This porchless house of about 11 m diameter evidently yielded little diagnostic pottery in its fills and the possibility is open that it belongs to a pre-Darmsden phase.

Further south in Essex, some useful site sequences have been recovered, those at Mucking North Ring and Loft's Farm being fully published (Bond 1988; Brown 1988). Loft's Farm has been particularly valuable in that three phase groups could be established on the basis of two stratigraphic successions (each comprising two phase groups) and their linkage by assemblage comparisons. The sequence thus runs:

	Main enclosure ditch	*External well 840*
1	Early ditch silts	
2	Later ditch silts	Early fill
3		Later fill

Brown places these changes within a timescale spanning the tenth to fifth centuries BC (Brown 1988). Only the first group here would conform to Barrett's plainware, but the nature of decoration changed from group 2 to group 3, the latter being allied to Cunliffe's Darmsden–Linton ware (Cunliffe 1968a).

It is the second phase group at Loft's Farm which provides a context for the original pit groups at Fengate. Champion has already suggested (1975, 135) that some of the Fengate material could date to the full Late Bronze Age, although on current evidence his dating (ninth–eighth centuries BC) seems a shade early, even for his putative early group. The present writer, however, feels that there may not be a valid distinction in chronological terms between the two pit groups defined by Hawkes and Fell (1945). At least some of the pottery more recently recovered at Fengate seems to belong to this stage, as recognised by Pryor (1984).

However, insofar as the modest-sized Stonea assemblage can be characterised, it does not give a close overall match for either Fengate or West Harling. A brief consideration of the main elements present is worthwhile.

The incidence of decoration can, as we have seen, give some notion of temporal position within the early first millennium sequence. One critical change was the application of decoration to fine tableware which had previously been embellished by a different aesthetic technique (plain burnishing). In general, incised decorated bowls are thought to date from the eighth century BC (calibrated) onwards (Barrett 1980, 308), but in time this will doubtless emerge to be an over simplification. In the relatively well dated sequence at Runnymede Bridge (Area 6), for instance, decorated fine wares seem to be added to the plainware repertoire before the close of the ninth century cal BC (Needham 1991, 377), but this did not lead to the immediate cessation of the plain burnished bowls that had dominated the early ninth century series on the site.

Decoration on coarse ware followed a similar course in terms of relative frequency. The predominant decorative forms involve various fingertip treatments and these are already present at low percentages in early PDR assemblages (i.e. Barrett's plainware), such as Aldermaston, Berks (Bradley *et al* 1980), or the earliest groups at Runnymede, units A–D (Longley 1991). Early fingertipping (or similar) seems almost invariably to be restricted to a single row per vessel, whereas the later developments involved frequent multiplication of rows (and sometimes columns) as well as a widening of the detailed techniques of execution, as seen classically in the Fens region at West Harling (Clark and Fell 1953).

With these points in mind, we can return to the Stonea assemblage. Although the different contexts do not necessarily relate closely together it is useful initially to outline noteworthy elements within the whole assemblage.

Amongst the finer wares one of the more striking features is the presence of at least five round-bodied bowls with outturned rims (nos 3–6, 10, 24). A sixth (uncatalogued) portion shows a pronounced round belly, but the rim is damaged. These vary in detailed profile and can be relatively deep (10). Extant bases (4, 5, 24) are neat but unelaborated. By contrast, carinated hollow-necked bowls, which are a frequent component of PDR assemblages (including some Early Iron Age assemblages, e.g. Gretton, Northants. Jackson and Knight 1985), are represented just by two rather weakly carinated specimens (21, 46). Vessels 9 and 14 have cylinder necks above more bulbous bodies, a form perhaps ultimately related to Urnfield styles. Internal bevels feature on a few vessels (9, 10, 14, 31, 44, 45, and a coarser rim, 26).

Virtually all the material considered so far is well made and several sherds retain traces of burnish. Coarser wares are dominated by vessels with angular shoulders/carinations of variable strength. Only a small jar (23) definitely lacks decoration, the rest carrying various fingertip treatments (11, 12, 32, 39, 51). Sherds 49 and 55 seem to belong to a distinct form, the convex-walled tub or jar, whilst 53 has a 'lid seat' above the neck and probably had a rounded shoulder/belly. Girth cordons such as 18 tend also to occur on round bellied jars. (There is another (uncatalogued) cordoned sherd from pit 920). Most rims in the assemblage are simple, either rounded or flattened. The strongly out-turned rim on 16 is noteworthy and resembles some at Burderop Down (Gingell 1992, 98, Fig. 72), although these seem consistently to have cordons sited immediately beneath the rim flange for which there is no indication on the Stonea sherd. Although Gingell attributes the Burderop sherds in question to the barrel urn class, they can probably be regarded instead as part of the associated PDR assemblage, which includes clear-cut PDR forms (*ibid.*, Figs 74–5), LBA metalwork and stone mould (*ibid.*, 109–11). The treatment of sherd 16 is not the same as on the Upper Thames/Chiltern pots with heavy out-turned rims (e.g. Harding 1972, Pl. 44).

Decoration is virtually absent on the finer wares; just one catalogued piece bears a single fine groove (42; occasional additional grooved sherds from the site might belong to this phase). On the coarser wares, a fair variety of decorative techniques is employed: fingertipping on shoulder/carination (11, 12, 32, 39, 51), neck (32, 38), rim interior (12), rim exterior (52), cabling on rim top (13, 53), slashes on rim exterior (51), *kerbschnitt* on shoulder (53), pits in neck (26), ?stabs on rim top (50) and a pie-crust moulded cordon (18).

There are indications that the Stonea assemblage does not represent a narrow chronological horizon. On the one hand, the variety of expression seen in finger decoration on the coarse wares would tend to point to a late PDR date. Furthermore, certain specific forms, such as 32, 51, 52 and 53, are best matched in assemblages regarded as typical of the LBA/EIA transition, circa late eighth–sixth centuries BC, notably West Harling. Features like the external rim decoration in particular seem to be diagnostic of this phase (nos 51–2). On the other hand, the fine ware bowls recovered from the site show neither decoration nor the specific beaded biconical form which seems to be important at many transitional sites, e.g. Staple Howe (Brewster 1963), West Harling (Clarke and Fell 1953), Petters B (O'Connell 1986; Needham 1990), Minnis Bay (Worsfold 1943). This specific form has a strong carination, the short upper body is straight or even marginally convex, and there is usually neat beaded definition of rim and sometimes also shoulder. The dating evidence from Petters points to the existence of this form by the eighth century cal BC (Needham 1990, 125, 140).

The round-bodied bowl form with thin walls and a small out-turned rim, which is the dominant fine-ware form at Stonea, can probably be regarded as distinct in concept from the carinated hollow-necked series. It seems, however, to be essentially contemporary for it can be found in several early PDR assemblages, amongst them: Puddlehill (Matthews 1976, 55, Fig. 18.6–7), Loft's Farm (Brown 1988, 265, Fig. 14, no. 22), Heybridge (Brown and Adkins 1988, 248, Fig. 11.9), Mucking North Ring (Barrett and Bond 1988, Fig. 23, nos 90 and 98), Runnymede Bridge (Longley 1991, 191, Fig. 88, P178), Weston Wood Area 2 (Russell 1989, 36, Fig. 23, no. 239; 25, Fig. 25, no. 313), Aldermaston (Bradley *et al* 1980, 238, Fig. 14, no. 62; 240, Fig. 16, no. 116) and Burderop Down (Gingell 1992, 102, Fig. 75.1). These round-bodied bowls should not be identified with ovoid or globular vessels dating essentially to the Middle Iron Age (amongst Knight's group 2 – Knight 1984), although occasionally profiles can be similar.

PDR carinated bowls are very varied in profile. The weakly carinated examples with only slightly concave necks at Stonea are paralleled by one from an important association at Beeston Regis, Norfolk (Lawson 1980a). This vessel had been used as a container for a Ewart Park phase hoard, circa late tenth–eighth centuries BC. A rim sherd found close to another Ewart Park hoard, at Aylesham, Norfolk (Lawson 1980b, 278, Fig. 5G), has a squat neck above a weak shoulder, apparently part of a wide bowl.

Internally bevelled rims, seen on several Stonea sherds, are present on PDR ceramics from at least the beginning of the ninth century BC. Applied cordons, particularly those sited in the necks of tripartite profiles, were very popular in the transitional period, but those placed on the body (as no. 18) seem to be present in small quantity in earlier assemblages.

The divergent Stonea pottery affiliations may best be resolved by distinguishing the different context groups. The pit group (3–20) has no sherds that need be regarded as particularly late; even the double fingertip treatment on 12 can be accepted as an early manifestation. At the same time the group does not seem to be especially early (although closed groups to compare with are a problem) and the most satisfactory date bracket would be around the ninth–eighth centuries BC. The ring gully and one post-hole inside it provided rather small assemblages, but they could be broadly contemporaneous. The silt layer lying between gully and pit contained little diagnostic, but vessel 32 can be regarded as representative of a later stage, circa eighth–sixth centuries BC. Consequently the material in this silt body should be regarded as either later or an accumulation over a longer time span. The relative chronology suggested ties in with the stratigraphy, whereby the ring ditch only appeared after the silt layer had been removed. It is of course possible that some of the material in the silt layer could have been reworked from a pre-existing surface. Late PDR material is important amongst the 'miscellaneous' contexts as well, namely 51–3, yet some or all of the finer bowls (44–6) could be earlier. The convex-walled vessels are unfortunately not diagnostic.

On current evidence the Stonea PDR ceramics can be placed within a ninth–sixth century BC bracket with indications that activity was spread through this period rather than being short-lived.

Evaluation of the Stonea PDR pottery in functional or social terms is made difficult by the very fragmentary nature of the settlement plan recovered. The larger context groups comprise an expected mixture of forms and quality of ware. However, the good proportion of fine tableware in both the pit group and the ring gully assemblage is worthy of note. The fine bowl sherds from miscellaneous contexts in immediate proximity (nos 44–6) seem to reflect the same trend. These suggest a derivation more from the consumption of food, than its storage, but this might be a very local bias dependent on the organisation of activities. One vessel (24) bears traces of charred food residues.

THE BRONZE AGE METALWORK AND METALLURGICAL DEBRIS

Stuart Needham   (Fig. 87)

CATALOGUE

1 Razor fragment   P 1982 6–2 117

Extant length 32 mm; extant width 17 mm; maximum thickness 3.0 mm; weight 3.5 g.

Mainly a good deep green patina; a few ruddy brown extrusions.

The fragment represents one side of a single-edged razor with remains of a ring handle, probably originally one of a pair. The ring has a thin subsquare section and a stump on the side is a remnant of a branch presumably linking two rings. The ring was cast in one with the blade, the top of which is strengthened on both faces with a crisp bead rib. One side of the blade is intact and describes a gently concave line. The blade is thinned by hammerworking a little over halfway down, as shown by slight faceting. The cutting edge has been lost due to damage.

A very fine web of casting flash survives in the angles between the ring and blade. It was common for such remnants to be left in relatively inaccessible places without hindering use of the object.

In detail the double-looped, single-edged razors of the Hallstatt C phase show a remarkable variety in the combinations of features employed (Jockenhövel 1980, Tf. 34 and 35). The Stonea fragment shows no signs of perforations and in its complete state would probably have resembled the example from Villeneuve St George, Val-de-Marne, France (ibid., 176, no. 672), with or without the central feature present on the handle there.

Stonea Grange Surface Collection.

2 Socketed axe fragment   P 1982 6–2 173

Extant length 78.5 mm; extant width at mouth 35.5 mm; breadth of mouth 33 mm; minimum intact breadth of loop 7.0 mm; weight 100.5 g.

Most of the surface carries a dark brown patina, but it is much pocked and chipped to dusty light green and ruddy brown surfaces.

Over half the original axe head has been reconstructed from four pieces. Most of the mouth is present and supports a neatly fashioned collar of squat trumpet type. This has a small underlining step, a concave profile and, where undamaged, a flat top. The loop has a D-shaped cross-section commonly found on faceted axes, whilst the meticulous removal of all traces of casting flash is also typical. The collar features and its simple octagonally faceted body place it with the class D1 axes defined in the Petters hoard (Needham 1990, 41).

Stonea Grange Surface Collection.

3 Socketed axe fragment   P 1982 6–2 174

Extant length 29.5 mm; extant width cutting edge 37 mm; maximum extant breadth 14 mm; extant depth socket 11 mm; weight 32.8 g.

A rather undulating grey-green surface with some iron-rich patches; the metal showing at the break is grey.

This is a badly damaged blade fragment with none of the cutting edge remaining intact. The lower body has a standard sub-rectangular section. This fragment cannot be classified but is consonant with LBA forms.

Stonea Grange Surface Collection.

4 Socketed axe or chisel fragment   ST 83 CCP, SF 482

Extant length 33 mm; extant width 41 mm; maximum thickness of mouth moulding 4.2 mm; weight 16.7 g.

Smooth milky green patina with occasional corrosion spots.

This fragment from the mouth of an axe has been somewhat distorted, presumably during its fragmentation. Hammermarks occur on the upper, bead-like moulding which has a flat top. Two original corners seem to be present, implying a sub-rectangular mouth shape. A slight ridge 18 mm lower defines the base of a deep 'trumpet' moulding. Although flattened, the face below bears corrugations which seem to derive from two (or more) vertical features. These are best interpreted as the ridges defining facets.

This could come from a faceted chisel (cf. no. 6) or a faceted axe with a deep trumpet moulding, a variant more normal in the north of Britain (e.g. Schmidt and Burgess 1981, nos 1225–30).

From disturbed silt layer (unit 1062), south-east of the ring gully (gully 1).

5 Socketed axe fragment   (Unillus.) ST 83+, SF 451

Extant length 16 mm; extant width 24.5 mm; maximum thickness of mouth moulding 6 mm; weight 7.6 g.

Olive patina remnants amongst green corrosion areas.

Small fragment from a socket encircled with a moderately heavy bulbous moulding; thus most likely from a socketed axe. A small bump on the inner lip probably indicates the position of a runner.

Topsoil find from 1983 excavation area.

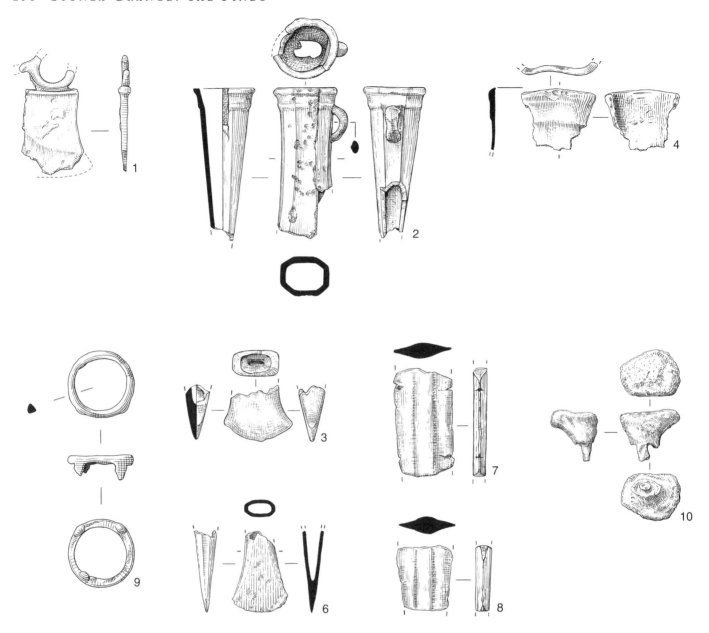

Fig. 87 Stonea Grange: Bronze Age metalwork, 1–3 and 6–8 from the Stonea Grange Surface Collection, 4, 9 and 10 from the excavations (scale 1:2, except 1 and 9 = 1:1).

6 Socketed chisel fragment   P 1982 6–2 175

Extant length 43 mm; width cutting edge 31 mm; extant depth of socket 27 mm; minimum extant width 18 mm; maximum extant breadth 11.5 mm; weight 21.3 g.

Rough surface, maroon and rich green.

Although the original surface seems to have been lost, causing loss of feature definition, traces of facets can be discerned on each of the four body angles. There is therefore no doubt that this fragment comes from a slender waisted and faceted form of chisel. The cutting edge subtends a very acute angle in profile, probably accentuated by hammering from about 25 mm up the blade. The blade tips

are damaged, but the rest of the edge was probably intact. The more intact side is narrow and flattish.

Late Bronze Age chisels come in a variety of forms in detail, but there are two main types: a) 'mortising chisels' with a long solid lower blade terminating in a narrow chisel edge (Coombs 1979, 214), a form which had a long ancestry on the continent (O'Connor 1980, 174); b) 'fully socketed' chisels (Burgess 1968, 40(h)), which have moderately broad blades, but are nevertheless much lighter-weight implements than the contemporaneous axes, and also lack the loop. The Stonea chisel belongs to this latter class which generally has an oval or faceted body section. This faceted variant can be matched for example at Carleton Rode, Norfolk (Norfolk Museums

Service 1977, Pl. VI.18), Wandsworth, Greater London, and in three finds from the Thames, two from Sion Reach and one from Bray (NBI).

Stonea Grange Surface Collection.

7 Sword fragment P 1982 6–2 176

Extant length 56.5 mm; maximum extant width 31 mm; maximum extant thickness 8.1 mm; weight 57.1 g.

Mostly dry green surface with scattered remnants of likely patina, black-green.

A sword blade fragment with a thick rounded midrib flanked by hollowed wings giving an eye-shaped cross-section overall. There are no traces of edge bevels. In its current state the edges are a little blunt and carry several notches, some of which are deep. The gentle taper of the fragment indicates that it is from the middle portion of a sword blade.

The cross-section seen on this piece is typical of Ewart Park type swords and can be found on some earlier types. It would not, however, be expected on a Hallstatt C sword.

Stonea Grange Surface Collection.

8 Sword fragment P 1982 6–2 177

Extant length 33 mm; maximum extant width 30.5 mm; maximum extant thickness 8.5 mm; weight 32.6 g.

Dark green-brown patina, small patches thinly flaked to brighter green dry surface. Patina over both breaks.

Sword blade fragment with thick rounded midrib outlined by vestigial steps down to hollowed wings. Faint traces only of broad edge bevels. Parts of cutting edges still patina-covered – thin, but not especially sharp; rest slightly chipped.

As with no. 5, this blade fragment is most likely to come from a Ewart Park type sword.

Stonea Grange Surface Collection

9 (?)Ring binding ST 82 BLL, SF 418

External diameter 18.2–19.0 mm; internal diameter 13.4–14.2 mm; maximum depth 6.7 mm; weight 1.5 g.

Fine olive green patina; tiny areas chipped.

A small circular ring with three roughly triangular spikes projecting from one face. A fourth spike is required to complete the symmetry, and there is a small stub in the expected position. However, it seems likely that this spike failed in the casting as no fractured surface is evident. The spikes and the face from which they project are partially as-cast surfaces with some rough working, but the perimeter of the ring, its upper and inner surfaces are smooth. The inner surface is bevelled inwards. All these features point to the most likely function of the ring being a decorative or reinforcing binding for the mouth of a hollow or solid cylindrical object. The spikes would have allowed the ring to be hammered or tapped into position, and the absence of one out of four would not seriously affect the functioning of the object.

From pit 920, unit 957. Phase I.

10 Casting jet ST 83 +

Maximum diameter of top 33 mm; height 25.5 mm; diameter of feeder at break 5.0 × 3.3 mm; weight 38.1 g.

Very dull brown-green surface, except pallid green on upper surface.

Roughly conical reservoir with oval cross-section and a somewhat dished lower end, off-centre, from which projects an oval-sectioned feeder. The upper surface is irregular and in part vesicular, presumably in its as-cooled state.

It is possible to rule out a derivation from casting certain objects, notably socketed axes, but otherwise impossible to attribute this piece on present evidence. It is not even certain that it is Bronze Age. The single, fairly slender feeder suggests the casting of a smallish bronze.

1983 surface find.

11 Probable crucible or mould fragment (Unillus.) ST 82 BGM

Height 16 mm, thickness 9 mm.

Consistent light grey fabric with coarse sand. One edge seems to be a rounded rim; curving profile below.

From unit 862, sondage into silt layer north of and beneath street 1 E/W.

12 Probable clay mould fragment (Unillus.) ST 82 ABQ

Length 26 mm, width 22 mm

Consistent grey fabric with dense coarse sand. Apparently one intact side with flattish contact face, which broadens from end to end of the piece. Neat concave face alongside is presumably matrix – suggests casting of tubular form, for example, a spearhead socket.

From topsoil/cleaning, blocks 2–4.

13 Probable clay mould fragment (Unillus.) ST 82 ABQ

Length 34 mm, width 25 mm.

Consistent grey fabric with dense coarse sand, including grains up to 3 mm across. Small surviving part of presumed contact face atop upstanding flange. Profile inside (presumed matrix) describes single faceted right angle, the facet tapers within the fragment. It is possible that this comes from one of two valves for casting a faceted socketed axe.

Context as no. 12.

DISCUSSION

Most of the metalwork considered here (seven of ten items) was found outside the archaeological excavations and thus offers little scope for contextual interpretation. A few comments may be made, however, about the general character of the material. All the identifiable objects can be attributed to the Late Bronze Age, indeed probably with an emphasis on the Ewart Park and Llyn Fawr stages. In recent years, these stages have been dated to c. 900–700 and 700–600 BC respectively, but the repercussions of much consolidated dating (dendrochronological and calibrated radiocarbon) in central Europe and Britain are pointing to slightly earlier beginnings, c. 950 and 750 BC respectively (Needham forthcoming).

Although there was little by way of direct associations, it would appear from independent assessment that the metalwork belongs to a similar timespan as the PDR pottery discussed above. The ring binding (no. 9), which but for the associated pottery would have been undatable, is a noteworthy addition to the growing repertoire of known LBA bric-à-brac.

The metalwork cannot be regarded as a useful archaeological assemblage because of the possibility of selective recovery and differential survival in the plough soil. The ring binding and the razor reflect the ornamental and personal implement components which seem to figure large in most Middle–Late Bronze Age settlement assemblages. More dominant, however, are intimations of metalworking – most directly in the casting jet and clay refractories (assuming their contemporaneity). Less certainly relevant are the fragmentary axes, swords and chisel. The extent of later damage is difficult to evaluate but it seems likely that at least some of these pieces (especially no. 4) were scrapped metalwork at the time of loss or deposition. This recalls an increasingly familiar pattern of such scrapped material on LBA sites, notably The Breiddin (Coombs 1991), Ivinghoe Beacon (Britton 1968), Petters Sports Field (Needham 1990) and others.

The refractories are abraded and poorly contexted. However, in morphological characteristics and fabric they compare well with known Bronze Age assemblages. Contact surfaces, indicative of clay bivalve mould technology (e.g. Hodges 1954; Needham 1980), can be tentatively identified on nos 12 and 13 and the presumed matrix shapes can be tentatively matched to certain bronze types having tubular sockets or faceted bodies respectively. The rounded rim on no. 11, if original, might suggest instead a crucible, although it is relatively thin-walled and lacks obvious 'slag' deposits.

In the context of this metalworking evidence it is noteworthy that a Late Bronze Age hoard, including five socketed axes and three pieces of ingot, was found somewhere near Stonea Grange Farm, presumably not far away (V. C. H. Cambs. I, 1938, 303; National Bronze Implements Index; Wisbech Museum). Another metalwork find provenanced to the Farm is a side-looped spearhead of Middle Bronze Age date (references as previous; Rowlands 1976, 363, no. 1232), and yet more finds have been reported subsequently from the immediate area, including a gold hair-ring (Pendleton 1985; Suffolk CC SMR).

IRON AGE POTTERY

Val Rigby   (Fig. 88)

EARLY IRON AGE POTTERY

Vessels 1–4 probably result from occupation in the sixth to second centuries BC. The vessels were handmade in fabrics with mixed inclusions of coarse sand, glauconite, grog and flint, in differing proportions. The sherds are small and abraded, and the sample is too small and disparate to illustrate any pattern.

1 ST 84, O   Rim sherd from jar with slight cabling on the top edge of the rim. The fabric includes grog and sparse flint up to 3 mm in diameter. Dark grey ware with rough and smeared surfaces. There is insufficient evidence to decide if the vessel had a rounded or carinated shoulder. Probably 6th–5th century BC.

From machine-cut trench O, 60–90 m from south-west end. Unstratified.

2 ST 83 CME   Rim sherd from a small, thin-walled shapeless bowl or jar. Abraded surfaces. Black ware with partially oxidised brown exterior. Probably 6th–4th century BC.

Residual in ditch 12, unit 1268 (post-medieval).

3 ST 83 CEI   Base sherd from a large jar. Fabric includes coarse sand, glauconite and flint; the base has a flint rough-cast finish. Oxidised orange ware with grey core. First half first millennium BC.

From gully 1, unit 1104. Phase I.

4 ST 84 Q 23, 1   Two rim sherds with rather different profiles from opposite sides of the same shouldered jar, with slightly defined neck. The fabric includes sand, grog and sparse flint; the interior was smoothed horizontally, the exterior has been textured with horizontal smearing. Probably 2nd century BC.

From machine-cut trench Q, unit 23, layer 1, silt make-up of building R15 (temple). Phase II?

LATE IRON AGE POTTERY

The group from ditch 69, pit 520 and silt layer 268 comprises sherds from four different wheel-thrown vessels in similar fabrics with mixed inclusions of coarse sand, clay pellets and grog. Small voids at the surfaces of nos 5 and 6 suggest that fine calcite may also have been present amongst the inclusions. The absence of flint is the most obvious characteristic which distinguishes the later from the earlier fabrics, and suggests that all materials were obtained from local resources. The fabric and forms belong to the Late Iron Age ceramic tradition of south-east Britain, and manufacture occurred between the late Augustan and the Neronian periods.

There is a marked difference in the quantity and condition of the sherds suggesting that they enjoyed different post-discard events before their final deposition. The most complete pot is no. 7: about half of the rim and shoulder circuit

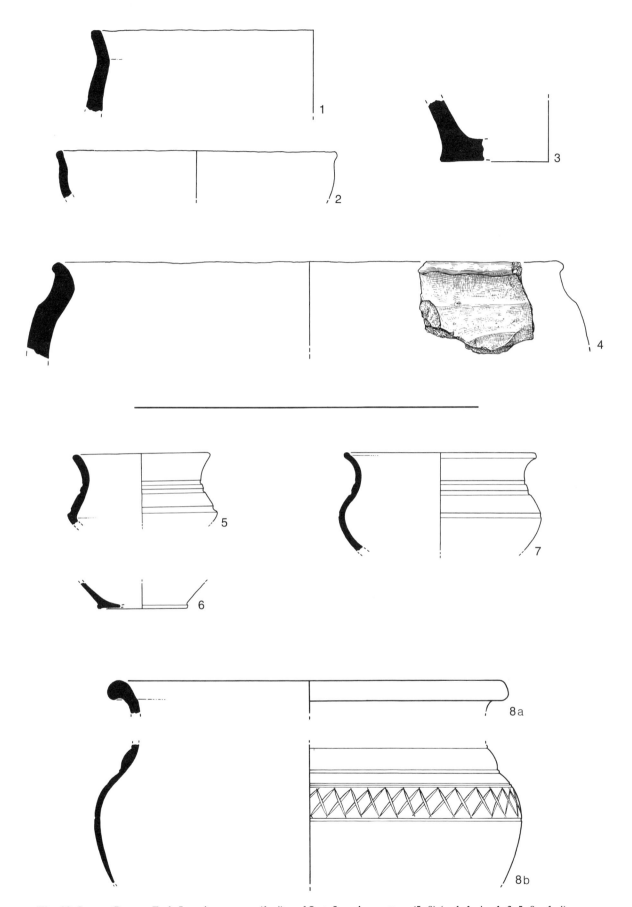

Fig. 88 Stonea Grange: Early Iron Age pottery (1–4), and Late Iron Age pottery (5–8) (scale 1–4 = 1:2; 5–8 = 1:4).

survives in the form of two large sherds, fragmented subsequently, from opposite sides of the vessel. Although in all there are 30+ sherds, none is from the area of the base. The sherds are all in good condition with little abrasion. There are 20+ sherds from no. 8: most are upper body sherds and appear to consist of fragmented non-conjoining sherds. The rim and shoulder do not join. Number 5 is represented by a single sherd, no. 6 by three sherds. The interior surfaces of nos 5, 6 and 8 are markedly abraded, although the exterior finishes have survived better. The only base (no. 6) does not belong to any of the rims.

5 ST 81 MQ   Carinated bowl with cordon at the waist. Uncontrolled firing, grey core, brown surfaces with a large black sooty patch on the outside. Burnished exterior.

From silt layer 268, block 1, north.

6 ST 83 CSP   Closed form. Partial oxidation, grey core, orange surfaces. Abraded.

From ditch 69, unit 1422. Phase II.

7 ST 83 CSP   Necked bowl with cordon at the neck base and a groove on the maximum girth. Dark brown ware, burnished from lip to groove, lower body matt.

Context as no. 6.

8 ST 82 ADG and ST 83 CSP   Rim and body sherds probably from the same necked storage jar. Burnt and discoloured fabric. Burnished rim and cordon, lower body matt. Decoration – deeply incised lattice.

8a and 8b from pit 520, Phase III. 8b from same context as nos 6–7.

IRON AGE METALWORK

Ralph Jackson   (Fig. 89)

1 Duck attachment   Length 20 mm   P 1982, 6–2, 2

A small copper-alloy attachment in the form of a sitting or swimming duck. The flat base has a simple tendril design cast in low relief. The eye-sockets, recessed circles, are proportionately large. They retain the stub of a tiny central pin which fastened an inlay, probably of coral, bone or enamel. A fragmentary thin elliptical rod or strut runs from the bird's tail to the back of its head. It was the mode of attachment, but too little of it remains to indicate its original appearance.

The tendril design is reminiscent of that on the cast bronze bracelet from Newnham Croft and suggests a date of late fourth/early third century BC or later.

Potter and Jackson 1982, 112, 115, Fig. 3.1.

Stonea Grange Surface Collection

2 Strap union   Length 46 mm, weight 55.8 g   P 1985, 10–3, 1

A side-looped two-way strap union formed of two opposed tip-touching crescents enclosing a circular ring with central perforation and flanked by two pillar-like strap bars. The central ring, plain on the back, has a prominent flattened ridge on the front ornamented with a circle of thirteen pellet-like bosses. The crescents are very plump, rather more convex on the front than on the plain back, and are not an exact pair – one is noticeably larger than the other. On the apex of each is the same low-relief, S-shaped, lobed scroll motif, the middle unit of which, with its pelleted rim, is a miniature version of the central ring. Pelleting extends also onto the rim of the round lugs of the strap bars, where it is 'sandwiched' between a pair of lightly incised lines. On the back of the rims the pellets and lines are worn almost entirely away, and wear is also evident on the full length of the inner face of both strap bars. The maximum dimensions of the strap that would have been admitted is 15 mm in width and 2 mm in thickness.

The object is in good condition, though the surface is extensively pocked with tiny corrosion craters. In common with many other Iron Age 'bronzes', the patina has a metallic grey, ?tin-rich, appearance. This is a fine example of the figure-of-eight form strap union which Taylor and Brailsford classify as Type I (Taylor and Brailsford 1985, 247). The tip-touching crescents with low-relief decoration may be seen on their Fig. 2, no. 5, from Danebury (Cunliffe 1984, 341–2, 345, Figs 7.5, 7.6, no. 1.35, dated c. 100 BC.); while the circle of pellet-like bosses can be paralleled in their Fig. 2, no. 8, from Glastonbury (Bulleid and Gray 1911, 299, E262, Pl. XLIV). However, the closest parallels are a pair of strap unions from Kirkburn, cart burial K5, which were found in direct association with a set of five terrets and are interpreted as yoke-end attachments, probably used to adjust the girth (Stead 1991, 47–51, Figs 41–2). They share with the present union the figure-of-eight form, the conjoined central units with rings of pellet-like bosses, and the pellet-rimmed lugs of the strap bars. Additionally, the S-shaped lobed scroll motif on the Stonea union may be compared to the similar device applied to the large terret in one of the Garton Station cart burials, GS6, (Stead 1991, 47–8, Fig. 39, no. 5, and 182, Fig. 99h). On stylistic grounds Stead regards the cart burials from Kirkburn, Garton Station and Wetwang Slack as broadly contemporaneous (ibid. 181), La Tène I, probably c. 200 BC (ibid. 179ff.). Some confirmation of this early date comes from the Deal burial, probably very early La Tène II, c. 200 BC, which includes a sword scabbard with both the pelleted circle motif and the S-shaped lobed scroll motif (I. M. Stead, personal communication).

Stonea Grange Surface Collection.

3 Terret   Height c. 50 mm   P 1985, 10–3, 2

Rather over half of the cast copper-alloy loop remains, with one stop and the corroded stub of the iron attachment bar. The loop has a raised rib running around its perimeter but is otherwise plain. It swells towards the stop, which is circular and cushion-shaped, with a groove incised around the rim facing the attachment bar. The bar is of vertical rectangular cross-section. Moderate wear is visible as a polish and slight facetting in the expected places – on the inner face of the side of the loop and the top of the stop. The areas of surviving original surface display a grey, tin-rich patina.

This is an example of Spratling's Group I 'simple form' terret (Spratling 1972, vol. 1, 25 ff.). It is not closely paralleled, though there is a similar example from Danebury (Cunliffe and Poole 1991, 332, Fig. 7.5, no. 1.96); and a simple terret from Glastonbury (Bulleid

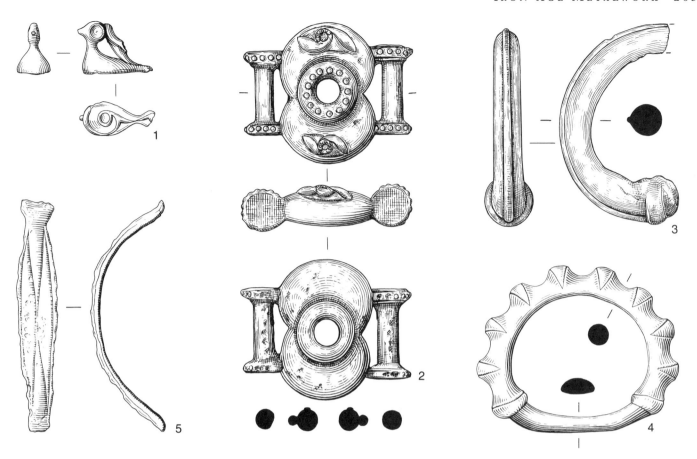

Fig. 89 Stonea Grange and Stonea Camp: Iron Age metalwork from the Surface Collections (scale 1 : 1).

and Gray 1911, 229, 231, Pl. XLIII, E8), of equivalent size, with similar stops and a double rib on the perimeter.

Stonea Grange Surface Collection.

4 Terret Height 44 mm, width 55 mm P 1982, 6–2, 1

Jennifer Foster writes: 'A cast bronze terret or reinring, very worn and slightly corroded but with much of the original surface remaining. The decoration consists of eight raised lobes around the loop, each outlined by two lines. Two knobs divide the loop from the bar on either side. The bar is unusually flat in section and slightly curved. The terret had obviously been heavily used prior to its loss. The top two lobes are particularly worn, and the entire inner surface is smoothed. The underside of the bar still has its original surface, showing clear filing marks where flashes from the casting were filed away. Despite the wear, it was possible to see that the decorative lines on either side of the lobes were cast in and not incised into the metal surface.

This terret is typical of the series of Late Iron Age/early Roman lipped terrets, so-called because of the protruding lobes often divided in the form of a pair of lips. The closest parallels to this example are two terrets from Hagbourne Hill (now in the British Museum) each with six knobs outlined by two lines; however, both terrets have iron bars. Most of the examples are unstratified, but a general date for the type of late 1st century BC to *c*. AD 50 is indicated by radiocarbon dates from Gussage All Saints, where moulds for casting lipped terrets were found with other debris in a pit (Foster 1980). This date would accord well with the lipped terret from Hod Hill, and that from Glastonbury.'

Potter and Jackson 1982, 112, 115, Fig. 3.2.

Stonea Grange Surface Collection.

5 Tankard handle Length 61 mm P 1981, 5–3, 1

An arched handle which splays from the terminals (both now broken) to its maximum width at the centre point. It is of concavo-convex cross-section with a smooth inner (convex) face and a lightly channelled outer (concave) face. The latter is elegantly ornamented with raised rims and an elongated incuse X-motif which runs the length of the handle and divides it into four slender cambered panels. Although the fastening plates are broken the handle arch is complete. The low ellipse would have accommodated the centre two fingers of an adult male hand grasping the vessel wall rather than the handle itself, the most likely mode of use of such handles (Jackson 1990, 45, no. 120).

The form and size of the handle are broadly paralleled by examples from Neath and Newstead (Corcoran 1952, 87, Fig. 1c; Pl. IX, 3; and 101, nos 20 and 25), and it is likely to date to the second half of the 1st century AD.

Stonea Camp Surface Collection. [Note that a wooden tankard stave was found in the Stonea Grange excavations – p. 550, no. 8.]

IRON AGE COINS

Amanda Chadburn   (Pls XXIII–XXIV)

INTRODUCTION

The Stonea area has produced an increasing number of Iron Age coin finds over recent years, many of which are of types traditionally ascribed to the Iceni, the local Iron Age tribe. Amongst the most significant finds are the hoard from Field Baulk, March, and a dense scatter of Iron Age coins from the Stonea Grange area. These and other Iron Age coin finds from the excavation and the general vicinity are discussed below, with the coin catalogues given at the end of the section.

The circumstances of the recovery of the Field Baulk hoard, and its pottery container are described in detail at p. 45.

METHODOLOGY AND CLASSIFICATION

All the coins in the catalogues are held by the Department of Coins and Medals of the British Museum, whose accession numbers are given in the text. The coins were conserved and photographed in-house, and weighed by the present author with an electronic balance after conservation. A full die study of the Field Baulk hoard has been undertaken (to be published elsewhere), which has enabled some of the previously unclassified coins to be identified further; this report therefore supercedes the preliminary published report on the hoard (Chadburn 1992).

Over recent years, a number of major reclassifications of British Celtic coins have been carried out, notably by Haselgrove (1987) and Van Arsdell (1989). However, for the Iceni neither new classification is entirely satisfactory in the light of the detailed die study (as can be seen from the concordance given in Table 5). The most useful classification still appears to be that of Allen (1970), and so this is used throughout the text with some minor alterations described below, and shown in Table 5.

Additionally, there are a number of early Face–Horse types which are not fully described in either Allen, Haselgrove or Van Arsdell, so the classification system of Gregory (1992) has been followed for these coins.

A concordance of the classification scheme used in the text with Haselgrove and Van Arsdell is given in Table 5. For a concordance of Allen's classification of Icenian coins with Mack and Evans, see Allen (1970, 25–33). Further concordances relating to other major classifications may be found in Van Arsdell (1989, 437–51) and Haselgrove (1987, ii, 262–3).

Table 5 Concordance of Icenian coin types

Obv die links	Type†	Allen number (1970)	Haselgrove number (1987)	Van Arsdell number (1989)
	Norfolk Wolf	—	EA 51	610
	Irstead 1/4 stater	Id	EA 71.1	628
	Early type	Ia	EA 61.1 EA 61.2	620
	Boar–Horse A	IIa	EA 62	655
	Boar–Horse B	IId	EA 72.1	657
	Boar–Horse C	IIe	EA 72.2	659
	Boar–Horse D (Cans Dvro)	IIf	EA 72.3	663
	Early Face–Horse B (after Gregory)	—	—	—
	Early Face–Horse Cc (after Gregory)	—	—	—
•	Normal Face–Horse A	IIIb	EA 73.2	790
•	Normal Face–Horse B/C	IIIc/d	EA 83.1/83.2	792, 794
	Early Pattern–Horse A	IVa	EA 61.2	679
	Early Pattern–Horse B	IVc	EA 71.1	675
	Anted	Vb	EA 81	710, 711
•	Ecen	VIa		730, 732
•	Ed(n)	VIb		734, 740
•	Ed(n) variant (after Chadburn)	VIc	EA 91.1	756, 754
	Symbol (after Chadburn)	VIb/c		750, 752
	Minims of Ecen/Ed(n)/ Symbol group	VId		736, 738 742, 744 683
	Ece A	VII	EA 91.2	758, 760
•	Ece B	VIII		762, 764
•	Ece B (reversed)	VIII	EA 91.3	766
•	Saenv	IXa		770
•	Aesv	IXb		775

† Mostly after Allen 1970 and used throughout text.

Early type stater

This type is now thought to be rather later in the series than other Icenian uninscribed gold issues, and its place within the series is under review (Chadburn 1991b). However, as this review is incomplete, Allen's nomenclature and classification are used here.

A new sub-type of this type was recovered, described below (Stonea Grange Catalogue No. 2), which appears to confirm the proposed later relative date for these 'Early Type' staters (*ibid.*), as the Y-headed horse on the reverse of this specimen is common amongst the later inscribed silver types (e.g. Ece B; Saenv; Aesv etc.).

Normal Face–Horse B/C

Allen's Normal Face–Horse B and C types have been amalgamated into a single group. The two face 'types' on the obverse form each end of a typological spectrum, and there is no clear distinction between types B and C, both of which show a head with a moustache. The reverse shows a horse which is identical in both B and C types.

Ed(n) variant

It is clear that the Ed(n) coins, are derived from the Ecen coins and are almost certainly meant to be the same type, but the legend on the reverse has been blundered (Allen 1970). The Ed(n) coins always show a horse on the reverse with a 'double' mane, and can only be distinguished from the Ecen types by the legend. When this is off-flan, a die study is the only method of distinguishing the two types, as the obverses have the same design. The legends vary between EDN and ED, although again these can be difficult to distinguish where part of the legend is off-flan.

However, two variants of the Ed(n) type are apparent. In the Field Baulk hoard, there are two reverse dies which appear to be degenerate types of the Ed(n) types.

Variant 1

The reverse die, exceptionally, appears to have a single N below the horse as a legend, which was mistaken by Allen for the top of a triangle symbol (see Allen number 153); see Fig. 90. (There are coins of Anted which similarly show only a single letter, T, beneath the horse, and which may also be interpreted as a degenerate legend type). Coins of this variant Ed(n) die have obverse die links with certain Ed(n) coins.

Variant 2

The reverse die shows a horse of the usual open-headed type, but the mane is blundered and looks rather like a Symbol 'single' mane at first glance (Fig. 90). The top of a letter – almost certainly an E – is visible and confirms that this die is not a blundered Symbol type. Additionally, the obverse is die-linked to other Ed(n) coins.

The Ed(n) variant type is incorrectly classified by Van Arsdell (1989) as two separate coin types both called Ecen Symbol (754 and 756), but in fact the reverses of 754 and 756 are die linked. Confusingly, Ed(n) variant coins can look similar to the Symbol coins but can generally be distinguished from them as the horse on the reverse has a 'double' mane, not a 'single' one (see also Fig. 91).

The Ecen, Ed(n) and Ed(n) variant types (and those classified Ecen/Ed(n)) could be regarded as a single group in which the legend becomes progressively more and more degenerate, as die links exist between these types.

Figures 90 and 91 show those parts of individual dies which are visible from a variety of specimens. The enclosing line therefore represents the extent of our knowledge of the die design, and not the shape of the coin flan.

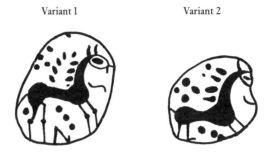

Variant 1   Variant 2

Fig. 90 Iron Age coins. Ed(n) variant: reverse die reconstructions (scale 2 : 1).

Symbol

When Allen defined his Symbols type he had few coins to work with. It is now clear that his Symbols group includes coins of Ecen and Ed(n), and that the symbols designs do not include I, which is, in fact, the top of a straight-legged triskeles, or just the line of three pellets (see Allen number 152). Of Allen's eight examples which he classifies as Symbols (numbers 152 to 159 inclusive), types 156 to 159 inclusive are Symbol types, but 152 and 155 are Ecen/Ed(n) types; 153 is an Ed(n) variant type as defined above, and 154 is an Ece A coin.

Of the five types classified by Van Arsdell as Ecen Symbol Type (750, 752, 754, 756, 758), only two types are Symbol (750 and 752). 754 and 756 are the Ed(n) variant type and 758 is an Ece A coin.

Currently only four reverse dies and two designs of this type are known, shown in Fig. 91: a straight-legged triskeles or inverted Y design; and a concave-sided triangle (often appearing unfinished in one die). This coin type has been named Symbol and should not be confused with Allen's Symbols type.

The symbols shown – the straight-legged triskeles and the triangle – show the importance of triplism to the die designers. Throughout the Icenian series, there are numerous different coin types which use triplism in their design, and this is a well-known aspect of Celtic iconography (Green 1986, 208–11).

These coins can be distinguished from the Ecen and Ed(n) types, as they always have a 'single' mane, unlike the other two types and the Anted silver coins, which all have 'double' manes. However, care must be taken in identifying this type, as sometimes part of a 'double' mane can lie off-flan. Sometimes a triple pellet motif can be discerned on the shoulder, although this has often worn away.

Straight-legged triskeles designs

Triangle designs

Fig. 91 Iron Age coins. Symbol: reverse die reconstructions (scale 2:1).

THE IRON AGE COINS FROM STONEA GRANGE: GROUP I (Pl.XXIII)

A large number of Iron Age and Roman coins held by the British Museum were found in the fields adjacent to the excavations by Mr. D. Amps, using a metal detector. They were found over several years, and the silver and gold coins were subject to two Treasure Trove inquiries. The coins broadly fall into two main groups of material: Late Iron Age and contemporaneous (Group I) and first to third century AD Roman coins with a mixture of later material (Group II – Shotter, p. 290). Group I consists of 59 Celtic and early Roman coins, including 16 certain Icenian issues, plated types or cores, and a further three types presumed to be new Icenian types. The coins were found dispersed over a wide area near Stonea Grange, casting some doubt as to whether they come from a hoard or hoards.

Table 6 Stonea Grange: coin type totals from Group I

Coin types	Totals	
Iceni: gold series		
Early Type stater – new sub-type (Cu alloy core)	1	
Iceni: gold series total	1	(2%)
Iceni: silver series – Boar–Horse		
Boar–Horse A	3	
Boar–Horse B	2	
Boar–Horse C (including one plated)	6	
Boar–Horse: new type 1	1	
Boar–Horse: new type 2	1	
Iceni: Boar–Horse total	13	(22%)
Iceni: silver series – Face–Horse		
Early Face–Horse types	2	
Normal Face–Horse A	1	
Normal Face–Horse B/C (including one core)	4	
Iceni: Face–Horse total	7	(12%)
Iceni: silver series – Pattern–Horse		
Early Pattern–Horse A	2	
Early Pattern–Horse B	2	
Anted (including one plated)	13	
Ecen	2	
Ed(n)	1	
Ecen/Ed(n)	3	
Minim of Ecen/Ed(n)/Symbol Group (plated)	1	
Ece A	1	
Ece B	1	
Iceni: Pattern–Horse: New type 1 (core)	1	
Iceni: Pattern–Horse: Unclassified (including one core)	2	
Iceni: Pattern–Horse total	29	(49%)
Other Celtic		
Gallo–Belgic: gold series		
Gallo–Belgic E (Cu alloy core)	1	
Corieltauvi		
Prototype gold stater: type D	1	
Potin		
Early type	2	
Trinovantes		
Andoco (Cu alloy unit)	1	
Addedomarus (Cu alloy unit)	1	
Roman		
Denarius of Augustus	1	
Miscellaneous		
Unidentified Celtic silver units	2	
Others total	9	(15%)
Grand total	59	(100%)

Description

The coins are generally in a poor condition, typical of coins derived from a ploughsoil. Their weights are generally low, perhaps partly as a result of long exposure to the soil and because of chipping, but in certain coins, partly due to circulation wear, too.

A relatively large number of plated coins and cores form part of this group; eight certain examples have been identified, and a number of others are poorly alloyed, or are very base (e.g. Early Pattern–Horse A, Stonea Catalogue no. 24). There must be a possibility that these eight coins represent contemporary forgeries: Stonea Catalogue nos 1; 2; 12; 19; 38; 45; 48; 50.

IRON AGE COINS FROM THE STONEA GRANGE EXCAVATION   (Pl. XXIV)

Two Icenian coins were recovered from the excavations at Stonea Grange, both from residual contexts. Both were Boar–Horse types. The first (catalogue no. 60) was found built into the north wall of the central block of building R1 (unit 243), perhaps placed there deliberately. It was in a very good, unworn condition, which is perhaps surprising as it is a relatively rare early type. The second (catalogue no. 61) was found in pit 563 with third century AD pottery. It is the more common Boar–Horse type of a later date than no. 60 and was slightly worn through circulation.

THE FIELD BAULK HOARD   (Pl. XXIV)

Description

The discovery of the Field Baulk hoard and the subsequent excavation of the area around the findspot is fully discussed elsewhere in this volume (pp. 45–8). It is the largest recorded Icenian hoard, containing 872 silver coins in total. (Originally the total number of coins was thought to be 860, but during conservation it was discovered that a number of coins were stuck together.) The next nearest it in terms of size is that from Lakenheath, Suffolk, which contained 479 Icenian and Roman coins. No Roman or other Celtic coins were associated with the Field Baulk hoard, although this is not necessarily unusual with Icenian coin hoards, as less than half recorded so far are associated with Roman coins, and few contain other Celtic coins.

The vessel which was found in association with the coins is discussed in detail elsewhere (p. 45), and is certainly the container of the hoard. A number of other Icenian coin hoards are associated with containers, such as the hoard at Freckenham, Suffolk, which was found in a small poorly-fired pot (Haselgrove 1987); the silver Fring hoard which was found with a concave-sided cup (Chadburn and Gurney 1991); and that at Honingham which was found with a Butt Beaker (Clarke 1956).

Composition

The hoard is composed of 17 recognisable or presumed new Icenian coin types, along with a few unclassifiable Boar–Horse, Face–Horse, and Pattern–Horse issues, detailed in the Field Baulk Catalogue. There are no minims, and all appear to be silver units of much the same weight and size. There are apparently seven plated coins and cores, which may represent contemporaneous forgeries (nos 17, 68, 96, 453, 591, 708, 829) and additionally, there are two brockages (nos 675 and 676, produced when a coin sticks in one of the dies, and impresses a reverse image on the next coin being struck), and one miscast coin (no. 674). A further coin, 530, appears to be a brockage which has been overstamped with an obverse die to correct the error.

Generally, the coins are in a very good state of preservation, owing no doubt to the circumstances of their deposition. While some coins are worn through circulation, they do not appear to have been subject to leaching through exposure to the soil, and the weights are therefore particularly useful and valid for statistical work.

Table 7 Field Baulk: composition of the hoard

Coin type	Number of coins	% of total
Boar–Horse A	4	
Boar–Horse B	4	
Boar–Horse C	25	
Boar–Horse D (CANS–DVRO)	1	
Boar–Horse unclassified (core)	1	
Boar–Horse total	35	4%
Normal Face–Horse A (including 1 plated)	42	
Normal Face–Horse B/C (including 1 plated)	129	
Unclassified Face–Horse	1	
Face–Horse total	172	20%
Early Pattern–Horse B	1	
Anted	193	
Ecen (including 1 plated)	157	
Ed(n) (including 1 core)	60	
Ed(n) variant	12	
Symbol	29	
Ecen/Ed(n) (including 1 plated)	10	
Ece A	73	
Ece B	74	
Ece B (reversed) (including 1 core)	23	
Aesv	11	
Saenv	16	
Iceni Pattern–Horse unclassified/brockages/miscast	6	
Pattern–Horse total	665	76%
Grand total	872	100%

Die links

There are die links between the Ecen, Ed(n), Ed(n) variant and Ecen/Ed(n) coin types, and these coins could therefore be considered as a single type (Ecen types) in which the die cutting and legend become more and more degenerate. However, they are here considered as separate coin types, the classification being based on the different reverse designs. The Symbol type is certainly related, but stands somewhat apart from them as the mane is different and there is no inscription. Its precise relationship to the Anted and Ecen types is unclear.

The obverse die links, which are apparent between several coin types, show they are related and may have been struck within a relatively short space of time:

1 Normal Face–Horse A and Normal Face–Horse B/C
2 Ecen and Ed(n)
3 Ed(n) and Ed(n) variant } a group related by die linking
4 Ece B and Ece B (reversed)
5 Aesv and Saenv

The coins of Aesv and Saenv are particularly interesting. The die study has shown that all Aesv and Saenv coins were struck from a single obverse die, as was tentatively suggested by Allen (1970, 33, but see, alternatively, 22). Additionally, it is clear from this hoard and from a study of other specimens (Chadburn 1991a) that the Aesv coins were all struck from the same pair of dies, whereas there were two reverse Saenv dies, and the single obverse die. It is also apparent from studying the die wear on the single obverse die, that all the Aesv coins appear to have been struck *after* the Saenv coins. The two types are therefore likely to be closely related, and may well be the product of the same moneyer and mint. No obverse die link with the Ece B series has yet been noted.

ALLEGED FINDS OF IRON AGE MATERIAL FROM THE STONEA AREA

Since 1978 there have been a number of alleged finds in this general area, which are worth mentioning both in view of their intrinsic importance, and in view of the significance they have for our understanding of the archaeology of the region. A number of these unpublished and unreported finds have found their way into museums or private collections, which lends some credibility to these reports.

Around the late 1970s and early 1980s, three coin hoards which included Iron Age coins were allegedly found in the general vicinity of Stonea Camp. The coins – although a little scattered – came from fairly discrete sites, and as no isolated coins were found, it seems clear that they really do represent hoard finds. No pots were apparently found.

One alleged hoard consisted of a mixture of Celtic coins, including gold staters of Cunobelin, and silver coins both of the Corieltauvi and of the Iceni. Such a hoard would be unusual, although the hoard at Chatteris contained Roman coins and coins of Tasciovanus (Burnett 1986a). However, another more recent alleged hoard apparently contained precisely this mixture of Celtic coins.

A second alleged hoard close by consisted of a mixture of Roman denarii, and Icenian silver coins. This hoard is paralleled by the hoard from Scole (Burnett 1986b) which similarly contained a mixture of denarii and Icenian silver coins.

The last hoard, further to the north, consisted of early asses, including a large number of 'good style' Claudian asses – presumably good style imitations. This, if true, would appear to be unique to the East Anglian region.

As well as these three hoards, other finds have been reported as found between the late 1970s and 1985 from Wimblington parish, which certainly have a bearing on our understanding of the archaeology of this region. The finds from this area allegedly include very large numbers of Celtic coins, perhaps as many as several thousand. Reported are at least three 'Norfolk Wolf' staters, an Early Type stater, a gold-plated stater inscribed ECEN, some gold Irstead quarter staters, and very large numbers of base cast potins. Also reported are large numbers of Icenian coins (including a silver Cans Dvro Boar–Horse coin) and early denarii, apparently about 25% of each being plated specimens. Around the early 1980s, a gold Celtic object or objects – but not torcs – were apparently found in this region too, and a Bronze Age gold lock-ring.

A gold-plated stater of Ecen exists in a private collection, and there is also one in the British Museum (accession number 1980, 5–41, 1). Five gold staters of Ecen have been recorded in 1992 trade publications and also in Van Arsdell (1992), so there are genuine gold staters of this type now known. A number of other Iron Age coins allegedly from these hoards have been reported in private collections. The gold lock-ring certainly exists, and has been fully recorded (Pendleton 1985). The existence of these finds gives a certain amount of credence to these reports, although of course they must be used with care.

SCIENTIFIC ANALYSIS OF THE IRON AGE COINS   M. R. Cowell

Introduction

The coins examined are from the Field Baulk hoard (acquired in 1983) and the Stonea Grange excavations (acquired in 1984); all are debased silver issues of the Iceni. Existing analyses of the Icenian coinage are confined mainly to the gold issues with very few examples of the silver ones. However, some recent semi-quantitative XRF analyses confirm that the issues are base with silver contents in the range 50–70% (RL File 4932). This hoard provides an opportunity to examine the composition of the series in more detail to investigate the relationship of the various types. The primary interest is the silver content (fineness) and whether there is evidence of debasement or systematic differences between types. A determination of the silver content will also assist in establishing the monetary relationship of the series with that of contemporary Roman denarii. The coins examined from the hoard include a number of examples of the uninscribed types (Boar–Horse and Face–Horse) and the assumed later types with inscriptions (e.g. Anted, Ecen, Aesv, Saenv etc.).

Analytical technique

The coins are particularly small, typically less than 10 mm in diameter and not more than 1 mm in thickness. Coins of this size are unsuitable for reliable X-ray fluorescence (XRF) analysis because the X-ray beam irradiates an area larger than could normally be prepared on the coin edge and any surface enrichment or internal corrosion could not be avoided. The size of the coins also rules out sampling and the use of techniques such as atomic absorption. Small artefacts can however be reliably analysed using energy dispersive X-ray analysis (EDX) in the scanning electron microscope (SEM).

Although the detection limits are generally higher by this technique than by XRF, in this instance only the major and minor element concentrations were considered important.

An area on the edge of each coin was polished to remove surface depleted layers of corrosion with the intention of exposing a section with a centre of uncorroded metal. The section was examined visually in the SEM and areas selected for analysis which appeared to have little or no corrosion. In practice three coins were considered to be too corroded to justify anything other than qualitative analysis. A further coin was slightly corroded and could only be analysed semi-quantitatively.

Several plated contemporary forgeries were also examined. These were prepared in the same manner and analysed both on the core and the plating.

All the analyses are listed in Table 8. The precision (reproducibility) for each element is approximately 1–2% for silver, 1–2% for copper and 10–50% for the remaining minor elements. As the results are scaled to total 100%, those coins that are corroded, and have consequently lost copper through leaching, are likely to show an apparent enhancement of the silver.

Table 8 SEM–EDX analyses of the Iron Age coins

BMRL	Cat/Reg	Description	Part	Cu	Ag	Sn	Pb	Au	Comments
37068y	1983, 3–30, 1	Early Pattern–Horse B		52	48	<0.5	<0.4	<0.3	
37069w	1983, 3–30, 18	Boar–Horse C		54	46	<0.5	<0.4	<0.3	
37070z	1983, 3–30, 23	Boar–Horse C		48	46	5.8	<0.4	<0.3	
37071x	1983, 3–30, 28	Boar–Horse A		56	42	1.5	<0.4	<0.3	
37072v	1983, 3–30, 30	Boar–Horse A		56	43	<0.5	0.6	<0.3	
37073t	1983, 3–30, 34	Boar–Horse B		48	52	<0.5	<0.4	<0.3	
37074r	1983, 3–30, 35	Boar–Horse B		49	51	<0.5	<0.4	<0.3	
37075p	1983, 3–30, 36	Boar–Horse D		49	51	<0.5	<0.4	<0.3	
37076y	1983, 3–30, 41	Face–Horse A		49	51	<0.5	<0.4	<0.3	
37077w	1983, 3–30, 54	Face–Horse A		51	48	1.5	<0.4	0.4	
37078u	1983, 3–30, 60	Face–Horse A		49	50	1.4	<0.4	<0.3	
37079s	1983, 3–30, 66	Face–Horse B/C		49	49	1.6	0.5	<0.3	
37080v	1983, 3–30, 75	Face–Horse A		49	50	1.5	0.5	<0.3	
37081t	1983, 3–30, 78	Face–Horse A		43	55	1.6	0.7	<0.3	
37082r	1983, 3–30, 88	Face–Horse B/C		48	48	3.8	0.4	0.4	
37083p	1983, 3–30, 89	Face–Horse B/C		45	54	0.8	0.4	<0.3	
37084y	1983, 3–30, 96	Face–Horse B/C	Plating	62	38	<0.5	<0.4	<0.3	Plated coin
37084y	1983, 3–30, 96	Face–Horse B/C	Core	98	0	2.0	<0.4	<0.3	Plated coin
37085w	1983, 3–30, 101	Face–Horse B/C		53	47	<0.5	<0.4	<0.3	
37086u	1983, 3–30, 106	Face–Horse B/C		50	50	<0.5	0.4	<0.3	
37087s	1983, 3–30, 109	Face–Horse B/C		41	59	0.7	<0.4	<0.3	
37088q	1983, 3–30, 113	Face–Horse B/C		51	47	1.6	<0.4	<0.3	
37089z	1983, 3–30, 213	Anted		59	41	<0.5	<0.4	<0.3	
37090r	1983, 3–30, 226	Anted		54	46	0.4	<0.4	0.3	
37091p	1983, 3–30, 268	Anted		52	47	0.8	<0.4	0.3	
37092y	1983, 3–30, 281	Anted		58	42	<0.5	<0.4	<0.3	
37093w	1983, 3–30, 405	Ecen		52	48	<0.5	<0.4	<0.3	
37094u	1983, 3–30, 493	Ecen		50	49	0.6	0.4	0.5	

Table 8 continued

BMRL	Cat/Reg	Description	Part	Cu	Ag	Sn	Pb	Au	Comments
37095s	1983, 3–30, 584	Symbol		52	47	0.7	<0.4	0.4	
37096q	1983, 3–30, 585	Symbol		58	42	0.4	<0.4	0.3	
37097z	1983, 3–30, 591	Ecen or Ed(n)	Plating	61	37	2.2	<0.4	<0.3	Plated coin
37097z	1983, 3–30, 591	Ecen or Ed(n)	Core	96	1	3.3	<0.4	<0.3	Plated coin
37098x	1983, 3–30, 670	Edn		52	47	0.6	0.6	0.5	
37099v	1983, 3–30, 671	Edn		50	49	0.7	0.4	<0.3	
37100r	1983, 3–30, 701	Ece A		51	49	<0.5	<0.4	<0.3	
37101p	1983, 3–30, 711	Ece A		48	51	0.7	0.5	<0.3	
37102y	1983, 3–30, 803	Ece B		55	44	0.6	<0.4	<0.3	
37103w	1983, 3–30, 806	Ece B		54	46	<0.5	<0.4	<0.3	
37104u	1983, 3–30, 827	Ece B rev		52	47	0.5	<0.4	0.5	
37105s	1983, 3–30, 829	Ece B rev	Core			<0.5	<0.4	<0.3	Corroded
37106q	1983, 3–30, 833	Ece B rev		52	48	<0.5	<0.4	<0.3	
37107z	1983, 3–30, 842	Aesv		49	50	0.6	<0.4	0.5	
37108x	1983, 3–30, 847	Aesv		52	48	<0.5	<0.4	<0.3	
37109V	1983, 3–30, 862	Saenv		52	47	0.5	0.4	<0.3	
37110Y	1983, 3–30, 864	Saenv		56	43	0.7	<0.4	0.4	
39392Z	1983, 3–30, 708	Ed(n)	Core	98	2	<0.5	<0.4	<0.3	
39393X	1982, 4–3, 1	Early Face–Horse B							Corroded
39394V	1982, 4–3, 2	New Icenian type							Corroded
39395T	1982, 4–3, 6	Icenian Pattern–Horse		40	60	<0.5	0.4	<0.3	Slight corrosion
39396R	1984, 2–22, 20	Early Pattern–Horse A		62	33	4.9	0.4	<0.3	

Discussion

All the unplated coins are essentially silver–copper alloys containing approximately 50% silver with often minor or trace amounts of tin, lead and gold. The lead and gold will have been introduced into the alloy with the silver. Lead was used in the refining process of cupellation and lead ore (argentifer-rous galena) was the usual source of silver in antiquity. Gold is associated with silver sources but is not removed by the refining process. The tin content of some of the coins is almost certainly associated with the copper and derived from the addition of some bronze to the alloy. Although not shown in Table 8 some coins also contain traces of antimony, not quantified but probably about 0.5%. This element has been found in Celtic bronze coinage at concentrations up to 2% (Northover, personal communication) and is presumably characteristic of some of the copper sources used.

The amounts of tin are rather variable but, relative to the copper content, they suggest the use of a bronze containing at least 10% tin. Tin is often found in the base gold coins of the Iceni and other issues (British L, British M etc.) but the proportions in these indicates the use of bronze with a rather higher tin content, possibly up to 20% (Cowell 1992). There is no consistent correlation between the tin content and coin type although the uninscribed issues generally contain higher concentrations than the inscribed issues.

The significance of differences in the fineness of the various types was investigated using Student's t-test. For clarity, the distributions of the groups tested are summarised below.

Type	Number	%Ag (mean)	Standard deviation
Boar–House	7	47.3	4.1
Face–Horse	12	50.7	3.6
Anted	4	44.0	2.9
Ecen	6	47.0	2.6
Ece, Aesv, Saenv	8	46.6	2.3
Boar–Horse + Face–Horse	19	49.4	4.0
Inscribed (Anted etc)	18	46.2	2.7

A test of the means of the two uninscribed issues (Boar–Horse and Face–Horse) showed no significant difference as did tests of pairs of the inscribed issues. However, a test of the two major groups, uninscribed and inscribed, did show a significant difference. The t-value (2.9 with 35 degrees of freedom) exceeds the 0.05 probability value of 2.0 which indicates that there is only a 5% probability of the difference resulting from chance.

There is therefore a small but significant decrease in fineness from the uninscribed to the inscribed issues. As there are sound typological reasons for considering that the uninscribed issues are earliest this result indicates a small debasement of the series. Whether this reduction was intentional and constituted a deliberately controlled standard cannot be deduced from these data, but it seems unlikely given the small magnitude of the decrease.

The overall fineness of these Icenian issues at about 48% silver is in fact almost exactly half that of the contemporary denarii which are typically in the range 96–97% silver

(Walker 1976). This could be an indication of a relative tariff of the two currency systems.

There are some contemporary forgeries in the hoard as a whole, mainly plated coins. The two plated coins which were examined are very similar in composition. Both are silver plated on a base metal core, the plating being carried out prior to striking probably by wrapping with foil and fusing it to the core. The core in both cases is a low tin bronze and the plating is base silver. The silver content of the plating is lower than that of the normal coins. In one case the plating alloy also includes some tin, probably through alloying with bronze.

DISCUSSION   Amanda Chadburn

1 The composition of the coin assemblages and their significance, and comparative data

The composition of the Field Baulk hoard is fairly typical of the many Icenian silver hoards which have been discovered over the last two centuries. However, it is the largest recorded to date and contains a proportionately higher number of rare types, such as Aesv and Saenv, and is significant for this reason.

About half the known Icenian hoards have been found to be mixed with Roman coins, so the fact that there are no Roman coins is not atypical. Other Celtic issues are rare in Icenian silver hoards, and the Field Baulk hoard follows the normal pattern here, as it contains no other Iron Age coins from other tribal areas.

The Field Baulk hoard is also important as it represents a third of the recorded Icenian coinage to date, and increases the number of recorded specimens by over half in some cases. The total number of Icenian coins recorded by Haselgrove in 1987 was 2674, which includes the Field Baulk hoard, whereas Allen in 1970 was only able to study 1150 specimens. In some cases, the hoard provides a larger number of coins

than Allen had altogether. For example, Allen studied 9 specimens of the coins of Saenv, whereas there are now 16 examples from Field Baulk alone.

The number of brockages is high for a hoard of this size, and would appear to be higher than normal brockage frequency for Celtic coins, and indeed for the Roman Republican series too (Goddard, personal communication and forthcoming). This would appear to indicate that the production of the numerous Pattern–Horse types at least, was rushed, and that they were produced in a short space of time.

Table 9 sets out the result of selected coin assemblages from the Icenian area. The most striking aspect is the similarity between the hoard profiles (the 'average' hoard profile does not include the Fring or Field Baulk hoards) and more especially between the Fring hoard and the Field Baulk hoard, which are virtually identical, despite the difference in their size.

However, there are some differences between the Field Baulk hoard and Allen's 'average' Icenian coin hoard. The Field Baulk hoard contains a higher proportion of Pattern–Horse types, and lower Boar–Horse and Face–Horse types. This may reflect a chronological or spatial variation in the hoarding patterns throughout the Icenian territory.

Another striking aspect of Table 9 is that the Field Baulk hoard and the coin assemblage from the Stonea Grange area vary considerably in composition, which almost certainly reflects the difference between the composition of hoards and those from settlement sites such as Saham Toney (Brown 1986).

Additionally, it is immediately obvious that there are strong similarities between the Stonea Grange and Saham Toney assemblages (where a similar number of Iron Age coins were recovered), and on the basis of the composition of the assemblage, it is probable that the Stonea Grange coins are site finds and not a hoard.

There are other factors in favour of the interpretation of the Stonea Grange coins as site finds. First, the coins were

Table 9 Proportions of Icenian coin types in selected findspots

	Boar–Horse %	Face–Horse %	Pattern–Horse %	Other Celtic %	Number of specimens
Allen's average Icenian hoard (Allen, 1970, 8)	7	30	60	3	—
Fring hoard, Norfolk	3	20	77	—	153
Field Baulk hoard, Cambs	4	20	76	—	872
Honingham hoard, Norfolk	6	25	69	—	340
Scole hoard, Norfolk (excluding denarii)	7	21	72	—	202
Saham Toney, Norfolk (settlement site: Iron Age coins only)	24	13	40	23	82
Stonea Grange, Cambs (Iron Age coins only, but not those from the excavations)	22	12	48	18	59

dispersed over a wide area, although this does not necessarily preclude them from being a hoard. The coins were in a poor condition, fragmentary and sometimes corroded, compared to those from other Icenian coin hoards such as Field Baulk. Clearly they had been dispersed for some years, if not from antiquity. Many genuine dispersed Icenian hoards such as that from Fring (Chadburn and Gurney 1991) are often in rather better condition, as the coins have been in the plough-soil only a relatively short period of time.

Second, and more important, the coins themselves do not look like the contents of a typical Icenian hoard. Many coins appear to be contemporary forgeries, and silver plated coins and new types are relatively common (15% are apparent for-geries at Stonea Grange as opposed to 0.8% from the Field Baulk hoard). In contrast, most Icenian hoards seem to have been carefully selected for good quality coins. The reports of the allegedly high numbers of plated coins discussed above (apparently amounting to about 25% of the totals recov-

ered) found in the area of Stonea Grange underline this contrast.

Similarly, there is a relatively high proportion of non-Icenian coins in the assemblage (12%), and the date range also varies widely from early coins such as the Gallo–Belgic E stater, Potin and the Norfolk Wolf stater, to presumed later coins such as Ecen and Ece B. This pattern is also found at other Icenian coin-using sites where a wide date range of coins are usually found. Most Icenian hoards do not contain such a wide date range, and no hoard found to date contains a tripartite mixture of gold, silver and bronze types, which is the composition of both the Stonea Grange assemblage and the Saham Toney assemblage.

Naturally, it is possible that the Stonea Grange assemblage could include a dispersed hoard of some material (e.g. the later silver issues), alongside which were found 'site' coins or further hoards dating to earlier periods. However, on the bal-ance of probability, we should conclude that all these coins

Table 10 Suggested dates for Icenian coin types

Obverse die links	Name†	Van Arsdell date	Haselgrove date	Allen date
	Norfolk Wolf	65–45 BC	{ 70–40 BC / 50–30 BC	—
	Irstead 1/4 stater	45–40 BC	20 BC–AD 10	—
	Early Type	45–40 BC	50–20 BC	c. 10 BC
	Boar–Horse A	35–25 BC	50–20 BC	c. 10–0 BC
	Boar–Horse B	35–25 BC	20 BC–10 AD	c. 0–10 AD
	Boar–Horse C	35–25 BC	20 BC–10 AD	c. 10–25/30 AD
	Boar–Horse D (Cans Dvro)	25–20 BC	20 BC–10 AD	c. 30 AD
	Early Face–Horse B (after Gregory)	—	—	—
	Early Face–Horse Cc (after Gregory)	—	—	—
⊶	Normal Face–Horse A	61 AD	20 BC–10 AD	c. 10–30 AD
⊶	Normal Face–Horse B/C	61 AD	10 AD–40 AD	c. 30–60 AD
	Early Pattern–Horse A	15–1 BC	50–20 BC	c. 0–5 AD
	Early Pattern Horse B	15–1 BC	20 BC–10 AD	c. 0–10 AD
	Anted	1–25 AD	10–40 AD	c. 25–47 AD
⊶	Ecen	25–38 AD	30–60 AD	c. 47–60 AD
⊶	Ed(n)	{ 45–50 AD / 38–40 AD	30–60 AD	c. 60/1 AD
⊶	Ed(n) variant (after Chadburn)	40–45 AD	—	—
	Symbol (after Chadburn)	40–45 AD	30–60 AD	c. 60/1 AD
	Minims of Ecen/Ed(n)/ Symbol group	{ 25–38 AD / 38–40 AD / 15–1 BC	30–60 AD	—
	Ece A	40–45 AD	30–60 AD	c. 50–60 AD
⊶	Ece B	{ 45–50 AD / 45–50 AD	30–60 AD	c. 50–60 AD
⊶	Ece B (reversed)	45–50 AD	30–60 AD	—
⊶	Saenv	50–55 AD	30–60 AD	c. 60 AD
⊶	Aesv	55–60 AD	30–60 AD	c. 61 AD

† Mostly after Allen 1970.

probably represent site finds which were lost within an activity area (presumably a settlement) over a number of years. Certainly they do not all come from a discrete hoard such as Field Baulk.

2 The date of the coin assemblages

There is some dispute as to absolute dates for the Icenian series, although the three major classifications given in Table 10 broadly agree on the relative ordering of the series. See Table 5 (p. 264) for the various classifications.

In his 1970 paper, Allen concluded that the majority of Icenian coin hoards were buried around the time of the Boudiccan rebellion. Since then the discovery of a number of hoards, such as Scole (Burnett 1986b), have tended to substantiate this, especially when one considers the similar hoard profiles which many of them have (see Table 9). The Scole hoard included a coin of Nero, dating to *c*. AD 61, and the Fring hoard was found in a Romanised pottery vessel which was dated to the mid-first century AD. The Field Baulk hoard seems no exception, and the dating of the beaker to *c*. AD 60–70 would fit in with a burial date of *c*. AD 60. The low proportion of presumed early Icenian issues, might also indicate a late deposition date.

Further work on the nature of Icenian hoards is still needed to clarify the date(s) of their deposition, and we should remember that earlier historical episodes, e.g. AD 47/48, and indeed the Conquest period in general, might also be suitable dates when native wealth was hoarded, as well as other times of unrest which were not documented. Indeed, there may have been some hoards where an owner was not able to retrieve his or her wealth, due to a variety of reasons which might have nothing to do with any political situation. Perhaps some of the gold Gallo–Belgic or Norfolk Wolf hoards might fit into such a category. However, in conclusion, the weight of the current evidence suggests that many of the Icenian silver hoards date to around the Boudiccan rebellion, and the Field Baulk hoard is likely to date to this period.

By contrast, the coins from Stonea Grange contain a relatively high proportion of presumed early issues, and this contrasts strongly with the Field Baulk hoard. If we accept Allen's broad chronology for Icenian coins, early Icenian issues (i.e. Boar–Horse A and B types, early Face–Horse and early Pattern–Horse A and B types) only represent 0.6% of the total number of coins in the Field Baulk hoard. (As there is some doubt about the date of the Early Type stater it was not included in these calculations.) This contrasts with a high proportion of early Icenian coins and other Early Iron Age coins from Stonea Grange (including the Gallo–Belgic and Potin coins), which made up over 24% of the total assemblage, although this will in part be a reflection of sample size. It seems clear that the Stonea Grange

assemblage dates back well into the mid first century BC and continues into the first century AD.

The coins from the excavation are residual, and therefore do not add anything to the arguments about the date of Icenian coins.

3 Metrology

Table 11 Field Baulk: mean weights for coin types in the hoard

Coin type	Mean weight (grams)	Number of coins
Boar–Horse A	1.09	4
Boar–Horse B	1.23	4
Boar–Horse C	1.19	25
Boar–Horse D (Cans-Dvro)	1.25	1
Normal Face–Horse A	1.26	41
Normal Face–Horse B/C	1.25	128
Early Pattern–Horse B	1.22	1
Anted	1.22	193
Ecen	1.25	156
Ed(n)	1.26	59
Ed(n) variant	1.25	12
Symbol	1.25	29
Ece A	1.25	73
Ece B	1.24	74
Ece B (reversed)	1.26	22
Aesv	1.17 †	11
Saenv	1.25	16

† 1.21 excluding chipped coin.

Most of the coin types in the Field Baulk hoard appear to have a mean weight of around 1.25 g. A similar exercise was not attempted for the Stonea Grange coins, because of their poor condition.

Some types are slightly lower in weight, for example the earlier types such as the early Pattern–Horse coins and the Boar–Horse coins. The Anted coins are also slightly lower in weight than some of the other Pattern–Horse types, and it is noteworthy that these are often worn. The differences in mean weights do not appear to be statistically significant at this stage, and were probably caused because of differential wear, with the earlier coins being the most worn.

Icenian silver coins are quite often found hoarded with Roman denarii (e.g. the Chatteris and Scole hoards, Burnett 1986), and the metallurgical and metrological results highlight some possible relationships between these two types. Allen (1970, 23) was convinced that a formal system existed between the Celtic and Roman coins, and speculated that it could have been 1 denarius to 3 Icenian silver units.

From the point of view of weight, this still seems to work, as the average weight of a Roman denarius at this period was *c*. 3.7 g (Walker 1976), and Van Arsdell (1987) has proposed a standard weight of 1.25 g for the Icenian silver unit. If this is correct, a ratio of 2.96 Icenian units to 1 denarius, or 3 : 1, may still hold good.

However, if the relationship depended on the amount of silver in the coin, then there would be a ratio of about 6 Icenian silver units to 1 denarius, as most Roman denarii of this date contained between 92–98% silver, whereas the Iceni units contain about 50% silver. Further work remains to be done to see if a formal relationship can be defined.

4 The distribution of Icenian coins and the evidence from the Stonea area

There are now strong indications from the numismatic and archaeological evidence that the March area falls within the main territory of the Iceni. This evidence includes the eight hoards which contain Icenian coins reported from the area around March, including Field Baulk itself; a hoard of 20 Iceni and Roman coins from Langwood Fen at Chatteris (Burnett 1986a), some 16 km from March; and further hoard finds reported from the vicinity of Stonea, although some of these are only alleged finds discussed above, and are not well recorded. However, the recorded numismatic evidence alone suggests that the area is not outside the main territory of the Iceni, and that, indeed, there is a concentration of activity here in the Iron Age. The difficulties of establishing tribal boundaries from numismatic evidence have been discussed in detail by Sellwood (1984b), but there does appear to be firm evidence that the Iceni were well established in this area. It is noteworthy that 84.5% of the Iron Age coin finds from Stonea Grange area were Icenian.

This is at variance with the provisional distribution patterns noted by Allen (1970) following Clarke (1956), who believed that the River Ouse formed the western boundary of the Icenian territory.

Additionally, the tripartite interpretation of the Icenian tribe, based on the three streams of coin types (Boar–Horse, Face–Horse and Pattern–Horse) each representing a *pagus*, also seems to be oversimplified (Allen 1970). For example, there are numerous Pattern–Horse coins in both the Fring and Field Baulk hoards, but the Breckland area of Norfolk has been suggested as their main distribution. The material from Stonea Grange, with a high proportion of early Pattern–Horse coins also suggests Allen may have been wrong on this point, and that the distribution of Pattern–Horse coins is more extensive than was previously thought. This is especially true as, for the hoards at least, there seems to be little difference in the distribution patterns of the three major silver types (see Table 9).

Similarly, Table 9 shows that both the Boar–Horse and Face–Horse types are under-represented at Field Baulk in relation to Allen's average hoard type. It is too early to say whether the distribution patterns deduced mainly from hoards still hold good, but evidence from Field Baulk, and numerous recent single coin finds would tend to suggest

not, and emphasise the provisional nature of earlier coin distribution studies.

5 Relationship to archaeological material and conclusions

The numbers of Iron Age coins from the Stonea Grange area are relatively high, although paralleled by the 82 Iron Age coins found at Saham Toney, Norfolk (Brown 1986). However, it should be remembered that many hundreds more were alleged to have been found from this vicinity, and this further suggests that the settlement was of high status. A number of other unpublished coin-using sites from Norfolk have similar coin assemblages (but with fewer numbers) varying widely in date, and containing relatively high numbers of plated coins and other tribal issues.

Other large assemblages of Iron Age coins are known from Romano-British temple sites such as Hayling Island, Harlow and Wanborough, and from high-status sites such as the *oppida* at Canterbury, Colchester and Silchester (Haselgrove 1987). Nearer East Anglia, 28 Iron Age coins were recovered from Puckeridge-Braughing, Hertfordshire, and 38 from the nearby Skeleton Green (Potter and Trow 1988). This latter complex was a high status settlement in the Late Iron Age with strong trading links with the Continent, and evidence of minting. Both the temple at Stonea Grange and the presence of other Iron Age finds suggest a settlement of some importance in the area, in addition to the Iron Age enclosure of Stonea Camp, which may never have been used for long-term settlement.

If we follow Allen's provincial dating of Icenian coinage, there is now strong numismatic evidence that the area may have been in use well before AD 47/8, and that occupation on the Stonea 'island' may date from at least the first century BC, even if the earthworks of Stonea Camp are later. The large amount of other Late Iron Age archaeological material from this area, which includes the terret-ring, a bronze duck probably embellished with coral, a large number of brooches (at least 20 of which are pre-Flavian) and other material such as pottery, seem to confirm the existence of a Late Iron Age high-status site on the Stonea 'island'. Indeed, such material would not be out of place at an *oppidum*.

Haselgrove (1988) has indicated that it can be demonstrated in an Iron Age context, that the pattern of coin supply to any location, and the intensity of occupation in each period, are critical variables in determining how well different coin types are represented in an assemblage. The relatively high numbers of earlier Icenian issues which may date to the later first century BC, and the lower numbers of the later issues (e.g. Ecen), may indicate on numismatic grounds that the floruit of the Stonea Grange settlement dates to the later first century BC.

Both the Field Baulk hoard and the Stonea Grange assemblage can now be viewed within a wider context, as it appears increasingly likely that this part of the Fens was a focus of activity in the Late Iron Age. The substantial number of coin hoards and individual coin finds, as well as the concentrations of other Late Iron Age archaeological material emphasises this, and indicates in particular the existence of high-status, coin-using settlement in the Stonea Grange area, perhaps reaching a peak of activity in the late first century BC/early first century AD.

CATALOGUES

1 The Group I coins from Stonea Grange
(Pl. XXIII)

The catalogue relates to British Museum accession numbers, and also indicates the Treasure Trove dates/episodes of recovery as the coins were found over several years. Stonea Ia (Amps I) includes accession numbers 1982, 4–3, 1 to 1982, 4–3, 8; Stonea Ib (Amps II) 1984, 2–22, 1 to 1984, 2–22, 36; Stonea Ic (Amps III) 1985, 10–37, 1 to 1985, 10–37, 8 and also 1985, 10–39, 1 and 1985, 10–39, 2. Five other Iron Age coins (nos 38, 53–6) found by Mr Amps were not declared Treasure Trove.

All coins are silver unless otherwise stated, and are grouped by type.

No mean weights are given because of the poor and chipped condition of many of the coins.

Gallo–Belgic E gold stater (core) – 1 coin

No.	Accession number	Weight (grams)	Notes
1	1985, 10–39, 2	1.69	Cu alloy core. Possible contemporary forgery. Reverse badly corroded

Iceni: Early Type gold stater (core) – 1 coin

No.	Accession number	Weight (grams)	Notes
2	1985, 10–39, 1	3.24	New sub-type. Cu alloy core: possible contemporary forgery. No trace of plate Obv: 2 back-to-back crescents with pellets in field Rev: Y-headed horse left (usually horses are open-headed and face right)

Iceni: Boar–Horse A – 3 coins

No.	Accession number	Weight (grams)	Notes
3	1984, 2–22, 6	0.91	Rev: die-linked to no. 4
4	1984, 2–22, 7	0.93	Rev: die-linked to no. 3
5	1984, 2–22, 8	0.75	

Iceni: Boar–Horse B – 2 coins

No.	Accession number	Weight (grams)	Notes
6	1984, 2–22, 9	0.76	Not die-linked
7	1984, 2–22, 10	0.69	

Iceni: Boar–Horse C – 6 coins

No.	Accession number	Weight (grams)	Notes
8	1984, 2–22, 11	0.90	
9	1984, 2–22, 12	0.91	
10	1984, 2–22, 13	0.94	Corroded
11	1984, 2–22, 14	1.18	Slightly corroded
12	1984, 2–22, 15	0.80	Ag plated unit with Cu alloy core. Possible contemporary forgery. Poor condition
13	1985, 10–37, 1	0.83	Poor condition

Iceni: Boar–Horse new types – 2 coins

No.	Accession number	Weight (grams)	Notes
14	1984, 2–22, 4	0.99	New type 1. (A die duplicate coin is known from Norfolk) Obv: stylised boar to right with upturned snout and bristles Rev: open-headed horse to right with triangles and wheel above
15	1984, 2–22, 5	0.91	New type 2 Obv: boar to right with bristles and pellet flower below Rev: open-headed horse to right with pellet flower below and wheel above

Iceni: Early Face–Horse – 2 coins

No.	Accession number	Weight (grams)	Notes
16	1982, 4–3, 1	0.51	Fragment. Sub-type B (after Gregory). Metal too corroded to analyse, but probably Ag half unit
17	1984, 2–22, 16	0.98	Sub-type Cb (after Gregory)

Iceni: Normal Face–Horse A – 1 coin

No.	Accession number	Weight (grams)	Notes
18	1985, 10–37, 2	1.13	

Iceni: Normal Face–Horse B/C – 4 coins

No.	Accession number	Weight (grams)	Notes
19	1982, 4–3, 3	0.97	Cu alloy core. Possible contemporary forgery

No.	Accession number	Weight (grams)	Notes
20	1984, 2–22, 17	0.88	Die duplicate to no. 21
21	1984, 2–22, 18	0.98	Die duplicate to no. 20
22	1985, 10–37, 3	1.01	

Iceni: Early Pattern–Horse A – 2 coins

No.	Accession number	Weight (grams)	Notes
23	1984, 2–22, 19	0.75	Not die-linked to no. 24
24	1984, 2–22, 20	0.98	Cu-rich alloy (see analysis)

Iceni: Early Pattern–Horse B – 2 coins

No.	Accession number	Weight (grams)	Notes
25	1984, 2–22, 21	0.84	Not die-linked to no. 26
26	1984, 2–22, 22	0.76	Chipped

Iceni: Anted – 11 coins

No.	Accession number	Weight (grams)	Notes
27	1982, 4–3, 4	0.72	Chipped
28	1982, 4–3, 5	0.96	Chipped
29	1982, 4–3, 7	1.04	
30	1982, 4–3, 8	0.80	Chipped and flan badly miscast
31	1984, 2–22, 25	0.84	
32	1984, 2–22, 26	1.01	
33	1984, 2–22, 27	0.96	
34	1984, 2–22, 28	0.94	
35	1984, 2–22, 29	0.83	
36	1984, 2–22, 31	0.54	Badly chipped
37	1985, 10–37, 5	1.09	
38		0.96	Corroded

Iceni: Plated Anted – 1 coin

No.	Accession number	Weight (grams)	Notes
39	1984, 2–22, 30	0.84	Ag plated. Possible contemporary forgery

Iceni: Ecen – 2 coins

No.	Accession number	Weight (grams)	Notes
40	1984, 2–22, 32	0.93	
41	1984, 2–22, 33	0.84	

Iceni: Ed(n) – 1 coin

No.	Accession number	Weight (grams)	Notes
42	1985, 10–37, 4	1.11	Die-linked to Field Baulk no. 604

Iceni: Ecen/Ed(n) – 3 coins

No.	Accession number	Weight (grams)	Notes
43	1984, 2–22, 34	0.85	Much Cu visible
44	1984, 2–22, 35	0.88	Much Cu visible
45	1985, 10–37, 7	1.10	

Iceni: Minim of Ecen/Ed(n) group (plated) – 1 coin

No.	Accession number	Weight (grams)	Notes
46	1984, 2–22, 24	0.49	Ag plated, inscribed ECE[. Possible contemporary forgery

Iceni: Ece A – 1 coin

No.	Accession number	Weight (grams)	Notes
47	1984, 2–22, 23	0.83	

Iceni: Ece B – 1 coin

No.	Accession number	Weight (grams)	Notes
48	1984, 2–22, 36	0.88	2 fragments, weight includes glue

Iceni: Pattern–Horse new type (core) – 1 coin

No.	Accession number	Weight (grams)	Notes
49	1985, 10–37, 8	1.17	New type 1. Possible contemporary forgery. Mane and mouth of horse composed of pellets. Cu alloy core. ?Y-headed; similar to Ece B types

Iceni: Pattern–Horse unclassified – 2 coins

No.	Accession number	Weight (grams)	Notes
50	1982, 4–3, 6	0.39	Obv: Back-to-back crescents Rev: Horse to left. Silver unit; metal slightly corroded (see analysis)
51	1985, 10–37, 6	0.85	Obv: back-to-back crescents. Rev: Open-headed horse to left. Cu alloy core. Possible contemporary forgery

Corieltauvi: Prototype gold stater: type D – 1 coin

No.	Accession number	Weight (grams)	Notes
52	1984, 2–22, 2	4.33	Previously unrecorded die (pers. comm. J. May) cf. 219, Pl. I in Allen 1963, and 805 in Van Arsdell 1989

Potin – 2 coins

No.	Accession number	Weight (grams)	Notes
53		2.70	Sn alloy unit. Class I (Allen); P1 (Haselgrove); 1428–3 (Van Arsdell)
54		3.45	Sn alloy unit. Class I (Allen); P1 (Haselgrove); 1428–3 (Van Arsdell)

Trinovantes: Andoco – 1 coin

No.	Accession number	Weight (grams)	Notes
55		1.69	Cu alloy unit. cf. 1871–1, Van Arsdell

Trinovantes: Addedomarus – 1 coin

No.	Accession number	Weight (grams)	Notes
56		1.21	Cu alloy unit. cf. 1615–1, Van Arsdell. (Possible reverse die link to 1615–1)

Unidentified Celtic – 2 coins

No.	Accession number	Weight (grams)	Notes
57	1982, 4–3, 2	0.60	Obv: unclassifiable ?animal Rev: Icenian open-headed horse to right Metal too corroded to analyse. Large flan but coin fragmentary. Probably an Icenian unit
58	1984, 2–22, 3	0.97	Celtic silver unit: Icenian new type? 2 fragments; weight includes glue Obv: blank with a small arc in one corner Rev: horse to right with pellet triangle and pellets in ring in field. Affinities to Whaddon Chase horse types, e.g. Van Arsdell 1500 and 1505

Early Roman – 1 coin

No.	Accession number	Weight (grams)	Notes
59	1984, 2–22, 1	3.56	Ag denarius of Augustus, c. 30 BC Obv: head to right Rev: Mercury seated on a rock playing lyre. CAESAR DIVI Ref. BMC 596 (identification by A. Burnett)

2 Iron Age coins from the Stonea Grange excavation (Pl. XXIV)

Catalogue number	Excavation code	Weight (grams)	Type (after Allen 1970)	Context
60	ST 81 LN, SF 120	0.90	Boar–Horse A	Building R1
61	ST 82 AFB, SF 397	0.70	Boar–Horse C	Pit 563

3 Iron Age coins from the Field Baulk hoard, by coin type (Pl. XXIV)

Boar–Horse A – 4 coins

Accession number	Weight (grams)
1983, 3–30, 28	1.09
29	1.10
30	1.09
31	1.07
Mean weight	1.09

Boar–Horse B – 4 coins

Accession number	Weight (grams)
1983, 3–30, 32	1.24
33	1.18
34	1.32
35	1.17
Mean weight	1.23

Boar–Horse C – 25 coins

Accession number	Weight (grams)	Notes
1983, 3–30, 2	1.28	
3	1.22	
4	1.21	
5	1.10	
6	1.20	
7	1.10	
8	1.22	
9	1.09	
10	1.22	
11	1.29	
12	1.17	
13	1.25	
14	1.23	
15	1.18	
16	1.02	
18	1.19	
19	1.06	
20	1.12	
21	1.20	
22	1.19	
23	1.28	

Accession number	Weight (grams)	Notes
1983, 3–30, 24	1.23	
25	1.17	Elongated flan
26	1.26	
27	1.31	
Mean weight	1.19	

Cans-Dvro (Boar–Horse D) – 1 coin

Accession number	Weight (grams)
1983, 3–30, 36	1.25

Boar–Horse unclassified – 1 coin

Accession number	Weight (grams)	Notes
1983, 3–30, 17	0.67	?Contemporary forgery. Possible core. Very worn

Normal Face–Horse A – 41 coins

Accession number	Weight (grams)	Notes
1983, 3–30, 37	1.28	
38	1.33	
39	1.22	
40	1.29	
41	1.29	
42	1.31	
43	1.19	
44	1.30	
45	1.22	
46	1.24	
47	1.26	
48	1.22	
49	1.28	
50	1.15	
51	1.28	
52	1.19	
53	1.28	
54	1.28	
55	1.22	
56	1.29	
57	1.28	
58	1.29	
59	1.40	Heavy
60	1.29	
61	1.25	
62	1.29	
63	1.21	
64	1.20	
65	1.25	
67	1.20	
69	1.26	
70	1.21	
71	1.28	

Accession number	Weight (grams)	Notes
1983, 3–30, 72	1.22	
73	1.23	
74	1.25	
75	1.16	
77	1.26	
78	1.30	
79	1.26	
80	1.29	
Mean weight	1.26	

Normal Face–Horse A (?plated) – 1 coin

Accession number	Weight (grams)
1983, 3–30, 68	1.17

Normal Face–Horse B/C – 128 coins

Accession number	Weight (grams)	Notes
1983, 3–30, 66	1.25	
81	1.28	
82	1.27	
83	1.27	
84	1.30	
85	1.26	
86	1.29	
87	1.29	
88	1.30	
89	1.29	
90	1.29	
91	1.30	
92	1.25	
93	1.28	
94	1.26	
95	1.25	
97	1.27	
98	1.28	
99	1.20	
100	1.17	
101	1.23	
102	1.26	
103	1.26	
104	1.27	
105	1.26	
106	1.26	
107	1.31	
108	1.29	
109	1.24	
110	1.24	
111	1.28	
112	1.25	
113	1.26	
114	1.27	
115	1.29	

Accession number	Weight (grams)	Notes
1983, 3–30, 116	1.21	
117	1.22	
118	1.26	
119	1.32	
120	1.25	
121	1.26	
122	1.28	
123	1.24	
124	1.21	
125	1.24	
126	1.25	
127	1.25	
128	1.26	
129	1.23	
130	1.20	
131	1.22	
132	1.26	
133	1.22	
134	1.26	
135	1.22	
136	1.26	
137	1.23	
138	1.25	
139	1.19	
140	1.30	
141	1.27	
142	1.28	
143	1.21	
144	1.27	
145	1.25	
146	1.33	
147	1.24	
148	1.25	
149	1.21	
150	1.24	
151	1.15	
152	1.25	
153	1.21	
154	1.27	Unusual Pb-coloured alloy, but coin is die-linked to other F–H B/C coins
155	1.28	
156	1.26	
157	1.25	
158	1.40	Heavy
159	1.27	
160	1.26	
161	1.28	
162	1.26	
163	1.22	
164	1.29	
165	1.27	
166	1.24	
167	1.26	
168	1.30	
169	1.28	
170	1.39	Heavy

Accession number	Weight (grams)	Notes
1983, 3–30, 171	1.24	
172	1.27	
173	1.16	
174	1.29	
175	1.24	
176	1.29	
177	1.27	
178	1.22	
179	1.23	
180	1.25	
181	1.27	
182	1.30	
183	1.23	
184	1.25	
185	1.31	
186	1.25	
187	1.21	
188	1.24	
189	1.21	
190	1.09	
191	1.24	
192	1.29	
193	1.24	
194	1.21	
195	1.18	
196	1.28	
197	1.24	
198	1.25	
199	1.27	
200	1.24	
201	1.23	
202	1.27	
203	1.05	Unusual Pb-coloured alloy. Coin is not die-linked to other F–H B/C coins
204	1.22	
205	1.25	
206	1.19	Elongated flan
207	1.26	
208	1.00	Unusual Pb-coloured alloy, but coin is die-linked to other F–H B/C coins
Mean weight	1.25	

Normal Face–Horse B/C (plated) – 1 coin

Accession number	Weight (grams)
1983, 3–30, 96	1.18

Normal Face–Horse unclassified – 1 coin

Accession number	Weight (grams)
1983, 3–30, 76	1.18

Early Pattern–Horse B – 1 coin

Accession number	Weight (grams)	Notes
1983, 3–30, 1	1.22	

Anted – 193 coins

Accession number	Weight (grams)	Notes
1983, 3–30, 209	1.25	Antedi type
210	1.21	Antedi type
211	1.23	Antedi type
212	1.23	Antedi type
213	1.29	
214	1.27	
215	1.15	
216	1.19	
217	1.24	
218	1.21	
219	1.22	
220	1.14	Elongated flan
221	1.16	
222	1.26	
223	1.25	
224	1.19	
225	1.04	
226	1.18	
227	1.22	
228	1.27	
229	1.22	Antedi type with elongated flan
230	1.20	
231	1.19	
232	1.26	
233	1.19	
234	1.31	
235	1.21	
236	1.21	
237	1.23	
238	1.25	
239	1.24	
240	1.20	
241	1.23	
242	1.27	
243	1.25	
244	1.21	
245	1.25	
246	1.27	
247	1.23	
248	1.21	
249	1.24	
250	1.25	
251	1.16	
252	1.22	Elongated flan
253	1.17	
254	1.14	Chipped on centre of flan
255	1.14	
256	1.04	
257	1.26	

Accession number	Weight (grams)	Notes
1983, 3–30, 258	1.22	
259	1.22	
260	1.35	
261	1.08	
262	1.25	
263	1.25	
264	1.21	
265	1.16	
266	1.18	
267	1.34	Slightly chipped and worn, but still heavy
268	1.23	
269	1.22	
270	1.20	
271	1.09	
272	1.21	
273	1.21	
274	1.27	
275	1.21	
276	1.05	
277	1.21	Elongated flan
278	1.23	
279	1.23	
280	1.19	
281	1.27	
282	1.23	
283	1.18	
284	1.23	
285	1.22	
286	1.22	
287	1.28	
288	1.21	
289	1.17	
290	1.24	
291	1.23	
292	1.28	
293	1.23	
294	1.25	
295	1.20	
296	1.21	
297	1.21	
298	1.25	
299	1.21	
300	1.30	
301	1.21	
302	1.26	
303	1.20	
304	1.27	
305	1.26	
306	1.28	
307	1.20	
308	1.24	
309	1.32	
310	1.20	
311	1.03	
312	1.24	
313	1.28	

Accession number	Weight (grams)	Notes		Accession number	Weight (grams)	Notes
1983, 3–30, 314	1.23			1983, 3–30, 371	1.20	
315	1.17			372	1.25	
316	1.25			373	1.19	
317	1.24			374	1.22	
318	1.39	Heavy		375	1.18	
319	1.21			376	1.29	
320	1.25			379	1.16	
321	1.22	Slightly mis-struck on reverse		380	1.68	Very heavy, but worn
322	1.23			381	1.21	
323	1.20			382	1.25	
324	1.21			383	1.22	
325	1.26			384	1.21	
326	1.28			385	1.27	
327	1.25			386	1.26	
328	1.28			387	1.25	
329	1.19			389	1.26	
330	1.16			390	1.24	
331	1.23			391	1.19	
332	1.23			392	1.23	
333	1.28			393	1.25	
334	1.09			394	1.23	
335	1.24			396	1.27	
336	1.23			397	1.24	
337	1.22			398	1.28	
338	1.22			399	1.30	
339	1.18			401	1.28	Some Cu visible
340	1.23			402	1.27	
341	1.23			403	1.18	
342	1.23			404	1.24	
343	1.18			516	1.26	
344	1.26			571	1.19	
345	1.25				—	
346	1.23			Mean weight (excluding chipped coins)	1.22	
347	1.22					
348	1.17					
349	1.24			Mean weight (all coins)	1.22	
350	1.17					
351	1.18					
352	1.32			*Ecen – 156 coins*		
353	1.25					
354	1.21			Accession number	Weight (grams)	Notes
355	1.21			1983, 3–30, 405	1.23	
356	1.15			406	1.27	
357	1.22			407	1.17	
358	1.21			408	1.32	
359	1.27			409	1.25	
360	1.29			410	1.25	
361	1.29			411	1.27	
362	1.23			412	1.29	
363	1.26			413	1.25	
364	1.18			414	1.22	
365	1.07			415	1.25	
366	1.12			416	1.22	Chipped
367	1.22			417	1.25	
368	1.27			418	1.23	
369	1.23			419	1.25	
370	1.15					

Accession number	Weight (grams)	Notes	Accession number	Weight (grams)	Notes
1983, 3–30, 420	1.25		1983, 3–30, 480	1.26	
421	1.27		481	1.24	
422	1.29		482	1.23	
423	1.30		483	1.30	
424	1.25		484	1.19	
425	1.14		485	1.26	
426	1.25		486	1.27	
427	1.23		487	1.24	
428	1.22		488	1.27	
429	1.24		489	1.26	
430	1.22		490	1.27	
432	1.26		491	1.27	
433	1.25		492	1.31	
434	1.27		493	1.28	
435	1.34		494	1.28	
436	1.25		495	1.26	
437	1.26	Some Cu visible	496	1.29	
438	1.17		497	1.29	
439	1.19		498	1.28	
440	1.24		499	1.29	
441	1.28		500	1.28	
442	1.26		501	1.30	
443	1.19		502	1.25	
445	1.27		503	1.24	
446	1.25		504	1.26	
447	1.27		505	1.22	
448	1.27		506	1.28	
449	1.21		507	1.25	
450	1.23		508	1.28	
451	1.25		509	1.24	
452	1.21		510	1.29	
454	1.22		511	1.24	
455	1.27		512	1.20	
456	1.25		513	1.26	
457	1.22		514	1.25	
458	1.20		515	1.26	
459	1.22		517	1.26	
460	1.30		519	1.25	
461	1.28		521	1.23	
462	1.27		523	1.27	
463	1.25		524	1.26	
464	1.26		525	1.28	
465	1.22		526	1.25	
466	1.30		527	1.25	
467	1.25		528	1.28	
468	1.27		529	1.26	
469	1.34		530	1.23	Overstamped brockage
470	1.26		531	1.28	
471	1.26		533	1.26	Double struck
472	1.26		534	1.20	
473	1.28		535	1.27	
474	1.22		536	1.24	
475	1.19		537	1.21	
476	1.26		539	1.30	
477	1.27		540	1.19	
478	1.25		541	1.30	
479	1.30		543	1.25	

Accession number	Weight (grams)	Notes		Accession number	Weight (grams)	Notes
1983, 3–30, 544	1.28			1983, 3–30, 608	1.29	
545	1.26			609	1.25	
546	1.27			610	1.32	
547	1.26			613	1.24	
548	1.23			614	1.23	
550	1.23			615	1.25	
552	1.24			617	1.27	
554	1.22			618	1.31	
556	1.20			619	1.31	
557	1.22			620	1.30	
558	1.34			624	1.30	
559	1.25			625	1.08	
560	1.29			627	1.28	
562	1.30			628	1.24	
563	1.18			629	1.29	
564	1.26			630	1.27	
567	1.28			632	1.30	
569	1.26			633	1.22	
570	1.27			634	1.25	
572	1.29			635	1.25	
574	1.26			638	1.28	
575	1.26			639	1.31	
576	1.27			640	1.21	
577	1.25			641	1.22	
597	1.03			642	1.25	
603	1.25			646	1.24	
659	1.06			647	1.24	
				649	1.24	
Mean weight (excluding chipped coin)	1.25			650	1.31	
				651	1.22	
Mean weight (all coins)	1.25			653	1.26	
				654	1.23	
				655	1.18	
				656	1.35	
				657	1.26	
				658	1.23	
				660	1.25	
				662	1.26	
				663	1.27	
				664	1.22	
				666	1.25	
				667	1.26	
				668	1.28	
				669	1.21	
				670	1.26	
				671	1.25	
				672	1.24	
				Mean weight	1.26	

Ecen (plated) – 1 coin

Accession number	Weight (grams)	Notes
1983, 3–30, 453	1.08	Rev: die cutting unusual

Ed(n) – 59 coins

Accession number	Weight (grams)	Notes
1983, 3–30, 444	1.26	
518	1.25	
532	1.33	
553	1.27	
555	1.28	
561	1.27	
594	1.27	
600	1.20	
601	1.24	
602	1.29	
604	1.26	
605	1.23	

Edn (core) – 1 coin

Accession number	Weight (grams)	Notes
1983, 3–30, 708	0.77	Cu alloy core; EDN. The D appears to have a crossbar

Ed(n) variant – 12 coins

Accession number	Weight (grams)	Notes
1983, 3–30, 599	1.29	
606	1.30	
612	1.14	Pb coloured alloy
616	1.35	
622	1.27	
626	1.24	
631	1.26	
636	1.27	
637	1.19	
644	1.24	
645	1.26	
652	1.23	
Mean weight	1.25	

Symbol – 29 coins

Accession number	Weight (grams)	Notes
1983, 3–30, 378	1.29	
520	1.22	
522	1.27	
538	1.32	
542	1.23	
549	1.23	
551	1.25	
565	1.29	
566	1.29	
568	1.25	
573	1.19	
578	1.26	
579	1.25	
580	1.24	
581	1.29	
582	1.25	
583	1.26	
584	1.25	
585	1.30	
586	1.13	
587	1.23	
588	1.26	
589	1.26	
590	1.27	
592	1.28	
593	1.21	
595	1.25	
596	1.24	
643	1.25	
Mean weight	1.25	

Pattern–Horse unclassified: Ecen or Ed(n) – 10 coins

Accession number	Weight (grams)	Notes
1983, 3–30, 388	1.22	Elongated flan
591	1.06	Plated

Accession number	Weight (grams)	Notes
1983, 3–30, 598	1.25	
607	1.32	
611	1.23	
621	1.24	
623	1.26	
648	1.28	
661	1.21	
665	1.32	

Ece A – 73 coins

Accession number	Weight (grams)	Notes
1983, 3–30, 677	1.24	
678	1.24	
679	1.24	
680	1.21	
681	1.28	
682	1.27	
683	1.09	
684	1.22	
685	1.22	
686	1.22	
687	1.26	
688	1.26	
689	1.23	
690	1.24	
691	1.24	
692	1.25	
693	1.26	
694	1.19	
695	1.27	
696	1.38	
697	1.25	
698	1.17	
699	1.24	
700	1.25	
701	1.27	
702	1.30	
703	1.29	
704	1.24	
705	1.20	
706	1.24	
707	1.27	
709	1.25	
710	1.23	
711	1.25	
712	1.28	
713	1.29	
714	1.26	
715	1.31	
716	1.20	
717	1.24	
718	1.29	
719	1.20	
720	1.20	
721	1.28	

Accession number	Weight (grams)	Notes	Accession number	Weight (grams)	Notes
1983, 3–30, 722	1.20	Elongated flan	1983, 3–30, 771	1.21	
723	1.26		772	1.23	
724	1.30		773	1.21	
725	1.27		774	1.29	
726	1.29		775	1.19	
727	1.29		776	1.14	
728	1.19		777	1.24	
729	1.25		778	1.23	
730	1.24		779	1.26	
731	1.30		780	1.26	
732	1.28		781	1.28	
733	1.13		782	1.27	
734	1.28		783	1.20	
735	1.21		784	1.26	
736	1.26		785	1.23	
737	1.26		786	1.18	
738	1.24		787	1.23	
739	1.22		788	1.30	
740	1.21		789	1.24	
741	1.22		790	1.25	
742	1.28		791	1.24	
743	1.31		792	1.26	
744	1.27		793	1.23	
745	1.26		794	1.24	
746	1.34		795	1.31	
747	1.18		796	1.27	
748	1.26		797	1.22	
749	1.28		798	1.21	
753	1.27		799	1.36	
Mean weight	1.25		800	1.01	
			801	1.27	Some Cu visible

Ece B – 74 coins

Accession number	Weight (grams)	Notes	Accession number	Weight (grams)	Notes
1983, 3–30, 377	1.19		802	1.25	
431	1.26		803	1.26	
750	1.25		804	1.31	
751	1.23		805	1.20	
752	1.25		806	1.30	
754	1.31		807	1.26	
755	1.26		808	1.26	
756	1.25		809	1.23	
757	1.27		810	1.25	
758	1.25		811	1.26	
759	1.27		812	1.26	
760	1.20		813	1.16	
761	1.21		814	1.24	
762	1.24		815	1.26	
763	1.23		816	1.26	
764	1.32		817	1.25	
765	1.23		818	1.25	
766	1.27		869	1.08	
767	1.26		870	1.24	
768	1.46	Heavy	871	1.25	
769	1.19		872	1.11	
770	1.26		Mean weight	1.24	
			Mean weight including Ece B (reversed)	1.25	

Ece B (reversed) – 22 coins

Accession number	Weight (grams)	Notes
1983, 3–30, 819	1.29	
820	1.26	
821	1.25	
822	1.25	
823	1.23	
824	1.30	
825	1.30	
826	1.31	
827	1.22	
828	1.22	
830	1.21	
831	1.22	
832	1.27	
833	1.28	
834	1.25	
835	1.27	
836	1.27	
837	1.20	
838	1.19	
839	1.26	
840	1.27	
841	1.29	
Mean weight	1.26	

Ece B (reversed) ?core – 1 coin

1983, 3–30, 829	0.76	?Core; possible contemporary forgery. Pb-coloured alloy. Too worn to die link

Saenv – 16 coins

Accession number	Weight (grams)	Notes
1983, 3–30, 852	1.20	
853	1.26	
854	1.23	
855	1.30	
856	1.22	
857	1.28	
858	1.24	
859	1.26	
860	1.28	
861	1.28	
862	1.24	
863	1.27	
864	1.25	
865	1.23	
866	1.22	
867	1.28	
Mean weight	1.25	

Aesv – 11 coins

Accession number	Weight (grams)	Notes
1983, 3–30, 842	1.28	
843	1.14	
844	1.23	
845	1.22	
846	1.21	
847	1.27	
848	1.19	
849	1.18	Some Cu visible
850	1.21	
851	0.84	Chipped
868	1.13	
Mean weight (excluding chipped coin)	1.21	
Mean weight (all coins)	1.17	

Iceni Pattern–Horse unclassified and Iceni Pattern–Horse brockages – 6 coins

Accession number	Weight (grams)	Notes
1983, 3–30, 395	1.24	Anted or Ecen or Ed(n)
400	1.10	Anted or Ecen or Ed(n) or Ece A (worn)
673	1.18	Ecen or Ed(n) or Anted
674	1.22	Pattern–Horse Unclassified (mis-strike)
675	1.16	Pattern–Horse Unclassified: brockage
676	1.19	Pattern–Horse Unclassified: brockage

Acknowledgements

I am most grateful to the following colleagues who have helped in various ways, by generously contributing unpublished material, by discussing this subject in general with me, or by criticising earlier drafts of this paper: Tim Potter, Jeffrey May, the late Tony Gregory, Colin Haselgrove, Andrew Burnett, John Kent, Melinda Mays and Dr J. Goddard.

ROMAN COINS

D. C. A. Shotter [Submitted 1988] (Fig. 92)

A THE COINS FROM THE EXCAVATIONS

This section consists of identification of the 61 Roman coins recovered in the excavations. A discussion of their significance will be found in section B, where consideration is given to the total sample of coins found in the area.

Catalogue

Abbreviations

Crawford   Crawford 1974
RIC   Mattingly *et al* 1923–
LRBC   Carson *et al* 1960
LW   Little worn
MW   Moderately worn
VW   Very worn

Republican – 1 coin

1   ST 84 DBM, SF 828
    Æ Denarius, M. Antonius   MW   32–31 BC
    Obv: ANT AVG IIIVIR RPC
    Rev: LEG XXIII   Crawford 544, 39
    From the uppermost fill (unit 1536) in latrine pit 1536.
    Early 3rd century AD.

Claudius – 1 coin

2   ST 83 CAW, SF 467
    Æ As (imitation)   MW   *c.* AD 50 +
    Obv: Head left
    Rev: Minerva   as *RIC* I².100
    From the fill of pit 1020, in which it was probably a residual find.

Vespasian – 7 coins

3   ST 80 unstratified, SF 2
    Æ Sestertius   VW   AD 69–79
    Surface find, beyond excavation edge, west of building R1.

4   ST 81 GS, SF 51
    Æ Sestertius   VW   AD 69–79
    From silt spread 155 beyond the south-east corner of building R1. 3rd or 4th century AD.

5   ST 82 AAA, SF 248
    Æ Sestertius   VW   AD 69–79
    From topsoil/cleaning, blocks 1a and 1b.

6   ST 82 ABS, SF 259
    Æ Dupondius   VW   AD 69–79
    From top layer (unit 483) of pit 483/918. Late 3rd/4th century AD.

7   ST 82 AZZ, SF 278
    Æ Denarius   MW   AD 74
    Obv: IMP CAESAR VESP A[
    Rev: [PONTIF MAXIM]   *RIC* 83
    From top layer (unit 705) of well 705. 3rd/4th century AD.

8   ST 84 DGZ, SF 810
    Æ Denarius   VW   AD 69–79
    Obv: IMP CAESAR VESP[
    From uppermost layer (unit 1668) of pits 1834, 1835/2007, 1850. 3rd century AD.

9   ST 84 EAK, SF 1093
    Æ As   VW   AD 69–79
    Obv:]VESP[
    From primary silt (unit 2086) of pit 2061. Early 3rd century AD.

Domitian – 1 coin

10 ST 82 AAB, SF 242
    Æ Dupondius   VW   AD 81–96
    From disturbed uppermost fill (unit 443) of well 446. Late 3rd century AD.

Nerva – 1 coin

11 ST 82 BCO, SF 316
    Æ Denarius   LW   AD 96
    Obv: IMP NERVA CAES AVG P M TR P COS II P P
    Rev: LIBERTAS PVBLICA   *RIC* 7
    From ditch 9, cut 4, unit 767. Late 3rd/4th century AD.

Trajan – 10 coins

12 ST 81 FV, SF 67
    Æ As (probably of Trajan)   VW   AD 98–117
    From silty clay spread (unit 134), south of Anglo-Saxon building S1. Late 3rd–4th century AD, with Anglo-Saxon pottery.

13 ST 81 JV, SF 90
    Æ Dupondius   VW   AD 103–11
    Obv:]NER TRAIANO[
    Rev: S P Q R OPTIMO PRINCIPI S C
    From building debris in shallow scoop (unit 203) south-east of building R1. Phase IV.

14 ST 81 MR, SF 166
    Æ Sestertius   VW   AD 103–17
    Obv:]AVG GER[
    From silt spread (unit 269), south-east of Anglo-Saxon building S1. 3rd century AD, with Anglo-Saxon pottery.

15 ST 82 AZZ, SF 274
Æ Dupondius   MW   AD 103–11
Obv:]AVG GER DAC P M [TR P COS V P P
Rev: [S P Q R OPTIMO PRINCIPI] S C

Context as no. 7.

16 ST 82 ABQ, SF 293
Æ Dupondius   VW   AD 99–100
Obv:]TRAIAN[
Rev: COS III[

From topsoil/cleaning (unit 481), above pit 997.

17 ST 83 CNA, SF 543
Æ As   VW   AD 98–117

From clay spread (unit 1288), above pit/ditch 69. Late 3rd–4th
century AD.

18 ST 84 DCC, SF 703
Æ Denarius   MW   AD 103–11
Obv: IMP TRAIANO AVG GER DAC [P M TR P]
Rev: (Arabia) COS V P P SPQR OPTIMO PRINCIPI
                                               RIC 142

From lower layer (unit 1551), of pit 1542. Mid 3rd century AD.

19 ST 84 DKF, SF 801
Æ Dupondius   MW   AD 103–117

From well 704/1663, unit 1722. Late 3rd/early 4th century AD.

20 ST 84 DXZ, SF 1076
Æ Dupondius   VW   AD 103–117

From pit 2021/2110, unit 2028. 3rd century AD.

21 ST 84 ECP, SF 1114
Æ As   MW   AD 98–99
Obv: IMP CAES NERVA TRAIAN AVG GERM P M
Rev: TR POT COS II S C   RIC 392ff.

From the surface fill of pit 2139.

Hadrian – 7 coins

22 ST 81 FF, SF 38
Æ Dupondius   MW   AD 134–8
Obv: HADRIANVS AVG COS III P P
Rev: AEQVITAS AVG S C   RIC 795

From topsoil/cleaning (unit 121), block 1a.

23 ST 81 HX, SF 83
Æ As   VW   AD 117–38
Rev: [   ] S C (In exergue)

From building R1, central block, north-east quadrant, robbing
debris (unit 182). Phase IV.

24 ST 81 JV, SF 93
Æ Sestertius   VW   AD 117–38
Obv: HADRIANVS[

Context as no. 13.

25 ST 82 AAA, SF 241
Æ Dupondius   MW   AD 117–38
Rev: [   ] S C

Context as no. 5.

26 ST 82 ACV, SF 305
Æ Sestertius   VW   AD 125–38
Obv: HADRIANVS AVGVSTVS
Rev: [   ] S C

From sinkage fill (unit 509) in ditch 74, cut 1. Late 3rd/4th century AD.

27 ST 84 DAC, SF 623
Æ Sestertius   VW   AD 117–38

From the upper fill (unit 1503) of pit 1503. ?3rd century AD.

28 ST 84 DVL, SF 938
Æ Dupondius   VW   AD 117–38

From pit 1967, unit 1967. Late 3rd–early 4th century AD.

Antoninus Pius – 9 coins

29 ST 80 AZ, SF 22
Æ Dupondius   MW   AD 138–61

From occupation debris (unit 23) west of the small hypocausted
room of building R1. 2nd–7th century AD.

30 ST 81 NL, SF 183
Æ Dupondius   MW   AD 153/4
Obv: ANTONINVS AVG PIVS[ ] TR P [XVII
Rev:] S C

From pit 170, unit 287. 3rd/4th century AD.

31 ST 81 KS, SF 197
Æ Dupondius   MW   AD 154–5
Rev:]COS IIII (Britannia bowed)

From occupation layer (unit 224), south of Anglo-Saxon building S1. 3rd or 4th century AD.

32 ST 81 LZ, SF 221
Æ Dupondius   MW   AD 138–61
Obv: ANTONINVS AVG[
Rev:] S C

From upper layer (unit 253) of gully 64, cut 1. Late 3rd–4th
century AD.

33 ST 81 KX, SF 231
Æ Sestertius   VW   AD 138–61
Obv:] AEL CAES HADR ANTON [
Rev:] S C

From ditch 54, cut 6, unit 228. Mid/late 3rd century AD.

34 ST 81 NC, SF 240
Æ Dupondius   LW   AD 140–4
Obv: ANTONINVS AVG PIVS P P TR P COS III
Rev: ANNONA AVG S C   RIC 656

From lower layer, south-west quadrant (unit 279), of the low rubbly mound sealing Anglo-Saxon building S1. Phase V.

35 ST 82 ADO, SF 335
Æ Dupondius   MW   AD 152–3
Obv: ANTONINVS AVG PIVS P P [TR P   (or 155–6)
Rev: LIBERTAS [COS IIII] S C   *RIC* 908 (or 950)

From oyster midden deposit (unit 527) south-east of building R4. 3rd century AD.

36 ST 83 CAA, SF 459
Æ Sestertius   LW   AD 143–4
Obv: ANTONINVS AVG PIVS P P TR P [COS III
Rev: IMPERATOR II S C   *RIC* 717

From topsoil/cleaning (unit 1000) above street 1 E/W at north-east corner of block 1.

37 ST 83 unstratified, SF 450
Æ Sestertius   MW   AD 145–61
Obv: ANTONINVS AVG PIVS P P [
Rev: (Salus?)

From machine spoil, east end of block 11.

Marcus Aurelius as Caesar – 2 coins

38 ST 80 AZ, SF 6
Æ Dupondius   MW   AD 145–61
Obv: AVRELIVS CAES [
Rev: [   ] S C

Context as no. 29

39 ST 83 CKL, SF 530
Æ Sestertius   MW   AD 151–61
Obv: AVRELIVS CAESAR AVG PII FIL [
Rev: [   ] S C (Minerva)

From ditch 14, cut 4, unit 1226. Post-medieval with residual Roman.

Faustina I – 3 coins

40 ST 81 NF, SF 172
Æ Dupondius   MW   AD 141+

From cobble surface (unit 282), north end of hard-standing, north-west quadrant block 1. Late 2nd century AD.

41 ST 83 CAN, SF 463
Æ Sestertius   LW   AD 141+
Obv: DIVA FAVSTINA
Rev: [AETERNITAS] S C

From ditch 13, cut 4, unit 1012 (residual). Phase VI.

42 ST 84 DNY, SF 823
Æ Dupondius   MW   AD 141+
Obv:] AVGVSTA
Rev: [   ] S C

From gully 24, south branch, cut 2, unit 1811. Early 3rd century AD.

Faustina II – 1 coin

43 ST 81 NK, SF 179
Æ Dupondius   MW   AD 145–61
Obv: FAVSTINA AVG PII AVG FIL
Rev: [   ] S C

From degraded mortar floor foundation (unit 286) of building R2. 3rd century AD.

Marcus Aurelius as Augustus – 2 coins

44 ST 84 DEK, SF 776
Æ As   MW   AD 161–80
Obv:]TR P X [

From unit 1606 in latrine pit 1536. Early 3rd century AD.

45 ST 84 DPI, SF 846
Æ Dupondius   MW   AD 161–80
Obv:]AVRELIVS [
Rev: [   ] S C (Mars)

From unit 1845 in pit 1994/gully 30. 3rd century AD.

Faustina II – 2 coins

46 ST 83 CCY, SF 475
Æ Sestertius   LW   AD 161–76
Obv: FAVSTINA AVGVSTA
Rev: IVNO S C   *RIC* (Marcus) 1645

From topsoil/cleaning within area of building R4.

47 ST 84 DAK, SF 625
Æ As   MW   AD 161–76
Obv: FAVSTINA AVGVSTA
Rev: [SALVTI AVGVSTAE S C]   *RIC* (Marcus) 1672

From area of recent agricultural disturbance (unit 1510) near pit 761.

Septimius Severus – 3 coins

48 ST 84 DIR, SF 782
Æ Denarius   MW   AD 193–8
Obv:]PERT[
Rev:]COS II

From gully 29, cut 10, unit 1709. 3rd century AD.

49 ST 84 DOK, SF 840
Æ Denarius (Geta)   LW   AD 198–212
Obv:]GETA CAES
Rev: PONT[

From gully 19, cut 5, unit 1822. Mid 3rd century AD.

50 ST 84 DTW, SF 1028
Æ Denarius (fragment)   LW   AD 193–218
From gully 18, cut 16, unit 1953. 3rd century AD.

Alexander Severus – 1 coin

51 ST 84 DIR, SF 780
Æ Denarius   LW   AD 226
Obv: IMP C M AVR SEV [ALEXAND AVG
Rev: P M TR P [V] COS II P P (Mars)   *RIC* 53
Context as no. 48.

Radiates – 3 coins

52 ST 82 AAG, SF 250
Æ Copy, probably of Tetricus I   MW   AD 271–3
Rev: Pontifical Instruments
From topsoil/cleaning (unit 448), block 5a.

53 ST 84 DAA, SF 626
Æ Copy, probably of Tetricus I   VW   AD 271–3
From topsoil/cleaning (unit 1501), block 6, just south-east of pit 1765.

54 ST 81 FY, SF 130
Æ Copy   VW   *c.* AD 270
From lower layer, north-west quadrant (unit 137) of the low rubbly mound sealing Anglo-Saxon building S1. Phase V.

Constantinian – 3 coins

55 ST 81 HJ, SF 66
Æ   LW   AD 323–4
Obv: CONSTANTINVS AVG
Rev: SARMATIA DEVICTA S̄T̄R̄   *RIC* (Trier) 429
From pit 170, uppermost layer (unit 170), 3rd/4th century AD.

56 ST 81 JK, SF 102
Æ   AD 330–5
Rev: [GLORIA EXERCITVS] 2 standards
From pit 132, unit 194. Late 2nd/early 3rd century AD. (Presumably residual.)

57 ST 80 AC, SF 3
Æ Copy   MW   AD 350 +
Rev: [FEL TEMP REPARATIO] Fallen Horseman
From pit 3, upper fill (unit 3). Phase V.

Valentinianic – 2 coins

58 ST 81 unstratified, SF 225
Æ   MW   AD 364–75
Obv: D N VALENS P F AVG
Rev: SECVRITAS REIPVBLICAE OF|I   *LRBC* II. 516
                                    CON
No context.

59 ST 83 unstratified, SF 452
Æ   MW   AD 364–75
Rev: [SECVRITAS REIPVBLICAE]
Topsoil find from north area of block 1.

Illegible – 2 coins

60 ST 83 CHA, SF 485
Æ As (probably Flavian)   VW   AD 69–96
From upper layer (unit 1168) above road ditches of street 1 E/W, north-east of Anglo-Saxon building S1. Phases V and VI.

61 ST 82 BLA, SF 386
Æ Fragments
From post-hole 947, south-east corner of building R6. Phase III.

Table 12 Stonea Grange: chronological distribution of coins from the excavations

			%				%
I	(–AD 41)	1	1.67	XII	(235–259)	–	–
II	(41–54)	1	1.67	XIII	(259–275)	3	5.00
III	(54–68)	–	–	XIV	(275–294)	–	–
IV	(69–96)	9	15.00	XV	(294–324)	1	1.67
V	(96–117)	11	18.33	XVI	(324–330)	–	–
VI	(117–138)	7	11.66	XVII	(330–346)	1	1.67
VII	(138–161)	15	25.00	XVIII	(346–364)	1	1.67
VIII	(161–180)	4	6.66	XIX	(364–378)	2	3.33
IX	(180–192)	–	–	XX	(378–388)	–	–
X	(192–222)	3	5.00	XXI	(388–)	–	–
XI	(222–235)	1	1.67				

B THE COINS FROM THE AREA AROUND THE EXCAVATIONS

The Roman coins recovered during the excavations have been described in Section A: discussion of them is now undertaken in conjunction with the approximately 900 Roman coins which were recovered from the area in recent years and acquired by the British Museum at various times. The coins contained groups that clearly comprised hoards and parts of hoards: they were declared in three groups: I) a group of 38 silver coins, ranging from Nero to Gordian III (238–44): reg. no. CM 1982–4–4; II) a group of 47 silver coins, ranging from Vespasian to Severus Alexander (222–35): reg. no. CM 1984–2–23; III) a group of 22 silver coins, with the same date range as group II: reg. no. CM 1985–10–38. Such coins are *not* included in this section.

A complete list of so many coins cannot be provided in the present context; they are thus shown distinguished by issuing authorities and denominations. In Tables 13a–c the additional figures in parentheses represent those coins recovered from the recent excavations.

The Roman coin lists

Table 13a Stonea: to AD 259

	Antoninianus	Denarius	Sestertius	Dupondius	As	Total
Republican		(1)				(1)
Caligula					1	1
Claudius				1	2(1)	3(1)
Nero					3	3
Vespasian		2(2)	1(3)	1(1)	5(1)	9(7)
Domitian				1(1)	1	2(1)
Nerva		(1)			1	1(1)
Trajan		2(1)	5(1)	7(5)	(3)	14(10)
Hadrian			14(3)	17(3)	10(1)	41(7)
Antoninus Pius		1	24(5)	23(10)	9	57(15)
M. Aurelius			29(1)	12(1)	4(2)	45(4)
Commodus			7	5		12
Septimius Severus		6(3)	1	1	2	10(3)
Caracalla		2				2
Macrinus				1		1
Elagabalus	1					1
Severus Alexander		3(1)	1			4(1)
Maximus			1			1
Gordian III	2			3		5
Philip	2			1		3
Valerian	2		1			3
Totals	7	16(9)	84(13)	73(21)	38(8)	218(51)

Table 13b Stonea: radiates (AD 259–94)

Gallienus	21
Postumus	12
Claudius II	42
Victorinus	15
Tetricus I	72(2)
Tetricus II	30
Unattributable	102(1)
Aurelian	2
Tacitus	1
Probus	2
Maximian	1
Carausius	11
Allectus	9
Total	320(3)

There were thus 294(3) radiates of the period to the collapse of the Gallic Empire (AD 273), 6 of the improved type, and 20 'British Empire' issues.

Table 13c Stonea: Post-Reform coins

	ÆR	Æ	Total
Diocletian		2	2
Maximian		3	3
Constantius I		1	1
Maxentius		1	1
Licinius		4	4
Constantine I		163(2)	163(2)
Constans		21	21
Constantius II	1	33(1)	34(1)
Magnentius		20	20
Decentius		1	1
Valentinian I } Valens }		60(2)	60(2)
Gratian	1	14	15
Magnus Maximus		2	2
Valentinian II		1	1
Theodosius		8	8
Arcadius		2	2
Totals	2	336(5)	338(5)

Table 14 Stonea: chronological distribution of Roman coin finds

		Casual finds	Excavation	Total	%
I	(–AD 41)	1	1	2	0.21
II	(41–54)	3	1	4	0.43
III	(54–68)	3		3	0.32
IV	(69–96)	11	9	20	2.13
V	(96–117)	15	11	26	2.78
VI	(117–38)	41	7	48	5.13
VII	(138–61)	57	15	72	7.69
VIII	(161–80)	45	4	49	5.24
IX	(180–92)	12		12	1.28
X	(192–222)	14	3	17	1.82
XI	(222–35)	4	1	5	0.53
XII	(235–59)	12		12	1.28
XIII	(259–75)	294	3	297	31.73
XIV	(275–94)	26		26	2.78
XV	(294–324)	53	1	54	5.77
XVI	(324–30)	6		6	0.64
XVII	(330–46)	133	1	134	14.32
XVIII	(346–64)	58	1	59	6.30
XIX	(364–78)	75	2	77	8.23
XX	(378–88)	7		7	0.75
XXI	(388–)	6		6	0.64
Totals		876	60	936	

Table 15 Stonea: Roman coins – annual loss rate per 1000 coins

I	Caligula	0.21
II	Claudius	0.31
III	Nero	0.21
IV	Vespasian	1.71
	Titus	–
	Domitian	0.20
V	Nerva	0.71
	Trajan	1.28
VI	Hadrian	2.56
VII	Antoninus Pius	3.21
VIII	M. Aurelius	2.62
IX	Commodus	0.99
X	Severans	0.59
XI	Alexander Severus	0.38
XII		0.51
XIII		18.67
XIV		1.39
XV		1.86
XVI		0.92
XVII		8.42
XVIII		3.32
XIX		5.48
XX		0.68
XXI		0.43

Table 16 Stonea: Roman coins – value in *asses* of coin-loss in periods I–XII

	As value	%
I	17	1.35
II	5	0.40
III	3	0.24
IV	95	7.55
V	116	9.21
VI	119	9.45
VII	207	16.44
VIII	155	12.31
IX	48	3.81
X	218	17.32
XI	68	5.40
XII	208	16.52

Discussion

The sample of over 900 coins represents as reasonably as possible those that have resulted from casual loss, with likely hoard coins excluded.

Initial occupation

Pre-Flavian coins are present in the sample and include issues such as that of Caligula and Claudian copies, which one would not normally expect to find on a site where occupation commenced as late as the last years of the first century AD or the early years of the second. This therefore would provide some numismatic support for Roman activity on the site before or around the middle of the first century (Shotter 1979).

The level and condition of Flavian issues would virtually rule out the possibility of any significant activity in the second half of the first century: indeed, the relatively low showing of Trajanic coins – at about the same level as the Flavian – suggests that we should look at Flavian and Trajanic issues as chronologically residual. The low rate of loss prior to Trajan's death, however, stands in marked contrast to the pattern of loss from the Hadrianic period onwards, with 20% of the total sample coming from periods VI–IX (AD 117–92); a peak is reached with the coins of Antoninus, which is even more sharply reflected in the coins from the excavation.

The clear implication of the chronological distribution of the coins is that we should look to the mid Hadrianic period as the beginning of a major phase of activity on the site; major occupation earlier in the Hadrianic period would probably have produced a somewhat larger figure of loss for Trajanic issues.

The denominational distribution of coins within these second century periods show a gradual shift towards higher denomination *Aes* coins, which is probably an indication of inflationary tendencies. There is not, however, any marked strength in the loss of *denarii*, which might have been expected had there been any real input into building activity on the part of legionary soldiers.

The coin evidence tends to support the idea that the site was established sometime in the 120s, and that the main constructional effort was put in by local rather than imported tradesmen and labourers. It should perhaps be noted, however, that if a substantial number of the *denarii* which have been classified as hoard coins were not to be so, then we might have to rethink the implications of a denominational distribution which put more weight on to *denarii*.

Later second/third centuries

It is normal to expect coin loss to decline numerically between the mid-second and mid-third centuries due to the effects of inflation when lower denomination *Aes* played a smaller part in the money economy. The greater use of higher denominations may well, as has been suggested (Table 16: Casey 1974), have led to greater effort being put into the recovery of lost coins. The numerical decline is more marked amongst the coins from the excavation and shows a falling away in the last few decades of the second century that is a commonly observed feature.

In other words, although coins of the later second and early third centuries are thinly represented, this cannot *by itself* be taken to indicate any particular trend in occupation. The fact, however, that the excavation produced very few such coins might suggest some physical movement of the more important areas to other parts of the site. There are, unfortunately, only the most general indications of the whereabouts of the find spots of those coins which have been casually recovered.

The mid third century (period XIII) accounts for a large proportion of the sample – slightly in excess of 30%, which is paralleled at a great many sites. It is noticeable that a marked proportion of period XIII coins are Gallic Empire issues and generally poor copies of them (Shotter 1978). In fact, over one third of all coins of this type could not be attributed to any particular prototype; this perhaps points to a local centre of manufacture. Again, however, it is striking that the excavation produced only a small proportion of such coins (5% of the excavated sample), suggesting that in the mid-third century the main centre of activity at the site was elsewhere than in the excavated area. It is clearly not, however, a reflection of activity over the site as a whole.

Post-Gallic radiates are generally relatively rare as Romano-British site-finds (Shiel 1977); these reformed radiates appear to have made little headway against the great mass of period XIII radiates and copies which must have continued to provide the bulk of coinage in circulation in the later third century – and even beyond (Shotter 1981).

We should note, however, that an exception to this is to be seen in British Empire issues of Carausius and Allectus: rather unusually, coins of Allectus bulk almost as strongly as those of Carausius.

The fourth century

As with coins of the third century, there is a striking difference in numbers of fourth century coins when we contrast those from the excavation and those recovered casually – 8% of the sample compared with 40%. This suggests a similar pattern as was observed in third century occupation, namely that whilst activity in general remained intense on the site, the excavated area itself was not the scene of major fourth century occupation (but see final paragraph below).

The volume of coin loss through the Constantinian and Valentinianic periods appears uniform, with no obvious weakness across the first three-quarters of the century. A considerable number of these coins, particularly within periods XVII and XVIII, are local copies of varying standard, and often small in size. A third of the coins of period XVIII are of the rebel Magnentius, which may indicate strength of support for the anti-Constantinian rebellion in the area.

Although the excavation did not yield coins later than the House of Valentinian, casual finds show significant numbers of issues of Valentinian II, Magnus Maximus, Theodosius and Arcadius, as are commonly noted on Fenland sites (Shotter 1981). It can be assumed from this, therefore, that the area remained under active occupation throughout the fourth century: in view of the wear exhibited by a number of the issues of periods XX and XXI, it would not be unreasonable to regard them as losses of the early years of the fifth century, or even later.

CONCLUSIONS

In summary, the general similarity in the chronological distribution of coin loss at Stonea and that recorded over a wider area of this part of the Fens is striking (Shotter 1981, 126), apart from coins of the Hadrianic period in which Stonea is markedly stronger. The presence of pre-Flavian *Aes* coinage on this, as on other Fen 'islands', is indicative of the activity that must have accompanied early Roman penetration of the area around the time of Prasutagus' death.

The level of Flavian and Trajanic losses is certainly not consistent with major Roman activity at these times, and the coins represent a small enough proportion of the sample to be considered residual. The Hadrianic period clearly represents a change in the nature of the site, with large losses of Hadrianic coins; as noted earlier the coin evidence would be consistent with this Hadrianic period of activity being concentrated into the second half of the reign. Thereafter, coin losses over the remainder of the second century are notable for their strength.

The most notable feature of third and fourth century coin loss is the discrepancy between the excavation assemblage and the casual coin finds. The latter clearly suggest a continuing strength of activity in the area, while the former appears to leave it as questionable whether the significance of the *excavated* part of the site was maintained. However, as discussed elsewhere (Jackson, this page), the topsoil coin sample from the excavated site, which would have incorporated many of the late issues, is an 'invisible' component of the collection of casual coin finds; and other archaeological evidence from the excavations points to a continuing occupation in the third and fourth centuries. This provides yet another example of the dangers of attempting to generalise about a large area from a small sample; we have to accept on the basis of the coin evidence that the fate of the excavated portion of the site does not provide a true reflection of Romano-British activity in this particular area of the Fenlands.

SOME OBSERVATIONS ON THE CONSEQUENCES OF METAL DETECTOR ACTIVITY AND ON THE POSSIBLE SIGNIFICANCE OF THE COIN DISTRIBUTION

Ralph Jackson

Over some 20 years prior to the excavations, a local resident, with the permission of the landowner, searched the fields of Stonea Grange Farm, primarily the large field to the south of the farmyard, with a metal detector. As the whole of the farm was under intensive arable cultivation, he had a considerable area of regularly-turned ploughsoil at his disposal, and the collection he amassed, the 'background noise' to the excavated settlement site, was both large and significant. Although it included a very few non-metallic items (Fig. 80, no. 11, p. 244; Fig. 177, no. 4, p. 487; Fig. 195, no. 31, p. 529), the great majority of objects were of copper alloy, with smaller numbers of lead and silver. It is greatly to be regretted that the finder did not record with any precision the findspot of individual objects. The collection, referred to throughout this report as the Stonea Grange Surface Collection, was ultimately acquired by the British Museum to complement the excavated assemblage. It comprises well in excess of 1000 objects, almost 900 of which are Roman coins.

The area of the 1980–4 excavations was not only within the metal-detector search zone but was fairly central to it. Furthermore, the finder recalled that many of his finds had come from that region. Thus, the Stonea Grange Surface Collection certainly incorporates the ploughsoil finds from the excavation area, though neither their identity nor their quantity can now be established. It is important to bear in mind this indefinable component of the Surface Collection, but more important still to register it as a negative

component of the excavation metalwork assemblage, where it has, perhaps, its most serious repercussions in the size and composition of the coin sample.

After establishing, by hand-digging the plough-disturbed topsoil in 1980, that there were virtually no finds and no useful archaeological information to be retrieved from the upper part of the ploughsoil, it was machined off to within a few centimetres of its base in the four subsequent excavation seasons. The ploughsoil base hand-removal and feature-top cleaning which followed the machining revealed a modest number of coins and other metal finds in what was the truncated upper stratigraphy of the site. Indeed, the majority of the excavated coin finds was from these contexts, from superficial occupation layers and from the uppermost fill of cut features. The upper plough-disturbed topsoil is, therefore, likely to have yielded a fairly considerable number of coins. As these would have belonged, in the main, to the later Roman phase of occupation it can be seen that their 'transfer' from the excavation coin assemblage to the Surface Collection is likely to have depleted very significantly the fourth century component of the former.

Another negative influence on the excavated coin sample, less discriminative, and perhaps acting as a partial counterbalance to the absence of the topsoil coins, was the loss of finds through criminal activity. For, in the 1982 season, and, despite precautions, again in 1983 and 1984, illicit metal-detectorists came to the site, under cover of darkness at night and in the early hours of the morning, and looted metal finds from the part-excavated levels and features. On the main site alone the number of observed illicitly dug holes from the three raids totalled over 60, of which 20 were in block 1 and 23 in block 9. Three of the latter had certainly contained copper-alloy coins, for corrosion products adhering to clods in the disturbed soil preserved their impression – indeed, in two cases so clear was the impression that it was possible to determine that the coin had been a sestertius. It is probable that a relatively great proportion of the remaining holes had contained coins and that perhaps as many as 30 coins were erased from the excavated assemblage in this way.

Despite the reduction in sample size and the probable chronological bias caused by these two agencies, in addition to the usual range of factors affecting distribution and loss/preservation processes, spatial analysis was attempted. Making allowance for circulation Shotter's chronological groups (p. 290) were clustered in order to approximate them to the site's Roman phases, and the distribution of the coins was plotted accordingly (Fig. 92). The resultant patterning shows possible trends in coin loss.

The sparseness of coins in Phase II, as with other evidence, indicates only a low level of activity in the first century (Phase II); but the position of the Claudian *as* copy (no. 2) in the north-east corner of block 1 is probably meaningful as it is adjacent to pit/ditch 69, with its first century

Fig. 92 Stonea Grange: the catalogued Roman coins from the excavations. Distribution by groups related approximately to site phases.

AD pottery (Fig. 88, nos 6–7) and close to the findspot of a pair of Colchester brooches (Mackreth cat. nos 1–2). In contrast is the overwhelming concentration of coins – over 80% – in the main Roman phase (Phase III). Equally striking, and, although tenuous, apparently significant, is the dramatic reduction in the loss of new coinage of the later second and early third century (Phase III later). This would appear to suggest a reduction, whether gradual or abrupt, in the volume of coin-using activity on the site in the latter part of Phase III, which is consistent with other evidence for a decline in the size and importance of the settlement at this time. Furthermore, while the coins in Phase III earlier are fairly evenly distributed between the official complex – building R1 and block 1 – and the residential areas – blocks 2–9 – there is an almost total absence of coins from the R1 complex and its environs in the later part of Phase III and in Phase III/IV. 85% of the coins of this period come from blocks 6–9. Though very few coins are involved it suggests that a reduced level of activity continued in the residential quarters after the demise of building R1 saw an end to all coin-using activity in block 1.

In Phase IV blocks 7–9 are devoid of coins and the modest number of finds is concentrated on the western side of the site. By this time the site of building R1 had been levelled and partially re-occupied by building R2, to which the coin activity may relate. In view of the relative eminence of this part of the site, with consequent severe plough damage, and the absence of the topsoil finds, it is certain that the low level of coin loss indicated by the excavation finds is more apparent than real.

BROOCHES

D. F. Mackreth   (Figs 93–101)

This report is organised in four sections:
1 Introduction: comment on the brooches in sections 2–4.
2 The brooches from the excavations.
3 The brooches from the area around the excavations.
4 The brooches from the area of Stonea Camp.

All brooches are of copper alloy, unless otherwise stated. They are numbered in a single series through the three chief sections of the report. This is to make cross-referencing easier as the main comments are made under the first occurrence of a type or variety.

1 INTRODUCTION

The chief interest in the collection lies in the comparisons between the three groups into which it is divided. These groups are: the brooches from the excavations; the surface collection around the excavations; and the surface finds in Stonea Camp. Two serious imbalances prevent a straight comparison. First, the difference in numbers of brooches in each group: 21 from the excavations, 74 from the area around and 13 from the Camp. This should mean that the first and last groups are not only more prone to distortion by absences, but their small numbers are not really statistically valid: the writer estimates that 50 is the lowest reasonable limit and collections of 100 or more offer a good basis for comparison. Only the number of surface finds from around the excavations, therefore, fulfils this criterion.

The second imbalance is the demonstrable difference between what the excavation produced and what was available to be picked up on the surface. The former has more of some classes of brooch than either one or both of the other groups. The relatively heavy representation of these particular classes can only partly be explained by arguing that they are equally present outside the excavation, but are in deep features untouched by ploughing. The chances that the bulk of these classes would be in such deep features are surely limited. On the grounds of probability alone, an equal proportion in each group should have remained in top-soil deposits to be churned up into the modern ploughsoil from which some 87 of the brooches come.

The chief types of brooch for immediate discussion are the Colchester (1–3, 23–5 and 96), the Rearhook (4–7 and 26), the Harlow (27–33), continental Late La Tène types (53–5 and 99–100), and the Aucissa–Hod Hill series (56–67 and 101–6). The earliest brooch, a La Tène I (22), is adventitious as far as the rest of the collection is concerned. Apart from that, the brooch evidence is against any major occupation before the first century AD, and nothing to suggest any occupation in the first two decades. At least three of the Colchesters (1–3) should have been on the site before AD 43/5 and may have been lost before then. The remaining four could also be as early, but probably equally had a chance to survive to, c. 50/5. None of the Late La Tène brooches belonging generally to the Nauheim and *Drahtfibel* tradition (13–16 and 47–8) shows any sign of being pre-Conquest and are common enough afterwards for them to be discounted. The only other group which *may* actually represent pre-Conquest occupation is the continental Late La Tène group, the Rosette–Langton Down family (53–5 and 99–100) and none belongs to the main Augustan–Tiberian series and all could have arrived after the Conquest.

The Colchester is best represented, as a percentage, in the excavation assemblage, and, although actual numbers may be meaningless, this is highlighted by the incidence of the Rearhook: one from the area around the excavation, none from Stonea Camp, but four from the excavation. As the Rearhook was the direct successor of the Colchester in the lands of the Iceni, perhaps it should be added to the Colchester and, hence, deduce that the centre of early occupation was close to the excavation. If the evidence from the excavation really represents the major early post-Conquest period, perhaps it may be used to place the majority of the group to

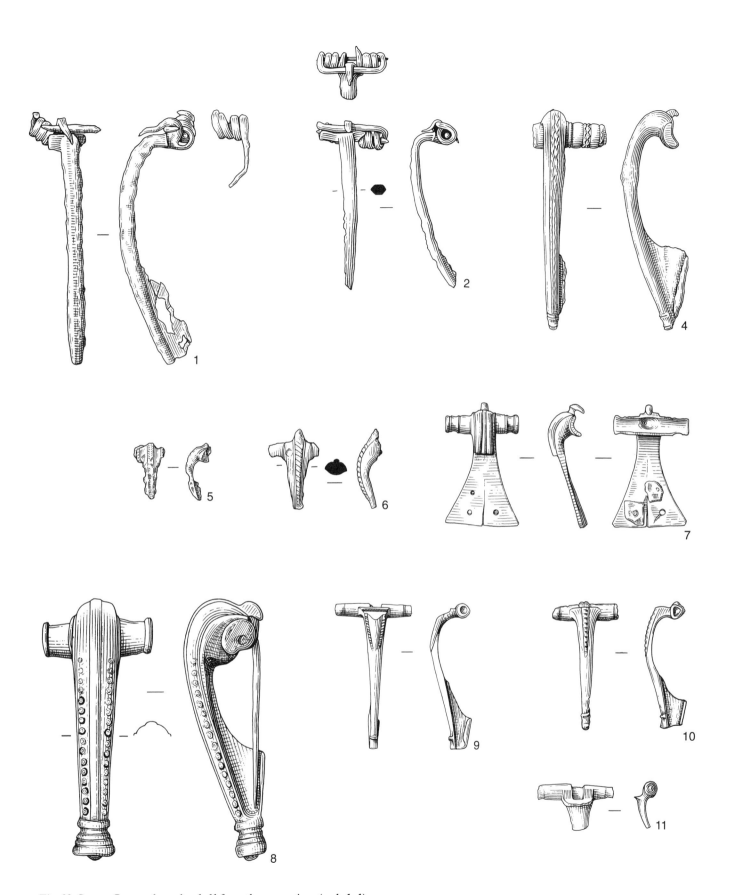

Fig. 93 Stonea Grange: brooches 1–11 from the excavations (scale 1 : 1).

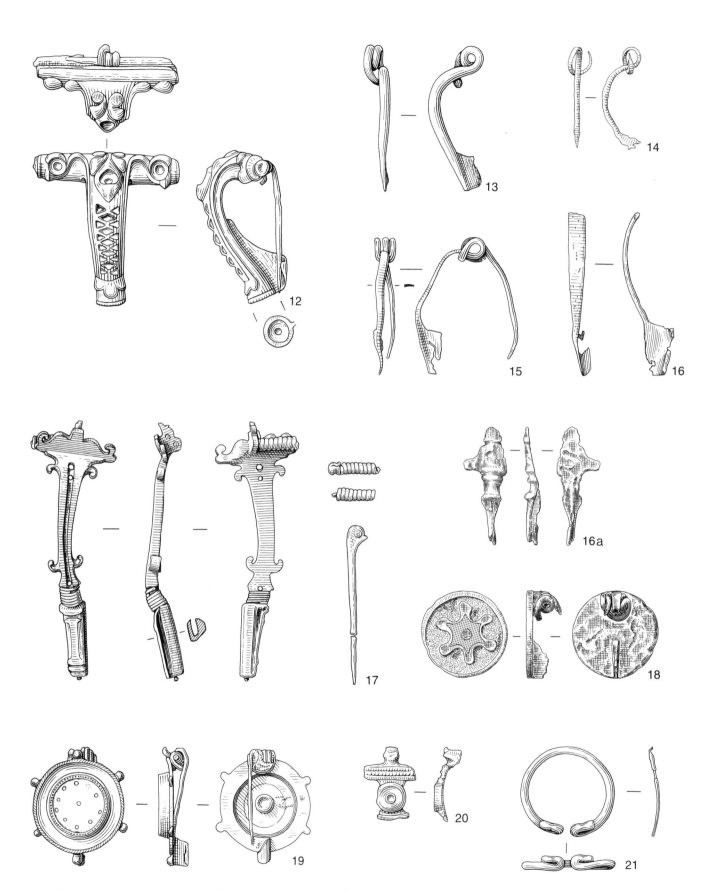

Fig. 94 Stonea Grange: brooches 12–21 from the excavations (scale 1:1).

which 13–16 and 47–8 belong in the same period, that is, before *c.* 60/5. However, this would leave out of account the Rosette and Langton Down brooches (99–100) from Stonea Camp which could be placed against the three (53–5) from the area around the excavations. In percentage terms, this could be said to go some way to counterbalance the general lack of 'early' brooches from Stonea Camp. But much also depends on supply.

Stonea seems to have been within the Icenian area of influence and from which it would seem that Augustan–Tiberian Rosette and Langton Down brooches were largely excluded. The successor of the Colchester in the lands to the south, the Harlow (27–33) may well also have been excluded. There are eight of these as opposed to the five examples of the 'native' brooch, the Rearhook (4–7 and 26). As some 'market penetration' of each type into the homeland of the other can be shown, a strict division on temporal grounds is not possible. However, while the Rearhook hardly survives the period AD 60–5, suggesting that its demise was related to the suppression of the Boudiccan revolt, the Harlow continued to at least *c.* 70–80. What the figures for each *may* show is that the bulk of the Harlows arrived after the defeat of Boudicca. The absence of any Harlow from the excavation may only be due to the small numbers of brooches recovered from that and, therefore, the finds from the surface around may be a better representation of types in the immediate area. A simple view of the assemblage from Stonea Camp would conclude that the absence of Harlows arises from abandonment of the Camp site as a result of the brutal Roman retaliation to the revolt, but there are so few brooches from the Camp that this would be a dangerous conclusion.

The truly unknown quantity is what the nature and intensity of the occupation of the Camp was. If brooches provide a guide, early occupation was mainly outside the Camp. However, the Aucissa–Hod Hill component in the collection from the Camp is hard to explain on these grounds. First, the Camp produced the only possible Aucissa (101). Second, including the Aucissa, there are 6 of the series from the Camp against the 12 from the area around the excavation, and only one from the excavation itself. Here, percentages probably mean something: 46% of the brooches from the Camp belong to the series as against 16% from the area around the excavation, and only 14% if the figures for the excavation and the surrounding area are combined. The actual percentage figure for the Camp can only partly be explained by noting that there so very few brooches later than the later first century AD (97, 107) that this throws the number of Hod Hills into relief. The date range given for the series is from the Conquest to *c.* 70/5 at the latest and they were passing out of use from *c.* 60. The prominence of the series in the Camp is further highlighted by the very small number of other early items there.

The high percentage of Aucissa–Hod Hills in the Camp could represent an unusual element in occupation there.

If the argument that the Harlow and the Rearhook were almost mutually exclusive and the arrival of most of the Harlows was after the collapse of the Boudiccan revolt, and that there had been a barrier against Rosettes, Langton Downs and related types, it could also be argued that the Hod Hill was also excluded until the times were propitious for its introduction: the arrival of the vengeful Roman army. This deduced barrier should have been a cultural one arising from the Iceni having been a client kingdom until the death of Prasutagus. It is worth more than a passing thought that the statistically improbable preponderance of Hod Hills in the Camp may mark where a detachment of the army had its quarters and once this left, the Camp was abandoned.

The other brooch types add little to knowledge of the site. The British brooches serve to show that the area within which the excavation lay continued in occupation into the third century while continental types carry the time forward to the end of the fourth century (93).

2 THE BROOCHES FROM THE EXCAVATIONS (Figs 93–4)

Colchesters

1 ST 84 DXK, SF 1127, length 66 mm   All the original surface is lost and the body is badly pitted. The chord of the eight-coil spring is held by a moderately long hook which has a concavity in its top and a thinner section for the last 2 mm. The damaged wings have no sign of any decoration. The bow has a hexagonal section and a very slight taper to the squared-off foot. Faint traces remain of a recess down the centre, possibly with a wavy ridge in it. The damaged catch-plate has the remains of fretting.

From the lower layer (unit 2014) in pit 2014, one of the earliest pits in block 9. Later 2nd century AD.

2 ST 83 CCY, SF 541a, length 45 mm   All the original surface is lost. The spring had eight coils. The hook is relatively short. The surviving wing may be plain. The hexagonal-sectioned bow has a more pointed foot than brooch 1. The catch-plate is missing.

From topsoil/cleaning, centre north bock 1 and block 11.

3 ST 83 CCY, SF 541b (*unillus.*), length 45 mm   All the original surface is lost. The spring is missing and what is left of the hook is short. The bow is eroded and what is left has a flat back with chamfers on the rear corners. Only the stub of the catch-plate survives.

Context as no. 2.

Unlike the others covered in this comment, 1 and 2 have faceted bows and 3 has facets down the back corners. Brooch 1 may also have decoration down the front. The remaining four, 23–5 and 96 are in such poor condition that their plain wings and generally round-sectioned bows may owe more to this than to their original appearance. So many Colchesters are in this state that it seems that the type was peculiarly susceptible to corrosion. It is a salutary lesson that the largest single group of aberrant decoration occurs in the King Harry Lane cemetery, St Albans, where the state of preservation was generally good (Stead and Rigby 1989, graves 53, 58, 69, 115, 152, 170, 177, 179, 189, 196, 202, 207, 259, 312, 337, 397, 420, 424, 433, 450, 464). Most Colchesters with faceted bows recorded by the present author run from Verulamium to the north as far as the Humber, although there is one from the Isle of Man (Gelling 1958, 94–5, Fig. 4, 1) and from North Wales (Prestatyn, excavations, K. Blockley, forthcoming). The dating from King Harry Lane is, for Phase 1, AD 1–40, graves 206, 242, 312; Phase 2, 30–55, graves 13, 128, 152, 339, 360, 399; Phase 3, 40–60, graves 112, 117, 204 (for comment on the dating of the phases in this cemetery, see Mackreth in Garrod and Atkin, forthcoming). From Braughing-Puckeridge there is one dated c. 10 BC–AD 20 (Mackreth 1981, 141, Fig. 68, 21), another was c. 25–40 (ibid., 136, Fig. 68, 15) and a third was c. 30–40 (ibid., 136, Fig. 68, 18). A fourth covered the general period c. 20 BC–AD 45 (Olivier 1988, 40, Fig. 18, 23). These lend some precision to the over-lapping phase dates of those from the King Harry Lane cemetery and practically all should be dated to before AD 45. The remaining four Stonea brooches display no early feature such as a nearly straight bow-profile or a finely fretted multiple-opening catch-plate and can only be given a general end-date of 50/5. The end of manufacture for Colchesters must be about 40 as it is pointed out under brooch 31 that the type to which those belonged should have come into being before the Conquest: the Colchester would hardly have continued in production.

Colchester Derivatives

The springs of the following four brooches were held in place by a rearward-facing hook behind the head of the bow.

4 ST 84 DQR North, SF 1052, length 58 mm The surviving wing has a bulbous moulding next to the bow, then two opposed wavy ridges formed by hand followed by a short plain section and, finally, two thin mouldings at the end. The bow has an arris down the back, a step down each side of the front. Down the middle is a recess containing a repeat of the wavy ridges. The foot is moulded with pairs of thin mouldings divided by a flute.

From basal layer (unit 1877) of pit 1695. Later 2nd/3rd century AD.

5 ST 80 CY, SF 19, length 15 mm A tiny brooch in very poor condition. What is left of the wings has a bead-row next to the bow, which has a flat back. The front seems to have concave edges with a sunken bead-row down the centre. The stub of the catch-plate shows that the full length of the bow survives.

From robbing debris (unit 68) in building R1 (central block, south-east quadrant). Phase IV.

6 ST 81 FW, SF 54 The lower bow is missing. The damaged wings appear to be plain. The bow has curved sides; and a central beaded ridge, bordered by thin flat surfaces, runs down from the stub of the rearward-facing hook.

From uppermost layer (unit 135) of well 135. Phase V.

7 ST 83 CAA, SF 464, length 33 mm Near the end of each wing is a pair of sunken ridges separated by a flute. The bow is straight-sided and short, has a step down each side and a buried ridge down the middle of the swelled front. Below a step is a plain fantail foot which has three holes almost certainly to fasten a separately-made catch-plate.

From topsoil/cleaning, block 11, east, and block 1, north-east.

The rearward-facing hook was not the only means by which the spring was secured: behind the left-hand wing of a brooch from Thetford (Mackreth 1991) was a well-preserved deposit of solder which bore the imprint of the spring (see also 26). This method of holding the spring defines the family to which these four brooches belong. The distribution of the type is of interest. It occurs in large numbers in Norfolk and Suffolk and is relatively frequently found in Essex and along the western margins of the Fens. Outliers occur, but usually in early and specialised deposits, often military. Little can be said about the distribution of individual decorative varieties although those with a fantail bow or foot like brooch 7 here tend to lie in south Norfolk and Suffolk. Some of the decorative tricks were copied by craftsmen along the western Fen edge and one version of the fantailed form was probably the origin of brooches such as 43 below.

The dating is: Bagendon, c. 43–50, two examples (Clifford 1961, 172, Fig. 31, 1, 4); Longthorpe, Claudian–Neronian (Dannell and Wild 1987, 87, Fig. 21, 10); Puckeridge, Station Road, 40–65 (Mackreth 1979, 38, Fig. 6, 10); Bagendon, 50–60 (Clifford 1961, 172, Fig. 31, 2); Colchester, 49–61, four examples (Hawkes and Hull 1947, 311–312, Pl. 91, 44, 46, Pl. 92, 51; Crummy 1983, 13, Fig. 8, 62), 50/55–60/1, two examples (ibid., 12, Fig. 6, 56, 57), 50–65 (ibid., 12–13, Fig. 7, 61), 61–c. 65 (Hawkes and Hull 1947, 311, Pl. 91, 45); Welwyn, Lockleys villa, before c. 60–70 (Ward-Perkins 1938, 352, Fig. 2, 1); 'The Lunt', Baginton, before 70–5 (Mackreth 1969, 108, Fig. 19, 3); Harlow, 80–100? (France and Gobel 1985, 79, Fig. 41–68).

There can be little doubt, on this evidence, that most examples had entered the ground by AD 65, and this is emphasised by the fact that none of the specimens known from Colchester appears to have come from a deposit of later date. The unusually precise dating, coupled with the distribution of the type, very strongly suggests that the Rear-hook type was specific to the Iceni, its cutoff date reflecting the retribution which fell upon the tribe on the suppression of Boudicca's uprising.

8 ST 81 NR, SF 187, length 69 mm The spring is held in the Polden Hill manner: an axis bar passes through the coils and through pierced plates at the ends of the wings, the chord being held by a rearward-facing hook behind the head of the

bow. Each wing has a moulding at its end. The junction with the bow is masked by a curved plate rising from the wings. The bow has a rounded top, a step down each side, a broad ridge down the middle and, on each side, a series of small bosses running to the foot, those running over the head having been worn away. The elaborate foot-knob runs all the way round and has, underneath, an annular flute from which projects a boss. The catch-plate is very upright and continues as a flange right to the top of the bow.

From occupation layer (unit 292), north-west block 1. 3rd century AD.

A member of a large family found mainly in the West Midlands, Wales and the southern Pennines, examples occur in the rest of Roman Britain. Its origins probably lie in the southern Severn valley. The characteristics of the family are, apart from the Polden Hill spring system, the short usually plain wings apart from the mouldings at the end, the way in which the top of the bow is humped over the wings, and the moulded 'plate' rising from the wings on each side of the head. The decorative repertoire is fairly extensive and those with the bossed ornament present here tend to be much larger, but often had cores extending down the body of the casting to cut down on the weight of metal used. The only major variation within the family is the substitution of a hinged-pin in a group centering on the southern Pennines.

The dating is: Derby, late first and early second century, three examples (Mackreth 1985a, 283–5, Figs 123–4, 4, 5, 10); Wroxeter, 80–120 (Bushe-Fox 1916, 23, Pl. 15, 5); Croft Ambrey, c. 75–160, *four* examples (Stanford 1974, 144, Fig. 67, 1, 2, 4, 5); Wroxeter, c. 85–130 (excavations, Dr G. Webster forthcoming); Verulamium, 115–30 (Frere 1972, 114, Fig. 20, 10); Derby, 120–50 (Mackreth 1985a, 283–5, Fig. 124. 8), 150–75 (*ibid.*, Fig. 123, 6); Watercrook, 120–90 (Potter 1979, 210, Fig. 84, 11); Wall, Staffs, Hadrianic–early Antonine (Gould 1967, 17, Fig. 7, 7); Caerleon, Hadrianic–Antonine (Brewer 1986, 170, Fig. 54, 5); Baldock, 150–80 (Stead and Rigby 1986, 113, Fig. 45, 83); Whitton, Glamorgan, before 160 (Jarrett and Wrathmell 1981, 169, Fig. 69, 12); Shakenoak Farm, Wilcote, Oxon, mid second to mid third century (Brodribb *et al* 1971, 118–19, Fig. 47, 70), before 180 (*ibid.* 1968, 95, Fig. 27, 7). Specimens dated later are obviously residual in their contexts. The earliest dated example *may* be the one from the Polden Hill hoard itself (BM, PRB 1846, 3–22, 125), although the brooch probably has more to say about the actual date of that than any amount of art-historical discussion, and one from 'The Lunt', Baginton, Warks, without a foot-knob, is earlier than c. 70–5 (Mackreth 1969, 107, Fig. 19, 1). The date-range, therefore, is securely from the last quarter of the first century to c. 150/75.

9 ST 81 PA, SF 184   The pin was formed by wrapping a piece of wire round an axis bar mounted in the wings. Each wing has a wide moulding at the end. The bow has a broad top with a step across it. Below this is a raised triangular boss with a beaded border along each side. The bow tapers to a simple foot-knob below a ridge. The catch-plate has a pin-groove.

From the ragstone cobble surface (unit 300) near the north-west corner of building R1.

10 ST 82 ABT, SF 336   A repeat of the last, but with a beaded ridge instead of the triangular boss.

From layer 484 in the north sump. Phase IV/V.

11 ST 84 DAC, SF 624   Similar to the previous two, the top of the bow has a cross-ridge with a slight peak in the middle.

From the upper fill (unit 1503) of pit 1503. Phase III/IV.

Brooches 9 and 10, and almost certainly 11 as well, belong to a small family employing a limited repertoire of motifs to great effect. Brooches 9 and 10 both have what may be regarded as the basic form, the wings, the bows stepped away from the wings, and the foot-knobs being characteristic. These elements, including the triangular boss and beaded ridge, are sometimes combined with a fantail foot with three dot-and-circle stamps (e.g. Wheeler and Wheeler 1936, 206, Fig. 43, 19; Kenyon 1948, 249, Fig. 80, 10). One from Brixworth (excavations, P. Woods, forthcoming) has a short round-ended wing on each side of the middle of the bow, each bearing a dot-and-circle. The distribution lies, in essence, between Leicester, including the adjacent parts of Warwickshire, and East Anglia, and from Lincolnshire down and into Hertfordshire.

The dating is: Bannaventa, late first–early second century (Dix and Taylor 1988, 334, Fig. 19, 3); Weekley, Northants, late first century – c. 175 (Jackson and Dix 1987, M76, Fig 323, 15); Verulamium, before 150, two examples (Wheeler and Wheeler, 1936, 206, Fig. 43, 17, 18); Derby, Antonine (Mackreth 1985a, 285, Fig. 125, 12); Leicester, up to c. 220 (Kenyon 1948, 249, Fig. 80, 10). Hardly an extensive body of information and the few which have been excluded cover the rest of the third and fourth centuries and were, therefore, residual finds. The indicated date-range is wide, from the late first century to the later second.

Headstud

12 ST 83 CCY, SF 540   The pin is made from wire, the axis bar being mounted in a tube fitted behind the curved wings. Each wing has a small moulding at its end. In relief on the front face are Celtic-style trumpets two of which embrace a raised annulus which may once have had enamel in it. The stud has two more trumpets above and rises to a peak at the back and front, the latter having a short vertical moulding. The bow has a flute along each side, a step along the border of the front which has a set of lozenge-shaped cells with infilling triangles containing traces of discoloured enamel. The foot has three petals around the top and a moulding at the base.

Context as nos 2–3.

There is no immediately obvious family to which this brooch can be assigned, but it is best paralleled in one which has the same style of pin-mounting system, proportions and basic decoration on the bow, but with a series of small projections down each side and a forward-facing knob (e.g. Dudley 1949, 189, Fig. 52, 4). Beyond the basic form, the family is eclectic and the stud can be replaced by a simple moulded decoration (e.g. Hurst 1985, 31, Fig. 12, 6), a crest (e.g. Blockley 1985, 142–3, Fig. 45, 20), a dog (e.g. Atkinson 1942, 203, Fig. 36, H16), a plain enamelled cell or a double stud (Butcher 1977, 59, Fig. 8, 20; 62, Fig. 10, 26). The enamelled cells are usually like those here. Occasionally there is a row of rectangular cells (e.g. Thorpe by Newark, Newark Museum, 23.53) or no enamel at all (Hull 1967, 60, Fig. 24, 231). Once it is accepted that the only unusual features on the present specimen are the form of the foot-knob and the abundance of relief decoration on the upper part, the only other feature of note is the stud on each wing, but this is fairly frequent on this type. The main distribution of the family is essentially Warwickshire through to the Humber, although they are to be found as far away as Kent and Scotland.

The dating is: 'The Lunt', Baginton, Warks, before 70–5, four from one pit (Mackreth 1973a, 66, Fig. 19, 1, 4, 6, and one unillustrated); Kinvaston, Staffs, with Neronian rubbish (Webster 1957, 102, Fig. 2, 8); Wall, Staffs, with Neronian rubbish (Gould 1967, 15, Fig. 7, 2); Harlow Temple, before 80 (France and Gobel 1985, 79, Fig. 41, 69); Crundale, Kent, a grave with two pots belong to the second half of the first century, and probably before 75 (Hume 1863, 64 and figure); Wroxeter, last quarter of the first century (Atkinson 1942, 203, Fig. 36, H16); Carlisle, late first century to 105/15 (Mackreth 1990, 107, Fig. 100, 3); Newstead, 80–c. 200/10 (Curle 1911, 323, Pl. 86, 23); Verulamium, residual in a primary floor dating to 105–15 (Frere 1972, 116, Fig. 30, 12), before 105–30 (ibid., 116, Fig. 29, 11). The remaining dated specimens come from basically late Roman contexts. The dating seems to be certain: c. 60/5 to c. 100. The two from Verulamium could show that they should have run into the early second century, but the second came from an undated pit and the first was incorporated into a flooring and the chances are that both ceased to be used in the first century and that none of the family remained in use by 100.

Late La Tène

13 ST 82 BLI, SF 388   Half the four-coil-internal-chord is present. The bow has a circular section and tapers to a pointed foot.

From occupation layer (unit 955) block 2, north. Phases III–V.

14 ST 84 DOY, SF 832   The internal-chord spring had three coils. The bow has a circular section. The catch-plate is missing.

From unit 1835 in pit 1835/2007. Late 2nd/early 3rd century AD.

15 ST 83 CAC, SF 458   The internal-chord spring has three coils. The bow has a slight rectangular section and tapers to a pointed foot.

From silts (unit 1002) in the north-east corner of block 1.

16 ST 83 CRD, SF 606   The spring is missing. The bow has a broad rectangular section and tapers to a pointed foot.

From silts (unit 1387) in the north-east corner of block 1.

None of these four has any feature which must date to before the Conquest. All are so simple that discussion of possible derivation from the Nauheim or *Drahtfibel* is superfluous. The three-coil springs of brooches 14 and 15 are of interest: the number of coils was not dependent on the amount of wire available, otherwise the four-coil system would hardly dominate in the way that it does. In three-coil brooches, the absent coil is always at the beginning of the spring, and the distribution favours south-east England, particularly Kent, Essex and Hertfordshire. There are outliers but these are sparse. Excavations in Canterbury have shown that it is the commonest form and it and the four-coil version virtually replace the Colchester Derivative. Examples in iron are known, but the distribution pattern is very heavily influenced by the location of modern excavation and discoveries. Even so, there seems to be an epicentre which lies in and immediately around Hertfordshire.

The full dating evidence available to the author for three-coil brooches is: Skeleton Green, Puckeridge, Herts, iron, c. 10 BC–AD 20, two examples (Mackreth 1981, 132, Fig. 66, 1, 3); Maiden Castle, Dorset, iron, c. 25–50 (Wheeler 1943, 252, Fig. 85, 34); Station Road, Puckeridge, Herts, iron, c. 25?–Claudius, +? (Partridge 1979, 35, Fig. 6, 3); Bagendon, 50–60 (Clifford 1961, 169, Fig. 30, 1); Baldock, 50–70 (Stead and Rigby 1986, 109, Fig. 40, 18); Chichester, Flavian (Mackreth 1978, 280, Fig. 10, 27, 25); Springhead, c. 100–40 (Penn 1964, 185, Fig. 4, 17); Chelmsford c. 150 (Drury 1988, 94, Fig. 62, 3); Verulamium, 150–60 (Frere 1984, 21, Fig. 5, 12); Baldock, 150–80 (Stead and Rigby 1986, 109, Fig. 40, 19); Colchester, 150–250 (Crummy 1983, 8, Fig. 2, 5); Baldock, late third century? (Stead and Rigby 1986, 109, Fig. 41, 37); Neatham, Hants, iron, third and fourth centuries (Millett and Graham 1986, 101, Fig. 70, 2); Colchester, 350–400 (Crummy 1983, 8, Fig 2, 9). Those found in third century or later contexts do not represent actual use in late Roman times. There is no surprise in finding that the iron examples favour a pre-Conquest and Conquest period floruit, but there seems to be a gap at the end of the first century. The number of dated examples is, perhaps, too small to argue from, so it is possible that the variety either passed out of manufacture before 100, or continued into the second century.

For four-coil brooches, the dating evidence is given for those with plain bows approximating to a lanceolate shape which *may* show that the Nauheim had been its parent. The dating is: Braughing, Herts, iron, c. 25 BC–c. AD 25

(Mackreth 1979, 103, Fig. 30, 3); Verulamium, Prae Wood, 5–35 (Wheeler and Wheeler 1936, 176, Fig. 24, 2); Bishopstone, Sussex, pre-Conquest (Bell 1977, 131, Fig. 63, 29); Verulamium, King Harry Lane cemetery, Phase 2, iron, before 55 and probably before 40 (Stead and Rigby 1989, 386, Fig. 177, 440, 2: Mackreth in Garrod and Atkin, forthcoming); Baldock, 25–50 (Stead and Rigby 1986, 109, Fig. 40, 25), 25–80 (*ibid.*, 109, Fig. 41, 28); Skeleton Green, probably pre-Conquest (Mackreth 1981, 138, Fig. 70, 32); Julliberrie's Grave, Chilham, Kent, mid first century, possibly pre-Conquest (Jessup 1939, 270, Fig. 3); Bagendon, iron, Claudian (Clifford 1961, 167, Fig. 29, 1); Richborough, Claudian ditch (Cunliffe 1968b, 78, Pl. 26, 9); Chichester, Claudian (Mackreth 1978, 280, *unillus.*), *c.* 43–60 (Mackreth 1974, 144, Fig. 8, 15, 12), pre-Flavian (Mackreth 1989b, 186–8, *unillus.*); Longthorpe, Cambs, Claudian-Neronian (Dannell and Wild 1987, 85, Fig. 21, 3); Chichester, 44–Flavian (Mackreth 1989b, 186–8, *unillus.*), 43–late Flavian (*ibid.*, *unillus.*); Colchester, 49–61, two examples (Hawkes and Hull 1947, 312, Pl. 92, 55, 56); Dorchester, Oxon. 50–70 (Frere 1962, 137, Fig. 27, 3); Verulamium, King Harry Lane cemetery, phase 3, three examples, one in iron, before 60 (Stead and Rigby 1989, 282, Fig. 93, 32.2; 310, Fig. 112, 134, 2; 354, Fig. 153, 315, 3); Silchester, not later than 60 (Boon 1969, 47, Fig. 6, 2); Colchester, 61–*c.* 65 (Hawkes and Hull 1947, 312, Pl. 92, 59); Fishbourne, 43–*c.* 75, two examples (Cunliffe 1971, 100, Fig. 37, 14, 19); Chichester, pre-Flavian (Mackreth 1989b, 186–8, *unillus.*); Kelvedon, iron, before 65? (Rodwell 1988, 67, Fig 53, 4); Canterbury, 60–90 (Frere *et al* 1982, 121, Fig. 59, 1); Baldock, 70–90 (Stead and Rigby 1986, 109, no. 34, *unillus.*); Verulamium, *c.* 75 (Frere 1972, 114, Fig. 29, 2); Fishbourne, construction of the palace, 75–80, two examples (Cunliffe 1971, 100, Fig. 37, 17, 18); Baldock, 70–90 (Stead and Rigby 1986, 109, Fig. 41, 33); Chichester, Flavian, two examples (Mackreth 1978, 280, Fig. 10.27, 25; Mackreth and Butcher 1981, 256, Fig. 10.1, 10), late Flavian, two examples (Mackreth 1989b, 186–8, *unillus.*); Gorhambury, before 75/100 (Neal *et al* 1990, 115, Fig. 121, 14); Richborough, Kent, 80–90 (Bushe-Fox 1949, 108, Pl. 25, 5); Maxey, Cambs, first century? (Crummy 1985, 164, Fig. 111, 3); Chichester, late first century–mid to late second, five examples (Mackreth 1989b, 186–8, *unillus.*), late first–early second century (Mackreth 1978, 10.27, 29); Baldock, 120–50 (Stead and Rigby 1986, 109, Fig. 40, 24); Dover, before 160/70 (Philp 1981, 155, Fig. 34, 95); Bignor Villa, second century (Frere 1982, 177, Fig. 26, 2); Verulamium, two examples, one in iron, second century (Stead and Rigby 1989, 17, Fig. 10, 6; 20, Fig. 12, 38); Chichester, Antonine (Mackreth 1989b, 186–8, *unillus.*), second century (Mackreth 1978, 280, *unillus.*), probably second–third century (*ibid.*, Fig. 10.27, 30); Neatham, iron, late second–early third century (Millett and Graham 1986, 118, Fig. 82, 301).

The message is clear: they begin well before the conquest and run strongly to about the end of the first century. Some

may have survived in use a little longer, but there is a marked fall-off in dating and any assigned to the middle of the second century or later should have been residual. All later examples have been excluded as they clearly were. Better dating for the three-coil spring variety will probably reveal the same date-range.

16a ST 83 CMB, SF 531   A 'Hod Hill' brooch in poor condition: the head, pin and one wing are missing; the foot and catch plate are fragmentary; the bow is distorted and the surface is badly eroded. No trace of tinning survives. The form of the upper bow is not entirely clear. It appears to have had a swelled front with cross-mouldings top and bottom. The small surviving wing comprises a terminal knob with basal ridge. The lower bow is slender, tapered and flat with a beaded cross-moulding at the top.

From ditch 3, cut 6, unit 1265. 3rd century AD.

For discussion, see brooch 67.

Unclassified

17 ST 81 LZ, SF 134 and 144   Silver, parcel-gilt. Behind the head-plate is a central lug with two holes, one above the other. The top of the lug has a hollow next to the head-plate and a nib away from that. The remains of the spring show that it was in two rows mounted on axis bars running through the lug, the complex chord system is not reconstructable, but presumably an upper one was seated in the hollow in the top of the lug. The assembly was kept in place by knobs on the ends of the axis bars. Each knob was gilded and shaped to a bulbous end rising from a basal moulding and each was made from preformed strip bent round the axis bar. The pin, however, was hinged and mounted on the lower axis bar. The head-plate is flat with a shaped top edge. In the middle is a square-topped projection with a scroll on each side. The bow has a rectangular section with a squared recess down most of its length. At the top are two holes through the bow with another at the bottom. The sides of the bow are shaped with an outward scroll top and bottom. The top of the bow splays out to join the head-plate, the bottom has a smaller splay above a waist bound with silver wire. The outer surface of the brooch above the wire is gilded. The foot has a cross-groove at the top and two at the bottom. The sides between are chamfered. Behind the foot is the squashed flap which once held the pin.

From unit 253 of gully 64, at least a part of which was probably an inserted grave. Late 3rd–4th century AD.

The basic form of the brooch is that of an early Crossbow. The chief features showing this are the bow, with the slot down the front (cf. Böhme 1972, Taf. 20, 809; *Oxoniensia* 14, 1949, 12, Fig. 1), and the foot with its chamfers and cross-grooves. The wire round the lower part of the bow had probably been fed through the bottom hole from the back so that it could lie in the groove and was secured in the lower of the top two holes at least. The wire round the base of the bow occurs on developed Crossbows (*Oxoniensia*, above; Johns *et al* 1980, 57, Fig. 3, c). The presence of a spring places it before the development of the chief varieties of early Crossbows. However, it is the multiple spring which is of interest, especially as it was purely ornamental. Brooch 88 is also discussed here as the full form also relates it to approximately the same stage of development and an example from Springhead dating later than the late second century shows that it could also , but not necessarily (e.g. Webster 1990, 297, Fig. 11), have a multiple spring. On the Springhead brooch, there was no connection between the two springs, the lower had a true sprung pin, the upper was wound round a knob on the head of the bow. Both springs were mounted on axis bars and fitted with knobs which were given the appearance of being continuations of the spring (Harker 1970, 143, Fig. 2, b[1]). Another of the 88 type from North Africa also has the multiple spring (Gerharz 1987, 98, Abb. 15, 123). Otherwise, multiple springs do not seem to be the mark of a single type. They tend to occur on brooches belonging to the lands east and north of the Rhine and Danube and also as far away as southern Russia (Kuchenbach 1954, Abb. 1, 5–7, Abb. 3, 3, 8, 10; Kovrig 1937, Taf. 13, 137, Taf. 40, 1; Kempisty and Okulicz 1965, Pl. 93, 1, 2; Almgren 109). If there is one feature they tend to have in common, it is that there is a very high proportion of bullion brooches and it seems more than likely, in default of better evidence, that multiple springs are an elaboration well suited to the taste of those who could afford precious metals, or wished to copy those who could. Despite the disparate dates of these examples, basically third to fifth century, the present example should not be later than *c*. 250, nor earlier than 200, a date which would also suit a silver brooch from Benwell and which also has the remains of a multiple false spring (Allason-Jones and Page 1988, 248–9, Fig. 2, 10). This brooch could be described as being related both to early Crossbows and to a series which parallel those to which brooch 88 belongs. It has a series of projecting studs down both bow and foot and these are to be found on cased sprung-pin brooches of the second half of the second century into the early third related to 88 (e.g. Bushe-Fox 1932, 78, Pl. 9, 13; Allason-Jones and Miket 1984, 96–8, no 18; Wheeler and Wheeler 1928, 164, Fig. 14, 17) as well as a group of early or proto Crossbows which can be shown to be basically before 250 as an example comes from Dura Europos (Frisch and Toll 1949, 60, Pl. 15, 114). The absence of wings attached to the top of the bow of the Benwell brooch suggests that the false spring was exposed in the manner to be found in Free Germany. In other words, the basic cultural zone of the relations of the present brooch and the general dating proposed are again emphasised.

Plate

18   ST 82 BDS, SF 324   The bilateral spring is mounted on a single pierced plate. The circular plate is recessed for enamel,

now a dirty khaki in colour. The reserved ornament consists of a central reserved spot with, around that, an inverted sexfoil with lobes on the cusps. There is no trace of any appliqué ornament.

From upper layer (unit 795) in pit 795. Late 3rd/4th century AD.

The following discussion also deals with brooches 69, 70, 71 and 107. Both 69 and 107 have the same design as 18 while 70 is very closely related and 71 almost certainly came from the same factory. The use of a sprung-pin mounted on a single pierced lug is a peculiarly British mark. Brooch 71 has its spring mounted between two pierced lugs, but this does not mean that it could not have come from the same workshop as the others as a brooch having the same design as 18, but with the double lug of 71 comes from Stockton, Wilts (Mackreth 1973b, Fig. 27) and another from Canterbury (excavations, T. Tatton-Brown, forthcoming) has a hinged pin. What none of the Stonea examples shows is the use of applied white metal trim, usually beading on the rim on the concentric zones on 18 and 71, and dished bosses or rosettes on the lobes of 18 and spots of 71. The use of similar trim on Horse-and-Rider brooches (see brooch 83) may show that those also came from the same factory: it may be doubted that such a specialised technique was used by a host of small workshops, each producing an individual design. The traces of the trim are vulnerable to damage, corrosion and, in the past, uncomprehending conservation practices, which has tended to obscure the sophistication of the effect: the flat enamel with its bold colouring shone through the holes in a silvery relief decoration. The continental brooches which are contemporary with the British ones have hinged pins and relied on a crisp finish with beading and cross-cuts decorating their mouldings.

Other designs belonging to the group are all circular with different reserved designs: a central dot-and-circle surrounded by six more (Neal 1974, 128, Fig. 55, 28); a central annulus with six semicircles rising from the outer border (Allason-Jones and Mckay 1985, 25, Fig. 44); a central dot-and-circle surrounded by a chevron with spots at the base of each outward-facing point (brooch 70 here); a central spot and six triangles springing from the outer border which has a set of rounded projections on the outside (Hattatt 1985, 142, Fig. 61, 526); a central spot in an open triskele each leg of which ends in a circular reserved area (Hull 1967, 62, Fig. 25, 257); a five-legged version of the last (Atkinson 1916, 35, Pl. 9, 30); other variations include ivy leaves and plain scrolls (Crummy 1983, 17, Fig. 14, 82; Hattatt 1985, 142, Fig. 60, 525; *ibid*., Fig. 60, 524); a narrow cell across the centre with two concentric ones on each side (Todd 1969, 89, Fig. 37, 8); a variety of annulus in the centre with spots around that, sometimes in an inner zone (brooch 71), sometimes with the outer edge scalloped, or with small triangles and spots (Kenyon 1935, 259, Fig. 12, 13; Cunliffe 1975b, 199, Fig. 109, 3; Allason-Jones and McKay 1985, 25, Fig. 43). One from Coventina's Well has the remains of a black glass cone which relates this ornamental series to the gilded oval or round brooches and their precursors (see brooches 78–81); a series of annuli or spots in the middle, concentric rings or spots and all on plates having projections around the periphery (Hattatt 1985, 145, Fig. 61, 529; Millett and Graham 1986, 101–3, Fig. 70, 4).

Individual designs are poorly dated, but an idea of the floruit can be gained by looking at all designs using trim, but zoomorphic forms are excluded, as discussion of brooch 83 shows that there may be other factors at work which distort the overall date of the school. The dating is: Newstead, 80 to *c.* 200/10, four examples (Curle 1911, 330, Pl. 89, 1, 6, 7, 14); Nettleton, late first–early second century (Wedlake 1982, 130, Fig. 54, 68); Overstone, Northants, up to mid second century (Williams 1976, 126, Fig. 13, 107); Ewhurst, Surrey, 120–200 (Hanworth 1968, 33, Fig. 14, 3); Watercrook, *c.* 120–200+ (Potter 1979, 211, Fig. 84, 15); Ilchester, late second century (Mackreth 1982, 247, Fig 116, 25); Hockwold cum Wilton, late second century?, three examples (Gurney 1986, 64, Fig. 40, 5–7); Colchester, before *c.* 250, two examples (Crummy 1983, 17, Fig. 14, 80, 82); Zugmantel, before 260 (Exner 1939, 103, Taf. 13, 4. III. 23); Vindolanda, with mid third century material (Bidwell 1985, 117–9, Fig. 39, 3); Chichester, third century (Mackreth 1978, 287, Fig. 10.28, 55); Colchester, *c.* 250–300 (Crummy 1983, 17, Fig. 14, 83); Verulamium, debris with late third-century coins (Wheeler and Wheeler 1936, 209, Fig. 45, 35); Canterbury, 270–90 (Frere *et al* 1982, 121, Fig. 59, 10); Gloucester, late third century? (Hurst 1986, 39, Fig. 22, 4); Lullingstone, with coins of Allectus (Meates 1987, 65, Fig. 24, 61). The evidence favours a second-century date, possibly not significantly before 125, for the introduction of the technique, its use running through into the third. Fourth-century items have been omitted. It is tempting to see the whole of the enamelled series predating the introduction of gilding on the common round or oval Plate brooches which had a special setting in the middle (see brooch 78), but the bulge in the dating towards the end of the third century in the examples listed above possibly shows that anamelled Plate brooches continued side by side with the gilded versions, not being completely superseded until near the end of the floruit of those.

19 ST 81 QP, SF 213 The spring is mounted as that on the last brooch. The circular plate has a cross-cut border and six equi-spaced bosses. In the centre is a raised platform with a cross-cut border recessed for enamel, now discoloured and partly missing. Enough remains, however, to show that there had been an outer row of inset glassy dots and some more uncertainly disposed in the middle.

From the uppermost layer (unit 336) of well 336. Late 3rd–4th century AD.

While the style of mounting the pin is British (see 18), the author has only recorded one other like this example with a sprung pin (Marney and Mackreth 1987, 133, Fig. 41, 17), the others having hinged pins. The standard continental literature has yielded only one example (Exner 1939, 115, Taf. 17, 2.III.56). Dating is difficult: Chichester, in a grave with a coin of Septimius Severus and Caracalla mounted in a ring (Butcher 1978, 288, Fig. 10.48, 1). However, if the type is British, it is probably related to the development by which brooches 79–81 arose from the type to which brooch 78 belongs. In which case, the Chichester example *may* not be too far away from its proper floruit.

20 ST 84 DTO, SF 948 The pin was hinged. The central, circular motif has an annular recess filled with decayed enamel. On the head side is a cross bar with beaded borders and having a set of punch-marks in the groove between these. From the middle of the bar rises a terminal whose sides sweep up to a cross-moulding from which projects a small boss.

From an upper layer (unit 1946) in pit 1915. Early 3rd century AD.

Undoubtedly made on the continent, these equal-armed brooches have slight variations: the central motif may be oval or square or lozenge-shaped. The British dating is very limited: Verulamium, 155–210 (Frere 1984, 29, Fig. 8, 84). The continental evidence is not much better and comes from Augst: one was found with pottery dated AD 50–75 and a coin of Vespasian (Riha 1979, 193, Taf. 63, 1651. However, if equal-armed brooches of slightly differing patterns are looked at, two belonged to the second half of the first century (*ibid.*, Taf. 62, 1639, Taf. 63, 1654) and another to the late first century and early second (*ibid.*, Taf. 63, 1643). The bias of the evidence is, such as it is, towards the second half of the first century into the second. On the whole, the use of enamel suits a period after *c.* 75 and it is debatable whether the example from Verulamium was still in use when lost.

Penannular

21 ST 82 AAE, SF 252 The ring has a circular section. Each terminal is turned back along the surface of the ring and is considerably worn, the ornamental details surviving only on the inside. Each end has a nick in the side with a deep concavity between. Marks on the ring suggest that the brooch had been made from rolled sheet metal.

From an upper layer (unit 446) of well 446. Mid 3rd century AD.

When brooches, like most Penannulars, were finished by hand, it is unwise to make fine distinctions between, say, waisting, as here, or mere chamfering. Therefore, the meagre dating evidence is drawn from round-sectioned brooches belonging to the same group and with no sign of zoomorphic tendencies like brooch 95, and from similar brooches in which the central face is concave on top (W in the list which follows): Maiden Castle, Dorset, 25–50 (Wheeler 1943, 264, Fig. 86, 8); Bagendon,

Tiberian–Claudian (Clifford 1961, 184, Fig. 36, 8); Hod Hill, before 50, three examples, one W (*BM Guide*, 22, Fig. 12, 49; Brailsford 1962, 13, Fig. 11, E17, E18: Richmond 1968, 117–19; Colchester, 49–61 (Hawkes and Hull 1947, 327, Fig. 59, 7); Longthorpe, Cambs, W. *c*. 45 to 60/5 (Frere and St Joseph 1974, 46, Fig. 24, 13); Waddon Hill, Stoke Abbott, Dorset, W, *c*. 50–60 (Webster 1981, 62, Fig. 25, 11); Prestatyn, W, 70–160, two examples (Mackreth 1989a, 98, Fig. 49, 26, 27); The Ditches, North Cerney, Glos., before the middle of the second century (Trow 1988, 50, Fig. 24, 25); Marshfield, Avon, burial, after 370, but may have been residual in the grave fill (Blockley 1985, 148, Fig. 46, 35); Nettleton, late fourth century (Wedlake 1982, 133, Fig. 55, 80). The balance of the evidence favours a floruit from before the Conquest well into the second century, but with most belonging to the first.

Unidentifiable

21a ST 84 Q23, 1, SF 1104 (*unillus.*)   The heavily corroded foot and catch-plate of a bow brooch. The slender bow is of plano-convex cross-section, the catch-plate a low triangle.

From occupation layer in trench Q, near the temple (building R15). Found with Iron Age pottery and Flavian samian.

3 THE BROOCHES FROM THE AREA AROUND THE EXCAVATIONS
(Figs 95–100)

La Tène I

22 P 1985, 10–3, 5   The spring and catch-plate are missing. The bow shows signs of becoming straight and has, on its upper surface, a groove on each side.

A member of Hull and Hawkes' (1987) Type IBb or ICb, the absence of the foot prevents certainty. However, if the 'hump' and length of the bow is a guide, it could be intermediate. The date-range covered by both types is from the fourth century BC to 250 BC (Hull and Hawkes 1987, 96–7, 123).

Colchesters

23 P 1982, 6–2, 41   In poor condition, the spring is missing. The hook may not have been much longer than it is now. The bow although distorted and without its lower end, shows in profile a sharp bend at the top with the rest having been more or less straight.

24 P 1982, 6–2, 39, length 49 mm   The spring had six coils and the hook is moderately long. The bow profile is a slack curve. The stub of the catch-plate suggests that there had been rectangular piercings.

25 P 1982, 6–2, 40, length 49 mm   The spring is missing and the bow is very badly wasted by corrosion.

For comment, see after brooch 3.

Colchester Derivatives

26 P 1985, 10–3, 7   The spring was held by a rearward-facing hook behind the head of the bow and was also anchored by solder behind the left-hand wing. Each wing has a sunken moulding at the end. The hook behind the head is carried down the front of the bow as a ridge. The catch-plate was separately made and fitted into a slot cut into the back of the bow.

For comment, see after brooch 7.

27 P 1982, 6–2, 44, length 38 mm   Behind the head of the bow is a vertical plate with two holes. The spring was secured to this by an axis bar passing through the coils and lower hole, the chord being held by the upper. Each wing is plain and roughly finished. The plate behind the head is carried over the top to form a skeuomorph of the hook of the Colchester. Down each side of the bow is a concave surface with rocker-arm ornament on the central flat face. The catch-plate has a pin groove, a circular hole blocked by casting 'flash' and a flange across the top.

28 P 1982, 6–2, 43, length 40 mm   A repeat of brooch 27, but without the flange on the catch-plate which has a triangular piercing.

29 P 1982, 6–2, 45, length 41 mm   A repeat of the last but with casting flash in the triangular piercing.

30 P 1982, 6–2, 48   The head only of a brooch of the preceding type.

31 P 1982, 6–2, 51   The bow only of a brooch of the same type as the preceding ones. The catch-plate has no piercing.

These five brooches are members of a major family made in hundreds and was the successor of the Colchester in the home territory of that type, although outliers are fairly numerous. Just as the Rearhook seems to have been the mark of the Iceni, the present type was commonly worn by the Catuvellauni and Trinovantes. Unlike the Rearhook, which has a great number of decorative varieties, the present family has few and there is some evidence that it was produced in standard sizes. The few variations comprise bead and reel wings; one or two grooves down the central phase in place of rocker-arm ornament; the hook continued as a ridge to the foot with, or without, rocker-arm ornament on each side; a step down each side with a swelled centre having a median groove. The dating derived from these is included in the following list and marked with the initial V.

The dating evidence, excluding those later than 200, is: Bromham, Beds, before 50 (Tilson 1973, 56, Fig. 28, 278); Verulamium, up to 50? (Wheeler and Wheeler 1936, 207, Fig. 44, 22), V, before 50/5 (Stead and Rigby 1989, 354, Fig. 154, 316, 4: Mackreth in Garrod and Atkin, forthcoming); Colchester, 32 to 50/5 (Crummy 1983, 12, Fig. 6, 50), V, *c*. 50/5 (*ibid.*, 12, Fig. 6, 48), 49–61, two examples (Hawkes and Hull 1947, 311, Pl. 91, 36, 37); Verulamium, V, 49–60 (Frere 1972, 114, Fig. 29, 6); Baldock, V, 50–70 (Stead and Rigby 1986, 112, Fig. 44, 79); Verulamium, *c*. 55–61 (Richardson 1944, 91, Fig. 4, 3); Derby, *c*. 55 to 80/5 (Mackreth 1985a, 281–3,

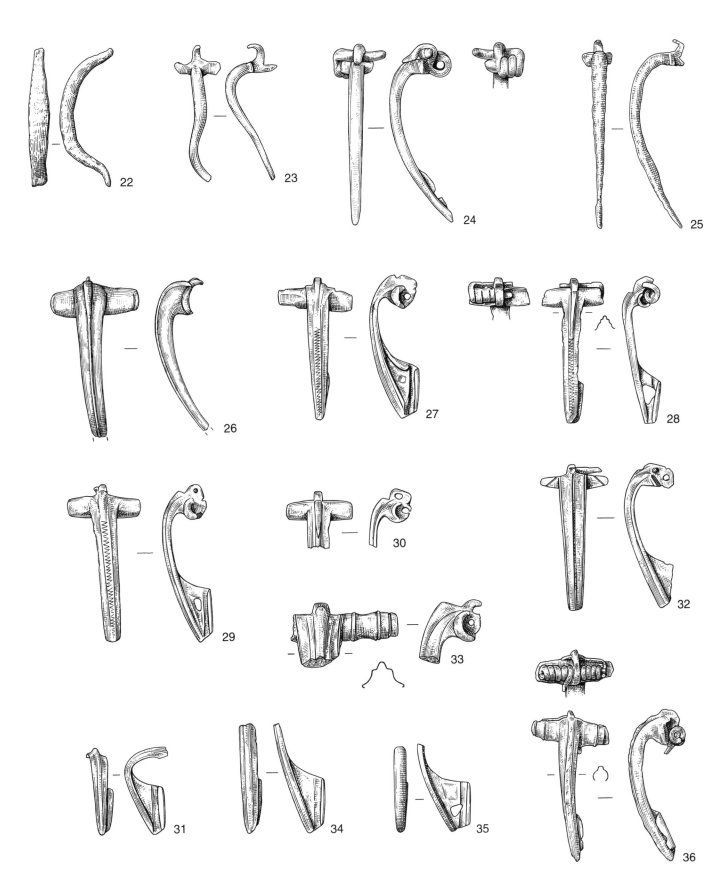

Fig. 95 Stonea Grange: brooches 22–36 from the Surface Collection (scale 1:1).

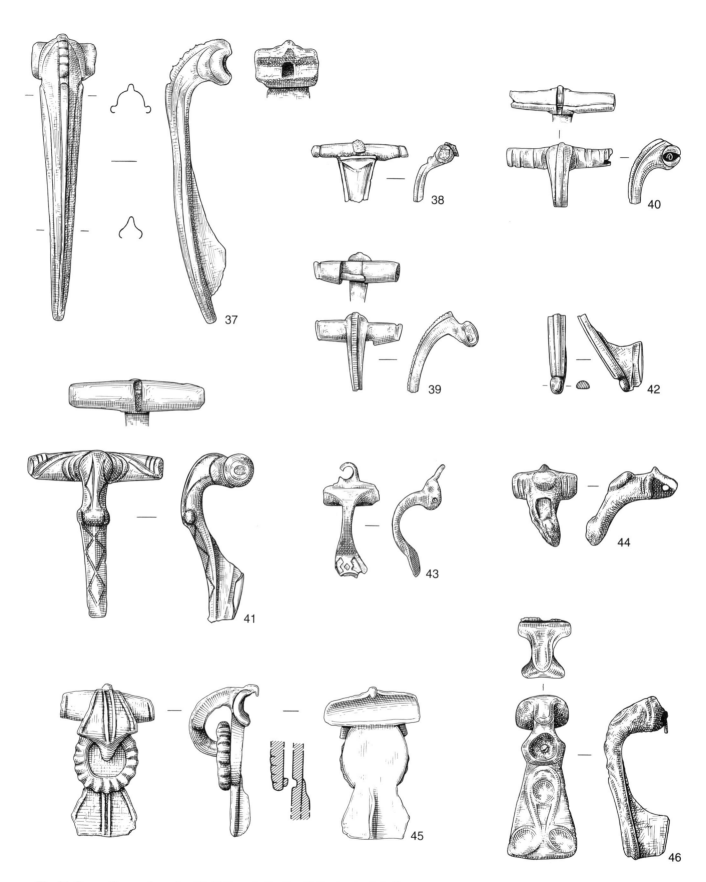

Fig. 96 Stonea Grange: brooches 37–46 from the Surface Collection (scale 1:1).

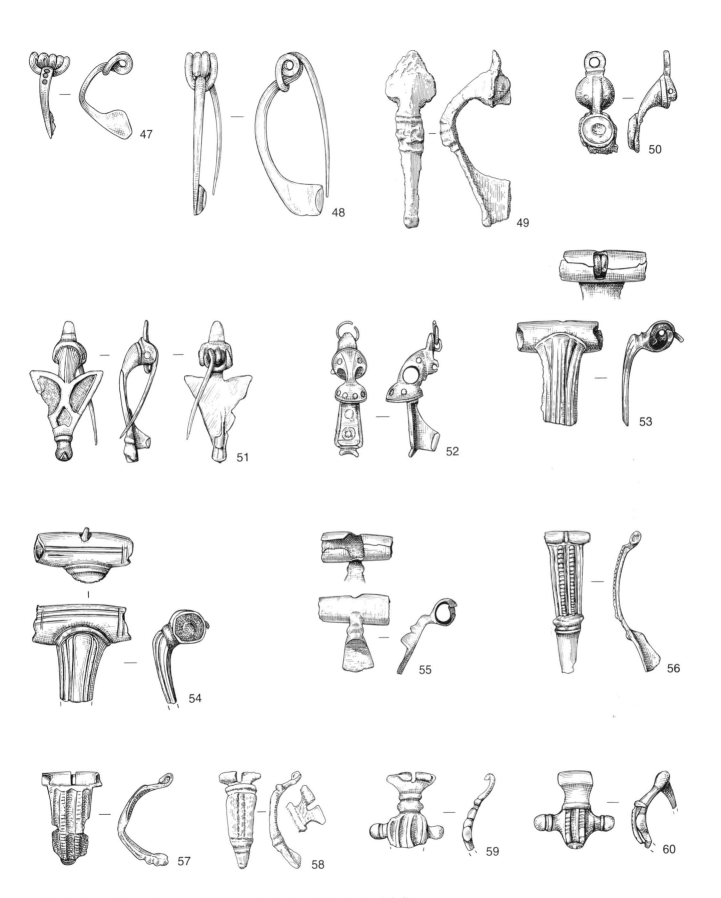

Fig. 97 Stonea Grange: brooches 47–60 from the Surface Collection (scale 1 : 1).

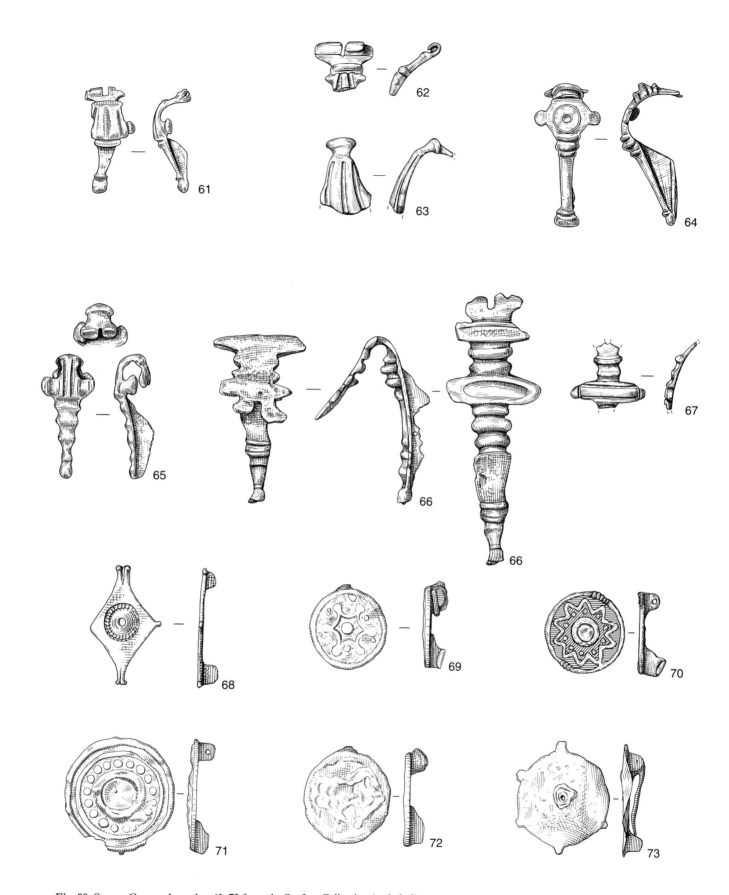

Fig. 98 Stonea Grange: brooches 61–73 from the Surface Collection (scale 1:1).

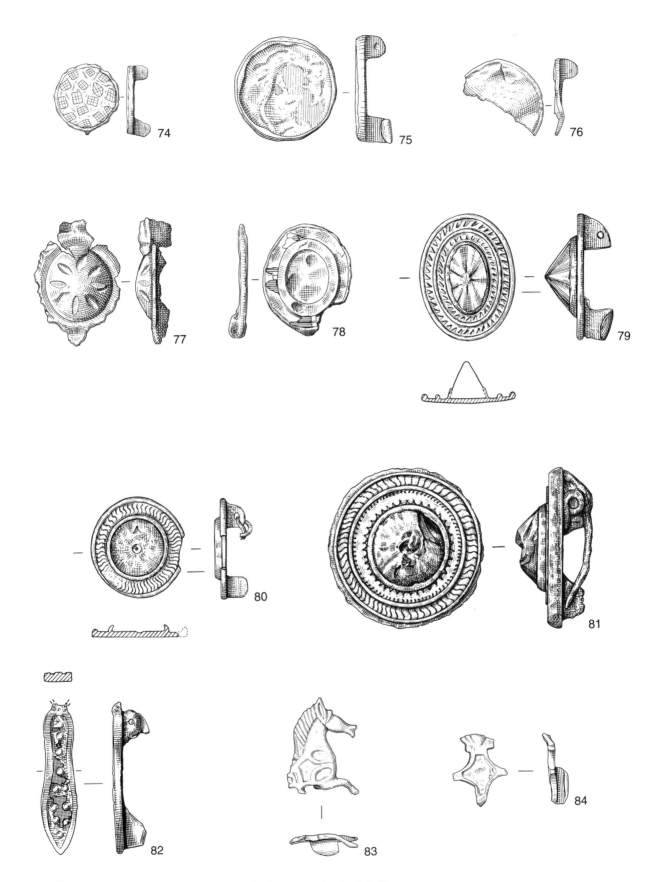

Fig. 99 Stonea Grange: brooches 74–84 from the Surface Collection (scale 1:1).

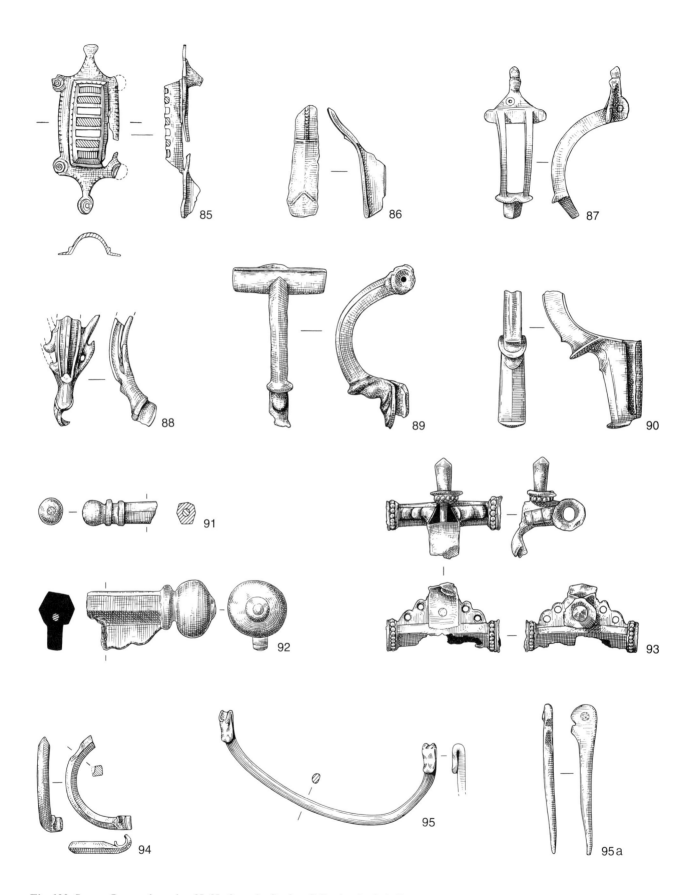

Fig. 100 Stonea Grange: brooches 85–95a from the Surface Collection (scale 1 : 1).

Fig. 123, 1); Verulamium, V, 60–1 (Frere 1984, 23, Fig. 6, 21); Colchester, 61–*c.* 65, two examples, one V (Hawkes and Hull 1947, Pl. 91, 38, 39); Kelvedon, mid–late first century? (Rodwell 1988, 57, Fig. 44, 21); Weekley, Northants, V, mid–late first century, two examples (Jackson and Dix 1987, M76, Fig. 23, 13, 14; Bancroft, V, Bucks, mid–late first century (Marney and Mackreth 1987, 129, 41, 10); Verulamium, V, 60–75 (Frere 1972, 114, Fig. 29, 8); 'The Lunt', Baginton, Warks, *c.* 70–80 (Mackreth 1969, 109, Fig. 19, 6); Fishbourne, *c.* 75–80, two examples, one V (Cunliffe 1971, 104, Fig. 39, 31, 33); Harlow, temple, before 80, four examples, two V (France and Gobel 1985, 78, Figs. 40, 50, 52, 57, 60); Baldock, V, 70–90 (Stead and Rigby 1986, 112, Fig. 44, 77); Springhead, V, 70–100 (Penn 1959, 48, Fig. 9, 3); Verulamium, 75–95 (Frere 1984, 23, Fig. 6, 24); Silchester, before 90/5 (Fulford 1989a, 127, Fig. 58, 1); Richborough, 80–100 (Bushe-Fox 1926, 43, Pl. 12, 2); Chichester, Flavian (Mackreth 1978, 274, Fig. 10. 26, 7); Chichester, V, late first century? (Mackreth 1989b, 185, *unillus.*); Nettleton, Flavian–Trajanic (Wedlake 1982, 125, Fig. 52, 46); Richborough, 80–120 (Bushe-Fox 1932, 77, Pl. 9, 10); Baldock, 80–120 (Stead and Rigby 1986, 112, Fig. 44, 73); Gorhambury, first century and late first–early second century (Neal *et al* 1990, 118, Fig. 122, 31, 32); Chelmsford, 90 to 120/30, two examples (Drury 1988, 94, Fig. 62, 7, 8); Verulamium, before 125 (Stead and Rigby 1989, 17, Fig. 10, 18), V, 130–50 (Frere 1984, 23, Fig. 6, 23), V, 150–70 (*ibid.*, 23, Fig. 6, 25); Lullingstone, late second century, two examples (Meates 1987, 64–5, Fig. 24, 59, 62).

Most examples date to before 75/80. There is so much crowding in the immediate post-Conquest period that it seems unlikely that none had been made before. That this might have been the case is shown by one from Skeleton Green whose stratigraphic position was ambiguous: it could have been earlier than the flood (Partridge 1981, 137, Fig. 69, 25). In that collection, it was the only Colchester Derivative and there was only one Hod Hill (*ibid.*, 141–2, Fig. 72, 55) which was said to have come from the latest pre-Roman land surface, but was not sealed by the flood. That these should be the *only* brooches belonging to the standard early post-Conquest suite argues for a closure *c.* 43/4. The chances are that the Skeleton Green brooch had been made before the Conquest.

32 P 1982, 6–2, 47   The spring is held as those in the preceding brooches. The wings have a nearly flat front face each with a diagonal groove. The skeuomorph hook is present, but the bow has a step down each side and a groove, and a line of rocker-arm ornament, down the centre of the swelled front.

33 P 1982, 6–2, 49   Only the head and one wing survives. The spring was held as before and there is a skeuomorph hook. The wing is moulded with a plain ridge next to the bow and one, possibly two, pairs of ridges divided by a shallow flute. The bow is similar to 27, but with bordering ridges.

Both of these are varieties of the preceding five and their dating has been included in the list after brooch 31.

34 P 1982, 6–2, 50   Only the lower bow survives. Down the centre runs a ridge relieved on either side by a flute. The catch-plate has a pin-groove.

35 P 1982, 6–2, 82   Only the lower bow is present. It is plain and has a squared-off foot. The catchplate has a pin-groove and two piercings, the upper of which is blocked by casting 'flash'.

Both of these were Colchester Derivatives but, without their heads, it is not possible to assign either to a particular group. Brooch 35 is likely to date to before 100 because of the piercings, in the catch-plate. Brooch 34 may also be earlier than 100 as it has a pin-groove.

36 P 1982, 6–2, 46, length 40 mm   The spring is held like those in brooches 27–31. Each wing has a pair of sunken ridges joined by a flute at its end. There is a ridge down the bow.

As this brooch is not a member of an established group, there are no parallels to provide a date and the brooch itself has no particular feature which helps either. It is likely to have been made and used during the period running from the middle of the first century to *c.* 150/75.

37 P 1982, 6–2, 53, length 77 mm   Although the wings are damaged, the spring had probably been held in the Polden Hill manner: an axis bar passed through the spring and through pierced plates at the ends of the wings; the chord held by a rearward-facing hook. The surviving stubs of the wings end in a single moulding, the rest appears to have been cut off. The hook was continued as a ridge, relieved by a step on each side, down the upper part of the bow, its profile showing signs of having been shaped into a series of alternating concave and convex curves separated by small nibs. The sides of the bow curve in at the top and the junctions with the wings are masked by curved mouldings rising from the wings. Lower down, each side of the bow has a strong moulding which runs to the foot.

Like many very large brooches, there is no group into which this one easily slots. In fact, there is no guarantee that the spring had not been held solely by a rearward-facing hook: the profile of the skeuomorph hook and the appearance of a concave-sided lozenge on the head of the bow are features found on Rearhooks (e.g. Crummy 1983, 13, Fig. 8, 62; Brown 1986, 21, Fig. 15, 78), but the masking of the junction of the bow with the wings is the mark of a large family of Polden Hills to which brooch 8 belongs. On balance, the large size better suits the latter and the date range would then be late first century to about 150. However, if it had been a Rearhook, it would date to before *c.* 65.

38 P 1982, 6–2, 56   The upper part only of a brooch of the same pattern as brooch 9.

39 P 1982, 6–2, 55   The upper part only of a brooch which had a wire pin like that of brooch 9. Each wing has a sunken moulding at its end. The top of the bow is stepped from the wings and has a broad beaded ridge down the centre.

40 P 1982, 6–2, 54   The top of a brooch with a hinged pin, whose axis bar had been inserted after casting. Each wing has a bulbous moulding at the end and then a pair of ridges joined by a shallow flute. Down the bow runs a beaded ridge.

The first of these two brooches has some resemblance to the family to which 38 belongs. This lies in the simply moulded wings, the beaded ridge down the upper part of the bow, the step on the head of the bow and in the way in which the pin was mounted. But the style of the wings and the proportions of the whole are sufficiently unlike for the relationship not to stand although it probably had the same date-range. Brooch 40, however, has no easily identifiable associations. The style of the decorated wings is not to be expected in the second century.

41 P 1982, 6–2, 71   The pin was hinged. Each wing has a long helical flute bordered by a ridge. Below this element a series of arcs spring from the bow. At the end of the wing is a curved groove which may be all that is left of a set rising from the end. The bow is divided by a cross-moulding on which there are two bosses. Above, is a central ridge on each side of which is a pair of steps forming a concave-sided lozenge lying across the bow. The lower bow has a slight taper to a squared-off foot. On the face is a series of grooves forming two and a half lozenges.

The author has not come across a parallel for this brooch. The helical groove on the wings and the concave-sided lozenge across the head of the bow are found on first-century brooches and are more typical of East Anglia than anywhere else. The diamond-pattern on the lower bow may be related to the enamelled lozenge and triangles found elsewhere, particularly the main varieties of Headstud, but the moulding across the bow has no obvious parallels. On balance, the likely date is the third quarter of the first century, perhaps running on a little, but it should not be second century.

42 P 1982, 6–2, 52   Only the lower bow is present. Down the middle runs a ridge to a step beneath which is a foot-knob.

Unclassified

43 P 1982, 6–2, 69   The pin was hinged. On the head is a cast-on loop. The wings are plain. The bow is well arched and curves out into the wings. There is a slighter splay at the bottom to join the fantail foot. This is damaged, but has part of an enamelled design in which there is a reserved voided lozenge joining the top of a reserved curve.

The full design of the fantail foot had a pelta in the bottom part (e.g. Hattatt 1982, 117–118, Fig. 49, 461) although other reserved designs are known (e.g. Stead 1980, 95, Fig. 61, 15) including an enamelled strip down the foot with reserved diamonds along it (e.g. Weston Blount, Bucks, private collection). All these are what may be called the developed form. There is a group which is unenamelled and whose pin is sprung and mounted in the Harlow manner (see brooch 27)

and one from Thetford (Hattatt 1982, 103, Fig. 42, 75) has a tinned or silvered finish. Another from Maxey, Cambs, has a groove and punched-dot line round the foot (Crummy 1985, 164, Fig. 111, 2). These features are more common in the first century and may mark stages in a transition from the design of brooch 7 to the hinged-pin form. There is a small group belonging to East Anglia and the southern Fens which has a hinged pin and bead-and-reel mouldings on the upper bow (Hattatt 1982, 169, Fig. 71a, 175c; *ibid.*, 1987, 116, Fig. 39, 931) which should also be first century and belong to a slightly different strand in the development of this fantailed type. Apart from a first-century one from Lullingstone (Meates 1987, 63, Fig. 24, 56), the rest could be said to be on the fringes of the Rearhook's main distribution and may have derived from an uncommon Rearhook variety. The distribution of those like 43 is along the west side of the Fens, although they occur as far away as Corbridge (Forster and Knowles 1911, 45, Fig. 29), which suggests that the origin of the type may well have been as outlined here.

Dating is difficult. Apart from the one from Maxey (see above) which is late first century–early second and that from Lullingstone, the only other dated example of an early form is from Gorhambury, which is only second century (Neal *et al* 1990, 117, Fig. 121, 16). An intermediate form from the Harlow Temple, still with a silvery finish, but with three triangular cells, was only before *c.* 175/200 (France and Gobel 1985, 76, Fig. 39, 18). For those like the present example, the dating is: Richborough, early second century (Bushe-Fox 1926, 43, Pl. 12, 4); Rudston, later than late second century (see above); Old Winteringham, Lincs, third century (Stead 1976, 198, Fig. 99, 10). Hardly an impressive list, but, following the general tenor of British brooch dating, the Richborough specimen should be within the real floruit and the enamelled series should follow the tinned or silvered ones in the later first century. The end-date is likely to be no later than 150/75.

Headstud

44 P 1982, 6–2, 70   The spring was mounted on an axis bar which ran through a pierced lug behind the head of the bow; the chord passing under a forward-facing hook of which the stump only survives. Each wing is stepped up to the bow. The circular stud seems to have an annular groove. The remnant of the rest of the bow has the top of a squared recess for enamel.

The sprung pin shows that this is typologically an early Headstud as it normally has a hinged-pin. The origins of the Headstud proper are a little obscure. We can begin with a brooch without a stud from Alcester, Warks (excavations, C. Mahany, forthcoming), which has a Colchester spring system and wings almost of the stepped type found on proper Headstuds, and a separately made foot-knob. Its date is unknown. Another unstudded brooch from Catterick (excavations, J. S. Wacher, forthcoming) also has a Colchester spring system, and wings which are fully stepped. The bow is rounded and runs down again to a separately made foot-knob. The next typological stage, was to make the spring separately and then to fasten it to the brooch in the way that had been done on the present specimen and on one from 'The Lunt', Baginton, Warks, dated to before *c.* 70–5 (Mackreth 1973, 66, Fig. 19, 9). It came from the same pit which produced four examples of the type to which brooch 12 belongs. The brooch from 'The Lunt' has the usual enamelled lozenge-and-triangle layout of the Headstud on its bow as well as the typical foot-knob. Perhaps the best dated of these unstudded brooches is one found in a hoard at Honley, Yorks, whose latest coins was AD 72/3 (Richmond 1925, 14, Figs 2 and 2a). A brooch which probably represents the transitional stage between those with no stud and those with one cast on is represented by an example from Leicester (Jewry Wall Museum, 116. 1962/966) which is very like the Honley brooch with a separately made foot-knob and a stud riveted through the bow.

So far, the only enamelling which has appeared in the discussion was on the brooch from 'The Lunt'. On brooch 44 there is the top of a square-ended cell. Both continuous strips and sets of rectangular cells are known and the slight evidence is that these are earlier than the standard Headstud types; not only are square or strip enamelling more common on sprung-pin Headstuds, but the dating evidence also points this way. An initial point of reference is the presence of square cells on some of the examples of the family to which Brooch 12 belongs and that had passed out of use by 100. The rest of the dating is really confined to one from Wall, Staffs, *c.* 60 to 80/5 (Gould 1964, 43, Fig. 18, 3) and another, possibly related to the Headstud, but with no stud and an elaborate ornament on the bow: Baldock, 55–90 (Stead and Rigby 1986, 67, Fig. 29, 10). The conclusion, on this evidence is that brooch 44 probably belongs to the period *c.* 65–85.

Aesica

45 P 1982, 6–2, 72   This brooch has already been published (Mackreth 1982).

46 P 1982, 6–2, 75   The pin was hinged. The design falls into three parts. At the top is a trumpet head covered with relief decoration in Celtic style. In the centre is a conical recess with a hole in its base set in a circular panel with a small excrescence on each side. The rest of the brooch is a fantail foot with a modified repetition of the decoration of the head.

Brooch 98 is included in this discussion. The elements which go to make up both brooches 46 and 98 can be directly paralleled on the Aesica and, in the terms discussed in 1982 (Mackreth 1982), are one-piece castings. Brooch 46 has system D and its dating was not discussed. When that note

was composed, the Stonea Brooch was the only one known to the author with a rearward-facing hook. Since then, apart from the strong possibility that brooch 98 had the same, there have been a number reported: Bergh Apton, Norfolk (Hattatt 1987, 370, Fig. 122, 1393); Weeting (Cambridge, Museum of Archaeology and Anthropology, *unnumbered*); Saham Toney, Norfolk, three examples (Brown 1986, 20, Fig. 12, 37, 38; 26, Fig. 16, 87); Carleton Rode, Norfolk, probably an unfinished item (NCM[2]); Ingoldisthorpe, four examples (NCM); North Creake, Norfolk (NCM); Ditchingham, Norfolk (NCM); Shotesham, Norfolk (NCM); Swanton Morley, Norfolk, (NLA[3]); Thetford, Norfolk, (Mackreth 1991, 124, Fig. 114, 28); Wicklewood. three examples, Norfolk (NCM); Wreningham, Norfolk (NCM); East Anglia (Hattatt 1987, 58, Fig. 21, 798); Eriswell, Suffolk (*ibid.*, 62, Fig. 23, 808); Farley Heath, Surrey (Hattatt 1985, 45, Fig. 20, 287); near Cambridge (*ibid.*, Fig. 20, 288); Cambridgeshire (Hattatt 1985, 45, Fig. 20, 289); Essex (*ibid.*, 48, Fig. 20, 294); Norfolk, three examples (*ibid.*, 46, Fig. 20, 292; Hattatt 1987, 63, Fig. 810, 811); near Salisbury (*ibid.*, 57–58, Fig. 21, 797); Mildenhall, Suffolk (*ibid.*, 63, Fig. 23, 811); Suffolk (Hattatt 1985, Fig. 20, 289A); Britain (*ibid.*, Fig. 20. 290); unprovenanced four examples (*ibid.*, 48, Fig. 20, 295; Hattatt 1987, 63, Fig. 23, 812–14). This relatively sudden access of new examples serves to emphasise the homeland of the rearhook method of holding the spring and, while none with a date is so far available, the discussion of the Colchester Derivative Rearhooks (see after brooch 7) indicates that there is little chance that the present brooch is later than 60–5. No parallel for 98 is known to the writer and, if it did not have a rearhook, the simulation of the basic characteristics of a Rosette should place it in the first century.

Brooch 46 has no useful parallel, and therefore no date. The ornament in relief does not serve to place the brooch securely either in the first or the second century and the central, rather small, rosette does not help either: witness the similar decoration on Hod Hill 64 and what may have been an enamelled derivative of that with an emaciated trumpet head often with projections on each side of the rosette like those here and on 64 (e.g. Butcher 1977, 64, Fig. 10, 30). Dating is exiguous: Thetford, before 61 (Mackreth 1991 above); Newstead, 80 to *c.* 200/10 (Curle 1911, 324, Pl. 86, 24); Camelon, either *c.* 80–90 or Antonine (Christison 1901, 406, Pl. A, 4: Hartley 1972, 5–6). The style of the piece does not suit the middle and later part of the second century. It is probable that brooch 46 belongs to the same general period, say, late first–earliest second century. One example of an enamelled Aesica has come to the author's notice: Halam parish, Notts (forthcoming); it is a two-part casting with the spring held in the Polden Hill manner (see brooch 8). The interest of the piece is, not so much that it has enamel, but that it also has appliqué white metal trim which should mean that it must be second century and probably after *c.* 125 (see brooch 18).

Late La Tène

47 P 1982, 6–2, 42   The spring has six coils and an internal chord. The bow has a more or less oval section and tapers to a pointed foot. On the upper part of the bow are five circular stamped recesses each with a boss rising from the base.

The author has only come across one reasonable parallel, from London and it is undated (*BM Guide*, 64, Fig. 24, 5). It *may* have the same date-range as the next brooch. Dating for the rare group of brooches with more than the usual four coils is remarkably common: Werrington, Cambs, *c.* 50/60 to 100 (Mackreth 1988, 91, Fig. 20, 2); Derby, *c.* 55 to 80/5 (Mackreth 1985a, 294, Fig. 128, 34); Weekley, Northants, mid–late first century (Jackson and Dix 1987, M78, Fig. 24, 21); Old Winteringham, before 75 (Stead 1976, 198, Fig. 100, 21); Fishbourne, *c.* 75–80 (Cunliffe 1971, 100, Fig. 37, 15); Chichester, late first–mid/late second century (Mackreth 1989b, 188, *unillus*.). They appear, on present evidence, to be first century and there is no particular reason to think that they should have lasted into the second.

48 P 1985, 10–3, 4   A standard four-coil-internal-chord brooch whose bow has a circular section.

Discussion of brooch 16 was confined to those which had lanceolate bows as these were easy to define. When it comes to rounded bows, the matter is different: some have a tendency to be oval and others have a flattened back without being actually flat. Nonetheless, it is probable that all had the same basic floruit as the others and this has not been tested.

The dating is: Werrington, first or second century BC to AD 50/60 (Mackreth 1988, 90–1, Fig. 20, 1); Gussage All Saints, Dorset, iron, first century BC to AD *c.* 75, four examples, two in iron (Wainwright 1979, 108, Fig. 82, 1006, 1038, 1056, 1070); Kelvedon, Essex, iron, first century BC–AD 43 (Rodwell 1988, 67, Fig. 53, 5); Verulamium, King Harry Lane cemetery, Phase 1, *c.* 15 BC–AD 30 (Stead and Rigby 1989, 342, Fig. 141, 270, 2: Mackreth in Garrod and Atkin, forthcoming); Kelvedon, Essex, iron, Tiberian to *c.* 40 (Rodwell 1988, 67, Fig. 53, 3); Ower Dorset, iron, before 25/30 two examples (Woodward 1987, 97, Fig. 52, 217, 219); Bagendon, iron, *c.* 20/5 to 43/5 (Clifford 1961, 168, Fig. 29, 5); Puckeridge, Station Road, iron, *c.* 25–Claudian, +?, two examples (Mackreth 1979, 35, Fig. 6, 1, 2); Silchester, iron, pre-Roman (Boon 1969, 47, Fig. 6, 1); Hod Hill, pre-Roman (Richmond 1968, 113, Fig. 56, 4); Skeleton Green, probably pre-Roman (Mackreth 1981, 138, Fig. 69, 31); Bishopstone, Sussex, iron, before 50 (Bell 1977, 131, Fig. 63, 30); Hod Hill, before 50 (Brailsford 1962, 7, Fig. 7, C18; Richmond 1968, 117–19); Gorhambury, 32–62 (Neal *et al* 1990, 115, Fig. 121, 1); Fishbourne, 43–*c.* 75 (Cunliffe 1971, 100, Fig. 37, 20); Verulamium, with Claudian sherds (Stead and Rigby 1989, 17, Fig. 10, 7); The Ditches, North Cerney, iron, 40–60 (Trow 1988, 46, Fig. 22, 12); Weston Favell, Northants, mid first century (Bunch and

Corder 1954, 224, Fig. 3); Thetford, iron, *c.* 45–61, two examples (Mackreth 1991, 123, Fig. 113, 21, 24); Bagendon, iron, 50–60 (Clifford 1961, 167, Fig. 29, 4); The Ditches, North Cerney, iron, Claudian–Neronian, two examples (Trow 1988, 46, Fig. 22, 13, 14); Puckeridge, Station Road, Claudian–Neronian (Mackreth 1979, 36, Fig. 6, 7); Bagendon, 50–60 (Clifford 1961, 169, Fig. 30, 2); Hardwick Park, Northants, mid first century (Foster *et al* 1977, 88, Fig. 89, 1); Baldock, 50–70 (Stead and Rigby 1986, 109, Fig. 41, 26); Verulamium, 50–75 (Wheeler and Wheeler 1936, 204, Fig. 43, 2), 60–140 (Frere 1984, 21, Fig. 5, 10), under Flavian building (*ibid.*, 21, Fig. 5, 11); 'The Lunt', Baginton, Warks, 64–75 (Hobley 1975, 34, Fig. 9, 7); Silchester, *c.* 65–100 (Cotton 1947, 143, Fig. 7, 1); Chichester, Flavian (Mackreth 1989b, 186–8, *unillus*.); Verulamium, 70–100, (Frere 1984, 21, Fig. 5, 13); Fishbourne, *c.* 75/80 (Cunliffe 1971, 100, Fig. 37, 16); Lullingstone, iron, first century (Meates 1987, 102, Fig. 47, 278); Hardwick Park, Northants, first century (Foster *et al* 1977, 90, Fig. 19, 3); Verulamium, 80–150 (Wheeler and Wheeler 1936, 204, Fig. 43, 1); Maxey, Cambs, late first–late second century, four examples, two in iron (Crummy 1985, 164, Figs 111–12, 5, 10, 11, 10); Newstead, 80 to *c.* 200/10 (Curle 1911, 318, Pl. 85, I,); Silchester, 100–20 (Cotton 1947, 143, Fig. 7, 3); Braughing, 100–50 (Olivier 1988, 37, Fig. 17, 10), 100–200 (*ibid.*, 36, Fig. 17, 5); Baldock, 120–50 (Stead and Rigby 1986, 109, Fig. 41, 40); Verulamium, 135–45 (Frere 1972, 114, Fig. 29, 1); Verulamium, before *c.* 150 (Stead and Rigby 1989, 17, Fig. 10, 3); Leicester, before 150/60 (Kenyon 1948, 249, Fig. 80, 3). Those dating entirely after 150 have been omitted. Most had entered the ground by 75/80, but there is a trail through to the early second century, if the latest date is taken, and a thinner one beyond *c.* 150. Perhaps 100 is a reasonable terminal date for most. The dating matches that for the lanceolate bows (see after brooch 16) and any dating to the middle of the second century and later should be residual.

Trumpets

49 P 1985, 10–3, 8   The sprung-pin was mounted between two pierced lugs. On the head is a protruberance which was probably once a cast-on loop. The trumpet head is thin with a central arris and runs up to a circular plate. The knop has a pair of cross-mouldings above and below three pairs of crude petals. The lower bow has a central arris and ends in what is now an ill-defined foot-knob.

This does not belong to a marked group and its date is likely to be part of the overall floruit of the Trumpet. The dating evidence has recently been discussed (Mackreth in Garrod and Atkin, forthcoming): the full range runs from before 75 to 150/75 with a few continuing later. In the present instance, the method of holding the spring should not be as early as 75 and the brooch is probably entirely second century.

50 P 1982, 6–2, 74   The spring was held as that in the last brooch. On the head is a cast-on loop rising from a simple pedestal. The trumpet head has a groove round the top, a white metal strip down the centre and a circular patch on each side. The knop is replaced by a disc with a raised central area recessed for enamel, now missing. In the centre is a reserved annulus. There is the trace of one of the four projections round the perimeter of the disc. The lower bow is missing.

'Plate-on-Bow' brooches came in three sizes and the present piece is a member of the smallest. All were tricked out with applied repoussé white metal decoration and so were probably contemporary with those Plate brooches using the same ornament (see under brooch 18). The disc is the common form of the plate on the bow and this seems to be the only form for the large size. This also has a proper foot-knob, but of two patterns: one with a hollow under for enamel (e.g. Richardson 1960, 208, Fig. 1, 16), the other fully moulded ending in a small boss (e.g. Wedlake 1982, 128, Fig. 54, 63). The middle and small sizes are much more varied: the plate may be replaced by a pelta (e.g. Buckland and Magilton 1986, 89, Fig. 20, 18) or an enamelled D (e.g. Hattatt 1985, 116, Fig. 48, 457). The foot is frequently replaced by a ring shaped to look like a penannular with the terminals ending in small lobes (e.g. Richardson 1960, 212, Fig. 2, 31). There probably is no chronological significance either in the displacement of the disc or in the form of the foot. The difference in size is probably more related to price than date.

There are so few dated specimens that the dating of each size cannot be considered separately: Camerton, 90–100 (Wedlake 1958, 224, Fig. 51, 19); Newstead, 80 to *c*. 200/10, two examples (Curle 1911, 324, Pl. 87, 26, 27); Camelon, *c*. 140–65 (Christison 1901, 401, Fig. 39: Hartley 1972); Wroxeter, mid second century (Kenyon 1938, 224, Fig. 15, 3); South Shields, *c*. 150 (Miket 1983, 113, Fig. 71, 84); Strageath, 158 (Frere and Wilkes 1989, 150–1, Fig. 76, 56); Springhead, second century to *c*. 175 (Penn 1957, 98, Fig. 14, 5); Scole, Norfolk, mid-Antonine–early third century (Rogerson 1977, 132, Fig. 54, 8); Leicester, before 180 (Kenyon 1948, 251, Fig. 81, 1); Verulamium, late second–early third century (Richardson 1944, 93, Fig. 4, 5); Camerton, 250–80 (Wedlake 1958, 224, Fig. 51, 18); Verulamium, before the late third century (Wheeler and Wheeler 1936, 207, Fig. 44, 30); Nettleton, late third century (Wedlake 1982, 128, Fig. 54, 63). Apart from the first example from Camerton, the dating matches fairly well that for the Plate varieties discussed under brooch 18 and the early Camerton piece should be discounted. The range in date, therefore, appears to be from the second century to the middle third. The initial date may not be before *c*. 125 again and the later third century dates should represent the time when the last survivors in use were entering the ground.

51 P 1985, 10–3, 11   The top of the brooch is similar to the last, but with a groove round the trumpet a little lower and no trace of the white metal roundels. The lower bow is in the form of a stylised fly. Each wing has a semi-circular cell for enamel, now missing, and there is another above the foot-knob which forms the head. There are traces of white metal on the wings.

A highly individual design, possibly emanating from the same workshops as the Plate and 'Plate-on Bow' brooches dealt with already. Its trumpet head and the use of appliqué ornament show that it was made in Britain. The numbers known are few and, as a consequence, the dating is sparse: Caerleon, 160–230 (Brewer 1986, 172, Fig. 55, 13). Although the only dated one to come to the writer's notice, it fits in well with the evidence available for brooches like 18 and 50.

Unclassified

52 P 1982, 6–2, 73   The spring was held as that in the preceding brooches. On the head is a tab, with chamfered corners, behind which is a loop which holds a ring. The trumpet head is the same as that on brooch 50, but the back turns down to join the central feature. This is a projection, circular in plan and with a flat underside, whose domed top runs up to the trumpet. On the forward edge of the projection are four white metal spots. The foot is a panel which flares out slightly towards the bottom. It has a bordering groove and two circular white metal excrescences in the middle. Under the panel is the top of a loop.

The upper part bears a marked relationship to the Trumpet and the types to which brooches 50 and 51 belong, but the 'knop' and the lower bow seemingly owe nothing to any British brooch type known to the author. There are, however, related forms on the continent called by Böhme the German Bow Brooch (Böhme 1972, 30–2). They are to be differentiated from 52 by the way in which the sprung pin is held: there is a single pierced plate behind the head of the bow with a notch in the top to hold the external chord (*ibid.*, Taf. 21, 849–864). The general type is exemplified by Almgren's 101 and its initial dating by Fischer (1966) is in the late Flavian and Trajanic period, perhaps a span from 80 to 120. The distribution as shown by Böhme (1972, Taf. 35) shows that the continental type discussed by her lies in two distinct zones, one along the German *limes* and the other along the river Elbe. So far, only one in Britain is known to the author: Corbridge (Haverfield 1911, 488–9, Fig 4). The chief difference between the group lying away from the frontier and that along the German *limes* seems to be in the spring: the former is equipped with a spring of exaggerated length.

The Almgren '101' group is marked by the use of white metal appliqué decoration and, as such, is the only major one which the author has identified on the continent as being in any way parallel with the use of the similar technique in Britain (see 18, 50 and 51). The British examples can be guaranteed to be native to Britain by virtue of their spring system. Böhme dates her examples from Saalburg and Zugmantel essentially to the first half of the second century (Böhme 1972, 32). The dating of the British type is: Newstead, 80–210 (Curle 1911, 318, Pl. 85, 2); Chichester, late first to mid/late second century (Mackreth 1989b, 188–9, *unillus.*); Dura Europos, mid second to mid third century (Frisch and Toll 1949, 41, Pl. 9, 23); Camerton, second century, probably Antonine (Wedlake 1958, 223, Fig. 52, 16); Leicester, up to *c.* 220 (Kenyon 1948, 251, Fig. 80, 15). Hardly the basis for a firm conclusion, it does not confirm a strict contemporaneity with Böhme's range and only faintly indicates the same time range as the other British brooches using applied white metal decoration already discussed.

Late La Tène

53 P 1982, 6–2, 37   The original surface is now missing. The spring-case is now plain. The bow is separated from the case by a cross-moulding and has normal reeded decoration, including the extra mouldings to fill out the splayed head.

54 P 1985, 10–3, 6   The same as the last, but more heavily worn.

Brooch 100 is included in this discussion. Both 53 and 54 are of the standard reeded pattern, but with no beading. The basic Langton Down, reeded and beaded, had developed by the last decade of the first century BC as one from Dangstetten shows (Fingerlin 1972, 217, Abb. 9, 3), otherwise the development of the type and the dating of its varieties is not easy. The King Harry Lane cemetery offers some valuable pointers. The reeded and beaded variety occurs four times in Phase 1 (Stead and Rigby 1989, graves 97.5, 287.5, 288.7, 309.5), twice in Phase 2 (*ibid.*, graves 255.2, 361.4) and twice in Phase 3 (*ibid.*, graves 68.6, 370.4), which suggests that it was most common early in the first century. The plain reeded pattern, on the other hand, appears in two graves in Phase 1 (*ibid.*, graves 71.3, 4, 413.3, 4) and in three graves in Phase 3 (*ibid.*, graves 47.4, 156.2, 4, 370.5) suggesting that it is later than the other, although two from Braughing dated Augustan–Tiberian (Olivier 1988, 45, 51, Fig. 19, 37, 41) show that the plain reeded type was well established by *c.* 25/30. The author has suggested (Mackreth in Garrod and Atkin, forthcoming) that the dating of the phases in the King Harry Lane cemetery is too late and that Phases 1–3 more probably cover the period *c.* 15 BC–AD 50.

The third main variety, to which 100 belongs, has a squared top and straight sides and is much less common, its incidence in the King Harry Lane cemetery being twice in Phase 1 (*ibid.*, graves 202.8, 287.6), twice in Phase 2 (*ibid.*, graves 289.3, 399.2) and once in Phase 3 (*ibid.*, grave 117.5) which suggests a falling off in manufacture and use towards the Conquest period. The evidence from Skeleton Green shows that there it was in use in the overall period 10 BC–AD 25 (Mackreth 1981, 133–4, Fig. 71, 43, 140, Fig. 71, 44, and possibly, 139, Fig. 71, 46) which would better suit the suggested redating of the King Harry Lane cemetery referred to above.

The dating evidence for when the common plain reeded brooch was passing out of use is more diffuse and has to rely on evidence from other sites: Baldock, first quarter first century (Stead and Rigby 1986, 113, Fig. 45, 87); Braughing, *c.* 20 BC–AD 45 (Olivier 1988, 45, Fig. 19, 37); Colchester, 10–43 (Hawkes and Hull 1947, 319, Pl. 94, 94), published as early Claudian, but could be earlier (Hull 1942, 61, Fig. 1, 6), 43/44–61, two examples (Hawkes and Hull 1947, 319, Pl. 94, 98, 102); Hod Hill, before 50 (Brailsford 1962, 8, Fig. 7, C29: Richmond 1968); Chichester, mid first century (Mackreth 1978, 286, Fig. 10.28, 50); The Ditches, North Cerney, Glos., mid first century (Trow 1988, 46, Fig. 22, 15); Colchester, 49–61, two examples (Hawkes and Hull 1947, 319, Pl. 94, 99, 101). All examples dated to the second century and later have been omitted. The Baldock and Braughing pieces are finely made recalling the care taken over the Dangstetten example (see above), otherwise, the rest are ordinary: unless those collected by the author have an uncharacteristic bias, all should have passed out of use by 60, the bulk having entered the ground by 50.

55 P 1982, 6–2, 57   The spring-case is plain. The bow has an angled step at the top, a cross-moulding in the middle and steps back to the top of the fantail foot.

This is the final devolved form of the *Léontomorphe* (Feugère 1985, 280. Type 18a4, Pl. 102, 1332). Feugère derives his dating from Augst where the relevant examples cover the Tiberian–Vespasianic period, but only three have dates and there is a marked residual element at Augst: it is doubtful if any are as late as 70/5. The British dating is: Verulamium, King Harry Lane cemetery, Phase 2, 30–55 (Stead and Rigby 1989, 362, grave 353.5) or before 40 (Mackreth in Garrod and Atkin, forthcoming); Hod Hill, before 50 (Brailsford 1962, 8, Fig. 8, C43); Bagendon, 43/5 to 47/52 (Clifford 1961, 196, Fig. 32, 9); Colchester, before 43–60 (Niblett 1985, 116, Fig. 74, 17); Longthorpe, Cambs, before *c.* 65 (Frere and St Joseph 1974, 44, Fig. 23, 6); Kelvedon, mid–late first century (Rodwell 1988, 57, Fig. 44, 24). This limited selection gives a maximum range of *c.* 30–65 and a closing date of 50/5 would suit all.

Hod Hills

All of these have the axis bar of the hinged pin housed in the rolled-over head of the bow.

56 P 1985, 10–3, 10   The upper bow has four ridges separated by flutes. The two middle ridges are beaded. The plain lower bow is topped by two cross-mouldings.

57 P 1982, 6–2, 61   A repeat of the last without the lower bow.

58 P 1985, 10–3, 9   The upper bow has a buried ridge in a swelled front with one cross-moulding above and two below. The lower bow, as it survives, seems to have been rounded in front.

59 P 1982, 6–2, 64   The upper bow consists of a rectangular panel of four vertical ridges under two cross-mouldings, and a wing on each side made up of a boss with a basal ridge.

60 P 1982, 6–2, 65   Similar to the last, the panel is narrower with two broad beaded ridges. The wings are the same and the cross-moulding above is very thin.

61 P 1982, 6–2, 62   The upper bow splays out towards the bottom. It has a thin beaded buried moulding in the middle, a broad ridge on each side, then a flute and a bordering ridge. Across the top is a beaded cross-moulding. The surviving wing is a simple bulbous boss. The lower bow is flat with a beaded moulding across the top and tapers to the usual two-part foot-knob.

62 P 1982, 6–2, 63   There were at least three mouldings down a panel splaying outwards to the bottom. There was either a small wing on each side, or two more mouldings.

63 P 1982, 6–2, 67   A fragment with a cross-moulding at the top and two or four mouldings splaying out towards the bottom.

64 P 1982, 6–2, 59   The upper bow is a circular disc with two annular grooves, a rounded wing on each side and triple cross-mouldings above and below. The lower bow has a slightly rounded front and a two-part foot-knob.

65 P 1982, 6–2, 60   Below two cross-mouldings, the upper panel has three vertical mouldings with a marked wing on each side. The lower bow is made up of four cross-mouldings above the two-part foot-knob.

66 P1982, 6–2, 58   The upper bow has two major cross-elements, the upper has a raised wavy ridge between bordering ridges, divided by two cross-mouldings. The lower bow has multiple cross-mouldings with a short flat face in the middle.

67 P 1982, 6–2, 66   The cross-element here has a broad central moulding between two narrow ones and has a boss at each end. There are two cross-mouldings above.

This discussion includes brooches 102–6. The Hod Hill arrives in great numbers with the Roman army. Amongst the early arrivals are those which show the transitional stage between the last members of the 'Aucissa' series and the first fully fledged descendants, but they are few and the eponymous site, which closed *c*. 50, had a large number of developed forms (Brailsford 1962, 9, Figs 8–9, C57–C80), enough to show that they had come into being before AD 43. None has been published from a guaranteed pre-Conquest context: one from Baldock was dated to the first quarter of the first century (Stead and Rigby 1986, 120, Fig. 47, 112), but as it would then predate its parent, must have been wrongly assigned. The only possible pre-Conquest Hod Hill known to the author comes from Skeleton Green (Mackreth 1981, 141–2, Fig. 72, 55), but was not in a properly sealed layer. There is, however, a small amount of Roman military equipment (Partridge 1981, 105, Fig. 54, 1–3) and the Hod Hill may have arrived with that. The distribution of the Hod Hill in Britain shows fairly conclusively that it was decreasing in numbers between 60 and 70 and so very few came from

lands taken into the Province in the 70s that virtually all must have ceased to be used by then.

The exception to this general rule is a small element amongst Hod Hills which developed on the continent and by the end of the first century was being decorated with enamel. The evolutionary stages are not clear. Very few, if any, have been securely identified in this country. The only possible one at Stonea is brooch 64, and none of the others has the very crisp detailing, proper beading and possibly a tendency to be larger than average, features which seem to be characteristic of the group.

Plate

68 P 1982, 6–2, 98   The pin was hinged. The plate is flat, shaped as a lozenge with concave sides. On the long axis, the ends bifurcate to turn out to form small circles. On the short axis, there was a small circle on the point; one is left. In the centre is a circular recess with an annular ridge and a hole in the middle.

This is the commonest design of a large family whose chief unifying feature is the circular recess, with its ridge. The bifurcated terminals is also frequent, but neither is a pre-requisite before a brooch can be included in the family. It is Feugère's Type 24 in which he notes six chief divisions (Feugère 1985, 184). The following can be added: the equal-sided version of the present design (Bushe-Fox 1949, 109, Pl. 25, 6) also with exaggerated terminals (Brailsford 1962, 13, Fig. 11, F5); a circular plate with a scalloped edge and punched-dot decoration (Kenyon 1948, 251, Fig. 82, 2); a circular version with a single bifurcated or other terminal, and sometimes with extra excrescences (Hattatt 1985, 126, Fig. 59, 509, 510; Brown 1986, 35, Fig. 24, 167); a crescent with a relief-modelled leaf attached (Crummy 1983, 288, Fig. 1, 2); a simplified version of the six bone bosses alternating with feathered motifs (Hattatt 1985, 138, Fig. 59, 513). The distributions of the six main types (Feugère 1985, Figs 48–52) show major concentrations in and around Augst and, although large-scale excavations are always likely to distort statistics, there is a possibility that Augst lay in the region of major production: Feugère gives 32 examples from Augst for his distributions, but there are at least 70 from there (Riha 1979, Taf. 57–9, 1502–68, Taf. 65, 1688, Taf. 66, 1708–11).

Feugère (1985, 344) dates the family to 30/40 to 60/70 drawing heavily on Augst (Riha 1979, 180–4, 199). The British dating is: Bagendon, 20/5 to 43/5 (Clifford 1961, 184, Fig. 36, 6); Hod Hill, before 50, three examples (Brailsford 1961, 13, Fig. 11, F2-F3, F5); Colchester, 43/4 to 48, two examples (Hawkes and Hull 1947, 326, Pl. 98, 177, 179); Lockleys villa, Welwyn, Herts, Claudian (Ward-Perkins 1938, 352, Fig. 2, 2); Colchester, 43–61 (Hawkes and Hull 1947, 325, Pl. 98, 170), 49–61, four examples (*ibid.*, 325, Pl. 98, 165, 172–4); Longthorpe, Cambs, Claudian–Neronian (Dannell and Wild 1987, 87, Fig. 21, 11); Waddon Hill, Stoke Abbott, Dorset, *c.* 50–60 (Webster 1981, 61, Fig. 25, 6); Colchester, 61+ (Hawkes and Hull 1947, 325, Pl. 98, 171); Richborough, pre-Flavian (Bushe-Fox 1949, 109, Pl. XXV, 6); Wroxeter, Flavian (Atkinson 1942, 208, Fig. 36, H86); Braughing 45–150 (Olivier 1988, 49, Fig. 21, 70); Colchester, before 100 (Crummy 1983, 17, Fig. 14, 85). All initially later than 100 have been omitted. The Wroxeter brooch, and another unstratified (forthcoming), could not have arrived there before 55/60. The message is clear: a closing date of *c.* 60 for specimens in use would be appropriate. As so many appear so very early after the Conquest, and as they were very widespread in central and north Gaul, there is a possibility that one or two may have arrived before the Roman army.

69 P 1982, 6–2, 95   A repeat of brooch 18, mid-blue enamel survives in the outer zone.

70 P 1982, 6–2, 94   The spring was mounted on a pierced lug behind the circular plate. The surface of this is recessed for enamel. The reserved design consists of a central annulus with, around that, a chevron of ten points with a reserved spot in the base of each. Red enamel survives in the inner zone and a medium blue in the outer. There are remains of beaded white metal appliqué.

71 P 1982, 6–2, 89   The spring is held between two pierced lugs. The circular plate has a reserved design of two rings with a series of close-set spots in the middle zone. No colour can be seen. The spots and the central reserved band have white metal surfaces.

72 P 1982, 6–2, 91   The pin was hinged. The plate is circular and has traces on the front face of once having had an applied repoussé sheet.

73 P 1982, 6–2, 92   The sprung pin is mounted between a pair of pierced lugs. The circular plate is plain except for a corroded dimple in the centre. Round the edge are six square-ended projections.

The first, 72, may have belonged to the type which has a variety of designs on the applied plate running from the so-called coin type (Goodchild 1941) to abstract patterns like the relatively common triskele (Brewer 1986, 170, Fig. 54, (9)). The type is not well dated and the indications cover most of the second century with some perhaps running into the third. No useful parallel for 73 is known to the author and only the most general of date-ranges can be proposed: from *c.* 100 into the third century.

74 P1982, 6–2, 96   The pin was hinged. The circular plate is recessed for red enamel containing random millefiore squares in blue and white arranged 3 × 3 with white in the corners.

75 P1982, 6–2, 90   A repeat of the last, but with only a little discoloured enamel left.

76 P1982, 6–2, 93   A repeat of the last, but with about half the plate missing.

Plain brooches like these are not particularly common and are said by Böhme to be centred in north Gaul and Belgium as well as the Rhineland (Böhme 1972, 38). They occur sporadically in Britain which suggests that they were of continental origin. The British dating evidence is meagre: Colchester, probably 150–300 (Crummy 1983, 17, Fig. 14, 81). To this can be added one from Tiefental, found in a grave of the first half of the third century (Exner 1939, 108, Taf. 14, 6.III.30), and two from Augst one of which was Flavian to early third century and the other was late second to early third century (Riha 1979, 191, no. 1625, Taf. 62, 1624).

77 P1982, 6–2, 99   The pin was hinged. The plate was circular. In the centre, and surrounded by a groove, is a shallow dome. On the top is a small boss set in a circular recess. Round the sides of the dome are eight leaf-shaped cells filled with deep blue enamel. Above the pin-fixing arrangement are the stubs of a cast-on loop. Part of a projection opposite survives.

A member of a fairly large family with hinged pins and made in Britain as hardly any are known on the continent (e.g. van Buchem 1941, Pl. XV, 19; Exner 1939, 114, Taf. 17, 3.III.53; Riha 1979, 187, Taf. 60, 1595). The standard design has two rows of triangles on the dome, and the rim usually has three projections with a tab above the pin mounting (Hawkes 1927, 181, Fig. 11, 3); but one row of triangles, either small or large, can occur (Hattatt 1985, 152, Fig. 63, 555); there can be a wide border with dot-and-circle ornament on projections (Wheeler 1930, 96, Fig. 29, 37) or a row of triangles and an indented edge (Hattatt 1985, 146, Fig. 61, 536). Other variations are known, but at present they are represented by few examples and none changes the basic shape of the brooch as represented by 77 here.

The dating is: Newstead, 80 to *c.* 200/10 (Curle 1911, 331, Pl. 89, 20); Wroxeter, *c.* 100 (Bushe-Fox 1913, 26, Fig. 10, 9); Carlisle, *c.* 110 to 120/30 (Mackreth 1990, 112, Fig. 101, 22); Harlow Temple, *c.* 120–200 (France and Gobel 1985, 80, Fig. 41, 82); Ravenglass, *c.* 130–200 (Potter 1979, 67, Fig. 26, 2); Strageath, 142–58 (Frere and Wilkes 1989, 151, Fig. 76, 57); Canterbury, mid second century (Williams 1947, 84, Fig. 9, 1); Camelon, 140 to *c.* 160/5 (Christison 1901, 405, Pl. A, 2); Alchester, third century plus (Hawkes 1927, 181, Fig. 11, 3). The few fourth-century examples have been omitted. The evidence suggests that the type was entirely second century in date, possibly not really surviving in use until the end of that century, and it is possible that the piece from Wroxeter was dated a little too early.

The following four brooches all had their sprung pins mounted on a single lug.

78 P1982, 6–2, 97   The oval plate has a central cell, now empty and, around that, traces of blue enamel alternating with white.

79 P1982, 6–2, 88   The oval plate was gilded on the front. The base metal has a reddish colour suggesting that it is copper designed for mercury gilding. In the central cell is a black glass cone. Around that are two recesses each with a band of stamped squares containing a reserved saltire. Only half the stamp was used to produce a series of Vs.

80 P1982, 6–2, 87   Like the last, with a tinned or silvered back as well as gilding, but circular, with an empty central cell and one outer zone filled with a band of stamped elongated Ss.

81 P1982, 6–2, 86   Gilded and tinned/silvered like the last, the central setting is a marbled green and yellow cone. In the inner of the two surrounding recesses are two stamps: S-shaped one used to create a single strand guilloche; and a half-circle to form a series of arcs with a dot on each cusp. The outer recess has a set of radial S-shapes.

All four belong to a single series with 78 belonging to the earlier part. Like the group to which brooch 18 belongs, they had applied white metal trim (Buckland and Magilton 1985, 89, Fig. 20, 19; excavations, T. Tatton-Brown, forthcoming). Almost all have their springs mounted as on brooch 78 and this system was used exclusively on the gilded and stamped series. The chief form of the beginning of the series is oval, usually with one zone around an empty centre. The enamel in the outer zone is frequently in two alternating colours. Some of the plain round two-zoned brooches discussed under 18 should possibly be assigned here as the gilded series has both oval and round forms with one or more zones around the middle. The central zone may have had a copper-alloy repoussé plate over it, like one from Dover dated c. 190–210 (Philp 1981, 150, Fig. 32, 73); or a separately made copper-alloy mount with a cast intaglio in the top (Atkinson 1916, 35, Pl. 9, 34), sometimes found separately (Hattatt 1987, 252, Fig. 79, 1207); or even a glass cone, commonly found on the gilded series (Hull 1967, 54, Fig. 22, 197). The dating of this end of the series is sparse: Nettleton, mid second century (Wedlake 1982, 128, Fig. 54, 64); Richborough, early–mid third century? (Bushe-Fox 1949, 117, Pl. 29, 48: Cunliffe 1968b, 243–4). The very poverty of the dating, despite the numbers known, could be a sign that the bulk actually date to after 150, and just possibly after 175 when dating of all kinds begins to falter: the example from Nettleton is dated by an associated coin which continued in common usage into the third century (see above). Slight support for such a view comes from the general consideration of Plate brooches with white metal trim (see brooch 18) in which there is a cluster of deposition dates at the end of the third century which does not fit with a general trend towards plain residuality after say 225. The common characteristic in the form of the gilded series is the raised central setting and the development of this can be seen to be happening in the enamelled series (Lechlade, Claydon Pike, forthcoming; Branigan 1977, 120, Fig. 26, 508, very poor illustration).

The gilded series is known in Britain by the score, but is uncommon on the continent. This detail, coupled with the sprung-pin, demonstrates that the type is entirely British. The commonest central decoration is the paste cone, but there are a few cast paste intaglios (a die for one of which was found near Brough-on-Humber (Henig 1984)), which serve to link this series to the enamelled one (e.g. Mackreth 1985b, 28, Fig. 11, 165; Hattatt 1985, 180, Fig. 73, 678). The stamps used in the outer zone or zones are usually the S or the relief saltire in a square, but also known are round ones with a central boss, pairs of lentoids to produce a wreath, a boss in a triangle, a saltire bisected by a bar, a boss in a D, a T with a boss in half a shield (Hattatt 1985, 181, Fig. 73, 643), arcs large and small, and a diamond. Alternatives to the cast intaglio and the conical boss in the central setting are a glass ring rather like a doughnut (Alcester, excavations, C. Mahany, forthcoming; Hattatt 1985, 182, Fig. 73, 645) or the extraordinary central metal cone finished with a boss and with five or six ribs radiating from it (Pitt Rivers 1887, 41, Pl. X, 5; Hattatt 1985, 152, Fig. 63, 548–51; Bidwell 1985, 126, Fig. 44, 93). Perhaps the most elaborate design is one with three zones round the centre, the inner and outer stamped, the middle one interrupted by four more settings for bosses (Dickinson 1979, Fig. 3, 12a; Mackreth 1985b, 28, Fig. 11, 167; Allason-Jones and McKay 1985, 25, Fig. 41).

There has been a tendency to ascribe the whole of the gilded series to the fourth century. In fact, although the dating is still relatively thin, there is enough evidence to provide a satisfactory floruit. The continental evidence is: Saalburg and Zugmantel, three examples (Böhme 1972, 110 No. 1133, Taf. 29, 1132, 1134). Both forts ceased to be occupied in 260. One from Augst was found with third-century pottery (Riha 1979, 88, Taf. 13, 309). Four come from the Netherlands, two were found in a cremation urn of a type dated to the second half of the second century and the third (van Es and Verlinde 1977, 80, Fig. 28, 28) and two were recovered from Tumulus V at Esch with other grave goods which indicate a date of 200–50, possibly 225–50 (van den Hurk 1977, 108–9, 122–3, Figs 25 and 26, Pl. IV, 3). The British evidence is: Manchester, c. 160–earliest third century (Bryant et al 1986, 65, Fig. 5.5, 3102); Dorchester, Oxon., post-Antonine? (Frere 1962, 137, Fig. 27, 8); Hockwold cum Wilton, late second century–late fourth? (Gurney 1986, 64, Fig. 40, 8); Brancaster, with third-century pottery (Hinchliffe and Green 1985, 44, Fig. 28, 5); Inworth, Essex, c. 250 plus (Going 1987, 81, Fig. 40, 2); Maxey, Cambs, late third–fourth century (Crummy 1985, 164, Fig. 111, 6); Fishbourne, before c. 300 (Cunliffe 1971, 106, Fig. 40, 43); Nettleton, 360–70 (Wedlake 1982, 148, Fig. 63, 5). All the British dating known or available to the author, save for examples from Anglo-Saxon graves, has been included and there should be no doubt that it covers the manufacturing period and the time when survivors-in-use were to be seen. Those later would have been residual in their contexts. These brooches were entering the ground mainly between 225/50 and 300, and should mark the period when survivors-in-use were being discarded. This allows a reasonable period for the type to have superseded the enamelled series which, on one view of what can be seen in the group discussed under brooch 18, ceased to be made more or less at the turn of the second into the third century. However, the evidence can also be used to show that the two ran in parallel for some time, even if the tenor is that the enamelled series began first. Those which are actually dated to the fourth century are negligible and the series should no longer be regarded as being fourth century.

82 P1982, 6–2, 101   The pin was hinged. The plate is in the form of a boot or shoe sole and is recessed for orange enamel set with small glass spots rising from the field to represent hobnails.

Enamelled brooches in the shapes of objects are not common and, of these, the boot or shoe sole is by far the most frequent. The distribution of this form, as Feugère (1985, Fig. 57) has shown, covers the whole of Gaul and upper Germany as well as Roman Britain. They appear to be most common in east Gaul, possibly reflecting manufacture somewhere in that region, althouh the distribution *may* only represent where the most extensively explored sites lie. The large number from Nor 'nour reflects the size of that assemblage which could have been the result of a shipwreck (Fulford 1989b). Feugère follows the examples from Augst when it comes to dating (Feugère 1985, 375–7) and these cover the Hadrianic–early third century period (Riha 1979, 203, Taf. 68, 1749–56) although an unenamelled one was dated Neronian–early Flavian (*ibid.*, 200, Taf. 66, 1727). The British evidence is: Verulamium, shield, 80–150, (Wheeler and Wheeler 1936, 209, Fig. 45, 34); Chichester, late first century to mid/late second (Mackreth 1989b, 192, Fig. 26.2, 84); Verulamium, 135–45 (Frere 1984, 29, Fig. 9, 50); Quinton, Northants, unenamelled, Hadrianic–Antonine (Friendship-Taylor 1979, 138, Fig. 63, 478); Shakenoak Farm, Wilcote, Oxon., second century (Brodribb *et al* 1973, 108, Fig. 53, 179); Cramond, purse, *c.*140–200+ (Rae and Rae 1974, 193, Fig. 14, 2); Caerleon, 160–230 (Brewer 1986, 172, Fig. 55, 14); Camerton, axe, 180–350 (Wedlake 1958, 232, Fig. 54, 55); Dover, flagon, 190–210 (Philp 1981, 150, Fig. 32, 71); Nettleton, axe, with a late third-century coin (Wedlake 1982, 130, Fig. 54, 71). They are all soles of footwear, unless otherwise given. This indicates the same general period, but the unenamelled ones could point to a late first–early second century origin.

83 P1982, 6–2, 103   Half a Horse-and-Rider brooch consisting of the front part of a horse with ears pricked and galloping to the right. The head is stylised with an open mouth, a dot for the eye and a band across the forehead. The mane is upright and represented by a series of vertical ridges. The body was enamelled, the reserved bands in the enamelled area may represent part of the animal's harness. All that is left of the rider is the leg in the form of a reserved band on the body and the foot projecting below the horse's belly.

The type represented here appears to be British and the common use of a sprung pin also points to this. The dating is: Hockwold cum Wilton, late second century? (Gurney 1986, 66–7, Fig. 41, 20), late second century–late fourth?, three examples (*ibid.*, Fig. 41, 18, 19, 22); Nettleton, with a

coin of 270–3 (Wedlake 1982, 132, Fig. 54, 73); Bannaventa, third–fourth century (Dix and Taylor 1988, 334, Fig. 19, 2); Durobrivae, Cambs, horse without rider, with third and fourth-century pottery (Butcher 1977, 54, Fig. 7, 12); Verulamium, 375–400 (Frere 1984, 29, Fig. 9, 52). An unenamelled one with a tinned or silvered finish from Ware, Herts, (excavations, C. Partridge, forthcoming) may indicate a late first–early second century origin, otherwise the dating, even if the number of examples is small, suggests that the late second century was the earliest time for their manufacture, and the five from the Lamyatt Beacon temple should date to the time when the temple was in use: late third century into the fifth (Leech 1986, 270, 316–19, Fig. 34, 6–10).

The relatively common association of this design with religious sites may mean that they had an unnaturally extended life. Eight came from the Hockwold cum Wilton temple where they were found with horses and riders on brooches decorated with repoussé plates and a brooch representing a bird of prey eating an animal. It was pointed out there that this suite had much in common with that from what had probably been a temple site at Cold Kitchen Hill, Brixton Deverill, Wilts (Mackreth 1986, 64–7, Fig. 41). Gurney, in discussing the Hockwold temple, concludes that it was no earlier than the late second century and continued well into the fourth century. He also suggests that items such as brooches of specialised design, which could have formed part of the 'regalia' of a priesthood, might equally have been votive and consigned to a special store (Gurney 1986, 88–91). The Lamyatt Beacon collection, however, should only date after the late third century which may favour the thought that they formed part of a priest's gear, assuming that the brooches had been manufactured much earlier.

The Hockwold brooches revealed discrete areas of surface corrosion and the suggestion was made that there had been a white metal appliqué ornament (Mackreth 1986, 66). Many of the Lamyatt Beacon Horse-and-Rider brooches also had the same effect, if the illustrations are to be relied on (Leech 1986, Fig. 34). That extra decoration was used has now been confirmed on a fragment of a horse of the same pattern as the Stonea one from Norfolk (Kessingland?, information from Norwich Castle Museum). Discussion under brooch 18 arrived at the conclusion that the use of that technique on other types of brooches was second century into the third. It is hardly likely that a very narrow range of enamelled brooches tricked out with applied white metal trim would have continued to be made after all others had been abandoned. This author prefers to see the Horse-and-Rider brooches as having been made at the same time as these others and for this group to have received special treatment because of its religious connotations.

84 P1982, 6–2, 102   Only the bottom of what seems to be a bow finished with a cross-moulding survives. The rest is a concave-sided lozenge recessed for blue enamel.

85 P1982, 6–2, 100   The pin was hinged. The basically rectangular plate has cross-cut borders and projections curving out
from the plate and finished with a boss. Each corner had a
semicircular projection with recessed ring-and-dot decoration. In the centre is a rectangular platform with a cross-cut
step at its base. On top are seven enamelled cells: red in the
middle, green/red/dull brown, on each side of that.

There is little that can be said about 84 as so little survives. How important it is to know what the rest of it may
have looked like is not known: the sub-division into intelligible groups of the general class of elaborate enamelled
brooches on the continent has not yet been done. The
dating from Augst may indicate the floruit: 50–late second
century (Riha 1979, 197, Taf. 65, 1694); first–second century
(ibid., 193, Taf. 62, 1636); late first century–150 (ibid., 195, Taf.
64, 1673); Flavian–late second century (ibid., 197, Taf. 65,
1692); 150–200 (ibid., 197, Taf. 65, 1699). Only those which
appear to have similar extravagant features have been
included. A second-century date seems appropriate. British
dating is meagre: Camelon, c.140–65 (Christison 1901,
404–5, Pl. A, 1).

Brooch 85 fares little better. Several brooch designs have
raised areas with cross-cutting along their borders and frequently have projections with dot-and-circle decoration.
Again, Augst has been used to provide what may be the largest body of reasonably well-dated items on the continent:
50–100 (ibid., 187, Taf. 60, 1596); 50–late second century
(ibid., 188, Taf. 61, 1603); second century–early third, two
examples (ibid., 187, Taf. 60, 1596, 1598). A badly damaged
brooch from Niederbieber is a very good parallel for brooch
85 and, from that site, dates between 190 and 260 (Gechter
1980, 590, 606, Abb. 10, 1). A maximum range running from
the late first century into the third is indicated. The British
dating, such as it is, supports this: Chichester, latter part of
second century (Down and Rule 1971, 113, Fig. 5.17.228K).

Unclassified

86 P1982, 6–2, 38   The top of the upper bow is missing. The rest
has a swelled front with a bead-row sunk down the middle. The
lower bow is recurved, has a slight splay towards the foot, a
central arris and a double chevron across the bottom.

A small brooch of the same family as the *Augenfibel*, but without the eyes, there are two basic patterns: that represented
by the present example, marked by the bead-row and the
chevron; the other is narrower, lacking ornament except for
the cross-moulding on the bow. The British dating for the
first is: Colchester, 49–61, two examples (Hawkes and Hull
1947, 321, Pl. 96, 120, 121); Towcester, c.100 (Lambrick 1980,
60, Fig. 12, 3); Baldock, 180–220, two examples (Stead and
Rigby 1986, 112, Fig. 42, 47, 48). For the second, it is: Baldock, 90–120 (ibid., 112, Fig. 42, 49). Clarity is lacking, but it
may be doubted that any were in use in the second century.
There is some uncertainty about the later stages of the

Augenfibel which has only partially been resolved by Kunow:
brooch 86 belongs to what has been described as Hofheim
Typ IId and been ascribed to Claudian–Neronian times
(Kunow 1980, 158) using, amongst others, English sites.
However, these do not allow close dating and more dated
pieces are needed before the floruit can be said to have been
established.

Divided Bow – Crossbow Series

87 P1982, 6–2, 76   The spring was mounted on a single pierced
lug. The head-plate is triangular with an elongated double
boss on top and a ring-and-dot on the front. The head-plate
rises from a crossbar, with rounded ends, joining the two thin
bars of the bow which sit on another crossbar whose front edge
has a hollow in its centre. Beneath that is a triangular-
sectioned bar.

Böhme dates these from the end of the second century
through the first half of the third (Böhme 1972, 26, Taf.
15–16, 655–97), although the number of dated specimens
seems rather small. One occurs at Niederbieber, which was
occupied between 190 and 260 (Gechter 1980, 590, 600, Abb.
6, 3), and this fits Böhme's range. The British dating is: Chichester, Antonine (Mackreth 1978, 286, Fig. 10.28, 53);
Carpow, earliest third century (Birley 1963, 206, Fig. 16, 4).
These also fall in the same range, but, bearing in mind the
development of the earliest Crossbows which can be dated
to before 260 from the large numbers found at Saalburg and
Zugmantel (Böhme 1972, Taf. 16–20, 698–779, 789–806), the
end of the range should perhaps be moved back to c.225.
This may affect thinking about when the type began, but
more evidence is needed.

88 P1982, 6–2, 68   The surviving part of the bow consists of a
rectangular bar with a ridge down the front and the remains of
openwork ornament on each side. Beneath is the triangular-
sectioned bridge with a markedly concave profile to the lower
bow of which only a fragment remains.

For the discussion of this brooch, see after brooch 17.

89 P1982, 6–2, 77   The spring was housed in an open-backed
case and held in place by an axis bar secured in the pierced
ends. The case is plain and has a slight step running along the
top. The bow has flat back and sides, an arris down the front
and a moulding near the bottom.

90 P1982, 6–2, 81   The bow section is rectangular with a buried
swell down to a slight projection above a concave surface.
There is a close repeat of the projecting moulding and bridge
on 89. The foot has a deep and wide chamfer on each side,
cross-cuts down the narrow front face and a simple moulding
at the bottom.

Although there is no guarantee that 90 had a spring, the
rest of the brooch shows that it is related to the same group
to which 89 belongs. The sprung pin of 89 places the brooch
before the introduction of the hinged pin (Böhme 1972, Taf.
13, 593; Taf. 17, 723; Taf. 13, 599: Taf. 17, 721; Taf. 13, 601; Taf.

16, 700). Böhme dates the sprung-pin type to the late second and the first half of the third century (*ibid.*, 24), the same as for brooch 87. For the hinged-pin type, the date she gives is basically the first half of the third century (*ibid.*, 27–8), but running on. However, her group includes a fairly large number with knobs at the ends of the wings and these should be the forerunners of those with three knobs. As it was suggested that the type to which brooch 87 belongs should, perhaps, be taken back a little, so the sprung pin should also be moved to give more time for the two sorts of hinged pin, those without knobs and those with. This is very much a construct, but the third century is notorious for its poor dating. The British evidence for the sprung-pin type is: Dover, probably lost in the first half of the third century (Philp 1981, 151, Fig. 22, 80); Brancaster, later than the late second century (Hinchliffe and Green 1985, 199–200, Fig. 86, 8); Caerleon, early third century (Wheeler and Wheeler 1928, 164, Fig. 14, 17); Housesteads, early third century (Birley and Charlton 1934, 195, Pl. 29, 2); Beauport Park, two examples, Sussex, before 250 (Brodribb and Cleere 1988, 259, *unillus.*); Kettering, with coins of the Gallic Empire and third century pottery (Dix 1987, 101–2, Fig. 7); and for the hinged-pin type without knobs at the ends of the wings: South Shields, *c.*170 (Miket 1983, 110, Fig. 70, 38); Dura Europos, before 256, seven examples (Frisch and Toll 1949, 60, Pl. 9, 31, 38; Pl. 11, 62, 63; Pl. 13, 84, 93; Pl. 15, 118); Birdoswald, after 253/61 (Richmond 1931, 132, Fig. 4, 2c); Colchester, before 300 (Crummy 1983, 15, Fig. 13, 73); Verulamium, before 300 (Wheeler and Wheeler 1936, 209, Fig. 44, 32). The example from South Shields is almost certainly wrongly dated. Brooch 90, despite its lack of a head, may be safely placed in the early and mid third century.

91 P1982, 6–2, 80 The left hand wing from a hinged-pin Crossbow has an octagonal section and a boss at the end rising from a double basal moulding. The front edge of the wing swings away to join the bow.

92 P1982, 6–2, 79 Again, only the left hand wing is left of a hinged-pin Crossbow, this time gilded. The section is octagonal and has a 'bracket' with a double ogee front edge attached to its front face. The knob on the end is onion-shaped and has basal moulding.

93 P1982, 6–2, 78 This brooch was carefully fabricated from gilded sheet metal. All that really survives are the wings and traces of the knobs. The axis bar of the hinged-pin was housed in hexagonal-sectioned wings. The knobs are lost, but the spike in the one on the head has a pointed top, suggesting that they had been onion-shaped. The basal mouldings are of beaded wire. The brackets on the front of the wings are deep and have three lobes, two of which have holes through them. The bow had a flat back, chamfered sides and a narrow front face.

The most recent systematic study of Crossbows made great use of coin-dated graves (Keller 1971). The progression is admirable from *Typ* 1 to *Typ* 4, but fails for *Typ* 5 (*ibid.*, Abb. 11, 12) and *Typ* 6. Unfortunately, the whole brooch is needed in order to be able to apply Keller's principles, and these three are fragmentary. Brooch 91 could be *Typ* 2 or 3 on the basis of the bracket and the slight onion-shaped knob, in which case the date-range would be 320–70. Brooch 92 would be *Typ* 1 because of the double mouldings next to the knob and Keller's date would be 285–315, but the knob itself is very weak and occurs with the double moulding at Saalburg (Böhme 1972, Taf. 21, 822), probably before 260: the later coins from the site are few and there was no pottery to go with them (*ibid.*, 9, n.9).

Brooch 93 is a member of Keller's *Typ* 6 as far as the length of each wing in proportion to the width of the bow allows a determination (*ibid.*, Abb. 11). The use of sheet-metal to reduce weight and prominent brackets are the marks of both *Typen* 5 and 6 and the foot would have had the C ornament common to both (e.g. Clarke 1979, 262, Fig. 32, 587; Hattatt 1985, 135, Fig. 58, 507). There is no evidence on the Stonea fragment that it had been fitted with a screwed terminal, which is more to be expected on *Typ* 6 than 5.

The breakdown in the coin-dating noted above is taken by Keller to have been a mark of the latest Roman period when coins were no longer minted in the same quantities and older coins were selected to make up the quantities needed (*ibid.*, 51–2). In Britain, the use of coins has received some attention and, whatever may have been the case on the continent, the state of affairs after the major House of Valentinian issues, which coincides with Keller's dating of his *Typ* 4 and provides the bulk of the dating in his sample for *Typ* 5 (*ibid.*, Abb. 12), is that there is a decline in coin use emphasised by the lack of copying (Reece 1973, 244). This should mean that the coins occurring with Keller's examples offer no real basis for redating his last two types to run, perhaps, parallel with others, on the grounds that these two types were a *functional* variation not related to chronology: the weak dating itself may be evidence for a late date. However, the very high proportion of pieces belonging to these two types, and late Crossbows in general, which were of, or made to look like, bullion is almost certainly related to status and it is just possible that the C motif of *Typen* 5 and 6 is a mark of this. In any case, brooch 93 should belong to the last quarter of the fourth century at least. Keller's arguments are that *Typ* 6 is from *c.* 400 to the middle of the fifth century (*ibid.*, 52). British dating of Crossbows of these types is, apart from Lankhills, Winchester, virtually non-existent. Lankhills produced one *Typ* 5 dated 350–90 (Clarke 1979, 260, Fig. 32, 257) and two *Typ* 6 dated 370–90 and 390–400 (*ibid.*, 261–2, Fig. 32, 447, 587). Typologically, neither of these two has the long foot which Keller's type-specimen would have us believe (Keller 1971, Abb. 11, 13) and the later one has the squat proportions ascribed to *Typ* 5.

Penannulars

94 P1982, 6–2, 85   The ring has a lozenge-shaped section. The remaining terminal was formed by coiling the beaten out end of the ring.

95 P1982, 6–2, 84   The D-sectioned ring has the curve at the top. The terminal is folded back along the surface of the ring, has a rounded end and a hollow chamfer on each side. Two cuts at the bend give a zoomorphic appearance.

Tightly coiled terminals at right angles to the plane of the ring tend to be a mark of the first two centuries AD. However, it is not certain what the chronological significance of differing ring-sections is. The limited evidence may be said to support the general date-range: Colchester, 43/4 (Hawkes and Hull 1947, 326, Fig. 59, 5); Longthorpe, Cambs, *c.* 45–65 (Frere and St Joseph 1974, 45, Fig. 24, 12); Harlow Temple, before 80 (France and Gobel 1985, 80, Fig. 41, 83); Camerton, up to the middle of the third century (Wedlake 1958, 234, Fig. 55, 63A).

Items such as brooch 95 can be classed as being zoomorphic in the sense that there seems to have been an attempt to provide 'ears', but whether there was a deliberate intention to produce a hound's or horse's head is beyond knowing, but if these similarities appear to us, it is likely that they were not lost on the producers and wearers. There is little real guidance about whether the D-shaped section of the ring is a chronological indicator. The dating evidence is: Moulton, Northants, round-sectioned, late third–fourth century (Hunter and Mynard 1977, 134, Fig. 19, 262); Verulamium, rectangular-sectioned, late fourth century (Kenyon 1935, 259, Fig. 12, 12). A more fully zoomorphic one from Barton Court was dated late Roman (Miles 1986, 5, D20, Fig. 103, 7). The dating is weak and points at best to the fourth century.

Brooch pin

95a P1982, 6–2, 83   A complete hinged pin.

4 THE BROOCHES FROM STONEA CAMP   (Fig. 101)

Colchester

96 P1981, 5–3, 7, length 48 mm   The broken spring has its start bent to form a loop to hold an axis bar through either the original spring or a replacement.

For comment, see after brooch 3.

Colchester Derivative

97 P1981, 5–3, 10   The pin was hinged. Each wing is plain, has an oval section and was wrapped round the axis bar of the hinged pin. The bow is sturdy and has two large flat-bottomed insets

at the top. The foot projects. The catch-plate has a pin-groove almost hidden by the return.

The insets on the bow are characteristic of a group found mainly in the East Midlands stretching down into Cambridgeshire and across to East Anglia. The origin of the insets – for enamel – is unknown, and the general lack of other ornament prevents much being said about the associations of the group. The dating is sparse: Leicester, up to 125–30 (Kenyon 1948, 249, Fig. 80, 7); Old Winteringham, third century (Stead 1976, 198, Fig. 100, 18). The Leicester example is likely to lie within the floruit.

Aesica

98 P1982, 5–3, 2   In very poor condition, the brooch was cast all in one piece. The spring had probably been held by a rearward-facing hook behind the head of the bow. The wings are now lost. The bow had been wide and has a beaded ridge down the middle. The bottom of the bow runs back sharply to meet the disc just above an oval defined by a square-topped ridge. The fantail foot has corrosion accretions on it and all that can be seen is a beaded border on the left and part of a ridge in the middle.

For comment, see after brooch 45.

Late La Tène

99 P1981, 5–3, 8   Rosette. There is a short bridge between the spring-case and the body of the brooch which is a simple plate with a disc at the top and a fantail foot, now missing, beneath. The disc has traces of having had a rivet through the middle for either an applied plate or an enamelled boss.

This postdates the full Augustan–Tiberian type from which the Aesica derived. As the type is probably no earlier than *c.* 30, British examples are likely to provide the best dating for the end of its floruit: Colchester, 43/4 to 48 (Hawkes and Hull 1947, 316, Pl. 94, 83); Bagendon, Claudian to 50/60 (Clifford 1961, 175, Fig. 32, 4); Chichester, Flavian–early second, could have had a hinged-pin (Mackreth 1978, 285, Fig. 10.28, 49). Later ones have been ignored. These few specimens could indicate that examples may have remained in use for 20 or so years after the Conquest. At Augst, two-thirds had passed out of use by the end of Claudius' reign (Riha 1979, 106, *Typ* 4.7) suggesting that the closing date should be shortened to 55/60 as the remaining third were probably all residual, there being a very high residual factor at this site.

100 P1981, 5–3, 5   Langton Down. The bow has a squared top. Down the front are three rounded ridges with a pointed one between each. There is a series of punched dots on each side of the latter.

For comment, see after brooch 54.

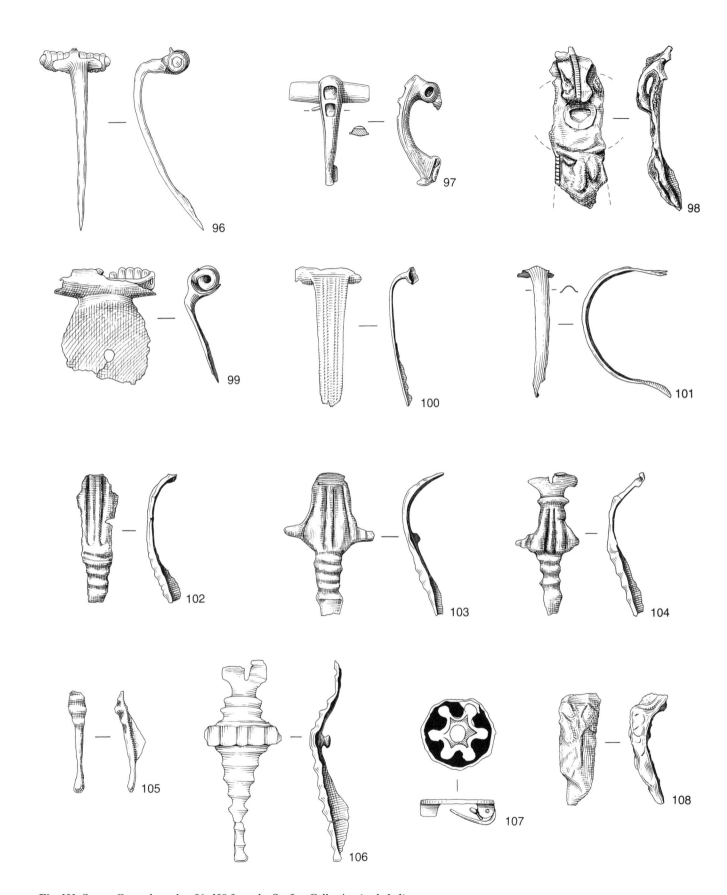

Fig. 101 Stonea Camp: brooches 96–108 from the Surface Collection (scale 1:1).

Aucissa–Hod Hill

All have or had rolled-over heads to house the axis bar of the hinged-pin.

101 P1981, 5–3, 9   Possibly an ordinary Aucissa, its poor condition prevents certainty. If so it is unlikely to have arrived much, if at all, before the Conquest, or to have lasted beyond 55 at the latest.

102 P1981, 5–3, 15   The upper bow has two broad flutes down it. The lower bow was probably fully cross-moulded.

103 P1981, 5–3, 3   The upper bow splays out towards the bottom and has a ridge down the middle and both sides. On each bottom corner is a wing. The lower bow has four cross-mouldings at the top above part of a shovel-shaped plate.

104 P1981, 5–3, 6   Like the last, but with a slightly different lower bow.

105 P1981, 5–3, 13   The lower bow has three cross-mouldings at the top.

106 P1981, 5–3, 4   The body of the brooch is almost entirely made up of cross-mouldings. There are two wide ones at the top, then an elongated element with six vertical ridges and a knob at each end. Beneath this are six more cross-mouldings narrowing down to a simple foot-knob.

For comment, see after brooch 67.

Plate

107 P1981, 5–3, 12   A repeat of brooch 18.

For comment, see after brooch 18.

Fragment

108 P1981, 5–3, 7   A fragment of a bow without head or foot, very heavily corroded. Possibly part of a Colchester Derivative.

Notes

1 I am grateful to Miss J. Vale of the Kent County Museums Service for checking the details for me.
2 All the brooches marked (NCM) come from private collections, the information being generously channelled to the author by Mr W. Milligan of the Norwich Castle Museum, to whom I give my thanks.
3 Information concerning brooches marked NLA was sent to the author from Norfolk Landscape Archaeology based at Gressenhall. My thanks go to the late Tony Gregory, and to Mr David Gurney.

FINGER-RINGS

Catherine Johns   (Figs 102–5)

Where all or most of the ring is present, the *internal* width is given, or the *internal* diameter where the form is effectively circular.

A FROM THE EXCAVATIONS   (Fig. 102)

1 Iron ring   Internal width *c*. 20 mm   ST 84 DXZ, SF 1070

The corrosion makes it difficult to perceive the exact form of the ring, but it can be assigned to the standard Henig II type of the 1st and 2nd century, with an expanded bezel area set with a gem and shoulders tapering smoothly into the rest of the hoop.

The 'gem' is in an opaque white vitreous material, and is very badly cracked and damaged. The original colour is unlikely to have been white, and it is highly probable that the surface was engraved or moulded with a device in intaglio in imitation of a hardstone gem, though no trace of it can now be seen. XRF analysis (BM Cons. CA 1993/11) indicated the presence of iron, lead, a minor amount of silicon and calcium, suggesting the 'gem' could be a lead-based glass or enamel.

From pit 2021/2110, layer 2028/2117. 3rd century AD.

2 Carnelian intaglio   14 × 11 mm   ST 80 BE, SF 11

The gem is slightly convex on both obverse and reverse. It has been chipped at the lower edge, and there is a flake missing from the front surface which affects the area in front of the engraved figure. This is a representation of Fortuna standing with a cornucopia and a patera. The type resembles a 2nd-century example from Newstead, Henig 1978, no. 335, as well as nos 157–66 in the Snettisham hoard, which was buried in the middle of the second century (Johns, forthcoming).

From late 2nd/early 3rd century AD furnace debris (unit 28) outside the north-west corner of the small hypocausted room of building R1.

3 Bronze ring   Internal width *c*. 15 mm   ST 81 NB, SF 169

The ring, which is of light and thin construction, is broken across the bezel and its shape has been distorted. The bezel is a sub-rectangular plate bearing rows of lines and beading in relief, probably an applied plate worked in repoussé. The ring is not easy to parallel or to date, though Henkel contains a distantly related example in silver (Henkel 1913, no. 363). The most likely date range is 2nd–3rd century.

From unit 278, cut 2, gully 64, a possible grave, dated late 3rd–4th century AD.

4 Bronze ring   Internal diameter *c*. 18 mm   ST 80 BF, SF 12

Rather over half of a simple, well-made, circular ring. The internal face is very lightly convex, the outer face more markedly so, and the sides flattened. These features and the size make it very probable that this was a simple, plain finger ring. Cf. Henkel 1913, nos 485, 498.

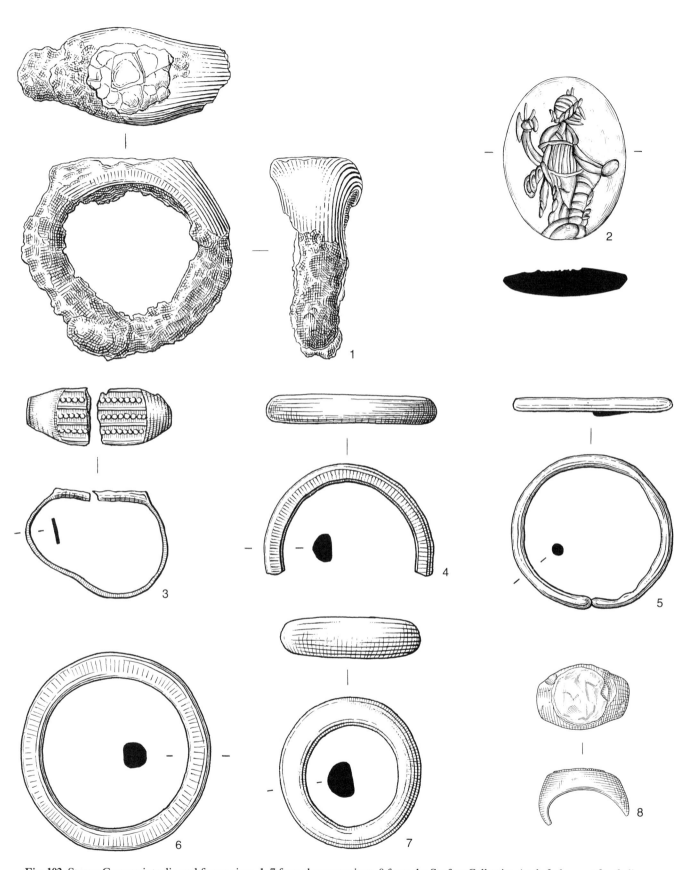

Fig. 102 Stonea Grange: intaglio and finger-rings, 1–7 from the excavations, 8 from the Surface Collection (scale 2 : 1 except 2 = 3 : 1).

From robbing debris in footing trench (unit 29), building R1, east wing, south side. 3rd or 4th century AD.

5 Silver ring   Internal width *c*. 18.5 mm ST 82 BAL, SF 307

A near-circular ring made from a plain, circular-sectioned wire, the rounded ends neatly butted. Cf. Henkel 1913, no. 315.

From unit 716 in fill of sinkage cone into top of fill of well 808. 5th–8th century AD.

6 Bronze ring
Internal diameter *c*. 20 mm ST 83 CCV, SF 465

A neatly-made circular ring of plump D-shaped cross-section.

From ditch 9, cut 2, top layer (unit 1067). 3rd–7th century AD.

7 Bronze ring   Internal diameter *c*. 13 mm ST 81 KS, SF 128

A small, heavy, slightly asymmetric, plain cast ring. The internal face is very lightly convex, the hoop of plump D-shaped cross-section.

From occupation layer (unit 224) in region of ovens 1 and 2. 3rd or 4th century AD.

B STONEA GRANGE SURFACE COLLECTION   (Figs 102–5)

8 Bronze ring, fragment with glass setting
Length 13 mm P1982, 6–2, 29

The circular bezel and part of the shoulders of a small ring set with plain glass. The shoulders have been bent inwards slightly, and the glass is cracked and damaged. The colour of the glass is mainly the standard light green, but there are patches of dark blue; these could, perhaps, be the result of corrosion of the underlying bronze.

The simple form is a variant of Henig II, and is probably to be dated to the 2nd century AD.

9 Bronze ring with enamel
Internal diameter 19 mm P1982, 6–2, 25

A simple circular ring in very good condition, expanding smoothly towards a circular bezel with raised concentric ring of bronze, the centre and border filled with enamel. The colour of the enamel has been lost by decomposition; probably both centre and outer circle were red, but there could have been two colours. Enamelled rings are not uncommon in the northern provinces. Those illustrated by Henkel (nos 1085–7) have more elaborate decoration, but Bushe-Fox 1949, nos 103–4 have concentric patterns, as do some examples from Colchester (Crummy 1983, Fig. 50). These are of different forms, however. The form of our ring suggests a 2nd century AD date.

10 Bronze ring with decorated bezel
Internal diameter 16 mm P1982, 6–2, 33

A small and very slender ring of circular shape, expanding towards the bezel which bears a raised lozenge-shaped panel with a beaded surface. This granulated appearance is now marred by corrosion.

The type can be closely paralleled in the Rhineland (see Henkel 877–81), while more robust examples, with applied 'granulated' panels are also known (Henkel 874–6). There are comparable pieces at Richborough (Bushe-Fox 1949, Pl. XXXV, 100), Carlisle (Padley 1991, 108, Fig. 69, 28), and, in France, at the Sources de Seine (Guiraud 1989, Fig. 55, 4). The type evidently does not occur in silver.

2nd–3rd century AD.

11 Bronze ring   Internal width 18 mm P1982, 6–2, 27

A Henig type II ring (back of hoop lost) with somewhat flattened shoulders and overall rather flimsy construction. The setting is lost, but traces of material, possibly adhesive, remain in the cell.

2nd–3rd century AD.

12 Silver ring, fragment   Length 18 mm P1982, 6–2, 24

The metal is a debased silver alloy with copper. The shoulder and the edge of the gem cell from a fairly developed Henig II/III. The setting contains a fairly thick (1 mm) layer of a gritty orange material, probably adhesive.

2nd–3rd century AD.

13 Bronze ring, fragment   Length 21 mm P1985, 10–3, 3

Bezel of a plain Henig type II or III ring, the gem lost.

2nd–3rd century AD.

14 Bronze ring with engraved nicolo
Internal width *c*. 16 mm P1982, 6–2, 26

The broad hoop, 13 mm wide at the bezel, is broken and disorted. It narrows towards the back, and is decorated with a pattern of punched lines and dots. The stone, which is dark blue with a lighter blue surface layer, is flat with bevelled edges, and is set almost flush with the surface of the hoop. It is very worn. The device engraved upon it is a small and stylised figure of Bonus Eventus.

The form of the ring is superficially similar to the standard Henig type II ring, but with its ribbon-like hoop and surface decoration it nevertheless belongs to a separate type. Henkel classifies it under 3rd-century forms; his no. 1240, from Heiligkreuz, is a close parallel and is set with a stone engraved with a seated Mercury. This, in turn, is almost identical with an unpublished ring from Colchester (BM, PRB, 1870, 4–2, 78). No parallels have been noted in silver.

Bonus Eventus is a frequent subject on Romano-British gems, e.g. Henig 1978, nos 190–202. It is the most common device in the series of engraved carnelians from the Snettisham Roman jeweller's hoard (Johns, forthcoming).

Late 2nd–3rd century AD.

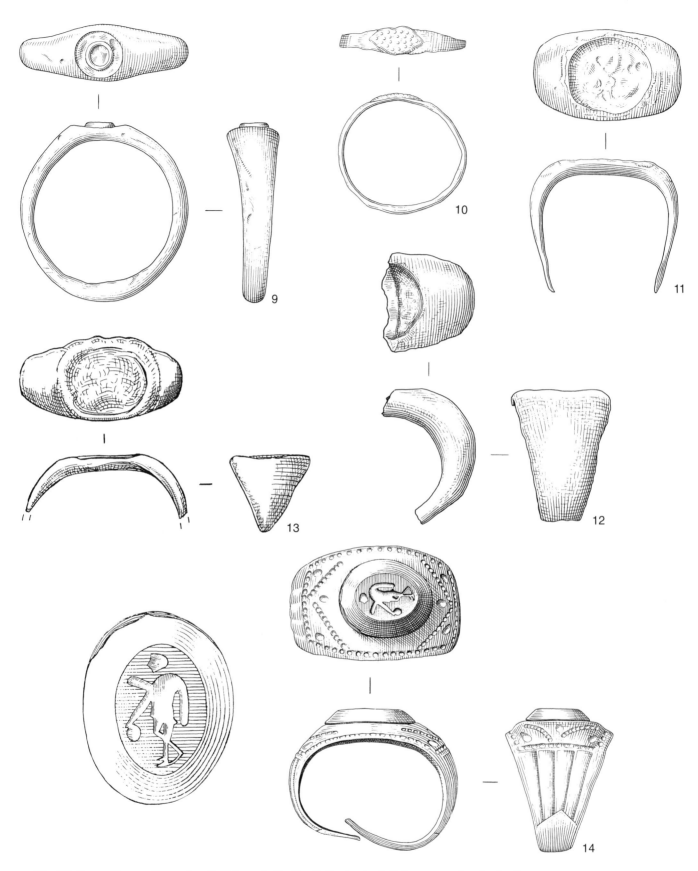

Fig. 103 Stonea Grange: finger-rings 9–14 from the Surface Collection (scale 2 : 1 except setting detail of 14 = 4 : 1).

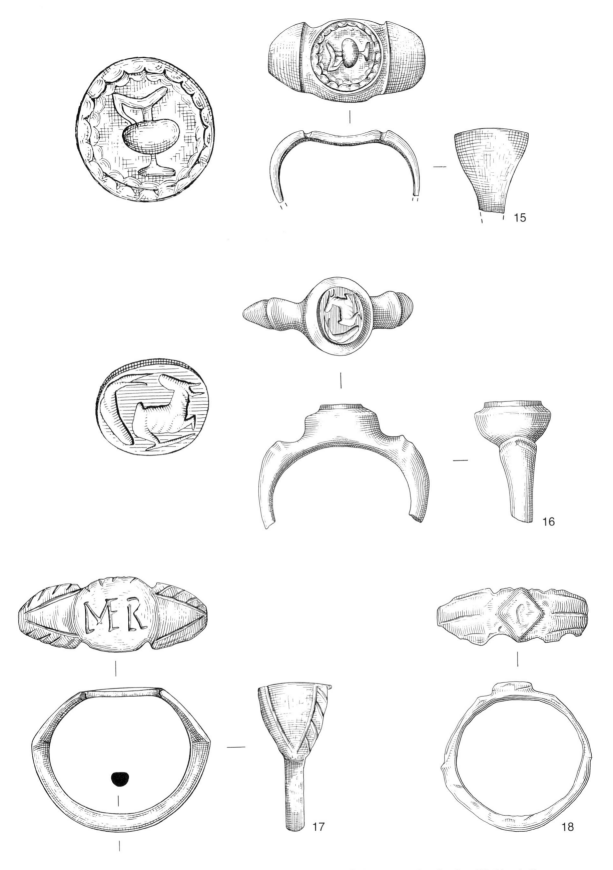

Fig. 104 Stonea Grange: finger-rings 15–18 from the Surface Collection (scale 2 : 1 except setting details of 15–16 = 4 : 1).

15 Bronze ring with relief-decorated bezel
Internal width 19 mm P1982, 6–2, 28

The ring has lost the back of the hoop. It is of light construction, with plain tapering shoulders, somewhat flattened. The internal border of the setting (not a separate collet) has a pie-crust edge and retains what may be a small separate bronze disc with a representation in relief, probably cast rather than repoussé, of a single-handled pedestalled beaked flagon or ewer within a beaded border.

The significance of a wine cantharus would clearly be Bacchic, but this ewer is more likely to be a sacrificial/funerary motif. A very fine early gem from Silchester (Henig 1978, no. 410) is a clear illustration of a sacrificial ewer, but has little in common with our somewhat crude rendering.

The use of metal settings ornamented in relief is most common in the late Empire, but the form of this ring suggests a late 2nd–3rd century AD date.

16 Silver ring with engraved carnelian
Internal width c. 17 mm P1982, 6–2, 22

The silver hoop, of which the back portion is lost, is slender and the slightly raised, transversely set oval bezel is flanked by 'hunched' shoulders of a distinctive type. They are hollowed next to the bezel, and then rise to form marked swellings before tapering into the hoop. The type is 3d in Guiraud's classification (Guiraud 1989). The carnelian setting has a flat surface, and the engraved device is of an animal, probably a goat, lying beside a tree.

The form is characteristic of the 3rd century AD. Henkel 1913, nos 1254 and 1258 provide parallels in bronze, and two silver examples from Britain are catalogued in Johns 1991, nos 19 and 20. The scene on the gem recalls two other examples from Britain, Henig 1978, nos 616 and 617, from York and Coleman Street, London, respectively. Though both are described as stags rather than goats, they are essentially the same scene.

17 Bronze ring with inscribed bezel
Internal width 19 mm P1982, 6–2, 36

The ring has a narrow square-sectioned hoop and triangular shoulders set at a marked angle. The bezel is roughly circular. The shoulders have an incised border of a line and a series of diagonals. On the bezel, MER is engraved in clear capitals (ME ligatured).

The form is a standard 3rd century AD one (a version of Henig VIII or Guiraud 3). Personal names sometimes occur on rings, but the names of deities are also recorded, and though they might in some cases have been intended as votives, they must surely have normally simply been protective and apotropaic in exactly the same way as the visual image of a god engraved on a gem. In this case, the abbreviation MER is certainly for Mercury. His name on rings occurs in the Rhineland (Henkel 374, 383, 394). In Britain, the enigmatic TOT rings are now plausibly interpreted as bearing an abbreviation of the Celtic god-name Toutatis (see M. Henig and J. Ogden, *Antiq. J.* 67 (1987), p. 366, on a silver TOT ring from Lincoln). Another silver TOT ring in the BM collections (P1988, 11–1, 1) is of similar form to the Stonea MER ring, though a little more decorative.

3rd century AD.

18 Bronze ring with raised bezel
Internal width 17 mm P1982, 6–2, 35

A small ring with a slender hoop and angled, narrow triangular shoulders bearing three deep grooves. The bezel is formed of a cast raised square set diagonally. It bears an amorphous motif in intaglio. For similar rings, typically 3rd century in their overall form, cf. Henkel 934 and 935 (but both have circular bezels).

19 Bronze ring with raised engraved bezel
Internal width 16 mm P1982, 6–2, 34

The form is Henig VIII, with angled shoulders and raised oval bezel. The shoulders are outlined with a shallow groove, and the bezel bears two fairly deeply cut curved lines, possibly SC, though it is not certain that they are letters.

3rd century AD

20 Bronze ring, fragment with glass setting
Length 13 mm P1982, 6–2, 30

The oval bezel survives, together with one small shoulder, a simple variant of the 'hunched' type, Henig Xb, Guiraud 3c. The setting is a domed oval light green glass with a longitudinal central groove. The 'coffee bean' form of the gem is evidently the same as that found in some military bronze fittings (cf. Oldensein 1976, Taf. 34, 267–72), and it is plausibly interpreted as a stylised rendering of the female genitals, in which case an apotropaic function is to be inferred, as in the case of phallic ornament.

3rd century AD.

21 Silver ring, fragment   Length 13 mm P1982, 6–2, 23

The bezel and shoulders of a small ring of 3rd century form (Henig VIII) with angled shoulders. The bezel is circular and undecorated. Henkel 388–9 are comparable.

3rd century AD.

22 Silver ring with decorated shoulders
Internal width 20 mm P1982, 6–2, 21

The ring has a square-sectioned hoop with triangular shoulders set at an angle and a large, flat rectangular bezel area measuring 19 × 13 mm which bears traces of solder. The shoulders have grooved and punched decoration whcih is very difficult to make out owing to wear and corrosion, but which is almost certainly based on stylised foliate patterns. The solder remnants on the bezel cover a circular area 11 mm in diameter. A raised box-bezel may originally have been attached or more probably, a metal plaque with decorated surface.

Rings of this type are of 3rd–4th century AD date. Parallels include three examples, all in silver, in the British Museum collections from Britain: one from Water Newton, Cambs (reg. no. 1882, 6–21, 116), which has no context; one from Grovely Wood, Wilts (1911, 10–26, 3), found with other rings, and possibly

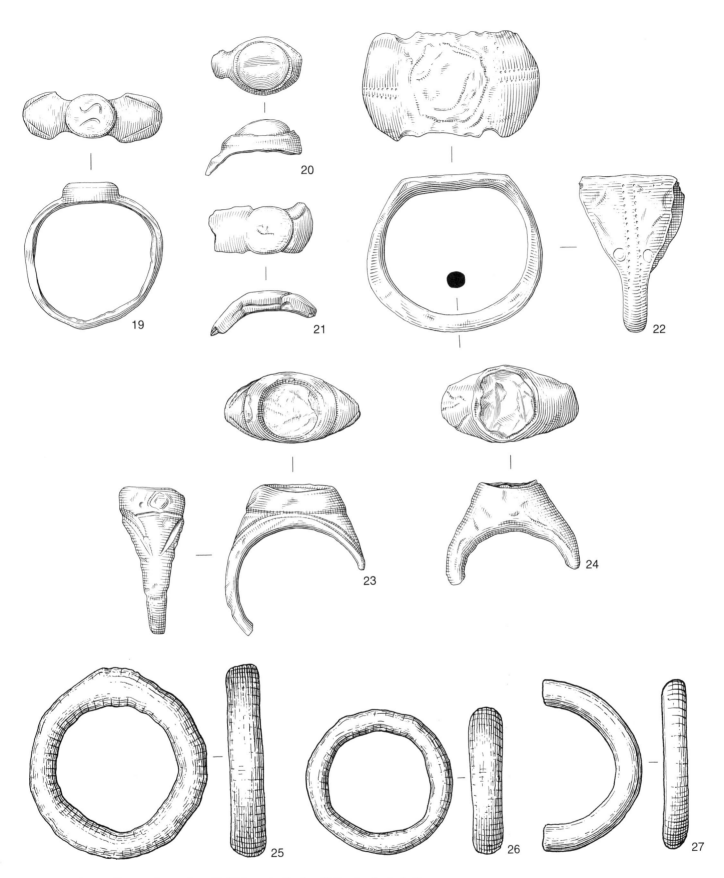

Fig. 105 Stonea Grange: finger-rings 19–27 from the Surface Collection (scale 2 : 1).

associated with one of two coin hoards of respectively early 4th century and late 4th century date; and one from Willersey, Glos. (P1969, 4–1, 1), associated with a hoard of siliquae deposited *c.* AD 363; see Carson 1971, 203.

3rd–early 4th century AD.

23 Bronze ring with glass setting
Internal diameter 16 mm P1982, 6–2, 32

The ring has lost about half of its slender hoop. The internal form is circular and the bezel tapers upward smoothly to a raised circular setting. A smoothly profiled groove surrounds the base of the setting and borders the shoulders. The bezel is set with plain, almost clear glass, now considerably damaged.

At first sight the form is reminiscent of the classic late Hellenistic Henig I, though there is a far greater taper towards the bezel: Guiraud form 1b is fairly close, but it is also linked with the early forms. It is possible to see some connection with the variants of Guiraud's form 4, in which the characteristic feature is that the bezel rises above the main line of the hoop. The mouldings around the shoulders and the bezel, breaking up the smooth line, distinguish our piece from the Republican type, but do not enable us to suggest a date with any confidence.

24 Bronze ring, fragment with glass setting
Internal width (incomplete) 15 mm P1982, 6–2, 31

The bezel and shoulders of another ring of the same type as no. 23. The grooves and mouldings appear to be absent, but the setting is also a plain glass gem, in this case a bright blue glass.

25 Bronze ring   Internal diameter 16 mm P1982, 6–2, 128

A small cast ring of rounded octagonal cross-section, with a small raised oval bezel.

26 Bronze ring   Internal diameter 14 mm P1982, 6–2, 129

A small, rather roughly-made ring of D-shaped cross-section. Possibly a finger-ring.

27 Bronze ring   Internal diameter 15 mm P1982, 6–2, 130

Half of a simple ring of rounded square cross-section.

BRACELETS

Catherine Johns   (Figs 106–7)

SNAKE JEWELLERY

Bracelets and rings in the form of snakes became very popular in the Hellenistic period, and continued to be a familiar type in Roman jewellery. The physical form of a snake lends itself well to the design of bracelets and finger-rings, and some of the popularity of such jewellery must have been due to the attractive appearance of the objects. However, snakes were regarded as beneficent creatures in Graeco-Roman mythology and symbolism, and this would have been the principal reason for the wearing of serpentiform ornaments. The snake was the companion of Asclepius, god of healing and medicine, and was connected with rebirth and regeneration. It also had chthonic connections, and could represent the spirits of the departed.

The species represented in jewellery of this kind is the Asclepian snake (*Elaphe longissima*), a large but non-venomous reptile which belongs to one of the most widespread families of snakes. The distinctive symmetrical pattern of scales on the head of the creature is carefully depicted in the most realistic jewellery, and becomes more and more simplified and stylised in later provincial products. There is a basic typological distinction (with separate histories) between the bracelets and rings which consist of a single snake with its head at one end and the slender pointed tail at the other, and those which are furnished with two snake-head terminals. In general, the former type often occurs in high-quality gold jewellery and is inclined to have quite realistic modelling, while the latter type becomes frequent in base metals and in very devolved stylised versions where the terminals are no longer immediately recognisable as snake-heads.

The snake bracelets from Stonea are all fragmentary, but there is no doubt that all are of the penannular two-headed type. The silver example retains some degree of realism, but the others are highly stylised and belong to a type which appears to have been common in Roman Britain. The finest and best-known British examples are a silver pair from Castlethorpe, Bucks (Marshall 1911, 2782–3), and five silver specimens are present in the Snettisham Roman jeweller's hoard found in 1985 and dated by coins to the middle of the second century AD. The stylised modelling of the snake's head, with the pattern of large scales, is generally rendered in low relief by casting, though some are simply engraved. There is often a flat border around the head which bears some additional punched or incised ornament, and in many of the finer examples, the animal's eyes are indicated, even though the head is almost two dimensional. The flattened hoop is sometimes decorated in a pattern which is intended to evoke the idea of scales, such as an incised lattice or a series of punched lines or curves, but other examples have geometric or scroll ornament which is quite unrelated to the concept of scaly reptile skin.

Simple base-metal snake bracelets were probably in use from the late first century to the fourth, and it is therefore impossible to assign close dates to the Stonea examples. A general Middle Empire period, second–third century, would probably cover all of them.

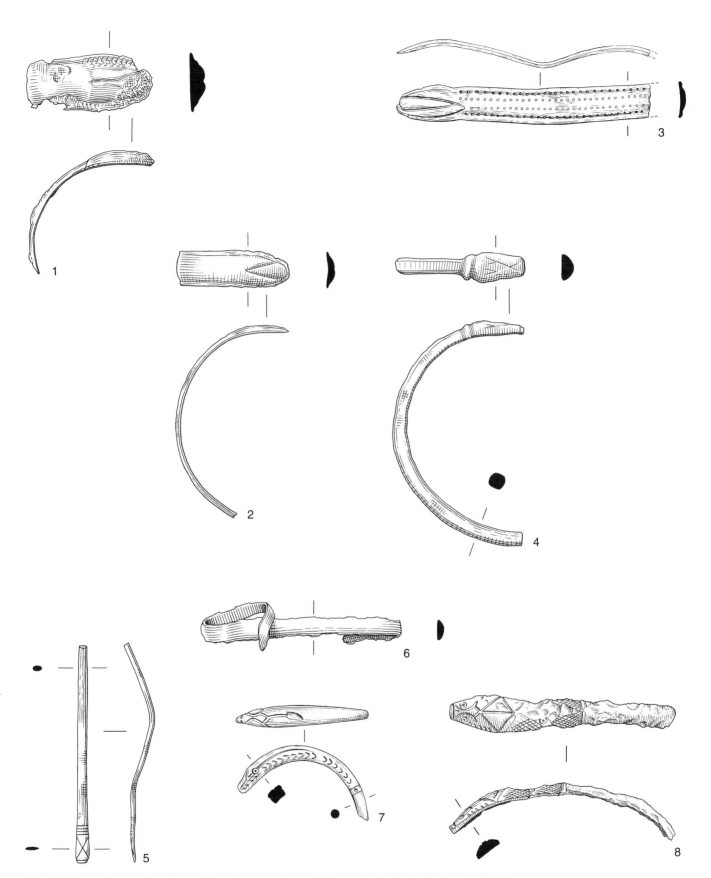

Fig. 106 Stonea Grange: bracelets 1–6 from the excavations, 7–8 from the Surface Collection (scale 1 : 1).

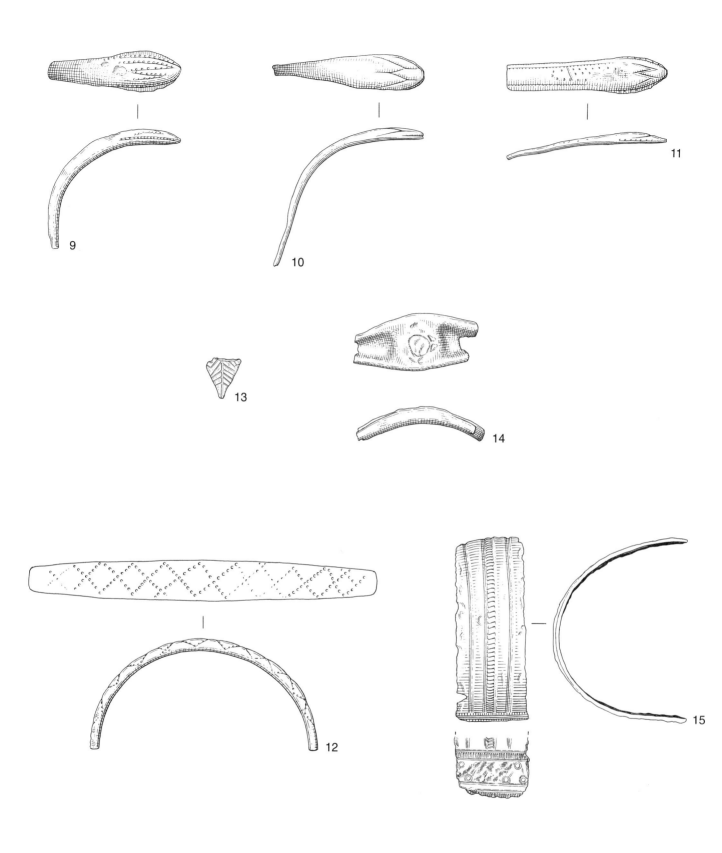

Fig. 107 Stonea Grange and Stonea Camp: bracelets from the Surface Collections (scale 1:1).

A BRACELETS FROM THE EXCAVATIONS   (Fig. 106)

1 Bronze penannular snake bracelet

Length 43 mm ST 81 FK, SF 40

One terminal and part of the hoop of a wide, flat snake bracelet. Patches of corrosion obscure some of the details of the head and the edges of the hoop are damaged, but the piece was originally a well-finished one. The stylised scales on the head are cast, and there is a plain raised border on each side of the hoop. Around the head is a border with fine diagonal punched lines. The hoop appears to be undecorated.

Found in a broken shell-gritted jar (FK) of ?mid/late 2nd century AD date, within the silty clay spread (unit 134) at the north-west of block 1.

2 Bronze penannular snake bracelet

Diameter c. 50 mm ST 81 NR, SF 188

A little less than half the bracelet survives. The hoop is plain, of low plano-convex cross-section with a neatly-channeled rim. The remaining terminal is only slightly wider than the hoop. The snake head is very devolved. The missing terminal would have been of the same form.

From grey silt spread (unit 292), north-west corner of block 1. 3rd century AD.

3 Bronze penannular snake bracelet

Length 69 mm ST 84 DBM, SF 829

A parallel-sided strip, of low plano-convex cross-section, with a neatly-channeled rim. The remaining terminal, hardly wider than the hoop, is a very stylised snake head.

In its dimensions and devolved form, this bracelet is similar to no. 2. However, unlike no. 2, the hoop has four lines of dot-punching to render the stylised snake skin.

From top layer (unit 1536) in latrine pit 1536. Early 3rd century AD.

4 Bronze penannular snake bracelet

Internal diameter c. 52 mm ST 81 HT, SF 86

About half of an ovoid penannular bracelet. The slender rod-like hoop has a lightly convex inner face and a faceted exterior, obscured by corrosion. Corrosion also obscures the detailed surface treatment of the surviving terminal. What remains is a stylised snake's head divided from the hoop by a ruff-like moulding. There are traces of criss-cross engraving on the head and a single engraved line emphasises the lightly arched blunt muzzle. The missing terminal would have been of the same form.

From gully 44, cut 2, top layer (unit 179). 3rd century AD.

5 Bronze bracelet   Length 57 mm ST 81 NC, SF 180

A distorted hoop fragment from an armlet of very slender oval cross-section. The hoop is plain. The surviving terminal is slightly expanded and flattened with incised decoration in the form of an elongated cross in a panel set between transverse grooves. Cf. e.g. Crummy 1983, Fig. 44, 1684, from the Butt Road site, Colchester.

From lower layer (unit 279), south-west quadrant of the low rubbly mound sealing building S1. 9th–10th century AD.

6 Bronze bracelet

Original length of strip 115 mm ST 82 BCZ, SF 320

A small, very distorted example, made from a plain strip of flat plano-convex cross-section, which tapers both ways to form two slender round-ended terminals. If the terminals originally butted, or nearly so, and the bracelet was of oval form, its dimensions would have been c. 40 × 30 mm.

From post-hole 777 of building S3. Phase V.

B BRACELETS FROM STONEA GRANGE SURFACE COLLECTION   (Figs 106–7)

7 Silver penannular snake bracelet

Length 37 mm P1982, 6–2, 104

One terminal and part of the hoop of a small silver snake bracelet. The terminal is cast as a three-dimensional head, complete with round eyes, and a very simple version of the standard stylised pattern on the skull. Punched crescents along the sides of the body are intended to suggest scales. Though much stylised and simplified, this is a more realistic representation than the very devolved flat snake heads which are so common in Romano-British jewellery.

8 Bronze penannular snake bracelet

Length 62 mm P1982, 6–2, 105

The bronze has a tin-rich surface which gives the impression of silver. The cross-section is a shallow triangle, giving a ridge or keel along the back of the snake, and the surviving stylised head is rendered with deeply engraved, not cast, details. Scales on the head and eyes are crudely indicated, and a lattice pattern and other engraved and punched ornament decorates the hoop.

Examination and analysis by N. Meeks (British Museum Research Laboratory, File no. 5297) demonstrated that the silver-coloured surface layer was attributable to tin sweat. That it was intentionally created seems possible, for, as Meeks comments: 'It has the desirable effect of producing a finished object with a durable silvery surface which does not require further tinning or silvering. The likeness to silver on a newly made object is deceptive.' On the subject of tin sweat, see Meeks 1993.

9 Bronze penannular snake bracelet

Length 46 mm P1982, 6–2, 107

Terminal and part of the hoop of a fairly solid and robust bracelet. The hoop is undecorated, and the simple cast mouldings of the head are emphasised by lines of punched dot ornament. There is a narrow flat border around the head.

10 Bronze penannular snake bracelet

Length 54 mm P1982, 6–2, 106

A simplified bracelet of slight construction: the hoop tapers to a width of only 3.5 mm. The snake head has simple cast mouldings without additional ornament, and there is no decoration on the hoop.

11 Bronze penannular snake bracelet

Length 43 mm P1982, 6–2, 108

This example has a flat ribbon-like hoop and simple head mouldings. The terminal has a narrow border ornamented with punched dots, and there are small crescentic punchmarks on the hoop between two lines of tiny dots.

12 Bronze penannular bracelet

Length 62 mm, max. width 9 mm P1982, 6–2, 109

About half of the hoop, both terminals lost. This is almost certainly a snake bracelet. The hoop is decorated with a continuous pattern of lozenges punched in dotted lines. The bracelet narrows towards the terminals.

13 Silver ?snake bracelet fragment

Length 11 mm P1982, 6–2, 111

A tiny broken terminal of silver. The tapered shape and engraved veined decoration are reminiscent of the terminals of devolved snake bracelets, but the piece is too small for certainty.

14 Bronze ?bracelet fragment

Length 34 mm, width 15 mm P1982, 6–2, 110

This object is of uncertain function, but a bracelet is a possible interpretation. If so, the form is analogous to a finger-ring, with a decorated feature at the broadest point of the hoop. There is a circular setting which apparently contains red enamel, possibly surrounded by a border of triangles, though it is difficult to establish whether these are intentional or the result of surface corrosion and damage.

C BRACELET FROM STONEA CAMP SURFACE COLLECTION (Fig. 107)

15 Bronze bracelet   Width 49 mm P1981, 5–3, 11

Rather over half of an ovoid penannular bracelet made from a flat parallel-sided sheet, 20 mm in width, with a finely-engraved design comprising grooves and hollowed channelling symmetrically flanking a central slender rope-like motif. One terminal survives with its decoration in a rectangular plate with milled edging set at right angles to the decorative scheme of the hoop. Though badly corroded the interior design appears to consist of a repeating tendril-like motif.

A 1st century type, cf. e.g. Colchester (Hawkes and Hull 1947, 333, Pl. C, no. 29), from a context dated *c.* AD 50–60; and Verulamium (Frere 1972, 119–20, Fig. 32, nos 30–1), from contexts dated AD 75–85 and AD 85–105.

GOLD LINKS

Catherine Johns (Pl. XXVa)

1 A rectangular openwork link. The rectangle incorporates a loop at each end, and is divided longitudinally by a straight bar. Each side is filled with an S-shaped wire volute, symmetrically disposed. The whole element is formed of the same rectangular-sectioned wire. Each end-loop carries a broken link of circular-sectioned wire, one being of noticeably thinner gauge than the other.

Overall length	30 mm
Length of link	19 mm
Breadth	10 mm
Weight	1.25 g

Metal composition (semi-quantitative XRF analysis): gold 89.7%; silver 8.7%; copper 1.6%.

Metal detector find from a field east of Stonea Camp, close to the findspot of the gold votive plaque to Minerva (see p. 220). Acquired by the British Museum, reg. no. P1992, 7–1, 1.

2 An elliptical element with a loop at each end, a central bar, and the spaces occupied by two C-scrolls back to back. In design it is obviously closely related to no. 1, and it, too, is formed of rectangular-sectioned wire, though the wire is a little more slender.

Length	24 mm
Breadth	11 mm
Weight	0.65 g

Metal composition (semi-quantitative XRF analysis): gold 90.3%; silver 8.2%; copper 1.5%.

Metal detector find from the field east of the Stonea Grange excavations. Acquired by the British Museum, reg. no. P1992, 7–1, 2.

DISCUSSION

Both metal composition and design suggest that the two links are closely related. Initially thought to be earring fragments, the more likely interpretation is that they are two elements from the same necklace, or two necklaces of very similar type.

One of the classic Roman jewellery types is the necklace of glass or hardstone beads strung on slender gold wires alternating with openwork gold links. Marshall (1911) 2730 is an example of the general type with emeralds and knot-of-Hercules links; a simpler version of the same type has been found in London (Johns 1976).

Much closer to the Stonea gold elements are the links in an unprovenanced necklace in Berlin (Greifenhagen 1975, Band II, Taf. 31, 2); this piece has flattened discoidal beads of red-brown glass with rhomboidal openwork links containing C-scrolls which are very close indeed to our elliptical link, No. 2. The clasp of the Berlin necklace is lost, so it is impossible to say whether the fastener might have incorporated a link of different shape.

Another similar necklace is recorded from Su Pidaccio, near Sassari in Sardinia (Pfeiler 1970, 66–7 and Taf. 13.). Pfeiler (Deppert-Lippitz) dates the type first to mid third century, and refers to two Romano-Egyptian mummy portraits of early Trajanic date which depict the type in wear.

A date some time in the second century AD is likely for these two small fragments from what was originally a high-quality piece of Roman jewellery.

Acknowledgement

We are grateful to David Gurney (Norfolk Landscape Archaeology), who alerted us to these discoveries and provided information.

OTHER COPPER-ALLOY OBJECTS

Ralph Jackson   (Figs 108–16; Pl. XXVb)

A FROM THE EXCAVATIONS   (Figs 108–12)

1 Hairpin   Length 65 mm ST 81 HZ, SF 89

A small, slender simple pin with a pear-shaped globular head.

Cf. Cool 1990a, Group 1.

From unit 184 of the low rubbly mound sealing building S1. 9th–10th century AD.

2 Hairpin   Length 64 mm ST 83 CIV, SF 491

A finely-made pin with spherical head. The circular-sectioned stem has a slight swelling just below its mid-point. The lower stem is bent and the pin tip is broken.

Cool 1990a, Group 2A, 1st–4th century AD.

From cleaning over building S1.

3 Hairpin   Length 60 mm ST 84 DDE, SF 796

An elegant example with slender, lightly tapered, circular-sectioned stem, the lower part broken. The head has a small moulded vase-shaped finial.

Cool 1990a, Group 3, 1st–3rd century AD. For a near-identical example from Tokenhouse Yard, London, see Wheeler 1930, 103, Pl. XLI, 4.

From top layer (unit 1577) of pit 1577. Late 2nd or 3rd century AD.

4 Hairpin   Length 59 mm ST 84 DBI, SF 627

A well-made pin with tapered, circular-sectioned stem, which is bent and broken. The head is broken at the neck above a pair of disc-mouldings.

Probably Cool 1990a, Group 3, 1st–3rd century AD.

From post-medieval disturbed layer (1533) in ditch 7, cut 1. Late 2nd/early 3rd century AD.

5 Hairpin   Length 128 mm ST 83 J4,5, SF 603

A well-made, but poorly preserved example with strongly tapered, circular-sectioned stem, blunt-pointed tip, and moulded head. The head is eroded and minus its finial. What remains are two crisply-cut disc mouldings surmounted by a drum-shaped moulding.

Probably Cool 1990a, Group 3, 1st–3rd century AD.

From well J4, layer 5. Late 3rd/early 4th century AD.

6 Hairpin   Length 120 mm ST 82 AAD, SF 245

A slender, circular-sectioned, tapered rod with a blunt point and a small, elegant, baluster-moulded head. The stem is now bent almost through a right angle.

Cool 1990a, Group 3, 1st–3rd century AD. Cf. Wheeler 1930, Pl. XLI, 4 from Tokenhouse Yard, London; Crummy 1983, Fig. 31, 511, from the Butt Road site, Colchester; Ruprechtsberger 1978, no. 370, from Lauriacum; and Bushe-Fox 1949, Pl. LIII, 198, from Richborough.

From contaminated spread (unit 445) east of building R1, east wing.

7 Pin   Length 32 mm ST 84 DWY, SF 1044

The head is large and rather more than a hemisphere. The stem is of rounded rectangular cross-section, tapered and broken.

Probably a Cool 1990a, Group 1 hairpin. Cf. Allason-Jones and Miket 1984, 3.517, from South Shields; and Down 1989, 218–9, Fig. 29.1, no. 10 from Chichester.

From top layer (unit 2003) of pit 2003. Late 2nd/3rd century AD.

8 Pin   (*Unillus.*) Length 99 mm ST 82 AAV, SF 326

A slender, circular-sectioned, tapered pin with a simple head. The shank is bent and broken and the end is missing.

From black soil spread (unit 461), south of building R1. 3rd century AD.

9 Pin   (*Unillus.*) Length 39 mm ST 81 GT, SF 57

A small, slender, circular-sectioned pin, the tapered tip virtually complete. The shank is broken at the head, the form of which is unclear. Immediately beneath are four lightly-incised girth rings.

From upper layer (unit 156) of well 135. 4th–7th century AD.

10 Pin   (*Unillus.*) Length c. 85 mm ST 82 ABQ, SF 269

A distorted slender pin in two pieces. One end is broken, the other ends in a coiled terminal.

From topsoil/cleaning (unit 481), blocks 2–4.

11 Pin/tack   (*Unillus.*) Length 22 mm ST 83 J4,1, SF 542

A small pin with a globular head. The tip of the diamond-sectioned stem is broken.

From top layer of well J4. Late 3rd/early 4th century AD.

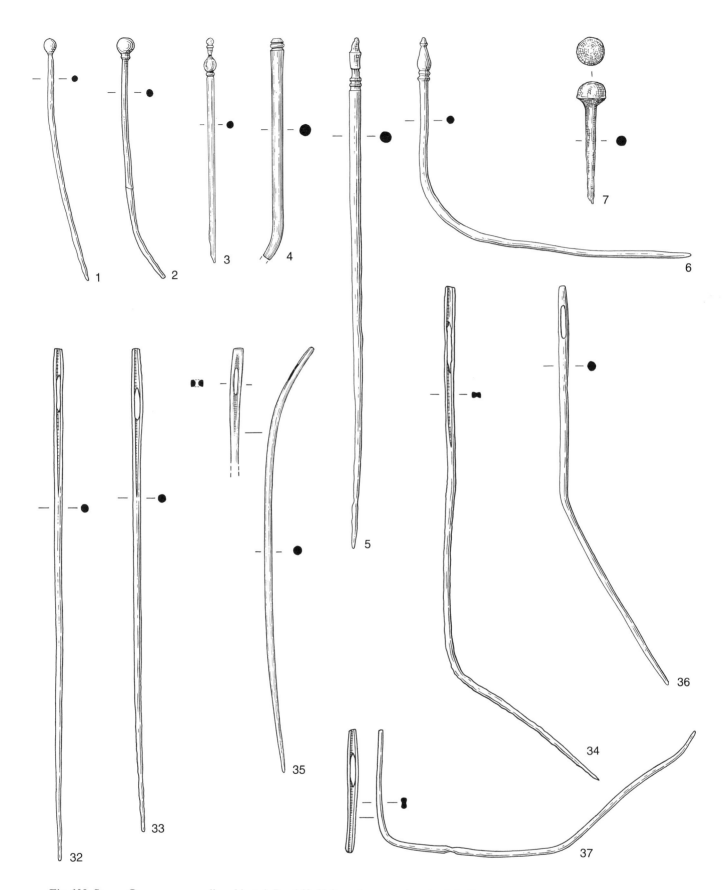

Fig. 108 Stonea Grange: copper-alloy objects 1–7 and 32–37 from the excavations (scale 1 : 1).

12 Pin/ligula (*Unillus.*) Length 80 mm ST 83 CCL, SF 479

Fragment. The pointed tip is complete, the thicker end broken. Probably the lower shank of a needle, pin or ligula.

From ditch 9, cut 2, unit 1058. 3rd century AD.

13 Pin/ligula (*Unillus.*) Length 68 mm ST 83 H8,3, SF 632

Fragment, as no. 12.

From layer 3 in large pit or ditch, H8. Late 3rd–4th century AD.

14 Pin/ligula (*Unillus.*) Length 62 mm ST 83 G7,1, SF 552

Fragment, as no. 12.

From ditch 15, cut 3, unit G7, layer 1. Early/mid 3rd century AD.

15 Pin/ligula (*Unillus.*) Length 65 mm ST 84 DEA, SF 740

Fragment, as no. 12.

From topsoil/cleaning (unit 1597), blocks 8 and 9 and east part blocks 3 and 4.

16 Pin/ligula (*Unillus.*) Length 58 mm ST 82 AAX, SF 365

Fragment, as no. 12.

From gully 42, cut 2, unit 463. Late 2nd/early 3rd century AD.

17 Pin/ligula (*Unillus.*) Length 50 mm ST 84 DGZ, SF 817

Fragment, as no. 12, with re-sharpened tip.

From layer 1668 above the pit cluster 1834 etc., west of centre block 9. Mid/late 3rd century AD.

18 Pin/ligula (*Unillus.*) Length 48 mm ST 83 CCV, SF 519

Fragment, as no. 12.

From ditch 9, cut 2, unit 1067. 3rd century AD.

19 Pin/ligula (*Unillus.*) Length 48 mm ST 84 DRN, SF 911

Fragment, as no. 12.

From basal layer (unit 1897) in well 1834. 3rd century AD.

20 Pin/ligula (*Unillus.*) Length 87 mm ST 84 DIF, SF 878

Fragment, as no. 12, broken at both ends.

From top layer (unit 1698) of pit 1698. 3rd or 4th century AD.

21 Pin/ligula (*Unillus.*) Length 74 mm ST 81 NK, SF 178

Fragment, as no. 20.

From degraded mortar floor (unit 286) of building R2. 3rd century AD.

22 Pin/ligula (*Unillus.*) Length 58 mm ST 84 DPX, SF 1037

Fragment, as no. 20.

From layer 1858 in pit 1695. Later 2nd/3rd century AD.

23 Pin/ligula (*Unillus.*) Length 48 mm ST 82 ABD, SF 364

Fragment, as no. 20.

From dark soil and ragstone spread (unit 469) in the region of building R3. Late 2nd century AD.

24 Pin/ligula (*Unillus.*) Length *c.* 45 mm ST 82 AHG, SF 414

Fragment, as no. 20.

From clay and ragstone spread (unit 616) south of building R1.

25 Pin/ligula (*Unillus.*) Length 41 mm ST 81 PV, SF 236

Fragment, as no. 20.

From occupation debris (unit 318) at south-west of the low rubbly mound sealing Anglo-Saxon building S1. 4th–7th century AD.

26 Pin/ligula (*Unillus.*) Length 38 mm ST 84 DBI, SF 701

Fragment, as no. 20.

Context as no. 4.

27 Pin/ligula (*Unillus.*) Length 33 mm ST 83 CAA, SF 472

Fragment, as no. 20.

From topsoil/cleaning (unit 1000), east end of block 11.

28 Pin/ligula (*Unillus.*) Length 31 mm ST 82 BAR, SF 315

Fragment, as no. 20.

From part of fill (unit 722) of sinkage cone into fill of well 905. 5th–8th century AD.

29 Pin/ligula (*Unillus.*) Length 29 mm ST 84 DPN, SF 872

Fragment, as no. 20.

From an upper layer (unit 1849) in well 1669. Mid/late 3rd century AD.

30 Pin/ligula (*Unillus.*) Length 27 mm ST 84 DBV, SF 709

Fragment as no. 20.

From ditch 15, cut 13, unit 1544. Early/mid 3rd century AD.

31 Pin/ligula (*Unillus.*) Length 17 mm ST 82 BHP, SF 383

Fragment, as no. 20.

From layer 889 in pit 483/918. Mid/late 3rd century AD.

32 Needle   Length 134 mm ST 83 CNC, SF 562

A complete example of normal form, in good condition. The slightly flattened head has a squared end and encloses a large slot-like eye countersunk on both faces in a grooved recess.

From a spit through gravels and silts (unit 1290), south side of street 1 E/W to the south-west of building S2.

33 Needle   Length 127 mm ST 83 H8, 1, SF 596

As no. 32.

From layer 1 in large pit or ditch, H8. 3rd/4th century AD.

34 Needle   Length 153 mm ST 83A, 26, 6, SF 1983A, 1

As no. 32, but bent.

From the north sump, layer A, 26, grid 6. Late 2nd–4th century AD.

35 Needle   Length 111 mm ST 81 LQ, SF 142

As no. 32, but bent.

From the denuded surface of street 1 E/W to the east of building S1. 5th–8th century AD.

36 Needle   Length 113 mm ST 82 BIP, SF 359

As no. 32, but bent.

From ditch 9, cut 3, unit 913. Late 2nd/early 3rd century AD.

37 Needle   Length 129 mm ST 83 CHR, SF 488

As no. 32, but bent.

From top layer (unit 1184) of pit 1184. Early 3rd century AD.

38 Needle   (*Unillus.*) Length 96 mm ST 82 ACV, SF 331

As no. 32, but bent, and head part-broken.

From sinkage (unit 509) into ditch 74, cut 1. Late 3rd/4th century AD.

39 Needle   (*Unillus.*) Length 91 mm ST 81 KS, SF 106

As no. 38.

From silty layer (unit 224) in vicinity of ovens 1 and 2. 3rd or 4th century AD.

40 Needle   (*Unillus.*) Length 100 mm ST 84 DKO, SF 941

As no. 32, but head damaged and lower stem broken.

From gully 33, cut 5, unit 1730. Late 2nd/early 3rd century AD.

41 Needle   (*Unillus.*) Length 71 mm ST 84 DRN, SF 910

As no. 32, but bent, and lower stem broken.

From basal layer (unit 1897) of well 1834. 3rd century AD.

42 Needle   (*Unillus.*) Length 48 mm ST 84 DEA, SF 728

As no. 40.

Context as no. 15.

43 Needle   (*Unillus.*) Length 56 mm ST 84 DWB, SF 1038

As no. 40, in two joining fragments.

From the uppermost layer (unit 1982) of pit 1982. Late 2nd/3rd century AD.

44 Scoop probe   Length 108 mm ST 83 CCV, SF 473

Only the stub of the broken scoop survives, but sufficient to show that it had the normal shallow V-shaped cross-section. A small squat baluster and double ring moulding divide it from the slender, finely faceted, circular-sectioned stem, which tapers to a large, elongated olivary terminal. A common toilet/cosmetic implement used also in medical kits.

Context as no. 18.

45 Scoop probe   (*Unillus.*)
Length 37 mm ST 84 DSF, SF 947

Only the damaged scoop and part of the necked junction with the stem survives. The scoop is of normal elongated form with gently keeled base and rounded V-shaped cross-section. The slender neck is of rectangular cross-section. No mouldings survive.

From an upper layer (unit 1914) in well 1914. 3rd century AD.

46 Ligula   Length 119 mm ST 84 Q16, 2, SF 1102

A plain example in good condition, complete except for the very tip of the pointed end. The gently tapered, finely faceted, circular-sectioned stem is slightly bent near the centre. The oval, discoidal, angled plate is a little larger than normal.

From foundation of floor Q16, south-west of the temple (building R15). Phase III/IV.

47 Ligula   Length 111 mm ST 82 ABX, SF 267

A plain, simple example, of normal form, with slender, tapered, circular-sectioned stem, now bent in three places. The pointed end is complete, the angled plate partly broken.

From ditch 9, cut 11, unit 487. 3rd century AD.

48 Ligula   Length *c.* 98 mm ST 84 DBL, SF 713 and 714

A simple, plain example of normal form. The lightly-tapered, circular-sectioned stem is bent and fractured. The pointed tip is complete but the small discoidal plate is broken.

From upper fill (unit 1535) of latrine pit 1535. 3rd century AD.

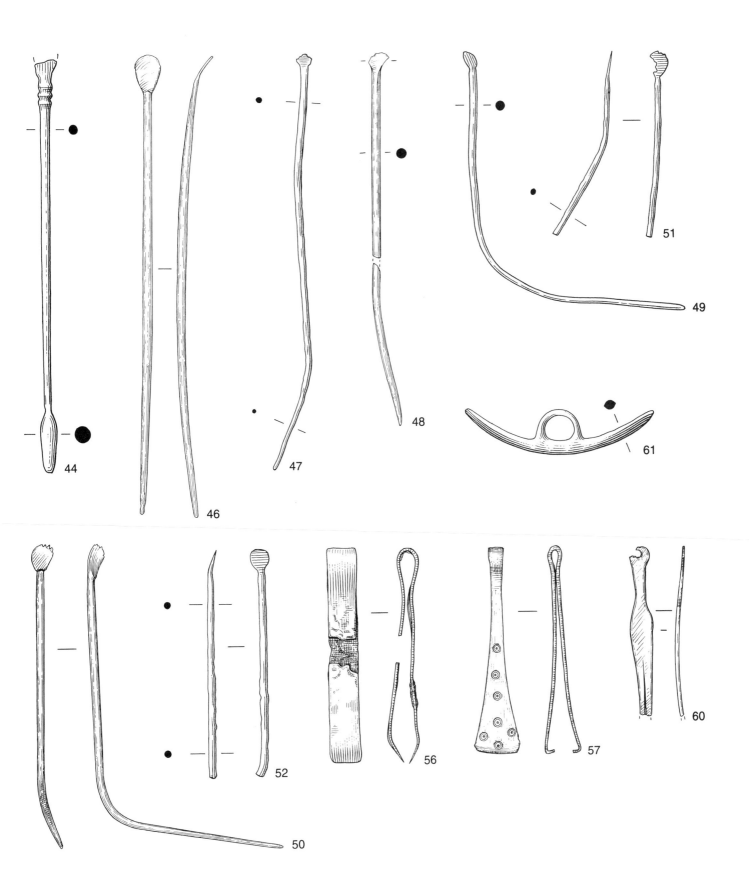

Fig. 109 Stonea Grange: copper-alloy objects 44, 46–52, 56–7 and 60–1 from the excavations (scale 1 : 1).

49 Ligula   Length 115 mm   ST 83 CCY, SF 546

A complete example, in good condition, but bent in two places. The circular-sectioned stem is plain and almost untapered with a steep-nosed blunt point at one end and a tiny angled discoidal plate at the other.

From topsoil/cleaning (unit 1070), centre block 11 and street 1 E/W

50 Ligula   Length 118 mm   ST 84 DTN, SF 1029

A complete, plain, well-preserved example, the lower stem bent almost to a right angle. A notable feature is the presence of three sharp teeth on the rim of the plate.

From layer 1945 in well 1914. 3rd century AD.

51 Ligula   Length 50 mm   ST 82 BHM, SF 353

The stem is very slender, of circular cross-section, bent and broken. The angled, ovoid disc-like plate is incomplete. Like no. 50 it has two or three tiny teeth on the rim of the plate.

From ditch 9, cut 4, unit 886. Late 3rd/4th century AD.

52 Ligula   Length 60 mm   ST 81 QP, SF 216

A slender, circular-sectioned rod, bent and broken at one end. The other end is gently tapered and flattened before expanding into the characteristic tiny, angled disc. This simple, plain example may have come from a toilet set.

From top layer (unit 336) of well 336. Late 3rd–4th century AD.

53 Ligula   (*Unillus.*)   Length *c.* 125 mm   ST 84 DPP, SF 848

A very distorted example with slender, lightly tapered oval-sectioned stem. The pointed tip is complete, but only the base of the small angled 'spoon' plate remains.

From layer 1851 in well 1836. Late 2nd/3rd century AD.

54 Ligula   (*Unillus.*)   Length 49 mm   ST 82 ABQ, SF 276

A slender, circular-sectioned rod, broken at one end. The other end is slightly flattened and terminates in the characteristic tiny angled disc, now slightly chipped.

Context as no. 10.

55 ?Ear scoop   (*Unillus.*)   Length 51 mm   ST 80 CV, SF 25

A slender, circular-sectioned rod, curved and broken at one end flattened and broken at the other. Probably a broken ear-scoop from a toilet set.

From robbing debris (unit 65), north-west quadrant of building R1 central block. Phase IV.

56 Tweezers   Length 58 mm   ST 81 LA, SF 117

A small tweezers with broad, square-ended, inturned jaws, made from a single undecorated strip, slightly waisted below the looped spring. Probably from a toilet set.

From basal layer (unit 231) of well 171/558. Late 3rd/4th century AD.

57 Tweezers   Length 53.5 mm   ST 81 FW, SF 174

Complete. The slender arms, now compressed, splay to broad, inturned, smooth, square-ended jaws. The looped head contributed to the 'spring' of the arms while providing an eye for suspension. The elongated triangular field on the outer surface of the arms is filled with a simple design comprising punched dot-and-ring motifs – seven on one arm, eight on the other.

One arm of another very similar tweezers is included in the Surface Collection, no. 110, p. 353. They are examples of a type which occurs both on late Roman and early Anglo-Saxon sites. Cf. e.g. Bushe-Fox 1949, 129, Pl. XXXVI, 114 and Brodribb *et al* 1972, 69, 71, Fig. 30, no. 135.

From the uppermost layer (unit 135) in well 135. Residual Roman finds with Anglo-Saxon pottery, 4th–7th century AD.

58 ?Tweezers/forceps   (*Unillus.*)
Length i) 64 mm; ii) 48 mm   ST 84 DWT, SF 1012

Two distorted fragments of slender, near parallel-sided strips, of flat rectangular cross-section. Their form and dimensions are similar to those of Roman tweezers and forceps, but there are many other possible uses.

From trowelling layer (unit 1999) above pit complex 2007 etc. 3rd century AD.

59 ?Tweezers   (*Unillus.*)
Length 42.5 mm   ST 82 AAG, SF 291

A slender rectangular-sectioned rod, in two pieces, broken at the narrow end. The other end is splayed and toothed. Possibly one arm of a tweezers.

From topsoil/cleaning (unit 448), blocks 5 and 5a.

60 Nail cleaner   Length 44 mm   ST 84 DEA, SF 729

A simple, unelaborate example made from a flat rectangular-sectioned strip. The suspension loop is incomplete and the forked end broken, but the characteristic groove makes the identification certain. From a toilet set.

Context as no. 15.

61 Cosmetic grinder   Length 53 mm   ST 82 AAG, SF 251

The solid, curved, pestle component of a centre-looped, two-piece cosmetic set. The crescentic, sub-circular-sectioned stem has a simple D-shaped suspension loop at the centre of its concave edge. One of its tapered tips has an asymmetric grinding facet on the convex edge.

For the function of these objects and a discussion of the type, see Jackson 1985. The mortar component of two further sets were found in the Stonea Grange Surface Collection (nos 112, 113, pp. 353–6). Context as no. 59.

62 Bead   Diameter 13 mm ST 84 DAA, SF 622

A low oblate bead with large circular eye. The wall, of plano-convex cross-section, is of rather irregular width. Cf. e.g. Bidwell 1985, 123, 126, Fig. 42, 59, from Vindolanda.

From topsoil, block 6 and block 5, south.

63 Bead or spacer   Length 26 mm ST 82 AZZ, SF 280

A hexagonal, barrel-shaped tube, one end now slightly distorted. Cf. Bushe-Fox 1949, 149, Pl. LV, 247, from Richborough; Bidwell 1985, Fig. 42, 57–8, from Vindolanda; Allason-Jones and Miket 1984, 3.1270, from South Shields; Kirk 1951, 28–9, Fig. 7, no. 5, from Woodeaton. Quita Mould (in Austen 1991, 194–5, nos 693–4) has postulated a military association for the type.

From top layer (unit 705) of well 705. 3rd/4th century AD.

64 ?Bead or ?collar   Length 28 mm ST 82 AZZ, SF 279

Part of a lightly tapered tube of circular cross-section internally, and hexagonal cross-section externally. Both ends appear complete. The broader end is plain; the narrower end terminates in a simple moulded rib. A little over half the tube is broken away longitudinally. Casting debris or the remains of some kind of fastening is present on the interior face.

Catherine Johns has drawn attention (personal communication) to the similarity between this object and certain amulet cases, though the better known examples are usually of gold.

Context as no. 63.

65 Scabbard slide   Length 106 mm ST 81 JF, SF 94

A complete example of normal form, made from a cranked, tapered strip. The crescent-shaped head and 'arrow-tipped' foot have neatly bevelled edges. Virtually all of the original surface has gone, but two small patches survive, one near the centre and the other at the upper shoulder. Both reveal lightly incised decoration – a series of at least three horizontal grooves on the shoulder, and a sinuous double groove running up the sides in the central region. At top and bottom of the belt slot are the corroded remains of the iron spikes/rivets which fastened the slide to its scabbard.

This type of scabbard slide is found in large numbers on the German *limes* and in Britain and dates to the early 2nd to 3rd century AD or earlier (See e.g. Bidwell 1985, 132–3, Fig. 47, no. 5). The majority were of iron, but the copper-alloy examples gave greater scope for decoration. The crescentic head of this example is paralleled by a slide from Zugmantel (Oldenstein 1977, Taf. 13, no. 58), while the remnants of its main zone of decoration conform to the curvilinear designs on iron slides based on a spiralling stem with tendrils, defined by Hundt (Hundt 1960).

From an upper layer (unit 190) in pit 132. 4th century AD.

66 Rosette mount   Diameter 19 mm ST 81 NX, SF 217

A military fitting comprising a lightly domed, circular rosette with ten petals. Attached to the concave back is a rectangular loop by which the mount was fastened to a leather strap, probably a piece of horse harness.

The rosette was a common motif on Roman military metalwork and was especially well-adapted to decorating the head of bosses, studs and other circular mounts. See e.g. Oldenstein 1977, Taf. 46, nos 483–4, Taf. 55, no. 678, Taf. 57, nos 704–11, and Taf. 62, nos 797–8.

From the fill (unit 297) of the east terminal of gully 44 (cut 1). 3rd century AD.

67 ?Belt mount   Length 48.5 mm ST 84 R24, 1, SF 769

An embossed binding made from thin, parallel-sided sheet, overlapped and riveted at the back. The front is decorated with a repousée ornament, comprising three irregularly spaced ringed bosses within a raised border. The binding, now slightly damaged, enclosed a space of *c.* 47 × 3 mm.

For a fragment of a near-identical mount from Chichester, Cattle Market site, cf. Down 1989, 202–3, Fig. 27.6, no. 93. Cf. also Jackson and Ambrose 1978, 219, 221, Fig. 57, no. 12, from Wakerley, dated Late Iron Age.

From the upper fill (layer 1) of ditch 87. Probably Phase III.

68 ?Pommel   Length 17 mm ST 82 ABQ, SF 362

A small egg-shaped mount, of concavo-convex cross-section, with a circular perforation. Perhaps the handle pommel from a knife or small dagger.

Cf. Bushe-Fox 1949, 107, Pl. I, 1. (Frontispiece). Context as no. 10.

69 Belt buckle   Length 29 mm ST 81 FF, SF 60

Part of the frame of a ?sub-rectangular belt buckle. Unfortunately, both ends are broken but the shape, dimensions cross-section and neatly stepped mouldings are characteristic of early Roman belt buckles.

For parallels amongst military belt buckles, see e.g. Grew and Griffiths 1991, esp. Figs 14–15.

From topsoil, block 1a.

70 ?Hinge plate   (*Unillus.*)
Length 24.5 mm ST 82 BCO, SF 318

A slightly distorted small plate, with gently tapered sides. The narrower end is complete and square-ended; the broader end is damaged but appears to have had originally a central slot flanked by a rolled strip – the seating for the buckle-tongue and hoop. A rivet passes through the plate near the narrow end. The form is similar to that of the strap and buckle fittings of Roman armour cuirasses (see e.g. Robinson 1975, 174ff.).

From ditch 9, cut 4, top layer (unit 767). Late 3rd–4th century AD.

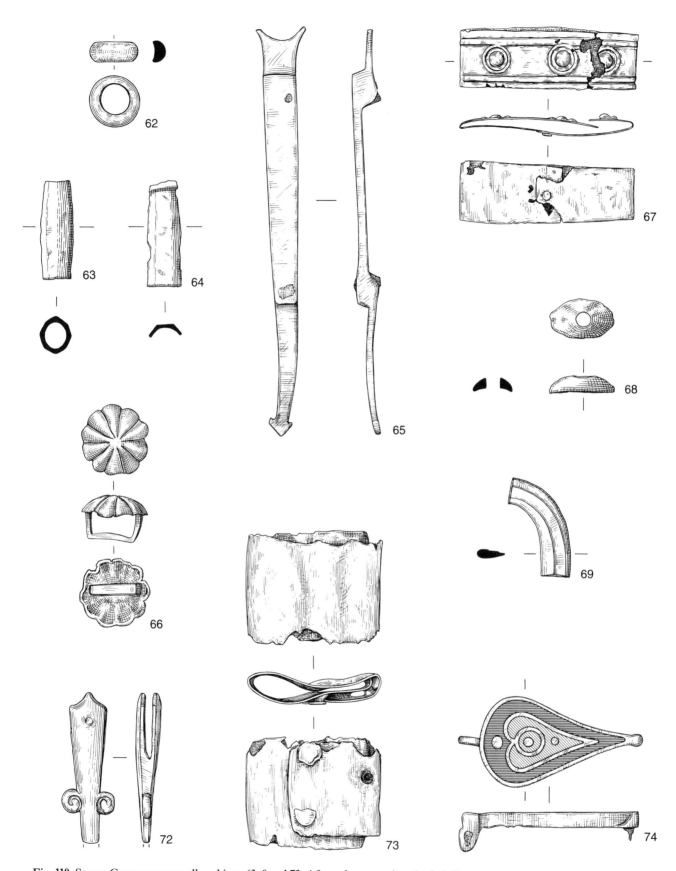

Fig. 110 Stonea Grange: copper-alloy objects 62–9 and 72–4 from the excavations (scale 1 : 1).

71 ?Chape (*Unillus.*)

Diameter *c.* 40 mm; thickness 7 mm ST 84 DEL, SF 733

A small distorted fragment of a curved, flat box-like object comprising a small part of the wall and fragments of the two flat faces. Perhaps part of a chape from a sword scabbard. ?2nd/3rd century? AD.

Cf. Cunliffe 1968b, Pl. XXXIV, 91–2; Allason-Jones and Miket 1984, 160–1, 3.401.

From fence slot (unit 1607), truncated by ditch 8, cut 4, unit 1594 (see no. 72 below). Late 2nd–3rd century AD.

72 Strap end   Length 37.5 mm ST 84 DDX, SF 721

A slotted, elongated triangular fitting, with a pair of small coiled projections. The narrow end is broken. The broader end has a neat, double-scalloped edge. Corroded fragments of the iron fixing pin block the small circular perforation in both faces near the broad end.

Cf. Allason-Jones and Miket 1984, 3.612, from South Shields; and no. 116, p. 356 (from Stonea Grange Surface Collection).

From ditch 8, cut 4, unit 1594. 3rd century AD.

73 Binding   Length 37 mm ST 84 DZX, SF 1088

A simple, quite crudely formed binding, originally enclosing an area *c.* 35 × 6 mm. but now somewhat distorted, crushed and chipped. A thin sheet, tapering in width from 29 to 26 mm, was wrapped round, overlapped, and riveted together with two simple, rather crude rivets. A third rivet hole appears not to have been utilised.

From pit 1943, unit 2074. Late 2nd–3rd century AD.

74 Seal box lid   Length 49 mm ST 81 KR, SF 116

A large leaf-shaped lid with the normal recessed underside and pierced hinge flange. The knobbed terminal preserves on its lower face the small pointed locating pin which ensured an accurate fit with the base. Within the stylised leaf-shaped border is a zone of blue enamel, which encloses a heart-shaped field filled with enamel of uncertain colour – it is now brown but was probably green originally. Within this is a circular blue zone with a central spot of enamel of the same appearance as that in the heart-shaped field. There is a further spot of this colour set into the outer blue zone, centrally above the heart.

This is an example of a very common type which dates to the 2nd–3rd century AD. Cf. e.g. Crummy 1983, Fig. 106, nos 2523, 2525; Allason-Jones and Miket 1984, 3.374; Holbrook and Bidwell 1991, Fig. 115, no. 94; Wheeler and Wheeler 1936, 211–12, Fig. 45, no. 53; Nash-Williams 1932, 85–6, Fig. 34, no. 46.

From an upper layer (unit 223) in ditch 9, cut 6. 3rd century AD.

75 Vessel handle

Length 148 mm; original diameter c. 120 mm ST 80 AW, SF 7

A slender twisted rod of rounded square cross-section, originally forming an arc, *c.* 120 mm in diameter. One end is now distorted and fragmentary; the other retains its tiny looped and knobbed terminal.

For an example of similar size and form from South Shields, see Allason-Jones and Miket 1984, 162–3, Fig. 3, 408. For handled vessels with a rim diameter of the appropriate size, but lacking their handles, see e.g. Radnoti 1938, Pl. X, 53 and Eggers 1951, Taf. 7, 66.

From burnt spread (unit 20), west of building R1. Phase III.

76 Vessel handle

Length 93 mm; original diameter *c.* 120 mm ST 81 FW, SF 44

A fragment, as no. 75. Both ends broken, but one preserves the beginning of its looped terminal.

From top layer (unit 135) of well 135, 4th–7th century AD.

77 Vessel handle   Length 111 mm ST 81 LS, SF 212

A fragment, as no. 76. Distortion prevents an accurate measurement of the diameter.

From burnt debris (unit 247) south of floor 139 of building R2. 3rd century AD.

78 ?Handle   (*Unillus.*) Length 43.5 mm ST 81 FF, SF 43

An elliptical fragment of slender twisted rod, broken at both ends. Probably part of nos 75–7, or similar.

From topsoil, block 1a.

79 ?Handle   Length 74 mm ST 84 DVD, SF 918

A very slender square-sectioned rod with a broken, tiny looped head. After a plain zone beneath the head the stem is neatly twisted. The lower end is broken.

From upper layer (unit 1960) of pit 1960. Late 2nd–3rd century AD.

80 Handle/hook   Length 141 mm ST 83 CHR, SF 486

A thin parallel-sided strip of flat rectangular cross-section. One end is broken. The other end terminates in a neat U-shaped hook with expanded 'serpentine' finials. The lack of any curvature of the strip poses a difficulty in interpreting the object as a vessel handle. Either it has been distorted – and it appears *not* to have been so – or a different function, perhaps as some form of hook, has to be envisaged.

Context as no. 37.

81 Handle terminal   Length 64 mm ST 82 ABQ, SF 258

The terminal is heavy, of D-shaped cross-section, with a plain, lightly convex internal face and plump convex exterior. It is decorated with a series of mouldings, three convex bands interspersed with two concave bands. The rod tapers rapidly from the terminal, and breakage has occurred at a narrow point. Two cut grooves at and near the broken edge appear to be features of re-use. Certainly, hammer facets on the external face of the terminal and both

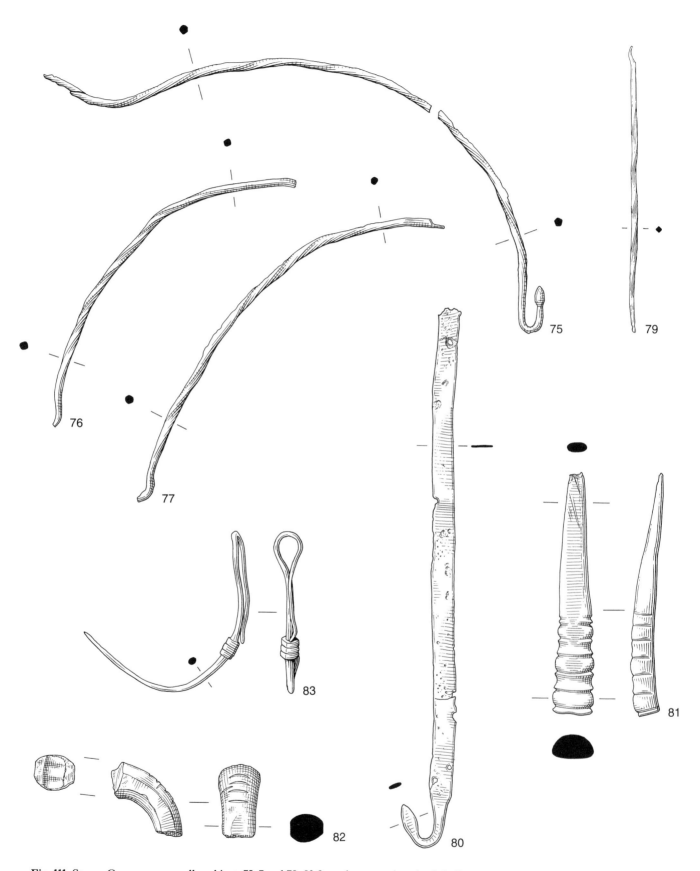

Fig. 111 Stonea Grange: copper-alloy objects 75–7 and 79–83 from the excavations (scale 1 : 1).

faces of the rod were presumably part of some secondary working after the object was broken.

Cf. Jackson 1990, 46, Pl. 13, no. 125; and Bushe-Fox 1949, 105, Pl. XLVIII, 219. Also no. 129, p. 357.

Context as no. 10.

82 ?Vessel handle

Length 26 mm; diameter: internal 20 mm, external 40 mm
ST 82 AZZ, SF 272

A small curved fragment of heavy cast bar, broken at both ends. The bar is tapered and of plump oval cross-section, with flattened sides. The inner (concave) face is worn; the outer (convex) face has a series of five rather irregular cut grooves. Breakage at the broader end has occurred at a point where a circular hole passes through the bar markedly off-centre. Perhaps a fragment of a jug handle, though the hole is difficult to explain.

Context as no. 63.

83 Hook   Length 42 mm ST 83 J4, 3, SF 585

A looped hook now apparently slightly distorted. The hook was made from a wire of rather irregular gauge and cross-section, by turning over one end and coiling it round the stem. The other end was bent into an open hook. There is wear on the inner face of the hook. Similar hooks were used on balances and steelyards, cf. e.g. Wheeler 1930, 85, Fig. 22, no. 2, a balance from London, Mansion House; and Neal 1974, 130–1, Fig. 56, no. 49, a loose hook from Gadebridge Park Roman villa.

From well J4, layer 3. Late 3rd/early 4th century AD.

84 Spoon handle   Length 101 mm ST 82 BAE, SF 281

A small example comprising a plain slender handle, of circular cross-section, which tapers to a point. The spoon bowl is broken, and only a fragment of the back of it survives at the plain stepped junction with the handle. The bowl is likely to have been fiddle-shaped or lute-shaped and the spoon is therefore probably of 2nd or 3rd century AD date. The handle stem is bent and is in two joining fragments.

Cf. e.g. Allason-Jones and Miket 1984, 3.322 and 3.335, from South Shields.

From an upper layer (unit 710) in pit 705. 3rd/4th century AD.

85 Pin/tack   Length 17 mm ST 84 DBV, SF 704

A small pin with rough circular-sectioned broken stem and crude flattened head, now bent.

From ditch 15, cut 13, unit 1544. Early/mid 3rd century AD.

86 Nail   (*Unillus.*) Length 13 mm ST 82 AAG, SF 289

A tiny nail or rivet, broken, with a rectangular cross-section and a simple flat head.

Context as no. 59.

87 ?Stud   (*Unillus.*) Diameter *c.* 27 mm ST 84 DEA, SF 738

Rather under half of a low-domed, plano-convex disc with neatly channelled rim, now distorted and broken. Perhaps a head of a large decorative stud.

Context as no. 15.

88 Ring   (*Unillus.*) Diameter 21 mm ST 83 CFC, SF 584

A small circular ring of rather irregular thickness and rounded diamond-shaped cross-section. A common type on Roman and Iron Age sites.

From grey silt, north-east block 2. 3rd century AD.

89 Ring   (*Unillus.*) Diameter 15 mm ST 82 ABS, SF 350

A small, neatly-made, circular ring of softened lozenge cross-section.

From top layer (unit 483) of pit 483/918. Late 3rd/4th century AD.

90 Ring   (*Unillus.*) Diameter 19 mm ST 84 DHA, SF 834

Rather over half of a small circular ring, made from rectangular-sectioned rod of slightly uneven thickness. No wear is visible. Possibly a ring terminal rather than a free ring.

From top layer (unit 1669) of well 1669. Mid/late 3rd century AD.

91 ?Billet   Length 42 mm ST 83 CNA, SF 641

A fragment of thick cast plate. The long curved edge is an original edge as, too, perhaps, the short edge opposite. The straight edge appears to have been cut, while the ragged concave edge is probably broken. Hammer facets are visible on the planar surfaces.

From clay spread (unit 1288) above pit/ditch 69. Late 3rd/4th century AD.

92 ?Ferrule   (*Unillus.*) Length 30 mm ST 81 KN, SF 113

A gently tapered tube, of oval cross-section, made from a sheet with overlapped edges. Both ends broken.

From upper fill (unit 220) of pit 170. 3rd/4th century AD.

93 ?Binding   (*Unillus.*)
Length 41 mm ST 84 EEF, SF 1161

A slender, tapered, grooved strip of semi-circular cross-section, broken at both ends. Probably a small channelled binding rather than a broken tube.

From post-hole 2178 on east side of building R10. Phase III.

94 Decorative strip   (*Unillus.*)
Length 30.5 mm ST 82 BDS, SF 322

A small slender sinuous strip with plano-convex cross-section and projecting ray-like motifs. Presumably a decorative appliqué.

From top layer (unit 795) of pit 795. Late 3rd/4th century AD.

B STONEA GRANGE SURFACE COLLECTION (Figs 112–16)

95 Minerva handle Height 69 mm P1982, 6–2, 5

A cast handle in the form of a small bust of Minerva. The goddess wears a *chiton* with an *aegis* in front. She has long wavy hair and wears an elaborate Corinthian helmet surmounted by a double crest on a rod-like support. The pedestal of the bust is a split trapezoidal plate with bevelled edges, which was the socket for an iron component, now represented only by a few traces of corrosion products.

Potter and Jackson 1982, 133, 115, Fig. 3.4.

Parallels are fairly numerous and include examples from Ospringe (Whiting 1923, 65–7, Pl. 5–6), Silchester (Pitts 1979, 97, Pl. 28, no. 219), Wilderspool (Thompson 1965, Fig. 20, 17). Wood-eaton (Kirk 1951, 40, no. 2, Pl. IV F), Nijmegen (Zadoks-Josephus Jitta *et al* 1969, 136–7, no. 59), Sarmizegethusa (Floca 1969, no. 22), Trier (Menzel 1966, 78–9 and Pl. 62, no. 188) and Zugmantel (*Saalburg Jahrbuch* 20, 1962, 73 nos ZM 1354, 1357 and 2044, Pl. 4, nos 1–3 and Pl. 5, nos 1–3).

Alone among these examples, that from the Ospringe cemetery was found with its iron component intact, albeit rather corroded. It consists of a long flat trapezoidal blade with its cutting edge on the broad end. This type of chisel-like blade may have been used for spreading the wax onto writing tablets (Gaitzsch 1984, 198–207). More probably, however, it was a razor (Boon 1991, 27ff). The Ospringe example came from a cremation (Group XI) with pottery dated to the mid 2nd century AD.

96 Minerva bust Height 29 mm P1982, 6–2, 7

A small bust with badly eroded patina. Despite the destruction of much of the original surface it is apparent that the workmanship was fairly indifferent and the features are lacking in clarity. Nonetheless, from the absence of a beard, the relatively slender neck, the form of the drapery and the remains of the crested helmet it is virtually certain that the bust was of Minerva.

Potter and Jackson 1982, 113, 115, Fig. 3.5.

97 ?Minerva/?Mars bust
Height 26 mm P1982, 6–2, 8

A small attachment in the form of a helmeted bust. The bust is a small plain triangle; the head displays little facial detail so that while the eyes and nose are prominent the slight chin has no indication of a beard and the mouth is not rendered; the helmet, though clearly a double-crested type, is also devoid of detail. There is a bar-like fastening flange behind the head.

For a near-identical example, dated 2nd century, from Caerleon see Nash-Williams 1932, 85–6, Fig. 34, no. 34; and for two similar but slightly larger and more detailed busts of Mars from Nijmegen, see Zadoks-Josephus Jitta 1973, 75, nos 127–8.

98 Figurine fragment Height 25 mm P1982, 6–2, 6

A broken double crest, probably from the Corinthian helmet of a figurine or bust of Minerva or Mars. The scalloped borders and incisions on the sides indicate the feathers. The size of the remaining crest fragment indicates a height of at least 150 mm if the complete object was a figurine. However, the quality and size of the crest find a close parallel in a fine bust of Minerva from Enns (Fleischer 1967, 44–5, Pl. 23, no. 28).

99 Animal figurine Length 21 mm P1982, 6–2, 138

Head of a horse or sheep, broken at the neck. Eyes, ears, nose and mouth are simply rendered as also skull shape and musculature. Corrosion and wear have undoubtedly coarsened the original workmanship and finish.

This fragment is tantalising in view of the fragments of the equine terracotta figurine (p. 486, no. 2) found in pit P10, near the temple.

100 Cockerel finial Height 29 mm P1982, 6–2, 9

A cast finial in the form of a cockerel on a pedestal. The modelling of the bird is good though stylised. The beak, comb and tail are all damaged. The legs are not rendered, and the bird rests upon a square-sectioned stem which projects from the moulded pedestal. The pedestal base has a small circular socket blocked with iron corrosion, implying that the cockerel surmounted an iron pin 3 mm in diameter. Perhaps a votive object.

Cf. Colchester (Hawkes and Hull 1947, Pl. C, no. 21, period IV, *c*. AD 50–60), Nijmegen (Zadoks-Josephus Jitta *et al* 1973, 31–2, no. 39), and Richborough (Cunliffe 1968b, 97–8, Pl. XL, no. 149).

101 Model axe Length 19 mm P1982, 6–2, 10

Although slightly damaged, the form of axe-head depicted is clearly the straight-sided shaft-hole axe typical of Roman woodworkers. The model incorporated an integral handle, most of which has broken away.

For a complete example of near-identical type in a group of models from Sussex, see *R-B Guide 1964*, 71–2, Fig. 37, 4, far right.

Of all the model objects from Roman Britain, axes are the most common. Of the 150 or so models known to Green (1976, 42–3), about a third were axes and she noted that of all types they were most often found in shrine contexts. In view of the presence of a temple and the discovery of a gold votive leaf at Stonea, it is likely that this model (as too, no. 102) is a votive object.

102 Model axe-head Length 19 mm P1982, 6–2, 11

A miniature but accurate version of a characteristic Roman axe-head with drooping triangular blade and squared-off butt. Realism extends to the shaft hole, a tapering oval, and to the absence of a handle which might suggest the axe-head was mounted on a wooden shaft. Alternatively, the object may have been intended for suspension, and this is implied by wear at the back of the eye. Like no. 101, it is probable that this was a votive object.

The great majority of Roman model axes are made with an integral shaft. However, there is a close parallel to the present object from the Roman cemetery at Poundbury (*Proc. Dorset Nat. Hist. & Archaeol. Soc.* 74, 1952 (1953), 98–9, Fig. 1), and another from the Lankhills Roman cemetery (Clarke, 1979, Grave 326, Fig. 87, no. 404 and pp. 326–7).

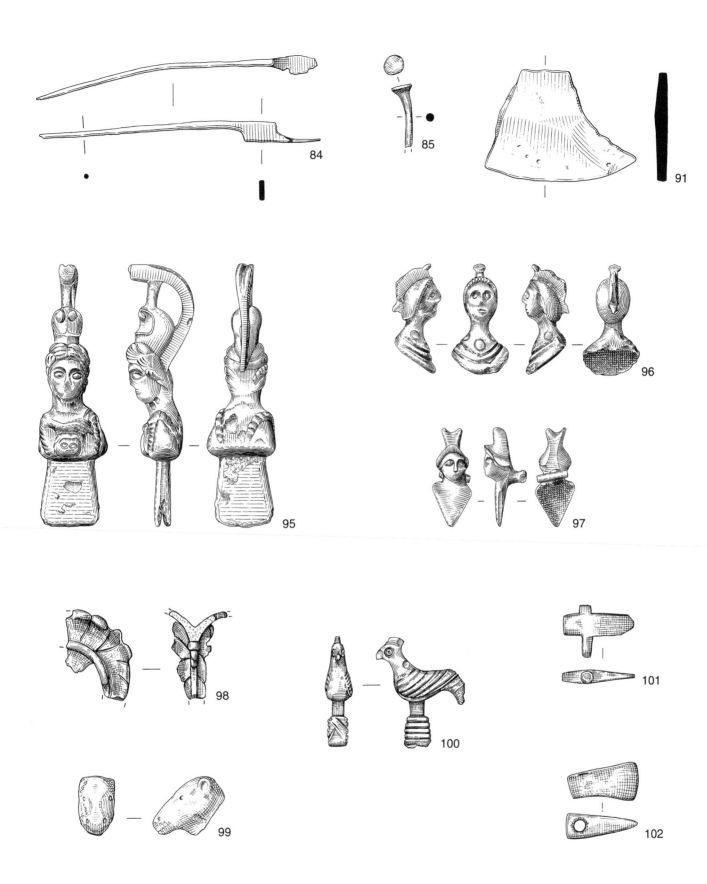

Fig. 112 Stonea Grange: copper-alloy objects 84–5 and 91 from the excavations, 95–102 from the Surface Collection (scale 1 : 1).

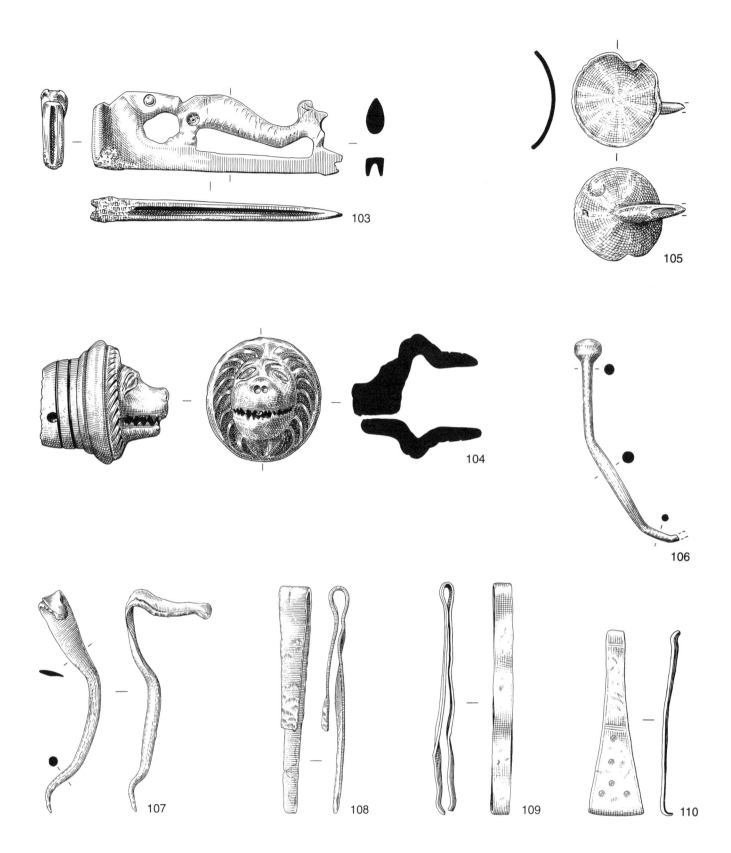

Fig. 113 Stonea Grange: copper-alloy objects 103–10 from the Surface Collection (scale 1:1).

103 Knife handle   Length 68 mm P1982, 6–2, 18

The copper-alloy handle of a clasp knife. The iron blade is missing but the iron hinge pin remains. The handle is finely made. It comprises a slotted bar, in which the blade edge (*c.* 55 mm long) was folded away, above which is a stylised dolphin confronting the fore-quarters of a seahorse. Both creatures have deep eye sockets, and the inset blue-green glass eyeballs remain in all but one case. The grooved, forked terminal was presumably functional. This type of folding knife is well known, though not particularly common. The figured motif is variable: most popular appears to have been the favoured Roman scene of a hound chasing a hare (e.g. Bushe-Fox 1949, Pl. XXXVI, 118, from Richborough; and Wheeler 1930, 78–9, Fig. 19, 4, from the River Thames at Hammersmith), but human erotic scenes are also known (e.g. C. M. Johns in Frere 1984, 58–9 and Fig. 23, 217, from fourth-century dark soil, Insula XXVIII 4).

Potter and Jackson 1982, 114, 115, Fig. 3, 3.

104 Lion-head terminal

Length 34 mm; max. diameter 33 mm P1982, 6–2, 20

Probably a fountain jet. A heavy, cast, lion-head protome on the end of a circular collar. A small hole in the collar indicates that the object was nailed/riveted to a projecting handle or pipe. A small hole passes through the lion's mouth from the interior. If connected to a pipe the terminal would have delivered a fine jet of water and such a use seems virtually certain. The lion's head motif was often chosen for round terminals. Some were jets or spouts, others decorative studs for boxes and others were used to secure ring handles. The form and degree of stylisation was very variable. For a selection of types, see e.g. Menzel 1966, Plates 54–5.

105 Spoon   Diameter of bowl 25 mm P1982, 6–2, 19

Round-bowled spoon. The handle, most of which is missing, forms a rat-tail junction with the bowl. The rim of the bowl, which is neatly bevelled, has been damaged at one point. There is no evidence of tin-plating.

Probably 1st–2nd century AD.

106 Pin

Length: present 59 mm; original at least 70 mm P1982, 10–3, 4

The lightly-flattened globular head has a double grooved neck-moulding. The shank is bent above and below a marked swelling. Its tip is broken.

This is an example of Cool's Group I Knob-headed pin, Sub-Group E, which has a marked concentration in East Anglia (Cool 1990, 151). Interestingly, the swollen shank feature also shows an East Anglian bias (*ibid*). The Group IE pins provide no dated context, but by analogy with the swollen-shanked pins in other better-dated groups, it may be suggested that some at least were in use in the 1st–2nd century AD.

107 Ligula/ear-scoop

Length: present 59 mm; original *c.* 90 mm P1982, 10–3, 6

A crushed and severely distorted small ligula, with a tubular stem and the normal small disc-like scoop. The end opposite the scoop, now a distorted tapered point, appears to have been originally a turned-over suspension loop, and it is probable that the object is an ear-scoop from a toilet set.

108 Tweezers   Length 60 mm P1982, 10–3, 5

A simple tweezers, made from a thin plain copper-alloy strip, with tapered arms and a broad looped head. Both jaws and part of one arm are broken, but the jaws were evidently of the narrow type. The workmanship is quite rudimentary. Probably epilation tweezers from a toilet set.

109 Tweezers   Length 61.5 mm P1982, 6–2, 13

The simplest form of tweezers, made from a thin, plain strip with inturned smooth jaws and a simple looped head. Probably epilation tweezers from a toilet set.

110 Tweezers   Length 49 mm P1982, 6–2, 14

Only one arm survives, broken at the suspension loop. The broad inturned jaw has a smooth edge. The elongated triangular field of the outer surface, emphasised by a peripheral engraved line, is divided midway by a double groove. A similar groove marks the base of the suspension loop, while a slightly asymmetric arrangement of five dot-and-ring motifs decorates the lower part.

Cf. no. 57, p. 344 from the excavation; a late Roman and early Anglo-Saxon type.

111 Nail cleaner   Length 33 mm P1982, 6–2, 120

The functional (forked) end of the leaf-shaped blade is broken. There is a row of dot-and-ring decoration down the axis of one face. Both this decoration and the mouldings beneath the small suspension loop are heavily worn implying long usage.

The form of decoration indicates a Late Roman date, 4th century or later.

112 Cosmetic grinder   Length 75 mm P1982, 6–2, 3

The grooved mortar component of a centre-looped, two-piece cosmetic set. The knobbed terminal is divided from the bow by a simple moulding. The large and elaborate bovid head has horns, ears, eyes and flared, flattened muzzle, with mouth and nostrils depicted. The deep round eye sockets were probably inset with coloured glass eye balls, though neither survives. The decoration on the bow comprises two bellied lines with a thin band of zig-zag between the upper line and the rim.

For the function of these objects and a discussion of the type see Jackson 1985, 166 Fig. 1, no. 60, and 185–6, no. 60. Potter and Jackson 1982, 112, 115, Fig. 3, no. 6. The excavation yielded a centre-looped pestle component (no. 61 above). However, it is not the pair to this mortar or to no. 113 below; therefore three sets are represented.

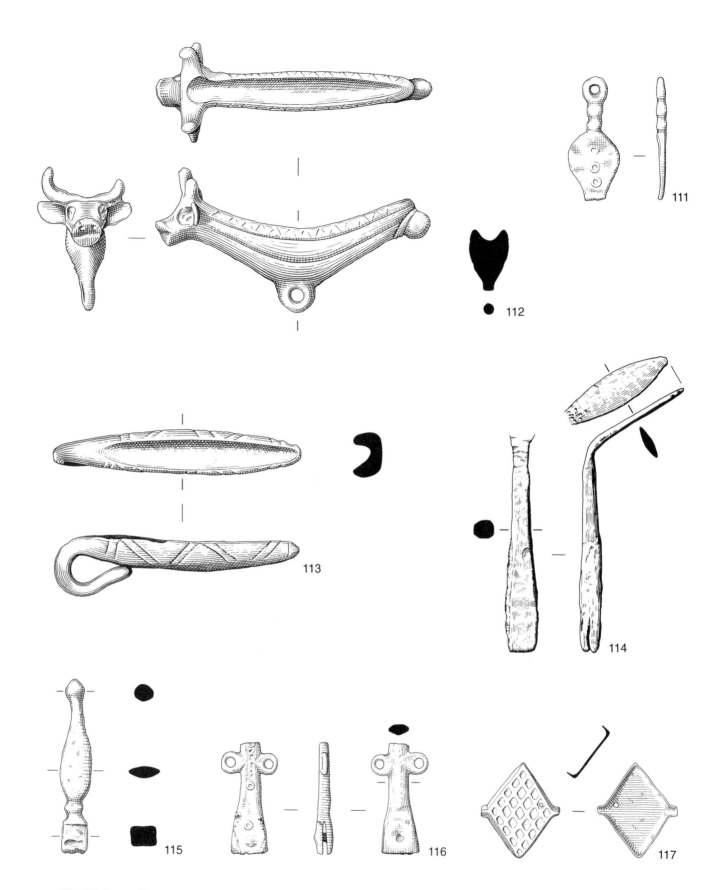

Fig. 114 Stonea Grange: copper–alloy objects 111–17 from the Surface Collection (scale 1 : 1).

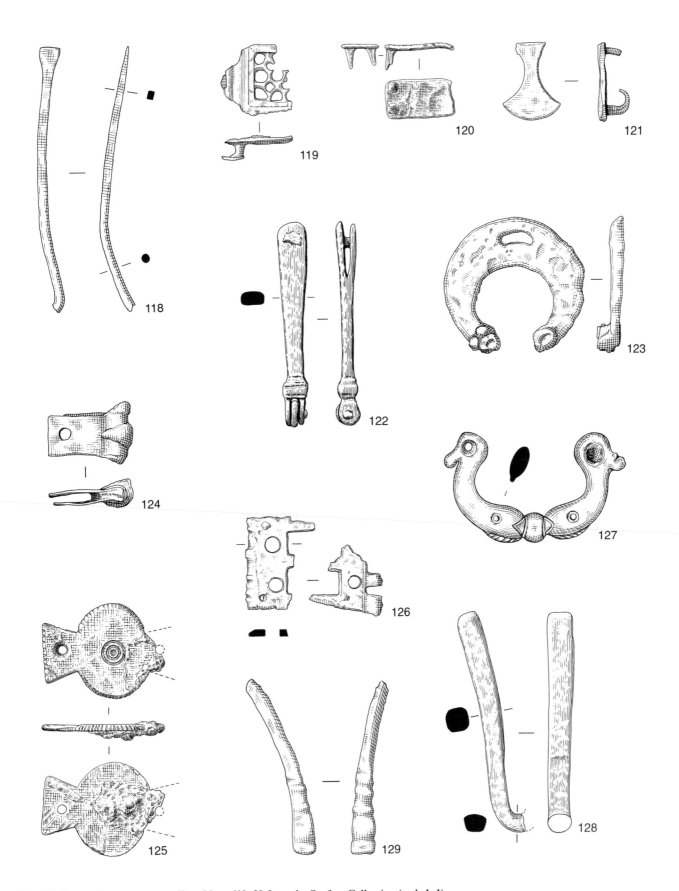

Fig. 115 Stonea Grange: copper–alloy objects 118–29 from the Surface Collection (scale 1:1).

113 Cosmetic grinder   Length 67.5 mm P1982, 6–2, 4

As no. 112, but a simpler end-looped example, with a plain terminal. The lightly curved bow has low walls decorated with paired zig-zag lines. The groove has a longitudinal wear facet which gives it a markedly asymmetric cross-section.

Jackson 1985, 166, Fig. 1, no. 19, 177, 179, no. 19.

114 Scalpel handle   Length 85 mm P1985, 10–3, 14

The leaf-shaped blunt dissector is small, with the normal low median ridge on both faces. It has been bent at the neck, apparently accidentally, and more probably recent than ancient. The neck is of chamfered rectangular (flat octagonal) cross-section and splays out to form the block-like rectangular-sectioned grip, which has grooved terminals. Within the grip is a simple split socket in which are corroded remains of the tang of the iron scalpel blade. There is no sign of decoration on the planar faces of the grip, though corrosion is particularly heavy there.

This is a slender example of the most common form of Roman scalpel handle, Jackson Type I (Jackson 1986, 133). The blade was probably of convex, bellied type, but for the range of known blade types, see Jackson 1990a, Fig. 1, nos 6–12.

115 Finial   Length 46.5 mm P1982, 6–2, 15

A ridged, leaf-shaped spatula with a knobbed terminal. At the proximal end a ring moulding separates the neck of the spatula from a grooved, rectangular plinth, the base of which is broken. Within the plinth there is a split socket, blocked with soil and ?iron corrosion. The function is uncertain, but there is a similarity with the leaf-shaped terminals of certain medical instruments, notably scalpel/needle handles.

116 Strap end   Length 29 mm P1982, 6–2, 118

A slotted, crinoline-shaped fitting with a pair of perforated circular projections. The narrow end is broken. At the broad end the tiny circular perforation is blocked with the corroded remains of the iron fixing pin. The two main faces differ in form: one is plain, with a low axial ridge; the other has a linear design of dot-and-ring and dot-punched decoration on a flattened axial zone with bevelled edges. The form of decoration indicates a late Roman date, 4th century or later.

Cf. no. 72 above.

117 Seal-box lid   Length 25.5 mm P1982, 6–2, 12

A small lozenge-shaped example divided into 25 enamel-filled cells. The central cell retains its red enamel and the four flanking cells are filled with yellow enamel. the remaining cells have lost most of their enamel, but the traces that survive indicate either turquoise or turquoise interspersed with light green. The angled bridge projection has broken away.

A five-by-five grid seems to be the norm for this type of lid. Cf. e.g. South Shields (Allason-Jones and Miket 1984, 152–4, nos 3.376 and 3.377).

118 ?Ligula or ?stylus   Length 70 mm P1982, 6–2, 133

A broken and distorted slender rod of circular cross-section changing to rectangular cross-section in the region of the simple flat wedge-shaped terminal.

119 Military belt plate, fragment
Width 19 mm (damaged) P1982, 6–2, 113

Part of a rectangular plate with broken moulded frame around an openwork design. The rearward fastening stud has a flat head which probably engaged in a slotted leather strap or belt. The patina is very grey (?tin-rich).

Oldenstein (1977, 193–7) dates this type later 2nd to mid 3rd century AD. For parallels, see Oldenstein 1977, Taf. 62–4; Cunliffe 1968b, 94, Pl. XXXV, 105–6; Nash-Williams 1932, 84–5, Fig. 33, nos 32–3, dated 2nd century; Wacher and McWhirr 1982, 113–4, Fig. 38, no. 126; and Allason-Jones and Miket 1984, 195–6, no. 634.

120 Belt fitting   Length 18 mm P1982, 10–3, 2

A small plain rectangular plate, broken at one end, with two projecting spikes on the underside at the complete end. Length of spikes 4.5 mm. Probably a belt stiffener from a military belt of the 1st or 2nd century AD.

Cf. Grew and Griffiths 1991, Belt Mount Type A3, 63, 66, Fig. 9, nos 54, 55, 57, from Hod Hill and Longthorpe; and Jackson 1990b, 31, Pl. 4, nos 43–5, from Camerton.

121 Military fitting   Length 21 mm P1982, 6–2, 115

A pelta-shaped mount with two rearward fastening spikes. One spike is broken, the other burred over, indicating that the mount was secured to a leather strap/belt c. 4 mm thick. The edges of the plate are neatly bevelled, and traces of white metal (probably tinning) remain on the outer face.

Cf. Oldenstein 1977, Taf. 53–5.

Probably 2nd–3rd century AD.

122 Strap-end   Length 53 mm P1985, 10–3, 15

A slender, club-shaped bar of rounded rectangular cross-section. The broad end, with rounded terminals, has a split socket perforated by an iron rivet, still in position. The narrow end terminates in a rectangular moulding surmounted by a simple hinge, which comprises two circular side flanges pierced by an iron hinge pin. The pin is in situ, as also the torn central hinge-plate of the missing movable copper-alloy component. Like many Roman military bronzes the object is tinned.

This is an example of a multiple-unit strap end. Less common than the single-unit type (see nos 72 and 116 above), examples have nonetheless been found in several forts on the German *limes* (Oldenstein 1977, 250, Taf. 37, 325–34). No precise chronology exists, though Oldenstein (*ibid.* 147) suggested a probable starting date after the mid 2nd century AD.

123 Harness mount   Width 39 mm P1982, 6–2, 123

A crescent-shaped stud or pendant, with a small slot for fastening to a leather strap. The crescent tips are embellished with a small drum-like terminal which may originally have held a decorative stud or inlay. The pitted and blistered corrosion has obscured much detail, but the front face is neatly finished with bevelled edges while the back face retains much of its as-cast surface.

124 Buckle-plate   Length 24 mm P1982, 6–2, 116

A small, simple buckle-plate made from a thin, undecorated strip folded back on itself. The gap implies a belt/strap thickness of *c*. 2 mm. Fragments of the small iron buckle and buckle pin survive.

125 Belt fitting

Width 25 mm; length: present 33 mm, original *c*. 38 mm
P1982, 10–3, 1.

A broken propeller-shaped plate, decorated on one face. The central oval unit is proportionately large. It has a bevelled and notched rim and a central incuse dot-and-double-ring motif. The remaining outer unit also has lightly-bevelled rims, the outermost of which is lightly-notched. It has a small circular perforation set a little off-centre. The other outer unit has broken across its perforation. The decorated surface and rims of the fitting display considerable wear.

This is a mount or stiffener from a late Roman belt set of copper-alloy fittings. The mounts vary somewhat in size, form, degree of decoration and number/position of attachment rivets. For a full discussion of the type, see Bullinger 1969. This example is probably from a narrow belt of the type in use in the middle and later 4th century AD. However, a date as early as the 3rd century has been postulated for the genesis of the propeller-shaped stiffener (*ibid.*, 77–8). British finds include: Richborough, 2 examples (Bushe-Fox 1928, 49, Pl. XXI, no. 52; Bushe-Fox 1949, 146, Pl. LIII, no. 209), Maryport, 4 examples (Bailey 1915, 169, Pl. XId), and single examples from Camerton (Wedlake 1958, Fig. 58, no. 12), Woodeaton (Kirk 1951, Fig. 7, no. 6), and Vindolanda (Bidwell 1985, 121–2, Fig. 41, no. 28).

126 Military belt buckle-plate, fragmentary

Width 24.5 mm P1982, 6–2, 114

Two pieces of an openwork plate with indented decoration on the edges. The openwork design originally comprised two or four rectangular openings flanked by four or six circular openings. Three of the four corner perforations for securing pins survive, as also part of the buckle hinge.

Mid–late 4th century AD. Late Roman belt buckle of Hawkes and Dunning Type IIA (Hawkes and Dunning 1961; Hawkes 1974; Jackson 1990b, 31–2, no. 46).

127 Drop handle   Length 50 mm P1982, 6–2, 19

A small drop handle in the form of two opposed dolphins with an ovoid object between their snouts. Their looped-back tails which secured the pins on which the handle pivoted, may also be viewed as stylised birds heads.

The handle is lightly encrusted with iron corrosion, and the dolphin's dorsal fins are badly chipped. It is also clear that it was well used: both faces are worn, one more so than the other, consistent with its function as a drop handle on a box, casket, cupboard or drawer.

128 Vessel handle   Length 60 mm P1985, 10–3, 16

A softened rectangular-sectioned rod, of slightly tapered and sinuous form. The broader end is complete and has a tiny dimple drilled into its end-face. The narrow end is fractured immediately beyond an angle-change, where its cross-section becomes plump D-shaped. There is an arc of wear-polish on the inner facer of the rod at the angle.

This is a broken terminal loop from the handle of a *situla*. Such handles have characteristically long upturned terminal loops, and this example has traces of wear in the expected position.

Cf. e.g. Cunliffe 1968b, 105, Pl. XLVIII, 219 from Richborough; and Jackson 1990b, 46, Pl. 13, no. 125, from Camerton. For the vessel types, see Radnoti 1938, Pl. IX, 45, 47; and den Boesterd 1956, Pl. VI, 147, 153, Pl. VII, 162.

129 Handle terminal(?)   Length 49 mm P1982, 6–2, 132

The terminal, of rounded rectangular cross-section, has bead-and-reel mouldings, with heavy wear on the inner (concave) face. The broken rod is narrow, of flat rectangular cross-section.

For references, see no. 81, pp. 347, 349.

130 Stud   Diameter 12 mm P1985, 10–3, 12

A small circular cell with gently inturned wall. Between the wall and a small central disc is a low recess originally filled with cerulean (sky blue) enamel, of which less than half now remains in situ. Over the entire back surface is the corroded remains of a white metal – almost certainly solder – by which means the stud was secured as a decorative mount.

Cf. e.g. Crummy 1983, Fig. 121, no. 3217, from Colchester.

131 Stud   Diameter 19 mm P1985, 10–3, 13

A heavy reel-shaped stud head, its upper face deeply sunk around a central small profiled knob. The rims of the reel are decorated with incised grooves. On the underside of the reel a small rectangular slot, clogged with corrosion products, marks the position of the missing pin shank which may have been of iron.

Such studs served a variety of purposes where a decorative head and functional shank were required. Cf. e.g. Crummy 1983, 124–5, Fig. 137, no. 4143, from Colchester; and for a discussion of the type, see Allason-Jones 1985.

132 Disc   Diameter 37 mm P1982, 6–2, 131

A heavy cast disc with turned mouldings and a lightly incised line around the circumference. One face has a recessed zone between the undercut rim and the centre moulding. The other face is heavily worn. Function unknown.

Fig. 116 Stonea Grange: copper-alloy objects 130–7 from the Surface Collection (scale 1 : 1).

133 Decorative boss Length 18 mm P1982, 10–3, 3

A small circular domed fragment in the form of a miniature shield boss. The flange has a grooved rim; the carinated *umbo* has a central knobbed projection. All edges are broken. Function uncertain, though possibly a damaged plate brooch, cf. Austen 1991, 184, Fig. 90, no. 630, from Old Penrith.

134 ?Engraving tool Length 39.5 mm P1982, 6–2, 134

A small strip, apparently complete, of tapered rectangular cross-section. The broad end has a bevelled ?working edge.

135 Ring terminal Length 28 mm P1982, 6–2, 119

A circular, disc-like terminal with rebated handle fragment. Function unknown.

136 Plate fragment Width 20 mm P1982, 10–3, 7

A near parallel-sided narrow plate fragment, broken at both ends, in one case across a circular perforation. One face is plain and unworked; the other has a neatly-applied light groove running along both long sides. The decorated face is also fairly heavily worn. Function uncertain. However, the general form, appearance and quality of workmanship are suggestive of Roman military metalwork, perhaps a belt plate, cf. Grew and Griffiths 1991, Belt Mount Type A2, 63, 66, Fig. 9, nos 48–51.

137 ?Statue fragment Length 28 mm P1982, 10–3, 8

An undiagnostic fragment of thick cast metal. Possibly statuary.

METALWORKING DEBRIS

Paul Craddock

Evidence of non-ferrous metallurgy in Phase III, albeit on a small scale, is provided by the base of a crucible (ST 84 DST, SF 1163; BMRL 44900X). This was found in block 8, at the south end of the central branch of gully 18 (cut 25, unit 1927), a Phase III context dated to the third century AD. The fragment is of a rather fine wheel-thrown white ware that has been given a rough coating of clay on the outside. Coated crucibles of this description are not uncommon in the Roman period, at least in the north-western part of the Empire, and have been studied by Bayley (1988), who notes a very similar example from Baldock (Foster 1986 Fig. 63, item 410). This was a small beaker-type crucible without pouring lip and with a narrow base. The upper parts of the Stonea example do not survive but the presence of metal between the outside of crucible and its clay coating suggests problems in pouring caused by the absence of a lip. The reasons suggested by Bayley for the clay coating on these crucibles include: to reduce the thermal shock when the crucible was placed in the fire; to increase the overall thermal capacity such that the crucible and contents would cool more slowly when removed from the fire; and generally to protect the inner crucible. Certainly crucibles inside clay coatings are rarely vitrified, and this is the case with the Stonea example.

The corroded metal runner between the inner crucible and its coating was analysed qualitatively by X-ray fluorescence (XRF: British Museum Research Laboratory File 6439). This showed the metal to be copper with tin and small quantities of zinc and lead. Alloys of this type were very common in Britain and Gaul (Craddock 1994).

IRON OBJECTS

Ralph Jackson (Figs 117–20, Pl. XXVb)

Soil conditions at Stonea were extremely unfavourable to the preservation of ironwork and, barring only a few objects from waterlogged contexts, the assemblage was at a very advanced stage of corrosion. Much had disappeared, and much that remained had laminated and disintegrated. Heavy accretions and surface depletion have hindered or rendered impossible identification of the surviving objects, with the result that the number of identifiable artefacts is not great. The vast majority of these are nails, as on most Romano-British sites. They have no special significance for the site and have been excluded from the report, as also have undiagnostic fragments of nailed and unnailed bindings, rods, bar and plate.

The remaining artefacts comprise an assemblage of just 80 catalogued objects, of which almost a half consists of keys, locks, door furniture and other structural ironwork. Despite the meagre size of the remainder all the main classes of Roman ironwork are represented, and there are some individually interesting and notable pieces, as, for example, the spade sheath (no. 16), the military buckle (no. 1) and the hairpin (no. 32). The specifically military component is small but significant, and it complements other objects and evidence for a military presence at the site in Phase III. Objects associated with transport are relatively numerous, but there is a rather surprising paucity of agricultural implements. However, the wooden rake-head (p. 547, no. 6) serves as a reminder that many such implements were made without metal parts. Knives, as is often the case, are the single most common object, and domestic and personal/toilet implements are also well represented.

Thus, while the ironwork assemblage is too small to permit a categoric assessment, its composition is entirely consistent with an interpretation as the debris of a proto-urban settlement in a rural setting.

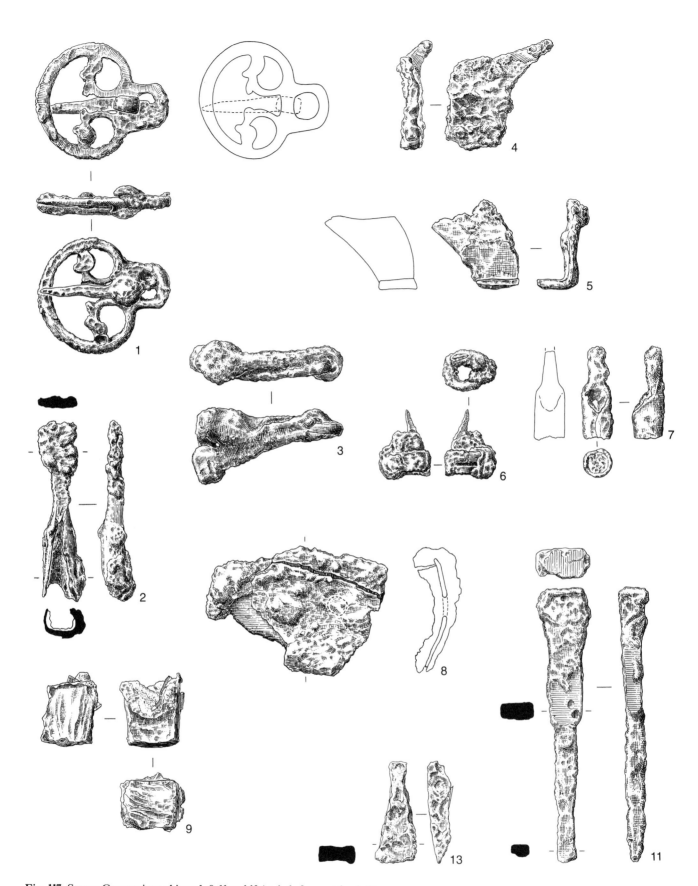

Fig. 117 Stonea Grange: iron objects 1–9, 11 and 13 (scale 1 : 2 except 1 = 1 : 1).

1 Military buckle   Length 3.6 cm ST 84 DVX, SF 693

A finely-made belt buckle with D-shaped hoop, of rounded triangular cross-section, in-filled with leaf-and-tendril struts. For the mode of attachment, discussion of the type, usually made of copper-alloy, and parallels from German fort sites see Oldenstein 1976, 213–16, Fig. 7 and Pls 75–6. British examples include those from Wroxeter (Bushe-Fox 1916, 32, Pl. XXI, Fig. 1, 2) and South Shields (Allason-Jones and Miket 1984, 193–4, nos 3.616–3.622). The type is of 2nd–3rd century AD date.

From a lower layer (unit 1978) in well 1678. Late 2nd–3rd century AD.

2 ?Spearhead   Length 9.6 cm ST 84 DKP, SF 820

A socketed blade of uncertain form. The open socket, which has a distinctly rectangular cross-section is damaged at the mouth, probably across the fastening nailhole. Too little of the blade survives to allow of certainty but the slender stemmed junction with the socket, which appears to meet the blade centrally, makes identification as a small spearhead probable.

From gully 32, cut 4, unit 1731. Early 3rd century AD.

3 Bridle bit
Length of links 8.1 cm and 8.0 cm ST 84 DQG, SF 877

A snaffle bit of the commonest Roman type, comprising two links of rounded square cross-section with a simple inner loop and collar-like side loop.

From occupation layer (disturbed silts) in the south-east quadrant of block 9. Late 2nd–3rd century AD.

4 Hipposandal, fragment
Height 6.1 cm ST 84 DBL, SF 711

One side-wing only, broken at the angle with the base plate. From an Aubert Type I hipposandal (see Manning 1985, 63–6).

From upper layer (unit 1535) in (?)latrine pit 1535. 3rd century AD.

5 Hipposandal, fragment
Height 4.2 cm ST 81 KE, SF 157

Side-wing of an Aubert Type I, as no. 4, with a small part of the broken base plate.

From gully 54, cut 5, unit 212. Mid/late 3rd century AD.

6 Ox-goad   Length 3.7 cm ST 84 DRA, SF 883

Normal type, with a two-turn spiral-coiled socket and a shorter slender spike.

From upper layer (unit 1885) of well 1885. 3rd century AD.

7 Ox-goad   Length 4.6 cm ST 81 GT, SF 181

A well-made example of the split tubular-socketed type of goad, rather less common than the coil-socketed type. The spike projects from one edge of the socket and has lost its pointed tip, which may have been down-turned to facilitate its use. Cf. Atkinson 1916, 52, no. 38, Pl. XV, 18, two examples from Lowbury Hill.

From an upper layer (unit 156) in well 135. Residual Roman finds with Anglo-Saxon pottery, 4th–7th century AD.

8 ?Pole-tip, fragment   Length 9.6 cm ST 81 HK, SF 97

A badly corroded fragment of heavy dished plate with no certain original edge surviving. X-radiography discloses a sub-rectangular perforation. Although other possibilities exist, the fragment is similar in general form and dimensions to three putative cart pole-tips from Newstead (Curle 1911, 288. Pl. LXV, 2–4) and a fourth example from Wilderspool (Jackson 1992, 82, Fig. 43, 8).

From well 171, uppermost layer (unit 171). Residual 3rd–4th century AD pottery with Anglo-Saxon sherds, 4th–7th century AD.

9 Axe-butt   Width 3.4 cm ST 82 BAW, SF 343

A heavily-corroded and laminated axe-head fragment, comprising the butt and roughly half of the shaft hole. The hammer-face of the butt is a very lightly domed rectangle. The butt is not diagnostic, and other than observing that the shaft hole was unlugged, the axe-head cannot be further classified. Its modest size is indicative of general carpentry or farm usage rather than tree-felling.

From ditch 71, cut 9, unit 726. Residual Roman and Anglo-Saxon finds in post-medieval ditch.

10 Drill-bit   (*Unillus.*) Length 4.2 cm ST 81 HM, SF 171

The heavy pyramidal head from a carpenter's bit. Breakage has occurred in the usual place, at the junction of head and stem.

From a shallow scoop (unit 173), probably recent disturbance, north of building R1. Phase VI.

11 Chisel   Length 14.4 cm ST 83 J1,1, SF 590

A solid-handled mortise chisel, complete except for the very end of the blade. The handle is rectangular-sectioned with a lightly domed head burred through use. Its junction with the narrower, square-sectioned stem is marked by sloping shoulders. Although the blade lacks its cutting edge, its plano-convex profile, formed by a bevel on one side, is characteristic of mortise chisels. Cf. Manning 1985, 23, Pl. 11, B39, from Hod Hill.

From pit J1, layer 1. Late 3rd/early 4th century AD.

12 ?Chisel   (*Unillus.*) Length 14.9 cm ST 84 DRA, SF 906

A rectangular-sectioned rod broken at one end. The complete end terminates in a lightly-domed head. The upper stem is of rounded rectangular cross-section. It tapers and splays to the lower stem, of crisper, flat rectangular cross-section. The end of what was probably a lightly-flared cutting edge is damaged. Probably a solid-handled paring chisel or small mortise chisel.

From the uppermost layer (unit 1885) of well 1885. 3rd century AD.

13 ?Wedge or ?chisel

Length 5.5 cm ST 84 P10, 1, SF 768

A small wedge-shaped block, apparently complete, with broad, blade-like edge. Perhaps a small wedge or a chisel for e.g. mosaic work. The object was fused by its corrosion products to the base of a shell-tempered jar.

From pit P10, layer 1. Early 3rd century AD.

14 ?Punch (Unillus.) Length 11.1 cm ST 84 DVZ, SF 1011

A carefully-made cigar-shaped rod, the upper stem of chamfered square cross-section, the lower stem of rectangular cross-section. The head is damaged and the end of the lower stem is broken, so certainty is lacking, but this is probably a craftsman's punch.

From an upper layer (unit 1980) in well 2020/pit 2022. 3rd century AD.

15 Pruning hook (Unillus.)

Length 6.5 cm ST 82 ABF, SF 254

A small socketed hook, badly corroded and lacking most of the curved blade. In view of its diminutive size (socket diameter 1.3 cm), the hook must have been used for light agricultural/ horticultural tasks.

From topsoil/cleaning, block 2.

16 Spade sheath Length c. 28 cm ST 84A II, 26, 11, SF A28

A heavily-encrusted iron sheath (blade-edge) in position on the wooden blade of a complete T-handled spade. This combination of wood and iron components is usual for Romano-British spades. However, although blades completely of iron were not used, it is quite probable that many spades were made entirely of wood. X-radiography clarified the form of the sheath, which has a curved edge and flared arms, grooved to receive the end and sides of the wooden blade. It is an example of Manning's Type 1b sheath, of which smaller examples are known from Runcton Holme, Norfolk, and from the probable late Roman Lakenheath Hoard, Suffolk (Manning 1985, 44–7, Fig. 10, Pl. 19, F10 and F11.) Amongst the encrusted corrosion products on the blade is a calcite-rich sandy concretion of a similar composition to the mortar used in the construction of building R1 (see pp. 524–5 for analyses). The accidental encumbrance of the blade with hardened mortar may have been the reason the spade was discarded, but the absence of the concretion from the wooden part of the blade argues against this. For discussion of the spade, see p. 547, no. 5.

From the northern sump cut II, grid 11, layer 26. Late 2nd–3rd century AD.

17 Knife Length 12.8 cm ST 84 DSY, SF 1062

A small socketed knife. X-radiography revealed a nailhole in the open socket. The small blade has a straight back and a convex cutting edge which slopes up to the tip. The tip is complete but part of the cutting edge is broken away. Though always a slender blade, it would originally have been slightly more bellied.

This type of small socketed knife is not common. It is Manning's Type 22 (Manning 1985, 116, Fig. 29) and similar examples are known from Colchester, London (ibid. 117–8, Q62–Q65, Pl. 56) and Baldock (Stead and Rigby 1986, 154–5, Fig. 67, 535).

From pit 1931/2091. Early 3rd century AD.

18 Knife Length 13.9 cm ST 80 DA, SF 21

A light, tanged knife with slender blade. The blade back, straight and comparatively thick, slopes down steeply to the blunt tip. The lightly convex cutting edge is rather damaged but evidently ran parallel to the blade back. The slender rectangular sectioned tang is set centrally to the blade. A slight vertical ridge coinciding with the stepped tang/blade junction marks the proximal end of the handle. Manning's Type 10 (Manning 1985, 113–4 and Fig. 28), dated 1st century AD onwards.

From robbing debris (unit 70) in footing trench of building R1, east wing, east side, centre. Phase IV.

19 Knife Length 10.2 cm ST 80 AA, SF 9.

Similar to no. 18, though the tang is a little broader and fragmentary and the end of the blade is lacking so the form of the tip is uncertain.

From topsoil over building R1.

20 Knife Length 5.6 cm ST 84 DEA, SF 771

A fragment of a tanged knife. Most of the thin rectangular-sectioned tang is missing, together with much of the deep, flat blade. However sufficient survives to identify it as an example of Manning's Type 24 (Manning 1985, 116, Fig. 29, 118–9, Pl. 56, Q72–Q84), with a sinuous back and a lightly hollowed heel.

From topsoil/cleaning above pit 1825/1967.

21 Knife Length 5.7 cm ST 84 DVY, SF 1054

Blade fragment, proximal end with stub of the tang; distal end lacking. Quite a broad blade, with a straight back and a parallel, straight cutting edge. The tang is joined to the blade back.

From lower layer (unit 1979) in pit 2022. 3rd century AD.

22 ?Knife (Unillus.) Length 8.9 cm ST 84 DVE, SF 928

A rectangular-sectioned rod with lightly convex sides and a squared terminal. Only the stub of the blade remains at the other end. It appears to have had a downward-angled back and a marked heel. This is probably the rod handle or bar-like tang from a stout knife, perhaps of Manning's Type 8 (Manning 1985, Fig. 28, 113, Pl. 54, Q25–Q27).

From gully 31, cut 8, unit 1961. Late 2nd/3rd century AD.

22a Knife (Unillus.) Length 12.1 cm ST 82 ACL, SF 308

Blade fragment of a large tanged knife lacking most of the tang and the upturned blade tip. The back is concave and the cutting edge convex. It is Manning's Type 1 cleaver (Manning 1985, Fig. 30).

From ditch 9, cut 12, unit 500. 3rd century AD.

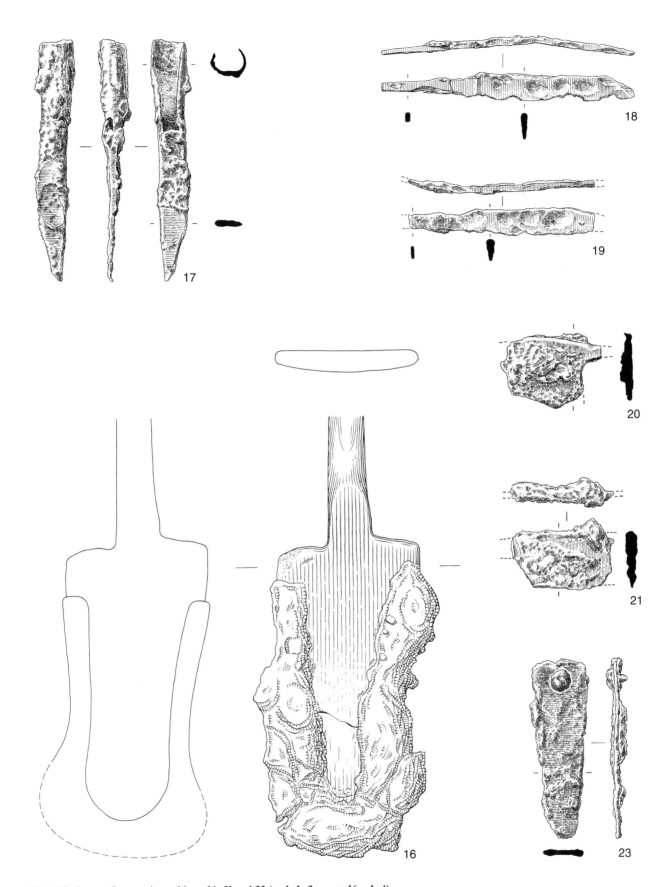

Fig. 118 Stonea Grange: iron objects 16–21 and 23 (scale 1:2 except 16 = 1:4).

23 Knife   Length 9.5 cm   ST 84 DRA, SF 892

An elongated triangular blade, of flat and very thin cross-section, with a straight back and damaged, lightly convex cutting edge which slopes up near the tip. The handle fastening appears to have been a handle-plate, but it is broken, probably across a nailhole, and only a single perforation remains, with a corroded nail in situ.

From upper layer (unit 1885) of well 1885. 3rd century AD.

24 Knife   Length 8.1 cm   ST 81 QP, SF 206

A short, deep blade from a clasp knife. The cutting edge is straight, or nearly so, the back convex, sloping gently down to the rounded tip. X-radiography revealed the characteristic broad offset tang, broken just short of the perforation for the pivot pin. In form and size very close to the blade of a complete example from Silchester (Boon 1974, Fig. 34, 15).

From uppermost layer (unit 336) of well 336. Late 3rd–4th century AD.

25 Knife   Length 11.1 cm   ST 81 KE, SF 147

Blade only, both ends broken. The cutting edge is straight, the back humped with a gentle convex slope down to the tip. The form appears not to be included in Manning's typology (Manning 1985, 108ff., Figs 28–9). Though the fragmentary state of the knife renders any identification uncertain, it may have been the blade of a clasp knife with slotted bone or wooden handle, cf. Boon 1974, Fig. 34, no. 15, from Silchester, and Bushe-Fox 1914, 22, Pl. X, Fig. 1, from Wroxeter.

Context and date as no. 5.

26 Ladle   Length 19.7 cm   ST 83 CML, SF 547

A complete example, with a shallow, slightly elliptical bowl and a comparatively short narrow handle of rounded rectangular cross-section. As usual on Roman ladles the junction of handle and bowl is strengthened by expanding the handle into a trapezoidal plate. A closely similar example from Winterton (Stead 1976, 222–3, Fig. 120, no. 187) came from a third century context.

From ditch 3, cut 6, unit 1274. 3rd century AD.

27 Flesh fork   Length 5.4 cm   ST 83 G4, 4, SF 497

Only the functional end survives with its characteristic double prong arrangement, and part of the handle stem. Flesh forks were sometimes combined with ladles, one at each end of the handle stem, but occur more frequently singly with a looped handle plate, cf. Manning 1985, 105, Pl. 51, P35, a complete example from London.

From well G4, layer 4. Mid 3rd century AD.

28 ?Lamp hanger   (*Unillus.*)
Length 15 cm   ST 84 DRO, SF 902

A slender rectangular-sectioned rod, broken at both ends. Approximately one half of the rod is spirally twisted. The end of the other

half is curved at the point of breakage. Too slight to be a rod component of a cauldron chain, this may have been part of a lamp hanger; cf. Manning 1985, 99–100, Fig. 26 and Pl. 45, P6.

From gully 29, cut 5, unit 1898. 3rd century AD.

29 Bucket handle   (*Unillus.*)   ST 84A, II, 26, 8, SFA, 29

From the north sump, cut II, layer 26, grid 8. Late 2nd–3rd century AD.

30 Bucket handle   Length 13.1 cm   ST 81 GP, SF 47

One hooked terminal and part of the hoop from a bucket handle, heavily corroded.

From hard-standing (unit 152), north of the intersection of gullies 48 and 49. Phase III.

31 Handle staple   Length 6.7 cm   ST 84 DCT, SF 734

A small example of normal Roman type. There is wear in the eye of the looped head. X-radiography revealed two small square nailholes in the plate, the end of which may be broken.

From unit 1567 in pit 1567. 3rd century AD.

[Finger-ring, see Finger-rings, no. 1, p. 327.]

32 Pin   Length 9.1 cm   ST 81 JQ, SF 139

A heavily corroded rod of circular cross-section. X-radiography revealed that this is an ornately decorated pin, sadly broken at both ends. The upper end retains a finely worked reel-and-baluster moulding, beneath which the stem tapers to a waist before expanding to a swelling above the tapered but incomplete lower end, presumably a hairpin. Such elaborate decoration is unusual on an iron pin and the present author knows of no obvious parallel.

From unit 199 of the low rubbly mound sealing building S1. 9th–10th century AD.

33 Stylus   Length 13.1 cm   ST 81 GA, SF 196

The badly corroded remains of what was once a well-made stylus, with long hourglass-shaped eraser. X-radiography revealed that the stem, now bent, retains no copper alloy inlaid decoration, often to be found on iron styli. Corrosion had destroyed the surface and erased any cut decoration that may have been present. As usual there is a marked swelling, to form a grip, just above the simple writing point.

From the mortar floor (unit 139) of building R2. Phase IV.

34 ?Strike-a-light   Length 8 cm   ST 81 FM, SF 74

A short, loop-headed rod of flat rectangular cross-section. The object is complete, though slightly distorted. The form and size are close to that of strike-a-lights (Feuereisen) from the late Roman

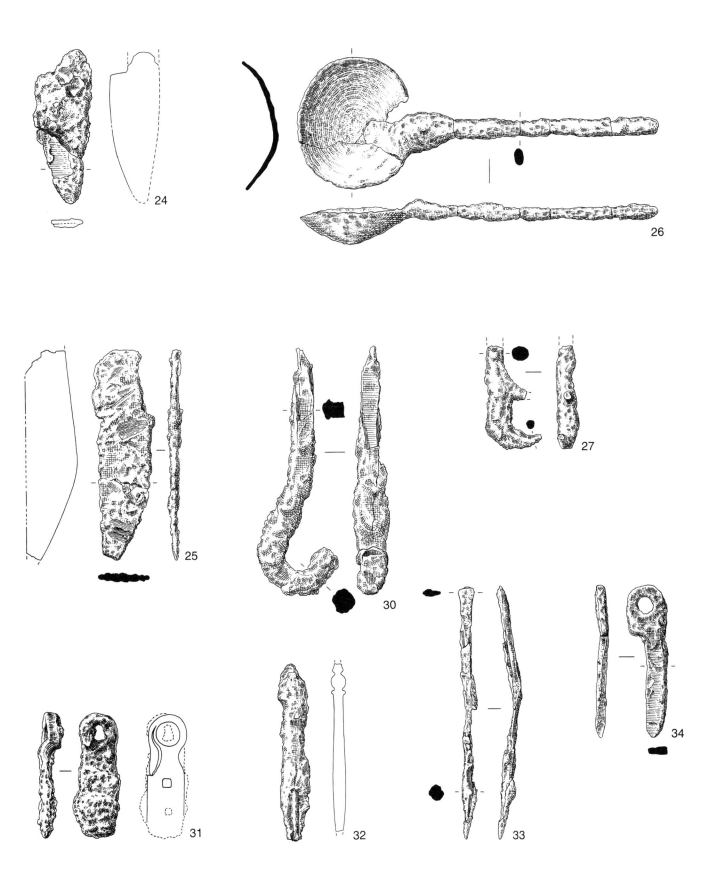

Fig. 119 Stonea Grange: iron objects 24–7 and 30–4 (scale 1 : 2).

cemetery at Keszthely-Dobogó, esp. grave 38 (Sági 1981, 19–20, Abb. 6.1, 7–9; 49–51, Abb. 33, 13.).

From unit 127 of the low rubbly mound sealing building S1. 9th–10th century AD.

35 Hobnailed shoe   (*Unillus.*) ST 84 DTB, SF 681

The shape of the shoe was revealed by a corroded mass of hobnails in a soil matrix. No patterning of the hobnails could be discerned.

From well 1914, unit 1934. 3rd century AD.

36 Hobnailed shoe   (*Unillus.*) ST 84 DIH, SF 775

A cluster of about 30 hobnails fused to the side of a rim sherd from a large grey-ware bowl. The hobnails preserve partially the curved outer edge of the shoe sole/heel, with a row of smaller nails round the perimeter and a mass of larger nails within.

From gully 21, cut 2, unit 1700. Early 3rd century AD.

37 Hobnailed shoe   (*Unillus.*)
Max. length 8.2 cm   ST 83 J1, 2, SF 595

Four clusters of hobnails corroded in position and preserving partially the shape of the shoe sole/heel. No patterning of the hobnails is observable.

From pit J1, layer 2. Late 3rd/early 4th century AD.

38 Hobnailed shoe   (*Unillus.*) ST 84 DVD, SF 920

Several fused clusters of hobnails with profile, incomplete, of shoe edge. Originally undoubtedly, the remains of a complete shoe.

From lower layer (unit 1960) in pit 1960. Late 2nd/3rd century AD.

39 Hobnailed shoe   (*Unillus.*) ST 84 DQR, SF 1050

About 15–20 hobnails fused in small clusters, one preserving part of the curve of the heel/sole of the shoe.

From basal layer (unit 1877) in pit 1695. Later 2nd/3rd century AD.

40 Hobnailed shoe   (*Unillus.*) ST 84 DXS, SF 1081

Seven small hobnails retrieved from the soil-stain of a shoe/sandal.

From basal layer (unit 2022) pit 2022. 3rd century AD.

41 Hobnails   (*Unillus.*) ST 84 DXX, SF 1087

A fused strip of seven hobnails.

From gully 18, cut 12, unit 2026. 3rd century AD.

42 Hobnails   (*Unillus.*) Head diameter 1.3 cm   ST 80 CS, SF 18

Twenty-three dome-headed hobnails.

From secondary silt (unit 63) in the small hypocausted room of building R1. Early 3rd century AD.

43 Hobnails   (*Unillus.*)
Head diameter 0.9 cm   ST 83 CDF, SF 514

Twelve dome-headed hobnails.

From ditch 9, cut 2, unit 1077. 3rd century AD.

44 Key   Length 25.3 cm   ST 82 AAK, SF 301.

A large T-shaped lift-key of normal form, with a rectangular plate and an anchor-shaped bit providing one tooth on either side of the stem. One tooth and the handle's suspension loop are broken.

From the uppermost layer (unit 451) of the north end of the sump. Residual Roman finds with post-medieval material.

45 Key   (*Unillus.*) Length 11.1 cm   ST 82 ACV, SF 328

An L-shaped lift key, badly corroded and laminated. The upper stem has a neat square cross-section and terminates in a rolled-over suspension loop. The slender rectangular-sectioned lower stem tapers to the bit, most of which is broken away.

From ditch 74, cut 1, uppermost layer (unit 509). Late 3rd–4th century AD.

46 Key   Length 8.2 cm   ST 82 AAA, SF 243

A slide-key of standard form, with rectangular handle plate and teeth cut into a straight rectangular bit. Corrosion has removed most of the surface and blocks the teeth. This type of key is often well finished, and the remains of a simple grooved moulding is visible on the sides at the junction of the handle plate with its looped head.

From topsoil over block 1b.

47 Key   Length *c.* 7 cm   ST 81 FR

A slide-key, as no. 46, but a little smaller, very heavily corroded and in poor condition. Drawn from X-ray plate.

From surface cleaning (unit 131) over upper fill of pit 132. Phase IV.

48 ?Latch lifter   (*Unillus.*)
Length over 30 cm   ST 84 DKA, SF 791

Although heavily corroded, laminated and shattered, the fragmentary remains display the characteristic shape of a latch lifter – flat handle plate dropping down to a long curved bow. The end of the bow, with its upturned tip, is missing, and the end of the handle plate is too encrusted to determine whether or not it had a suspension loop.

From gully 32, cut 3, unit 1717. Early 3rd century AD.

49 Looped head   (*Unillus.*) Length 4.1 cm   ST 81 FS, SF 80

A collar-like looped terminal on the end of a fragmentary rectangular-sectioned rod. Probably a key handle.

Context and date as no. 68.

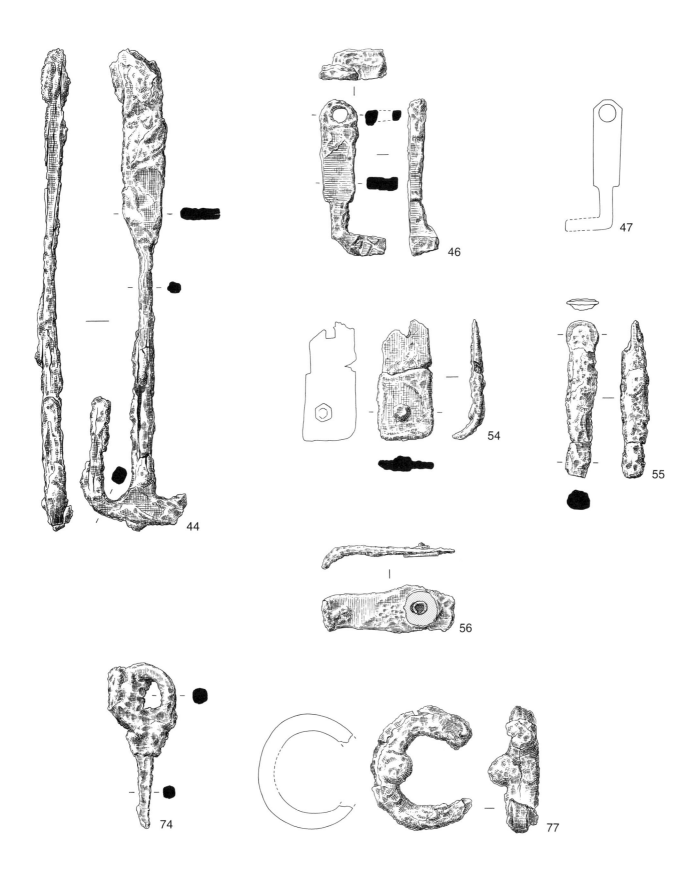

Fig. 120 Stonea Grange: iron objects 44, 46–7, 54–6, 74 and 77 (scale: 1:2).

50 Looped head   (*Unillus.*) Length 3.9 cm   ST 81 LZ, SF 129

A neatly-made broken loop of slender square-sectioned rod. Perhaps the looped terminal of a key or latch-lifter.

From upper layer (unit 253) of gully 64, cut 1. Late 3rd–4th century AD.

51 ?Lock bolt   (*Unillus.*) Length 6.4 cm   ST 81 HT, SF 96

A small rectangular-sectioned bar with a rod-like projection at one end. The other end is broken. Form and size very similar to the lock bolts of the type of tumbler lock operated by L-shaped slide-keys.

From upper layer (unit 179) gully 44. 3rd century AD.

52 Hinge   (*Unillus.*) Length 14.8 cm   ST 84 DEE, SF 722

A U-shaped drop-hinge. The U-curve is narrowed and thickened to a rounded square cross-section. The arms, now fragmentary, were probably originally of equal length. They taper towards their tip. One preserves three blocked nail-holes; the other has two but probably originally three.

Cf. Meates 1987, 94–5, Fig. 41, no. 231, from the Lullingstone villa.

From ditch 8, cut 7, unit 1601. 3rd century AD.

53 ?Hinge   (*Unillus.*) Length 11.4 cm   ST 80 AZ, SF 24

A rectangular-sectioned bar, tapered at one end and U-curved at the other, both ends broken. The narrowed, thickened curve is characteristic of Roman drop-hinges.

Context and date as no. 66.

54 ?Hinge strap or nailed binding
Length 6.3 cm   ST 81 FM, SF 82

A parallel-sided or gently-tapered strip with two perforations, one of which is blocked with the remains of a nail. Both ends fragmentary. the curving of one end appears original and the object may have been a corner binding or a hinge strap.

From unit 127 of the low rubbly mound sealing building S1. 9th–10th century AD.

55 ?Window bar   Length 8.2 cm   ST 83 CCV, SF 469

A rounded rectangular-sectioned rod terminating in a discoidal flange with central perforation in which is the remains of a nail corroded in position. The other end is broken. The presence of the nail rules out the possibility that this was a knife or key handle but is consistent with identification as a window bar. Although it differs from the characteristic strap-and-star arrangement of the type of window grille most often found in the northern provinces (Manning 1985, 128 and Pl. 60 R17–R18), it is not dissimilar to the simpler lattice grilles still in situ in windows at Pompeii and Herculaneum.

From the top layer (unit 1067) of ditch 9, cut 2. 3rd–7th century AD.

56 Binding/mount   Length 7.4 cm   ST 84 P10, 1, SF 752

A flat parallel-sided strip, broken at one end just beyond an angled curve. The other end, which may be complete, is hammer-flattened and splayed around a perforation, in which are the corroded remains of an iron nail/stud with a large sub-circular tin–lead alloy disc, presumably either a decorative washer or solder. The nail head is missing. The object is too fragmentary to permit of certainty, but the combination of a decorative stud and an angled binding are suggestive of a fitting from a box, chest or door.

From pit P10, layer 1. Early 3rd century AD.

57 Corner bracket/angle binding   (*Unillus.*)
Width 2.1 cm   ST 84 DVG, SF 936

A small example, broken at both ends.

From occupation layer (unit 1963) over pit complex 1989, 1990 etc, south-west block 9.

58 Binding/hinge   (*Unillus.*)
Length 4.9 cm, width 2.1 cm   ST 84 DIC, SF 1021

A narrow parallel-sided nailed strip bent over to form an equal-armed binding or simple hinge strap.

From the uppermost layer (unit 1695) in ?latrine pit 1695.

59 Binding   (*Unillus.*) Length 6.7 cm   ST 84 DSC, SF 934

A heavy rectangular binding of plano-convex cross-section, broken at one end. The complete end is squared-off. A single perforation survives, with nail corroded in position, its tip bent over. Probably a binding or hinge strap from a door.

From gully 34, cut 2, unit 1911. Late 2nd/early 3rd century AD.

60 Binding/plate   (*Unillus.*)
Length 9.3 cm, width 4.9 cm   ST 84 DXQ, SF 1066

A broad, parallel-sided plate made from very thin sheet, broken at one end and either complete or cut at the other. X-radiography revealed no nailholes. Of many potential uses a binding or strengthening plate for a box, chest, door etc. is probable.

From well 2020, unit 2020. Late 2nd–3rd century AD.

61 T-clamp   (*Unillus.*)
Width 8.1 cm (original *c.* 9.2 cm)   ST 80 AB, SF 1

A stout, but badly corroded example lacking the end of one arm and most of the stem.

From dereliction debris (unit 2) above building R1. Phase IV.

62 T-clamp   (*Unillus.*) Length 6.1 cm   ST 80 AB, SF 36

Fragment, the apex of the T only, badly laminated.

Context and date as no. 61.

63 T-clamp (*Unillus.*) Length over 8 cm ST 80 CV, SF 23 and 30

Fragments from the head and stem of one or more large T-clamps, now badly laminated and broken.

From robbing debris (unit 65), north-west quadrant of building R1.

64 T-clamp (*Unillus.*) Length 5.3 cm ST 80 CV, SF 20

Fragment, laminated and deeply-fissured, comprising the top of the stem and the truncated remains of both arms.

Context and date as no. 63.

65 T-clamp (*Unillus.*) Length 9.5 cm ST 80 DN, SF 32

Lower stem only, badly corroded.

From surface of natural clay (unit 82) beneath robbed foundation of building R1, south-east quadrant. Phase III/IV.

66 T-clamp (*Unillus.*) Length 5.3 cm ST 80 AZ, SF 29

Laminated stem fragment.

From occupation debris (unit 23), west of building R1. 2nd–7th century AD.

67 T-clamp (*Unillus.*) Width 6.6 cm ST 84 DDP, SF 712

A stout example with short broad arms lacking the lower stem.

From basal layer (unit 1587) of pit 1567. 3rd century AD.

68 ?T-clamp (*Unillus.*) Length 5.4 cm ST 81 FS, SF 88

Stem, spiked terminal fragment only.

From top layer (unit 132) of pit 132. 4th century onwards.

69 Joiner's dog (*Unillus.*) Length 8.1 cm ST 84 DIF, SF 858

Normal broad, shallow, U-shaped form. The body is lentoid, the spikes short.

From upper layer (unit 1698) in pit 1698. 3rd or 4th century AD.

70 Joiner's dog, fragment (*Unillus.*) Length 7.2 cm ST 84 DEA, SF 741

From topsoil, blocks 8–9 and 3–4 east.

71 Split spiked-loop (*Unillus.*) Length 4.6 cm ST 84 DSS, SF 927

A small example of normal type with a looped head and everted spikes, both now broken short. Often used to secure ring-handles to woodwork – doors, chests etc.

From an upper layer (unit 1926) in well 1885. 3rd century AD.

72 Split spiked-loop (*Unillus.*) Length 4.3 cm ST 84 DYW, SF 1079

Looped head only, lower stem and spikes lacking.

From building R12, east unit, post-hole 2049.

73 Ring-headed spike (*Unillus.*) Length 8.9 cm ST 82 ADM, SF 332.

A looped spike, with circular head and sinuous stem. Complete.

From ditch 9, cut 8, unit 525. 3rd century AD.

74 Ring-headed spike Length 8.7 cm ST 84 DOK, SF 870

A looped spike, with large circular head and tapered, rectangular-sectioned shank, the tip broken.

From gully 19, cut 5, unit 1822. Mid 3rd century AD.

75 Loop-headed spike (*Unillus.*) Length 8.4 cm ST 81 FN, SF 59

A complete but slightly distorted example

Cf. Manning 1985, R27–R33, and probably used to anchor a securing ring.

From the hard-standing (unit 128) north of building R1. 2nd–7th century AD.

76 Looped head (*Unillus.*) Length 3.8 cm ST 81 FW, SF 53

A small looped terminal fragment, as no. 50.

From top layer (unit 135) of well 135. 4th–7th century AD.

77 Ring Diameter *c.* 6.5 cm ST 81 GP, SF 46

A large broken annular ring, of rounded square cross-section, with the corroded remains of what may once have been the looped head of a split pin or split spiked-loop. If so the ring was probably used as a handle or tethering point.

Context and date as no. 30.

78 Ring (*Unillus.*) Diameter 4.5 cm ST 84 DYC, SF 1080

A plain ring made from a slender rod of rounded rectangular cross-section.

From gully 19, cut 2, unit 2031. Mid 3rd century AD.

79 Scrap (*Unillus.*) Length 4.4 cm ST 81 FV, SF 64

A cut fragment of heavy bar of plano-convex cross-section.

From silty clay occupation layer (unit 134), north-west quadrant block 1.

Phase IV/V.

80 ?Cramp (*Unillus.*) Length 13.4 cm ST 84 DOT, SF 819

A curved rectangular-sectioned rod with hooked end, broken at the other end. Possibly a joiner's dog or cramp, but perhaps a vessel handle or latch lifter.

From layer (unit 1831) above gully 27, cut 2. 3rd century AD.

IRONWORKING DEBRIS

Paul Craddock

The smelting and working of iron produce considerable quantities of durable debris, slags etc. as well as other evidence such as blackening of the soil. At Stonea small amounts only of the debris of iron working were recovered. These pieces were all isolated finds in contexts which otherwise had no evidence for iron production. Thus, they are almost certainly not in their primary context but do suggest that ironworking was taking place somewhere on site.

The pieces were all visually examined and qualitatively analysed in the British Museum Research Laboratory (File 6439). The analyses, which were performed on unprepared surfaces by X-ray fluorescence (XRF), were carried out principally to look for evidence of non-ferrous metalworking. None was found beyond a very faint trace of lead in no. 2. The soils at Stonea are calcareous and this accounts for the presence of calcium and of strontium, and the titanium is also likely to come from the soil. The potassium is likely to originate from charcoal or wood ash, while the traces of manganese are likely to come from the iron.

All the fragments are slags or vitrified clays which could all belong to either the primary smelting, or the smithing stage, where the iron, either as blooms or as forged billets, was hammered to shape on an anvil with frequent annealing in a hearth. The general absence of sizeable solid lumps of tap slag suggests that most of these fragments were associated with smithing rather than primary smelting.

1 ST 81 FW, BMRL 44910T Small lump of dense slag, 100 g, iron with silicon, calcium and titanium. Could be from either iron smelting or smithing.

From top layer (unit 135) of well 135. Phase IV/V. 4th–7th century AD.

2 ST 81 JT, BMRL 44901V Fragment of gassy, partially vitrified material, containing iron with calcium, potassium, strontium and a faint trace of lead. This could be associated with iron smithing. The lead content is too small to be of any significance.

From the upper fill (unit 202) of gully 54, cut 5. Phase IV. Mid/late 3rd century AD.

3 ST 81 LQ, BMRL 44902T Fragment of gassy, partially vitrified material containing iron and silicon with calcium, strontium, potassium, and manganese. This could be associated with iron smithing.

From the denuded surface (unit 245) of street 1 E/W, east of Anglo-Saxon building S1.

4 ST 81 MR, BMRL 44903R Two pieces of burnt red clay with some vitrification, containing iron and silicon with some calcium, potassium and titanium. Partially vitrified material containing iron with silicon, titanium, calcium, strontium and potassium. These pieces could be from a smithing hearth.

From a spit (unit 269) through the silts south-east of Anglo-Saxon building S1. Phase IV–V.

5 ST 81 ND, BMRL 44904T Rather light fragment of partially vitrified material containing iron and silicon. Probably from a hearth lining.

Context as no. 4, unit 280. Phases IV–V.

6 ST 81 NY, BMRL 44906W A fragment of heavily vitrified dross containing iron, silicon, calcium, strontium and potassium. This could come from smithing operations.

From gully 64, cut 2, unit 298. Phase IV. Late 3rd–4th century AD.

7 ST 81 QC, BMRL 44907U A partially vitrified fragment containing iron and silicon with some calcium, strontium, titanium and potassium. This could come from smithing operations.

From the upper fill (unit 325) of oven 2. Phase IV. 3rd/4th century AD.

8 ST 81 QP, BMRL 44908S A partially vitrified fragment containing iron and silicon with some calcium, strontium, titanium and potassium. This could come from smithing operations.

From the top layer (unit 336) of well 336. Phase IV onwards. Late 3rd–4th century AD.

9 ST 82 ABF, BMRL 44909Q Partially vitrified fragment containing iron with calcium, silicon, strontium, potassium, titanium and traces of manganese. This could come from a smithing operation.

From topsoil, north-east quadrant of block 1.

In conclusion, the few scattered fragments of burnt and partially vitrified material centred on the north-west quadrant of block 1 indicate that either iron smelting or smithing, more probably the latter, was carried on somewhere in the vicinity in Phase IV, though not actually in any of the areas excavated as the concentration of debris is far too small. Understandably, such activity was kept well away from the Phase IV dwelling areas to the south and east.

LEAD OBJECTS

Ralph Jackson (Figs 121–3)

A FROM THE EXCAVATIONS (Fig. 121)

The malleability and ductility of lead make it a readily reusable metal and mitigate against the survival intact of lead objects. Accordingly, the excavation assemblage includes no complete object, and the fragmentary nature of the pieces renders difficult their identification. The majority of the catalogued items are pieces of cut sheeting, clippings, and

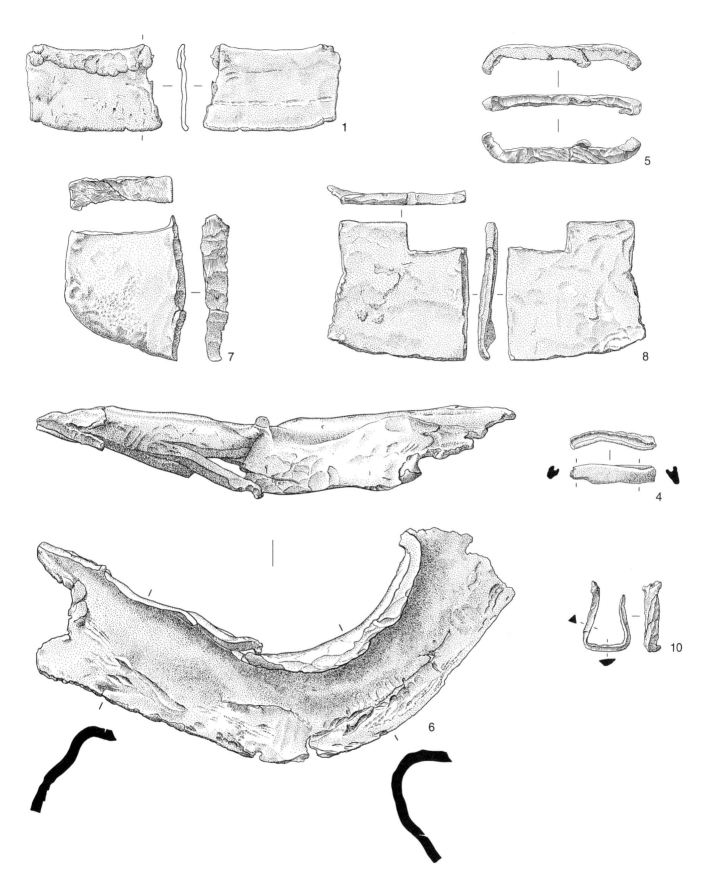

Fig. 121 Stonea Grange: lead objects 1, 4–8 and 10 from the excavations (scale 1 : 2).

fused lumps, over 80% of which were found within or in the close vicinity of the R1 building complex. Many of those contexts are dereliction/destruction deposits, and it seems probable that the lead fragments are, in the main, the chopped-up or melted remains of piping, flashing and other waterproofing linings, removed from the building after its demise.

1 ?Vessel rim

Length 78 mm, original diameter *c.* 200 mm, weight 63.8 g
ST 82 BDL, SF 323

Sheet fragment, with one complete curved edge with beaded rim. The opposite edge is broken, possibly on the line of a carination, while the two short edges are cut. In its final form this was a piece of scrap metal, with the beaded rim hammered back on itself. Originally it may have been part of a flanged dish. Cf. Frere 1984, 65, Fig. 27, no. 242, of pewter.

From upper layer (788) in well 808. 3rd century AD.

2 ?Vessel base (*Unillus.*)
Diameter 44 mm, weight 43.7 g ST 81 NX, SF 209

Base fragment of a small thick-walled ?pot cut up for scrap.

From the east terminal (cut 1) of gully 44. 3rd century AD.

3 ?Finial (*Unillus.*) Length 46 mm, weight 18.1 g ST 82 AAE

An L-shaped moulded strip of rounded rectangular cross-section, broken at one end. Function unknown, but perhaps a decorative fitting.

From the upper layer (446) of well 446. South of stone building complex R1. Mid/late 3rd century AD.

4 ?Window leading
Length 47 mm, weight 16.6 g ST 80 AA, SF 10

A strip, now distorted, of wedge-shaped cross-section, with a U-sectioned groove let into the thicker side. One end appears complete; the other is rebated and broken. Function uncertain, but the size and form of the groove corresponds to the dimensions of the edges of the thinner panes of window glass from the stone building complex R1, for which it could have been a seating.

From topsoil in the region of building R1.

5 ?Cramp or ?rivet
Length 87 mm, weight 29.5 g ST 81 FF, SF 69

A roughly-cut rectangular-sectioned U-shaped rod with turned over ends, and an off-centre flange.

From topsoil in the region of building R1.

6 ?Waterproof lining
Length 260 mm, thickness 4–5 mm, weight 926.2 g
ST 81 KF, SF 107

An arched, flanged fragment of thick sheet, with coarse cutting marks where it was hacked away from its original position and cut up for scrap. Perhaps part of an outlet/inlet waterproofing from a lead-lined tank or bath.

From well 135, unit 213. Later 3rd century AD.

7–8 Scrap: two pieces   ST 81 LS, SF 133

7 Length 66 mm, weight 424.3 g

A trapezoidal piece cut from the corner of a billet/ingot, 9–13 mm thick. Each of the two cut edges appears to have been cut with a different tool. The long, clean, cut-facets on the longer edge imply the use of a heavy blade, perhaps an axe. The striated appearance of the cut face on the shorter edge, on the other hand, was more probably caused by a toothed blade, i.e. a saw.

8 Length 73 mm, weight 202.6 g

A sub-rectangular piece cut from a hammered sheet 3–6 mm in thickness. One edge is ragged and was probably broken by bending to-and-fro. The other edges were cut, two bearing a marked 'step' which resulted from being cut from both planar faces. The function of/reason for the rectangular notch is not clear. The possibility that it was detached to give the piece a chosen unit of weight gains little support from the weight measurement which corresponds only to $7\frac{1}{2}$ Roman ounces (203.25 g using the conversion 27.1 g per *uncia*).

From a charcoal-rich spread (unit 247) south of building R1. Phase IV.

9 Scrap (*Unillus.*)
Length 121 mm, weight 261.5 g ST 84 DCP, SF 914

A heavy, broken and distorted amorphous fragment with hammer-marks and cutting marks. The cutting marks are nearly identical to those on the shorter edge of no. 7, and were probably made by a toothed blade.

From the fill of ?latrine pit 1563. 3rd century AD.

10 Off-cut   Length 38 mm, weight 11.1 g ST 80 BA, SF 28

An irregular clipped strip bent to a rough U-shape. It is not clear whether this distortion was intentional/functional or whether the object was simply a piece of scrap.

From destruction deposit (unit 24) in the small hypocausted room of building R1. Late 2nd/early 3rd century AD.

11 Off-cut (*Unillus.*)
Length 48 mm, weight 23.8 g ST 81 MG, SF 156

A distorted, tapered clipping, with cut marks on one face.

From amorphous rubbish spread 260, south of building R1. Phase IV.

12 Off-cut (*Unillus.*) Length 61 mm, weight 10.8 g ST 82 AHR

A distorted ribbon-like clipping of flat triangular cross-section. Cut marks are visible on one face.

From the timber slot in the south side of the shaft of well 446. Late 2nd/3rd century AD.

13 Off-cut (*Unillus.*)

Length 185 mm (unrolled), weight 45.7 g ST 82 ABF, SF 255

A 'concertinaed' rough clipping.

From topsoil/cleaning, blocks 2/3.

14 Off-cut (*Unillus.*)

Length 36 mm, weight 4.3 g ST 81 KB, SF 170

A small fragment.

From gully 44, cut 2, unit 209. Late 2nd century AD.

15 Off-cuts (*Unillus.*)

Length 48 mm, 36 mm, 31 mm, 22 mm; weight 15.5 g ST 82 AAA

Four fragments of slender clippings.

From topsoil/cleaning, block 1a/1b.

16 Off-cut (*Unillus.*)

Length 41 mm, weight 3.4 g ST 81 FN, SF 49

A very slender clipping, distorted.

From the metalled surface (unit 128) north of building R1. Phases III–V.

17 Off-cut (*Unillus.*)

Length 39 mm, weight 4 g ST 81 FG, SF 61

A slender triangular-sectioned clipping fragment.

From robbing/dereliction debris, south side of south room, building R1. Phase IV.

18 Off-cut (*Unillus.*)

Diameter 13 mm, weight 2.7 g ST 82 AFZ, SF 369

A small coiled tapered clipping.

From ditch 9, (cut 11), unit 585, south-east of building R1. 3rd century AD.

19 Off-cut (*Unillus.*)

Length 33 mm, weight 10.9 g ST 81 HB, SF 202

A fragment of clipped, semi-coalesced strip.

From sub-circular stone setting 163, south of building R1. Phase IV.

20 Off-cut (*Unillus.*)

Length 41 mm, weight 7.8 g ST 80 BA, SF 35

A J-shaped stepped 'segmented' clipping of trapezoidal cross-section, with cutting marks on the flat lower face.

Context as no. 10.

21 Off-cut (*Unillus.*)

Length 49 mm, weight 9.5 g ST 82 AAV, SF 422

A sinuous clipping of trapezoidal cross-section, as no.20.

From black soil spread south of building R1. 3rd century AD. Phase III/IV.

22 Off-cut (*Unillus.*)

Length 41 mm, weight 6.4 g ST 81 FG, SF 39

A slender curved strip of semi-circular cross-section. The convex face preserves the cast surface, the flat face bears stepped cutting marks.

Context as no. 17.

23 Off-cut (*Unillus.*)

Length 49 mm, weight 7.4 g ST 84 DPW, SF 1086

A very corroded piece in two fragments.

From gully 18, cut 20, unit 1857. 3rd century AD.

24 ?Packing (*Unillus.*)

Thickness 9 mm, weight 1.9 g ST 83 J4,2, SF 581

A small fragment sandwiched between the corroded remnants of thin copper-alloy sheet.

From well J4, layer 2. Late 3rd/early 4th century AD.

25 Strip (*Unillus.*)

Length 38 mm, weight 11.4 g ST 81 PY, SF 195

An L-shaped rod of rectangular cross-section. Function not apparent.

From oven 1, unit 321. Phase IV.

26 Rod (*Unillus.*) Length 55 mm, weight 19.8 g ST 82 AFY

A short length of rounded triangular-sectioned rod, tapered at one end, broken at the other, with a small slot near the broken end. Function unknown.

From ditch 9 (cut 9) unit 584, south-east of building R1. Late 3rd/early 4th century AD.

27 Sheet (*Unillus.*)

Length 51 mm, thickness 6 mm, weight 72.8 g ST 80 AC, SF 4

Irregularly cut fragment with hammer and cut markings.

From upper layer (unit 3) of pit 3. Phase IV/V. 4th–7th century AD.

28 Sheet   (*Unillus.*)

Length 23 mm, thickness 1–2 mm, weight 2.9 g ST 80 AA, SF 5

Small irregular bent and cut fragment with a thickened edging.
Context as no. 4.

29 Sheet   (*Unillus.*)

Length 21 mm, thickness 1 mm, weight 3.3 g ST 81 GN, SF 78

Small irregular strip fragment, bent.
From robbing debris, (unit 151), building R1, north-west quadrant.
4th century AD.

30 Sheet   (*Unillus.*)

Length 56 mm, thickness 2 mm, weight 30.7 g ST 81 FF, SF 70

Distorted irregular fragment with torn edges.
Context as no. 5.

31 Sheet   (*Unillus.*)

Length 59 mm, thickness *c.* 2 mm, weight 29.4 g ST 82 AEF

Distorted and corroded fragment with irregular edges and surfaces.
From fill of pit 543, north-east of building R1. 3rd century AD.

32 Sheet   (*Unillus.*)

Length 106 mm, thickness 1.2 mm, weight 37.7 g ST 81 HJ, SF 91

Fragment, with one original, but irregular long edge and one torn
long edge.
From upper fill (unit 170) of pit 170, north of building R1. 3rd/4th
century AD.

33 Sheet   (*Unillus.*)

Length 68 mm, thickness 0.2–0.4 mm, weight 5.5 g
ST 82 AGV, SF 404

An elongated triangular fragment of very thin sheet, with one
?original edge and two long cut edges. In thickness reminiscent
of *defixiones*, but not inscribed.
From basal layer (605) of pit 171/558, north-east of building R1. Late
3rd/4th century AD.

34 Sheet   (*Unillus.*)

Length 41 mm, thickness *c.* 2.5 mm, weight 14.5 g ST 81 HT, SF 165

A small distorted fragment with one thickened edging. The other
edges are ragged.
From gully 44, cut 2, unit 179. 3rd century AD.

35 Sheet   (*Unillus.*)

Length 56 mm, 34 mm; weight 29 g ST 82 AAE, SF 264

Two irregularly-shaped fragments.
Context as no. 3.

36 Fused lump   (*Unillus.*)

Length 56 mm, weight 87.8 g ST 80 CJ, SF 17

An irregularly-shaped coalesced puddle with a small globule fused
to the surface.
From robbing debris, building R1, south-east quadrant. 4th century AD.

37 Fused lump   (*Unillus.*)

Diameter *c.* 100 mm, weight 375 g ST 81 GT, SF 73

A large sub-circular lump, now distorted, of plano-convex cross-
section comprising several semi-coalesced fragments fused
together, perhaps in a small, shallow bowl-shaped hearth.
From upper layer (156) in well 135. 5th–7th century AD. (Residual
Roman and Anglo-Saxon.)

38 Fused lump   (*Unillus.*)

Length 60 mm, weight 39.8 g ST 81 LS, SF 125

An irregular-shaped lump comprising several fragments of thin
sheet (*c.* 0.9 mm) fused and compressed together. Mortar adheres
to one face.
From charcoal-rich spread (unit 247) south of building R1. Phase
IV.

39 Fused lump   (*Unillus.*)

Length 78 mm, weight 114.7 g ST 81 LS, SF 126

As no. 38; another, larger, more contorted fragment of the same
mass.
Context as no. 38.

40 Fused lump   (*Unillus.*)

Length 62 mm, weight 41.1 g ST 84 DVY, SF 695

A folded, irregular-shaped lump of distorted, semi-coalesced sheet
(*c.* 1.5 mm) with ragged edges.
From layer 1979 in pit 2022. 3rd century AD.

41 Fused lump   (*Unillus.*)

Length 49 mm, weight 30.7 g ST 82 AAI, SF 265

An irregular-shaped lump of distorted and roughened semico-
alesced sheet.
From gully 41, cut 2, unit 450. Late 2nd/early 3rd century AD.

42 Fused lump (*Unillus.*)

Length 58 mm, weight 55.4 g ST 81 LF, SF 135

A semi-coalesced puddle with ragged edges.

From a heavily burnt spread south of building R1. Phase IV.

43 Fused lump (*Unillus.*)

Length 51 mm, weight 29.5 g ST 81 HB, SF 203. As no. 42.

Context as no.19.

44 Fused lumps (*Unillus.*)

Length 93 mm, 51 mm; weight 329.5 g ST 82 AAV, SF 300

Two irregularly-shaped puddles.

Context as no. 21.

45 Fused lump (*Unillus.*)

Length 103 mm, weight 103 g ST 81 TP, SF 229

An irregular-edged and distorted semi-coalesced puddle.

From robbing debris, building R1, south room. Phase IV.

46 Fused lump (*Unillus.*)

Length 24 mm, weight 4.8 g ST 81 HB, SF 205

A tiny fragment.

Context as no. 19.

47 Fused lump (*Unillus.*)

Length 46 mm, weight 29.3 g ST 81 HB, SF 204

An L-shaped fragment.

Context as no. 19.

48 Fused lump (*Unillus.*)

Length 61 mm, weight 28.7 g ST 82, AAG

An irregular sinuous puddle of melted and semi-coalesced lead.

From topsoil/cleaning, south-east of building R1.

49 Fused lump (*Unillus.*)

Length 25 mm, weight 5.2 g ST 84 DYZ, SF 1165

A small fragment.

From the upper layer (2052) of pit 2052. Late 2nd/3rd century AD.

50 Fused lump (*Unillus.*)

Length 102 mm, weight 54 g ST 83 CLM, SF 532

An amorphous serpentine puddle of melted lead.

From ditch 12, cut 5, unit 1251. Post-medieval.

51 Fused lump (*Unillus.*)

Length 49 mm, weight 13.8 g ST 80 AA, SF 8

A part-melted, narrow, rod-like fragment.

Context as no. 4.

B STONEA GRANGE SURFACE COLLECTION (Figs 122–3)

52 ?Sealing Length 31.5 mm, weight 26.2 g P 1982, 6–2, 170

A slug-shaped lead object of D-shaped cross-section. A fragmentary rectangular border on the convex face encloses at least three illegible numerals or letters. Raised 'squiggles' on the flat face may also be the remnants of characters.

Cf. a 2nd century military lead sealing from Leicester (*RIB* II.i; 2411.79).

53 Steelyard weight

Diameter 45–7 mm, weight 345.5 g P 1982, 6–2, 150

Biconical lead weight, with corroded remains of the iron suspension loop. It was not necessary for a steelyard weight to represent an exact unit of weight. Nevertheless, it is likely that this weight was intended to approximate to one *libra* (*c.* 325 g). On lead weights, see e.g. Jackson 1990b, 52–3.

54 Steelyard weight

Diameter 41 mm, weight 210.5 g P 1982, 6–2, 151

Biconical lead weight, with corroded remains of the iron suspension loop. Ancient 'doodling' includes scratched cross-hatching (upper face) and an unintelligible incised inscription (lower face). In addition there is a grooved number VI with cursory seriphs, on the upper face. This number cannot easily be accommodated as a weight descriptor – 6 *unciae* would correspond to a metric weight of only *c.* 162.5 g. In any case, as noted at no. 53, exact units of weight were not required for a steelyard.

55 Steelyard weight

Diameter 35 mm, weight 156.7 g P 1982, 6–2, 152

Biconical lead weight, lacking its iron suspension loop. The weight corresponds approximately to half a *libra* (6 *unciae* being only 5.9 g underweight using the conversion 325 g/*libra*.

56 Steelyard weight

Diameter 44–6 mm, weight 299.1 g P 1982, 6–2, 153

A worn and damaged, biconical, lead weight, with corroded remains of the iron suspension loop on the truncated upper face. The upper face and one side were damaged in antiquity and a corroded iron stub on the circumference may be the remains of a replacement suspension loop. The present weight corresponds quite closely to 11 *unciae* (10 g overweight), and, bearing in mind the damage sustained, the weight may originally have been intended as an approximate 1 *libra* unit.

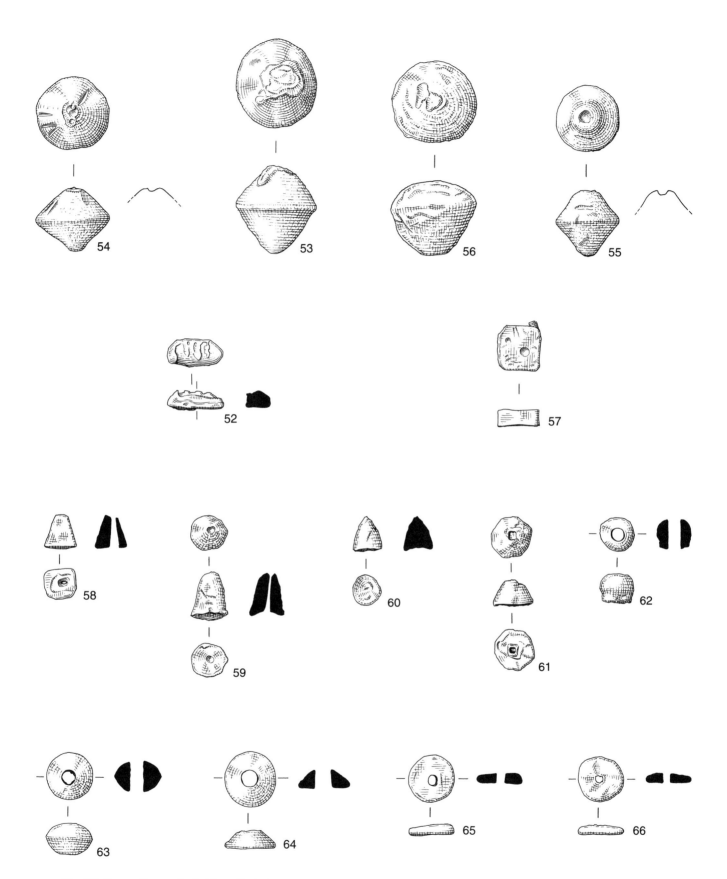

Fig. 122 Stonea Grange: lead objects 52–66 from the Surface Collection (scale 1 : 2).

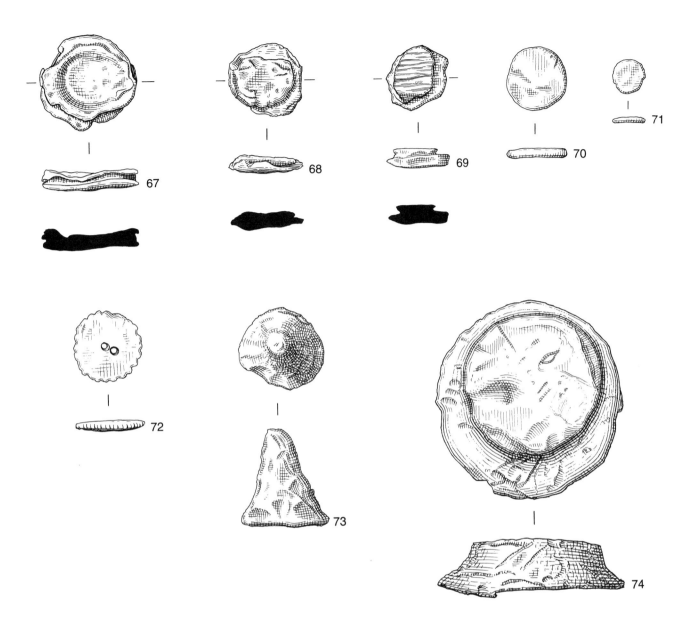

Fig. 123 Stonea Grange: lead objects 67–74 from the Surface Collection (scale 1 : 2).

57 ?Weight

Width 23.5 mm, thickness 10 mm, weight 49.9 g P 1982, 6–2, 168

A square lead block with bevelled corners and two shallow 'dimples' on one planar face. Two corners are damaged. Probably a weight. it is only 4.3 g underweight for a 2 *unciae* unit, a discrepancy which could easily be accounted for by the damage sustained to the corners. It is tempting to regard the two 'dimples' as symbols for the unit of weight.

For a near identical object, also 2 *unciae*, see Frere 1984, 66–7, Fig. 28, no. 246, from Verulamium; and for a copper-alloy weight of the same type, see Cunliffe 1968, 105, Pl. XLVII, no. 213, from Richborough.

58 ?Foot/?support

Height 18.5 mm, weight 25.3 g P 1982, 6–2, 154

A small pyramidal lead object with flat 'base' and vertical perforation. Function unclear. For similar, though conical, objects from Camerton, see Jackson 1990b, 53, and Pl. 17, nos 190–2.

59 ?Foot/?plumb-bob

Height 24 mm, weight 40.3 g P 1982, 6–2, 155

A small, perforated, bell-shaped, lead object with concave 'base'. Function unclear. Ref. as no. 58.

60 ?Foot/?support

Height 18 mm, weight 21.0 g P 1982, 6–2, 156

A small sub-conical lead object with concave 'base'. Function unclear. For a similar object from Camerton, see Jackson 1990b, 54 and Pl. 17, no. 200.

61 ?Packing/?reinforcement

Diameter 22 mm, weight 25.6 g P 1982, 6–2, 157

A low truncated lead cone, quite roughly made, with vertical perforation. The perforation is partially blocked with the corroded remains of a square-sectioned iron shank. Probably the packing for a decorative hollow copper-alloy boss or stud.

For a similar object from South Shields, see Allason-Jones and Miket 1984, 331, 333, no. 8.97; and for an in situ example of similar form and dimensions from Chichester, see Down 1978, 305–6, Fig. 10.39, no. 119.

62 ?Weight or ?packing

Diameter 18 mm, weight 25.7 g P 1982, 6–2, 158

A sub-spherical lead object with flanged 'base' and large circular vertical perforation. Function unclear.

63 ?Spindle-whorl or ?weight

Diameter 25 mm, weight 50.6 g P 1982, 6–2, 159

A finely made compressed biconical lead weight or small flywheel with vertical circular perforation.

64 Spindle-whorl

Diameter 28–9 mm, weight 35.8 g P 1982, 6–2, 160

A well-made, low truncated, lead cone with bevelled rim and large circular perforation. The taper of the perforation, 9.5 to 8.7 mm, is consistent with identification as a spindle-whorl.

For a near-identical example from Fishbourne, see Cunliffe 1971, 144–5, Fig. 66, no. 8.

65 ?Spindle-whorl/small flywheel

Diameter 25 mm, weight 24.7 g P 1982, 6–2, 161

A rather roughly made lightly plano-convex lead disc with central perforation.

66 ?Spindle-whorl/small flywheel

Diameter 24 mm, weight 10.2 g P 1982, 6–2, 162

A crudely made, lightly concavo-convex, lead disc, with central perforation.

67 Repair patch

Diameter 49–53 mm, weight 116.8 g P 1982, 6–2, 163

A large lead patch run in to an ovoid hole c. 39 × 41 mm, presumably in the base of a pottery vessel.

68 Repair patch

Diameter 39–40 mm, weight 57.1 g P 1982, 6–2, 164

A smaller lead patch, as no. 67.

69 Repair patch

Diameter 37 × 31 mm, weight 52.8 g P 1982, 6–2, 165

A small, but thick lead patch, as no. 67. The inner face is impressed with concentric circles; the outer face has taken the impression of ?coarse wood grain when the lead was poured.

70 Disc   Diameter 33 mm, weight 37.9 g P 1982, 6–2, 166

A roughly flattened, lead disc, possibly a counter.

71 Disc   Diameter 17.5 mm, weight 6 g P 1982, 6–2, 167

A small, crudely made, lead disc, possibly a counter.

72 Perforated disc

Diameter 39 mm, weight 45.2 g P 1982, 6–2, 169

A well-made, but slightly damaged, lead disc with double perforation, slightly off-centre, and blunt-toothed, cog-like circumference. The object is slightly thicker at the centre than the edge. Function uncertain.

73 ?Foot or ?spacer

Height 52 mm, weight 224.7 g P 1982, 6–2, 171

A large, sub-conical, lead object. Mortar is present on the sides and the flat face implying some kind of structural function, and the shape is reminiscent of the corner projections on *tegulae mammatae*.

74 ?Plinth   Diameter 105 mm, weight 1368 g P 1982, 6–2, 172

A very heavy and somewhat lop-sided lead plinth.

GLASS

Jennifer Price   (Figs 124–35; Pl. XXVIa)

DISCUSSION

1 Glass vessels

During the excavations at Stonea Grange at least 537 fragments of vessels, 6 objects and more than 1300 pieces of window glass were found.

The vessel glass falls into two broad categories: tablewares, and household and storage vessels. There is a complete absence of cast and decorated mould-blown wares. All the forms were free-blown, with the exception of the prismatic bottles, which were blown into body and base-moulds. No fragments from polychrome vessels were recorded. The dominant colour overall was blue-green, accounting for 262 fragments (48.80%) of which 170 came from at least 18 table and household vessels and 92 from at least 10 bottles. Also prominent was colourless or greenish colourless, accounting for 97 fragments (18.06%) from at least 22 table vessels and 2 Mercury bottles. The remainder (178 fragments – 33.14%) was strongly coloured; 172 fragments came from 3 or 4 yellow-brown vessels, 2 came from 1 or 2 yellow-green vessels, 2 came from a 'black' vessel, 1 from a dark green vessel and 1 from a dark green-blue or peacock blue vessel. Most of the unusually large number of yellow-brown pieces come from 2 partly reconstructable vessels (nos 4–6) from ditch 9.

The range of tablewares is not very extensive. The quality of the glass is good, though not particularly luxurious, and the vessel forms are well-known. Many of them are likely to have been used for serving and consuming liquids. Drinking cups are the commonest vessels present; at least 20 colourless and 3 blue-green specimens have been identified. There are also 2 yellow-brown, 2 colourless and 6 blue-green jugs of different forms, and at least 5 large bowls, 1 yellow-brown and 4 blue-green. Apart from 2 colourless and greenish-colourless Mercury bottles, all of the household and storage vessels are blue-green. The majority of these are cylindrical and prismatic bottles, though a few jars and unguent bottles are recognisable.

The glass assemblage belongs to the early second to early third century AD. The range of glass vessels indicates that glass was used at Stonea from the second quarter of the second century to the first quarter of the third century or thereabouts, and within this period of approximately a century there appear to be two distinct groups of tableware. Some forms were in widespread circulation by the beginning of the period, such as the cylindrical bowls and conical jugs (nos 4–7, 36–40, 45–8) which were already in production during the last third of the first century, and the drinking cups with cracked-off rims and wheel-cut linear decoration (nos 8–11) which occur from the beginning of the second century. All these are likely to have gone out of use around

the end of the third quarter of the second century, whereas forms such as the cylindrical drinking cups with fire-rounded rims (nos 13–30, 32–4), jugs with pouring spouts (nos 31, 49–54) and cylindrical bottle with wheel-cut decoration (no. 12) make their first appearance during the third and fourth quarters of the second century and continued into the third century. The evidence from the findspots at Stonea, and from other Romano-British sites, suggests that there was comparatively little overlap between the two groups. By contrast, the commonest containers, square bottles (nos 61–71), were present throughout the period, though they are likely to have gone out of production by the end of the second century.

There is a very little evidence that broken fragments of glass were re-worked for secondary purposes at Stonea. Only three pieces show signs of grozing.

a Strongly coloured tablewares (Figs 124–5, nos 4–7)

Numbers 1–3 are small body fragments and the vessel forms have not been identified. Number 1 is a small, thin-walled convex body fragment, from a dark green vessel, possibly an unguent bottle. Although it comes from a third century AD level, it is very likely to be a first century vessel, as dark green glass mostly occurs in the Claudian and Neronian periods in Britain, as at Kingsholm, Gloucester (Price and Cool 1985, 48, no. 40).

The dating of no. 2 is more ambiguous. Peacock blue blown vessels are occasionally found in second century contexts. For example, there is a globular flask with horizontal wheel-cut lines at Pentre Farm, Flint (Price 1989a, 77 and 81, no. 2, Fig. 29), and fragments of bowls at Cosgrove, Northants, and King Harry Lane, Verulamium (Price 1989b, 48, Fig. 26.279). Alternatively, in view of its context, the fragment may belong to the post-Roman period. A few peacock blue vessel fragments probably dating from the seventh to ninth century are known at Caister on Sea (Price and Cool 1993, 152, no. 139), York Minster and Flixborough (unpublished – information from Professor V. I. Evison).

Dark yellow-brown glass, appearing black (no. 3), was occasionally used for cast bowls and plates in the first century, but not often for blown vessels. Most of the blown pieces known in Britain have been noted among groups of second century glass. The finds are usually very fragmentary, though several forms of bowls, drinking cups, jars and jugs are known from Colchester (Cool and Price 1995, nos 615, 694, 713, 1480, 1485), the Lanes, Carlisle (Price and Cottam, forthcoming, nos I5, I8, I12) and Castleford (unpublished). Some burials in the lower Rhineland have produced 'black' vessels; for instance, a globular jar with wheel-cut lines and a bowl with scalloped rim-edge and opaque blue marvered trails came from barrow 3 at Esch, North Brabant (van den Hurk 1976, 224–5, nos 26–7, Figs 68–9), and a globular flask and a shallow bowl with saucepan handle were

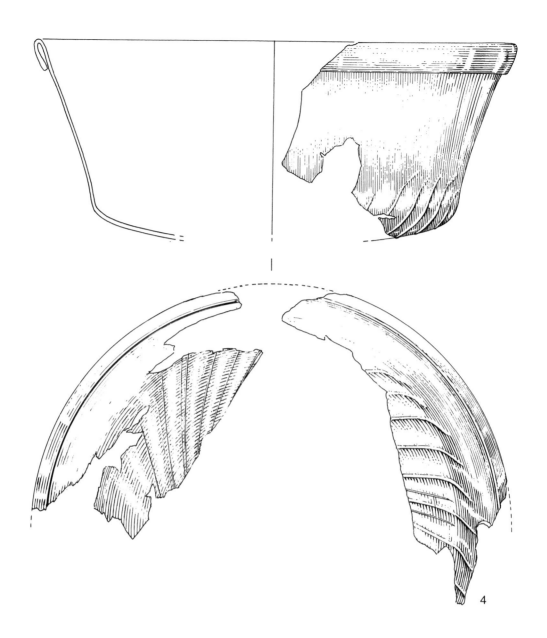

Fig. 124 Stonea Grange: glass bowl 4 (scale 2:3).

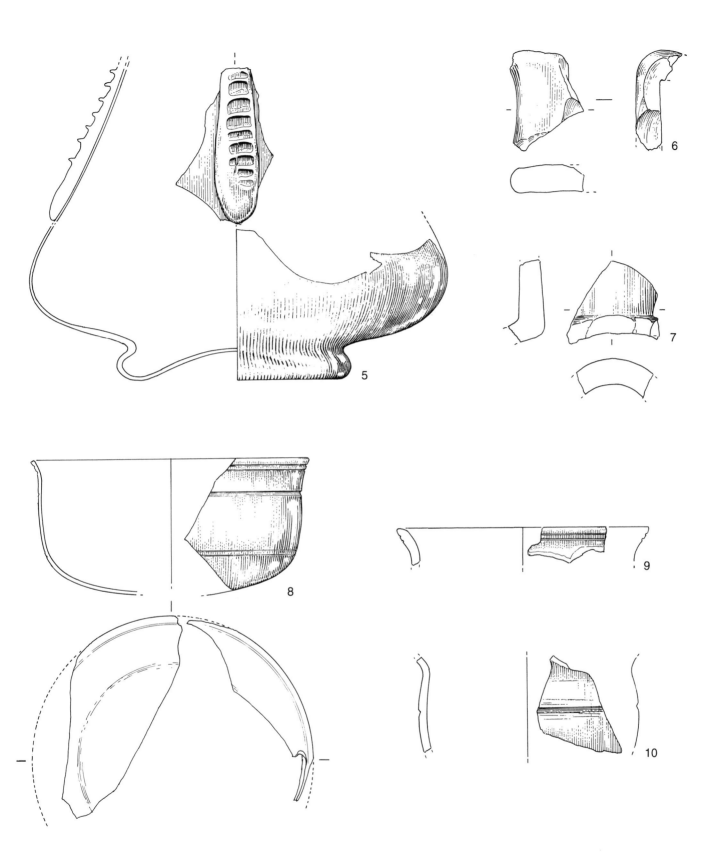

Fig. 125 Stonea Grange: glass vessels 5–10 (scale 1:1).

found in sarcophagus II at Stein, Houterend, in Limburg (Isings 1971, nos 19 and 78, Figs 1 and 4, Pl. 1).

The only other strongly coloured vessel fragments in the Stonea assemblage are the yellow-brown and yellow-green vessels represented by nos 4–7. Two yellow-brown vessels, a deep cylindrical bowl with tubular rim and diagonal ribs on the lower body (no. 4), and a conical jug with open base-ring and angular ribbon handle with central rib and scored trail (nos 5–6), are reconstructable, but the others are represented only by neck or body fragments, and may come from one of several types of jugs or jars.

Large tubular-rimmed bowls with undecorated or ribbed cylindrical bodies, wide bases and applied true base-rings were in widespread use in the north-west provinces from the later first to at least the middle of the second century AD (Isings 1957, form 44), and were probably produced in the region. Most of the bowls were made in bluish-green glass, though some were strongly coloured, and a very few had opaque white marvered splashes on the body.

The bowls are common finds on settlements in Britain, and they are often present in large numbers. Some are known in Neronian and early Flavian contexts, as at Kingsholm, Gloucester (Price and Cool 1985, 43–4, no. 17, Fig. 17) and Fishbourne (Harden and Price 1971, 351–2, no. 66, Fig. 140), but many more occur in the later first and second centuries. For example, at Verulamium, 35 examples came from insulae XIV, XVIII, XX, XXI, XXII, XXVII and XXVIII, of which 17 came from contexts predating AD 150, and 6 more from contexts dating between AD 150 and AD 175 (Charlesworth 1972, 199–200, Fig. 74.6–11; Charlesworth 1984, 151–3, nos 53–70, Fig. 62.21–9), and others, including a polychrome fragment, came from King Harry Lane (Price 1989b, 47–8, Fig. 26.274, 286–7).

Some bowls were in use in the third quarter of the second century AD, as a pit deposit dated by samian to AD 160–70 at Felmongers, Harlow, Essex, contains substantial fragments of one yellow-brown and two bluish-green specimens (Price 1987, 188, 202, nos 4–6, Fig. 1).

Strongly coloured glass vessels are generally thought to belong to the early and middle first century AD, and to have largely disappeared by the late first century, but yellow-brown and yellow-green vessels were in circulation until the third quarter of the second century, as at Felmongers, Harlow, where the bowl mentioned above, a conical jug and a small ovoid jar were found (Price 1987, nos 4, 20, 23), and at Park Street, Towcester, where five conical jugs and discoid jugs or jars were found in a pit dated to AD 155–65 (Price 1980, 66, nos 7–11, Figs 15–16).

Yellow-brown bowls with vertical or diagonal ribs on the body above and below the carination, as on the Stonea bowl, are known from a late Flavian or Trajanic pit at Hemel Hempstead (Charlesworth 1974–6, 117, Fig. 64A), and from Mount Batten, Plymouth. The Mount Batten bowl was destroyed during the Second World War, but a drawing

survives (Cunliffe 1988, 95, no. S25, Fig. 53), so it is possible to identify the vessel as a tubular-rimmed cylindrical bowl with diagonal ribbing on the body, and as a blown vessel rather than a cast or sagged bowl of Hertford Heath type as suggested by Cunliffe. Rim fragments from five similar tubular-rimmed bowls (nos 36–40) were also found.

There are two yellow-brown jugs (nos 5–7). One, represented by nos 5–6, has a conical body, open base-ring and concave base, and an angular ribbon handle with central rib and vertical handle trail with pinched projections. Conical-bodied jugs with folded rims, long necks, simple concave bases or open base rings and concave bases, and angular ribbon handles with central rib and vertical trail (Isings 1957, Form 55), are found in the north-west provinces from the third quarter of the first century AD to the middle of the second century. Like the tubular-rimmed bowls, they were almost certainly produced in the region.

These jugs are very frequently found in Romano-British settlements, and sometimes in burials. They appear in Neronian contexts, and are common finds in the Flavian, Trajanic and Hadrianic periods. Examples with simple concave bases continued in use until the third quarter of the second century, as one was found in the pit deposit at Felmongers, Harlow (Price 1987, 193–5, 204, no. 20, Fig. 3). It is not clear whether conical jugs with open base-rings and concave bases were produced as early as those with simple concave bases. One from a burial at Colchester is dated to AD 69–96 (May 1930, 287–8, grave 8f, Pl. XC), but most examples have come from Hadrianic or Antonine deposits, such as the Hadrianic burials at Lower Runham, Kent (Monkton 1979, 120, Fig. 3) and Huntington (Harden 1968, 308, Pl. 80a). Others are known from an early–mid second century context in the Castleford vicus (unpublished) and from the pit at Park Street, Towcester (Price 1980, 66, no. 9, Fig. 15).

Numbers 46–7 come from two blue-green conical jugs, though whether they had simple concave bases or open pushed-in base-rings and concave bases is not known.

Number 7 is likely to come from a jug with a very short neck, but nothing is known about the body, base or handle. Jugs with very short necks include the dark blue globular-bodied jug from Shefford, Cambridgeshire (Fox 1923, 213, 216, Pl. 26.2), a yellow-brown conical jug from Alcester (Price and Cottam 1994, 224, 228, no. 10, Fig. 104) and a blue-green fragment from Fishbourne (Harden and Price 1971, 360–1, no. 93, Fig. 142).

b Colourless tablewares (Figs 125–8, nos 8–31)

Thirteen fragments from at least five colourless vessels with horizontal wheel-cut lines were found (nos 8–12), most of which are likely to come from drinking vessels. Colourless cups or beakers with curving cracked-off and ground rims, cylindrical, biconical or convex bodies, and tubular pushed-in base-rings, separately blown feet or simple concave bases,

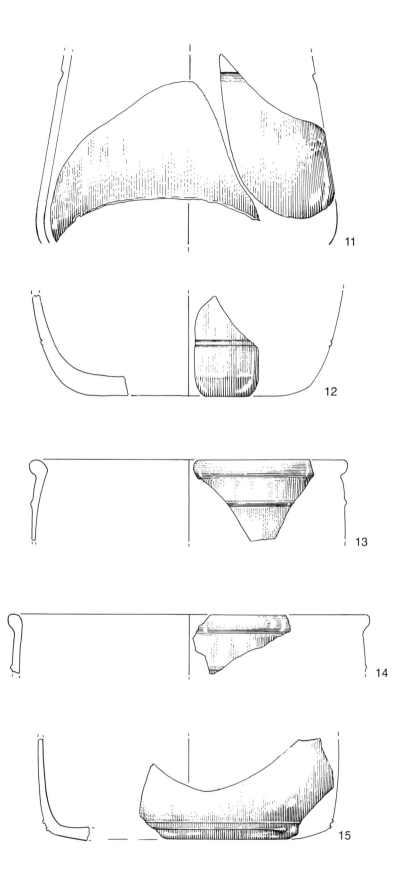

Fig. 126 Stonea Grange: glass vessels 11–15 (scale 1 : 1).

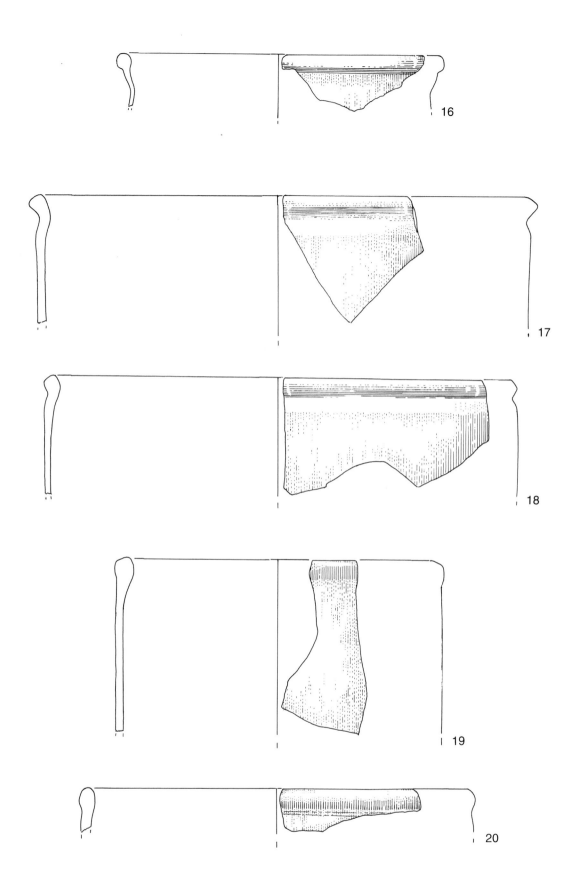

Fig. 127 Stonea Grange: glass vessels 16–20 (scale 1 : 1).

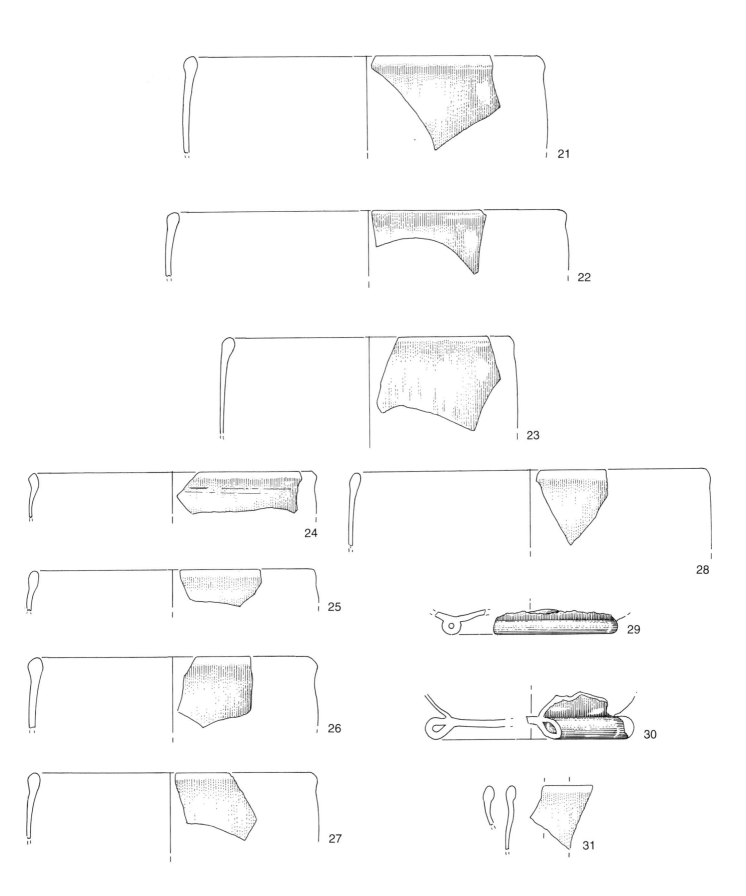

Fig. 128 Stonea Grange: glass vessels 21–31 (scale 1:1).

and horizontal wheel-cut lines arranged singly or in bands on the body, are commonly found in second century AD contexts in Britain. Some appear at the end of the first or beginning of the second century, but most occur in Hadrianic and Antonine contexts, and they disappear rapidly after *c.* AD 165–70. They dominate the glass drinking vessel assemblages of the period, often being recorded in quite large numbers. For example, there are at least 6 examples at Felmongers, Harlow (Price 1987, 188–91, nos 8–11, 13–4, Fig. 2), at least 13 from Verulamium (Charlesworth 1972, 206–8 xiii. 3–4, 6, Fig. 77.43–4, 46; Charlesworth 1984, 155–6 nos 93–102, fig. 63.45–53) and more than 30 from Castleford (unpublished).

The form of no. 8 is unusual; it is a shallow cylindrical cup with a convex lower body tapering in, apparently to a small flat or concave base, and may be compared with cylindrical cups from Castlecary, on the Antonine Wall (Charlesworth 1959a, 48, Fig. 7.6) and from Burial XXXIII at Skeleton Green (Charlesworth 1981, 268–9, Fig. 105.3). Alternatively, it is possible that no. 8 had a separately blown foot, in which case it would resemble a shallow cup from a pit dated to *c.* AD 160–80 in Southwark (Townend and Hinton 1978, 389, no. 114, Fig. 176).

The rim fragment (no. 9) is too small for the form to be precisely identified. It might come from a biconical cup similar to no. 11, or from a cylindrical cup. Three biconical cups were found in the Antonine pit at Felmongers, Harlow (Price 1987, 188–9, 202–3, nos 8–10, Fig. 2) and others are known from mid second century contexts at Castleford (unpublished), from a pit dated to AD 150–60 at Alcester (Price and Cottam 1994, 224–5, no. 11, Fig. 104) and elsewhere. More nearly cylindrical examples are known from insula XIV at Verulamium (Charlesworth 1972, 206–8, xiii 3, Fig. 77.43 – dated to AD 150–155/60), and Crundale, Kent (Charlesworth 1959a, 49, Pl. II). The convex cup (no. 10) is very like fragments from Fishbourne (Harden and Price 1971, 346, 348 no. 56, Fig. 140 – AD 100–270) and insula XXI at Verulamium (Charlesworth 1984, 155, no. 95, Fig. 63.47 – AD 170–80), and may have resembled the globular cup from a second century cremation burial at Fordstreet, Braughing (Harden 1977, 102, Fig. 43.23, Pl. IXb).

The remaining colourless fragment with wheel-cut lines, no. 12, is part of the lower body and base of a more robust cylindrical vessel, and may be from a bottle, rather than a drinking cup. Colourless cylindrical bottles with horizontal wheel-cut lines on the body, which often tapers in above the flat or slightly concave base, and an angular ribbon handle applied to the shoulder and attached to the neck, occur in the north-west provinces in the later second and early third centuries. Examples are known from Maastricht-Himmel, Gulpen and Heerlen in Limburg (Isings 1971, 33, no. 108, Fig. 6; 34, no. 111, Fig. 7; 84–5, no. 198, Fig. 21) and elsewhere.

In Britain the most complete example known was found at Hauxton, Cambridgeshire, probably in a burial (Harden 1958, 12, 14–5, no. 2, Fig. 6, Pl. IIIb), and others have come from Corbridge (Charlesworth 1959a, 54, Fig. 10.1) and elsewhere. They seem to have been in use in the later second century AD, though few have come from closely-dated contexts.

More colourless cylindrical cups with fire-rounded rims and double base-rings (nos 13–28) were found at Stonea than any other form of tableware. Sixteen examples were identified from the rim and body fragments, three decorated with unmarvered horizontal trails (nos 13–15) and thirteen without decoration.

These cups are very common indeed in the north-west provinces in the late second and early third century (Isings 1957, Form 85b). They completely dominate the assemblages of the period in Britain, and are found in very large numbers at many sites; for instance, 7 trailed and 39 undecorated examples were noted from Colchester (Cool and Price 1995, nos 465–533), at least 30 undecorated examples were found at Blackfriars Street, Carlisle (Price 1990, 170–2, nos 22–30, Fig. 161), and at least 61 were noted at Piercebridge (unpublished).

The date of introduction of the form seems to occur in the third quarter of the second century. One rim fragment was found in the Antonine pit group from Felmongers, Harlow (Price 1987, 192–3, 204, no. 19, Fig. 2), and several others are known from contexts dated to *c.* AD 140–80 at Castleford (unpublished). They were at the height of their popularity in the last quarter of the second century and first quarter of the third century; and remained in use until the middle of the third century. Late deposits include three from burials dated to AD 220/30–270/80 at Brougham, Cumbria (Cool 1990b, 170, Fig. 1.1) and two from contexts dated to *c.* AD 235 and later at Vindolanda (Price 1985, 207, nos 11 and 11b, Fig. 7).

Numbers 29–30 come from vessels with tubular base-rings. Number 29 may be the outer ring from a cylindrical cup of Isings form 85b, but no. 30 is likely to come from a different form, perhaps a small bowl, like the two examples from Hauxton (Harden 1958, 12–13, 15, nos 3–4, Fig. 7, Pl. IIIc–d).

The last fragment of colourless tableware (no. 31) comes from the rim of a jug with a pouring spout; it will be discussed in connection with nos 49–54 below.

c **Blue-green tablewares** (Figs 129–32, nos 32–59)

The range of blue-green tablewares includes three cylindrical cups (nos 32–4), a small bowl or jar with everted fire-rounded rim (no. 35), five bowls with tubular rims (nos 36–40), two conical jugs with pinched handle trails (nos 46–7) and four jugs with pouring spouts (nos 49–52), while the unguent bottle or flask (no. 57), and the two bath flasks (nos 58–9) have been classified as household wares. The tubular

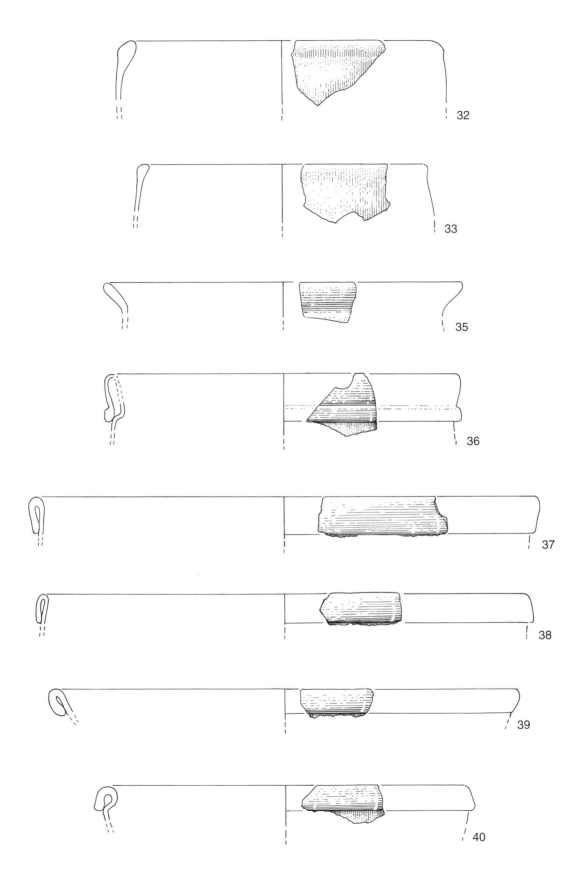

Fig. 129 Stonea Grange: glass vessels 32–3 and 35–40 (scale 1 : 1).

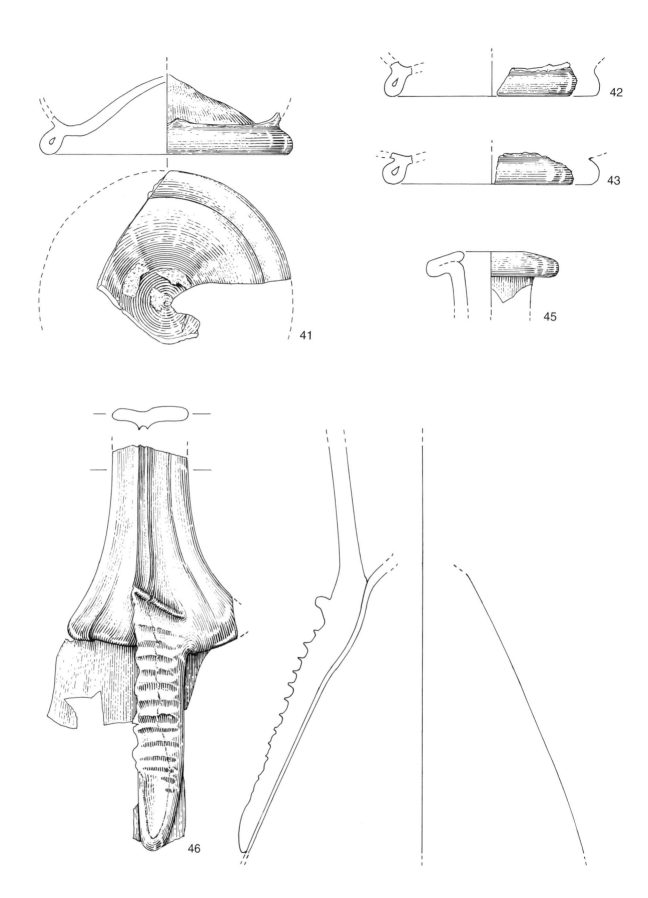

Fig. 130 Stonea Grange: glass vessels 41–3 and 45–6 (scale 1:1).

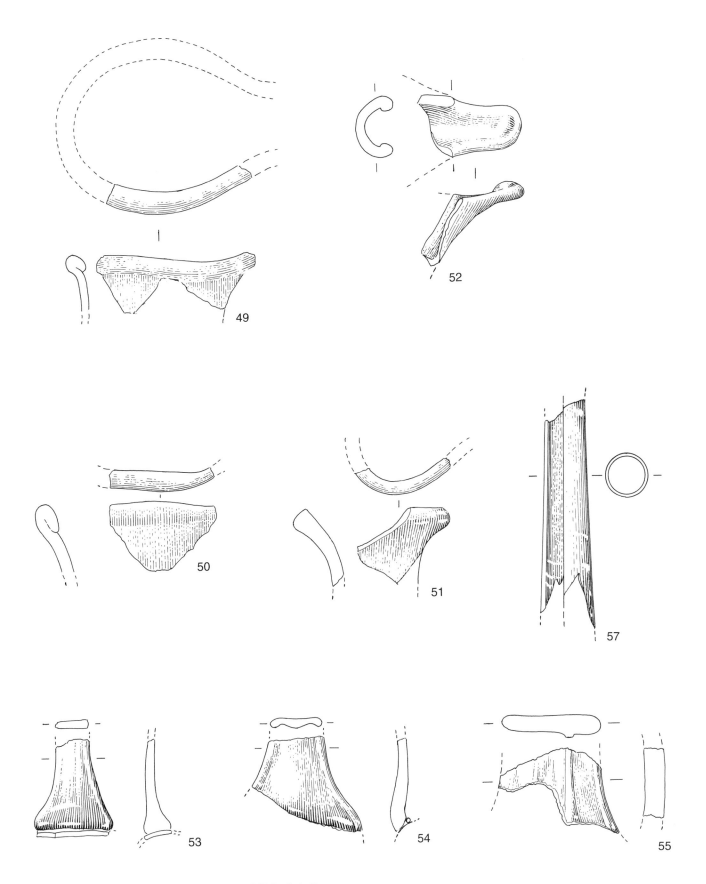

Fig. 131 Stonea Grange: glass vessels 49–55 and 57 (scale 1:1).

base-rings with concave bases (nos 41–4), handles (nos 53–6) and body fragments probably belong to vessel forms represented by more diagnostic fragments.

The cylindrical cups are very similar in form to the colourless ones discussed above (Isings Form 85b), and are almost certainly contemporary with them, but they are not found so frequently or in such large numbers. Rim and body fragments are known from Towcester (Price and Cool 1983, 116, 119, no. 9, Fig. 46), Vindolanda (Price 1985, 209, nos 24–5, Fig. 77), Blackfriars Street, Carlisle (Price 1990, no. 41), Birdoswald and Piercebridge (both unpublished).

The everted fire-rounded rim (no. 35) is not easy to identify, and no close parallels have been recognised. Many varieties of small jars and bowls with such rims were in use in Britain in the first to third centuries AD, as at Colchester, where many broadly comparable vessels have been found, usually in very small pieces (Cool and Price 1995, nos 693, 713–5, 832–8).

The fragments from bowls with tubular rims have already been discussed in connection with no. 4, though the presence of rims which have been rolled inwards before being bent out and down (nos 36 and 40) is noteworthy.

The conical jugs (nos 46–7) have already been discussed in connection with nos 5–7. The other identifiable jugs in the Stonea assemblage have oval-shaped mouths with either rolled–in or fire-rounded edges, and pulled-out pouring spouts. Five have been identified, four being blue-green (nos 49–52) and one colourless (no. 31). None survives with more than a small part of the mouth and neck, but by comparison with other Romano-British finds, the bodies of the jugs are likely to have been either globular or discoid, with a ribbon handle applied to the upper body and attached to the mouth and rim (nos 53–4), and sited opposite to, or at 90° to, the spout. At least one jug (no. 54) had unmarvered trails on the upper body, and some of the convex body fragments with unmarvered spiral trails may come from jugs of this kind.

The jugs were widely used in the north-west provinces in the later second and early third centuries AD and are often found in Britain, as at Colchester (Thorpe 1935, 21, Pl. VIIIa), Combe Down, near Bath (Scarth 1864, 96, Pl. XLIV), Verulamium (Charlesworth 1984, 165–6, nos 235–9, 245, Fig. 67.99–100, 104) and the legionary bathhouse drain at Caerleon (Allen 1986, 108, no. 57, Fig. 42).

The neck fragment (no. 57) appears to come from an unguent bottle or flask. Although close identification is not possible, the piece may belong to a tall unguent bottle with a low, wide reservoir. These vessels, which sometimes have impressed stamps on their bases, were in use in the second century in many parts of the Roman world, and have often been recorded in Britain. Four came from the Antonine pit at Felmongers, Harlow (Price 1987, 196–7, 205–6, nos 28–32, Fig. 4) and examples are known from Verulamium (Charlesworth 1984, 167, no. 273, Fig. 68.126), Southwark (Brailsford 1958, 44, no. 13, Pl. XII) and elsewhere.

The handle and shoulder fragment (no. 58) and the lower body and base fragment (no. 59) very probably come from bath flasks. These vessels have folded rims, short necks, globular bodies and two small looped handles, often called dolphin handles. They occur in large numbers throughout the Roman world from the Neronian period until at least the middle of the third century (Isings 1957, form 61). They were used to contain oil for bathing, and were fitted with rings and chains or handles for carrying and for securing the stopper. Many of the attachments were probably made of perishable materials such as cord or leather, but metal attachments sometimes survive, as on two blue-green bath flasks, one fragmentary and the other complete, now in the Museum of London (Guildhall Museum 1908, 76, nos 17 and 23, Pl. 8.1 and 4).

Bath flasks are often found in large numbers in the deposits accumulated in the drains of bathhouses. For instance, in the drain deposit dating from c. AD 160–230 at the legionary bathhouse at Caerleon, 16 pieces were catalogued, representing 8 blue-green and 5 colourless vessels, and a further 166 blue-green fragments (53 from rims and handles, 102 from bodies and 11 from bases) were also recorded (Allen 1986, 104–9, nos 32–42, 52–6, Figs 41–2). A smaller number came from the legionary bathhouse drain at Church Street, York (Charlesworth 1976, 15–6, nos 32–42 Fig. 12), and others have been noted in drains elsewhere. At least 14 examples were recorded during the excavations in Colchester between 1971 and 1985 (Cool and Price 1995, 157–60, nos 1190–1209). None of these were found in drains, though three specimens deposited in horticultural contexts at Balkerne Lane around AD 300 may have been derived from drain clearance at a nearby bathhouse.

Most bath flasks are difficult to date very closely. The basic form usually remains the same throughout the period of production, although some changes in the formation of rims and handles may have chronological significance; Allen (1986, 104–5) has identified a second century group of small, carelessly-made bath flasks with thin walls and flimsy handles. The Stonea fragments are from thick-walled, competently made bath flasks; the handle and base are both common forms, and closely comparable with examples from Caerleon (Allen 1986, nos 35–6 and 41–2), and Colchester (Cool and Price 1995, nos 1197–9 and 1208).

d Bottles (Figs 132–5, nos 60–71)

i COLOURLESS

Apart from no. 12, which may come from a cylindrical bottle with wheel-cutting on the body, there are three body fragments (no. 60) which may come from two small colourless containers with a folded rim, long neck and narrow square-sectioned body blown into a mould. These are often called Mercury bottles or flasks, because the bases of some of

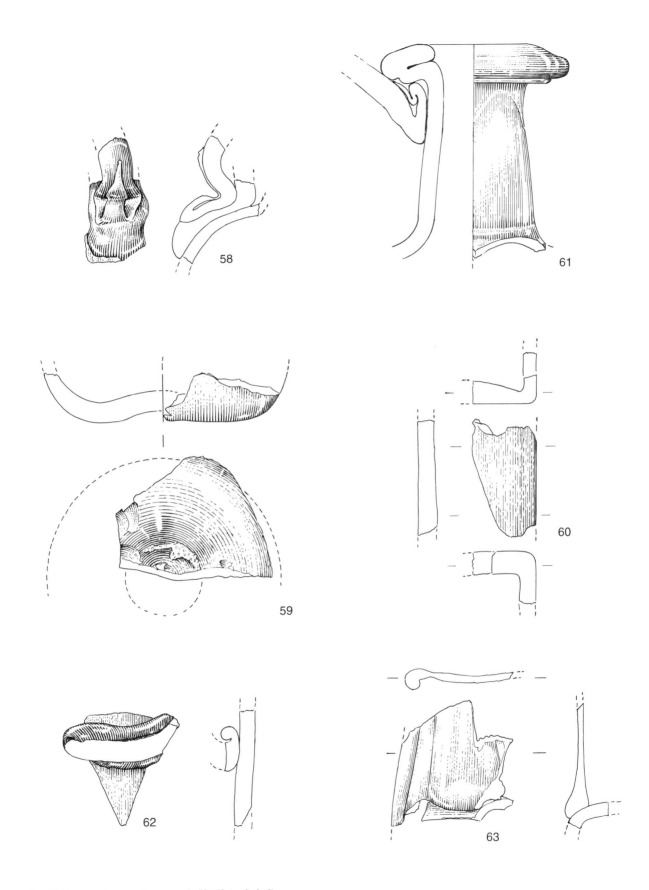

Fig. 132 Stonea Grange: glass vessels 58–63 (scale 1:1).

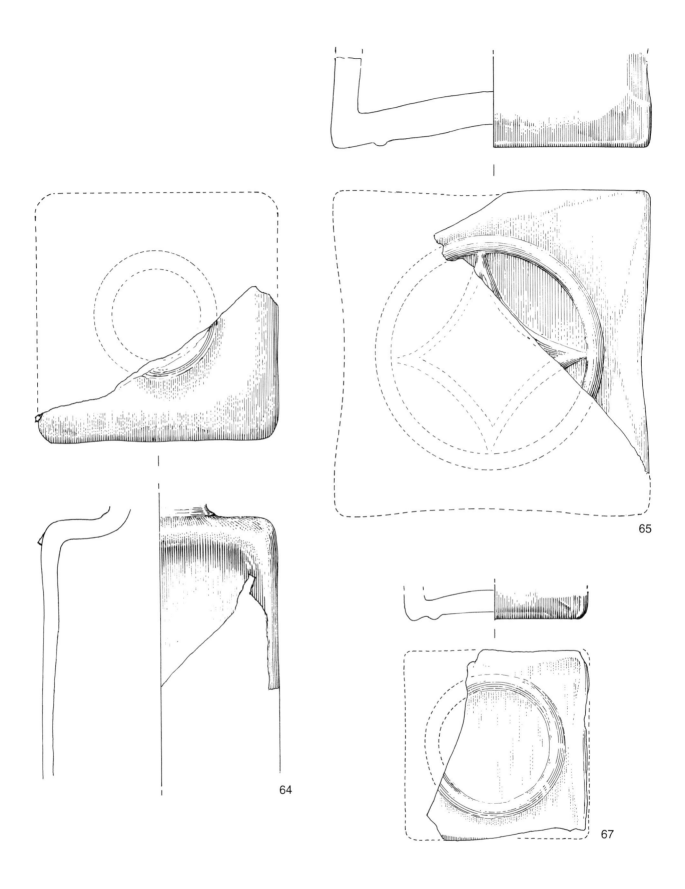

Fig. 133 Stonea Grange: glass vessels 64, 65 and 67 (scale 1 : 1).

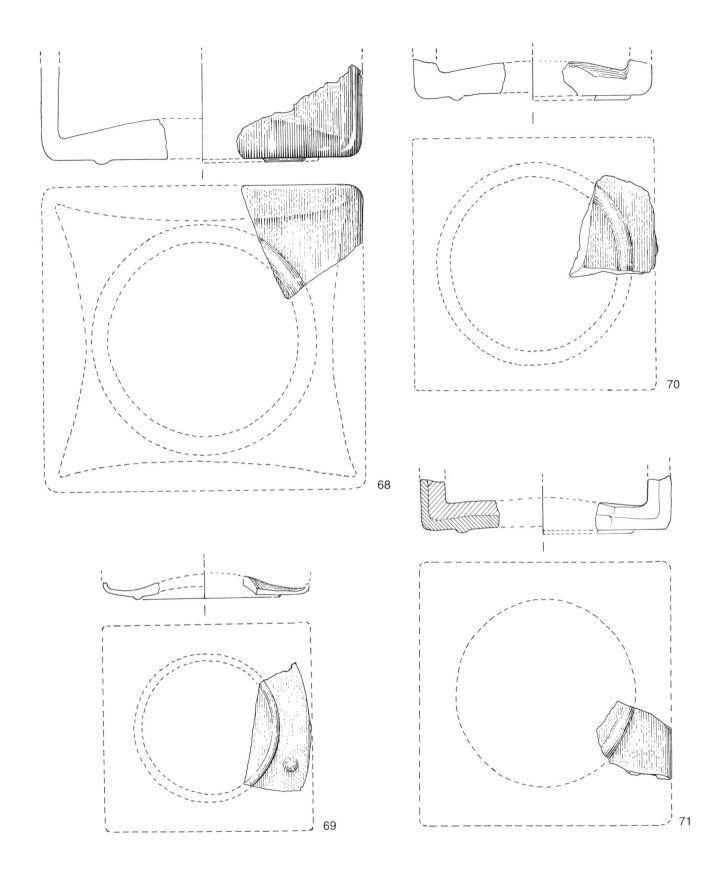

Fig. 134 Stonea Grange: glass vessels 68–71 (scale 1 : 1).

them have a raised design incorporating a figure thought to represent that deity. The vessels are widely known in later second and third century contexts in north-west provinces (Isings 1957, form 84).

In Britain, a few examples have been recorded from burials, but most are known from settlements, as at Fishbourne (Harden and Price 1971, 358 no 87, Fig. 142). The Romano-British finds have been discussed recently in connection with the Colchester fragments (Cool and Price 1995, 153–4, nos 1182–3). In addition, small body fragments are known from Witcombe villa, Gloucestershire (unpublished) and Caldecotte, near Milton Keynes (Zeepvat, Roberts and King 1994), and a piece with an hexagonal, rather than square, section came from the late second to early third-century drain deposit at Caerleon (Allen 1986, 113, no. 77a, fig 43).

ii BLUE-GREEN

Ninety-two fragments from blue-green bottles were found (nos 61–71). This amounts to 17.3% of the vessel glass assemblage (or 24.47% if the two fragmentary yellow-brown vessels, nos 4–6, are each treated as one fragment). In either case, this is a smaller proportion of bottle glass than is usual among groups of second century glass in Britain. For example, at King Harry Lane, Verulamium, more than 49.25% of the vessel fragments were bottles (Price 1989, 50) and high percentages of bottle fragments have been recorded at several sites in Carlisle (Annetwell Street – 44%, unpublished; Blackfriars Street – 45%, Price 1990, 163 and 175; Castle Street – 53%, Cool and Price 1991, 166; Lanes – 48%, Price and Cottam forthcoming, 243). It thus appears that Stonea was receiving a lower volume of commodities in glass bottles than many other Romano-British settlements, despite the presence of a good range of contemporary glass tablewares.

It has not been possible to estimate the number of bottles very accurately. There are at least three square and a further four different square or other prismatic bottle bases (nos 65–71), one hexagonal bottle and two cylindrical bottles, making a total of ten, but many more are likely to be represented by the fragments.

Blue-green cylindrical and square bottles were manufactured in very large numbers in the Roman world during the later first and second centuries AD (Isings 1957, forms 50–1). They were produced in a wide range of sizes, and functioned primarily as containers for the transport and storage of liquid to semi-solid foodstuffs, though the larger specimens were sometimes re-used as cremation urns.

In Britain, cylindrical bottles were very common in the late first century, but disappeared in the early second century (see Price 1990, 175, for a discussion of cylindrical bottles). Square bottles were also common in late first century contexts, and they became the principal bottle form of the second century. Charlesworth argued that the production of square bottles ceased soon after AD 130 (Charlesworth

1966, 30). More recent finds, however, have shown that many new basal designs appear after this time, and that the bottles remained in common use until the end of the second or early third century, so production is likely to have continued until the late second century. Hexagonal bottles were never as common as the cylindrical and square bottles; most of them appear to have been in use in the late first to early second century, but some have been noted in mid-late second century contexts.

All forms of one-handled bottles have similar rims, necks, shoulders and handles. The cylindrical bottles have undecorated concave bases, whereas mould-blown prismatic bottles almost always have raised basal designs, which frequently consist of geometric patterns. All the base designs at Stonea (nos 65–71) include at least one concentric circle; no. 65 also has four arcs inside the circle, forming a hollow-sided lozenge, and no. 69 has a raised pellet near to one edge. Concentric circles occur on the vast majority of square bottle bases, and have been noted on virtually all Romano-British sites. The combination of a circle surrounding a hollow-sided lozenge is less common, though several broadly comparable examples are known from Fishbourne (Harden and Price 1971, 364, no. 100, Fig. 143), and Catterick and Lincoln (unpublished).

2 Objects of glass   (Fig. 135, nos 72–7)

A small number of glass objects, five beads and one reworked circular disc, were recorded during the excavations at Stonea (nos. 72–7).

The small, dark blue, annular bead with three opaque yellow spirals (no. 72) came from a late third or fourth century deposit in well 1667, although is likely to have been produced before then. Much larger dark blue annular beads with yellow spirals have been noted in late pre-Roman Iron Age contexts in Britain (Guido 1978, class 6, 53–7, Pl. I. 6c), and a smaller one is known from an undated context at Worthing (Guido 1978, Group 2, 60 and 123, Fig. 18 right), but otherwise it has been difficult to find parallels for this piece.

The two monochrome small annular beads (nos 73–4) are respectively dark blue and dark yellow-green appearing black. Undecorated annular beads in these and other colours are very long-lived. They have been found in pre-Roman Iron Age, Roman and post-Roman contexts (Guido 1978, group 6, 65–9), the blue ones (Group 6 [ivb]) being much commoner than the black ones (Group 6 [ix]).

The remaining two beads (nos 75–6) are not found in pre-Roman contexts. The globular bead probably comes from a segmented bead (Guido 1978, 91–3, Fig. 37. 1–3), a type known in the second to fourth and later centuries, though blue-green examples have not often been recorded. Dark green cylindrical rod beads are known in first century contexts, though most of them are found in the third and fourth centuries (Guido 1978, 95, Fig. 37. 4).

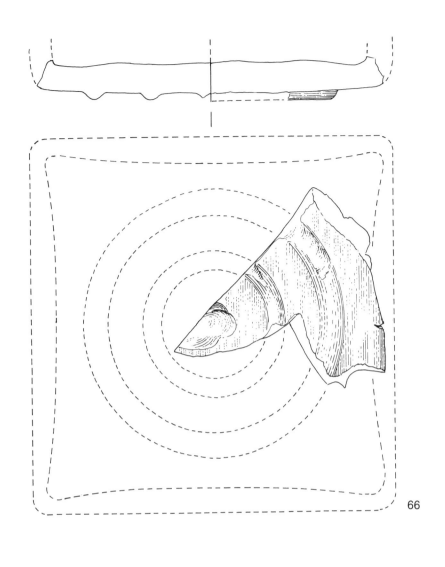

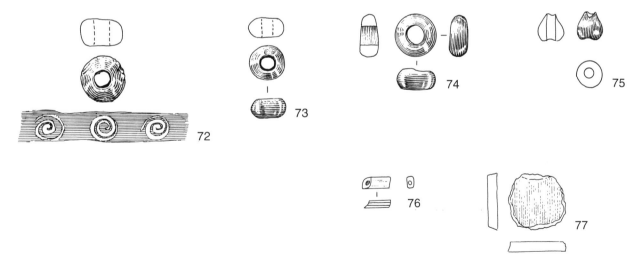

Fig. 135 Stonea Grange: glass vessel 66, beads 72–6 and counter 77 (scale 1:1).

The reworked circular disc (no. 77) was formed from a broken piece of a matt-glossy window pane. Similar objects have been recorded on other Romano-British sites, and it is often assumed that they were shaped for use as counters or gaming pieces. It is noteworthy that none of the more usual plano-convex glass counters was found at Stonea, as these are quite often found on settlements in the first and second centuries.

3 Window glass   (Pl. XXVIa)

The excavations produced more than 1300 fragments of translucent blue-green, greenish colourless and colourless glass with one flat and matt surface and one slightly uneven and glossy surface. The thickness of the fragments varies considerably from 2 mm or less at the middle to 4.5 mm or more at the rounded edges. In addition, some fragments show straight grozed edges cut from larger pieces. Traces of mortar survive on either the matt or the glossy surface of some edge pieces.

The fragments come from square or rectangular sheets of glass, which almost certainly functioned as window panes, though similar sheets may occasionally have been used for wall decoration or internal screens. The combination of matt and glossy surfaces, the uneven thickness of the fragments, the layering effect visible in the sections, and the tooling and stretching marks on the glossy surface near the thick rounded edges and in the corners, are characteristic features of the kind of window glass which appeared in the Roman world in the first half of the first century AD. This occurs in Britain very soon after the Claudian invasion, in contexts dated to AD 49–61 at Camulodunum (Harden 1947, 306) and to AD 45–60 in insula XXVII at Verulamium (Charlesworth 1984, 171, no. 318). It has been found on a wide variety of military sites, towns and rural settlements occupied in the first to third centuries, particularly in association with the hot and warm-rooms of bathhouses and with some residential buildings, where it appears to have functioned both to admit light and to prevent heat from escaping.

The method of manufacture of this window glass was the subject of some controversy at one time. Harden argued that all Romano-British window glass was made by blowing elongated cylindrical gathers, cutting them open longitudinally and flattening them into sheets (Harden 1961, 41–52). However, Boon's study of finds from Caerleon and elsewhere in Wales made a convincing case for window glass with flat and matt and uneven and glossy surfaces being produced by casting or pouring hot glass into shallow stone or wood trays (Boon 1966), and this is now widely accepted (for example, see Harden 1974). Without exception, all the Stonea Grange finds belong to the cast category examined by Boon.

Cylinder-blown window glass, which has two glossy surfaces and is thinner and of more even thickness than cast window glass, appears to have been produced from the third century onwards, although fragments have occasionally been noted in earlier contexts. For instance, pieces from Neronian, Flavian and second century contexts have been recorded at Exeter (Charlesworth 1979, 230).

Blown window glass became common in Britain in the late third and fourth centuries, but cast window glass also continued in use. It is noteworthy that few, if any, buildings constructed before the fourth century have windows glazed *only* with cylinder-blown glass, and buildings occupied during the late third and fourth century often contained both blown and cast panes, as in the wooden cottage-like structure at Grandford, near Stonea (Potter and Potter 1982, 11), building A at Frocester Court, Gloucestershire (unpublished; information from E. G. Price) and elsewhere. It is not clear whether cast, matt-glossy window glass was still made in the late Roman period, or whether the panes were very long-lived. After windows were glazed, there may not have been any reason to change the type of window glass until the panes in place were broken. It is quite possible that some window panes remained in position for 200 years or more, and where alterations were made to a building, the glazed windows in the new phase might well have been the re-used panes from an earlier phase.

Fishbourne, which produced the largest quantity of cast, matt-glossy window glass recorded in Britain, provides an illustration of this point. About 18 kg of blue-green, greenish and colourless fragments were found, the largest deposit coming from the floor of room N9 in the North Wing (Harden and Price 1971, 367–8). This deposit belonged to the last phase of occupation of the North Wing, and was very considerably affected by the fire which destroyed Fishbourne in c. AD 280–90 (Cunliffe 1971, 188). The panes, some of which retained traces of mortar on the edges, had been removed from their settings and were being stored, perhaps during renovations or alterations. This glass was thus almost certainly in use until the late third century, and may well have been used in the building since its construction in the first century. In view of the date of destruction of Fishbourne, it is noteworthy that no fragments from blown window panes were recorded.

The 1300 plus window fragments at Stonea (the second largest cast matt-glossy group from Roman Britain) covered an area of 8390 cm^2 and weighed 6.8 kg. The glass was recorded in more than 350 contexts widely distributed across the site. Pieces came from shallow scoops, floors, post-holes, wall trenches, rubble deposits, boundary ditches, pits, wells, latrines and other features, in blocks 1–10, and in trenches AA, H, O and P to the east and north-east of the main excavation.

The fragments were not deposited uniformly throughout the excavated area, and there was considerable variation both in the quantity of glass found and in the average size of the fragments (see Plate XXVIa and the information summarised in the Appendix, p. 406). By far the greatest concentration of finds occurred in block 1, in and around building R1. Approximately 150 contexts containing window glass were noted inside or in the vicinity of this building, and these contexts contained the largest quantities of glass and most of the biggest fragments from the site, including almost all the groups of fragments covering areas of more than $100\,cm^2$. Elsewhere, much less glass was found: 25 contexts were noted in block 2, under 20 in each of blocks 3–8 and 10, and 41 in block 9, the remainder coming from the sump and outlying trenches, topsoil and unstratified deposits. In particular, some large fragments came from the fill of well 1836 and the adjacent section of gully 35, in the north-east corner of block 4, outside the timber building R7; and a considerable concentration of fragments came from pits, latrines and gullies in block 9.

In view of the concentration of window glass in and around the building, it is virtually certain that building R1 had several glazed windows. The window panes were probably installed at the time of the construction of the building during the second quarter of the second century, around AD 140, and they appear to have been broken in the early third century, around AD 220–30. Within the central block, fragments were found close to the west, north and south walls, which may suggest that these contained windows glazed with at least one colourless and several blue green and greenish colourless panes, and finds in similar positions in the south room suggest that the west and south walls there also contained glazed windows.

However, the broken window glass does not appear to have remained where it fell. Instead, it was removed and collected up, before being either buried in various features outside the building, none of which contain fragments of only one pane, or incorporated into deposits of rubble which were then used to infill. It sems likely that the material found within the building was redeposited and so cannot be associated directly with any particular wall. It would therefore be futile to attempt any estimate of the number of glazed windows, or of their positions within the building.

Whether the window glass fragments in other parts of the site originated from the disposal of debris from building R1 or whether one or several other structures also had glazed windows is not known. There is no observable difference between the window panes represented by the finds adjacent to building R1, and the panes in block 3, or 9, or from trench P in the vicinity of the Romano-Celtic temple (building R15), more than 250 metres to the north-east of building R1. This might be taken to indicate that they all came from the same building, though other explanations, such as production at about the same time, or by craftsmen working in a common tradition, or using similar raw material, are equally likely. As the distribution of other materials does not indicate that debris from building R1 was deposited throughout the settlement, the most reasonable interpretation of the wide spread of finds of window glass and the distinct local concentrations may be that buildings with glazed windows existed in several parts of the settlement.

The very large quantity of window glass at Stonea is quite remarkable. Such window glass occurs most commonly in wealthy rural residences, as at Fishbourne, or in bathhouses, as in the legionary fortress baths at Caerleon, where 4 kg of blue green and colourless fragments were found, mainly in the upper fill of the drain (Allen 1986, 116), and in bathhouse at Catterick, where the area of window glass amounted to $3320\,cm^2$ (Baxter and Cool 1991, 128). Clearly, building R1 at Stonea was provided with a considerable number of glazed windows, a feature which supports other evidence for a rather lavishly appointed and imposing structure. On a more modest scale, at least some of the buildings in block 9 (buildings R10–R14) and blocks 3–4 (buildings R6–R7) were probably furnished in part, if not throughout, with glazed windows.

Nothing is known about where the Stonea finds or any other cast, matt-glossy window panes were produced. It is generally accepted that the process of casting was comparatively simple and that the panes are likely to have been made close to the buildings in which they were to be fitted, rather than transported over long distances. Most of the Stonea panes were probably made from recycled blue-green vessel fragments or from blocks of raw glass, though in some cases attempts were made to decolourise the glass.

Of the total area of the surviving fragments ($8390\,cm^2$), and the total weight (6.801 kg), $6371\,cm^2$ and 5.207 kg come from blue-green panes, and $2019\,cm^2$ and 1.594 kg come from greenish colourless and colourless panes. Too many uncertainties exist for it to be possible to establish the number of panes represented even approximately, and the calculation of minimum numbers is also very problematic. No information about the size of the individual panes has survived, though no. 78 (Pl. XXVIa), the larger reconstructed fragment from pit 170 which preserves one rounded edge, comes from a pane measuring at least $283 \times 241\,mm$ (that is, at least $682\,cm^2$). If this is taken as the standard size for a pane, and if all the blue-green fragments found at Stonea were joined together, they would cover an area equivalent to at least ten panes, while the greenish colourless and colourless fragments would cover an area equivalent to at least three panes.

Few cast, matt-glossy window panes in Britain are complete enough for their overall dimensions to be established, but it is clear that they were produced in a range of sizes. The excavation of the bathhouse at Garden Hill, Hartfield, East Sussex, produced one nearly complete pane measuring $255 \times 235\,mm$ and one fragmentary pane measuring $275 \times 215+\,mm$ (Harden 1974), and fragments from the main drain of the bathhouse at Red House, Beaufront near Corbridge, were reconstructed to form a pane measuring at least $600 \times 600\,mm$ (Charlesworth 1959b, 166). The variation in dimensions also occurs elsewhere in the Roman world; a fragmentary, unprovenanced, pane in the Department of Greek and Roman Antiquities, British Museum (1958.2–28.1) measures $535 \times 355\,mm$, one from Pompeii measures

330 × 270 mm, and four others, set in a wooden frame in the tepidarium of the baths of the villa of Diomedes, also at Pompeii, each measure 268 × 268 mm (Harden 1974, 281).

Traces of mortar suggest that many of the panes at Stonea were fixed by their edges into an aperture or on to a frame. All the panes may have been attached in this manner, though pieces without evidence for the presence of mortar might have been fitted into wooden or metal frames. It is not possible to determine whether the panes were set individually into apertures or whether several panes were fitted into frames which were in turn fitted into apertures, though the fragments with grozed edges show that some panes were cut from larger cast sheets, in the same manner as the Garden Hill pane.

Finally, it is surprising that such a large quantity of window glass fragments has survived at Stonea, because the settlement continued in occupation after the windows were broken, and broken glass would have been recyclable. Although some collection for recycling is very likely to have taken place at the time of breakage or soon afterwards, because otherwise it would surely have been possible to reconstruct at least some of the panes, this does not seem to have been pursued very rigorously. The quantity of fragments deposited in pits and other features as part of a phase of rubbish disposal is in marked contrast to the situation usually recognised on Romano-British sites, where broken window glass is very scarce, having been collected either for re-use in the same settlement, or for transfer to a local glass working centre.

Acknowledgements

I would like to thank Rachel Tyson and David Wraight whose careful and thorough work in measuring, plotting, recording and weighing the Stonea window pane fragments has greatly assisted the preparation of this report.

CATALOGUE

All measurements are in millimetres.

Abbreviations

Dims	Dimensions
T	Thickness
PH	Present height
D	Diameter
BD	Base diameter
RD	Rim diameter

Strongly coloured   (Figs 124–5, pp. 380–1)

1   ST 81 KR (*Unillus.*) Body fragment. ?Unguent bottle. Dark green. Small bubbles, black specks. Thin-walled convex side.
   Dims 25 × 11; T 0.75.
   From an upper layer (unit 223) in ditch 9, cut 6. 3rd century AD.

2   ST 81 GT (*Unillus.*) Body fragment, ?small bowl. Dark green-blue (peacock blue). Small bubbles, black specks. Rim edge missing, vertical, slightly convex side.
   PH 20.5; T 2–2.5.
   From upper layer (unit 156) of well 135. 4th–7th century AD.

3   ST 84 DGT, SF 662 (*Unillus.*) Two joining body fragments. Dark yellow-brown, appearing black. Dull, distorted by heat.
   Dims 20.5 × 21.5; 19 × 17; T 1.
   From well 704/1663, unit 1663. Late 3rd/early 4th century AD.

4   ST 82 ADY, SF 334a 150 + small rim and body fragments, cylindrical bowl with tubular rim. Yellow-brown. Dull, patches of weathering, pitted. Many small bubbles and black specks. Vertical rim, edge bent out and down to form oval tube, concave upper body, strong carination, wide flat lower body tapering in. Diagonal ribs on lower body.
   PH 73; RD 220; T 1–2.5.
   From ditch 9, cut 8, unit 536. Late 2nd/early 3rd century AD.

5   ST 82 ADY, SF 334b Thirteen fragments, joined in three pieces, handle, body and base of conical jug. Yellow-brown. Heavily weathered on outside surface. Part of vertical handle trail with scored horizontal lines applied to straight side expanding out, curved carination above slightly convex lower body tapering in to open pushed-in base ring and domed base. Wear on base ring.
   PH (lower body) 43; BD 64; T 0.75–2.
   Context as no. 4.

6   ST 82 AFR, SF 407 Handle fragment, jug, yellow-brown. Dull, grainy surface. Lump of colourless sand or grit on outside surface. Angular ribbon handle, central rib.
   Dims 25 × 20; max T 7.5.
   From ditch 9, cut 10, basal layer (unit 578). Late 2nd/early 3rd century AD.

Also, *unillustrated*:

a   ST 82 AAO, SF 419a Fragment, body, streaky colour.
   Context as no. 70.

b   ST 84 DNM, SF 839 Fragment, convex body.
   From gully 19, cut 3, unit 1800. Mid 3rd century AD.

c   ST 84 DPW, SF 882 Fragment, convex body.
   From gully 18, cut 20, unit 1857. 3rd century AD.

d   ST 84 DEA, SF 665 Fragment, lower body above base ring.
   Context as no. 20.

e   ST 81 GX Small body fragment, vertical rib.
   Context as no. 21.

f ST 84 DZZ, SF 1132 Yellow-green. Small body fragment, vertical rib.

From occupation layer (unit 2076) south-east block 9. 3rd century AD.

g ST 83 CFB, SF 527 Yellow-green. Small body fragment.

From silts, north-east block 2. 3rd century AD.

7 ST 84 DER, SF 720 Neck fragment, thick walled ?flask or ?jug, yellow-brown. Dull, strain cracks. Change of angle below rim, short cylindrical neck, tooling marks at junction with shoulder.

PH 23; T 5.0–5.5.

From ditch 8, cut 5, unit 1613. 3rd century AD.

Also, *unillustrated*:

a ST 82 ABX Fragment, convex body.

From ditch 9, cut 11, unit 487. 3rd century AD.

b ST 83 CMB Fragment, convex body.

From ditch 3, cut 6, unit 1265. 3rd century AD.

Colourless: horizontal wheel-cut lines
(Figs 125–6, pp. 381–3)

8 ST 82 AGO, SF 419b and ST 82 ACE, SF 294 Four fragments, three joining, rim and body, low cylindrical cup. Greenish tinge. Little visible weathering. Few small bubbles. Small curved rim, edge cracked off and ground flat, vertical side, rounded carination, convex lower body tapering in. Two narrow lines on rim, broad line on upper body, two narrow lines above carination, abraded band on lower body.

PH 35; RD 80; T 1–3.

From ditch 9, cut 9, basal layer (unit 599). Late 2nd/early 3rd century AD. And from ditch 9, cut 11, unit 494. 3rd century AD.

9 ST 83 CAN, SF 507 Rim fragment, ?cup. Dull, pitted, strain cracks. Curved rim, edge cracked off and ground, upper body expanding out. Two narrow lines below rim.

PH 11; RD 70; T 2.

From ditch 13, cut 4, unit 1012 (residual). Phase VI.

10 ST 83 CDA, SF 477 Body fragment, cup. Dull, pitted. Curved rim (edge missing), convex upper body. One line on upper body.

Dims 25 × 22; max. D approx. 60; T 2.

From ditch 3, cut 5, uppermost layer (unit 1072). 3rd century AD.

11 ST 83 CPP, SF 598 and ST 83 CPS, SF 597 Two body fragments, biconical cup. Few small bubbles, black specks. Straight side expanding out above carination. Broad line on upper body.

PH 43; body D approx. 80; T 2.0–2.5.

From ditch 2, cut 4, units 1350 and 1353. 2nd–3rd century AD.

12 ST 83 J4(1), SF 576 Lower body and base fragment, ?cylindrical cup or bottle. Greenish tinge. Dull, pitted. Straight sides tapering in, flat base. Two close-set narrow lines above base.

PH 25; BD–; T 2.0–5.5.

From top layer of well J4. Late 3rd/early 4th century AD.

Also, *unillustrated*:

a ST 83 ACR, SF 409 Convex body fragment. Three close-set narrow lines.

From gully 50, cut 1, unit 506. 3rd century AD.

b ST 82 AEW Convex body fragment. Three close-set lines.

Dims 27 × 24 × 1.5.

From well 171/558, uppermost layer (unit 558) Phase V.

c ST 84 DEA, SF 724. Convex body fragment. One narrow line.

Dims 14.5 × 16 × 1.

Context as no. 20.

d ST 84 DEA, SF 658 Melted body fragment. Two close-set narrow lines.

Dims 25.5 × 24 × 1.

Context as no. 20.

e ST 84 DXT, SF 1068 Body fragment; abraded band.

Dims 30 × 14.5 × 1.

From pit 2023, unit 2023. Early/mid 3rd century AD.

f ST 84 EDR, SF 1130 Straight body fragment, curved carination. Abraded band.

Dims 19 × 12 × 1.5.

From fill (unit 2165) in gully 24, cut 2 and gully 29, cut 11. 3rd century AD.

g ST 81 NX Two straight body fragments. Two wheel cuts.

Dims 34 × 21 × 1.

From the fill (unit 297) of the east terminal of gully 44 (cut 1). 3rd century AD.

h ST 83 J4(1), SF 576 Lower body fragment. Two close-set lines.

Context as no. 12.

Colourless: trails   (Fig. 126, p. 383)

13 ST 84 DGZ, SF 821 Rim fragment, cylindrical cup. Dull, pitted, strain cracks. Small bubbles. Vertical rim, edge fire rounded and thickened, vertical side. Horizontal unmarvered trail on upper body.

PH 22; RD 90; T 1.0–1.5.

From layer 1668 above the pit cluster 1834 etc., west of centre, block 9. Mid/late 3rd century AD.

14 ST 84 DOY, SF 837 Rim fragment, cylindrical cup. Slight pitting, strain crack. Small bubbles. Vertical rim, edge fire rounded and thickened, vertical side. Horizontal unmarvered trail on upper body.

PH 15; RD 100; T 1.5–2.

From pit 1835/2007, unit 1835. 3rd century AD.

15 ST 84 DXG, SF 1089 Body fragment, cylindrical cup. Dull, pitted, strain cracks. Some bubbles. Vertical side, curved carination, flat lower body. Two horizontal unmarvered trails at carination.

PH 25; body D approx. 86; T 2.0–3.5.

From pit 1633, unit 2011. Late 2nd century AD.

Also, *unillustrated*:

a ST 84 DGN, SF 774 Body fragment. Horizontal unmarvered trail.

Dims 23.5 × 11.5 × 1.5.

Context as no. 27.

Colourless: undecorated   (Figs 127–8, pp. 384–5)

16 ST 84 DVD, SF 919 Rim fragment, cylindrical cup. Dull, light pitting, strain crack.

PH 15; RD 90; T 1.5.

From upper layer (unit 1960) of pit 1960. Late 2nd–3rd century AD.

17 ST 84 DTZ, SF 1057 Rim fragment, cylindrical cup. Dull, pitted. As 16.

PH 42; RD 140; T 2.0–2.5.

From gully 18, cut 15, unit 1956. 3rd century AD.

18 ST 84 DWA, SF 1060 Rim and three body fragments, cylindrical cup. Greyish tinge. Dull, slightly pitted. Some bubbles. As no. 16.

PH 30; RD 130; T 1–2.

From gully 29, cut 6, unit 1981. 3rd century AD.

19 ST 83 JI(2), SF 594 Rim fragment, cylindrical cup. Pitted. Small bubbles. As no. 16.

PH 46; RD 90; T 1.5–3.

From pit J1, layer 2. Late 3rd/early 4th century AD.

20 ST 84 DEA, SF 739 Rim fragment, cylindrical cup. Dull, some pitting. Some bubbles. As no. 16.

PH 12; RD 110; T 2.5.

From topsoil/cleaning (unit 1597) blocks 8 and 9 and east part blocks 3 and 4.

21 ST 81 GX, SF 123 Rim fragment, cylindrical cup. Greenish. Dull patch; small bubbles. As no. 16.

PH 24; RD 100; T 1–2.

From well 135, unit 159, 4th–7th century AD.

22 ST 82 BKD, SF 360 Rim fragment, cylindrical cup. Dull, light pitting, strain cracks. As no. 16.

PH 16; RD 120; T 1–2.

From well 905, unit 926. Late 3rd century AD.

23 ST 81 KR Rim fragment, cylindrical cup. Light pitting; few bubbles. As no. 16.

PH 24; RD 80; T 1.0–1.5.

Context as no. 1.

24 ST 81 unstratified Rim fragment, cylindrical cup. Light pitting, iridescent weathering; small bubbles. As no. 16.

PH 11; RD 80; T 1.5.

25 ST 84 DHA, SF 833 Rim fragment, cylindrical cup. Some pitting; small bubbles. As no. 16.

PH 9; RD 80; T 1.5.

From top layer (unit 1669) of well 1669. Mid/late 3rd century AD.

26 ST 83 J4(1), SF 534 Rim fragment, cylindrical cup. Dull, some pitting. As no. 16.

PH 18; RD 80; T 2

Context as no. 12.

27 ST 84 DGN, SF 668 Rim fragment, cylindrical cup. Dull, pitted. As no. 16.

PH 16; RD 80; T 1.5.

From trowelling layer (unit 1657) over gully 29, cut 8, unit 1712. Mid 3rd century AD.

28 ST 84 DWX, SF 1039 Rim fragment, cylindrical cup. Greenish tinge. Dull, pitted. As no. 16.

PH 19; RD 110; T 1.5.

From basal layer (unit 2002) in pit 1996. 3rd century AD.

29 ST 81 SV, SF 220 Base fragment, cylindrical cup. Dull, pitting. Wide lower body, tubular base ring, flat base (broken at edge of inner base ring).

PH 4; BD 46; T 1.

From silts (unit 364) at the east of building S1 enclosure. 4th century AD.

30 ST 81 HV, SF 87 Base fragment, cup or bowl. Dull, iridescent weathering. Wide diagonal lower body. Outsplayed tubular base ring, concave base.

PH 11; BD 60; T 1.

From unit 180 of the clay platform to the south of building R1. ?3rd century AD.

31 ST 82 AAG, SF 304 Rim fragment, jug with pouring spout. Dull, weathered. Small oval bubbles in neck. Rim edge rolled in, funnel mouth, cylindrical neck.

PH 17; RD–; T 1.0–1.5

From topsoil/cleaning (unit 448), block 5 and 5a.

Bluish green: undecorated   (Figs 129–32, pp. 387–91)

32 ST 83 CNC, SF 583 Rim fragment, cylindrical cup. Dull, weathered. Some bubbles. Vertical rim, slightly inturned edge fire rounded and thickened, vertical side.

PH 18; RD approx. 90; T 1.5.

From a spit (unit 1290) through gravels and silts, south side of street 1 E/W, to the south-west of building S2.

33 ST 83 J4(1), SF 535 Rim fragment, cylindrical cup. Some bubbles. Vertical rim, edge fire rounded and thickened, vertical side.

PH 16; RD 80; T 1.

Context as no. 12.

34 ST 81 PQ (*Unillus.*) Small rim fragment, ?cylindrical cup. Dull. Vertical rim, edge fire rounded and thickened, vertical side.

PH 7; RD –; T 1.5.

From silt (unit 314) to west of hard-standing in block 1. ?Late 2nd century AD.

35 ST 84 DTW, SF 1056 Rim fragment, ?cup or jar. Some bubbles. Rim bent out diagonally, edge fire rounded, change of angle to body.

PH 9; RD approx. 100. T 1.5.

From gully 18, cut 16, unit 1953. 3rd century AD.

36 ST 81 GT, SF 77 Rim fragment, bowl. Dull. Vertical tubular rim, edge rolled inwards, then bent out and down to touch straight upper body.

PH 16; RD approx. 96; T 1.

Context as no. 2.

37 ST 82 BNC, SF 394 Rim fragment, bowl. Vertical tubular rim, edge bent out and down to touch upper body. Broken edge carefully grozed.

PH 11; RD 140; T 1.

From pit 997, unit 997. ?Later 3rd century AD.

38 ST 84 DVX, SF 1082 Rim fragment, bowl. Vertical tubular rim, edge bent out and down to touch upper body.

PH 8.5; RD approx 135; T 1.

From a lower layer (unit 1978) in well 1678. Late 2nd–3rd century AD.

39 ST 81 FN, SF 84 Rim fragment, bowl. Dull. Slightly out-turned tubular rim, edge bent out and down to touch upper body.

PH 10; RD approx. 130; T 1.

From the hardstanding (unit 128) north of building R1. 2nd–7th century AD.

40 ST 82 ABF, SF 341 Rim fragment, ?bowl. Inturned tubular rim, edge rolled inwards, then bent out and down to touch upper body, straight side tapering inwards.

PH 12; RD approx. 105; T 1.

From topsoil/cleaning, block 2.

41 ST 81 MR, SF 163 Lower body and base fragment, ?bowl or jug. Some bubbles. Lower body tapering in, tubular base ring, high concave base with central 'kick'. Pontil scar. Wear on base ring.

PH 19; BD 70; Pontil scar D 19; T 1–3.

From spit (unit 269) through disturbed silts, north side block 1. Phases IV–V.

42 ST 81 MR, SF 175 Lower body and base fragment, ?bowl or jug. Lower body tapering in, tubular base ring. Wear on base ring.

PH 9; BD approx. 45; T 1.5.

Context as no. 41.

43 ST 82 ABT, SF 346 Base fragment, ?bowl or jug. As 42. No wear on base ring.

PH 8; BD 58. T 1.5.

From rubble layer 484 in the sump. Phases IV–VI.

44 ST 84 DRP, SF 1073 (*Unillus.*) Base fragment ?bowl or jug. As 42, with diagonal base ring. Wear on base ring.

PH 8; BD –; T 1.5.

From well 1678, unit 1899. 3rd century AD.

Body fragments, *unillustrated*:

a ST 84 DGZ, SF 805 Carinated fragment, probably from cylindrical bowl.

Context as no. 13.

b ST 84 DGZ, SF 804 Lower body fragment, probably from cylindrical bowl.

Context as no. 13.

c ST 84 DGZ, SF 664 Small fragment.

Context as no. 13.

45 ST 84 DEA, SF 1042 Rim and neck fragment, ?jug or flask. Dull. Vertical bubbles in neck. Horizontal folded rim, edge bent out, up and in and flattened on top, narrow cylindrical neck. Surfaces slightly distorted by heat.

PH 15; RD 36; neck D approx. 18; T 3.

Context as no. 20.

46 ST 84 DGZ, SF 809 and SF 818 Twenty six body, base and handle fragments (many joining), conical jug. Dull, bubbles and black streaks in handle and trail. Slightly convex upper body expanding out, concave base (edge missing). Straight ribbon handle with central rib applied to upper body, claw attachment and vertical trail with 15 scored projections in low relief extending down body.

PH (handle fragment) approx. 116; T 0.7–1.

Context as no. 13.

47 ST 83 JI(1), SF 578 (*Unillus.*) Handle trail fragment, jug. Part of vertical trail, three scored projections in low relief.

PH 12.

From pit JI, layer 1. Late 3rd/early 4th century AD.

48 ST 84 EAR, SF 1094 (*Unillus.*) Base ring fragment, ?jug or jar. Wide lower body tapering in, constriction above open base ring.

PH 13; BD approx. 80; T 1.

From gully 18, cut 13, unit 2093. 3rd century AD.

49 ST 84 DNP, SF 813 Rim fragment, jug with pouring spout. Rolled rim, edge bent inwards, part of almond shaped mouth with raised spout, neck tapering in.

PH approx. 16; length of fragment 42; T 1.25.

From the fill (unit 1803) of pit 1803. Mid–late 3rd century AD.

50 ST 84 DEA, SF 737 Rim fragment, jug with pouring spout. Some bubbles. Unevenly rolled rim, edge bent in and flattened, part of almond shaped mouth, neck tapering in.

PH 21; length of fragment 35.5; T 2.5.

Context as no. 20.

51 ST 84 DIC, SF 1010 Rim fragment, jug with pouring spout. Very bubbly, black specks. Rim edge fire rounded. Part of almond shaped mouth, neck tapering in.

PH 21; T 3.

From uppermost layer (unit 1695) in ?latrine pit 1695. 3rd/4th century AD.

52 ST 81 MD, SF 132 Rim fragment, jug with pouring spout. Some bubbles. Rim edge fire rounded. Part of elongated and raised spout from almond shaped mouth. Pincer mark at lip of spout, neck tapering in.

PH approx. 17; T 1.5.

From the fill of gully 62 (unit 257). 4th–7th century AD.

53 ST 81 FV, SF 85 Body and handle fragment, jug. Some bubbles. Wide convex upper body, lower attachment of plain ribbon handle.

PH 24.5; T 1.

From silty clay occupaton layer (unit 134), north-west quadrant block 1. Phase IV/V.

54 ST 84 DVG, SF 940 Handle fragment, jug with trailed decoration. Some bubbles. Small part of upper body with fine unmarvered horizontal trail, lower attachment of plain ribbon handle.

PH 25.5.

From occupation layer (unit 1963) over pit complex 1989, 1990 etc. south-west block 9.

55 ST 84 DMM, SF 789 Handle fragment, jug or bottle. Straight ribbon handle with faint vertical ribs.

PH 27; W 28+.

From pit 1776, unit 1776. 3rd century AD.

Body fragments with trails, *unillustrated*:

a ST 82 AFC, SF 406 Fragment.

From ditch 9, cut 10, uppermost layer (unit 564). 3rd century AD.

b ST 83 J4(2), SF 601 Fragment.

From well J4, layer 2. Late 3rd/early 4th century AD.

c ST 84 DRW, SF 861 Three fragments, globular body.

From gully 31, cut 7, unit 1905. Late 2nd/3rd century AD.

d ST 84 DWX, SF 1040 Fragment, globular body.

Context as no. 28.

e ST 84 DHA, SF 833 Fragment.

Context as no. 25.

Undecorated body fragments, *unillustrated*:

f ST 84 DQY, SF 1001 Fragment.

From layer (unit 1883) in pits 1906, 1907 and gully 30. Late 2nd/early 3rd century AD.

g ST 84 DIG, SF 816 Fragment.

From gully 18, cut 23, unti 1699. 3rd century AD.

h ST 84 DOX, SF 849. Two fragments.

From well 1834, unit 1834. 3rd century AD.

i ST 84 DEA, SF 654 Fragment.

Context as no. 20.

j ST 81 ST Fragment.

From the fill (unit 363) of pit 363.

k ST 84 DPW, SF 888 Fragment.

Context as no. 6c.

l ST 84 DRR, SF 923 Fragment.

From well 1678, unit 1901. 3rd century AD.

m ST 84 DOX Fragment.

Context as no. 55h.

56 ST 84 DVF (*Unillus.*) Small handle fragment, ?jug or bottle. Small part of angular ribbon handle with at least two vertical ridges.

Dims 7.5 × 18.

From uppermost layer (unit 1962), in pit 1962. Late 2nd/early 3rd century AD.

57 ST 84 ECG, SF 1111 Neck fragment, ?unguent bottle. Very bubbly. Narrow cylindrical neck expanding out.

PH 59; neck D 11, 5.0–13.5; T 1.

From pit 2106, unit 2131. ?Late 2nd/3rd century AD.

58 ST 83 G4(8), SF 539 Body and handle fragment, bath flask. Convex shoulder expanding out, lower attachment of small dolphin shaped handle applied to shoulder, drawn up neck (now missing), then bent out and down to form small aperture and attached to shoulder.

PH 26; T 2.5.

From well G4, layer 8. Early 3rd century AD.

59 ST 82 AAQ Base fragment, ?jug or bath flask. Very bubbly, many streaks. Thick-walled convex body and small concave base. Pontil mark at centre of base.

PH 12; BD approx. 30; T 4–6.

From gully 41, cut 5, unit 457. Late 2nd/early 3rd century AD.

Neck fragments, *unillustrated*:

a ST 84 DPX, SF 682 Fragment.

From layer 1858 in pit 1695. Later 2nd/3rd century AD.

b ST 84 DPS, SF 1034 Fragment.

Context as no. 61.

c ST 84 DEA, SF 659 Fragment.

Context as no. 20.

d ST 84 DBH, SF 628 Fragment.

From gully 21, cut 1, unit 1532. Early 3rd century AD.

e ST 84 DBH, SF 630 Fragment.

Context as no. 59d.

f ST 84 DVE, SF 929 Fragment.

From gully 31, cut 8, unit 1961. Late 2nd/3rd century AD.

g ST 84 DPS, SF 1036 Fragment.

Context as no. 61.

h ST 84 DNT, SF 665 Fragment.

From general trowelling (unit 1807) over block 7 and 8.

i ST 83A (26)/7/, SF 3 Fragment.

From the northern sump, layer A, 26, grid 7. Late 2nd–4th century AD.

j ST 82 BDS Fragment.

From top layer (unit 795) of pit 795. Late 3rd/4th century AD.

k ST 84 DYD, SF 1084 Fragment.

From gully 19, cut 4, unit 2032. Mid 3rd century AD.

Base fragments, *unillustrated*:

l ST 84 DRP, SF 689 Five fragments, 4 convex body, 1 concave base.

Context as no. 44.

m ST 83 CRD, SF 610 Fragment, thick concave base, pontil mark.

From occupation layer (unit 1387), centre north, block 1. Late 2nd–3rd century AD.

n ST 84 DRA, SF 896 Fragment, thick concave base, pontil mark.

From upper layer (unit 1885) of well 1885. 3rd century AD.

o ST 82 BIV Fragment, thick concave base, centre missing.

From upper layer (unit 918) in pit 483/918. 3rd century AD.

p ST 83 J4(4), SF 611 Fragment, thick concave base, pontil mark.

From well J4, layer 4. Early 3rd century AD.

Bottles: colourless   (Fig. 132, p. 391)

60 ST 82 AAG Body fragment, small prismatic vessel (?Mercury bottle). Dull, strain cracks. Part of two thick-walled vertical sides, right angle.

PH 31; max width of side 17; T 3.5–6.

Context as no. 31.

Also, *unillustrated*:

a ST 83 CKE, SF 528 Greenish tinge. Body fragment.

From ditch 4, cut 4, unit 1220. Early 3rd century AD.

b ST 81 KN Greenish tinge. Shoulder fragment.

Context as no. 63.

Bottles: bluish green   (Figs 132–5)

61 ST 84 DPS, SF 850 Two fragments, rim, neck and handle. Dark bluish green. Dull, bubbly. Horizontal folded rim, edge bent out, up, in and flattened on top, cylindrical neck, shoulder expanding out. Folded upper attachment of ribbon handle on neck and rim edge.

PH approx. 55; RD 50; T 4.

From ?latrine pit 1695, unit 1854. Later 2nd/3rd century AD.

Rim fragments, *unillustrated*:

a ST 82 AFE Fragment.

From ditch 9, cut 7, uppermost layer (unit 566). 3rd century AD.

b ST 83 CPB Fragment.

From ditch 10, cut 1, unit 1337. Phase IV.

c ST 84 DAA, SF 660 Fragment.

From topsoil (unit 1501), block 6 and block 5, south.

62 ST 82 BIQ, SF 382 Neck and handle fragment. Iridescent weathering. Cylindrical neck, folded upper attachment of ribbon handle.

PH 30; neck D approx. 30. T 4.

From well 808, unit 914. Late 2nd–3rd century AD.

Neck fragments, *unillustrated*:

a ST 82 AAG Fragment.

Context as no. 31.

b ST 83 J4(1), SF 533 Fragment.

Context as no. 12.

c ST 83 CCV Fragment.

From ditch 9, cut 2, unit 1067. 3rd century AD.

d ST 84 DNP, SF 814 Fragment.

Context as no. 49.

63 ST 81 KN, SF 112. Shoulder and handle fragment. Iridescent weathering. Many bubbles in handle. Curved shoulder, lower attachment of straight ribbon handle with edge rib and broad central ridge.

PH 31; T 3.5.

From upper fill (unit 220) of pit 170. 3rd/4th century AD.

Shoulder fragments, *unillustrated*:

a ST 84 DVF, SF 1055 Fragment.

Context as no. 56.

b   ST 84 DEA, SF 744 Fragment.

Context as no. 20.

c   ST 84 DIV, SF 793 Fragment.

From gully 29, cut 9, unit 1712. 3rd century AD.

d   ST 83 JI(1), SF 577 Fragment.

Context as no. 47.

e   ST 84 DDV, SF 715 Fragment.

From pit 1592, unit 1592. Phase III/IV.

f   ST 82 ADM Fragment, prismatic bottle.

From ditch 9, cut 8, unit 525. 3rd century AD.

g   ST 81 LZ Fragment, prismatic bottle.

From upper layer (unit 253) of gully 64, cut 1. Late 3rd–4th century AD.

Handle fragments, *unillustrated*:

h   ST 84 DDA, SF 710 Fragment.

From ditch 7, cut 1, unit 1573. Late 2nd/early 3rd century AD.

i   ST 84 DEA, SF 723 Fragment.

Context as no. 20.

64   ST 80 AZ, SF 13 Three fragments, neck, shoulder and body, square bottle. Iridescent weathering. Tooling marks at base of neck, flat shoulder, parts of three vertical sides, two with concave areas below shoulder. Scar of handle with multiple reeding on shoulder.

PH approx. 74; width of sides 63; T 3–4.

From occupation debris (unit 23), west of building R1. 2nd–7th century AD.

Square and prismatic body fragments, *unillustrated*:

a   ST 82 BLH, SF 441 Fragment.

From ditch 9, cut 1a, unit 954. Late 2nd/early 3rd century AD.

b   ST 84 DOT, SF 697 Fragment.

From layer (unit 1831) above gully 27, cut 2. 3rd century AD.

c   ST 82 AGZ, SF 398 Fragment.

From building R2, ash and clay surface (unit 609). Late 2nd century AD.

d   ST 81 HK Fragment.

From well 171, uppermost layer (unit 171). Residual 3rd–4th century AD pottery with Anglo-Saxon sherds. 4th–7th century AD.

e   ST 84 DKF, SF 671 Fragment.

From well 704/1663, unit 1722. Late 3rd/early 4th century AD.

f   ST 84 DEA, SF 663 Fragment.

Context as no. 20.

g   ST 81 KQ Fragment.

From well 171, unit 222. Late 3rd–4th century AD.

h   ST 83 H8(1) Fragment.

From layer 1 in large pit or ditch, H8. 3rd/4th century AD.

i   ST 81 NC Fragment.

From lower layer, south-west quadrant (unit 279) of the low rubbly mound sealing Anglo-Saxon building S1. Phase Va.

j   ST 84 DIC, SF 1016 Fragment.

Context as no. 51.

k   ST 83 J4(1) Two fragments.

Context as no. 12.

l   ST 84 DWY, SF 1047 Fragment.

From top layer (unit 2003) of pit 2003. Late 2nd/3rd century AD.

m   ST 84 DPS, SF 1033 Fragment.

Context as no. 61.

n   ST 84 DRS, SF 915 Fragment.

From uppermost fill (unit 1902) of well 1914. 3rd cenury AD.

o   ST 84 DRM, SF 899 Fragment.

From gully 18, cut 22, unit 1896. 3rd century AD.

p   ST 83 G8(1), SF 498 Fragment.

From the fill of gully 18, cut 6.

q   ST 83 CMT, SF 605 Fragment, burnt.

From gully 53, cut 2, unit 1282. Late 3rd–4th century AD.

r   ST 84 DLC, SF 799 Fragment.

From well 1602, unit 1743. Later 2nd/3rd century AD.

s   ST 81 FM Fragment.

From unit 127 of the low rubbly mound sealing building S1. 9th–10th century AD.

t   ST 82 AET Fragment.

From ditch 9, cut 5, basal layer (unit 556). Early 3rd century AD.

u   ST 84 DYS, SF 1077 Fragment.

From building R12, post-hole 2046. Phase III/IV.

v   ST 84 DPS, SF 690 Fragment.

Context as no. 61.

w   ST 84 DEP, SF 779 Fragment.

From pit 1611, unit 1611. Early/mid 3rd century AD.

x   ST 84 DPS, SF 1035 Fragment.

Context as no. 61.

y   ST 84 EAS, SF 1124 Fragment.

From pit 2094, unit 2094. 3rd century AD.

z   ST 84 DYC, SF 1078 Fragment.

From gully 19, cut 2, unit 2031. Mid 3rd century AD.

aa ST 82 ABF Fragment.

Context as no. 40.

ab ST 82 ACV Fragment.

From sinkage (unit 509) into ditch 74, cut 1. Late 3rd/4th century AD.

ac ST 81 KS Fragment.

From silty layer (unit 224) in vicinity of ovens 1 and 2. 3rd or 4th century AD.

ad ST 84 DTA, SF 1097 Fragment.

From the fill (unit 1933) of pit 1933. Phase V.

ae ST 84 EBP, SF 1121 Fragment.

From gully 24, cut 5, unit 2115. 3rd century AD.

af ST 84 DAA Fragment.

Context as no. 61c.

ag ST 84 DGY Fragment.

From uppermost layer (unit 1667) in well 1667. Late 3rd/4th century AD.

ah ST 84 DEA Fragment.

Context as no. 20.

ai ST 82 BBC Fragment.

From upper fill (unit 732) of pit 736/737. 3rd century AD.

aj ST 81 KB Fragment.

From gully 44, cut 2, unit 209. Late 2nd century AD.

ak ST 84 DYC Fragment.

Context as no. 64z.

al ST 84 DIC, SF 841 Fragment.

Context as no. 51.

am ST 81 HV Two fragments.

Context as no. 30.

an ST 84 DPS, SF 850 Fragment.

Context as no. 61.

Cylindrical bottle fragments, *unillustrated*:

ao ST 81 LR Base fragment.

From pit 170, unit 246. ?3rd century AD.

ap ST 84 AA16(1), SF 1175 Body fragment.

From ?pit AA16, unexcavated.

Hexagonal bottle fragments, *unillustrated*:

aq ST 84 DNP, SF 814 Body fragment.

Context as no. 49.

65 ST 84 DYA, SF 1072 Base fragment, square bottle. Dark bluish green. Dull. Some round bubbles. Two vertical sides, concave base. Raised basal design. Concentric circle surrounding hollow sided lozenge.

PH 22; T 2.5–7.5.

From gully 18, cut 10, unit 2029. 3rd century AD.

66 ST 81 MG, SF 158 and ST 81 QQ, SF 210 Five base fragments, three joining, square bottle. Vertical side, concave base. Raised basal design. Two concentric rings and central pellet.

Dims 59 × 52; D (rings) 66 and 38; T 7.5.

From amorphous rubbish spread 260, south of building R1. Phase IV. And from slumped clay (unit 337) over south edge of metalled surface north of building R1. Late 2nd century AD.

67 ST 84 DBR, SF 746 Base fragment, square bottle. Dull. Some small bubbles. Three sides, concave base. Raised basal design. Concentric ring. Patches of wear on edges and corners of base.

PH 6; width of side 50; T 2–6.

From the uppermost layer (unit 1541) of pit 1541. 3rd century AD.

68 ST 84 DTZ, SF 1046 Base fragment, square or rectangular bottle. Two vertical sides, concave base. Raised basal design. One concentric ring. Band of wear at edges of base.

PH 22; Dims 29 × 31; T 4.5–9.

Context as no. 17.

69 ST 83 CIB, SF 490 Base fragment, square or rectangular bottle. Vertical side, concave base. Raised basal design. One pellet outside narrow concentric ring. Small thin-walled vessel.

Dimensions 33 × 19; T 1.5–2.

From lower fill (unit 1193) of pit 1184. Early 3rd century AD.

70 ST 82 AAO, SF 344 Base fragment, prismatic bottle. Vertical side, concave base. Raised basal design. One concentric ring. Some wear on base edge.

Dims 27 × 24; T 6–7.

From gully 41, cut 4, unit 455. Late 2nd/early 3rd century AD.

71 ST 81 HJ Base fragment, prismatic bottle, pale bluish green. One vertical side, concave base. Raised basal design. Concentric ring.

Dims 29.5 × 20.5, T 4.5–6.5.

From upper fill (unit 170) of pit 170, north of building R1. 3rd/4th century AD.

Objects (Fig. 135, p. 395)

Beads

72 ST 84 DPM, SF 866 Annular bead. Dark blue ground, three opaque yellow spirals. Wide perforation.

H 7; max. D 12; perforation D 4.7.

From well 1667, unit 1848. Late 3rd/4th century AD.

73 ST 83 CKA, SF 492 Annular bead. Dark blue. Wide perforation. Wound bead. Complete.

H 4.5; max. D 9; perforation D 4.

From ditch 4, cut 5, unit 1216. Mid/late 3rd century AD.

74 ST 82 ADW, SF 337 Annular bead. Dark yellowish green, appearing black. Wide perforation. Wound bead. Complete.

H 4.2–5; max. D 11.3; perforation D 6.

From slump (unit 534) into ditch 74, cut 1. Late 3rd/4th century AD.

75 ST 81 QQ , SF 200 Small globular bead, perhaps from segmented bead. Bluish green. Small perforation, one end twisted and broken.

H 7.8; max. D 7.8; perforation D 2.

From slumped clay (unit 337) over south edge of metalled surface north of building R1. Late 2nd century AD.

76 ST 82 BFE, SF 349 Cylindrical bead. Dark green. Side flattened. Small perforation, Broken at one end.

L 7.1; T 3.6 × 2.2; perforation D 1.5.

From pit 830, unit 830. Late 2nd/3rd century AD.

Counter or gaming piece

77 ST 84 DIS, SF 1160 Fragment of matt-glossy window glass reworked into roughly circular roundel for secondary use. Grozed edges.

Dimensions 14.4 × 15.7; T 3.

From unit 1710 in mixed silt 1689, north-west block 9. Phase III/IV.

Window glass   (Pl. XXVIa)

78 ST 81, NJ Twenty joined fragments, matt-glossy window pane, part of one side surviving. Blue-green. Bands of small bubbles, some black streaks. Matt surface very smooth, dull and pockmarked, glossy surface smooth and even in interior, becoming uneven and thicker towards rounded edge. Smooth surface scratched, in lines parallel to rounded edge; evidence for mortar on matt surface near to rounded edge. Star-shaped breaks in the pane suggest that it was hit by a sharp object in at least two places, one close to the rounded edge and the other in the middle of the pane.

Max. dims 283 × 241; T 2.5–4.5; area 414.7 cm^2; weight 340.9 g.

From pit 170, unit 285. 3rd/4th century AD.

79 ST 81, MA Five joined fragments, matt-glossy window pane, part of two sides and corner surviving. Blue green. Bands of bubbles, black streaks and details of surfaces, as no. 78; evidence of tooling on the glossy surface where the glass has been pushed to form the rounded corner.

Max. dims 132 × 197; T 2.5–4.5 mm; area 120.4 cm^2; weight 118.1 g.

From pit 170, unit 254. 3rd/4th century AD.

More than 1300 fragments of matt-glossy window glass were recorded. Lists containing details of the assemblage have been lodged in the site archive. See also following Appendix.

APPENDIX: SUMMARY LIST OF LOCATIONS OF PRINCIPAL DEPOSITS OF WINDOW GLASS

Block 1

Including the boundary ditch (ditch 9) on the east side. Window glass in 154 contexts.

Principal deposits

1 Inside the central block of building R1 – 12 contexts:

a 43 blue-green fragments, 383.7 cm^2, 272.4 g;
b 39 greenish colourless fragments, 231 cm^2, 200.4 g;
c 3 colourless fragments, 16.5 cm^2, 13.4 g, representing a minimum of three panes.

The position of the finds suggests that this building had glazed windows on the north, west and south walls. However, it is difficult to judge whether the glass has been deposited close to where it fell, or whether it was redeposited as part of the rubble infill; the only large deposit [ST 80, BD; context 27, bag 12] was found in the rubble infill in the apse.

2 Inside the north range and east wing of building R1 – 5 contexts:

a 8 blue-green fragments, 23.1 cm^2, 14.3 g;
b 4 colourless fragments, 8.3 cm^2, 5.6 g, representing a minimum of two panes.

These are small fragments in wall footings, a shallow scoop and in the clay floor.

3 In the small hypocausted room on the south-west corner of building R1 – 4 contexts:

a 95 blue-green fragments, 668 cm^2, 458 g;
b 5 greenish colourless fragments, 55 cm^2, 36.3 g, representing a minimum of two panes.

Most of these fragments belong to the destruction and abandonment of the small hypocaust; the largest group [ST 80, BA; context 24, bag 11] was found in the destruction deposit, and another [ST 80, BE context 28, bag 9] came from the furnace area. In ST 80, DS [context 86, bag 21], five blue-green fragments were found below the hypocaust, in the primary silt on the old ground surface.

4 In the south room of building R1 – 3 contexts:

a 1 blue-green fragment, 12 cm^2, 7.7 g;
b 5 greenish colourless fragments, 36 cm^2, 33 g, representing a minimum of two panes.

All the finds occur on the west and south sides of this room which may indicate that the west and south walls had glazed windows, unless the fill in which they were found was brought from elsewhere.

5 North of building R1

a Pit 170 – 7 contexts:
48 blue-green fragments, 672.1 cm^2, 573.3 g;
14 greenish colourless fragments, 79.5 cm^2, 60.6 g;
6 colourless fragments, 21.5 cm^2, 17.5 g, representing a minimum of three panes.

Two large pieces of blue-green window pane (catalogue nos 78–9) have been reconstructed from fragments found in several different contexts within this pit, indicating that the glass was broken *before* the fragments were deposited in the pit. Both pieces are very similar in colour, quality and thickness, and they are likely to come from the same window pane. In particular, they both contain a dark band of small bubbles. It is possible that they could be linked along one edge, which would increase the length of one side of the pane to 412 mm, though this is far from certain.

b Area of ragstone cobbles to the north of building R1 (pit 170 is within this area) – 9 contexts:
23 blue-green fragments, 139.5 cm^2, 112.9 g;
22 greenish colourless fragments, 50.0 cm^2, 45.4 g;
6 colourless fragments, 18.0 cm^2, 11.3 g, representing a minimum of three panes.

These deposits are very small, apart from one [ST 81, FN, context 128, bag 293] which contained 37 small pieces.

6 West of building R1

a Pit 132 and the surface above:
3 blue-green fragments, 26 cm^2, 24.8 g;
2 colourless fragments, 5 cm^2, 4.2 g, represents two panes. Very small deposits.
b Stone-lined drain (gully 49):
10 blue-green fragments, 39 + cm^2, 31 + g;
1 colourless fragment, 2.5 cm^2, 1.7 g, representing a minimum of two panes. Very small deposits.
c Occupation debris:
47 blue-green fragments, 152 cm^2, 201.4 g;
5 greenish colourless fragments, 15 cm^2, 9.7 g, representing a minimum of two panes.

This group may be derived directly from windows in the west wall of building R1, though the fragments are more likely to have been redeposited with the occupation debris.

7 South of building R1

a Gully 44 – 5 contexts:
23 blue-green fragments, 133 cm^2, 87.6 g;
1 colourless fragment, 3.5 cm^2, 2.9 g, representing a minimum of two panes.
b Block 1b enclosure gully (gully 41) and interior gully (gully 42) – 5 contexts:
14 blue-green fragments, 75.5 cm^2, 60.8 g;
2 colourless fragments, 7.0 cm^2, 4.4 g, representing at least two panes.

These are small deposits, though it is noticeable that one [ST 82, AGQ, gully 42, context 601, bag 263] contained more fragments than the other four.

c Well 446 – 6 contexts:
27 blue-green fragments, 208 cm^2, 164.6 g;
1 colourless fragment 11.5 cm^2, 10.5 g, representing a minimum of two panes.

It is interesting that window glass was found in several of the upper layers of the well but not in the bottom three, suggesting that it had already been abandoned at the time of deposition of the glass.

Otherwise, there is a scatter of fragments in the ragstone and clay spreads.

8 North-west of building R1

a Well 135 – 7 contexts:
15 blue-green fragments, 47.0 cm^2, 37.9 g;
6 colourless fragments, 36.8 cm^2, 27.3 g;
4 greenish colourless fragments, 18.5 cm^2, 18.7 g, representing a minimum of three panes.

Mostly rather small fragments, found in all the layers of the well except the bottom one.

9 North-east of building R1

a Well 171/558 – 5 contexts within fill:
11 blue-green fragments, 55.5 cm^2, 46.9 g;
6 colourless fragments, 48 cm^2, 44.7 g;
3 greenish colourless fragments, 31 cm^2, 34.6 g, representing a minimum of 3 panes.

Otherwise, there are single fragments in three other pits and gullies.

10 Boundary ditch (ditch 9) to east and south-east of building R1 – 22 contexts:
44 blue-green fragments, 228.8 cm^2, 173.3 g;
17 colourless fragments, 206.0 cm^2, 172.5 g;
12 greenish colourless fragments, 56.0 cm^2, 43.2 g, representing a minimum of three panes.

All these are very small groups.

11 Features at north of block 1, to the south of street 1 E/W – 17 contexts scattered in the road gravel, and in pits and post-holes, some relating to the Anglo-Saxon buildings:
> 30 blue-green fragments, 128.7 cm^2, 105.5 g;
> 7 colourless fragments, 31.0 cm^2, 24.4 g;
> 5 greenish colourless fragments, 7.0 cm^2, 5.8 g, representing a minimum of three panes.

The sump

A few fragments of blue-green, greenish colourless and colourless window glass were found, but this was not much used as an area for dumping the broken panes.

Block 2

Twenty-five contexts.

Single fragments were found in the boundary ditch (ditch 9), and in beam slots, post-holes and pits. There is a concentration of fragments in ditch 9 and pits to the east of the modern dyke.

a Boundary ditch [ditch 9, contexts 726, 765, 766]:
> 5 blue-green fragments, 34.5 cm^2, 24.3 g;
> 3 colourless fragments, 34 cm^2, 33.0 g, representing a minimum of two panes.

b Pit 483/918 [contexts 918, 483, 864, 892, 922]:
> 5 blue-green fragments, 32 cm^2, 28.4 g;
> 1 greenish colourless fragment, 16.0 cm^2, 13.7 g;
> 5 colourless fragments, 38.5 cm^2, 37.3 g, representing a minimum of three panes.

c Pits 794, 795 [units 794, 795, 824]:
> 3 blue-green fragments, 11 cm^2, 8.7 g;
> 1 colourless fragment, 1.5 cm^2, 1.2 g, representing at least two panes.

Blocks 3 and 4

Thirteen contexts.

1 Finds in vicinity of buildings R7 and R6:

a Well 1836 and gully 35, north-east of block 4 – 5 contexts [1740, 1836, 1851, 1855, 1856]:
> 9 blue-green fragments, 160 cm^2, 145.8 g;
> 4 greenish colourless fragments, 30 cm^2, 20.0 g;
> 1 colourless fragment, 11.0 cm^2, 9.4 g, representing a minimum of three panes.

b Pit 736/737, south-west corner of block 3 – 2 contexts [732, 736]:
> 2 blue-green fragments, 9 cm^2, 6.9 g.

Otherwise, there are single fragments in gullies, fence-lines etc.

Block 5

Twelve contexts.

Pits 1567, 1525 and 1776, south-west block 5 – 5 contexts:
> 17 blue-green fragments, 83 cm^2, 78.1 g;
> 2 colourless fragments, 9.0 cm^2, 6.5 g, representing a minimum of two panes.

Finds in the top and upper layers of pits.

Otherwise, there is a marked absence of glass in the pits in this area.

Block 6

Thirteen contexts.

a Pit 1577 – 1 context:
> 5 blue-green fragments, 32 cm^2, 28.4 g.

Otherwise, single fragments from ditches, latrines and other pits.

Block 7

Nine contexts.

a Well 1885 – 2 contexts:
> 6 blue-green fragments, 48.0 cm^2, 33.3 g;
> 1 colourless fragment, 3 cm^2, 2.1 g, representing at least two panes.

Otherwise, there are one or two fragments in pits and ditches.

Block 8

Nineteen contexts.

Widely scattered deposits in pits and gullies. No concentrations of fragments.

Block 9

Forty-one contexts.

More window glass was found in this block than elsewhere on the site, except in block 1. The distance between the two areas suggests that the block 9 fragments may derive from glazed windows in the timber buildings within the block (buildings R10–R14). Some pieces occurred in gullies, and some came from 16 pits and latrines in this area.

The largest concentration came from ?latrine pit 1695 adjacent to building R13 – 3 contexts:
> 26 blue-green fragments, 241.5 cm^2, 210.0 g;
> 2 colourless fragments, 12.5 cm^2, 10.0 g, representing at least two panes.

Block 10

Six contexts.

The finds came from features exposed in machine-cut trench J.

Well J 4 (contexts +, 1, 7)
    5 blue-green fragments, 19.0 cm², 15.5 g;
    4 colourless fragments, 28.0 cm², 23.5 g, representing at least two panes.

SAMIAN WARE

Catherine Johns   (Figs 136–41)

Abbreviations

Déch	Déchelette 1904
Dr	Dragendorff 1895
O	Oswald 1936/7
Ricken/Fischer	Ricken and Fischer 1963
Rogers	Rogers 1974
CGP	Stanfield and Simpson 1958

The selection of decorated samian sherds for illustration and description in final excavation reports is often made on a variety of quite different, even contradictory, criteria, and they are seldom explained. Some sherds may be included because they are exceptional and rare, while others are catalogued because they are common and typical; yet others may be unimportant as samian, but are described because they are from significant contexts. Decorated sherds which are large and well-preserved, good 'drawable' pieces, are also often included even if they are of little interest in themselves. They can be helpful for users of the report who may be trying to match smaller sherds from similar vessels.

The 44 sherds catalogued were selected from some 300 decorated sherds (catalogue nos. 45 and 46 are technically plain vessels). The inclusion of four sherds of Dr 29 (nos 1–4) was on the basis of their extreme rarity on the site, and East Gaulish decorated bowls are also statistically over-represented compared with the Central Gaulish majority, though not to anything like the same extent. Numbers 5, 37 and 41 were complete enough for their full scheme of decoration and profile to be drawn, and this in itself is a reason for their importance, though no. 41, a stamped bowl by IANVS of Rheinzabern, would have warranted inclusion even if it had been very fragmentary.

The general impression given by the catalogue is of an overwhelming preponderance of typical Antonine Lezoux ware, and this is a fair reflection of the assemblage as a whole, which is very homogeneous; the vast majority of the vessels were, indeed, made in Central Gaul in the Antonine period. The virtual absence of first century AD ware from South Gaul and the complete absence of Trajanic Central Gaulish products is a very striking feature.

From the total of approximately 3000 sherds of plain samian forms, only four sherds are definitely first-century South Gaulish, and a further two may be. Of the decorated forms, five sherds are from South Gaulish bowls of form Dr 29, but two, or possibly three, of these are from the same vessel. There are no South Gaulish examples amongst the potters' stamps.

The forms represented in the plain samian are those which are to be expected at this period, with large numbers of Dr 31 and Dr 33. There are a few sherds of Dr 27, but all are of typically late profile. The flanged bowl Dr 38 is present in some numbers, as are the late forms Walters 79 and 80 and the closely related types Ludowici Tg and Tx. Ludowici Th, another Walters 79 variant, also occurs. Dr 36 and Dr 45, plus the mortarium form Dr 45, one or two sherds of Dr 42 and one example of the unusual hybrid form of Dr 15/31 sums up the whole assemblage. On plain forms alone, without a single decorated sherd or potter's stamp, the Antonine dating would be obvious.

The size and condition of the sherds is very variable, though we may note in passing that the South Gaulish fragments are all very small and worn. One site context deserves special mention because of the condition of the sherds and their size. This is P 10, a deposit fully discussed elsewhere (pp. 219–20). The samian from this group stands out, with very large sherds bearing, in many cases, little or no signs of use. There is just one exception, a large portion from a small Dr 38 which was heavily worn and also broken and riveted before it was discarded. The range of types present in the pit closely reflects the range on the site as a whole, including several examples of Walters 79. Ten potters' stamps derive from P 10, nos 3, 37, 55, 58, 65, 67, 77, 81, 93 and 95: all are Central Gaulish, and all have a date-range falling within the second half of the second century AD. The large size and good condition of the sherds supports the interpretation that P 10 was filled at one time in some form of clearing or tidying operation, rather than serving as a disposal area for rubbish over an extended period.

1 **Dr 29 SG**   ST 82 AAG

Upper zone fragments with scroll containing a seven-rayed rosette and a small bird facing right.

Flavian.

From topsoil/cleaning, block 5.

2 **Dr 29 SG**   ST 82 ADW

Upper zone, a scroll with eight-rayed rosettes, and small beads bordering a narrow central moulding.

(Sherds probably from the same vessel in ST 82 BEI)

Flavian.

From ditch 74, cut 1, unit 534 (sinkage fill). Late 3rd/4th century AD.

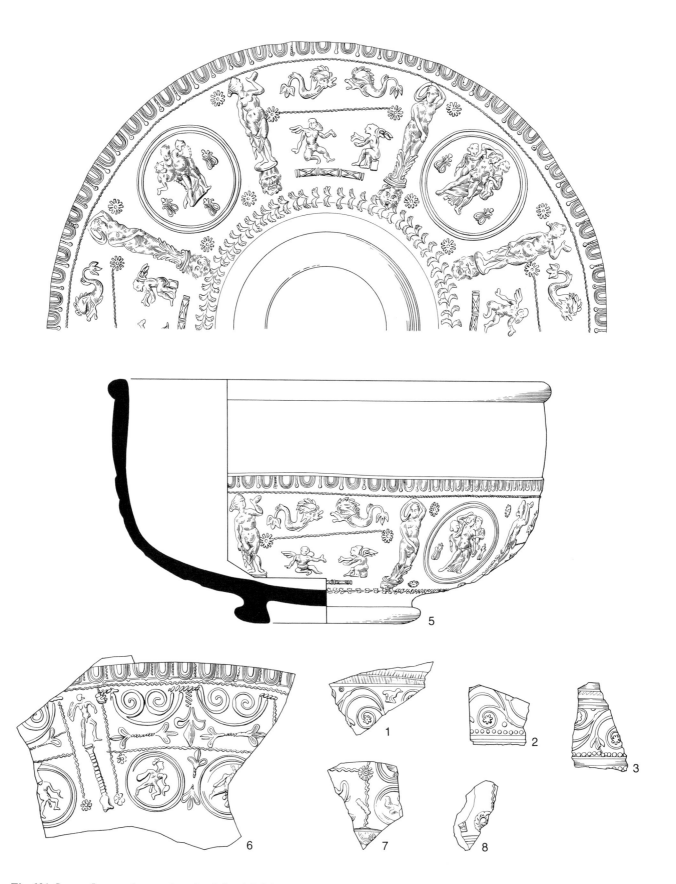

Fig. 136 Stonea Grange: decorated samian 1–3 and 5–8 (scale 1 : 2).

3 Dr 29 SG ST 82 ACV

Upper zone, a scroll with a small triple leaf and rosette. Possibly from the same bowl as no. 2 above.

Flavian.

From ditch 74, cut 1, unit 509 (sinkage fill). Late 3rd/4th century AD.

4 Dr 29 SG (*Unillus*.) ST 84 DGQ

A small upper-zone sherd with a scroll incorporating a very blurred leaf and a seven-pointed rosette.

Flavian.

From occupation level (unit 1867), south-east quadrant of block 9.

Late 2nd/3rd century AD.

5 Dr 37 CG ST 84 DON (SF 767, 691)

Most of a fairly large bowl (rim diameter 24.4 cm) which was broken in antiquity and repaired with rivets. The ware is of good quality and the moulding sharp and fresh. The design is loosely organised and may be described as semi-panelled, with caryatid dividers and double medallions. The ovolo is double-bordered with a corded, ring-tipped tongue, Rogers B 109 (ovolo 2 of Butrio). The horizontal border is a very fine wavy line. There is a basal wreath consisting of a bifid leaf, Rogers K 35, which is attributed to Butrio, plus Paternus II, Albucius and Servus I. In the field are eleven-rayed rosettes, Rogers C 213, recorded for Butrio and X-11. Rogers notes the fact that different drawings of this detail are not consistent in the number of rays: he himself draws the rosette with ten, but he may have been following the drawing in *CGP* rather than an actual vessel. It is often difficult to be certain of such details unless the moulding is unusually sharp.

The latticed column, Rogers P 3, was a common detail employed by several potters. Within the medallions is a stylised leaf derived from South Gaulish designs, Rogers G 144. It is not noted as a type used by Butrio; the workshops given are those of Avitus, P-1, P-8 and P-10. The figure-types are as follows: Venus/caryatid on mask, O 305; male caryatid, O 1201; dolphin to the right, O 2382; dolphin to the left, O 2392; flying cupid, O 440; seated cupid, O 444. In the medallions are the groups of a drunken Silenus supported by satyrs, O 561 and a drunken Bacchus supported by satyrs, O 557: the latter is slightly reduced in size when compared with the Oswald drawing, though it corresponds with the example from Cirencester illustrated in *CGP*, Pl. 60: 697.

The bowl may be assigned to the workshop of Butrio. The general scheme of decoration, with caryatid dividers and horizontally-divided panels, has much in common with *CGP* Pl. 61: 681, from Lezoux.

Hadrianic.

From unit 1825, pit 1825. 3rd century AD.

6 Dr 37 CG ST 84 DXK, DFE

Sherds in a rather poor ware with a very confused scheme of decoration. There are narrow vertical panels and horizontally-divided panels containing festoons and small double medallions. There are echoes of some late South Gaulish designs.

The ovolo is partly obscured by the guideline beneath it, but is certainly double-bordered with a corded tongue. In spite of the fact that Rogers 228 is drawn with a plain tongue, this may be the same one, used by a number of Hadrianic potters including the group of Quintilianus, Avitus and Vegetus. All the borders are wavy lines. The details include plain spirals in festoons, Rogers S 7 and S 37 (X-9, Medetus/Ranto, P-5), a segmented column, Rogers P 10 (X-5, X-9), rosettes, Rogers C 172 (Avitus, Quintilianus), and a fleur-de-lys, Rogers G 88 (Vegetus, Laxtucissa, X-5).

Neither the small warrior on the column nor the armed pygmy in the medallions can be precisely matched in Oswald. The general style indicates one of the Hadrianic groups of potters which include the various Quintilianus styles and Avitus/Vegetus. Note the similar use of very small figures on several sherds illustrated in *CGP* Pls 63–4.

Hadrianic.

From two nearby pits in block 9: pit 2014, unit 2014. Later 2nd century AD. Well 1625, unit 1625. 3rd/4th century.

7 Dr 37 CG ST 84 DIV

A small fragment with bold wavy lines demarcating the panels. The wheel-rosette Rogers C 297 forms a junction, and an astragalus is placed diagonally over a vertical border. A very small double medallion contains a tiny stylised dolphin, O 2407A, and the adjacent small panel contains a vase, Rogers T 8. All the details are typical of Gelenus.

Hadrianic.

From gully 29, cut 9, unit 1712. 3rd century AD.

8 Dr 37 CG ST 83 CCB

A small fragment in good-quality ware with sharp moulding and a glossy slip. All that survives of the design is a bold zigzag border and the edge of a curled acanthus frond. This latter could be Rogers G 349, used by Avitus. The fabric suggests a Hadrianic date.

Hadrianic.

From ditch 9, cut 1b, unit 1049. Late 2nd/early 3rd century AD.

9 Dr 37 CG ST 83 CNL

A small bowl with blurred and rather rough moulding. The ovolo is a distinctive single-stamp impression, narrow, with a long, possibly corded bead-tipped tongue on the left. The border is a wavy line, and the decor is of festoons and tassels containing small rings, and a kneeling cupid, O 403. The ovolo is difficult to match exactly: Rogers B 80 and B 244 are possibilities (assigned to Cettus and Austrus respectively). The figure-type is recorded for Austrus and Lalus/X-6, as well as Ioenalis and later Blickweiler and Heiligenberg potters. The general decoration recalls work of Austrus and X-5 and X-6, but Austrus or an associate seems most likely. He did occasionally use wavy lines (e.g. *CGP*, Pl. 94: 1, 3, 5).

Hadrian-Antonine.

From ditch 10, cut 2, unit 1298. Phase IV(?)

Fig. 137 Stonea Grange: decorated samian 9–17 (scale 1 : 2).

10 Dr 37 CG   ST 84 W 10, 1

A small sherd with a double basal line and panels divided by astragalus borders. Part of a double medallion can be seen in one panel; in the next, the legs of a figure are preserved above the rosette-and-feather, Rogers U 140 (Ariccus, Laxtucissa, Paternus and Quintilianus). The figure-type is a man in a short tunic moving to the right, probably the bestiarius O 1073 without his spear, which is known to be an optional addition. A similar decor with this figure is attributed to the style of Laxtucissa in *CGP*, Pl. 100: 25.

Antonine.

From trench W, pit W 10, layer 1.

11 Dr 37 CG   ST 84 DVY, DXA; ST 82 BBV

Several sherds in a rather poorly-finished fabric. There is a double basal line, as seen in many designs of Hadrianic to early Antonine date, and the borders are of distinctive rectangular beads with tiny eight-pointed rosette junctions. The ovolo has a thin, plain tongue with a flattened, or perhaps bifid, tip: possibly Rogers B 211 ('potier inconnu'). The borders may be identified as Rogers A 15 (used by Atilianus, Avitus, Austrus, Catussa, Iuliccus I, Primulus, Vegetus, X-6, P-2, P-10, P-17, and P-18); the rosettes are not in Rogers. Of the figure-types, the dolphins to left and right are not in Oswald, and the kneeling cupid with jug and bowl is a smaller variant of O 504. The dancer with one end of her stole missing is basically O 355, recorded on the work of Laxtucissa, Censorinus, Geminus, Acaunissa and Advocisus, but it is also reduced in size. The workshop remains uncertain, but the date is likely to be early Antonine.

From pit complex 2022, unit 1979. 3rd century AD. Redeposited clay layer 2005, north end block 9. Early 3rd century. Well 730, unit 749. 3rd/4th century.

12 Dr 37 CG   ST 83 H 8, 3, H 8, 1

Several sherds from a bowl with panels divided by bold bead-rows. The border junctions are larger beads. The ovolo is imperfectly impressed, with the tongue invisible in some areas, but it seems to be a corded one. The dancing cupid in the main surviving panel is O 384, and according to the index of types in *CGP*, was used by Acaunissa. The Pan mask, a very common type, is O 1214, and the tree or trophy motif in the narrow panel is Rogers Q 42, used by a number of Hadrianic and Antonine potters.

Antonine.

From trench H, feature H 8, a large pit or ditch, layers 1 and 3. Late 3rd/4th century AD.

13 Dr 37 CG   ST 84 P 10, 1, SF 760

Several sherds from a bowl which has been broken and repaired in antiquity with lead rivets. The panelled design includes the standard stamp of Advocisus (ADVOCISI) set vertically alongside a panel border (stamp catalogue no. 3). The ovolo has a corded tongue, and is probably Rogers B 103. It is combined with neat bead-rows. The decoration includes plain double festoons containing a bear running to the left, O 1627 and the very common small panther to the right, O 1518, placed below the festoon. The two figure-types which remain in the narrow panels are the half-draped Venus, O 339 and a small fully draped female figure with right arm extended.

Antonine.

From pit P 10, layer 1. Early 3rd century AD.

14 Dr 37 CG   ST 84 DIV

A sherd from a small bowl with a neat panelled design. The ovolo Rogers B 12, a single-bordered one with a corded, rosette-tipped tongue. It is very similar to B 28, an ovolo of Trajanic origin which was also used later. B 12 was employed in the work of Criciro, Divixtus and others. The bead-rows with segmented ring junctions are typical of the style of Divixtus (e.g. *CGP*, Pl. 116: 8). The panther within the double medallion is O 1518, a very common type, and the caryatids appear to be O 1199, though Oswald has drawn them as female figures, and these are certainly male. Style of Divixtus.

Antonine.

From gully 29, cut 8, unit 1712. 3rd century AD.

15 Dr 37 CG   ST 84 DXA

A fragment with a small ovolo with corded, ring-tipped tongue over a rather fine bead border. This is Rogers B 102 (Advocisus, Priscus/ Clemens, P-19). Beneath is a miniature siren playing the double flute, O 862A, and a double-arrow detail, Rogers U 104, which is attributed to Advocisus and Divixtus.

Antonine.

From redeposited clay layer 2005, north end block 9. Early 3rd century AD.

16 Dr 37 CG   ST 84 DNY

A basal fragment with bead-rows and a bead junction, one panel containing a small double medallion with a hare to the right, O 2057; the style is typical of Divixtus.

Antonine.

From gully 24, south branch, cut 2, unit 1811. Early 3rd century AD.

17 Dr 37 CG   ST 82 AAO

A freestyle design: the ovolo has a corded tongue whose tip could be a trifid one or a rosette. Below it is a fairly fine wavy line border. The principal surviving figure-type is a large lion to the left, O 1450, with the snake-and-rock motif O 2155. The ovolo might be Rogers B 47, used by Criciro, and the overall style is consistent with his work, e.g. *CGP*, Pl. 118: 17.

Antonine.

From gully 41, cut 4, unit 455. Late 2nd/early 3rd century AD.

18 Dr 37 CG   ST 84 DVZ

The lower part of a bowl with a fine animal freestyle scene. The ovolo is large and slightly squared, with a corded, ring-tipped tongue; there is a bold, even bead-row border. It is Rogers

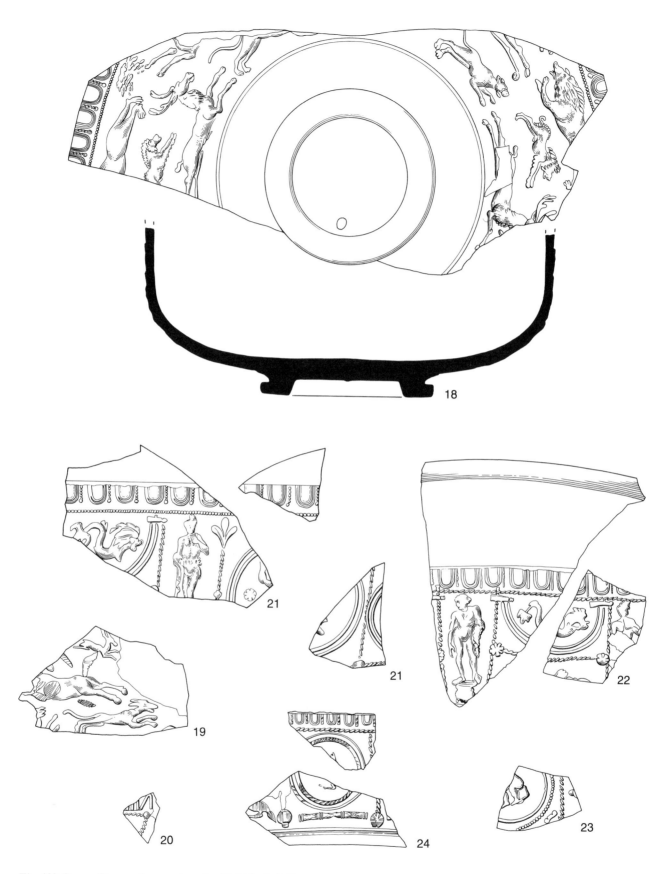

Fig. 138 Stonea Grange: decorated samian 18–24 (scale 1 : 2).

B 105/106. (Surely the same ovolo with different degrees of wear on the cording of the tongue?) It is a standard ovolo of Paternus II and associates. The figure-types are a large stag running to the right, O 1822o, a small boar to the right, O 1642, a lioness to the right, O 1508 and a bear to the left, O 1617. The bear is incorrectly drawn in Oswald, but an accurate version may be seen on the bowl stamped by Paternus illustrated as *CGP*, Pl. 106: 22. There is also part of a hoofed animal, perhaps another stag, to the left. Only one non-figural detail can be seen, the upper part of a tree just beneath the ovolo, Rogers N 13. This is listed for Butrio, Ianuaris II/Paternus I, Iustus and Laxtucissa.

Antonine.

From well 2020/pit 2021 complex, unit 1980. Late 2nd/early 3rd century AD.

19 Dr 37 CG   ST 83 CCV

An animal freestyle including a horse to the left, O 1911, a large hound to the right which cannot be matched exactly, and the tiny stag or goat to the right, O 1732. In the field are the small twists which appear on *CGP*, Fig. 30, 18, but are omitted by Rogers. For similar schemes of decoration incorporating these elements, see *CGP*, Pl. 106: 21, 22, vessels stamped by Paternus.

Antonine.

From ditch 9, cut 2, uppermost layer (unit 1067). 3rd century AD.

20 Dr 37 CG   ST 82 BGK

A tiny sherd with roped panel borders and part of the large Paternus stamp, cf. *CGP*, Pls 104–7.

Antonine.

From pit 860, uppermost layer (unit 860). 3rd/4th century AD.

21 Dr 37 CG   ST 83 CPG, CMT

A bowl with panelled decoration and a large double-bordered ovolo with a beaded, bent-tipped tongue. The horizontal line is beaded, while the panel dividers are rope borders. The ovolo is Rogers B 234, one of the typical features in designs by Iustus. One of the panel borders has a large triple leaf at the top which cannot be matched exactly. In the narrow vertical panel is a figure of Pan playing pipes, O 709A, and in a double festoon, a dolphin to the right, O 2384.

Antonine.

From gully 53, cut 2, unit 1282 and from post-hole 1342 which cuts it. 3rd–4th century AD.

22 Dr 37 CG   ST 82 AFR, ACE, ABQ

Sherds from a bowl with a large squarish ovolo with a plain slender tongue, Rogers B 258. All the borders are roped, and there are astragalus and rosette junctions. The figure-types are the standing man on a mask, O 538, a dolphin to the right, O 2385, and the pipe-playing Pan, O 709A. The design is extremely close to that of the stamped Mercator II vessel from Corbridge illustrated in *CGP*, Pl. 145: 4.

Antonine.

From ditch 9, cut 10, basal layer (unit 578), and from ditch 9, cut 11, unit 494. Late 2nd/early 3rd century AD. And from topsoil/cleaning, block 2.

23 Dr 37, CG   ST 83 CEK

A small sherd with a roped panel border and a double medallion, the outer ring of which is beaded; possibly Rogers E 18. There is a small, plump astragalus in the spandrel, and within the medallion, a seated cupid, O 444. This figure was used by Paternus and associated potters, and also occurs on a stamped Dr 30 by Mercator II (*CGP*, Pl. 145: 2).

Antonine.

From ditch 14, cut 5, unit 1105. Phase VI.

24 Dr 30 CG   ST 84 DXA, EAO

Two small sherds from the same vessel. The ovolo is very small and square and has a corded tongue attached on the right side. It is Rogers B 259, used only by Mercator II. The borders are corded, and there is a double medallion whose inner ring is also corded, not in Rogers. Below the medallion the latticed column, Rogers P 3. The large eight-pointed rosettes at the base of the vertical borders are Rogers C 171, another exclusive Mercator II detail.

Antonine.

From redeposited clay layer 2005, north end block 9. Early 3rd century AD. And from the nearby well 2020, unit 2090. Late 2nd–3rd century AD.

25 Dr 37 CG   ST 82 AGK

The bowl has a large, square double-bordered ovolo with a thick corded tongue and a fine bead-row border. It is difficult to identify, but could possibly be Rogers B 156, used by Iullinus. The decor consists of a large scroll with a leaf, Rogers H 30, attributed to Paternus II, and a small corded ring, probably Rogers E 76, used by the same potter. The figure-types are two birds, the complete one probably O 2295A, and in a lower concavity of the scroll, Silenus and a nymph, O 552.

Antonine.

From ditch 9, cut 9, unit 595. Late 3rd/early 4th century AD.

26 Dr 37 CG   ST 82 AAG, AAQ

Several sherds from a bowl with a somewhat haphazard panelled design. The ovolo is a large one with a thick corded tongue, and all borders are neat bead-rows. The ovolo is Rogers B 164, characteristic of Iullinus. The large acorn used in the upper part of the narrow panels is Rogers U 87, a detail also employed mainly by this potter. The pedestalled bowl containing fruit is not catalogued by Rogers, and may well be peculiar to Iullinus. The identifiable figure-types are a small caryatid, close to O 1199, the cockerel O 2342 and the stag or goat O 1732. The cupid holding aloft a cup is probably O 378.

Antonine.

From gully 41, cut 5, unit 457. Late 2nd/early 3rd century AD. And from topsoil/cleaning block 5a.

Fig. 139 Stonea Grange: decorated samian 25–35 (scale 1 : 2).

27 Dr 37 CG ST 84 DQN

The decoration is based on panels and medallions. The ovolo is either Rogers B 164, typical of Iullinus, or B 153, a slightly larger ovolo used by Casurius and Servus. The horizontal border is a wavy line, but the panel borders are bead-rows: Servus II used wavy-line borders, cf. *CGP*, Pl. 131. The rosette in the field is Rogers C 171, employed only by Mercator II, while the distinctive astragalus is Rogers R 60, used by Mercator and some other potters. The large naturalistic leaf is Rogers H 18, a Doeccus type. Doeccus also used the dolphin figure-type O 2384. The bird with raised wings is O 2316 (Servus, Mercator, Paternus).

Antonine.

From layer 1873 above pit cluster 1973/4/5/6, south side block 9. Late 2nd/3rd century AD.

28 Dr 37 CG ST 84 DBL

A well-made vessel with panels demarcated by very bold and open zig-zag lines without any border junction motifs. The ovolo is either Rogers B 164 or B 153, with the same range of possibilities as no. 27 above – Iullinus, several Servi/Serverus. One detail, the angled balustrade Rogers U 263, is typical of Iullinus, whose work does sometimes include wavy lines, cf. *CGP*, Pl. 127: 34. The figure-type is a small Pan walking to the right, O 717, used by a number of Antonine potters. Above the balustrade is part of a cigar-shaped 'twist', probably that illustrated in *CGP*, Fig. 37, 2, as a detail used by Severus. It is not included in Rogers. *CGP*, Pl. 128: 3, from Colchester, attributed to the style of Severus, is very similar to our sherd.

Antonine.

From latrine pit 1535, unit 1535. 3rd century AD.

29 Dr 37 CG ST 82 ADM

A small sherd with a freestyle hunting design. The ovolo is probably Rogers B 153, assigned to Servus, Banuus, Casurius, Iullinus and Severus: beneath it is a neat bead-row. The 'twists' in the field are *CGP*, Fig. 37, 2 (Severus), and the figure-types are a bestiarius, O 673, a bear, O 1630, a lion to the right, O 1497b, a small leopard, O 1510, and the hare or rabbit, O 2116. The scheme of decoration is virtually the same as that on *CGP*, Pl. 128: 2, stamped SEVERI.

Antonine.

From ditch 9, cut 8, unit 525. Late 2nd/early 3rd century AD.

30 Dr 37 CG ST 81 PV, SF 228

A small sherd from a panelled design including the small stamp of Cinnamus (CINNAMI retrograde; stamp catalogue no. 20). The stamp is set vertically in a narrow panel between leaf-tips, a device seen on many stamped Cinnamus designs. The bead-rows are neat, and there is part of a small double festoon or medallion with the front paw of an animal.

Antonine.

From occupation debris (unit 318), north-west block 1. Phase IV/V.

31 Dr 37 CG ST 84 DKZ

A sherd with panelled decoration divided by roped and beaded borders, and an ovolo made unclear by the plain horizontal line which underlies it. The ovolo may be Rogers B 223, a Cinnamus ovolo also used by Pugnus and Casurius, which is also found with the rim-stamp *Cintusmus* (*CGP*, Pl. 164: 6). The stylised leaf-tuft in a festoon is Rogers G 8, also attributed to 'Cintusmus' and Pugnus: it is set over an arrow motif, not in Rogers, but present on *CGP*, Pl. 155: 25 (Pugnus). That sherd also features the caryatid, O 1206, and the guideline beneath the ovolo.

Antonine.

From layer 1740, above the gully and pit cluster, south-east corner block 3. Late 2nd–3rd century AD.

32 Dr 37 CG ST 84 DGB

A bowl with freestyle decoration featuring a series of figures. The ovolo is not clear, but may well be Rogers B 144, used by Cinnamus and several others. The large eight-petalled rosette, if it is Rogers C 51 (it might be C 52) is also used by Cinnamus, as is Venus leaning on a pillar, O 322 and Vulcan without his tongs, O 66.

Antonine.

From occupation layer 1646, over layer 2005, north block 9. Phase III/IV.

33 Dr 37 CG ST 84 DRR

A vessel with Cinnamus ovolo 3, i.e. Rogers B 143. The panel borders are neat bead-rows. A large plain festoon contains a running boar to the left, O 1666, over the tiny centauress O 735A; in the adjacent panel is a large satyr with wineskin and drinking-horn, O 625, a typical X-2 figure-type not usually seen on later stamped Lezoux ware. The boar, though used by a number of Antonine potters, also originated with the Trajanic products of X-2. In the field are small rings and leaf-tips. The bowl can be assigned to the style of Cinnamus.

Antonine.

From well 1678, unit 1901. 3rd century AD.

34 Dr 37 CG ST 84 DZZ

A tiny fragment with a lion overpowering a boar, O 1491. This figure-type was used by Libertus and Butrio and by several Antonine potters, amongst them Cinnamus, to whom this sherd is probably to be attributed.

Antonine

From occupation layer 2076, south-east block 9. 3rd century AD.

35 Dr 37 CG ST 82 AZT

A small sherd with a leaf-scroll incorporating the leaf Rogers J 86 and a small ring. The design is close to the signed Cinnamus bowl *CGP*, Pl. 162: 62.

Antonine

From gully 40, unit 700. Late 3rd/early 4th century AD.

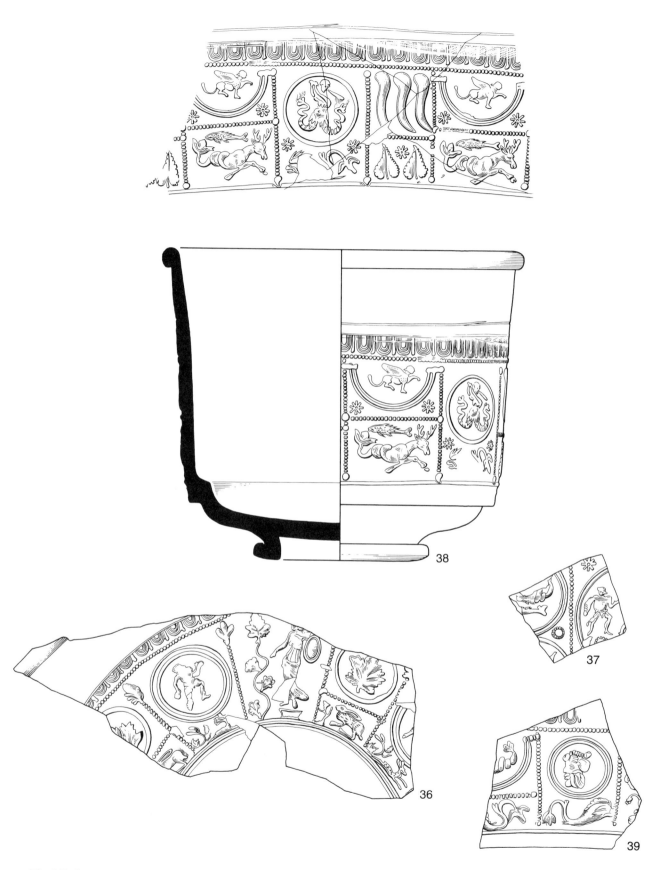

Fig. 140 Stonea Grange: decorated samian 36–9 (scale 1:2).

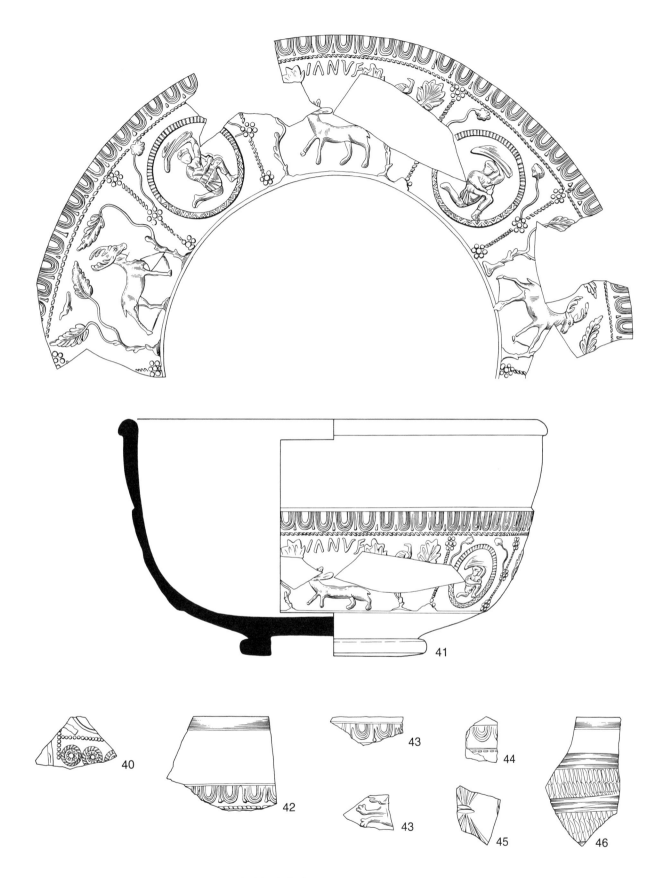

Fig. 141 Stonea Grange: decorated samian 40–6 (scale 1 : 2).

36 Dr 37 CG　ST 84 EBX

A bowl with a panelled design and small, plain-tongued ovolo, Rogers B 160, used by Doeccus. There are bold beaded borders with three different junction motifs, a stylized leaf, Rogers J 149, attributed to Doeccus, Belsa and Carantinus, a small rosette and a triple-lobed motif. The rosette and triple leaf cannot be identified with certainty. A small double medallion contains a leaping figure, O 687, which is found on the work of Doeccus and Q. I. Balbinus; a naturalistic leaf, Rogers H 74 or 110 (Doeccus, Servus III) is set in a small single medallion. The figure of Minerva in a large panel is O 126B, noted only for Iustus and Cettus, but she is flanked by a 'tree', wavy line carrying another Doeccus leaf, Rogers H 134 and a smaller variant of a shuttlecock motif, Rogers G 259, used by several potters including Doeccus. The other figure-types are a hare facing left, O 2119 or O 2116, and a small running stag, probably O 1732A. The tiny vine-scroll beneath the medallions appears to be omitted by Rogers, but may be a reversed version of his M 28.

Antonine.

From basal layer (unit 2122) in pit 2121. 3rd century AD.

37 Dr 37 CG　ST 84 DXC

A small sherd from a bowl with panels and medallions of different sizes. The bead-row is bold and regular. In a spandrel between two medallions is a small corded or segmented ring, perhaps Rogers E 58, used by Doeccus and others: a rosette in the next panel, Rogers C 167 or C 170 is also found on designs from his workshop, as is the small male figure O 687. There are two marine creatures in the medallion on the left, the upper unidentifiable, the lower a fish to the left, O 2418.

Antonine

From pit 1835/2007, unit 2007. 3rd century AD.

38 Dr 30 CG　ST 84 DOK, SF 672

The greater part of a Dr 30 bowl in the style of Doeccus, with neat, bold, but rather coarse moulding. The ovolo is Rogers B 161, used only in the style of Doeccus. Small double festoons contain the sphinx, O 853, and in the panel beneath is a marine stag to the right, O 54, and a fish to the left, O 2418. The marine theme continues with the large triton O 19 in a plain medallion above a dolphin swimming left, O 2393. The remaining panel in the three-panel repeat has three volutes or curved gadroons above, Rogers U 152 and a pair of heart-shaped leaves. The leaves do not appear to be in the usual repertoire of Doeccus, perhaps Rogers J 77. The overall design and layout are typical of Doeccus.

Antonine.

From gully 19, unit 1822. Late 2nd–mid 3rd century AD.

39 Dr 30 CG　ST 83 A, 26 E

This is a small sherd from another Dr 30 bowl in the style of Doeccus. The ovolo is his smaller one, Rogers B 160, and the panels are defined by bold-rows with bead and astragalus junctions. In the full-depth panel, a small double medallion contains the Pan mask O 1214; below the medallion is a dolphin to the right, apparently not the same as O 2384, the obvious counterpart to O 2393, which is used in a small lower panel to the left. Above the latter is a double festoon containing a sea-horse O 33. The narrow panel on the right of the sherd has a decorative stand, Rogers Q 6, as used on *CGP*, Pl. 152: 1, which is in the style of Doeccus with the rim-stamp of Moxivs.

Antonine.

From the sump, layer 26, cut I, grid 6. Mid–late 3rd century AD.

40 Dr 37 CG　ST 84 DQL

A small sherd with a narrow horizontal panel containing a series of three elaborate 'Catherine-wheel' rosettes. These could be Rogers C 98 or 99; the inner rosette has eleven spokes, which would make it C 98, a type used in the styles of Cinnamus, Iustus and Pugnus. The nature of the design, however, looks more reminiscent of Doeccus, e.g. *CGP*, Pl. 148: 14. C 99 should have only eight spokes in the centre.

Antonine.

From gully 31, cut 4, unit 1871. Late 2nd century AD.

41 Dr 37 EG　ST 82 BKL, BLF, BKB, BKO

Most of a very fine and well-made bowl with the stamp of Ianus of Rheinzabern. The fabric is very orange in colour, with a good, glossy surface and sharp moulding. The stamp IANVF (the final letter is probably a ligured SF) is placed horizontally beneath the ovolo border in a large panel containing a doe walking to the left and looking back, between two trees. The stamp is no. 33 in the catalogue of stamps. The decoration is typical for this potter, classified by Ricken (Ricken 1942) as Ianuarius I. The ovolo is Ricken/Fischer 1963 E 19, with a boldly corded horizontal border. The large seven-beaded rosettes are Ricken/Fischer O 42. The smaller panel contains the kneeling warrior beneath his shield, M 211, within a decorated medallion, K 48. The larger panels have a stag walking to the right, T 83, and the doe to left, T 78. Both animals are between trees made up of simple lines and leaves, P 90 and P 47. Trees of this kind can be seen in other designs by the potter, e.g. Ricken 1942, Taf. 5, 12 and Taf. 7, 1–10.

Antonine.

From ditch 9, cut 3, lowest fill (units 924, 933, 936, 952). Late 2nd/early 3rd century AD.

42 Dr 37 EG　ST 80 AZ

A small rim sherd with the ovolo of Ianus of Rheinzabern, Ricken/Fischer E 19, with a corded horizontal line.

Antonine.

From occupation debris (unit 23), west side of building R1. Phases III–V.

43 Dr 37 EG　ST 82 ABE, ABF

Two very small sherds from the same vessel, one with an ovolo which appears to have a thin plain tongue, the other with a running lion, its front paws at a characteristic divergent angle. This characteristic is not evident in Oswald's drawing, O 1483, but can be seen clearly in Ricken/Fischer, their type T 5. The lion was used by Ianus, see, for example, Ricken 1942, Taf. 3, 10.

Antonine.

From gully 50, cut 3, unit 470. 3rd century AD. And from topsoil/cleaning blocks 2–3 and north-east block 1.

44 Dr 37 EG ST 81 ABQ

A tiny sherd with part of a double-bordered tongueless ovolo and a dashed-line border below a plain line. The source is uncertain, but it is probably one of several tongueless Rheinzabern ovolos, e.g. Ricken/Fischer E 58, 63 or 66.

Antonine.

From topsoil/cleaning, block 2.

45 Déch 72 CG ST 82 AZT

A plain samian vase with incised ('cut-glass') decoration. This is a very small fragment from such a vase.

Context as no. 35.

46 Dr 30 variant, probably EG ST 82 AAV

Another 'plain' vessel, a cylindrical beaker with all-over rouletting, as Oswald and Price Pl. LXXV, 13.

Antonine.

From occupation layer (unit 461) south of building R2. 3rd century AD.

SAMIAN POTTERS' STAMPS

Brenda Dickinson (Figs 142–3)

Each entry gives: excavation number, potter (i, ii, etc., where homonyms are involved), die number, form, reading of the stamp, site of manufacture, date. The parenthesised letters indicate:

(a) Stamp attested at the pottery in question.
(b) Potter, but not the particular stamp, attested at the pottery in question.
(c) Assigned to the pottery on the evidence of fabric, distribution and, or, form.

1 ST 82 AED, SF 338 Advocisus 2a′ 38 ADVOCIS Lezoux (a). *c*. AD 160–90.

From gully 67, unit 541. Mid/late 2nd century AD.

2 ST 84 DAA, SF 621 Advocisus 2a′ 38 or 44 ADVOCIS Lezoux (a). *c*. AD 160–90.

From topsoil, block 6 and block 5, south.

3 ST 84 P 10,1, SF 760 (For illustration see Decorated Samian cat. no. 13, p. 412–13). Advocisus 8a 37 [A]DVOCI[SI] Lezoux (a). A small bowl, mended in several places with large rivets. *c*. AD 160–90.

From pit P10, layer 1. Early 3rd century AD.

4 ST 82 ABQ, SF 260 Aestivus 2a 33 [A]IIS[TIVI:M] Lezoux (b), *c*. AD 160–90.

From topsoil/cleaning, block 2.

5 ST 84 DPF, SF 836 Aestivus 6a 31 AIST [IV]I·M Lezoux (b). *c*. AD 160–90.

From gully 36, cut 9, unit 1842. 3rd century AD.

6 ST 84 N+, SF 743 Aestivus 6a 31 AISTIVI·M Lezoux (b). *c*. AD 160–90.

From block 10, topsoil trench N, south.

7 ST 82 BHP, SF 443 Aestivus 6a 33 AISTIVI·M Lezoux (b). *c*. AD 160–90.

From pit 483/918, unit 889. Mid/late 3rd century AD.

8 ST 84 DWC, SF 1002 Aeternus 2a 33 AETERNIM retr. Lezoux (c). *c*. AD 160–85.

From uppermost layer (unit 1983) of pit 1984. Early 3rd century AD.

9 ST 83 CCY, SF 509 Annius ii 4a 33? [AN]NIVSF Lezoux (b). *c*. AD 130–50.

From topsoil/cleaning, block 1, north and block 11, centre.

10 ST 84 DIC, SF 1015 Antiquus 2a 31 AN[T]ICVI Lezoux (b). *c*. AD 150–70.

From uppermost layer (unit 1695) in ?latrine pit 1695. 3rd/4th century AD.

11 ST 84 EBK, SF 1151 Atticus ii 2b 31 A·T·T·I C·I·M Lezoux (b). *c*. AD 150–70.

From pit 2021/2110, unit 2110. 3rd century AD.

12 ST 82 AGO, SF 374 Attillus v 9a 31 ATTILLVS Lezoux (b). *c*. AD 160–80.

From ditch 9, cut 9, basal layer (unit 599). Late 2nd/early 3rd century AD.

13 ST 84 DIC, SF 1014 Aventinus ii 1a 33 [AVENT]INI·M Lezoux (a). *c*. AD 150–80.

Context as no. 10.

14 ST 84 DEA, SF 651 Beliniccus i 11a 31 [BEΛINIC]IM retr. Lezoux (a). *c*. AD 135–65.

From topsoil/cleaning, blocks 8 and 9, and blocks 3 and 4, east.

15 ST 84 DPE, SF 1152 Briccus 3b 27 [BR]ICCI·M Lezoux (c). *c*. AD 145–60.

From gully 18, cut 5, unit 1841. 3rd century AD.

16 ST 81 MA, SF 168 Burdo 6a 27 (slightly burnt) BVꓤDOF Lezoux (b). *c*. AD 140–60.

From pit 170, uppermost layer (unit 254). 3rd/4th century AD.

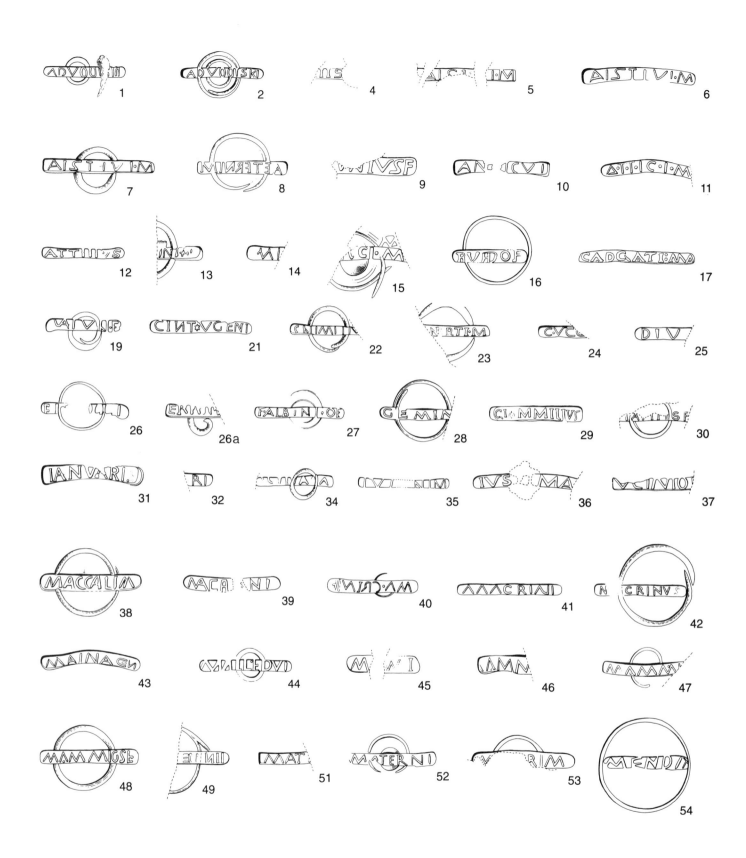

Fig. 142 Stonea Grange: samian potters' stamps 1–2, 4–17, 19, 21–32, 34–49 and 51–4 (scale 1:1).

17 ST 82 AGO, SF 375 Cadgatis 1a 33 (almost complete, with slightly worn footring) CΛDGΛTI:MΛ Lezoux (a). *c.* AD 150–80.

Context as no. 12.

18 ST 82 BCQ, SF 429 (*Unillus.*) Carussa 3c′ – [CΛ]RV[⟨Λ⟩] Lezoux (b). *c.* AD 160–90.

From pit 841, layer 769. 3rd/4th century AD.

19 ST 83+, SF 478 Catullus ii 6a 33 CATV(L)LI·F Lezoux (b). *c.* AD 160–90.

1983, unstratified.

20 ST 81 PV, SF 228 (For illustration see Samian Ware cat. no. 30, p. 417) Cinnamus ii 5b 37 [CIN]NAMI retr. Lezoux (a). *c.* AD 150–80.

From occupation layer (unit 318), north-west block 1. 3rd/4th century AD.

21 ST 84 DQG, SF 869 Cintugenus 3a 33 CIT·VGENI Lezoux (c). *c.* AD 150–80.

From occupation layer (unit 1867), south-east bock 9. Late 2nd–3rd century AD.

22 ST 82 BGO, SF 421 Clemens iii 3b or b′ 33 (slightly burnt) CΛIIMII[NƧ] (with original or recut N) Lezoux (b). *c.* AD 160–90.

From pit 483/918, unit 864. Mid/late 3rd century AD.

23 ST 83 G4,4, SF 526 Cobnertus iii 1a 18/31R [COB]NERTI·M Lezoux (a). *c.* AD 150–65.

From well G4, layer 4. Early 3rd century AD.

24 ST 84 DQV, SF 1171 Cuccillus i 6a 31 C·VCC[IL·LI] Lezoux (b). *c.* AD 150–80.

From well 1669, unit 1880. Mid/late 3rd century AD.

25 ST 83 H+, SF 521 Divixtus i 10a 31 DIV[IXTI] Lezoux (b). *c.* AD 150–80.

From topsoil, trench H.

26 ST 81 LT, SF 124 Elvillus 1a 31R (grooved for a rivet and with fairly worn footring) EL[VI]LLI Lezoux (a). *c.* AD 160–90.

From ditch 9, cut 6, basal layer (unit 248). 3rd century AD.

26a ST 84 DKZ, SF 677 Ericus 1a 33 ERICI[M] Lezoux (c). *c.* AD 130–60.

From well 1836, uppermost layer (unit 1740). Late 2nd/3rd century AD.

27 ST 84 DQR, SF 1051 Flo-Albinus 4a 33 F·AΛBINI·OF Lezoux (b). *c.* AD 150–80.

From pit 1695, basal layer (unit 1877). Later 2nd/3rd century AD.

28 ST 84 DZZ, SF 1131 Geminus vi 7a 33 GEMIN[I·] Lezoux (b). *c.* AD 160–200.

From occupation layer (unit 2076), south-east block 9. 3rd century AD.

29 ST 84 DRT, SF 908 Giamillus ii 9a 33 GIAMMILLVS Lavoye (c). Antonine.

From well 1669, basal layer (unit 1903). Mid/late 3rd century AD.

30 ST 82 AZV, SF 268 Habilis 5d 33 HABILISF Lezoux (b). *c.* AD 150–80.

From pit 701, unit 701. 3rd century AD.

31 ST 84 DNY, SF 825 Ianuaris ii 6a 31 IANVARIS Lezoux (b). *c.* AD 150–70.

From gully 24, south branch, cut 2, unit 1811. Early 3rd century AD.

32 ST 84 W9,2, SF 751 Ianuarius ii 5a 33 [IAVA]RI Lezoux (b). *c.* AD 125–55.

From ditch 76, W9, layer 2. Phase III, but with modern disturbance.

33 ST 82 BKL (For illustration see Decorated Samian cat. no. 41, p. 419–20). Ianus ii (Ludowici-Ricken's Ianu(arius) I) 3a 37 IANVF (. . . SF?) Heiligenberg (a), Rheinzabern (a). A Rheinzabern bowl, to judge by the decoration. *c.* AD 160–90.

From ditch 9, cut 3, unit 933. Late 2nd/early 3rd century AD.

34 ST 83 CCP, SF 480 Icttiama 1a 33 ICTTIAΛ Lezoux (a). *c.* AD 155–85.

From occupation layer (unit 1062), north-east block 2. Phase III to recent.

35 ST 82 AGO, SF 373 Iullinus ii 3d 31 IVLLINIM Lezoux (b). *c.* AD 160–90.

Context as no. 12.

36 ST 81 HL+, SF 109 Iustus ii 2b 31 IVSTIMA Lezoux (a). *c.* AD 160–90.

From building R1, east wing, interior, sub-floor natural clay surface, east side (unit 172). 3rd century AD.

37 ST 84 P10,1, SF 764 Lucinus 1a′ 31 __VCIΛIO[F] Lezoux (b). *c.* AD. 160–90.

Context as no. 3.

38 ST 84A 36,2, SF 1984A, 36 Maccalus 3a 33 MACCALIM Lezoux (a). *c.* AD 160–200.

From grid-square 2 of the basal layer (unit A,36) of the north sump.

39 ST 82 BHT, SF 354 Macrianus 4a 31 ΛCRIANI Lezoux (c). *c.* AD 150–80.

From ?timber slot 893, north of building R5. Phase III.

40 ST 84 DOB, SF 666 Macrinus ii 6a 33 MΛ·CRINI*FE* retr. Lezoux (b). *c.* AD 125–50.

From pit complex 1814, unit 1814. 3rd century AD.

41 ST 84 DQR, SF 1049 Macrinus iii 5b 31 MACRIΛI Lezoux (a). *c.* AD 150–80.

From ?latrine pit 1695, basal layer (unit 1877). Later 2nd/3rd century AD.

42 ST 84 DIC, SF 1005 Macrinus iii 7a 33 MACRINVS Lezoux (a). *c*. AD 150–80.

From ?latrine pit 1695, context as no. 10.

43 ST 83 J4,2, SF 587 Mainacnus 5a 31R (approximately half-complete) MAINACИ Lezoux (b). *c*. AD 160–200.

From well J4, layer 2. Late 3rd/early 4th century AD.

44 ST 81 MA, SF 185 Malledo 6a 33 MΛLLEDVI Lezoux (b). *c*. AD 155–85.

Context as no. 16.

45 ST 83+, SF 555, and G4,4, SF 522 Malliacus 2b 31 M[ΛLLI]ΛCIF Lezoux (b). *c*. AD 135–65.

From topsoil; and from well G4, layer 4. Early 3rd century AD.

46 ST 84 DEA, SF 736 Mammius 1a′ or, more probably, 1a″ 33 \ΛMM[I] (from a die giving first MΛMMI·ᴑF, then \ΛMMI·ᴑF and finally \ΛMMI) Lezoux (a). *c*. AD 160–80.

From topsoil/cleaning, as no. 14.

47 ST 84 DWQ, SF 1008 Mammius 8a 33 MΛMM[I] Lezoux (a). *c*. AD 150–80.

From pit 1996, unit 1996. 3rd century AD.

48 ST 84 DVY, SF 1059 Mammius 11a, 18/31-31, with heavily-worn footring MΛMMIGSŁ Lezoux (b). *c*. AD 150–80.

From pit 2022, unit 1979. 3rd century AD.

49 ST 81+, SF 192 Marcellinus ii 2a 33 [MARC]ELLIIᚺ Lezoux (a). *c*. AD 160–200.

1981, unstratified.

50 ST 84 DPG, SF 1181 (*Unillus*.) Maternus iv 1a 31 [MAT]ERИI Lezoux (b). *c*. AD 160–80.

From gully 36, cut 7, unit 1843. 3rd century AD.

51 ST 84 DKS, SF 811 Maternus iv 1a 31R MAT[ERИI] Lezoux (b). *c*. AD 160–80.

From gully 30, cut 4, unit 1734. 3rd century AD.

52 ST 84 DPN, SF 867 Maternus iv 1g 33 MATERNI Lezoux (b). *c*. AD 150–180.

From well 1669, unit 1849. Mid/late 3rd century AD.

53 ST 82 BKP, SF 384 Maturus ii 1b 33 MΛTVRI·M Lezoux (b). *c*. AD 150–80.

From ditch 9, cut 1a, uppermost layer (unit 937). 3rd century AD.

54 ST 83 H7,1, SF 574 Menda 1b 33 MEИDΛ Argonne (c). Antonine.

From trench H, gully H7, layer 1. 4th century AD.

55 ST 84 P10,1, SF 761 Mox(s)ius ii 1a 31 MOXIVS·F Les Martres-de-Veyre (c). *c*. AD 130–60.

Context as no. 3.

56 ST 83 CRM, SF 608 Muxtullus 1a 31 ·MVXTVLLI·M Lezoux (b). *c*. AD 150–80.

From post-hole 1395, north-east block 2.

57 ST 84 DXB, SF 1058 Muxtullus 2a 33 MVXTVΛIM Lezoux (a). *c*. AD 150–80.

From well 2020, unit 2006. Late 2nd–3rd century AD.

58 ST 84 P10,1, SF 765 Muxtullus 3a 38 MV + TVΛΛI·· Lezoux (b). *c*. AD 155–85.

Context as no. 3.

59 ST 84 DFR, SF 894 Muxtullus 3a 33 MV + TV[ΛΛI··] Lezoux (b). *c*. AD 155–85.

From gully 32, cut 1, unit 1637. Early 3rd century AD.

60 ST 81 ABQ, SF 257 Namilianus 3a 33 NΛMILIANI Lezoux (b). *c*. AD 160–200.

Context as no. 4.

61 ST 84 DIC, SF 1020 Osbimanus 7a 18/31R or 31R [OS]BIMΛI· Lezoux (b). *c*. AD 150–80.

Context as no. 10.

62 ST 84 DYD, SF 1085 Ottonus Incomplete 1 31 (slightly burnt) OTTONIᛕ Lezoux (c). Antonine, probably after AD 160.

From gully 19, cut 4, unit 2032. Mid 3rd century AD.

63 ST 84 EBV, SF 1123 Pater ii 4a 33 PAꞱ³R Lezoux (b). *c*. AD 130–155.

From occupation layer (unit 2120) centre east block 9. Late 2nd–3rd century AD.

64 ST 84 DES, SF 727 Paterclinus 1a 31 PΛTERCLINIOF Lezoux (a). *c*. AD 150–80.

From post-hole 1614, north-east block 9.

65 ST 84 P10,1, SF 753 Paterclinus 3a 38 PΛTERCLINIM Lezoux (a). *c*. AD 150–80.

Context as no. 3.

66 ST 82 AEE, SF 339 Paterclinus 4a 79 or Ludowici Tg PΛTER-CLINI Lezoux (a). *c*. AD 160–80.

From ditch 9, cut 5, unit 542. 3rd century AD.

67 ST 84 P10,1, SF 762 Paternus v 6a 79 [P·A·ꞌ·E·]RNI Lezoux (b). *c*. AD 160–95.

Context as no. 3.

[For Paternus, see also Samian Ware cat. no. 20, p. 415].

68 ST 83+, SF 563. Paullus v 8b 33 PΛV·ΛΛI Lezoux (b). *c*. AD 160–200.

1983, unstratified.

69 ST 84 DEA, SF 784 Paullus v 8b 33 PΛV·ΛΛI Lezoux (b). *c*. AD 160–200.

From topsoil/cleaning, as no. 14.

70 ST 82 ABQ, SF 367 Primanus iii 3c′ 31R [PRIM]ANI·M Lezoux (b). *c*. AD 160–200.

Context as no. 4.

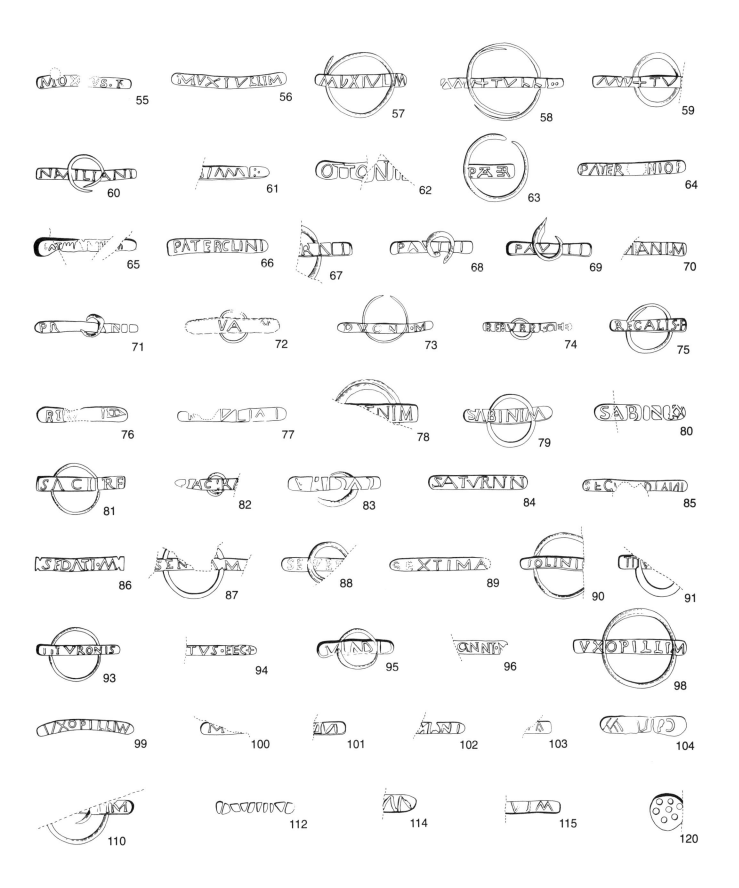

Fig. 143 Stonea Grange: samian potters' stamps 55–91, 93–6, 98–104, 110, 112, 114–15 and 120 (scale 1 : 1).

71 ST 81 FV, SF 110 Primanus iii 6h 33 PR(IMΛ)NI Lezoux (b). *c.* AD 160–200.

From occupation layer (unit 134), north-west block 1. Phases III–V.

72 ST 81+, SF 191 Privatus iii 1a 33 (PRI)VA(TIΛ) Lezoux (a). *c.* AD 160–200.

1981, unstratified.

73 ST 82 AGH, SF 417 Pugnus ii 1a 33 PVGNI·M(Δ) Lezoux (b). *c.* AD 145–75.

From ditch 9, cut 7, unit 593. 3rd century AD.

74 ST 84 EBV, SF 1122 Reburrus ii 3a 33 REBVRRI·OF Lezoux (a). *c.* AD 145–70.

Context as no. 63.

75 ST 84 DVZ, SF 943 Regalis i 4a 33 REGALIS·F Lezoux (b). *c.* AD 150–80.

From well 2020, unit 1980. Late 2nd–3rd century AD.

76 ST 82 BHL, SF 355 Regalis i 8a 31 RIIGΛLI☐☐ Lezoux (a). *c.* AD 150–80.

From the upper layer (unit 885) of pit 885. 3rd century AD.

77 ST 84 P10,1, SF 758 Regulianus 3a 33 RIICVLIΛI Lezoux (b). *c.* AD 160–90.

Context as no.3.

78 ST 81 ABR, SF 271 Reogenus 1b? 33 (burnt) [RIIOG]ENIM Lezoux (a). *c.* AD 150–80.

From occupation layer (unit 482), block 2, north. 3rd/4th century AD.

79 ST 81 HJ, SF 76 Sabinus viii 8b 33 SABINIM Lezoux (b). *c.* AD 160–85.

From pit 170, uppermost layer (unit 170). 3rd/4th century AD.

80 ST 83A,4, SF 1983A,20 Sabinus viii 13a 31 SΛBINI◇I Lezoux (a). *c.* AD 155–85.

From layer A, 4 in the north sump. Phase IV/V.

81 ST 84 P10,1, SF 763. Sacer iii 2a 33 (almost complete, with slightly worn footring) SΛCIIRF Lezoux (c). Mid to late Antonine.

Context as no. 3.

82 ST 83 CRD, SF 607 Sacirapo 1a or a′ 33 SACIRA[P⟨O⟩] Lezoux (a). *c.* AD 125–50.

From occupation layer (unit 1387), centre north block 1. Late 2nd–3rd century AD.

83 ST 82 BHR, SF 423 Sacirus ii 6c 33 SΛCIRV retr. Lezoux (a). *c.* AD 130–60.

From post-hole 891 in street 1 E/W, north of block 2.

84 ST 82 ACV, SF 310 Saturninus ii 1a 33 SATVRNIN Lezoux (b). *c.* AD 160–200.

From sinkage fill (unit 509) in ditch 74, cut 1. Late 3rd/4th century AD.

85 ST 83 CDA, SF 484 Secundianus 1a 33 SECV()DIAI Lezoux (c). *c.* AD 160–90.

From ditch 3, cut 5, uppermost layer (unit 1072). 3rd century AD.

86 ST 82 AGN, SF 380 Sedatus iv 2a 18/31 or 31 SEDΛTI·M (in an ansate panel) Lezoux (a). *c.* AD 125–50.

From ashy dereliction deposit (unit 598), south of building R1. Late 2nd–3rd century AD.

87 ST 82 BBQ, SF 314 Senila 1a 33 SEN(IL)A·M Lezoux (c). *c.* AD 150–70.

From well 705, unit 745. 3rd/4th century AD.

88 ST 84 DEA, SF 719 Severus iv 6b or b′ 33 SEVER[V·S·⟨F⟩] Lezoux (b). *c.* AD 130–55.

From topsoil/cleaning, as no. 14.

89 ST 82 BGS, SF 352 Sextus v 4d 33 SEXTIMA Lezoux (a). *c.* AD 160–200.

From well 905, uppermost layer (unit 868). 3rd/4th century AD.

90 ST 84 ECO, SF 1115 Solinus Incomplete 1 33 SOLINI[Lezoux (b). *c.* AD 160–200.

From gully 25, cut 1, unit 2138. Late 2nd/early 3rd century AD.

91 ST 81 LT, SF 145 Tituro 1a 33 TITV[RONISQF] Lezoux (a). *c.* AD 160–90.

Context as no. 26.

92 ST 82 AET, SF 420 (*Unillus.*) Tituro 1a 31 TITVRONISQF Lezoux (a). *c.* AD 160–90.

From ditch 9, cut 5, basal layer (unit 556). Early 3rd century AD. Adjacent to nos 91 and 26.

93 ST 84 P10,1, SF 766 Tituro 5b Ludowci Tx TITVRONIS Lezoux (b). *c.* AD 160–90.

Context as no. 3.

94 ST 84 DOB, SF 812 Titus iii 10a 31 [TI]TVS·FEC+ Lezoux (b). *c.* AD 150–70.

From upper layer (unit 1814) in pit complex pit 1814 etc. 3rd century AD.

95 ST 84 P10,1, SF 759 Vindus ii 2a 33 (almost complete, with worn footring) VINDI Lezoux (c). Mid or late Antonine.

Context as no. 3.

96 ST 82 BLN, SF 389 Vosecunnus 1a 18/31 [VOSE]C\NNI·M Lezoux (c). *c.* AD 140–70.

From post-hole 959, east side of building R6. Phase III.

97 ST 84 DXZ, SF 1071 (*Unillus.*) Uxopillus 4a 33 VXOPILLI·M Lezoux (a). *c.* AD 150–70.

From pit 2021/2110, unit 2028. 3rd century AD.

98 ST 82 ECT, SF 1126 Uxopillus 4a 33 VXOPILLI·M Lezoux (b). *c.* AD 150–70.

From occupation layer (unit 2143) within north end of building R8. Phase III+.

99 ST 82 BBQ, SF 340 Uxopillus 4b 31 VXOPIΛΛIW (sic) Lezoux (a). *c.* AD 160–80.

Context as no. 87.

Unidentified

100 ST 83 CDO, SF 512 M[on form 33, Central Gaulish. Antonine.

From ditch 11, cut 3, unit 1085. Mid/late 3rd century AD.

101 ST 83+, SF 564]Δ on form 38 or 44, Central Gaulish. Antonine.

1983, unstratified.

102 ST 83 H7,1, SF 575]MΛNI on form 31, Central Gaulish. Antonine.

Context as no. 54.

103 ST 83 CAA, SF 561]A on form 31, Central Gaulish. Antonine.

From topsoil/cleaning, block 11 east.

104 ST 81+, SF 71 CIIVIΛΛ retr. on form 33, Central Gaulish. Antonine.

1981, unstratified.

105 ST 81 JQ, SF 155 (*Unillus.*) C[on form 31, Central Gaulish. Antonine.

From the upper layer (unit 199), south-east quadrant of the low mound sealing the south side of building S1. 9th–10th century AD.

106 ST 81 HT, SF 235 (*Unillus.*)]VP[on form 33, Central Gaulish. Antonine.

From gully 44, cut 2, uppermost layer (unit 179). 3rd century AD.

107 ST 82 BKM, SF 361 (*Unillus.*)]MT[on form 33, Central Gaulish. Antonine.

From ditch 9, cut 1, uppermost layer (unit 934). Phases IV–V, with modern contamination.

108 ST 84 EDS, SF 1177 (*Unillus.*)]CCIOM? on form 38 or 44, Central Gaulish. Antonine.

From gully 30, cut 7, unit 2166. 3rd century AD.

109 ST 84 DVE, SF 1178 (*Unillus.*) IV[on form 31, Central Gaulish. Antonine.

From gully 31, cut 8, unit 1961. Late 2nd/3rd century AD.

110 ST 84 DGW, SF 807]TIM on form 33, Central Gaulish. Antonine.

From gully 35, cut 7, unit 1665. 3rd century AD.

111 ST 84 DZZ, SF 1156 (*Unillus.*) CO..[on form 38, Central Gaulish. Antonine. With graffito X inscribed under the base after firing.

Context as no. 28.

112 ST 84 DOY, SF 880 /\\/IIN on form 33, Central Gaulish. Antonine.

From pit 1835/2007, unit 1835. 3rd century AD.

113 ST 83 CDL, SF 515 (*Unillus.*)]/\\\\ on form 79 or Ludowici Tg?, but with the underside of the base rising slightly at the centre. Central Gaulish. Mid to late Antonine.

From topsoil/cleaning, block 11, west.

114 ST 82 BAE, SF 290]NV retr? on form 31, Central Gaulish. Mid to late Antonine.

From well 705, unit 710. 3rd/4th century AD.

115 ST 82 AGK, SF 371]VIM on form 31R, Central Gaulish. Mid to late Antonine.

From ditch 9, cut 9, unit 595. Late 3rd/early 4th century AD.

116 ST 84 DWA, SF 1179 (*Unillus.*) ·AΛ[on form 31R, Central Gaulish. Mid to late Antonine.

From gully 29, cut 6, unit 1981. 3rd century AD.

117 ST 84 DQS, SF 1182 (*Unillus.*)]I[on form 31R (with heavily-worn footring), Central Gaulish. Mid to late Antonine.

From ?well 1667, unit 1878. Late 3rd/4th century AD.

118 ST 84 DEA, SF 742 (*Unillus.*)]M on form 31R, Central Gaulish. Mid to late Antonine.

From topsoil/cleaning, as no. 14.

119 ST 80 BA, SF 15 (*Unillus.*)]ΛIΛΛ[on form 31R, Central Gaulish. Mid to late Antonine.

From building R1, small hypocausted room, destruction deposit (unit 24). Early 3rd century AD.

120 ST 84 DGE, SF 1027 A seven-beaded rosette, on form 33, East Gaulish. Probably Argonne ware and Antonine.

From gully 34, cut 1, unit 1649. Late 2nd/early 3rd century AD.

121 ST 81 HY, SF 99 (*Unillus.*) C[on form 38 or 44?, East Gaulish. Antonine or first half of the 3rd century AD.

From topsoil, south-east block 1.

122 ST 84 DOK, SF 1180 (*Unillus.*). /[or]/ on form 31, East Gaulish. Antonine or first half of the 3rd century AD.

From gully 19, cut 5, unit 1822. Mid 3rd century AD.

STAMPS ON COARSE WARES

Val Rigby   (Fig. 144)

1 ΛBICCIΛS or ΛBIILIΛS   ST 82 AEE

Central stamp; burnished circle. Bowl closely copying Dragendorff 31. Fine-grained, smooth textured matrix; dark grey with paler surfaces; burnished finish.

From ditch 9, cut 5, unit 542. 3rd century AD.

Abiccias/ Abelias Die 1A1 − see no. 2 below.

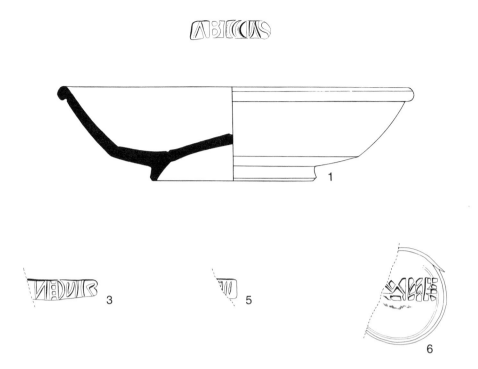

Fig. 144 Stonea Grange: stamps on coarse wares 1, 3 and 5–6 (scale 1:1 except vessel 1 = 1:2).

2 ΛBICCIΛS or ΛBIILIΛS (*Unillus.*)
ST 84 DVY North, SF 1031

Central stamp. Small carinated cup with tall functional foot-ring, probably a copy of Dragendorff form 33. Fine-grained, smooth textured matrix with fine black clay pellets; grey-black core with paler grey surfaces; abraded, no finish survives.

From pit cluster 2022, unit 1979. 3rd century AD.

Abiccias/Abelias Die 1a1 – the same die as no. 1 above and a cup found on the site of the military works depot at Longthorpe, Cambs (Rigby 1987, Fig. 36, 2, where the stamp is incorrectly deciphered and illustrated upside down). The discovery of three examples within 50 km suggests a local source, probably near Durobrivae, in the Lower Nene Valley potteries, where most of the common wares found at Stonea were produced.

Bowl no. 1, complete when discarded, was found in an upper layer of ditch 9 with other pottery dated to the early 3rd century, and cup no. 2 was also found with third century pottery. The context of the Longthorpe stamp was undated. A date of manufacture in the second half of the 2nd century seems likely, and this gains support from the fact that the bowl copies almost exactly its samian prototype and therefore should have been made after AD 120.

3 [. .]VIEDVIIC or [. .]VIEDVIIL, possibly ..VANEDIVEL(OS); if retrograde then CIIVDENV..   ST 84 DBR, SF 705

Central stamp; single burnished circle. Bowl with tall foot-ring probably copying Dragendorff 31. Fine-grained dense matrix with occasional white shell and dark argillaceous inclusions; light blue-grey with traces of a burnished finish.

From the uppermost layer (unit 1541) of pit 1541. 3rd century AD.

..anedivilos Die 1A1. Full name not recorded and no known parallels for the die. The fabric suggests a source where shelly clay was available, and the form, a date of manufacture in the 2nd century.

4 [. .]INEDO (*Unillus.*) ST 84 N1,1, SF 1168

An uncertain reading.

Central stamp; probably a small bowl or cup. Fine-grained soapy-smooth matrix; brown, with traces of burnished finish.

From block 10, trench N, base of ploughsoil.

..inedo Die 1A1. Full name not recorded, and no known parallels. The smooth fabric is typical of stamped and stamp-decorated vessels which are commonly found on sites in the region of the Ouse–Nene–Welland river system (Stead and Rigby 1986, Table 16, 243–55). Similar fabrics were produced at West Stow, Suffolk, which is fairly close to Stonea, but although more than 30 stamps were found, all are closely related bordered Marks, and no Names occurred (Rigby 1989, 86–9). Late 1st to mid 2nd century AD.

5 IIB[. . .] or IID[. . .]   ST 83 CIB, SF 489

Central stamp. Bowl with tall functional foot-ring, form unknown. Fine-grained soapy smooth fabric; dark grey-black, with paler outer surface; highly burnished finish.

From lower fill (unit 1193) of pit 1184. Early 3rd century AD.

Stamp too fragmentary for identification. From a similar source, and with the same date range as no. 4.

6 Decorative stamp   ST 83 CEG, SF 510

Multi-motif block die. Central stamp – a single incised circle. Open form, variant unknown. Colour-coated ware with cream matrix and brown slip: a typical product of the Lower Nene Valley potteries.

From post-medieval disturbed layer (unit 1102) in block 11, east.

No more than three potter's Marks or Names have been recorded on colour-coated wares made in the Lower Nene Valley. Occasionally, as in this case, a decorative die was preferred. The large block stamp combines at least two rectangular motifs, each lacking a cartouche, which produces a pattern in reserve. Dies without a cartouche were usually confined to decorative stamps and were impressed either centrally or radially on the base inside, or outside, or both. A similar multi-motif block stamp, found at the kiln site at Stanground, has been used to decorate the exterior of a drinking cup (Dannell 1973, Fig. 1, 3). It is likely that the Stonea vessel was originally stamp-decorated rather than simply stamped with the potter's Mark.

STAMPED MORTARIA

Kay Hartley   (Figs 145–8)

Note: the black vesicular material mentioned with mortaria attributed to the Nene valley or Northants, will be ironstone or iron slag.

1 CICUR (O/US)   ST 83+, SF 508

Diameter c. 31 cm. A mortarium, which has been fired extremely hard, probably mainly in a reducing atmosphere. Thick outer skin grey, fabric then buff-cream with grey core. Inclusions: moderate, ill-sorted, mostly black vesicular (probably refired pottery) with few quartz. The poorly impressed stamp,]ICVR[, is from the only known die of Cicur(o/us), who worked in the Mancetter–Hartshill potteries probably AD 150–80.

1983, Unstratified.

2 GRATINUS   ST 82 AEQ, SF 376

Diameter c. 36 cm. Fine-textured, cream fabric. Inclusions: moderate quartz, fewer red-brown. The stamp is from the most commonly used die of Gratinus who worked in the Mancetter–Hartshill potteries c. AD 130–60+. Worn.

From the sump, north-west quadrant, layer 553. Early/mid 3rd century AD.

3 IUNIUS   ST 82 AAV, SF 295 and AAA, SF 244

Diameter 35 cm. About half of the rim survives. The intended colour is probably the buff apparent near the spout but the rest of the fabric is pink. Inclusions: abundant, fairly well-sorted, quartz. Trituration grit: included flint and quartz. Both of the potter's stamps survive and the most obvious reading is IVNII retrograde, for the genitive form of Iunius. This is a different potter from the maker of no. 4. His mortaria are also recorded from Brockley Hill (3), Braughing, London, Radlett, Verulamium and Ware. His fabric indicates manufacture in the potteries by Watling Street, south of Verulamium, which included workshops at Radlett and Brockley Hill, where he may well have worked. His work undoubtedly belongs to the first half of the second century, perhaps later than AD 110. Very heavily worn.

SF 244 and 295, joining. SF 295 from unit 461, black soil spread, block 1a. 3rd century AD. Phase III/IV. SF 244 from topsoil in same region.

4 IUNIUS   ST 81 FB, SF 55

Diameter 31 cm. Hard, fine-textured, cream fabric. Inclusions: very moderate, sporadic tiny quartz with few larger red-brown and black. No trituration grit survives. The stamp reads]NIVS, retrograde, and is from one of the dies of Iunius who worked in the Mancetter–Hartshill potteries. AD 150–80.

From unit 117, ashy spread, south of the small hypocausted room of the R1 building complex. Late 2nd century AD. Phases III–V.

5 ?MAURIUS   ST 82 ABQ, SF 263

Diameter c. 27 cm. Hard, fine-textured, cream fabric. Inclusions: fairly frequent, quartz (milky, transparent, pink), with some opaque red-brown and black and large cream ?grog pellets. The poorly and incompletely impressed stamp may read]AM[. Only one other stamp, from Wroxeter, is fairly certainly by the same potter, although the die is a different one. It is possible that they are retrograde stamps of Maurius but only further examples will clarify this point. This mortarium can be attributed to the Mancetter –Hartshill potteries, AD 140–80 (probably later than AD 150). Heavily Worn.

From topsoil/cleaning, block 2.

6 MESSOR   ST 81 NL, SF 189

Diameter 39 cm. Fine-textured, pale creamy brown fabric. Inclusions: fairly frequent tiny quartz, flint, black ?slag and red-brown with moderate and ill-sorted larger inclusions composed of the same materials. Trituration grit: flint, quartz, red-brown and black ?slag. The potter is Messor who worked at Colchester, c. AD 130–70. For further details, see Symonds, forthcoming (Colchester).

From layer 287 in pit 170. 3rd/4th century AD.

7 SARRIUS   ST 82 AGN, SF 396

Diameter 30 cm. Hard, very fine-textured, cream fabric. Inclusions: very few, small, quartz and rare opaque red-brown material. Trituration grit: few survive, included red-brown, probably re-fired pottery. The stamp is from the most commonly used die of Sarrius, the most prolific stamper of mortaria in the second century. Sarrius worked c. AD 140–70. This is a product of his Mancetter–Hartshill workshop, which was probably active throughout his career although he had two other workshops further north, which had smaller outputs.

From unit 598, ashy destruction/dereliction layer south of R1 building complex. Late 2nd–3rd century AD. Phase III/IV.

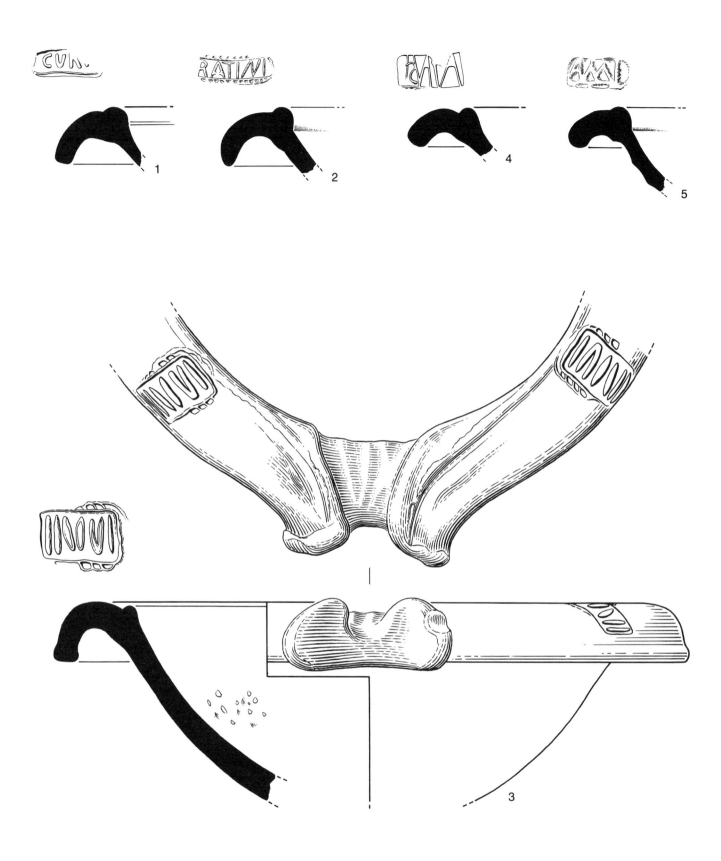

Fig. 145 Stonea Grange: stamped mortaria 1–5 (scale 1 : 2).

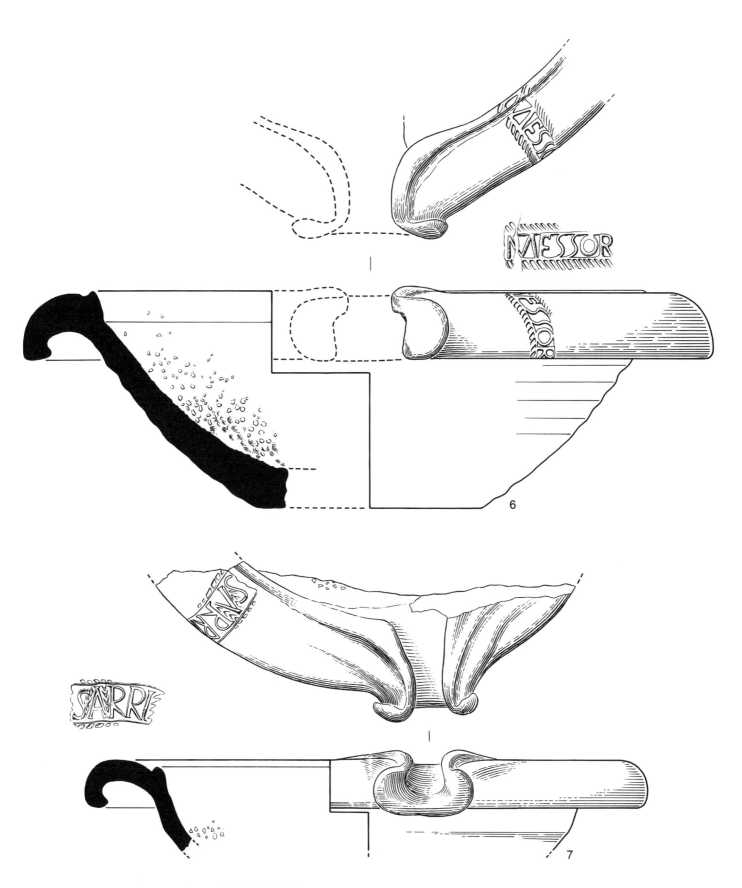

Fig. 146 Stonea Grange: stamped mortaria 6–7 (scale 1:2).

8 VARINNA   Stonea Grange 1963

Diameter 31 cm. Very hard, drab cream fabric. Inclusions: fairly frequent, ill-sorted, red-brown sandstone which stains the fabric, with few quartz. No specific trituration grit survives. Discoloured at one end. The retrograde stamp gives the name Varinna. Mortaria of his are now recorded from Ashton, Northants; Godmanchester; Stonea (2) (see no. 9 below); Water Newton; Sibson cum Stibbington; and Northants, ?Duston. The distribution points to an origin in the Nene Valley and Dr D. F. Williams, when examining the Sibson example, also favoured this source. Varinna's rim-profiles would best fit the period AD 140–80.

Surface find at TL 451936, in 1963.

9 VARINNA   ST 84 EBH, SF 1095

Diameter 34 cm. Hard fabric; orangy at surfaces with thick cream-buff core and pinky brown slip. Inclusions: fairly frequent, ill-sorted, transparent, milky and pink quartz, black (vesicular), and red-brown. Trituration grit: quartz, black vesicular, and red-brown sandstone. The broken stamp is probably from the same die of Varinna as no. 8; the bottom of the final]NA is preserved. Heavily worn.

From ditch 18, cut 13, unit 2108, Phase III.

10 VEDIACUS   ST 84 DOZ, SF 675

Diameter 34 cm. Burnt, and heavily worn. Micaceous and fine-textured fabric. Thick surface skin, pale grey with pink tinge in parts; very thick black core. Inclusions: sparse, large cream with some red-brown and black. No specific trituration grit survives. Heavily worn. The incomplete, two-line stamp reads]D≠ACVS/]ICIT.

From unit 1836, pit 1836. Late 2nd/3rd century AD.

11 VEDIACUS   ST 83A 26, 6, SF 1983A, 6

Diameter 28 cm. Very hard fabric, grey throughout with buff-brown surface slip. Inclusions: frequent, well-sorted, quartz only visible at ×20 magnification, with much larger, sparse, vesicular black, red-brown and yellowish material. Trituration grit: few red-brown survive. The broken two-line stamp reads VIIDI/IIII I for Vediacus/fecit, II used for E. Heavily worn. This is a second mortarium of Vediacus. His distribution points to a workshop in the upper Nene Valley. His rim-profiles were undoubtedly produced within the period AD 140–80, probably later than AD 150. See Frere 1984, 289, no. 99 for further details.

From the sump, layer A, 26, grid 6. Late 3rd century AD.

12 VIRAPIUS   ST 81 MC, SF 149

Diameter 27 cm. Hard, cream fabric with thick pink core. Inclusions: fairly frequent and well-sorted quartz with rare, larger red-brown ?sandstone. Trituration grit included red-brown ?sandstone, black ?slag or ironstone and probably quartz. Buff-cream slip. Virapius certainly used a kiln at Snettisham in Norfolk but the fabric of the mortaria from this kiln undoubtedly differs from most, if not all, of the rest of his work. Other mortaria of Virapius are noted from Braughing; Earith, Hunts; the Holbeach area; and

Werrington, near Peterborough. Some activity in the Nene Valley/Cambridgeshire would be a possibility and further finds should eventually clarify this matter. His rim-forms leave no doubt that his optimum date is AD 150–80. Worn.

From gully 64, cut 1, unit 256. Late 3rd–4th century AD.

13 ?VIRAPIUS   ST 80 BJ

Incomplete rim-section. Very hard, sandwich fabric, pale grey at surface enclosing brownish-buff around a core of pale grey. Inclusions: abundant, fairly well-sorted quartz, with rare black, red-brown and cream. Buff-brown slip. Trituration grit: included red-brown material. Unfortunately the stamps are too fragmentary for certain identification but they may be the ends of two stamps of Virapius impressed along or slightly diagonally on the flange. If so, they are not from the same die as no. 12 but from his second die. Stamping along the flange was very unusual in Britain in the second century AD but Virapius is one of the few potters, who sometimes did this. Made in the East Midlands, probably in the Nene Valley/Cambridgeshire area; possibly quite local to Stonea. Probably AD 140–80. Heavily worn.

From R1 building, central block, south-east quadrant, unit 32, robbing debris. 4th century AD.

14 ...SCII..   ST 82 AER, SF 370

Diameter 27 cm. Off-white fabric. Inclusions: fairly frequent, mainly quartz (pink and transparent), and cream grog (up to 6 mm), rare red-brown sandstone. Trituration grit: mixed, up to 5 mm, mainly brown and red-brown sandstone with some opaque white quartz, and possibly a few igneous fragments. Self-coloured. Well-worn and slightly singed. The incompletely impressed stamp, reading]??SCII?, is from the same die as no. 15.

From well 446, unit 554. Late 2nd–3rd century AD.

15 ...SCII..   ST 84 DPQ, SF 676

Diameter c. 31 cm. Three flange fragments, two joining, in cream fabric with a thick pink core. Inclusions: fairly frequent, pink quartz with fewer red-brown sandstone, cream grog and tiny black fragments. Self-coloured. The stamp is from the same die as that on no. 14.

From pit 1814, layer 1852. 3rd century AD.

The interpretation of the stamps on the two mortaria, nos. 14 and 15, is uncertain but they probably read]VSCII retrograde or]ASCII, left to right with blind A. Other stamps from the same die are known from Lincoln (Darling 1984, 70, Fig. 19, no. 4), Margidunum and Mancetter. The potter probably worked in the Mancetter–Hartshill potteries within the period AD 140–80 and these two examples have spouts likely to be later than AD 150. There is a possibility that the die concerned belonged to Bruscius but only the discovery of further stamps can clarify this point.

16 ...?...   ST 82 BBY, SF 432

Diameter c. 22 cm. Fine-textured, brownish-cream fabric with thick orange-pink core. Inclusions: moderate, smallish, mostly quartz

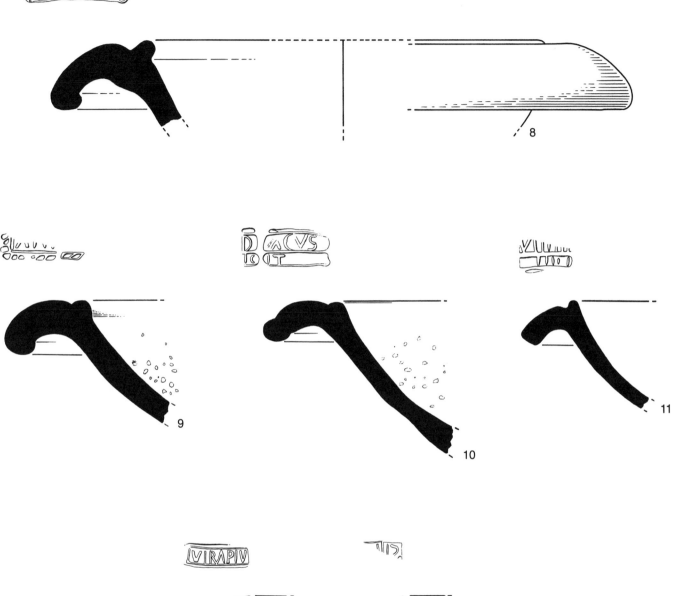

Fig. 147 Stonea Grange: stamped mortaria 8–13 (scale 1:2).

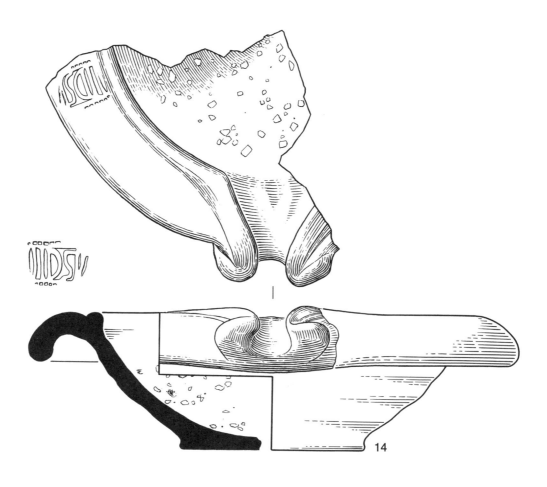

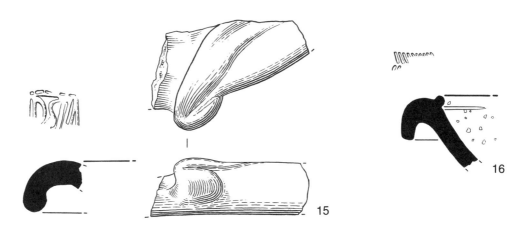

Fig. 148 Stonea Grange: stamped mortaria 14–16 (scale 1 : 2).

with rare red-brown and black. Trituration grit: flint, quartz and rare red-brown. The broken stamp is of herringbone type but is too fragmentary to be identified. The fabric and form clearly indicate a product of the Colchester potteries AD 140–70.

From ditch 71, cut 8, unit 752. Post-medieval.

AMPHORAE

S. J. Keay and C. Carreras   (Figs 149–50)

The five seasons of excavations at the Grange site have provided a good assemblage of amphora sherds. The following types were distinguished:

TYPOLOGIES

1 Dressel 20   (Class 25, Peacock and Williams 1986)

A large globular amphora produced along the Guadalquivir Valley (southern Spain) in at least 70 different centres (Ponsich 1970; 1974; 1991. Remesal 1986). It was distributed chiefly in the western Roman Empire and its main content was olive oil (Dressel 1899; Condamin *et al* 1976; Curle 1911). In Britain and Germany it is the most common amphora from the middle of the 1st to the middle of the 3rd century AD. This suggests that the olive oil may have been supplied by the state to the Roman legions (Remesal 1986). This form is usually stamped on the handle and some of them bear painted inscriptions (*tituli picti*) which have been interpreted as fiscal controls. This type occurred in fabrics 1 (41.7%), 2 (14.97%), 3 (23.52%), 5 (0.53%), 6 (13.90%), 8 (1.60%) and 10 (3.20%).

Rims 1 (J4,2), 2 (DIV), 3 (DON), 4 (SV), 5 (DXB), 6 (J4,1)

Handle 7 (ADM)

Bases 8 (J4,1), 9 (DXS)

2 Gauloise 7   (Class 31, Peacock and Williams 1986)

A small, globular amphora with pulley-wheel rim and short furrowed handles, ending in a base with thick footring. This type was produced in different areas of the Mediterranean region such as Tarraconensis, Spain; Baetica, Spain (Rodríguez Almeida 1989); and Velaux, France (Laubenheimer 1985). However, the samples from Stonea are basically from southern France. The main content is not certain, though wine or fish sauce have been suggested for the Gaulish amphorae. It has a widespread distribution in the western Roman Empire from the late Augustan to the first half of the 2nd century AD (Laubenheimer 1985). It occurred only in fabric 4.

Base 10 (LT).

3 Gauloise 4   (Class 27, Peacock and Williams 1986)

A thick, rounded rim with flat grooved handles and flat base are the main features of this type. It was produced in Languedoc (southern France) and the principal content was wine (Laubenheimer 1985). The distribution of this amphora includes the whole western Roman Empire from the mid 1st to the 3rd century AD. It is the second most common amphora in Britain, where it is usually found in contexts after AD 61 (Peacock 1978). It occurred in fabrics 4 (40%), 7 (50%), 19 (3.33%), 12 (3.33%) and 17 (3.33%).

Rims 11 (AEE), 12 (KC), 13 (BGN), 14 (DVA), 15 (BKX), 16 (DKS), 17 (DTT), 18 (DWP), 19 (AEE)

Handle 20 (DEA)

4 Dressel 2/4 (Italian)
(Class 10, Peacock and Williams 1986)

This type of wine amphora is characterised by a pronounced variation on the shoulder and long bifid handles. There were different production areas in the Mediterranean such as Campania (Italy), Latium (Italy), Etruria (Italy), Catalonia (Spain), Baetica (Spain) and southern and central Gaul. The samples from Stonea are Italian since the fabric contains black sand which is a typical feature of volcanic areas such as Campania. It had a widespread distribution in the western Roman Empire between *c*. 50 BC to the later 2nd or early 3rd century AD (Arthur and Williams 1992). It occurred only in fabric 14.

Not illustrated.

5 Eastern   (Classes 39–49, Peacock and Williams 1986)

The Stonea samples did not provide any form for these amphora sherds which were assigned an origin in the eastern Mediterranean on the basis of the fabric. Therefore it is difficult to specify either a production area or a date range for them. It occurred only in fabric 16.

Handle 21 (AAW).

6 New Amphora type

Number 22. A substantially complete piriform amphora (from unit 892 in pit 483/918) with a low concave rim, pronounced handles with circular profile and a ring-foot. It is characterised by a series of post-cocturam graffiti (see p. 491). The type is unparalleled, with the nearest shape being a complete vessel from Lenzburg (Ettlinger 1977, 13, Fig. 3). This appears in a third century context, but may well be residual. It occurred in fabric 18.

7 Miscellaneous

In addition, there were a number of unidentified sherds; these occurred in fabrics 9, 11, 13, 15 and 20.

QUANTIFICATION

Different measurement units (Orton 1982; Keay 1984; Tomber 1988; Orton 1989) were used to analyse the amphora assemblage in order to discover possible supply trends. These measurement units were weight, sherd count, EVE (rim), handles and bases. As may be observed in Table 17, some units such as EVE and bases misrepresent the types since the assemblage is relatively small. The most reliable unit of assessment is weight, which in this case produces results identical to those produced by sherd count.

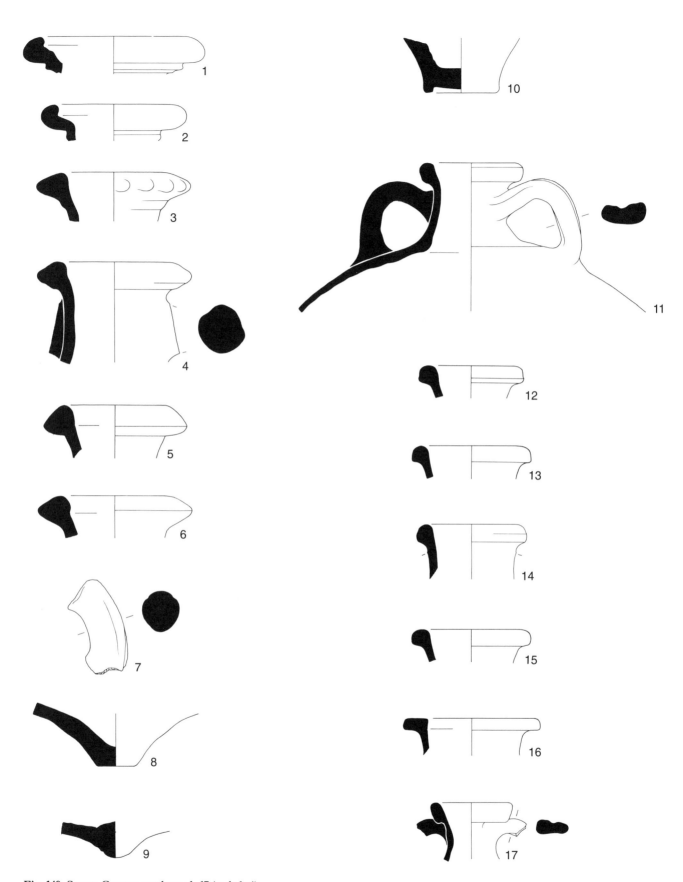

Fig. 149 Stonea Grange: amphorae 1–17 (scale 1:4).

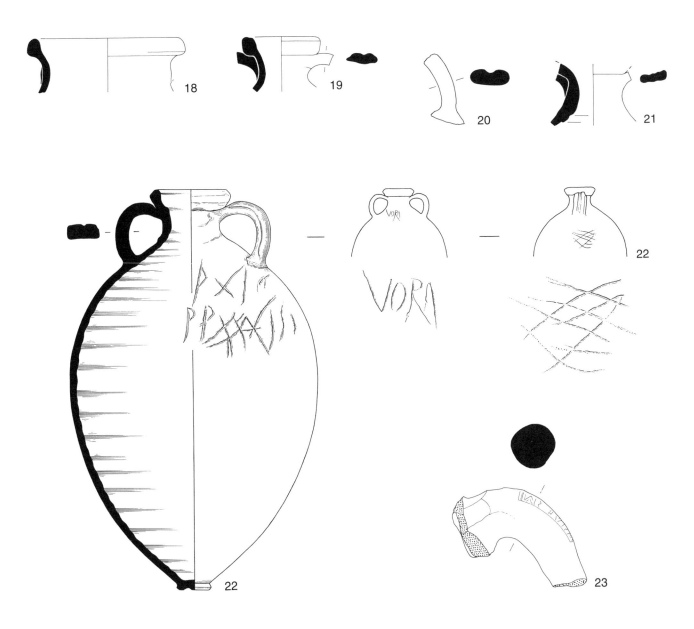

Fig. 150 Stonea Grange: amphorae 18–23 (scale 1:4 except simplified views of 22).

Table 17 Stonea Grange: comparison of the different measurement units used to analyse the amphora assemblage

Units	Weight (g)	Sherds	EVE (%)	Handle	Base
Dr 20	42 101.61	368	94	8	3
Gaul 7	654	8	–	–	1
Gaul 4	4 076.5	43	204	3	–
Dr 2/4	11	2	–	–	–
Eastern	200.8	1	–	1	–
Unrecog.	5 794.4	56	–	2	1
Totals	52 838.56	479	398	14	5

Table 18 includes the percentage of each amphora type according to the weight and sherd units. The percentages quite closely match other assemblages in Britain, of second century AD date such as Chichester, Winchester or Leicester. Dressel 20 normally comprise between 70% and 90% of those assemblages while the Gauloise 4 is the second most common type. The remaining types are basically residual in the second century AD contexts, as at Stonea. The main difference between the Stonea assemblage and the others is the absence of fish-sauce amphorae. This is the third most important type of the period, but it is not present at Stonea.

Table 18 Stonea Grange: percentage of each amphora type according to the weight and sherd units

Percentage	Weight (g)	Sherds
Dr 20	79.67	76.8
Gaul 7	1.23	1.67
Gaul 4	7.71	8.97
Dr 2/4	0.02	0.41
Eastern	0.38	0.2
Unrecog.	10.96	11.69

AMPHORA STAMP

Number 23. Only one amphora stamp was recovered from the excavations. It was on the handle of a Dressel 20 amphora. This was very worn, making a certain identification difficult. However it is possible that it may read: P.IVL.ITFILI....

The closer parallels are PIVLICRISPI, PIVLRECTI or IVLTEREN, all of Flavian–Trajanic date.

Note: the stamp is so worn as to render useless any attempt at a drawing.

DATING EVIDENCE

As has been noted, the amphora assemblage from Stonea seems to suggest a second century AD supply to the site. However, a low percentage of these amphora sherds were found in stratigraphic contexts of this period. Most of them were recovered from third and fourth century layers; therefore the problem was to assess whether they were residual or not. Table 19 shows the amphora percentage for each chronological phase defined by the site stratigraphy.

Table 19 Stonea Grange: amphora percentages for site chronological phases

Phases	Early 2nd cent	Late 2nd cent	3rd/4th cent	Post-Roman
Dr 20	1.87%	17.04%	76.17%	4.9%
Gaul 4	1.72%	9.37%	88.90%	–
Italian	–	–	100	–

The chronology of the assemblage was assessed on the basis of an analysis of the Dressel 20 rims and the amphora stamp.

1 Amphora Stamp

If the interpretation above is correct, this was of Flavian–Trajanic date or later.

2 Dressel 20 Rims

Seven Dressel 20 rims were available to provide some dating evidence. Martin-Kilcher (1983, 1987) defined a typological evolution of the Dressel 20 amphora rims according to well-dated layers at Augst and Kaiseraugst (Switzerland) and supported to some extent by the evidence from Alsace and Lorraine (Baudoux 1990). It has been suggested that the classification is not very accurate since some rim types belonging to different phases were found in the same shipwreck (Nieto *et al* 1989). However, it is clear that the basic division into first, second and third century types is consistent enough. Three Stonea rims correspond to early types: 25 (cat. 1), 32 (cat. 3) and 17 (cat. 2) date to the first half of the second century AD. The remaining four rims are types of the second half of the second century; 35 (cat. 5, 6) and 36 (cat. 4; the other is not illustrated).

It is evident, therefore, that this is a homogeneous assemblage, of second century date. Supply ended with the demise of the R1 building complex *c.* AD 200. Since many of the sherds occurred in later contexts, however, their size was measured to test for residuality (cf. Bradley and Fulford 1980; Tomber 1988; Evans and Millett 1992). The histogram shows the frequency of weights of the sherds. The *x*-axis represents the number of sherds with same range of weight, while the *y*-axis provides the weight in grams for each group.

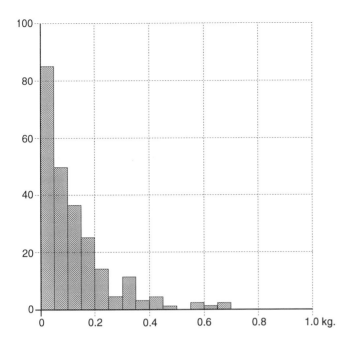

Only three samples weighed more than 1 kg and only eight more than 500 g. The majority of weights fall in a range between 0 and 100 g (50.82%), whilst the second most numerous group is between 100 and 200 g (31.81%). Therefore, on account of the small size of the sherds, it can be concluded that the amphora assemblage may have been residual in the stratigraphic context where it was found.

FABRICS

The petrological analysis of the amphora fabrics provided 20 different types which are described below, based on a macroscopic analysis with the aid of a ×10 hand lens.

1 Soft to hard, orange/pink to brown/buff fabric, with a smooth fracture and a very common ground scatter of quartz crystals (*c.* 0.5 mm). Other inclusions were frequent calcite, occasional grog, ironstone and mica. These were all sub-rounded to angular.

2 Hard to very hard, fine-grained grey to buff fabric, with fairly common lime inclusions (0.75 mm) and rare quartz (2.5 mm) and ironstone.

3 Hard to very hard, grey/buff fabric with frequent air holes. Probably a variant of fabric 2.

4 Hard to very hard, light brown/buff fine-grained fabric with a smoothish fracture. Occasional lime inclusions were present together with a fine scatter of mica.

5 A soft to hard fabric made from a very finely elutriated clay of orange/red (outside) and grey (inside) colour. Occasional lime inclusions (0.75 mm) and rare ironstone and quartz.

6 A hard version of fabric 1.

7 Similar to fabric 4 except for a higher tenor of lime inclusions (up to 4.00 mm).

8 A very fine-grained light brown/buff fabric. Mica was the only visible inclusion.

9 A hard, fine-grained fabric with a hackly fracture and laminar lime inclusions and occasional air holes.

10 A very fine fabric of a pink to light buff colour and a very hackly fracture. Inclusions were very common and included red to grey grog, quartzite and quartz grains. All were well sorted and ranged up to 5.00 mm.

11 A very hard fine-grained, well-elutriated clay with occasional air holes. A range of sub-angular/rounded moderately sorted inclusions were present, comprising quartz (very common), calcite (quite common), lime (rare) and biotite mica (rare).

12 A hard, buff/light brown fabric with a hackly fracture. Sub-angular lime and clay grog inclusions were frequent, while unsorted quartz was rather rare.

13 A hard, light pink/buff clay with a 'honey-combed' texture and hackly fracture. There were frequent subangular quartz inclusions, which were well sorted, as well as rarer red/grey grog.

14 A soft to quite hard, finely elutriated pink-buff fabric with a hackly fracture. Medium sorted subangular black volcanic minerals were common, whilst there were occasional clay, mica and lime inclusions.

15 A very hard, well-elutriated clay of an off-white colour with a hackly fracture. The fabric contained common poorly sorted subangular quartz grains, together with rarer red grog and black inclusions.

16 A very hard, light brown/buff, well-elutriated clay with a hackly fracture with a white/cream exterior wash. There were very common subangular quartz grains present, together with ironstone and limestone reaction rims.

17 A hard, poorly elutriated, pinkish clay with a light buff core and hackly fracture. There were very common well sorted subangular quartz grains present, quite common sub-angular black inclusions and rare orange grog.

18 A soft to medium hard fabric of light buff/pink colour and well elutriated clay with a smoothish fracture. There were no visible inclusions, except for a scattering of mica, occasional red clay particles and occasional large lumps of quartzite (4–5 mm) breaking through the outer body wall.

19 Similar to fabric 7 except that it is characterised by the presence of dark coloured inclusions.

20 A soft, fairly fine elutriated clay of an orange (outside)/ grey (inside) colour, with a smooth/hackly fracture. Quite frequent quartz and rare lime inclusions were present.

Table 20 Stonea Grange: summary of weights and percentages of each amphora fabric

Fabric	Weight (g)	Percentage
1	18 747.46	36.08
2	7 559.85	14.54
3	11 695.10	22.43
4	1 199.40	2.50
5	18.80	0.03
6	6 936.60	13.34
7	3 196.09	6.15
8	519.90	1.00
9	1 384.10	2.66
10	887.20	1.70
11	347.30	0.67
12	170	0.34
13	31.40	0.06
14	11	0.03
15	116.10	0.22
16	200.8	0.38
17	102.40	0.19
18	3 362.30	6.47
19	121.90	0.23
20	44.90	0.08

CONCLUSIONS

The amphora assemblage represents a second century AD supply, which seems to finish by the end of that century. It may correspond to the period of the Hadrianic settlement which was abandoned *c.* AD 200. Notwithstanding the continuous occupation of Stonea during the third and fourth centuries, there is no sign of amphora imports during this period.

The reason for such a drastic end in the amphora imports may be due to a change in the nature of the population of the site in the third century AD. Products such as olive oil or wine may not have been appreciated by the new dwellers, who may have had other substitutes in their diet (Carreras 1991; forthcoming). It may also indicate that the new population had a lesser purchasing power and could not afford these imports.

As a final hypothesis, the end of amphora imports may be related to the possible administrative role of the site. Research in amphora distributions shows that products such as olive oil may have been part of a long distance trade underwritten by the Roman State to provide supplies to the Army and its administrative staff in distant provinces (Remesal 1986; Carreras 1991).

OTHER ROMAN POTTERY

Fiona Cameron [Submitted 1987] (Figs 151–73)

In this section, the Roman pottery other than the samian, the stamped mortaria, the amphorae and certain pieces of figured coloured coat are considered. It should be noted that the text was completed early in 1987.

TYPE SERIES   (Figs 151–58)

Nene Valley fabrics

The Nene Valley potteries, which seemed to have supplied most of the sites in the Roman Fenland, were producing a variety of vessels from approximately the second quarter of the second century AD, right through to the fifth century. A type series for these wares with a discussion of the chronology has already been published by Peterborough Museum (Howe *et al* 1980), and many of the forms and fabrics have been adequately dealt with in that book (hereinafter referred to as the *NV Guide*). However, since its publication, a great deal of work has been done by the Nene Valley Research Committee at Peterborough, in particular on the site at Chesterton. Although this report has not yet been published, the new information which has come from this site has been made available to provide parallels for the pottery from Stonea. Since the site at Chesterton had a good deal of independent dating evidence, whereas Stonea has very little, this has been particularly valuable. Where the dates given for certain types in the *NV Guide* have been superseded with the help of the evidence from Chesterton, these more recent dates have been used here.

Nene Valley Colour-coated wares (NVCC)   (Figs 151–2)

BEAKERS

Type 1   Bag-shaped beaker with a plain rim (*NV Guide* nos 44 and 45) ST 83A Layer 4. (residual in Phases IV–VI). This type is dated in the *NV Guide* to the later 2nd–early 3rd century AD, although at Chesterton it appears to go back to the mid 2nd century.

Type 1.2   As Type 1, with underslip barbotine decoration (not illustrated).

Type 1.3   As Type 1, with underslip barbotine scales (not illustrated).

Type 2   Bag-shaped beaker with cornice rim. SY. Phase III.

Type 2.2   As Type 2, with grooved decoration. ADY. Phase III.

Type 2.3   As Type 2, with rouletted decoration (*NV Guide* no. 32). NJ. Phase IV.

Type 2.4   As Type 2, with underslip barbotine applied scales. AAO. Phase III.

Type 2.5   As Type 2, with rough-cast decoration. DDM. Phase III.

Type 2.6   As Type 2, with stylised floral underslip barbotine decoration (*NV Guide* no. 29). BA. Phase IV.

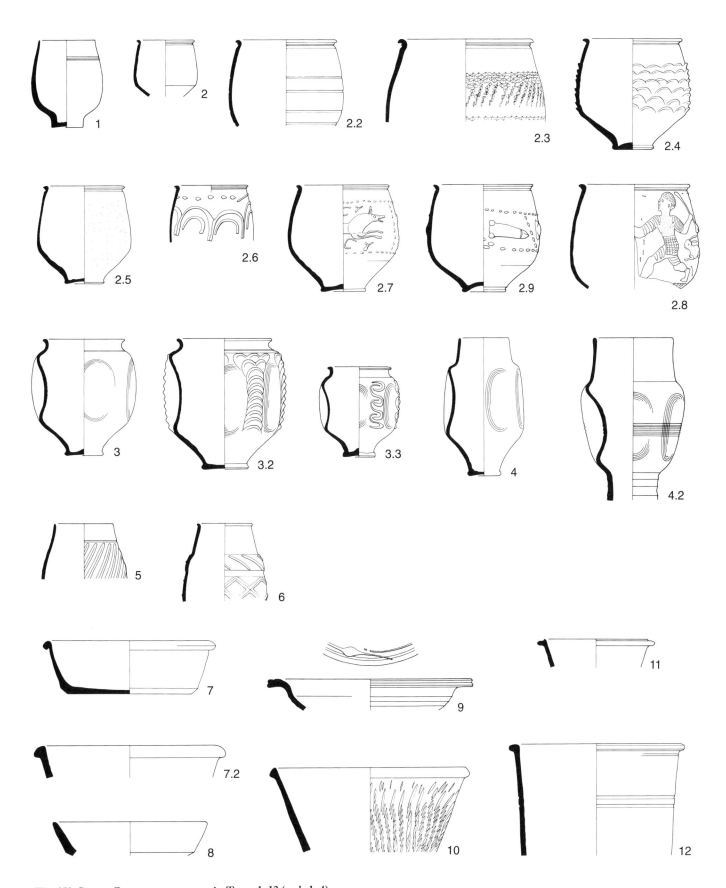

Fig. 151 Stonea Grange: pottery vessels, Types 1–12 (scale 1:4).

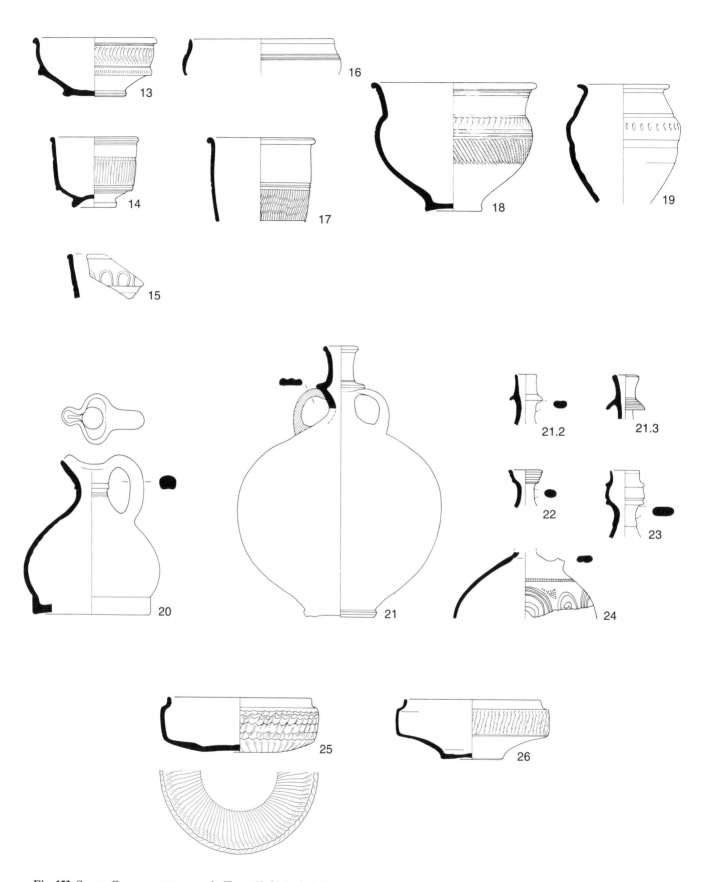

Fig. 152 Stonea Grange: pottery vessels, Types 13–26 (scale 1:4).

Type 2.7 As Type 2, with underslip barbotine hunting scene. (*NV Guide* no. 26). AGL. Phase III. Cf. the discussion by Johns, p. 483, no. 12.

Type 2.8 As Type 2, with underslip barbotine figured scene (*NV Guide* no. 28). KB. Phase III. Cf. the discussion by Johns, p. 479, no. 3.

Type 2.9 As Type 2, with underslip barbotine phalli. J1, layer 1. Phase IV. Cf. the discussion by Johns, p. 481, no. 6.

All the examples of this type in the *NV Guide* and at Chesterton seem to belong to the late 2nd to early 3rd century AD, and the different types of decoration appear to be more or less contemporaneous.

Type 3 Indented beaker with everted rim (*NV Guide* no. 40). AEE. Phase III.

Type 3.2 As Type 3, with underslip barbotine applied scales. P10, layer 1. Phase III.

Type 3.3 As Type 3, with underslip barbotine scrolls (*NV Guide* no. 36). FV. Phase IV/V.

This type is dated to the late 2nd to early 3rd century AD in the *NV Guide* and at Chesterton.

Type 4 Indented beaker with funnel-neck (*NV Guide* nos 42 and 43). KE. Phase IV.

Type 4.2 As Type 4, with a taller neck and foot and grooved decoration. BKO. Phase III.

This type generally belongs to the mid to late 3rd century AD from the dating of the *NV Guide* and at Chesterton. The elongated version is probably slightly later in date, i.e. late 3rd.

Type 5 Beaker with white overslip decoration. CDB. Phase IV.

A close parallel for this type at Chesterton is dated to the mid 3rd century AD, and it was from this period that overslip barbotine decoration became common.

Type 6 Beaker with white overslip barbotine decoration. AFN. Phase III/IV.

Type 6.2 As Type 6, but with stylised floral overslip white decoration (not illustrated).

There is no very close parallel for this form in the *NV Guide* but it seems to be related to the 'pentice-moulded' beakers (nos 55–7) which are dated to the 4th century AD. The nearest parallels at Chesterton are also late 3rd to 4th century.

DISHES

Type 7 Pie-dish with sloping sides. BA. Phase IV.

This type does not appear in the *NV Guide* but is dated to the later 2nd or 3rd century AD at Chesterton. The same form in NVGW (*NV Guide* nos 17 and 18) is dated to the 2nd or 3rd century, so that the same form must have been produced at the same period in the two different fabrics.

Type 7.2 Pie-dish. J1, layer 1. Phase IV.

This heavier and thicker version of Type 7 is dated at Chesterton to the late 3rd or early 4th century AD.

Type 8 Plain-rimmed dish with sloping sides. H8, layer 3. Phase IV.

This type does not appear in the *NV Guide*, but at Chesterton the closest parallels are dated to the later 2nd century AD.

Type 9 Dish, imitation of samian form Dr 36. BKO. Phase III.

This type is dated by the *NV Guide* (no. 81) to the late 3rd to mid 4th century AD, although at Chesterton it seems to be slightly earlier, i.e. early to mid 3rd century.

BOWLS

Type 10 A deeper version of Type 8, with rouletted decoration. LT. Phase III.

There is no direct parallel for this type in the *NV Guide*, but a similar vessel at Chesterton, but without the rouletting, is dated to the late 3rd to early 4th century AD.

Type 11 Flanged bowl. CMT. Phase IV.

Type 11.2 Flanged bowl with painted decoration on the rim (not illustrated).

This type is dated to the 4th century AD both in the *NV Guide* (no. 79) and at Chesterton.

Type 11.3 The larger version. Although more common on the site, the sherds are too small to merit illustration.

Type 12 Deep, straight-sided bowl with rim. DOX. Phase III.

This type has no parallel in the *NV Guide*, but a similar vessel at Chesterton is dated to the second half of the 2nd century AD.

CUPS

Type 13 Imitation samian cup. ABS. Phase IV.

Type 14 Imitation samian cup. G4, layer 4. Phase III.

Type 15 Imitation samian cup. ACE. Phase III/IV.

The dating of these three types is very problematic, since close parallels occur neither in the *NV Guide* nor at Chesterton. However, other imitations of the samian forms in this fabric are dated in the *NV Guide* (nos 80–4), and at Chesterton, on the whole, to the 4th century AD.

Type 16 Small bowl or cup. AZ. Phase III onwards.

This type does not appear in the *NV Guide* or at Chesterton, but may well be an early version of the Castor box (Type 25/26), although it lacks the rouletted decoration. If this is the case, this type probably dates to the later 2nd century AD.

Type 17 Deep cup or bowl with rouletted decoration. CGH. Phase III.

This seems to be of the same general type as Type 12, although the rim here is more rounded and there is rouletting on the lower half of the body. It should therefore be a later 2nd century AD type, as the context implies.

JARS

Type 18   Wide-mouthed jar or bowl with rouletted decoration. FL. Phase IV/V.

This type, although not rouletted, is dated in the *NV Guide* (no. 77) and at Chesterton, to the 4th century AD.

Type 19   Jar with slashed cordon. DBH. Phase III.

This type appears much more frequently in its NVGW version. Although there is no parallel in this fabric either at Chesterton or in the *NV Guide*, the NVGW versions (*NV Guide* no. 2) are dated to the 2nd century AD in both cases. It is possible, as seems to be the case with some NV forms, that the colour-coated version is produced in the 3rd or 4th century after the grey ware version has died out. With this type, however, it would seem more likely that the NVGW and NVCC versions are contemporaneous.

FLAGONS

Type 20   Pinched-neck flagon with flat base and single handle. AFN. Phase III/IV.

A close parallel for this vessel is *NV Guide* no. 64, dated to the 4th century AD, but at Chesterton, this type of pinched-neck has been dated to the 3rd century, which is the date given in the *NV Guide* for the NVGW version of this form (*NV Guide* no. 14). Where this type has been used here as the dating criterion for a given context, the earlier date has been accepted, but it is worth noting that it may in fact, be later.

Type 21   Disc-necked flagon, double-handled. GX, JX, KF. Residual in Phase IV/V.

The same problem arises with this type as with Type 20, in that the *NV Guide* dates it to the 4th century AD (no. 67) whereas at Chesterton the type seems to be 3rd century.

Type 21.2 (CDC. Phase III/IV) and 21.3 (BKO. Phase III) are versions of the disc-necked type and are therefore probably of the same date.

Type 22   Ring-necked flagon. H7, layer 1. Phase IV.

A similar form at Chesterton is dated to the 3rd century AD.

Type 23   Flagon neck. BHB. Phase III/IV.

There is no parallel for this form either at Chesterton or in the *NV Guide*, but it may be generally related to the disc-necked type.

Type 24   Flagon with white overslip barbotine decoration. DRB. Phase IV.

Although the rim form of this example is unknown, the narrowness of the neck makes it likely that it was a disc-neck or something similar. The white overslip decoration, by analogy with similar vessels at Chesterton and in the *NV Guide*, would date it to the late 3rd or early 4th century AD.

CASTOR BOXES

Some examples of this form may date to earlier or later periods; but in general the smallest versions are late 2nd to early 3rd century AD, and the larger ones go into the 4th century. However, these two Castor boxes have been illustrated as examples of the general type.

Type 25   Castor box with flat base. EAS. Phase III/IV.

This version without a foot is not paralleled in the *NV Guide*, but at Chesterton a similar vessel is dated to the mid to late 3rd century AD.

Type 26   Castor box with foot. AGO. Phase IV.

A larger version of this form is dated in the *NV Guide* (no. 89) to the 4th century, but being smaller it may be a little earlier. This would fit in with a parallel from Chesterton, which is dated to the mid to late 3rd century AD.

Nene Valley Grey ware (NVGW)   (Figs 153–4)

JARS

Type 27   Jar with slashed cordon. BEP. Phase IV.

This type of jar is dated in the *NV Guide* (no. 2) and at Chesterton to the 2nd century AD. (Cf. type 19 for the NVCC version)

Type 27.2 Jar with plain cordon. AFR. Phase III.

This version of Type 27, with the undecorated cordon, must be of the same date.

Type 28   Wide-mouthed bowl or jar, with neck. A, 32. Phase III.

According to the *NV Guide* this type (no. 11) is basically 3rd century AD, although it seems from Chesterton that it begins in the late 2nd century.

Type 28.2 Smaller version of Type 28 and presumably of similar date. ADM. Phase III/IV.

Type 29   Wide-mouthed bowl or jar without neck, with rouletted decoration on shoulder. P10, layer 1. Phase III.

Type 29.2 Variation of Type 29. CPG. Phase IV.

This neckless version of Type 28 seems from parallels at Chesterton to be slightly later and to belong entirely to the 3rd century AD.

Type 30   Wide-mouthed, neckless jar, with flanged rim and rouletted decoration on the shoulder. P10, layer 1. Phase III.

This form does not appear in the *NV Guide* but a close parallel at Chesterton is dated to the early 2nd century AD.

Type 31   Large jar with hooked rim and rouletted decoration on the shoulder. BIX. Phase III.

Similar vessels occur at Chesterton although smaller in size, and these are dated to the late 2nd to 3rd century AD.

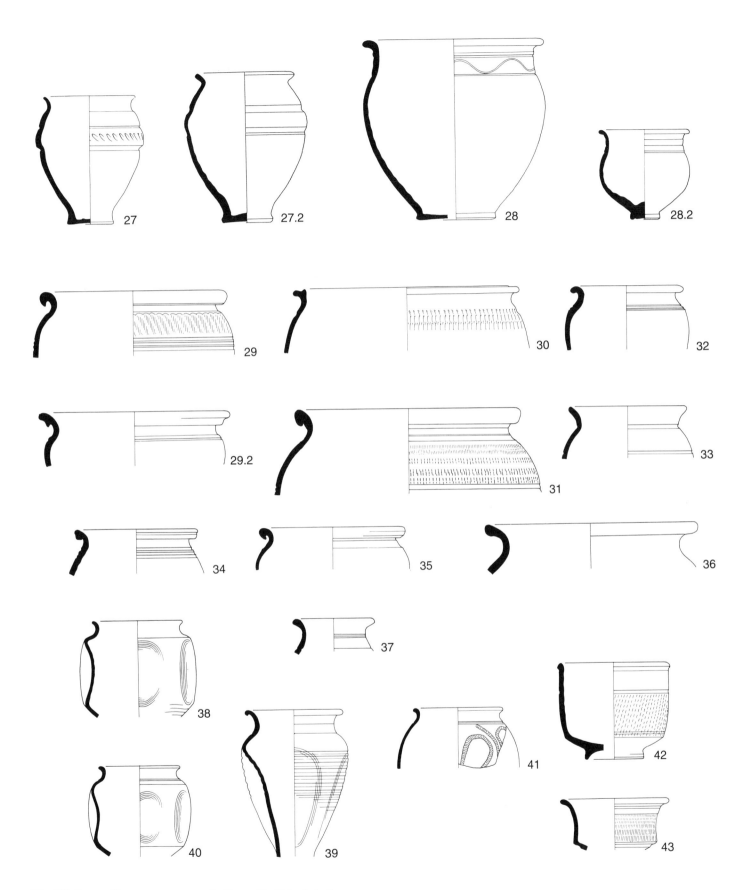

Fig. 153 Stonea Grange: pottery vessels, Types 27–43 (scale 1 : 4).

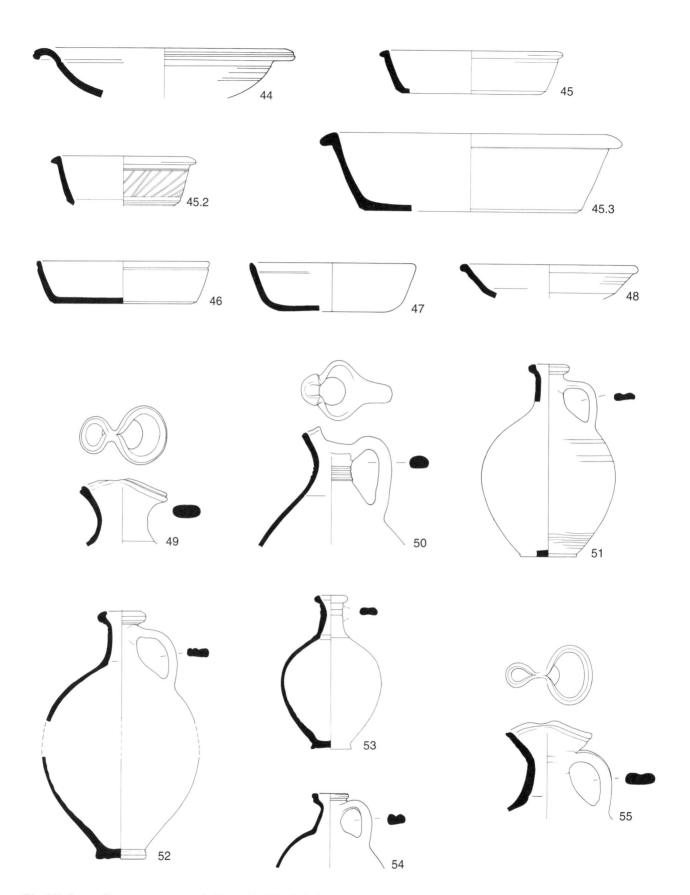

Fig. 154 Stonea Grange: pottery vessels, Types 44–55 (scale 1:4).

Type 32   Small jar with everted rim and grooves on shoulder. SY. Phase III/IV.

This type at Chesterton is dated to the later 2nd to 3rd century AD.

Type 33   Small jar with everted rim. CDC. Phase III/IV.

A similar vessel at Chesterton is dated to the 2nd half of the 2nd to 3rd century AD.

Type 34   Jar with grooved rim. AGN. Phase III/IV.

This sort of form is more commonly seen in NVSC ware, or one of the other buff wares, and in both fabrics seems to date to the late 2nd century AD.

Type 35   Jar with hooked rim. CCV. Phase IV.

A close parallel to this form cannot be found in the *NV Guide* but vessels of the same general type at Chesterton are dated to the late 2nd to 3rd century AD.

Type 36   Large jar with everted rim. BHP. Phase III/IV.

The nearest parallels to this rim form are to be found among the other grey wares at Chesterton, where they belong to the late 2nd or 3rd century AD.

Type 37   Narrow-mouthed jar. CMT. Phase IV.

Similar vessels at Chesterton are generally dated to the 3rd century AD.

BEAKERS

Type 38   Indented beaker with everted rim. BIZ. Phase IV.

This is a NVGW version of Type 3 NVCC, and may well be contemporaneous, i.e. late 2nd to 3rd century AD.

Type 39   Large indented beaker with everted rim and grooves on the body. BFC. Phase IV.

The NVCC version of this type in the *NV Guide* (no. 41) is dated to the early 3rd century AD, and this type may be of the same date, although it probably lasts for a good deal of the 3rd century.

Type 40   Indented beaker with horizontal cordons. BCO. Phase IV.

Parallels for this vessel are hard to find; a similar vessel with the horizontal folds can be found at Chesterton in the late 2nd to 3rd century, which also seems to fit in with the dates of the more conventional indented beakers.

Type 41   Beaker with roller-stamped decoration. DWL. Phase III.

This type is probably an imitation of a closed samian form such as Déchelette 72, and so probably dates, like the other NVGW imitations of samian forms (Types 42 and 43), to the late 2nd to early 3rd century AD.

Type 42   Small cup with rouletted decoration; imitation samian Dr 30, (?). P10, layer 1. Phase III.

Type 43   Small cup with rouletted decoration, imitation samian Dr 33, (?). AGK. Phase IV.

The samian imitations in NVGW at Chesterton are dated to the late 2nd to early 3rd century AD.

DISHES

Type 44   Shallow dish, imitation of samian form Dr 36. CCV. Phase IV.

Parallels for this type at Chesterton and in the *NV Guide* (no. 15) date to the late 2nd to 3rd century AD.

Type 45   Pie-dish. NX. Phase III/IV. (*NV Guide* no. 18).
Type 45.2 As 45 with burnished line decoration. BA. Phase IV.
Type 45.3 Much larger and heavier version of Type 45. (*NV Guide* no. 17). AGK. Phase IV.

This is one of the most common types found on the site and is dated both by the *NV Guide* and at Chesterton to the mid 2nd to late 3rd century AD. The fact that this form has such a long life-span probably accounts for its ubiquity. Rim forms do vary considerably, but how this relates to their chronology is difficult to establish.

Type 46   Dog-dish with grooved rim. SP. Phase IV.

This type is dated in the *NV Guide* (no. 20) to the 2nd and 3rd centuries AD, and more precisely at Chesterton to the later 2nd to 3rd century.

Type 47   Dog-dish with plain rim. CCV. Phase IV.

This type is dated in the *NV Guide* (no. 19) to the 2nd and 3rd centuries AD, and more precisely at Chesterton to the 3rd century.

Like Type 45, Types 46 and 47 are long-lived and, probably for this reason, occur very frequently on the site.

Type 48   Dish or bowl, imitation of samian form Dr 31. AGN. Phase III/IV.

This appears in the *NV Guide* as no. 16, dated to the later 2nd to 3rd century AD.

FLAGONS

Type 49   Pinched neck flagon. DWL. Phase III.

NV Guide no. 14, dated to the 3rd century AD.

Type 50   Pinched-neck flagon. BHP. Phase III/IV.

This is similar to Type 49 although a closer parallel can be seen in NVCC types. The date, however, is probably also the 3rd century AD.

Nene Valley Self-coloured ware (NVSC)   (Figs 154–5)

FLAGONS

Type 51   Flagon. BA. Phase IV.

Type 52   Flagon. DOO. Residual in Phase IV.

Type 53   Flagon. BA. Phase IV.

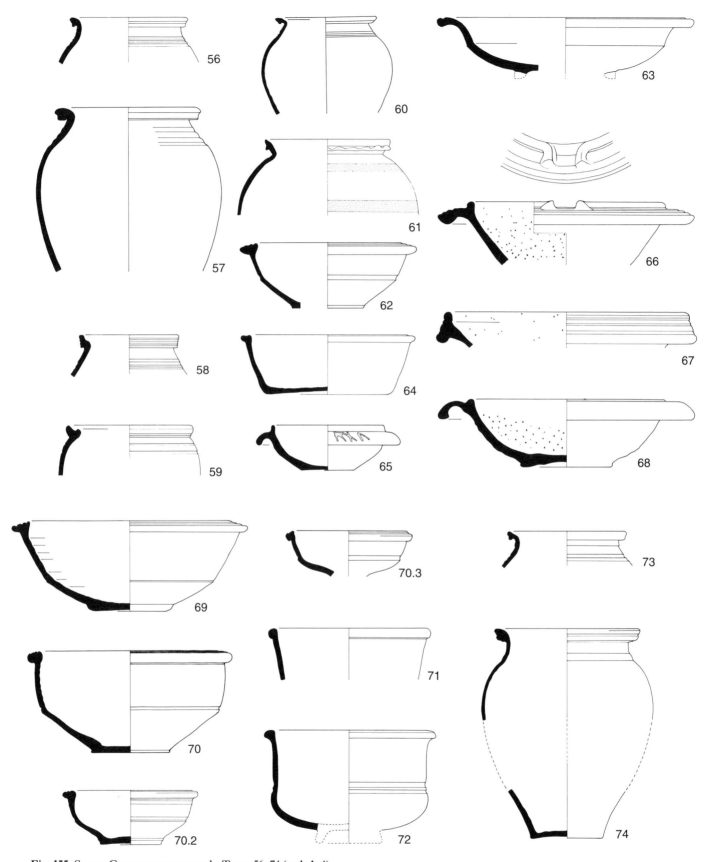

Fig. 155 Stonea Grange: pottery vessels, Types 56–74 (scale 1:4).

Type 54 Flagon. BA. Phase IV.

The main differences between these vessels are the variations in the rim forms; but from parallels at Chesterton they can all be dated to the second half of the 2nd century AD.

Type 55 Pinched-neck flagon. DVZ. Phase III.

This is the NVSC version of Types 20 (NVCC) and 49 (NVGW). If the NVGW version of the 3rd century AD was superseded by the NVCC version in the later 3rd to 4th century, then this one may be the earliest of the three. It seems likely that this type, like most of the NVSC vessels, dates to the second half of the 2nd century. The body shape of these flagons is fairly basic and the pinched neck is a very simple means of forming a spout. This is altogether a larger and more basic sort of vessel than, for instance Types 51 to 54 – more of a jug and less of a flask, and perhaps kitchen rather than tableware.

JARS

Type 56 Jar with bifid rim. ACC. Phase III.

Type 57 Large jar with grooved rim. BKT. Phase IV.

Type 58 Jar with multi-grooved rim. AGL. Phase III.

Type 59 Jar with lid-seating. DSS. Phase III/IV.

Type 60 Jar with fine bifid rim. AFR. Phase III.

Type 61 Jar with frilled decoration on rim. DRZ. Phase III.

All these jars except Type 61 have late 2nd century AD parallels at Chesterton. It is likely that Type 61 is of a similar date.

Type 62 Carinated bowl with reeded rim. J4, layer 7. Phase III.

Type 63 Large carinated bowl with reeded rim and raised foot. CKB. Phase III.

These reeded-rim bowls are common on many Fenland sites, and similar vessels are dated to the late 2nd century AD at Chesterton.

Type 64 Bowl with slight flange on rim. ACE. Phase III/IV.

Parallels for this type are harder to find, but it may well be of a similar date to Types 62 and 63.

Type 65 Small flanged bowl with orange or brown painted decoration on the rim. SV. Phase IV.

In the *NV Guide* (no. 99) this type is dated to the 2nd to 4th century AD, but at Chesterton it is dated to the later 2nd to mid 3rd century.

MORTARIA

Type 66 Mortarium with reeded rim and black ironstone grits. CMS. Phase IV. (*NV Guide* no. 103).

Type 67 Mortarium with upright reeded rim and black ironstone grits. ABS. Phase IV.

Type 68 Mortarium with plain rim and black ironstone grits. BA. Phase IV. (*NV Guide* no. 101).

Little is known of the date of these NV mortaria – no date is offered for them in the *NV Guide*, and no examples seem to have occurred at Chesterton.

Gritty buff ware   (Fig. 155)

This is a distinctive, although not very common, fabric which has a grey core with buff or cream surfaces. It contains abundant quartz grits and is fired very hard, which gives it a harsh surface texture which distinguishes it from the other buff fabrics which are common in the Roman Fenland. The forms which most often occur in this fabric are reeded-rim bowls and bifid rimmed jars. At Chesterton, these forms seem to belong to the second half of the second century AD, although at Verulamium (Frere 1972, Fig. 106) and in the north of England (Gillam 1970, Types 214–17), they begin to appear as early as the later first century AD.

BOWLS

Type 69 Carinated bowl with reeded rim. NX. Phase III/IV. Cf. Type 62.

Type 70 Carinated bowl with reeded rim and foot. BA Phase IV. Cf. Type 63.

Type 70.2 Smaller version of Type 70. DOO. Residual in Phase IV.

Type 70.3 As 70.2, with variation of rim form. G4, layer 8. Phase III.

Like Types 62 and 63 (above) these vessels are probably later 2nd century AD in date.

Type 71 Deep bowl with bead rim. PY. Phase IV.

There are no parallels for this Type at Chesterton or in the *NV Guide*, but it probably has a similar date to Types 69 and 70, i.e. later 2nd century AD.

Type 72 Deep bowl with foot-ring. P10, layer 1. Phase III.

Of the same general type as *NV Guide* no. 100 which is dated to the 2nd century AD. Type 71 may be of similar date.

JARS

Type 73 Jar with bifid rim. AZ. Phase III onwards. Cf. Type 56, dated later 2nd century AD.

Type 74 Large jar with bifid rim. CS. Phase III. Cf. Type 57, dated later 2nd century AD.

Shell-gritted ware   (Figs 156–7)

It seems likely that much of the shell-gritted ware, which is so common on Fenland sites, was actually produced in the Nene Valley although this has not been proven as yet. Shell-gritted vessel types are notoriously difficult to date and the

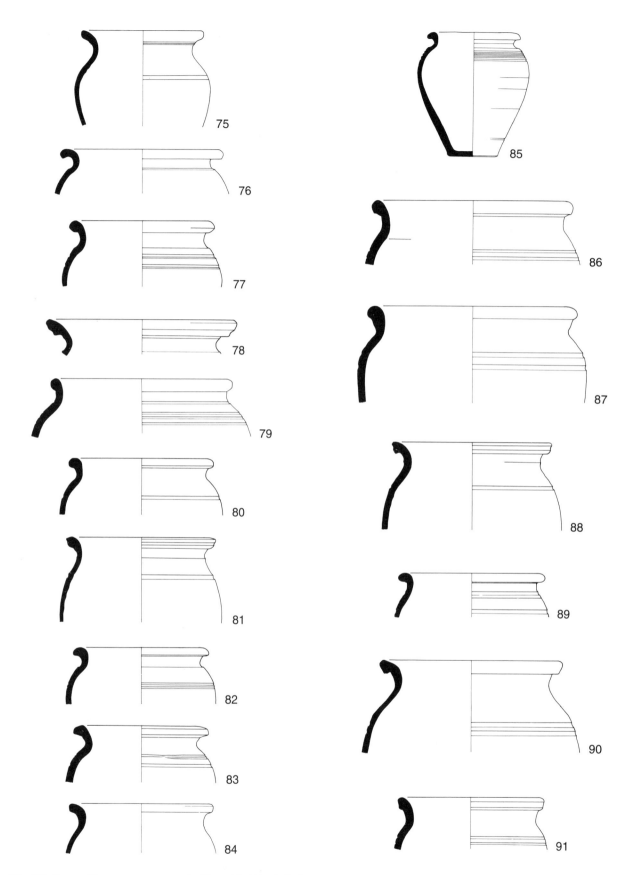

Fig. 156 Stonea Grange: pottery vessels, Types 75–91(scale 1:4).

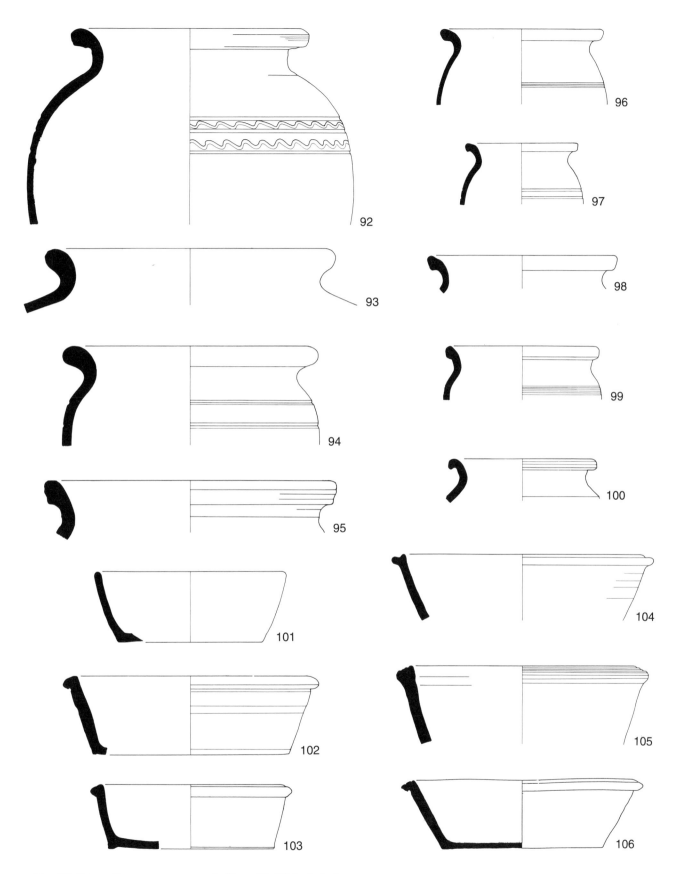

Fig. 157 Stonea Grange: pottery vessels, Types 92–106 (scale 1:4).

ware as a whole seems to span the entire Roman period. Some attempt has been made here to illustrate the more common types found on the site but these types have not been used as dating evidence for features unless there is absolutely no alternative, since their dating seems so uncertain. The types here have been arranged in three groups, as far as possible corresponding to the dating of reasonable parallels at Chesterton.

MID TO LATE SECOND CENTURY AD

Type 75, KE. Phase IV; Type 76, SP. Phase IV; Type 77, NJ. Phase IV; Type 78, ABS. Phase IV; Type 79, AAV. Phase IV; Type 80, BKT. Phase IV; Type 81, BKO. Phase III; Type 82, BIZ. Phase IV; Type 83, BIZ. Phase IV; Type 84, CCV. Phase IV; Type 85, ADY. Phase III.

THIRD CENTURY AD

Type 86, AZ. Phase III onwards; Type 87, AGO. Phase IV; Type 88, BKO. Phase III; Type 89, CML. Phase III/IV; Type 90, CMS. Phase IV; Type 91, AGN. Phase III/IV.

LATE THIRD TO FOURTH CENTURY AD

Type 96, KE. Phase IV; Type 97, CCV. Phase IV; Type 98, AZ. Phase III onwards; Type 99, AZ. Phase III onwards; Type 100, ACE. Phase III/IV.

The very large storage jars are even harder to date than the smaller cooking pots, but where a dated parallel occurs at Chesterton, it has been quoted.

Type 92   CS. Phase III. Chesterton 2nd century AD.

Type 93   BIZ. Phase IV. Chesterton 2nd century AD.

Type 94   CCV. Phase IV.

Type 95   BIN. Phase IV.

DISHES AND BOWLS

None of the types here have close parallels at Chesterton, apart from Type 101 which is probably 3rd century AD.

Type 101   Dog-dish. MS. Phase ?III/?IV.

Type 102   Large pie-dish. BIZ. Phase IV.

Type 103   Dish with slight flange. CIB. Phase III.

Type 104   Flanged bowl. BCO. Phase IV.

Type 105   Bowl with grooved or reeded rim. BIZ. Phase IV.

Type 106   Bowl with grooved rim. AFN. Phase III/IV.

Horningsea ware   (Fig. 158)

The kilns at Horningsea (Walker 1912) produced the very large grey ware storage jars with the characteristic combed

decoration and wide everted rims, which are also found on most Fenland sites of the Roman period. The date of these kilns was estimated by the excavator to start in the first century AD and to go on into the fifth, although it is not always clear on what evidence these estimates were based. On Nene Valley sites these vessels seem to occur mainly in third century contexts (information from J. R. Perrin), and at Stonea they are normally found in contexts which probably belong to the third century. It seems likely, therefore, that while the Horningsea kilns may have been producing pottery as early as the 1st century, it was not being traded further afield on any significant scale until the early third century. Although the rim forms of these jars do not vary a great deal, a selection of them has been illustrated here.

Type 107, AEQ. Phase III; Type 108, P10 layer 1. Phase III; Type 109, BIZ. Phase IV; Type 110, ACE. Phase III/IV; Type 111, PY. Phase IV; Type 112, LT. Phase III; Type 113, SP. Phase IV; Type 114, AAV. Phase IV.

GROUPS   (Figs 159–73)

The following groups, selected as key or typical, have been fully discussed and illustrated. Abbreviated summaries of the pottery groups from other contexts are to be found within the relevant context descriptions elsewhere in the report.

Pits and wells   (Figs 159–62)

Well 336   Phase III (Fig. 159)

SP/359   Upper layers. Date: late 3rd/4th century AD.

1 Dish: NVCC: Imitation of samian Dr 36, White fabric with brown colour-coat. Type 9.
2 Dish: NVGW. Type 45.
3 Dish: NVGW. Variation of Type 45.
4 Dish: NVGW. Type 46.
5 Dish: NVGW. Type 47.
6 Dish: NVGW. Type 47.
7 Flanged bowl: NVSC, with orange painted decoration on flange. Type 65.
8 Large jar: Horningsea ware. Type 107.
9 Large jar: Horningsea ware. Type 109.
10 Reeded-rim bowl: sandy buff fabric with pale yellowish slip. Cf. Type 69.
11 Jar: pale orange fabric with pale brownish slip. Cf. Type 74.
12 Jar: dark grey shell-gritted fabric. Type 76.

The upper layers of this feature are dated by the presence of no. 1 and of a sherd of NVCC jar or Castor box of late 3rd to 4th century AD date. The NVGW dishes are long-lived types which may be as late as the late 3rd century, as are the Horningsea jars. Numbers 7, 10 and 11, however, are contemporary with the main fill of the well and are, therefore, residual in this context.

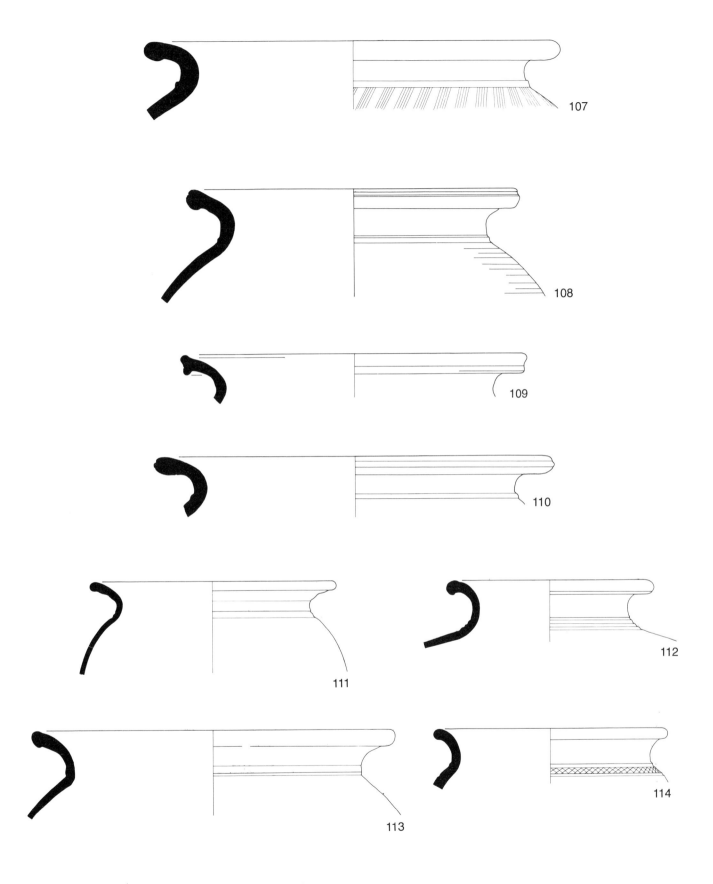

Fig. 158 Stonea Grange: pottery vessels, Types 107–14 (scale 1 : 4).

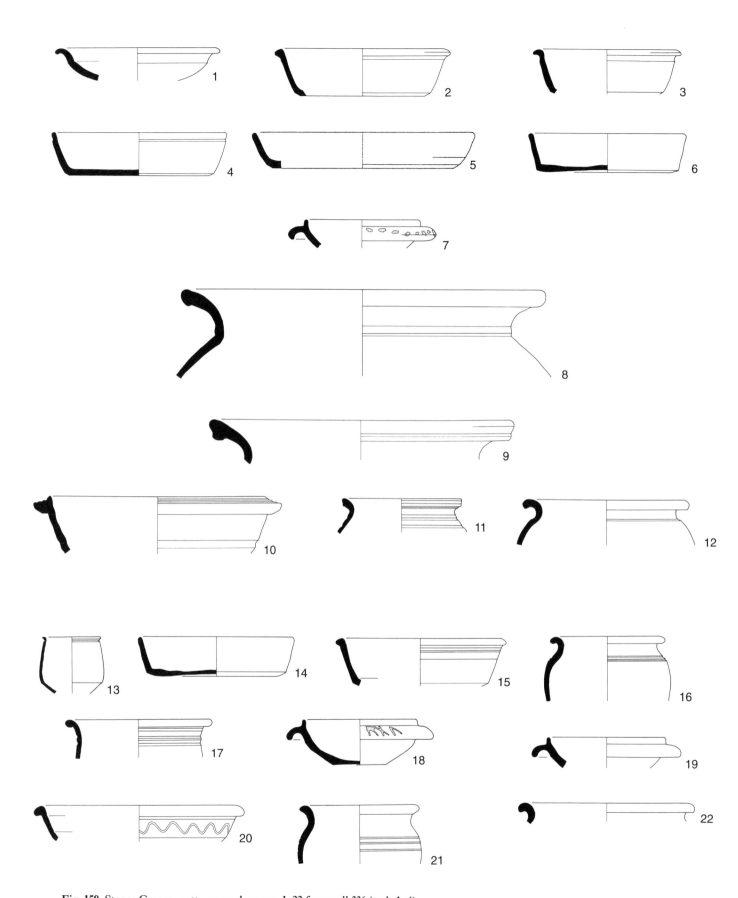

Fig. 159 Stonea Grange: pottery vessel groups, 1–22 from well 336 (scale 1 : 4).

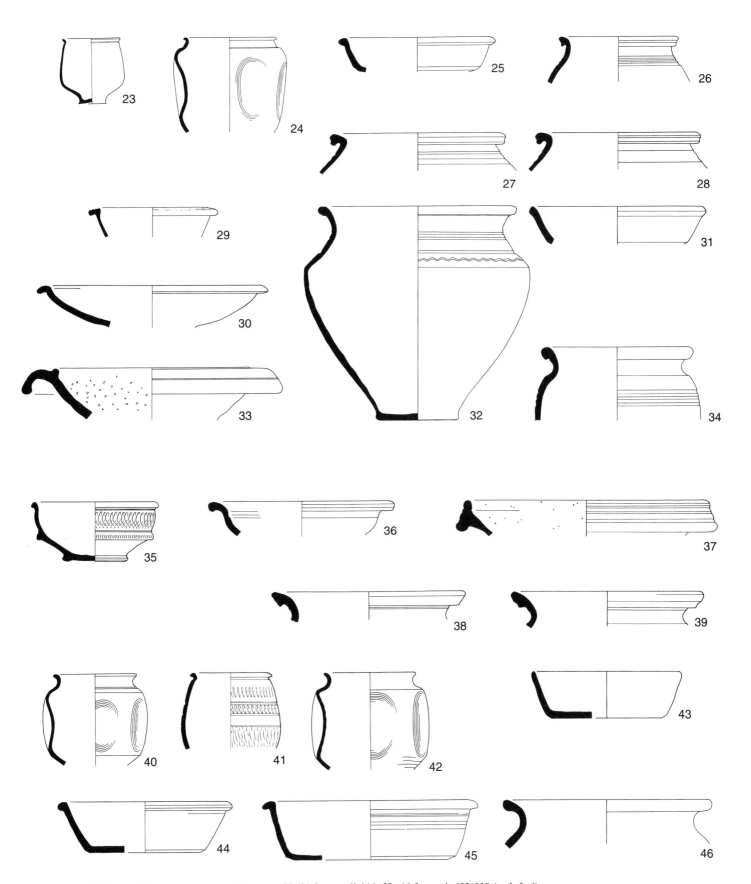

Fig. 160 Stonea Grange: pottery vessel groups, 23–34 from well 446, 35–46 from pit 483/918 (scale 1:4).

SY/367 Fill of well. Date: late 2nd/3rd century AD.

13 Beaker: NVCC, white fabric with pale brown colour-coat. Type 2.
14 Dish: NVGW. Type 47.
15 Dish: NVGW. Type 45/45.3.
16 Jar: NVGW. Type 32.
17 Wide-mouthed jar: NVGW. Type 28.
18 Flanged bowl: NVSC with orange painted decoration on flange. Type 65.
19 Flanged bowl: NVSC with traces of orange painted decoration on the flange. Type 65.
20 Dish: grey fabric with burnished line on exterior. Cf. Type 45.
21 Jar: reddish shell-gritted fabric with reduced patches.
22 Jar: Dark grey shell-gritted fabric.

The vessels from the fill of the well are of a consistently late 2nd/3rd century AD date, given that the NVGW dishes are of types which began to be produced during this period.

Well 446 Phase III (Fig. 160)

The upper layer of this well (AAE/446) is dated to the mid 3rd to 5th century, by the presence of an Oxford ware mortarium of Young Type W. C. 7.

23 Miniature beaker: NVCC, white fabric with dark brown colour-coat. Type 2.
24 Indented beaker: grey fabric with orange surfaces and dark brown colour-coat. Probably produced at Colchester. Cf. Type 3.
25 Dish: NVGW. Type 45.
26 Jar: NVSC, buff fabric with grey-buff slip. Type 56.
27 Jar: gritty buff fabric. Type 74.
28 Jar: gritty buff fabric. Type 74.
29 Reeded-rim bowl: gritty buff fabric. Type 69.
30 Dish: fine, micaceous dark grey fabric. Imitation London ware.
31 Dish: sandy grey fabric with orange-brown colour-coat.
32 Wide-mouthed jar: fine sandy grey fabric with darker surfaces.
33 Mortarium: soft, slightly coarse whitish fabric with ironstone inclusions; only impressions of the gritting remain. Cf. Type 68.
34 Jar: dark grey shell-gritted fabric.

The vessels from the layers which make up the main fill of this well have been dealt with as a group as they appear to be consistently late 2nd/3rd century AD.

Pit 483/918 Phase III/IV (Figs 160–1)

ABS/483 Upper layers.

35 Bowl/cup: NVCC, grey fabric with dark grey colour-coat. Type 13.
36 Dish: NVCC, pale orange fabric with brown colour-coat. Cf. Type 9, although a closer parallel at Chesterton is late 3rd century AD.
37 Mortarium: ?NVSC, fine buff fabric with ironstone gritting. Type 67.
38 Jar: brown shell-gritted fabric.
39 Jar: dark grey shell-gritted fabric. Cf. Type 98 although closer parallels at Chesterton are dated to the 4th century.

In addition, this layer contained sherds of NVCC flagons (Type 20/21) and beakers which are usually late 3rd/4th century AD in date. Thus, a late 3rd/4th century date for these upper layers seems likely.

Fill of pit

40 Indented beaker: NVCC, white fabric with brown colour-coat. Type 3.
41 Beaker: NVCC, white fabric with dark brown colour-coat and rouletted decoration. Cf. Types 2.2/2.3.
42 Indented beaker: NVGW. Type 38.
43 Dish: NVGW. Type 47.
44 Dish: NVGW. Type 45.3.
45 Dish: NVGW. Type 45.3.
46 Wide-mouthed jar: coarse NVGW. Type 36.
47 Jar: NVGW.
48 Pinched-neck flagon: NVGW. Type 50.
49 Flanged bowl: sandy orange fabric with grey core and white slip on exterior.
50 Flanged bowl: sandy orange fabric with grey core and white slip on exterior.
51 Bowl: fine dark grey fabric. Imitation London ware.
52 Large jar: Horningsea ware. Type 109.
53 Mortarium: gritty cream fabric, blackened in places. Cf. Type 68.
54 Jar: fine grey fabric, with white inclusions. Cf. Type 28.
55 Jar: fine hard, grey fabric.
56 Jar: sandy grey fabric with paler grey surfaces.
57 Bowl with grooved rim: red-brown shell-gritted fabric with dark grey exterior. Type 106.
58 Bowl with grooved rim: brown shell-gritted fabric with orange interior surfaces. Type 106.
59 Jar: buff shell-gritted fabric with dark grey exterior. Cf. Type 89.
60 Jar: brown shell-gritted fabric with dark grey surfaces. Type 83.
61 Jar: red-brown shell-gritted fabric, blackened on rim. Cf. Type 88.
62 Jar: red-brown shell-gritted fabric with dark grey surfaces.
63 Bowl: dark grey shell-gritted fabric with brown interior surfaces. Cf. Type 102.
64 Jar: dark grey shell-gritted fabric with brown interior surfaces. Cf. Type 81.
65 Jar: orange shell-gritted fabric. Type 82.
66 Jar: orange shell-gritted fabric with dark grey exterior surfaces.
67 Storage jar: red-brown shell-gritted fabric with dark grey core. Type 93.
68 Storage jar: pale red-brown shell-gritted fabric. Type 95.

In addition to the vessels illustrated, the fill of the pit also included sherds from NVCC flagons (Types 20/21) and Castor boxes (Types 25/26) and the majority of the pottery is therefore 3rd century AD. There are some vessels, however, such as nos 40, 41 and possibly 49 and 50, which may be earlier in date and therefore residual.

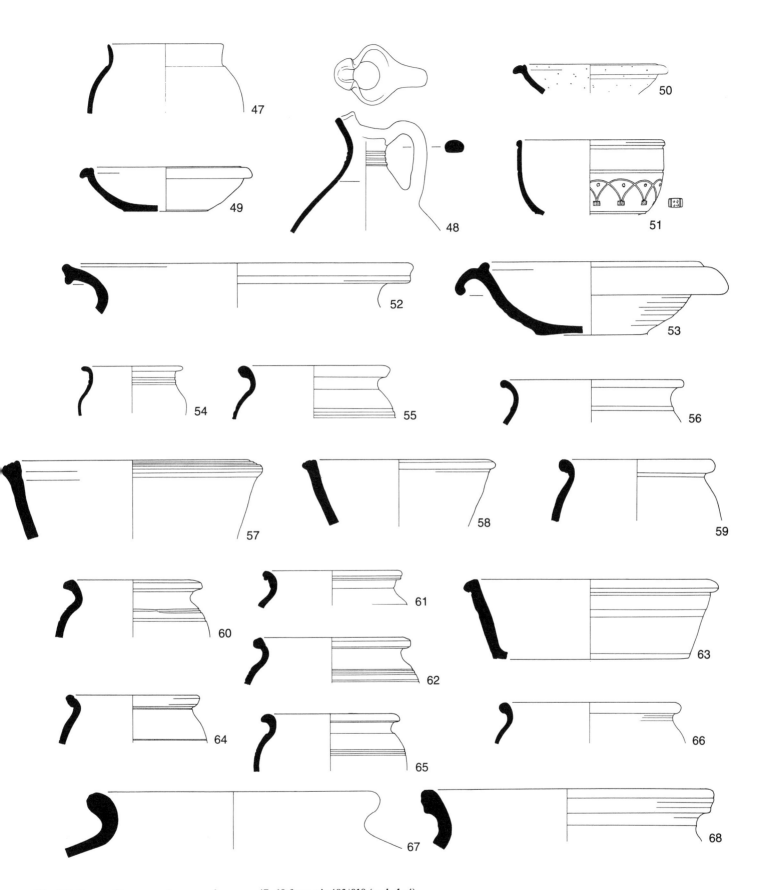

Fig. 161 Stonea Grange: pottery vessel groups, 47–68 from pit 483/918 (scale 1:4).

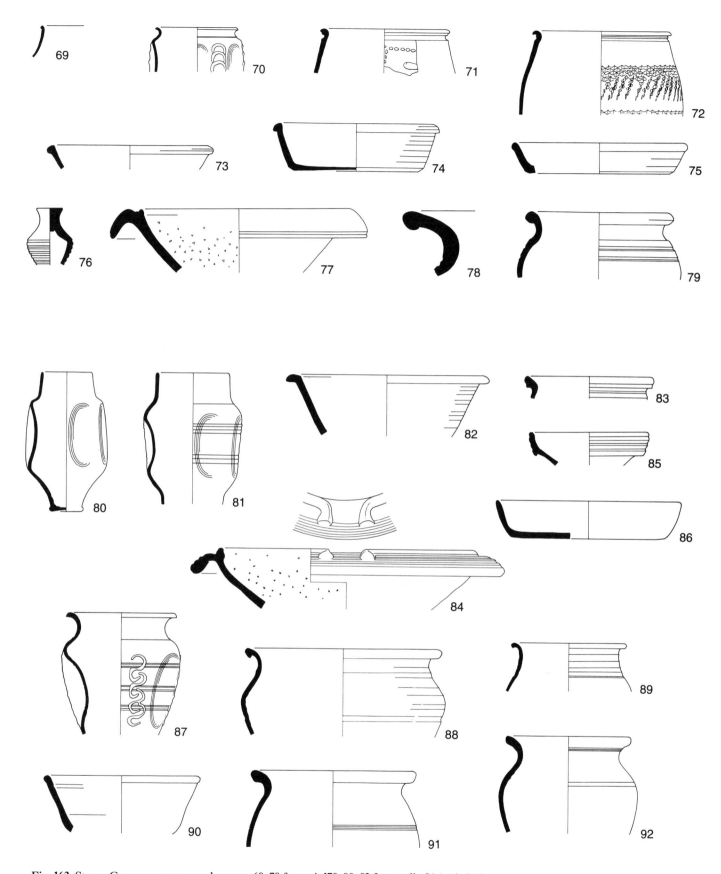

Fig. 162 Stonea Grange: pottery vessel groups, 69–79 from pit 170, 80–92 from gully 54 (scale 1:4).

Pit 170   Phase III, later (Fig. 162)

69 Beaker: fine, soft orange fabric with glossy dark brown colour-coat. Probably imported from Central Gaul.
70 Indented beaker: NVCC, white fabric with dark brown colour-coat and underslip barbotine applied scales. Type 3.2.
71 Beaker: NVCC, pale orange fabric with pale brown colour-coat and underslip barbotine decoration. Cf. Type 2.7/2.8/2.9.
72 Beaker: NVCC, off-white fabric with dark brown colour-coat and rouletted decoration. Type 2.3.
73 Dish: NVGW. Type 45.
74 Dish: NVGW. Type 45.
75 Dish: NVGW.
76 Unguent jar: fine off-white fabric with reduced patches and traces of cream slip.
77 Mortarium: soft fine buff fabric with red ironstone inclusions and mixed grits.
78 Large jar: Horningsea ware. Type 107.
79 Jar: brownish shell-gritted fabric with reduced patches. Type 77.

Most of the pottery from the fill of the pit is of 3rd or 4th century AD date, although the vessels illustrated here are only from the third and fourth layers. There is also a certain amount of residual late 2nd century material, which probably includes nos 70 and 71.

Ditches and gullies   (Figs 162–70)

Gully 54   Phase IV (Fig. 162)

80 Indented beaker: NVCC, white fabric with dark brown colour-coat. Type 4.
81 Indented beaker: fine, soft orange fabric with traces of orange colour-coat. ?NVCC. Type 4.2
82 Bowl: NVGW. Type 45.3.
83 Jar: fine pale orange fabric with pale grey-brown slip. ?NVSC. Type 57.
84 Mortarium: NVSC, white fabric with traces of buff slip, black ironstone grits. Type 66.
85 ?Flagon: fine sandy pale pink fabric.
86 Dish: BB1-type fabric, with finely burnished surfaces.
87 Large indented beaker: fine sandy grey fabric with barbotine decoration. Cf. Type 39.
88 Wide-mouthed jar: grey fabric with white inclusions. Cf. Types 28 or 29.
89 Wide-mouthed jar: fine, soft pale grey fabric with orange core. Cf. Type 28.
90 Bowl: very sandy pale grey fabric.
91 Jar: brown shell-gritted fabric, reduced in patches. Type 96.
92 Jar: reddish shell-gritted fabric, reduced on exterior.

The pottery from this gully has been dated to mid/late 3rd century AD, but there is a certain amount of residual late 2nd century material also included, e.g. 83, 85.

Gully 53   Phases IV and ?V (Fig. 163)

93 Small flanged bowl: NVCC, white fabric with dark brown colour-coat. Type 11.
94 Narrow-mouthed jar: NVGW. Type 37.

95 Mortarium: fine, sandy buff fabric with black ironstone grits. NVSC, Type 66.
96 Large indented beaker: fine sandy grey fabric with orange margins and grey/orange/brown colour-coat. Cf. Type 39.
97 Dish: sandy grey fabric. Cf. Type 46.
98 Dish: fine grey fabric.
99 Dish: sandy grey fabric with white inclusions. Cf. Type 45.
100 Wide-mouthed jar: fine, soft grey fabric with white inclusions. Cf. Type 28.
101 Jar: red-brown shell-gritted fabric. Type 90.
102 Jar: reddish shell-gritted fabric.

The pottery from this gully has been dated to the late 3rd to 4th century AD but the majority of the vessels illustrated here are of long-lived 3rd century types, which makes it difficult to distinguish any residual material.

Gully 44   Phase III (Fig. 163)

103 Beaker: NVCC, white fabric with dark brown colour-coat and underslip barbotine figured scene. Type 2.8. Cf. the discussion by Johns, p. 479, no. 3.
104 As above, fragment.
105 Dish: NVGW. Type 45.
106 Dish: NVGW. Type 45.
107 Jar: NVGW. Cf. Type 27.
108 Flanged bowl: NVSC, buff fabric with pale brown slip and dark brown painted decoration on the flange. Type 65.
109 Reeded-rim bowl: gritty buff fabric with reduced exterior. Type 69.
110 Mortarium: very sandy cream fabric with traces of self-coloured slip. Only impressions of the gritting remain.
111 Dish: very sandy grey fabric with darker surfaces.
112 Jar: reddish shell-gritted fabric. Cf. Type 80.

The main fill of this gully belongs to the later 2nd century AD, while the upper layers have been dated to the 3rd century. Only nos 103 and 104 are actually from the main fill; the remainder of the vessels illustrated, although they come from the upper layers and are therefore residual in their context, are, nevertheless, characteristic of the material from the main fill and have been illustrated here for this reason.

Ditch 9   Phases III and IV (Figs 164–70; Pl. XXVIIIa)

Cut 11 (ACE)   Date: 3rd century AD.
113 Cup/bowl: NVCC, grey fabric with grey colour-coat. Imitation samian. Type 15.
114 Narrow-mouthed jar or flagon: NVGW. Cf. Type 37.
115 Dish: NVGW. Type 45.
116 Flanged bowl: NVSC, soft buff fabric. Type 64.
117 Dish: sandy grey fabric. Cf. Type 45.
118 Large jar. Horningsea ware. Type 107.
119 Large jar. Horningsea ware. Type 108.
120 Jar: orange shell-gritted fabric with grey core. Type 100.

Number 116 is probably late 2nd century AD in date and, therefore, residual.

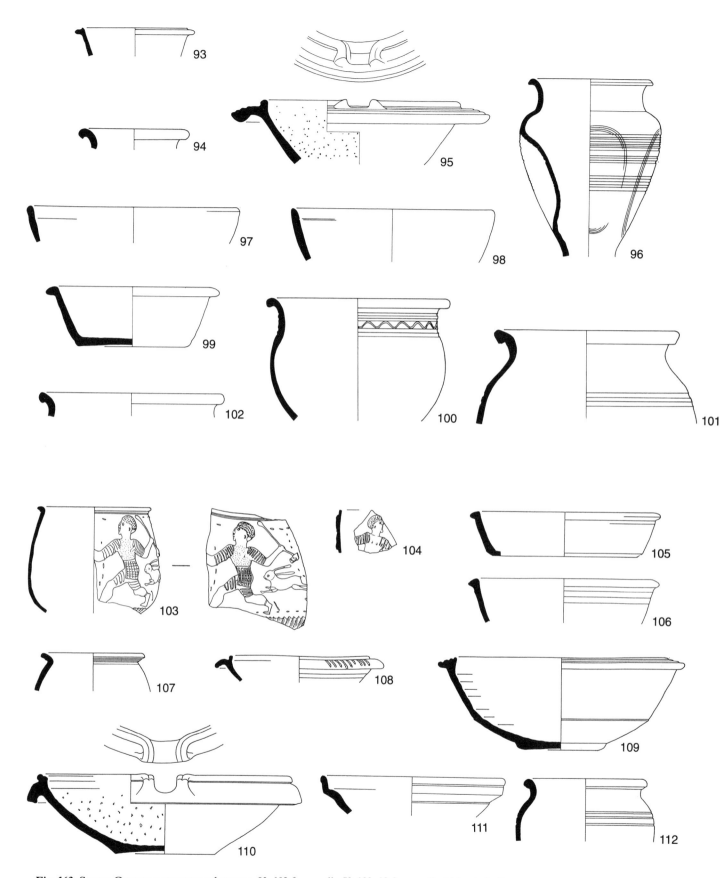

Fig. 163 Stonea Grange: pottery vessel groups, 93–102 from gully 53, 103–12 from gully 44 (scale 1:4).

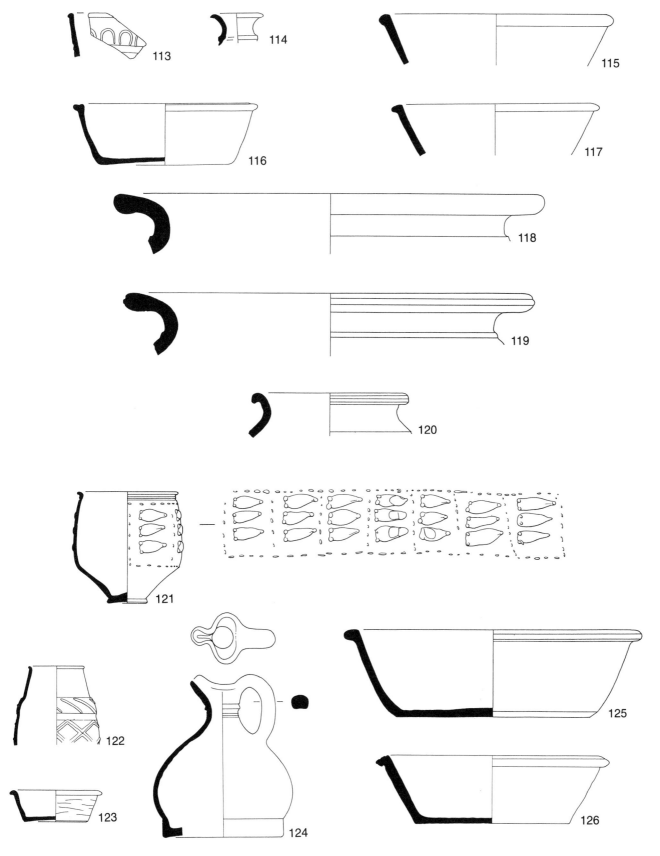

Fig. 164 Stonea Grange: pottery vessel groups, 113–26 from ditch 9 (scale 1 : 4).

Cut 10, upper layer (AFN)   Date: 3rd century AD.

121 Beaker: NVCC, white fabric with dark brown colour-coat and underslip barbotine decoration in form of phalli. Type 2.9. Cf. the discussion by Johns, p. 481, no. 5.

122 Beaker with cordon: NVCC, white fabric with brown colour-coat and white overslip barbotine decoration. Type 6.

123 Miniature pie-dish: NVCC, buff fabric with brown colour-coat. Cf. Type 7/7.2.

124 Pinched neck flagon: NVCC, white fabric with dark brown colour-coat. Type 20.

125 Dish: NVGW, Type 45.

126 Dish with grooved rim: orange-red shell-gritted fabric. Type 106.

The overall date for the material in this layer is 3rd century AD, probably the latter part as no. 122 is probably a late 3rd/4th century type. Number 121 is probably contemporary with the lower layers which are late 2nd/3rd century and is therefore residual.

Cut 10, lower layer (AFR)   Date: late 2nd/3rd century AD.

127 Large beaker: NVCC, white fabric with brown colour-coat. Type 2.

128 Cordoned jar: NVGW. Type 27.2.

129 Jar: ?NVSC, white fabric with yellowish slip. Cf. Type 60.

130 Flagon: fine sandy pale pink fabric with white exterior. Cf. Types 51/53.

Cut 9 (AGO, AGK)   Date: late 3rd/4th century AD.

131 Castor box: NVCC, white fabric with dark brown exterior and pale brown interior colour-coat. Type 26.

132 Slashed cordon jar: NVCC, pale orange fabric with orange-brown colour-coat. Type 19.

133 Beaker: ?NVGW, hard sandy grey fabric with dark grey colour-coat and underslip barbotine decoration. Cf. Type 2.6.

134 Cup: ?NVGW, Imitation London or samian ware, soft, fine grey fabric with darker surfaces. Type 43.

135 Dish: NVGW. Type 45.

136 Jar: sandy cream fabric with reduced surfaces. Cf. Type 56.

137 Flanged bowl: fine, soft orange fabric. Cf. Type 64.

138 Dish: fine grey fabric, with stamp on interior. Imitation London ware/samian. Cf. the discussion by Rigby, p. 427, no. 1.

139 Flanged bowl: fine soft grey fabric with slightly darker surfaces.

140 Jar: gritty grey fabric with orange core.

141 Wide-mouthed jar: fine soft grey fabric with large black and white inclusions. Cf. Type 28.

142 Large jar: gritty dark grey fabric with rusticated decoration.

143 Jar: dark grey shell-gritted fabric with brownish interior surface.

144 Jar: dark grey shell-gritted fabric with brown interior surface.

145 Jar: dark grey shell-gritted fabric with buff patches. Type 87.

Although the overall date for this cut is late 3rd/4th century AD, dictated by the presence of later material, the majority of the vessels shown here are earlier in date and therefore residual in this context.

Cut 8, upper layer (ADM)   Date: 3rd century AD.

146 Beaker/Hunt Cup: NVCC, white fabric with grey colour-coat. Type 2.6.

147 Small wide-mouthed jar: NVGW. Type 28.2.

148 Dish: NVGW. Type 45.3.

149 Dish: NVGW. Type 47.

150 Jar: NVGW.

All of these vessels may be 3rd century AD, which is the date of the layer, but no. 147 may be a little earlier and therefore contemporary with the lower layers of this cut.

Cut 8, lower layer (ADY)   Date: late 2nd/3rd century AD.

151 Beaker: NVCC, white fabric with brown colour-coat. Type 2.2.

152 Flagon: fine pink fabric with cream exterior surface. Cf. Type 51.

153 Flagon: sandy buff fabric with pale grey core. Cf. Type 52.

154 Reeded-rim bowl: gritty buff fabric with ironstone inclusions. Type 70.

155 Jar: off-white fabric with abundant white inclusions. Type 74.

156 Jar: sandy buff fabric with pale grey core and pale brown slip and abundant white inclusions. Type 74.

157 Dish: NVGW. Type 45.

Cut 7, lower layer (AGL)   Date: early 3rd century AD.

158 Beaker/Hunt Cup: NVCC, white fabric with dark brown colour-coat and underslip barbotine decoration. Type 2.7. Cf. the discussion by Johns, p. 483, no. 12.

159 Flagon or jar: ?NVSC, buff fabric with pale brown slip on exterior. Type 58.

160 Jar: ?NVSC, sandy cream fabric.

161 Flagon: fine cream fabric with ironstone inclusions and traces of pale brown slip on exterior. Cf. Type 52.

162 Dish: NVGW, Type 45/45.3.

163 Jar: soft pale brown fabric with grey surfaces.

164 Jar: dark grey shell-gritted fabric.

Cut 6   Date: 3rd century AD.

165 Bowl: NVCC, pale orange fabric with orange colour-coat and rouletted decoration. Type 10.

166 Large jar: Horningsea ware. Type 107.

167 Jar: dark grey shell-gritted fabric.

Cut 5, upper layer (AEE)   Date: 3rd century AD.

168 Indented beaker: NVCC, white fabric with dark brown colour-coat. Type 3.

169 Indented beaker: NVCC, white fabric with dark brown colour-coat. Type 3.

170 Wide-mouthed jar: NVCC, pale grey fabric with dark grey-brown colour-coat. Type 18 or 28 (NVGW).

171 Bowl: NVGW. Type 45.3.

Numbers 168 and 169 are probably residual in this context, but contemporary with the lower layers.

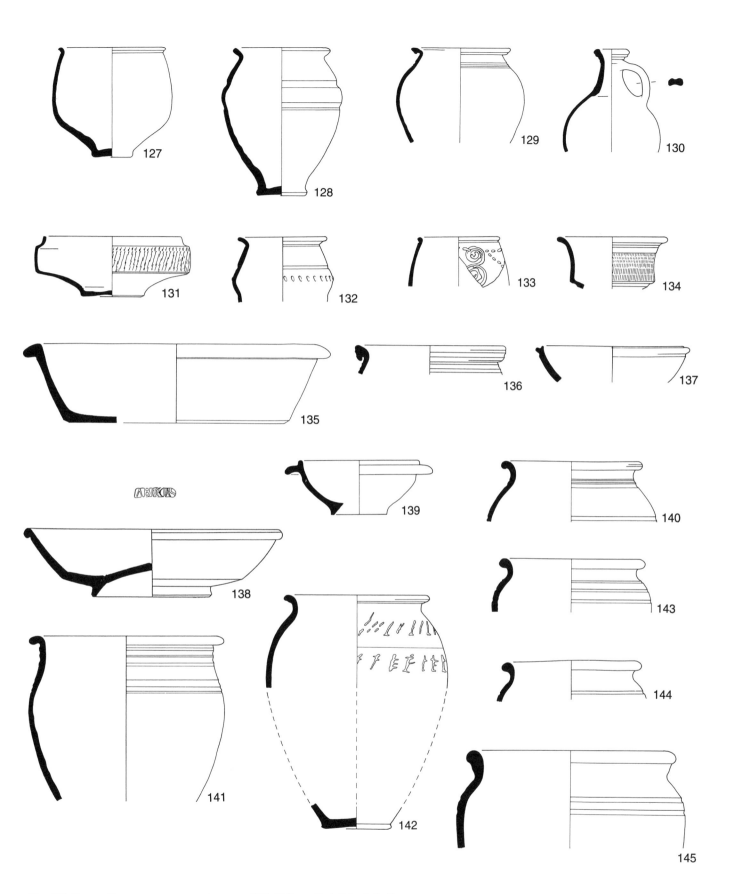

Fig. 165 Stonea Grange: pottery vessel groups, 127–45 from ditch 9 (scale 1:4).

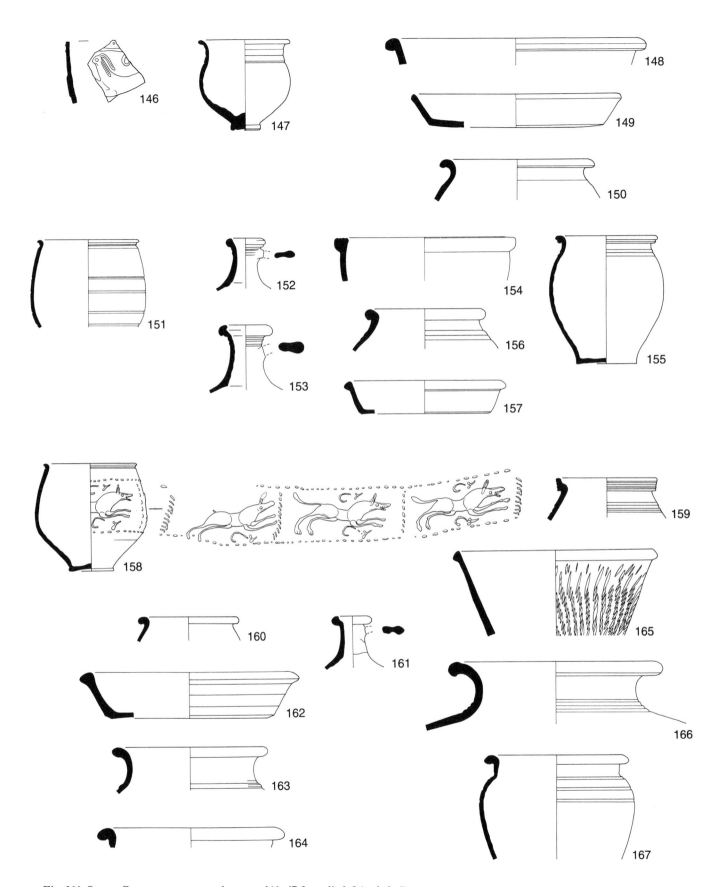

Fig. 166 Stonea Grange: pottery vessel groups, 146–67 from ditch 9 (scale 1:4).

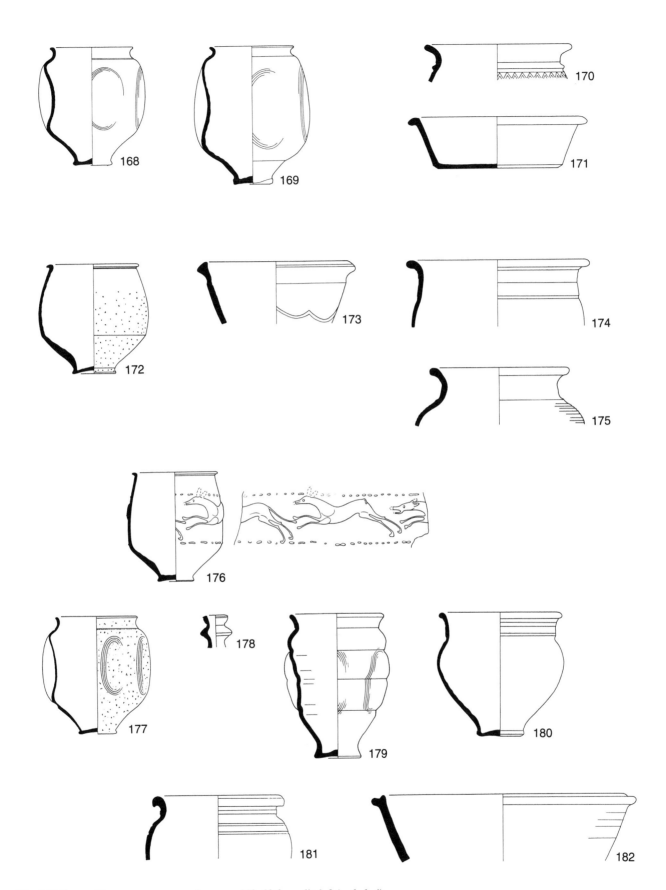

Fig. 167 Stonea Grange: pottery vessel groups, 168–82 from ditch 9 (scale 1:4).

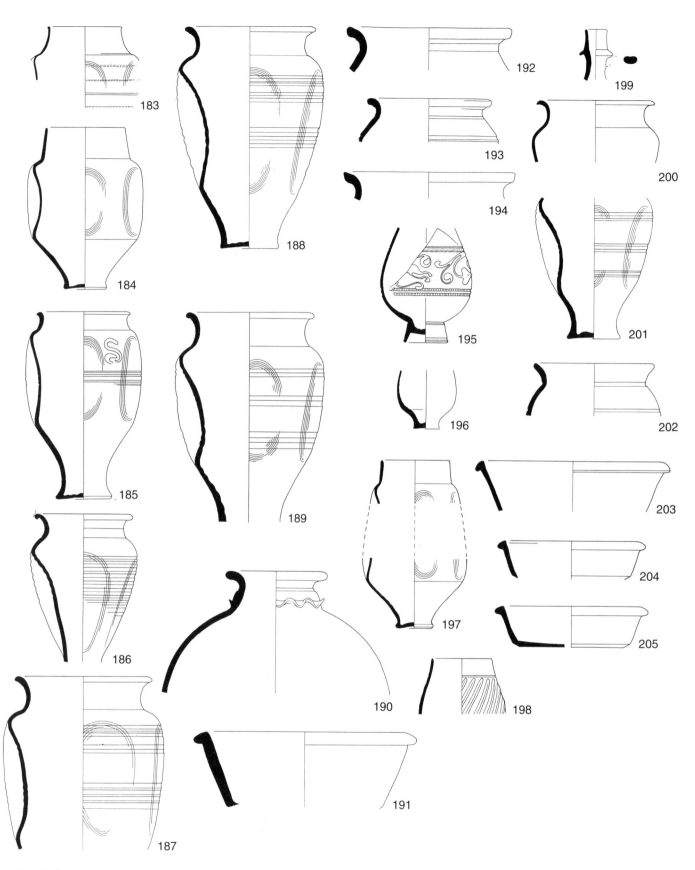

Fig. 168 Stonea Grange: pottery vessel groups, 183–205 from ditch 9 (scale 1 : 4).

Cut 5, lower layer (AET) Date: early 3rd century AD.

172 Beaker: NVCC, white fabric with brown colour-coat and rough-cast decoration. Type 2.5.
173 Bowl: NVGW, with burnished line on exterior. Cf. Type 45.2.
174 Wide-mouthed jar: NVGW. Type 28.
175 Jar: very sandy grey fabric with buff core.

Cut 4, upper layer (BCO) Date: late 3rd/4th century AD.

176 Beaker/Hunt Cup: NVCC, white fabric with dark brown colour-coat. Type 2.7. Cf. the discussion by Johns, p. 485, no. 13.
177 Indented beaker: brown fabric with dark grey colour-coat. Possibly made at Colchester.
178 Flagon: sandy pale orange fabric with brown colour-coat. Cf. Type 21. Possibly made at Colchester.
179 Indented beaker: NVGW, with raised cordons. Type 40.
180 Small wide-mouthed jar: NVGW. Type 28.2.
181 Jar: dark grey shell-gritted fabric.
182 Flanged bowl: dark grey shell-gritted fabric. Type 104.

Much of the material from this upper layer is residual (e.g. nos 176, 177 and possibly nos 179 and 180) in this context, but contemporary with the lower layer.

Cut 3, upper layers (BCN, BFC) Date: late 3rd/4th century AD.

183 Indented beaker: fine soft orange fabric with glossy black colour-coat. Central Gaulish ware.
184 Indented beaker: cream fabric with dark brown colour-coat. ?NVCC Type 4.
185 Indented beaker: NVGW with barbotine decoration. Type 39 but cf. Type 3.3.
186 Indented beaker: NVGW. Type 39.
187 Indented beaker: fine grey fabric with black and white inclusions. Cf. Type 39.
188 Indented beaker: fine pale grey fabric with large white inclusions. Cf. Type 39.
189 Indented beaker: ?NVGW. Type 39.
190 Large narrow-mouthed jar: sandy orange fabric with grey core and white slip, with frilled cordon round the neck.
191 Dish: dark grey shell-gritted fabric with orange interior. Type 102.
192 Jar: buff shell-gritted fabric with grey core.
193 Jar: orange shell-gritted fabric, reduced in patches.
194 Jar: buff shell-gritted fabric with grey core.

The upper layers of this cut have been dated to the late 3rd/4th century AD by other material not illustrated here, and much of this group may be residual, but contemporary with the lower layers (see nos 231–6 below). However, the grey-ware indented beakers are probably one of the many types which seem to have been produced throughout the 3rd century and may therefore belong to either context.

Cut 2 Date: 3rd century AD.

195 Beaker: fine orange fabric with glossy dark brown colour-coat and underslip barbotine decoration. Central Gaulish ware.

196 Small beaker: NVCC, white fabric with dark brown colour coat. Type 1.
197 Indented beaker: NVCC, white fabric with pale brown colour-coat. Type 4.
198 Beaker: NVCC, white fabric with red-orange colour-coat and white overslip barbotine decoration. Type 5.
199 Disc-necked flagon: NVCC, white fabric with orange colour-coat. Type 21.
200 Indented beaker: NVGW. Type 39.
201 Indented beaker: NVGW. Type 39.
202 Jar: NVGW. Type 33.
203 Dish: NVGW. Type 45.
204 Dish: NVGW. Type 45.
205 Dish: NVGW. Type 45.
206 Dish: NVGW. Type 47.
207 Dish: NVGW. Type 47.
208 Wide-mouthed jar: NVGW. Type 29.
209 Dish: NVGW. Imitation samian Dr 36. Type 44.
210 Jar: fine sandy off-white fabric with reduced exterior. Cf. Type 57.
211 Jar: fine sandy buff fabric with reduced patches. Cf. Type 57.
212 Jar: sandy orange fabric with grey core and white slip on exterior.
213 Mortarium: NVSC, fine buff fabric with yellowish-buff slip. Type 66.
214 Indented beaker: fine grey fabric. Cf. Type 39.
215 Wide-mouthed jar: very fine grey fabric. Cf. Type 28.
216 Wide-mouthed jar: grey fabric with orange core and white inclusions. Cf. Type 28.
217 Dish: sandy grey fabric. Cf. Type 47.
218 Flanged bowl: soft, very sandy grey fabric.
219 Jar: sandy grey fabric with white inclusions. Cf. Type 34.
220 Jar: sandy pale grey fabric with darker surfaces.
221 Jar: brownish shell-gritted fabric. Cf. Type 88.
222 Jar: brownish shell-gritted fabric.
223 Jar: brownish shell-gritted fabric.
224 Jar: brownish shell-gritted fabric. Type 97.
225 Jar: brownish shell-gritted fabric. Type 84.
226 Jar: dark grey shell-gritted fabric.
227 Jar: dark grey shell-gritted fabric.
228 Jar: pale brown shell-gritted fabric.
229 Jar: dark grey shell-gritted fabric with brown interior surfaces.
230 Large jar: reddish shell-gritted fabric. Type 94.

Numbers 196, 202, 209 and 219 are probably residual in this context, and contemporary with the lower layers of this cut which have been dated to the late 2nd/3rd century AD.

Cut 3, lower layer (BKO) Date: 3rd century AD.

231 Indented beaker: NVCC, white fabric with dark brown colour-coat. Type 4.2.
232 Disc-necked flagon: NVCC, white fabric with dark brown colour-coat. Type 21.3.
233 Dish: NVGW/NVCC, grey fabric with dark grey colour-coat. Type 9.
234 Jar: dark grey shell-gritted fabric with brown patches. Type 81.
235 Jar: red-brown shell-gritted fabric with grey core. Cf. Type 88.
236 Bowl: dark brown shell-gritted fabric.

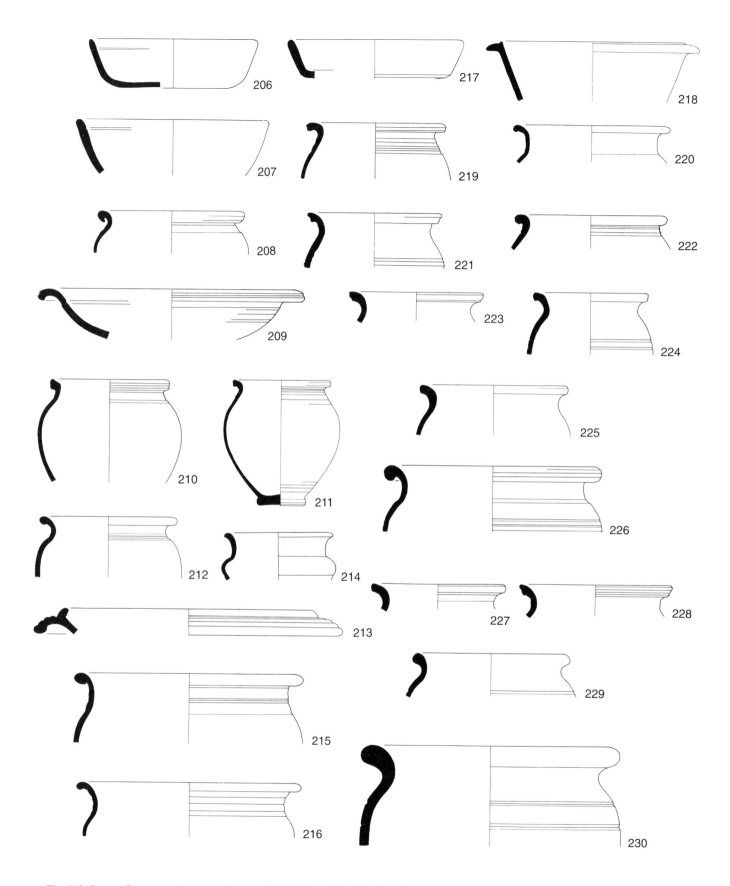

Fig. 169 Stonea Grange: pottery vessel groups, 206–30 from ditch 9 (scale 1:4).

Fig. 170 Stonea Grange: pottery vessel groups, 231–9 from ditch 9, 240–8 from well J4, 249–55 from pit P10 (scale 1:4).

Cut 1b, upper layer (CEE)

237 Indented beaker: fine sandy orange fabric, possibly mica-dusted.
238 Dish: NVGW. Type 45.
239 Mortarium: fine white fabric.

Other features   (Figs 170–3)

Well J4   Phase III (Fig. 170)

Lower layer – 7   Date: early 3rd century AD.

240 Wide-mouthed jar: NVGW, with rouletted decoration. Type 30.
241 Reeded-rim bowl: ?NVSC. Type 62.
242 Jar: fine sandy buff fabric with reduced exterior. Cf. Type 57 or 74.
243 Dish: fine grey fabric with mica-dusted surfaces.
244 Dish: fine dark grey fabric.
245 Jar: fine sandy grey fabric. Cf. Type 34.
246 Wide-mouthed jar: fine orange fabric with pale grey surfaces.
247 Jar: pale grey shell-gritted fabric.
248 Bowl: dark grey shell-gritted fabric. Type 101.

Pit P10   Phase III, later (Figs 170–1)

Fill of pit   Date: early 3rd century AD.

249 Beaker: NVCC, white fabric with dark brown colour-coat. Type 2.
250 Indented beaker: NVCC, white fabric with dark brown colour-coat and underslip barbotine scales. Type 3.2.
251 Beaker: NVCC, white fabric with dark brown colour-coat. Type 2.
252 Beaker: hard orange fabric with green-brown metallic colour-coat. Continental import – possibly from Trier.
253 Dish: NVGW, Type 45.
254 Dish: NVGW. Type 47.
255 Wide-mouthed jar: NVGW. Type 30.
256 Jar: NVGW.
257 Wide-mouthed jar: NVGW, with rouletted decoration on shoulder. Type 29.
258 Flagon: ?NVSC, pale orange-pink fabric with brownish-yellow slip.
259 Flagon: fine buff fabric with large white inclusions. Cf. Type 84.
260 Jar: gritty buff fabric with self-coloured slip. Cf. Type 59.
261 Jar: buff fabric with grey core and self-coloured slip. Cf. Type 59.
262 Carinated bowl: gritty buff fabric with self-coloured slip. Type 72.
263 Cup/bowl: ?NVGW, fine hard grey fabric with rouletted decoration. Type 42.
264 Cordoned jar: ?NVGW. Type 27.2.
265 Jar: brown fabric with finely burnished black surfaces.
266 Wide-mouthed jar: sandy orange fabric with grey core and surfaces.
267 Wide-mouthed jar: sandy grey fabric with orange stripes showing through burnished grey surfaces. Cf. Type 28.

268 Large jar: Horningsea ware, Type 108.
269 Jar: brownish shell-gritted fabric with wavy line on exterior.
270 Jar: brownish shell-gritted fabric.
271 Jar: brownish shell-gritted fabric.

Building R1, small hypocaust   Phase III (Figs 172–3)

Destruction deposit (BA)   Date: early 3rd century AD.

272 Beaker: NVCC, white fabric with dark brown colour-coat. Type 2.
273 Beaker: NVCC, pale orange fabric with red-orange colour-coat and underslip barbotine decoration. Type 2.6.
274 Beaker: very fine, soft orange and grey fabric with grey-brown colour-coat and rough-cast exterior. Cf. Type 2.5. Continental import.
275 Flagon: NVSC, buff fabric with buff-grey slip. Type 51.
276 Flagon: NVSC, buff fabric with yellowish-buff slip. Cf. Type 52/3.
277 Flagon: NVSC, very pale pink fabric with pale yellowish slip. Type 52.
278 Flagon: NVSC, buff fabric with pale brown slip. Cf. Type 51/52.
279 Flagon: NVSC, whitish fabric with pale yellow-buff slip. Type 51/52.
280 Flagon: sandy buff fabric with brown slip.
281 Flagon: ?NVSC, fine buff fabric with self-coloured slip. Type 54.
282 Flagon: very hard, coarse dark grey fabric with buff exterior surfaces. Cf. Type 53.
283 Flagon: ?NVSC, fine pink and buff fabric with pale yellow-brown slip. Type 53.
284 Reeded-rim bowl: gritty buff fabric. Type 69/70.
285 Reeded-rim bowl: gritty buff fabric. Type 69/70.
286 Reeded-rim bowl: gritty buff fabric. Type 69/70.
287 Jar: gritty buff fabric, reduced on rim. Type 74.
288 Mortarium: very sandy dark grey fabric with buff surfaces.
289 Mortarium: ?NVSC, fine white fabric with red ironstone grits. Type 68.
290 Slashed cordon jar: NVGW, Type 27.
291 Dish: NVCC, white fabric with dark brown colour-coat. Type 7.
292 Dish: NVGW, with burnished diagonal lines. Type 45.2.
293 Dish: NVGW, Type 46.
294 Jar: soft sandy grey fabric with darker surfaces.
295 Jar: sandy grey fabric.
296 Jar: very fine micaceous grey fabric with burnished lines.
297 Jar: sandy grey fabric. Cf. Type 34.
298 Large jar: Horningsea ware. Type 107.
299 Jar: dull orange-brown shell-gritted fabric. Type 81.
300 Jar: brownish shell-gritted fabric.
301 Jar: grey shell-gritted fabric with brown core.
302 Lid: red-orange shell-gritted fabric with pale brown surfaces.
303 Jar: grey shell-gritted fabric.
304 Jar: pale brown shell-gritted fabric with grey core.
305 Jar: red-brown shell-gritted fabric. Cf. Type 92.
306 Storage jar: dark red shell-gritted fabric with pale brown surfaces. Type 93.

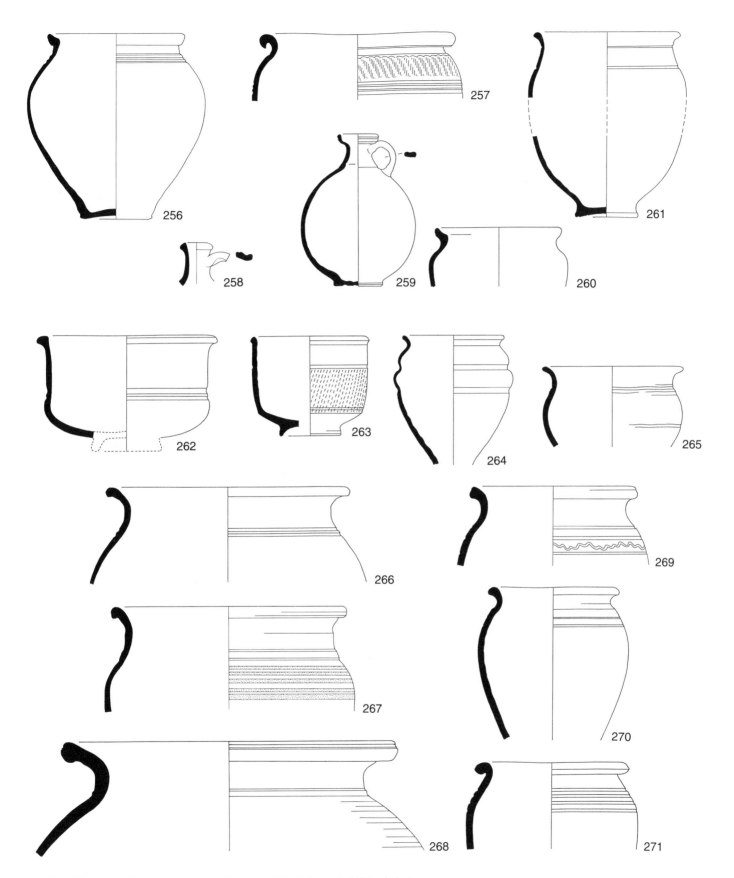

Fig. 171 Stonea Grange: pottery vessel groups, 256–71 from pit P10 (scale 1 : 4).

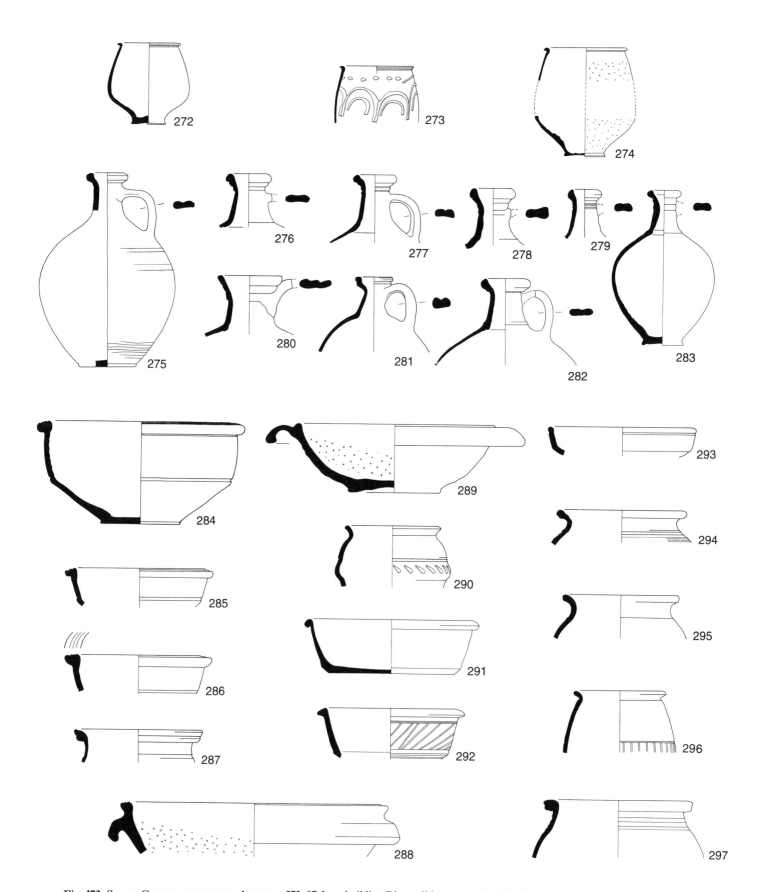

Fig. 172 Stonea Grange: pottery vessel groups, 272–97 from building R1, small hypocaust (scale 1 : 4).

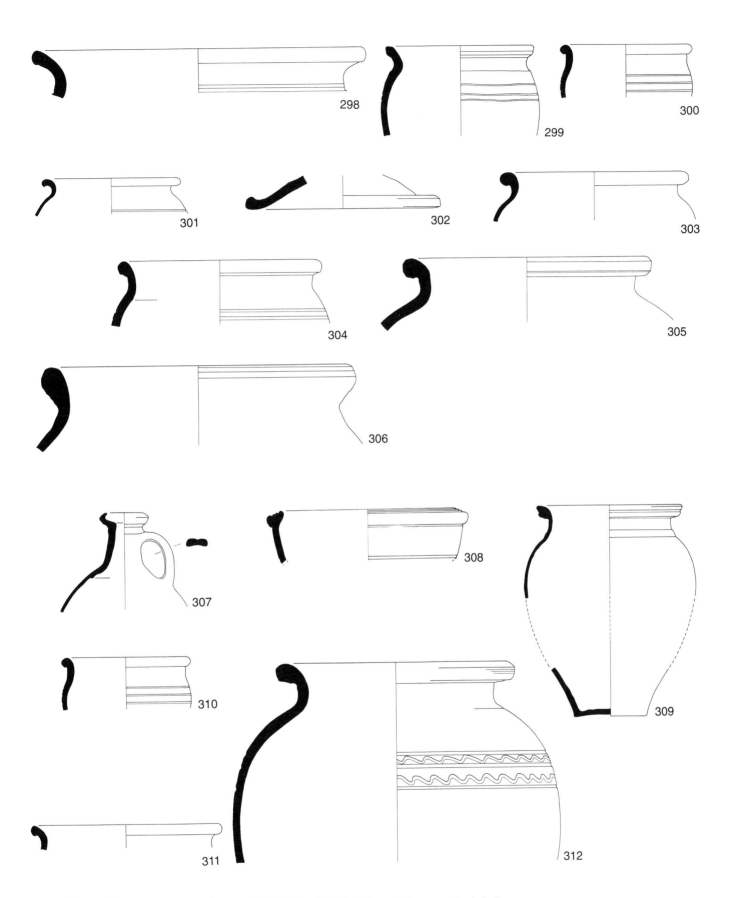

Fig. 173 Stonea Grange: pottery vessel groups, 298–312 from building R1, small hypocaust (scale 1:4).

Secondary silt (CS)   Date: early 3rd century AD.

307 Flagon: fine sandy off-white fabric. Cf. Type 52.
308 Reeded-rim bowl: sandy buff fabric with pale yellowish slip. Type 62/63.
309 Jar: gritty buff fabric with self-coloured slip and reduced patches on exterior. Type 74.
310 Jar: dark grey-brown shell-gritted fabric.
311 Jar: red-brown shell-gritted fabric.
312 Storage jar: red-brown shell-gritted fabric with wavy lines on exterior. Type 92.

DISCUSSION

The categories

The Roman pottery assemblage from the site has been quantified by weight and Tables 21–9 show the amounts of each ware in grams as well as the percentage of the total. The identification of the fabrics was made macroscopically or with a 1×10 hand lens. It should be noted at this point that it was not possible to quantify the material from the final season of excavation in 1984. However, an examination of the pottery which was undertaken for dating purposes did not reveal any significant differences from the previous seasons. This observation is supported by the fact that the categories of pottery and wares which were chosen for the quantification of the material from the first season's work still held good for the final season. Many of these categories are actually identifiable wares, some of which have been discussed in the Type Series. The remainder, however, require some explanation.

Where possible imported colour-coated wares have been identified as either *Rhenish* or *Central Gaulish*, insofar as Rhenish ware is taken to be a hard fine red and/or grey fabric with greenish/brown metallic colour-coats, whereas Central Gaulish ware is taken to be a softer orange fabric with a glossy black colour-coat. Specialists in either of these wares may well disagree with these identifications, and it is also possible that further examples of these wares have been included in the category of *Other Fine* wares. *Mica-dusted* vessels are rare but occur in a variety of fabrics and forms so they have simply been categorised according to this surface treatment. The *London type* ware probably comes from the Nene Valley kilns but since this attribution is not certain for all examples, they have been quantified separately. The category of *Other Fine* may include some stray examples of imported colour-coated wares and even unidentified Nene Valley ware. It also includes a number of wares of varying degrees of fineness, of which there are too few examples to merit a separate category, but which are clearly table wares. It is notoriously difficult to differentiate between isolated sherds of colour-coated vessels made in the Colchester kilns from those of the Nene Valley, and whilst examples of Colchester ware are probably rare, where

they do occur they will have been included in this category. In adopting this category, as well as those described as *Other Oxidised* and *Other Reduced*, it has seemed safer to include any sherds whose area of origin is in any way uncertain here, rather than to risk giving an unrealistic bias in favour of the better-known wares, for the purposes of statistics. These categories may also include sherds of wares which may be identifiable as, for instance, 'rusticated ware', but which occur in such insignificant amounts that they do not merit individual quantification.

Flagons and *Mortaria* have been quantified as types rather than wares for two reasons. Firstly, it was possible that a spatial analysis of the types of vessels found on the site as a whole might have yielded some useful information although, in fact, this proved not to be the case. Secondly, both types occur in a variety of wares which are not always identifiable and are often in quantities too small to be worth quantifying separately. Where either of these types occurs in *Nene Valley Self-coloured* ware, they have been included in that category. The category given as *BB types* may, like the London-type category, include Nene Valley imitations of BB fabrics, but it has proved impossible to differentiate between these and the many imitations of both BB1 and BB2 which are to be found in Roman Britain.

The assemblage

Table 21 shows the percentages of the various wares from the site as a whole, and in Tables 22–8 the material is divided up by phase. There is a certain amount of material from the site which does not belong to any particular phase and this is given in Table 29. Thus, Table 21 represents the sum of the material in Tables 22–9 and therefore includes all the Roman pottery found on the site, other than in initial machine clearance.

From Table 21 it can be seen that the better-known of the Nene Valley fabrics account for 27.56% of the total assemblage. If the shell-gritted wares, which were probably also made in the Nene Valley are added to this, the total is then 50.2%. The unidentified fine, oxidised and reduced wares amount to 36% of the assemblage and the total of identifiable wares which are not from the Nene Valley, only amounts to 13.8%. The only one of these latter which occurs in any significant quantities is Horningsea ware – 8.47%. It should be noted, however, that the Nene Valley and shell-gritted wares, and to a slightly lesser extent, Horningsea, were being produced over a long period of time, unlike the 'Gritty Buff' ware, for instance, which accounts for a much higher percentage of the material in one particular time.

The context

The pottery assemblage from Stonea Grange differs in a number of important ways from those of other sites in the area. In his discussion of pottery in the Roman Fenland, Hartley describes the Fenland as 'the main market of the Nene Valley kilns' (Hartley 1970) and this certainly holds true for Stonea Grange. However, he also observes that there is a scarcity in the Fenland of amphorae and any other imports (apart from samian) and a lack of 'any appreciable indication of far-reaching trade'; that storage jars are common (both Horningsea and shell-gritted); and that flagons are also scarce.

Two other Roman sites have been excavated in the general area of Stonea Grange in recent years, at the Golden Lion Inn, March (Potter 1975–6) and at Grandford (Potter and Potter 1982), although they were in no way comparable in sample size. Table 30 shows which of the wares found at Stonea Grange also occurred on these sites. In addition, an analysis has recently been made (Cameron 1987) of Roman pottery from the Fenland survey which deals with 35 sites in the parishes of Borough Fen, March, Whittlesey, Thorney and Eye. Table 31 shows the number of sites out of these 35 where each of the wares occurred. Although pottery collected during a field-survey may not be truly representative of the site by comparison with an assemblage of excavated material, it is interesting to note that Hartley's observations hold true, not only for the field survey sites but also for the Golden Lion Inn and Grandford sites. At Stonea Grange, however, although the assemblage is dominated by Nene Valley wares and the instance of storage jars is high, the quantities of amphorae (Keay and Carreras, pp. 435–40), flagons, black-burnished wares and Continental colour-coated vessels signify important differences which doubtless reflect the unusual nature of the site.

Table 21 Stonea Grange: other Roman pottery – whole-site ware quantification

Ware	%	Weight (g)	Ware	%	Weight (g)
Rhenish	0.04	225	Gritty Buff	0.74	4 670
C Gaulish	0.12	750	Other Oxidised	9.16	58 092
Nene Valley CC	8.01	50 780	Horningsea	8.47	53 690
Mica-dusted	0.11	695	Nene Valley Grey	17.95	113 850
London type	0.19	1 205	BB types	0.30	1 870
Other Fine	0.51	3 211	Other Reduced	26.33	166 965
Flagons	0.93	5 925	SG (cooking pots)	14.14	89 685
Mortaria	2.92	18 535	SG (storage jars)	8.50	53 890
NV Self-coloured	1.60	10 175			
			Totals	100.02	634 213

Table 22 Stonea Grange: other Roman pottery – ware quantification, Phase II/III contexts

Ware	%	Weight (g)	Ware	%	Weight (g)
Rhenish			Gritty Buff	13.11	80
C Gaulish			Other Oxidised	13.11	80
Nene Valley CC	1.64	10	Horningsea	14.75	90
Mica-dusted			Nene Valley Grey		
London type			BB types	9.84	60
Other Fine	1.64	10	Other Reduced	44.26	270
Flagons	1.64	10	SG (cooking pots)		
Mortaria			SG (storage jars)		
NV Self-coloured					
			Totals	99.99	610

Table 23 Stonea Grange: other Roman pottery – ware quantification, Phase III contexts

Ware	%	Weight (g)	Ware	%	Weight (g)
Rhenish	0.05	150	Gritty Buff	0.86	2 470
C Gaulish	0.20	585	Other Oxidised	9.45	27 292
Nene Valley CC	7.30	21 070	Horningsea	7.02	20 270
Mica-dusted	0.14	395	Nene Valley Grey	16.68	48 145
London type	0.28	805	BB types	0.17	480
Other Fine	0.46	1 336	Other Reduced	28.93	83 510
Flagons	1.24	3 590	Rusticated	0.32	910
Mortaria	2.42	6 985	SG (cooking pots)	13.78	39 785
NV Self-coloured	1.92	5 545	SG (storage jars)	8.79	25 360
			Totals	100.01	288 683

Table 24 Stonea Grange: other Roman pottery – ware quantification, Phase III/IV contexts

Ware	%	Weight (g)	Ware	%	Weight (g)
Rhenish			Gritty Buff	1.31	340
C Gaulish			Other Oxidised	11.12	2 880
Nene Valley CC	5.65	1 465	Horningsea	2.70	700
Mica-dusted	0.89	230	Nene Valley Grey	16.75	4 340
London type	0.31	80	BB types	3.05	790
Other Fine	0.29	75	Other Reduced	21.19	5 490
Flagons	0.12	30	SG (cooking pots)	22.42	5 810
Mortaria	4.52	1 170	SG (storage jars)	8.22	2 130
NV Self-coloured	1.47	380			
			Totals	100.01	25 910

Table 25 Stonea Grange: other Roman pottery – ware quantification, Phase IV contexts

Ware	%	Weight (g)	Ware	%	Weight (g)
Rhenish	0.01	10	Gritty Buff	0.48	500
C Gaulish	0.10	100	Other Oxidised	9.40	9 770
Nene Valley CC	10.45	10 860	Horningsea	9.50	9 870
Mica-dusted	0.06	60	Nene Valley Grey	18.03	18 735
London type	0.12	120	BB types	0.43	450
Other Fine	1.03	1 070	Other Reduced	24.02	24 950
Flagons	0.91	945	SG (cooking pots)	14.83	15 405
Mortaria	3.46	3 590	SG (storage jars)	6.64	6 900
NV Self-coloured	0.54	560			
			Totals	100.01	103 895

Table 26 Stonea Grange: other Roman pottery – ware quantification, Phase IV/V contexts

Ware	%	Weight (g)	Ware	%	Weight (g)
Rhenish			Gritty Buff		
C Gaulish			Other Oxidised	7.04	1 840
Nene Valley CC	10.03	2 620	Horningsea	10.41	2 720
Mica-dusted			Nene Valley Grey	18.37	4 800
London type	0.04	10	BB types		
Other Fine	0.65	170	Other Reduced	24.57	6 420
Flagons	0.27	70	SG (cooking pots)	10.03	2 620
Mortaria	5.43	1 420	SG (storage jars)	13.17	3 440
NV Self-coloured					
			Totals	100.01	26 130

Table 27 Stonea Grange: other Roman pottery – ware quantification, Phase V contexts

Ware	%	Weight (g)	Ware	%	Weight (g)
Rhenish			Gritty Buff	0.44	100
C Gaulish	0.09	20	Other Oxidised	5.56	1 275
Nene Valley CC	7.98	1 830	Horningsea	8.02	1 840
Mica-dusted	0.04	10	Nene Valley Grey	22.46	5 150
London type	0.04	10	BB types		
Other Fine	0.35	80	Other Reduced	25.68	5 890
Flagons	0.35	80	SG (cooking pots)	10.94	2 510
Mortaria	5.23	1 200	SG (storage jars)	12.47	2 860
NV Self-coloured	0.35	80			
			Totals	100.00	22 935

Table 28 Stonea Grange: other Roman pottery – ware quantification, Phase VI contexts

Ware	%	Weight (g)	Ware	%	Weight (g)
Rhenish	0.15	5	Gritty Buff	2.05	70
C Gaulish			Other Oxidised	12.15	415
Nene Valley CC	10.69	365	Horningsea		
Mica-dusted			Nene Valley Grey	26.94	920
London type			BB types		
Other Fine			Other Reduced	31.92	1 090
Flagons			SG (cooking pots)	5.56	190
Mortaria	6.15	210	SG (storage jars)	4.10	140
NV Self-coloured	0.29	10			
			Totals	100.00	3 415

Table 29 Stonea Grange: other Roman pottery – ware quantification, unphased contexts

Ware	%	Weight (g)	Ware	%	Weight (g)
Rhenish	0.04	60	Gritty Buff	0.68	1 110
C Gaulish	0.03	45	Other Oxidised	9.11	14 840
Nene Valley CC	7.71	12 560	Horningsea	10.61	17 280
Mica-dusted			Nene Valley Grey	19.49	31 760
London type	0.11	180	BB types	0.06	90
Other Fine	0.29	470	Other Reduced	24.15	39 345
Flagons	0.74	1 200	SG (cooking pots)	14.34	23 365
Mortaria	2.43	3 960	SG (storage jars)	8.02	13 060
NV Self-coloured	2.21	3 600			
			Totals	100.02	162 925

Table 30 Comparison of Roman pottery types found at excavated sites in the Stonea region

Ware	Stonea Grange	Golden Lion	Grandford
Samian	×	×	×
NVCC	×	?	×
NVGW	×	?	×
NVSC	×	?	?
Mortaria	×	×	×
Flagons	×	–	×
Horningsea	×	×	×
Shell-gritted	×	×	×
London	×	–	×
Amphorae	×	×	–
Imported fine	×	–	×
Oxford	×	–	×

×	Present
?	Possibly present, not identified
–	Absent

NVCC	Nene Valley Colour-coated
NVGW	Nene Valley Grey
NVSC	Nene Valley Self-coloured

Table 31 Distribution of Roman pottery types by sites within parishes of Borough Fen, March, Whittlesey, Thorney and Eye

Ware	Borough Fen	March	Whittlesey	Thorney	Eye
Samian	1	13	1	2	0
NVCC	1	12	4	1	4
NVGW	1	18	4	3	4
NVSC	0	3	1	0	0
Mortaria	0	7	1	1	2
Gritty Buff	0	4	0	0	1
Flagons	0	2	0	0	0
Horningsea	0	8	0	1	1
Shell-gritted	1	15	4	3	3
Oxidised	1	14	4	1	2
Reduced	1	21	4	3	5
London	0	1	1	0	0
Total of sites	1	21	4	3	6

NVCC   Nene Valley Colour-coated
NVGW Nene Valley Grey
NVSC   Nene Valley Self-coloured

DECORATED COLOUR-COATED WARE

Catherine Johns   (Figs 174–6; Pls XXVIb–XXVII)

The 15 vessels described below are incorporated in the full pottery report in the normal way, but they have been singled out here for specific study of their decoration. My approach to this subject is wholly art-historical, taking account not only of the subject-matter of the decoration but also of the individual styles of the potters, insofar as it can be discerned. This aspect of Romano-British (and other provincial Roman) pottery deserves more attention than it has yet received. My aim is to provide pointers for further work which may eventually combine with other methods of analysis, including scientific study of fabrics, to refine our knowledge of manufacturing sources and chronology.

Many researchers, going back to Charles Roach Smith in the nineteenth century, have taken an interest in the sometimes very obscure subject-matter of the scenes which incorporate human or divine figures, and have hoped that a better understanding of them would substantially augment our knowledge of Romano-British life and religious customs. In recent years, the theme has been explored anew by Graham Webster (Webster 1986, 1989, 1991), while Maggi Darling has also speculated upon the processes behind the creation of the more elaborately decorated vessels, touching on such matters as the source of models for some of the motifs, and the question of whether these complex pieces were made to special order or were part of a potter's standard repertoire (Darling 1989).

These are all questions of undoubted interest and importance, but they cover only a part of the additional information which might be obtained from a careful study of the decoration of these colour-coated vessels. Attempts to distinguish the hands of different decorators, or at least the products of different *officinae*, in the manner which has long been familiar to students of Greek painted pottery and *terra sigillata*, have the potential to provide an extremely valuable additional basis for classification. Comments on stylistic idiosyncrasies have indeed been made on occasion, notably by the present author (Johns 1981, 90), and by Anne Anderson in a discussion of Continental barbotine wares (Anderson 1981); the idea is also alluded to by Rex Hull in his discussion of the Colchester colour-coated products (Hull 1963, 93, col. 2), but no progress has been made on the subject.

Stylistic analysis has probably been avoided not only because it is unfashionably art-historical but also because the published examples of suitable decorated sherds form a very limited sample, and the quality of published illustrations is too variable to provide a sound basis for valid comparisons. Many of the published drawings are reproduced at a small scale which, while adequate for illustrating the profile of the vessel, is unsuitable for analysis of the decorative motifs. This problem can gradually be overcome by systematic work and proper publication. The other factor which might confuse stylistic judgements is the need to distinguish between characteristics which are the direct result of the potters' personal styles and preferences and those which arise naturally from the physical requirements of the barbotine technique. More practical experiment would obviously be of value, though the results of this approach should always be evaluated cautiously; the fact that a process can be executed in a certain way does not always prove that the same method was used in antiquity. In general, if the principles and a broad framework for classification were to be laid down, it would become progressively easier to fit new finds into it. An attempt to lay the basis of such work is undoubtedly worthwhile.

Barbotine decoration, the technique of creating low relief designs by trailing thick clay slip onto the surface of the pot, has often been compared with piping designs in sugar icing on cakes and other foodstuffs; Ludowici made the comparison long ago in his description of barbotine-decorated samian ware from Rheinzabern (Ludowici 1901–5, 243), and in general the analogy seems to be a valid one. At least one researcher, Richard Landy, has successfully experimented with the method on pottery with the aim of reproducing the appearance of Roman colour-coated beakers, though unfortunately he says little in his publication about the equipment he used (Landy 1984–5). Although a mixture of clay and water will not behave in exactly the same way as a mixture of egg-white and sugar, some important observations can nevertheless be made on the basis of extensive experience of piped decoration using substances other than clay. One of the most fundamental is that the best results are obtained by a decorator who is able to work quickly. The warmth of the hands and the seepage of moisture through the piping bag – assuming it is made of a permeable material – alters the consistency and flow of the mass being piped. The fluidity of the material must be closely controlled, and it is possible that pot decorators, like cake decorators, used a stiffer mix for fine lines and a softer one for larger areas of low relief. Landy mentions the importance of achieving a shrinkage rate in drying and firing which is consistent with the body of the vessel. The shape as well as the size of the nozzle or tube is important, and though a very wide range of effects can be created using only a circular outlet cut straight across, angled and flattened forms can greatly facilitate the work. The angle of the nozzle against the surface of the pot will vary according to whether smooth areas, lines or raised dots and circles are required. Turntables are not essential, but they are very helpful, and we can probably assume that they were used. Since only one hand is normally needed to control the piping bag and nozzle, a hand-turned wheel is all that is necessary. Finally, after the main decoration has been piped, it is possible to use styli or brushes to add detail, or to emphasise or smooth out relief (cf. the use of a fine sharp point on the torso of the human figure, Fig. 174, no. 3).

My reason for spelling out somewhat obvious points about the methods which may have been used is to underline the fact that there are many opportunities for an artisan to develop distinctive individual traits, and careful examination of a sufficiently large number of beakers with complex decoration should reveal some of these.

For our purpose, the content of the scenes may usefully be divided into four broad categories: (a) human figures (including gods/goddesses), (b) phallic themes, (c) animals, (d) vegetal/abstract motifs; these may overlap considerably in some cases, though as it happens, in our group from Stonea they are mutually exclusive. I have not discussed the few examples of coloured-coated ware from the site which fall into class (d), with foliate scrolls or scale decoration. The decorative schemes could be classified under quite different headings, e.g. subject-areas such as mythology, gladiatorial, hunting-scenes, erotica, but I have preferred a simpler range because many of the more detailed scenes are intrinsically difficult to classify, and because it is a comparison of the treatment of individual motifs, human, animal or other, which is likely to prove most fruitful in defining style.

Scenes with human figures   (Fig. 174; Pl. XXVIb)

Most of the points arising from the study of the decoration on beakers 1–4 are noted in the individual descriptions. Number 3 stands out as a skilfully decorated and distinctive vessel with enough characteristic features to make the decorator's style potentially recognisable elsewhere. The dotted hair (and animal pelt), the added point of slip forming the chin and the small curved line for the ear are likely to be repeated in all human figures created by this decorator. Ears are completely omitted in many barbotine human figures, for example that on the curious sherd from Grandford (Johns 1981, Fig. 6, 5; Webster 1989, Fig. 2, 24). The subject of the decoration on no. 3, whether it is a hunt or an arena performance, places it in the mainstream of this class of Romano-British art. The other sherds are all frustratingly small, making them difficult to compare with others either stylistically or thematically, though nos 1 and 2 are representations of gods and therefore belong to another well-established subject area.

Phallic decoration   (Figs 174–5; Pl. XXVIIa)

The seven examples (nos 5–11) from Stonea are all phallic in the strict sense, that is, phalli apparently form the sole decoration. This theme should be distinguished from erotic scenes which feature human participants, such as the examples from Horsey Toll, Saffron Walden and South Shields (Johns 1982, 94–5; Turnbull 1978, 202–3), even though the latter may include disembodied phalli as space-fillers. It is not possible for us to judge how the more elaborate bawdy scenes would have been perceived by the Romano-British owner of such a pot. They may illustrate stories or sayings which are unknown to us, they may have been primarily humorous, or they may have been concerned above all with the serious symbolic significance of phallic imagery. Almost certainly they were less embarrassing to the contemporary viewer than they tend to be to us.

Stylised phalli alone are easier to classify. The place of this theme in Roman symbolism is quite clear, and whatever additional values might have been placed upon it (including, no doubt, humour), the underlying significance of phallic representations concerns good fortune and power over harmful influences (Johns 1982, ch. 3; Turnbull 1978). Designs such as those on the phallic pots from Stonea must have been intended principally to ensure good luck for the user. It is perhaps worth drawing attention, with all due caution, to the findspots of these vessels within the excavated area: with one exception (no. 5) they all come from the contiguous areas blocks 8, 9 and 10. This observation is certainly insufficient to form a basis for any theories about the nature and usage of either the buildings or the pottery, but attention to the distribution of such vessels within a site might eventually be useful, even if it were only to demonstrate that there are no significant patterns.

The catalogue entries describe fully the marked difference in style between the beaker with the winged phalli, no. 11, and the others. Even within this small sample of seven vessels, we can attribute nos 5, 6, and 7 to the same hand, nos 8 and 9 to the same workshop, if not the same potter, no. 10 to a different decorator, and no.11 to yet another artisan and in all probability another pottery. It is worthy of note that the difference in decorative style and technique of this last example is reinforced by some variation in form and fabric from the norm represented by the other vessels.

Animals   (Fig. 176; Pl. XXVIIb)

'Hunt cups' featuring hounds chasing deer or hares are the most common figured scenes on Romano-British barbotine-decorated vessels. The theme is also favoured on Continental pottery of the same type, including samian with barbotine relief. Superficially they all look rather alike, but there are many small characteristics which should eventually make it possible to distinguish different hands. Our three fairly complete examples, nos 12–14, are undoubtedly the work of at least two different potters. It is very unlikely that a decorator who normally depicted the body of an animal in one single sweep of the nozzle would on other occasions choose to emphasise the form by using three. Other details vary between the vases, such as the presence or absence of dots indicating teeth, and the differing treatment of legs; one artist created limbs with some feeling of structure and clearly depicted paws or hooves, while the other produced bonelessly curved legs tapering to amorphous blob-like feet. It is possible, though not certain, that our nos 13 and 14 were decorated by the same hand. We can be sure that no. 12 is the work of a different person.

In her study of Continental beakers, Anderson linked vessel-form with both the themes and the style of the decoration, and assigned these to chronological phases (Anderson 1981): we need much more analysis of this kind before all the variables (fabric, form, theme and style of decoration) and all the possible reasons for them (source, date, individual artisan) can be organised and understood.

CATALOGUE

1   A small sherd from a large beaker; the fabric is fairly thick, and has a greyish core and light red surface which shows through the matt grey slip. All that remains of a single figure in the decoration is the upraised right arm and two attributes. The hand grasps a very stylised thunderbolt, rendered as a short double-ended trident, of which only one end survives. Over the forearm is a fall of drapery, the folds indicated by an applied zigzag line, further embellished with small decorative dots. Near the elbow is part of a curved object which is almost certainly a wheel.

The figure evidently represents Jupiter Taranis, with the attributes of *fulmen* and wheel. The thunderbolt can be compared with that brandished by a deity, presumably Jupiter, on an indented beaker from Great Chesterford (Roach Smith 1857, 91; Webster 1989, Fig. 7, 59c), while the drapery over the arm is stylistically related to the drapery of the Mars on another indented beaker, from Lothbury, London (Walters 1908, M. 2483 (BM no. 1871, 7–14, 18, P&RB); Webster 1989, Fig. 7, 60; Going 1981, 316). Beakers ornamented with a series of standing gods and goddesses are often of the indented or 'folded' form, the hollows providing suitable niches for the figures, but this Stonea example is from a plain bag-shaped beaker. Nevertheless, we may take it that it belongs to the god-beaker class, with images of several deities standing in a line with appropriate attributes.

Since so little of the figure is present, it is difficult to identify any specific stylistic traits which might help to define the work of this particular decorator, except perhaps for the treatment of the drapery with its added lines and tiny dots. In our present state of knowledge, one could certainly postulate a connection between the decorator of this vessel and of the Lothbury Mars sherd, but it would be stretching the evidence to attribute them to the same hand.

ST 84 DOK, SF 854. From gully 19, cut 5, unit 1822. Mid 3rd century AD.

2   A sherd from a large beaker in a very pale grey fabric with a matt black slip. The only recognisable features surviving are the legs, from the knees down, of a large standing figure. Two adjacent bumps are unidentifiable. The legs are crossed at the ankles, and no shoes or other garments are indicated. It is reasonable to assume that this, too, is a sherd from a god-beaker, but there is no evidence for identification of the deity. In classical art, Bacchus is quite commonly depicted standing with legs crossed, but the sherd from Lothbury cited above (Walters 1908, M. 2483) is decorated with a figure of Mars who stands in just this manner.

Insofar as style can be detected at all, we may note that the limbs are very simply rendered without much attempt to delineate muscles. Compared with some other work (see no. 3 below), the legs are slender.

ST 83 J4, 1. From well J4, layer 1. Early 3rd century AD.

3   Four sherds from a large beaker in fine, thin buff ware, with a slightly metallic slip varying from brownish-black to a chestnut colour. The decoration, including human and animal figures, is applied above a band of rouletting, and there is a ground line and some panel divisions of widely spaced, very fine dashes: the spaces demarcated by these panel borders are not respected by the applied figures.

The principal surviving figure is virtually complete, a man running to the left followed by a running hare. Two smaller sherds bear the head and shoulders of another man to the right, and part of the head and body of an animal running left, probably a hound. A fourth tiny sherd has some lines which cannot be interpreted.

Both human figures wear protective binding on the upper arms and legs similar to that used by charioteers and gladiators. This is represented by fine transverse lines from shoulder to elbow and on the lower body and thighs. In addition, the main figure has vertical lines superimposed from waist to groin, and an overall texturing of tiny stabbed holes on the chest. A transverse line above the ankles shews that he is wearing boots. Protective clothing of this kind incorporating leather strapping or binding was not worn by ordinary *bestiarii* in the arena, nor, one might suppose, was it normal equipment for huntsmen. Webster discusses the matter of clothing in hunting scenes in some detail (Webster 1989, 3–5) but there are still many unanswered questions. As yet we can say only that the

Fig. 174 Stonea Grange: barbotine-figured pottery 1–4 and 7–10 (scale 1:2).

equipment shewn in these Romano-British scenes does not always correspond to what we would expect on the basis of other Roman art, including the many amphitheatre and hunting scenes to be found on Gaulish sigillata, which is as provincial a product as the pottery we are considering here.

We do not know whether a scene such as this depicts a staged *venatio* in the arena, an actual hunt in open country, or a mythological or ritual scene with a hunting element, nor whether the clothing is a confused and inaccurate rendering of reality, the result of artistic licence, or a faithful image of what was worn on the relevant occasions in Roman Britain.

To return to our main figure, his twisted pose appears at first sight to present his back to the viewer, but in addition to the dotted texturing referred to above, his nipples are added as

applied dots (one is lost, but its position is visible). This indicates not only that the hunter's body is twisted towards rather than away from the viewer, but also that he is not wearing an upper garment, an inference supported by the absence of a line across the throat representing the neckline. What, then, does the dotted texture represent? Does it indicate body hair? The other figure has no such patterning, though there are a few very slight scratched lines above the nipples which might not even be intentional. The attribute held by the more complete huntsman is hardly a normal weapon of the chase, for in his left hand he brandishes a hammer with a very long shaft. The hammer-head is carefully formed, and is embellished with three small raised points which seem to have no functional significance.

There are several distinctive details of style and technique which can be seen on the human figures. The hair is treated as a close-set series of raised dots on a smooth base. The eyes are large round points, and the low-set ears are single small curved lines. The chins are large added blobs of slip. No attempt has been made to define the fingers on the hand which grasps the hammer. The legs of the more complete figure are short and have greatly emphasised calves and small, slender feet.

The running animal which is partly preserved on another small sherd is covered with short piped lines which depict a shaggy or bristly coat. The line of the back survives, together with the cheek, an oval eye and part of a pricked ear, but the muzzle has broken away. At first sight, the rough coat suggests a boar, but there is no crest and the proportions of body and neck are more consistent with the shape of a dog or wolf. If a dog, it could well be one of the very large Celtic hounds, which had rough coats resembling that of the Irish Wolfhound. Hounds on colour-coated beakers are usually left smooth. The hare on the largest sherd is quite simply rendered without any distinctive features.

ST 81 KB; 81 MG, SF 153; 81 KA, SF 108; 81 FH. From gully 44, cut 2, various layers. Later 2nd–3rd century AD. (One sherd – 81 FH – from topsoil).

4 A sherd in a ware with a pink core, graduating to a pale grey on the interior and buff on the exterior. The matt slip is light orange.

The surviving decoration depicts the neck, torso and part of one leg of a figure transfixed through the upper body by an arrow. The thickness of the ware and the direction of the throwing grooves indicate the orientation of the body, which is falling forward. The point of the arrow emerges through his chest, and short lines at the back of the figure must be intended to depict falling drops of blood.

The interpretation of this individual presents great difficulties, and without additional sherds from the vessel it will probably remain impossible to identify him. He appears to have a long pointed beard, and his body is evidently naked, but the incomplete leg which is preserved is that of an animal, implying that the figure is a Pan or satyr. Added lines which divide the legs from the torso make no sense as clothing, but if the figure is indeed naked, it is extremely odd that there is no indication of his genitals. This would be possible if we had here the human part of a centaur, but against that interpretation is the fact that the upflung leg is surely an animal's *hind* leg. A row of raised dots along this leg is a distinctive, though mysterious, detail.

Unless another beaker is found which has comparable decoration, all that can be said at present is that the figure may be a Pan, and that he is presumably taking part in a scene of hunting or battle.

ST 84 DMX, SF 798. From upper fill (unit 1786) of pit 1786. Late 2nd/3rd century AD.

5 A restored bag-shaped beaker, complete but for a few small sherds. Where visible, the fabric is buff with some reddish highlights visible through the matt brownish-black slip.

The decoration consists of seven panels demarcated by a border of dashes above and below and vertical lines of dashes;

each panel contains three stylised phalli, one above the other, facing right.

Phallic ornament has been found on a number of Romano-British colour-coated vessels, and is well represented at Stonea itself with seven examples. The significance of the motif needs no detailed discussion here (see e.g. Johns 1982), but it should be noted that we do not yet have any way of knowing whether decoration of this kind was universally acceptable or was specially selected for particular purposes.

Stylistically, the vessel is highly distinctive. Each phallus consists of a single broad trail of clay tapering sharply to a pointed tip which is emphasised by a final small blob, plus two small vertically-applied blobs at the other end to represent the testicles. In one panel only, all three motifs have additional transverse lines near the tip to indicate the glans. Overall, the decoration gives the impression of having been carried out rapidly according to a very familiar and standardised routine, and the degree of stylisation is so extreme that some knowledge of the comparanda is needed to recognise the motifs as phalli at all. It is reasonable to infer that the potter had reduced the number of movements necessary to depict a phallus to the minimum, and that this was the result of producing many pots with such decoration: the presence of three more examples of his work at Stonea helps to confirm this.

ST 82 AFN, From ditch 9, cut 10, unit 574. 3rd century AD.

6 More than half of a beaker of similar size, form, fabric and decoration to no. 5 above.

A narrow band of panels has lines of dashes above and below, but as is often the case, the dividers between the panels are diagonal rather than vertical, sloping from upper left to lower right. Each panel contains one phallus to the right, larger than those on no. 5 and depicted with slightly more attention to detail, but essentially in the same somewhat slapdash style. The proportions are more naturalistic, and in particular, the glans is fairly normally shaped and is demarcated from the rest of the organ by a clear, straight transverse line. The way in which the piping tube has been used to finish the tip of each phallus has left a slight raised line and point at the end. The testes are shown in precisely the same manner as those on the previous pot, as two tiny and widely spaced blobs at the back 'corners' of the motif.

There can be little doubt that this vessel is from the hand of the same potter who fashioned no.5.

ST 83 J1, 1. From pit J1, layer 1. Late 3rd/early 4th century AD.

7 A small sherd in buff ware with a matt brownish-orange slip, probably from just below the rim. If so, the incomplete motif is of a phallus facing to the left. There is no trace of dotted borders. Though it is such a small sherd, this too can be attributed to the same Nene Valley potter as the two preceding vessels. We have only the base of a phallus with one small testicle placed in the same way as we have seen on nos 5 and 6. It seems likely that this overall scheme of decoration would also have contained rows of phalli.

ST 84 DWY, SF 1048. From the upper fill (unit 2003) of pit 2003. Late 2nd/3rd century AD.

8 A small sherd, the interior slip in a dull light orange-brown, and the exterior dull black with some oxidised highlights, decorated

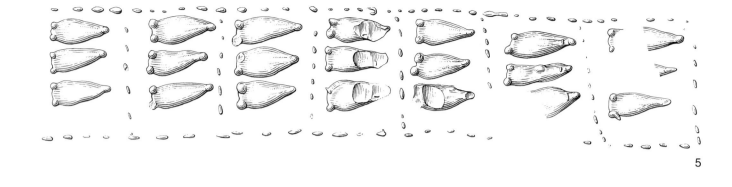

5

6

11

Fig. 175 Stonea Grange: barbotine-figured pottery 5–6 and 11 (scale 1:2).

with the front part of a phallus set more or less horizontally. The sherd evidently belongs to a beaker with decoration similar to that of no. 6 above, and the technique and style are also very close, although the relief of the motif is higher.

Though the diagnostic area of the testicles is missing, the very similar treatment of the glans suggests that this is another example of the work of the craftsman who made the preceding beakers.

ST 84 DST. From gully 18, cut 25, unit 1927. 3rd century AD.

9 A small sherd in buff ware with a light golden-brown slip. The design appears once more to consist of diagonally bordered panels containing phalli to the right, but the work is rather more careful and finished than that of the four examples above, and it is not possible to assign this sherd confidently to the same source.

The panel borders consist of fairly small dots rather than the carelessly variable dashes of nos 5 and 6, and the phallus, of which we have only the tip and part of the shaft, is larger and somewhat more carefully shaped. The glans lacks the longitudinal ridge seen on no. 6, and the transverse line is carefully curved. This phallus could simply be an example of more careful work by the same potter; in the absence of the diagnostic small, widely spaced testicles we cannot be sure. It might also be a product by another decorator, but it is very closely related to the other four pots.

ST 83 J4, 1. Context as no. 2.

10 A sherd in very thick buff fabric, probably from a rather larger beaker than the previous examples. The slip is blackish with the usual tan or orange-brown shadings around the barbotine relief. The surviving decoration consists of the greater part of a small, well-defined phallus to the right and three areas where the relief has broken away from the surface; these almost certainly represent parts of additional phallic motifs. One is a rounded area immediately below the testicles of the extant phallus and probably represents a testicle belonging to another phallus in line with the preserved one, while the other areas would seem to indicate another vertical row of phalli behind the first. The decor is therefore like that of no. 5, through without the dividing lines forming panels.

The style in which the phallus is depicted is distinctly different from that seen on nos 5–7 above; the glans area is broken away and cannot be compared, but the testicles, instead of being schematically rendered as small points, are clearly defined rounded projections, producing a far more naturalistic image.

ST 84 DEA. From topsoil/cleaning (unit 1597), blocks 8 and 9.

11 The greater part of a beaker in fine red ware with a brownish-black slip. The ornament consists of a single zone of phallic decoration with two plain phalli alternating with two phallus-birds. There is no ground line, but there is an upper border of short dashes. Between the main motifs are ivy leaves on long curving stems.

This vessel is exceptionally well-made, thin-walled and hard-fired, more rounded in profile than the other complete beakers with phallic motifs and decorated in an elegant and assured style. Apart from the convention whereby the shaft

and tip of the phallus is seen in side view and the testicles almost in frontal view, the phalli are naturalistic, and are furnished with well-placed curved ridges dividing the shaft and glans: while the identification of the motifs on no. 5 could prove difficult for anyone unfamiliar with Roman imagery, there could be no possible doubt in the case of this pot, even though two of the motifs have been embellished with the fantasy additions of stylised wings and birds' legs.

The personification of phalli as animals, especially birds, is found throughout the Roman Empire in a variety of media. Several examples have been recorded from Britain, the closest parallel to our pot being a sherd from a colour-coated vessel from Colchester (Hull 1963, Fig. 53, 1) with a phallus-bird. The extraordinary chariot-racing scene on the Saffron Walden beaker (Johns 1982, 94, Fig. 78; Webster 1989, Fig. 2, 16) is relevant insofar as it depicts zoomorphised phalli, bird-legged but apparently wingless, and there are other phallic beakers from Colchester (e.g. Hull 1963, Fig. 54, 2, with ivy-leaf space-fillers) which clearly belong to the same general class.

Our potter's mastery is well demonstrated in the leaves which form space-fillers. Their triple-lobed form is itself phallic, though whether this is a conscious echo of the main theme is uncertain, since it is the normal form for stylised ivy-leaves in barbotine decoration, and the confident curves of the stems are precisely judged to create a good balance of space and ornament. The wings of the phallus-birds are simplified into slender fringed lines, in both cases reaching right up to the rim. The wings do not override the dotted border, however, because the border has been added after the phallus-birds, and gaps have been left to accommodate their wings. One of the phallus-birds is standing still, while the other appears to be walking.

Much more work is required before we can make detailed and valid comparisons between the style of this potter and of others who produced phallic and erotic ornament on Romano-British colour-coated wares. For the present, we can say only that the skills of the artisan who produced our no. 11 were far superior to those of the potters who made the other phallic beakers described here, and that there are some indications that the Colchester potteries provide better parallels for his work than the Nene Valley.

ST 84 DRN. From the base layer (unit 1897) of well 1834. 3rd century AD (see no. 15).

12 An almost complete beaker with a simple chase scene: three dogs running to the right are framed within dashed-line borders top and bottom and vertical panel dividers. Small stylised leaves on curved stems form space-fillers above and below the hounds. The fabric is buff with a brownish-black slip and some dull red shewing through in places.

Two of the hounds have open jaws, and their teeth are indicated by dots. The animals' bodies are formed in three stages, the centre of the body being the first unit in fairly low relief, with the haunch and hind leg overlying it at the back, and the shoulder and neck, tapering into the head, forming a second applied layer at the front. The forelegs, the far hind leg and the tail, ears, eye etc. are added. The result is a variable height of relief which gives noticeable modelling to the figure. The long ears of two of the hounds are piped so that the nearer ear overlies the further to increase the perspective effect. The long legs

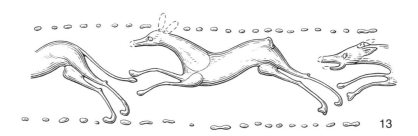

Fig. 176 Stonea Grange: barbotine-figured pottery 12–14 (scale 1 : 2).

are thin and sketchy, and the slender long tails thicken slightly at the tip with the final stroke of the piping nozzle. No collars are shewn. The overall effect is of strong, well-muscled animals.

A similar technique in applying animal bodies may be seen in several Colchester products (e.g. Hull 1963, Fig. 51, 8, Fig. 53, 8), as far as can be ascertained from the drawings.

ST 82 AGL. From ditch 9, cut 7, base layer (unit 596). Early 3rd century AD.

13 The greater part of a beaker of somewhat slender form with a chase scene. The fabric is buff and the slip black, shading abruptly to reddish-brown a little way below the decoration. The decorated frieze is a very simple one of three animals running to the left between upper and lower dashed-line borders. One animal is completely preserved, but the others lack their front and hind parts respectively.

The animal represented by head, neck and forelegs is a hound: its jaws are open, and its ears laid back. No teeth are depicted. The other incomplete animal is also a dog, with a long thin tail. Between them is another running creature which at first sight could be a dog, but on the basis of its large raised ears which go through the upper border (both ears are now lost, but their position can be seen clearly), and its tiny tail it should perhaps be interpreted as a hind. Treatment of the body, legs and feet is the same in all cases.

The style of the animals differs from that seen on no. 12 above. The head, neck, haunch and the whole of the nearer hind leg are formed in one sweep of the nozzle, the other legs and the tail and ears being added afterwards. The proportions are long and slender, and the height of the relief fairly constant. While the figures look highly stylised, they are extremely skillfully executed, conveying a tremendous sense of movement.

ST 82 BEY, BCO. Joining sherds, from pit 794, unit 824, late 3rd/4th century AD; and from the nearby ditch 9, cut 4, top layer (unit 767), late 3rd–4th century AD.

14 The greater part of a beaker in pale buff ware, the slip shading from dull dark grey to a pale orange near the foot and on the interior. The decorated zone contains three animals, two almost completely preserved, the third represented only by its hindquarters. There are dashed-line borders above and below and between the animals.

The completely preserved animal is a hind: she has a very long head, pricked ears, a disproportionately long neck and short body, and very long legs which taper to single slender lines. There is no tail, and the hocks are emphasised by tiny added points of slip. Though the mouth is not open, the lower jaw and lower line of the head is marked. Following the hind is a stag, preserved except for the far antler. The form is naturally very similar, though the stag's body is longer.

Of the third animal, we see only the hind legs and long, slender tail, and part of the front legs. From the tail, and from the logic of the decoration, it must be a hound.

Stylistically, there is an overall similarity between this decoration and that of no. 13. One would hesitate to attribute them to the same hand, but it would be possible to envisage the same decorator producing them at different times: the form of the heads cannot be directly compared in detail, but seems similar, the forms of body, neck, shoulders and haunches are depicted in

the same way, and in particular the legs, single curving lines, the hocks shown only as added lines, tapering to undifferentiated feet, are close.

ST 84 DIA. From unit 1693, an occupation layer above pit cluster 1960, 1982 etc. at the south of block 9.

15 (*Unillus.*) A sherd in pale fabric with a brown slip on both surfaces. The profile is fairly straight. The surviving decoration consists of a fairly broad horizontal body in low relief with an oval swelling superimposed at the left-hand end. The interpretation of this is uncertain. It could be a large phallic motif, but it seems rather more likely to be part of an animal moving to the left, the raised area of relief corresponding with the attachment of the foreleg to the body.

ST 84 DQC. From middle layer (unit 1863) of well 1834. 3rd century AD (see no. 11).

TERRACOTTAS

Catherine Johns   (Fig. 177; Pl. XXI)

The site produced fragments from four moulded objects made of fired clay. Two of these, nos 1 and 2 below, come from Central Gaulish white pipeclay figurines of well-known types; no. 3 is in a buff fabric which was originally lead-glazed and is likewise of Central Gaulish manufacture; while no. 4, though in a darker clay with a light slip, is a mould-made figurine which clearly belongs to the same general class as the pipeclay examples.

The principal manufacturing sites for pipeclay statuettes were in the Allier Valley and adjacent areas of Central Gaul and in the Rhine–Mosel region around Cologne and Trier: both of these areas were major pottery production centres making a range of ceramics including terra sigillata and lamps, and operating extensive export trades. Technologically there are certain features common to sigillata, lamp and statuette production, above all the use of moulds. The names of artisans and workshops are found on both moulds and final products in the pipeclay statuette industry, just as they are on samian and lamps, but the precise connections between these ceramic industries is not understood, and as yet the statuettes have not been as fully studied as the related industries.

The two most useful general references are Rouvier-Jeanlin 1972 and van Boekel 1987: the former catalogues the collections of the Musée des Antiquités Nationales at St Germain, and the latter is a corpus of finds from the Netherlands. They cover a good range of Central Gaulish and Rhine–Mosel types respectively. Figures from both areas are found in Britain, though Central Gaulish imports predominate. The origins can be distinguished in part by typological means, but it is also worth noting that the Central Gaulish figurines were made in fired-clay moulds while the Rhine–Mosel examples were nearly always produced in plaster (gypsum) moulds. Air bubbles formed in plaster during drying leave characteristic raised globules on the surface of the completed ceramic cast. Central Gaulish figures are generally carefully finished and have a polished surface (see van Boekel 1987, 216–31).

The most typical subjects for Gallo-Roman pipeclay statuettes are Venuses and mother-goddesses. Figures of other deities exist, as do a variety of animals, especially birds. The principal function of terracotta models was religious, though their presence in some children's graves suggests that they may have been used as playthings on occasion: though purpose-made toys have existed in most societies, children have also always played with items which were not originally intended for that purpose. In the case of the grave from Arrington (Cambridgeshire) which contained a fine group of terracottas including a Cologne mother-goddess, the items would hardly have been appropriate playthings, since the occupant of the grave was a sadly handicapped infant less than a year old (Taylor 1993). It is worth noting that the Stonea horse (no. 2) is from a site context which may have ritual meaning.

Though both the pipeclay figures from Stonea are very fragmentary, they can be fairly closely identified. This is not the case with no. 3, the basal fragment in a buff ware. While it is almost certainly from a zoomorphic vase made of lead-glazed Central Gaulish ware, it is not easy to match its form, and the suggestion made in the entry below is by no means certain. Small containers of this type were probably designed to contain scent or unguents, but they, too, are known from the graves of children, e.g. the Colchester example (May 1930, Pl. LXXV). The white, cream or buff body finished in an amber-to-brown or greenish lead glaze was also used in Central Gaul for some mould-made vessels decorated, like ordinary samian ware, in low relief, and the dating of these falls into the first century AD rather than the second.

The remaining terracotta, no. 4, is even more difficult to date and parallel. The fabric is not immediately recognizable, but because of the technique of manufacture and the shape of the pedestal, a Central Gaulish origin seems likely.

1 Mother-goddess   Height 3.8 cm, width 2.7 cm   ST 82 BAE

A roughly triangular fragment from a mould-made figure in a fine, hard white clay with a smooth, but not lustrous, exterior surface. There is one large rounded quartz grit visible, and there are sparse very small flakes of mica. The decoration consists of flattish vertical ribs with incised chevron patterns marked upon them, a stylized rendering of basketry.

The fragment is from the back of a statuette of a mother-goddess seated in a basketwork chair and nursing either one or two infants. There is considerable diversity in the range of mother-goddess figurines, and unfortunately the Stonea fragment is too undiagnostic for us to be able to assign it to one of Rouvier-Jeanlin's principal types (Rouvier-Jeanlin 1972), let alone to a specific mould.

It may be worth noting that the fine complete mother-goddess from Welwyn (Rook 1973, Pl. 1A; British Museum, P1981, 11–2, 1)

displays a similar treatment of the wickerwork. The Welwyn figure belongs to Rouvier-Jeanlin's Type IIB, and is very close indeed to her catalogue no. 369. This might, therefore, be some guide to the original appearance of the Stonea example.

2nd century AD.

From an upper layer (unit 710) in well 705. 3rd/4th century AD.

2 Horse   ST 84 P10, 1, SF 1157

(a) Neck fragment, 3.8 × 3 cm
(b) Near foreleg, length 5.3 cm
(c) Off hind leg, length 5 cm
(d) Part of near hind leg, length 3.2 cm.

The fabric is fine, hard and creamy-white. The external surfaces are polished and lustrous, though this burnishing is less evident on the inner surfaces of the legs, which are not formed in a mould but hand-modelled. The legs have broken away where they were luted on to the mould-made body.

Fragment (a) is from the base of the horse's neck on the near (left) side. A raised band crossing it just above the shoulder is probably a rein, though it could be a breast-band associated with a saddle. A small segment of the upstanding mane survives, marked with straight incised lines. Fragment (b) consists of the near foreleg from its attachment to the body to the fetlock, where the profile starts to expand towards the hoof. It is a fairly featureless tapering shape, without any indication of the knee. Fragment (c) is almost the whole of the off hind leg from the point of attachment to just above the fetlock. The leg is schematically but quite effectively formed, with the hock indicated simply by pinching the clay into a flattened angle. Fragment (d) is the lower part of the other hind leg, from just beneath the hock.

Though there must be some uncertainty as to whether the line across the neck is a rein or a breast-band, taken in combination with the treatment of the mane and the form of the legs, the Stonea horse compares well with Rouvier-Jeanlin's nos 983–5. The comparison must be tentative, but we can positively state that the Stonea horse is not the same as any of the others illustrated in Rouvier-Jeanlin. Fragmentary pipeclay horses from Canterbury and Wroxeter (Jenkins 1962, Pl. I) and another example from Canterbury (unpublished) can also be excluded as close parallels.

Rouvier-Jeanlin no. 983 originally had a side-saddle rider, although this was an addition, not part of the same mould. The rider would almost certainly have been Epona.

2nd century AD.

From the main fill (layer 1) of the shaft of pit P10, adjacent to the temple (building R15). Early 3rd century AD.

3 Fragment of lead-glazed vase
Height 2.5 cm, width 4.1 cm   ST 83 CAA, SF 500

A basal fragment in a light buff ware with quartz grits of very variable size and some minute flakes of mica. There is a very small patch of surviving amber-coloured lead glaze, and other greyish and brownish surface accretions may well be decayed remains of glaze.

The fragment is from a mould-made object with a narrow oval base and a profile which flares outwards. It is likely to be from a zoomorphic vase or flask, one of the typical products in this

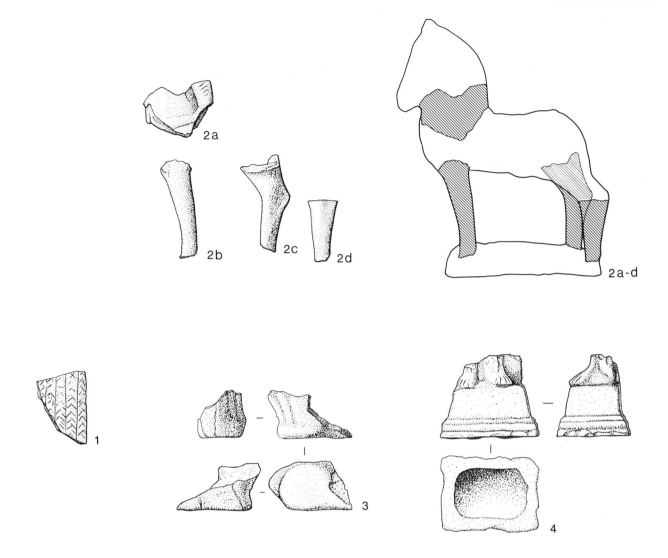

Fig. 177 Stonea Grange: terracottas, 1–3 from the excavations, 4 from the Surface Collection (scale 1:2).

lead-glazed Central Gaulish ware. The Stonea fragment is clearly not from one of the reclining animal figures (e.g. lions, deer and hares), but may be from an upright figure such as one of the seated monkeys; Rouvier-Jeanlin no. 1075 is comparable, as are two of the figures in the famous child's grave from Colchester (May 1930, Pl. LXXV, 251–2).

1st–2nd century AD.

From topsoil/cleaning, eastern end block 11.

4 Pedestal and feet

Height 4.4 cm, width 5.4 cm P1982, 6–2, 139

The feet of a standing human figure set on a rectangular pedestal, mould-made in a very hard greyish-brown clay with a light buff slip. Very small flakes of mica are present.

The pedestal base is rectangular, tapering inwards and provided with step-like mouldings at the base. It is hollowed out on the underside. Attached to the top are the bare feet of a human figure, the left foot slightly advanced, with an amorphous support, possibly drapery, behind it.

Since this figure is not a pipeclay one, it may be futile to seek a close parallel amongst the Allier Valley statuettes. However, the pale slip suggests that the figurine was intended to resemble the pipeclay examples, and it is in fact possible to find fairly similar pieces, in particular Rouvier-Jeanlin no. 542, an un-identified male figure set on a rectangular pedestal very like the Stonea example. The micaceous fabric may well be Central Gaulish.

?2nd century AD.

Stonea Grange Surface Collection.

POTTERY COUNTERS AND MISCELLANEOUS CERAMICS

Ralph Jackson   (Fig. 178)

For counters of bone and stone, see pp. 532 and 522.

1 Counter   Diameter 28–30 mm ST 83 CCY, SF 474

Wall sherd, grey ware, with ground edge.

Topsoil/cleaning, block 1, north-east and block 11, centre.

2 Counter   Diameter 20 mm ST 84 DPW, SF 857

Wall sherd, grey ware, with ground edge.

From gully 18, cut 20, unit 1857. 3rd century AD.

3 Counter   Diameter 19 mm ST 83 G8,1, SF 523

Wall sherd, NVGW, with well-formed ground edge and abraded inner surface.

From the fill of gully 18, cut 6. 3rd century AD.

4 Counter   Diameter 20–22 mm ST 83 CHR, SF 495

Wall sherd, NVGW, with carefully chipped edge.

From upper layer (unit 1184) in pit 1184. Early 3rd century AD.

5 ?Counter rough-out   *(Unillus.)*
Diameter 28 mm ST 81 SY, SF 237

NVCC base. For pottery counter rough-outs, see Crummy 1983, 93 ff.

From well 336, unit 367. Late 2nd–3rd century AD.

6 Counter   Diameter 20–20.5 mm ST 84 DYA, SF 692

A well-formed circular disc showing signs of long/heavy usage. *Terra sigillata* Central Gaul, 2nd century AD.

From gully 18, cut 10, unit 2029. 3rd century AD.

7 Counter   Diameter 20–22 mm ST 83 G4,1, SF 551

Wall sherd, with carefully chipped edge. *Terra sigillata*, Central Gaul, 2nd century AD.

From well G4, layer 1. Late 3rd/4th century AD.

8 Counter   Diameter 19.8–20.5 mm ST 84 DOK, SF 1162

A roughly chipped disc. *Terra sigillata*, Central Gaul, 2nd century AD.

From gully 19, cut 5, unit 1822. Mid 3rd century AD.

9 Counter   Diameter 23–27 mm ST 84 DST, SF 699

A roughly-formed ovoid disc. *Terra sigillata*, Central Gaul, 2nd century AD.

From gully 18, cut 25, unit 1927. 3rd century AD.

10 Counter   Diameter 13 mm ST 84 DOR, SF 685

A small circular example with chipped edge. *Terra sigillata*, Central Gaul, decorated vessel, probably a Dr 37 bowl, 2nd century AD.

From layer (unit 1829) above gully 27, cut 1. Late 2nd/early 3rd century AD.

11 Pierced counter   Diameter 21–23 mm ST 81 FM, SF 79

Wall sherd, probably Oxford ware. The edge is chipped, ground and worn. The small 'hourglass' perforation is rudimentarily cut approximately centrally. Possibly Anglo-Saxon use of a Roman sherd as a neck ornament.

From layer 127, above Anglo-Saxon building S1. Phase Va.

12 Pierced roundel
Diameter 43 mm ST 83 A,26,6, SF 1983 A,9

NVCC base. The outer surface is completely unworn and the perforation has been made at a point where the base had cracked three ways in firing. This suggests the pot was a waster and that the base was immediately adapted to alternative use. Although the five-sided perforation is slightly off-centre, the roundel may have been used as a spindle whorl. Diameter of perforation 5 mm.

From sump layer A, 26, grid 6. Late 3rd century AD.

13 Pierced base   Diameter 74 mm ST 83 J4,1, SF 544

NVGW base, fragmentary. Both inner and outer surfaces are fragmented, but show no sign of abrasion or controlled chipping. In addition to the completed hourglass piercing, which is markedly off-centre, there are two incipient perforations. Probably the base of a flower pot rather than a roundel.

From well J4, layer 1. Late 3rd–early 4th century AD.

14 Spindle-whorl   Diameter 29–30 mm ST 84 DAA, SF 620

A perforated ovoid disc made from a wall sherd of coarse grey ware. The edge is slightly damaged. The perforation is slightly off-centre.

From topsoil, block 6 and block 5, south.

15 Spindle-whorl   Diameter 35 mm ST 81 JS, SF 95

Slightly under half of a fine buff-ware spindle-whorl. The base is plain and lightly convex, while the inward-sloping convex side and flattened top are embellished with concentric incised lines, three on the side, one on the top. The perforation, which tapers very slightly from base to top, is set a little off-centre, a deliberate feature, perhaps, intended to increase momentum.

From unit 201 of the low rubbly mound partially sealing building S1. Phase Va.

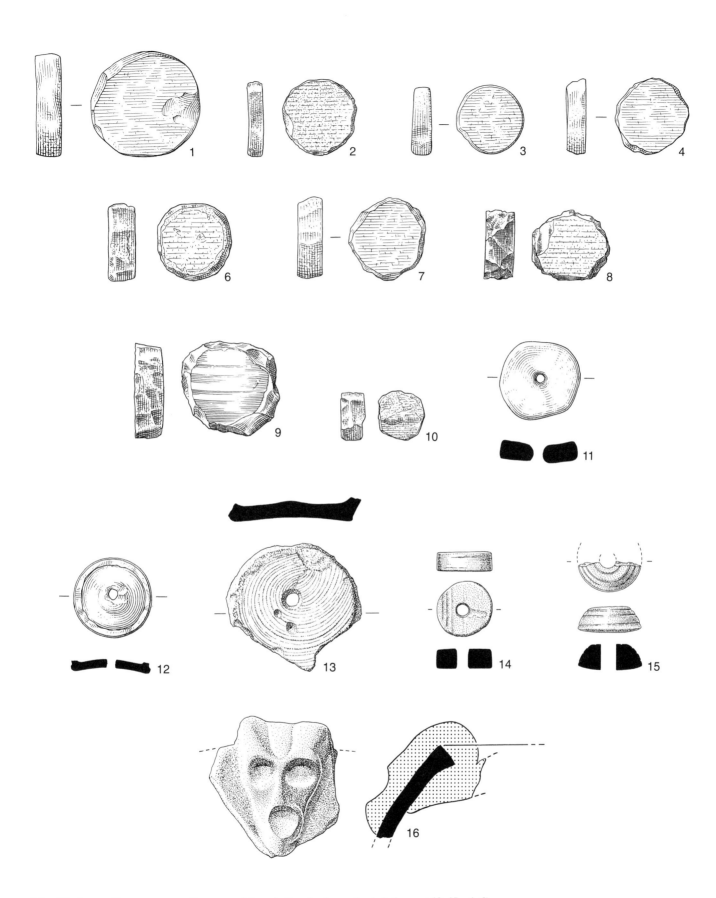

Fig. 178 Stonea Grange: pottery discs, roundels, spindle-whorls etc. (scale 1 : 1 except 12–15 = 1 : 2).

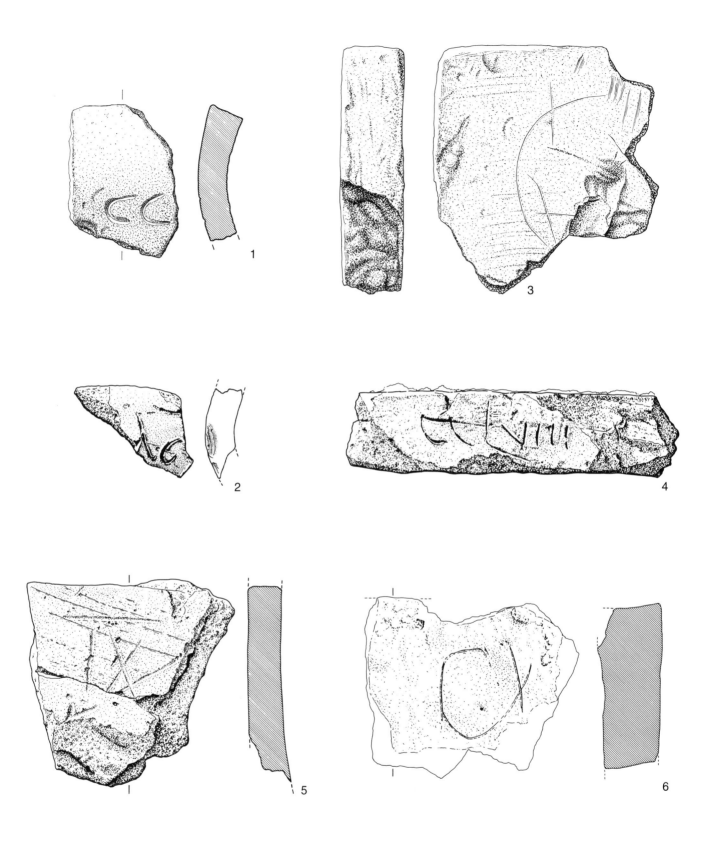

Fig. 179 Stonea Grange: graffiti on tile 1–6 (scale 1 : 2).

16 Face-mask handle Height 37 mm ST 81 FM, SF 45

Val Rigby writes: 'Face-mask applied to the upper end of a folded strap-handle, on the inside of the rim of a vessel of unknown form. Fine-grained sandy matrix, with sparse white (?shell) inclusions; light orange ware, traces of a pale cream slip or wet-hands 'slurry' finish. The vessel may be a hanging bowl (cf. Gillam 174) or a jug (cf. Gillam 60). The latter is more likely because jug handles were more frequently decorated than any other vessel type. The face is triangular, with rudimentary features, upon which no detail survives, probably as a result of abrasion. The handle is folded over the edge of the rim in such a way that the straps give the impression of curved ram's horns, perhaps to indicate the horned god Cernunnos or Mars. The vessel was possibly made somewhere in the Lower Nene Valley potteries.

Neither the mask nor the form can be closely paralleled. A sherd decorated with the bust of a horned goddess was found at Richborough (Bushe-Fox 1949, Pl. LXII, 347), and there is a series of grotesques on a vessel from Kiln III, at Caistor, Norfolk (Atkinson 1932, Pl. XII, Fig. 6, 46).'

From unit 127 of the low rubbly mound partially sealing building S1. Phase Va.

GRAFFITI

T. W. Potter (Fig. 150, p. 437; Figs 179–80)

The following notes are based on observations by Mr M. W. C. Hassall, to whom we are most grateful.

TILE (Figs 179–80)

1 ST 81 JH, SF 101

Imbrex, incised before firing: CC[.... Probably a batch number, 200 or more. The manufacture of 220 tiles by one man in one day does not appear to be uncommon: Tomlin 1979, 236. Tomlin, *ibid.* 239, also points out that such batch numbering is, however, infrequently attested in Britain. Cf. also no. 4 below.

From pit 132, unit 192. Late 2nd/early 3rd century AD (but probably residual).

2 ST 81 LX

Imbrex, incised before firing. ...]MC[... or ...]AC[... If an A, there is no horizontal bar.

Residual in gully 61, unit 251. 5th–7th century AD.

3 ST 82 AAV, SF 416

Pila, incised before firing: X. Perhaps not a number.

From building R2 occupation layer, unit 461. 3rd century AD.

4 ST 83 A,4, SF 83 A,21

Floor tile, incised on the side of the tile, before firing: CCLVIII. A batch total, 258; as no. 1 above.

From the north sump, layer 4. Phase IV/V.

5 ST 82 ABT

Tile, incised before firing: IX.

From the north sump, layer 484. Phase IV/V.

6 ST 80 AZ

Tile, incised before firing: CX.

From occupation debris, unit 23, west of building R1. Phases III–V.

7 ST 80 AZ

Imbrex, incised before firing: X.

Context as no. 6.

POTTERY (Figs 150, 180)

8 ST 82 BHS, SF 440

A substantially complete amphora of unparalleled form. (For illustrations of the pot and its graffiti, see Keay and Carreras, Fig. 150, p. 437, no. 22.) Graffiti, scratched after firing:

a) PXI
b) PPXXXIII
c) VORII (on shoulder, on other side of vessel).
d) Diagonal criss-cross design (on shoulder).

a) *p(ondo) xi*; b) *p(lena) p(ondo) xxxiii*; c) *Vore* or *Vore(a)e*.

a) 'Weight 11' [lb]; b) 'weight full 33' [lb].

Cf. from Saunderton (Buckinghamshire) a graffito on a jug in yellow ware: TPX[ ]/PPXX[: *t(esta) p(ondo) x* [ ] *p(lena) p(ondo) xx* [ ] (*JRS* 29 (1939), 229, no. 15); cf. also *CIL* xv, 4851, 4852, 4853 (on amphorae); also *CIL* xiii, 10008, 52: *p(ondo) i s(emis)*, *p(lena) p(ondo) iii*.

The actual weight of the reconstructed amphora is 3360.6 g; its estimated weight, if complete, would be about 3400 g. Various figures are suggested for the value of the Roman pound (cf. Johns and Potter 1983, and references) as follows:

Roman pound (g)	Approx. weight of amphora (Roman pound)
318.9	10.66
324.25	10.48
327.45	10.37

Given that the estimated weight is approximate (based on weighing other sherds which roughly make up for the missing pieces), the correspondence between the empty weight written on the vessel, XI, and the estimated weight in Roman pounds is striking.

From pit 483/918, unit 892. 3rd century AD.

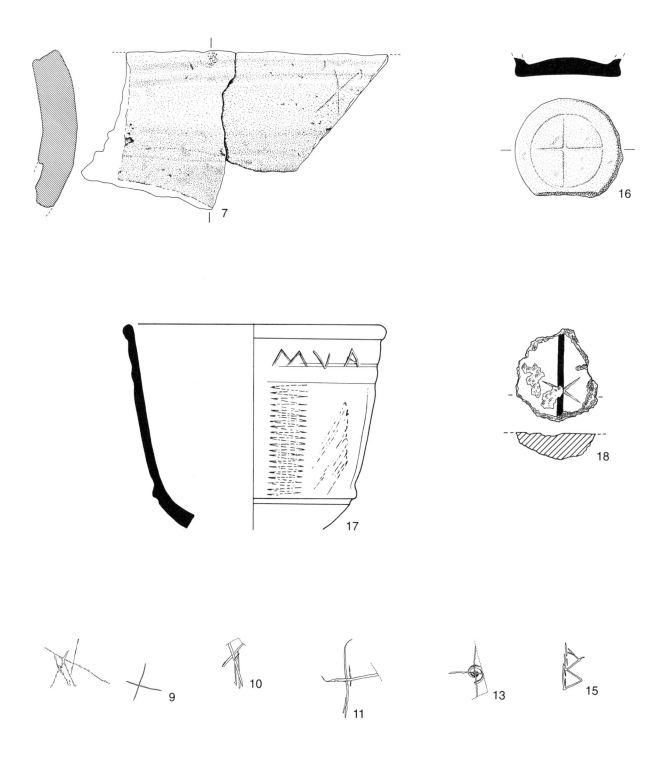

Fig. 180 Stonea Grange: graffiti on tile 7, pottery 9–11, 13, 15–17 and plaster 18 (scale 1 : 2 except 9–11, 13 and 15 = 1 : 1).

9 ST 84 DOE, SF 674

Two graffiti on the wall of a samian Dr 33 (CG, Antonine):
a) Very faintly XX (rather than XIX).
b) X or + (perhaps a mark of ownership).
From pit 1577, unit 1817. Late 2nd–3rd century AD.

10 ST 83 JI,I, SF 569

Graffito on the exterior of the foot-ring of a samian Dr 33 (CG, 2nd century AD): X[... Conceivably part of a number.
From pit JI, I. 3rd–4th century AD.

11 ST 84 DNY, SF 826

Graffito on the underside of a samian base, within the footring (Dr 37, CG, Antonine): X.
From gully 24, south branch, cut 2, unit 1811. Early 3rd century AD.

12 ST 84 DQV, SF 884

Graffito (not illustrated) on the underside of a rough-cast colour-coat beaker: X.
From pit 1669, unit 1880. Mid/late 3rd century AD.

13 ST 84 DZZ, SF 1156

Graffito on the underside of a samian base: X. [See also Dickinson cat. no. 111.]
From occupation layer (unit 2076), south-east block 9. 3rd century AD.

14 ST 84 DTQ, SF 1164

Graffito (not illustrated) on a sherd of NVCC: X.
From pit 1915, unit 1948. Early 3rd century AD.

15 ST 82 ACV, SF 329

Graffito on the underside of a samian base within the foot-ring (Dr 18/31, CG, Antonine): B.
From sinkage (unit 509) into ditch 74. 3rd–4th century AD.

16 ST 81 FW, SF 162.

Graffito on the underside of a base in NVGW: +.
From well 135, uppermost fill (unit 135). Residual Roman with early Anglo-Saxon pottery. 4th–7th century AD.

17 ST 84 DQF, SF 678

Graffito below the rim on the exterior of a London-type bowl: MVA.
From pit 1814, basal layer (1866). 3rd century AD.

PLASTER

18 ST 81 FN, SF 122

On a fragment of painted plaster: X. [See also Jackson, p. 498, cat. no. 37.]

From the hard-standing (unit 128) to the north of building R1 and pit 170. 3rd century AD on.

PAINTED PLASTER

Ralph Jackson   (Figs 181–4)

The following catalogue is a brief selection from a large assemblage of painted plaster, none of which was found in situ or in an undisturbed fallen context. Most of it derives from building R1 and is in a very fragmentary state. For, what had not fallen from the ceilings and walls of the building after its desertion in the early 3rd century AD was rapidly hacked away by those quarrying the building for stone and timber. The plaster, with tile and mortar debris, was left in heaps and was subjected to erosion and further fragmentation by weathering and by sorting in subsequent stone-robbing episodes. Nevertheless, despite the small size and poor condition of the surviving fragments it is possible to infer that the interior decor of building R1 included simple red and white panelling, marbling, speckling, coloured frameworks, geometric designs, and figured scenes and landscapes. In addition, there are simple mouldings from wall and wall–floor junctions, from window/door embrasures and, probably, from pilasters and niches.

There is some uniformity in the backings, the majority of which comprise either a whitish sandy coat with grit and crushed tile inclusions or a yellowish sandy coat with grit inclusions. Several fragments (e.g. 10, 20, 25, 27, 31) combine both these backings, with a plaster skim sandwiched between them. They presumably indicate two phases of wall decoration, though in no case is it possible to determine whether or not the earlier, sandwiched, surface is painted. The decoration of the secondary surface included maroon and white panelling, maroon and grey panelling, green-on-white framework, and marbling. These two phases of decoration echo the two main structural phases of building R1 but a concordance between them cannot be established.

While it is very probable that all the plaster found within block 1 (sections i–ii below) derived from building R1, the same assumption cannot be made for the fragments found elsewhere. The remains found in blocks 9 and 4 (nos 40–4), for example, may have belonged to any of the adjacent timber buildings.

Key to Figs 181–4

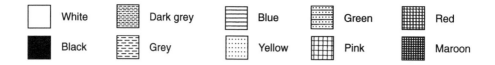

White	Dark grey	Blue	Green	Red
Black	Grey	Yellow	Pink	Maroon

i FROM BUILDING R1 (Figs 181–3)

1 ST 80 AA

An angle-moulding, with an irregular trail of black blobs. The pink backing has crushed tile inclusions.

From topsoil over building R1.

2 ST 80 AA

Four yellow spots and a black stripe on a white ground. Backing as no. 1.

Context as no. 1.

3 ST 80 AA

A straight division of red and white. The creamy backing has grit and finely crushed tile inclusions.

Context as no.1.

4 ST 80 AA

A straight division of red and white. The yellow sandy backing has grit inclusions.

Context as no.1.

5 ST 80 AA

A straight division of black and white. The backing consists of two layers: the upper, $c.$ 7 mm thick, a fine creamy sandy coat; the lower, at least 9 mm thick, a yellow sandy coat with grit inclusions.

Context as no. 1.

6 ST 80 AA

Part of a green motif on a white ground. The backing consists of three layers: 1) and 2) both $c.$ 11 mm thick, a creamy coat with grit and finely-crushed tile; 3) a yellow sandy coat, at least 7 mm thick.

Context as no. 1.

7 ST 80 AK

A yellow ground with two narrow black stripes set at right angles. The yellow sandy backing has grit and crushed tile inclusions.

From building R1, central block, upper robbing debris/levelling (unit 10). Phase IV/V.

8 ST 80 AK

Three parallel narrow brown-black stripes amongst indefinable pink (and other) paintwork on a white ground. The very thin plaster skim coats a creamy sandy backing.

Context as no. 7.

9 ST 81 FX

A straight division between maroon and white grounds, the latter badly eroded. The creamy backing, $c.$ 20 mm thick, seals another plaster skim over a yellow sandy backing at least 9 mm thick. This replastering presumably represents two phases of wall decoration.

From building R1, central block, robbing debris/levelling (unit 136). 4th century AD.

10 ST 80 BD

Grey veining on an off-white ground, with a very smooth and carefully-finished surface. The marbling is probably in imitation of cipollino. The backing, $c.$ 16 mm thick, is creamy with much crushed tile and seals a thin plaster skim over a yellow gritty base coat, perhaps the remains of an earlier decor.

From building R1, central block, robbing debris/levelling in apse (unit 27). Phase IV.

11 ST 80 BD

Two non-joining fragments. White ground splattered with small red spots and splashes. The yellow gritty backing, at least 19 mm thick, is the same as the base coat of no. 10.

Context as no. 10.

12 ST 80 BD

The straight interface of white and yellow bands is overpainted with a maroon stripe, and there is the edge of a second parallel maroon stripe at the other edge of the 20 mm wide yellow band. The backing and base coat are as no. 10.

Context as no.10.

13 ST 80 BD

A straight interface of black and white, the latter with indefinable traces of over-painting.

Backing as the base coat of no. 10.

Context as no. 10.

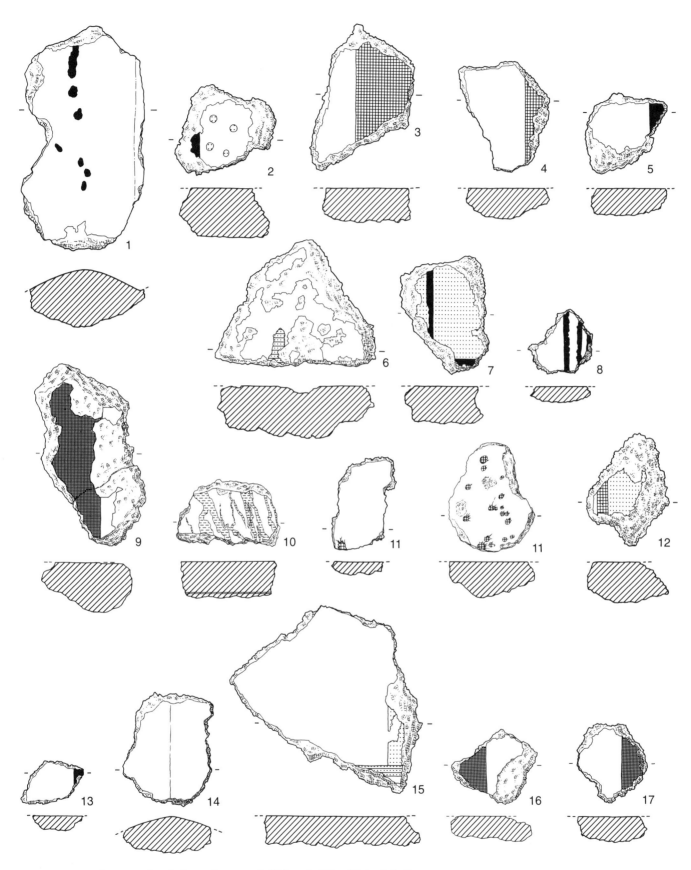

Fig. 181 Stonea Grange: painted plaster fragments 1–17 from building R1 (scale 1:2).

14 ST 80 BD

Angle-moulding with creamy-buff (?self-coloured) surface. The white sandy backing has grit and crushed tile inclusions.

Context as no. 10.

15 ST 80 CV

Right-angle intersection of a green stripe and a yellow band demarcating a panel with white ground and traces of red and other paint. The pinkish-white sandy backing, 7 mm thick, seals a white base coat of similar thickness, with coarse grit and crushed tile inclusions and grass/straw impressions.

From building R1, central block, north-west corner, robbing debris (unit 65). Phase IV.

16 ST 81 HQ

A straight division of maroon and white grounds, with indistinct traces of pink and other colouring in the latter. The backing is sandy yellow.

From building R1, central block, north-west quadrant, robbing debris (unit 176). Phase IV.

17 ST 80 DK

A straight division of maroon and white grounds. Decor and backing very similar to no. 16 and possibly from the same decorative scheme.

From building R1, central block, north-east quadrant, robbing debris (unit 79). Late 3rd–4th century AD.

18 ST 80 AM

A maroon stripe flanked by a yellow band/stripe with a white ground on either side. Traces of pink in the larger surviving area of white ground hint at more elaborate decoration. The backing is yellowish and sandy with straw/grass impressions.

From building R1, central block, north-east quadrant, robbing hollow in top of north wall (unit 12). Phase IV.

19 ST 81 FT

The end of a thin white brush stroke on a black ground. The relatively thick plaster skim covers a creamy-yellow sandy backing with grit inclusions.

From building R1, central block, east side, rubble on sub-floor foundation (unit 133). Phase III/IV.

20 ST 80 BJ

A straight division of maroon and white grounds, with plaster-finishing marks on the surface. The creamy sandy backing c. 16 mm thick, has crushed tile and grit inclusions. Beneath it is a plaster skim with the remains of a yellow sandy backing with grit inclusions, the remains of an earlier decor.

From building R1, central block, south-east quadrant, upper robbing debris (unit 32). 4th century AD.

21 ST 80 CJ

An angle-moulding, perhaps from a window embrasure. The narrower surviving face is painted maroon (with prominent brush-marks) and this colour encroaches onto the second face where it forms a straight interface with a buff ground. On the latter are the indistinct remains of grey veining with white and brown motifs, probably in imitation of marble. The backing is yellowish and sandy.

From building R1, central block, south-east quadrant, robbing debris (unit 55). 4th century AD.

[A smaller fragment of identical type and colour was found in unit 65. For context see no. 15 above.]

22 ST 80 CJ

A broad green stripe with prominent brush marks on a white ground. The backing comprises three rather indistinct sandy coats – yellow, pinkish, creamy-white – with a clearer division between the fourth yellow sandy coat.

Context as no. 21.

23 ST 80 CT

A grey ground overpainted with a diagonal pink/red stripe and a yellow band or stripe. The backing is fine sandy yellow.

From building R1, central block, south-east quadrant, robbing debris (unit 64). 3rd or 4th century AD.

24 ST 81 KH

Two non-joining fragments with a green ground overpainted with dark blue-black and white. The design is too faint and fragmentary to interpret but was evidently complex, probably a pastoral or maritime scene. Many brush strokes are visible. The backing is a thick homogeneous creamy sandy coat.

From building R1, central block, south-east quadrant, robbing debris (unit 215). 4th century AD.

25 ST 80 BC

A green stripe on a white ground. The backing comprises two layers of a creamy-white sandy coat which seal a plaster skim over a yellow sandy base coat with grit inclusions.

From building R1, south room, robbing/dereliction debris (unit 26). 3rd–7th century AD.

26 ST 80 BC

A straight division of maroon and white. The pinkish-cream sandy backing has grit and crushed tile inclusions.

Context as no. 25.

27 ST 80 BW

A straight division of maroon and white grounds with plaster finishing marks on the surface and 'pull' marks on the white ground adjacent to the maroon border caused by removal of the paint-mask-

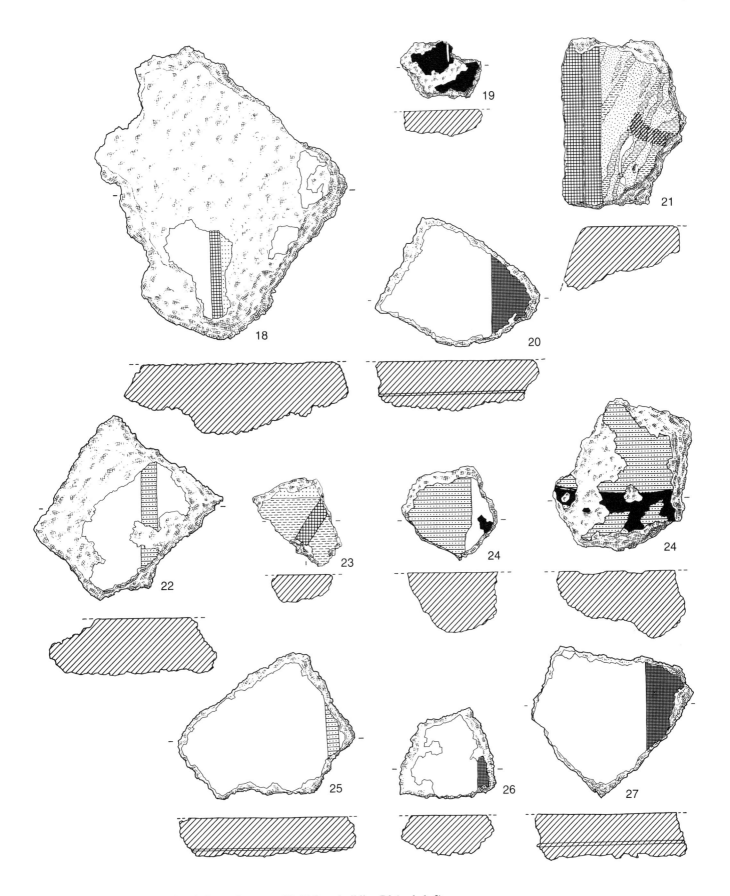

Fig. 182 Stonea Grange: painted plaster fragments 18–27 from building R1 (scale 1:2).

ing device from the wet plaster surface. The backing and decor are identical to no. 20.

From building R1, south room, robbing/dereliction debris (unit 43). Phase IV/V.

28 ST 80 AD

A maroon stripe on a white ground. The creamy sandy backing has grit and sparse crushed tile inclusions and straw/reed impressions.

From building R1 east wing, west side, north end, robbing debris (unit 4). 4th century AD.

29 ST 80 CE

Angle-moulding. A quarter-round moulding, probably from a wall-floor or corner angle. The only rudimentarily finished surface has been painted red. The creamy white backing has coarse grit and crushed tile inclusions.

From building R1, west range, robbing debris (unit 51). Phase IV.

30 ST 80 BX

Fragment from an outer angle – niche, embrasure, pilaster etc – slightly greater than a right angle. The edge is maroon, flanked on one face by a red ground, and on the other face by a discontinuous red band and a white ground. The coarse creamy-white sandy backing has profuse grit and crushed tile inclusions.

From building R1, west range, south end, upper robbing debris (unit 44). 3rd century AD.

31 ST 80 BX

A straight division of maroon and grey grounds. The backing is identical to no. 20.

Context as no. 30.

32 ST 80 CQ

Red paint on a white ground. There appear to be at least two parallel stripes but they may be brush marks in an eroded red ground. The backing is as no. 30.

From building R1, west range, robbed wall footing, south end (unit 61). Phase IV.

33 ST 80 AC

A straight interface of white and green. The latter has a darker green (over-painted) line at the junction. The creamy sandy backing has grit inclusions.

From building R1, central block, pit 3, upper fill (unit 3). 4th–7th century AD.

34 ST 80 AN

A badly-eroded yellow motif on a white ground. The creamy-white backing has coarse grit inclusions.

Context as no. 33, but lower fill (unit 13). 4th–7th century AD.

ii FROM THE ENVIRONS OF BUILDING R1   (Fig. 183)

35 ST 81 HJ

Tiny fragment from a complex decor, comprising a curved red stripe with yellow beyond the convex side and yellow, lighter red and pink, all eroded, within the inner curve. The whitish backing has quite coarse grit and crushed tile inclusions.

From pit 170, uppermost layer (unit 170). 3rd/4th century AD.

36 ST 81 MK

A thin black stripe on a white ground with indefinable ?yellow patches. The surface is well smoothed and the stripe precisely painted. The creamy-white backing is fine and sandy.

Context as no. 35, but basal layer (unit 263). Early 3rd century AD.

37 ST 81 FN, SF 122

Another fragment, identical in decor and backing to no. 36, but with the addition of an incised cross on the black stripe. The cross was lightly-cut into the wet plaster and was presumably a setting-out mark for the design.

From the hard-standing (unit 128) to the north of building R1 and pit 170. 3rd century AD on.

38 ST 81 FW

The eroded remains of a complex decor. What survives is the interface of red and white grounds with traces of overpainted yellow, brown and pink. The backing comprises c. 5 mm of a yellowish fine sandy coat on c. 20 mm of a coarser whitish sandy base coat.

From well 135, uppermost layer (unit 135). 4th–7th century AD.

39 ST 81 FM

A broad grey stripe, with lightly scored marking-out line on one side, on a white ground. The plaster surface is markedly rippled, probably a 'combed' surface, with no attempt to smooth. The backing is thin – c. 9 mm and quite coarse – a whitish sandy coat with profuse crushed tile. From unit 127 of the low rubbly mound sealing building S1. 9th–10th century AD.

iii FROM VARIOUS CONTEXTS   (Figs 183–4)

40 ST 84 DPZ

Two non-joining fragments from the same decor, both with severely eroded surface. The larger piece has the straight interface of yellow and white grounds, the junction marked by a deeper yellow stripe. The smaller piece follows the same arrangement, but the yellow ground is badly faded. It also has a grey band/ground whose edge was marked out with a shallow channel. The backing is extremely coarse – a cream and white sandy coat with profuse coarse grit and crushed tile inclusions.

From well 1667, unit 1860.

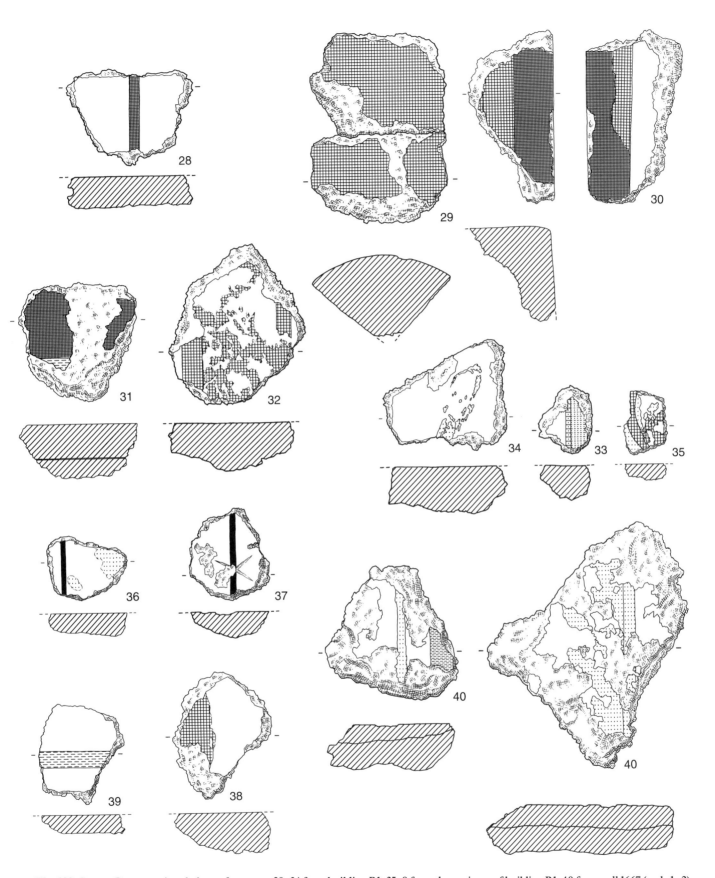

Fig. 183 Stonea Grange: painted plaster fragments 28–34 from building R1, 35–9 from the environs of building R1, 40 from well 1667 (scale 1 : 2).

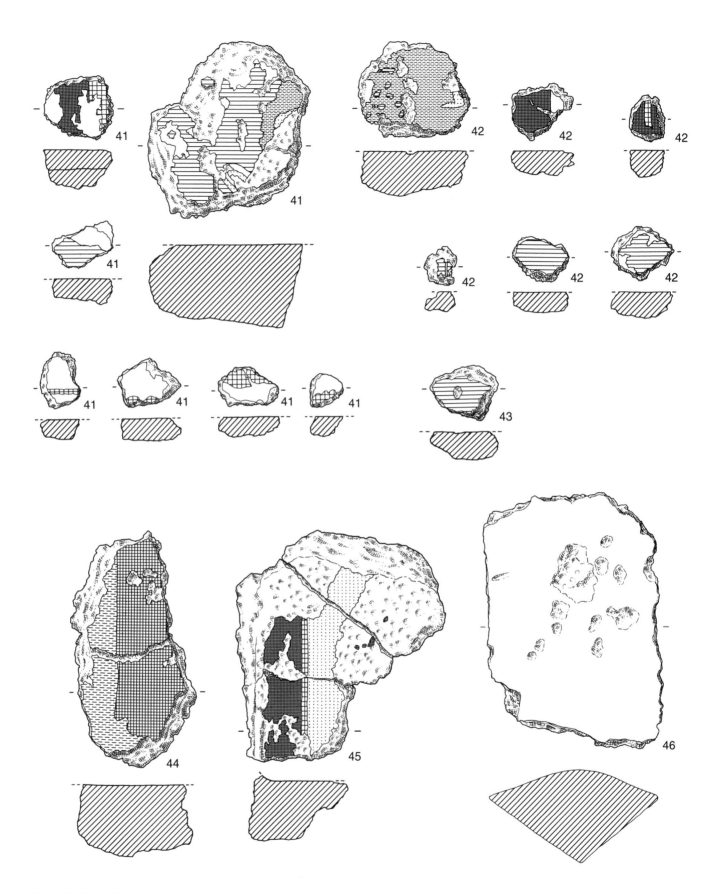

Fig. 184 Stonea Grange: painted plaster fragments 41–6 from various contexts (scale 1:2).

41 ST 84 DRP

Many non-joining fragments (seven illustrated) from a complex polychrome scene, probably figured. Colours represented are maroon, pink, yellow, green, light blue, mid-blue, grey, black and white. The backing is a white sandy coat with fine gravel inclusions, *c.*10 mm thick, on a yellow sandy base coat with coarser gravel inclusions.

From well 1678, unit 1899. 3rd century AD or later.

42 ST 84 DRR

More non-joining fragments (six illustrated) from the same decor as no. 41. Colours represented include white on a light blue ground, pink on a maroon ground, blue on a grey ground and an interface of white and maroon. The backing is as no. 41.

From well 1678, unit 1902. 3rd century AD or later.

43 ST 84 DKZ, SF 900

Light blue ground, of the same hue as parts of nos 41 and 42. The backing is pinkish and sandy with very fine crushed tile and grit inclusions.

From well 1836, uppermost layer (unit 1740). Late 2nd/3rd century AD.

44 ST 84 DKI

A gently curving interface of red and grey grounds. The backing is thick and coarse, a whitish sandy coat with coarse crushed tile inclusions.

From the fill (unit 1725) of pit 1725. Mid/late 3rd century AD.

45 ST 84A, 26, 3, SF1

Panel border, with pink-edged maroon band adjacent to a buff-yellow ground. The plaster retains an angle change at the edge of the maroon band. The thick backing is a medium-coarse sandy coat with grit and crushed tile inclusions.

From the sump, layer A, 26, grid square 3. 3rd–4th century AD.

46 ST 81+

Angle-moulding, with the eroded remains of two, probably self-coloured, plaster surfaces. The backing is whitish and sandy with profuse coarse grit and crushed tile inclusions. The angle adopted by the backing is distinctly greater than 90° and the moulding is therefore more likely to have come from a wall junction than a wall–floor junction.

From building R1, unstratified.

EGYPTIAN BLUE

Mavis Bimson and Ralph Jackson

Nine sub-spherical balls or fragments of blue frit were found in the excavations. They were visually examined in the British Museum Research Laboratory by Mavis Bimson, who checked three (nos 1, 3, 4) by X-ray diffraction analysis (XRD). All nine were confirmed as examples of the artificial glassy pigment known today as Egyptian Blue (BMRL File no. 5668).

The manufacture of little balls (*pilae*) of this material, a calcium–copper silicate known in antiquity as *caeruleum*, is described by Vitruvius (VII, 11, 1) in a chapter of the section on colours which follows his accounts of stucco and wall painting. For this reason, modern commentators usually associate Egyptian Blue with wall-painting (e.g. Atkins 1971; Boon 1974, 211; Davey and Ling 1982, 220–2; Gower 1984; Ling 1991, 208–9). While it undoubtedly was employed as a pigment in mural decoration, it may not have been used exclusively as such. For example, spatial analysis of the finds at Augst (Riha 1986, 97–8 and Fig. 34) demonstrated that there, Egyptian Blue pellets were found in the residential areas as well as the artisan quarters, a distribution which led Riha (*ibid.* 97) to postulate a cosmetic use, namely as eyeshadow. The very much smaller Stonea sample also shows an interesting distribution: all nine finds came from rubbish and debris generated by houses in blocks 3, 8 and 9; none came from or around building R1, the only excavated building of the settlement known to have had painted plaster decoration.

The pieces were found in the following contexts.

1 ST 82 BGK, SF 410 A complete small ball, maximum diameter 13 mm.

From block 3, pit 860, upper layer (unit 860). 3rd/4th century AD.

2 ST 84 DWI, SF 1022 A complete small pellet, maximum dimension 9 mm.

From block 9, pit 1989, unit 1989. Late 2nd century AD.

3 ST 84 DRV, SF 907 A sub-triangular fragment, maximum length 16 mm, of what was originally probably a plump rhomboid 'ball'.

From block 9, south side, layer above pit and gully complex (unit 1904). 3rd century AD.

4 ST 84 DRV, SF 922 A tiny fragment.

Context as no. 3.

5 ST 84 DQC, SF 885 Small fragment.

Block 9, well 1834, unit 1863. 3rd century AD.

6 ST 84 DEA, SF 730 Pellet fragment.

From block 9, north-east corner, cleaning over street 2 N/S.

7 ST 84 DWQ, SF 1007 A tiny fragment.

From block 9, pit 1996, unit 1996. 3rd century AD.

8 ST 84 DGN, SF 661 A tiny fragment.

From block 9, layer 1657, above gully 29. Mid 3rd century AD.

9 ST 84 DWD, SF 945 A tiny fragment.

From block 8, pit 1984, unit 1984. Early 3rd century AD.

TILE AND BRICK (Figs 185–8)

In the years immediately prior to the first season of excavation at Stonea Grange, a number of studies had drawn attention to the potentially useful information that could be evinced from Roman brick and tile (McWhirr 1979). In particular, there was an appreciation of the need to seek information from the plainer range of ceramic building materials as well as from the more accessible categories – impressed, inscribed and roller-stamped tiles. Since the plain wares generally comprise a high percentage (and, more critically, often very large quantities and bulk) of the brick and tile assemblage, it was essential to adopt, or devise, a strategy that would maximise results without committing disproportionate resources, either in recording, processing or storage.

It was already evident, from surface finds, that Stonea Grange would yield a considerable quantity of brick and tile, and that in a region otherwise virtually devoid of those materials in the Roman period (cf. Potter and Potter 1982). It was hoped, therefore, that quantification and analysis of the assemblage would shed light on manufacturing, production and trade patterns, as well as on methods and types of building. With these aims in mind a proforma sheet was developed in order to maintain a uniform recording system throughout the excavation. The form, by the excavators, was revised and improved by Mr Michael Stone, who was taken on as site assistant to deal specifically with the on-site brick and tile quantification and analysis and, subsequently, to prepare a report on the results. The quantifying information on the proforma comprised: tile type, fabric, weight, thickness, any complete dimensions, presence of side or end, tegula flange height, further information, whether retained. A total of 17 842 tile fragments were washed, examined and quantified in this way. Certain pieces, such as box flue tiles, complete lengths, and examples with finger-marked 'signatures', were retained for further research, while the majority of processed fragments were reburied on site at the end of each season. This permitted a total record combined with a rational retention/storage policy.

Unfortunately, despite the provision of illustrators' time and other resources and assistance, Mr Stone failed to produce a report, other than the following fabric descriptions. Apart from the considerable wasted time and effort of various people that this has caused, it has, still more seriously, deprived us of the very information that we had carefully planned to retrieve. It is a most regrettable situation, which

is only partly compensated by the excellent reports on tile petrology by Dr Freestone (pp. 508–10) and on imprinted tiles by Dr Legge (pp. 510–15).

TILE FABRIC DESCRIPTIONS

All tile excavated on site was examined in a consistent manner by creating a fracture which was examined by a ×10 hand lens. At the end of the excavations, 21 individual fabrics had been isolated.

Samples of tile fabrics were submitted to I. C. Freestone of the British Museum Department of Scientific Research, who carried out a thin-sectioning programme which resulted in the petrology report (see pp. 508–10). Fabrics 19, 20 and 21 were identified towards the end of the excavation and only occur in small numbers and small fragments which were deemed unsuitable for thin-sectioning.

Site handling of the tile suggested that some of the fabrics could be grouped, implying common sources, such as fabrics 1, 10 and 11. The petrology report has confirmed the groupings, and the fabrics are therefore discussed in these groups.

The fabric groups

Group 1 F1, F8, F10, F11, F12, F13, F18
      2 F2, F6, F14, F15, F16, F17
      3 F3A, F3B
      4 F4, F5
      5 F7
      6 F9
      7 F19
      8 F20
      9 F21
   10 Unassigned tiles

Group 1

F1 Very hard slightly sandy red to orange fabric on surface. The firing reduced the centre of the fabric to grey. The clay matrix contains limestone, sand and silt with layers of lighter clay and voids. This fabric is most common on the site in a wide range of tile products. Roof furniture predominated.

F8 Very hard to slightly soft sandy orange-red fabric, similar to fabric 1 and fabric 13 but with more limestone particles on the surface. Limited range of tile products. Samples in this fabric are mostly brick.

F10 Very hard and often over-fired grey to red-purple fabric. Similar to fabric 1 and fabric 11, the clay matrix containing large inclusions and voids. This fabric is mostly utilised for the production of bricks.

F11 Very hard slightly sandy orange-red fabric with a reduced core. Almost identical to fabric 1 except that

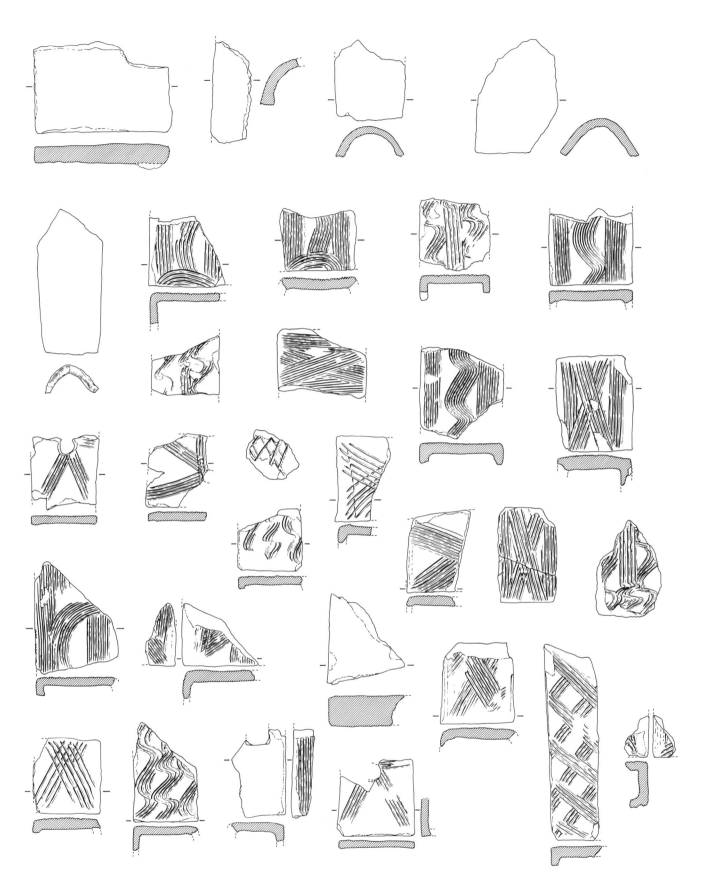

Fig. 185 Stonea Grange: box flue-tiles, *imbrices*, etc. (scale 1:8).

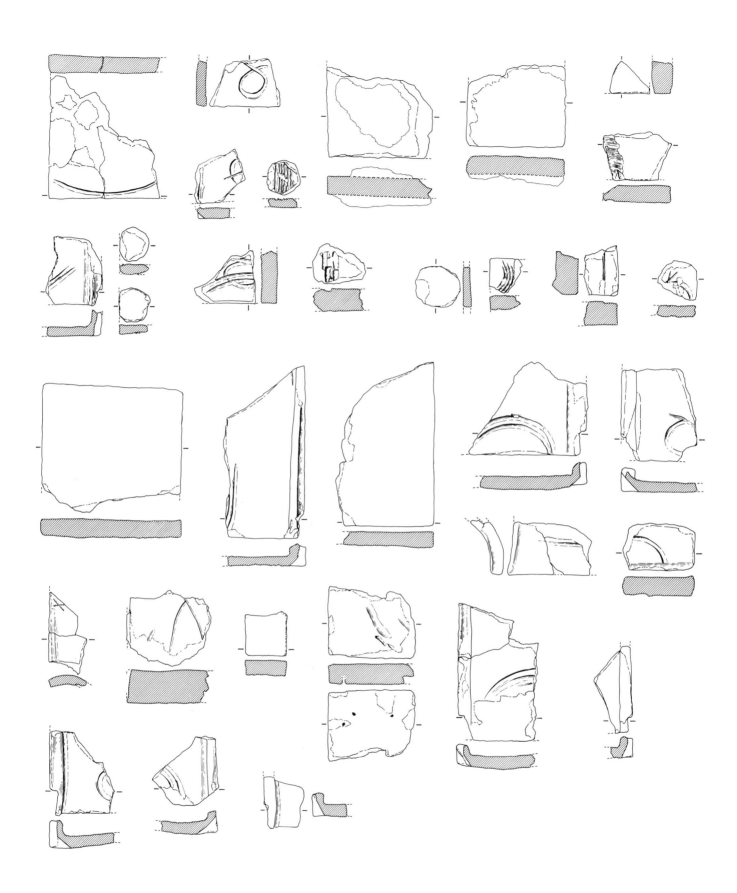

Fig. 186 Stonea Grange: *tegulae*, bricks etc. (scale 1:8).

the stone inclusions and voids are larger suggesting less clay preparation as this fabric is usually used in production of large bricks.

F12 Very hard slightly sandy over-fired red to brown fabric. Very similar to fabrics 10 and 11. Tiles in this fabric produced a limited range of products.

F13 Very hard well-finished and well-fired orange fabric similar to fabric 8 and fabric 13. Tiles in this fabric are mostly roof furniture.

F18 Very hard well-fired slightly sandy orange-red fabric similar to fabric 13 but has no reduced core. Limited range of products and mostly occurs as roof furniture.

COMMENTS

The range of tiles in this fabric group when linked to the amount of tile from the site suggests a large nucleated producer. During the excavations comparisons were made with coarse pottery which suggest that the Nene Valley and the Oxford clays may be the source of this tile producer.

Group 2

F2 Hard well-fired cream to orange-red fabric. In the fracture clay streaks are common along with quartz and sand. This is a common fabric produced in a wide range of products with roof furniture predominating.

F6 Hard to soft crumbly yellow to green fabric. This fabric is under-fired and low in numbers and is probably a variant of fabric 16.

F14 Hard to soft slightly sandy orange fabric with numerous surface indents and voids in the matrix. Some examples are wasters and this could be the same as fabric 2. This fabric mostly occurs as roof furniture.

F15 Very hard well-made and well-fired orange fabric. Products are mostly in roof furniture.

F16 Hard to slightly soft sandy orange fabric similar to fabric 2 and fabric 15.

F17 Hard orange fabric with numerous voids in the clay matrix and surface. Not a common fabric. Similar to fabric 15 and to examples of bricks and roof tiles on barns in the excavation area, suggesting local manufacture (see below).

COMMENTS

Comparison to local post-medieval to modern products suggests that group 2 tiles were made from the local Ampthill clay.

Group 3

F3A/F3B Very hard slightly soapy brown to grey-black fabric. In fracture large quantities of fossil shell and limestone are visible. Examination of tiles on site suggested 2 groups (A and B), which was also borne out by petrology. This could be taken no further. This fabric is very distinct and occurs in a wide range of products. Comparison to other sites suggests that these shelly tiles are produced from the shelly marls and Blisworth clays in the region of Harrold in Bedfordshire (see report by John Cooper, p. 507).

Group 4

F4 Hard sandy orange-red fabric slightly under-fired. Visually similar to tiles from Eye (see below).

F5 Almost the same as fabric 4 but slightly over-fired.

Group 5

F7 Very hard red to salmon fabric, well-fired, and similar to fabric 4 and fabric 5 and Eye tiles.

Group 6

F9 Very hard poorly-fired tile in an orange to red fabric with voids, inclusions and shale.

Group 7

F19 Very hard purple to grey fabric. May relate to tiles in group 1, particularly fabric 12. Tiles in this group have not been thin-sectioned.

Group 8

F20 Very hard and crumbly red to brown fabric with iron and quartz and yellow streaks in the matrix. This fabric has not been thin-sectioned.

Group 9

F21 Hard to soft white to cream fabric with little in the way of inclusions in the clay matrix. This fabric has not been thin-sectioned.

Eye fabrics

Mr Stone's attention was drawn by David Hall to a site in the parish of Eye some 5 km to the north-west of Stonea Grange.

Fig. 187 Stonea Grange: bricks, *tegulae*, etc. (scale 1:8).

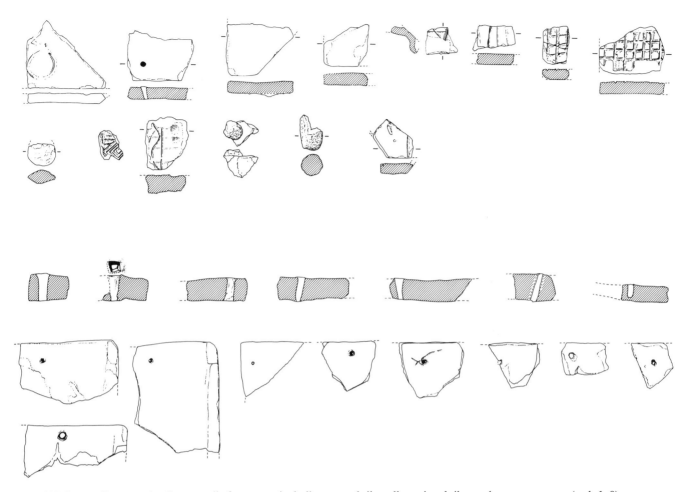

Fig. 188 Stonea Grange: miscellaneous tile fragments, including pegged tile, roller-printed tile, *tegulae mammatae*, etc. (scale 1 : 8).

Field inspection of the site revealed tiles, some of which were wasters, suggesting production at this spot. Two samples were submitted for petrology to check whether they would fit any of the tiles from Stonea.

Eye fabric 1   Hard slightly sandy orange fabric with a reduced grey core. Visually similar to fabric 1 and fabric 18.

Eye fabric 2   Hard sandy orange fabric with no core reduction visually similar to fabric 18.

The tile petrology report (Freestone, pp. 508–10) clearly shows that Eye tiles were not present on the Stonea site in any significant quantity, probably because they were produced before the Hadrianic period.

REPORT ON SAMPLES OF GROUP 3, FABRIC 3 TILE   John Cooper

All the samples (S1–S10) are of essentially similar composition of shelly clay of Upper Jurassic age, either of Oxford clay or more probably of the local Ampthill clay. The shell fragments (the result of the clay being pounded) are mostly of ostreid (gryphaeid), pectinid and other bivalves, with a few fragments of the shells of punctuate brachiopods. Only one bivalve is readily identifiable, the umbonal region of the pectinid *Oxytoma* in sample S4.

Some of the samples (S1, S3, S5) are blacker internally than others, suggesting an origin from a slightly different clay horizon with more carbonaceous plant material within the Oxford or Ampthill clay, or it may be the result of differing kiln temperatures.

One sample (S9) contains the mould of a contemporary (Roman) grass or straw stem as an accidental inclusion.

TILE PETROLOGY

Ian Freestone

INTRODUCTION

Thirty-six tiles from Stonea, along with two wasters from the kiln site at Eye, were examined in thin section. The predominant inclusion in much of the tile is quartz-rich sand, and the qualitative attributes (presence/absence of inclusion types) available to subdivide the material into fabric groups are limited. It was therefore necessary to base the classification to a significant extent upon textural characteristics, in particular the density of inclusions and their grain-size distribution. Textural analysis has become well established in ceramic studies over the past decade or so, and has been reviewed by Freestone (1991).

The procedure adopted in the present investigation was as follows. Tile fabric groups were initially established on the basis of the qualitative observation of inclusion grain size, density and type, with the aid of black-and-white photomicrographs taken at a constant magnification. It was found that the differences were such as to give broad confidence that the major groups were discrete with respect to one another. These groups were then tested for internal consistency and for further subdivisions by quantitative grain-size analysis using a Kontron MOP-Videoplan semi-automatic image analyser (Middleton, Freestone and Leese 1985). The analysis was based upon the measurement of 150, 100 or (in the case of fabric Group 2 where quartz grains are sparse) 50 quartzose grains selected using the ribbon/area method (Middleton *et al*, *op. cit*). It was found possible to establish six fabric groups in this study. Measurement parameters were tailored for each group to optimise the number of grains sampled. Group 1 was measured at a magnification of $\times 100$ with a lower limit of $20\,\mu m$; Groups 4, 5 and the tile from Eye were measured at $\times 40$ with a lower limit of $62.5\,\mu m$, and Group 2 was measured at $\times 40$ with a lower limit of $100\,\mu m$. Grain-size histograms were derived and compared for each tile, and summary data for the mean diameter, standard deviation, skewness and kurtosis produced. In general, it was found that the mean diameter and standard deviation were the most useful measurements for the comparison of groups. Skewness and kurtosis were found to show large within-group fluctuations and were less helpful, as anticipated by Leese (1982).

THE FABRICS

Group 1 (Includes excavator's F1, F8, F10–F13, F18)

This group is characterised by the presence of abundant, sub-angular quartz of silt to very find sand grade. Rounded fragments of shale 0.5–1.00 mm maximum dimension are scattered throughout the fabric and some limestone fragments are present in some sections. Poor mixing of the silt/sand and clay fractions has resulted in patches and streaks which are very rich in quartz. Grain-size analysis (Table 32) indicates that the quartz in these areas has the same characteristics as that in the fabric as a whole. Thus this fabric is likely to have been produced by the homogenisation of a clay showing clay and quartz-rich lamellae.

The heterogeneity which results from the poor mixing of the two-component (quartz-rich and clay-rich) raw material resulted at first in the establishment of two fabric groups, differing in the amount of quartz that the thin sections appeared to contain. However, grain size distributions of all tiles analysed in this group shows that the characteristics of the inclusions form a well-defined group with a narrow range of mean diameters (Table 32).

Group 2 (Includes excavator's F2, F6, F14–F17)

This group is again rather variable internally but certain common features indicate that it represents a single clay source. However, this source was heterogeneous with respect to the relative proportions of non-plastic inclusions.

The diagnostic feature of this fabric is the presence of large voids, typically $c.1\,mm$ in size and often greater, which have the lenticular and/or 'arrowhead' or 'swallow-tail' form of simple or twinned crystals of gypsum (selenite). Some of these voids have been partially refilled with sparry, acicular calcite growing from the margins. It appears that the clay originally contained crystals of gypsum which on firing would have converted to the water-free form, anhydrite. This was later dissolved out by groundwater during burial, leaving the moulds of the original gypsum crystals. Redistribution of the calcite during burial has resulted in the partial infilling of the voids.

Other characteristics of Group 2 include the presence of finely divided calcite in the clay matrix, scattered fine quartz sand and sparse shell fragments ranging from very fine to coarse grade. The apparent concentration of the calcite in streaks gives a variegated appearance to the tile fabric in hand specimen. This is due to the critical effect that calcite can have on the colour of fired clay due to the incorporation of deeply coloured iron oxides into pale or colourless calcium iron silicates.

A list of the tiles assigned to Group 2 is given in Table 33 with a presence/absence chart for the principal inclusions. The diagnostic voids after gypsum are not present in every section due to their sparse distribution. Therefore, in order to render the group membership more robust, grain-size data are reported for the quartzose inclusions. These show that the tiles form a coherent group and reinforce the group membership of some of the tiles which show no evidence of original gypsum.

The evidence for original gypsum in this group suggests that it was produced from the Ampthill clay, which outcrops locally and which, according to Chatwin (1961) commonly contains crystals of selenite (gypsum).

Group 3   (Includes excavator's F3A, F3B)

This fabric is characterised by the presence of abundant fragments of fossil shell. Less common limestone fragments suggest that it may have been derived from a partially lithified shell-bed in a clay. One example (ST 82 ADY) appears slightly different from the others on the basis of the proportion of shell and the nature of the matrix and is only tentatively assigned to this group.

Sherds in Group 3: ST 80 AA F3; ST 82 ACL, AD2, ACE (a), (b), ADY.

Group 4   (Includes excavator's F4, F5)

This fabric is characterised by the presence of around 8% fine quartz sand with no other diagnostic inclusions. In some respects it resembles the wasters from the kiln at Eye, so a textural analysis was carried out to compare them. Results for the two samples from Eye and for the two examples of Group 4 tile are given in Table 34. The Eye sherds are slightly coarser than those of Group 4 and there is a small difference in all grain-size parameters. However, this difference could be more apparent than real, due to the small numbers of samples analysed. It remains possible that Group 4 tile is a product of the Eye kiln, but unproven without further analysis.

Group 5

Represented by only one of the tiles examined (ST 81 NL T/S 1), this fabric contains around 3% quartz sand with a mean diameter of 0.12 mm, significantly finer than the Group 4 tile and the Eye wasters.

Group 6

Again represented by only one tile in the analytical sample (ST 81 NL T/S 4), this fabric is characterised by abundant coarse fragments of shale with sparse quartz sand.

CONCLUDING REMARKS

Of the 36 samples examined, 32 fall into Groups 1–3, while Groups 4–6 are represented by 4 tiles. Thus three or more kilns produced most of the tile for the building. The kiln at Eye may have produced one of the minor groups (Group 4), but this is not proven. Although there are a number of fabric groups, this need not imply that tile was imported over a long distance. For example, John Cooper reports (p. 507) that, on the basis of the fossils it contains, Group 3 is likely to originate in the Ampthill clay, the same formation which has been suggested as the raw material for Group 2 on mineralogical grounds. Given that deposits of boulder clay also occur in the vicinity, it is possible that the bulk of the tile represents local production.

Table 32 Stonea Grange: Roman tile – mean diameters and standard deviations for tiles assigned to Group 1, based on samples of 100 grains

	Tile number	Mean diameter (µm)	Standard deviation
1	ST 81 NL T/S 6	61	28
2	ST 81 NL T/S 6	61	27
3	ST 81 MA T/S 3	63	42
4	ST 80 BD16	60	34
5	ST 80 BD19	67	41
6	ST 81 + T/S 8	66	35
7	ST 81 + T/S 9	60	29
8	ST 81 + T/S 10	64	36
9	ST 81 NL T/S 5	61	28
10	ST 81 + T/S 7a	63	41
11	ST 81 + T/S 7b	65	45
12	ST 82 ACE F18	62	31

Analyses 1 and 2 are clay and silt-rich areas from the same tile, 10 and 11 are repeat analyses of the same section.

Table 33 Stonea Grange: Roman tile assigned to Group 2, with presence/absence chart and results of grain-size analysis on selected sections

Sample number	Gypsum moulds	Calcite	Quartz >0.1 mm	Variegated clay	Mean diameter (μm)	Standard deviation	Skewness
ST 80 BD12	?	×	×	×	224	87	0.81
ST80 BD15	×	×	×	×	214	116	1.40
ST 80 BD17	×	×	×	×	218	92	0.47
ST 81 NL T/S2	×	×	×	×	222	91	0.73
ST 80 BD18	–	×	×	×	195	78	1.07
ST 82 ABT F15	×	×	×	×	256	141	1.82
ST 82 ACE F15	×	×	×	×	211	79	0.48
ST 82 ABT F14	–	×	×	?	221	109	1.98
ST 82 ACE F14	×	×	×	–	229	98	1.56
ST 80 BA F6	×	×	×	×	240	95	1.36
ST 82 ABT F16	?	×	×	×	216	100	1.54
ST 80 BD20	–	×	×	–	184	83	1.63
ST 82 ABQ F17 (a)	×	×	–	×	–	–	–
ST 82 ABQ F17 (b)	×	×	–	–	–	–	–
ST 80 BD13	×	×	–	×	–	–	–
ST 80 BD14	×	×	×	×	–	–	–

Table 34 Stonea Grange: Roman tile – results of textural analysis on quartz grain distributions in tile wasters from Eye and in Fabric Group 4

Tile number	Mean diameter (μm)	Standard deviation	Skewness	Kurtosis	Percentage quartz
Eye 1983 S17	157	93	1.2	0.89	2.7
Eye 1983 17	177	93	1.0	0.64	8.6
ST 80 AD F5	147	73	1.3	1.5	8.7
ST 80 BC F4	149	79	1.6	2.6	7.5

IMPRINTED TILES

Tony Legge   (Fig. 189; Pl. XXVIIIb)

THE TILES

The Stonea tiles were made by a variety of means. In some, the clay was thrown into a shallow mould of the desired form, and then struck off flush with the sides of the mould leaving the tile with one smooth surface in contact with the mould and one striated surface. These tiles were inverted when put out for drying, leaving the smoother side uppermost, on which the prints are found. Other tiles were formed in a mould that was placed on a sanded surface, leaving the underside rough and impressed with sand grains, while the upper surface is striated. Some were made by a further technique which left both surfaces showing strickle or wiping marks.

The measurements given below are approximate; the variable shape of the fragments is expressed only as the approximate maximum length and breadth of the fragment at right angles to this. Similarly, the variable fabric meant that thickness measurments are at best approximations to a variable form.

THE PRINTS

Most of the prints listed below are from domestic mammals; cats, dogs and caprines (sheep or goat). These are all digitigrade mammals; that is, walking on the toes. In cats and dogs, each phalanx is supported by a leathery pad (toe pads) behind which is the main pad. The different gaits in the cat of walking, trotting and leaping result in different tracks. In the faster gaits, most impulsion is provided by the toe pads and these will be more deeply marked. In walking and trotting, the hind paw prints commonly overlap with those of the fore paw and are said to 'register'. This is also so for dogs, except that the paw prints less often overlap. In dogs, the faster gait is a gallop. In sheep and goats, the common gaits are a walk or slow trot. In the slower gaits, the hoof prints commonly are registered.

CATALOGUE

Where possible, measurements of the prints are given following Bang and Dahlstrom 1972, 12–13.

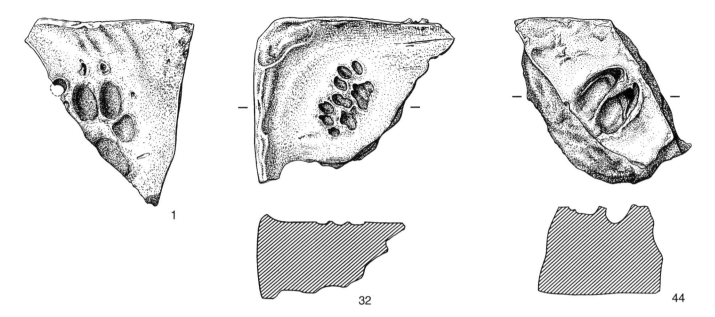

Fig. 189 Stonea Grange: animal prints in tile. Dog (1), cat (32), sheep/goat (44) (scale 1 : 2).

DOG

1 ST 80, AZ S31 (Fig. 189)

Margin fragment of a thin tile, 100 × 92 mm, 18 mm thick. Part of a well marked paw impression of a large dog, the impression made at a normal walking gait.

From ashy spread south and west of building R1, small hypocausted room. 4th–7th century AD.

2 ST 84A, III, 28, 2 S37 (Pl. XXVIIIb)

Irregular fragment of a thick tile, 115 × 85 mm, 38 mm thick. Deeply impressed print from a large dog made on soft clay, walking gait. The print is broken through, but can be estimated at 55 mm wide. The print is partly obscured by a rather smudged second paw print. Print on smooth surface.

From the sump, cut III, layer 28, spit 2, south end. Late 2nd–3rd century AD.

3 ST 84, EBP S33

Small fragment of tile 85 × 70 mm, 21 mm thick. Part of a deeply impressed paw print from a large dog. Print on smooth surface.

From gully 24, cut 5, unit 2115. 3rd century AD.

4 ST 81, FN S53

Margin fragment of a thick tile, 130 × 75 mm, 47 mm thick. On the tile margin, a deeply impressed paw print from a large dog, broken through, showing three anterior pads with claw impressions. Print on smooth surface, lower sanded.

From the cobbled surface (unit 128) north of building R1. Phase III on.

5 ST 80, AD S52

Irregular tile fragment, 75 × 55 mm, 33 mm thick. Part of a paw print from large dog, showing faint claw marks on anterior toe pads. Broken through. Print on smooth surface.

From robbed wall-footing (unit 4), building R1, east wing. 4th century AD.

6 ST 82, ACL S16

Fragment of coarse gritted tile, 80 × 120 mm, 22 mm thick. A double dog paw print, not quite registered, but probably fore and hind of the same animal. Width: fore paw 57 mm, hind paw 38 mm. A possible, very blurred human thumb print between the paw prints and a break prevent length measurments. Print on struck surface.

From ditch 9, cut 12, unit 500. 3rd century AD.

7 ST 81, TG S19

Large piece of coarse sandy tile, 170 × 200 mm, 37 mm thick. Two paw prints, probably from different dogs. One is broken through, but obviously large, showing the intermediate pad and 1 toe pad, while the second is faint and much smaller, showing the intermediate pad and the proximal pads. Print on struck side.

From the cobbled surface (unit 375) north of building R1. Phase III on.

8 ST 82, AAG S15 (Pl. XXVIIIb)

Small fragment of tile, 60 × 70 mm, 21 mm thick. Two overlapping footprints from a medium sized dog, one of the fore foot and one of the hind. The clay was partly dry, and light claw prints show only one pad from the front paw and four from the hind. Dog footprints are registered in this way during normal walking. Print on struck surface.

From topsoil/cleaning (unit 448), block 5.

9 ST 82, AAD S54 (Pl. XXVIIIb)

Corner fragment of a thick tile, 123 × 95 mm, 37 mm thick. Deeply impressed paw print of a small dog, broken through, and showing the two anterior toe pads with well marked claw prints and one lateral toe pad. Width can be estimated at 35 mm. Print on smooth surface.

From debris (unit 445) on mortar surface 449, east of building R1, east wing. Phase III on.

10 ST 80, BZ S60

Small corner fragment of thick tile, 90 × 110 mm, 30 mm thick. Two rather faint registered footprints of a small dog, at walking pace. Print on smooth surface.

From debris (unit 46) on mortar surface beyond south-east corner of building R1. 3rd or 4th century AD.

11 ST 80, DK S44

Corner fragment of small tile, with cut chamfer at edge. 140 × 113 mm, 22 mm thick. Faint registered paw prints of small dog. Both surfaces smooth.

From robbing debris (unit 79), building R1, north-east quadrant. Late 3rd–4th century AD.

12 ST 81, FR S48

Irregular tile fragment, 70 × 70 mm, 24 mm thick. Faint paw print of dog with claw tip impressions, 34 mm wide. Print on struck surface; lower is sanded.

From pit 132, unit 131. 3rd century AD.

13 ST 81, MA S47

Margin fragment of a thin tile, 70 × 60 mm, 16 mm thick. Part paw print of a small dog, with claw tip impressions. Walking gait.

From pit 170, unit 254. 3rd/4th century AD.

14 ST 80, AZ S27

Irregular fragment of tile, 90 × 160 mm, 40 mm thick. Small, faint paw print of small dog; intermediate and two toe pads. Print on struck side.

Context as no. 1.

15 ST 81, KS S39

A corner fragment from a large tile, 115 × 90 mm, 55 mm thick. Two deeply impressed paw prints, with deep claw marks. The prints are obscured by their partial registration. Probably of a small dog, at a fast gait. Print on struck side, lower sanded.

From layer, unit 224, north-west corner block 1. 3rd or 4th century AD.

16 ST 80, BA S4

Small fragment of a tile, 60 × 80 mm, 40 mm thick. Part of a paw print, deeply impressed into wet clay, with clear claw impressions. Probably small dog, possibly running. Print on smooth surface.

From layer 24, building R1, small hypocausted room. Late 2nd–early 3rd century AD.

17 ST 84, DVY S20

Irregular tile fragment, 100 × 120 mm, 24 mm thick, of a coarse sandy texture. Two faint paw prints, probably of a small dog. Print on smooth surface.

From pit 2022, unit 1979. 3rd century AD.

18 ST 81, MA S12

Almost whole tile, missing one corner, 180 × 200 mm, 35 mm thick. Registered fore and hind paw prints of dog; the tile is broken through the prints. Print on smooth surface.

Context as no. 13.

19 ST 84, DQA S61

Fragment of margin from an *imbrex*, 150 × 170 mm, 18 mm thick. Registered paw prints of a dog on the upper surface, made on fairly dry clay. The impression was broken through when the tile was fragmented. Print on upper surface, lower sanded.

From gully 35, cut 6, unit 1861. 3rd century AD.

20 ST 83A, 12 S14

Small fragment of tile, 60 × 90 mm, 31 mm thick. Medial part of a dog paw print, deeply impressed into wet clay. Print on struck surface.

From the sump, layer 12. 1st–3rd century AD.

21 ST 82, AAN S45

Corner fragment from a thick tile, 142 × 136 mm, 43 mm thick. Tip of a paw print of a dog, showing the two anterior and one lateral pads, with claw impressions. Made at walking pace. Print on smooth surface, lower sanded.

From gully 41, cut 3, unit 454. Late 2nd/early 3rd century AD.

22 ST 83A, 4 S21

Corner fragment of a thick tile, 80 × 140 mm, 36 mm thick. Part of a dog paw print made into very soft clay, the tile broken through the print. Print on struck surface.

From the sump, layer 4. Phases IV–VI.

23 ST 80, AA S2

Fragment of tile with faint paw print of a dog. Print on smooth surface.

From topsoil (unit 1), above building R1.

24 ST 80, BD S49

Irregular tile fragment, 80 × 55 mm, 17 mm thick. Part of a faint paw impression of a dog. Print on smooth surface.

From robbing debris/levelling (unit 27), building R1, south-west quadrant. Phase IV.

25 ST 81, MA S28

A small tile fragment, 80 × 100 mm, 40 mm thick. Three indentations are possible human finger impressions, with part of a faint dog paw print. Print on struck side.

Context as no. 13.

26 ST 80, AA S1

A small, irregular tile fragment, 150 × 70 mm. Part of a faint paw print of a dog. Print on struck surface.

Context as no. 23.

27 ST 80, BD S50

Margin fragment of a tile, 111 × 75 mm, 32 mm thick. Partial faint paw prints, registered, probably of a dog. Print on smooth surface.

Context as no. 24.

28 ST 82, AAE S55

Irregular margin fragment of a tile, 85 × 65 mm, thickness variable, 30 mm at margin. Partial faint paw print, probably of a dog.

From well 446 (unit 446). Late 2nd-3rd century AD.

29 ST 81, FE S7

Small fragment of a thin tile, 25 × 55 mm, 22 mm thick. Partial print of a ?dog paw, showing two pads and fur marks. Smooth surface.

From robbing debris (unit 120), building R1, south-west quadrant. Phase IV.

30 ST 82, ADS S17

Small fragment of grey tile, 70 × 100 mm, 38 thick. Part of a faint impression of a (?)dog paw print, made on the almost dry clay. Print on struck surface.

From ditch 9, cut 5, unit 531. Late 3rd century AD.

31 ST 82, ABT S22

Small fragment of tile, 70 × 100 mm, 30 mm thick. A group of faint paw marks. Two are fairly clear and one is smudged, showing drag marks of the claws; the latter possibly from a dog startled into motion. Print on struck side.

From the sump, unit 484. Phases IV–VI.

CAT

32 ST 80, AZ S32   (Fig. 189)

Corner fragment of a thick tile, 117 × 87 mm, 45 mm thick. A double paw print of a cat, registered, representing the fore and hind paw impressions made at a normal walking gait.

Context as no. 1.

33 ST 80, + S6

Irregular fragment of tile, 100 × 140 mm, 24 mm thick. Two paw prints, partly registered, of a domestic cat. The hind paw print obscures that of the fore paw. Only the toe pads are impressed. Width (hind) 22 mm. Print on struck surface.

From building R1, E/W section cleaning, unstratified.

34 ST 82, BKM S42

Margin fragment of tile, 144 × 112 mm, 24 mm thick. One clear and one faint paw print of a cat. The well marked print is 32 mm wide and 28 mm long. Print on smooth surface.

From layer 934, above ditch 9, cut 1a. Phases V–VI.

35 ST 81, DJ S40   (Pl. XXVIIIb)

Corner fragment of thick tile, 120 × 100 mm, 36 mm thick. Deeply impressed prints of cat paws, one fore (32 mm wide) with an overlapping hind print. The partly registered prints are characteristic of a walking gait, obviously made on very wet clay. Print on struck surface, lower sanded.

From robbing debris (unit 78), building R1, north-east quadrant. Phase IV.

36 ST 81, FX S35

Corner fragment of a tile, 90 × 68 mm, 38 mm thick. Light paw print of cat, at the margin of the tile. The print is 28 mm wide, 28 mm long. Print on smooth surface.

From robbing debris/levelling (unit 136), building R1, north-west and north-east quadrants. 4th century AD.

37 ST 82, ADL S41   (Pl. XXVIIIb)

Small fragment of thick tile, 120 × 110 mm, 44 mm thick. Single well impressed paw print of a cat, with only the four anterior toe pads marked. 27 mm wide. The single print and the presence of faint claw tip marks suggest a rapid gait. Both surfaces struck.

From well 446 (unit 524). Late 2nd–3rd century AD.

38 ST 81, KS S51   (Pl. XXVIIIb)

Corner fragment of a tile, 85 × 80 mm, 35 mm thick. Two deeply marked paw prints of a cat, registered. The toe pads are deeply impressed, the main pad faintly impressed, suggesting a rapid gait. Print on struck surface.

Context as no. 15.

39 ST 81, MA S29

Margin fragment of a tile 110 × 180 mm, 33 mm thick. Two paw prints of cat, registered at walking pace. The hind print partly obscures the fore. Print on struck side.

Context as no. 13.

40 ST 82, ABT S56

Small margin fragment of tile, 115 × 65 mm, 20 mm thick. Two or three overlapping paw prints of a cat, at walking pace, possibly made from two directions. Print on smooth surface.

Context as no. 31.

41 ST 84, ECH S34

Irregular fragment of thick tile, 70 × 65 mm, 38 mm thick. A faint impression of the fore part of the anterior pads of a cat. Print on smooth surface, lower sanded.

From layer (unit 2132) over gully complex, south-east block 8. Late 2nd–3rd century AD.

42 ST 80, BA S10

Corner fragment of tile, 150 × 140 mm, 34 mm thick. Faint impression of paw print of cat, partly obscured by adhering mortar. Print on smooth surface.

Context as no. 16.

43 ST 81, KN S43

Corner fragment of an *imbrex*, 190 × 121 mm, 27 mm thick. Faint paw print on upper surface, showing three anterior pads only, Small, probably a cat. Print on struck surface, lower sanded.

From pit 170, unit 220. 3rd/4th century AD.

CAPRINES

44 ST 80, CE S30   (Fig. 189)

Small margin fragment of a very thick tile, 90 × 60 mm, 46 mm thick. The fragment bears a well-marked caprine hoof impression, probably of a sheep, deeply marked in soft clay. Normal walking gait.

From robbing debris, building R1, west range. Phase IV.

45 ST 80, BF S11   (Pl. XXVIIIb)

Tile fragment 170 × 90 mm, 23 mm thick. Imprint of caprine hoof, into fairly dry clay. Only the outer margins of the hoof were impressed; the rather pointed hoof tips suggest that the animal was a sheep. Length 30 mm, width 30 mm. Plaster encrustations over surface.

From robbed wall footing (unit 29), building R1, east wing. 3rd or 4th century AD.

46 ST 81, VY S26   (Pl. XXVIIIb)

Irregular fragment of thick tile, 80 × 90 mm, 40 mm thick. One well marked hoof print, probably of lateral hoof, of caprine. Print on struck surface, but strickle marks evident on both surfaces.

From well 336, unit 412. Late 2nd–3rd century AD.

OTHER

47 ST 81, FE S8

Fragment of thick tile, 70 × 100 mm, 42 mm thick. Four rather faint impressions, probably of human fingers, near to broken margin. Print on struck surface.

Context as no. 29.

DISCUSSION

Forty-six animal prints could be identified, most with confidence. Including those where the identification could be only made with some slight doubt, there are 31 prints of dogs, 12 prints of cats and 3 from caprines, probably all from sheep. The dogs show a considerable variability in size, though this is not easily judged from tile prints. The size of the print varies according to the softness of the clay, in which a larger print will be made in a softer matrix. There is also shrinkage during the drying and firing of the tile. The speed of the animal in question also influences the result; a fast gait will create a deeper impression, though usually from the anterior part of the paw. The cat paw prints are from small animals, almost certainly those of domestic cats. The wild cat is considerably larger than the domestic form and while the Fen basin would have provided some areas of refuge in which wild animals could survive into Roman times in greater numbers than in more accessible areas, it is unlikely that a seasonally wet habitat would have been attractive to this species.

Obviously domestic cats and dogs had ready access to the tile yards and appeared to have wandered at will over the drying tiles. Most appear to have had a leisurely gait, with only a few specimens showing indications of fast motion. Even where this is evident the causes may have come from the animals themselves rather than from the intervention of the tile manufacturers.

The frequency of the species represented on the Stonea tile fragments can be compared with those from Silchester (Cram and Fulford 1979):

Species	Stonea	Silchester
Horse	0	1
Cattle	0	6
Caprine	3	22
Dog	31	35
Cat	12	8
Bird	0	7
Human	1(?)	25

The two assemblages show some differences, most notably in the absence of hoof prints from large domestic mammals at Stonea, and the smaller proportion of caprines at this site. At Silchester, both sheep and goat hoof prints were identified. Two of the three caprine prints from Stonea were only partial, but the rounded hoof tips and the contour of the hoof suggest that sheep were the more likely identification.

The Silchester caprine imprints include those of juveniles, leading to the conclusion that the tiles were made in spring or early summer. The season of birth cannot be assumed among domestic mammals in earlier times, as this can quite easily be manipulated for special reasons. However, on at least one Roman site, that of the Harlow Temple, seasonal birth among the caprines could be demonstrated due to the coincidence of certain age classes, a pattern which could only have been created under a regime of spring births (Legge and Dorrington 1985).

STONE OBJECTS

Ralph Jackson and Sylvia Humphrey (Petrology)   (Figs 190–3)

Forty-two of the catalogued objects were examined by Sylvia Humphrey (British Museum Research Laboratory, File no. 6255), with a view to determining rock types and, where possible, to comment on likely sources. In most cases it was possible to identify the rock types macroscopically, but X-ray diffraction analysis (XRD) and thin-sectioning were employed where necessary. The results indicated that certain types of stone were imported (either as roughouts or finished articles) from recognised non-local sources to provide specialised types of artefact. These stones include Niedermendig lava and also, probably, the Millstone Grit of northern England, both popular materials for the production of milling stones. Similarly, the majority of the whetstones are of Kentish Ragstone. A number of the less specialised artefacts consist of locally available materials, for example the quartzite pebbles with worn faces, which may have been collected from local glacial deposits.

MILLING STONES   (Fig. 190)

MILLSTONE GRIT

Numbers 1–8 consist of a coarse pinkish, feldspathic sandstone, some containing quartz pebbles. Numbers 3–5 were selected as being representative of the varieties within the group and were analysed by X-ray diffraction. Comparison with several potential sources of Millstone Grit and Coal Measures sandstones from the Sheffield area suggests that these particular stones may have been derived from at least two horizons of the Millstone Grit. Visually, all of the stones included in this group are rather similar. The sizes of some of the fragments makes it unlikely that they were made from locally obtained, erratic boulders derived from glacial drift.

1 Upper stone, fragment   Diameter c. 45 cm ST 82 ABP

The grinding face is very worn and only the faintest trace of parts of two harps of furrowed dressing is visible. There is a flattened band c. 4 cm wide around the edge of the skirt, the outer part of which is unworn. The upper surface and side are neatly dressed with pocking. The stone may have broken at or near the eye, but nothing remains of the hopper or handle seating.

From ditch 71, cut 1, unit 480. Post-medieval recutting of a Phase III ditch.

2 Upper stone, fragment
Diameter c. 45 cm ST 82 BLH, SF 436

The grinding face is very worn, but remains of dressing furrows are visible in two places. The upper surface and side have a rough, pocked dressing. No evidence survives to indicate the form of the handle or the hopper.

From ditch 9, cut 1a, unit 954. Late 2nd/early 3rd century AD.

3 Upper stone, fragment
Diameter c. 45 cm ST 83 CAB, SF 503

The grinding face is very worn, and rotary striations are visible, especially nearer the centre. The upper surface and side are roughly dressed and retain no evidence of the form of handle or hopper. The stone is broken near the eye which must have been 10 cm or less in diameter.

From topsoil/cleaning, block 11 east, block 2 north.

4 Upper stone, fragment   Diameter c. 45 cm ST 82 AER

The lightly-worn grinding face preserves parts of two harps of furrowed dressing set approximately at a right angle to each other. The upper surface and side are roughly dressed with pocking, and part of a chased groove remains on the upper surface. Its function is unclear and it may be a feature of re-use.

From well 446, unit 554. Late 2nd–3rd century AD.

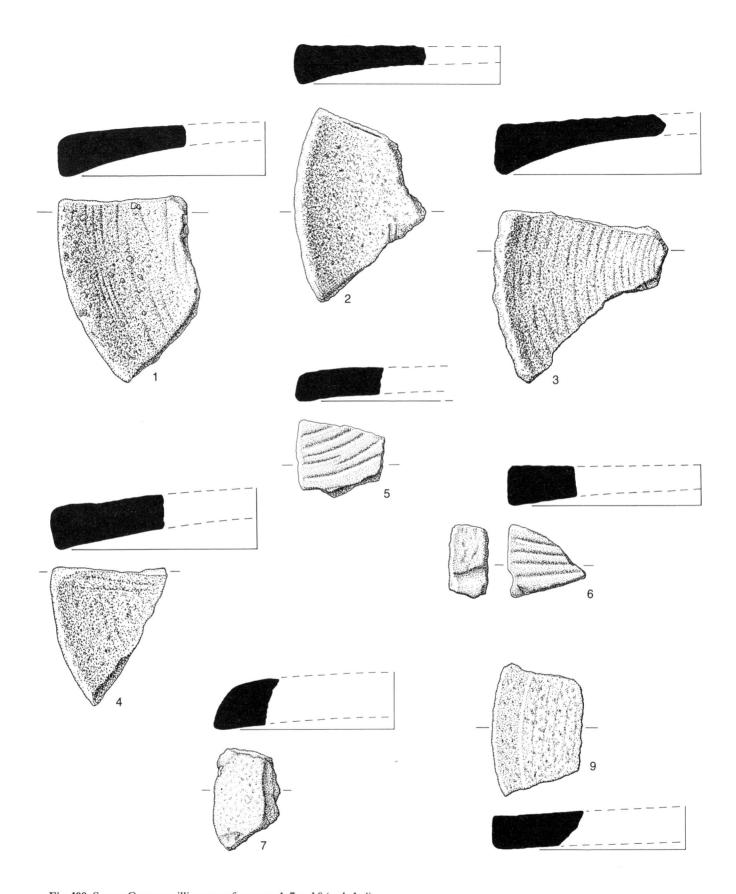

Fig. 190 Stonea Grange: milling stone fragments 1–7 and 9 (scale 1:4).

5 Upper stone, fragment
Diameter *c*. 40 cm ST 83A, 26, 5, SF 1983A, 24

The fragment is from the edge of a slim stone (thickness 2.9 cm). The worn grinding face preserves part of a harp comprising at least seven radiating elliptical furrows. The side is roughly dressed, but the upper surface is very smooth and may have been used secondarily as a sharpening stone.

From sump layer A26, grid 5. Late 3rd century AD.

6 Upper stone, fragment
Diameter *c*. 42 cm ST 83 CNA, SF 571

The worn grinding face preserves part of a harp comprising at least four converging furrows. The upper surface and side have a rough, pocked dressing. A vertical slot in the side of the stone is an intentional feature, presumably part of the seating for an iron hoop handle. It has a small patch of wear-polish on one side of its lower edge.

From clayspread (1288) above layer 1421 of ditch 69. Late 3rd–4th century AD.

7 Upper stone, fragment
Diameter *c*. 40–45 cm ST 84 EEI, SF 1133

The fragment is from the edge of a very thick stone, with roughly sloping side. No furrows are visible on the worn grinding face. The upper surface is irregularly dressed but quite smooth.

From building R10, post-hole 2181. Phase III.

8 Lower stone, fragment   (*Unillus.*)
Length 14.5 cm ST 83 J4,1, SF 639

From well J4, layer 1. Late 3rd/early 4th century AD.

NIEDERMENDIG LAVA

Numbers 9–11, 14–15 and 22 were examined macroscopically and were found to consist of a fine grey vesicular lava. The samples are all very similar in hand specimen, and probably originate from the same geological source. No. 11 was examined in thin section. This rock consists of microphenocrysts of aegirine–augite (typically less than 1 mm in diameter), in a fine grained groundmass of feldspar, clinopyroxene and an opaque ore mineral. The aegirine–augite is pleochroic (in shades of green to almost colourless), and strongly zoned. Rare, rounded, quartzitic inclusions and very rare nepheline phenocrysts are also present. This rock matches closely samples of Niedermendig lava from the Tertiary volcanic area of Northern Germany.

Because of the crumbly nature of the lava quern fragments, it has seldom been possible to measure or estimate the diameter. Thickness and weight measurements have been substituted.

9 Lower stone, fragment
Diameter 42 cm, weight 659.2 g ST 84 DPO, SF 891

The well-worn grinding face has a flat band *c*. 2.5 cm wide around the edge of the skirt. Beyond this zone the face is lightly domed. No furrows are visible. The side (3.4 cm thick) is dressed with engraved vertical striae, now rather worn, while the lower surface is flat and unremarkable.

From the fill (unit 1850) of pit 1850. Later 2nd/3rd century AD.

10 Lower and ?upper stone, fragments   (*Unillus.*)
Weight 171.9 g ST 84 DRK, SF 912

Two small fragments, the larger from a lower stone, with a diameter of *c*. 42 cm. No furrows are visible on the grinding face. The smaller fragment appears to be from the edge of an upper stone of similar diameter.

From gully 29, cut 2, unit 1894. 3rd century AD.

11 ?Lower stone, fragment   (*Unillus.*)
Diameter *c*. 40 cm, weight 498 g ST 83 CDY, SF 504

Outer edge fragment, 3.8 cm. thick.

From post-medieval layer 1094, block 11, east.

12 Fragment   (*Unillus.*)
Thickness at least 5 cm, weight 134.3 g ST 82 ACE

From ditch 9, cut 11, unit 494. 3rd century AD.

13 Many fragments   (*Unillus.*)
Thickness *c*. 3.9 cm, weight 425 gm ST 82 BAI

From unit 714, fill of sinkage cone into the fill of well 808. 4th–8th century AD.

14 Fragment   (*Unillus.*)
Thickness *c*. 3 cm, weight 89.1 g ST 83 CHR, SF 559

From upper layer (unit 1184) in pit 1184. Early 3rd century AD.

15 Fragment   (*Unillus.*)
Thickness *c*. 3 cm, weight 30.8 g ST 83 CIB, SF 556

From basal layer (unit 1193) in pit 1184. Early 3rd century AD.

16 Many fragments   (*Unillus.*) Weight 790 g ST 81 LX

From the fill (unit 251) of gully 61. 5th–7th century AD.

17 Many fragments   (*Unillus.*) Weight 267 g ST82 AAE

From upper layer (unit 446) of well 446. 3rd century AD.

18 Many fragments   (*Unillus.*) Weight 247 g ST 82 BAD

From oven 7, surface debris in the chamber (unit 709). Phase IV.

A larger fragment was also found in the collapsed superstructure of the same oven (unit 768), and it is probable that they were part of a milling stone, residual from Phase III, that was given a secondary use as a structural component of the oven.

19 Many fragments   (*Unillus.*) Weight 200 g ST 82 BEI

From gully 35, cut 3, unit 810. 3rd century AD.

20 Fragments   (*Unillus.*) Weight 145 g ST 81 JS

From unit 201 of the low rubbly mound sealing Anglo-Saxon building S1. 9th–10th century AD.

21 Fragments   (*Unillus.*) Weight 39 g ST 81 FM

Context as no. 20, unit 127.

22 Fragments   (*Unillus.*) Weight 38 g ST 83 CPY, SF 638

From post-hole 1358.

23 Fragment   (*Unillus.*) Weight 17 g ST 82 ABT

From rubble layer 484 in the sump. Phases IV–VI.

RUBBING AND GRINDING STONES
(Fig. 191)

Numbers 24–5 and 27–30 consist of micaceous sandstone. This material is probably from several, non-local sources. Three fine-grained quartzite pebbles (nos 31–3) are of uncertain (but non-local) geological provenance. It is possible that these materials were obtained from local glacial or other drift deposits.

24 Re-used ?architectural fragment
Length 20.5 cm ST 82 BKO, SF 434

A broken slab of micaceous sandstone used as a mortar and a sharpening stone. The fragment, worn and damaged, retains parts of two faces and two corners. Tooling on one corner defines a rudimentary boss and there is a possible worn grooved moulding adjacent to this. These may have been part of the decor of a capital from a small column or pilaster. Whatever its original function, the stone was subsequently re-used as a mortar or grinding stone. That this use was heavy and prolonged is evident from the deep hollow on both planar faces. In fact the stone was probably completely worn away at the thinnest point. It may be at this stage that the stone was converted to a sharpening block: whetting grooves are present on both dished planar faces.

From ditch 9 cut 3, until 936. Late 2nd/early 3rd century AD.

25 Sharpening stone   Length 10.1 cm ST 82 AFN, SF 433

An irregularly-shaped fragment of micaceous sandstone. The main planar face is lightly dished through wear and also has a series of oblique, narrow whetting grooves of varying depth. The lower planar face is partly-ground, as also is an arc of one edge.

From ditch 9 cut 10, unit 574. 3rd century AD.

26 Rubbing stone   Length 9.8 cm ST 81+

A rectangular tablet of fine quartzite. The size and general form are reminiscent of Roman stone cosmetic palettes. Those, however, are normally rather thinner and of softer stones. Additionally, there is no tell-tale dishing of the main planar surface. That face is flat and smooth, with a distinct wear polish, which is present also on both long sides, and the irregular bevelled lower planar face. The short ends are irregularly bevelled and ground. One of the long sides is 'rippled' with wear grooves consistent with use as a whetting surface. For a similarly enigmatic small stone slab from Gadebridge Park Roman villa, see Neal 1974, 194–5, Fig. 85, no. 711.

Unstratified (surface find).

27 Rubbing stone/pestle
Height 9.6 cm ST 83 CDQ, SF 501

A large ovoid pebble, of indurated micaceous sandstone, with a distinct wear facet on one end.

From ditch 12, cut 2, unit 1087. Post-medieval.

28 Rubbing stone   (*Unillus.*)
Length 11.1 cm ST 83 CAD, SF 525

A truncated wedge-shaped piece of micaceous sandstone. This is a fragment of a quern upper stone, with rough upper face, and partly smoothed side. the lower (grinding) face has been dished through re-use as a whetting or grinding surface.

From ditch 71, cut 10, unit 1003. Post-medieval.

29 Rubbing stone   (*Unillus.*)
Length 8.0 cm ST 83A, 26, 2, SF 1983A, 31

A rounded pebble, of cross-bedded micaceous sandstone, with several wear-facets around the circumference.

From sump layer A, 26, grid 2. Late 3rd century AD.

30 ?Rubbing stone   (*Unillus.*)
Length 11.2 cm ST 83 CHK, SF 554

An irregular fragment of micaceous sandstone, with at least two prepared faces and a third which appears to have been used as a grinding/whetting surface.

From ditch 4, cut 1, unit 1177. Late 2nd/early 3rd century AD.

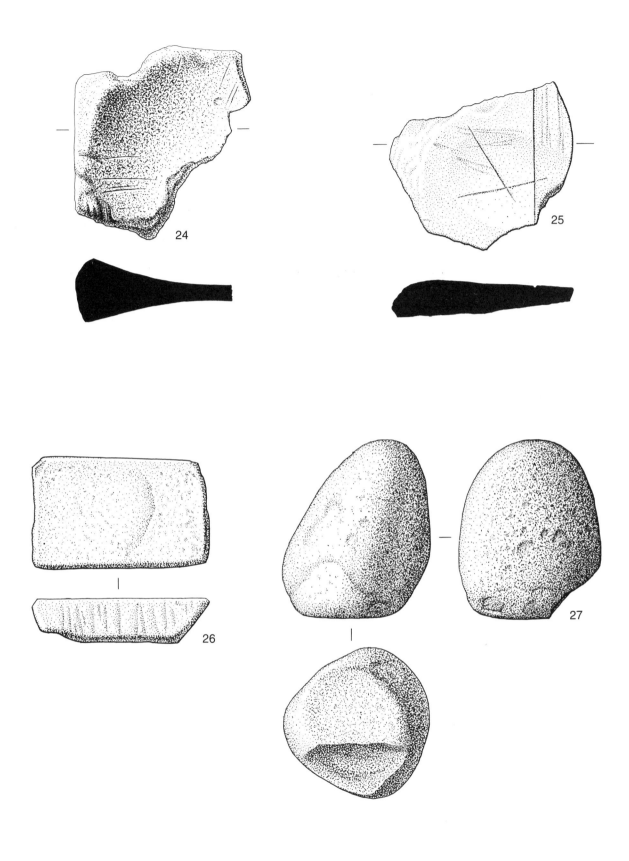

Fig. 191 Stonea Grange: worked stone objects 24–7 (scale 1 : 2 except 24 = 1 : 4).

31 ?Rubbing stone   *(Unillus.)*
Length 6.3 cm ST 82 BLH, SF 437

A rounded quartzite pebble with one flattened (?worn) face.
Context as no. 2.

32 Rubbing stone   *(Unillus.)*
Length 6.3 cm ST 83 CML, SF 568

As no. 31.

From ditch 3, cut 6, unit 1274. 3rd century AD.

33 ?Rubbing stone   *(Unillus.)*
Length 8.7 cm ST 83A, 26, 9/6, SF 1983A, 30

As no. 31.

From sump layer A, 26, grid 9/6. Late 3rd century AD.

WHETSTONES   (Fig. 192)

Of the ten whetstones examined, eight (nos 35–42) have been identified in hand specimen as Kentish Ragstone (from the Hythe Beds of Kent), partly on the basis of shape and general dimensions which are very characteristic for whetstones made of this material. A small quantity of material was scraped from each piece, and a brisk effervescence on the addition of dilute acid confirmed the presence of calcareous material, which is a significant component of Kentish Ragstone. One example (no. 41) is slightly darker in colour than the other specimens of Kentish Ragstone; this feature together with its slightly larger dimensions suggests that it may not belong to this group. Whetstone no. 43 is mudstone. It is laminated, and slightly calcareous. Number 44 is a fissile sandstone.

KENTISH RAGSTONE

34 Whetstone, broken   Length 4.7 cm ST 80 BA

A well-made, tapered pestle-shaped example, with neatly-formed flat end-face and plump, rounded rectangular cross-section. Slight dishing of the planar faces and 'rippling' of the lateral faces are products of wear.

From destruction deposit 24 over the small hypocausted room of building R1. Early 3rd century AD.

35 Whetstone, broken   Length 4.4 cm ST 81 NR

A well-made example of tapered plump rectangular-sectioned rod. The planar faces are flat, the lateral faces lightly convex, and the corners rounded-off. There is little sign of wear. The complete end face is worked flat. Like the broken end it is unworn, and the stone was probably discarded after breakage.

From occupation layer 292, north-west corner block 1. 3rd century AD.

36 Whetstone, broken   Length 5.1 cm ST 82 AZY, SF 303

A slender example of rounded rectangular cross-section. Dishing of the planar faces and a more marked waisting of the lateral faces are products of wear.

From top layer (unit 704) in pit 704. Late 3rd/4th century AD.

37 Whetstone, fragment
Length 3.1 cm ST 82 ABF, SF 262

A well-made 'cushion'-shaped example of plump, rounded rectangular cross-section. The planar faces are lightly convex, the lateral faces more markedly so: both show signs of wear. The prepared end face also appears to have wear facets.

From topsoil/cleaning, block 2.

38 Whetstone, fragment   Length 4.1 cm ST 81 HJ, SF 232

The waisted shape is a product of heavy wear on the lateral faces.

From top layer (unit 170) in pit 170. 3rd/4th century AD.

39 Whetstone, broken
Length 8.0 cm, originally *c*. 10 cm ST 83 CNA, SF 573

A flat, tabular example of lightly softened, rectangular cross-section. One of the planar faces retains, almost unworn, a ?calcareous stratum along which the stone was cut. The other planar face and the two lateral faces are markedly hollowed through whetting. The complete end face is partially worked. The other end, broken in antiquity, shows no sign of wear and the stone may have been discarded after the breakage.

Context as no.6.

40 Whetstone, broken
Length 6.2 cm ST 84 DIQ, SF 1125

The original unworn cross-section, where it is visible beneath the end face, is a plump rectangle with rounded corners. Whetting has reduced all four lateral and planar faces, and especially heavy wear on one of the planar faces has sharpened the corners. Although the stone was once longer, much of the wear appears to have occurred after breakage, and there is an angled wear facet on both end faces.

From gully 33, cut 3, unit 1708. Late 2nd/early 3rd century AD.

41 Whetstone   Length 5.8 cm ST 82 AGN, SF 438

An unusually short, stout example of softened rectangular cross-section with marked dishing through wear on the planar and lateral faces. The end faces are unworn, and the fact that neither is fractured demonstrates that the stone was always short and is not a re-used fragment of a longer stone.

From ashy destruction/dereliction deposit (unit 598) to south of building R1. Late 2nd/early 3rd century AD.

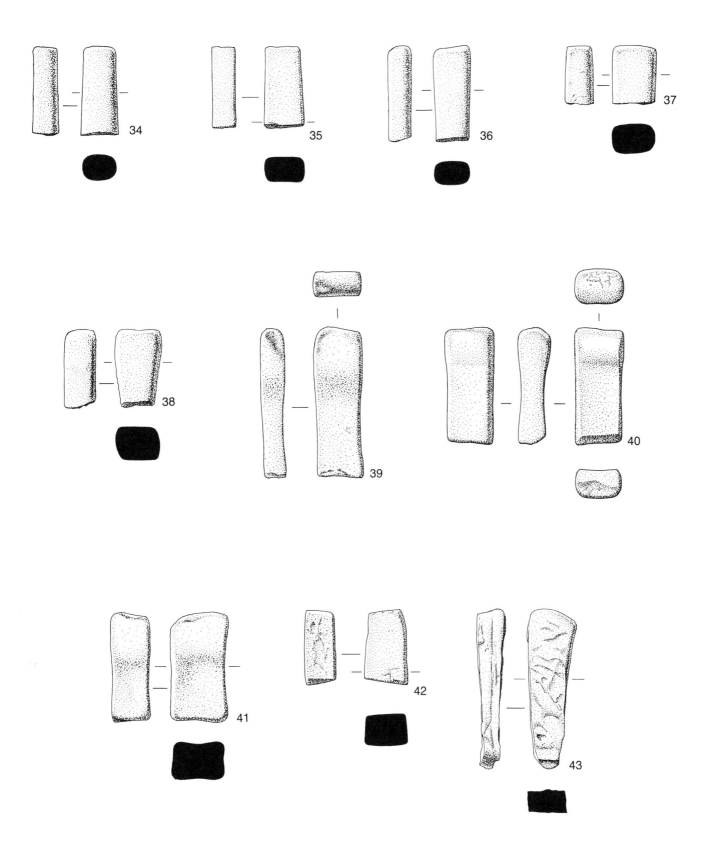

Fig. 192 Stonea Grange: whetstones 34–43 (scale 1 : 2).

42 Whetstone, fragment

Length 4.0 cm ST 83 CMT, SF 631

A tapered rod of rectangular cross-section. The complete end face is worked flat and the corners are un-bevelled. All the faces are worn, but not heavily. The broken face has been ground, which suggests re-use of a broken stone.

From gully 53, cut 2, unit 1282. Late 3rd–4th century AD.

OTHER STONE

43 Whetstone, of fine grey mudstone

Length 8.5 cm ST 81 MW, SF 233

The surface of both planar faces has sheared away. The lateral faces are smooth, and the concavity of one is probably a result of usage.

From unit 273, part of layer 127 which seals Anglo-Saxon building S1. Phase Va.

44 ?Whetstone, of fissile sandstone   (*Unillus*.)

Length 11.7 cm ST 83A, +, 7, SF 1983A, 28

A natural, sausage-shaped pebble, which may have been utilised as a whetstone. Though both planar faces have sheared away along bedding planes, the lateral faces appear to have a wear-polished surface.

From sump, grid 7 unstratified.

ARCHITECTURAL AND MISCELLANEOUS   (Fig. 193; Pls XXI, XXIIb)

Number 50 is an oolitic limestone. This rock is Jurassic in age, and has an extensive outcrop from Dorset to Yorkshire, outcropping locally near Peterborough; nos 51–2 (and probably 53) consist of a single variety of limestone; nos 47 and 55 are a micaceous sandstone, no. 55 fissile; no. 49 is sandstone; and no. 48 is probably Kentish Ragstone, with abundant small flakes of mica defining the bedding planes.

45 Gaming counter   Diameter 1.95 cm ST 81 HT, SF 164

A finely-made domed counter of marble, probably pavonazzetto. (This identification and the following references by courtesy of Dr Susan Walker, personal communication). Cf. Mielsch 1985, 59, Taf. 18, Nr. 606, 611.

The decorative effect of the green and purple veining on a milky-white background has been exploited to the full. There is a centring dimple on the flat face.

Pavonazzetto, known in antiquity as *marmor phrygium, marmor synnadicum* or *marmor docimium*, came from the marble quarries of central Phrygia, notably from Docimium, some 50 km north of Synnada, the chief ancient city of the region (Fant 1989, 3–5). The earliest known use of pavonazzetto in Rome was at the very end of the 1st century BC in the Forum of Augustus, but already by the death of Augustus it had become one of the most prized of

coloured marbles, and the quarries at Docimium were under imperial control (*ibid.* 7–8). As late as Diocletian's Price Edict of AD 301 *lithos Dokimenos* was still the most costly listed marble (*ibid.* 10). In Britain, as has been shown (Pritchard 1986), some two-thirds of the continental marble veneers and ornamental stones of Roman London came from the east Mediterranean. Pavonazzetto was prominent (*ibid.* Fig. 13) and appears to have reached a peak in the 2nd and early 3rd century AD.

The Stonea counter was perhaps made from an offcut or waste from the manufacture of wall veneers, and its height, 1.05 cm, corresponds to the maximum thickness of the illustrated London pavonazzetto veneer fragments (*ibid.* Fig. 11).

While it may have been brought to Stonea as a finished artefact it may alternatively have been manufactured on site, which might be taken as indirect, possible, evidence for the former presence of wall veneers. Certainly, the desire for, if not firm evidence of, such veneers is demonstrated by a fragment of wall plaster painted in imitation of cipollino marble (Fig. 181, no.10).

From the top layer (unit 179) of gully 44 (cut 2), south of building R1. 3rd century AD.

[For bone and ceramic counters, see pp. 532 and 488.]

46 ?Gaming counter   Diameter 1.8 cm ST 81 FW, SF 58

A naturally-occurring small disc of flint which may have been used as a counter. It has a creamy-white patina.

From top layer (135) of well 135. 4th–7th century AD.

46a ?Gaming counter

Length 3.45 cm ST 84 DYA, SF 696

A small limestone tablet cut, quite rudimentarily, to a rectangle. One planar face bears an incised eight-rayed star; the other face is lightly dished through use as a whetstone.

From gully 18, cut 10, unit 2029. 3rd century AD.

47 Disc, in two joining pieces

Diameter 7.5 cm ST 80 BA and ST 81 SS, SF 223

A pale ginger-brown, banded micaceous sandstone disc. One face has been ground very smooth and also has a shallow dished groove which may have been a product of whetting. The circumference is carefully cut and partially ground; it is worn away at one point. Function uncertain, but two similar, though centrally perforated, objects from Vindolanda were tentatively identified as pot lids (Bidwell 1985, 153–4, Fig. 58, nos 7–8). Whatever its function(s) the present stone is likely to have been selected for its 'glittery' appearance.

From 1) old ground surface (unit 362) beneath the small hypocausted room of building R1; and 2) the destruction deposit (unit 24) above it. Late 2nd/early 3rd century AD.

48 ?Palette, fragment   Length 6.7 cm ST 83 H8, 1, SF 635

A fragmentary, lightly curved, thin slab of Kentish Ragstone in two joining pieces (modern break). The concave planar face is hardly

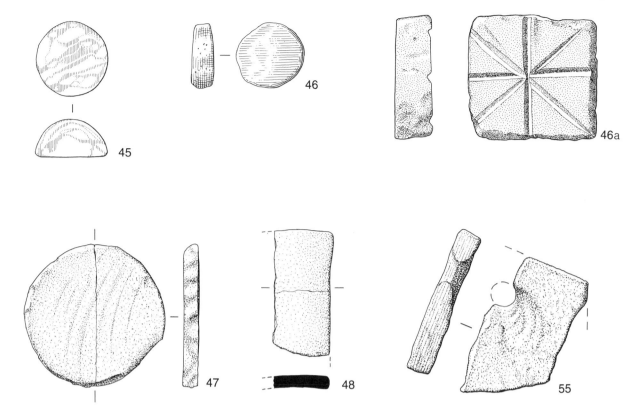

Fig. 193 Stonea Grange: worked stone objects 45–8 and 55 (scale 45–46a = 1 : 1, 47–55 = 1 : 2).

worked at all; the convex face is ground smooth as are one of the long sides and one of the short sides (both incomplete). The ground long side is lightly 'rippled' through (?)secondary use as a whetting stone.

From top layer of ?ditch/?pit H8. 3rd/4th century AD.

49 Small block (*Unillus.*) 6 × 3 × 5+ cm ST 83 CKL, SF 570

A broken rectangular sandstone block. No wear marks visible. Function uncertain, though possibly architectural, e.g. an *opus sectile* element.

From ditch 14, cut 4, unit 1226. Post-medieval, with residual Roman.

50 Carved fragment (*Unillus.*)
c. 12 × 10 × 10.5 cm ST 83A, 4, SF 1983A, 22

A fragment of worked oolitic limestone, with grooves and projecting parts visible, but too small, irregular and poorly preserved to permit certain identification. It was probably part of an architectural decoration or statuary.

From sump layer A, 4. 3rd/4th century AD.

51 Tesserae (Pl. XXI)
Average size 3.5 × 2.8 × 2.2 cm ST 84 P10,1, SF 1105

Fifteen limestone cubes and blocks of slightly varying size and shape. Two have deliberately rounded or angled edges.

From pit P10, layer 1. Early 3rd century AD.

52 Tessera (*Unillus.*) 2.8 × 2.5 × 2.4 cm ST 84 DXQ, SF 1075

A limestone cube, with mortar on one face. The opposing face is worn smooth. Coarse mosaic or border work. The same rock type, and very similar in character to the group of tesserae, no. 51, above.

From layer 2020 in pit 2020. Late 2nd–3rd century AD.

53 Tessera (*Unillus.*) 3.8 × 2.7 × 2.2 cm ST 82 BAE

Another, as no. 52.

From the upper fill (unit 710) of well 705. 3rd/4th century AD.

54 Tessera (*Unillus.*) 2.6 × 2.5 × 2.4 cm ST 80 BA

A worn ?mudstone cube, with mortar adhering to all but one face.

Context as no. 34.

55 Roofing slate, fragment

Length 8.9 cm ST 83 CDO, SF 481

Part of a thin slab of fissile micaceous sandstone split along the bedding planes. One top edge and part of one of the sides remain, as also rather over half of the peg/nail hole, of circular 'hourglass' form, diameter 1.3 cm. For complete examples of such slates, see Neal 1974, 191, 193, Fig. 83; and Holbrook and Bidwell 1991, 282–4, Fig. 137.

From ditch 11, cut 3, unit 1085. Mid/late 3rd century AD.

56 Voussoir (Pl. XXIIb)

Length 19 cm, thickness *c*. 11 cm ST 83A, 4, SF 1983A, 27

A semi-complete tufa voussoir, with marked taper.

Context as no. 50.

57 Facing stone (Pl. XXIIb)

Length 41.5 cm, height *c*. 7 cm, depth 16.5 cm ST 80 BD

A rectangular block of limestone dressed on the front face and sides, less regularly worked on the upper and lower faces, and possibly broken on the back face. This is probably a complete facing stone from either the foundation or superstructure of the central block of building R1. It was the most complete single block to have been found in the dereliction debris.

From building R1, apse, robbing debris/levelling (unit 27). Phase IV.

NON-ARTEFACTUAL ROCK TYPES

Adrian Challands

The site yielded a large quantity of rock fragments, most of which probably derived from the debris of building R1. Samples of the various types found in the 1983 excavations were selected and were macroscopically examined with the following results.

Phase III contexts

Lincolnshire limestone (Barnack rag) ST 83 CHR; CML; A, 26, 10; A, 28, 8.

Blisworth limestone (Previously Gt. Oolite limestone) ST 83 CND; G4,8; A, 26, 8.

Sandstone/millstone grit ST 83A, 26, 11.

Collyweston (Tile) ST 83 CMB; CDR; G4,9; A, 28, 9.

Phase IV contexts

Lincolnshire limestone ST 83 G4,2; J4,5.

Blisworth limestone ST 83 H8, 1; J4,1; J4,5.

Cornbrash limestone ST 83 CNL.

Millstone grit ST 83 J4,5.

Sandstone ST 83 H8,3.

Quartzitic pebble ST 83 CEE.

Collyweston (Tile) ST 83 CMT; H8,3; J4,1.

Phase IV/V context

Blisworth limestone ST 83 CMS.

Phase VI contexts

Lincolnshire limestone ST 83 CGZ; CKL; CHC; CMX; CFR.

Millstone grit ST 83 CII; CNM.

Northampton sand ST 83 CHC; CIQ.

Quartzitic pebble ST 83 CIE.

Chalk ST 83 CEC.

Collyweston (Tile) ST 83 CKL; CME; CQO; CSQ.

MORTAR SAMPLES

Andrew Middleton

INTRODUCTION

Samples of mortar from three different construction phases, together with a sample of the mortar-like concretion adhering to the blade of the wooden spade from the sump were analysed using X-ray diffraction (XRD), optical microscopy (samples 139/GA and ST 84A 28 only) and scanning electron microscopy (SEM) with energy-dispersive X-ray analysis (EXDA). The aim of the investigation was to characterise the mortars; in particular to establish whether mortars from the different phases of construction are distinctive. A list of the samples analysed is given in Table 35.

RESULTS AND DISCUSSION

Analytically the mortars fall into three groups, distinguished on the basis of their physical characteristics and mineralogical composition.

1 The first group includes two samples, 139/GA (Phase IV) and ST 84A 28 (material adhering to wooden spade). Both are relatively 'solid' materials and 139/GA can be seen to include fragments of crushed ceramic material up to about 1 cm long. Thin-section analysis indicates that some, at least, of these ceramic fragments have a fabric similar to one of the groups of tiles from Stonea

Table 35 Stonea Grange: list of mortar and mortar-like samples analysed

Sample number	Laboratory number	Description	Phase	'Analytical group'	XRD	SEM
2/AB	27618Z	Fragment of N–S wall, building R2	IV	2	√	√
58/CM	27619X	Layer in soakaway (gully 48)	III	2	√	–
93/EA	27620P	Wall footing, building R1, W range	IIIa	3	√	–
96/ED	27621Y	Lower mortar surface from 'raft' foundation of building R1	III	2	√	√
139/GA	27622W	Remains of mortar floor, building R2	IV	1	√	√
438/XB (a)	27623U	Core sample of wall footings, building R1, central block	III	2	√	–
438/XB (b)	24505X	Core sample of wall footings, building R1, central block	III	2	–	√
439/XC (a)	27617Q	Core sample of N range footings, building R1	IIIa	3	√	√
439/XC (b)	24504Z	Core sample of N range footings, building R1	IIIa	3	–	√
ST 84A 28	24008V	Concretionary material on spade	III	1	–	√

(Freestone, pp. 508–10, Fabric Group 2) – both have distinctive 'swallow-tail' shaped voids left after the dissolution of gypsum from the original raw clay (probably Ampthill clay). ST 84A 28 lacks the ceramic inclusions.

Both samples contain relatively angular sand (typically <0.5 mm in diameter, but including grains up to several millimetres across, especially in ST 84A 28), which is sparse in 139/GA but common in ST 84A 28.

ST 84A 28 is considerably altered with extensive replacement of the matrix by iron sulphide, presumably during burial under waterlogged conditions.

2 The samples in this group include 438/XB (a) and (b) (Phase III), 96/ED (Phase III), 58/CM (Phase III) and 2/AB (Phase IV); all are rather friable materials, much less sound than the two samples of group 1. They are lime-rich aggregates containing 'sand' and 'gravel' in varying proportions. In the SEM, the sand-grade grains (<2 mm) are seen to be generally coarser and better rounded than in the group 1 samples.

The calcareous matrices of samples 96/ED and 438/XB (b) have been partially replaced by iron-rich deposits, presumably during burial.

3 Samples 439/XC (a) and (b) (Phase IIIa), and 93/EA (Phase IIIa) are brown in colour and very friable. Analysis indicates that they contain very little lime and are aggregates of gravel and silty clay, rather than lime-based mortars.

CONCLUSIONS

Sample 139/GA (Phase IV) appears to be a good quality mortar containing deliberately added pozzolanic material (crushed tile). In some respects, its texture resembles that of the material from the wooden spade but the latter appears to lack the fragments of crushed tile. Some, at least, of the crushed ceramic material in 139/GA was derived from local tile having a distinctive fabric produced from a clay which originally contained crystals of gypsum (probably the Ampthill clay – see Freestone, pp. 508–10).

Samples 2/AB, 96/ED, 438/XB (a) and (b) and 58/CM (Phases III and IV) may also be lime mortars although they lack the crushed ceramic inclusions of 139/GA and are clearly considerably less durable materials.

Samples 93/EA and 439/XC (a) and (b) (Phase IIIa) are probably aggregates of clay and gravel rather than lime mortars.

OBJECTS OF WORKED BONE AND ANTLER

Stephen Greep [Submitted 1986] (Figs 194–201)

The excavations at Stonea produced a typical assemblage of Roman material, hairpins and needles being the most common forms. Of those types which are datable within the Roman period (principally the hairpins), at least 45% are in apparent residual contexts, a figure comparable with that at the Marlowe Car Park Excavations, Canterbury (Greep 1995). The small number of gaming-counters is unusual in an assemblage of this size but there are more needles than one would expect, and the presence of other textile working equipment, such as the unusually large number of points, the perforated ovicaprid metatarsal, and the weaving tablet, should be noted. As a whole the assemblage falls between what would usually be interpreted as urban and rural.

HAIRPINS (Figs 194–5)

Hairpins are the most common type of bone artefact recovered from sites throughout the Roman period. They may be divided typologically and chronologically between those forms with tapering (earlier Roman) and swelling (later Roman) stems. The function and chronology of hairpins is discussed in detail elsewhere (Greep 1995, 1113–21), and the typology given there is followed below. In addition to those pins listed below, a number of stems of tapering form (Type A) were recovered but only one further swelling stem (Type B).

TYPE A1   (Fig. 194)

Pins with a thick, flat head, sometimes slightly pointed, and a tapering stem. A mid Roman type, mostly 2nd–3rd century AD (Greep 1995, 1114).

1 Pin, broken   (*Unillus.*) Length 68 mm ST 81 FY, SF 154

From lower layer, north-west quadrant (unit 137) of the low rubbly mound sealing Anglo-Saxon building S1. Phase Va.

2 Pin, broken   (*Unillus.*) Length 96 mm ST 81JQ, SF 137

Context as no. 1, but upper layer, south-east quadrant (unit 199).

3 Pin, broken   Length 65 mm ST 82 AEW, SF 368

From well 171/558, uppermost layer (unit 558). Phase V.

4 Pin, broken   (*Unillus.*) Length 63 mm ST 82 AFN, SF 366

Two joining fragments.
From ditch 9, cut 10, unit 574. 3rd century AD.

5 Pin, complete   (*Unillus.*)
Length 113 mm ST 83 CDA, SF 476 and ST 83 CAN, SF 446

Two joining fragments.
From ditch 3, cut 5, unit 1072. 3rd century AD; and from ditch 13, cut 4, unit 1012 (residual). Phase VI.

6 Pin, broken   Length 59 mm ST 81 HP

From clay and mortar spread, north-west corner block 1. 2nd century AD.

7 Pin, broken   Length 52 mm ST 84 N2,2, SF 770

From gully 78, cut N2, layer 2. 3rd century AD.

8 Pin, near-complete   Length 101 mm ST 84 DLE, SF 794

From gully 68, lower fill (unit 1745). Late 2nd–early 3rd century AD.

9 Pin, broken   Length 68 mm ST 84 DOK, SF 673

From gully 19, cut 5, unit 1822. Mid 3rd century AD.

9a Pin, complete   Length 97 mm ST 84 DFS, SF 806

From ?latrine pit 1638, upper layer (unit 1638). Late 2nd–early 3rd century AD.

10 Pin, broken   Length 101 mm ST 83 J4,5, SF 592

Some file marks are still visible on the stem but this is not an unfinished pin.
Two joining fragments.
From well J4, layer 5. Late 3rd/early 4th century AD.

TYPE A2.1   (Fig. 194)

Pins with a plain conical head and a pointed stem. This form dates to *c.* AD 40–200/250 (Greep 1995, 1116–17).

11 Pin, complete   Length 100 mm ST 81 NC, SF 167

Context as no. 1, but south-west quadrant (unit 279).

12 Pin, broken   (*Unillus.*) Length 29 mm ST 81 FB, SF 56

From ashy spread (unit 117), south of the small hypocausted room of building R1. Late 2nd century AD.

13 Pin, broken   Length 102 mm ST 84 DPI, SF 855

From gully 30, cut 11, unit 1845. 3rd century AD.

TYPE A2.2   (Fig. 194)

Pins as Type A2.1, above, but with a series of grooves cut beneath the head. The date range for this form is similar to that of Type A2.1, *c.* AD 40–200/250 (Greep 1995, 1116–17).

14 Pin, complete   (*Unillus.*)
Length 73 mm ST 81 KB, SF 176

Single groove.
From gully 44, cut 2, unit 209. Late 2nd century AD.

15 Pin, broken   (*Unillus.*) Length 49 mm ST 81 JA, SF 198

Single groove.
From robbing debris (unit 185), building R1, central block, north-east quadrant. 4th century AD.

16 Pin, broken   Length 62 mm ST 83 G4,4, SF 496

Single groove.
From well G4, layer 4. Early 3rd century AD.

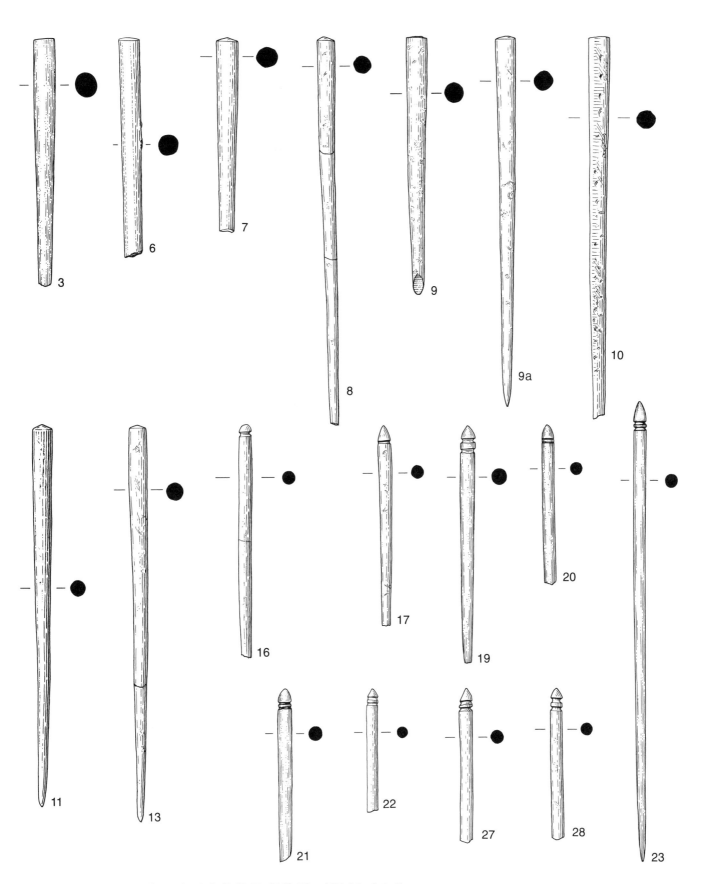

Fig. 194 Stonea Grange: bone pins 3, 6–11, 13, 16–17, 19–23 and 27–8 (scale 1 : 1).

17 Pin, broken   Length 53 mm ST 84 DOZ, SF 881

Single groove.

From well 1836, unit 1836. Late 2nd/3rd century AD.

18 Pin, broken   (*Unillus.*) Length 45 mm ST 81 MW, SF 199

Single collar.

Context as no. 1, but north baulk (unit 273).

19 Pin, broken   Length 63 mm ST 82 BMF, SF 391

Single collar.

From building R5, beam slot 976. Late 2nd century AD.

20 Pin, broken   Length 43 mm ST 82 BLI, SF 390

Single collar.

From silty occupation layer (unit 955) in the region of buildings R5 and S3. Phases III–V.

21 Pin, broken   Length 46 mm ST 80 AZ, SF 34

Single collar.

From occupation debris (unit 23), west of building R1. Phases III–V.

22 Pin, broken   Length 33 mm ST 82 ABF, SF 342

Single collar.

From topsoil (unit 471), block 1, north-east.

23 Pin, complete   Length 121 mm ST 80 BA, SF 33

Single collar.

From destruction deposit (unit 24) in the small hypocausted room of building R1. Early 3rd century AD.

24 Pin, broken   (*Unillus.*)
Length 82 mm ST 83 G4,4, SF 493

Single collar.

Context as no. 16.

25 Pin, broken   (*Unillus.*) Length 62 mm ST 81 MG, SF 151

Single collar.

From occupation debris (unit 260) sealing gully 44 west of building R2. 3rd century AD.

26 Pin, broken   (*Unillus.*) Length 58 mm ST 81 NC, SF 182

Context as no. 11.

27 Pin, broken   Length 42 mm ST 84 DKY, SF 886

Single collar.

From ?latrine pit 1638, basal layer (unit 1739). Late 2nd–early 3rd century AD.

28 Pin, broken   Length 40 mm ST 84 DKI, SF 917

Single collar.

From the fill (unit 1725) of pit 1725. Mid/late 3rd century AD.

TYPE A3   (Fig. 195)

All other Type A pins. These should all have been manufactured in the period *c.* AD 40–200/250.

29 Pin, broken   Length 44 mm ST 82 BAI, SF 311

Crudely shaped pin with a conical head and a single groove. Possibly unfinished and residual in this context.

From upper layer (unit 714) of sinkage cone in the top of pit 808. 4th century AD, but Phase V.

30 Pin, broken   Length 60 mm ST 82 BAE, SF 285

The sightly bulbous conical head is decorated with a band of trellis within two grooves. Tapering stem and therefore within type A pins, though the bulbous head is more reminiscent of later Roman forms.

From well 705, unit 710. 3rd/4th century AD.

31 Pin, broken   Length 36 mm P1982, 6–2, 16

The head comprises a cone, an inverted bell and a collar above a tapering stem.

Stonea Grange Surface Collection.

32 Pin, broken   Length 49 mm ST 83 CCP, SF 511

Pin with a rounded, conical head above three collars. A variant of Type A2.2. These forms are recorded throughout Britain, although they are never common (e.g. Greep, forthcoming).

From occupation layer (unit 1062), north-east block 2. Post-medieval disturbance.

33 Pin, complete   Length 121 mm ST 84 DHA, SF 838

The head comprises a series of five collars above a ball and two further collars. Tapering stem.

From the uppermost layer (unit 1669) in well 1669. Mid/late 3rd century AD.

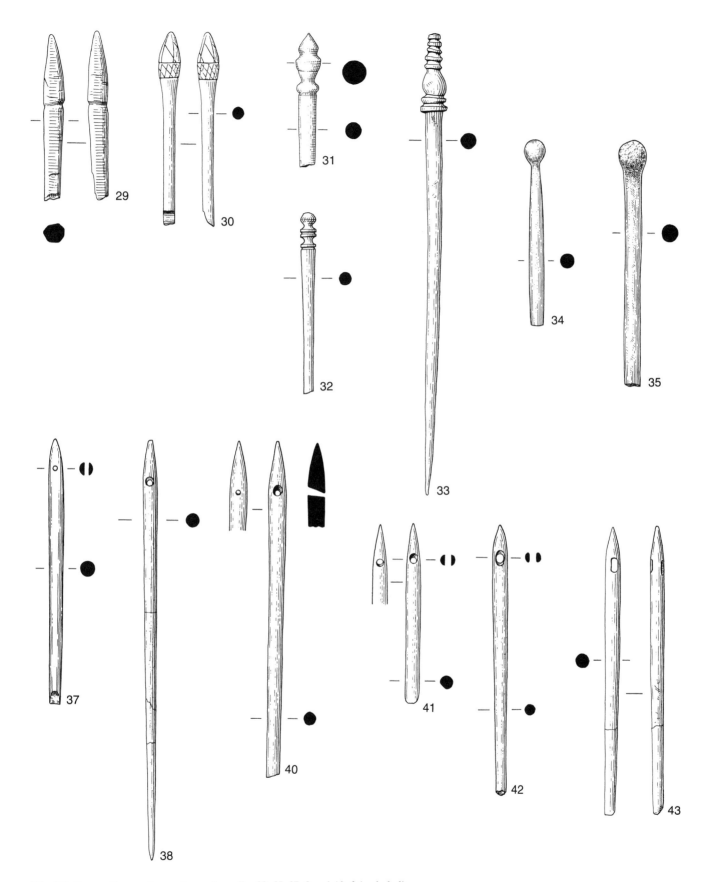

Fig. 195 Stonea Grange: bone pins and needles 29–35, 37–8 and 40–3 (scale 1:1).

TYPE B1

Pins with simple oval or round heads and a swelling stem. A late Roman type datable to *c.* AD 150/200–400 (Greep 1995, 1117–18).

34 Pin, broken   Length 49 mm ST 82 BAM, SF 306

From well 705, unit 717. 3rd/4th century AD.

35 Pin, broken   Length 64 mm ST 82 BHP, SF 387

Irregular example.

From pit 483/918, unit 889. Mid/late 3rd century AD.

36 Pin, broken   (*Unillus.*) Length 22 mm ST 81 FN, SF 48

From metalled surface (unit 128) north of building R1. Phases III–V.

NEEDLES   (Figs 195–6)

A wide variety of bone needles are found during the Roman period. They appear most commonly on earlier Roman sites (first–mid third century), but it is not possible yet to date individual forms. For a discussion of the typology and function of Roman bone needles, see Greep 1995, 1122–5.

TYPE 1

Needles with a single round eye (Greep 1995, 1122–3).

1.1 With a pointed head of oval section.
1.2 With a squared-off head of flattened oval section (not represented at Stonea).

TYPE 1.1   (Fig. 195)

37 Needle, broken   Length 69 mm ST 82 ABF, SF 297

Stained green. The staining of needles is an early Roman technique, occasionally found on needles of this type. On the use of staining to decorate hairpins and needles, see Greep (forthcoming).

Context as no. 22.

38 Needle, complete   Length 110 mm ST 83 G4,4, SF 499

Context as no. 16.

39 Needle, broken   (*Unillus.*)
Length 90 mm ST 81 KB, SF 173

Stained green. See comments to no. 37.

Context as no. 14.

40 Needle, broken   Length 89 mm ST 84 DKI, SF 803

Slight green tinge, ?stained.

Context as no. 28.

41 Needle, broken   Length 48 mm ST 84 DGZ, SF 824

From layer 1668 over pits 1834, 1835, 1850. 3rd century AD.

42 Needle, broken   Length 72 mm ST 84 DCA, SF 706

From unit 1549 in pits 1567 and 1588. 3rd century AD.

TYPE 2

Needles with a figure-of-eight eye (Greep 1995, 1122–3).

2.1 With pointed head of oval section.
2.2 With squared or slightly rounded head (not represented at Stonea).

TYPE 2.1   (Fig. 195)

43 Needle, broken   Length 75 mm ST 81 QQ, SF 207

From slumped clay (unit 337) over south edge of metalled surface north of building R1. Late 2nd century AD.

TYPE 3

Needles with a rectangular eye (Greep 1995, 1123).

3.1 With pointed head of oval section.
3.2 With 'rectangular'-shaped head pared flat.

TYPE 3.1   (Fig. 196)

44 Needle, broken   (*Unillus.*)
Length 64 mm ST 83 J4,5, SF 591

Context as no. 10.

45 Needle, broken   Length 52 mm ST 84 DIC, SF 842

From ?latrine pit 1695, uppermost layer (unit 1695). 3rd/4th century AD.

46 Needle, broken   Length 59 mm ST 84 DIC, SF 1017

Context as no. 45.

47 Needle, complete   Length 112 mm ST 84 DPS, SF 1030

Context as nos 45–6, but layer beneath (unit 1854). Later 2nd/3rd century AD.

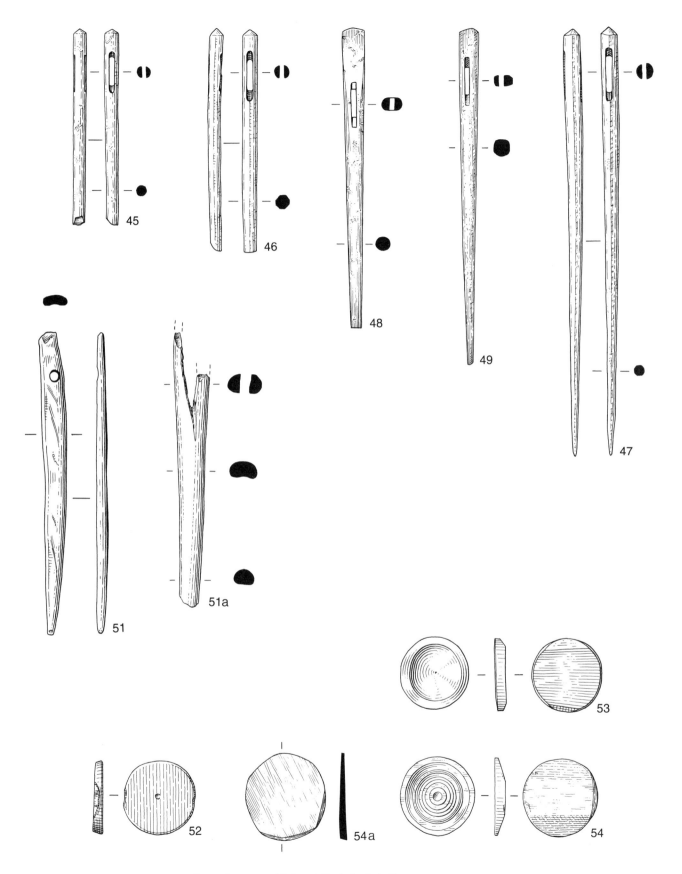

Fig. 196 Stonea Grange: bone needles and counters 45–9 and 51–4a (scale 1:1).

TYPE 3.2 (Fig. 196)

48 Needle, broken   Length 79 mm ST 80 BF, SF 14

From building R1, east wing, robbing debris in footing trench, south side, east end (unit 29). Later 2nd/3rd century AD.

49 Needle, near-complete

Length 88 mm ST 82 BHB, SF 405

Tip broken.

From pit 860, unit 876. 3rd/4th century AD.

50 Needle, broken   (*Unillus.*)

Length 51 mm ST 81 JH, SF 100

From pit 132, unit 192. Phase IV.

OTHER NEEDLES   (Fig. 196)

51 Needle, near-complete

Length 81 mm ST 82 BCT, SF 321

Crude needle with a single, round eye.

From the uppermost sealing layer (unit 772) of silted well 808. 3rd century AD.

51a ?Needle, broken   Length 73 mm ST 84 DVH

A tapered crude ?needle, broken across the eye and the shank.

From trowelling layer over pits 1986, 1987 and gully 29.

GAMING COUNTERS   (Fig. 196)

Examples of the three main types of Roman gaming counter were recovered from the excavations. For a detailed discussion of those forms and their chronology, see Greep 1995, 1125–7.

[For stone and ceramic counters, see pp. 522 and 488.]

52 Counter

Diameter 19.5 mm, thickness 3 mm ST 81 JX, SF 193

Type 1 gaming counter, with flat obverse and reverse surfaces. This form belongs to the early Roman period and may be dated *c*. AD 40–200/250.

From well 135, unit 205. Later 3rd century AD.

53 Counter

Diameter 19.5 mm, thickness 3.5 mm ST 83 CAA, SF 456

Type 2 gaming counter. The obverse surface is countersunk; the reverse is flat, with two bevelled edges. The reverse also has three inscribed circles, presumably to denominate value. This form was introduced in the 2nd century AD, possibly continuing into the later Roman period.

From topsoil/cleaning (unit 1000), block 11, east and block 2, north.

54 Counter

Diameter 20.5 mm, thickness 3 mm ST 84 N2,2, SF 1099

Type 3 gaming counter, decorated with concentric circles on the obverse surface. The reverse is flat, with two broad bevels. This form continues throughout the Roman period.

Context as no. 7.

54a Disc

Diameter 22 mm, thickness 1–2 mm ST 82 BIN, SF 357

Possibly a blank for a gaming counter, although perhaps rather too thin; and clearer evidence of the manufacturing processes involved would suggest otherwise (e.g. Greep 1990, Fig. 93, 18).

From pit 483/918, lower layer (unit 911). Mid/late 3rd century AD.

POINTS   (Figs 197–8)

Points manufactured from ovicaprid metapodials and tibia are most commonly found in Iron Age contexts (e.g. Cunnington and Cunnington 1923, Pls 8–9) but continue into the Roman period, where they are found particularly on sites of a rural nature (e.g. Stead 1980, Fig. 69, 74–6). It is the relatively large quantity from a Roman site rather than their presence here which is unusual.

The function of these objects has been the subject of much discussion. They are most usually referred to as 'gouges' (Wheeler 1943, 304) but other suggested uses include dart-heads (Childe 1952, 158–9), spear-points (Roes 1963, 34–5; Beveridge 1930–1, Fig. 16), pegs (Stead 1968, 170), awls (Young and Richardson 1959–60, Fig. 13, 37), socketed knives (Wainwright 1979, Figs 88–9) and, most typically, pin beaters (Crowfoot 1945). They have usually been classified according to type of bone utilised and working processes, though the recent study of the Danebury finds (Sellwood 1984a, 382–7) concentrates on wear patterns as a means of classification. Sellwood supports a use as pin beaters for some of the Danebury finds, though a use in hide dressing is postulated for others (Sellwood 1984a, 387). It seems probable that these objects were multipurpose tools, most typically with textile manufacturing associations. Only a programme of micro-wear analysis (cf. Semenov 1964) and experimentation is likely to determine the full range of functions.

55 Point, broken

Length 81 mm (Pl. XXI) ST 84, P10,1, SF 756

Point manufactured from an ovicaprid tibia.

From ?votive pit P10, layer 1. Early 3rd century AD.

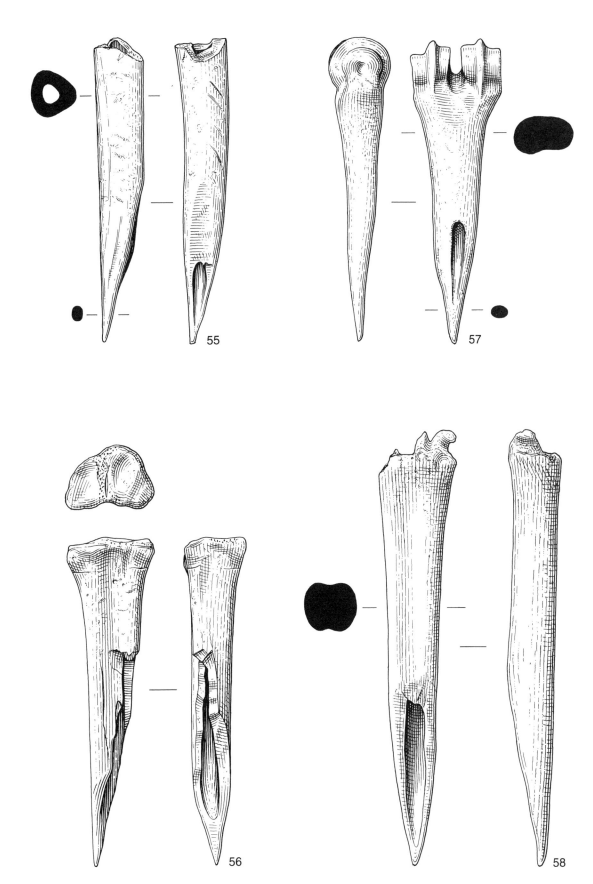

Fig. 197 Stonea Grange: bone points 55–8 (scale 1 : 1).

56 Point, complete   Length 87 mm ST 83 G8,1, SF 565

Point manufactured from an ovicaprid metapodial.

From gully 18, cut 6, unit G8, layer 1. 3rd century AD.

57 Point, complete   Length 80 mm ST 84 O62,1, SF 1103

Point manufactured from an ovicaprid metapodial.

From ditch 84, cut 1, layer 1. 3rd century AD.

58 Point, complete   Length 115 mm ST 81 FW, SF 50

As no. 57.

From well 135, uppermost layer (unit 135). 4th–7th century AD.

59 Point, fragment   Length 59 mm ST 81 JQ

Tip only, similar to nos 55–8.

Context as no. 2.

60 Point, fragment   Length 62 mm ST 83 BAI

As no. 59.

Context as no. 29.

61 Point, complete   Length 112 mm ST 81 SP, SF 234

As no. 57.

From well 336, unit 359. Late 3rd–4th century AD.

OTHER ROMAN OBJECTS   (Figs 198–201)

62 Weaving plate
Width 30 mm, height 27 mm ST 82 AGN, SF 378

Small triangular weaving plate, with well-worn perforations. Though most commonly used in sets (e.g. Wild 1970, 72–5) weaving tablets are usually found as isolated examples. The triangular forms are the most common (e.g. Crummy 1983, Fig. 72, 2006) but few are closely dated. On present evidence they would seem to belong principally to the later Roman period in Britain. However, three from London (unpublished, British Museum) may be from Walbrook deposits of 1st–mid 2nd century date and an example from Scole, Norfolk (Rogerson 1977, Fig. 86, 16) is dated Trajanic–mid Antonine.

From ashy dereliction deposit (unit 598) south of building R1. Late 2nd–3rd century AD.

63 Ligula, broken   Length 63 mm ST 82 BAX, SF 312

Bone ligula with a small, flat oval plate. These forms are common, but few are from dated contexts. An example from Canterbury (Greep 1995, 1132–3, Fig. 495, no. 930) is from late third–fourth century deposits, but there are earlier examples from Staines (Crouch and Shanks 1984, Fig. 51, 36), of Hadrianic–mid Antonine date, and

from Lincoln (unpublished, Lincoln Archaeological Trust), which is Antonine–3rd century.

From well 705, unit 727. 3rd/4th century AD.

64 Scoop probe   Length 125 mm ST 82 BCT, SF 317

Double ended implement with a small bowl at one end and a probe at the other. This form is most typically found in bronze (e.g. Milne 1907, Pl. XII), but there is a similar bone example from York (unpublished, Yorkshire Museum).

Context as no. 51.

65 ?Gaming piece
Length 38 mm, thickness 4.5 mm ST 84 DSC, SF 935

Pointed, oval-shaped object, decorated on two faces with ring-and-dot ornament, seven on one planar face and four on one side. This is one of a small group of numbered bone plates (e.g. Passmore 1922, Pl. 1, 12) which may be oval, diamond-shaped or square. A use in gaming seems likely, but all the known pieces have been found singly, never in sets, and it is difficult to suggest to which game they belong. Only one comparable piece, a square plate numbered on all sides, from Verulamium (Frere 1984, Fig. 32, 286), is dated (c. AD 180–200).

From gully 34, cut 2, unit 1911. Late 2nd/early 3rd century AD.

66 Peg   Length 21 mm ST 84 DOE, SF 683

Small bone peg. Similar pegs, though rather better manufactured, have been found in association with bone 'toggles' at Wroxeter (Bushe-Fox 1914, Pl. 9, Fig. 1, 3), Watercrook (Potter 1979, Fig. 88, 94) and Malton (unpublished, Malton Museum), but no 'toggles' have yet been recorded at Stonea.

From pit 1577, unit 1817. Late 2nd or 3rd century AD.

67 ?Awl   Length 103 mm ST 84 DEA, SF 657

Horse metapodial, showing some signs of possible wear, perhaps as an awl. Tip broken.

From topsoil/cleaning (unit 1597) blocks 8 and 9; and 3 and 4 east.

68 ?Handle   Length 67 mm ST 81 NC

Ovicaprid metapodial, with a single hole drilled at the top. Broken.

Context as no. 11.

68a Worked metapodial
Length 134 mm ST 84 DPN

Ovicaprid metatarsal with a perforation at the distal end. This is an example of a well-known group of worked and perforated metapodia which are more normally found in pre-Roman contexts, although there is good evidence for the continuation of the form throughout the Roman era. The type was very common

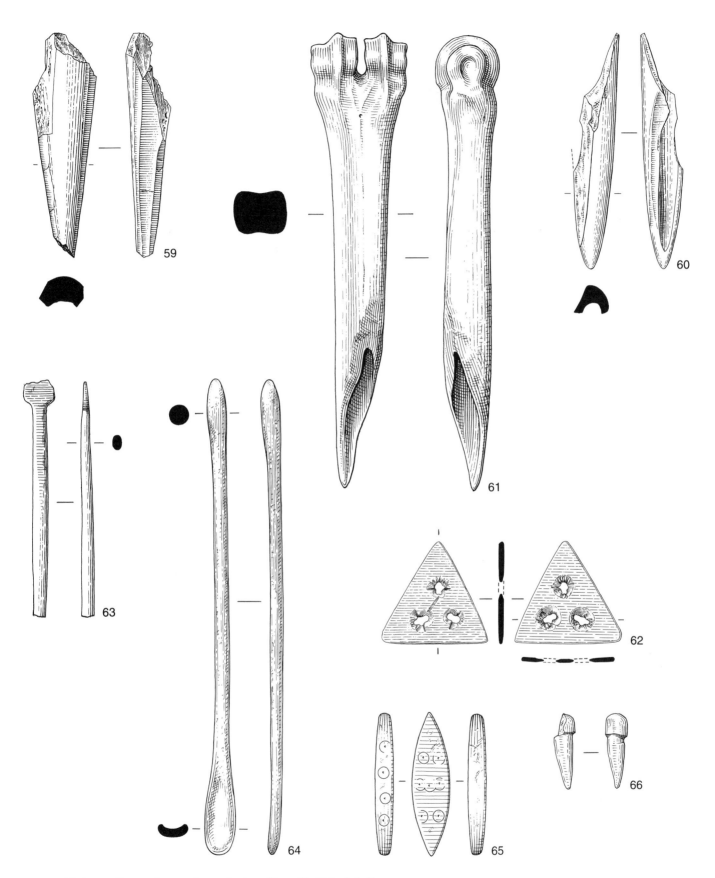

Fig. 198 Stonea Grange: bone points and other objects 59–66 (scale 1:1).

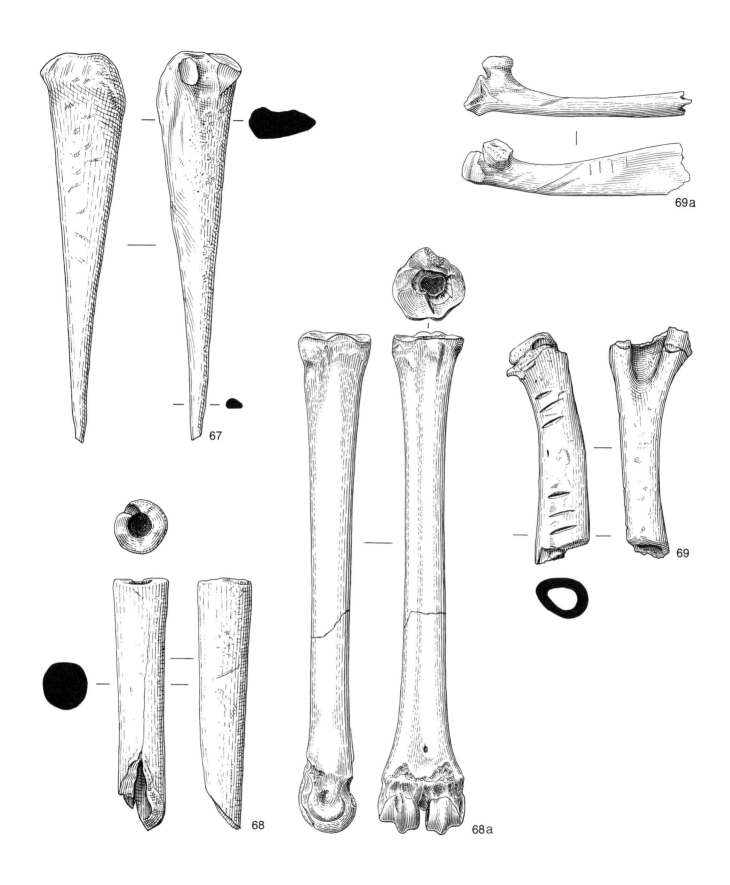

Fig. 199 Stonea Grange: bone objects 67–9a (scale 1:1).

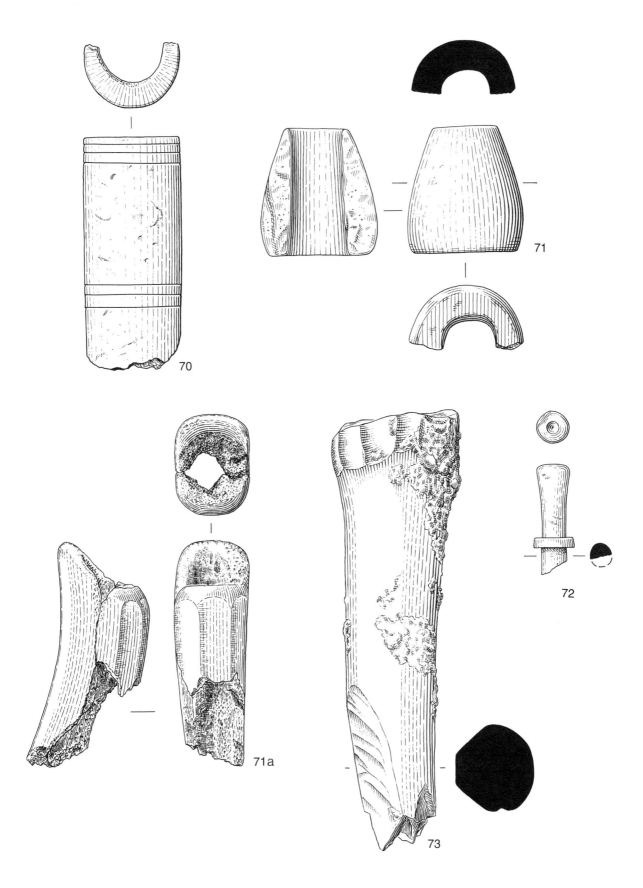

Fig. 200 Stonea Grange: bone objects 70–3 (scale 1:1).

at Glastonbury and Meare where Bulleid and Gray (1917, 426–7; following Pitt-Rivers 1888, Pl. CXVII) suggested that these objects may have been used as 'bobbins'. The interior of a shaft of one from Glastonbury contained a bronze spindle (Bulleid and Gray *op. cit.*, 426) and an example from Manching is similarly interpreted (Jacobi 1974, 62–3 and Taf. 81.1617). The type is, however, best regarded as being of uncertain function, but is probably related to other perforated metapodia.

During the Roman period these forms are rare. There are examples from Flavian–Trajanic contexts at Cowbridge (unpublished excavations) and in late Roman contexts at Poundbury (unpublished), suggesting that they may last throughout the Roman period, although more securely stratified examples are clearly required.

From well 1669, unit 1849. Mid/late 3rd century AD.

69 ?Tally   Length 59 mm ST 84 DEA, SF 718

?Ovicaprid tibia, with two groups of three knife-cuts, possibly used as a tally. Broken.

Context as no. 67.

69a ?Tally   Length 62 mm ST 82 BMT, SF 393

Bone marked similarly to no. 69, with a series of cuts. If other than butchering marks, function uncertain.

From beam slot 989 of building R5. 3rd or 4th century AD.

70 ?Handle   Length 62 mm ST 84 DIC, SF 835

Lathe-turned bone cylinder, decorated with two groups of three lines. Broken. Possibly a handle.

Context as no.45.

71 Object of unknown function
Length 35 mm ST 83 CKL, SF 529

Plain bone cylinder, split centrally. Uncertain function.

From ditch 14, cut 4, unit 1226. Residual Roman material in post-medieval ditch.

71a ?Handle   Length 59.5 mm ST 82 AZW

Section of antler tine, hollowed, its surface worked smooth and facetted. Probably a simple handle.

From gully 36, cut 2, unit 702. 3rd century AD.

72 ?Handle   Length 30 mm ST 84 DGL, SF 844

Lathe-turned terminal, broken, but possibly the top of a small handle as at Richborough (Cunliffe 1968b, Pl. XLIX, 241.).

From gully 27, cut 1, unit 1655. Late 2nd/early 3rd century AD.

73 Object of unknown function
Length 117 mm ST 81 MQ

Bone, displaying knife-cuts. Probably a waste product.

From silty occupation layer (unit 268), north-west block 1. 3rd century AD.

74 Comb fragment   Length 22 mm ST 81 FQ, SF 222

Fragment of a retaining plate from a double-sided composite comb, decorated with two sets of three parallel lines.

From gravel metalling (unit 130) at the west end of street 1 E/W. 3rd or 4th century AD onwards.

SAXON OBJECTS   (Fig. 201)
CIGAR-SHAPED PIN-BEATERS

Double ended 'cigar-shaped' pin-beaters are common finds of the Saxon period (cf. MacGregor 1985, 188–9), although they are first seen in Roman contexts (Wild 1970, Table k). They are most typical in earlier, pagan, contexts but last throughout the Saxon period.

75 Pin-beater, complete
Length 78 mm ST 81 FM, SF 103

Context as no. 1, but upper layer (unit 127). Phase Va.

76 Pin-beater, complete
Length 115 mm ST 81 FV, SF 68

From silty-clay (unit 134), south of Anglo-Saxon building S1. Phase IV/V.

COMBS
77 Comb, fragmentary   Width 34 mm ST 81 FW, SF 52

Fragments of a double-sided, composite comb manufactured in antler. One retaining plate is rather highly polished and does not possess the usual marks from cutting the teeth. However, other parts of the comb do not appear unfinished and the plate may have been a replacement.

Context as no. 58.

PIERCED OYSTER SHELLS

Caroline Cartwright   (Fig. 201)

Four perforated valves of oyster (*Ostrea edulis*) from three contexts were submitted for examination to ascertain whether the perforations were of human or gastropod manufacture (British Museum Research Laboratory, File no. 6458, no. 45240W).

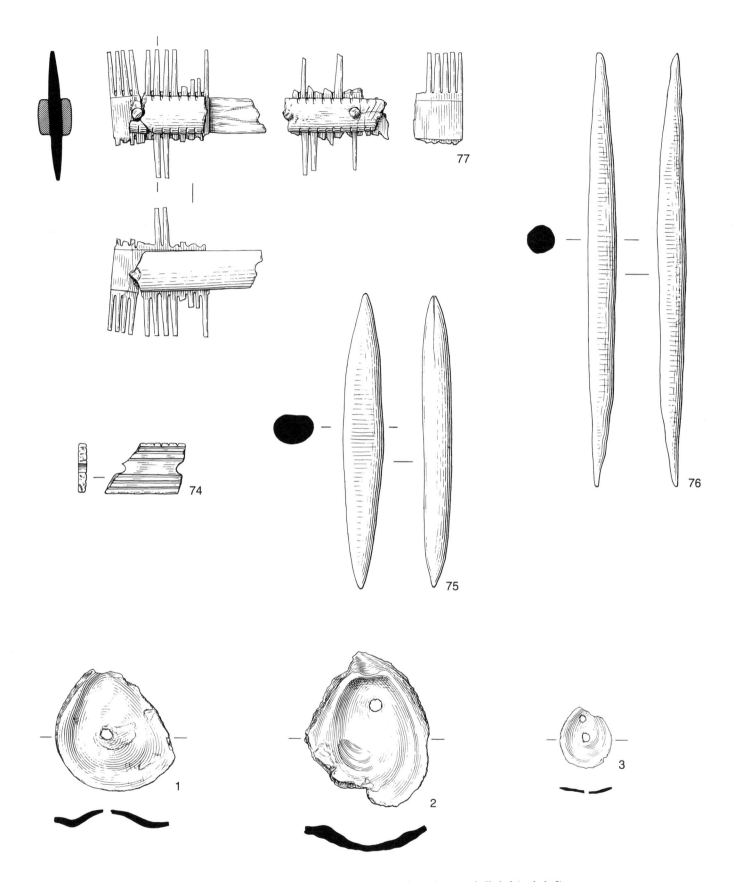

Fig. 201 Stonea Grange: bone combs and pin-beaters, 74–7 (scale 1:1), and perforated oyster shells 1–3 (scale 1:2).

1 ST 82 ADF, SF 427

Upper oyster valve (6.5 cm long) with central perforation. Examination of the perforation shows pecking and fracture indicative of artificial piercing. At the hinge there is a half notch which may be a human-made perforation that has fractured.

From gully 53, cut 1, unit 519. Late 3rd–4th century AD.

2 ST 82 AEN, SF 426

Lower oyster valve (8.4 cm long) with a perforation placed 3.5 cm along the long axis measured from the hinge. The perforation has been evenly pecked or drilled at a point on the valve where the more substantial hinge area becomes apparent. The depth of the perforation, c. 6 mm, suggests that durability of the perforation was an important factor.

From the uppermost layer (unit 550) of slump into the top of ditch 74. Late 3rd/4th century AD.

3 ST 82 BLH, SF 425

Two fragments of upper oyster valves. The larger, an almost intact valve (3.2 cm long), shows two artificial perforations whose neat sides and clean piercing indicates the use of a sharp metal or bone implement. The smaller of the two perforations, near the hinge, would not support more than organic cord or thread passing through it. The slightly larger central perforation is also shallow and may possibly have functioned as a double threading device.

The second fragment is a small, incomplete portion of inner nacreous lining of upper oyster valve which appears to have become detached from the parent valve described above (although the diameter of the perforation is smaller).

From ditch 9, cut 1a, unit 954. 3rd century AD.

CONCLUSION

There are several marine gastropods capable of piercing marine or estuarine bivalves such as oysters and mussels. Any consideration of perforations in marine molluscs must therefore take into account the morphology of the perforations. In the case of the Stonea oyster valves, there is no indication of secretion and boring of the shells by marine gastropods; all perforations exhibit the pecking, fracture or drilling typical of artificial piercing.

It cannot be assumed that all the perforations on the Stonea oyster valves are for one purpose. Those perforations which have been made into the thicker parts of the shell could withstand a more robust use, such as can be seen for the medieval period in Sussex, where the use of nailed oyster valves has been postulated as temporary roof repairs on domestic buildings (Freke 1976). Numbers 1 and 2 could have been used in this manner. However, the valve (and fragment) from no. 3 would not support the insertion of a nail and the valve is much smaller than the two former examples. It could have been used decoratively, either threaded on a cord or possibly attached to a garment.

LEATHER FOOTWEAR

Michael Rhodes   (Figs 202–3)

The surviving leather items were found in the sump, where organic preservation was generally excellent. They are all of cattle hide and comprise parts of four shoes, and a few waste pieces possibly from the manufacture of nailed-shoe uppers. Given the extent of the excavations, this is less leatherwork than might be expected, and we must conclude that much was lost in antiquity, due to drying out of the pits and ditches (For confirmation, see Iron Objects, cat. nos 35–43, p. 366).

The paucity of the leatherwork is counterbalanced by its considerable interest, in that it extends our knowledge of shoe designs and offers some clues as to the people who lived and worked at Stonea in Roman times. Besides the shoemakers' waste, it includes the nailed shoe of a woman or youth, another nailed shoe of a kind associated in particular with military sites in the north of England, and a pair of men's one-piece shoes of a type regarded as belonging to the native end of Romano-British footwear. These one-piece shoes are heavily worn and crudely made, and, given that they were found in the sump together with a number of workmen's tools, it is possible that they were discarded at the same time and by the same workman.

CATALOGUE

For definitions of the terminology used in the following descriptions, see Thornton (1973) and Rhodes (1980).

1 ST 84A, I, 29/31, 5, SF A, 34; I, 31, 2, SF A, 31; and I, 36, 5, SF A, 35

Fragments of a matching pair of one-piece shoes. These were men's shoes, based on their heavy construction (the hide is c. 5 mm thick) and their length (around 290 mm). Ignoring any possible longitudinal shrinkage, this is the equivalent of size 9½ on the English Shoe-Size Scale.

Although only the inner halves have survived, the shoes were clearly of identical size and design. Each was laced to the foot using four pairs of semicircular loops – of which only those on the inner edges have survived – and by a matching pair of ankle loops, represented by the inner loop of the left shoe. This inner ankle loop widens towards the end, where there is a single lenticular eyelet with a decorative incised line running parallel to its forward curve. The cut edges of the shoes are chamfered and rounded, and score lines on the grain surface around the edge of the tread are suggestive of guidelines.

Both shoes bear evidence of very heavy use. The wearer had bunions on both feet, revealed by large bulges between the second and third loops on the inner sides of the shoes. They were worn until they were in holes and had to be patched. The evidence for this comprises pairs of 3 mm long, oval awl holes that were used to attach an oval repair piece under each heel and another under the treads. Fragments of a 2.5 mm wide leather thong used to attach the patches survive on the left shoe of the pair.

Originally, both shoes had an invisible butted heel seam, probably sewn with gut or a strong thread. The evidence comprises a series of 2 mm diagonal, lenticular awl holes *c.* 8 mm apart, which penetrate from the butt edge of the leather to the inside of the shoe. These awl holes extend also around the heel curves of the sole, where they are 3 mm apart. After a period of use, however, the back seams were crudely reinforced or replaced as evidenced by pairs of oval thong slots, 3–5 mm wide – three pairs down the back of the heel and three more around the heel curve. These were stitched with 3.5 mm wide leather thongs, remains of which are still visible in the holes. The crude but efficient character of these repairs suggests that they may have been effected when the heels were patched.

From two adjacent grid squares, 2 and 5, in the north sump, cut I, layers 29/31, 31 and 36. Mid 2nd to early 3rd century AD.

Discussion

Unlike the other common varieties of Roman footwear, one-piece shoes seem to be a hybrid form with native as well as classical precursors. Some are of high quality hide and are decorated with elaborate open-work patterns. Such shoes are classical in feel and hark back to the Greek *carbatina*. At the other end of the scale are more crudely made and less highly decorated examples, which may represent the continuation into the Roman period of a native shoemaking tradition. The shoes currently under discussion, with their thick leather, simple semicircular loops and a virtual absence of decoration, lie very firmly at the 'native' end of the spectrum.

There are no close published parallels to the cutting pattern used for these particular shoes. This is unremarkable, since one-piece shoes vary a great deal in style and sophistication of manufacture and with further systematic research may one day form a basis for the differentiation of regional costume. The widely spaced arrangement of side loops is especially unusual. Crudely made shoes with semicircular side loops are known, for example, from the late 1st to early 2nd century fort at Newstead (*Trimontium*) (Curle 1911, Pl. XX, no. 3), and from a 2nd to 4th century context at Shakenoak Farm (Brodribb *et al* 1973, no. 10). In both instances, however, the loops are close together so that the top edge of the shoe takes on the form of a wavy line.

The execution of the repair, although crude, is perhaps better than might be expected of a purely amateur effort. One-piece shoes were generally discarded once the soles had worn through, but there are numerous surviving examples that had been repaired by thonging patches to the underside (e.g. Rhodes 1980, no. 646; Brodribb *et al* 1973, Fig. 74, no. 1). The use of thonging as a means of repairing the back seam is consistent with a later Roman date. During the 1st and 2nd centuries, back seams were usually stitched with thread or gut, but thonging was occasionally used as an alternative in late Roman shoes (Turner and Rhodes 1992, 85).

On the basis of more elaborate examples from London, the present author has previously suggested that one-piece shoes may have been intended for indoor use (Rhodes 1980, 127). However, in view of the growing numbers of strongly made and heavily worn native-style shoes, they must now be regarded as general-purpose footwear. This interpretation can only be reinforced by the pair under discussion, which may have been discarded with a number of workmen's tools.

2 ST 82 AAK

The lower half of a right nailed shoe, comprising a sole, middle sole and insole, a fragment of heel stiffener, and a few scraps of upper. The sole is around 285 mm long, which, ignoring any possible longitudinal shrinkage, is the equivalent of shoe size 9 on the English Shoe Size Scale.

As is usual in shoes of this kind, most of the upper has deteriorated beyond recognition. The only parts to survive comprise two pieces from the tips of ankle loops, which show that the ends of the loops were decorated with a series of parallel incisions.

To judge from the holes, the hobnails were arranged in a single outer row, with three nail rows in the tread, and three more under the heel. The nail-heads were *c.* 9 mm across.

The middle sole was attached to the insole with a thin leather thong, pieces of which still adhere to the insole. This thong was threaded through six pairs of thong slots: one each at the rear and front of the heel, and four more arranged in a diamond pattern under the tread. Clear impressions of the lasting margins show that the shoe was of *calceus* construction, wherein the lasting margins (outer edges) of a closed or semi-closed upper were attached between the sole layers. The outer thong slots were apparently positioned so that the thonging could be tacked into the lasting margins.

Residual, in the uppermost fill (unit 451) of the north sump, which contained finds relating to Phases III–VI.

Discussion

The most distinctive feature of this shoe is the diamond arrangement of the thong slots. The significance of this feature has recently been discussed in connection with a nailed shoe found on the Grewelthorpe bog body (Rhodes 1991). The Grewelthorpe shoe also has a similar nailing pattern. It differs only in one minor respect, namely that it lacks a middle sole, which was sometimes added to provide some additional strength. The nailing pattern is especially associated with male shoes, which in this instance is seemingly confirmed by the shoe's large size (*idem.*).

To avoid unwarranted repetition, the reader is referred to the discussion of the Grewelthorpe shoe for details of other parallels, and their dating and distribution. It must here suffice to say that on present evidence shoes with a diamond thong-slot pattern are unknown on the Continent

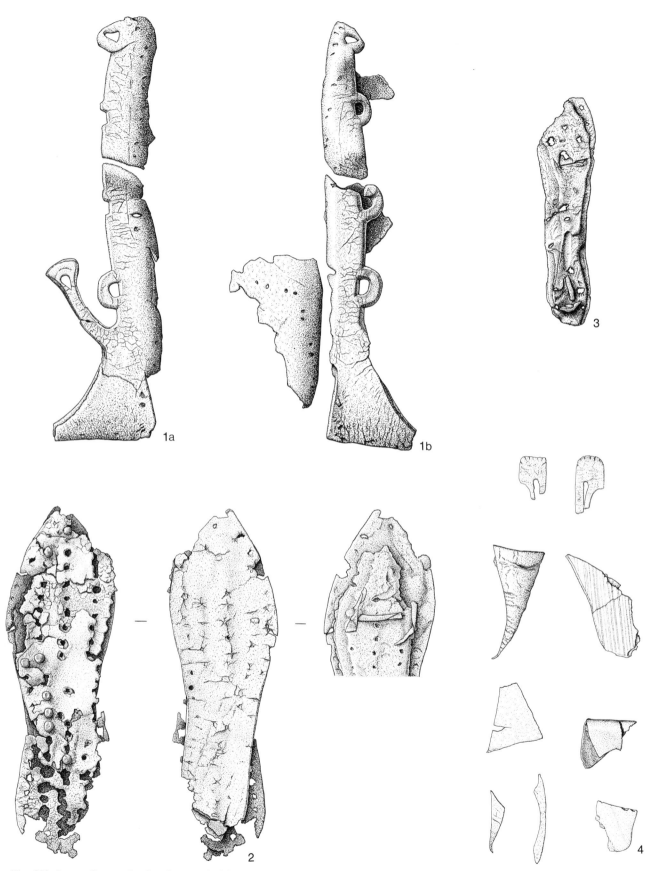

Fig. 202 Stonea Grange: leather footwear 1–4 from the sump (scale 1:3).

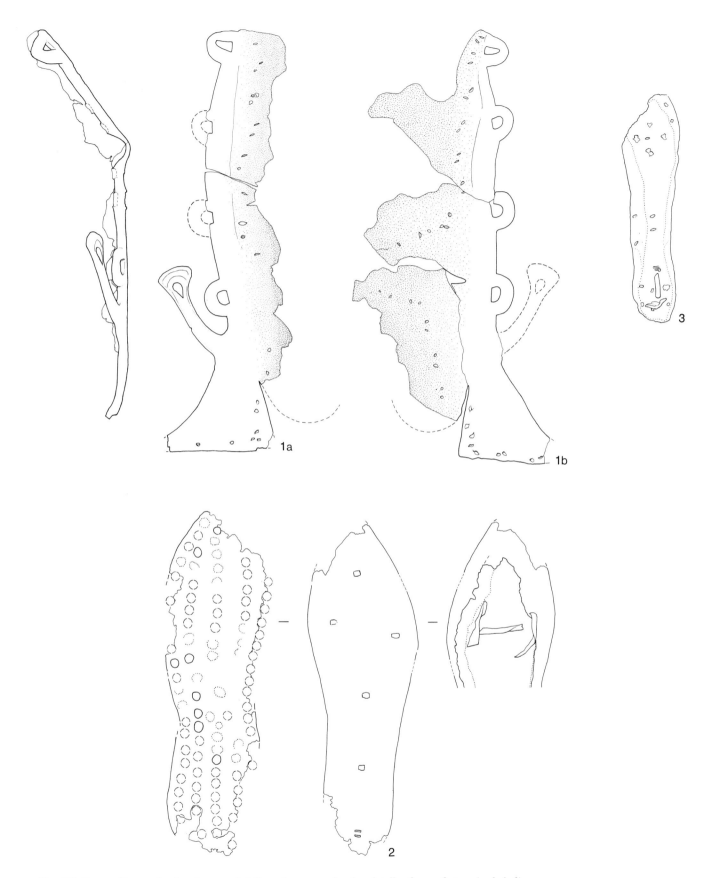

Fig. 203 Stonea Grange: leather footwear 1–3 from the sump, showing details of manufacture (scale 1:3).

and, apart from Caerleon and now at Stonea, have hitherto been found almost exclusively in the north of England. On this basis, the diamond pattern is regarded as characteristic of a regional variety of nailed shoe, which on present evidence was produced at least from the late 1st to the mid 3rd century. It is tempting to link the variety with military sites, but since most north of England sites have military connections, and since Grewelthorpe man was not wearing military garb, it would be safer to say that such shoes were manufactured by shoemakers who supplied large quantities of them to the military. Within Britain, the earliest military shoes were generally of *caliga* construction, but by the mid 2nd century, shoes of *calceus* construction were favoured, presumably because they offered better protection in wet and cold weather (Rhodes 1980, 114).

The upper fragments are too deteriorated to be certain of the shoe's original appearance. The two surviving ankle loops are, nevertheless, consistent with an upper of *calceus* construction. We may cite, for example, one of the military *calceii* from the Antonine fort of Hardknott (*Mediobogdum*), which – albeit more strongly built – offers a clue as to the general appearance of this shoe before burial (Charlesworth and Thornton 1973, no. 1).

3 ST 84A, I, 26, 1, SF A, 10

Middle sole from a right nailed shoe which, on account of its small size and light nailing must have been worn by a woman or youth. To judge from the nail holes, the nailing pattern comprised a single, widely spaced nail row around the edge, with one or two nails along the centre line at the waist and under the heel, and four placed in a diamond under the tread. Shoes with a somewhat similar nail pattern have been found in a late 1st century context in London (Rhodes 1980, no. 515), and in a 2nd to 4th century context at Shakenoak Farm (Brodribb *et al* 1973, nos 2 and 4). Such a simple pattern might, nevertheless, have been adopted at different times by numerous different shoemakers.

Lasting margins on the underside of the middle sole indicate that the shoe was of *calceus* construction. Three pairs of long slots down the centre line indicate where the sole was thonged to the insole. The end of the thong survives near the heel, where it widens to prevent it from being pulled through the slots.

From grid square 1 in the north sump, cut I, layer 26. Late 3rd century AD.

4 ST 84A, SF A, 15, 18, 24 and 30

Seven triangular leather scraps in thin cattle hide, perhaps from the manufacture of nailed shoe uppers. Regular impressions on one fragment are probably accidental rather than decorative.

From four different contexts in the north sump, dating from the late 2nd to late 3rd century AD.

WOODEN ARTEFACTS

Ralph Jackson   (Figs 204–8; Pls XXIX–XXX)

1 Writing tablet

(Fig. 204; Pl. XXIX) ST 84A II, 26, 7, SF 84A, 26

A complete and well-made stylus tablet of ash, in good condition, with one plain and one recessed face. It is Type 1 in Padley's classification (Padley and Winterbottom 1991, 210–11) and measures overall 162×99 mm. The recessed writing area measures 137×83 mm and has a raised rim on all four sides. In one of the long side rims are two small fastening holes symmetrically disposed, 85 mm apart and 36 mm from the corners. Rim thickness 6–7 mm. Recess thickness 5–6 mm.

Dr Alan Bowman writes: 'There is no trace of incision on the back. The recessed face, on which no wax survives, has remains of about fifteen lines of incised writing where the stylus has penetrated the wax. The tablet was used according to the normal letter format, with the broad dimension as the width and the writing running along the grain of the wood (Bowman and Thomas 1983, 37–40). The traces of the last line are comparatively clear compared with the rest, which suggests that the tablet may have been re-used and that there are remains of at least two texts.' Despite intense and prolonged examination of the tablet involving ultra-violet lighting and infrared and other specialised photography in both an unconserved (wet) and conserved (dry) state, it proved impossible to decipher any of the text.

The use of ash wood for all four stylus tablets from Stonea is noteworthy, for most of the surviving British examples are made of silver fir (R. S. O. Tomlin, 209–10 in Padley and Winterbottom 1991). As the latter appears not to have been native to Britain, it is assumed that the tablets (or their raw material) were imported. Many, indeed, were probably 'incoming mail' subsequently re-used within the province. Those from Stonea, on the other hand, may well have been made in Britain, if not in the immediate vicinity of the site. The presence of fastening holes in the complete tablet indicates that it was once part of a hinged diptych or triptych, but it had certainly become detached, and probably re-used, by the time of its disposal. Its dimensions differ from those of the other Stonea tablets, and no two form a matching pair. There are no securing notches cut into the rim, but for a possible alternative mode of binding see no. 3 below.

From the north sump, cut II grid square 7, layer 26. 3rd–4th century AD. Phase III/IV.

2 Writing tablet   (Fig. 204) ST 84A II, 29, 9, SF 84A, 33

A broken but well-preserved tablet of ash, with one recessed and one plain face. There is a raised rim on all three remaining sides of the recessed face. Overall length 179 mm; maximum surviving width 80 mm; rim thickness 4–5.5 mm. Recessed area: length 156 mm; maximum surviving width 70 mm; thickness 2.5–3.5 mm.

Like no. 1, this is a well-made tablet with neatly bevelled edges. The recessed face retains a marked manufacture facet, but this would not have been visible when the bed of wax was in place. In addition to a few damaged or degraded areas the smooth surface of the tablet is broken by a number of tiny dimples. Some of these are quite irregular and probably fortuitous, but seven are of identical

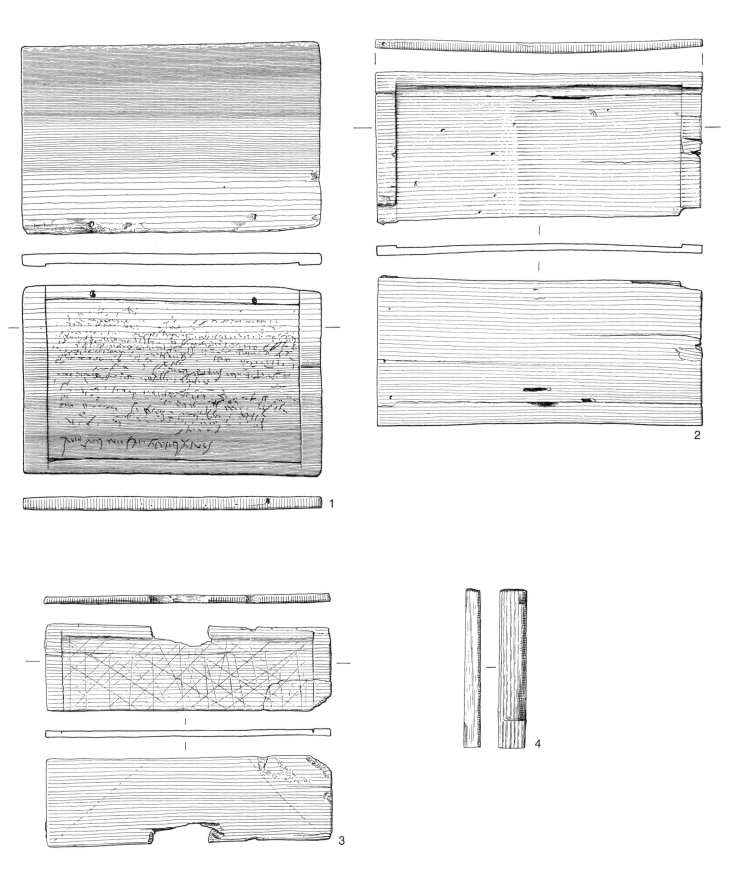

Fig. 204 Stonea Grange: wooden writing tablets 1–4 from the sump (scale 1:2).

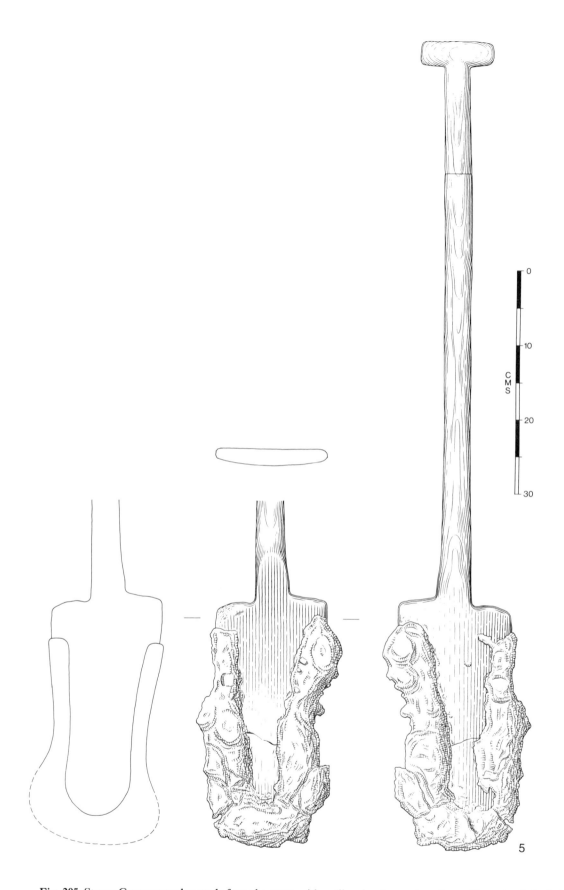

Fig. 205 Stonea Grange: wooden spade from the sump, with outline drawing to show form of iron sheath (scale 1:5).

form – tiny 'pits' made with a blunt-pointed solid tip. There seems little doubt that they were made with a stylus point, and the three on the recessed face may have occurred accidentally. However, a linear group of three (originally more, perhaps) near the edge of one of the short sides of the plain face was clearly intentional as, too, a single example at the corresponding end of the remaining long side edge. A function as collation marks or a code to signify contents etc. seems probable. The tablet had certainly been used, for there are traces of several lines of illegible incised writing near the broken edge. They follow the wood grain and run almost the entire breadth of the recessed area, as on no. 1, but extend no further than *c*. 17 mm from the broken edge. Other than the three dimples there is no trace of incision or ink writing on the back.

From the north sump, cut II, grid square 9, layer 29. Late 2nd–early 3rd century AD. Phase III.

3 Writing tablet   (Fig. 204) ST 83A I, 26, 2, SF 83A, 7, W 419

A broken and quite badly degraded tablet of ash, with one plain and one recessed face. There is a raised rim on all three remaining sides of the recessed face, but it is decayed and collapsed in most places and has suffered excavation damage on the long side. Overall length 155 mm; maximum surviving width 46 mm; maximum surviving rim thickness 4.5 mm. Recessed area: length 136 mm; maximum surviving width 39 mm; thickness 2.5–3.5 mm.

The recessed face is covered with scored lines. That they were not simply a key for the wax bed is indicated by the fact that they were applied in at least two sets, and it may be concluded that they were caused by scoring through texts in the wax. The density of the scoring and relatively poor preservation of the wood render it impossible to discern any trace of incised writing.

There is no trace of ink or incised writing on the plain back, but a straight line has been scored across both surviving corners in an approximately symmetrical arrangement. Each line is 'shadowed' by a less certain impressed line *c*. 13–14 mm away towards the corner. Their function/significance is unclear, but they recall the elasticated bindings of some modern notebooks, and it is possible that they were connected with the securing together of two or more tablets.

From the north sump, cut I, grid square 2, layer 26. 3rd–4th century AD. Phase III/IV

4 Writing tablet   (Fig. 204) ST 84A W 6224

A fragment from the corner of an ash tablet, comprising one end of a long side rim and the edge of the adjacent recessed face. Like nos 1–3, the back is plain. Surviving length 85 mm. Rim thickness 8–9 mm.

From the north sump.

5 Spade
(Fig. 205; Pl. XXX) ST 84A, II, 26, 11, SF 84A, 28

A complete wooden spade, overall length 1086 mm, made from a single piece of ash. The circular-sectioned T-handle (length 105 mm) is integral with the shaft, which is also of circular cross-section except in its lower part where it is flattened towards the blade. The blade (maximum dimensions 340 × 160 × 23 mm) is long, slender and tapered, with a flat face and lightly convex back. Its edge and sides are strengthened and sharpened by an iron spade sheath, now badly corroded but originally close-fitting (see p. 362, no. 16 for discussion of the iron sheath). There is a marked disparity in the height and shape of the blade shoulders, but it is not clear whether this asymmetry was a quirk of manufacture or a product of uneven wear. It is perhaps significant that the lower (?worn/?damaged) shoulder is on the side which would have been used as a tread by a right-footed person. Although the blade is relatively long and narrow, it is not excessively so, and the spade was probably not a specialised type but a general-purpose tool, as much for construction work as for agricultural/horticultural use.

While iron spade sheaths, a Roman period introduction to Britain, are quite commonly found on the more 'Romanised' sites, both military and civilian (Rees 1979, 322–6, Figs 108–21; Manning 1985, 44–7, Pls 17–19), the wooden parts of spades are rarely preserved and at best usually comprise only degraded fragments. Complete examples are exceedingly rare, and the single-piece construction of the Stonea spade is, seemingly, as yet unparalleled. The rather motley array mustered by Rees (*ibid*. 320–2, 417–9, and Figs 106–7) is, for the most part, made up of undiagnostic fragments or broken blades from composite tools. There is nothing approaching the size of the Stonea spade which is a notable and significant addition to the known range of Roman tools and implements.

From the north sump, cut II, grid square 11, layer 26. Late 2nd–3rd century AD.

6 Hayrake   (Fig. 206) ST 82 ADZ

A broken rake, in three joining fragments, comprising rather more than half of the clog with snapped tines and the stub of the handle. All these components are made of ash wood.

The clog, of rectangular cross-section (*c*. 37 × 26 mm), is perforated by a row of circular holes, of which four complete ones remain. They measure 9–11 mm in diameter. The three in the complete half of the clog are equally spaced 63 mm apart, while the pair flanking the handle junction are 79 mm apart. The clog is broken across the fifth hole, one side of which is preserved. It, too, lay 63 mm from its surviving neighbour. It may safely be assumed that there was one further hole in the missing part of the clog and that the object was a six-tined rake.

The wooden tines are all snapped, but their circular-sectioned base remains tightly dowelled into three of the holes. That adjacent to the handle junction on the broken side preserves its neatly finished, lightly domed head. Their form and spacing correspond to those of the pre-modern traditional British hayrake, the preferred wood for which was also ash.

The handle has a maximum surviving length of 170 mm and a sub-circular cross-section 30–31 mm in diameter at its broken end. It tapers towards the junction with the clog, and its upper surface and sides are pared away respectively *c*. 65 mm and 35 mm from the clog to reduce it to a plump D-shaped cross-section. Adjacent to the clog the lower surface, too, was steeply trimmed to complete the conversion of the round handle to the rectangular tenon required to fit the mortise cut through the clog. Ten millimetres of the tenon projects from the distal end of the mortise hole. An

Fig. 206 Stonea Grange: wooden hayrake from the sump, with outline drawing to show constructional details (scale 1 : 2).

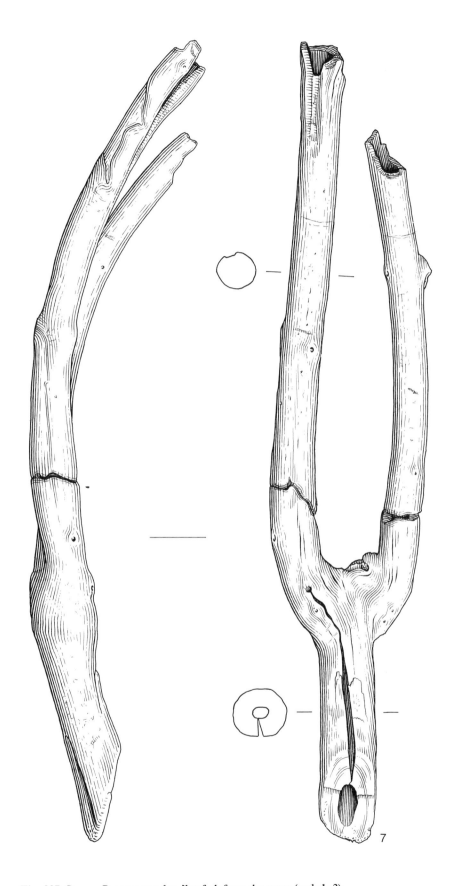

7

Fig. 207 Stonea Grange: wooden ?hayfork from the sump (scale 1:2).

iron nail was driven through the joint, and the shape of its disc head is preserved as a stain of corrosion products on the lower face of the clog. It is not clear whether this was an original feature or a repair, though the seemingly close fit of the joint would suggest the former. A marked bevelling of the leading lower angle of the clog may also be a feature of manufacture. More probably, however, it is a wear facet produced by use, in the expected position.

Assuming symmetry, the overall length of the clog would have been *c.* 450 mm: projection from the centre of the handle junction yields a measurement of *c.* 460 mm; while a measurement taken from the mid-point between the central pair of tines gives a length of 445 mm. By comparison with pre-modern hayrakes the size is fairly modest as, too, is the number of tines. However, it is in accord with other evidence for Roman rakes and may be compared to a seven-tined rakehead from a 1st century AD context at Newstead (Curle 1911, 283 Pl. 61, 7), length *c.* 330 mm; a six-tined rakehead from Saalburg (Jacobi 1897, 444, Fig. 69, 1, Pl. 80, 2), length 350 mm; and a fragmentary example of similar proportions from Borough Hill, Daventry (Manning 1985, 59, Pl. 25, F63). The Newstead and Borough Hill clogs are of oak, while the handle of the latter is of field maple or sycamore. Both the Saalburg and Newstead heads were mortised directly onto their handles in the same way as the Stonea rake, which implies that neither the split handle mode of attachment nor the pair of half-moon bow strengtheners, both common features of pre-modern rakes, were favoured by Roman rake-makers. However, it would be incautious to draw firm conclusions from the very limited evidence presently available. Such caution is highlighted by the present find: hitherto prominence has been given to the iron-tined type of wooden rake, often with the tacit assumption that it was the normal Roman form. The examples from Newstead, Saalburg and Borough Hill are, indeed, all of this type, and where less favourable conditions prevail the iron tines alone (usually between 110 and 170 mm long) have been found in some numbers on Roman sites. It is probable that the composite rake was a Roman introduction to Britain (Manning 1985, 59; Rees 1979, 484–5 and 737–40). However, the Stonea example underlines the importance of the waterlogged context and emphasises the ubiquity of wooden implements in antiquity and the careful choice of species often evident in their manufacture.

From unit 537 (= A, 26) in the north sump. 3rd–4th century AD. Phase III/IV.

7 ?Hayfork (Fig. 207) ST 82 AEQ, W26

Maximum length 430 mm. Prongs: length 310 mm, 260 mm.

A naturally forked piece of ash roundwood, broken at both ends. The absence of the tips of the gently curved prongs and, therefore, of any definite signs of use, prevent certainty, but size and form of the object as well as its stratigraphic proximity to the rakehead (no. 6) are in favour of identification as a pitch fork. The oblique cutting of the stem (32 mm diameter at the break) may have been done to retrieve the greater part of the handle shaft, presumably an eminently re-usable straight pole.

The tanged or socketed iron heads of two-pronged pitchforks are not uncommon finds from Roman Britain, and socketed iron tips, believed to be guards for the prongs of wooden forks, have also been found at several sites (Rees 1979, 482–4, 734–40 and Figs 251–5). However, no unequivocal surviving example of a Romano-British wooden pitchfork has yet been identified, despite the fact that they must have been the norm – Rees (*ibid.* 483) noted that wooden hayforks remained commoner than those of iron until the 19th century.

From unit 553 in the north sump. ?3rd century AD. Phase III.

8 Tankard stave (Fig. 208) ST 83 G4, 8, SF 548, W18

A very thin, gently tapered slat of ash wood, height 174 mm, thickness 3–4 mm. Both ends and the sides in the broader part are complete, but there is damage to the narrower part of the sides. The inner face at both ends is marked by a distinct bevel, while adze marks are visible on the outer face, especially in the narrower section. There are three tiny circular piercings: 1) 4 mm below the broad edge; 2) 71 mm below the broad edge and 11 mm from the nearest side; 3) 65 mm above the narrow edge and 4 mm from the nearest (damaged) side. It is very probable that a fourth piercing would have been present in the missing part of the narrow edge.

The extreme thinness, modest height and internal bevels distinguish this stave from those of buckets, barrels and tubs and identify it as part of a straight-sided, tapered tankard or measure. Furthermore, the rudimentary finish of the exterior surface implies a sheet bronze cladding or binding, and this is further suggested by the piercings: those at the ends would have held the rivets which secured rim and base bindings, while rivets in those in the body of the stave would have secured panels or sheet. From the absence of other staves and the metal fittings it may be inferred that the vessel had been broken and/or dismantled for scrap prior to deposition.

For staves of this size and type on tankards of the 1st century BC–3rd century AD, see Corcoran 1952. The complete examples display a variety of profiles and it is uncertain whether the Stonea vessel tapered towards its rim or its base, though the former seems more probable. While the object may have had a purely domestic function an official use as a dry measure, for corn or other agricultural produce, similar to the late 1st century AD bronze *modius* from Carvoran (Haverfield 1916; and *Archaeologia Aeliana* (4), 34, 1956, 130) should not be ruled out. The Carvoran measure is 310 mm high, but the height and degree of taper of the Stonea vessel correspond very closely to those of a bronze *modius* from Herculaneum in the Naples National Archaeological Museum (Inv. no. 6331. Haverfield 1916, 90–2, Fig. 4).

From well G4, primary silt (layer 8). Early 3rd century AD. [See p. 263, no. 5, for a bronze tankard handle from Stonea Camp.]

9 Bucket base or barrel head
(Fig. 208) ST 84A I, 31, 3, W5708

A broken discoidal plate of oak, diameter 130 mm, thickness 11 mm. Despite the loss of approximately one third of the disc and a little damage sustained on excavation, the object is identifiable as a single-piece base or end-plate from a small stave-built bucket, cask or tub. Its edge, characteristically, is chamfered on one face only to ensure a close-fitting joint in the croze groove at the end of the staves.

For many well-preserved stave-built buckets with identical, though larger, base-plates, found in a probable late 4th century AD context near the bottom of well 1 at Dalton parlours villa, see Morris 1990. One of the three small barrel heads from Carlisle,

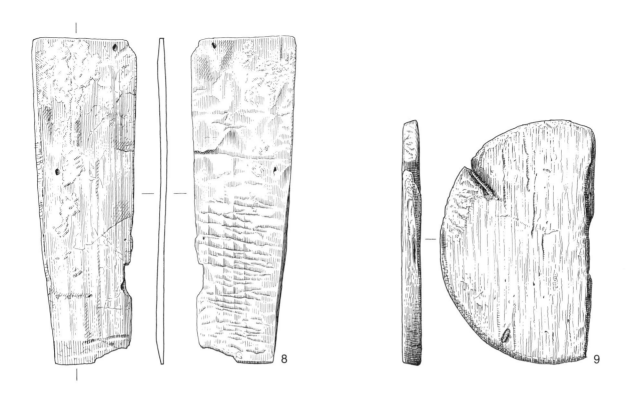

Fig. 208 Stonea Grange: wooden tankard stave (8), bucket base (9), and twisted binding (10) (scale 1:2).

Castle Street (Padley and Winterbottom 1991, 208, no. 790), from a mid–late 2nd century AD context, is of the same size, though thinner than, the Stonea plate. It is also of oak, as are most of the Dalton Parlours base-plates.

From the north sump, cut I, grid square 3, layer 31. Mid 2nd century AD on. Phase III. [Other bucket fragments from the sump include an iron bucket handle – p. 364, no. 29.]

10 ?Bucket binding or handle
(Fig. 208) ST 82 AGS, SF 381

Three twisted willow withy strands twisted together. They retain their bark, and their combined thickness is *c.* 25 mm. The broken and frayed ends give the object its present penannular form (external diameter *c.* 170–180 mm), but it is possible that originally it comprised a small circular hoop. Despite the modest size – internal diameter *c.* 120–30 mm – it could have been a binding from the tapered section of a narrow stave-built bucket (For one of suitable dimensions, see Feugère *et al* 1992, 62–3, no. 125, a tall, slender bucket of the 1st century AD from Saintes.) Certainly, its well-bottom context favours that identification, while the bucket base-plate from the sump (no. 9) also has a diameter of just 130 mm. Alternative uses include handle or rope fragment. For another twisted withy strand, from the sump, W 1201, see Fig. 222, p. 569.

From well 446, primary basal silt (unit 603). Phase III.

WATERLOGGED WOOD FROM THE SUMP

Caroline Cartwright   (Figs 209–28)

TECHNIQUES OF RECOVERY, CONSERVATION AND SAMPLING ON SITE

In Britain, waterlogged organic remains on archaeological sites are perhaps most well known from peat, e.g. the Neolithic and Bronze Age trackways of the Somerset Levels, and from certain urban contexts such as cesspits, latrines and wells. Increasing attention is being paid to other categories of waterlogged deposits on archaeological sites of all periods, particularly where the opportunity exists for comparison with non-waterlogged features on the same site complex. Such an opportunity exists with the organic and charred remains from the Stonea Grange excavations.

The techniques of recovery of the large quantity of waterlogged wood and other organic remains at Stonea were, in part, dictated by the depositional condition of the material. Excavation revealed a wide variety of waterlogged organic fragments including wooden artefacts, planks, pegs, chips and other woodworking debitage, withy bundles, withy ties, bark, nuts, fruits, pine cones and a large quantity of brushwood. In order to recover the range of carpenter's debris as well as artefacts, techniques of recovery included an elaborate system of scaffolding to keep the excavators and

conservators off the fragile material and a constant system of spraying to retain moisture in the material to be lifted (Pl. XVIa). Detailed plans and photographs documented the material in situ. Characterisation of the varied range of waterlogged remains required full analysis of the entire assemblage, but a selective programme of conservation was necessary to represent accurately the overall quality and content. The following policy guidelines were adopted:

1 All the artefacts were retained and conserved.

2 A full range of fragments which exhibited particular woodworking techniques was retained and conserved.

3 A representative sample of larger items, such as the planks, have been retained for the present time, pending the possible acquisition of larger freeze-drying facilities.

4 A representative sample of the other organic material such as withies, bark, fruits, pine cones etc. has been retained and conserved.

5 Certain of the withy bundles have been retained intact and conserved for possible display.

6 After full analysis and documentation, unmodified fragments of brushwood (roundwood) were discarded, but any modified fragments which, for example, exhibited cut, slashed, sawn or charred ends were retained and conserved.

7 Any items not falling into any of the above categories, but which displayed unusual features, have been retained and conserved.

8 Constant monitoring of the range of conserved items over the next decade is being carried out jointly with the Organics Section of the British Museum Department of Conservation.

As the analysis of the waterlogged assemblage proceeded alongside the conservation of the above-mentioned selected categories, a responsive approach was adopted to the details of the polyethylene glycol freeze-drying methods employed. It rapidly became apparent that certain woods responded differently to the treatments; PEG dispersal within the cellular structure appeared not to be uniformly related to the varying sizes of the vessels, parenchyma, fibres and other anatomical features of woody taxa. In other words, in a taxon such as *Quercus* (oak) which commonly exhibits large vessels (in the early wood of the growth ring cycle), the dispersal of PEG was not necessarily more efficient than within a taxon such as *Corylus* (hazel) with smaller, more dispersed vessels. Nor does the reverse hold true. Clearly there are many factors which need to be taken into account, such as the cellular degradation of the wood fragments, features such as tyloses (commonly found in oak) which may obstruct vessel cavities, infestation of the wood cells by fungal hyphae, as well as those variables introduced by the PEG and freeze-drying methods themselves.

The main waterlogged feature of the Phase III settlement consisted of a huge pit, some 10 m square and up to 3.5 m deep in places (see p. 87ff. and Pl. XVI). A second pit was located to the south of the primary one. Both appear to have been filled rapidly, and may have acted as sumps. Many of the wooden artefacts derive from the lowest levels and the sides of this large pit; the bulk of the unworked roundwood fragments, woodworking debris (chips and offcuts), withy bundles, planks, bark and other macrobotanical material being deposited in an apparently haphazard manner. The analysis of waterlogged wood which follows below, concentrates on the contents of the large pit. It seems highly probable that a large proportion of the timber preserved by waterlogging relates to the construction of building R1 (and possibly to other structural features also). Apart from the use of wood for artefacts, other wooden features within the Phase III settlement include posts, staves, fencing and planking. The posts and staves are usually of ash (*Fraxinus* sp.), oak (*Quercus* sp.) or sometimes hazel (*Corylus* sp.). Fencing often utilises birch (*Betula* sp.), in addition to the aforementioned species. The planking, some of which may have been for scaffolding purposes, is frequently oak or ash.

Ash was often used for the timber-lining of wells, latrines and tanks, but as will be seen, the dependence on ash (*Fraxinus* sp.) is noteworthy for all categories of finds in the Stonea assemblage. Trees and shrubs provided an assortment of material for fuel – both domestic and industrial – and the processes involved in selecting specific timber for these purposes, are discussed in detail below. Furthermore, some woodland management (particularly coppicing) may be inferred from the quantified results. As with the other environmental specialist reports (French, pp. 639–54, and van der Veen, pp. 613–39) the results from the analysis of the waterlogged and other organic remains can be used to build up a picture of the palaeoecology. However, although selection of timber can be postulated with some conviction, no assumption can be made that the relative proportions of timbers necessarily present an exact ecological 'mirror' of the past. For example, the overall dependence on ash (*Fraxinus* sp.) does not necessarily mean that ash was the dominant tree of the surrounding environment; it may mean that ash was preferentially selected for its particular properties and suitability for structural timbers (Figs 209a–c).

PROPERTIES OF TIMBERS

Some of the woody taxa most frequently present in the Stonea assemblage are discussed here.

Ash (*Fraxinus* sp.) is a durable and heavy timber which can exhibit close and straight grain. It is both tough and flexible and has commonly been used for handles and hafts for artefacts, frames, oars, curved hoops for barrels and a range of domestic utensils. It has a number of structural uses and, as fuel, provides a high temperature, clear, steady burn.

Oak (*Quercus* sp.) is renowned for its strong and durable character. The heartwood is strong and heavy, and is very much preferable to the less stable sapwood. Seasoning oak is essential to avoid splitting, particularly in constructional timbers such as frames for houses, planks, floors and roof joists.

Hazel (*Corylus* sp.) has been extensively used in its young growth form as coppiced lengths. The wood is flexible and long-lasting, with a wide range of uses for items requiring elasticity.

Birch (*Betula* sp.) has a fine-grained texture which takes a satiny finish when planed and sanded. The wood is hard and tough, and the bark also has uses, as in the manufacture of vessels and canoes, as a roofing material, and, in rolls, for making tapers.

Willow (*Salix* sp.), like hazel, is most frequently used as young growths (of one to two years), i.e. osiers. Thin willow strips are often plaited in basketry.

Alder (*Alnus* sp.) is most frequently used where the timber is to be kept wet, such as river revetments. When dry, the wood may be rather weak and soft, but it is sometimes turned for small items where durability and strength are less important.

Blackthorn/sloe (*Prunus spinosa*) has been used extensively for hedging. Its spikes may be used in combs for the carding of flax, and for fish-hooks. Sloe fruits have a number of culinary applications.

Traveller's Joy (*Clematis vitalba*) produces slender stems which are used, peeled, for basketry. The inner bark may be useful for straining whey from curd.

Hawthorn (*Crataegus* sp.) wood is very hard and close-grained. It makes a fine substitute for box (*Buxus* sp.) for engraving and carving.

WATERLOGGED WOOD ANALYSIS. WOOD TECHNOLOGY

Over 98 000 pieces of waterlogged wood (including bark fragments) were analysed from the large waterlogged feature (Fig. 209a). Of these, 91 689 were unworked roundwood fragments. Figures 209b–c summarise the main trees and shrubs represented in the unworked material. Figures 209c–d and 210–11 provide the details of stem diameter range in each taxon. Much of the data will be used later to discuss the environmental reconstruction and possible woodland management systems (see pp. 577–83). Even at this point, although the focus in this section is on worked pieces, debitage and artefacts, it is important to note the high values for ash (*Fraxinus* sp.), hazel (*Corylus* sp.) and oak (*Quercus* sp.).

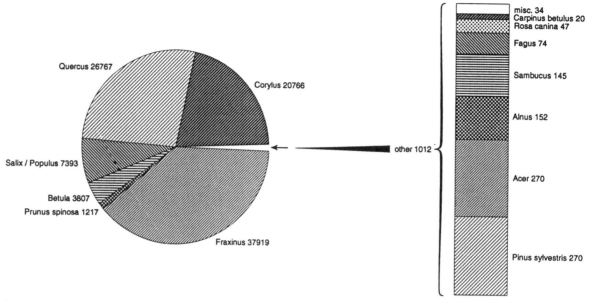

a.

Primary group (total 97,869)

Quercus 26767
Corylus 20766
Salix / Populus 7393
Betula 3807
Prunus spinosa 1217
Fraxinus 37919
other 1012

Secondary group (total 1,012)

misc. 34
Carpinus betulus 20
Rosa canina 47
Fagus 74
Sambucus 145
Alnus 152
Acer 270
Pinus sylvestris 270

b.

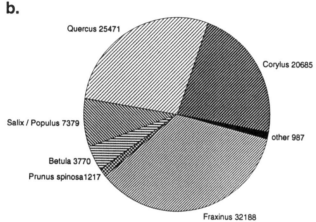

Quercus 25471
Corylus 20685
Salix / Populus 7379
Betula 3770
Prunus spinosa 1217
Fraxinus 32188
other 987

c.

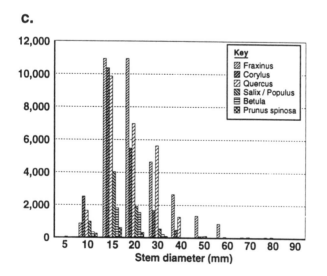

Key
Fraxinus
Corylus
Quercus
Salix / Populus
Betula
Prunus spinosa

Stem diameter (mm)

d.

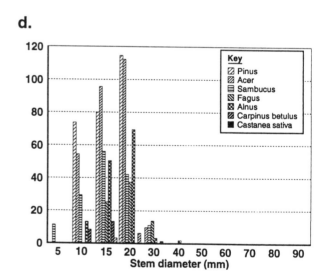

Key
Pinus
Acer
Sambucus
Fagus
Alnus
Carpinus betulus
Castanea sativa

Stem diameter (mm)

Fig. 209 Stonea Grange: waterlogged wood from the sump. a) Summary of combined wood categories. b) Unworked roundwood fragments, total. c) Unworked roundwood fragments, primary group (vertical axis = fragments). d) Unworked roundwood fragments, secondary group.

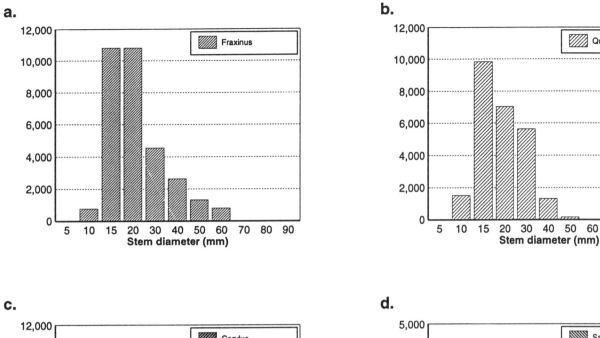

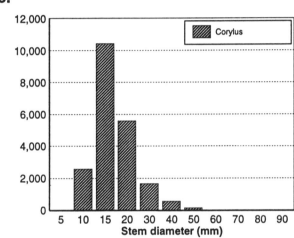

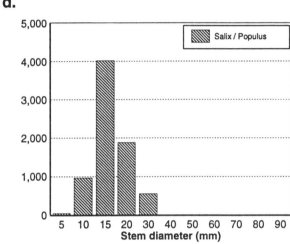

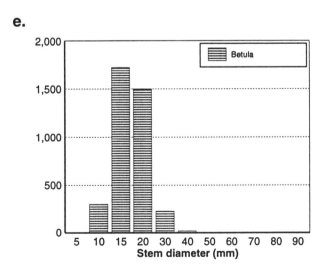

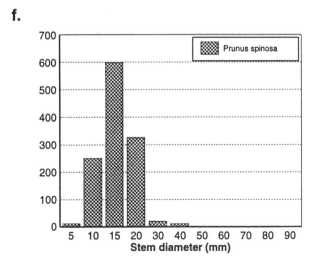

Fig. 210 Stonea Grange: waterlogged wood from the sump, unworked roundwood fragments, primary group – a) ash, b) oak, c) hazel, d) willow/poplar, e) birch, f) blackthorn (vertical axis = fragments).

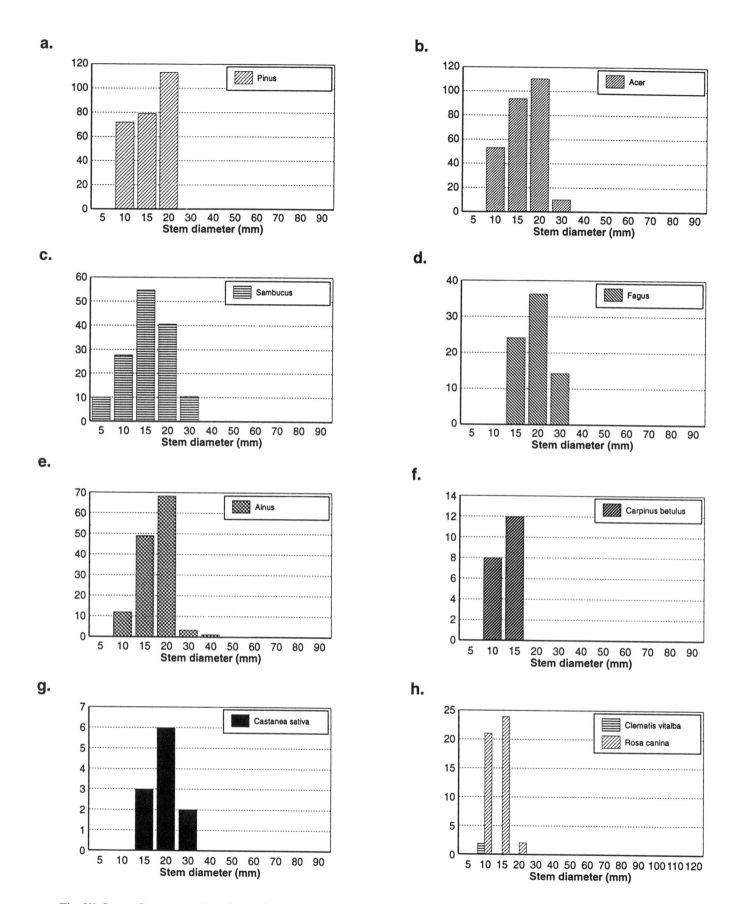

Fig. 211 Stonea Grange: waterlogged wood from the sump, unworked roundwood fragments, secondary group – a) pine, b) field maple, c) elder, d) beech, e) alder, f) hornbeam, g) sweet chestnut, h) Traveller's Joy and dog rose (vertical axis = fragments).

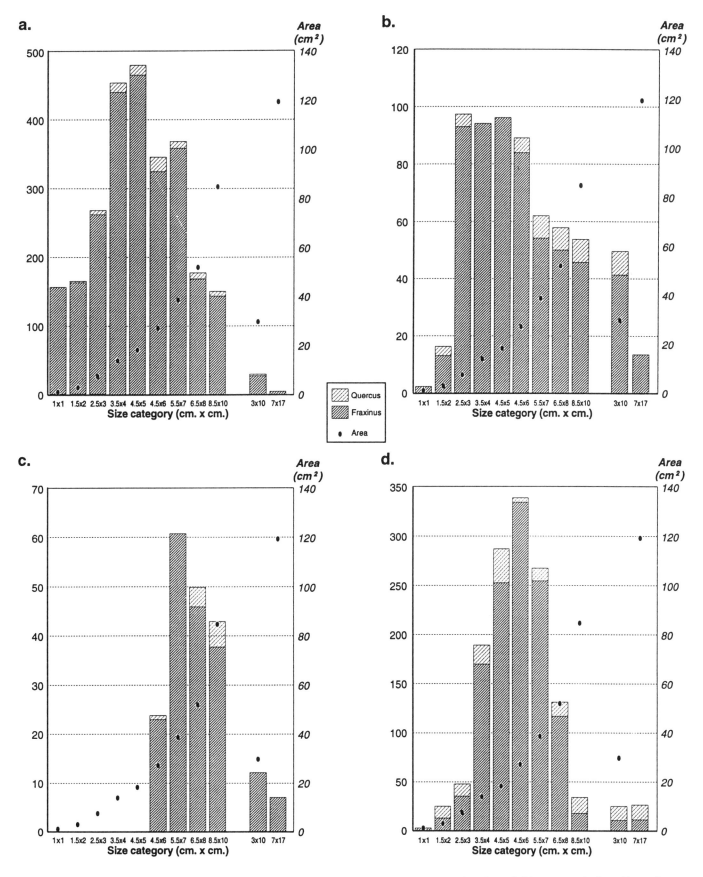

Fig. 212 Stonea Grange: waterlogged wood from the sump, ash (*Fraxinus* sp.) and oak (*Quercus* sp.) – a) wood chips, one main facet; b) wood chips, two main facets; c) wood chips, three main facets; d) offcuts.

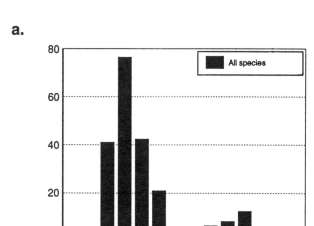

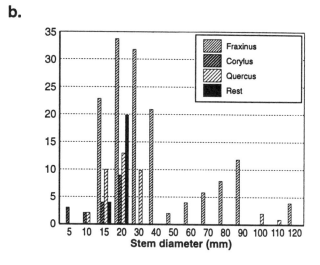

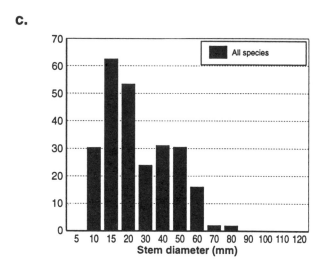

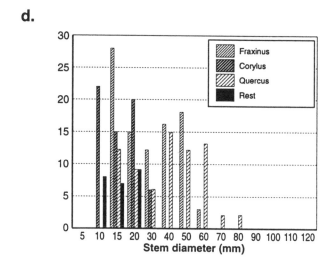

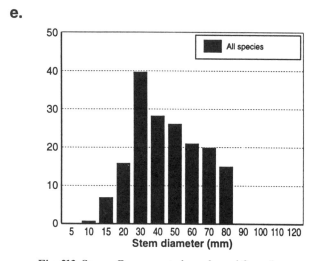

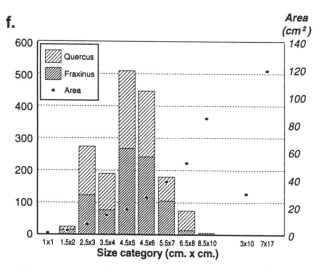

Fig. 213 Stonea Grange: waterlogged wood from the sump – a, b) roundwood fragments, one diagonally cut end; c, d) roundwood fragments, two diagonally-cut ends; e) roundwood fragments, radially-split (half-sectioned); f) bark fragments, ash (*Fraxinus* sp.) and oak (*Quercus* sp.).

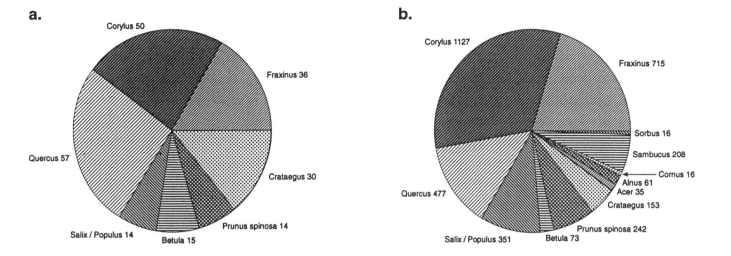

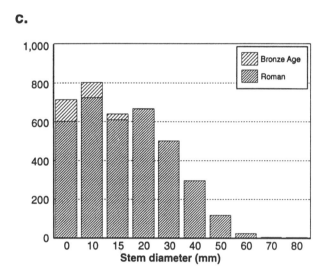

Fig. 214 Stonea Grange: charcoal fragments – a) Late Bronze Age contexts, b) Roman contexts, c) Late Bronze Age and Roman contexts.

The fragmentation of the waterlogged pieces needs some comment. If the large waterlogged feature was rapidly filled with waste material, woodworking debris and miscellaneous (roundwood) branches cut from woodland stands as a part of management practices, there would be no reason to assume a particular significance in the orientation of the fragments. Detailed plans and photographs of the material in situ reveal the 'unstructured' nature of some of the elements, whilst others, such as the withy bundles, appear to remain fairly intact. The condition of the wood varies in terms of overall preservation. Furthermore, despite best attempts by all concerned, a certain percentage has suffered further fracturing on lifting. Adjoining fragments of a roundwood piece were frequently bagged together and are clearly identifiable as such. However, where fragmentation has occurred, either in antiquity or more recently, adjoining pieces may be difficult or impossible to locate. Therefore, the decision was made to enumerate fragments for the analysis to facilitate correlations. This fragmentation problem means that roundwood *lengths* are virtually meaningless for the unworked pieces.

The presence of such a large quantity of wood is remarkable; indeed one may query why it had not been used as firewood. Part of the answer could lie in the fact that larger roundwood (branch) fragments may well have provided the required timber for domestic or industrial fuel. The trimmings, which might comprise a large quantity of smaller roundwood and twigs (such as we find in the large waterlogged feature) remains as superfluous to requirements, after fuel, structural and artefactual wood preparation has been completed.

A THE DEBITAGE

i Chips

Over 3400 wood chips were excavated and analysed. In order to characterise their features, their facets were studied under the microscope, evaluated and enumerated. A series of chip classes and categories emerged, primarily based on facetting, shape and area. A spectrum of chip facetting exists from short, steep removals to broad, flat, shallow faces. Caution must be exercised, however, as the nature of the archaeological context in which this material was deposited has resulted in much fragmentation, abrasion and wear, in addition to that produced by woodworking, function and use. Axe 'signatures' (such as have been recognised for the Somerset Levels trackways assemblages), adze cuts, knife, saw, chisel, wedge and plane marks (amongst others) have been sought. Many of these details have not been as diagnostic as one might anticipate, partly as a result of the aforementioned factors.

Figures 212a–c give details of the relative proportion of timbers used in each chip size category. Inevitably certain chips fall outside these parameters. Where significant, these are described below. Although useful in terms of characterising the chip assemblage, one should not necessarily assume that these chip features have the same significance as, for example, the patterns of flaking (specifically predetermined) on a flint tool. The chips are waste products after all, and whilst they may yield valuable technological information relating to the methods and techniques of tree felling and timber preparation, it is through the overall size categorisation that significant trends emerge. Each blow of an axe into a tree-trunk may yield three or four chips, depending on the strength and angle of the blow, the axe edge and the properties of the timber. Dressing, shaping, splitting, shaving, honing and carving of the wood not only involve a range of woodworking tools, but may produce characteristic debitage. The illustrations of the range of debitage (and artefacts) depict the variety of techniques used, (including the direction and sequence of facets) both for 'typical' pieces and unusual items. Not all fragments are described in detail here; this level of information is held on archive.

The properties of various timbers play a crucial role in selection for specific function, and it seems highly likely that, from the earliest times, people would have been aware of these varying properties. Figure 212a shows the prime use of ash (*Fraxinus* sp.) – being 96.7% of the total (2606) in the chip class which has one main facet. Examples of this class are illustrated in Fig. 215 (chip number 5983 and five of the chips in chip scatter number 6147). Many of the chips in this class have been split along the rays. In other words, after a trunk or branch has been cut across transversely, the rays which are then displayed ('fanning out' at right angles to the growth rings) have been used as markers for axial splitting. In this way an even grain is produced in the finished product. Not all of the examples illustrated in this chip class (or others) are confined to the radially split element. Where possible the grain orientation has been indicated by the illustrator – particularly where it is significant that a tangential or a transverse split or cut is present. Whilst grain orientation is noteworthy, it is not surprising that tree felling and timber preparation should necessitate chip and waste product removal from many directions.

Oak (*Quercus* sp.) represents 2.9% in this 'one main facet' chip class and the remainder consists of a few chips of willow/poplar (*Salix/Populus*), field maple (*Acer* sp.) and birch (*Betula* sp.) Figure 212a concentrates on the chip-size ranges for ash and oak only. High values are seen for chip sizes 4.5 × 5 cm and 3.5 × 4 cm; both are mainly represented by ash.

Categories 5.5 × 7 cm and 4.5 × 6 cm are also well represented, and are also almost entirely composed of ash. This class concentrates on chips with one main facet. However, there are certain chips which exhibit one cut face but not as a clean cut. The axe or adze blow may have been deflected or repeated in the same place. In consequence a step-like main cut may be produced, e.g. chip numbers 5240, 5983, N/N1

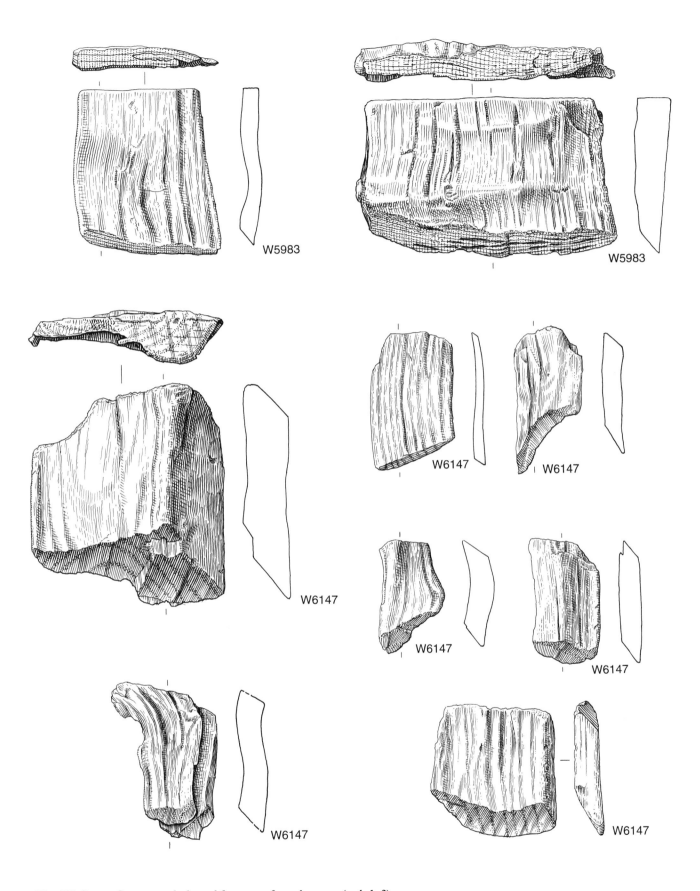

Fig. 215 Stonea Grange: worked wood fragments from the sump (scale 1 : 2).

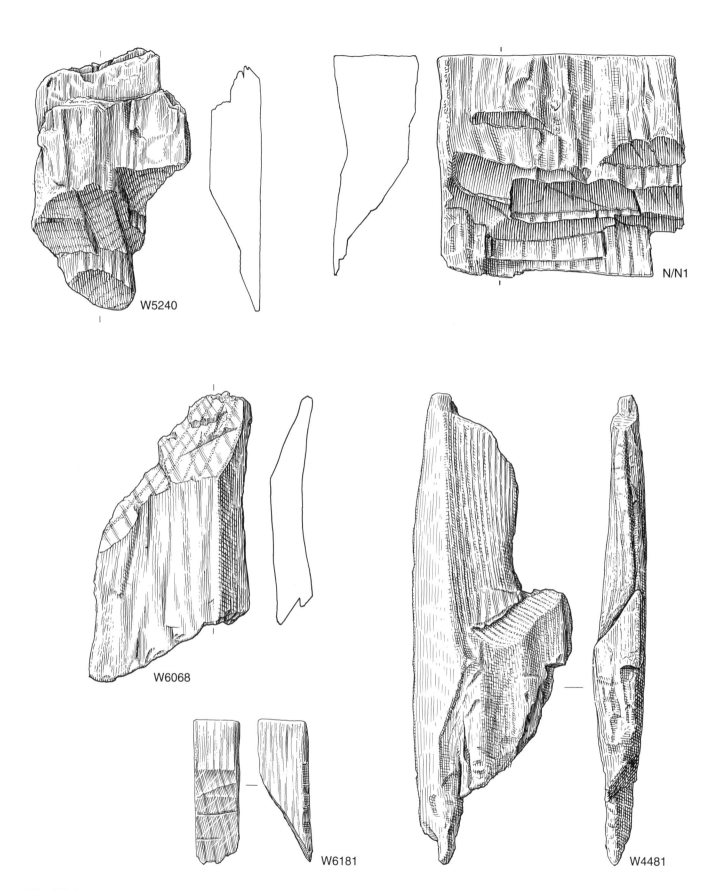

Fig. 216 Stonea Grange: worked wood fragments from the sump (scale 1 : 2).

and 6068 (Figs 215–16) (the latter is not radially split). It must be stressed therefore, that the designation 'one main facet' is used to signal a main cutting event on that particular item; it is not intended to be applied in the narrow sense. The 'one facet' may be a direct cut into the wood, or may have been produced as a detached surface facet consequent to a blow or axe-cut elsewhere on that area of wood, e.g. chip number 4481 (Fig. 216). Frequently, the 'one facet' is a diagonal cut, resulting in a wedge-shaped end to the chip, e.g. numbers 6181 and 6041 (Figs 216–17), the second of which also has preliminary dorsal 'nibbling'. Within the artefact category (Section Bi, pp. 571–4) certain pieces are designated as 'wedges' (e.g. wood number 1, Fig. 223); there may be some overlap in use between those apparently predetermined in shape to be wedges and those wedge-like chips which could well have served a similar function. Furthermore, the distinction between the 'wedge' category and shaped or pointed stake, post or peg ends is made on the nature and distribution of the facets, the dimensions of the fragments and the condition of the other surface of the piece concerned. Examples are wood numbers 6205, 31, 1202 and 5464 (Figs 224–7). Unfinished pieces in this category include wood number 486 (Fig. 225) and chip number 6148 (Fig. 217).

Figure 212b comprises a total of 632 chips which exhibit two main facets (or cutting events), e.g. chip numbers 22, 4794, 2951, 1685, 6191, and 80 (Fig. 217). Only ash (93%) and oak (7%) are present. The chip-size 2.5 × 3 cm is almost entirely ash; 4.5 × 5 cm and 3.5 × 4 cm are entirely so. In the 4.5 × 6 cm category, a small amount of oak is present with the ash. These four categories have the highest representation. This chip class also exhibits the step-like facetting described above, e.g. chip number 6074 (Fig. 217) and one of the chips from chip scatter 6147 (Fig. 215). Wedge-like, diagonally-cut end(s) are sometimes present, e.g. two of the chips from chip scatter number 6147 (Fig. 215), chip numbers 6230, 6201, 24, 1206, and 6162 (Fig. 218). Some unusual chips are present, e.g. chip number 4B, an oak chip with worn and abraded facets and a small circular depression on the transverse face (Fig. 218). Certain of the chips in this class have squared-off or quasi-geometric shapes, either produced through preshaping, wear-use or abrasion. These may also exhibit the scalar and/or wedge-like facets, e.g. chip numbers 66, 4793, 9, 33, and 6225 (Figs 218–9). In some instances, wear-usage, abrasion or damage may mask possible function as an artefact e.g. wood numbers 6002, 6050, 6132, 6180, 32, and N/N4 (Fig. 219). Chips resulting from the cutting of small roundwood lengths include some of those in the ADZ group (Fig. 220). Also in this ADZ group are larger chips and offcuts which appear to result from adze usage on the timber. Characteristic long, thin 'peels' are chipped away. (Fig. 220, ADZ). It may be noted here that this technique may be used, as an alternative to splitting, wedging or chiselling, to produce shingles, thin

'board' suitable for tablets, (barrel) staves, slats and frames (see Fig. 227, wood numbers 5402 and 4983, and Section B, pp. 571–7).

Not surprisingly, the chip class which has three or more main facets, tends to favour the larger chip-size categories, i.e. 4.5 × 6 cm upwards (Fig. 212c). Out of 197 chips in this class, ash constitutes 94.9% and oak 5.1%. The peak occurs in the 5.5 × 7 cm chip-size range. Examples include chip numbers 4133, 4248, and 5160 (Fig. 220). This chip class also exhibits some step-like facetting (described above), e.g. on chip numbers 37, 5147, and 5154 (Figs 220–1). Wedge-like, diagonally-cut surface(s) are sometimes present, e.g. chip numbers 6206, 6229, 6059, 4973, and 2083 (Figs 220–2). Certain of the chips in this class also have squared-off or quasi-geometric shapes. These may exhibit as well the scalar and/or wedge-like facetting, e.g. chip number 5945 (Fig. 222). Here, too, in some instances, wear-usage, abrasion or damage may mask possible functions as an artefact, e.g. wood numbers 266 (Fig. 222), 1437 (Fig. 224) and 4688 (Fig. 223).

ii Offcuts

Differentiation between chips and offcuts is based on size, shape and facetting of the fragments. In terms of dimensions, the offcuts fall within the suggested chip-size categories but have a general lack of facetted surfaces, other than the obverse and reverse as a planar face. Some of the offcuts appear to be the by-products of woodworking of planks, structural timbers and larger timber items. A total of 1387 offcuts which fall into the chip-sized categories comprise 89% ash (*Fraxinus* sp.) and 11% oak (*Quercus* sp.) (Fig. 212d). Highest frequencies occur in the 4.5 × 6 cm, 4.5 × 5 cm and 5.5 × 7 cm categories respectively; ash predominating throughout.

iii Cut roundwood

As previously discussed, roundwood lengths can infrequently be relied upon for diagnostic information. However, roundwood with one or two cut ends falls within the overall debitage category – not necessarily as by-products of structural or artefactual woodworking – but possibly as trimming of larger roundwood branches for a variety of uses. Aspects of woodland management or gardening (such as pruning) are also possibilities. Figures 213a–b summarise the stem diameter range for all woody taxa exhibiting roundwood fragments with one diagonally-cut end. A total of 226 roundwood fragments is present, of which 64.7% is ash (*Fraxinus* sp.), 16.8% oak (*Quercus* sp.), 7.9% hazel (*Corylus* sp.), 5.3% birch (*Betula* sp.) and 5.3% alder (*Alnus* sp.). The cut end may be axe-cut, sawn or knife-cut. No clear examples of sawn ends are present. Most seem to be axe-cut, e.g. wood number 26 (Fig. 207). Wood number 486 (possibly an

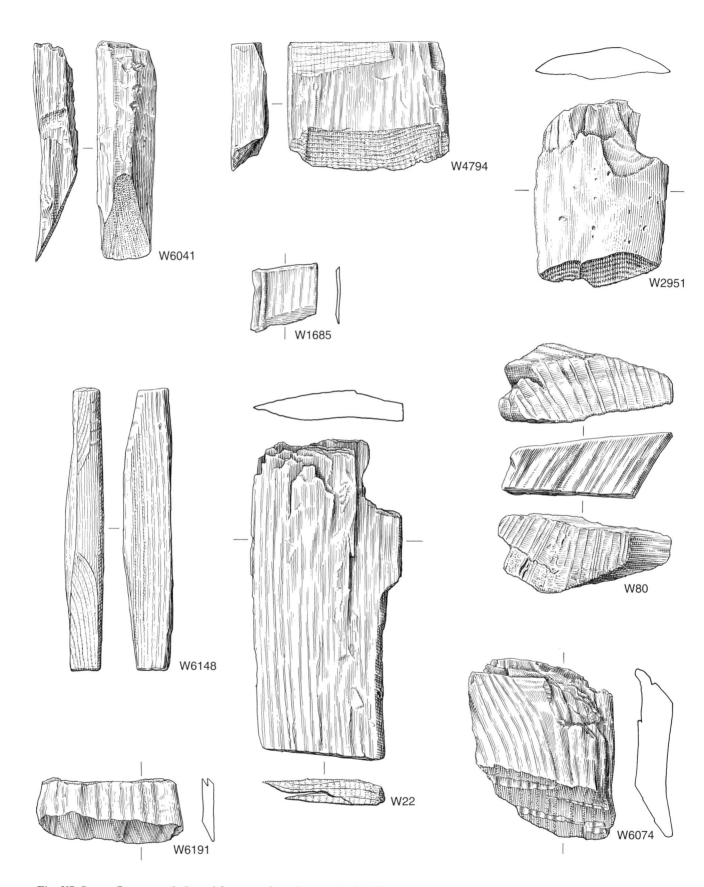

W6041

W4794

W2951

W1685

W6148

W80

W6191

W22

W6074

Fig. 217 Stonea Grange: worked wood fragments from the sump (scale 1:2).

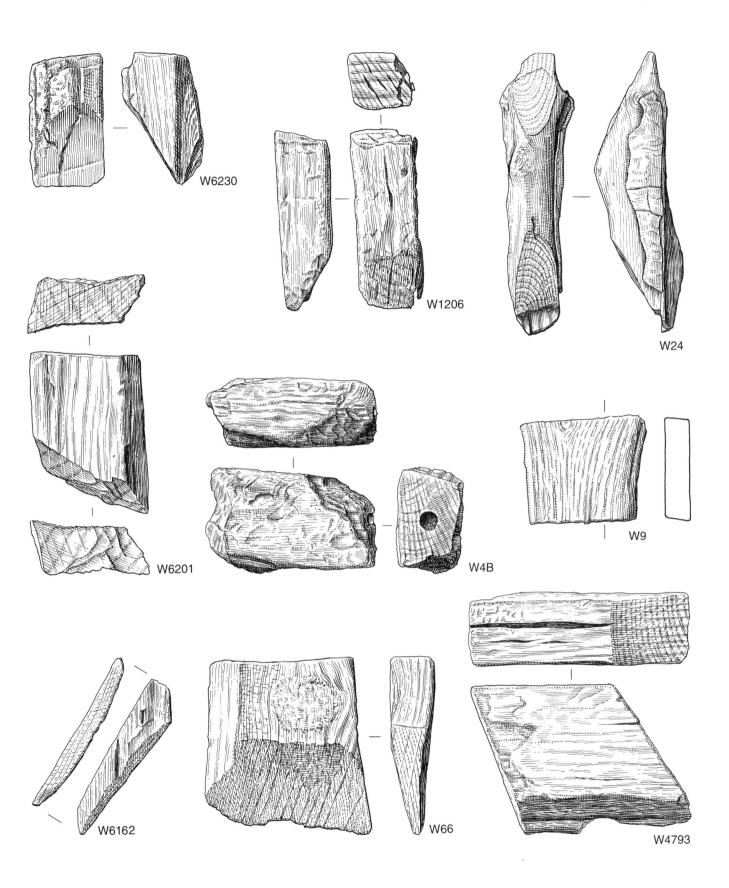

Fig. 218 Stonea Grange: worked wood fragments from the sump (scale 1 : 2).

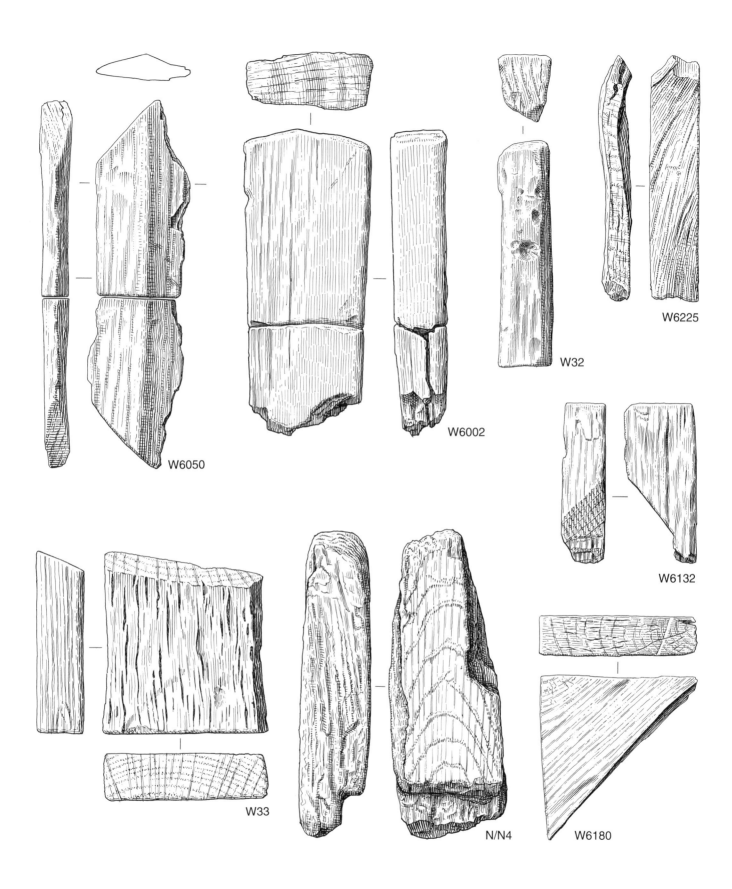

Fig. 219 Stonea Grange: worked wood fragments from the sump (scale 1:2).

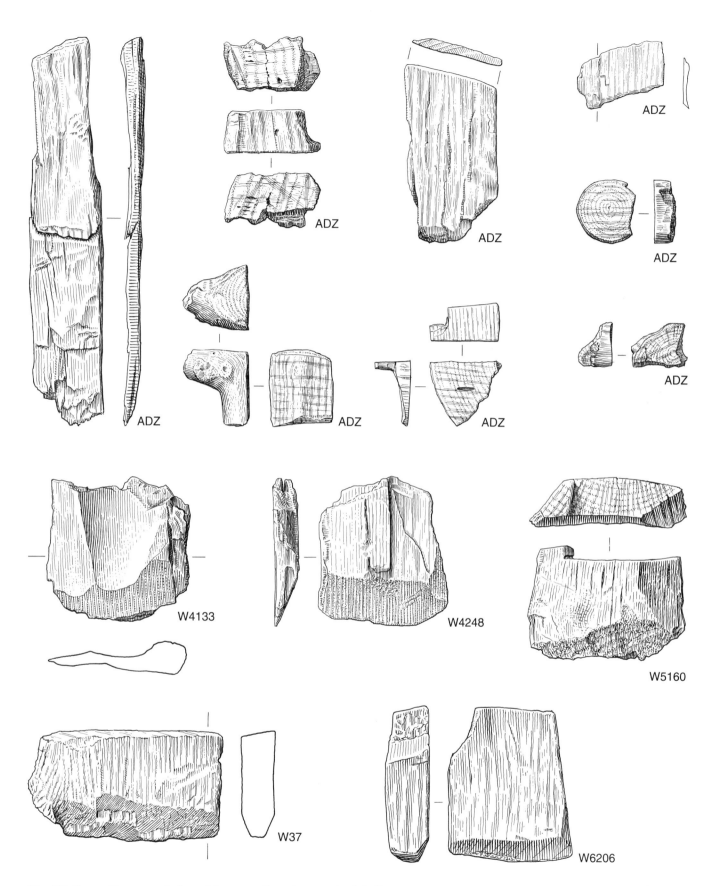

Fig. 220 Stonea Grange: worked wood fragments from the sump (scale 1:2).

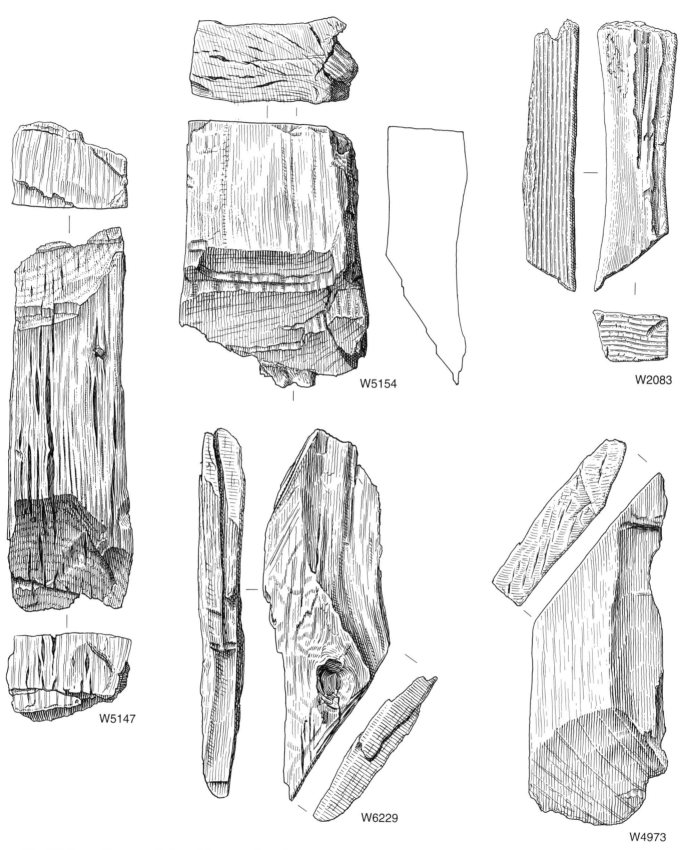

W5154

W2083

W5147

W6229

W4973

Fig. 221 Stonea Grange: worked wood fragments from the sump (scale 1 : 2).

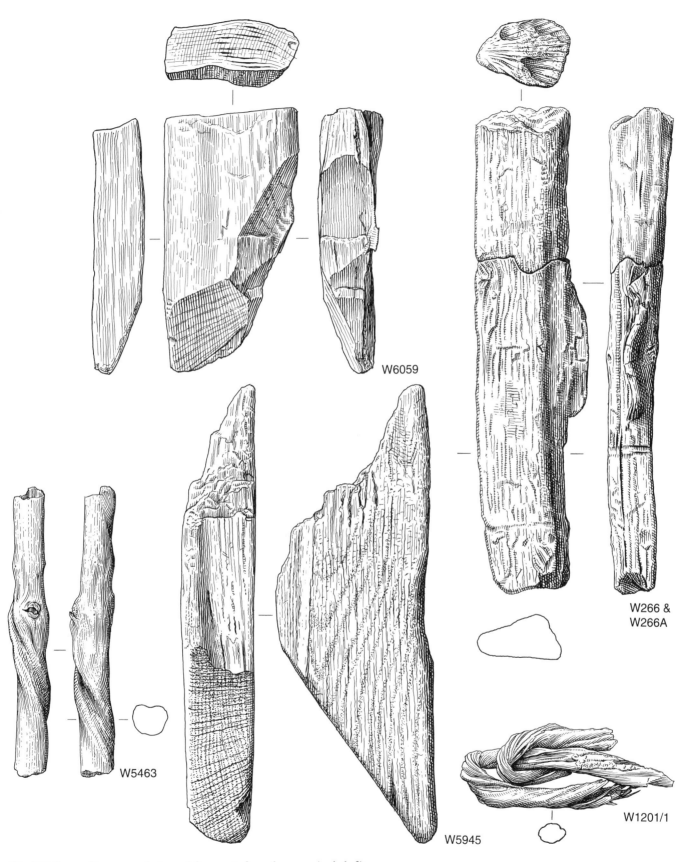

W6059

W266 &
W266A

W5463

W5945

W1201/1

Fig. 222 Stonea Grange: worked wood fragments from the sump (scale 1 : 2).

unfinished stake end) appears to have knife-cuts producing the facetted surfaces (Fig. 225). This hazel fragment did not respond well to the PEG and freeze-drying treatment; the illustrated splitting is attributable to this problem.

Highest occurrences are seen for the 20 mm stem diameter measurement, for all the taxa concerned (33.6% of the total). High values are also recorded for ash and oak roundwood fragments with 30 mm stem diameter measurement, and for ash, oak, hazel and alder roundwood fragments with 15 mm stem diameter measurement. It seems likely therefore that coppicing, pruning and trimming of hazel and ash wands by a single-bladed cutting implement produced this category of waste material.

Similar mechanisms may have operated for those roundwood fragments with two diagonally-cut ends. Figures 213c–d summarise the stem diameter range for all taxa. A total of 250 fragments comprises 36.8% ash (*Fraxinus* sp.), 28.4% oak (*Quercus* sp.), 25.2% hazel (*Corylus* sp.), 4.8% birch (*Betula* sp.), 2.8% willow/poplar (*Salix/Populus*) and 2% alder (*Alnus* sp.). The peak value (24.8%) falls within the 15 mm stem diameter category in which ash, hazel and oak predominate and birch and alder are present. The 20 mm stem diameter category constitutes 21.2% of the total, with hazel, ash, oak, birch and alder present in order of diminishing frequency. Stem diameters measuring 40 mm, 50 mm and 10 mm form 12.4%, 12% and 12% respectively. In the 40 mm and 50 mm categories, ash and oak alone are present. The 10 mm category sees a high proportion of hazel, and a lesser quantity of birch, alder and willow/poplar. Coppicing, trimming and pruning all appear to be evidenced by the relative proportions of the taxa and their dimensions.

A total of 174 roundwood fragments have been half-sectioned by radial splitting. Fig. 213e summarises the details for all taxa. Ash constitutes 59.2% of the total, followed by oak at 32.8%, birch at 6.3% and willow/poplar at 1.7%. Peak value occurs in the 30 mm category (ash, oak and birch). No freshly fractured or split roundwood has been included in this class of waste product. No fragments which exhibit cut, slashed, sawn or charred ends are included here either; these are included in worked fragment categories.

The final element in the debitage or waste product range comprises bark fragments. Perhaps one of the most difficult categories to evaluate, it nevertheless has a significant presence. A total of 1712 bark fragments has been categorised into chip-size ranges. Figure 213f summarises the ash and oak totals – 50.2% and 49.5% respectively. The remainder consists of pine bark fragments (probably *Pinus sylvestris* – Scots pine) at 0.3%. There is no great significance in the size range values as the fragmentation factor associated with the bark will have been so variable. Bark-stripping, prior to the shaping and planing of structural timbers, is an automatic primary task. In addition to the above-mentioned

bark fragments, 1.3% of the wood chips and worked roundwood retain a bark surface, e.g. numbers 24 (Fig. 218) and 6205 (Fig. 227). The latter example serves to illustrate also the problem of bark retention on the wood generally. The conditions of burial of the entire waterlogged assemblage have tended to encourage the detachment of bark from the wood. Bark retention during the PEG and freeze-drying conservation treatment was also particularly problematic. Nevertheless, the indications are that a significant proportion of the timber arrived on site with adherent bark. Figure 213f, however, does not necessarily reflect the degree of bark stripping carried out intentionally, prior to further modification of the wood.

iv Other macrobotanical material

Wood and other macrobotanical material which does not easily fit into categories as described above or artefact categories below will be summarised in this section. This includes both modified, utilised, raw and waste material.

Withy bundles. Stick bundles

Six largely intact withy bundles and other stick bundles were retrieved from the large waterlogged feature (e.g. wood number 2184). Although the bundle itself retained its general form in the soil, the individual osiers, withies or sticks often exhibit fragmentation. Most frequently the withies and osiers are of willow (*Salix* sp.), although there is some representation of hazel and ash in the stick bundles.

Twisted withy strands

Twisted withy strands (occasionally in situ around stick and withy bundles) are present in small quantities. Wood number 1201 illustrates a twisted willow strand (Fig. 222). Opened out, this withy coil measures 22.5 cm and is torn at both ends. Its maximum stem diameter is 10 mm. All examples are willow (*Salix* sp.). Such withy strands could provide a variety of uses such as bucket handles, ropes, netting, bindings.

Wood number 5463 (Fig. 222) is a short length of ash roundwood featuring a spirally-indented impression in the surface of the wood. The fragment does not retain any bark. It is possible that ivy (*Hedera helix*) could have twisted a strand around the fragment tightly enough to have created this indented surface even under the (presumably once-present) bark. Alternatively, this fragment may have been used for twisting withy ties for the purpose of securing a withy or stick bundle. Ivy has not been found in the waterlogged wood or charcoal assemblages, but it is a common component of mixed deciduous woodland, and is present in the Stonea pollen record (van der Veen, pp. 636–8).

Coppice stools

Bases (or stools) of trunks from which coppice shoots spread have been recorded in situ (e.g. wood number 5149); some examples were lifted. All are hazel (*Corylus* sp.).

Pine cones

Five examples of Scots pine cones (*Pinus sylvestris*) were retrieved from the waterlogged wood assemblage (Pl. XXXII); a representative sample has been conserved.

Fungi

A range of puffballs and bracket fungi from the waterlogged assemblage has been conserved (Pl. XXXII). [See also van der Veen, pp. 638–9.]

Oak galls, acorns, fungal hyphae and insect infestation in oak heartwood

A small quantity of oak galls and acorns from *Quercus* spp. was retrieved and conserved (Pl. XXXII). Their presence reinforces the overwhelming evidence from the roundwood for timber being brought to the site as a raw material for subsequent preparation and fabrication; apart from timber selection and felling within the woodland environment, little off-site woodworking is indicated. Some of the larger fragments of oak heartwood display considerable encroachment into the woody tissue by fungal hyphae, and in some cases, infestation by insects.

Hazelnuts, fungal hyphae in hazel wood

A small number of hazelnuts (some charred) were retrieved and conserved (Pl. XXXII). Some larger fragments of hazel contain abundant fungal hyphae which penetrate particularly through the ray cells.

Ash keys, fungal hyphae and insect infestation in ash heartwood

The waterlogged feature preserved a number of ash keys as well as a small amount of fungal and insect infestation in larger fragments of ash heartwood.

Fruitstones and thorny twigs

Stones and thorny twigs from blackthorn (sloe) (*Prunus spinosa*) were recovered in association with the waterlogged roundwood fragments. Samples have been conserved (Pl. XXXII).

B THE ARTEFACTS [See also pp. 544–52]

The modified wood and artefacts have been illustrated in such a way as to provide as much detail as possible both about the item's dimensions, and about woodworking techniques. In the instance of a facetted item, the direction and sequence of the blows may be 'read' by studying the detail of the illustration. Where possible, the grain of the wood itself has been indicated, but care has been taken not to obscure woodworking or use-wear detail. Where necessary, the text reinforces the salient information. In the case of smoothed, abraded or worn pieces, the text supplements the illustrated information. Other modifications such as charring, cutting, shaping or conjoining are pin-pointed.

i Utilitarian items

Certain of the modified wood pieces, either through constant wear, or as a result of abrasion in their burial environment are problematic to interpret. Their function may not be immediately apparent, or indeed they may have been subjected to secondary usage. Whilst terms such as bung, stopper, dowel, peg, wedge and so on may be used for convenience, it should not be assumed that these are used in a way which excludes other possibilities.

Bungs and stoppers

Wood number 6099 (Fig. 223), made on a fragment of oak roundwood, is one such item. The upper and lower ends are slightly curved, possibly through use, and display the transverse plane of the wood structure. The longitudinal surface has a partially flattened, almost waisted, section. Both this item and wood number 6055 (Fig. 223) may be termed a bung or stopper.

Item 6055 consists of a fragment of ash roundwood with the upper surface exhibiting a flattened but irregular transverse plane of the wood (The top view of the illustration shows a split which is attributable to freeze-drying.) The lower end of the piece is roughly facetted around part of the circumference to produce a blunt point. Both 6099 and 6055 have a worn or abraded surface, although the former shows a more comprehensive wear surface than the latter.

Wood number 5741 (Fig. 223) could be interpreted as a square bung although other functions are certainly possible. This slow-grown oak fragment has not been split to produce clean-grained faces. An almost tangential longitudinal split has been produced. The illustrated section of the upper end surface clearly shows the transverse arrangement of vessels and rays (in semi-schematic form). Its square form has sub-rounded corners, possibly as a result of usage. The upper surface has an old, irregular fracture which would not necessarily impede its function.

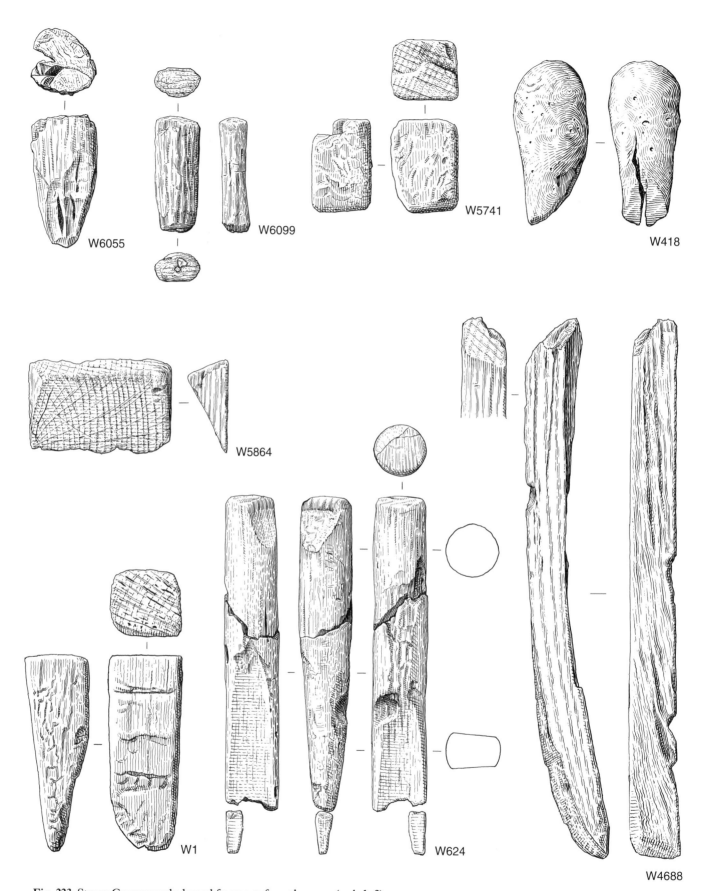

Fig. 223 Stonea Grange: worked wood fragments from the sump (scale 1:2).

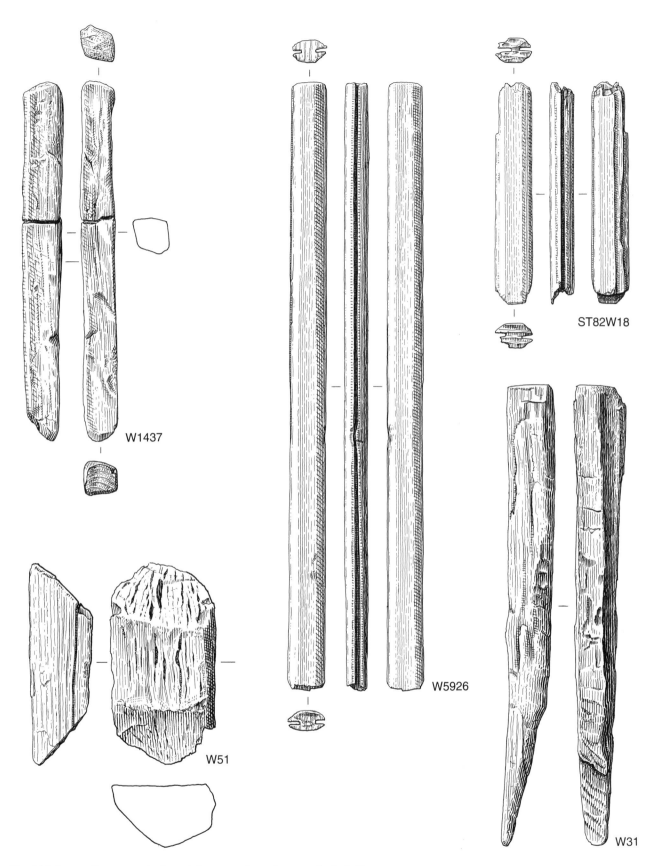

W1437

ST82W18

W5926

W51

W31

Fig. 224 Stonea Grange: worked wood fragments from the sump (scale 1:2).

Wood number 418 (Fig. 223) consists of an ash 'burr', a naturally-rounded area of abnormal growth, modified in this instance, with a diagonal cut at the base. It is only included in this section on the grounds that its natural shape may have encouraged further rounding and smoothing through use as a stopper. However this is highly conjectural.

Wedges

As already stated above, the division between items specifically shaped to function as wedges, those items of debitage such as chips and offcuts which display wedge-like cuts which could have been used as wedges, and those offcuts, which, as a by-product of carpentry, have arbitrary wedge-like features, is a difficult one to make. In some respects the distinction may be a semantic one – wedges are undoubtedly used for a variety of purposes – not least of which is the preliminary splitting of timber with wedges and hammers or mallets. Division has been suggested in this report (by the inclusion of certain items under particular headings), but overlap amongst these items must be considered.

Wood number 5864 (Fig. 223) consists of a fragment of ash, whose dorsal, wedge-shaped surface has abraded, sub-rounded edges. Some small batter marks and surface damage (not recent) is present on the dorsal surface. The wedge form is unequal in dimensions. The ventral surface is flattened with an abraded surface of minor irregularity.

Wood number 1 (Fig. 223) consists of a fragment of ash roundwood which had been facetted and abraded. The stepped facetting is confined to half of the object to produce a wedge-like end. The blunting form of end-damage at the base, together with the flattened upper surface, suggests use as a wedge which may have been hammered. Alternatively the wedge-like form could have been produced as secondary usage of a fractured stake, but the width of the piece argues against this.

Wood number 624 (Fig. 223) consists of a well-worked fragment of oak roundwood. The upper (transverse) end has been carefully worked to enhance the natural roundness of the stem diameter. This upper surface is slightly dished and worn as though it had been repeatedly struck by a mallet. A fracture scar which has left a diagonal break across one third of the transverse surface, may also have resulted from mallet blows. The shaft of the piece shows smoothing and wear-usage, possibly attributable to gripping in the hand and to functional application. The lower end develops a slightly concave wedging on both sides (though rather more pronounced on one). The lower extremity has been fractured, and only a small, abraded fragment remains. Areas of slight charring are visible.

Reference has already been made to the problematic nature of wood number 1437 (Fig. 224), a fragment of roughly squared-off oak roundwood. This fractured piece displays an approximately diagonal, semi-rounded upper transverse end. The lower end has a sub-rounded wedged appearance. There are many categories into which this item could be placed, but damage and abrasion mask its precise attribution.

Wood number 51 (Fig. 224) is another item which bridges two classificatory groups. This ash roundwood fragment displays a double wedging on the dorsal face. The ventral face retains the planar surface of the longitudinal section of the roundwood. The double wedging consists of a series of slightly stepped facets which produce a rather rough form. The object seems likely to have been more useful as a bung than as a wedge.

Slotted frames

Wood numbers 5926 and 18 (Fig. 224) consist of an interesting series of fragments, which, function aside, may be described as slotted frames. The illustrations show the fine crafting involved in producing the slots, which match more exactly in the 5926 example. Apart from the carefully excised slot cuts, both of the longitudinal surfaces are smoothly bevelled. These fragments are ash roundwood, cut both with and against the grain. Number 5926 has a smoothed and rounded upper transverse cut, whereas the lower end and both ends of number 18 have been fractured. Careful examination has confirmed that the slotting is not a natural feature, such as might result from the pith rotting away in young stems.

?Furniture

Wood number 4688 (Fig. 223) consists of a slightly curved fragment of oak. The upper end (as illustrated) has irregular, diagonally-snapped facets revealing the transverse section of the wood. The longitudinal surfaces are partially squared, but have sustained some edge damage. The lower edge has a small chisel-like bevel which creates a wedged point.

ii Structural items

Stakes, poles, posts, fencing, sticks

The section on cut roundwood (pp. 563–70) has already signalled the difficulty of division amongst fragments which have been specifically modified as stakes, poles etc. and those fragments of cut roundwood which, although 'technically' may be classified as wood-felling or woodworking waste, could well have been used as structural items.

Wood numbers 5460, 5462 and 5464 (Fig. 225) have all been modified. All were probably part of the same object and have holes which originally contained iron nails. The discoidal shape of the nailheads are preserved as corrosion stains around the nailholes.

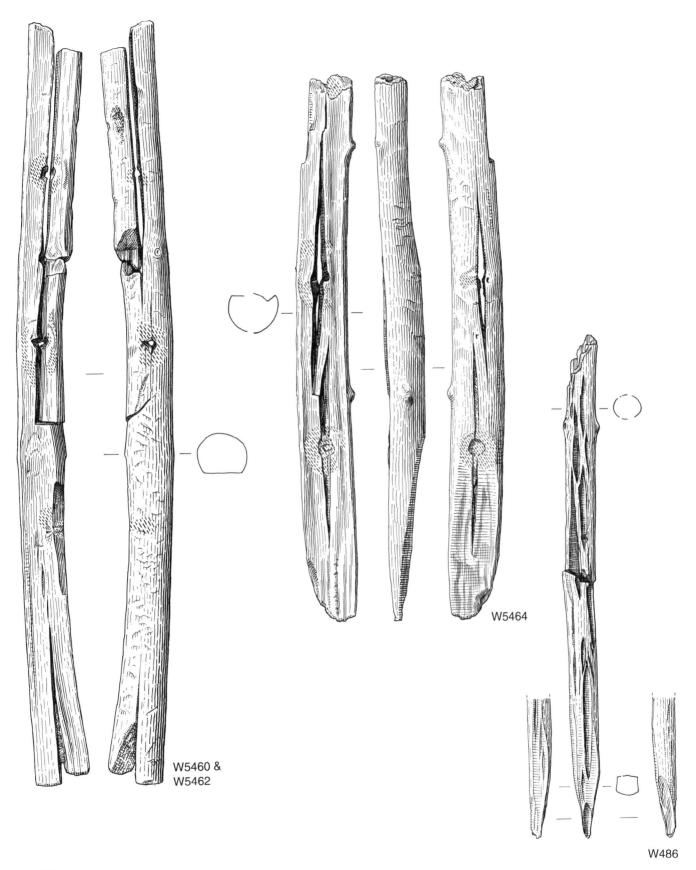

W5460 &
W5462

W5464

W486

Fig. 225 Stonea Grange: worked wood fragments from the sump (scale 1 : 2).

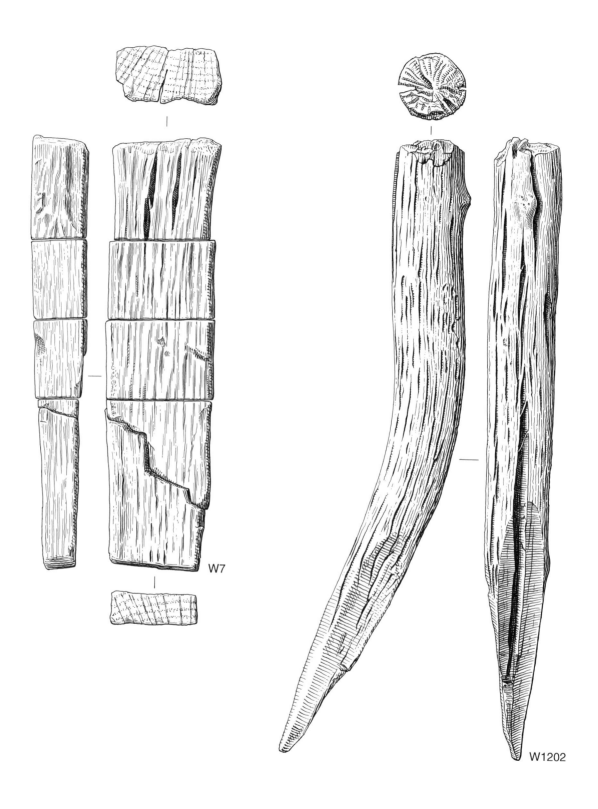

Fig. 226 Stonea Grange: worked wood fragments from the sump (scale 1 : 2).

Wood number 486 (Fig. 225) may represent an unfinished example within this structural category. The partially-facetted lower end of a narrow fragment of this hazel stick or stake, does not appear to display any traces of use or abrasion. The upper transverse end has suffered a recent fracture, and the stick has not responded well to freeze-drying.

Wood number 31 (Fig. 224) consists of a fragment of ash roundwood with a partially squared section. The upper end has been flattened and has a slight bevel in one direction. The lower end has a wedge-shaped taper to a flattened rounded point. Both the upper and lower ends suggest possible use as a short stake.

Wood number 1202 (Fig. 226) consists of a fragment of a long stake made of hazel roundwood. The upper end has been snapped and the full length of the stake is therefore unknown. The lower end has one main cut facet, diagonally splitting the roundwood to bring it to a point. Use wear on this point has abraded the surface. Freeze-drying has resulted in some recent splitting.

Wood number 6205 (Fig. 227) consists of a fragment of ash roundwood with some bark still adhering to it. The upper transverse end has been snapped in antiquity. The fragment has a pronounced natural angled curve, which, however, has not prevented its lower end being modified to a slightly curved point. This stake-like lower end comprises a primary diagonal cut to reduce the area of roundwood, and secondary smoothing or use abrasion which has resulted in a sub-rounded form. If it is not a structural item, it may be a dibber or a similar gardening or agricultural tool.

Wood number 281 (Fig. 228) is a curiosity whose classification in some respects spans both utilitarian and structural categories. It consists of an ash 'staff' (made from roundwood), roughly tapered from a knob-like 'head' to a roughly cloven, partially-pointed base. The head has been lightly trimmed to produce a domed shape. Although there is a small central flat facet at the apex of the dome, no batter marks, indicating mallet or hammer blows, are present. The lightly facetted dome shape could have functioned as a grip or palm rest, although it must be noted that the item is rather short to be classified as a staff. The distal end is not easily interpreted either. It comprises a forked or cloven terminal, unfortunately partially fractured and thus of unknown length. It is therefore difficult unequivocally to propose a structural function for this object, whilst the damage to the forked end is too great to establish whether or not it functioned as a tool haft.

Fence posts, poles, stakes, house posts and the like may not necessarily be preserved in recognisable form. Fence posts could consist of lightly trimmed branches or saplings, which, after fragmentation, may be difficult to identify in the large waterlogged wood assemblage. Similarly poles, stakes and house posts could be overlooked. There is a frequent tendency to sharpen or char the ends of such items to facilitate driving into the ground or prepared post-hole. These items may not survive well in the archaeological record because of the high wear and tear resulting from their function.

Slats, shingles, boards, linings

During the course of the excavation, over six fragments of thin oak and ash wood were described as shingles (e.g. wood numbers 2504, 5402 and 4983). There is an obvious overlap here, with, for example, barrel or bucket staves, and writing tablets, and small fragments may be difficult to attribute precisely if they are very abraded.

Wood numbers 5402 and 4983 (Fig. 227) are illustrated here. The latter has sustained both modern and ancient fracture and damage. Splitting along the rays is helpful in the production of thin shingles.

Planks

Large sections of oak and ash planks were excavated. Width measurements range from 17 to 26 cm, and over 4 m of these scaffolding planks have been recorded. Thirteen shorter oak plank fragments (13.5 to 37 cm in length by 10 to 12.6 cm in width) and one half-sectioned ash plank fragment are also present. Wood number 7 (Fig. 226) (sawn into four sections and fractured) consists of a squared-off portion of timber, possibly associated with the plank assemblage.

WOODLAND MANAGEMENT AND ECOLOGY

i Unworked roundwood fragments

Primary tree grouping

Over 91 000 fragments of unworked roundwood were excavated and analysed. Figures 209b–c summarise the primary group of trees utilised. Figures 210a–f provide individual histograms according to taxon. Of the 91 689 unworked roundwood fragments, ash (*Fraxinus* sp.) represents 35.1%, oak (*Quercus* sp.) follows with 27.8% and hazel (*Corylus* sp.) with 22.5%. Willow/poplar (*Salix/Populus*) constitutes 8.6% of the total, birch (*Betula* sp.) 4.1% and blackthorn (*Prunus spinosa*) 1.3%.

Figure 210a exhibits the high values of the 15 mm and 20 mm stem diameter measurement categories for unworked ash (*Fraxinus* sp.) roundwood fragments. A diminishing curve follows for the 30 mm, 40 mm, 50 mm and 60 mm categories. The latter is matched by the 10 mm category. Only two fragments represent the 70 mm stem diameter size. As suggested earlier in this section, it is possible that the focus on smaller roundwood amongst such taxa as

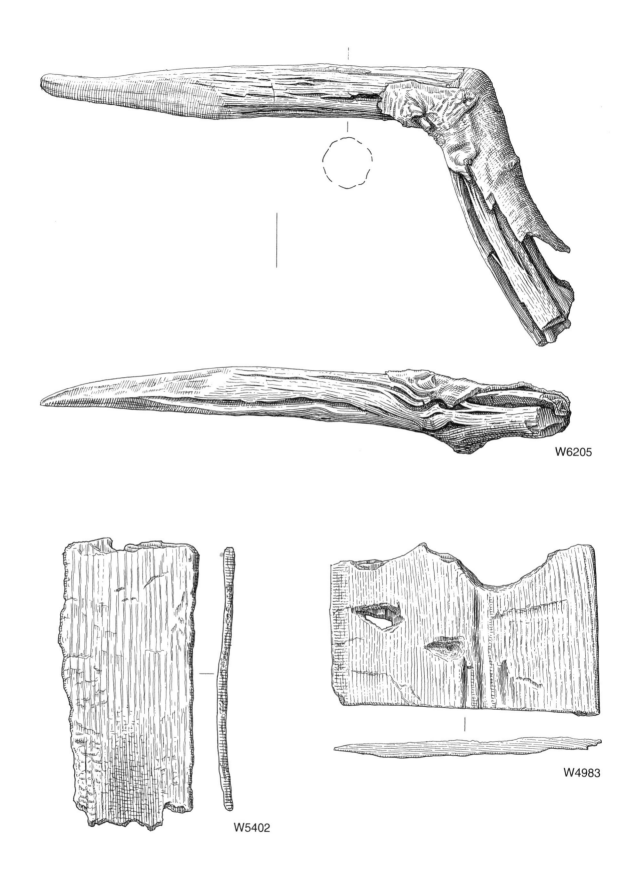

W6205

W5402

W4983

Fig. 227 Stonea Grange: worked wood fragments from the sump (scale 1:2).

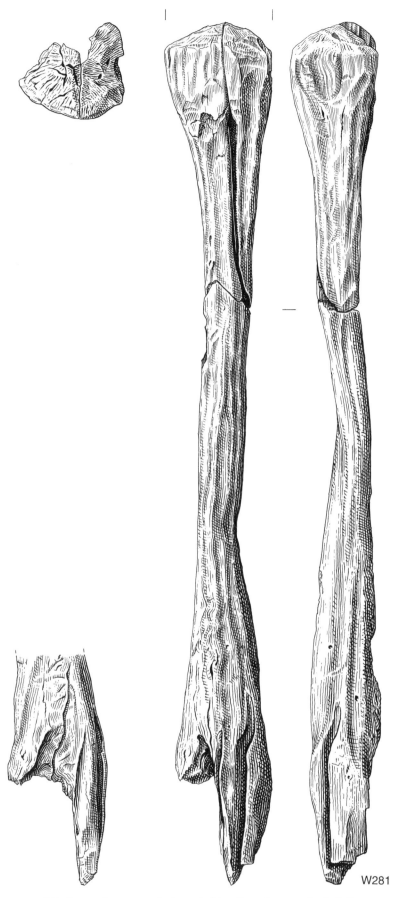

W281

Fig. 228 Stonea Grange: worked wood object from the sump (scale 1:2).

hazel, ash, willow/poplar and birch, combined with the selection of examples such as blackthorn roundwood, reflects

i coppicing activities for the production of narrow, straight wands and sticks for use in fencing, hedging, hurdles, wattles (and other elements for timber buildings), traps, basketry, wickerwork, screens, osiers and the myriad uses of withies;

ii trimming of woodland trees, hedges and shrubs (on both living and felled timber);

iii the by-products of the trimming of larger roundwood prior to use as fuel, structural timber, transport vehicles or artefacts.

Figure 210b provides the breakdown for oak (*Quercus* sp.) unworked roundwood fragments. A similar patterning to that of ash may be detected, with probably similar causation. Figure 210c for hazel (*Corylus* sp.) has a marked peak (50.2%) for the 15 mm stem diameter range, falling to 26.5% for the 20 mm category. Clustered on either side are broadly comparable values for the 10 mm and 30 mm categories (12.1% and 7.9% respectively). In the coppicing hypothesis suggested above, (i) seems most feasible, with elements of (ii) and (iii) also possible. Though considerably smaller in quantity, the values for willow/poplar (*Salix/Populus*) in Fig. 210d, mirror that of hazel. The birch (*Betula* sp.) histogram (Fig. 210e) shows high values for both the 15 mm and 20 mm categories, which, combined, amount to 85.7%. Birch is a relatively fast-growing coloniser of waste ground and open scrub or acid heathlands. As such, it would provide a ready source of narrow sticks, pliable fencing raw material, or light disposable frames. The final taxon in the primary tree grouping is blackthorn (*Prunus spinosa*). Figure 210f demonstrates the now-familiar peak for the 15 mm category, flanked by 20 mm and 10 mm in terms of relative abundance. The shrubby characteristics of blackthorn are used to their full advantage here; stout, thorny stems providing ideal hedging possibilities.

Secondary tree and shrub grouping

Figure 209d summarises the secondary grouping of trees and shrubs within the 'unworked roundwood fragments' category. The remaining 0.6% comprises field maple (*Acer* sp.) 0.29%, (Scots) pine (*Pinus* cf. *sylvestris*), elder (*Sambucus* sp.), alder (*Alnus* sp.), beech (*Fagus* sp.), dog rose (*Rosa canina*), hornbeam (*Carpinus betulus*), guelder rose (*Viburnum opulus*), sweet chestnut (*Castanea sativa*), whitebeam (*Sorbus* sp.), walnut (*Juglans regia*) (probably an import or a more recent fragment), dogwood (*Cornus* sp.) and Traveller's Joy (*Clematis vitalba*). Study of Figs 211a–e and g – the histograms for pine, field maple, elder, beech, alder and sweet chestnut – show a familiar pattern, where the 15 mm and 20 mm categories vie for peak values. Figures 211f (hornbeam) and 211h (dog rose), however, display 15 mm and 10 mm as peak values.

ii The woodland

The importance of woodland as a source of raw materials (animal and human foodstuffs, fuel, fodder and building materials) has sometimes been overlooked as an essential attribute of the rural and urban economic structure alike. The 'farming' of woodland to produce reliable resources may equal the more 'visible' system of agriculture. In Britain, evidence from Neolithic and later period settlements suggests a level of forest clearance for agriculture in key regions. Whilst woodland clearance for roads, military installations and settlements might still be necessary in the Roman period, the balance of trade, economy and maintenance of the resources of the surrounding environment had to be nurtured by careful management. Close proximity to fuel supplies for the Roman pottery industries, for example, seem to have outstripped the need to be within a central (urban) market area. Systems of land divisions and holdings could equally feasibly be applied to tracts of woodland, both having considerable economic potential and value, and timber being a recognised trade item. Market gardens and orchards too should not be undervalued.

If there were not a question of the selection preferences for timber on the part of the occupants of Stonea, the relative frequencies of the woody taxa could be viewed as a proportionate representation of the environment of the site. Recent research by Rodwell and others (Rodwell 1991) has characterised a number of British vegetation communities. Woodlands are assigned W designations followed by a number. For easy reference, these W numbers are used here. Such studies of present plant communities suggest potential models for the recognition of the impact of coppicing on hazel, ash and oak in *Fraxinus excelsior–Acer campestre–Mercurialis perennis* (W8) and *Quercus robur–Pteridium aquilinum–Rubus fruticosus* (W10) woodlands, and also for oak in *Quercus petraea–Betula pubescens–Oxalis acetellosa* (W11) and *Quercus petraea–Betula pubescens–Dicranum majus* (W17) woodlands (Rodwell 1991). These models document the distinctive plant communities which develop after coppicing, how replanting affects the woodland character and how neglect of woodland management develops a response in the plant communities. The nature of botanical variation amongst mixed deciduous and oak–birch woodlands could be reflected, at least to some degree, in the components of the assemblage represented by the 'unworked roundwood fragments' category (Figs 209b–11h).

A recognisable fen carr and alder–willow–birch fen woodland community is modelled by Rodwell and others (Rodwell 1991) as *Salix cinerea–Betula pubescens–Phragmites australis* woodland (W2) with *Alnus glutinosa* in the canopy. *Rubus fruticosus*, *Rosa canina* and *Myrica gale* may be present in the understorey. Certain other species may achieve local dominance, for example at Wicken Fen (Cambridgeshire) where *Frangula alnus* and *Rhamnus catharticus* form major additional elements of the woodland. (Godwin 1936; Godwin *et al* 1974). (Neither *Frangula* nor *Rhamnus* is represented in the waterlogged wood or charcoal assemblages from Stonea, however). Some fen woodland subcommunities may contain occasional well-grown oak (*Quercus robur*) and ash (*Fraxinus excelsior*) trees interspersed among shorter willow and birch, with guelder rose (*Viburnum opulus*) and hawthorn (*Crataegus monogyna*) forming part of the underbrush. Secondary colonisation of fen woodland may include blackthorn (*Prunus spinosa*), but considerable variation in local fen communities in terms of tree and shrub heights coupled with tree and shrub cover, produces a mosaic of vegetation. Should such fen woodland communities be the major source for the Stonea wood, it is clear that particular processes and/or careful management of certain woody taxa would be necessary, in order to sustain the dominant use of ash, oak, hazel and to some degree birch and willow.

Whilst it is entirely possible to list ash, field maple, hazel, birch and oak as components of the *Fraxinus–Acer–Mercurialis* woodland with subcomponents including hornbeam, whitebeam, dogwood, elm, lime, sycamore and holly, such a woodland community favours heavy, base-rich, moist soils. Hawthorn, elder and blackthorn may favour the more free-draining soils within *Fraxinus–Acer–Mercurialis* woodland subcommunities. Alder, willow (both of which coppice well) and guelder rose may feature on moister soil. Some dog rose may occur in the field layers of certain subcommunities. Utilisation of such managed woodlands with their frequent features of coppiced undergrowth, principally ash, hazel, field maple and oak as coppice-with-standards (Rodwell 1991) must therefore have relied on a co-operative effort on the part of the inhabitants of Stonea. This co-operative mechanism has to nurture carefully those areas within the Stonea 'exploitation zone' which have suitable soils, perhaps with base-rich ground water, to sustain woodland of these characteristics. Alternatively, the co-operation has to extend to a rather more far-reaching trade or marketing system with areas which are naturally more conducive to such woodland communities.

Beech (*Fagus sylvatica*) is poorly represented in the Stonea wood assemblage. Beech dominates at least three woodland communities in Britain today, designated as *Fagus sylvatica–Mercurialis perennis* (W12), *Fagus sylvatica–Rubus fruticosus* (W14) and *Fagus sylvatica–Deschampsia flexuosa* (W15) by Rodwell (1991). Interestingly, for W12, Rodwell notes: 'Coppiced stands are rare: *Fagus* pollards well but it produces rather weak coppice shoots or it is perhaps more prone to disease when coppiced and is only very occasionally seen as the dominant in coppice underwood forms of the community.' (Rodwell 1991, 217; Rackham 1980; Peterken 1981) Free-draining, calcareous, base-rich soils are favoured by W12 beech woodlands, principally on limestones, whilst W14 beech woodland occurs on lower base-status brown-earths. At the other end of the spectrum, W15

tolerates infertile, base-poor, usually free-draining lowland soils.

Turning towards those plant communities in which oak predominates, such as *Quercus robur–Pteridium aquilinum–Rubus fruticosus* (W10), *Quercus petraea–Betula pubescens–Oxalis acetosella* (W11), *Quercus* spp. *–Betula* spp.*–Deschampsia flexuosa* (W16) and *Quercus petraea–Betula pubescens–Dicranum majus* (W17) woodlands (Rodwell 1991), W10, W11 and W17 provide the best candidates for a considerable coppice component. Only in W11 is there also likely to be a moderate hazel coppice fraction and a small ash coppice component.

None of these alternatives has to be mutually exclusive. The inhabitants of Stonea may well have been tapping into the resources of a number of wood, scrub and fenland plant communities. After all, pine is also present in the Stonea assemblage; usually a clear indicator of acid soils. Sweet chestnut usually takes place within *Quercus–Pteridium–Rubus* woodland (W10) (Rodwell 1991). Many of the above species, rejuggled in relative proportions, form the basis of a variety of documented woodland and scrub community descriptions according to the soil characteristics. It is the human selection and management factor which must override one-to-one matching of the relative frequencies of the taxa, as illustrated by the Stonea wood, with the modular presentations of modern woodland and scrub communities, invaluable though that documentation may be.

The extent to which woodland management practices comprised thinning-out of top branches on trees, cutting back to ground level to produce coppiced wood and ensuring no particular tree or shrub was overexploited, cannot be accurately quantified for the Stonea wood assemblage. There is a noticeable amount of forked roundwood branch fragments (an illustrated example, wood number 26 (Fig. 207) has one diagonally cut end). Such cut forked branch fragments (ash, oak and hazel) tend to substantiate the suggestion of thinning-out tree crowns and lower branches also. Some of the smaller roundwood ash, hazel, oak and birch fragments exhibit heel scars where the branches and twigs have been torn off a larger branch. It is relevant to reiterate here that a certain amount of this sort of information has been lost due to the high fragmentation factor present in the material. Some oak, hazel and ash root material is present. It is not impossible that such trees could have been growing within the Stonea settlement, but an alternative explanation invokes the uprooting of saplings for use as poles, stakes or fence posts.

Analysis of the assemblage of roundwood fragments shows a trend towards spring and autumn felling, but the character of the archaeological context of the material again cautions against overinterpretation or overreliance on possible quantification of the wood. The seasoning of timbers by allowing them to dry out, usually involves splitting large branches and stacking in such a manner as to encourage the free circulation of air. Planks may be seasoned by radial splitting to avoid warping, although some swelling or shrinkage is possible. Where longitudinal splitting or cleaving of wood is not possible, burning may provide an alternative method. Axes, adzes and wedges are the most common woodworking felling and splitting tools used to prepare wood for stacking and seasoning.

A small amount of partial charring is present on some of the Stonea wood, mainly on ash and oak unworked round-wood fragments and on a few unmodified fragments of oak heartwood. A few small ash chips have been slightly charred also. There is no evidence of regular burning of larger timbers as an alternative tree-felling method, although such evidence may remain principally on the site of the felling episode within the woodland, or alternatively have become detached and become 'anonymous' within the rest of the charcoal assemblage.

iii The charcoal

Useful comparisons may be made between the charred and the organic components of the large waterlogged feature, although the former is significantly smaller in quantity than the latter (Fig. 214a–c). Analysis and interpretation of the charred remains follows below – for both the Roman and the earlier pre-Roman phases of the site. Certain elements of the transport and deposition of charcoal fragments always require careful interpretive attention. Charcoal fragments may arrive in archaeological features through a variety of depositional agencies (including earthworm activity, percolating water and so on) – hence the reliance on the part of the archaeologist and environmental specialist alike on 'closed contexts' where sealed deposits ensure a closer association of environmental with artefactual material. Charcoal and other (charred) plant remains from contexts such as post-holes, (rubbish) pits, latrines, cesspits, ditches, gullies and wells, consequently present a series of interpretational problems. One cannot automatically be sure exactly where the material derives from, when or how it was transported to and deposited in the context. Charcoal in a post-hole, for example, may represent the in situ remnants of the original wooden post (possibly later charred), but could equally well have become trapped in the post-hole structure through dispersal mechanisms at any point in the feature's infill. This may not necessarily even be representative of the main habitation phases of the site.

With these caveats in mind therefore, a cumulative histogram has been presented for the charcoal from such features during the Late Bronze Age occupation of the site (Fig. 214a and c), and a similar breakdown for that of the Roman phases of settlement (Fig. 214b–c). The different taxa may represent the same range of elements as the waterlogged wood, i.e. artefacts, woodworking debris, fencing, planks, linings, withies, staves, posts etc. After charring and/or fragmentation, such utilisation is more difficult to pin-point. Coupled with the

problems posed by their provenance in particular kinds of contexts (pits, post-holes, ditches and the like), one may make more general rather than specific suggestions about their use and function. Hearth or kiln contexts may provide closer associations for determining selection of timbers for fuel. Relative frequencies may, however, yield a useful comparative yardstick against which to compare the relative frequencies of the (waterlogged) wood, when attempting palaeoecological reconstructions.

A further complication is introduced by the fact that under the same conditions of burning certain taxa fragment more readily than others. Some may even be entirely consumed – to be present in the archaeological record only in the form of an ashy powder. This reinforces the value of comparisons with non-charred organic assemblages – a particularly rare occurrence on most archaeological projects.

Turning to the details of the charcoal assemblages – relative frequencies for all taxa in both the Bronze Age and Roman phases are summarised in Fig. 214. The Bronze Age phases comprise a total of 216 fragments. Ideally, quantification of charcoal would not depend on the counting of charcoal fragments, as fragmentation may occur as a result of a variety of factors. Counting fragments may therefore be fairly meaningless, as it is not clear exactly what is being evaluated. Alternative procedures may include the expression of relative charcoal percentages by weight – an attempt to introduce an 'objective' standard. This method is not feasible for the charcoal from Stonea, as the charcoal fragments derive from waterlogged and non-waterlogged features alike. Any attempts to air or oven-dry the waterlogged material might introduce yet another set of variables to render the results unreliable. Another alternative method of expressing relative proportions of charcoal fragments quantitatively involves the measurement of charcoal volume within a given constant of sediment. This, again, is not suitable for the waterlogged and non-waterlogged range of contexts. Despite disadvantages, the Stonea charcoal fragments have therefore been enumerated and used in comparative terms on this basis.

Charcoal from Bronze Age contexts (Fig. 214a and c) collectively reveals oak (*Quercus* sp.) as the highest value with 26.4%, followed by hazel (*Corylus* sp.) at 23.1%. Ash (*Fraxinus* sp.) represents 16.7%, hawthorn (*Crataegus* sp.) 13.9%, birch (*Betula* sp.) 6.9%, blackthorn (*Prunus spinosa*) and willow/poplar (*Salix/Populus*) each 6.5%. The stem diameters of the fragments indicate small roundwood and twigs. High values in all taxa for the 5 mm stem diameter category, amounts to 50.9% of the total. The 10 mm stem diameter category accounts for 34.7%. Hazel, ash, oak and willow/poplar fragments constitute the 20 mm stem size (0.9%). It is interesting to note that although hawthorn falls well within many of the mixed deciduous plant communities (in ecological terms), it is first seen at Stonea as charcoal not wood.

Domestic hearth residues may contain this range of small diameter roundwood as kindling material. Larger logs are frequently entirely consumed in high temperatures at the centre of a fire. A similar mechanism may operate in industrial contexts such as pottery kilns, ovens, furnaces and so on. Much of the heavy-duty fuel is consumed and remains only as ashy powder, whereas stoking material, kindling and fuel around the perimeter of the features may escape total combustion. There is an increasing need for the evaluation of charcoal distribution in a spatial sense on archaeological sites, to allow for more detailed recognition of spatial patternings according to contexts. In turn, this may lead to an increasingly fine-tuned interpretation of the charred assemblage. Not all archaeological contexts are suitable for this sort of analysis, because of the problems of movement of charcoal and redeposition, but more studies of such 'context-related variation' amongst charred assemblages remains a research objective for the subject.

Figure 214b summarises the collective charcoal frequencies from Roman contexts. A total of 3474 fragments was recovered. Hazel holds the highest value with 32.4% of the total. Ash accounts for 20.6% and is followed by oak with 13.7%. The remainder comprises willow/poplar 10.1%, blackthorn 7%, elder 6%, hawthorn 4.4%, birch 2.1%, alder 1.7%, field maple 1%, whitebeam 0.5% and dogwood 0.5%.

A similar situation exists for the charcoal assemblage from Roman contexts as for the wild plants range from this period (van der Veen, pp. 613–39), in that a wider variety of taxa is encountered compared with the Late Bronze Age period. For the charcoal, this may partly be attributable to greater quantities. Nevertheless, it is useful to note how closely van der Veen's wild plant listings concur with the charcoal. Both contain hazel, elder, hawthorn, blackthorn, and ash. However, no blackberry (*Rubus fruticosus*), box (*Buxus sempervirens*) or sweet gale (*Myrica gale*) charcoal is present in these Roman contexts.

Figure 214b summarises the cumulative totals for the main woody taxa as plots for the charcoal assemblage compared with the waterlogged wood (Figs 209a–b). As a general comparative point of reference, the results are self-evident, but the difficulties of fine correlation or contrast are too great to sustain reliable statements. Charcoal fragments may be produced through a variety of deliberate or accidental activities, and may become incorporated in archaeological layers through a complex series of depositional processes. Detailed interpretation of the fragments depends heavily, therefore, on contextual information and on the security of close associations with archaeological material in an undisturbed stratigraphic matrix. The value of the Stonea situation lies in the wealth of comparative (and to some degree corroborative) information from the waterlogged wood assemblage, against which the charcoal results may be placed in focus. In other words, if the charcoal alone had been available for analysis, a restricted interpretation would have had to follow. On account of the extensive and detailed information from the waterlogged wood assemblage, however, the range of application and use of the timber may be placed on a more secure foundation of interpretation.

Acknowledgements

During the period of primary analysis of the waterlogged wood, I should like to acknowledge the staff of the British Museum Organics Conservation section, particularly John Lee, who provided a constant source of information about the conservation treatment of the Stonea waterlogged assemblage, and a productive working environment. I should like to thank Meredydd Moores for producing the wood illustrations and for taking so much trouble to illustrate the direction and sequence of facetting on the wood chips and artefacts in a self-explanatory fashion. My grateful thanks go also to Morven Leese for helpful discussion and practical input regarding the quantitative presentation of the data. I am indebted to Sheridan Bowman for reading a draft of this report and making many vital critical suggestions. Finally, I should like to express a long-standing acknowledgement to Geoffrey Dimbleby who provided me with an early source of inspiration in vegetation studies.

HUMAN BONES

Janice Conheeney   (Fig. 229; Pl. XIVb)
[See also Stallibrass, pp. 589, 594]

LOCATION AND PROBABLE DATE

Human bone from six locations was examined. Three post-holes of building R10 had bone deposits adjacent to them (Fig. 71, p. 193). The building was dated later second to early third century AD. Two other deposits came from the uppermost fill of possible latrine pits: pit 1563, the single fill of which was dated to the third century; and pit 1695, the uppermost fill of which was dated to the third or fourth century. The bone from pit 1695 was burnt. The final deposit, a single femur head, was recovered from a ditch fill of the early third century AD.

TREATMENT OF THE DEPOSITS

As association between the deposits was only likely for the post-hole burials, given the differences in dating, each context has been dealt with individually. Where possible, measurements were taken and the preservation of that particular bone described to indicate the probable accuracy of the measurement.

Age estimates were arrived at using diaphysis length following Johnston (1962) and the stage of dental development after Ubelaker (1989). It must be stressed that the ages derived in this way are estimates of the development age of the individual and are not true chronological ages. They should be used as a guide to the range of ages present at Stonea and give the level of development of each individual relative to others at the site. The error inherent in both of the ageing methods used, i.e. that they are based on American Indian data and White American/American Indian mixed data respectively and were applied to a European population here, should also be borne in mind.

The bones were also examined for pathological changes and congenital abnormalities.

1 2173 (EEA)   (Fig. 71, p. 193; Fig. 229)

This was the post-hole burial to the west side of building R10. The remains were those of a fairly complete, articulated infant with the exception of the cranium, most of which was missing. The body was north–south aligned with the head end to the south. Following Sprague's definition (1968) the upper legs were semi-flexed, the lower legs flexed and both legs were more or less together. One arm was bent in front of the body and the other arm was disarticulated. From the position of the limbs and the grouping of the vertebrae and ribs it appeared that the infant was lying on its right side. After in situ drawing, the bones were lifted individually.

The bones

The condition of the bone was reasonably good although most shafts were broken into two or three pieces and the diaphysis ends were eroded. The bones consisted of:

3 tiny fragments of cranium.
Left medial clavicle with about half the shaft.
Left and right humerus.
Left and right ulna.
Left and right innominates (all 3 parts).
Left and right femur.
Left and right tibia.
Left and right fibula shafts with both ends missing.
2 left and 4 right thoracic vertebral unfused arches.
4 left and 1 right lumbar vertebral unfused arches.
15 vertebral bodies.
49 very fragmentary pieces of rib.
6 probable metacarpals.
3 probable metatarsals.
1 unknown metacarpal/metatarsal.
4 hand phalanges.

It was of interest that the missing parts of the skeleton – one and a half clavicles, two scapulae and the cervical vertebrae – were all the upper part of the skeleton which fits with the skull being missing. Otherwise the skeleton was practically complete except for parts of the hands and feet which would be very easy to miss while excavating.

Measurements

Table 36 Stonea Grange: infant burial 1, measurements

	Left Condition	Length (mm)	Right Condition	Length (mm)
Femur	Complete, quite good	81	2 pieces, very eroded proximal end	83
Tibia	Complete, quite good	72	Complete, but slightly eroded ends	71
Fibula	Shaft, no ends	–	2 pieces, no ends	–
Humerus	2 pieces, proximal end quite damaged	71	Complete, distal end slightly damaged	71
Ulna	Compete, distal end quite damaged	65	2 pieces, damaged distal end	–
Radius	2 pieces, not complete	–	3 pieces	c. 58
Widest part of ilium	Complete	35.5	Broken edge	—

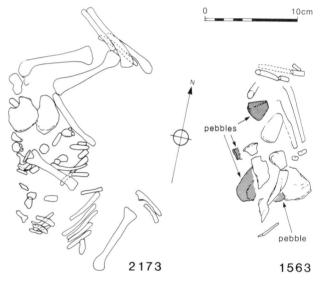

Fig. 229 Stonea Grange: infant burials, cat. nos 1 and 4 (scale 1:4).

Age

Johnston's figure for diaphysis length in millimetres for the quoted age group is given in parenthesis following the age estimation.

Femur length	New born to 0.5 years (78.84 ± 7.23)
Tibia length	New born to 0.5 years (69.28 ± 6.33)
Humerus length	New born to 0.5 years (67.66 ± 5.94)
Radius length	New born to 0.5 years (55.05 ± 4.24)
Ulna length	New born to 0.5 years (63.70 ± 4.74)

As all measurements taken here (see Table 36) fell within the upper range of length given by Johnston for that age group, the infant was probably 3–6 months old rather than new born to 6 months. However, it must be noted that Johnston was working on an American sample, so caution should be exercised in attempting too precise an estimate.

From stage of fusion evidence, the two halves of the vertebral or neural arches had not yet fused, which usually occurs between 1 and 3 years (Bass 1987), confirming that the infant was certainly below 3 years.

Pathology

One right and one left lumbar vertebral arch (which could well be a pair) had a tiny foramen each on the inferior surface of the bend between the pedicle and the lamina. There was also possible very slight pitting on the medial end, dorsal surface of two ribs, although poor preservation made this difficult to affirm.

There was no other pathology or congenital defects.

2 2178 (EEF)   (Fig. 71, p. 193; Pl. XIVb)

This was the more northerly post-hole burial of the two on the east side of building R10. After photography, the burial was lifted as a soil block. Unfortunately, this had dried out so many of the bones were disturbed and loose where the soil had cracked and moved, and nearly all had several recent breaks due to the same cause. This particularly applies to the cranium which consisted of 107 fragments, the average size of which was less than 1 cm square and many were very tiny indeed. Viewing the burial in the block, it appeared to be the remains of one articulated infant which had been recorded previously as being north–south aligned with the head to the south. The arms were too disturbed to comment on but the remainder of the body appeared to be lying on the right side facing east. The upper legs were tightly flexed and the lower leg flexed (after Sprague 1968).

Other than their fragmentary state, the bones were in a reasonably strong condition. Therefore, in order to examine them in more detail, the loose bones were picked off, any loose soil was dry sieved using a 1.5 mm mesh, and finally all the concreted deposits were wet sieved at the same mesh size as this appeared to be the only way to break down these hardened lumps without causing further fractures to the bones.

The bones

Cranium: 107 fragments; most parts represented. Notable absences were the maxilla and the left petrous part of the temporal bone.

Mandible: 7 fragments, unfused symphysis.

Left and right humerus.
Left and right radius.
Left and right ulna.
Left and right femur.
Left and right tibia.
Left and right fibula.
Right ischium.
Left medial clavicle with about half of the shaft.
4 vertebral bodies.
1 right and 1 left cervical vertebral unfused arch.
9 right and 9 left thoracic vertebral unfused arch.
3 right and 1 left lumbar vertebral unfused arch.
5 scraps of unidentified vertebrae.
58 fragments of rib (including a complete right first rib).

7 metacarpals.
4 hand phalanges.
5 metatarsals.
3 foot phalanges.
4 unidentified fragments metacarpals/metatarsals.
1 unidentified epiphysis.
2 fragments which could be scapula.

There was noticeably no ilium but as much tinier bone was recovered it was unlikely that this was lost due to the sieving process.

Dentition

2 upper central incisors, *c.* half of the crown formed.
2 upper lateral incisors, *c.* third of the crown formed.
3 lower incisors, *c.* half or two thirds of the crown formed.
1 canine tip.
3 complete cusp tips for molars.
2 3-cusp completed molars.

Measurements

Table 37 Stonea Grange: infant burial 2, measurements

	Left Condition	Length (mm)	Right Condition	Length (mm)
Humerus	2 pieces, not good join	68	2 pieces, distal end missing	–
Femur	2 pieces	79.5	At least 5 pieces, proximal end crushed	–
Tibia	2 pieces, good condition	68	At least 3 pieces and distal end crushed but measured *in situ*	68

Age

Humerus length   New born to 0.5 years (67.66 ± 5.94).
Femur length   New born to 0.5 years (78.84 ± 7.23).
Tibia length   New born to 0.5 years (69.28 ± 6.33).

The stage of development of the dentition indicated an age of birth ± 2 months. Given the length measurements placing the infant in the middle of Johnston's range, the two pieces of evidence were combined to give an age estimate of birth to 3 months. This very young age was also confirmed by the unfused mandibular symphysis as this union is usually completed by 1 year of age.

Pathology

There were no noticeable pathological changes or congenital defects.

3 2177 (EEE)   (Fig. 71)

This burial was positioned to the south of no. 2, immediately inside the south-east corner of building R10. The remains were those of an articulated infant, fairly complete, though lacking the cranium. The body was north–south aligned lying on its right side with the head to the south. The legs were flexed as no. 1. After in situ photography, the bones were lifted individually.

The bones

The bones were in a reasonably good condition and comprised *c*. 60% of the skeleton. They consisted of:

Mandible.
Right humerus.
Left distal humerus.
Right proximal ulna and radius.
Left radius.
Left and right femur.
Left and right tibia.
Left and right fibula.
Right ilium.
Left and right pubis.
Left and right medial clavicle.
Right head and edge of scapula.
1 left rib, 1 right rib and multiple fragments.
3 cervical vertebral unfused arches.
1 sacral vertebra.

Dentition

1 lower central incisor
1 lower lateral incisor

Measurements

Table 38 Stonea Grange: infant burial 3, measurements

	Left Condition	Length (mm)	Right Condition	Length (mm)
Tibia	Good, complete	67.0	Good, complete	66.5
Ilium	–	–	Good, complete	34.0

Age

Tibia length, left   New born to 0.5 years (78.84 ± 7.23)
Tibia length, right   New born to 0.5 years (78.84 ± 7.23)

The stage of development of the single assessable tooth indicated an age of birth ± 2 months, while the evidence of diaphysis length and stage of fusion (mandibular symphysis) gave an age estimate of under 1 year. The combined evidence suggested a newborn infant, within the bracket birth to 3 months.

Pathology

None

4 1563 (DCP)   (Fig. 229)

This was reportedly an articulated burial with north–south alignment, head to south, from the surface fill of the possible latrine pit 1563. However, from the field drawing this did not appear to be the case; the remains appeared to be disarticulated.

The bones

Again the bones were in quite good condition although fragmented. The cranium had been lifted mainly as a block so a similar procedure was followed to free the bones as that for infant no. 2.

43 cranial fragments with most parts represented and including the maxilla and mandible.

Distal two thirds right humerus.
Right and left radius.
Right and left ulna.
Proximal two thirds right tibia.
Distal third left tibia.
(these tibiae definitely did not unite)
9 metacarpals.
8 hand phalanges.

Dentition

Left and right mandible, unfused.
Right maxilla.
2 upper central incisors, half crown.
1 upper lateral incisor, probably right, half crown.
2 upper first molars, cusps completed.
2 lower first molars, cusps completed.
2 second probably lower molars, 3 cusps formed.
2 canines, crown half formed.

Measurements

Table 39 Stonea Grange: infant burial 4, measurements

	Left Condition	Length (mm)	Right Condition	Length (mm)
Radius	Complete, 2 pieces proximal end slightly damaged	54.5	Complete, 2 pieces	54
Ulna	Complete, 2 pieces	61	Complete, 3 pieces	62

Age

Radius   New born to 0.5 years (55.05 ± 4.24).
Ulna   New born to 0.5 years (63.70 ± 4.74).

The measurements taken here were slightly to the lower end of Johnston's range indicating that the infant was probably 0–3 months. This was confirmed by the age estimate derived from dental development which was birth ± 2 months. That the mandibular symphysis had not yet fused also agreed with this young age.

Pathology

There were no pathologies or congenital defects.

5 1574 (DDB)

This was a single fragment, the proximal third of a left femur diaphysis found in the fill of ditch 20, (only *c.* 13 m distant from the position of no. 4 above). To judge from size and form the infant was very similar in age to infant no. 1, i.e. 3–6 months, although it must be stressed that this was a very crude estimate with no other evidence to confirm it.

There was no pathology.

6 1695 (DIC)

This was a deposit of burnt bone from the possible latrine pit 1695. No information was recorded on its position in the ground.

All the fragments were a blue-grey and white colour which indicates that all the parts were burnt with a similar efficiency, probably at temperatures greater than 800 °C, and the large portion of white colouration suggested that prolonged exposure to these high temperatures, and a good oxygen supply, were maintained (Ubelaker 1989).

The bones

Fragment of proximal articular surface of tibia. Appeared to have been fully fused, i.e. adult.

Ischial tuberosity, probably right. Epiphysis was fused on, therefore adult. Also 1 fragment of probably right acetabulum and 5 other fragments of probable pelvis.

2 pieces of cranium, one possibly root of zygoma, one a fragment of petrous part of temporal bone.

1 fragment of long bone cortex of a thickness which suggested humerus.

16 fragments of larger long bones, e.g. possibly femur or tibia.

7 fragments of thinner cortex probably fibula or humerus, maybe radius or ulna.

19 unidentifiable fragments, most of which were lumps of cancellous matter or tiny and thin fragments of cortex.

The fragments ranged from a couple of millimetres square to the largest at *c.* 3 cm square. The squareness of the majority of pieces despite the absence of transverse fracturing suggested that the remains may possibly have been smashed up, although this could be accidental damage due to handling of brittle, burnt bone. Altogether 5 g of fragments were unidentified of a total deposit of 95 g, i.e. 5.3% of the deposit remained unidentified.

There was nothing to suggest that there was more than one adult present in the deposit. There was no indication of the sex of that adult. The bone was so efficiently burnt and with the absence of any diagnostic landmarks, it was conceivable that not all may be human. However, the general size and form would allow the identifications given above. If correct most areas of the skeleton were represented, that is, the deposit was not made up of only part of a body.

CONCLUSION

The remains of six individuals were recovered but apart from infants 1–3 the burials were not associated. The individuals were one adult represented by burnt bone, three infants of birth to three months and two infants of three to six months. It was of interest to note the similarity in orientation and position of the three posthole burials, although the infants differ slightly in age. The possible latrine pit burial 1563 was also positioned in a similar manner.

ANIMAL BONES

Sue Stallibrass   (Figs 230–3; Pl. XXXI)

1 HAND-RECOVERED MATERIAL

Methods of recovery

Most of the material excavated at Stonea was recovered during trowelling by hand. In addition, some was recovered from bulk samples that were wet sieved through 500 μm mesh. The botanical material from these samples is reported upon by Marijke van der Veen (pp. 613–39). The first part of this report is concerned only with the hand-recovered material, the second part with the residues from wet-sieved samples.

The standard of recovery by hand was very high, with small fragments forming a considerable portion of the collection (see below). During hot weather, the indurated nature of the sediments led to the fragmentation of many bones during excavation. Whilst this has resulted in the loss of some information due to the destruction of measurable parts of some bones, the inclusion of most of the small pieces of broken bones further suggests that the excavators were diligent in their recovery of small fragments.

Methods of recording

Two methods of recording of animal bones have been used for this collection. Approximately half of the collection (8580 fragments) were recorded individually for archaeological and zoological traits. The archaeological traits include aspects of preservation, fragmentation, and butchery (see below for full details). The zoological traits include tooth eruption and wear, epiphyseal fusion and metrical data. This 'sample' was considered sufficient for the investigation of archaeological and taphonomic variables, considering the time-consuming nature of the method, and is referred to as the 'detailed sample'.

For the other half of the collection (10 096 fragments), only the zoological data were recorded routinely (1438 fragments). This is referred to as the 'selective sample'.

The databases were recorded using SPSSX on mainframe computers. For the whole collection, any unusual aspects were noted by hand.

The material

Most of the animal bones come from contexts assigned to Phases III and IV (second/third century AD and third/fourth century, respectively). Table 40 presents the distribution of fragments identified from the detailed sample, and Table 41 presents the distribution of species identifications for the recorded fragments in the selective sample. The numbers of bones identified from prehistoric and post-medieval contexts are very small, and are not considered further in this report.

Preservation

Table 42 presents data on preservation states for fragments in the detailed collection belonging to Phases III, IV and V.

Most of the bones (c.96%) are quite well preserved. They have intact surfaces which retain any traces of cutmarks, gnawmarks, periosteal alterations etc., and which can be used for accurate anatomical measurements. The remaining 3–4% are slightly eroded, mainly due to abraded edges, and may be residual. Most of the bones appear to have been preserved by rapid burial, although a significant minority (11–13%) have been chewed, probably by dogs. This implies that relatively fresh bones were available to carnivores prior to burial. Only 2–4% of the bones show signs of burning. Butchery marks are quite infrequent, especially for the smaller species such as sheep and pigs compared to cattle (6% and 7% compared to 12%, respectively). Two types of butchery were recorded: 1) if a fragment has been chopped through, and 2) if it bears cutmarks on its surface. About one quarter of the bones are cracked and this probably relates to the high degree of fragmentation. Most of the cracked fragments could not be identified to species level.

Table 40 Stonea Grange: animal bones – distribution of species by period in the collection recorded in detail

Phase	III 2nd/3rd century	IV 3rd/4th century	V Anglo-Saxon	VI Post-medieval	Unknown	Totals
Cattle	419	1294	325	15	125	2178
Sheep/goat	496	1271	410	36	92	2305
(Sheep)	(6)	(5)				(11)
(Goat)		(3)	(1)			(4)
Pig	127	340	72		44	583
Horse	20	48	14	2	4	88
Dog	44	22			7	73
Cat	2		1		1	4
Roe deer	1					1
Deer species	2	2				4
Hare	2	2				4
Human	4	13	3	1		21
Cattle-sized	225	615	239	4	39	1121
Sheep-sized	331	908	376	47	59	1720
Pig-sized	92	215	107	5	16	435
Unidentified mammal	3	2				5
Fowl	3	8	1			12
Duck cf. mallard	5					5
Skylark	2					2
Turdus sp.	2					2
Wader	1					1
Goose-sized bird	1			1		2
Fowl-sized bird	3	6				9
Frog/toad	1	1				2
Totals	1786	4748	1548	110	338	8580

Table 41 Stonea Grange: animal bones – distribution of species by period in the collection recorded for selected measurements and/or ageing

Phase	I Prehistoric	III 2nd/3rd century	IV 3rd/4th century	V Anglo-Saxon	Totals
Cattle	5	153	212		370
Sheep/goat	2	227	220		489
(Sheep)		(38)	(48)		(86)
(Goat)		(3)			(3)
Pig	1	65	75	*	141
Horse		6	8		14
Dog		85	17		102
Hare		1	3		4
Human		8	2		10
Cattle-sized		28	12		40
Sheep-sized		7	12		19
Pig-sized		1	1		2
Unidentified mammal			1		1
Watervole		14			14
Field vole		7			7
Apodemus sp.		5			5
Water shrew		1			1
Common shrew		8			8
Fowl		41	43		84
Goose		4	1		5
Goose (cf. greylag)		12	1		13
Duck cf. mallard		20	33		53
Mallard-sized duck		1			1
Widgeon-sized duck			1		1
Teal		1	3		4
Cormorant		4			4
Shag		1			1
Wader			1		1
Turdus sp. (cf. song thrush)		1			1
Warbler-sized passerine		1			1
House-sparrow		1			1
Small dove		1			1
Owl (cf. barn owl)		7			7
Raven		6	1		7
Crow/rook		2			2
Jackdaw		10			9
Red kite		1			1
Eagle (cf. white-tailed)			1		1
Swan/crane-sized bird			1		1
Fowl-sized bird			5		5
Unidentified bird		1			1
Frog/toad		1			1
Totals	8	735	695	*	1438

(*n*), the number of specimens identified to species level, is included within the overall total for sheep/goat.

* Part of a complete articulated skeleton.

Table 42 Stonea Grange: animal bones – preservation states for cattle, sheep/goat and pig fragments in the detailed collection

	Eroded	Chewed	Burnt	Chopped	Cutmarked	Cracked
Romano-British (Phases III + IV)						
Cattle	4%	3%	3%	4%	12%	29%
Sheep/goat	2%	3%	3%	1%	6%	25%
Pig	1%	2%	2%	2%	7%	25%
Anglo-Saxon (Phase V)						
Cattle	4%	12%	1%	3%	7%	22%
Sheep/goat	3%	13%	1%	1%	4%	16%
Pig	3%	10%	3%	0%	6%	22%

Table 43 presents the rates of breakage for fragments from the detailed collection of Phases III, IV and V.

Table 43 Stonea Grange: animal bones – fragmentation rates for bones from the detailed sample

Phase	III 2nd/3rd century	IV 3rd/4th century	V Anglo-Saxon
<25% complete	65%	69%	76%
26–50% complete	18%	17%	13%
51–75% complete	6%	6%	4%
76–99% complete	4%	4%	3%
100% complete	6%	5%	5%
<50 mm in length	45%	55%	97%
51–100 mm in length	42%	36%	3%
101–150 mm in length	11%	6%	<1%
>150 mm in length	2%	2%	<1%

The patterns of completeness are extremely similar for Phases III and IV, although the absolute lengths vary. The greater proportions of smaller fragments in Phase IV cannot be explained by the ratio of cattle to sheep and pig fragments, but may be due to the relatively smaller numbers of cattle-sized fragments in Phase IV (see Table 40).

Table 42 shows how the preservation of the bones of the three main species in the Anglo-Saxon deposits compares with that of the Romano-British material. Overall, the rate of erosion, burning, cracking and cutting are very similar for all three species. The main difference concerns the rate of chewing (by dogs). The bones of all three species show much higher rates in the Anglo-Saxon deposits (10–13%, compared to 2–3%). This is despite the rarity of bones identified as dog in the Anglo-Saxon layers. Presumably, although live dogs must have had relatively free access to the bones of domestic animals, they themselves were usually left where they died, or were disposed of away from the main areas of rubbish dumping. An exception is the complete skeleton of a large dog in pit 504 (see below).

Table 43 shows the rates of breakage for Phases III–V using bones from all species. The Anglo-Saxon bones tend to be slightly more fragmented than those in either of the Romano-British collections (76% retain less than one quarter of their original length, compared to 65% and 69% for the Romano-British collections). The absolute lengths show a greater degree of difference between the periods: 97% of the fragments in the Anglo-Saxon deposits are less than 50 mm long (compared to 45% and 55% in the second-fourth century). It is quite possible that these greater degrees of fragmentation in the Anglo-Saxon collection are due to the element of residuality in the material. The comparable rates of erosion for the Romano-British and Anglo-Saxon collections cannot be used to argue for or against this hypothesis. They simply indicate that none of the material was exposed to subaerial weathering for any significant length of time prior to burial (or reburial).

The greater degree of fragmentation in the Anglo-Saxon collection compounded with the smaller absolute numbers of bone fragments ($N = 1551$ compared with $N = 2521$ for the second/third century and $N = 5443$ for the third/fourth century) means that the numbers of bones suitable for measurement or ageing analysis are much reduced compared to the Romano-British collections.

Context types

The animal bones in the detailed collection derive from a variety of context types including ditches, gullies, wells, pits, stake- or post-holes, middens, general external deposits, stone surfaces and occupation layers. There are few differences in the types of preservation associated with different context types. Bones from drains tend to be less fragmented, but these form a very small proportion of the overall collection. The sump material has particularly good preservation due to waterlogging of the deposits and contains several bird bones (see the list of species from the selectively-recorded collection, Table 41).

The species

The vast majority of the fragments identified to species derive from the three main domestic animals: cattle, sheep and pigs.

Of the sheep/goat bones, most are probably from sheep rather than goats. Only seven goat bones were identified out of the whole assemblage (both detailed and selective samples), whereas 97 bones were identified as sheep.

Other species identified from the hand-recovered material include horse, dog, hare, deer and cat, domestic fowl (chickens), wild and/or domestic geese and ducks, and various wild birds ranging in size from a warbler-sized passerine to the white-tailed (sea) eagle.

Patterns of husbandry in the Romano-British phases

The term 'sheep' will be used throughout this section, although it should be remembered that a few goats may be included in this category.

The detailed sample (see Table 44) has similar proportions of cattle:sheep:pig in the two main Roman phases. Cattle plus sheep make up 88% or 89% in roughly equal proportions, with a slight reduction in the relative proportion of sheep through time. By comparison with King's (1988) survey of different types of Romano-British collections, the collections from the two main Roman phases at Stonea both fall into the range of un-Romanised settlements, mainly due to the high proportion of sheep bones (see King, 1988, Fig. 6.4). The effect of varying the recording method can be seen by comparing the proportions in the detailed sample with those in the selective sample at Stonea. In the latter, the proportions of pig bones are both increased slightly from 12% to 15%, whilst the proportion of sheep is very much greater in the second/third century collection (51%) than in any of the other three. However, King's survey used bone reports that tended to use recording methods closer to those utilised in the detailed sample, and so these are probably the better comparison for his survey. His survey suffers from his having to work with data that were not collected consistently between sites, but the main conclusions were that 1) pre-existing patterns of exploitation that emphasised sheep husbandry were replaced by more 'Romanised' patterns that laid greater emphasis on cattle; and 2) later Roman sites also tended to have more pig remains than earlier sites. The proportions of sheep bones at Stonea, therefore (equal to or greater than the proportions of cattle bones) are more like the Iron Age sites and would suggest that the people living at Stonea were relatively un-Romanised in their lifestyles. The site's proximity to the Fenland Causeway means that the inhabitants must have had contact with Romanised ways of life through travellers passing through the area. Whether or not they chose to emulate Roman customs must be investigated through their use of Roman style artefacts, building styles etc.

Table 44 Stonea Grange: animal bones – proportions of the three main domestic species in Phases III–V.

	Detailed sample						Selective sample			
Phase	III 2nd/3rd century		IV 3rd/4th century		V Anglo-Saxon		III 2nd/3rd century		IV 3rd/4th century	
	N	%	N	%	N	%	N	%	N	%
Cattle	419	40	1294	45	325	40	153	34	212	42
Sheep	496	48	1271	44	410	51	227	51	220	43
Pig	127	12	340	12	72	9	65	15	75	15
Totals	1042		2905		807		445		507	

The emphasis on sheep raising is slightly surprising, considering that the surrounding pastures may have been damp. Damp pastures could have given rise to two problems for sheep: 1) footrot and 2) liver fluke (cf. French, p. 653). It is possible that the sheep were resistant to footrot, like the modern Romney Marsh sheep. Although liver fluke can be a serious hazard for flocks of mature sheep, who develop the full effects of infection, young animals may, in fact, enjoy an initial 'bloom' due to the stimulation of the liver. If the animals are culled young, they do not develop the full effects and may serve to 'clean up' the pastures by being removed from the land before they re-infect it with the next stage of the fluke's life cycle.

Sheep can be utilised for a variety of purposes during their lives, and these uses may be reflected in the age distributions at which they were slaughtered. They can be important producers of dairy foods (milk, cheese, buttermilk etc.) as well as supplying annual crops of wool. Their dung forms an important source of manure for arable crops and they are often integrated into mixed farming systems.

Two methods of ageing have been used: one based on the sequence of tooth eruption and wear following the methods of Grant (1982), the other based on the sequence of epiphyseal fusion of different bones in the skeleton (based on Silver, 1969). Figure 230a presents the Mandibular Wear Scores (MWS) (sensu Grant 1982) for sheep/goats. Mandibles with a tooth missing or damaged post-mortem have had their MWS estimated by comparison with the complete jaws, and are probably accurate to within one or two points on the scale. Rates of tooth wear vary according to several factors including genetic predisposition and intake of grit in the diet (which can relate to stocking rates/overgrazing etc.). The fact that the complete jaws show very close correlations of overall score with individual tooth wear stages suggests that the sheep derive from a single flock (or closely-related breeding stock) on a uniform type of pasture with relatively standard stocking rates. In an urban situation, where sheep deriving from several flocks in different areas may be represented, the individual tooth wear stages often show much greater variation when compared to the overall scores (personal observation).

Figure 230a is bimodal, with the main peak of scores lying between 30 and 43 and a smaller peak representing younger animals with scores between 2 and 14. The Mandibular Wear Scores are an expression of relative wear states rather than absolute ages, and do not translate directly into ages. However, some points on the scale can be calibrated with modern tooth eruption ages (Silver 1969). The MWS for jaws with the first molar just erupting (c. 3 months) is 6–7, that for the second molar (9–12 months) is 17–18 and that for the third molar (18–21 months) is 28–9. In addition, the fourth permanent premolar erupts at 21–4 months, and the MWS for these jaws is 32–3. By tying in these MWS and tooth eruption ages, the ages at death can be estimated:

12 at <3 months, 1 at 3 months, 26 at 3–9 months, 1 at 9–12 months   (40 in first year)

21 at 12–18 months, 2 at 18–21 months, 15 at 21–4 months (38 in second year)

53 over 24 months   (53 at more than 2 years)

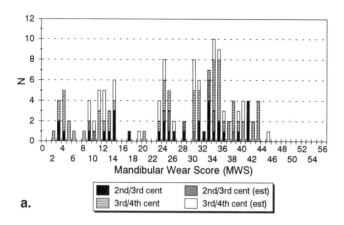

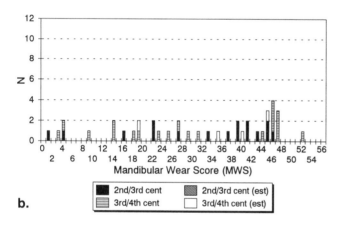

a.

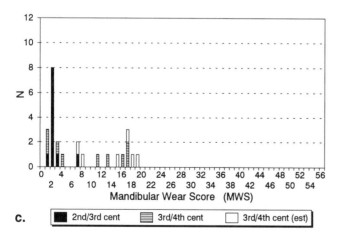

b.

c.

Fig. 230 Stonea Grange: animal bones – Mandibular Wear Scores of a) sheep/goat, b) cattle, c) pig.

The peaks of deaths appear to have occurred during the neonatal period and (assuming a spring season for birth) during the first summer/autumn, the second spring/summer and the second winter. It is not possible to suggest how old the adult (over 2 years old) animals were when they died by using tooth eruption and wear data, but it is clear that only 40% survived this far, and that there is not a predominance of particularly old animals (which would have MWS of c. 40–8).

The peak of deaths during the neonatal period could have two explanations: 1) they were unavoidable deaths incurred in the local flock (even modern shepherds suffer considerable neonatal losses); or 2) they were imported as luxury items for their ultra-young meat. These two possibilities are considered further, using the butchery and epiphyseal fusion data (below).

The later peaks of deaths emphasise the importance of young animals. Those in their first year would not even have supplied a crop of wool before they died. Those in their second year would have provided one crop of wool, but are unlikely to have been used for breeding if they were to be killed during their second spring/summer, as they would have lost condition prior to slaughter. The high proportion of animals killed at less than two years (60%) emphasises the importance of prime lamb and mutton i.e. meat. The older animals are likely to be the breeding ewes. A small amount of milk might have been provided by these, but dairying is unlikely to have been a major role of the sheep flocks. All of the animals would have provided dung during their lives, of course, and all of them would have provided skins/fleeces as well as meat when they were slaughtered.

The mandibles can be used to estimate relative numbers of animals, to check the species ratios estimated by fragment numbers. Table 45 presents the numbers of mandibles from cattle, sheep and pigs. Only those that are complete enough to have Mandibular Wear Scores (whether observed or estimated) have been counted.

Table 45 Stonea Grange: animal bones – numbers of mandibles with Mandibular Wear Scores

Phase	III		IV		V
	2nd/3rd century		3rd/4th century		Anglo–Saxon
Cattle	17	24%	23	18%	0
Sheep/goats	44	61%	87	70%	4
Pig	11	15%	15	12%	3
Totals	72		125		7

When these figures are compared with Table 44 (the numbers of identified fragments of cattle, sheep and pig) it is clear that the mandibles demonstrate a much higher proportion of sheep/goats than was suggested by the fragment

Table 46 Stonea Grange: animal bones – Minimum Numbers of Elements for the three major species

	Cattle	Sheep	Pigs	Totals
		2nd/3rd century		
Mandible	17	44	11	72
Scapula (glenoid)	10	8	4	22
Distal humerus	9	10	9	28
Proximal radius	13	13	3	29
Proximal metacarpal	14	34	2	50
Pelvis (acetabulum)	9	12	3	24
Distal femur	11	6	9	26
Distal tibia	13	24	2	39
Astragalus	9	5	1	15
Calcaneum	7	12	3	22
Proximal metatarsal	12	31	2.5	45.5
		3rd/4th century		
Mandible	23	87	15	125
Scapula (glenoid)	20	20	4	44
Distal humerus	19	27	8	54
Proximal radius	25	20	12	57
Proximal metacarpal	18	40	2.5	60.5
Pelvis (acetabulum)	16	24	6	46
Distal femur	35	24	15	74
Distal tibia	21	39	6	66
Astragalus	16	5	1	22
Calcaneum	13	14	13	40
Proximal metatarsal	29	45	2	76
		Anglo-Saxon		
Mandible	4	11	5	20
Scapula (glenoid)	4	4	0	8
Distal humerus	3	8	0	11
Proximal radius	3	4	1	8
Proximal metacarpal	3	5	0	8
Pelvis (acetabulum)	2	5	1	8
Distal femur	2	5	2	9
Distal tibia	3	2	1	6
Astragalus	3	1	1	5
Calcaneum	4	5	1	10
Proximal metatarsal	6	5	0	11

Note: For pigs, lateral metapodials have not been counted, and the numbers of metapodials III plus IV have been halved, to make the frequencies comparable to those of sheep and cattle.

numbers. The proportions of sheep/goats are raised from 43–51% to 61–70%. This emphasises the 'non-Romanised' nature of the husbandry pattern even further.

Butchery marks are quite scarce on sheep bones (see Table 42), but butchery must have taken place to remove the head and feet, and to subdivide the carcasses into usefully-sized joints for cooking. In particular, it is noticeable that the numbers of animals represented by mandibles are far larger than those indicated by any other element. Table 46 presents minimum numbers of elements for the major parts of

the skeleton for the three main species. Sheep have very high numbers of mandibles, followed by high numbers of proximal metapodials and distal tibiae. The same pattern is present in each of the two main Roman phases. The distal metacarpal fuses at 18–24 months (Silver 1969). The ratio of fused to unfused sheep metacarpals in Phases III plus IV is 18:12. This suggests that 60% of the bones derive from animals killed at less than two years old i.e. the same ratio as demonstrated by the mandibles. The 'over-representation' of head and foot bones of sheep indicate that sheep were being raised by the inhabitants of Stonea, killed and butchered in situ, and then the carcasses (headless and, sometimes, footless) exported to other sites. The local small towns, especially Durobrivae, are the most likely consumer sites to have received meat produced at Stonea.

Sample sizes for the other elements are much smaller, but similar investigations of the fusion states of the distal humeri (fusion age 10 months) and proximal tibiae (fusion age 3–3.5 years) give very similar ratios. Of the 42 distal humeri with fusion evidence, 27 (64%) are fused, 5 (12%) are partially fused, and 10 (24%) are unfused. For the 14 proximal tibiae with fusion evidence, 5 (36%) are fused, 5 (36%) are unfused and 4 (29%) are extremely young and likely to be from animals that died when they were neonatal, or only a few weeks old. The Mandibular Wear Scores show that 30% of the mandibles come from animals that died before they reached about 9 months of age, compared to 36% that failed to reach 10 months, according to the humeri. This consistent pattern of ageing, using different parts of the skeleton, suggests that the exported carcasses (whose head and foot bones were left behind at the site) were a fair representation of the animals slaughtered. That is, there is no evidence for the home consumption of old mutton in preference to the exported prime meat carcasses.

Table 47 demonstrates the effect of element representation on the relative frequencies of the three main species. The mandibles show that sheep were very important (61% and 70% in Phases III and IV, respectively) but the other elements fail to reveal this importance. Table 47 shows the percentage representations using the proximal radius and the distal femur. These elements have been chosen because they are the two most frequent elements that are not part of the head and feet butchery debris.

Table 47 Stonea Grange: animal bones – relative proportions of the three major species using different skeletal elements

Phase	III						IV					
	2nd/3rd century						3rd/4th century					
	Cattle		Sheep		Pigs		Cattle		Sheep		Pigs	
	N	%	N	%	N	%	N	%	N	%	N	%
Mandible	17	24	44	61	11	15	23	18	87	70	15	12
Prox. radius	13	45	13	45	3	10	25	44	20	35	12	21
Distal femur	11	42	6	23	9	35	35	47	24	32	15	20

Tables 46 and 47 suggest that all parts of the cattle skeletons are relatively evenly represented. There is no obvious pattern of 'missing' parts. Frequencies of elements of sheep and pigs, however, are quite variable. For the most part, this seems to be explicable in terms of the butchery pattern described for sheep, together with a lack of smaller bones of the skeleton due to recovery bias. Pig metapodials are much smaller than those of sheep and cattle and so are unlikely to have been recovered in large numbers, even if present. However, the similar numbers of elements for pig mandibles, distal humeri and distal femora suggest that whole skeletons of pigs are represented rather than any biased butchery debris.

The Mandibular Wear Scores for cattle are plotted in Fig. 230b. The overall numbers are far fewer than for sheep (a total of 40 for the two phases, including estimated scores), although the actual range of scores is greater (0–52). The scores are very evenly spread out, with a small cluster around 45–7. These jaws come from animals whose teeth had worn down almost to the gumline. These animals may have died of old age, or been culled when they ceased to be productive. Calibration of Mandibular Wear Scores with tooth eruption stages gives the following 'fixed points' on the graph: MWS = 5 (5–6 months), MWS = 17 (15–18 months), MWS = 29 (24–30 months). Like sheep, cattle can be used for a variety of purposes whilst still alive, including dairying and traction. A dairy herd would be indicated if there were clusters of jaws from very young and very old animals. Although there are a few jaws from very young calves, the numbers are insufficient to support an interpretation of dairying (although, of course, their mothers may well have been milked adventitiously). A meat economy would have left a death assemblage from mainly juvenile/young adult animals (c. 2.5–3.5 years old). There is definitely no cluster of jaws in this age range.

Cattle are usually kept on into old age for one of two reasons: traction or breeding/dairying. The aged animals indicated by the small cluster of jaws with Mandibular Wear Scores of 41–52 were probably utilised for one or both of these purposes during their lives. The rest of the animals represented by mandibles probably had unavoidable deaths due to natural causes, or were culled due to undesirable traits such as barrenness. A few may have been killed for meat but this was not a major role for the herd.

The greater frequency of butchery marks on the cattle bones compared to those on the sheep bones (see Table 42) probably reflects the larger size of cattle carcasses. These require a higher degree of subdivision in order to comprise suitably-sized joints of meat for cooking, and are also more likely to be filleted.

Figure 230c presents a graph of the Mandibular Wear Scores for pig jaws. Two facts are immediately clear: 1) the overall numbers are considerably less than those for sheep and cattle (N = 26); and 2) all of the scores come from young animals, with a preponderance (14 out of the 26) of

neonatal jaws (MWS = 0–4). Calibrating the MWS with tooth eruption ages gives the following 'fixed points' on the graph: MWS = 7 (4–6 months), MWS = 16 (7–13 months). None of the jaws in Fig. 230c have their third molar erupted (17–22 months). This pattern is slightly difficult to interpret. A high proportion of neonatal piglets could indicate either indigenous losses or the importation of luxurious suckling pig. The additional presence of foetal pig remains supports the interpretation of unavoidable indigenous deaths, although the lack of jaws from old breeding sows is surprising. It is possible that older animals were sold on, either as breeding stock or as complete carcasses (which could have been processed by smoking or salting).

This interpretation may seem a case of special pleading, but it is highly unlikely that foetal piglets were imported to the site. Their remains occur in several contexts, sometimes as isolated bones, sometimes as complete or partial skeletons. The pig has a gestation period of approximately 115 days. Using Prummel (1989), the following ages since conception were estimated from lengths of longbones: from the sump: four foetal piglets that died at 85, 87, 88 and 89 days, plus a neonatal piglet that died at 120 days; and from pit 1577 (context 1817): two foetal piglets of 82 and 89 days. Context 1817 also contained remains of a neonatal human infant, supporting the notion that the piglet was disposed of as an unwanted death, and is not evidence of a high status diet. Remains of neonatal piglets of 148 and 157 days were found in a possible latrine, pit 1638 (context 1739) and in the rubble associated with building R1. Very young piglet bones (a few weeks old) were found in well 135 (context 135) and in well 1836 (context 1740). These remains are evenly spread between the two main Roman phases.

Human neonatal infants had a similar distribution. Their remains were recovered from a well and two pits (contexts 1853, 1817 and 2125), latrine pits 1536 and 1563, and context 318 (but see also Conheeney, pp. 583–7).

Apart from foetal and neonatal remains, there were very few partial or complete burials of the three main species. No sheep burials were found. One young male cattle skeleton was recovered from gully 29 (context 1723). The animal was 3–5 years old when it died (longbones all fused, vertebrae not fused) and it does not appear to have been eaten. This animal may have been considered unfit to eat; it does not appear to be a ritual deposit.

None of the animal bones indicates anything other than general domestic rubbish or accidental farming losses. Even pit P10 (the 'votive pit') contained general food debris, indistinguishable from the rest of the collection.

Types of Romano-British livestock: sizes, sexes and morphology

The conformation of the animals is unremarkable for the Romano-British period. The cattle are similar to the 'Celtic

Table 48 Stonea Grange: animal bones – cattle metacarpal measurements (in mm)*

Bp Proximal breadth	SD Midshaft diameter	Bd Distal breadth	BFd Dist. breadth at fusion line	Max. depth of medial condyle	GL Greatest length	Withers height $(GL \times 6.12)$†
			2nd/3rd century			
48.4	25.5					
49.2	26.8					
50.1	29.4					
54.3						
56.4	31.8	54.1	52.1	29.5	191	1169
61.7						
65.6	36.9					
66.9	38.8					
68.2	39.3					
			3rd/4th century			
		52.8	47.8	28.9		
		51.4		29.4		
		55.1	49.9	31.1		
		61.2				
		58.1	53.1	31.5		
		60.4		30.5		
		55.2	48.8	30.4		
		54.0	51.3	29.5		
		54.1	49.4			
		54.9				
47.5	25.0					
48.0	26.0					
49.8	25.1					
51.7						
52.6	32.7	56.8		29.3	196	1200
53.3						
53.9	31.5	54.0	51.3	27.3	200	1224
54.6	30.8	54.8		29.0	192	1187
57.9	33.3					
58.0	34.9					

Summary statistics for Bp and Bd measurements

	2nd/3rd century	3rd/4th century
	Bp	Bp
N	9	10
Mean	57.9	52.7
Minimum	48.4	47.5
Maximum	68.2	58.0
Standard deviation	7.47	3.45
Coefficient of variation	12.90	6.55

	2nd/3rd century	3rd/4th century
	Bd	Bd
N	1	13
Mean	54.1	55.6
Minimum		51.4
Maximum		61.2
Standard deviation		2.72
Coefficient of variation		4.89

* Measurements defined in von den Driesch 1976.
† Zalkin 1960.

Table 49 Stonea Grange: animal bones – cattle metatarsal measurements (in mm)*

Fusion	*Bp*	*SD*	*Bd*	Maximum depth distal condyles	*GL*	Withers height (*GL* × 5.47)†
			2nd/3rd century			
		16.0				
		20.6				
		22.5				
		23.8				
DF		24.0				
		25.3				
DF			50.7	28.0		
	39.4	20.4				
DF	43.4	25.3			214	1171
	44.1					
	44.8	23.4	50.4	26.9	204	1116
	46.9					
	47.6	26.2				
DF	48.8		52.4			
DF	57.3		62.6			
			3rd/4th century			
		15.4				
		21.0				
		21.8				
		22.2				
		23.3				
DF			51.2			
DF			53.4	28.8		
DF			58.4			
	33.1	15.9				
DF	38.3	23.0				
	41.9	25.2				
DF	42.2	21.6	46.6	26.7	212	1160
	42.5	23.7				
DF	43.8	25.8	52.7	30.4	216	1182
DUF	44.7	20.3	45.7		(169)	
	45.1					
	45.5	23.8				
	46.2					
	46.5	22.7				
	46.8	26.4				
	47.1	24.8				
DF	47.1	24.8				
	49.1	30.4				
	52.9					
	57.0	32.0				
			Anglo-Saxon			
DF		25.3	51.6			
DF		26.3	52.5			
DF			54.0			
DF			54.4	29.5		
	46.4	25.2				

* Measurements defined in von den Driesch 1976.
† Zalkin 1960.
DF   Distal fused
DUF   Distal unfused

continued

Fusion	Bp	SD	Bd	Maximum depth distal condyles	GL	Withers height (GL × 5.47)†

Summary statistics for *Bp* and *Bd*

	2nd/3rd century	3rd/4th century	Anglo-Saxon
	Bp	*Bp*	*Bp*
N	8	17	1
Average	46.5	45.3	46.4
Minimum	39.4	33.1	46.4
Maximum	57.3	57.0	46.4
Std dev.	4.90	5.14	
CV	10.53	11.36	
	2nd/3rd century	3rd/4th century	Anglo-Saxon
	Bd	*Bd*	*Bd*
N	4	6	4
Average	54.0	51.3	53.1
Minimum	50.4	51.6	51.6
Maximum	62.6	58.4	54.4
Std dev.	5.01	4.29	1.13
CV	9.28	8.36	2.12

shorthorn' cattle that predominated in Britain throughout the Iron Age and Romano-British period. Several horned skull fragments were found, but no polled examples. There are too few cattle horncore measurements for any analysis of horncore morphology to be undertaken.

Tables 48, 49 and 50 give measurements for cattle metacarpals, metatarsals and astragali respectively. All other elements produced very few measurable examples.

All four complete metacarpals in Table 48 give breadth:length ratios that Howard (1962) ascribes to the range normal for female *Bos longifrons* (the Celtic cow). All of the examples happen to be Romano-British. Similarly, all four (Romano-British) complete metatarsals give female shape indices. It is probable that the majority of the metapodials derive from females, although a few of each element are probably from males. Plotting the distal breadth (*Bd*) measurements of the two elements on a histogram (not illustrated), shows a cluster of measurements with two or three outliers indicating ratios of 11/12 females to 2/3 males (*N* = 14 for each element). This sex ratio may support the suggestion made in relation to the mandibular ageing pattern that aged animals were culled once they had ceased to be productive. Male cattle are unlikely to have been kept on into old age except for one or two breeding bulls and, possibly, a few oxen for traction (although cows can equally be used for draught purposes provided that the strength required is not excessive and they are not heavily pregnant or suckling).

The actual measurements of the metapodials are similar to those from other Romano-British sites (Luff 1982) including the nearby settlement at Grandford (Stallibrass 1982). The sample sizes at Stonea for any one phase are small, and

any difference between the mean sizes of bones in Phase III and Phase IV are either very slight, or could be due to small sample bias. There is no trend for the later Roman cattle bones to be substantially larger (or smaller) than those from the earlier Roman phase, and the small sample of Anglo-Saxon cattle metatarsals is indistinguishable from the Roman collections.

Similarly, the astragalus measurements do not show any size trend through time, and are very similar to those for astragali from another roadside settlement at Wilcote in Oxfordshire (Hamshaw-Thomas and Bermingham 1993). Any changes in cattle type that may have occurred during the Romano-British period are, perhaps, most likely to be evidenced at major livestock breeding centres such as villas, or at sites with high status food deposits rather than at roadside settlements such as Stonea or Wilcote.

Table 51 and Fig. 231b present data on calculated withers heights for cattle, using Matolcsi's factors in von den Driesch and Boessneck (1974). The sample size is very small, but there does appear to be a slight indication that the cattle became slightly bigger in the later phase. The four withers heights estimated for bones from the second/third century AD range from 1.05 to 1.17 m, whilst the seven for the third/fourth centuries range from 1.08 to 1.22 m. This slight difference cannot be ascribed to a change in the sex ratio, since even the greatest height in Fig. 231b derives from a bone (a metacarpal) estimated to be from a female. However, this interpretation must remain entirely speculative until greater sample sizes are available for statistical testing.

Several horned sheep skull fragments were recovered. Some of the horncores are very robust, and probably derive

Table 50 Stonea Grange: animal bones – cattle astragalus measurements (in mm)*

	Bd	GLl Greatest lateral length
2nd/3rd century		
	38.3	62
	39.2	62
	39.4	
	40.6	67
	41.1	65
	42.3	64
	46.8	
3rd/4th century		
		60
		61
	34.9	59
	35.7	56
	35.9	60
	37.7	
	38.5	
	39.2	64
	39.3	62
	39.7	
	40.0	
	40.4	63
	41.9	63
	42.7	67
	44.1	71
	49.3	75
Anglo-Saxon		
	37.2	60
	38.2	61

Summary statistics for *Bd* and *GLl*

	2nd/3rd century Bd	3rd/4th century Bd	Anglo-Saxon Bd
N	7	14	2
Average	41.1	40.0	37.7
Minimum	38.3	34.9	37.2
Maximum	46.8	49.3	38.2
Std dev.	2.63	3.63	
CV	6.40	9.08	

	2nd/3rd century GLl	3rd/4th century GLl	Anglo-Saxon GLl
N	5	12	2
Average	64	63	
Minimum	62	56	60
Maximum	67	75	61
Std dev.	1.90	5.09	
CV	2.97	8.03	

* Measurements defined in von den Driesch 1976.

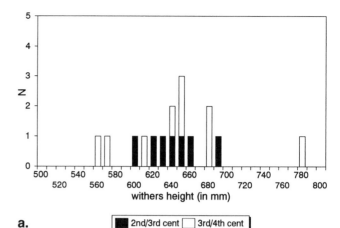

a.

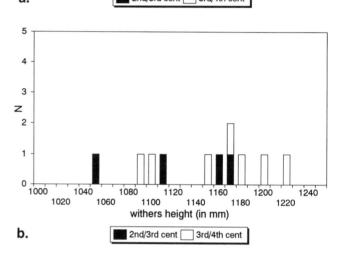

b.

Fig. 231 Stonea Grange: animal bones – withers heights of a) sheep/goat, b) cattle.

from rams rather than ewes. One skull fragment was recovered with slight bumps where the horncores should grow. Although the fragment was from an immature skull (unfused sutures), it would appear that the horns were going to be vestigial. No fully polled (hornless) examples were found. The presence of male sheep remains is also suggested by the size of one or two of the bones. A massive sheep metacarpal was found in gully 19 (context 1822). This bone is definitely from a sheep not a goat, and has a total length of 159 mm. A similarly massive metacarpal was found in the sump. It is distally unfused and has a diaphyseal length of 123 mm.

Table 51 and Fig. 231a present the calculated withers heights for Phases III and IV combined, using the lengths of all available (fused) sheep longbones and the factors given by Teichert in von den Driesch and Boessneck (1974). The outlying height of 780 mm is calculated from the particularly massive metacarpal mentioned above. The sample size is small, but the distribution appears to be normal, and there is no difference between the second/third century and third/fourth century collections, excepting that the range is greater for the later phase.

Table 51 Stonea Grange: animal bones – withers heights of sheep and cattle (in mm)*

Element	GL	Factor	Withers height
SHEEP			
2nd/3rd century			
Metacarpal	121	4.89	592
Metacarpal	126	4.89	616
Metacarpal	128	4.89	626
Metacarpal	129	4.89	631
Metacarpal	131	4.89	641
Metacarpal	134	4.89	655
Metatarsal	151	4.54	686
3rd/4th century			
Metacarpal	113	4.89	553
Radius	141	4.02	567
Metatarsal	133	4.54	604
Metatarsal	139	4.54	631
Metacarpal	131	4.89	641
Metacarpal	133	4.89	650
Metatarsal	149	4.54	676
Metacarpal	139	4.89	680
Metacarpal	159	4.89	778
Anglo-Saxon			
Metatarsal	146	4.54	663

Summary data for sheep withers heights

	2nd/3rd century	3rd/4th century	Anglo-Saxon
N	7	9	1
Average	635	642	663
Minimum	592	553	
Maximum	686	778	
Std dev.	27.63	63.48	

Element	GL	Factor	Withers height
CATTLE			
2nd/3rd century			
Radius	243	4.3	1045
Metatarsal	204	5.4	1102
Metatarsal	214	5.4	1156
Metacarpal	191	6.1	1165
3rd/4th century			
Humerus	227	4.77	1083
Radius	255	4.3	1097
Metatarsal	212	5.4	1145
Metatarsal	216	5.4	1166
Metacarpal	192	6.1	1171
Metacarpal	196	6.1	1196
Metacarpal	200	6.1	1220

Summary data for cattle withers heights

	2nd/3rd century	3rd/4th century
N	4	7
Average	1117	1154
Minimum	1045	1083
Maximum	1165	1220
Std dev.	48.05	46.17

* Measurements defined in von den Driesch 1976.

Tables 52–5 present measurement data for sheep/goat metacarpals, metatarsals, humeri and tibiae respectively. There are no indications of any goat bones in the measured collections. The measurements of second/third and third/fourth century sheep/goat metacarpals are indistinguishable from each other, and there are too few Anglo-Saxon examples for any meaningful comparison to be made. Of the metacarpals that could be ascribed to species, all eleven are from sheep. Figure 232a presents a histogram of the midshaft diameters of all of the third/fourth century examples of measured metacarpals (only those bones retaining additional measurements are listed in Table 52). The figure shows a normal distribution of measurements with, perhaps, a small outlying group of larger bones. This might indicate a preponderance of females or the presence of two types of sheep or simply a natural range of individual variation.

The metatarsal measurements (Table 53) also show no differences between the collections from the two main Romano-British phases. The standard deviations of the summary statistics are low and would support an interpretation of the bones deriving from a single population. This would suggest that a) the bones all derive from sheep with no admixture of goat bones, b) that all of the sheep derived from a local population and c) that there was no improvement in livestock type during the Romano-British phases.

The sheep/goat humerus measurements are presented in Table 54 and Fig. 232b. The figure shows how the measurements from all three phases (i.e. both of the Romano-British phases plus the Anglo-Saxon phase) appear to derive from a single population. Again, there is no suggestion of any inadvertent mixing of goat with sheep bones, nor of any improvement of the livestock. The three smallest measurements (two Anglo-Saxon and one from the second/third century) all derive from animals that were immature, the fusion line of the distal epiphysis still being visible. It is possible, therefore, that these three bones had not yet reached their potential full size. All of the other bones are well fused at the distal epiphysis (proximal fusion data are not preserved on any of these bones).

The sheep/goat tibia measurements (Table 55) again demonstrate the similarity between the sizes of the sheep bones from the two main Romano-British phases.

Overall, these sheep/goat and cattle measurements are similar to those from several sites in southern England (e.g. Chichester Cattlemarket: Levitan 1989) including the nearby site of Grandford (Stallibrass 1982). Measurements from Roman sites further north, however, show that sheep and cattle tended to be slightly smaller than at the more Romanised, southern sites (Stallibrass, in prep.).

Since the pig bones are nearly all immature, it is not possible to estimate the sizes of the adult animals.

The sex ratios of the pig bones have been estimated using mandibular canines. Loose teeth and empty alveoli have been counted in addition to canines in situ in the jaw. None

Table 52 Stonea Grange: animal bones – sheep/goat metacarpal measurements (in mm)*

Specific identifi-cation	Fusion	Bp	SD	Bd	Max. depth medial condyle	Min. depth medial condyle	GL
				2nd/3rd century			
Sheep	DF			24.0	14.5	11.0	
	DF						121
Sheep	DF		13.1	23.5	15.5	11.1	126
			13.6	25.4	16.1	11.7	
		18.2	11.8				
		18.2	11.8				
Sheep	DUF	19.8	11.8				
		20.6	10.4				
Sheep		20.8	12.3				
		21.1					
	DF	21.3	12.4	23.9	15.2	11.0	129
		21.4	11.3				
		21.5					
		21.6					
		21.9	12.9				
Sheep	DF	22.0	13.0	24.4	15.3	10.2	128
		22.2	13.9				
		22.3	15.6				
	DUF	22.6	13.3				
		23.3	15.3				
Sheep	DF	23.5	13.5	24.8			134
	DF	23.5	13.8	24.9	16.2	11.0	131
		23.9	14.1				
	DUF	23.9	15.0	27.8			

Summary data for sheep/goat metacarpal measurements

N		20	19	8	6	6	6
Average		21.7	13.1	24.8	15.5	11.0	128
Minimum		18.2	10.4	23.5	14.5	10.2	121
Maximum		23.9	15.6	27.8	16.2	11.7	134
Std dev.		1.60	1.34	1.26	0.57	0.44	4.06

Specific identifi-cation	Fusion	Bp	SD	Bd	Max. depth medial condyle	Min. depth medial condyle	GL
				3rd/4th century			
	DF			22.6	15.5	10.3	
	DF		14.2		16.7	10.9	
		18.4	11.8				
		19.2	12.4				
		19.9					
		20.5	11.9				
	DUF	20.5	12.9				
Sheep	DF	20.5	13.4	23.2			139
		20.8	13.5				
	DUF	21.0	13.8	22.4			
		21.1	14.6				
		21.2	13.4				
		21.5	12.6				
	DF	21.8	11.8		14.9	10.7	113
Sheep	DFsg	21.8	13.7	25.7	15.6	11.0	133
		21.9	12.1				
		21.9	12.9				
		21.9	13.0				
		22.0	13.4				
Sheep		22.0	12.7				
		22.3	13.3				
		22.5	13.9				

Table 52 continued

Specific identifi-cation	Fusion	Bp	SD	Bd	Max. depth medial condyle	Min. depth medial condyle	GL
		22.6	13.6				
		22.7					
		23.1	13.5				
		23.1	14.4				
	DF	23.4	14.2	24.5	15.5	10.7	131
		23.8	15.5				
		24.3	13.2				
		24.7	16.4				
Sheep	DF	25.2	16.5	28.0	18.4	13.4	159
Sheep	DF		13.6	25.4	16.1	11.7	
		22.3	15.6				
	DF			26.3	17.3	12.0	
		19.8	12.4				

Summary data for sheep/goat metacarpal measurements

N		31	31	8	8	8	5
Average		21.9	13.6	24.8	16.3	11.3	135
Minimum		18.4	11.8	22.4	14.9	10.3	113
Maximum		25.2	16.5	28.0	18.4	13.4	159
Std dev.		1.53	1.20	1.83	1.08	0.94	14.81

				Anglo-Saxon			
			13.0				
			13.3				
		21.1	14.6				

* Measurements defined in von den Driesch 1976.
DF   Distal fused
DUF   Distal unfused
DFsg   Distal fusing

Table 53 Stonea Grange: animal bones – sheep/goat metatarsal measurements (in mm)*

Fusion	Bp	SD	Bd	Max. depth medial condyle	Min. depth medial condyle	GL
			2nd/3rd century			
DUF		10.1	22.1	13.9	8.8	
DF		10.6	21.7			
DFvis	16.9	10.6	22.3	14.7	9.8	132
DUF	18.4	10.2	21.6			113
	18.5	11.5				
	19.0	10.8				
DUF	19.3	11.9				
DFsg	19.5	12.2	23.3	16.4	11.0	148
	19.6	10.2				
DUF	19.6	12.0				
DF	20.2	10.9	23.2	15.2	9.6	141
DF	20.2	11.2	24.0	16.6	10.5	151
DUF	20.3	11.6				
DUF	20.4	11.5				

Table 53 continued

Fusion	Bp	SD	Bd	Max. depth medial condyle	Min. depth medial condyle	GL
DUF	20.6	11.3				
	20.6	12.4				
DUF	20.7	10.6				
DUF	21.7	13.3				

Summary data for sheep/goat metatarsal measurements

	Bp	SD	Bd	Max. depth medial condyle	Min. depth medial condyle	GL
N	16	18	7	5	5	5
Average	19.7	11.3	22.6	15.4	9.9	137
Minimum	16.9	10.1	21.6	13.9	8.8	113
Maximum	21.7	13.3	24.0	16.6	11.0	151
Std dev.	1.05	0.84	0.84	1.02	0.76	13.67

3rd/4th century

Fusion	Bp	SD	Bd	Max. depth medial condyle	Min. depth medial condyle	GL
DF				15.7	10.3	
DUF		9.2	20.4			
DUF		10.2				
DF		14.8	25.2	17.0	11.3	
DUF	16.7	9.5				
	16.9	10.4				
	17.3	10.0				
	18.3					
DF	18.4	11.2	22.0	15.0	9.5	135
	18.7	14.0				
DF	18.8	10.9	23.0	15.7	9.9	139
	18.9	10.4				
	18.9	11.7				
	19.0	11.4				
	19.0	12.0				
	19.1	11.3				
	19.1	11.4				
	19.1	11.9				
	19.2	11.6				
	19.3					
DFvis	19.3	11.1	23.9	15.3	10.0	133
	19.4	12.2				
	19.4	12.2				
DUF	19.5	10.5	22.7			81
	19.9					
	19.9	12.0				
	20.6	13.0				
DFvis	20.8	11.5	24.0	16.4	11.1	114
DF	20.9	12.8	24.7	16.8	10.8	149
	21.7	14.4				
	24.1	13.0				

Table 53 continued

Summary data for sheep/goat metatarsal measurements

Fusion	Bp	SD	Bd	Max. depth medial condyle	Min. depth medial condyle	GL
N	27	27	8	7	7	6
Average	19.3	11.7	23.2	16.0	10.4	125
Minimum	16.7	9.2	20.4	15.0	9.5	81
Maximum	24.1	14.8	25.2	17.0	11.3	149
Std dev.	1.44	1.36	1.46	0.70	0.62	22.33
Anglo-Saxon						
DF	21.7	13.9	26.5	17.6	11.5	146

* Measurements defined in von den Driesch 1976.
DF   Distal fused
DUF   Distal unfused
DFvis   Distal fusion line visible
DFsg   Distal fusing

Table 54 Stonea Grange: animal bones – sheep/goat humerus measurements (in mm)*

Fusion	SD Midshaft diameter	Bd Distal breadth	BT Trochlea breadth	GHT Greatest trochlea height
2nd/3rd century				
	11.5			
DF	11.6			
DUF	12.2			
	12.2			
DUF	12.4			
	13.2			
	14.9			
	15.8			
	16.2			
DF	16.2			
DF		29.7	26.6	17.4
DF			27.7	16.5
DF		30.6	30.0	17.9
3rd/4th century				
DUF	10.3			
DFvis	10.7	25.1	23.5	15.2
DUF	10.8			
	11.0			
	11.0			
	11.4			
	11.4			
DUF	11.6			
	12.2			
DF	12.2			
	12.4			
	12.6			

Table 54 continued

Fusion	SD Midshaft diameter	Bd Distal breadth	BT Trochlea breadth	GHT Greatest trochlea height
	12.6			
	12.8			
	12.9			
DF	13.1	30.9	28.5	18.7
	13.2			
	13.5			
	13.5			
	13.5			
	13.6			
DF	13.6			
	13.7			
DF	13.8	26.5	26.3	16.8
	13.9			
DF	14.2			
DF	14.2	30.3	29.0	19.7
DF	14.3	28.6	27.0	17.0
	14.5			
	14.9			
DF	15.0		28.3	
DF			28.5	19.2
DF		28.3	28.7	17.0
DF		29.4	29.2	18.9
DF	15.0		29.3	19.4
DF	15.2	29.3	28.1	17.6
	15.6			
DF	16.2	32.7	30.7	20.1
DF	17.3	33.7	31.6	20.9
DF	18.4	33.6	31.3	19.8

Summary statistics for 3rd/4th century
(using fully fused bones only)

N	10	13	
Average	30.3	29.0	
Minimum	26.5	26.3	
Maximum	33.7	31.6	
Std dev.	2.27	1.47	

Anglo-Saxon

Fusion	SD	Bd	BT	GHT
DUF	9.4			
DUF	9.9			
DFvis		26.6	25.2	15.8
DFvis	11.9		25.6	15.6
	12.2			
DF	14.5	29.4	27.9	17.7
DF	15.9	32.4	30.2	18.4

* Measurements defined in von den Driesch 1976.
DF   Distal fused
DUF   Distal unfused
DFvis   Distal fusion line visible

Table 55 Stonea Grange: animal bones − sheep/goat tibia measurements (in mm)*

Fusion	SD	Bd	Dd Distal depth
Prehistoric			
	12.5		
	12.6		
2nd/3rd century			
DUF	8.7		
	11.6		
	12.2		
	12.3		
	12.6		
DUF	12.9		
DF	12.9		
	13.1		
	13.3		
	13.3		
	13.5		
	13.7		
DUF	13.8		
	14.6		
	14.7		
	14.9		
	16.0		
DF	16.7		
DF		21.4	15.1
DF		23.4	18.7
DF	13.4	23.7	19.0
DF	12.8	24.0	
DF	14.5	26.4	19.8
DF	14.7	26.5	19.2
DF		26.5	19.6
DF		26.6	20.9
DF	15.0	26.6	21.1
DF		26.6	22.1
DF	15.6	26.7	20.1
DF	13.8	27.2	20.6
DF	15.4	27.4	20.8
DF		32.7	26.5

Summary statistics for 2nd/3rd century

N	14	13	
Average	26.1	20.3	
Minimum	21.4	15.1	
Maximum	32.7	26.5	
Std dev.	2.50	2.42	

3rd/4th century			
DF	13.8	23.1	
DF	14.3	23.2	
DF	13.3	23.6	18.5
DF	13.1	23.9	18.7
DF	13.2	23.9	18.9
DF		24.1	19.2

Table 55 continued

Fusion	SD	Bd	Dd Distal depth
DF	13.5	24.2	18.9
DF	14.4	24.3	19.6
DF	14.2	24.4	21.2
DF	13.4	24.5	19.2
DF		24.9	17.0
DF	19.6	25.1	
DF		25.3	19.5
DF	14.9	25.4	19.6
DF	15.5	25.4	20.6
DF		25.6	19.9
DF	13.8	27.2	20.2
DFvis		27.2	22.2
DF	15.6	27.3	22.1
DF	15.9	27.5	21.0
DFvis	15.8	27.7	21.4
DF	15.1	27.9	21.3
DF	14.4	28.2	20.7
	16.3	28.3	22.2
DF		29.3	19.8
DF	16.5	29.7	

Summary statistics for 3rd/4th century

N		26	22
Average		25.8	20.1
Minimum		23.1	17.0
Maximum		29.7	22.2
Std. dev.		1.92	1.32

	Anglo-Saxon
DUF	10.3
	10.5
	11.5
	11.9
	12.4
	12.8
	13.6
	13.9
PFvis DF	14.0
	14.4
	14.8
	14.9
DUF	14.9

* Measurements defined in von den Driesch 1976.
DF   Distal fused
DUF   Distal unfused
DFvis Distal fusion line visible
PFvis Proximal fusion line visible

of the loose teeth comes from the same context as any of the empty alveoli and so it is unlikely that any individual has been double counted. The sample size for Phase III is very small: two males and two females. Using the associated

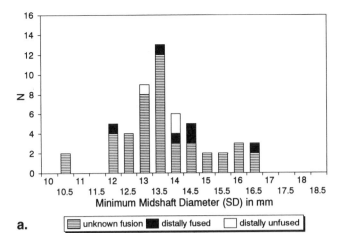

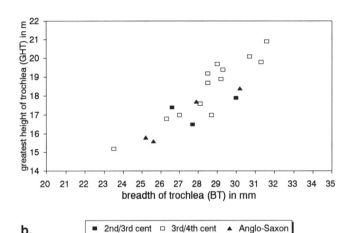

Fig. 232 Stonea Grange: animal bones – a) sheep/goat metacarpal midshaft diameters (third/fourth century AD); b) sheep/goat humerus distal trochlea breadth and height.

tooth eruption evidence it is possible to state that one of the female teeth comes from an individual that died at less than 4–6 months of age. In Phase IV, the sample size is rather larger: fifteen males and one female. Again, using associated tooth eruption data, it is possible to suggest that one of the male canines comes from an individual that died at about 12–16 months of age, whilst two more males died at over this age, probably sometime in their second year of life.

The overall ratio for the combined Romano-British phases is: 17 males to only 3 females. This heavy bias in favour of males (particularly young males) is consistent with a husbandry system that culls young pigs for meat. However, such a culling practice requires the presence of some older females, in order to maintain the stock, and no such remains have been identified in the collection. Whether they were disposed of elsewhere on the site, or sold off cannot be ascertained from this evidence. The alternative hypothesis (that young pig carcasses were imported to the site) was rejected earlier due to the presence of foetal and neonatal pig remains at the site (see above).

Congenital abnormalities and pathology of the Romano-British livestock

Congenital abnormalities in the dentition of cattle have been noted at many Romano-British sites, and the material from Stonea is no exception. Six of the 21 cattle mandibles (29%) from Phases III and IV that retain the portion of bone in which the second premolar (P_2) should occur are lacking the tooth. In none of the cases does the tooth appear to have been lost post-eruption. This abnormality has no effect on the health or diet of the animals, but may indicate a 'founder effect' of a recessive gene that became expressed in cattle herds throughout Britain during the Romano-British period. It is interesting to note that the incidence of cattle jaws congenitally lacking P_2 drops significantly in the medieval period, when regional types of cattle appear. Although the lack of P_2 has been suggested as being due to nutritional disturbances during the developmental stage of the teeth, there is no apparent reason why this should be a common problem in the Romano-British period but not in the medieval period, nor is there any corroborative evidence of malnutrition from the cattle bones at Stonea.

In fact, the overall levels of health of all of the livestock represented in the Romano-British phases at Stonea were very high.

The age distribution of cattle bones shows that overwintering of stock was no problem, some of the animals living well into maturity through several winters. Only 19 of the 2078 cattle bones show external signs of pathology, and by far the commonest type of pathology observed relates to osteoarthritis, the effects of which are often associated with old age. Various joints have been affected, almost all of them in the feet (one astragalus, one calcaneum, one other tarsal, five metapodials and three phalanges). One hip has also been affected. Apart from the osteoarthritic alterations, only one other bone is abnormal, and this is a mandible from an extremely aged animal. The Mandibular Wear Score is 52 and the teeth have very uneven wear. However, neither this bone nor any of the other jawbones show any examples of abscesses or ante-mortem tooth loss.

The sheep bones show a similarly good level of husbandry. Again, there is one sheep/goat mandible from a very aged individual, whose teeth were unevenly worn but still healthy when the animal died. There is one sheep/goat maxilla with slightly misaligned teeth and there are two sheep metacarpals with evidence of periostitis on their shafts, probably from ossified bruises.

Three pig maxillae have the lateral roots of some of their cheek teeth protruding slightly through the bone, which is a common trait in Romano-British pig skulls (personal observation) and may not have affected the animals during their lives.

Summary of the Romano-British livestock husbandry

Evidence from the bones of the three main domestic species at Stonea suggests that the livestock economy was heavily dependent on the raising of sheep (with a few goats). The sheep were mainly slaughtered at young ages, almost certainly for meat rather than for any other products. Many of the slaughtered sheep were butchered at the site, and the post-cranial carcasses exported, probably to neighbouring small towns in the region. Pigs were also raised for meat, but appear to have been for home consumption. It is possible that mature pigs were exported complete, since no trace of older, breeding sows were found in the excavated portion of the site. In contrast, the cattle were raised probably for general farm purposes such as traction, with dairy products a minor 'sideline'. Most of the cattle deaths were probably unavoidable rather than intentional, although a few may have been slaughtered for home consumption (probably because they were considered unsuitable for anything else, rather than because they had been raised with meat production in mind).

The collection of animal bones from second–fourth century deposits at Stonea forms an interesting comparison with collections from other sites in the region, particularly since it is dominated by the bones of sheep. This was also the case at Maxey (Halstead 1985), Braughing-Puckeridge (Fifield 1988) and Grandford (Stallibrass 1982). This consistency emphasises the importance of sheep in this area during the Roman period. However, the sheep were clearly put to different uses at the different sites. Whereas most of the bones at Grandford derive from mature adult sheep, presumably kept for wool, those at Stonea and Maxey derive mainly from young sheep, that must have been bred primarily as a meat supply. The Stonea sheep were clearly bred with a market in mind, for many of them were slaughtered and butchered at the site and then their carcasses exported elsewhere. Whether this was the case at Maxey, as well, cannot be judged, since the post-cranial material was not examined.

King (1988) has emphasised the importance of sheep at non-Romanised sites but this, perhaps, is an over-simplification that does not take into account regional factors. The land around Stonea is clearly productive sheep land: not only are the collections from both main Romano-British phases dominated by the remains of sheep, but so, too, are the smaller collections from the Anglo-Saxon and post medieval periods (see Table 40). Other evidence at Stonea, particularly that relating to material goods such as metalwork and pottery, demonstrates that the inhabitants had strong links with Roman markets, and were not an isolated 'backwater in the Fens'. Potter (1989b) has suggested that the settlement at Stonea was a consumer rather than a producer site, due to the lack of evidence for industrial activities. The animal

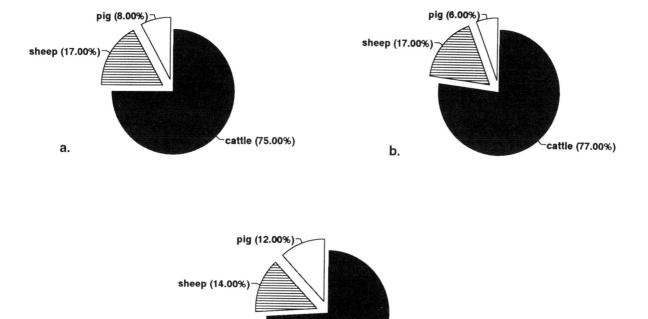

Fig. 233 Stonea Grange: animal bones – relative meatweights from cattle, sheep and pigs, a) second–third century, b) third–fourth century, c) Anglo-Saxon.

bones, however, demonstrate clearly that the people living at Stonea were producing a highly marketable commodity: prime meat from lambs and sheep and, possibly, from pigs too. The Stonea people themselves probably ate the animals that died incidentally or which needed to be culled. In particular, this would have included the cattle (each of which would have provided considerably more meat than any of the sheep carcasses).

Ratios of meatweights provided by the three main domestic species have been calculated from estimates of Minimum Numbers of individuals based on numbers of mandibles. Figure 233 shows that cattle probably provided three-quarters of the meat available from livestock in both of the main Romano-British phases, despite the fact that cattle were the least likely species to have been raised primarily for meat provision. Even when the 'extra' mandibles thought to belong to sheep whose carcasses were exported are included, mutton would have provided only 17% of the meat, and pork (from pigs raised specifically to provide meat) contributed a mere 6–8%. Whilst sheep might have provided the most lucrative trading stock (meat, wool, skins for parchment, and sheepskins), it is the cattle that were most important in terms of food for the inhabitants of the settlement.

Patterns of husbandry in the Anglo-Saxon phase

Table 44 presents the relative distribution of fragments of the three major domesticates (cattle, sheep and pigs) from the Anglo-Saxon and Romano-British deposits recorded in detail (the only Anglo-Saxon animal bones in the selectively recorded sample derive from a pig burial in pit 1933, see below). It is clear that there was no major change through time in the relative abundance of the three species. Fragments identified as sheep (and/or goat) outnumber those of cattle, and these two species dominate the collection. This is 'normal' for Anglo-Saxon collections in Britain (Maltby 1981).

Documentary and archaeological sources suggest that sheep became important economically during the Anglo-Saxon period as suppliers of wool. When a flock is managed for wool production, the kill-off pattern reflects the fact that most animals (whether male or female) are kept for several years, until the quality of their fleece declines. In contrast to a flock culled for meat, therefore, the age range for a population raised for wool should show a heavy bias towards adults. The collection of mandibles and loose teeth from Anglo-Saxon deposits at Stonea is extremely small, but is sufficient to indicate that it is highly *unlikely* that the flock was kept for wool production. Three mandibles have Mandibular Wear Scores (MWSs) of 4, 35 and 40, and a fourth can be estimated at MWS 11. Using the calibration of MWS with chronological age established for the Romano-British collections, these jaws represent one very young lamb of less than 3 months, one lamb of 3–9 months, one young adult of just over 2 years and one more mature adult. Since preservation biases tend to act against the recovery of complete juvenile jaws, the ratio of all deciduous and permanent last premolars has been used to increase the sample available for interpretation. The permanent tooth (P_4) replaces the deciduous tooth (dp_4) at 21–4 months. The Anglo-Saxon deposits at Stonea produced 5 dp_4 s and 3 P_4 s, indicating a slight predominance of animals of less than 2 years old. The Anglo-Saxon deposits at West Stow, Suffolk (Crabtree 1989) produced an extremely large sample of sheep/goat jaws. Unlike the deposits at North Elmham or Hamwih, for which a wool producing economy has been postulated, juvenile jaws outnumbered jaws from mature adults and Crabtree concluded that there was no evidence for wool production at West Stow. She found that the ratio of jaws from animals below and above 2 years of age was 63:37% (i.e. the same as at Stonea). Using six stages of wear, comparable to that used by Bourdillon and Coy (1980) for the Hamwih material, 45% of the West Stow jaws are from animals less than 1 year old. The comparable ratio at Stonea is 63%.

Despite the very low numbers of suitable jaws and teeth from Stonea, it seems clear that the kill-off pattern resembles that of the Romano-British collections, and emphasises the role of Stonea as a meat producing site. The resemblance could be due to a high degree of residuality (which remains unproven), but this seems unlikely for two reasons: i) the collections do differ in other ways (see below), which would not be expected if the material was residual; and ii) it is improbable that the Anglo-Saxon deposits should only contain residual material with no 'fresh' input. Another East Anglian site (Sedgeford, Norfolk: Clutton-Brock 1976) also produced an Anglo-Saxon assemblage that was dominated by sheep bones from young animals. This was probably a small country hamlet and Clutton-Brock contrasts the site with the townships of Thetford (Norfolk) and Hamwih, where the age distributions do suggest that the sheep were raised primarily for wool. The landscape around Stonea might not be suitable for the largescale sheep runs that are usually required for wool production, which tends to be an extensive rather than intensive form of animal husbandry. The land might have been used more profitably in other ways. In addition, sheep kept for wool need to be kept for several years, in order to provide several clips of fleece. If the soils were infested with liver fluke, this might have been a serious hindrance to the husbandry of adult sheep.

Table 46 presents the Minimum Numbers of Elements for the major bones of the body, and illustrates the paucity of material from the Anglo-Saxon deposits compared to those dating to the second–fourth centuries. The number of sheep mandibles is, again, notably higher than those for any other element of sheep, although the disparity is not as marked as it is in both of the Romano-British collections, and is not matched by the numbers of metapodials. Mandibles tend to preserve well and are easily recovered during excavation, so the data may represent whole carcases rather than a mixture of carcases and primary butchery waste.

Typically, the pigs are represented more by mandibles than by any post-cranial element, which is probably due to the fact that many of the pig bones are from juveniles, and these tend to preserve less well than mandibles.

The sex ratio of pig canines ($N = 3$), using the same system for calculations as for the Romano-British material, is three males to zero females. One of these males was a young individual buried in pit 1933. The tooth eruption data indicate that the pig's age at death was greater than 7–13 months but less than 17–22 months, and the post-cranial fusion evidence supports this (i.e. more than 1 year old: acetabulum fused; but less than 2 years old: distal tibia unfused).

The cattle elements are very evenly represented and probably also derive from whole carcases.

Using the minimum numbers of elements to estimate Minimum Numbers of Individuals for the three major species, and converting these into relative amounts of meat, it is clear that meat from cattle would still have provided three quarters of the total, just as it appears to have done in both of the main Romano-British phases (see Fig. 233). The main difference seen in the Anglo-Saxon estimates is the greater importance of pork, which reverses the trend begun in the later Roman period. In the Anglo-Saxon estimates, pork almost equals lamb/mutton in terms of meatweights.

The paucity of measurable bones precludes a comparison of livestock types between the Romano-British and Anglo-Saxon periods. Only one bone can be used to estimate withers heights for any species. This is a sheep metatarsal with a length of 146 mm which converts to an estimated withers height of 663 mm. This is within the range of the Romano-British collection (see Table 51).

There are no externally pathological bones of sheep/goat or cattle in the Anglo-Saxon material. One pig mandible has the P_4 rotated and impacted on the M_1. This is a common abnormality in domestic pigs (whose teeth are quite often crowded in the jaw) and this case shows no sign of any infection. There are only three examples of cattle mandibles retaining the portion where P_2 should be, and all three have the P_2 erupted as normal.

Summary of the Anglo-Saxon livestock husbandry

Overall, the collection of animal bones from the Anglo-Saxon deposits suggests that the settlement continued to be a self-supporting, modest rural community raising sheep (mainly for meat), cattle and pigs. Unlike the Romano-British period, however, there may have been little surplus for export, and in contrast to several other Anglo-Saxon sites in south-east England, there is no evidence that the sheep were being raised for wool production.

Minor species

Occasional bones of horse were scattered throughout deposits of all phases, usually contributing approximately 1% of the fragments recorded in any one phase. None of these bones was found in articulation and all appear to have been part of the normal 'incidental' rubbish at the site.

None of the horse bones from any of the phases has been chopped through, but three of the 102 Romano-British bones (all from Phase IV) bear cutmarks. Two of these are scapula fragments, and may indicate that meat was occasionally filleted off the bone. Although horseflesh was not usually eaten by Romanised people, taboos may have been broken occasionally, or the meat simply used to feed the dogs. The third bone bearing cutmarks is a proximal metatarsal fragment. In this instance, it is unlikely that meat removal was involved, as there is extremely little meat on the metapodials. Instead, it is more likely that the cutmarks resulted from the removal of the hide (for tanning) or the removal of the bone itself (for craftworking).

The other species of domestic animal that was found throughout the site at Stonea is the dog. Some of the dog bones were found as isolated fragments in general rubbish deposits, but several partial or complete skeletons were also found. Dogs of all ages are represented, from neonatal puppies through juveniles to mature adults.

Measurements of complete (fully mature) longbones indicate a range of sizes, including many small, bandy-legged animals. Shoulder heights have been calculated following Harcourt (1974) and are presented in Table 56. They range from 0.24 to 0.72 m. One of the dog bones from the sump (context 29) is a baculum (penis bone) and indicates the presence of a large male dog. Most of the dogs (even the small, bandy-legged variety) were probably working animals rather than pets. They were most probably used for herding livestock, for guarding livestock and other property, and for hunting wild animals.

Some of the dogs incurred injuries during their lives. Although people sometimes break dogs' bones by kicking them or throwing stones at them, it is thought likely that at least some of the injuries sustained by the Stonea dogs were incurred 'during the course of duty'. Herded cattle often kick

Table 56 Stonea Grange: animal bones – estimated shoulder heights for dogs (in mm)*

Context	Element	GL	Estimated shoulder height
2nd/3rd century			
1243	Radius	166	547
1733	Humerus	106	337
1733	Radius	103	347
1733	Humerus + radius		341
1733	Femur	114	345
2820	Humerus	79	
2820	Humerus	79	244
2820	Ulna	85	244
2820	Femur	82	243
2820	Femur	81	245
2820	Tibia	79	241
2820	Femur + tibia		242
2860	Tibia	100	301
2950	Humerus	102	323
2950	Humerus	103	327
2950	Radius	97	328
2950	Radius	97	328
2950	Humerus + radius		326
2950	Humerus + radius		324
2950	Ulna	116	329
2950	Ulna	117	331
2950	Femur	111	336
2950	Radius	94	318
3111	Humerus	153	498
3111	Radius	156	516
3111	Humerus + radius		506
3111	Femur	167	511
3150	Radius	109	366
3rd/4th century			
563	Radius	126	420
563	Femur	137	417
213	Humerus	73	224
Anglo-Saxon			
504	Humerus	209	690
504	Humerus	209	690
504	Radius	201	659
504	Radius	201	659
504	Humerus + radius		672
504	Femur	232	716
504	Tibia	232	687
504	Tibia	234	693
504	Femur + tibia		703

* Factors used are those of Harcourt 1974.

out at the dogs snapping at their heels, and sometimes they make contact and break the dogs' bones. The most commonly affected elements are those of the front of the body (e.g. the head and forelimbs), which tend to be closest to the hooves. In contrast, maltreatment by people often results in broken ribs (none of which were noted in the Stonea material).

The pathological specimens of dog bones at Stonea include one maxilla with a slight bony growth, three broken radii and a broken femur (all from the two main Romano-British phases). Plate XXXIa shows an unusual healed fracture of a dog's radius and ulna found in context 1733 (a third century layer in well 1625). In dogs, the radius and ulna are two full-length, separate bones. In this instance, both bones were broken through at the midpoint but, when the breaks healed, the proximal ulna fused onto the distal radius. The proximal radius then fused onto the ulna/radius at the join, leaving the distal ulna as a vestigial projection. The healed join appears to have been quite healthy, although the individual would have lost some of the ability to rotate the forearm, which might also have been slightly foreshortened. The other two forearm breaks relate only to radii. When this bone is broken on its own, the ulna acts as a splint, and both broken radii appear to have healed well.

The most serious break involved a femur of a dog (see Pl. XXXIb) in context 1756, a late second/third century layer in gully 23. This bone was broken through in the midshaft region, and never healed properly. A broken femur (thigh bone) is extremely painful, as the strong thigh muscles pull the broken edges across each other, causing them to tear through the surrounding tissue. Sometimes the broken edges protrude through the skin, making the damaged area prone to infection. Plate XXXIc shows how the limb was shortened by the muscle pull following the break (compare the left and right femora). It is also clear that the break became infected, and that this infection spread to the lower vertebrae and to the knee joints (see the lumbar vertebrae and the proximal tibiae in Plate XXXIc). Plate XXXIb reveals that the two halves of the broken femur never fused back together, despite the proliferation of new bony growth. The midshaft became, in effect, a new joint, although it is possible that the dog did not use the leg very much since it was probably very painful. The absence of a fully healed break, and the presence of secondary infections suggests that the dog died as a result of the broken leg, possibly through blood poisoning caused by the infection.

An Anglo-Saxon dog skeleton from context 504 in pit 504 is extremely large and strongly built. Estimates of its shoulder height (based on various longbones) range from 0.66–0.72 m. Similarly large dog skeletons have been found at other Anglo-Saxon sites, the upper end of the size range being slightly larger in the Anglo-Saxon period than in the Romano-British period (Harcourt 1974). The Stonea dog was probably male since the bones are all very robust, with

pronounced muscle attachments. It was quite old when it died: all of the epiphyses are fused and the teeth are well worn. On both mandibles the P_2 and the M_3 are missing. In all four cases, it is possible that the teeth erupted but were subsequently lost but, if so, the alveoli have healed over very well. There is plenty of space in the jaws where the teeth would be expected, and so overcrowding cannot be a cause of their absence. It is possible that all four teeth never erupted and are missing congenitally. Although the premolars are all well spaced, the P_4 and M_1 in both mandibles overlap slightly. There is no evidence for any pathology anywhere on the skeleton, apart from a slightly raised area of bone on one of the metatarsals, which might be the result of a bruise (the blood lost can become ossified), but might equally have been caused by over-exertion of a muscle at its insertion. The animal obviously led a long, healthy and active life. Although the sizes of the bones might suggest that the skeleton is that of a wolf rather than of a domestic dog, the facts that the animal was very old, was buried complete and had not been skinned all suggest that it was, in fact, a very large, strong dog, such as might have been used as a hunting dog (for wild boar, deer, etc.) or as a guard dog.

The bones of cat are less usual at Roman sites, but do occur occasionally. It is not possible to suggest whether the Stonea examples are from wild or domestic cats (see also Legge, pp. 513–14).

The wild species of mammal represented in the hand-recovered collection include deer (roe deer and, possibly, red deer) and hare in the two main Romano-British phases. Bones of these species commonly occur in small numbers at Romano-British sites. There are no bones of wild boar at Stonea in any of the phases. Wild boar bones are often scarce or absent on British sites apart from some high status medieval sites where hunting was a favoured pastime. Their absence at Stonea does not necessarily imply that the area had been deforested.

Bones of domestic fowl (chickens) and geese normally occur at Roman and later sites in Britain, and are not remarkable here. Some of the ducks and geese represented at Stonea may have been kept as domestic stock and some may have been caught by wildfowlers (the bones of early domestic ducks and geese are almost impossible to distinguish from those of mallard and greylag). Given the proximity of the site to wetlands, it is probable that wild and domestic ducks and geese interbred.

The other species of bird represented at Stonea tend to reflect the proximity of wetlands and open water, or to be scavengers often associated with human habitations. A humerus of a white tailed (sea) eagle was found in context 1869 (an early third century layer in gully 30). White tailed eagles were widespread in Britain in the Roman period, when they were still found close to water inland as well as at coastal sites (they did not die out in Britain as a breeding species until the eighteenth century AD: Reid-Henry and

Harrison 1988). Their bones have been found at various Romano-British sites, both rural and urban (Parker 1988). It is possible that they were hunted for their wing feathers. A neck vertebra from a very large bird of crane or swan size probably also represents a large waterbird.

The sump contained some excellently preserved water-logged material, including many bird bones. Whether the concentration of bird bones in the sump is due to a) better preservation, b) differential recovery techniques, c) a larger bulk of material excavated or d) a genuine concentration of bird bones cannot be resolved. O'Connor (1986) noted a concentration of bird bones in the bath drains at Caerleon, and Stallibrass (1991) noted a similar concentration of bird bones in drains at the Roman fort in Carlisle. The birds represented in the sump at Stonea include (besides the 'usual' fowl, duck and goose) bones of more or less complete skeletons of cormorant, raven, jackdaw and owl. The corvid species (raven and jackdaw) may have been commensals or pets, and all of the birds could have provided food for people.

Other bird species identified at Stonea include red kite (a common scavenger at settlement sites, that only became rare in Britain due to persecution in the eighteenth and nineteenth centuries) a small dove, and various passerines including house sparrow and a thrush species (probably song thrush). These birds could have been accidental deaths, accruing 'naturally' in the deposits, but it is equally possible that they formed occasional parts of people's diets. The skylark indicates the presence of open grassland in the vicinity of the site, whilst the thrush would have required bushes or trees (which could have occurred in patches of scrub or in hedgerows, as well as in woodland).

In the Anglo-Saxon collections, bones of wild mammals and birds are scarce or absent. This might be due to archaeological factors such as context type, or to small sample size, or it could be a genuine scarcity reflecting a different lifestyle.

2 THE RESIDUES FROM WET-SIEVED SAMPLES

Three hundred and eighty-nine small bags of material sorted from residues from wet-sieved sediment samples were examined for faunal remains. Two thirds of the bags ($N = 250$) derive from Romano-British deposits and 12% ($N = 48$) from Anglo-Saxon deposits. A further 32 (8%) derive from a variety of prehistoric contexts. Most of the remaining contexts are not firmly dated.

The sizes of the samples processed are insufficient to undertake quantification analyses that might redress the bias against the recovery of very small bones that is unavoidable in hand-recovered collections. However, the fact that so many samples were taken, from all of the major periods, does permit useful qualitative studies of the smaller species whose remains were deposited at the site.

Much of the material could not be identified to species level, so broad classes were recorded on a presence/absence basis (see Table 57). These classes are: mammal, small mammal, bird, frog/toad and fish bones, plus marine shells. For the purposes of this study, the 'small mammal' category includes any mammal of water-vole size or smaller, whilst any mammal of rabbit size or larger has been classified as 'mammal'.

Apart from two isolated winkle shells, the marine shells are from oysters and mussels. Shells of both of these species are well distributed throughout the Romano-British deposits, occurring in one third of the samples in both main phases. This contrasts strongly with the prehistoric and Anglo-Saxon samples, in which marine shells occurred in only 3% and 13% respectively. It is difficult to interpret this contrast, however, since the types of context sampled tend to differ between the periods. Many of the prehistoric and Anglo-Saxon contexts were small features such as postholes, which would not be expected to be as rich in finds as

Table 57 Stonea Grange: animal bones – distribution of faunal remains in the wet-sieved sample residues

Period	Total number of residues containing material N	Mammal bone* N	$\%$	Bird bone N	$\%$	Small mammal bone* N	$\%$	Frog/toad bone N	$\%$	Fish bone N	$\%$	Marine shell N	$\%$
Undated	49	21		1		10		4		3		6	
Prehistoric	32	14	44			4	13	3	9	4	13	1	3
2nd/3rd century	153	94	61	31	20	38	25	20	13	39	25	50	33
3rd/4th century	97	62	64	22	23	32	33	10	10	22	23	31	32
Anglo-Saxon	48	26	54	3	6	10	21	4	8	2	4	6	13
Medieval	1												
Post-medieval	6	4	67			3	50	1	17				
Recent	3	2	67	1	33								

*Water-vole and smaller mammals are categorised here as 'small mammal', whilst hare and larger mammals are categorised here as 'mammal'.

general occupation layers and pits, which occurred more commonly in the Romano-British phases. Although the paucity of marine shells in the prehistoric and Anglo-Saxon samples may be due to an absence of evidence rather than genuine evidence of absence, the frequent occurrence of cockle and mussel shells in the Romano-British samples does indicate that contacts and trade with coastal areas were a standard part of the way of life for the people living at Stonea.

It is interesting, therefore, to note that the fish remains do not indicate the same importance for marine resources. The fish bones are often unidentifiable to species level due to the loss of diagnostic parts and almost all consist of small vertebrae (of about 5 mm diameter). Salmonids (the trout and salmon family) and eels are definitely represented, plus at least one carp. Small estuarine species such as dabs may be present, but there are no bones from any large or deep sea fish. The presence of fish bones in one quarter of the second/third century and third/fourth century samples demonstrates that fish, like shellfish, were a standard part of the diet, but it is unlikely that they contributed a major portion of the meat compared to the larger mammals such as cattle and sheep. Chewed fish bones, that could have been eaten by people or by dogs, were recovered from samples from context 1535 (a third century deposit from a latrine) and context 1342 (a third century post-hole), indicating the presence of faecal material in these deposits.

Bones of frogs and toads occur in about 10% of the samples from each of the major periods. They may represent food remains but, perhaps, are more likely to indicate simply that a negative feature (such as a post-hole) remained open long enough to act as a pit-fall trap. Frogs and toads often fall prey to raptors and carnivorous mammals, but the bones at Stonea did not occur in dense clusters (as might be expected for owl pellet remains), nor do they appear damaged or acid etched (as would be expected from carnivore faeces), and they are interpreted here as being most likely to represent occasional natural deaths.

The bones of small mammals (voles, mice and shrews) are present in various frequencies of samples from the prehistoric to Anglo-Saxon phases (see Table 58). They occur in 13%

of the prehistoric samples, one fifth of the Anglo-Saxon samples, one quarter of the second/third century samples and one third of the third/fourth century samples. As with the frog/toad bones, their presence may be due to accidental deaths rather than any actions by humans. Although the small mammals may have been food for carnivores, the relative completeness of their bones argues against any interpretation of consumption by humans, and the lack of any acid etching suggests that owls are the only likely predators to have deposited the bones. Again, the general distribution of small mammal bones (i.e. ubiquitous but in small numbers) suggests that most of the deaths were pitfall accidents.

There are two samples that contain material that is interpreted as being likely to derive from owl pellets, due to the concentration of their remains. The sample from context 494 (a layer in ditch 9 dated to the late third/early fourth century) produced a comparatively large number of small mammal bones together with several small acid-etched fragments of larger mammal bone and very little else. The small, acid-etched fragments probably represent faecal material, although it cannot be said from the bones whether they have been eaten by humans or some other species, such as dogs. The small mammal mandibles indicate Minimum Numbers of: 13 field-voles (*Microtus agrestis*), 1 bank-vole (*Clethrionomys glareolus*), 5 common shrews (*Sorex araneus*) and 1 woodmouse (*Apodemus sylvaticus*). Teeth and post-cranial material indicates the presence of one water-vole (*Arvicola terrestris*) as well.

The sort from a sample from context 574 (another layer in ditch 9, also dated to the late third/early fourth century) also consisted almost entirely of small mammal bones, although the occasional larger mammal bones were not acid-etched in this sample. The mandibles indicate Minimum Numbers of: 10 field voles, 3 common shrews and 1 woodmouse. Again, loose teeth and post-cranial material indicate the presence of one water-vole. In this sample, two bird bones from small passerines (perching birds) were also present. The two humeri are from one bird the size of a bunting or finch and from another similar to a small corncrake. These birds might also have fallen prey to a raptor, although consumption by humans is also possible.

The woodmouse remains are all of the size of *Apodemus sylvaticus* and there is no obvious indication of the presence of any yellow-necked mice (*A. flavicolus*), which is notably larger in its adult form. Unfortunately, no skulls with upper incisors were present that could have been used for metrical determination.

There are no indications of the presence of any house mice (*Mus domesticus*) at the site, although woodmice are well known as commensals in rural areas, particularly during the winter months, and these could have been a nuisance in foodstores.

Similarly, there are no bones attributable to rat, although these have been found at some urban sites dating to the

Table 58 Stonea Grange: animal bones – approximate numbers of individuals of small mammals recovered from wet-sieved sample residues

		Pre-historic	2nd/3rd century	3rd/4th century	Anglo-Saxon
Field vole	*Microtus agrestis*	3	14	26	3
Common shrew	*Sorex araneus*	1	8	10	
Woodmouse	*Apodemus sylvaticus*	2	4	5	
Water-vole	*Arvicola terrestris*		4	5	2
Bank-vole	*Clethrionomys glareolus*		1		
Mole	*Talpa europaea*			1	

Romano-British period, particularly those which acted as ports (such as London and York). Black rats like warm, dry living conditions and, although these may have obtained at the site of Stonea itself, rats might have had problems reaching the site.

Overall, the frequencies and identifications of small mammal remains at Stonea are extremely interesting. Despite the location of the site on a small rise in an otherwise very low-lying area of land that might have been expected to have been very wet in many places, the identifications are overwhelmingly of small mammals that live in open grassland or scrub/woodland. No water shrews (*Neomys fodiens*) were found and water-voles were far outnumbered by field-voles, whose preferred habitat is rough (ungrazed) grassland. The second most commonly occurring species is the common shrew, which also likes thick grassland or greater ground cover such as scrub, hedgerows and deciduous woodland. There is no trend through time for any major changes in habitat, field-voles dominating the suite of small mammals in all four major periods (see Table 58). Bones of mole (*Talpa europaea*) and bank-vole were recovered in single instances.

Most of the bird bones could not be identified to species due to the facts that a) many of the bones recovered are phalanges (toe bones), which are not easily distinguishable between species, and b) many of the other bones are from juveniles. Many of the juvenile bones may well derive from domestic chickens.

Of the bones of larger mammals (hare size or bigger), the vast majority are unidentifiable fragments of bones of cattle size or sheep size, and almost certainly derive from the animals already represented in the hand-recovered collections. Two partial skeletons were recovered. One is of a very young piglet in context 1739 (a late 2nd century deposit in a possible latrine, pit 1638). The upper first molar is erupted but not yet in wear and the vertebral bodies are unfused. Its age at death was probably about 3–4 months. Part of a small to medium sized dog was recovered from context 1743 (a late second/early third century layer in well 1602). The fusion and tooth eruption data suggest that it was between 8–15 months old when it died.

Acid etched bone fragments indicating the presence of faecal material were recovered from a variety of contexts from all periods, although it is not possible from the bones to state whether dogs or people deposited the material (for probable dog faecal material, see Cartwright pp. 612–13).

Summary of the wet-sieved material

Overall, the material from the wet-sieved samples has revealed several aspects of the site that were not apparent from the hand-recovered collections. The small mammal species show that the surrounding countryside contained considerable tracts of open rough grassland, probably with patches of scrub or hedgerows. Very few of the small mammals are likely to have lived in damp or wet habitats. This environmental evidence appears to remain unchanged from the prehistoric to the Anglo-Saxon periods. The fish bones are ubiquitous but are all from small fish, probably mainly salmonids (trouts and/or salmon) and eels. There are no examples of large sea fish, even though the marine mollusc shells of oysters and mussels demonstrate that links with the coast were well established, particularly in the Roman period. The presence of faecal material in several samples can be used to discuss levels of hygiene at the site.

3 SUMMARY OF THE ANIMAL BONES

Animal bone material from Stonea has been studied in three groups. About 9000 fragments of hand-recovered animal bones were recorded in detail for taphonomic and zoological data, whilst a further 10 000 fragments were studied for zoological data alone. In addition, nearly 400 bags of material from samples wet-sieved through 500 µm mesh were scanned for information on small species and faecal material.

Most of the animal bones date to the two main Romano-British phases of occupation (Phase III: second–third century and Phase IV: third–fourth century), with a significant minority deriving from Anglo-Saxon contexts (Phase V: fifth–seventh century). For various reasons, the Anglo-Saxon material is thought to include little residual material.

The overwhelming majority of the identified bones derive from the three main domestic species: sheep, cattle and pigs, all of which appear to have been well looked after. In terms of numbers of individuals, sheep were the dominant species in all three main phases, whilst cattle produced by far the greatest quantities of meat. This is despite the fact that cattle appear to have been kept for anything but meat (this simply being a 'perk' when an animal ceased to be more useful alive). Cattle were slaughtered in small numbers, and were probably kept for general purposes around the settlement such as traction, plus a little milk supply from breeding cows.

In the two main Romano-British phases, the sheep appear to have been kept as a commercial enterprise, with many individuals being slaughtered at the site (at a prime age for meat supply) and their butchered carcases exported elsewhere. Being a roadside settlement near the Fen Causeway, Stonea had good communications, and the nearby small town of Durobrivae may have been a local market for mutton, skins and fleeces. Although pigs were raised primarily for meat for home consumption, they only contributed less than 10% of the total meatweight provided by the domesticates. Wild species of mammals and birds contributed almost nothing to the diet in terms of meatweights, although their distinctive flavours may have been valued, and the sport involved in their occasional capture may have been enjoyed. Domestic chickens were kept, and some of the ducks and geese represented at the site may have been domestic.

Interestingly, apart from the scavenging species, the wild birds at Stonea tend to be indicators of wetlands, whereas the small mammals strongly indicate the presence of rough grassland. This apparent discrepancy may be due to differences in habitat locations, the small mammals deriving from the immediate vicinity of the site and the birds coming in, or being brought in, from further afield. The remains of freshwater fishes indicate that people at Stonea were exploiting local water sources, and the presence of marine mollusc shells shows that they had some links with coastal areas, although it is significant that no deep sea fish remains were found at the site.

None of the species represented in the Romano-British phases are particularly remarkable, although two of the birds (white-tailed eagle and red kite) have become nationally or locally extinct following post-medieval persecution, and the lack of black rat suggests that this species could only colonise British sites if given a port of entry plus suitable living conditions.

Remains of dogs and horses were found in many of the Romano-British contexts. The horses were probably used as pack animals or, possibly, for traction. It is possible that horseflesh was occasionally eaten. The dogs varied in size from small to large and were probably all kept as working dogs. Fractures of long bones indicate that dogs sometimes incurred injuries, either whilst working or through maltreatment.

The material from the Anglo-Saxon phase is very similar to that from the Romano-British deposits. It is particularly interesting to note that sheep continued to be the most numerous species represented and that they continued to have been raised for meat (albeit for home consumption, without a surplus for trade and exchange). This contrasts with some other East Anglian and southern British sites where the age distribution of sheep mandibles suggests that wool was the main product sought from sheep. There may be a distinction between urban and rural livestock husbandry during the Anglo-Saxon period, or a complex system of supply and demand whereby only certain age categories were sent (on the hoof) to urban markets.

Although the post-medieval material from Stonea has not been studied in detail, it is clear that sheep continued to be an important part of the local economy. Independent analysis of the (scarce) ageing evidence for post-medieval sheep bones and teeth by Walsham (1996) demonstrates that they continued to be raised primarily for meat, even though the size and conformation of the animals had changed. Although ground levels and water-table levels have probably fluctuated since the Romano-British period, the current land-use around the site of Stonea may not be fundamentally different (in terms of livestock farming) to that of two millenia ago.

PARASITE OVA

Marijke van der Veen

Eggs of the parasitic intestinal nematodes *Trichuris* (whipworm) and *Ascaris* (maw-worm) have been found frequently in archaeological deposits (Jones 1982, 1985). The analysis of these ova provides important evidence for the occurrence of these common intestinal diseases in the past, and also serves as an indicator of the presence of ancient faeces in archaeological sediments (Jones 1985). Since the presence of mineralised seeds in the latrine (pit 1536, context 1606) suggested the presence of cess, it was felt important to test these deposits for the presence of parasite ova.

Two samples from the latrine deposits (1606 and 1816) and a sample from a well (well 2020, context 2090) were submitted for analysis to Andrew K. G. Jones (Environmental Archaeology Unit, University of York). He examined the sample using the 'Stoll' method for faecal samples (Jones 1985, 109), but, unfortunately, no parasite ova were found in any of the samples. While parasite ova can be fairly durable in archaeological deposits, they do gradually decay (A. Jones, in litt.). The botanical evidence suggests that the preservation conditions were poor, so that the parasite eggs might simply not have been preserved. It is, of course, also possible that the people using the latrine did not suffer from this intestinal disease.

In addition to these latrine samples, a number of possible coprolites from various contexts were submitted to Andrew Jones. They were found during the excavation and come from contexts 1721 (well 704/1663), 1828 (gully 27), 2090 (well 2020) and 1979 (pit 2022). Andrew Jones reported that, on the basis of their general shape and inclusions (small pieces of bone), they were all almost certainly dog excrement. They were disaggregated in dilute HCl and concentrated with magnesium sulphate. None yielded parasite ova on detailed examination (A. Jones, in litt.). It is not clear whether this is a true absence, or an absence caused by poor preservation. For further coprolite material, see Cartwright, following.

COPROLITES

Caroline Cartwright

In addition to the samples just described (van der Veen, Parasite ova) ten other putative coprolite fragments were recovered from four Phase III contexts and were submitted for examination (British Museum Research Laboratory File no. 6548, no. 45239T).

1 ST 84 DOQ

An incomplete circular fragment (2.5 cm diameter) of possible faecal origin was examined using incident light optical microscopy. A small sample was disaggregated for identification of the particles. The fragment is coarse in texture and contains numerous sub-rounded fragments of partially digested bone. Large areas of charred parenchymatous tissue are present. The calcareous matrix is fine in areas close to the 'skin' of the fragment but mostly coarse, almost vesicular, in the main body of the coprolite. The nature of the matrix and the predominance of bone fragments suggests that the material is indeed faecal in origin and probably from a dog.

From the lower fill (unit 1828) of gully 27, cut 2. Late 2nd/early 3rd century AD.

2 ST 84 DRF

A roughly circular possible coprolite, 2.7 cm in diameter, was partially disaggregated for identification. Coarse in texture with numerous bone pieces, this fragment displays a highly calcareous matrix with large, sub-rounded quartz grains. A small quantity of charred parenchymatous tissue is present. Although many more quartz grains are present in this fragment than in no. 1, the matrix and inclusions suggest this is also of canid origin.

From the lower fill (unit 1890) of well 1834. 3rd century AD.

3 ST 84 N2,1

Three small fragments, possibly belonging to one 'torpedo'-shaped coprolite 3.5 cm long × 1.5 cm in diameter. The constituents of the fragments closely resemble those described for no. 1. and suggest dog faeces.

From the upper fill of gully 78. 3rd century AD.

4 ST 84 N2,2

Five conjoining fragments of a possible coprolite of roughly 'torpedo' shape 3.8 cm long × 1.6 cm in diameter. The matrix and included bone particles match those of the probable dog faeces (no. 3) from the upper fill of the same feature.

From the lower fill of gully 78. 3rd century AD.

All the material submitted has a considerable quantity of partially digested bone fragments in a calcareous matrix. Most fragments are coarse textured, often open and almost vesicular in places. Variable quantities of charred parenchymatous cell tissue are present. These may represent tuberous and other plant materials possibly present in hearth or rubbish pit areas subsequently scavenged by dogs. Only fragment no. 2 is significantly different insomuch as it contains numerous large quartz sand grains. This, too, may be the result of buried or scavenged bones being dug up and consumed by the dog. None of the bone inclusions was identifiable to animal species although there is some evidence that mostly medium-sized mammal bones may be present. No fish bone could be recognised. This is not surprising as even during modern experiments in feeding fish to dogs and examining the resultant faeces, it was found that a larger number of bones had been digested and those present in the faeces were unrecognisable (Jones 1984).

PLANT REMAINS

Marijke van der Veen   [Submitted 1986]   (Figs 234–8; Pl. XXXII)

Part I Carbonised seeds

PART I CARBONISED SEEDS

1 Sampling

From 1981 onwards the sampling for plant remains, molluscs, and small animal bones was an integral part of the excavation strategy (during 1980 the excavations had concentrated on the foundations of the stone tower). Initially, an attempt was made to collect a sample from every feature, but the large increase in the scale of the excavations forced us to accept the more realistic policy of collecting a representative sample from each type of feature: pits, ditches, gullies,

Table 59 Stonea Grange: plant remains – overall sample statistics for carbonised plant remains

Phase	No. of litres sieved	No. of contexts sieved	No. of contexts sterile	No. of contexts analysed	No. of litres analysed	Total no. of seeds	No. of seeds per 1 litre
I	243	33	10	23	185	419	2.3
I/II	92.5	6	2	4	87	88	1
II	54	4	2	2	36	21	0.6
III	1820.5	129	44	85	1399.5	2654	1.9
III/IV	309.5	16	4	12	262	207	0.8
IV	1429.5	99	19	80	1227.5	2983	2.4
IV/V	252	16	3	13	225	141	0.6
V	490.5	64	29	35	295	260	0.9
Unphased or contaminated	351	38	–	–	–	–	–
Totals	5042.5	405	113	254	3717	6773	1.8

wells, post-holes etc. Large ditches or gullies were often sampled at more than one section, and the different fills in pits, ditches etc. were, obviously, separately sampled. Large contexts were sometimes sampled more than once.

During the 1981–4 seasons 405 contexts were sampled, representing 5042.5 litres of sediment. During the post-excavation work it became apparent that not all contexts could be adequately dated and that some were contaminated by modern material. The samples from these contexts were, consequently, omitted from the analysis. Table 59 lists the overall sample statistics for each phase. The figures in Table 59 indicate that the number of contexts analysed and the total amount of soil sieved for each of the two main Roman phases of occupation (i.e. Phases III and IV) are very similar indeed. The numbers for the minor phases of occupation (i.e. I/II and V) are much smaller, reflecting the fact that those settlements lay on the edge of the main excavated area.

2 Methods

The aim was to have a standard sample size of two buckets of sediment, i.e. about 20 litres. However, many contexts were smaller than that, especially the post-holes, and the sample size varied accordingly. In Table 60 the average sample volumes are given for each type of context and phase.

All samples were sieved on site. During the 1981 season a simplified 'Siraf' flotation machine was used (Williams 1973), using a 0.5 mm mesh sieve to collect the plant remains and a 1 mm mesh sieve to collect the small animal bones. During the subsequent seasons the samples were processed by hand, using manual flotation (with a 0.5 mm mesh), after which the residues were washed over a 1 mm mesh to retrieve the small bones. The reason for this change in method was the improvement of the recovery rate of the seeds. With the 'Siraf' type flotation machine it was apparent that many seeds were in suspension in the water, but did not float to the surface and hence were not all recovered. With manual flotation, the entire water content of the bucket is poured through a 0.5 mm mesh sieve, ensuring a much higher recovery rate. The molluscs behaved like seeds in the sieving process and were all collected in the 0.5 mm mesh sieve. The flots were air-dried, wrapped in tissue paper, and stored in plastic bags. The residues were air-dried and then examined for small animal bones, any remaining seeds, small finds, etc. The number of seeds found in the residues was negligible.

The sorting of the flots was carried out in the laboratory, with the help of a microscope. Magnifications of ×10 to ×15 were required to pick out the seeds and molluscs from the remaining organic matter. For the identification of the seeds magnifications of ×15–×100 were used. The identifications were made by comparison with modern reference material, seed manuals (Beijerinck 1947; Berggren 1969 and 1981) and floras (Clapham et al 1962; Godwin 1975; Perring et al 1964), and by consultation with colleagues. Nomenclature follows Clapham et al 1962.

3 Results

Because of the very large number of contexts analysed it was not possible to present a table listing the results for each individual context. Instead, the results are presented as follows: Table 60 gives the sample information for each of the main phases and presents the seed density for each of the feature types. Table 61 gives the total number of seeds for each taxon for each of the phases, while Table 62 gives the average number of seeds for each taxon expressed per 10 litres of sediment, in order to facilitate inter-phase comparison. In the following sections the results of the analysis are described for each of the main phases of occupation. For this purpose the results from Phases I, I/II, and II have been combined. The results from Phases III/IV and IV/V have been listed in Table 61. As they confirm the evidence

Table 60 Stonea Grange: plant remains – sample information of carbonised plant remains for each of the four main phases

PHASE I/II

	Sterile	Post-holes	Pits	House gullies	Ditches	Wells	Spreads	Latrines	Total minus sterile	Total
No. of contexts sampled	14*	17	5	5	2	–	–	–	29	43
No. of litres of soil sieved	81.5	109	95	68	36	–	–	–	308	389.5
Average sample volume in litres	5.8	6.4	19	13.6	18	–	–	–	10.6	9.1
Total number of seeds	0	362	94	51	21	–	–	–	528	528
No. of seeds per litre of soil	0	3.3	1	0.8	0.6	–	–	–	1.7	1.4

* 14 sterile contexts = 8 post-holes, 1 pit, 2 gullies, 3 ditches.

PHASE III

	Sterile	Post-holes	Pits	Gullies	Ditches	Wells	Spreads	Latrines	Total minus sterile	Total
No. of contexts sampled	44*	8	24	21	11	11	3	7	85	129
No. of litres of soil sieved	421	44	275.5	422	192	248	54	164	1399.5	1820.5
Average sample volume in litres	9.6	5.5	11.5	20	17.5	22.5	18	23.4	16.5	14
Total number of seeds	0	37	1018	352	79	955	7	206	2654	2654
No. of seeds per litre of soil	0	0.8	3.7	0.8	0.4	3.9	0.1	1.3	1.9	1.5

* 44 sterile contexts = 11 post-holes, 19 pits, 2 gullies, 10 ditches, 2 wells.

PHASE IV

	Sterile	Post-holes	Pits	Gullies	Ditches	Wells	Spreads	Ovens	Total minus sterile	Total
No. of contexts sampled	19*	–	33	12	10	3	3	19	80	99
No. of litres of soil sieved	202	–	474.5	192	139	45	48	329	1227.5	1429.5
Average sample volume in litres	10.6	–	14.4	16	13.9	15	16	17	15	14.4
Total number of seeds	0	–	1369	211	825	31	51	497	2983	2983
No. of seeds per litre of soil	0	–	2.9	1.1	5.9†	0.7	1.1	1.5	2.4	2.1

* 19 sterile contexts = 2 post-holes, 5 pits, 1 gully, 7 ditches, 3 spreads, 1 oven.
† This figure is entirely caused by the high number of seeds in context 509 (762 seeds in 12 litres). The corrected figure (excluding this sample) is 0.5.

PHASE V

	Sterile	Post-holes	Pits	Gullies	Ditches	Wells	Spreads	Ovens	Total minus sterile	Total
No. of contexts sampled	29*	24	7	2	–	1	1	–	35	64
No. of litres of soil sieved	195.5	178.5	62.5	18	–	24	12	–	295	490.5
Average sample volume in litres	6.7	7.4	8.9	9	–	24	12	–	8.4	7.7
Total number of seeds	0	231	21	5	–	2	1	–	260	260
No. of seeds per litre of soil	0	1.3	0.3	0.3	–	0.1	0.1	–	0.9	0.5

* 29 sterile contexts = 25 post-holes, 1 pit, 2 gullies, 1 well.

Table 61 Stonea Grange: plant remains – total number of carbonised seeds for each phase

Phase	I	I/II	II	III	III/IV	IV	IV/V	V
No. of contexts	23	4	2	85	12	80	13	35
No. of litres sieved	185	87	36	1399.5	262	1227.5	225	295
Cereals								
Triticum spp. (wheat)	52	12	•	30	4	57	7	12
Triticum spp. (hexaploid) (wheat)	•	•	•	51	2	124	•	5
Triticum aestivo/compactum type (bread/club wheat)	•	•	•	3	•	9	•	3
Hordeum vulgare (six-row hulled barley)	26	6	•	74	4	113	11	4
Avena sp. (oat)	4	•	•	5	•	2	•	•
Secale cereale (rye)	•	1	•	•	•	•	•	•
Cerealia indet.	208	18	4	205	14	452	17	61
Chaff								
Glume bases *Triticum* spp.	67	27	11	269	2	487	2	8
Glumes *Triticum* spp.	3	•	•	•	•	•	•	•
Rachis internodes *Triticum* spp. (brittle rachis)	2	2	•	19	•	43	•	1
Rachis internodes *Hordeum vulgare*	•	1	•	42	•	2	•	2
Awn fragment *Avena* sp.	1	•	•	•	•	•	•	•
Culm nodes cereals/large grasses	1	•	•	114	23	45	3	5
Chaff indet.	1	•	•	3	•	1	•	•
Other crop plants								
Linum usitatissimum L. (flax)	•	•	•	3	1	3	1	•
Vicia faba L. (celtic bean)	•	1	•	12	•	•	•	•
Pisum sativum L. (pea)	•	•	•	1	•	1	•	•
Lens culinaris (lentil)	•	•	•	1	•	1	•	•
Large legumes indet.	•	•	•	22	•	39	•	•
Ficus carica L. (fig) (not carbonised)	•	•	•	4	•	•	•	•
Trees & shrubs								
Corylus avellana L. (hazel)	3	•	•	6	1	7	1	1
Fraxinus excelsior L. (ash)	•	•	•	25	•	1	•	•
Sambucus nigra L. (elder)	•	•	•	2	3	4	•	•
Prunus cf. *spinosa* L. (blackthorn, sloe)	•	•	•	1	•	•	•	•
Crataegus monogyna Jacq. (hawthorn)	•	•	•	1	•	•	•	•
Crataegus sp. (hawthorn)	•	•	•	•	•	1	•	•
Buxus sempervirens L. (box)	•	•	•	1	•	•	•	•
Myrica gale L. (sweet gale)	•	•	•	2	•	•	•	•
Rubus fruticosus agg. (bramble)	•	•	•	1	•	•	•	•
Plants of wet ground								
Cladium mariscus (L.) Pohl (giant sword sedge)	2	•	2	563	60	306	24	19
Scirpus maritimus/lacustris (sea club-rush/bulrush)	•	•	•	151	7	165	7	4
Scirpus tabernaemontani C. C. Gmel (glaucus bulrush)	•	•	•	47	2	39	5	•
Eleocharis cf. *palustris* (L.) Roem. & Schult (common spike rush)	•	•	•	105	•	17	1	6
Carex spp. (sedges)	•	•	1	34	4	87	10	8
Carex flava type (sedge)	•	•	•	8	1	1	•	•
Carex nigra group (sedge)	•	•	•	•	•	2	•	•
Juncus sp. (capsule) (rush)	•	•	•	2	•	2	•	•
Culmnodes *Phragmites/Cladium*?	•	•	•	10	•	7	•	•
Stem fragments *Phragmites/Cladium*	•	•	•	+++	•	+	•	•
Sparganium sp. (bur-reed)	•	•	•	2	•	•	•	•
Najas marina L. (holly-leaved naiad)	•	•	•	•	•	1	•	•
Hydrocotyle vulgaris L. (pennywort)	•	•	•	2	•	•	•	•
Stellaria palustris Retz. (marsh stitchwort)	•	•	•	3	•	2	•	•
Galium palustre L. (marsh bedstraw)	•	•	•	3	•	•	•	•
Rumex hydrolapathum Huds (great water dock)	•	•	•	1	•	•	•	•
Ranunculus flammula L. (lesser spearwort)	•	•	•	1	•	•	•	•

Table 61 continued

Phase	I	I/II	II	III	III/IV	IV	IV/V	V
No. of contexts	23	4	2	85	12	80	13	35
No. of litres sieved	185	87	36	1399.5	262	1227.5	225	295
Arable & waste land weeds								
Ranunculus acris L. (meadow buttercup)	·	·	·	·	·	1	·	·
Ranunculus repens L. (creeping buttercup)	·	1	·	·	·	·	·	·
Ranunculus sp. (ac/bul/rep)	·	·	·	11	·	6	·	·
Papaver rhoeas/dubium (poppy)	·	·	·	7	1	5	·	1
Brassica campestris L. (wild turnip)	·	·	·	5	·	30	·	·
Raphanus raphanistrum L. (wild radish)	·	·	·	2	·	1	·	·
Viola sp. (violet)	·	·	·	1	·	·	·	·
Silene alba (Mill.) E. H. L. Krause (white campion)	1	·	·	·	·	·	·	·
Stellaria media (L.) Vill. (chickweed)	·	·	·	2	·	3	1	·
Stellaria sp.	·	·	·	·	1	·	·	·
Caryophyllaceae indet.	·	·	·	2	·	1	·	·
Montia fontana, spp. *chondrosperma* (Fenzl) S. M. Walters (blinks)	·	·	·	4	·	3	·	1
Chenopodium album L. (fat hen)	1	1	·	13	·	15	·	·
Chenopodium sp.	3	1	·	11	·	7	·	2
Atriplex hastata/patula (orache)	·	·	·	24	1	6	1	·
Chenopodiaceae indet.	·	·	·	·	·	2	·	·
Vicia/Lathyrus (vetch)	·	·	·	44	4	85	1	6
Leguminosae indet. (small seeded)	1	·	·	71	19	78	5	7
Potentilla sp. (tormentil)	·	·	·	·	·	1	·	·
Conium maculatum L. (hemlock)	·	·	·	5	·	3	·	9
Polygonum aviculare agg. (knotgrass)	2	·	·	11	·	4	·	·
Polygonum convolvulus L. (black bindweed)	2	·	·	1	·	14	·	·
Polygonum lapathifolium L. (pale persicaria)	3	·	·	·	·	1	·	·
Polygonum persicaria L. (red shank)	7	1	·	2	·	1	·	·
Polygonum sp.	·	·	·	2	·	5	·	1
Rumex acetosella agg. (sheep's sorrel)	·	·	·	18	·	3	·	1
Rumex spp. (docks)	3	1	·	122	8	126	14	23
Polygonaceae indet.	2	·	·	·	·	3	·	1
Urtica dioica L. (stinging nettle)	·	·	·	7	·	·	·	·
Lithospermum arvense L. (corn gromwell)	·	·	·	1	·	2	·	·
Hyoscyamus niger L. (henbane)	·	·	·	1	·	3	·	·
Rhinanthus cf. *minor* L. (yellow rattle)	·	·	·	1	·	1	·	·
Odontites/Euphrasia	·	·	·	4	·	4	·	1
Mentha arvensis/aquatica (mint)	·	·	·	9	·	1	·	·
Prunella vulgaris L. (self heal)	·	·	·	2	·	1	1	1
Stachys palustris L. (marsh woundwort)	·	·	·	1	·	·	·	·
Plantago major L. (great plantain)	2	·	·	5	·	9	1	1
Plantago lanceolata L. (ribwort plantain)	·	·	·	7	2	8	·	·
Galium aparine L. (goosegrass)	·	·	·	17	1	27	·	1
Galium sp.	·	·	·	3	·	·	·	·
Anthemis cotula L. (stinking mayweed)	·	·	·	·	·	3	·	·
Tripleurospermum maritimum (L.) Koch (scentless mayweed)	2	·	·	4	·	9	·	·
Arctium sp. (burdock)	·	·	1	5	·	·	·	·
Centaurea sp.	·	·	·	1	·	1	·	·
Crepis capillaris (L.) Walh. (smooth hawk's beard)	·	·	·	1	·	·	·	·
Arrhenatherum elatius. var. *bulbosum* (Willd.) Spencer (onion couch)	·	·	·	·	·	1	·	·
Sieglingia decumbens (L.) Berh. (heath grass)	·	·	·	1	2	·	·	·
Bromus sp. (bromegrass)	6	4	·	32	·	109	·	15
Small grasses	·	1	·	59	1	38	·	5
Gramineae indet.	10	8	2	102	11	145	2	23
Indeterminate	4	2	·	204	28	196	26	22
TOTALS	419	88	21	2654	207	2983	141	260

Table 62 Stonea Grange: plant remains – average number of carbonised seeds in 10 litres of sediment for each of the main phases of occupation

Phase	I/II	III	IV	V
Cereals				
Triticum spp. (wheat)	++++	++	++	++
Triticum spp. (hexaploid) (wheat)	•	++	+++	++
Triticum aestivo/compactum type (bread/club wheat)	•	+	+	+
Hordeum vulgare (six-row hulled barley)	+++	++	+++	+
Avena sp. (oat)	+	+	+	•
Secale cereale (rye)	+	•	•	•
Cerealia indet.	++++++	++++	+++++	++++
Chaff				
Glume bases *Triticum* spp.	++++	++++	+++++	++
Glumes *Triticum* spp.	+	•	•	•
Rachis internodes *Triticum* spp. (brittle rachis)	+	+	++	+
Rachis internodes *Hordeum vulgare*	+	++	+	+
Awn fragment *Avena* sp.	+	•	•	•
Culm nodes cereals/large grasses	+	+++	++	++
Chaff indet.	•	+	+	•
Other crop plants				
Linum usitatissimum L. (flax)	•	+	+	•
Vicia faba L. (celtic bean)	+	+	•	•
Pisum sativum L. (pea)	•	+	+	•
Lens culinaris (lentil)	•	+	+	•
Large legumes indet.	•	+	++	•
Ficus carica L. (fig) (not carbonised)	•	+	•	•
Trees & shrubs				
Corylus avellana L. (hazel)	+	+	+	+
Fraxinus excelsior L. (ash)	•	++	+	•
Sambucus nigra L. (elder)	•	+	+	•
Prunus cf. *spinosa* L. (blackthorn, sloe)	•	+	•	•
Crataegus monogyna Jacq. (hawthorn)	•	+	•	•
Crataegus sp. (hawthorn)	•	•	+	•
Buxus sempervirens L. (box)	•	+	•	•
Myrica gale L. (sweet gale)	•	+	•	•
Rubus fruticosus agg. (bramble)	•	+	•	•
Plants of wet ground				
Cladium mariscus (L.) Pohl (giant sword sedge)	+	+++++	++++	+++
Scirpus maritimus/lacustris (sea club-rush/bulrush)	•	+++	+++	+
Scirpus tabernaemontani C. C. Gmel (glaucus bulrush)	•	++	++	•
Eleocharis cf. *palustris* (L.) Roem. & Schult (common spike rush)	•	+++	+	++
Carex spp. (sedges)	+	++	+++	++
Carex flava type (sedge)	•	+	+	•
Carex nigra group (sedge)	•	•	+	•
Juncus sp. (capsule) (rush)	•	+	+	•
Culmnodes *Phragmites/Cladium*?	•	+	+	•
Stem fragments *Phragmites/Cladium*	•	+++	+	•
Sparganium sp. (bur-reed)	•	+	•	•
Najas marina L. (holly-leaved naiad)	•	•	+	•
Hydrocotyle vulgaris L. (pennywort)	•	+	•	•
Stellaria palustris Retz. (marsh stitchwort)	•	+	+	•
Galium palustre L. (marsh bedstraw)	•	+	•	•
Rumex hydrolapathum Huds (great water dock)	•	+	•	•
Ranunculus flammula L. (lesser spearwort)	•	+	•	•

Table 62 continued

Phase	I/II	III	IV	V
Arable & waste land weeds				
Ranunculus acris L. (meadow buttercup)	+	•	•	•
Ranunculus repens L. (creeping buttercup)	•	+	+	•
Ranunculus sp. (ac/bul/rep)	•	+	+	+
Papaver rhoeas/dubium (poppy)	•	•	+	•
Brassica campestris L. (wild turnip)	•	+	++	•
Raphanus raphanistrum L. (wild radish)	•	+	+	•
Viola sp. (violet)	•	+	•	•
Silene alba (Mill.) E. H. L. Krause (white campion)	+	•	•	•
Stellaria media (L.) Vill. (chickweed)	•	+	+	•
Caryophyllaceae indet.	•	+	+	•
Montia fontana, spp. *chondrosperma* (Fenzl) S. M. Walters (blinks)	•	+	+	+
Chenopodium album L. (fat hen)	+	+	+	•
Chenopodium sp.	+	+	+	+
Atriplex hastata/patula (orache)	•	++	+	•
Chenopodiaceae indet.	•	•	+	•
Vicia/Lathyrus (vetch)	•	++	+++	++
Leguminosae indet. (small seeded)	+	++	+++	++
Potentilla sp. (tormentil)	•	•	+	•
Conium maculatum L. (hemlock)	•	+	+	++
Polygonum aviculare agg. (knotgrass)	+	+	+	•
Polygonum convolvulus L. (black bindweed)	+	+	+	•
Polygonum lapathifolium L. (pale persicaria)	+	•	+	•
Polygonum persicaria L. (red shank)	++	+	+	•
Polygonum sp.	•	+	+	+
Rumex acetosella agg. (sheep's sorrel)	•	+	+	+
Rumex spp. (docks)	+	+++	+++	+++
Polygonaceae indet.	+	•	+	+
Urtica dioica L. (stinging nettle)	•	+	•	•
Lithospermum arvense L. (corn gromwell)	•	+	+	•
Hyoscyamus niger L. (henbane)	•	+	+	•
Rhinanthus cf. *minor* L. (yellow rattle)	•	+	+	•
Odontites/Euphrasia	•	+	+	+
Mentha arvensis/aquatica (mint)	•	+	+	•
Prunella vulgaris L. (self heal)	•	+	+	+
Stachys palustris L. (marsh woundwort)	•	+	•	•
Plantago major L. (great plantain)	+	+	+	+
Plantago lanceolata L. (ribwort plantain)	•	+	+	•
Galium aparine L. (goosegrass)	•	+	++	•
Galium sp.	•	+	•	•
Anthemis cotula L. (stinking mayweed)	•	•	+	•
Tripleurospermum maritimum (L.) Koch (scentless mayweed)	+	+	+	•
Arctium sp. (burdock)	+	+	•	•
Centaurea sp.	•	+	+	•
Crepis capillaris (L.) Walh. (smooth hawk's beard)	•	+	•	•
Arrhenatherum elatius. var. *bulbosum* (Willd) Spencer (onion couch)	•	•	+	•
Sieglingia decumbens (L.) Berh. (heath grass)	•	+	•	•
Bromus sp. (bromegrass)	++	++	+++	++
Small grasses	+	++	++	++
Gramineae indet.	+++	+++	+++	+++
Indeterminate	++	++++	++++	+++

+	0.001–0.14 seeds per 10 litres	++++	1.5–3.4	
++	0.15–0.54	+++++	3.5–5	
+++	0.55–1.4	++++++	5+	

from Phases III, IV and V without offering new information, they are not discussed further.

Phase I/II

A total of 29 contexts were analysed from this period, 17 of which were post-holes. Of the 528 seeds found, 331 were cereal grains, 116 chaff fragments, 1 celtic bean, 3 hazelnut shell fragments, and 77 seeds of herbaceous species. Most of the cereal grains were badly preserved; the wheat grains could not be identified to species level (*Triticum* sp.). The barley grains belonged to *Hordeum vulgare*, six-row hulled barley (many lateral grains, ridges on the dorsal surface, and an angular cross-section). Because of the absence of the flowerbases the oat grains could not be identified to species level (*Avena* sp.). One grain of *Secale cereale*, rye, was found. The majority of the cereal grains were so badly preserved that they could not even be identified to genus level (i.e. Cerealia indet.).

Although the wheat grains were too badly preserved to identify them to species level, the glume bases indicated the presence of both emmer (*Triticum dicoccum*) and spelt wheat (*Triticum spelta*). On the basis of the venation pattern and the angles of the glume faces, the presence of both emmer and spelt wheat could be established, both occurring in similar quantities. The morphological characteristics of emmer glume bases are: the strongly developed primary keel, a fairly prominent secondary 'keel', and poorly developed tertiary veins. The angle between the glume faces on either side of the primary keel is less than 90°, while the angle on either side of the secondary 'keel' is distinct, but obtuse. Glume bases of spelt wheat possess a prominent primary keel, but the secondary 'keel' cannot easily be distinguished from the strongly developed tertiary veins. The angle between the glume faces on either side of the primary keel is greater than 90 degrees, while the glume faces on either side of the secondary 'keel' form an almost smooth curve (G. Hillman, personal communication). The measurements of the glume widths at the level of spikelet articulation (measurement B, Helbaek 1952) are presented in Fig. 234 and also indicate the presence of two species.

One other crop plant was found in the samples, i.e. *Vicia faba*, celtic bean. The only other food plant present was *Corylus avellana*, hazelnut, of which three small shell fragments were found.

Apart from *Cladium mariscus*, sedge, or giant-sword sedge, all other herbaceous plants were species frequently found in charred plant assemblages, and are common weeds of arable and waste places. The achenes of scentless mayweed (*Tripleurospermum maritimum*) were identified as sub-species *inodorum* on the basis of the presence of round oil glands (cf. Clapham *et al* 1962). The grass caryopses were so fragmented that no attempt was made to identify them to genus. The remains of *Arctium* consisted of the inside part

of the achene. The plants of *Cladium mariscus* will have grown in a reed-swamp at some distance from the site. The weeds would suggest that the soils used for agriculture were rich in mineral nitrogen, circum-neutral and well-drained (neither wet, nor dry).

Phase III

A total of 2654 seeds were found for this phase. The plant assemblage was dominated by plants of wet ground, like *Cladium mariscus, Scirpus* spp. etc. While the number of contexts analysed was much higher than in the previous phase, the number of cereal grains found was similar, i.e. 368.

The wheat grains have been divided into three categories, i.e. *Triticum* spp., when the grains were too badly preserved to be identified to species level; *Triticum* spp. (hexaploid), when the grains were relatively flat, with rounded ends, and with relatively straight sides; and *Triticum aestivo/compactum*, when the grains were very short, broad and compact, and have a maximum width just above the embryo. Most of the *Triticum* spp. (hexaploid) grain probably belonged to *Triticum spelta*. The barley grains belonged to *Hordeum vulgare*, six-row hulled barley. The oat grains could not be identified to species level.

The venation pattern on the glume bases and the angles of the glume faces indicated that most of the glume bases belonged to *Triticum spelta*, spelt wheat, but there were still a few glumebases of emmer wheat (*Triticum dicoccum*) present as well. The measurements of the width of the glume bases at the level of spikelet articulation is given in Fig. 234, which shows a shift to the right of the diagram compared with the measurements of Phase I/II, indicating the move from the narrower emmer to the broader spelt.

A surprisingly large number of culm nodes or straw nodes of cereals were found in the samples. It is generally assumed that it is impossible to distinguish the culm nodes of cereals from those of large grasses, but when they occur in charred plant assemblages with other cereal remains, they are usually taken to represent cereal straw nodes (but see discussion below).

In addition to the cereals, evidence for five other crops was found. Three seeds of flax (*Linum usitatissimum*) were present. The seeds of flax are usually underrepresented in charred plant assemblages (they are much less likely to get charred than cereals) and their presence, combined with the presence of flax pollen (see Part III, pp. 636–8), suggests that flax was an important crop. Unfortunately, it is not possible to tell from the seeds whether the plant was used for its fibre (linen), or for the oil content of the seeds (linseed oil).

Three different pulse crops were found: celtic bean (*Vicia faba*), pea (*Pisum sativum*), and lentil (*Lens culinaris*). The lentil probably represents an imported crop (see discussion section). There were a large number of fragments of legumes which could not be identified. The low numbers of the

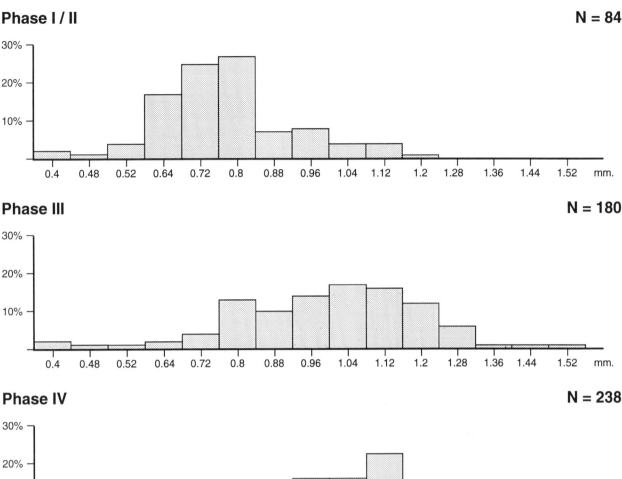

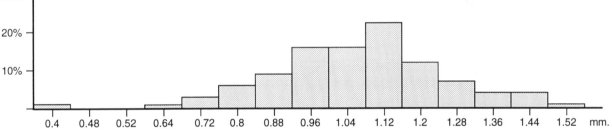

Fig. 234 Stonea Grange: plant remains – glume widths of the carbonised glume bases of *Triticum* spp., measured at the level of spikelet articulation.

pulses does not mean that they formed an unimportant crop, however; it is a common feature of charred plant assemblages that pulses are underrepresented.

The presence of fig pips (*Ficus carica*) in a latrine is also mentioned here, although the seeds were not preserved by carbonisation, but by waterlogging of the soil. Like the lentils, they were probably a luxury food item.

Eight species of small trees or shrubs were found. The presence of carbonised ash keys (*Fraxinus excelsior*), and of a charred box leaflet (cf. *Buxus sempervirens*) is unusual. If preserved at all, they are usually found in waterlogged contexts.

As already mentioned above, the samples are dominated by plants of wet ground. The most common plant in this category is *Cladium mariscus*, giant-sword sedge, followed by *Scirpus maritimus/lacustris*, sea club-rush/bulrush, *Eleocharis* cf. *palustris*, spike-rush, *Scirpus tabernaemontani*, glaucus bulrush,

and *Carex* spp., sedges. The seeds of *Scirpus maritimus* and *Scirpus lacustris* are very difficult to distinguish from one another. The seeds in these samples are very varied in shape and size, which might suggest that they belong to *S. maritimus* (van Zeist, personal communication). *Scirpus tabernaemontani* is also known as *Schoenoplectus tabernaemontani* (C. C. Gmel.) Palla, or as *Scirpus lacustris*, subsp. *glaucus*. A number of very large culm nodes were found. Initially it was thought that they belonged to *Phragmites communis*, reed, but comparison with *Cladium* nodes now suggest they are more likely to belong to *Cladium*, but the identification is very uncertain. The nutlets of *Carex*, sedge, are notoriously difficult to identify, and they have not been identified further, with the exception of two types.

In addition to these fen species, there is a large range of weeds from arable and waste places. Their ecological requirements suggest the use of a wider range of soil types than in the previous phase (see discussion section). The weeds indicate the presence of soils ranging from acid to neutral, from poor to rich in mineral nitrogen, but with adequate moisture levels (i.e. neither too wet nor too dry).

Phase IV

The plant assemblage from this phase is very similar to that of Phase III. While the number of cereal grains and chaff fragments is higher than in Phase III, the same range of species is present: *Triticum spelta* and *Hordeum vulgare*, with only a trace of *Triticum aestivo/compactum* and *Avena* sp. The evidence from the glume bases indicates that emmer wheat (*Triticum dicoccum*) is no longer present (see also Fig. 234).

As in Phase III, the category of 'other crop plants' includes flax, peas, and lentils. No celtic beans were found, but there are a large number of legume fragments. They may include fragments of *Vicia faba*. Unfortunately, fragments of cotelydons of large legumes are very difficult to identify. Again, one lentil was found, but no figs were recorded for this period.

The ranges of trees and shrubs, and plants of wet ground, is slightly smaller than in Phase III, but the species found also occurred in Phase III. The range of weeds is again very similar, and does not need any further discussion here.

Phase V

As with the prehistoric occupation on the site, the Anglo-Saxon settlement was located towards the northern edge of the excavated area. The plant assemblage recovered from this phase is rather small, only 260 seeds in total. The cereals account for one third of the assemblage. *Triticum* spp. (hexaploid), almost certainly spelt wheat, *Hordeum vulgare* and *Triticum aestivo/compactum*, are again the cereal species present. The venation pattern and the angles of the glume faces of the glumebases that were well enough preserved all belonged to spelt wheat. The number of glumebases found was insufficient to draw up a histogram of the measurements of their widths.

No other crop plants were found and, apart from one small fragment of hazelnut shell, no other food plants were found. Only a relatively small number of waterplants was found (*Cladium mariscus*, *Scirpus maritimus/lacustris*, *Eleocharis* cf. *palustris* and *Carex* spp.). The range of weed species was restricted, as in Phase I/II, but unlike Phase I/II there are a number of species indicative of poor and slightly acidic soil conditions.

4 Discussion

1 Crop plants

During each of the four phases of occupation the main crop plants identified were wheat and barley. In the Late Bronze Age two glume-wheats were present, *Triticum dicoccum*, emmer, and *Triticum spelta*, spelt wheat. In the first main Roman period (Phase III) emmer was still present, but only as a very small component, while in the later Roman period (Phase IV) it had disappeared completely (see also Fig. 234). Spelt wheat was the dominant wheat species in the Roman period. The free-threshing wheat *Triticum aestivo/compactum*, bread/compact wheat, was present during the Roman and Anglo-Saxon periods, but only in very small numbers. Its relative importance is difficult to assess.

The increase in spelt wheat at the expense of emmer wheat at Stonea mirrors similar developments in other parts of the country (Green 1985; Jones 1981; Murphy 1991). Although it has been suggested that free-threshing wheat had become the dominant wheat species by the Anglo-Saxon period (Jones 1981), the evidence from Stonea, and also from other East Anglian sites (Murphy 1985), indicates that in that region the cultivation of spelt continued into the Anglo-Saxon period, implying that the shift from glume-wheat to free-threshing wheat had not been simultaneous across Britain; the shift from emmer to spelt seems to show a similar regional variation.

Unfortunately, it was not possible to establish whether the few oat grains found belonged to the cultivated or the wild species of oat. The occurrence of rye, *Secale cereale*, in Phase I/II is remarkable. Although only one grain was found the dating evidence is reasonably secure. The history of rye as a crop plant in Britain is still far from clear. Rye has usually been regarded as a Roman or Late Iron Age introduction into Britain, but recently a number of Early Bronze Age pollen records of rye have come to light, suggesting a far greater antiquity for rye in Britain than originally thought (Chambers and Jones 1984). The paucity of early macrofossil records makes it difficult to interpret these pollen records, but this might be a consequence of inadequate recovery techniques. The application of large scale flotation of a wide range of contexts on excavations (as at Stonea) might soon redress this imbalance. Early rye records are now known from Myrehead, Scotland (Barclay and Fairweather 1984: early first millennium bc), Asheldham Camp, Essex (tentative identification, Murphy 1991: Iron Age), and this find at Stonea (Late Bronze Age).

Interestingly, the context that produced this early record for rye also produced an early record for celtic bean, *Vicia faba*. Most British records of celtic bean are from Iron Age sites (Jones 1981), but a few Late Bronze Age records are now known as well, i.e. Lofts Farm and Frog Hall Farm, Fingringhoe, Essex (Murphy 1991) and Black Patch, Sussex (Hinton 1982); and one late Neolithic record from Ogmore, West Glamorgan (Hillman 1981a).

The presence of celtic beans (*Vicia faba*), pea (*Pisum sativum*), and flax (*Linum usitatissimum*) in the Roman period at Stonea compares well with records for other Roman sites in Britain.

Both the lentils (*Lens culinaris*), and figs (*Ficus carica*) found in the Roman period are regarded as imported crops, probably from the Mediterranean region. The presence of lentils and figs is quite unusual as the two species are not only rarely found in Britain, but, more significantly, are almost exclusively confined to urban or military sites. Lentils have been found in Roman London and possibly in Roman Colchester (Willcox 1977; Murphy 1984; Straker 1984), and also in Isca (Caerleon) (Helbaek 1964). Figs are commonly found in urban deposits, such as Roman London, York, Colchester and Carlisle (Willcox 1977; Kenward and Williams 1979; Donaldson and Rackham 1984; Murphy 1984). There is a certain amount of discussion in the literature about the question of whether these crops could physically have been grown in Britain (Willcox 1977; Straker 1984), but they are here regarded as imports from the Mediterranean region. The fact that they are almost exclusively found in urban contexts would seem to confirm this interpretation. However, it is not suggested that the people of Stonea obtained these luxury food items directly from the Mediterranean; it is more likely that they came via one of the Roman towns in Britain. The presence of these species at Stonea would, therefore, seem to confirm the unusual character of the site. The only exception to the urban and military character of the findspots for lentils is the record of lentils at Maxey, a native farmstead on the fen-edge, although the identification is only tentative (Green 1985, 230). The lentils at Maxey are thought to have come in as an imported crop or as a crop contaminant. There is, in fact, no evidence for crop production at Maxey (Green 1985).

The range of crop plants found at Stonea and the changes through time in this range seem in general to mirror the developments known from other parts of Britain. Unfortunately, it was not possible to say exactly when the shift from emmer to spelt took place, as no Iron Age assemblages were recovered, but it must have been sometime in the Early Iron Age. The shift from spelt to bread/compact wheat must have taken place after *c.* AD 700, as spelt was still present in the Anglo-Saxon assemblage at Stonea. The early records for rye and celtic bean, and the finds of lentil and fig demonstrate the importance of large scale flotation programmes on site.

2 Use of wild plants

In contrast to the Late Bronze Age and Anglo-Saxon periods, a wide range of wild plants other than weeds of arable and waste places, was found in the Roman period. These wild plants can be divided into two categories: firstly, the wild trees and shrubs (see also Cartwright, pp. 552–83); and secondly, the plants of wet ground.

The first category consists of hazelnut (*Corylus avellana*), elderberry (*Sambucus nigra*), blackberry (*Rubus fruticosus*), hawthorn (*Crataegus monogyna*), blackthorn or sloe (*Prunus spinosa*), ash (*Fraxinus excelsior*), box (*Buxus sempervirens*) and sweet gale (*Myrica gale*). The fruits of hazelnut, elderberry, blackberry, sloe and hawthorn could have been either eaten or used in the preparation of beverages. The presence of carbonised ash keys and a carbonised leaflet, probably of box, is very unusual, but waterlogged ash keys have also been found (see Part II, pp. 629–36; Cartwright, p. 571). It is not clear whether the ash keys were used for a specific purpose, or just became incorporated in the assemblage by accident. Box leaves and seeds are strongly purgative and have been used herbally as a blood purifier and against rheumatism (Polunin 1976). Box leaves have been found on other Roman sites, but always in waterlogged conditions (A. Hall, personal communication). Sweet gale has in the past been used as bedding material; the stems give off a sweet resinous smell when bruised. The plant was also used, often instead of hop, as a flavouring and preservative in beer, especially in Danish and north German beer (Behre 1984). There is no evidence here for a connection of sweet gale with brewing activities.

All plants in this category, with the exception of sweet gale, could have grown very close to the site as part of some scrub woodland or in hedgerows, or even as individual trees around the settlement.

The second category is that of plants of wet ground. They can be divided into two subgroups, i.e. plants of reed-swamps, fens and ponds, growing in still, standing water (such as *Cladium mariscus*, *Scirpus* spp. and *Phragmites communis*), and plants of wet ground, ditches and fen meadows (such as *Carex* spp., *Juncus* spp., *Eleocharis*, *Stellaria palustris*, *Ranunculus flammula* etc.).

None of these species could be interpreted as weeds of arable fields, nor are they likely to have grown on the site itself (except possibly in the ditches; see Part II, pp. 629–36). The most likely explanation for their presence (especially as they are charred), is that they were brought to the site for a particular purpose. Considering the species present, they probably represent raw materials for thatching and litter. *Cladium mariscus*, giant sword-sedge, is the dominant species in this category. It is a natural component of the Fenland vegetation, preferring a depth of a few centimetres of water. Its leaves grow to a length of up to 3 m. Their durability exceeds that of cereal straw and reed, and consequently it has been a very important raw material for thatching in the Fens (Godwin 1978). *Phragmites communis*, reed, has probably been a more widespread source of thatch in the Fens (Godwin 1978), but, unfortunately, its presence has not been conclusively recorded at Stonea. There are a number of very large culm nodes that originally had been interpreted as belonging to *Phragmites*, but it now appears that they might belong to *Cladium* instead. Culm nodes are a category of plant remains that is insufficiently studied, and the absence of identification criteria makes their identification virtually impossible at the moment. There are also a large number of smaller culm nodes present in the samples.

They have provisionally been identified as culm nodes of cereal straw, but they might, equally, belong to *Phragmites*.

The *Scirpus* spp. and *Eleocharis* were probably cut for litter and brought to the site for that reason (some of the gullied enclosures on the site have been interpreted as possible stock compounds). The *Carex* spp. and the other herbs (*Stellaria palustris, Galium palustre, Ranunculus flammula* etc.) were probably brought in with the cut litter. Both the old thatch and the used litter must have been used as fuel in the settlement fires and become carbonised in that way.

3 Weeds

The weeds present in the samples provide information regarding the range of vegetation habitats utilised and the soil conditions prevalent in the fields where the crops were grown. The exploitation of the fenlands (reed-swamps and fen meadows) for the harvest of raw material for thatch and litter has been discussed above. Here the other herbacious species are considered.

One way of arranging the ecological information of the weed seeds is by arranging the species according to their phytosociological associations. Phytosociology attempts to classify plants into sensible vegetation units, providing some fixed points in the vegetational continuum. Plants are classified according to their most typical community today, with recognition of the fact that they can also grow outside that community (Ellenberg 1979; Greig 1988, 1990).

One major problem with applying phytosociological classifications to British data is the fact that no such classification of British species exists, forcing us to use data based on observations from Central Europe (Ellenberg 1979). A second problem is that, as yet, little research has been done on the historical development of present-day plant communities. They might not have existed in their present-day form in the periods archaeobotanists deal with (but see Greig 1988 and 1990). Thirdly, as the state of preservation of the carbonised plant remains from archeological sites is not always optimal, several species might be excluded from the classification, which might make it unrepresentative. Much more research is needed before we can decide on the usefulness of phytosociology in archaeobotany. Here, the classification of the Stonea data will be briefly discussed.

When we apply the classification of Ellenberg (1979) to the Stonea data, the weeds are classified into two separate groups. First, the group of weeds of disturbed ground (group 3), to which 20 species belong; and second, the group of grassland herbs (group 5), to which 8 species belong. A further 16 species could not be classified as they were inadequately identified, illustrating the third problem mentioned above.

The grassland group can be subdivided into two classes: firstly, the herbs of acid grassland (Nardo-Callunetea, 5.1), with *Rumex acetosella* and *Sieglingia decumbens*, and secondly,

the herbs of neutral grassland (Molinio-Arrhenatheretea, 5.4), with *Plantago lanceolata, Prunella vulgaris, Arrhenatherum elatius, Stachys pallustre, Rhinanthus* cf. *minor* and *Crepis capillaris*. However, *Rumex acetosella* and *Stachys pallustre* do also occur on cultivated ground (Clapham *et al* 1962), and *Arrhenatherum elatius* spp. *bulbosum* is a very obnoxious arable weed in Britain. *Rumex acetosella, Sieglingia decumbens, Plantago lanceolata, Prunella vulgaris* and *Arrhenatherum* tubers have commonly been found in British charred plant assemblages associated with cereal crops, suggesting that they did occur as arable weeds in the past. This suggests that we should be careful in applying these classifications uncritically to our archaeobotanical data (but see below). The range of species present would suggest that there is some grassland component present in the Stonea assemblage, but that it is less important than the group of weeds of disturbed ground, which includes all the arable weeds. A real problem associated with this interpretation, however, is the fact that it has not been possible to identify the seeds of the Gramineae and Leguminosae families to specific level. Both these groups include arable and grassland species.

In addition to classifying the central European plants into communities, Ellenberg (1979) has also provided information on the ecological behaviour of the plants, such as their reaction to three climatic factors (light, temperature, and continentality) and three soil factors (moisture, pH and nitrogen levels). The behaviour of plants to these factors is less likely to change through time than their association with certain plant communities, which makes this information more appropriate for archaeological data, although caution is required. Here the three soil factors will be discussed.

Ellenberg has expressed the ecological behaviour of the plants in numerical values on a scale of 1 to 9, with indifferent behaviour indicated with an x. In Fig. 235 the indicator values for moisture (M), acidity (R) and nitrogen (N) have been presented for each of the four phases of occupation. The values for the plants of wet ground (as listed in Table 61) are given as well. Their values are the shaded areas on the histograms.

The first thing to notice in Fig. 235 is the very large number of species displaying an indifferent behaviour towards these soil factors (i.e. frequent occurrence of values for x). Also, because of the bad state of preservation of the seeds and the resulting low level of identification of a number of the species, the values given are only of those species adequately identified.

The values for the moisture requirements show that there is very little change through time. In Phase I/II the values range from 3 to 7, i.e. from dry to moist. *Cladium mariscus* (value 10), preferring shallow water, is the only exception. The values for the two main Roman periods are very similar, with a peak for values 4 and 5; but note the high number of species for values 8–10, representing the plants of wet ground, such as *Cladium mariscus* and *Scirpus*

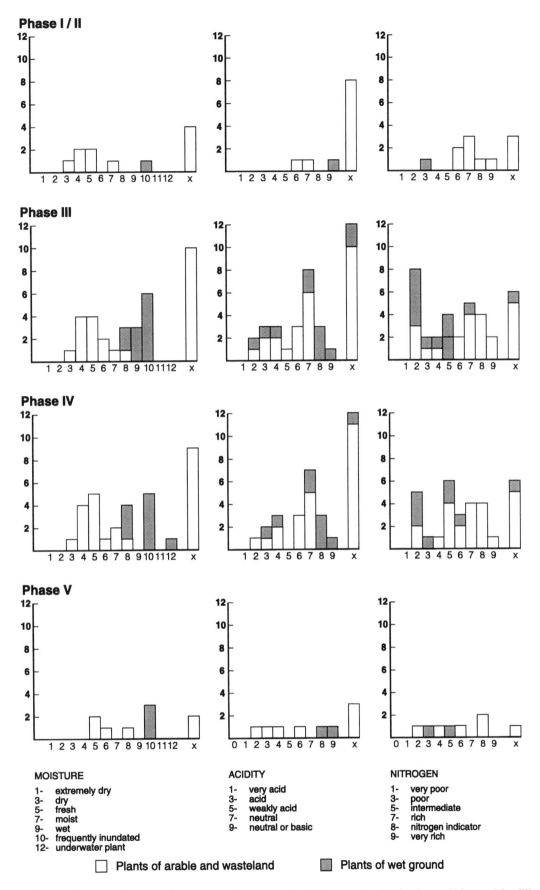

Fig. 235 Stonea Grange: plant remains – number of species for each of the indicator values for the three soil factors (after Ellenberg 1979). The value *x* stands for indifferent behaviour.

maritimus/lacustris. The values for Phase V are very much the same, but the number of species available was very small.

The figures for the pH values of the soils do show some changes through time. In Phase I/II only neutral values were present (but note the very small number of species that could be plotted). In the two main Roman and Anglo-Saxon phases there are quite a few values for acid soils. These values refer to *Rumex acetosella, Sieglingia decumbens, Prunella vulgaris, Crepis capillaris, Montia fontana* and *Raphanus raphanistrum*. Interestingly, two of these species were classified as acid grassland species (*Rumex* and *Sieglingia*) and two as neutral grassland species (*Prunella* and *Crepis*). This indicates the problem of too rigid a classification into groups. In fact, in Britain, *Rumex acetosella, Sieglingia* and *Prunella* do also occur on neutral or base-rich soils, while *Montia* and *Raphanus* are not excluded from calcareous soils (Clapham *et al* 1962).

The soils on Stonea 'island' are circum-neutral to slightly basic because of the base-rich ground water (C. French, personal communication). There are three possible explanations for these values. First, the values for Phase I/II are unrepresentative because of their low numbers, and there is no real change through time. Second, the change is real and the Roman period sees an increase in the soil types used. Third, the species in question, though normally behaving as acidity indicators, could here have grown on neutral soils. In each of these alternatives it does not necessarily mean that these acid soils were used for arable land. In fact, four of the six species in question were classified as grassland species, and one (*Montia*) grows along stream sides etc. All these species could have grown on the grassland growing on the peat surrounding Stonea 'island'. This grassland would almost certainly have been weakly acid to acid.

The nitrogen values show a similar picture, i.e. a small range of values in Phase I/II (mainly values for high nitrogen levels), while in the two main Roman and Anglo-Saxon periods the values range from poor in nitrogen to very rich in nitrogen. The high values for nitrogen probably indicate the presence of manure deposits and/or fertilisation of the fields with animal manure. The species indicating low levels of mineral nitrogen are the same as those indicating acid conditions (i.e. *Rumex acetosella, Sieglingia decumbens, Rhinanthus* cf. *minor, Crepis capillaris* and *Montia fontana*). The fairly large numbers of members of the Leguminosae family would also suggest that at least some of the arable soils were suffering from nitrogen depletion.

There is some evidence for slightly brackish soil conditions in the presence of *Scirpus maritimus, Scirpus tabernaemontani*, and *Najas marina*. All of them can tolerate brackish conditions, but they do not necessarily require permanently saline conditions. They could well have grown on marine silts that are slowly becoming desalinated. These species will have grown at some distance away from Stonea 'island'.

4 Contextual information

The most striking aspect of the plant remains from Stonea is the very low density of seeds in the soil for all phases (the average varying from 0.9 to 2.4 seeds per litre of soil) (see also Tables 59 and 60). There are very few contexts with a large number of seeds; most of them have only a few or none. The proportion of sterile contexts, not containing any plant remains at all, is very high (i.e. 32, 34, 24 and 45 percent resp. for the four phases of occupation). In all phases most of the seeds came from a few contexts only.

In Phase I/II there were only three contexts with more than 50 seeds (i.e. contexts 1359, 1368 and O33/1), two of which are post-holes and the third a pit. The seeds from these contexts amounted to 66% of the total for the entire phase. The seed density for these three contexts was 8.9 seeds per litre, instead of 1.7 for the total. The plant assemblages from the two postholes were dominated by cereal grain; the pit contained roughly equal quantities of cereals, chaff and weed seeds.

In Phase III there were 16 contexts with more than 50 seeds (i.e. 6 wells, 5 pits, 2 latrines, 2 gullies and one 'votive' pit). The number of seeds from these 16 contexts was 74% of the total. The average seed density was 5.9 seeds per litre of soil, as against 1.9 for the total. None of these contexts was dominated by cereal grains; the highest proportion of cereals in a context (23 percent) was found in a pit (1569), which was dominated by weed seeds. One context was dominated by chaff fragments (76%), while 6 (3 pits, 1 'votive' pit, 1 latrine and 1 gully) were dominated by weed seeds, but also contained large numbers of plants of wet ground. Cereals and chaff fragments only occurred in very small numbers in these contexts. In 8 contexts the plants of wet ground were the dominant category (i.e. 5 wells, 1 pit, 1 latrine and 1 gully), but these contexts usually also contained large numbers of weeds.

Consequently, it is difficult to explain the composition of the plant assemblage in terms of crop processing activities alone. There is evidence for a great deal of mixing of different types of refuse, i.e. crop processing refuse and refuse of burnt thatch and litter. The fact that so much material was found in the wells suggests that these wells, probably towards the end of the occupation period, were acting as receptacles for refuse, rather than functioning as wells. There are a very large number of pits on the site. Most of them are probably refuse pits, but only 5 out of the 43 pits sampled contained large quantities of plant remains. In fact, 19 of them did not contain plant remains at all.

In Phase IV there were 11 contexts with more than 50 seeds (6 pits, 1 pit/well, 1 gully, 1 ditch, and 2 ovens). Together they contained 70% of the total numbers of seeds, and the seed density was 9.3 seeds per litre of soil, instead of 2.4 for the total. The two ovens and two of the pits contained high percentages of cereal grain (47–90%), virtually no chaff and few weed seeds. The oven, with 47% cereals, also contained 42% of plants from wet ground. One context (ditch 74, unit 509) contained 67% chaff, 18% weeds, 11% cereals, and 4% 'waterplants'. Three contexts were dominated by weed seeds (2 pits and 1 gully), and one by 'waterplants'. Two contexts had roughly equal quantities of weeds and 'waterplants' (1 pit and 1 gully). The samples were not as dominated by plants of wet ground as in the previous phase, but they did maintain a firm presence. Context 735 (oven 5), containing 47% cereals, 42% 'waterplants', and 10% weeds, shows how a direct contextual relationship between feature type, function and crop processing product are difficult to find. In most cases, again, we see a mixture of different types of refuse.

In Phase V only one context contained more than 50 seeds, i.e. context 739, a post-hole of building S3 containing 139 seeds or 53% of the total. The density of seeds was 11.9 seeds per litre, as against 0.9 for the entire phase. While the context was dominated by weed seeds (49%), it also contained 42% cereals.

It is not very easy to generalise on the basis of this information, other than that the density of seeds does not appear to be directly related to feature type. While pits and wells are more obvious receptacles for refuse, there were post-holes in Phases I/II and V with large quantities of seeds. And while certain pits did contain large numbers of seeds, there were also many pits that contained either very few seeds or none at all. This fact emphasises the importance of sampling all features available, rather than selecting certain feature types. The two most striking aspects of the Stonea seed assemblages are, first, the very low numbers of seeds present and, second, the large amount of plant remains other than cereals, chaff and weed seeds, i.e. the large amount of thatching and litter material in comparison with the very small quantity of refuse of crop processing activities.

Surprisingly, there is very little evidence for the use of *Cladium* etc. for thatching in Phases I/II and V, even though the archaeological evidence suggests a continuation of post-built wooden structures. Their absence might be explained by the fact that neither the plant assemblages of Phase I/II nor Phase V can be regarded as representative; the settlements of these phases were only partially excavated.

5 Consumption versus production?

One further aspect of the plant assemblage needs discussing here, and that is the role of the arable products in the overall economy of the settlement. The archaeological evidence suggests that during the Roman period two main phases of occupation can be recognised. The first one (Phase III) is believed to have been a planned town, while the second (Phase IV) probably represents a farming complex of modest size. If this is indeed the case then we might expect

the plant assemblages from these two phases to show different characteristics, which might be explained by differences in the role the arable products played on the settlement, i.e. consumption versus production. The question as to whether we can tell from the inherent characteristics of carbonised plant assemblages if the cereal crops found were locally produced or not, is discussed in detail in van der Veen (1991). Here that discussion is briefly summarised.

One way of answering the question of production or consumption is to study which parts of the cereal plant were found on site. The presence of cereal grains alone does not prove that the crops were locally grown, but only that the cereals formed part of the diet. The most useful evidence for production is the presence of by-products from the earliest stages of crop processing (Hillman 1981), i.e. of those stages that are only carried out on production sites: threshing, raking, first winnowing and coarse sieving. The most characteristic by-product from these stages is cereal straw. Unfortunately, culm nodes of cereal straw not only occur rarely in charred plant assemblages, but they are also indistinguishable from culm nodes of the larger grasses. Thus, although a large number of culm nodes are present at Stonea in Phases III and IV (114 and 45 respectively) it is not possible to prove that they belong to cereal straw rather than a large grass, such as *Phragmites*. The number of culm nodes is, in fact, unusually high considering the number of cereal grains and chaff fragments. This could mean that cereal straw was imported for bedding or thatching, and that some or all of the culm nodes belong to wild grasses rather than cereals.

Another method for trying to answer this question has been suggested by Jones (1985). He argued that producer sites are characterised by large quantities of plant remains (i.e. high seed densities), and by very large quantities of cereal grain, while consumer sites are characterised by very small quantities of plant remains (i.e. low seed densities), and by an assemblage dominated by weed seeds, with only relatively small quantities of chaff and very few cereal grains. He has represented these two assemblages visually by plotting the samples onto triangular diagrams displaying the relative proportions of cereals, chaff and weed seeds (Fig. 236). The Stonea data have been plotted in the same way (Fig. 237). The three categories have been counted as follows. Grain – each grain counts as one; fragments of grain are combined to make up one. Chaff – each glume base, rachis internode and culm node count as one (thus, a spikeletfork consisting of two glume bases and a rachis internode still attached, counts as three). Weeds – each weed seed counts as one, but seeds from the category 'plants of wet ground', as listed in Table 61, (and of course from 'trees and shrubs' and 'other crop plants') have been excluded from the count.

The assemblage from Phase I/II (Fig. 237) consists of high proportions of cereal grain and relatively high proportions of

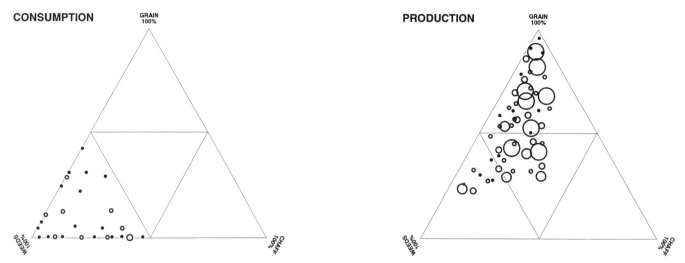

Fig. 236 Stonea Grange: plant remains – assemblages characteristic of producer and consumer settlements (after Jones 1985, Fig. 4.5). Every circle represents one sample; its size represents the seed density in the deposit. See key on Fig. 237.

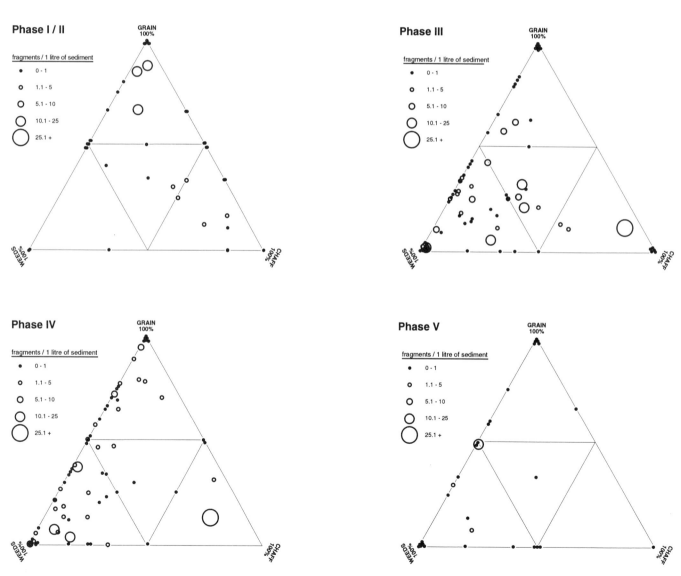

Fig. 237 Stonea Grange: plant remains – relative proportions of carbonised cereal grain, chaff fragments and weed seeds, according to site phases. Each circle represents one sample.

chaff. Although there are great dissimilarities, the assemblage is most like the producer-assemblage.

The assemblage from Phase III (Fig. 237) is dominated by weed seeds. Most of the samples contain high proportions of weed seeds, low proportions of chaff, and very small proportions of cereal grain. The samples with more than 50% cereal grain are all very small, containing only one or two cereal grains and little or nothing else. This assemblage is most like the consumer-assemblage, but there are some differences. First, there are some samples with more than 50% cereal grain (the model has none), and the seed density, though low, is higher than in the model.

The assemblage of Phase IV (Fig. 237) is very similar to that of Phase III, i.e. dominated by weed seeds. The proportions of chaff are low, many samples containing no chaff at all, and there is little cereal grain. Again, the assemblage is more like the consumer-assemblage than the producer-assemblage, but there are differences. First, the seed density is quite a bit higher, and second, there is a substantial number of samples with a high proportion of cereal grains (more than in Phase III).

The assemblage for Phase V (Fig. 237) is too small to be representative, but it would appear to be similar to those of Phases III and IV.

The real problem with interpreting these assemblages is the fact that the model of consumer versus producer settlements is too simplistic. Producer settlements can be small-scale subsistence farming units or large-scale surplus production units. Consumer settlements can be either small-scale pastoral settlements or large urban complexes. And even these four examples are only fixed points on a continuous scale. The producer-assemblage in the model is probably a surplus-production assemblage; leaving aside the question of what a subsistence-producer assemblage would look like. At the present moment the model is not detailed enough to provide that sort of information, but it is not impossible that the assemblages of Phase III and IV (or at least of Phase IV) could represent small-scale subsistence production.

While the present methods and models available are unable to give us very specific answers regarding our question of the role of the arable husbandry in the overall economy of the site, it is clear that the Late Bronze Age settlement is likely to have been a farming complex. Phase III is more difficult to interpret, but there is no evidence for the large scale storage of cereal grain which is characteristic of either large urban complexes or large 'manorial' type farms (Hillman 1981b). The settlement of Phase III is more likely to have been a small-scale consumer site or possibly, a small producer site producing only a very small amount of cereal products for subsistence only. The settlement of Phase IV was also either a small-scale consumer settlement, or a subsistence farming complex. The evidence for Phase V was too incomplete to allow an interpretation.

At this stage it is obviously important to consider the other environmental and archaeological information. The molluscan data did not include any evidence for arable fields, but this is largely a product of the fact that the samples all came from within the settlement site, and are, therefore, unlikely to have picked up evidence from outside the actual settlement (French, pp. 639–54). The soils on the 'island' are perfectly suitable for agriculture, being a sandy loam, free-draining, and easily tilled (the equivalent to Grade 2/3 modern arable land) (C. French, personal communication). The prevalent types of soil condition, as indicated by the weed seeds, are compatible with those found on the Stonea 'island', which would suggest that if the crops were brought in from another settlement, that settlement is likely to have been nearby.

Unfortunately, the information from the animal bone analysis (Stallibrass, pp. 587–612), was not available at the time of writing this section.

The archaeological material does not include any evidence for arable tools, such as ploughs etc., but the lay-out of the settlement and the types of building present suggested that Phase III was a small town and Phase IV a farming unit of modest size. Phases I/II and V are, on the basis of the archaeological evidence, likely to have been farming units.

PART II WATERLOGGED SEEDS

1 Introduction

Although situated in the Fenland, Stonea is in essence a 'dry' site, positioned on a gravel 'island' within the peat fens. Consequently, most of the deposits excavated did not possess the anaerobic conditions required for the preservation of waterlogged plant remains. However, a few features, mainly those that were cut deep enough to have reached the water-table, did contain plant remains preserved by waterlogging. The analysis of these plant remains is discussed in this section.

A number of samples (15) contained so few seeds (i.e. less than 50) that they were excluded from the analysis. There are only a few samples for each of the phases, and none for Phase I/II. The presentation of the results is by feature type, i.e. the sump, the pits, the latrine and the wells.

2 Methods

The extraction of the seeds was arrived at in two different ways. First, when a deposit was recognised in the field as containing waterlogged plant remains, a sample of about 5 litres was collected during the excavation, and stored for future analysis. Of these samples, usually a 1 litre subsample was analysed in the laboratory, but in the case of the samples from the sump only 0.5 litre was analysed due to the extreme richness of these deposits. These subsamples were washed through a stack of sieves with mesh sizes of 3.35, 1.7, 1.0, 0.5 and 0.3 mm. The residues were kept wet, and were sorted under the microscope.

The second extraction method was flotation. Manual flotation, using a 0.5 mm mesh sieve, was carried out in the field during excavation for the collection of carbonised plant remains. Some deposits subjected to water flotation did, in fact, contain waterlogged seeds, such as the deposits from the wells and pits, hence their very much larger sample volume. As these samples were processed using a 0.5 mm mesh sieve, some very small seeds might have been lost. The exact sample volumes are listed in the tables.

While in most samples all seeds were sorted, identified and counted, the seeds of *Sambucus nigra* and *Rubus fruticosus* occurred in such great numbers in the well samples that counting was stopped after 500 seeds.

For the identification, the same methods were used as for the carbonised seeds (see p. 614).

3 Results

1 The sump

The so-called sump represents a huge pit, about 10 m square, filled largely with organic deposits. From two sections through these organic deposits samples were collected for botanical analysis (see Fig. 238). A sequence of pollen samples was also collected (see pp. 636–8). The two columns of samples represent roughly the same sequence, although the deposits are somewhat changeable in nature. The top layer (layer A,26) was only sampled once. The bottom three layers (A,28, A,29 and A,32) belong to Phase III/IIIa; the top layer is dated to Phase IV. The results of the analysis are given in Table 63.

The deposits in the sump were very rich in seeds and fruits, with, on average, just over 900 seeds per 500 ml of sediment. The plant remains found can be divided into three categories: trees and shrubs; water plants/plants of wet ground; and plants of disturbed ground.

The trees and shrubs found were ash (*Fraxinus excelsior*), maple (*Acer campestre*), hawthorn (*Crataegus monogyna*), sloe (*Prunus spinosa*), willow (*Salix* sp.), dogwood (*Thelycrania sanguinea*), elder (*Sambucus nigra*), wild rose (*Rosa* sp.) and bramble (*Rubus fruticosus*). They all occur in relatively large quantities, with the exception of willow, which is generally underrepresented in the archaeobotanical macrofossil record (but note its persistent occurrence in the pollen record: see Part III, pp. 636–8; see also Cartwright, pp. 552–83).

The second category of plants found in the sump is that of the waterplants and plants preferring wet ground. They represent plants that will have grown in the pit itself when it held standing water, such as crowfoot (*Ranunculus*

subgenus *Batrachium*), starwort (*Callitriche* sp.), dropwort (*Oenanthe aquatica*) and duckweed (*Lemna* sp.). Celery-leaved crowfoot (*Ranunculus sceleratus*), and gipsywort (*Lycopus europaeus*) suggest the presence of very muddy, nitrogen-rich conditions.

The third category is that of weeds of disturbed ground. While there are a large range of species in the group, they occur usually only in small numbers, with the exception of stinging nettle (*Urtica dioica*), hemlock (*Conium maculatum*) and docks (*Rumex* spp.), which all again suggest nitrogen-rich sediments. Most of the species in this category are commonly found in association with settlement areas, as they thrive in conditions where the original vegetation has been disturbed.

2 Pits and wells

Only eight samples from pit fills contained waterlogged plant remains. In contrast to the fills of the sump, the pit fills were not very organic in nature; most consisted of a rather heavy clay. The number of seeds was considerably lower, with only just over 100 seeds per sample (with the exception of context 2001, a layer in well 1885). The results are listed in Table 64.

The plants have again been divided into three categories. In the trees and shrubs category elder and bramble seeds were present in all samples, though in relatively low numbers. Context 2001 contained, in addition to the elderberries and blackberries, some remains of ash, maple, wild rose, and sweet gale (*Myrica gale*).

The pit fills also contained a wide range of waterplants and plants of wet ground, though most occur only in very small numbers. Giant sword-sedge (*Cladium mariscus*) is an exception in that it occurs in abundance in one sample (context 2001, from well 1885). This does not mean that the plant grew locally on the site, but probably represents the dumping of some waste material of thatching. We have seen (p. 623) that *Cladium* was a likely source for roofing material for the wooden buildings on the settlement. The presence of water-plantain (*Alisma plantago-aquatica*), sea arrow-grass (*Triglochlin maritima*), and possibly sea club-rush (*Scirpus lacustris/maritimus*) indicates the presence of some brackish water.

The third category of weeds of disturbed ground shows a similar range to that of the sump. Stinging nettle (*Urtica dioica*) occurs again in large numbers.

3 Latrines

Two flotation samples were collected from one of the latrines (pit 1536). The results are listed in Table 65. Considering the size of the sample volume (24 litres each) the number of waterlogged seeds found is very low (about 6 per

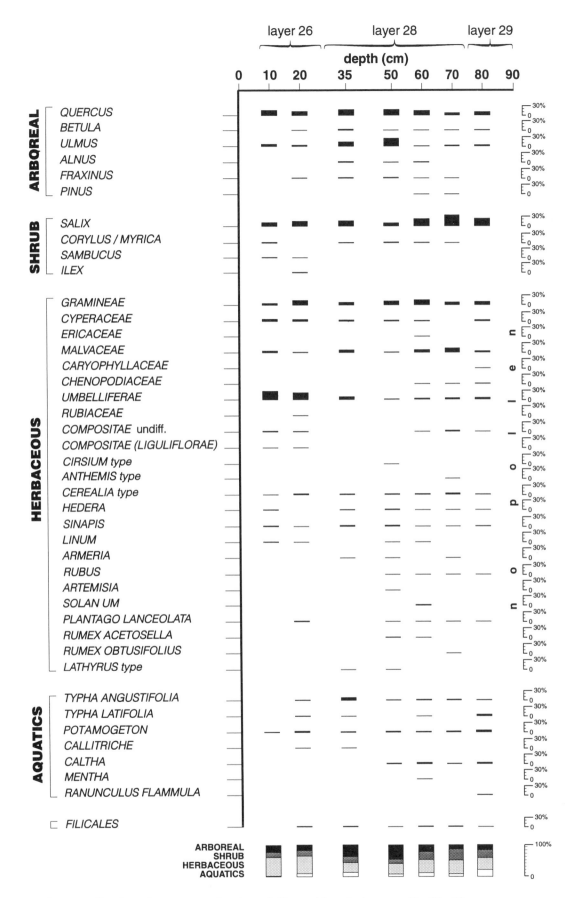

Fig. 238 Stonea Grange: pollen from the sump, sample column A. For position of column, see Fig. 35, p. 91.

Table 63 Stonea Grange: plant remains – waterlogged plant remains from the sump

Phase	III/IIIa						IV
Sample	DD	GG	CC	FF	BB	EE	AA
Layer	32	32	29	29	28	28	26
Volume (litres)	0.5	0.5	0.5	0.5	0.5	0.5	0.5
Trees & shrubs							
Fraxinus excelsior L. (ash), keys	•	1	14	15	41	14	1
Fraxinus excelsior L. (ash), leaf scars	•	•	1	2	51	20	12
Acer campestre L. (common maple)	•	•	8	12	1	•	5
Prunus spinosa L. (sloe)	•	1	5	•	13	2	6
Crataegus monogyna Jacq. (hawthorn)	•	•	•	•	3	1	7
Sambucus nigra L. (elder)	26	654	139	517	44	14	29
Thelycrania sanguinea (L.) Fourr. (dogwood)	•	•	•	•	8	1	17
Salix sp. (willow)	•	•	•	•	•	•	•
Rosa sp (wild rose), thorns	37	9	173	65	162	110	9
Rosa sp. (wild rose), seeds	1	•	•	•	5	1	1
Rubus fruticosus agg. (bramble)	1	32	129	46	296	92	125
Waterplants & plants of wet ground							
Ranunculus sceleratus L. (celery-leaved crowfoot)	2	3	758	515	63	69	1
Ranunculus, subgenus *Batrachium* (DC) Gray (crowfoot)	29	4	•	•	1	2	903
Callitriche sp. (starwort)	12	•	•	•	•	•	•
Oenanthe aquatica (L.) Poir. (fine-leaved water dropwort)	•	•	•	•	•	•	414
Lycopus europaeus L. (gipsy-wort)	•	6	46	74	4	7	3
Lemna sp. (duckweed)	•	•	•	•	•	•	24
Cladium mariscus (L.) Pohl. (giant sword-sedge)	•	1	•	•	•	•	•
Carex spp. (sedges)	•	•	•	•	•	•	3
Isolepis setacea (L.) R.Br. (bristle scirpus)	2	•	•	•	•	•	•
Plants of disturbed ground							
Ranunculus repens L. (creeping buttercup)	•	•	•	•	•	1	•
Papaver argemone L. (long prickly-headed poppy)	•	•	•	•	•	1	•
Brassica sp.	1	•	•	•	•	•	•
Stellaria media (L.) Vill. (chickweed)	•	5	•	2	•	•	•
Montia fontana spp. *chondrosperma* (Fenzl) Walters (blinks)	1	1	•	•	•	•	•
Chenopodium album L. (fat hen)	•	•	•	•	•	•	1
Atriplex hastata/patula (orache)	5	3	•	•	•	•	•
Chaerophyllum temulentum L. (rough chervill)	•	4	•	•	•	•	•
Conium maculatum L. (hemlock)	12	34	56	4	•	25	•
Umbelliferae indet.	•	•	3	•	4	27	•
Bryonia dioica Jacq. (bryony)	•	•	•	•	1	•	•
Polygonum aviculare agg. (knotgrass)	2	•	1	•	•	•	•
Polygonum lapathifolium L. (pale persicaria)	5	•	•	•	•	•	•
Rumex obtusifolius L. (broad-leaved dock)	7	•	•	1	•	•	•
Rumex conglomeratus Murr. (sharp dock)	9	7	5	9	•	•	•
Rumex spp. (dock)	24	6	33	10	1	•	2
Urtica dioica (stinging nettle)	71	39	81	•	5	13	4
Hyoscyamus niger L. (henbane)	•	•	•	•	•	1	1
Solanum dulcamara L. (woody nightshade)	•	3	7	•	13	7	10
Solanum nigrum L. (black nightshade)	•	4	•	•	•	•	•
Prunella vulgaris L. (self heal)	•	•	•	•	•	1	•
Galeopsis tetrahit agg. (hemp-nettle)	•	•	•	•	•	•	4
Labiatae indet.	•	•	•	•	•	•	2
Plantago major L. (great plantain)	3	•	•	•	•	•	•
Bidens cernua L. (nodding bur-marigold)	•	•	3	•	•	•	•
Carduus sp. (thistle)	1	•	•	•	•	•	•
Cirsium sp. (thistle)	9	4	3	•	3	2	4
Lapsana communis L. (nipplewort)	•	•	•	•	•	•1	•
Sonchus asper (L.) Hill. (sow-thistle)	9	8	1	•	•	•	14

Table 63 continued

Phase	III/IIIa						IV
Sample	DD	GG	CC	FF	BB	EE	AA
Layer	32	32	29	29	28	28	26
Volume (litres)	0.5	0.5	0.5	0.5	0.5	0.5	0.5
Sonchus oleraceus L. (milk-thistle)	·	4	·	·	·	·	·
Compositae indet.	·	·	·	·	·	1	·
Gramineae indet.	·	2	·	·	2	8	·
Mosses	+	+	+	+	+	+	+
Indeterminate	24	10	16	6	17	17	7
TOTALS	293	845	1485	1278	738	437	1610
				6686			
Cladocerum ephippia (waterflea)	4	·	·	·	·	76	46

Table 64 Stonea Grange: plant remains — waterlogged plant remains from pits and wells

Phase	III/IIIa			III/IV	IV		
Context	1954	2001	J4.7	2090	1886	1912	1584
Volume (litres)	1	1	1	1	1	1	45
Trees & shrubs							
Fraxinus excelsior L. (ash), keys	·	2	·	·	·	·	·
Acer campestre L. (common maple)	·	1	·	·	·	·	·
Sambucus nigra L. (elder)	3	3	5	7	5	6	3
Rosa sp. (wild rose), thorns	·	5	·	·	·	·	·
Myrica gale L. (sweet gale)	·	29	·	·	·	·	·
Rubus fruticosus agg. (bramble)	12	1	2	2	·	3	5
Waterplants & plants of wet ground							
Ranunculus flammula L. (lesser spearwort)	·	1	·	·	·	·	·
Ranunculus subgenus *Batrachium* (DC) Gray (crowfoot)	·	·	2	·	·	·	54
Ranunculus sceleratus L. (celery-leaved crowfoot)	·	2	·	2	·	·	·
Oenanthe aquatica (L.) Poir. (fine-leaved water dropwort)	·	·	·	·	·	·	4
Oenanthe fistulosa L. (water dropwort)	1	2	·	·	·	·	·
Hydrocotyle vulgaris L. (pennywort)	1	12	1	4	·	·	·
Mentha aquatica/arvensis (mint)	3	2	2	2	1	·	·
Alisma plantago-aquatica L. (water-plantain)	·	2	·	·	1	·	·
Potamogeton sp. (pondweed)	·	1	·	·	·	·	·
Lemna sp. (duckweed)	·	·	·	·	·	·	4
Cladium mariscus (L.) Pohl. (giant sword-sedge)	2	313	2	12	·	·	·
Eleocharis cf. *palustris* (L.) Roem. & Schult. (spike rush)	3	7	·	·	·	1	·
Scirpus lacustris/maritimus (bulrush/sea-club rush)	3	9	·	·	·	2	·
Carex spp. (sedges)	5	36	4	10	2	1	·
Cyperaceae indet.	·	4	·	2	·	·	·
Juncus sp. (rush), capsule + seeds	37	110	·	·	2	13	·
Triglochlin maritima L. (sea arrow-grass)	·	25	·	·	·	·	·
Plants of disturbed ground							
Ranunculus acris L. (meadow buttercup)	·	1	·	1	·	·	·
Ranunculus repens L. (creeping buttercup)	·	8	·	1	·	1	·
Ranunculus ac/bul/rep indet.	1	2	·	·	·	·	1
Stellaria media (L.) Vill. (chickweed)	·	1	1	·	·	·	2
Agrostemma githago L. (corn cockle)	·	2	·	·	·	·	·
Montia fontana spp. *chondrosperma* (Fenzl) Walters (blinks)	·	·	·	·	·	1	·
Atriplex hastata/patula (orache)	·	27	3	·	·	3	1
Chenopodium album L. (fat hen)	·	1	·	·	·	1	·

Table 64 continued

Phase		III/IIIa			III/IV	IV		
Context		1954	2001	J4.7	2090	1886	1912	1584
Volume (litres)		1	1	1	1	1	1	45
Chenopodiaceae indet.		•	•	2	•	•	•	•
Linum catharticum L. (purging flax)		•	1	•	•	•	•	•
Filipendula ulmaria (L.) Maxim. (meadow sweet)		•	2	•	•	•	•	•
Aphanes arvensis agg. (parsley piert)		1	•	•	•	•	•	•
Potentilla reptans L. (creeping cinquefoil)		11	•	•	•	•	•	•
Potentilla sp. (cinquefoil)		•	2	1	4	1	•	•
Apium graveolens L. (wild celery)		•	•	•	6	•	1	•
Conium maculatum L. (hemlock)		•	•	•	1	1	5	•
Daucus carota L. (wild carrot)		2	1	•	•	•	•	•
Umbelliferae indet.		1	3	4	1	•	•	4
Polygonum aviculare agg. (knotgrass)		•	1	•	•	•	•	1
Rumex acetosella agg. (sheep's sorrel)		•	1	9	2	•	•	•
Rumex spp. (dock)		•	16	7	1	2	32	•
Urtica dioica L. (stinging nettle)		22	47	2	175	54	144	6
Urtica urens L. (small nettle)		2	2	•	•	•	•	2
Solanum nigrum L. (black nightshade)		•	•	•	•	•	1	1
Prunella vulgaris L. (self heal)		•	2	•	1	•	•	•
Labiatae indet.		•	•	•	2	•	•	•
Plantago major L. (great plantain)		•	•	•	•	•	•	1
Arctium sp. (burdock)		•	•	•	•	•	1	•
Carduus sp. (thistle)		•	1	•	•	•	•	•
Cirsium sp. (thistle)		•	1	•	•	•	2	•
Leontodon sp. (hawkbit)		•	3	•	•	•	•	•
Eupatorium cannabinum L. (hemp agrimony)		•	3	•	•	•	•	•
Compositae indet.		•	4	•	•	•	•	•
Gramineae indet.		1	2	•	3	•	•	1
Mosses		•	+	•	•	•	•	•
Indeterminate		3	3	•	3	1	6	•
TOTALS		114	704	47	242	70	224	90
					1491			

litre). The preservation conditions were insufficient; the fill consisted of a clayey deposit with no visible organic remains. The waterlogged seeds found are similar to those found in the pits, i.e. elderberries, blackberries, stinging nettle, and a few other ruderals. However, these two samples also contained some more interesting material in the form of four fig pips (*Ficus carica*), which indicates that luxury food items were imported. These fig pips have already been discussed (p. 623).

In addition to the flotation samples, two separate samples were collected from the pit 1536 latrine deposits for analysis in the laboratory. While the sample from context 1816 did not contain any plant remains, context 1606 contained a large number of mineralised grains and seeds (see Table 65). As most mineralised material does not float they had not been recovered in the flotation samples. The seeds consist of an inorganic material, and are pale brown or dark yellow in colour. The preservation is probably due to a calcium phosphate replacement that must have taken place during burial in the soil (Green 1979). The phosphate and calcium could have originated from human faecal material. Mineralised seeds are often associated with garderobes and cess pits, so their presence in a latrine at Stonea need occasion no great surprise.

The mineralised seeds were dominated by cereal grain, most of which were rather fragmented. The numbers in the table represent whole grain equivalents, and not individual fragments. Spelt wheat (*Triticum spelta*) was the main species present; only three barley grains (*Hordeum vulgare*) were found. The presence of sloe stones (*Prunus spinosa*) and *Rubus* drupelets is interesting as it would suggest that they were eaten. The relatively high number of grasses (*Bromus* and Gramineae) compares well with the high numbers of these species in the carbonised assemblage.

As the occurrence of mineralised seeds in one of these deposits indicated that the deposits contained cess, the samples were also analysed for the presence of parasite eggs (see p. 612).

Table 65 Stonea Grange: plant remains – waterlogged and mineralised seeds from latrine 1536

Phase	III/IIIa		
Context	1536	1606	1606
Volume (litres)	24	24	1
			minera-lised
Crop plants			
Triticum cf. spelta (spelt wheat)	•	•	92
Hordeum vulgare (six-row, hulled barley)	•	•	3
Cerealia indet.	•	•	87
Ficus carica (fig)	3	1	•
Trees & shrubs			
Sambucus nigra L. (elder)	56	93	•
Corylus avellana L. (hazel)	•	•	1
cf. Prunus spinosa L. (sloe)	•	•	4
Rubus fruticosus agg. (bramble)	38	13	•
Rubus sp. drupelets	•	•	9
Plants of wet ground			
Scirpus lacustris/maritimus (bulrush/sea club-rush)	1	•	•
Isolepis setacea (L.) R.Br. (bristle scirpus)	•	1	•
Plants of disturbed ground			
Stellaria media (L.) Vill. (chickweed)	•	7	•
Chenopodium album L. (fat hen)	4	16	•
Chenopodium sp.	•	4	•
Potentilla reptans L. (creeping cinquefoil)	1	1	•
Umbelliferae indet.	•	•	1
Polygonum aviculare agg. (knotgrass)	•	•	2
Urtica dioica L. (stinging nettle)	28	17	•
Urtica urens L. (small nettle)	3	11	•
Bromus sp. (bromegrass)	•	•	15
Gramineae indet.	•	•	5
Indeterminate	2	1	8
TOTALS	136	165	227
		528	

4 Well 135

Four samples were available from well 135. The most striking characteristic was the very large number of elderberry and blackberry seeds. They occurred in such large numbers that counting was stopped after 500 seeds were recovered. Context 205 probably contained something like 10 000 elderberry seeds!

The samples from contexts 205 and 213 contained buds of oak (Quercus sp.). This species had not been found in any other deposit, but oak pollen was consistently present

Table 66 Stonea Grange: plant remains – waterlogged seeds from well 135

Phase	IV	IV	IV	V
Context	214	213	205	159
Volume (litres)	12	24	48	24
Trees & shrubs				
Quercus sp. (oak), buds	•	1	29	•
Sambucus nigra L. (elder)	8	500+	500+	500+
Thelycrania sanguinea (L.) Fourr. (dogwood)	•	16	7	•
Rosa sp. (wild rose), thorns	•	2	•	•
Rubus fruticosus agg. (bramble)	6	500+	500+	•
Plants of wet ground				
Lycopus europaeus L. (gipsy wort)	128	48	3	•
Carex spp. (sedges)	5	20	2	•
Cladium mariscus (L.) Pohl. (giant sword-sedge) *carbonised	•	•	1	•
Cyperaceae indet.	•	2	•	•
Plants of disturbed ground				
Ranunculus repens L. (creeping buttercup)	1	•	•	•
Chenopodium album L. (fat hen)	•	•	•	3
Atriplex hastata/patula (orache)	2	•	•	•
Conium maculatum L. (hemlock)	3	264	53	•
Aethusa cynapium L. (fool's parsley)	•	•	•	2
Umbelliferae indet.	•	•	1	•
Polygonum aviculare agg. (knotgrass)	1	•	•	•
Rumex obtusifolius L. (broad-leaved dock)	3	•	•	•
Rumex spp. (dock)	•	18	2	•
Urtica dioica L. (stinging nettle)	•	7	•	•
Urtica urens L. (small nettle)	•	•	•	3
Atropa bella-donna L. (deadly nightshade)	•	8	53	•
Solanum nigrum L. (black nightshade)	•	1	•	•
cf. Stachys palustris L. (marsh woundwort)	•	4	37	•
Glechoma hederacea L. (ground ivy)	•	3	3	•
Carduus sp. (thistle)	•	1	•	•
Cirsium/Carduus (thistle)	•	6	•	•
Eupatorium cannabinum L. (hemp agrimony)	•	•	32	1
Gramineae indet.	•	•	•	1
Triticum sp. (wheat) *carbonised	•	1	•	•
TOTALS	157	1402	1223	510
		3292		
Cladocerum ephippia (waterflea)	3	1	•	•

in the sump and well deposits (see Table 67; see also Cartwright, pp. 552–83). Fruits of dogwood (*Thelycrania sanguinea*) and thorns of a wild rose (*Rosa* sp.) were also found (see Table 66).

The number of plants of wet ground is remarkably small, compared to the other features. The range of ruderals matches that of the other samples.

4 Discussion

The conditions on the site were not favourable to the preservation of waterlogged plant remains, with the exception of the sump, where the preservation was excellent. Consequently, the information available originates from only a few deposits that were wet enough to allow some preservation. The information is not, therefore, comparable for all phases. No information is available for the prehistoric period, and for the Anglo-Saxon period only four samples from two wells were recovered. The following discussion is, therefore, based on qualitative information gained, rather than on a quantitative analysis.

It is very difficult to interpret the results from these samples on the basis of an individual feature. The origin of the plant remains found in the sump is not clear, although a large amount of the plants probably grew in the pit itself. The pit appears to have acted as a receptacle for a range of organic material; not just seeds and fruits, but even a whole tree trunk (ash), in addition to wood debitage, artefacts, etc. The deliberate dumping of these materials will have disturbed any natural sedimentation process. It is very difficult to detect any clear changes from the bottom to the top of the fill, although there is some evidence that layers 32 and 26 developed when there was standing water in the pit, while layers 29 and 28 might represent more muddy conditions. There are many species which indicate the presence of high levels of nitrogen, probably decaying organic matter, manure, etc.

The plant remains found in the pits suggest that these contained standing water, at least for part of the time, possibly seasonally. The presence of *Alisma*, *Triglochlin*, and *Scirpus* indicates the presence of some brackish conditions, but this might represent no more than a short-lived flooding.

The absence of any real waterplants in some wells might suggest that by the time those wells came into disuse, they no longer held much water. They might have been deliberately filled in. The very high numbers of elderberry and blackberry seeds would suggest that elder and bramble were growing in close proximity to well 135.

The mineralised seeds from the latrine form an important find because of their direct association with human food consumption. The number of wheat grains in the latrine sample is, in fact, larger than the total number of wheat grains for Phase III in the carbonised assemblage.

The most striking aspect of the results is the fact that, apart from the latrine, none of the samples contained food plants. While the sump was clearly used for the dumping of a variety of domestic refuse, such as pottery, shoes, wooden artefacts, etc., no food refuse was dumped into this pit. The same is true of the other pits and the wells, which would suggest that the disposal of domestic food refuse was not haphazard, but took place in a highly organised manner, probably onto specifically designated middens, which were, unfortunately, not found in the excavated area (although a midden-like deposit was found in trench P – see French, pp. 221–3, building R15 (the temple)).

The wide range of ruderals found in the samples compares well with results from other sites, and we could envisage most of the species growing in and around the settlement. Excepting block 1, there is no evidence that the settlement was extensively paved, so there will have been plenty of suitable habitats for these plants to grow. Some might, of course, have blown in from slightly further afield.

The consistent presence of a range of waterplants and plants of wet ground suggests that the water-table at the settlement site must have been fairly high, causing a number of features to be at least seasonally waterlogged. There is no evidence for any changes through time in this, but it must be stressed that the available samples do not form a representative assemblage.

The consistent and ubiquitous presence of a large range of trees and shrubs in all the samples suggests that there was a considerable number of trees and shrubs growing on the settlement, and indicates the presence of some old scrubland and/or the existence of hedgerows in the immediate vicinity of the settlement. During the first main Roman period (Phase III) the following species were recorded: ash, maple, willow, hazel, sloe, hawthorn, elder, dogwood, wild roses, sweet gale and bramble. During the later Roman period (Phase IV) the range is slightly smaller, but this might well be a sampling problem: oak, ash, maple, sloe, hawthorn, elder, dogwood, wild roses and bramble. During the early Anglo-Saxon period (Phase V) the number is even smaller, but that is certainly due to sampling problems: oak, elder, dogwood and bramble. While there is ample evidence for individual trees and shrubs in the settlement, and scrubland nearby, the landscape around the site must have been an open one, with only small patches of woodland (see also the pollen evidence, pp. 636–8; and Cartwright, pp. 552–83).

PART III POLLEN

1 Introduction

A number of pollen samples were collected from the waterlogged features. The extraction, identification and counting of the samples was carried out by Anne Blackham (Norfolk College of Art and Technology, King's Lynn). Due to the poor preservation conditions, a number of the samples

Table 67 Stonea Grange: plant remains – pollen analysis of a column from the lower part of the sump, and two well deposits

	Sump layer 26				Sump layer 28								Sump layer 29		Well 135		Well 808	
	10 cm		20 cm		35 cm		50 cm		60 cm		70 cm		80 cm		Layer 205		Layer 914	
	Counted to 100 grains		Counted to 200 grains		Counted to 200 grains		Counted to 200 grains		Counted to 200 grains		Counted to 200 grains		Counted to 200 grains		Counted to 100 grains		Counted to 200 grains	
	Actual count	% of total	Actual count	% of total	Actual count	% of total	Actual count	% of total	Actual count	% of total	Actual count	% of total	Actual count	% of total	Actual count	% of total	Actual count	% of total
Arboreal																		
Quercus	15	15.0	23	11.5	33	16.5	33	16.5	28	14.0	14	7.0	19	9.5	7	7.0	13	6.5
Ulmus	7	7.0	8	4.0	27	13.5	51	25.5	2	1.0	6	3.0	7	3.5	–	–	4	2.0
Alnus	–	–	–	–	6	3.0	2	1.0	3	1.5	–	–	–	–	1	1.0	–	–
Fraxinus	–	–	1	0.5	1	0.5	5	2.5	6	3.0	4	2.0	–	–	–	–	–	–
Betula	–	–	2	1.0	7	3.5	1	0.5	2	1.0	2	1.0	4	2.0	–	–	–	–
Pinus	–	–	–	–	–	–	–	–	1	0.5	1	0.5	–	–	2	2.0	–	–
Shrub																		
Salix	12	12.0	31	15.5	33	16.5	20	10.0	46	23.0	67	33.5	48	24.0	4	4.0	8	4.0
Sambucus	2	2.0	1	0.5	–	–	–	–	–	–	–	–	–	–	–	–	–	–
Corylus/Myrica	3	3.0	–	–	3	1.5	5	2.5	3	1.5	2	0.5	–	–	1	1.0	2	1.0
Ilex	–	–	1	0.5	–	–	–	–	–	–	–	–	–	–	1	1.0	–	–
Herbaceous																		
Gramineae	6	6.0	29	14.5	17	8.5	26	13.0	32	16.0	18	9.0	21	10.5	32	32.0	69	34.5
Cyperaceae	7	7.0	11	5.5	7	3.5	5	2.5	3	1.5	–	–	8	4.0	17	17.0	36	18.0
Compositae undiff.	3	3.0	3	1.5	–	–	–	–	2	1.0	8	4.0	2	1.0	–	–	7	3.5
Anthemis type	–	–	–	–	–	–	–	–	–	–	1	0.5	–	–	–	–	–	–
Umbelliferae	28	28.0	46	23.0	18	9.0	4	2.0	8	4.0	9	4.5	11	5.5	8	8.0	41	21.5
Malvaceae	6	6.0	3	1.5	–	–	4	2.0	17	8.5	28	14.0	10	5.0	1	1.0	1	0.5
Ericaceae	–	–	–	–	–	–	–	–	1	0.5	–	–	–	–	–	–	–	–
Chenopodiaceae	–	–	–	–	–	–	–	–	1	0.5	2	1.0	4	2.0	–	–	4	2.0
Cerealia type	1	1.0	7	3.5	6	3.0	5	2.5	5	3.0	9	4.5	4	2.0	2	2.0	4	2.0
Plantago lanceolata	–	–	6	3.0	–	–	1	0.5	1	0.5	2	1.0	2	1.0	1	1.0	–	–
Rubus	–	–	–	–	–	–	1	0.5	1	0.5	2	1.0	2	1.0	–	–	–	–
Sinapis	3	3.0	2	1.0	7	3.5	8	4.0	1	0.5	2	1.0	4	2.0	–	–	2	1.0
Solanum	–	–	–	–	–	–	–	–	5	2.5	–	–	–	–	–	–	–	–
Hedera	2	2.0	–	–	4	2.0	5	2.5	2	1.0	2	1.0	2	1.0	–	–	–	–
Rumex acetosella	–	–	–	–	–	–	3	1.5	1	0.5	–	–	–	–	2	2.0	–	–
Rumex obtusifolius	–	–	–	–	–	–	–	–	–	–	1	0.5	–	–	–	–	–	–
Linum	2	2.0	1	0.5	–	–	1	0.5	1	0.5	–	–	–	–	–	–	–	–
Armeria	–	–	–	–	1	0.5	1	0.5	–	–	1	0.5	–	–	3	3.0	–	–
Compositae (Liguliflorae)	1	1.0	1	0.5	–	–	–	–	–	–	–	–	–	–	4	4.0	2	1.0
Rubiaceae	–	–	1	0.5	–	–	–	–	–	–	–	–	–	–	–	–	–	–
Lathyrus type	–	–	–	–	1	0.5	1	0.5	–	–	–	–	–	–	–	–	1	0.5
Artemisia	–	–	–	–	–	–	1	0.5	–	–	–	–	–	–	–	–	–	–
Cirsium type	–	–	–	–	–	–	1	0.5	–	–	–	–	–	–	–	–	–	–
Caryophyllaceae	–	–	–	–	–	–	–	–	–	–	–	–	1	0.5	1	1.0	1	0.5
Aquatics																		
Potamogeton	2	2.0	10	5.0	6	3.0	7	3.5	6	3.0	7	3.5	13	6.5	6	6.0	1	0.5
Caltha palustris	–	–	–	–	–	–	6	3.0	10	5.0	4	2.0	10	5.0	–	–	2	1.0
Mentha aquatica	–	–	–	–	–	–	–	–	1	0.5	–	–	–	–	–	–	–	–
Typha angustifolia	–	–	4	2.0	17	8.5	3	1.5	5	2.5	5	2.5	4	2.0	–	–	–	–
Typha latifolia	–	–	3	1.5	2	1.0	–	–	1	0.5	–	–	11	5.5	–	–	1	0.5
Callitriche	–	–	1	0.5	1	0.5	–	–	–	–	–	–	–	–	–	–	–	–
Ranunculus flammula	–	–	–	–	–	–	–	–	–	–	–	–	3	1.5	–	–	–	–
Spores																		
Filicales	–	–	3	1.5	2	1.5	2	1.0	4	2.0	3	1.5	1	0.5	6	6.0	1	0.5
Pteridium	–	–	–	–	–	–	–	–	–	–	–	–	–	–	1	1.0	–	–

contained insufficient pollen to merit reporting. Only the results from the sump deposits and from two well samples are presented here (see Table 67 and Fig. 238).

2 Methods

Samples were collected from the organic fills of the sump at 10 cm intervals (except at 35 and 95 cm) (see Fig. 238). The pollen was extracted using standard methods of preparation. A total of 200 pollen grains was counted for each sample, apart from the sample at 10 cm and context 205 (only 100 grains each). The pollen diagram has been constructed using the percentage of total pollen for each depth. The percentage of arboreal to non-arboreal pollen (AP/NAP) has also been included.

3 Results

1 The sump

Apart from the bottom sample at 95 cm, all samples contained pollen. Arboreal species and shrubs are consistently present, and take up about 20% of the total. At 50 cm the arboreal species increase (with a dramatic rise for *Ulmus*). A small number of aquatics is present in all samples, normally taking up between 5 to 10% of the total. Only at 80 cm is this percentage higher, i.e. 19%. The herbaceous species maintain a dominance throughout the section with the Gramineae (grasses) making the largest contribution. The very high values for Umbelliferae at 20 and 10 cm match very well with the very high number of *Oenanthe aquatica* seeds in the macrofossil record. Cereals are present in all but one sample and even flax is recorded, corroborating the presence of flax in the carbonised seed assemblage (see p. 620).

2 The wells

The pollen recovered from these two samples (Table 67) gives information not unlike that from the sump. There are records for oak, elm, alder, pine, willow, hazel/sweet gale and holly. The absence of pollen from *Sambucus*, elder, and low values for *Rubus*, bramble, is surprising considering the very high number of elderberry and blackberry seeds found in this deposit.

4 Discussion

It is extremely difficult to interpret pollen evidence from archaeological features. While pollen diagrams from natural deposits such as lake sediments or peat bogs can be interpreted as representing changes in the surrounding vegetation, this is not possible with pollen diagrams such as

this one from the sump. The pollen found in this feature probably represents only a few pollen from the surrounding landscape; most will originate from the plants growing in and around the pit, and from pollen adhering to material deliberately thrown in. The peak in arboreal pollen at 50 cm probably represents the dumping of wood debitage, rather than an increase in the amount of woodland around Stonea.

The presence of cereal grains is interesting, but, unfortunately, does not provide definitive proof of cereal growing by the inhabitants of the settlement, especially as pollen of arable weeds occurs only in low values. Cereal pollen can adhere to the lemma and palea of cereal grains, and can in this way be introduced into a deposit with the grain (Robinson and Hubbard 1977). As no cereal grains were found within the macrofossils of these deposits, this possibility can be ruled out here. But it is a well-known fact that the husking of cereals (which can take place both on a producer-site and a consumer-site) can release large quantities of pollen into the air (Robinson and Hubbard 1977; Vuorela 1973). The cereal pollen in these deposits could, therefore, have originated either from a nearby arable field, or from the nearby husking of cereal grains.

To summarise: the pollen evidence, like the macrofossil record, suggests that the landscape around the settlement was fairly open, with patches of woodland and old scrubland in the vicinity. Oak and willow, which were only sparsely recorded in the macrofossil assemblage, were consistently present. Elm, alder, birch, pine and holly are species only recorded in the pollen rain.

PART IV MISCELLANEOUS

1 Fungi (Pl. XXXII)

A large number of puff-balls were found in the waterlogged deposits of the sump. They were found as a cache of about 70 specimens in a small hollow in a tree trunk of ash, which had fallen (or was thrown) into the sump. They were dark brown, almost black in colour, and had a leathery appearance. There were both elongated (3.5 × 1.8 cm) and rounded (2.5 × 2 cm) specimens; they looked a bit like 'empty date skins'.

Several of them were sent to Dr D. A. Reid (The Herbarium, Royal Botanical Gardens, Kew), who very kindly offered the following comments: While the specimens were definitely of fungal nature, they were totally devoid of any internal structures or spores. As a result it was only possible to suggest that, superficially, they resembled puff-balls of the genus *Bovista*, but to confirm this one would have to demonstrate the typical dendroid capillitial hyphae of the gleba which is characteristic of this genus. Unfortunately, none was preserved.

Puff-balls of the *Bovista* genus have been found in other archaeological contexts: Stanwick, North Yorkshire (Wheeler 1954), Vindolanda, Northumberland, Skara Brae,

Orkney, and Scole, Norfolk (Watling and Seaward 1976). All these finds are dated to the Late Iron Age or Roman period.

Because a puff-ball lacks rooting mycelial cords to anchor it, it is loosened at maturity from its substrate and transported by wind. In this way, mature fruit-bodies could have rolled into a settlement in much the same manner as autumnal leaves (Watling and Seaward 1976, 170).

The presence of such a large number of puff-balls at Stonea is puzzling, especially as they were found as a cache in a hollow of a tree trunk. This would suggest that they were purposely gathered, rather than blown in accidentally. There is no known ecological association between ash trees and *Bovista* puff-balls. The Stonea find is certainly the largest so far recorded. The other finds consist of only a few puff-balls each, although at Skara Brae 13 were found (Watling and Seaward 1976).

Watling and Seaward (1976) have put forward a number of suggestions for possible use of the puff-balls by humans, such as the use as a haemostatic, for cauterization, as tinder, or even as a hallucinogenic. They do, however, admit to the highly speculative nature of their suggestions.

The organic deposits of the sump also produced several pieces of bracket fungus.

Acknowledgements

First of all I would like to thank all those who carried out the flotation of the samples on site. I am also grateful to Anne Blackham, Andrew Jones and Dr D. A. Reid for their specialist contributions; to Jon Scholes for sorting the waterlogged samples; to Allan Hall, Jacqui Huntley, Jan Peter Pals, Mark Robinson, Philippa Thomlinson and Prof. W. van Zeist for their help with the identifications and for their advice on the interpretation; to Charly French and Peter Murphy for their comments on an earlier draft; and to Yvonne Beadnell for originating Fig. 235.

MOLLUSCAN ANALYSIS

Charles French [Submitted 1986] (Fig. 239)

INTRODUCTION

Eighty-three samples contained sufficient numbers of molluscs to warrant analysis out of a total of 481 samples (or 17.25%). These samples were from 55 contexts out of a total of a possible 422 contexts (or 14.1%). Some 35 600 molluscs were identified and counted from these samples from four years of excavation (1981–4). Sample contexts include ditches, gullies, pits, wells and ovens.

All the samples were wet-sieved on site (see van der Veen, p. 614). The standard sample size examined was 3–5 kg. The molluscs were picked out from the dried flot samples, identified and counted (after Evans 1972). Although each wet-sieved sample was examined, if there were less than 50 individuals present the results were not normally tabulated.

The results are presented in terms of absolute numbers by sample by phase (Table 68), by gross percentages for each ecological group in tabular form (Table 69) and in summary histogram form (Fig. 239) (after Boycott 1934, 1936; Ellis 1969; Evans 1972; Sparks 1961, 1964; Sparks and West 1959, 1970). The absolute numbers of molluscs found in the sump are given separately in Table 70. A summary of the molluscan species in each ecological group is given in Table 71. The results are discussed in approximate chronological order by phase in feature type groups. In the discussion which follows general comments will be made about the environment in the immediate vicinity of the feature, as well as possible micro-environments created by the archaeological features themselves. Also, molluscan assemblages from certain features or groups of features will be examined in more detail where appropriate.

Molluscs have been preserved mainly because of the waterlogging of many features by basic ground-water. As a result of the intensive drainage of this part of the Fenlands since the eighteenth century AD and particularly since World War 2, most features on Stonea 'island' are above the local ground-water table and are therefore subject to drying out, at least seasonally. This factor, plus the circum-neutral nature of the soil once it ceases to be waterlogged, has undoubtedly caused the poor preservation of molluscs in many features across the site. Nevertheless, the past use of some features may have created habitats unsuitable for molluscan life at the time of deposition, and may account for the absence of molluscs in some features. Also, a low ground water table at the time of the molluscs' inclusion in the infill of some shallower features may not have created a suitable environment for the preservation of the molluscs.

DISCUSSION

Phase I/II

The shallow ditch O12,1 (gully 80) is dominated by the catholic species *Trichia hispida* (84%) (Tables 68–9), to the virtual exclusion of most of the other species otherwise present. It may occur in a variety of habitats, but it is often abundant in damper places such as marsh or meadow (Boycott 1934; Ellis 1969). Pit O9,1 produced a small assemblage of molluscs, dominated by the open-country *Vallonia* species (37%), *Trichia hispida* (22%) and the freshwater slum species *Lymnaea truncatula* (18.6%). This assemblage differs very little from those in Phase III.

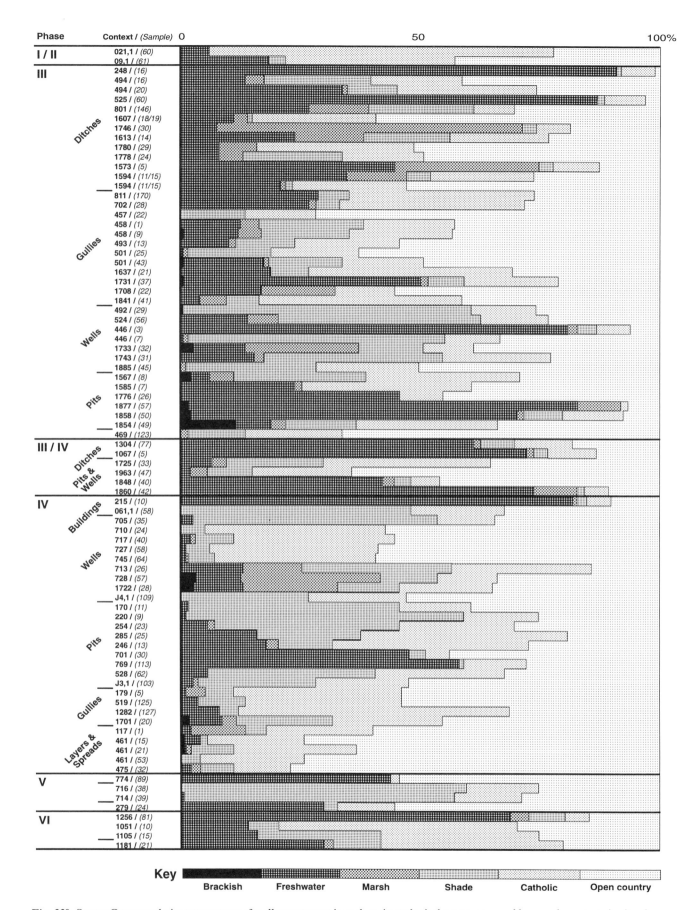

Fig. 239 Stonea Grange: relative percentages of molluscs present in each main ecological group, arranged by sample contexts in site phases.

Table 68 Stonea Grange: molluscan analysis – absolute numbers of molluscs in each context

Context	O12,1	O9,1	248	494	494	525	801	1607	1746	1613	1780	1778	1573	1594	1594	811	702	457	458	458	493	501	501
Sample	60	61	16	16	20	60	146	18/19	30	14	29	24	5	11/15	11/15	170	28	22	1	9	13	25	43
Valvata cristata Müller	–	–	–	–	–	–	–	–	–	–	–	–	–	–	–	–	–	–	–	–	–	–	–
Hydrobia ventrosa (Montagu)	–	–	–	–	–	–	–	–	–	–	–	–	–	–	–	–	–	–	1	–	–	–	–
H. ulvae (Pennant)	–	–	–	–	–	–	–	–	–	–	–	–	–	–	–	–	–	1	–	–	–	–	–
Viviparus piscinalis (Müller)	–	–	–	–	–	–	–	–	–	–	–	–	–	–	–	–	–	–	–	–	–	–	–
Bithynia leachii (Sheppard)	–	–	–	–	–	–	–	–	–	–	–	–	–	–	–	–	–	–	2	11	2	–	–
Aplexa hypnorum (Linnaeus)	–	–	–	–	–	18	6	1	–	14	5	4	19	8	1	–	–	–	–	–	–	–	–
Lymnaea truncatula (Müller)	11	11	5	8	3	30	24	38	10	15	7	6	6	2	91	47	105	–	123	120	61	2	60
L. palustris (Müller)	–	–	14	3	5	39	3	–	–	–	–	–	–	–	–	–	–	–	3	4	–	–	–
L. stagnalis (Linnaeus)	–	–	18	–	–	–	2	–	–	–	–	–	–	–	–	–	–	–	–	8	–	–	–
L. peregra (Müller)	–	–	–	1	–	8	1	–	–	–	–	–	–	–	–	–	–	–	3	–	1	–	–
Planorbis planorbis (Linnaeus)	–	–	–	–	–	–	1	–	–	–	–	–	–	–	–	–	–	–	–	2	1	–	–
Anisus leucostoma (Millet)	1	–	530	40	103	1146	2	10	18	140	15	3	82	90	27	2	2	–	54	108	31	–	1
A. vortex (Linnaeus)	–	–	–	–	–	–	–	–	–	–	–	–	–	–	–	–	–	–	–	–	–	–	–
Bathyomphalus contortus (Linnaeus)	–	–	–	–	1	–	–	–	–	–	–	–	–	–	–	–	–	–	4	1	–	–	–
Gyraulus albus (Müller)	–	–	2	–	–	–	–	–	–	3	–	–	1	–	–	–	–	–	2	2	–	–	–
Armiger crista (Linnaeus)	–	–	–	–	–	–	–	–	–	–	–	1	–	–	–	–	–	–	–	–	–	–	–
Hippeutis complanatus (Linnaeus)	–	–	–	–	–	–	–	–	–	–	–	–	–	–	–	–	–	–	2	2	–	–	–
Planorbarius corneus (Linnaeus)	–	–	–	–	–	–	–	1	1	–	–	–	–	5	–	–	–	–	2	1	–	–	–
Carychium minimum Müller	–	–	–	15	1	8	3	–	–	–	–	–	–	–	–	–	1	–	2	–	1	–	–
C. tridentatum (Risso)	–	–	–	28	8	1	32	3	10	131	–	34	8	15	9	3	–	6	339	332	108	76	40
Succinea putris (Linnaeus)	–	–	–	–	4	4	–	1	–	6	–	–	–	–	–	–	1	–	–	–	–	1	1
S. oblonga Draparnaud	–	–	–	–	–	1	–	–	3	21	37	–	3	13	3	–	1	2	–	1	–	–	–
Oxyloma pfeifferi (Rossmässler)	–	–	–	–	–	–	–	–	–	–	–	–	–	–	–	–	–	–	–	–	–	–	–
Succinea/Oxyloma spp.	–	–	–	–	1	16	11	8	205	65	22	5	61	33	3	–	–	1	6	–	–	3	2
Cochlicopa lubrica (Müller)	–	1	8	–	5	11	1	12	2	8	5	–	3	4	19	3	–	–	13	16	5	11	10
C. lubricella (Porro)	–	–	–	–	–	–	–	–	–	–	3	–	–	–	–	–	9	–	–	–	–	–	–
Cochlicopa spp.	8	7	4	5	20	31	12	94	15	135	102	18	17	56	78	10	29	1	55	48	23	33	22
Vertigo antivertigo (Draparnaud)	–	–	–	–	–	–	–	–	–	–	–	–	–	–	–	–	–	–	57	87	12	–	–
V. substriata (Jeffreys)	–	–	–	–	–	–	–	–	–	–	–	–	–	–	–	–	–	–	–	–	–	–	–
V. pygmaea (Draparnaud)	–	2	–	–	1	2	1	28	8	8	2	3	–	1	30	1	–	1	12	13	17	4	4
V. moulinsiana (Dupuy)	–	–	–	–	–	–	–	–	–	–	–	–	–	–	–	–	–	–	–	–	–	–	–
V. alpestris Alder	–	–	–	–	–	–	–	–	–	–	–	–	–	–	–	–	–	–	–	1	–	–	–
V. angustior Jeffreys	–	–	–	–	–	–	–	–	–	–	–	–	–	–	–	–	–	–	–	–	–	–	–
Vertigo spp.	–	–	–	–	–	1	1	–	–	–	–	–	–	–	5	–	–	–	9	5	2	2	–
Pupilla muscorum (Linnaeus)	–	1	–	–	–	1	1	5	2	–	1	–	1	–	2	–	–	1	2	4	2	2	–
Lauria cylindracea (Da Costa)	–	–	–	1	–	–	–	–	–	–	–	–	–	–	–	–	–	–	–	–	–	–	–
Vallonia costata (Müller)	–	6	6	90	56	34	–	–	–	–	–	–	–	–	–	26	80	9	34	14	41	263	126
V. pulchella (Müller)	5	1	1	7	6	1	9	100	14	72	46	23	13	37	83	4	10	22	252	318	184	13	13
V. excentrica Sterki	–	4	–	21	7	4	–	3	12	–	10	–	–	–	6	4	5	1	9	40	19	5	4
Vallonia spp.	8	11	–	40	13	–	31	121	31	75	120	54	18	35	204	7	17	19	356	407	239	55	32
Acanthinula aculeata (Müller)	–	–	–	1	–	–	–	–	–	–	–	–	–	–	–	–	–	–	–	–	–	–	–
Punctum pygmaeum (Draparnaud)	–	–	–	–	–	–	–	1	–	–	1	–	–	–	–	–	–	–	1	–	–	2	2
Discus rotundatus (Müller)	–	1	–	21	3	–	–	–	–	–	–	–	–	–	–	–	–	–	–	–	–	–	–
Vitrina pellucida (Müller)	–	–	–	–	–	–	–	–	–	–	–	1	–	–	–	–	–	–	–	–	–	–	–
Vitrea contracta (Westerlund)	–	–	–	–	–	–	–	–	–	1	–	–	–	–	–	–	–	1	–	–	–	–	–
Nesovitrea hammonis (Ström)	–	–	–	–	–	1	–	–	–	–	–	–	1	–	–	–	–	–	–	–	–	–	–
Aegopinella pura (Alder)	–	–	–	–	–	–	–	–	–	–	–	–	–	–	–	–	9	–	–	–	–	2	1
A. nitidula (Draparnaud)	–	–	4	6	1	14	–	–	–	–	–	–	–	–	–	4	1	–	–	–	–	1	5
Oxychilus cellarius (Müller)	–	1	1	2	6	6	–	–	–	–	–	–	–	–	–	1	1	1	2	–	1	3	–
Oxychilus spp.	–	–	2	18	16	5	–	–	–	–	–	–	–	–	–	1	8	–	2	–	1	5	6
Zonitoides nitidus (Müller)	–	–	–	–	–	–	–	–	–	–	–	–	–	–	–	–	3	–	–	–	–	–	–
Deroceras sp.	–	–	–	–	–	–	–	–	–	–	–	–	–	–	–	–	–	–	–	–	–	–	–
Euconulus fulvus (Müller)	–	–	–	4	1	–	–	–	–	–	–	–	–	–	–	–	–	–	–	2	2	–	1
Marpessa laminata (Montagu)	–	–	–	–	–	–	–	–	–	–	–	–	–	–	–	–	–	–	–	–	–	–	–
Clausilia bidentata (Ström)	–	–	–	7	–	–	–	–	–	–	–	–	–	–	–	–	–	1	–	–	–	–	–
Balea perversa (Linnaeus)	–	–	–	–	–	–	–	–	–	–	–	–	–	–	–	–	–	–	–	–	–	–	–
Helicella itala (Linnaeus)	–	–	–	–	–	–	–	–	–	–	–	–	–	–	–	–	–	–	–	–	–	–	–
Trichia hispida (Linnaeus)	173	13	25	69	69	43	–	4	–	7	5	9	4	1	23	52	109	9	232	300	181	60	34
Helicigona lapicida (Linnaeus)	–	–	–	–	–	–	–	–	–	–	–	–	–	–	–	–	–	–	–	–	–	–	–
Cepaea nemoralis (Linnaeus)	–	–	–	–	–	–	–	–	–	–	–	–	–	–	–	–	–	–	–	–	–	–	–
C. hortensis (Müller)	–	–	1	–	1	7	–	–	–	–	–	–	–	–	–	1	–	–	–	–	–	–	–
Cepaea spp.	–	–	–	–	1	2	–	–	–	–	–	–	–	–	–	1	2	–	–	–	1	–	–
Helix aspersa Müller	–	–	–	–	–	1	–	–	–	–	–	–	–	–	–	–	–	–	–	–	–	–	–
Sphaerium corneum (Linnaeus)	–	–	–	–	–	–	–	–	–	–	–	–	–	–	–	–	–	–	–	–	–	–	–
Pisidium personatum Malm	–	–	–	–	–	–	–	–	–	–	–	–	–	–	–	–	–	–	–	–	–	–	–
P. subtruncatum Malm	–	–	–	–	–	–	–	–	–	–	–	–	–	–	–	–	–	–	–	–	–	–	–
P. nitidum Jenyns	–	–	–	–	–	–	–	–	–	–	–	–	–	–	–	–	–	–	–	–	–	–	–
Ostrea edulis Linnaeus	–	–	1	–	–	–	–	–	–	–	–	–	–	–	–	–	–	–	–	–	–	–	–
Mytilus sp.	–	–	1	–	–	–	–	–	–	–	–	–	–	–	–	–	–	–	–	–	–	–	–

Table 68 continued

| Context | 1637 | 1731 | 1708 | 1841 | 492 | 524 | 446 | 446 | 1733 | 1743 | 1885 | 1567 | 1585 | 1776 | 1877 | 1858 | 1854 | 469 | 1304 | 1067 | 1725 | 1963 | 1848 | 1860 |
Sample	21	37	22	41	29	56	3	7	32	31	45	8	7	26	57	50	49	123	77	5	33	47	40	42
Valvata cristata Müller	–	–	–	–	–	–	–	–	–	–	–	–	–	–	–	–	–	–	–	–	–	–	–	–
Hydrobia ventrosa (Montagu)	–	1	–	–	–	–	–	2	–	–	–	–	–	–	–	5	10	–	–	–	–	–	–	–
H. ulvae (Pennant)	–	–	–	–	–	–	–	–	–	–	–	–	–	–	–	3	–	–	–	–	–	–	–	–
Viviparus piscinalis (Müller)	–	–	–	1	–	–	–	–	–	–	–	–	–	–	–	–	–	–	–	–	–	–	–	–
Bithynia leachii (Sheppard)	–	–	–	–	–	–	–	–	–	–	–	–	–	–	–	–	–	–	–	–	–	–	–	–
Aplexa hypnorum (Linnaeus)	–	–	–	–	–	–	10	–	–	–	–	–	–	7	–	–	–	–	42	38	–	–	–	–
Lymnaea truncatula (Müller)	–	43	11	11	–	–	29	1	1	8	–	1	2	308	59	6	2	–	36	46	28	2	107	8
L. palustris (Müller)	–	–	–	–	–	–	1	–	–	–	–	–	–	–	–	–	–	–	–	1	–	–	–	–
L. stagnalis (Linnaeus)	–	–	–	–	–	–	2	–	–	–	–	–	–	–	–	–	–	–	–	–	–	–	–	–
L. peregra (Müller)	–	–	5	–	–	–	1	–	–	–	–	–	–	–	–	–	–	–	1	1	–	–	–	–
Planorbis planorbis (Linnaeus)	–	–	–	–	–	–	–	1	–	–	–	–	–	–	–	–	–	–	2	2	–	–	–	–
Anisus leucostoma (Millet)	10	52	6	–	–	–	497	1	8	–	–	15	1	362	97	3	–	–	249	149	7	–	806	149
A. vortex (Linnaeus)	–	–	–	8	–	–	–	–	–	–	–	–	–	–	–	–	–	–	–	–	–	–	–	–
Bathyomphalus contortus (Linnaeus)	–	–	–	1	–	–	–	–	–	–	–	–	–	–	–	–	–	–	2	–	–	–	–	–
Gyraulus albus (Müller)	–	–	–	–	5	–	–	–	–	–	–	–	–	–	–	–	–	–	–	–	–	–	–	–
Armiger crista (Linnaeus)	–	–	–	–	–	–	–	–	–	–	–	–	–	–	–	–	–	–	1	2	1	–	152	66
Hippeutis complanatus (Linnaeus)	–	–	–	–	–	–	–	–	–	–	–	–	–	–	–	–	–	–	–	–	–	–	–	–
Planorbarius corneus (Linnaeus)	–	–	–	–	–	–	–	–	–	–	–	1	1	–	–	–	–	–	–	3	–	–	–	–
Carychium minimum Müller	–	–	–	1	–	–	12	2	–	–	–	–	1	–	–	–	–	–	8	1	5	–	2	–
C. tridentatum (Risso)	–	1	–	2	232	22	13	585	7	–	14	6	–	3	1	5	3	14	31	9	31	5	40	2
Succinea putris (Linnaeus)	–	–	1	–	1	–	1	2	–	–	1	–	–	–	5	2	–	–	–	–	12	–	30	–
S. oblonga Draparnaud	–	–	1	–	–	–	2	–	–	–	–	–	–	1	21	–	–	–	–	–	–	–	12	26
Oxyloma pfeifferi (Rossmässler)	–	–	–	–	–	–	–	–	–	–	–	–	–	–	–	–	–	–	–	–	–	–	–	–
Succinea/Oxyloma spp.	–	–	20	12	–	–	–	–	–	–	1	1	–	–	20	–	–	–	–	2	–	1	25	–
Cochlicopa lubrica (Müller)	–	1	–	16	9	1	6	28	1	–	–	–	3	8	–	6	7	–	7	–	22	4	18	–
C. lubricella (Porro)	–	–	–	7	1	1	–	18	–	–	–	–	–	–	–	–	–	–	–	–	–	–	–	–
Cochlicopa spp.	4	5	8	27	45	7	10	41	1	–	8	4	24	22	7	2	14	3	28	7	90	7	54	3
Vertigo antivertigo (Draparnaud)	–	3	–	–	–	–	–	17	1	–	1	–	–	–	–	3	2	–	–	–	–	1	–	–
V. substriata (Jeffreys)	–	–	–	–	–	–	–	–	–	–	–	–	–	–	–	–	–	–	–	–	–	–	–	–
V. pygmaea (Draparnaud)	4	4	–	1	4	11	–	6	5	1	2	2	1	5	3	5	–	2	10	–	1	4	86	2
V. moulinsiana (Dupuy)	–	–	–	5	–	–	–	–	–	–	–	–	–	–	–	–	–	–	–	–	–	–	–	–
V. alpestris Alder	–	–	–	2	–	–	–	–	–	–	–	–	–	–	–	–	–	–	–	–	–	–	–	–
V. angustior Jeffreys	–	–	–	1	1	–	–	2	–	–	–	–	–	–	–	–	–	–	–	–	–	–	–	–
Vertigo spp.	–	–	–	–	–	–	–	–	–	–	–	–	–	–	–	–	–	–	–	–	–	–	–	–
Pupilla muscorum (Linnaeus)	4	15	1	1	1	–	3	1	18	1	–	8	1	3	2	–	11	3	14	8	–	1	–	–
Lauria cylindracea (Da Costa)	–	–	–	4	–	–	–	1	–	–	–	–	–	–	–	–	–	–	–	–	–	–	–	–
Vallonia costata (Müller)	2	1	26	94	125	12	28	316	1	10	35	1	–	–	–	–	1	1	12	2	182	22	175	6
V. pulchella (Müller)	3	13	19	13	24	1	3	94	7	–	13	4	27	89	12	6	11	42	20	14	2	12	456	14
V. excentrica Sterki	1	–	–	1	2	1	2	3	–	–	1	–	–	–	2	–	4	2	2	–	1	1	20	1
Vallonia spp.	2	7	25	9	14	–	4	55	–	–	17	3	–	205	13	–	–	44	38	22	7	16	401	9
Acanthinula aculeata (Müller)	–	–	–	11	1	–	–	10	–	–	1	–	–	–	–	–	3	–	–	–	–	–	–	–
Punctum pygmaeum (Draparnaud)	–	–	–	5	–	2	8	–	–	–	1	–	–	–	–	–	–	–	3	–	–	–	2	–
Discus rotundatus (Müller)	–	–	–	21	1	–	–	32	–	1	5	2	–	–	–	–	–	2	–	–	1	1	–	–
Vitrina pellucida (Müller)	–	–	–	2	–	–	1	–	–	–	–	–	–	2	–	–	–	–	2	–	4	–	–	–
Vitrea contracta (Westerlund)	–	–	–	51	4	–	–	51	–	–	1	–	–	–	–	–	–	–	–	–	–	–	–	–
Nesovitrea hammonis (Ström)	–	–	–	5	1	–	–	7	–	1	–	–	–	–	–	–	–	–	–	–	–	–	–	–
Aegopinella pura (Alder)	–	–	–	–	19	3	–	24	1	–	1	–	–	–	–	–	–	–	–	–	–	–	–	–
A. nitidula (Draparnaud)	–	2	–	10	4	–	5	3	–	1	3	–	–	–	–	–	–	–	–	–	40	1	33	2
Oxychilus cellarius (Müller)	–	5	–	2	19	6	3	18	4	6	4	5	–	–	2	2	3	1	1	–	8	–	8	–
Oxychilus spp.	4	5	–	5	23	4	4	31	–	2	–	–	–	–	–	1	5	–	1	–	28	–	5	–
Zonitoides nitidus (Müller)	–	–	–	–	–	–	–	–	–	–	–	–	–	–	–	–	–	–	–	1	–	–	–	–
Deroceras sp.	–	–	–	–	–	–	–	–	–	–	–	–	–	–	–	–	–	–	–	–	–	–	–	–
Euconulus fulvus (Müller)	–	–	–	1	–	–	–	–	–	–	–	–	–	–	–	–	–	–	–	–	–	–	–	–
Marpessa laminata (Montagu)	–	–	–	–	–	–	–	3	–	–	–	–	–	–	–	–	–	–	–	–	–	–	–	–
Clausilia bidentata (Ström)	–	–	1	5	2	–	10	–	–	9	8	–	–	–	–	–	1	–	–	–	1	2	–	–
Balea perversa (Linnaeus)	–	–	1	–	–	–	–	–	–	–	–	–	–	–	–	–	–	–	–	–	–	–	–	–
Helicella itala (Linnaeus)	–	–	–	–	–	–	–	–	–	–	–	–	–	–	–	1	–	–	–	–	–	–	–	–
Trichia hispida (Linnaeus)	18	29	8	77	30	6	19	70	6	8	22	15	–	32	1	13	2	26	32	27	79	7	70	9
Helicigona lapicida (Linnaeus)	–	–	–	–	–	–	–	–	–	–	–	–	–	–	–	–	–	–	–	–	–	–	–	–
Cepaea nemoralis (Linnaeus)	–	–	–	–	–	–	–	–	–	–	–	–	–	–	–	–	1	–	–	–	–	–	–	–
C. hortensis (Müller)	–	–	3	4	–	–	10	–	–	3	–	–	–	–	–	–	–	–	–	–	–	–	–	2
Cepaea spp.	–	–	1	1	–	–	–	6	–	1	–	–	–	–	–	–	–	–	–	–	1	–	1	–
Helix aspersa Müller	–	–	–	–	+	–	–	–	–	–	–	–	–	–	–	–	–	–	–	–	–	–	–	–
Sphaerium corneum (Linnaeus)	–	–	–	–	–	–	–	–	–	–	–	–	–	–	–	–	–	–	–	–	–	–	–	–
Pisidium personatum Malm	–	–	–	–	–	–	–	–	–	–	–	–	–	–	–	–	–	–	–	–	–	–	–	–
P. subtruncatum Malm	–	–	–	–	–	–	–	–	–	–	–	–	–	–	–	–	–	–	–	–	–	–	–	–
P. nitidum Jenyns	–	–	–	–	–	–	–	–	–	–	–	–	–	–	–	–	–	–	–	–	–	–	–	–
Ostrea edulis Linnaeus	–	–	–	–	–	–	–	–	–	–	–	–	–	–	–	–	–	–	–	–	–	–	–	–
Mytilus sp.	–	–	–	–	–	–	–	–	–	–	–	–	–	–	–	–	–	–	–	–	–	–	–	–

Table 68 continued

Context	215	O61,1	705	710	717	727	745	713	728	1722	J4,1	170	220	254	285	246	701	769	528	J3,1	179	519	1282	1701
Sample	10	58	35	24	40	58	64	26	57	28	109	11	9	23	25	13	30	113	62	103	5	125	127	20
Valvata cristata Müller	26	–	–	–	–	–	–	–	–	–	–	–	–	–	–	–	–	–	–	–	–	–	–	–
Hydrobia ventrosa (Montagu)	–	–	–	–	–	–	–	–	–	–	–	–	–	–	–	–	–	–	–	–	–	–	–	12
H. ulvae (Pennant)	–	–	–	–	–	–	–	–	2	–	–	–	1	–	–	2	–	–	–	–	–	–	–	–
Viviparus piscinalis (Müller)	–	–	–	–	–	–	–	–	–	–	–	–	–	–	–	–	–	–	–	–	–	–	–	–
Bithynia leachii (Sheppard)	–	–	–	–	1	–	–	9	1	2	–	–	–	–	–	–	–	–	–	–	–	–	–	–
Aplexa hypnorum (Linnaeus)	–	–	–	–	–	–	–	–	–	–	–	–	–	–	–	–	4	–	–	–	–	–	–	–
Lymnaea truncatula (Müller)	3	–	4	–	1	–	4	2	–	–	–	3	2	4	8	46	75	57	1	9	–	3	6	16
L. palustris (Müller)	4	–	–	–	–	–	–	–	–	–	–	1	–	–	–	–	–	–	–	–	–	–	–	–
L. stagnalis (Linnaeus)	3	–	–	–	–	–	–	–	–	–	–	–	–	–	–	–	–	–	–	–	–	–	–	–
L. peregra (Müller)	423	–	–	–	–	–	–	–	–	–	–	–	1	–	1	6	–	–	–	–	1	–	–	–
Planorbis planorbis (Linnaeus)	43	–	–	–	–	2	–	–	–	–	–	–	–	–	–	1	–	–	–	–	–	–	–	–
Anisus leucostoma (Millet)	1535	–	3	–	1	–	2	4	4	5	–	6	1	8	–	–	2	41	5	–	1	–	1	28
A. vortex (Linnaeus)	–	–	–	–	–	–	–	–	–	–	–	–	–	–	–	–	–	–	–	–	–	–	–	–
Bathyomphalus contortus (Linnaeus)	–	–	–	–	–	–	–	–	–	–	–	1	–	–	–	–	–	–	–	–	–	–	–	–
Gyraulus albus (Müller)	–	–	–	–	–	–	–	–	–	–	–	2	–	–	–	–	–	–	–	–	–	–	–	–
Armiger crista (Linnaeus)	208	–	–	–	–	–	–	–	–	–	–	–	–	–	1	–	–	–	–	–	–	–	–	4
Hippeutis complanatus (Linnaeus)	–	–	–	–	–	–	–	–	–	–	–	–	–	–	–	–	–	–	–	–	–	–	–	–
Planorbarius corneus (Linnaeus)	51	–	–	–	–	–	–	1	1	–	–	–	–	–	–	–	–	–	–	–	–	3	–	2
Carychium minimum Müller	4	–	–	–	–	–	–	2	2	–	–	1	–	2	–	–	–	–	–	–	–	–	–	–
C. tridentatum (Risso)	5	–	74	2	5	5	8	10	–	6	37	103	69	7	1	19	1	3	3	45	12	1	1	15
Succinea putris (Linnaeus)	–	–	–	1	–	–	2	11	5	–	–	–	–	–	–	–	–	–	–	–	–	–	–	1
S. oblonga Draparnaud	4	–	–	–	–	–	–	–	5	–	–	–	–	–	–	–	–	–	–	–	–	–	–	8
Oxyloma pfeifferi (Rossmässler)	–	–	–	–	–	–	–	–	–	–	–	–	–	–	–	–	–	3	–	–	–	–	–	–
Succinea/Oxyloma spp.	–	–	–	–	–	–	–	–	1	–	–	–	–	–	–	–	–	2	–	–	–	–	–	10
Cochlicopa lubrica (Müller)	11	1	3	2	6	5	24	5	2	4	–	19	16	9	3	27	2	1	2	3	30	–	–	27
C. lubricella (Porro)	–	–	1	–	–	–	–	–	–	–	–	–	–	–	–	–	–	–	–	–	12	–	–	–
Cochlicopa spp.	11	3	18	5	11	34	107	13	2	3	9	14	11	11	5	34	4	4	10	17	30	1	–	73
Vertigo antivertigo (Draparnaud)	–	–	–	–	–	–	–	2	7	12	–	–	–	–	–	–	–	–	–	–	2	17	–	–
V. substriata (Jeffreys)	–	–	–	–	–	–	–	2	–	–	–	–	–	–	–	–	–	3	–	–	–	–	–	–
V. pygmaea (Draparnaud)	2	–	11	–	3	4	4	6	14	10	–	3	1	2	–	3	–	–	2	3	1	8	1	4
V. moulinsiana (Dupuy)	–	–	–	–	–	–	–	–	–	–	–	–	–	–	–	–	–	–	–	–	2	–	–	–
V. alpestris Alder	–	–	–	–	–	–	–	3	–	–	–	–	–	–	–	–	–	–	–	–	–	–	–	–
V. angustior Jeffreys	–	–	–	–	–	–	1	2	–	–	–	–	–	1	–	–	–	3	–	–	–	–	–	–
Vertigo spp.	–	–	–	–	–	–	–	–	–	–	–	–	–	–	–	–	–	–	–	–	–	–	–	–
Pupilla muscorum (Linnaeus)	7	–	–	1	1	1	1	–	3	10	–	4	3	1	1	12	5	–	–	–	32	–	–	5
Lauria cylindracea (Da Costa)	1	–	–	–	–	–	–	–	–	–	–	–	–	1	–	–	–	–	–	–	–	–	–	1
Vallonia costata (Müller)	219	20	23	41	49	57	320	6	2	3	42	132	70	31	4	53	2	–	31	91	123	8	5	310
V. pulchella (Müller)	19	–	20	11	14	34	37	1	1	2	10	90	5	11	3	5	22	17	6	28	50	6	13	10
V. excentrica Sterki	12	–	2	1	2	1	17	1	–	–	–	17	1	5	2	1	3	6	1	4	11	4	1	–
Vallonia spp.	24	–	30	4	11	64	100	1	1	–	11	45	9	12	–	2	41	23	–	54	29	18	6	3
Acanthinula aculeata (Müller)	2	–	7	–	1	–	–	–	–	–	1	12	4	1	1	–	–	1	–	–	1	–	–	–
Punctum pygmaeum (Draparnaud)	1	–	1	–	–	–	1	1	–	–	–	1	4	–	–	–	–	–	–	–	10	–	1	–
Discus rotundatus (Müller)	13	13	3	–	1	–	3	–	–	–	2	80	35	27	3	2	–	–	2	2	2	–	–	1
Vitrina pellucida (Müller)	–	–	–	–	–	–	2	1	–	–	1	1	2	–	–	1	–	–	–	1	–	1	–	6
Vitrea contracta (Westerlund)	14	1	13	–	–	–	–	–	–	–	4	28	20	9	1	–	–	–	–	–	1	1	–	–
Nesovitrea hammonis (Ström)	–	–	7	–	–	–	–	–	–	–	–	1	–	2	–	–	–	–	–	–	–	–	2	–
Aegopinella pura (Alder)	–	–	4	–	–	–	–	–	–	–	–	9	18	3	1	7	–	–	7	2	1	–	–	–
A. nitidula (Draparnaud)	2	–	2	2	3	–	6	1	–	4	–	9	6	2	–	2	2	–	–	9	–	3	–	75
Oxychilus cellarius (Müller)	10	4	7	–	1	1	5	8	5	–	–	24	17	10	1	4	–	–	5	6	6	1	–	15
Oxychilus spp.	11	3	6	1	1	5	11	10	1	–	1	20	17	10	3	1	2	–	7	10	10	2	–	33
Zonitoides nitidus (Müller)	–	–	–	–	–	–	–	–	–	–	–	–	–	–	–	–	–	–	–	–	–	–	–	–
Deroceras sp.	–	–	–	–	–	–	–	–	–	–	–	–	–	–	–	–	–	–	1	–	–	–	–	–
Euconulus fulvus (Müller)	–	–	–	–	–	–	–	1	–	–	–	–	–	–	–	–	–	–	–	–	–	4	–	2
Marpessa laminata (Montagu)	–	–	–	–	–	–	–	–	–	–	–	–	–	–	–	–	–	–	–	–	–	–	–	–
Clausilia bidentata (Ström)	3	9	5	–	–	1	3	–	–	–	–	50	21	15	1	–	–	–	6	3	1	–	–	–
Balea perversa (Linnaeus)	–	–	–	–	1	–	–	–	–	–	–	–	–	–	–	–	–	–	–	–	–	–	–	–
Helicella itala (Linnaeus)	–	–	–	–	–	–	–	–	–	–	–	1	1	1	2	–	–	–	–	–	–	–	–	–
Trichia hispida (Linnaeus)	126	8	8	31	33	58	155	16	4	8	2	69	17	27	14	57	3	17	16	35	101	25	44	69
Helicigona lapicida (Linnaeus)	–	–	–	–	–	–	–	–	–	–	–	2	–	–	–	–	–	–	–	–	–	–	–	–
Cepaea nemoralis (Linnaeus)	1	–	–	–	–	–	1	–	–	–	–	2	–	1	–	3	–	–	–	–	–	–	–	–
C. hortensis (Müller)	–	–	–	–	–	–	1	–	–	–	–	4	–	4	–	1	–	–	–	–	–	–	–	–
Cepaea spp.	–	–	–	–	–	–	1	–	–	–	–	–	–	–	–	–	–	8	–	–	1	–	1	2
Helix aspersa Müller	+	–	–	–	–	–	–	–	–	–	–	–	8	–	4	–	–	–	–	–	–	–	–	–
Sphaerium corneum (Linnaeus)	6	–	–	–	–	–	–	–	–	–	–	–	–	–	–	–	–	–	–	–	–	–	–	–
Pisidium personatum Malm	8	–	–	–	–	–	–	–	–	–	–	–	–	–	–	–	–	–	–	–	–	–	–	–
P. subtruncatum Malm	5	–	–	–	–	–	–	–	–	–	–	–	–	–	–	–	–	–	–	–	–	–	–	–
P. nitidum Jenyns	1	–	–	–	–	–	–	–	–	–	–	–	–	–	–	–	–	–	–	–	–	–	–	–
Ostrea edulis Linnaeus	–	–	–	–	–	–	–	–	–	–	–	+	+	–	–	–	–	–	–	–	–	–	–	–
Mytilus sp.	–	–	–	–	–	–	–	–	–	–	–	–	–	–	–	–	–	–	–	–	–	–	–	–

Table 68 continued

Context	117	461	461	461	475	774	716	714	279	1256	1051	1105	1181
Sample	1	15	21	53	32	89	38	39	24	81	10	15	21
Valvata cristata Müller	–	–	–	–	–	–	–	–	6	–	–	–	–
Hydrobia ventrosa (Montagu)	–	–	–	–	–	–	–	–	–	–	–	–	–
H. ulvae (Pennant)	–	1	1	–	–	–	–	–	–	–	–	–	–
Viviparus piscinalis (Müller)	–	–	–	–	–	–	–	–	–	–	–	–	–
Bithynia leachii (Sheppard)	–	–	–	–	–	–	–	–	–	–	–	–	–
Aplexa hypnorum (Linnaeus)	–	–	–	–	–	–	–	–	5	–	–	–	–
Lymnaea truncatula (Müller)	4	–	–	–	–	11	–	–	1	16	14	1	256
L. palustris (Müller)	–	–	–	–	–	–	–	–	–	–	–	–	–
L. stagnalis (Linnaeus)	–	–	–	–	–	–	–	–	–	–	–	–	–
L. peregra (Müller)	2	–	–	–	–	–	–	–	–	–	–	–	–
Planorbis planorbis (Linnaeus)	–	–	–	–	–	–	–	–	–	–	–	–	–
Anisus leucostoma (Millet)	13	6	2	–	–	7	–	1	21	51	–	5	–
A. vortex (Linnaeus)	–	–	–	–	–	–	–	–	–	–	–	–	–
Bathyomphalus contortus (Linnaeus)	–	–	–	–	–	–	–	–	–	–	–	–	–
Gyraulus albus (Müller)	–	–	–	–	–	–	–	–	–	–	–	–	–
Armiger crista (Linnaeus)	–	–	–	–	–	–	–	–	1	–	–	4	–
Hippeutis complanatus (Linnaeus)	–	–	–	–	–	–	–	–	–	–	–	–	–
Planorbarius corneus (Linnaeus)	–	–	–	–	–	–	–	–	–	–	–	12	–
Carychium minimum Müller	123	–	–	–	–	–	–	–	–	3	–	–	14
C. tridentatum (Risso)	22	3	–	5	–	–	43	117	1	9	2	30	57
Succinea putris (Linnaeus)	–	–	–	–	–	–	–	–	–	–	–	–	–
S. oblonga Draparnaud	–	–	–	–	–	–	–	–	–	–	–	–	–
Oxyloma pfeifferi (Rossmässler)	–	–	–	–	–	–	–	–	–	–	–	–	–
Succinea/Oxyloma spp.	1	–	–	1	–	–	–	–	–	1	–	–	–
Cochlicopa lubrica (Müller)	39	1	1	6	–	–	–	11	5	–	–	1	6
C. lubricella (Porro)	–	–	–	4	–	–	–	–	–	–	–	–	–
Cochlicopa spp.	28	4	5	21	–	1	6	16	2	–	14	9	51
Vertigo antivertigo (Draparnaud)	–	–	–	1	–	–	–	–	–	–	–	–	–
V. substriata (Jeffreys)	–	–	–	–	–	–	–	–	–	–	–	–	1
V. pygmaea (Draparnaud)	31	–	–	4	–	–	3	3	2	1	1	–	7
V. moulinsiana (Dupuy)	3	–	–	–	–	–	–	–	–	–	–	–	–
V. alpestris Alder	–	–	–	–	–	–	–	–	–	–	–	–	–
V. angustior Jeffreys	–	–	–	–	–	–	–	–	–	–	–	–	–
Vertigo spp.	3	–	–	–	–	–	–	–	–	–	–	–	–
Pupilla muscorum (Linnaeus)	22	21	11	9	–	–	–	–	20	–	–	–	1
Lauria cylindracea (Da Costa)	–	–	–	–	–	–	–	–	–	–	–	–	–
Vallonia costata (Müller)	156	29	50	10	–	–	2	33	2	–	25	28	133
V. pulchella (Müller)	102	63	128	35	–	5	2	31	8	5	2	–	14
V. excentrica Sterki	51	2	7	–	–	3	5	1	14	–	–	–	–
Vallonia spp.	290	29	83	22	–	14	10	30	6	9	–	7	16
Acanthinula aculeata (Müller)	–	–	–	–	–	–	6	9	–	–	–	–	–
Punctum pygmaeum (Draparnaud)	2	–	–	–	–	–	–	2	–	–	1	–	19
Discus rotundatus (Müller)	1	–	2	2	–	–	1	18	1	–	–	–	–
Vitrina pellucida (Müller)	1	–	1	–	–	–	–	–	–	–	–	–	12
Vitrea contracta (Westerlund)	–	–	4	–	–	–	–	8	–	–	–	–	–
Nesovitrea hammonis (Ström)	–	–	–	–	–	–	–	–	–	–	–	–	–
Aegopinella pura (Alder)	2	–	–	–	–	–	–	3	–	–	–	–	–
A. nitidula (Draparnaud)	1	–	–	–	–	–	–	1	–	–	2	–	–
Oxychilus cellarius (Müller)	1	2	20	2	–	–	2	7	1	–	–	6	–
Oxychilus spp.	10	1	7	–	–	–	2	1	–	–	–	–	–
Zonitoides nitidus (Müller)	–	–	–	–	–	–	–	–	–	–	–	–	–
Deroceras sp.	–	–	–	–	–	–	–	–	–	–	–	–	–
Euconulus fulvus (Müller)	–	–	–	–	–	–	–	2	–	–	–	–	–
Marpessa laminata (Montagu)	–	–	–	–	–	–	–	–	–	–	–	–	–
Clausilia bidentata (Ström)	–	–	2	–	–	–	–	19	–	–	–	–	–
Balea perversa (Linnaeus)	–	–	–	–	–	–	–	–	–	–	–	–	–
Helicella itala (Linnaeus)	–	–	–	–	–	–	–	–	–	–	–	–	–
Trichia hispida (Linnaeus)	191	33	85	19	–	–	6	18	4	5	32	36	261
Helicigona lapicida (Linnaeus)	–	–	–	–	–	–	–	–	–	–	–	–	–
Cepaea nemoralis (Linnaeus)	–	–	–	–	–	–	–	–	–	–	–	–	–
C. hortensis (Müller)	–	–	–	–	–	–	–	1	–	–	–	–	–
Cepaea spp.	1	–	–	–	–	–	2	1	–	–	–	–	–
Helix aspersa Müller	–	–	–	–	–	–	–	–	–	–	–	–	–
Sphaerium corneum (Linnaeus)	–	–	–	–	–	–	–	–	–	–	–	–	–
Pisidium personatum Malm	–	–	–	–	–	–	–	–	–	–	–	–	–
P. subtruncatum Malm	–	–	–	–	–	–	–	–	–	–	–	–	–
P. nitidum Jenyns	–	–	–	–	–	–	–	–	–	–	–	–	–
Ostrea edulis Linnaeus	–	–	–	–	–	–	–	–	+	–	–	–	–
Mytilus sp.	–	–	–	–	–	–	–	–	–	–	–	–	–

Table 69 Stonea Grange: molluscan analysis – relative percentages of molluscs in each ecological group

Context	O12,1	O9,1	248	494	494	525	801	1607	1746	1613	1780	1778	1573
Sample	60	61	16	16	20	60	146	18/19	30	14	29	24	5
Marine	–	–	+	–	–	–	–	–	–	–	–	–	–
Brackish	–	–	–	–	–	–	–	–	–	–	–	–	–
Freshwater	5.8	18.6	91.0	13.5	34.0	86.5	27.05	11.55	8.15	23.4	7.65	8.0	45.2
1) Slum	5.8	18.6	85.8	12.5	32.2	82.0	18.05	11.1	7.85	22.0	6.25	5.55	34.9
2) Catholic	–	–	5.2	1.0	1.8	3.25	2.75	–	–	0.4	–	–	0.8
3) Ditch	–	–	–	–	–	1.25	4.85	0.2	–	2.0	1.4	2.45	7.5
4) Moving water	–	–	–	–	–	–	1.4	0.2	0.3	–	–	2.45	2.0
Marsh	–	–	–	3.9	0.6	2.0	12.5	2.55	63.5	14.45	7.95	4.9	29.35
Land	94.2	81.4	8.7	82.6	65.4	11.5	60.45	85.9	28.35	62.15	84.4	87.1	25.45
Shade-loving	–	3.4	1.25	20.4	10.4	1.9	22.2	0.7	2.8	18.75	–	20.85	3.2
Rupestral	–	–	–	2.1	–	–	–	–	–	–	–	–	–
Punctum group	–	–	–	1.0	0.3	–	–	0.25	0.3	–	0.55	0.6	–
Catholic	87.85	35.6	6.2	19.3	29.35	6.6	9.0	25.45	6.7	20.4	32.75	16.55	9.5
Open-country	6.35	42.4	1.25	40.8	25.35	3.0	29.25	59.2	18.55	23.0	51.1	49.1	12.75
Totals	206	59	623	386	329	1434	144	432	357	704	351	163	252

Table 69 continued

Context	1594	1594	811	702	457	458	458	493	501	501	1637	1731	1708	1841
Sample	11/15	11/15	170	28	22	1	9	13	25	43	21	37	22	41
Marine	–	–	–	–	–	–	–	–	–	–	–	–	–	–
Brackish	–	–	–	–	–	–	0.2	–	–	0.3	–	0.5	–	–
Freshwater	35.1	21.3	29.2	27.2	–	12.45	14.05	10.2	0.4	16.7	19.2	50.8	17.0	3.8
1) Slum	32.3	21.1	29.2	27.2	–	11.3	12.35	9.8	0.4	16.7	19.2	50.8	13.15	3.8
2) Catholic	–	–	–	–	–	0.9	0.5	0.2	–	–	–	–	3.85	–
3) Ditch	2.8	0.2	–	–	–	–	0.1	–	–	–	–	–	–	–
4) Moving water	–	–	–	–	–	0.25	1.1	0.2	–	–	–	–	–	–
Marsh	12.65	1.4	–	1.75	–	4.15	4.75	1.3	0.9	0.8	–	1.6	15.5	4.85
Land	52.25	77.3	70.8	71.05	100	83.4	81.0	88.5	98.7	82.2	80.8	47.1	67.5	91.35
Shade-loving	5.25	1.6	5.8	4.5	10.6	22.0	18.05	12.3	16.35	14.25	7.7	6.95	–	6.55
Rupestral	–	–	–	–	2.65	–	+	–	–	–	–	–	–	0.7
Punctum group	–	–	–	–	–	+	0.1	0.2	0.35	0.8	–	–	–	–
Catholic	21.4	21.45	39.0	37.5	15.25	19.1	19.8	22.3	19.25	18.1	42.3	18.7	12.5	42.9
Open-country	25.6	54.25	26.0	28.05	71.5	42.3	43.05	53.7	62.75	49.05	30.8	21.45	55.0	41.2
Totals	285	559	168	393	76	1569	1843	938	545	365	52	187	129	289

Table 69 continued

Context	492	524	446	446	1733	1743	1885	1567	1585	1776	1877	1858	1854	469
Sample	29	56	3	7	32	31	45	8	7	26	57	50	49	123
Marine	–	–	–	–	–	–	–	–	–	–	–	–	–	–
Brackish	–	–	–	–	2.45	–	–	1.7	–	–	1.0	2.0	12.35	–
Freshwater	–	13.8	80.9	0.2	11.0	15.1	–	3.45	23.95	45.95	81.75	68.2	6.2	–
1) Slum	–	–	78.8	0.12	11.0	15.1	–	1.7	22.65	44.95	81.75	68.2	6.2	–
2) Catholic	–	5.5	0.3	–	–	–	–	–	–	–	–	–	–	–
3) Ditch	–	7.4	1.5	0.6	–	–	–	–	–	1.0	–	–	–	–
4) Moving water	–	0.9	0.3	–	–	–	–	1.7	1.3	–	–	–	–	–
Marsh	0.3	6.4	2.1	0.35	23.45	1.9	0.7	5.15	1.3	0.15	9.0	1.3	3.7	1.4
Land	99.7	79.8	17.0	99.45	63.1	83.0	99.3	89.7	74.75	53.9	8.25	29.8	77.75	98.6
Shade-loving	55.15	36.7	4.05	51.95	14.7	18.9	16.9	25.8	–	0.45	0.6	5.3	13.55	11.95
Rupestral	3.0	4.5	–	1.65	–	16.95	6.6	–	–	–	–	2.65	1.2	–
Punctum group	1.8	1.8	–	1.1	–	1.9	3.65	1.7	–	–	–	–	–	–
Catholic	14.3	13.8	6.95	11.5	9.8	22.65	22.05	32.75	36.0	9.0	1.55	14.35	29.6	20.4
Open-country	25.45	23.0	6.0	33.25	38.6	22.6	50.1	29.45	38.75	44.45	6.1	7.5	33.4	66.25
Totals	669	109	667	1430	81	53	136	58	75	687	515	151	81	142

Table 69 continued

Context	1304	1067	1725	1963	1848	1860	215	O61,1	705	710	717	727	745
Sample	77	5	33	47	40	42	10	58	35	24	40	58	64
Marine	–	–	–	–	–	–	–		–	–	–	–	–
Brackish	–	–	–	–	–	–	–		–	–	–	–	–
Freshwater	61.4	72.55	6.55	2.3	42.6	74.6	82.0	–	2.8	–	2.1	0.7	0.75
1) Slum	52.6	58.2	6.35	2.3	36.5	52.5	54.5	–	2.8	–	1.4	0.7	0.75
2) Catholic	0.7	1.2	0.2	–	6.1	22.1	22.8	–	–	–	–	–	–
3) Ditch	8.1	11.95	–	–	–	–	2.4	–	–	–	0.7	–	–
4) Moving water	–	0.9	–	–	–	–	2.3	–	–	–	–	–	–
Marsh	1.5	1.2	3.1	3.5	2.75	8.7	0.3	–	–	–	0.7	–	0.35
Land	37.1	26.25	90.35	94.2	54.65	16.7	17.7	100	97.2	100	97.2	99.3	98.9
Shade-loving	6.1	2.7	19.6	6.95	3.45	1.35	1.8	33.8	43.2	5.2	7.5	4.65	4.15
Rupestral	–	–	0.2	2.3	–	–	0.2	14.5	4.8	–	–	0.7	0.35
Punctum group	0.9	–	0.7	–	0.1	–	+	–	3.2	–	–	–	0.35
Catholic	12.35	10.15	34.8	20.9	5.7	4.6	5.2	19.35	11.95	38.0	34.2	36.25	35.35
Open-country	17.75	13.4	35.05	64.05	45.4	10.75	10.5	32.25	34.05	57.0	54.8	58.4	58.7
Totals	542	335	551	86	2503	299	2833	62	252	100	146	276	813

Table 69 continued

Context	713	728	1722	J4,1	170	220	254	285	246	701	769	528	J3,1	179	519
Sample	26	57	28	109	11	9	23	25	13	30	113	62	103	5	125
Marine	–	–	–	–	+	+	–	–	–	–	–	–	–	–	–
Brackish	–	3.125	2.6	–	–	+	–	–	+	–	–	–	–	+	–
Freshwater	12.9	9.375	10.55	–	1.7	1.1	5.6	16.0	18.0	47.9	58.0	5.6	2.6	1.0	3.65
1) Slum	5.15	6.25	6.65	–	1.2	0.8	5.6	12.8	15.0	45.55	58.0	5.6	2.6	0.2	3.65
2) Catholic	–	–	–	–	0.5	0.3	–	3.2	2.0	–	–	–	–	0.2	–
3) Ditch	–	–	–	–	–	–	–	–	–	2.35	–	–	–	–	–
4) Moving water	7.75	3.125	3.9	–	–	–	–	–	–	–	–	–	–	0.6	–
Marsh	12.9	29.625	19.9	–	0.13	–	1.4	–	2.5	–	–	–	0.6	4.0	–
Land	74.2	56.325	66.95	100	98.0	98.0	93.0	84.0	79.0	52.1	42.0	94.4	96.8	94.5	96.35
Shade-loving	29.25	12.45	13.3	36.6	36.0	51.0	30.7	19.4	11.2	3.55	1.75	28.95	21.5	4.4	8.55
Rupestral	–	–	–	0.8	8.5	6.0	7.0	3.2	–	–	–	6.5	1.2	0.2	–
Punctum group	1.9	–	–	0.8	0.4	1.65	0.9	–	0.3	–	–	–	2.8	1.0	1.2
Catholic	29.3	12.5	19.95	9.5	13.8	14.35	24.2	42.0	40.6	5.3	13.0	27.1	19.3	35.7	32.9
Open-country	14.0	32.925	33.7	52.6	39.3	25.0	30.2	19.4	26.9	43.25	27.25	38.35	52.0	53.2	53.7
Totals	116	64	75	120	754	360	215	62	306	169	169	107	342	469	82

Table 69 continued

Context	1282	1701	117	461	461	461	475	774	716	714	279	1256	1051	1105	1181
Sample	127	20	1	15	21	53	32	89	38	39	24	81	10	15	21
Marine	–	–	–	–	–	–	–	–	–	–	+	–	–	–	–
Brackish	–	1.65	–	0.6	0.2	–	–	–	–	–	–	–	–	–	–
Freshwater	8.3	6.95	1.8	3.1	0.45	–	2.2	43.9	–	0.3	30.0	69.15	14.4	15.8	30.0
1) Slum	8.3	6.1	1.6	3.1	0.45	–	2.2	43.9	–	0.3	23.0	62.6	14.4	4.35	30.0
2) Catholic	–	0.55	0.2	–	–	–	–	–	–	–	0.8	1.85	–	2.85	–
3) Ditch	–	–	–	–	–	–	–	–	–	–	6.2	4.7	–	–	–
4) Moving water	–	0.3	–	–	–	–	–	–	–	–	–	–	–	8.6	–
Marsh	–	2.6	11.5	–	0.45	–	2.2	–	–	–	–	3.75	–	–	1.65
Land	91.7	88.8	86.7	96.3	98.9	100	95.6	56.1	100	99.7	70.0	27.1	85.6	84.2	68.35
Shade-loving	1.2	19.3	3.8	1.55	8.55	3.9	7.7	–	53.35	44.9	3.0	8.5	4.5	26.0	6.65
Rupestral	–	0.15	–	–	0.45	–	–	–	6.65	8.1	–	–	–	–	–
Punctum group	2.4	1.1	0.3	–	0.2	–	–	–	–	4.4	–	–	1.05	–	3.65
Catholic	57.1	23.75	23.3	20.2	26.05	22.3	11.1	2.45	15.55	13.6	11.5	4.6	50.0	33.1	37.55
Open-country	31.0	44.5	59.3	74.55	63.65	73.8	76.8	53.65	24.45	28.7	55.5	14.0	29.95	25.1	20.5
Totals	84	720	1100	193	445	103	90	41	90	345	95	107	94	139	850

Table 70 Stonea Grange: molluscan analysis – absolute numbers of molluscs from the sump

Layer	32	32	29	29	28	28	28
Sample	DD	GG	CC	FF	BB	EEa	EEb
Aplexa hypnorum (Linnaeus)	–	–	–	–	–	–	1
Lymnaea truncatula (Müller)	–	–	–	7	–	–	–
L. stagnalis (Linnaeus)	–	–	2	1	5	4	–
Anisus leucostoma (Millet)	4	1	3	5	–	–	5
Armiger crista (Linnaeus)	4	30	–	1	–	–	3
Carychium tridentatum (Risso)	–	1	–	–	–	–	–
Succinea putris (Linnaeus)	2	–	–	1	–	–	–
S. oblonga Draparnaud	5	–	1	–	–	–	–
Succinea/Oxyloma spp.	26	–	–	–	–	–	3
Cochlicopa lubrica (Müller)	–	1	–	3	–	–	–
Cochlicopa spp.	–	3	–	–	–	–	–
Pupilla muscorum (Linnaeus)	–	–	2	2	–	–	–
Vallonia costata (Müller)	–	2	–	–	–	–	2
V. pulchella (Müller)	1	–	–	–	–	–	–
Aegopinella nitidula (Draparnaud)	2	–	1	–	–	–	1
Trichia hispida (Linnaeus)	–	–	1	1	–	–	–
Cepaea sp.	–	1	–	–	–	–	–
Totals	44	39	10	21	5	4	15

Table 71 Stonea Grange: molluscan analysis – the molluscan species in each ecological group

Ecological group	Species
Marine	*Ostrea edulis*
	Mytilus sp.
Brackish	*Hydrobia ventrosa*
	H. ulvae
Freshwater	
1) Slum	*Lymnaea truncatula*
	Anisus leucostoma
	Pisidium personatum
2) Catholic	*Lymnaea palustris*
	L. peregra
	Armiger crista
	Gyraulus albus
	Bathyomphalus contortus
	Hippeutis complanatus
	Sphaerium corneum
	Pisidium subtruncatum
	P. nitidum
3) Ditch	*Valvata cristata*
	Aplexa hypnorum
	Anisus vortex
	Planorbis planorbis
4) Moving water	*Valvata piscinalis*
	Bithynia leachii
	Lymnaea stagnalis
	Planorbarius corneus

Table 71 continued

Ecological group	Species
Marsh	*Carychium minimum*
	Succinea putris
	S. oblonga
	Oxyloma pfeifferi
	Zonitoides nitidus
	Vertigo antivertigo
	V. moulinsiana
	V. angustior
Land	
Shade-loving	*Carychium tridentatum*
	Discus rotundatus
	Aegopinella pura
	A. nitidula
	Vitrea contracta
	Oxychilus cellarius
	Vertigo substriata
Rupestral	*Lauria cylindracea*
	Acanthinula aculeata
	Clausilia bidentata
	Balea perversa
	Helicigona lapicida
	Vertigo alpestris
Punctum group	*Punctum pygmaeum*
	Euconulus fulvus
	Vitrina pellucida
	Nesovitrea hammonis
Catholic/Intermediate	*Cochlicopa lubrica*
	C. lubricella
	Trichia hispida
	Cepaea nemoralis
	C. hortensis
	Helix aspersa
Open-country	*Vallonia costata*
	V. pulchella
	V. excentrica
	Pupilla muscorum
	Helicella itala
	Vertigo pygmaea

Table 72 Stonea Grange: molluscan analysis – the sample volumes by context arranged in phase order

Phase	Context	Litres of soil	Totals
I/II	O12, 1	21	
	O9, 1	24	45 l.
III	248	24	
	494 (sample 16)	24	
	494 (sample 20)	24	
	525	36	
	801	4	
	1607 (samples 18 + 19)	48	
	1746	24	

Table 72 continued

Table 72 continued

Phase	Context	Litres of soil	Totals
	1613	24	
	1780	24	
	1778	18	
	1573	24	
	1594 (samples 11 + 15)	48	
	811	6	
	702	12	
	457	12	
	458 (sample 1)	12	
	458 (sample 9)	24	
	493	24	
	501 (sample 25)	12	
	501 (sample 43)	12	
	1637	24	
	1731	24	
	1708	18	
	1841	24	
	492	24	
	524	8	
	446 (sample 3)	12	
	446 (sample 7)	42	
	1733	21	
	1743	24	
	1885	24	
	1567	24	
	1585	24	
	1776	15	
	1877	24	
	1858	24	
	1854	21	
	469	21	834 l.
III/IV	1304	12	
	1067	6	
	1725	18	
	1963	18	
	1848	24	
	1860	24	102 l.
IV	215	24	
	O61, 1	9	
	705	12	
	710	12	
	717	12	
	727	9	
	745	12	
	713	12	
	728	12	
	1722	24	
	J4, 1	4	
	170	24	
	220	24	
	254	24	
	285	24	

Table 72 continued

Phase	Context	Litres of soil	Totals
	246	24	
	701	12	
	769	6	
	528	15	
	J3, 1	6	
	179	24	
	519	12	
	1282	18	
	1701	24	
	117	24	
	461 (sample 15)	24	
	461 (sample 21)	24	
	461 (sample 53)	8	
	475	12	471 l.
V	774	6	
	716	12	
	714	12	
	279	24	54 l.
VI	1256	12	
	1051	12	
	1105	12	
	1181	12	48 l.

Phase III   (Mid second to early third century)

The large 'boundary' ditch (ditch 9)
(Cut second century; filled second–fourth century)

Of the 12 sections excavated, samples from 4 of them contained sufficient numbers for analysis – 248, 494 (2 samples), 525, 801 – (Tables 68–9). Context 248 is the primary ditch fill; both 494 and 525 are units of secondary ditch fill; and context 801 is from the upper secondary fill.

The ditch was under the influence of freshwater throughout, although subject to periodic drying-out and stagnation. Freshwater species comprise from 13.5% to 91% of the assemblages in the ditch. The most abundant species is *Anisus leucostoma* (85%, 10%, 31%, 80%), which is able to resist drying conditions (Beedham 1972). Its very high frequencies in contexts 248 (85%) and 525 (80%) probably reflect sectors of the ditch which contained shallow, standing water, particularly during the accumulation of the primary and lower secondary fills. In context 801 the greater abundance of *Lymnaea truncatula* (16.6%), plus the presence of some marsh species (12.5%), indicates more marshy conditions as the ditch became infilled.

Ditch 9 also contains a substantial assemblage of land molluscs. Species with a variety of ecological habitat preferences are present, but are generally dominated by open-country species (1–40%) with the intermediate or catholic species (6–29%) and shade-loving species (1–22%) present to a lesser extent. There is nothing to indicate the existence of actual woodland in the vicinity, rather damp, open ground with tall grass and little or no bare ground. But the presence of *Discus rotundatus* (0–5%) and various species of Zonitidae (1–7%) plus a few rupestral species (0–2%) may indicate some localized scrub conditions alongside the ditch, as well as leaf litter and fallen branches entrapped within the abandoned ditch as it gradually infilled.

Vallonia costata is the most common terrestrial species present (1–23%). Although it is able to tolerate a wide range of mainly open habitat conditions, it may be found in shaded habitats (Evans 1972). In this case its presence may indicate damp, grass-covered ground with perhaps some localised shading provided by the ditch itself and/or a small scrub element alongside the ditch. The shade-loving species *Carychium tridentatum* tends to be indicative of tall, damp grass (Evans 1972) and is relatively common in the ditch (0–22%), and especially in context 801. The catholic snail *Trichia hispida* (11–21%) is often more abundant in damper habitats, which explains its greater abundance in the secondary fill ditch contexts, e.g. 494.

Considered together the molluscan assemblages from ditch 9 indicate a naturally vegetated ditch with mainly grass covered upper sides and edges. The ditch is relatively clean, except for some leaf litter perhaps, but contains varying amounts of very slow-moving to stagnant water subject to drying out. The ditch is situated in a generally open environment, but possibly there may be a few scrubby trees and bushes in the vicinity of the ditch.

Other ditches

Sample contexts 1607 and 1746 are from the lower fill (fence-line) in ditch 8, and sample contexts 1613 and 1778 are from secondary fill in ditch 8 and ditch 15, respectively. Some freshwater slum species are present, although in lesser abundance (5–22%) than in ditch 9. A few marsh species are also present (2.5–14.5%), although they are unusually common (63.5%) in context 1746. Nevertheless most of the marsh species were juvenile examples and therefore only identifiable to the *Succinea/Oxyloma* family, but they are probably mainly *Succinea putris* and *S. oblonga*, both of which are peculiar to marsh habitats (Evans 1972).

Shade-loving species occurred in similar abundance to those found in ditch 9 (1–21% and 2–22%, respectively). In both cases *Carychium tridentatum* predominates and is often the only species present (Tables 68–9). It is indicative of tall, damp grass growing both in the ditches and to either side, and it may be frequently found in marsh habitats (Evans 1972).

Catholic (7–25%) and the open-country species (18.5–59.5%) make up the bulk of the assemblages. *Cochlicopa lubrica* and *Trichia hispida* both tolerate a wide variety of habitat conditions, but may also be found in marsh habitats.

Vallonia pulchella is the most abundant open-country species present, and it too is able to tolerate wet conditions.

The overall impression from these samples is of wet, almost marshy conditions in the ditches, which in turn are set in a damp and open environment.

Samples contexts 1573 and 1594 were the primary fill of ditches 7 and 8, respectively. The snail assemblage indicates shallow, poor water conditions with a considerable marsh element in the ditches, set in a damp, open environment. Sample context 1780 was the upper fill of ditch 8. Its molluscan assemblage indicates relatively drier and more open conditions.

The enclosure gullies, blocks 1, NE, 1b and 4
(Cut second century; filled third century)

The molluscan assemblages from these three groups of features (contexts 811, 702, 457, 458, 493, 501) indicate generally similar environments to each other and to that suggested above for the ditch contexts.

The presence of some freshwater slum species, particularly in gullies 36 and 50, indicates that very poor, shallow water conditions pertained in them. The slightly greater variety of catholic freshwater species in gully 41 may suggest slightly better and more varied water conditions, but perhaps of a short-lived nature.

In all three contexts land snails predominate, and especially the open-country *Vallonia* species. The greater abundance of *Vallonia pulchella* in gully 41 may be due to its greater tolerance of wetter habitats than either *V. costata* or *V. excentrica* (Evans 1972). On the other hand, the greater abundance of *V. costata* in gullies 36 and 50 and the boundary fence-line may suggest a less damp but more sheltered habitat. The slightly greater presence of various Zonitidae in these same contexts may indicate some localised shaded conditions, perhaps by smaller shrubs or bushes. In contrast to this, the greater abundance of *Carychium tridentatum* in gully 41 suggests a greater presence of tall, damp grass and/or leaf litter than in the immediate vicinity of the other two gullies.

Other gullies

The molluscan assemblages and environmental inferences from the gully contexts 1637 and 1731 (gully 32), 1708 (gully 33) and 1841 (gully 18) differ only slightly from those in the ditch contexts (Tables 68–9). In general, the variety and abundance of species are less rich than in the ditches, probably because the shallow gullies were not as preferable as habitats. With the exception of sample context 1731, the gullies were drier and less marshy than the ditches. The virtual absence of *C. tridentatum* indicates the absence of tall grass in the vicinity, and/or some ground disturbance making the gullies less suitable habitats. Open-country species dominate the assemblage (21–55%), with *Vallonia costata* often as abundant as *V. pulchella*, which is also suggestive of slightly drier conditions (although still damp) in the gullies than in the ditches.

Wells

Well 446 (contexts 492, 524, 446) is dominated by land molluscs (Tables 68–9), presumably after the well had ceased to be used as such and was gradually becoming infilled.

In sample context 492 the assemblage is dominated by shade-loving species (57%) with a few rupestral species (3%) present (Table 69). The well probably created the damp, shaded and sheltered environment favoured by the shade-loving species, in effect acting as a refuge habitat. Consequently the assemblage is a poor indicator of the nature of the surrounding environment. *V. costata* is the most abundant open-country species (11–19%), probably because it is able to tolerate damp, shaded conditions.

In sample contexts 524 and 446 there are indications of increasing wetness in the disused well. The dominance of *Anisus leucostoma* in 446, sample 3 (74.5%) indicates shallow standing to stagnant water conditions, subject to drying out.

As the well became all but infilled and relatively dry, the molluscan assemblage became dominated by *C. tridentatum* (41%) and *V. costata* (22%). They suggest the establishment of damp grass cover at sometime later in the third century AD.

Other well contexts (1733, 1743, 1885) of this phase indicate similar micro-environments. The lower fills (contexts 1733 and 1743) of wells 1625 and 1602, and the upper fill (context 1885) of well 1885 provided a damp and very sheltered micro-habitat in which shade-loving and rupestral species could live, as well as the sometimes shade tolerant open-country species *V. costata* (Tables 68–9).

Pits

Pit contexts 1567 (pit 1567), 1585 (pit 1585/1515) and 1776 (pit 1776) contain assemblages which vary little from the other features of this phase (Tables 68–9). Context 1567 may provide a very sheltered, shaded and relatively dry micro-environment, whereas contexts 1585 and 1776 contain some freshwater.

Latrine pit 1695 comprises contexts 1877 (lower fill), 1858 (secondary fill) and 1854 (upper secondary fill). The first two stages of infilling are dominated by freshwater slum species – 82% and 68%, respectively (Tables 68–9). As conditions became drier and less sheltered, open-country and catholic species became predominant, e.g. in 1854. The considerable presence of *Pupilla muscorum* in context 1854 suggests the presence of some bare ground in the vicinity.

The sump

Seven samples from the sump contained molluscs (Table 70), but they were too few in numbers to warrant analysis. The very low abundance, from 5 to 44 individuals, is probably due to the feature being an unsuitable habitat for snails rather than to poor preservation. This could have been the result of a variety of factors. The sump may have been so full of organic debris that high acidity and poor oxygenation made it unsuitable for molluscan life. Also, the feature may not have been open for a sufficiently long period to have enabled colonization by snails. Alternatively, the ground surface conditions may have been too unstable and bare to provide suitable habitats for molluscs.

Miscellaneous

The building R3 occupation debris (context 469) is dominated by terrestrial molluscan species (98.6%) (Tables 68–9). The open-country species predominate (66%), in particular *Vallonia pulchella* (29.5%), along with the catholic species *Trichia hispida* (18%) (Tables 68–9). This assemblage suggests a relatively damp and open habitat.

Summary of the environment in Phase III

Throughout this period (second/third centuries), in whatever type of feature, the suggested site environment is generally consistent.

The almost ubiquitous presence of freshwater slum species is indicative of a high local ground water table, and the presence of shallow, standing to stagnant water in many features. Ditches and gullies would have been essential for drainage. Conditions in many features, especially in some pits may have been somewhat marshy with reeds and stagnant, very shallow water.

The surrounding environment was generally open and damp. A few patches of bare ground probably existed, but tall grass was probably commonplace. There may have been some localised scrub, for example as shrubs or small trees growing adjacent to ditches. Collapsed building debris and deep, sheltered features such as wells may have provided suitable microhabitats for rupestral and other shade-loving species.

Phase III/IV (Mid second to late third century)

The suggested local environment varies little from that indicated in Phase III, although there are slight indications of relatively drier ground conditions.

Ditches

The upper secondary ditch fill contexts 1304 (ditch 6) and 1067 (ditch 9) contain a variety of freshwater snails which tolerate varying water conditions and indicate water flow and volume in the ditches. In 1067 the freshwater slum species

Anisus leucostoma (44.5%) and *Lymnaea truncatula* (13.5%), as well as the ditch-living freshwater species *Aplexa hypnorum* (11%) predominate (Tables 68–9). Nevertheless, there are a few freshwater molluscs which are more catholic in habitat preferences, for example *Lymnaea palustris*, *L. peregra* and *Armiger crista*, plus a few examples of *Planorbarius corneus*, which prefer more flowing-water habitat conditions. The land molluscs (26%) are dominated by a few open-country (13%) and catholic species (10%) (Tables 68–9), again giving an indication of the generally open background environment.

Pits and wells

Contexts 1725 (Pit 1725) and 1963 (Pits 1989, 1996) contain similar molluscan assemblages (Tables 68–9) which indicate damp, relatively sheltered but open habitats. Few freshwater slum species are present (0–6%). The assemblages are dominated by the catholic species *Trichia hispida* (8–19%) and the open-country species (35–74.5%), and in particular *Vallonia pulchella* and *V. costata*, with a minor presence of shade/shelter-loving species.

In contrast well 1667 (contexts 1848 and 1860) was much wetter. The freshwater slum species comprise 36.5% and 52.5% of the assemblages, and especially in the lower fill. Otherwise the habitats were similar to those in the other pits of this phase.

Phase IV (Third to fourth century)

Robbing debris, buildings R1 and R15

Context 215 of the robbing debris of building R1 contained the greatest abundance of molluscs of any sample (Tables 68–9). As in the primary fill of ditch 9 (cut 6, context 248), it is dominated by freshwater molluscs (82%), and in particular the freshwater slum species *Anisus leucostoma* (54.5%). Nevertheless there are considerable numbers of other freshwater species less able to tolerate such poor water conditions. For example, the catholic freshwater species *Lymnaea peregra* (14.9%) and *Armiger crista* (7.3%) are relatively common. The former species is able to tolerate a wide range of habitat conditions, while the latter species may be found on water plants, both in stagnant and flowing waters (Beedham 1972). This assemblage suggests the existence of a pool of stagnant to standing water, with possibly some water plants growing in the robbed foundations.

The terrestrial species are few (17.7%) and mainly the open-country species *V. costata* (7.7%) and the catholic species *T. hispida* (4.4%). It is probable that they were living on the upper, open sides of the robber trench.

The presence of limestone building stone and mortar in the vicinity would have probably made this trench, and the water held in it, very lime-rich. This base-rich habitat and

the waterlogged conditions at the time of deposition, may account for the enormous abundance of molluscs.

The robbed cella wall footing of building R15 (context O61,1) is dominated by terrestrial molluscan species and in particular *Discus rotundatus* (21%) and *V. costata* (32%) (Tables 68–9). They suggest a very localised habitat of damp leaf litter and tall grass in this feature.

Wells

The snail assemblages in well 705 (contexts 705, 710, 717, 727, 745) probably reflect the environment of the feature, just as in the other wells and deeper pits. Sample context 705 is dominated by shade-loving species (Tables 68–9) whereas in the remaining samples these species comprise only 4–7.5% of the assemblages. Instead, the assemblages are dominated by *Trichia hispida* (19–31%) and *Vallonia costata* (20–41%). *V. pulchella* is also present in low frequencies. Although damp throughout, the habitat conditions within the well probably became less sheltered and shaded and more open and drier as the well infilled.

The molluscan assemblages in well 704/1663 (contexts 713, 728, 1722) suggest relatively marshy conditions (Tables 68–9). In samples 713 and 728, marsh species comprise 13% and 31% of the assemblages respectively, of which the obligatory marsh species *Succinea putris*, *S. oblonga* and *Vertigo antivertigo* comprise 11% and 27%, respectively. *Vertigo pygmaea*, which may also live in marshy conditions, is present in relatively high frequencies (5% and 20%, respectively). The freshwater slum species *Anisus leucostoma* is also present (3.5% and 6%, respectively). The remainder of the assemblages suggest a mixed environment of damp, open but sheltered conditions. These assemblages are probably indicative of the habitat created by the disused well, with reed and other aquatic plant growth both in the well and on its sides. The presence in sample context 713 (8%), and to a lesser extent in 728 and 1722, of *Bithynia leachii* (Table 68), which favours quiet, slowly moving water (Beedham 1972), may represent an element of overspill from the adjacent large boundary ditch (ditch 9).

The shade-loving species *Carychium tridentatum* is very common (30.5%) in another well context of this phase (J4,1), as is the open-country species *V. costata* (35%) (Tables 68–9). Together these species indicate a damp, grass/leaf litter habitat in the upper fill of the disused well.

Pits

The five samples (contexts 170, 220, 254, 285 and 246) from pit 170, situated just to the north of building R1, are all dominated by land snail species (79–98%) (Tables 68–9). The only freshwater snail occurring in any numbers is the slum species *Lymnaea truncatula*, and mainly in the upper fill

(246) (15%). It is able to live out of shallow water in damp habitats such as damp grass (Beedham 1972). Otherwise, the assemblage is dominated by shade-loving species (11–51%) and to a lesser extent by catholic (14–42%) and open-country species (19–39%) (Tables 68–9).

C. tridentatum and *Discus rotundatus* are the most common shade-loving species present. The former prefers to live in tall grass or leaf litter and dislikes ground disturbance of any kind, and the latter prefers leaf litter (Evans 1972). The presence of other shade-loving species such as *Oxychilus cellarius* and *Vitrea contracta*, which may inhabit collapsed wall debris (Evans and Jones 1973), possibly reflects the nearby demolished Roman building and/or the ragstone make-up scatter surrounding the feature, as well as the presence of tall grass and leaf litter. *V. costata* is the predominant open-country species. Although it may be found in damp habitats, it generally prefers drier open habitats than *V. pulchella*.

The other pit contexts of this phase 701 (pit 701), 769 (pits 826, 841), 528 (pit 528) and J3,1 (pit J3) contain assemblages of snails which suggest that they contained shallow, stagnant water, which was subject to drying out, set in an open environment (Tables 68–9).

Gullies

Four gully contexts of this phase (179, 519, 1282, 1701) were analysed (Tables 68–9). All four gullies held a small amount of shallow, standing water. They were set in a generally open environment, although gully context 1701 may have enjoyed some very localised shelter and/or shading as suggested by the variety of shade-loving species present (19.3%).

Layers and spreads

The amorphous ashy spread (context 117) outside building R1 is dominated by land molluscs (87%) (Tables 68–9). The three species of *Vallonia* present (54%) and *Pupilla muscorum* (2%) suggest the presence of damp grass, possibly with some broken ground in the vicinity. Damp ground surface conditions are further indicated by the presence of the marsh species *Carychium minimum*.

Like context 117, the three samples from the burnt spread (context 461) of building R2 are all dominated by terrestrial species of molluscs (96–100%) (Tables 68–9). Open-country species predominate (63.5–74.5%), with some catholic species (20–26%) and a few shade-loving species (1.5–8.5%) and freshwater molluscs (0–3%) (Tables 68–9). Again, damp and open, probably grass-covered conditions are indicated.

Context 475, a dark soil spread north of the sump, is similarly dominated by land molluscs (95%) (Tables 68–9). The three species of *Vallonia* (72%) and *P. muscorum* (4%) suggest the presence of damp grass, perhaps with some broken

ground in the vicinity. Damp ground surface conditions are also indicated by a few examples of the freshwater slum species *Anisus leucostoma*.

Although the origins and mode(s) of deposition of these 'spreads' of material are unknown, they may indicate slightly lower lying areas of the former ground surface in which freshwater-eroded material (plus the derived freshwater snails) was deposited, possibly during periods of alluviation in the immediate vicinity of the site, and/or remnants of the contemporary soil.

Phase V   (Fifth to seventh century)

The very limited assemblage in pit 774 (context 774) is dominated by the freshwater slum species *Lymnaea truncatula* (26.8%) and *A. leucostoma* (17.1%), and the open-country species (53.6%), in particular *Vallonia pulchella* (12%) and *V. excentrica* (7%) (Tables 68–9).

Both sample contexts 716 and 714 are from the infill of a post-hole of building S3 cut into the tertiary fill of an earlier pit (well 808). They are dominated by shade-loving species, and in particular *Carychium tridentatum* (48%, 34%) (Tables 68–9). There is also a considerable rupestral element (6.5%, 8%) with *Acanthinula aculeata* and *Clausilia bidentata* present. Other intermediate/catholic and open-country molluscs are present in low numbers, and generally indicate damp and open conditions.

As in many of the other pit and well feature contexts, the assemblages probably reflect the damp, relatively shaded and sheltered environment of the disused feature. In particular, the abundance of *Carychium tridentatum* may be due to high local humidity (Evans 1972) within the feature, and closely appressed leaves and vegetation.

Context 279, occupation debris associated with building S1, contains a molluscan assemblage generally similar to those found in the earlier spread contexts 117, 461, 469 and 475 (above). Land species predominate (70%), with the abundant *Vallonia* species (32%) and *Pupilla muscorum* (21%) indicating the presence of damp grass with patches of bare ground. Damp ground conditions are also suggested by the presence of *Anisus leucostoma* (22%) and *Valvata cristata* (6%) (Tables 68–9).

From this rather slender evidence one can suggest little about the environment of the period, although it appears to have changed little from the previous phase.

Phase VI   (Seventeenth to nineteenth century)

The molluscan assemblage from the fill of post-medieval ditches 12, 13 and 14 (contexts 1256, 1051, 1105 and 1181) suggests that, like Phase V, there was little difference then from the third/fourth centuries AD nature of the site (Tables 68–9). The ditches sometimes held shallow, stagnant water, with generally open and damp surrounding conditions.

CONDITIONS

Sampling

Before discussing the ecological and environmental aspects of the molluscan analysis, a few points must be made about the sampling strategy. With hindsight it would have provided more information and less processing work to have disassociated the molluscan sampling from the macrobotanical sampling programme. Potentially it would have provided better ecological evidence if only the larger linear features and wells had been sampled for molluscs, and sampled more intensively and at more frequent intervals. Nevertheless, the wet-sieving strategy covered the whole range of features and deposits extensively, and gives strength in numbers to the ecological interpretations suggested.

Ecology

Three main groups of molluscs were present at Stonea Grange during the Roman period. First, freshwater slum species are a common occurrence in most of the excavated features. They have a preference for, or tolerance of, poor water conditions such as small bodies of water subject to drying, to stagnation, and to considerable temperature variations (Sparks 1961).

In particular, the freshwater slum species *Lymnaea truncatula* is the specific intermediate host of the liver fluke, *Fasciola hepatica*, found as adults in sheep (Beedham 1972). Although there is no direct evidence that the site was used for grazing, if sheep grazed here or in the vicinity they would have been exposed to the liver fluke parasite (cf. Stallibrass, pp. 591, 606).

Second, there are molluscs, namely species of *Succinea/Oxyloma* and other obligatory marsh species and those not so restricted, which are more terrestrial in habitat preferences and live on vegetation at or above the level of the water and on the sides of the feature.

Third, a variety of terrestrial molluscs are found in the features, and are probably indicative of the immediate surroundings of the feature. Naturally the mixture and range of habitats represented in the features present problems, but several general conclusions about the environment of the site can be made.

The presence of *Succinea/Oxyloma*, *Vallonia* and often *Vertigo pygmaea*, which are generally indicative of open habitats, probably suggests the absence of a dense growth of trees and shrubs within the area of the site, but does not preclude their growth altogether.

Despite the often considerable presence of shade-loving species, there are no real obligatory woodland species present. But the sufficiently consistent presence of several species of the Zonitidae is suggestive of a minor scrub element in the vicinity, possibly along ditch edges and on the fen edge to the south.

The normally open-country species *Vallonia costata* often occurs in great abundance in association with the shade-loving species. It, in contrast to the other species of *Vallonia*, is probably better able to tolerate a slightly more shaded environment.

The common and consistent presence of *Carychium tridentatum* and *Vallonia costata* indicate the existence of much long grass growing in and around the disused and abandoned features. Neither tolerate disturbance, so it is probable that the area was not subject to heavy grazing, and certainly not to cultivation. Also, the latter species may occur in association with man as a synanthropic species.

When *Vallonia pulchella* is more abundant than *V. costata*, both the conditions within the feature and the immediate surroundings are probably more open, somewhat damper and perhaps slightly marshy in nature. But one cannot rule out the possibility that some form of competition between both species is at work within similar habitats and is affecting their relative population sizes.

Many of the features probably also contained leaf litter, branches and possibly rock rubble/building debris. This may also account for the presence of some of the shade-loving species, and in particular the rupestral species such as *Clausilia bidentata*.

The absence of snails in the vast majority of sample contexts (85.9%) is probably a reflection of the circum-neutral soil/subsoil conditions, and the absence of waterlogging with base-rich water, as the surface of the 'island' on which the site is situated rises north-eastwards. Also, the density of human occupation in some areas may have made conditions unsuitable for molluscan life.

Environment

In summary, the immediate environment of the site is probably one of damp grassland with occasional patches of bare ground, possibly with a scattered, minor scrub element throughout the second, third and fourth centuries AD. Low-lying areas and abandoned features probably held water intermittently, with marshy conditions in places.

The wells generally contained assemblages of molluscs with high relative frequencies of shade-loving and rupestral species which are probably only indicative of the localised, damp and shaded, refuge habitat in the abandoned wells. But these features were set in an open environment.

Although the site must have almost always been damp, there is some indication that it was becoming increasingly damp and wet in the later second and early third centuries AD, and then became relatively drier in the later third and fourth centuries AD. Nevertheless, in some cases this observed phenomenon may be more a function of the higher sample location in the feature than relatively lower or higher local ground-water levels.

Undoubtedly some of the variations seen in the composition of the freshwater molluscan species may be due to the rises and falls of the local ground water table, which may often have been of a seasonal nature. This in turn would have been affected by the greater movements of both brackish and fresh water in the surrounding fen. There is some evidence for the deposition of alluvial flood silts over parts of the site, both prior to the Roman occupation, during the early/middle third century AD and later during the early medieval period (see French, pp. 221–3; Hall 1987).

In the Saxon period very few snails were present in the excavated features. This was probably caused by the lack of waterlogging, which in circum-neutral soil conditions led to poor preservation of the molluscs once present. Nevertheless, this suggests that the 'island' of Stonea may have been relatively drier and therefore even more suitable for human occupation. The general absence of large drainage ditches attributable to this period, in contrast to the Roman period, may provide corroborative evidence.

The few brackish water molluscs present in a variety of Roman period contexts on the site need not imply tidal influence on site, but it does indicate the proximity of brackish water conditions. Indeed tidal conditions existed in the nearby Roman canals, and the presence of saltern sites indicate contemporary marine conditions in the adjacent fen (Hall 1987). The few marine bivalves present indicate that they were probably brought to the site as food.

The major caveat with respect to all of the foregoing conclusions is that the potential mixing effects of freshwater movement over the area of the site and within the larger features is unquantifiable. Species from several habitats in a relatively small area may have become intermixed by water action, therefore giving a 'death assemblage' which is a 'mosaic' collection of molluscs from different surrounding habitats, plus those species indicative of the 'in situ' environment. But the large number of features examined and the relative consistency of the results gives credence to the suggested nature of the environment of Stonea Grange during the Roman period.

Acknowledgements

I would like to thank Dr T. W. Potter, Ralph Jackson, Dr I. H. Longworth, Dr F. M. M. Pryor, D. N. Hall and Dr M. van der Veen.

ANGLO-SAXON POTTERY

Andrew Russel   [Submitted 1988]   (Fig. 240)

In 1982 the author, as part of research towards a higher degree, examined the pottery considered to be Anglo-Saxon which had been recovered up to and including the 1981 excavations. The pottery was divided into a number of fabrics and samples were taken for petrological analysis. This revealed a total of 10 fabrics (Russel 1984).

The total assemblage was examined again in 1985 when the excavations had finished. The pottery recovered between 1982 and 1985 had enabled the excavators to define more clearly the date range of the ceramics and it was possible to eliminate petrological fabrics 5, 6, 7 and 10 from the Anglo-Saxon period. This confirmed the author's suspicions that fabrics 1 to 4 were the Anglo-Saxon component. Petrological fabrics 8 and 9, too, are probably not Anglo-Saxon.

The larger quantity of pottery recovered in the post-1982 excavations had added one new fabric that was certainly of Anglo-Saxon date and two more to the uncertain group. None of these fabrics has been examined in thin section. Nine fabrics will be discussed here. Fabrics 1 to 4 are the same as the petrological fabrics assigned those numbers, fabrics 5 and 6 are the petrological fabrics 9 and 8 respectively. Fabrics 7, 8, and 9 are the new fabrics, defined only at a macroscopic level.

FABRIC DESCRIPTIONS

Measurements given are maximum dimensions in millimetres.

Fabric 1

Clay matrix with well-sorted, fine quartz component, and a coarser component of sub-angular to rounded grains (0.5). Inclusions of well-rounded chalk, ooliths (0.75), fragments of oolitic limestone (1) and large scattered fragments of igneous rock (2.75).

Fabric 2

Silty clay matrix with an unsorted fine quartz component. The coarser component consists of unsorted sub-angular quartz grains (0.5), derived from a quartz sandstone with a ferruginous cement. Inclusions of iron-rich clay-pellets (2.5) and igneous rock fragments (1.25). Chalk and oolitic limestone (2) are present but quantities vary from sample to sample.

Fabric 3

Clay matrix with an abundant, unsorted fine quartz component, and a coarse component (0.75) derived from a quartz sandstone with a calcareous cement. Occasional inclusions of rounded chalk and shell (2.25).

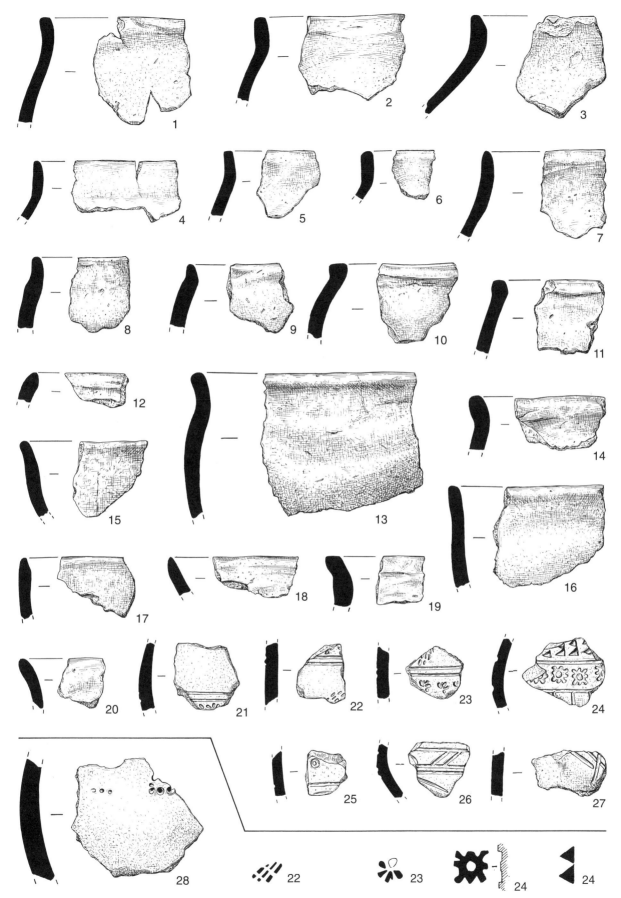

Fig. 240 Stonea Grange: Anglo-Saxon pottery (scale 1:2 except decorative details = 1:1).

Fabric 4

Silty clay matrix with very few fine quartz grains but a coarser component of scattered sub-rounded quartz grains (0.75). The fabric is distinguished by the presence of abundant particles of oolitic limestone. These appear either as single or broken ooliths (0.75), or fragments of oolitic limestone (1.75). Two sub-fabrics may be present to judge by the thin sections. Sample 26 contains fragments of fossil shell (0.25) in addition to the oolitic material whereas sample 6 has fragments of granitic rock (1.25) present. A sample of two sections is too small to judge the population variability, but the similarity of the clay matrices points to a similar source.

Fabric 5

Silty clay matrix with a sparse, well-sorted, fine quartz component and an abundant, rounded, coarse component (0.25) of quartz grains and iron compounds.

Fabric 6

Fine silty clay matrix, almost quartz free, with large grains of quartz (2). Many of the larger grains are composite fragments of rock consisting of up to 20 smaller grains.

Fabric 7

Macroscopically a medium sandy clay with no distinctive inclusions.

Fabric 8

Macroscopically a medium sandy clay containing many red and black iron compounds. Possibly related to fabric 5.

Fabric 9

Macroscopically a silty clay containing much crushed sandstone. As such may well be related to fabric 6.

CONCLUSIONS FROM PETROLOGICAL ANALYSIS

All the fabrics were probably made from clays gathered from glacial till deposits. Samples were taken from the deposits below the archaeological layers and these were found to contain rounded chalk, shell fragments and fragments of calcareous sandstone. No evidence of oolitic or shelly limestone was seen, so the potters probably did not obtain their clays from the immediate locality. Variations in the till occur abruptly and randomly and a distant clay source need not be assumed in order to account for the difference between the pottery and the clays nearest to hand. The thin sections of the Stonea pottery were compared with those from other sites of a similar date in Cambridgeshire. There was no similarity with the pottery at Grantchester, Cambridge, Linton or Waterbeach. All these sites are some distance from Stonea and it may well be more fruitful to examine the fabrics of Anglo-Saxon pottery to the west of Stonea for evidence of ceramic exchange.

FABRIC AND FORM

The author has put forward (1984) a proposal that East Anglian Anglo-Saxon rim forms can be divided into categories that relate to their function, and that their function can be seen as a determining factor in the choice of fabric. The number of Anglo-Saxon rims from Stonea is small, 30, and many of the rim sherds are rather small to be completely certain of the category; but it does seem that all the rims except four belong to type 2, a short upright rim rising from a globular body. Such rims are the most common type in the large Grimstone End, Suffolk, assemblage and were usually coarsely tempered. A cooking or general-purpose function has been suggested. Fabrics 1 to 4 all contain considerable quantities of tempering material and were probably used predominantly for such purposes. The four rims that do not belong to type 2 (e.g. cat. nos 8, 11, 16) are straight upright rims of type 3, large open, bucket-shaped vessels, which had no specific purpose.

The finer clays of fabrics 3 and 7 (in which no rim sherds were found but two neck sherds indicate everted rims of type 1) would have been best suited for storage and it is such vessels that are most commonly decorated in East Anglian assemblages.

DISTRIBUTION OF FABRICS

In terms of the distribution of the Anglo-Saxon pottery the site can be divided into two areas, east and west, with a mostly blank area between them. This blank area coincides with the open tract to the north of the Roman masonry building R1. The lack of Anglo-Saxon sherds from this area may well be due to the corresponding scarcity of negative features of the Roman period in the upper fills of which Anglo-Saxon sherds could become buried.

Fabrics 1 and 2 were found predominantly in the western half of the site but with a scatter in the east. Fabrics 3 and 4 were found only in the west half apart from three sherds found close to each other in contexts 171 and 504. Fabric 7 was found only in the north-east quarter of the excavated area in close relationship with the timber buildings.

The widespread distribution of cooking pot fabrics 1 and 2, which probably had a common source, suggests that they may well have been used by the occupants of all the buildings. This is in strong contrast with storage vessel fabrics 3 and 7, whose mutually exclusive distributions may represent production of vessels by and for two groups, who wished to maintain or reinforce a real or imagined difference between them by a deliberate choice of decoration and clay source.

DATING

Accurate dating of such an assemblage is difficult. The Stonea pottery consists mostly of one rim type, and a chronological seriation of rim types for the Anglo-Saxon period has yet to be proved. The rim types rather reflect the function of the vessel. As the rim type most commonly found at Stonea is long-lived, it is therefore difficult to seek dated parallels in the domestic or funerary pottery in this country or on the Continent. At Wijster pots with globular bodies and short cylindrical necks similar to those found at Stonea were in use throughout the life of the settlement, c. AD 1–450 (van Es 1967).

The decorated sherds provide more possibilities for dating, but they are so small that it is impossible to be sure of the vessel's form or decorative scheme. It is possible that cat. no. 26 is from a carinated vessel of *Schalenurnen* type (van Es 1967), normally considered to be a fifth century type. The stamps used to decorate the pottery could provide further clues but there are problems here too. The stamps used on cat. nos 21, 22 23 and 25 are very common. On the other hand, stamp cat no. 24a is unique, and the same appears to be the case with stamp cat. no. 24b (see Briscoe, this page).

A firm date for the Anglo-Saxon occupation cannot therefore be given. The small number of sherds and the few structures point to a short period of occupation, but all that can be said is that it took place in the early Anglo-Saxon period, between AD 400 and 650.

ANGLO-SAXON POTTERY STAMPS

Teresa Briscoe   (Fig. 240)

With two exceptions, discussed below, the stamps are of common types, so that not a great deal can be learned from them.

22 (CAM/180/55) This sherd has two stamps, a rosette stamp (Briscoe type A 5ai) and a round grid stamp (Type A 3a) (CAM/180/56). Both these are common stamp types. The A 3a stamp is very lightly impressed so that it is not possible to identify the grid with any certainty. The 'teeth' which made the negative impressions are unusually long and thin.

23 This is quite likely part of the same pot as no. 22. The A 5ai stamp (CAM/180/57) is only partly present, but shows similar rounding of the outer segments to that on no. 22.

The grid stamp (CAM/180/58) is even more fragmentary than the round grid (180/56) on no. 22. Its form suggests a rectangular grid (Type C 2a) but it may well have been made by the same die as that used for the round stamp but manipulated differently by the potter.

24a, b This sherd has the two unusual stamps referred to above.

The first (24a) (CAM/180/51) is unique. It could have been made by a metal 'holder' with a central raised peg to which something was fixed. The outline projections are not completely uniform.

A similarity between the outlines of this stamp and the two stamps, always occuring in tandem, which come from the Wilbrahams and Girton Cemeteries, also in Cambridgeshire, may be made. (*Myres Corpus* fig. 149 nos 198 and 2732) (Arch. nos GWI 34, LWI 58 and GIR 371). These fall into my type M lav, but the Stonea stamp has been placed in M laiv. The second stamp (CAM/180/52) is an uncommon type. There are only 16 other examples in the Archive, out of a total of some 5000 casts. The distribution is fairly wide. The nearest parallel is that from West Stow, Suffolk (West 1985).

25 The simple ring stamp (Type A 1bi) (CAM/180/53) is a very common type.

28 This sherd also has two stamps on it.

The grid stamp (CAM/180/60) is really too small to be identified with certainty, but I would suggest that it could be diamond shaped and therefore fall into my type F 2a.

The second stamp is a very small comb impression (Type N1a) (CAM/180/59). It consists of three very small dots in line, but has a less number of tooth marks than usual. It is a common type of decoration.

List of illustrated Anglo-Saxon sherds   (Fig. 240)

1 (FW)	Fabric 4	From well 135, uppermost layer (unit 135).
2 (FN)	Fabric 3	From hard-standing (unit 128), north of building R1.
3 (BAF)	Fabric 3	Intrusive in the fill of pit 711.
4 (AAG)	Fabric 1	Burnished. From topsoil/cleaning, blocks 4 and 5.
5 (FM)	Fabric 2	From unit 127 of the low rubbly mound sealing building S1.
6 (HZ)	Fabric 2	From unit 184 of the low rubbly mound sealing building S1.
7 (FY)	Fabric 3	From unit 137 of the low rubbly mound sealing building S1.
8 (JQ)	Fabric 1	From unit 199 of the low rubbly mound sealing building S1.
9 (GT)	Fabric 2	From well 135, upper layer (unit 156).
10 (HZ)	Fabric 2	Context as no. 6.
11 (CHN)	Fabric 1	Residual in ditch 12, cut 3, unit 1180.
12 (JS)	Fabric 2	From unit 201 of the low rubbly mound sealing building S1.
13 (Sump 28, grid 11)	Fabric 1	Intrusive in the north sump, layer 28, grid square 11.
14 (FM)	Fabric 2	Context as no. 5.
15 (FY)	Fabric 4	Context as no. 7.
16 (FY)	Fabric 2	Context as no. 7.
17 (CMK)	Fabric 8	From layer above road ditches, north-east of building S1.
18 (CMS)	Fabric 8	From gully 53, cut 3, unit 1281, south of building S2.

19 (FM)   Fabric 2   Context as no. 5.
20 (FY)   Fabric 2   Context as no. 7.

Stamped sherds

21 (ABQ)   Fabric 7   From topsoil/cleaning, blocks 2 and 3, region of buildings S3 and S4.
22 (AAA)   Fabric 7   From topsoil/cleaning, blocks 1a and 1b.
23 (CET)   Fabric 7   From the fill (unit 1114) of gully 56, within building S2.
24 (FM)   Fabric 2   Context as no. 5.
25 (FM)   Fabric 2?   Context as no. 5.
26 (FM)   Fabric 2   Context as no. 5.
27 (GT)   Fabric 2   Context as no. 9.
28 (ABF)   Fabric 2?   From topsoil/cleaning, block 1, north-east quadrant.

ANGLO-SAXON METAL OBJECTS

Leslie Webster   (Fig. 241)

1 Pin   Length 41.5 mm ST 81 FM, SF 75

Copper-alloy pin with head of inverted pyramidal form, separated from the slender, hipped shaft by a square-sectioned collar. Each of the vertical faces of the head has three punched dot-and-circle motifs in a column: the top of the head has incised cross-hatched decoration.

Small hipped dress or veiling pins are a common and distinctive Anglo-Saxon pin type, first appearing in female graves of the mid 7th century, continuing through the 8th century, but apparently declining in popularity in the 9th. The characteristic swelling or 'hipping' of the shank is designed to inhibit slippage. Middle Saxon pins, in general, share a country-wide distribution occurring on a wide spectrum of urban and rural occupation sites, as well as in considerable quantities on known Anglo-Saxon monastic sites, such as Whitby and Barking Abbeys (Graham-Campbell 1990, 181–3; Webster and Backhouse (eds) 1991, 82, 88–90 and *passim*.).

This specimen's simple, crisply faceted and collared head, and dot-and-circle decoration are among the characteristic features of the general type; and the less common head form can be paralleled by, for example, three examples from Whitby (Peers and Radford 1943, Fig. 14, 63).

From the north-west quadrant (unit 127) of the upper layer of the Phase Va low mound, which partially seals Anglo-Saxon building S1.

2 Strap-end   Present max. length 47 mm P 1982, 6–2, 144

Copper-alloy strap-end in two joining fragments, having been bent back and broken. It is inlaid with niello, and has extensive traces of solder on the back and on one lateral edge. The purpose of this is unclear, but it is not impossible that it may represent some attempt at covering the entire copper-alloy surface, forming a silvery contrast to the niello inlay. The split end (upper half now wholly missing) terminates in three projections, two containing vestiges of rivets. Traces of two secondary rivets at the site of the break indicate an ancient repair. Only the lower parts of the central decorative panel survive, themselves badly damaged: traces of niello

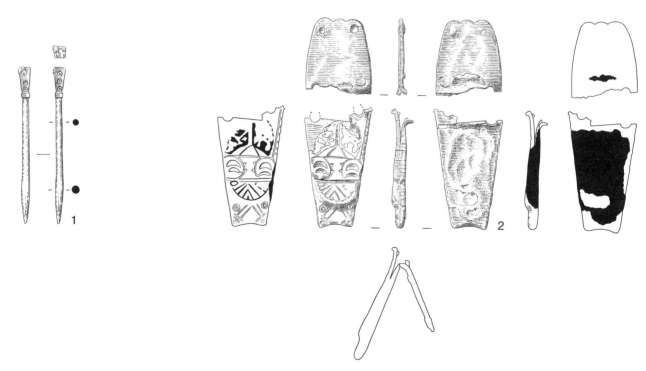

Fig. 241 Stonea Grange: Anglo-Saxon copper-alloy pin and strap-end (scale 1:1).

indicate a design based on at least two fields of now illegible Tre-whiddle-style ornament. The strap-end terminates in a foreshortened animal-head with rounded ears, prominent nostrils defined like the eyes by dot-and-circle motifs, and a bulging brow with traces of niello inlaid in a linear pattern.

The split-end construction, lentoid outline and animal-head terminal place the strap-end in a well-known Anglo-Saxon group, which dates predominantly to the 9th century. However, the distinctive foreshortened head with bulging brow and projecting nostrils relates it to a very rare sub-class, represented by a more elaborate silver example from Hertfordshire (Webster and Backhouse 1991, cat. no. 194, p. 234) and a gold and silver pair found recently at Ipsden Heath, Oxfordshire (MacGregor 1994). The relatively large breadth and overall length of these strap-ends is a feature increasingly apparent among late 9th century specimens.

From Stonea Grange Surface Collection

Examination and analysis by S. La Niece (British Museum Research Laboratory, File no. 6424) yielded the following results:

1 Metal composition: Semi-quantitative X-ray fluorescence analysis (XRF) on the broken edge identified the alloy as bronze (copper and tin) with a few per cent of lead.

2 Inlay material: X-ray diffraction analysis of the inlay material identified metallic silver and cuprite (Cu_2O) but no sulphides.

Although the inlay now consists of silver, it may originally have been niello which has reverted to the metallic form, perhaps as a result of heating for the solder work (see below).

3 A thick silvery layer partly covers the back of the strap-end and has run over one edge to the front. XRF analysis identifies this as an alloy of tin and lead (approximately 50:50), i.e. it is a soft solder. Its purpose is not obvious but it is unlikely to have been an original feature and was probably a repair or, perhaps, a feature of re-use.

[For other Anglo-Saxon objects, see Iron Objects, cat. nos 32 and 34, p. 364; and Objects of Worked Bone, cat. nos 75–7, p. 538.]

PHASE VI FINDS

The Phase VI finds assemblage is essentially domestic and rural comprising mainly household refuse – broken crockery and other ceramics, wine glasses and bottles, clay pipes, and metal dress fittings and articles of domestic equipment – together with a few items associated with horses. Characteristic of the Fenland region are the two bone sledge runners of eighteenth-nineteenth century date; and local trade is represented by the bottle seal of I. Batterham and the button stamped by Mappen of Wisbech.

POST-MEDIEVAL POTTERY

David Gaimster

Ditch 12

Level 1

Transfer-printed ware   1800–1900
    Cut 6, unit 1170.
Staffordshire scratchware, blue   1740–70
    Cut 6, unit 1170.
Post-medieval redware   1600–1800
    Cut 6, unit 1170; cut 10, unit 1196.

Level 2

Transfer-printed ware   1800–1900
    Cut 2, unit 1087; cut 3, unit 1180; cut 7, unit 1053; cut 8, unit 1172; cut 9, unit 1357.
Creamware   1770–1900
    Cut 8, unit 1172; cut 9, unit 1357.
English brown stoneware   1670–1900
    Cut 8, unit 1172; cut 9, unit 1357; cut 12, unit 1056; cut 13, unit 1268.
Chinese porcelain   1650–1900
    Cut 12, unit 1056.
Staffordshire scratchware, blue   1740–70
    Cut 9, unit 1357.
Staffordshire white salt-glazed stoneware   1720–70
    Cut 5, unit 1227; cut 10, unit 1221; cut 12, unit 1056; cut 13, unit 1268.
Post-medieval redware   1600–1800
    Cut 1, unit 1167; cut 2, unit 1087; cut 3, unit 1180; cut 5, unit 1227; cut 7, unit 1053 cut 8, unit 1172; cut 9, unit 1357 – including slip-decorated ware; cut 10, unit 1221 – including slip-decorated ware; cut 11, unit 1299; cut 12, unit 1056; cut 13, unit 1268.
English/Dutch tin-glazed ware   1600–1800
    Cut 2, unit 1087; cut 10, unit 1221; cut 12, unit 1056.
Staffordshire slipware   1600–1800
    Cut 1, unit 1167.
Westerwald stoneware   1600–1800
    Cut 9, unit 1357; cut 12, unit 1056.
Frechen stoneware   1550–1650
    Cut 13, unit 1268.

Level 3

Staffordshire coarseware   1650–1800
    Cut 12, unit 1089.
Post-medieval redware   1600–1800
    Cut 2, unit 1145; cut 7, unit 1098.
English/Dutch tin-glazed ware   1600–1800
    Cut 4, unit 1200.
Post-medieval black-glazed ware   1600–1700
    Cut 2, unit 1145; cut 12, unit 1089.

Level 4

English brown stoneware   1670–1900
   Cut 9, unit 1373.
Chinese porcelain   1650–1900
   Cut 9, unit 1373.
Staffordshire mottled brown glazed ware   1700–1800
   Cut 10, unit 1269.
Post-medieval redware   1600–1800
   Cut 5, unit 1251; cut 9, unit 1373 – including slip-decorated ware;
   cut 12, unit 1097.
English/Dutch tin-glazed ware   1600–1800
   Cut 9, unit 1373.
Westerwald stoneware   1600–1800
   Cut 9, unit 1373.

Ditch 13

Level 1

Transfer-printed ware   1800–1900
   Cut 1, unit 1016; cut 3, unit 1054.
Pearlware   1800–1900
   Cut 3, unit 1054; cut 5, unit 1069.
Staffordshire chamberpots   19th century
   Cut 3, unit 1054.
Creamware   1770–1900
   Cut 1, unit 1016; cut 3, unit 1054; cut 4, unit 1012 – includes
   encrusted tankard.
English brown stoneware   1670–1900
   Cut 2, unit 1143.
Chinese porcelain   1650–1900
   Cut 5, unit 1069.
Post-medieval redware   1600–1800
   Cut 2, unit 1143; cut 3, unit 1054 – including slip-decorated
   ware; cut 4, unit 1012; cut 5, unit 1069.
English/Dutch tin-glazed ware   1600–1800
   Cut 3, unit 1054; cut 4, unit 1012; cut 5, unit 1069.
Frechen stoneware   1550–1650
   Cut 2, unit 1143.

Level 2

Transfer-printed ware   1800–1900
   Cut 1, unit 1051; cut 2, unit 1146.
Creamware   1770–1900
   Cut 1, unit 1051; cut 2, unit 1146.
Post-medieval redware   1600–1800
   Cut 2, unit 1146.

Level 3

19th/20th century wares
   Cut 1, unit 1182.
Post-medieval redware   1600–1800
   Cut 2, unit 1133.

Ditch 14

Level 1

Creamware   1770–1900
   Cut 3, unit 1017.
Chinese porcelain   1650–1900
   Cut 3, unit 1017.

Pit 1267

Creamware   1770–1900
Chinese porcelain   1650–1900
Post-medieval redware   1600–1800

Pit 1285

Staffordshire white salt-glazed stoneware   1720–70

Pit 1173

Transfer-printed ware   1800–1900
Staffordshire white salt-glazed stoneware   1720–70
Post-medieval redware   1600–1800

Post-hole 1015

English brown stoneware   1670–1900
Post-medieval redware   1600–1800

LATE MEDIEVAL AND POST-MEDIEVAL METALWORK

David Gaimster   (Figs 242–3)

All objects are of copper-alloy unless otherwise stated.

DRESS FITTINGS   (Fig. 242)

1 P 1985, 10–3, 19   Length 39 mm

Strap mount, with two iron rivets, the plate cast with a floral design
in low relief. Mid 16th century. (For attachment to leather, strap-
work.)

Stonea Grange Surface Collection.

2 P 1982, 6–2, 143   Length 37 mm

Dress-hook, cast with a floral design in low relief. Probably 17th to
early 18th century.

Stonea Grange Surface Collection.

3 P 1982, 6–2, 126   Diameter 30 mm

Belt stud, cast as an openwork rosette, with traces of gilding on
upper surface, the reverse cast with staples for attachment to the
leather. 16th century.

Stonea Grange Surface Collection.

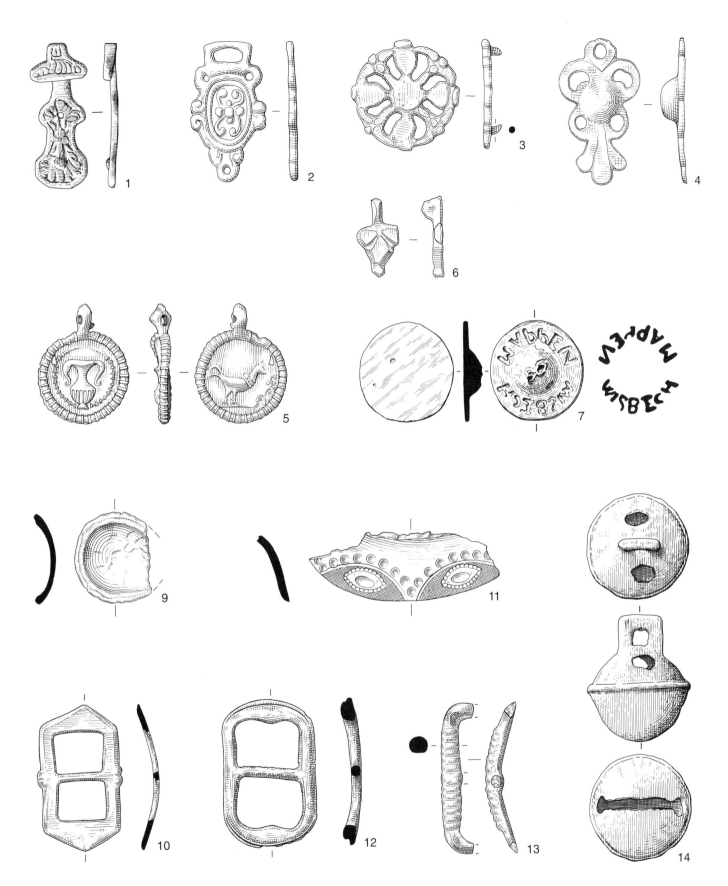

Fig. 242 Stonea Grange: late medieval and post-medieval metal objects 1–7 and 9–14, from the Surface Collection (scale 1 : 1 except 11 = 2 : 1).

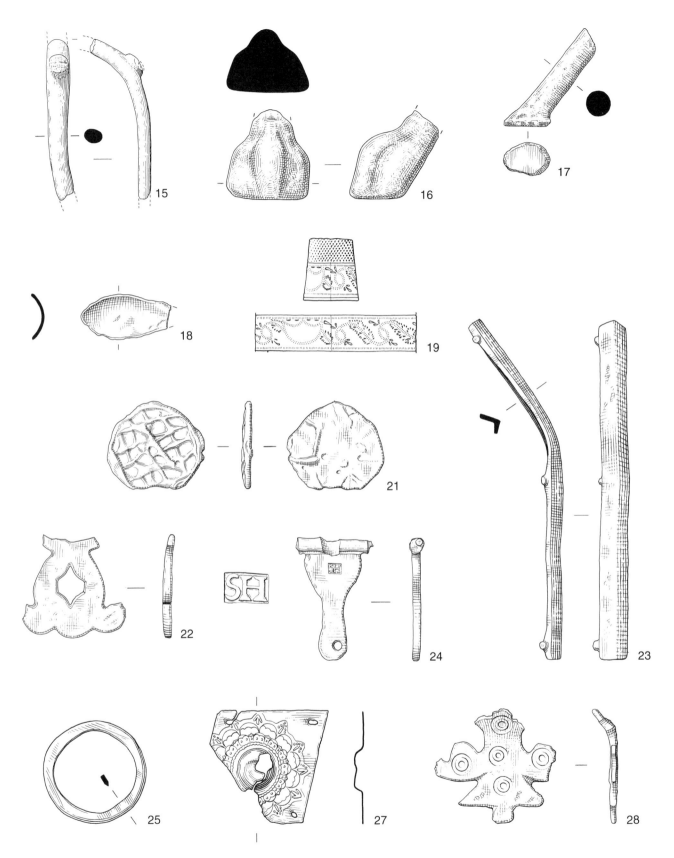

Fig. 243 Stonea Grange: late medieval and post-medieval metal objects 15–19, 21–5 and 27–8, from the Surface Collection and the excavation (scale 1:1 except 16–17 = 1:2, and detail of 24 = 3:1).

4 P 1982, 6–2, 127   Length 38 mm

Cast openwork mount with raised central boss and trefoil terminal. Probably 17th century.

Stonea Grange Surface Collection.

5 P 1982, 6–2, 121   Diameter 25 mm

Disc pendant, with beaded rim and circular suspension loop, cast in a grey metal (probably a lead-based alloy). The relief decoration comprises on one side an urn, on the other a bird. Probably 18th century.

Stonea Grange Surface Collection.

6 P 1982, 6–2, 122   Length 21 mm

Fragment of a decorative mount, cast with lozenge compartments, with traces of gilding on upper surface. Probably 15th to 16th century.

Stonea Grange Surface Collection.

7 P 1985, 10–3, 18   Diameter 26 mm

Button, thin disc type, with shank missing. Around the perimeter of the underside is the retrograde stamp of the maker: MAPPEN WISBECH. Mid to late 19th century.

Stonea Grange Surface Collection.

8 ST 83 CKM, SF 560   (*Unillus.*)   Diameter 19 mm

A small tinned disc button, complete with its wire eye in the squat bell-shaped back-face. 19th century.

From ditch 12, cut 5, unit 1227.

9 P 1982, 6–2, 146   Width 22 mm

Fragment of an 'ampulla', cast in a lead-alloy. Probably 14–15th century.

Stonea Grange Surface Collection.

10 P 1982, 6–2, 141   Length 38 mm

Rectangular buckle with extended triangular ends. Probably 17th century.

Stonea Grange Surface Collection.

11 P 1982, 6–2, 148   Length 26 mm

Fragment of shoe-buckle with stamped decoration. 18th century.

Stonea Grange Surface Collection.

12 P 1982, 6–2, 140   Length 39 mm

Buckle with double D-shaped loops. 17th century.

Stonea Grange Surface Collection.

13 P 1982, 6–2, 142   Length 40 mm

Fragment of a rectangular buckle with a beaded frame. 17th century.

Stonea Grange Surface Collection.

HORSE EQUIPMENT   (Figs 242–3)

14 P 1985, 10–3, 17   Height 34 mm

Rumbler bell with a square suspension loop and raised horizontal cordon around the waist. Copper-alloy pellet still extant. Early 17th century.

Stonea Grange Surface Collection.

15 P 1985, 10–3, 20   Height 45 mm

Spur, shank fragment with terminals and rowell-box missing. Late 17th to early 18th century.

Stonea Grange Surface Collection.

DOMESTIC EQUIPMENT   (Fig. 243)

16 P 1982, 6–2, 137   Width 44 mm

Cast foot of large cauldron. 15th or 16th century.

Stonea Grange Surface Collection.

17 P 1982, 6–2, 136   Length 68 mm

Cast foot and leg of skillet or ewer. 15th or 16th century.

Stonea Grange Surface Collection.

18 P 1982, 6–2, 147   Length 26 mm

Small spoon bowl, roughly cast. Late medieval/early post-medieval.

Stonea Grange Surface Collection.

19 ST 83 CDX, SF 518   Height 17 mm

Silver thimble, open-ended tubular band with tapering sides. Upper body with machine-made, densely-spaced indentations. Below with hand-stamped and punched floral swag motif. Probably early 19th century.

From north-east corner block 1, spit dug over ditches 12, 10 and 4 (unit 1093).

20 ST 83 CAA   (*Unillus.*)

Three dress pins with wound-wire heads. Probably late 17th to 18th century.

From topsoil/cleaning, block 11, east.

21 P 1982, 6–2, 145   Length 27 mm

Token, probably a lead-based alloy. Geometric relief design on obverse.

Stonea Grange Surface Collection.

22 P 1982, 6–2, 125   Length 29 mm

Furniture fitting, cast openwork design. Probably 18th century.

Stonea Grange Surface Collection.

23 P 1982, 6–2, 135   Length 93 mm

Binding strip of box or casket. Probably 17th or 18th century.

Stonea Grange Surface Collection.

24 P 1982, 6–2, 149   Length 33 mm

A hinged mount, probably a book-clasp, with the letters SH stamped in a rectangular cartouche. Probably 19th century.

Stonea Grange Surface Collection.

25 ST 83 CAA, SF 461   Diameter 27–28 mm

A roughly-made oval ring of irregular flat hexagonal cross-section. The inner face is worn, the outer face still bears coarse file marks.

From topsoil/cleaning, block 11, east.

26 ST 83 CAA, SF 513   (*Unillus.*) Diameter 27 mm

Another example, as no. 25.

Context as no. 25.

27 ST 83 CAA, SF 462   Width 30 mm

Copper-alloy lozenge mount, cast in relief with a floral border surrounding a central raised roundel. One corner missing. Nail perforations at each of the surviving corners. Probably early 19th century.

Context as no. 25.

28 P 1982, 6–2, 124   Length 33 mm

Fragment of a decorative mount or fitting. Function and date uncertain.

Stonea Grange Surface Collection.

POST-MEDIEVAL GLASS

David Gaimster   (Figs 244–6)

BOTTLE GLASS (Figs 244–6)

1–5 ST 83 CMF

Neck, base and body fragments of thick, dark green bottle glass. English, *c.* 1725–50.

From ditch 12, cut 10, unit 1269.

6–8 ST 83 CKF and CAD

Neck and base fragments of thick dark green bottle glass. English, *c.* 1700–50.

Nos 6–7 from ditch 12, cut 10, unit 1221 (CKF).
No. 8 from ditch 71, cut 10, unit 1003 (CAD).

9 ST 83 CHC

Neck and base fragment of thick, dark green bottle glass. English, *c.* 1700–30.

From ditch 12, cut 6, unit 1170.

10 ST 83 CGY, SF 558

Bottle seal, thick green glass, stamped with the legend *I* Batterham 1771. The personal seal of I. Batterham, believed to have been a builder, according to S. Ruggles-Brise, *Sealed Bottles*, London (1949), p. 84. Further seals of I. Batterham and J. Batterham in Wisbech Museum (1768 and 1770 for the latter).

From spit dug over ditches 12, 10 and 4, north-east corner block 1, unit 1166. Immediately east of the context for cat. no. 15.

11 ST 83 CCC

Cylindrical pharmaceutical phial with flanged rim and rounded basal kick in thin green glass. *c.* 1700–50.

From spit dug over ditches 12, 6, 2, 13 and 14, west of gully 1. Unit 1050 (CCC).

12 ST 83 CCI

Cylindrical pharmaceutical phial in thin green glass, *c.* 1750–75.

From ditch 12, cut 12, unit 1056.

VESSEL GLASS (Fig. 246)

13–14 ST 83 CPX and +

Wine-glass fragments with angular baluster stems in clear lead-crystal. *c.* 1750–1800.

No. 13 from ditch 12, cut 9, unit 1357 (CPX).
No. 14 ST 83 unstratified.

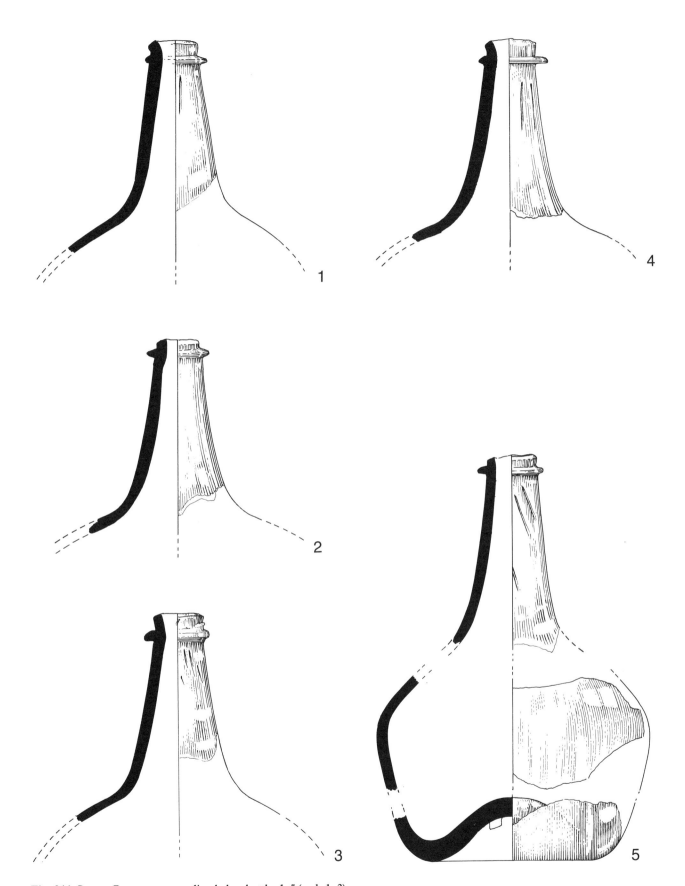

Fig. 244 Stonea Grange: post-medieval glass bottles 1–5 (scale 1 : 2).

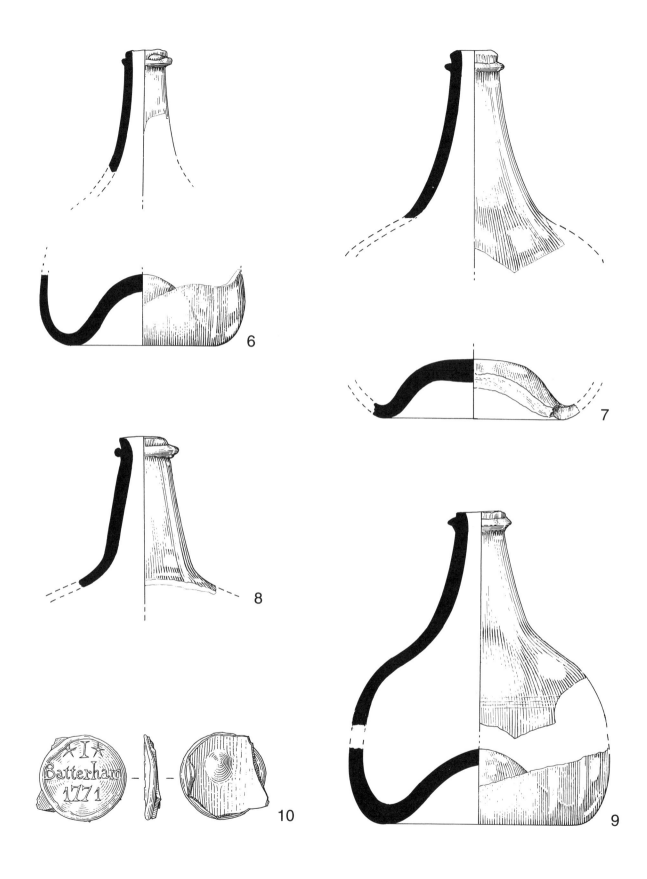

Fig. 245 Stonea Grange: post–medieval glass bottles 6–9 and bottle seal 10 (scale 1 : 2).

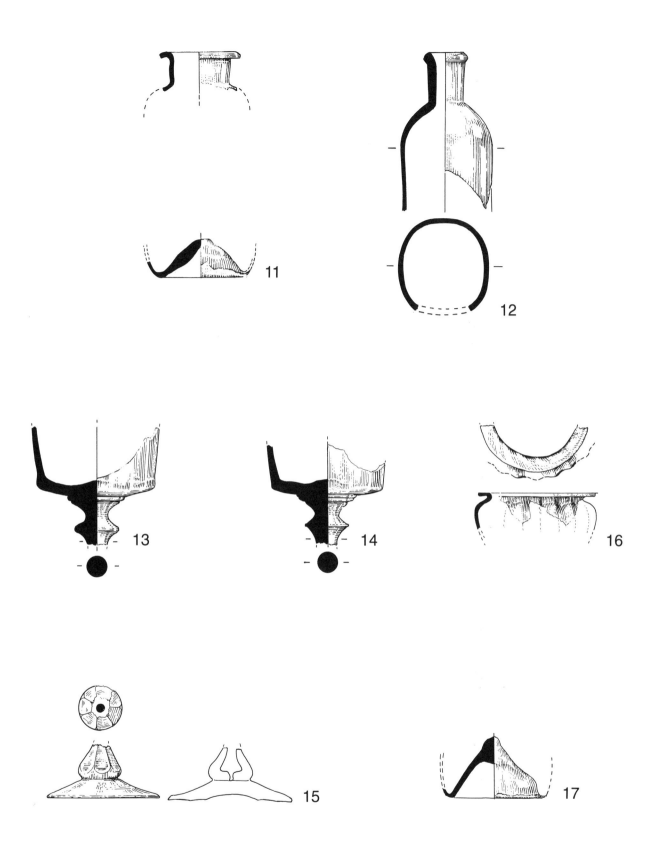

Fig. 246 Stonea Grange: post-medieval glass phials 11–12, wine-glasses 13–15 and beaker 16–17 (scale 1 : 2).

15 ST 83 CDX

Foot fragment of baluster-stem wine glass in clear lead-crystal. Facetted stem, *c.*1750–75.

From spit dug over ditches 12, 10 and 4, north-east corner block 1, unit 1093. Immediately west of the context for cat. no. 10.

16 ST 83 CQO

Beaker with flanged rim in fluted, thin, transparent green glass. *c.*1600–50.

From ditch 12, cut 9, unit 1373 – as cat. no. 11.

17 ST 83 CQO

Base, with lightly fluted conical kick, in thin, transparent green glass, of the same hue as no. 16, and possibly its base.

Context as no. 16.

POST-MEDIEVAL BONE OBJECTS

Virginia Smithson (Fig. 247)

SLEDGE-RUNNERS

In the following descriptions the anterior and posterior surfaces of the radii correspond to the underside and upper side of the runners; the proximal and distal ends of the bones have been designated as the front and back.

1 Sledge-runner, bone   ST 83 CGB, SF 524

Horse radius with fused shaft of ulna, left side. Proximal end chopped; articular surface partially removed, single chop mark evident on posterior surface. Lateral tuberosity chopped, medial side slightly smoothed. Distal end chopped; articular surface partially removed, lateral and medial protruberances trimmed. Each end perforated by a 15 mm diameter hole drilled through the shaft. A small crack radiates from the proximal hole along the long axis of the bone's anterior surface, which is flattened by wear, scored with longitudinal striations, and heavily abraded at the proximal end. Posterior surface roughly smoothed at both ends; head of ulna snapped off, top of remaining shaft pared down and filed, the marks extending onto the surface of the radius. Length of bone 358 mm; minimum distance between holes 264 mm.

From ditch 12, cut 2, unit 1145, level 3. 17th–18th century.

2 Sledge-runner, bone   ST 83 CDQ, SF 517

Horse radius with fused shaft of ulna, left side. Proximal end chopped; articular surface removed, two transverse chop marks visible. Lateral tuberosity roughly cut down and filed. Distal end chopped; articular surface removed, lateral and medial protruberances trimmed. Each end perforated by a 15 mm diameter hole drilled through the shaft. From the proximal hole a crack

issues down the length of the shaft's anterior surface, which is flattened by wear, and marked with longitudinal striations. Posterior surface roughly smoothed; head of ulna snapped off, top of remaining shaft pared down and filed, bottom of shaft obliterated by post-depositional damage. Length of bone 324 mm; minimum distance between holes 238 mm.

From ditch 12, cut 2, unit 1087, level 2 (layer above that in which runner no. 1 was found). 18th–19th century.

Bone sledge-runners are made from either horse mandibles or cattle or horse long bones, mainly metapodials or radii. They are similar to bone skates (also made from metapodials and radii), but can be recognised by their different methods of attachment (MacGregor 1985, 141–6). Skates generally were fastened to the foot by leather straps, threaded through a transverse hole at the front and plugged into an axial hole at the back. Runners have vertical holes, front and back, accommodating nails or pegs which fixed them to the sledge. The diameter of the holes and absence of staining from metal nails might suggest that the Stonea runners were secured by wooden pegs. Further modification of the bones was required to facilitate their attachment as runners to the sledge base: in mature horses the ulna fuses to the posterior surface of the radius, and on both of the present examples the head of the ulna, which normally stands proud, was totally removed and the upper part of the remaining shaft whittled and filed flat.

Shape also assists in differentiating between runners and skates. Unlike skates, many of which are upswept and shaped to a point at the front, presumably to improve performance, the Stonea runners have blunted ends, probably indicating that speed was not an important function. The front and back of the runners are not immediately distinguishable, but two longitudinal cracks originating from the peg-holes sited at the proximal ends of the radii may be stress fractures, caused by impact on the front of the runner. The degree of abrasion on the proximal ends, particularly on runner no. 1, which is also slightly upswept, lends support to the theory that it was the proximal end of the bone which formed the front of the runner.

The natural lengthwise curve of the radius dictates the use of the bone's anterior surface as the underside of the runner. Microscopic examination of the anterior surface of nos. 1 and 2 shows a wear pattern comparable to those recorded for skates (MacGregor 1975), demonstrating that the runners were used on ice. Runner no. 2, which has the larger crack, shows no signs of burnishing and must have been used less than no. 1, which has heavier striations and some 'ice polish'.

According to MacGregor (1975), sledges with bone runners were used by Fen wildfowlers to cross frozen water whilst stalking birds, the sledge being propelled by the use of iron tipped poles, and he cites various nineteenth century sources in support of this. The Fenland distribution of the

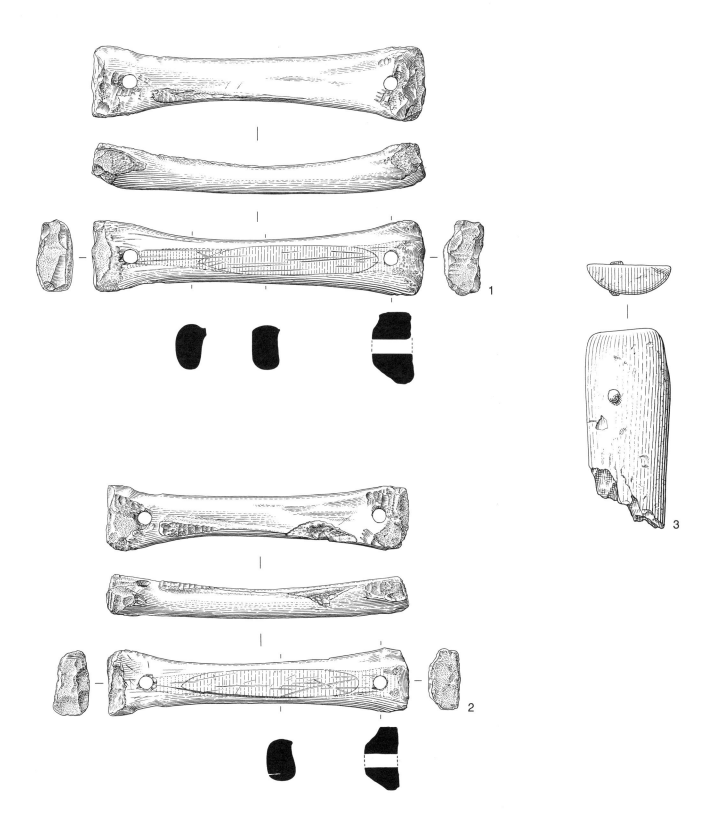

Fig. 247 Stonea Grange: post-medieval bone sledge-runners 1–2 and handle plate 3 (scale 1 : 4 except 3 = 1 : 1).

runners listed by MacGregor, a recently discovered example from Kings Lynn (Lindy Brewster, personal communication), and the two Stonea examples strengthen this argument. Sledges of this type may have been fairly common. Certainly two sledges are represented by nos 1 and 2: the radii are not from the same animal and the discrepancy in size, distance between peg-holes, and degree of wear also indicate that they are not a pair.

It is not known when such sledges were first used in this country, but stratified runners from Continental sites imply a pre-Conquest origin, while ethnographic reports from the Continent reveal use up until the early years of this century. Unfortunately none of the known finds from England can be securely dated, apart from the present examples, which were found in post-medieval layers dating to the eighteenth–nineteenth century.

3 Handle plate, bone   ST 83 CDQ, SF 506

Lightly tapered bone handle plate, probably from a knife. It has a low plano-convex cross-section and a squared-off butt. One small iron rivet remains in situ, and breakage of the plate has occurred across a second. Length 53 mm.

Context as no. 2.

6
DISCUSSION AND CONCLUSIONS
T. W. Potter

The intention of this final chapter is to draw together the diverse strands in the narrative of previous pages, and to attempt to integrate the evidence of excavation and fieldwork within a broader context. The conclusions must be recognised for what they are: tentative hypotheses, reached from the cutting of a few small windows into a huge and diverse sequence of ancient landscapes. Indeed, it is not always easy to appreciate just how sparse our available data are. Despite a long and distinguished tradition of fieldwork that extends back to the days of Fox (1923), and which has now been greatly extended by the work of the Fenland Project team (Hall and Coles 1994), there is still a dearth of excavation within the heartland of the Fens. Both the Haddenham and the Fengate-Maxey projects concern the fen edge as much as the Fens themselves, and there remains as symptomatic of the whole that extraordinary statistic that by 1981 only one barrow had been excavated within the Fenland proper (Lawson *et al* 1981, Fig. 46). The Roman landscape has suffered from a similar neglect, ironically, since the Royal Geographical Society Survey (Phillips 1970) both exploited the data brought to light through the destructive processes of modern ploughing and pan busting, and focused attention upon the key issues that excavation might resolve. Yet, until recently, excavation of Roman sites was largely confined to a few small-scale, amateur investigations (Potter 1981), none of which post-dated the publication of the Royal Geographical Society Memoir.

That this situation is changing is beyond dispute. The discovery of Flag Fen and its associated post alignments is a most signal contribution to our knowledge of the Bronze Age (Pryor 1992), while the excavations at Langwood Hill, near Chatteris, and Wardy Hill, near Coveney (Taylor and Evans 1993; Evans 1992) have shed much light upon the Iron Age settlement in the region, previously thought to have been an archaeological blank. Likewise, there has been some limited investigation of Romano-British features (e.g. Leah 1992, Macaulay and Reynolds 1993), although hardly on a scale commensurate with a landscape whose importance was manifest in the 1930s, and spelt out in a volume of international significance by Salway, Hallam and others in 1970. One anticipates with relish the stripping and study of one of the more ordinary Romano-British settlements, now so well known through observation from the air.

It is important to preface the remarks that follow in this way, since the comparatively extensive nature of the Stonea project may well have the effect of exaggerating disproportionately the conclusions drawn from the work. Stonea *appears* an unusual site in many respects, but this observation must be qualified because of the lack of comparable excavated data from within the Fenland region. It is tempting, for example, to regard the exemplary quality of the aerial photographs as an indication that most major features of the Roman landscape have been detected; yet, the Grange site, although known as a sherd scatter, totally escaped identification in this way, despite the magnitude of some of the buried features, and it was left to David Hall's inspired programme of fieldwalking to reveal the existence of the stone structures. It follows that there may be other sites of comparable interest and importance, especially within the Roman Fenland, which have eluded notice. This is more likely to be true of the 'islands' of the central and southern Fenland, where certain subsoils appear somewhat inimicable to the registration of crop marks and there is often an overlay of later settlement. We may legitimately wonder, for example, whether Ely may mask a major Roman site, thus helping to explain the otherwise somewhat incongruous appearance of a vast cathedral within a very modestly sized town. Indeed, March must conceal much of interest, given the wholly unexpected discoveries of prehistoric, Iron Age and early Roman date from Field Baulk and Estover (pp. 45–8 and pp. 49–60). Only in the silt fens is the aerial coverage likely to be more representative, although even here places such as Whaplode Drove seem to overlie Roman sites of apparently exceptional character, the finds including an altar and a 'building of some pretensions for the Fens' (Phillips 1970, 302).

Likewise, the discovery at Stonea Grange of both a major Late Bronze Age settlement (a period represented in the Fens by frequent finds of metalwork, but little more: Hall and Coles 1994, 89f.), and an early Anglo-Saxon farm or hamlet, can be interpreted in different ways. They may indeed show that it was regarded as a favoured place in which to live; but, despite the intensity of ground and aerial survey, they could equally demonstrate the difficulty of identifying sites of these periods. Many Fen 'islands' may in time prove to have been occupied at these times, and by inhabitants of equal or greater 'status'. Only Stonea Camp and probably its Roman successor are likely to remain as sites within the Fenland that are perceived as being of exceptional archaeological importance.

These therefore are some of the caveats to be borne in mind when evaluating the results of the Stonea excavation. To these must be added the fact that the 'island' of Stonea covers an area of about 300 ha (740 acres), excluding the high ground of Fincham and Ancaster Farms, which is topographically separate, and was also densely settled in the Roman period. This huge landscape has been examined at only four points: the Golden Lion Inn; the barrow close to Stonea Camp; Stonea Camp itself; and at the Grange where some 8 ha (20 acres) were sampled by trenching, and about one hectare investigated completely. In total, therefore, less than 3% of the island has been studied through excavation, a figure which further underlines the need for a cautious appraisal of the results, and judicious use of the hypotheses that are here developed.

There is one further introductory paragraph to add. Another major achievement of the Fenland Project has been to refine hugely our understanding of the Flandrian deposits. The picture that has emerged hitherto is of extraordinary complexity, and the definitive publication, by Waller, promises a still more radical rethink. It is, however, not available at the time of writing, and for this reason comment on environmental changes within the region has been here severely restricted. The excavations at Stonea do make some contribution to the debate, but it is a task of the future to set these findings within a broad framework. They are not easily interpreted, as will be seen; nevertheless, an awareness of the delicate balance between wetter and drier conditions must remain a constant backdrop to our interpretation of the lives of the people who for so long occupied this remote patch of land.

PALAEOLITHIC TO *c.* 2000 BC (Fig. 248)

Palaeolithic flint tools are not infrequently found in the central and southern Fens, and Stonea is no exception. Two fine Acheulean handaxes in a fresh condition are known, as well as a number of flakes (Hall 1992, 63; Ashton, pp. 36, 38). But without evidence for *in situ* chipping floors, we must be wary of regarding these as testimony of occupation. Such objects not infrequently occur in later contexts, and were perhaps collected as curios or items with a perceived ritual import. There may indeed have been a presence in the region at some points during the Palaeolithic, but to suggest that Stonea was amongst the places that were frequented would be to stretch the available testimony much too far. It is a conclusion that is underlined by the apparent absence of Mesolithic material from the 'island'. Some objects may belong to the later phases of the Mesolithic, in common with finds from the area collected by Mr. F. M. Walter (Middleton

1990); but the record from Stonea and the central Fens as a whole indicates that it was only in the Neolithic that occupation properly began.

The one excavated site definitely of this period lies just to the east of Stonea Camp. Here the very partial examination of a barrow in 1961–2 showed that it was preceded by rich Neolithic levels, which contained over 600 sherds, some of them large and unabraded (Potter 1975–6). In addition, two wooden posts, both of which had rotted *in situ*, were identified, as well as two substantial pits. Although only eight animal bones were found, it was inferred that this was a domestic site, occupied in the Final Neolithic. Stratified above this was a charcoal-rich layer of limited extent with two Beaker sherds, and it is now known that the whole area around the barrow is prodigal of worked flint of Neolithic and Early Bronze Age type. Some are associated with a palisaded ring ditch, 10 m in diameter, within Stonea Camp itself (Malim 1992) and, as will be seen below, a ritual component to the landscape of this part of the 'island' at Stonea is highly probable.

Stonea as a whole has yielded a good deal of surface evidence (including polished stone axes) for Neolithic activity elsewhere on the 'island' (Hall 1992, 63), and the Grange site produced two sherds and some flints of Neolithic type (including a leaf-shaped arrowhead). The major discovery, however, came from aerial reconnaissance over Stonea Grange, undertaken in 1984, which disclosed the faint cropmarks of a pair of parallel ditches heading south-eastwards towards the barrow excavated in 1961–2 (Pl. IX). Further study of other photographs (Pl. VIII) suggested that the feature changed alignment to the north, passing through the main excavation site at the Grange, where the more easterly ditch was identified at two places. Thereafter its northerly course is lost.

A section was cut across the parallel ditches at a point roughly halfway between the Grange site and the barrow. The east ditch was identified only with great difficulty, principally because it was filled with a sterile yellow clay, closely resembling the material through which it had been dug. It proved to be some 3.80 m wide and a metre deep, and was flat-bottomed. The angle of lenses of silt and pebbles in the fill suggested that the spoil had been banked up on the west, i.e. the interior of the feature. The west ditch could not be located at all, reflecting the much less distinct nature of the crop-mark, which may indeed indicate that there were a number of interruptions along its course.

The total length of the feature is at least 500 m, with the change of alignment taking place about 300 m from the south end. The width between the ditches is about 13 m. These dimensions are by no means incompatible with the range of measurements for the most obvious analogy for the Stonea ditches, namely the Neolithic cursus. Topping (1982), in his study of the Scorton cursus in Yorkshire, cites the following series of figures:

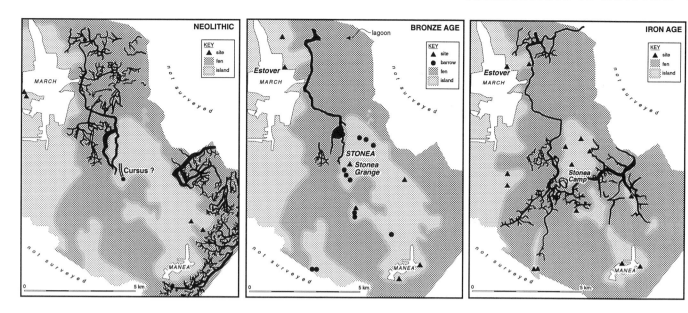

Fig. 248 Occupation on and around the 'island' of Stonea in the Neolithic, Bronze Age and Iron Age (after Hall 1987 and 1992).

	Minimum	Maximum	Average	
Length (m)	91+	19 811	2087.1	(sample 16 sites)
Breadth (m)	10.9	128	54.1	(sample 15 sites)
Ditch width (m)	1.5	3.8	2.9	(sample 8 sites)
Ditch depth (m)	0.43	2.28	1.1	(sample 7 sites)

These measurements suggest that only in its narrow breadth is Stonea to some extent atypical, although North Stoke (10.9 m) and Llandegai (12.2 m) provide parallels. Moreover, there are also many other respects in which the Stonea ditches may be compared with cursus monuments, and it is worth setting these out. Immediately striking is the fact that the majority of the known examples are sited on gravel terraces and terminate close to rivers. There are important exceptions, notably on the chalk downlands and in the Yorkshire Wolds, and it may be that the picture is distorted by the favourable crop marks that the gravels tend to produce. However, Stonea's low-lying position in a generally wet environment (Hall 1992), is consistent with this overall picture, and the notion that these rivers were in some sense sacred is an attractive one (Hedges and Buckley 1981, 11).

There are also many features of the form and layout of the Stonea ditches which find close comparison with other cursus monuments. Changes in alignment are commonly encountered, as are crop marks which register discontinuous lines; indeed, as Hedges and Buckley (1981, 13) point out, causewayed ditches are by no means uncommon, a possible explanation for the seemingly broken west ditch at Stonea. Moreover, not only is the bank, where apparent, always on the inside of the ditch (as at Stonea), but the ditch fill is almost invariably sterile. In our case, on so densely settled an area, this is in itself an argument for an early date, and the east ditch, where it crosses the Grange site, is indeed

demonstrably older than the Roman settlement. Finally, as Hedges and Buckley (1981, 15) stress, cursuses always occur with other monuments: 'frequently found are long, oval or round barrows, "long mortuary enclosures", and henge monuments. Although strict contemporaneity is yet to be proven at any site, the regular relationship of these monuments does portray an area of sanctity'.

At Stonea, there is certainly no shortage of prehistoric monuments, especially round barrows. There may have been several within the area of Stonea Camp itself (Phillips 1948), although Malim's excavation referred to above showed that at least one was a ring ditch containing a palisade. To the north, the crop-marks of two are visible on aerial photographs of the Grange field, and a further three are known to the north east (Hall 1987, M10, 11; 1992, Wb 9). Other groups occur on the high ground of Jenny Grays Farm, to the south-east (Hall 1992, Wb 3), and on Honey Hill to the south. Thus, while the density of barrows appears to be far less than that on the southern part of the Chatteris 'island' (Hall 1992, 89), or at Haddenham, Borough Fen and Maxey (Hall and Coles 1992; Pryor and French 1985), the concentration would seem to be significant.

The barrow near Stonea Camp with the underlying Neolithic deposits, alluded to above, is here of interest. It contained two burials of the Early Bronze Age, within the excavated part, and was some 20 m in diameter. However, replotting of the crop-marks has now shown that it lay within, but on one side of, a much larger ring ditch, with a diameter of about 35 m. This would be entirely consistent with its being a henge monument, and it may be that the Neolithic finds relate to this ditch. This is potentially of some importance, given that the Stonea Camp cursus (if that is what it is) does appear to be aligned upon it.

Indeed, careful study of the aerial photographs suggests that there *may* have been a rectangular terminal a short distance to the north of the barrow, conceivably not unlike that at Springfield Lyons, Essex (Hedges and Buckley 1981, 4).

Nevertheless, whatever the precise plan of the terminal, ring ditches situated at the end of cursus monuments are well attested with, for example, clear examples at Fornham All Saints in Suffolk (Hedges and Buckley 1981, Fig. 5), and at Scorton, Yorkshire (Topping 1982, Fig. 1). Still more elaborate is the huge enclosure recently revealed at Godmanchester, also at the end of a cursus (Parker Pearson 1993, 65). On the strength of these analogies, we can certainly postulate a not dissimilar ceremonial complex at Stonea, despite the limited scope of our investigation. Assigning a terminology for it is not, however, without its difficulties. We must surely agree with Hedges and Buckley (1981, 14) that 'the collective term "cursus" is being used to describe sites which may be quite different in form and function', and bear in mind Pryor's distinction between cursuses which were a) continuously used, as in Dorset; b) short-lived, single-period sites, as at Barnack; and c) long-lived sites, used and extended episodically (Pryor and French 1985, 300–1). Further to this, Bradley (1984, 44) has underlined the close morphological relationship between cursus monuments and bank barrows, suggesting that both were roughly contemporary developments which were 'elaborations of the funerary sites of the early Neolithic'. It may indeed be that the very narrow cursus-like features, such as Llandegai (Houlder 1968) and Stonea, were in fact some form of bank barrow.

In terms of absolute chronology, Stonea makes no real contribution to the question of the dating of cursuses. Bradley (1987a) notes that most radiocarbon assessments fall in the second half of the third millennium bc, with 'a few indications that this tradition was in existence by the middle of the third millennium bc (1984, 44). Pryor and French (1985, 304) suggest that, although the Maxey cursus is cut by henge features in the West Field, 'elsewhere there is good reason to believe the cursus alignment still held significance in Beaker times'. Thus, the Stonea cursus (if that is what it is) could well be roughly contemporary with the pottery from beneath the 1961–2 barrow, a group which Kinnes (in Potter 1975–6) describes as 'Final Neolithic', although a few pieces may be older, and there are in addition some sherds of Beaker.

By way of summary, we can conclude that in the mid to late Neolithic, the 'island' of Stonea began to emerge as a centre of activity, which may well – as at Etton (Pryor 1987) – have combined settlement with 'ceremonial' functions. Pryor and French (1985, 300) have attempted to argue against the emergence of territorial 'central places' in the period in East Anglia, pointing to the multiplication of causewayed enclosures in particular regions, such as that around Peterborough, and at the overlapping sites at Fornham All Saints in Suffolk. If, however, occupation was only sporadic at such sites (as Pryor and French themselves suggest) and communities were relatively mobile, then the *clusters* of sites may well represent territorial foci: for topographical considerations alone imply that there must have been differences in economic strategy between communities exploiting lands on or close to the Fen edge, and those inhabiting the Fens proper (assuming year-round occupation). Within the Fenland, the relationship with the wetlands is intimate and continual, whereas those on the Fen edge can take advantage of both low-lying and upland environments. It follows that the Fen 'islands' could have emerged as 'central places' at a relatively early stage in the region's prehistory, and especially in the Neolithic, with its capacity for agriculture. Indeed, we must not forget the fine group of Beaker pottery (Longworth, pp. 56–8) and other signs of occupation, that by chance emerged from the investigation at Estover, on the north side of March.

Moreover, Stonea may well have acquired a certain 'sanctity' early in its history of human occupation, and, given the apparent prominence of its later prehistoric and Roman archaeology within the context of the Fenland, it is germane to bear this in mind. We are not able to postulate continuity of settlement throughout later prehistory, but the introspective nature of the Fenlander is seemingly eternal, and encourages long memories: Stonea's selection as the site of major Iron Age and Roman centres may indeed be an echo of the more distant past.

THE SECOND MILLENNIUM BC (Fig. 248)

The present excavation revealed very few signs of occupation after the initial centuries of the second millennium, apart from a few stray items in residual contexts. The only clearly identifiable feature was a small pit, with a lens of dark grey silt, containing sherds perhaps of Middle Bronze Age type; this was sealed by a yellowish silt, which could have been waterlaid, but may point to little more than localised flooding. From Stonea as a whole, there is a spearhead of Middle Bronze Age type (Rowlands 1976, no. 1232), and sherds of a collared urn are said to have come from a barrow (Longworth 1984, no. 125); but the overall record is scant. Certainly, nothing has so far been found that might parallel the remarkable system of fields and droveroads discovered at Fengate (Pryor 1984), and which appear to span the millennium. Some Bronze Age field systems are now known in the Fens, notably a series of enclosures with some pretension to rectangularity in Block Fen between Chatteris and Mepal (*Fenland Research* 8 (1993), 1f.); but they are a far cry from the ordered layout of Fengate, and are most notable for their considerable extent.

It is possible, indeed likely, that something of the sort found at Block Fen will eventually come to light at Stonea. David Hall (1987, 1992) recorded a number of scatters of flints of general Bronze Age type, and it would be surprising were there to have been no settlement, whether transient or permanent, on the 'island' in the Middle Bronze Age and earlier part of the Late Bronze Age. One is reminded, however, of the scarcity of evidence for actual settlement at Fengate in this period, which hints at the elusiveness of such sites. There seem to have been only small foci of occupation, with few finds (Pryor 1984). Similarly, the 'island' of Chatteris, while prodigal of metalwork that represents all phases of the Bronze Age (Hall and Coles 1994, 79), has yielded only five flint scatters generally datable to this period (Hall 1992). There are enigmas here in the archaeological record which are likely to be resolved only by large-scale excavation. Nevertheless, we now know that around 1363 BC work began on building the remarkable timber platform at Flag Fen, linked by an alignment of posts with the field system at Fengate (Pryor 1992). The latest timbers are dated to 967 BC indicating a remarkable longevity of accretions to the structures. Whatever its purpose, it must have been of high importance in the political geography of the region, a factor which needs to be borne in mind in evaluating the site hierarchies of this period.

THE FIRST MILLENNIUM BC AND FIRST CENTURY AD   (Fig. 248)

While an unurned cremation, in the Deverel–Rimbury/ Ardleigh tradition, is likely to date to before 1000 BC, the first major concentration of settlement known from the excavations at Stonea Grange probably began in the ninth century BC. The evidence for structures was confined to the north-east part of the main area. Here was a ring ditch, 13 m in diameter; an adjacent, dense but incomprehensible cluster of post-holes; and a large pit or well. However, the indications from the machine-cut trenches and surface finds are that occupation extended onto the rather higher ground to the north and east, where sherds cover several hectares. Moreover, aerial photographs, using infrared film, show traces of what appear to be the east and south sides of a circular enclosure, with a diameter in the order of 300 m (Fig. 19, p. 62). As it was recognised only after the close of the fieldwork, no sections were excavated; but one might wonder whether, if not illusory, it could belong to the group of very early 'hillforts', characterised by rather slight defences (as is probably the case here), and spacious interiors (Cunliffe 1991, 346).

That, however, is speculation. What is certain is that the excavated and surface finds in combination point to a community with access to considerable sources of wealth. This is evinced both by the pottery and the metalwork. The ceramic assemblage, which is in the Post Deverel–Rimbury tradition, shows a significant proportion of burnished wares, sufficient to be noteworthy (Needham, pp. 245–57), and spans the period between the ninth and sixth centuries BC, with no

obvious sign of a gap. The metalwork falls within the same chronological bracket, and forms a striking collection. It includes fragments of socketed axes (4), swords (2), a chisel and a razor. All appear to have been scrap items, destined for reworking, as is implied by the discovery of a casting jet, and pieces of three moulds or crucibles, the latter in excavated contexts. To this evidence should be added the record of a Late Bronze Age gold 'lock-ring' (T. Gregory, personal communication), now published by Pendleton (1985), who also lists other metal detector finds of the period, amongst them socketed axes (3), cake and part of a knife. The presence of one or more founders' hoards cannot be ruled out, not least because the moulds were incorporated in excavated deposits. Finally, we should recall the earlier discovery near Stonea Grange of a hoard of five socketed axes and three ingots (Clark 1938, 303).

Cumulatively, these finds would appear to portray a settlement of some size and importance. Even though so very little is known of its layout and buildings, there are more than a few hints of the emergence of a major regional centre, where metalwork was manufactured, recalling contemporary developments (but not, on present indications, the plan) at sites like Springfield Lyons and Mucking (the 'South Rings': Etté 1993). Within the main excavated area, it was also clearly a de novo foundation, although whether this was an expansion from an unlocated nucleus of the Middle Bronze Age, or the result of an external intervention, is a matter that remains conjectural. As noted above, there were certainly no earlier field systems to be blotted out, as seems to have been the case at Mucking; but it is intriguing that settlement began at around the time of the demise of the sites at Fengate and Flag Fen (Pryor 1992), where waterlogging was becoming increasingly prevalent (French 1992). Indeed, the protracted, very large-scale investigations of the Peterborough area as a whole, have yielded remarkably little of the period of the Stonea Late Bronze Age settlement (Pryor and French 1985, 306). Similarly, finds of LBA metalwork apart, the Fenland as a whole has provided little diagnostic evidence for occupation (Hall and Coles 1994, 89–90), a picture that, in the light of the discoveries at Stonea, can now be seen as misleading.

The Late Bronze Age populace at Stonea Grange was certainly practising agriculture, as is evident from the botanical record. The plant remains, whilst not abundant, attest the cultivation and threshing of emmer and spelt wheat, as well as barley and oats. In addition, there are indications, that rye and Celtic beans may also have been grown, unusually for this period (van der Veen, pp. 616–20). Animal bones were found in insufficient quantity to furnish any valid picture, although numerically cattle occur most frequently (unlike all subsequent periods on the site, where sheep predominate). To judge from somewhat sparse botanical and molluscan data, damp meadowland certainly featured in the environs, on which to pasture the livestock.

The onset of wetter conditions in the Fens during the first millennium BC is dramatically illustrated at Stonea Grange. The Late Bronze Age settlement was blanketed with a layer of pale-grey, largely stone-free, silt, in the base of which were sherds perhaps of the sixth century BC (Fig. 22, p. 66). Thereafter, the artefact record from the main excavation remains a blank until the first half of the first century AD, when a few features were cut into the presumably now dried-out silts. Subsequently, the main Roman road was laid out in the second century AD over them, confirming the stratigraphical sequence and providing a secure *terminus ante quem*.

Examination of the silts for diatoms yielded a sparse assemblage, dominated by *Hantzshia amphioxys*, indicating 'a marginally wet environment at the inland limit of brackish water influence' (Alderton 1983–4, 21). This is not inconsistent with evidence from Manea, where Hall and Switsur (1981) showed that a roddon became tidal after 605 ± 45 bc (Q-2113), a date obtained from peat beneath the roddon silts. However, more recent work on the silts to the north of March indicate that they may be of quite late date in the Iron Age (Waller 1988, 338–9), and it is premature to comment any further upon the broader stratigraphical relationship of the deposits at Stonea until Waller has published his final synthesis of the environmental data.

Two aspects of the grey silts at Stonea do however require emphasis. Where they were best conserved, namely on the north side of the main excavation in an area protected from ploughing by the presence of the Grange, they were some 0.70 m in depth, and attained the exceptional height of 3.83 m AOD. This is well above figures that are normally cited for the top of the 'Iron Age' silts, 3–3.60 m AOD (Hall and Switsur 1981, 78), and may indicate purely local factors at work. Moreover, they were distributed only over the north part of the site, coinciding with the limits of the Late Bronze Age settlement. They were definitely *not* represented further south, as areas of undamaged stratigraphy (e.g around the Roman stone building, R1) clearly showed; this is despite the fact that the old ground surface averaged between 3.27 and 3.33 m AOD, i.e. well below the top of the flood silts. It follows that something must have blocked the spread of water onto this area, not inconceivably a bank around the Late Bronze Age site. But other explanations are possible, and the matter is rendered still more complex by deposits encountered in trenches to the north-east, as we shall see. All that can be safely concluded is that flooding is likely to have played a part in the abandonment of the Late Bronze Age Settlement, and that there was no subsequent activity on the main site at Stonea Grange until Roman times.

The Iron Age

Finds of both metalwork and pottery support the notion that there was occupation at Stonea Grange, whether continuous or intermittent, for much of the Iron Age. The objects include a fine attachment in the form of a duck of *c.* 300 BC, a strap union of *c.* 200 BC, a La Tène I brooch (fourth–third centuries BC), two Late Iron Age terrets, and a rich coin record dating from the mid first century BC onwards. The pottery covers a similar range. Whilst most of the metalwork is not closely provenanced, the sherds indicate that the main focus of occupation (leaving aside for the moment the question of Stonea Camp) lay to the north and east of the main excavation.

This is rather higher ground, with a Roman building, identified as a temple (see pp. 214–21) standing at about 4.25–4.35 m AOD, and the subsoil being *c.* 3.75 m AOD. Exploratory trenches in this area revealed the bases of numerous features, especially pits and ditches, cut into the natural clay and silts. However, they were so shallow in depth that they must have been dug from a much higher level, presumably well above the 3.83 m AOD reached by the flood silts on the main site. Pottery was not prolific, and the sample of features excavated was small; but sufficient was found to suggest that this area was densely occupied during the Late Bronze Age and the Iron Age (as the sheer number of features also implies).

The deposits overlying the subsoil comprise a dark grey silty material, reaching up to a metre in depth, which has been studied by French (pp. 221–3). He concludes that the lower part represents reworked midden material, while the overlying layer is alluvial in origin. He would regard the latter as of late Anglo-Saxon or medieval date, but there is no direct evidence for this. All that can safely be said is that the Roman temple sealed midden-like deposits, and that the bulk of the finds are of Late Bronze Age and Iron Age date. But it must be frankly admitted that we do not properly understand the stratigraphical sequences in this area, and it would undoubtedly repay more extensive investigation.

The one structure, the Roman temple apart, disclosed by this work comprised a line of post-holes, and a possible beam slot, revealed in a sondage beneath the temple forecourt. They were on the same alignment as that of the temple, and could well mark the site of an Iron Age precursor. However, they only survived as very shallow features cut into the subsoil, and the one certainty is that they predate the second century AD.

It was a signal achievement of the Fenland Project to identify abundant evidence, hitherto unsuspected, for Iron Age settlement on many of the Fen 'islands'. Hall (1987, Fig. 22; 1992, 67) recognised Iron Age material at no fewer than eight sites at Stonea, while at Langwood Hill, Chatteris, Evans has investigated a settlement of some 8 ha, with evidence of occupation throughout the Iron Age and into the Romano-British period (Taylor and Evans 1993, 169). In the Early Iron Age, there may have been as many as 100 buildings, and an extensive field system is also known. Likewise, Haddenham has yielded impressive evidence particularly for Middle Iron Age occupation, on a site with a longevity of monuments that is very comparable to Stonea (Evans and Serjeantson 1988). Extending over an area of some 5 ha, this too must have been a significant place in the Iron Age political geography of the region. However dimly perceived through the archaeological record, the signs are of emerging regional centres, existing within an increasingly fragile environment and, one imagines, in a degree of competition.

Where the populace of Stonea stood in the hierarchy (if such existed), is an interesting matter of conjecture. The finds of metalwork affirm the presence of individuals of relatively high status in both the Late Bronze Age and in the Iron Age, conceivably living within the very large enclosure provisionally identified on aerial photographs. To infer from this that Stonea may already have been rising to a degree of regional pre-eminence is to press the evidence much too hard; but it would provide a context for the construction of Stonea Camp, a very large and exceptional monument both in the Fens and in East Anglia as a whole.

The Camp has already been discussed in some detail (Chapter 2, pp. 27–44), and it is unnecessary to rehearse this at length again. The conclusion that begins to emerge, especially from the investigations of Malim (1992), is that it may have originated as a religious centre enclosed by a bank and ditch in the second century BC. No buildings or pits have been identified, and there is virtually no refuse. It would seem to have been surrounded by thick oak forest in this early period, which could also have ritual connotations, and the ditches contained dismembered human remains, including a skull bearing sword cuts. Subsequently, the form of the enclosure was modified and, later again, a double arc of banks and ditches inserted on the island side in a by now cleared landscape. These final works could have been an attempt to fortify the position in the face of the Roman army that, according to Tacitus, stormed an Icenian position in the wake of the revolt of AD 47. A skeleton found in a ditch belongs on radiocarbon dating to this time, and the very small group of pottery, Roman coins and other metalwork from the Camp also falls within the Claudio-Neronian period. They would not be inconsistent, indeed, with short-lived military occupation, in the view of Shotter and Mackreth (pp. 35–6).

It may be, on the other hand, that the correlation with Tacitus' account of the taking of the Icenian encampment should be rejected, and a rather different stance taken. The wealth of Iron Age coins from Stonea as a whole shows that it was emerging as a commercial centre from the mid first century BC, if not before. The earliest Icenian issues are represented, and overall coins of that tribe dominate the sample, amounting to 88%. When taken in conjunction with other Icenian coin hoards from the region, like those from Field Baulk (p. 45) and Langwood Hill (Potter 1989b, 156), it is evident that the central Fens lay in Iceni territory.

It is moreover interesting that the group of finds from Stonea Camp belong entirely to the period of the Icenian client kingdom. This is precisely the main period of the enigmatic site at Fison Way, Thetford. Gregory's (1991) remarkable investigation showed that this was a place of considerable importance, very probably with a ceremonial role, if not the residence of a member of the Icenian royal family (although the paucity of finds does not support the latter interpretation). It was demolished in the early 60s, under military supervision, and presumably in the aftermath of the Boudiccan uprising. It is not impossible, therefore, that both Fison Way and Stonea Camp operated as regional foci during the reigns of Antedios and Prasutagus, and were destroyed with the imposition of direct Roman rule in AD 61. Certainly, there are clear signs that the latest ramparts at Stonea Camp were slighted, conceivably explaining the presence on the site of, for example, types of brooch that are commonly found in military contexts.

Proof may indeed one day emerge that the central Fens was briefly placed under army control at this time, perhaps based on a fort at Grandford (Potter 1981, 85), where military metalwork has now been identified. Moreover, we should not forget the signs from sites like Estover and Field Baulk that there may have been much more settlement on 'islands' like March in the Claudio-Neronian period than was suspected even 25 years ago (Salway 1970, 8). Similarly, as the plough has bitten more deeply into the deposits at Flaggrass, pottery of this age has also been dragged to the surface. There may have been a quite substantial population in the region, although one which fell sharply in the repercussions that followed Boudicca's insurrection. For, the general dearth of Flavian samian, and the burial of the Field Baulk coin hoard in a pot of *c.* AD 60–70, must surely mark a Roman intervention with repercussions that were to last for a generation or more.

STONEA GRANGE IN THE ROMAN PERIOD

A few features and finds belong to the first century AD (Phase II), amongst them a substantial ditch, some possible slots, a pit and a hearth, perhaps for metalworking. They belong in the main to the period *c.* AD 40–60, and thus are an echo of what seems to have been, on artefactual evidence, the principal phase of activity at Stonea Camp. Thereafter, as noted above, the archaeological record is largely a blank for the next 70 to 80 years or so: there are a few finds of Flavian–Trajanic date, but structural evidence is entirely lacking. It was in effect a green-field site that the Romans were to develop.

The foundation date of the new settlement cannot be closely established on stratigraphical grounds. Tell-tale deposits had long since been erased, or yielded no objects.

Nevertheless, the assemblage from the site leaves no doubt that it was in the period between *c.* AD 130 and 150 that the site was laid out. Indeed, the best reading of the evidence, as indicated by the coins, is that the decision was taken in the later Hadrianic period, and had been implemented by early Antonine times. This, as Salway (1970, 9) stressed, is entirely consistent with the picture from the Fenland as a whole, a view that has not been modified as a result of recent work (e.g. Cameron in Hall 1987, 68–9). The region would appear to have been developed as the result of a single initiative, conventionally regarded as Imperially-inspired. One must here eschew images like those recorded by Felix in his eighth-century *Life of St Guthlac*, where the Fens are described as a 'wide wilderness', with 'immense marshes, now a black pool of water, now foul-running streams' (Darby 1974, 8). Although such regions did harbour ague and malaria, the Romans knew well enough the economic advantages of developing them. They had learnt much about managing environments of this sort from their Etruscan neighbours (Ward-Perkins 1962), and were in time to turn vast wetland areas like the Po Valley into regions of celebrated bounty (Pliny, *Nat. Hist.* iii, xvi; Strabo v, 1, 2). Hadrian was amongst those who were acutely aware of the potential of seemingly marginal terrain. His works are recorded in central Italy (*Liber Coloniarum*, 233), in Africa (Kehoe 1988) and in the Kopais Basin in Greece (Fossey 1979; Potter 1989b, 159), and his reorganisation of the system of procurators brought, for example, much benefit to Egypt (Crawford 1976, 53). The impact of such activities often achieved wide recognition. Thus, the North African rhetorician Tertullian, writing in the early third century, could observe how 'famous marshes have been blotted out by fair estates, forests have been conquered by ploughed fields, wild beasts have been put to flight by flocks of sheep, the sands are sown, the rocks planted, the marshes drained... everywhere there are houses, people, organised government, life' (*De Anima* xxx, 3). Hadrian's initiative might well have inspired a similar eulogy.

Whatever the precise status of the Fenland in the second century (and we must debate this further below), an intervention by Hadrian is entirely consistent with other evidence. It matches his activities in other provinces, and he will likely have seen this then sparsely inhabited region as he journeyed northwards in AD 122. Whilst the construction of the new frontier will have delayed the development of the Fens (for the army was surely involved, given its long tradition of canal digging: e.g. Tacitus, *Annals* 2, 8), by late Hadrianic times, with the Wall completed, the opportunity was there. Indeed, one must not forget Salway's important point that there may have been an economic link between the two (Salway 1981, 189). The Vindolanda tablets clearly imply the existence of sophisticated mechanisms of supply, over long distances; the Fenland could certainly have been the source for commodities such as wool, meat, salt and oysters, all of which are referred in the documents (Bowman and Thomas 1994, tablets 192.4; 186.10; 299, i, 3). Much must have been acquired locally (Bowman 1994, 72), but more distant (and perhaps Imperially-owned) sources may well have been exploited. At the very least, this provides one possible context for the development of the Fenland region.

If the foundation of the settlement at Stonea Grange coincides neatly with the main period of development of the region as a whole, then its character is decidedly different from that of other known sites in the Fens. It would seem that, from the first, there was a blueprint which envisaged a layout based on *pedes Monetales*. The principal unit was a square of 50 *p.M.* (rather than, for example, a half *actus*) but with street widths of 15 *p.M.* except for the *decumanus*, which averaged 30 *p.M.* As on Hadrian's Wall (although much more markedly), there was however a lack of rigour in its application. Two slightly divergent grids were employed, resulting in blocks in the east part of the site which were not rectangular, and even the main street took a course that was more sinuous than straight. Nevertheless, while the overall plan may smack of compromise and adaptation, an underlying design can be clearly discerned (Fig. 67, p. 137).

The use of mensuration is unusual in the Fens. This was not a centuriated landscape, postdating the main time when the *agrimensores* were active in parcelling out newly developed regions (Castagnoli 1958; Frederiksen 1959; Dilke 1971). Some field systems were fairly regularly laid out, like the celebrated example near Christchurch (Salway 1970, Pl. VIII; see also Silvester 1991, Pl. XII, Straw Hill Farm, near Downham); but they do not correspond to units of Roman feet (Hallam 1970, 64–7). One exception may be the Roman site at Rookery Farm, near Spalding, which is some 200 × 250 *p.M.* (*c.* 58 × 75 m: *J. Roman Stud.*, 45 (1955), Pl. XX); it was provided with its own approach road, and one wonders whether it was built by an army veteran. It is, however, very much the exception in its meticulous planning.

Another feature of the layout of the settlement at Stonea Grange is the evident separation of domestic buildings in the east 'compound', from the block where the great stone complex, R1, was to be constructed. The probability is that a wooden fence originally divided the two areas, but this was soon converted into a ditch as drainage requirements became more apparent. The R1 building is remarkable in a number of respects. It originated as a stone structure, probably intended to be 50 *p.M.* square, with an apse to the west, positioned slightly off-centre. The stone had been transported over a distance of at least 40 km from quarries in the Peterborough area, largely if not entirely by water: Hall's identification (1987, 42) of a canal between Flaggrass, on the north-east side of the March 'island', and Stonea is a most significant discovery, and it was surely built to facilitate the movement of the building materials.

It was originally thought that there was a portico on the east side of the structure (Fig. 249; Potter and Whitehouse

1982), for some traces were identified of what appeared to be a construction trench. However, a more rigorous assessment of the evidence suggests that, if such a portico was planned, then its foundations were never laid. Even so, the building was handsomely embellished. Despite the most thorough work of demolition and robbing, it is possible to demonstrate that it was provided with a hypocaust, with a *praefurnium* to the south, and floored in mosaic. The walls were decorated with painted plaster, the designs including red and white panels, landscape and figured scenes, other geometric motifs and imitation marbling, especially a sophisticated version of cipollino. Marble veneer may also have been employed, there being a piece of pavonazetto, from central Phrygia in Asia Minor (although it was later worked into a counter). Some architectural elements survived, amongst them a tufa voussoir and a possible piece of capital, as well as vast quantities of tile (some rendered white, as though for a chequer-board effect). Window glass was particularly abundant (and, curiously, not recycled), forming the second largest collection from a Romano-British site, only being exceeded by that from the palace at Fishbourne. A very considerable number of glazed windows is implied. In short, however fragmentary the evidence, there can be no doubt that this was a highly impressive building.

A number of attempts have been made over the years, all by different artists, to offer some sort of reconstruction (Figs 64–5, p. 134; Pl. XXIIa). None can be regarded as anything more than highly speculative, given that so little has survived; but it has seemed necessary to try. They were from the first inspired by two factors. One was an on-site conversation with an architect, R. D. Andrews, who took the view that so strongly founded a building could have stood to a considerable height. The other was what seemed to be a close parallel in terms both of ground-plan and date with a structure at Le Mura di Santo Stefano, near Anguillara, just to the north of Rome (Lyttleton and Sear 1977). Likewise a building of architectural pretension, it still stands three storeys, and over 17 m high; as at Stonea, the walls are 1.20 m thick, although they are strengthened internally with buttresses.

In the light of this still attractive parallel, it seemed reasonable to reconstruct the original stone building (later to be modified) as a tower-like structure. Rising high in the flat Fenland landscape, it would have been visible for miles (as is Ely Cathedral today), as impressive a statement of Roman power and authority as one could want. A lower building is not out of the question (and is favoured in the most recent reconstruction: Fig. 66, p. 135); but, whatever the height, the intention was surely to create an imposing architectural image.

Tall buildings were no novelty in the Imperial period. The so-called 'Temple of Janus' at Autun (Duval and Quoniam 1963) is one obvious example, as is the curious structure at Centum Cellas in Portugal, which measures 11.34 × 8.52 m, and still stands to a height of 22 m (Belo 1970). Similarly,

the *cellae* of Romano-Celtic temples are commonly restored as tower-like features. That at Hemel Hempstead, for instance, had an estimated height of 15.50 m and, like Stonea, belongs in all probability to the Hadrianic period (Neal 1984, 197). Towers also occurred in domestic complexes, especially villas. The Younger Pliny is at pains to evoke the pleasures of the *turris* in his Laurentian villa, by the sea near Ostia (ii, 17.9), while Hadrian had a high *belvedere*, the Torre di Roccabruna, in his villa at Tivoli (De Franceschini 1991, 577f.) Likewise, in discussing the Sette Bassi villa (*c.* AD 140–60) on the Via Latina near Rome, Ward-Perkins (1981, 210) concluded that 'tower-like residential blocks two and three storeys high are a feature of several other wealthy second-century villas on the periphery of Rome'.

It is probably far-fetched to suggest on such meagre surviving evidence that the layout of the original stone building at Stonea Grange was influenced by metropolitan fashions; but the possibility cannot be wholly ignored, especially if the development of the Fenland came about through Imperial initiative (Potter and Whitehouse 1982). Moreover, if the building presents an appearance which, in its context, is faintly absurd, then this is very much in the spirit of the age. The letters of Pliny the Younger, written while Governor of Bithynia between AD 111 and 113, are full of reports about urban extravagance, impracticable schemes, wasted money and shoddy work. 'The theatre at Nicaea, Sir,' he writes (x, 39), 'is more than half built but it is still unfinished, and has already cost more than ten million sesterces…I am afraid that it may be money wasted. The building is sinking and showing immense cracks.' Similar problems applied to the construction of a new gymnasium, and to projects at other cities like Prŭsa and Nicomedia.

Seen in this light, the errors in the street grid, and the sheer extravagance of the stone building make more sense. There are more than a few echoes here of a high-level decision to build the settlement and, presumably, to provide resources: Hadrian, for example, gave 65 000 denarii for a drainage scheme around Coroneia in Boeotia (Reynolds *et al* 1986, 140). However, the implementation of the work at Stonea was shoddy, and the plan essentially impracticable. Indeed, there is evidence for this in that the tower building was rapidly modified. The original entrance, which must have been on the east side opposite the apse (itself perhaps intended to house a statue), was blocked off by the construction of a hall-like building, measuring 16.25 × 10.1 m externally (the 'east wing'). Other rooms were added to the north and west sides, and a small hypocausted room to the southwest. All were constructed in stone, and one wonders whether the tower was not completed to its intended height, so that the stone could be redeployed. Certainly the original design was greatly modified.

We must speculate about the function of the building complex somewhat later, when more of the evidence has

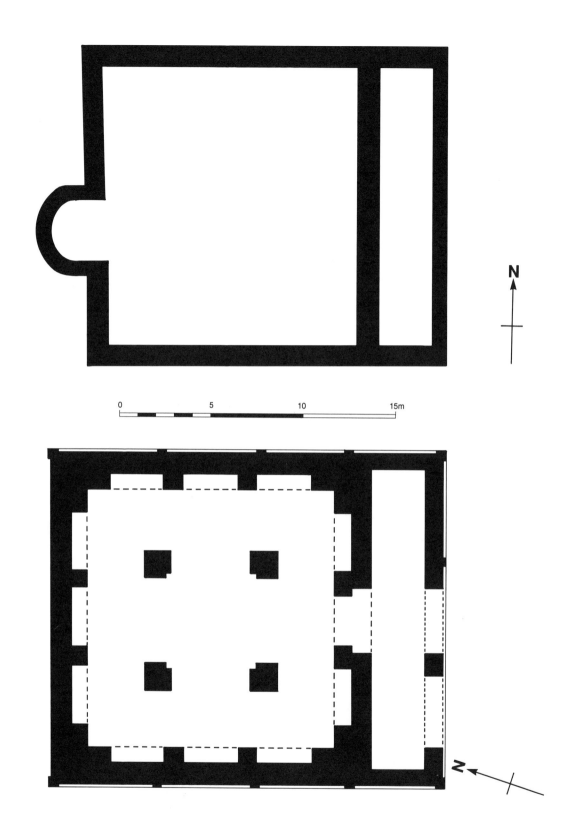

Fig. 249 Restored plans of Stonea building R1, foundations (top), and Anguillara, ground level.

been examined. It is nevertheless already clear that it corresponds with no very obvious model, either in Britain, or elsewhere. What is certain is that, in front of it to the north, lay a large reserved space: only approximately rectangular, and lacking a boundary on the west side, it measured some 60×40 m. The main road through the site formed the northern limit, and over that stretch was not provided with a drainage ditch along the south side; access to this piazza was evidently intended.

There are sufficient indications to show that the piazza was provided with an all-weather surface of mortar (or even flagstones), laid upon a hardstanding of limestone chips. Features were eventually to encroach upon this space, especially two wells along the west side; but it is clear that this area was from the first intended as reserved ground. Coin loss was not infrequent, however, and it is perhaps not unreasonable to compare it with the forum of a Roman town; one might envisage a series of temporary wooden stalls around the perimeter. By contrast, the area behind the stone buildings was divided into two fenced blocks, with at least one timber building; given that the *praefurnium* lay in the more northerly, they should probably seen as housing the services for the main stone complex. There was one well, with *opus signinum* steps (a notable feature on this site), although rubbish pits were completely absent. Most remarkable, however, was the massive feature measuring in all some 27×10 m, and up to 3.2 m in depth, that we have described as the 'sump'. Filled with organic matter (including more than 98 000 pieces of wood), it proved to be a botanical cornucopia, as the various specialist reports make clear. Much of the wood was unworked, and probably derived from clearance of the surrounding landscape; a substantial length of the trunk of an ash tree was amongst the debris. Nevertheless, the assemblage also provides eloquent testimony of construction in progress. Debitage was abundant, with all sorts of offcuts, and there were planks, perhaps for scaffolding, pegs, posts, staves and bundles of withies, probably for walls of wattle and daub. There were also elements from buckets and barrels and, most remarkably, a complete wooden spade with an iron sheath, seemingly encrusted with mortar. Likewise exceptional is a pair of much repaired workmen's shoes, of native rather than Roman type. Comparable to the modern 9½ shoe in size, they were clearly discarded as no longer fit to wear, and must surely indicate the use of British artisans.

Wooden artefacts were otherwise generally rare in the deposits, although there were three writing tablets of the wax type, and from third–fourth century levels a hayrake and a possible hayfork. Given that a later second-century drainage ditch was cut through the lower organic fills, it is reasonably certain that the constructional debris derives from the building of the stone complex, the fences demarcating the plots and perhaps other structures. No timber proved suitable for dendrochronological dating, but a late

Hadrianic–early Antonine context is entirely plausible on the basis of the pottery. The original purpose of this massive excavation is, however, extremely hard to fathom. Whilst it did function as a sump, this was surely not the initial intention. One possibility is that it represents the first stage in the construction of a building, a bathhouse being an obvious candidate, given that none can otherwise be identified. Yet, while this is consistent with the rectangularity of the feature, and its alignment with the stone buildings, it does not account for its considerable depth, and sloping sides. In short, it remains enigmatic although, on a site where changes in plan are so extremely evident, this is not entirely surprising. Confused and incompetent instructions could easily have been responsible, as is very much the import of Pliny's letters from Bithynia.

The east part of the main Grange site presents a sharp contrast with block 1. Virtually every block (2–9) yielded evidence for tightly packed wooden buildings, together with wells, latrines and rubbish pits. Two groups of pits, in blocks 5 and 5a, convey the impression of communal areas of refuse disposal; but it is the neatness of the arrangement of the features (certainly in the mid second century) that is so striking. In particular, the rows of pits, especially in blocks 3 and 4, are not unreminiscent of practices on military sites, as at Inchtuthil (Pitts and St Joseph 1985, 227f), although they are not unknown on civilian sites such as Baldock (Stead and Rigby 1986, 47). Thus their significance is essentially for orderly behaviour, although to a degree that would seem to be unusual.

The buildings themselves call for little comment. All were made of wood, with a hint from a few finds that wall-plaster may occasionally have been used. This was especially the case in block 9, which also yielded window glass and where the overall range of finds was much richer than elsewhere. Individual post-holes rather than wall-trenches were the norm, although they provided exasperatingly difficult to identify in the plough-scarred clays. As a result, it is impossible to say anything very meaningful about the overall dimensions or internal arrangements. The indications are that buildings R6 and R7 may have consisted of two large and one small room (and were probably provided with some glazed windows), but R10, which measured 4.5×5 m, had no obvious internal divisions. It does seem clear, however, that they were largely roofed not with tile, but with thatch: on the evidence of the seeds, giant sword-sedge was most commonly employed, a traditional technique in the Fens (Godwin 1978, 145f.). The contrast between the stone-built complex of block 1, and the cottage-like structures to the east was surely striking, as two of the reconstructions have sought to bring out (Figs 64–5, p. 134).

Despite its planned layout, the settlement at Stonea Grange does not seem to have grown to any size. To the east of the boundary of block 1, occupation extended for only some 120 m before apparently petering away, and it also faded out in the machine-cut trenches to the south. On the west side there were virtually no features while, surprisingly, even the area on the north side of the main road likewise appeared to be a blank. However, 140 m to the north-east of the main *decumanus*, a circular ditched enclosure some 50–60 m across was identified from the air in 1984. It proved to contain a Romano-Celtic temple, set on one side of what is most plausibly regarded as the boundary of the temenos; an off-central position for the cult building is indeed normal in Romano-Celtic sanctuaries (Lewis 1966, 134–5).

Although it was possible only to establish the main features in some exploratory trenches, it would seem to be a building of considerable interest. Raised on a low eminence, the *cella* was almost certainly of masonry construction, surrounded by a timber portico. The use of earthfast wooden columns is most unusual, and only the temple (perhaps of Abandinus) at Godmanchester can be cited as a parallel (Green 1986; Wilson 1980, 25). What is much more remarkable, however, is that there was, if correctly interpreted, a double row of timber columns along the south-west side, creating a form of *pronaos*. This would seem to be a unique feature in such temples. In front was a rectangular area of mortared hardstanding which, although initially interpreted as the floor of another building (Potter 1989b, 165), is better seen as a raised forecourt. This gives a very unusual orientation for the temple, since an easterly position was normally preferred for the entrance (Lewis 1966, 32–3); but this is probably explained by a requirement to face the main settlement.

One cannot of course reconstruct the building in any detail; but the double row of columns in the *pronaos* could well have supported some sort of wooden pediment, lending an appearance that would recall a classical temple. Its raised position is also relevant here, being likewise in a Roman tradition. This is entirely in line with current interpretations of a widespread class of Romano-Celtic temples with frontal extensions to the *cella* and ambulatory, and sometimes steps leading to a podium (Wilson 1975, Horne 1986). Much of the discussion has centred round the 'Grange-des-Dîmes' temple at Avenches in Switzerland (Verzàr 1978). The reconstructions of course vary in detail; but consistent is the presence of a high tower-like *cella*, with a colonnaded facade including a pediment. It may seem audacious to postulate something similar at Stonea, but the pointers are in that direction. Furthermore, there is evidence (see below) that it was provided with a tessellated floor, and that the windows were glazed, all suggesting a building of some pretension.

This apparent combination of classical and 'Romano-Celtic' features seems very much in harmony with the mixture of architectural traditions on the main site. Moreover, the stratified pottery makes it clear that the temple was built and in use only in Phase III, as with the stone-built complex, R1. Its siting so far away would however be

puzzling were it not for the fact that, as noted previously, a sondage through the foundation deposits of the hardstanding in front of the temple yielded evidence of earlier timber structures on an almost identical alignment. They cannot be precisely dated, but there was both Mid–Late Iron Age pottery and Flavian samian (which is otherwise of extraordinary rarity). To infer the existence of an earlier shrine has decided attractions, especially in view of the fact that many Romano-Celtic temples are now known to have had similar origins (Drury 1980; Woodward 1992).

The temple was provided with a link to the main site by a curving gravelled road, which joined with the *decumanus*. Between 3 m and 5 m in width, it may have formed a processional way to what was probably the principal sanctuary of the settlement. That said, the cult building was not particularly large, some 7 × 11.5 m, and falls towards the bottom range of Woodward's size classification (1992, 36). Curiously, it did not yield any votive objects within or around the temple, although there was a pit within the *cella*, conceivably for a sacred bush (Lewis 1966, 44). Admittedly, excavation was very partial and plough damage severe; metal-detecting has also played its part (see pp. 26, 220, 294–6). But the implication is that most cult and votive objects were systematically removed when the building was pulled down in the early third century. Some confirmation of this is provided by the contents of a pit, P10, situated some 28 m to the south of the temple. The pit itself was unusual, being more or less vertically sided, although shafts of this sort do occur in ritual contexts (Wait 1985). It was at least 1.40 m deep, and 1.10–1.40 m in diameter, and within it was a remarkable assemblage of whole or semi-complete pottery vessels, many of them of samian. There were also flagons, amphorae and much animal bone, suggesting that this may have been the service for ceremonial feasting (although with no special emphasis in food terms). In addition, a number of limestone tesserae were found, closely resembling examples found in the 'Crew Yard at Stonea Grange Farm', and presented to Wisbech Museum in 1855; if from the temple this implies that it had a mosaic floor, as was normally the case (Lewis 1966, 34). Sherds of window glass also occurred, suggesting the presence of glazed windows: this is a less common feature (although one should bear in mind the prodigious quantities of window glass from the site as a whole), but is not without parallel (Lewis 1966, 38). Finally, and most strikingly, were several fragments of a pipeclay figurine of a horse; whilst hardly decisive evidence, this does allow for the possibility that Epona was worshipped in the temple. These finds were deposited as a single dump, early in the third century. This action is therefore contemporaneous with the destruction of the temple, reinforcing the notion that the objects were the property of the sanctuary, and were buried when it was deconsecrated. That it also coincides with the demolition of the stone-built complex, R1, on the main site further implies that the two events were

Fig. 250 Gold votive leaf and bronze bust of Minerva from Stonea (scale − leaf 2 : 1, bust 1 : 1).

closely linked; the removal of patronage seems the likeliest explanation.

Objects with religious connotations are a not inconspicuous element of the collection from Stonea Grange, especially amongst the surface finds. Particularly notable are three certain, and two possible bronze busts of Minerva, together with a gold votive plaque, dedicated to the goddess (Figs 113, 250). The plaque can only have come from a temple (Johns in Potter 1981, 101f.). A ring inscribed MER for Mercury and a miniature bronze cockerel are no more than very thin hints that this most popular of deities might have

been venerated, but two model bronze axes are common votive finds on sanctuary sites. There is also a single horse-and-rider brooch, a type that is likewise frequent in religious contexts, as for example at Hockwold on the eastern Fen edge, and which are sometimes regarded as priestly regalia (Gurney 1986, 89). A mother goddess figurine was in addition discovered in a well in block 3.

Apart from the figurine none of these finds has a precise location. However, we know from the late Mr Tony Gregory (whose sources were excellent) that the area around the temple and adjacent ballast pit were especially prolific in finds, not least Iron Age coins, and unless we are to postulate a second sanctuary, it is reasonable to suppose that they derive from the one excavated by ourselves. The high proportion of items associated with Minerva is here of great interest. Bronze figurines of the goddess are not in fact particularly common in Britain; Green (1976, 22–3) cites only 'eighteen or so', and the pages of the journal *Britannia* would suggest that the list has not been significantly extended since then. Stonea's probable five examples very much stand out as a statistic.

Minerva was worshipped in a variety of contexts in Britain, as befits a goddess who was not only one of the Capitoline Triad, but who might also undertake other roles, including being patron of craftsmen and a healer of the sick. Using mainly Green's two catalogues (1976, 1978) we see that, the sanctuary at Bath apart, she is particularly well represented in the major towns (Canterbury, Chichester, Cirencester, Colchester, Silchester, Verulamium and especially London); some minor towns (Godmanchester, Ilchester, Kenchester); in many military contexts (cf. *RIB*); and in a few more rural sanctuaries (Harlow: Henig 1989, 220; Lamyatt Beacon: Leech 1986; Maiden Castle: Green 1986, 200; and Woodeaton: Green 1976, 177–8). She is also found at some industrial sites (Castor; Stibbington; Wakerley: Jackson and Ambrose 1978, 213–15), presumably as patroness of the artisans; and in burial contexts, as at Ospringe (Whiting *et al* 1931, Pl. 55). On the Continent, there is evidence for her in only about 13 Romano-Celtic temples, interestingly occurring once with Epona (Nuit-Saintes-George) and once with a pipeclay horse, perhaps of Epona (Trier, temple P: Horne and King 1980). The association of Minerva and Epona (together with other deities) is also to be found on a inscription from the fort at Auchendavy in Scotland (*RIB* 2177).

This list is not intended to be comprehensive (and leaves aside temple hoards like that from Felmingham Hall: cf. generally Toynbee 1964, 77–82); but it does establish the broad pattern. Evidence for the veneration of Minerva occurs quite frequently in 'official' centres, and in military contexts, but much less commonly in ordinary Romano-Celtic shrines. One must be careful not to read too much into this, given the lack of context for the finds (nor indeed into the possible link with Epona); but it could be unsatisfactory to ignore the possibility that the somewhat classicising temple at Stonea was dedicated principally to Minerva, as one of the State deities of Rome. The implications of this tentatively advanced suggestion will be explored further below.

The material culture in the second century

The assemblage of finds is large, supplemented as it is by a metal-detector collection of some 900 coins and more than 100 objects. Whilst Mr Amps' discoveries are not closely located, they come from the Grange site, and may reasonably

be used to cast light upon the nature of the settlement there. It should be noted, however, that the excavated refuse derives almost entirely from the area outside the block (1) with the stone buildings; some casual losses of military metalwork apart, discussed in the following section, we cannot therefore meaningfully separate it from the finds in the adjoining compound of wooden structures. Moreover, whilst we have not attempted any very sophisticated comparison of the finds from different blocks in the compound (especially the pottery), few obvious variations have emerged. Further research may show that these in fact existed; but that is a task for the future.

There are very few exotic objects in the collection. The items associated with the cult of Minerva, especially the gold plaque, are an exception, as are the gold links from one or more second-century necklaces: the latter might well derive from a burial. Similarly the small bronze lion-head terminal, probably from a fountain jet (cat. no. 104), and the fragment of bronze possibly from a statue (cat. no. 137) are also notable, and are very likely to be associated with the stone buildings. Moreover, the pieces of bronze which derive from vessels (eight certain or probable in the excavated assemblage alone), strike one as a significant component; none was found at Grandford (Potter and Potter 1982), and even at a rich villa like that at Gorhambury, they were relatively rare (Neal *et al* 1990, 131). These may therefore hint at some occupants of higher status, certainly in a Fenland context.

The other bronzes are mostly normal components of a Romano-British site. They include pins, needles, ligulae, tweezers, nail cleaners, cosmetic grinders, spoons, seal box lids, rings, bracelets and a large collection of brooches. Conspicuously lacking are high-quality pieces. There are only five silver rings (out of 27), two of them of the third–fourth centuries, and two silver bracelets (out of 14). The three gemstones are commonplace pieces of craftmanship. Moreover, the mid second century 'Snettisham jeweller', a rather average craftsman working less than 65 km away, does not seem to have found a market for his wares at Stonea. The impression is of some wealth, but of a limited kind.

The ironwork is likewise largely unexceptional. The paucity of agricultural tools is noteworthy (although there are some in wood), as is the relatively high proportion of transport elements. This is consistent with the provision of good communications (both a road and a canal), and very much in harmony with an interpretation which envisages a market role for the site, albeit mainly by individuals of no very elevated status.

More striking is a collection of seven lead weights (certain or possible) with values ranging from *c.* 2 *unciae* to one Roman pound. There is also a lead sealing. Whilst none derives from an excavated context, these must surely testify to commercial transactions. By way of comparison, both Verulamium (Frere 1972, 124) and Gorhambury (Neal *et al* 1990, 130) yielded a mere six, and Colchester (Crummy 1983, 101) only three, lending added significance to the number from Stonea. There is also the attractive interpretation that the wooden tankard stave found in the sump may have been from a *modius*. To this must be added the evidence for coin loss, which by Fenland standards was prolific at Stonea, not least in the second century. By contrast, excavated sites like Hockwold (Salway 1967) and Coldham (Potter 1965) yielded not a single coin, the Golden Lion Inn, Stonea (Potter 1975–6) just one (a surface find), and Norwood, March (Potter 1981) only two, but both of the fourth century. Whilst larger settlements in the central Fens such as Grandford (Potter and Potter 1982) and Flaggrass (Phillips 1970, 221) undoubtedly shared in a coin-using economy in the second century (and later), in its pattern of coin-loss, the Stonea Grange site stands out as exceptional, a further affirmation of its commercial role.

The pottery is here of some interest. Although the bulk derives from the Nene Valley kilns, it nevertheless represents a much more diverse assemblage than is normal on a Fenland site. With a total of about 3000 sherds, samian is quite common. Grandford, for example, yielded fewer than 300 sherds, even though prolific in pottery and a deeply stratified site. However, we should note that the proportion of decorated samian sherds from Stonea amounts only to 10%, a figure well below the 30% recorded for the legionary fortress at Usk, and Insula XIV at Verulamium (Tyers 1993). Moreover, a not insignificant proportion had been mended with lead rivets, like a Hadrianic decorated bowl by Butrio, which must surely have arrived in the baggage of one of the first settlers. The implication may be that supply – or demand – was sporadic.

The inhabitants did nevertheless have some access to Continental colour-coat vessels and, uniquely for the Fenland, to small quantities of black burnished, the ware that so dominates the assemblages from military sites, as well as the central Midlands. They also acquired decorated colour-coat cups, from both the Nene Valley and Colchester, where the emphasis upon phallic motifs is notable, and hints strongly at Romanised tastes (and are totally lacking at Grandford and at most other Fenland sites). Likewise, amphorae with a total of nearly 500 sherds, are a not insignificant component when seen in a Fenland context. As with the rest of the province, oil amphorae from Spain (Dressel 20) comprise the bulk (75%); but there are also wine containers from southern Gaul and Italy and even amphorae from the east Mediterranean. Garum was not imported, but the fish bones from the site remind us that local production would not have been problematic.

Keay and Carreras (pp. 435–40) make the point that the Roman State may have tried to ensure the provision of olive oil for the army and administrative units in the more peripheral provinces. Given that other finds support the idea of a military presence (see below), this might well provide a context for the sherds of amphorae and black-burnished ware. While not especially numerous, their presence does acquire significance when compared with other Fenland and Fen-edge sites. Thus none was identified at Grandford, Norwood or Coldham, and there was only a single Dressel 20 rim at the Golden Lion Inn, Stonea (Potter 1975–6, 41). Similarly, the three sites of Feltwell (a villa), Hockwold (a temple) and Denver (where salt was produced) yielded only 41 sherds of amphorae between them, 31 (somewhat curiously, in view of its nature) from Denver (Gurney 1986). Amphorae are in fact conspicuous by their rarity in the Fens, and black-burnished wares by their absence, as has been long emphasised (Hartley and Hartley 1970; see also Gurney 1991). Even the fact that Stonea represents a comparatively large assemblage does not really alter the picture, since it became obvious at a very early stage in the excavation that amphorae, in particular, were far from uncommon.

The vessel forms are also of interest. Flagons and mortaria are more frequent than on most Fen sites, arguably reflecting Romanised practices of eating and drinking. But most striking is the high proportion of storage vessels, whether in shell-gritted ware (8.79%) or from the Horningsea kilns (7.02%). This is also a feature of the assemblages from Grandford (Potter and Potter 1982, 40), and seemingly of many Fenland sites, especially in Cambridgeshire, although not apparently in Norfolk (Hartley and Hartley 1970, 168; Gurney 1991, 145). That the transport of goods was a significant factor in the local economy would appear to be implicit in these figures.

The study of the glass (Price, pp. 379–409) further reinforces this picture of a community with signs of greater affluence than other second-century settlers in the Fens, but not conspicuous wealth. While there is some good-quality glass, there are no real signs of luxurious elements (although two bath-flasks hint at a building that was not identified). Significantly, bottles amounted to only 17.13%. This is a figure that is markedly lower than other Roman sites such as Verulamium and Carlisle, where between 44% and 53% represents the norm. The conclusion that many fewer of the commodities carried in these bottles were reaching Stonea is in striking harmony with the comparatively low proportion of decorated samian, the modest quantity of amphorae and the rather average quality of the jewellery. Despite the apparent grandeur of the stone buildings, most of the inhabitants of the settlement were in provincial terms far from grand.

A military presence?

There are several pointers towards an army involvement on the site at Stonea Grange during the second century. Most conspicuous are a number of items of metalwork, mainly in bronze, with unmistakable military connections (Pl. XXVb). Amongst them are two belt-buckles (no. 169; iron catalogue no. 1); a belt-plate (no. 119); a belt-stiffener (no. 120); and a possible belt-mount (no. 67). There is also a strap-end (no. 122); a rosette mount (no. 66); and a pelta-shaped mount (no. 122). A hinge-plate (no. 70) is much less certainly military in its associations, as is a possible fragment of a chape (no. 71). But there can be no doubt about a scabbard-slide (no. 65), and there is what may be a pommel (no. 68). There is also a fragment of a possible iron spearhead (no. 2). It may be significant that, four metal-detector finds apart, which cannot be located precisely, the objects derive almost entirely from block 1 or 1a; the adjoining blocks 3 and 4 (where the carefully laid-out wooden buildings and orderly rows of rubbish pits would not be out of place on a military site); and the bottom of the well that served the otherwise more elegantly decorated building, R13. Nor must one forget the leather shoe from the sump, which, as Rhodes (p. 541, no. 2) has shown, was a type supplied to the army in Britain on a very large scale.

The occurrence of military metalwork of second and third century date on civil sites in Britain and elsewhere is not wholly unusual (e.g. Dawson 1990, 10). Bishop (1991) has listed examples from the following towns and 'small towns' in Britain, with the number of pieces in parenthesis: Aldborough (4), Chelmsford (4), Chichester (4), Cirencester (9), Colchester (12), Exeter (2), Scole (3), Silchester (6), Verulamium (7), Wickford (3). Items of this period have also occasionally been identified on villas; Gorhambury (Neal *et al* 1990, 113f.) for example yielded a scabbard-slide and mounts, while Dalton Parlours near York produced four or five military items (Wrathmell and Nicholson 1990, 81). At the latter, however, there is evidence, especially the reported discovery of stamped tiles of the Sixth Legion, to suggest that it was owned by a veteran.

The carrying of arms by civilians was of course prohibited by the *Lex Julia de vi publica* (*Digest* xlviii, 6, 1); weapons could only be used for hunting and self-defence on journeys. Thus the occurrence of objects such as belt-fittings and scabbard-slides should therefore be testimony that army personnel were present on a site (although see Brunt 1975). Moreover, it is generally argued that a sparsity of such items does not necessarily mean that there were only a few soldiers: it was a duty to maintain military gear to a high standard and casual loss can be assumed to have been minimal, and was certainly punished. Most finds of army equipment derive therefore from 'closure deposits', buried at the time of the evacuation of a fort or fortress, or from collections of material that was due for repair or recycling (Bishop 1985; Jackson 1990b, 22). It is a point quite neatly made by deposits of the second-third centuries in a guardchamber at the fort at Watercrook near Kendal. Apart from a large collection of chain mail, associated with smithing deposits and thus evidently being recycled, there were few, if any, items of personal military equipment (although two arrowheads, three calthrops and many other items had been dropped). This is despite the fact that the room had been used

for cooking, and was generally rather squalid in appearance and without proper floors (Potter 1979, 157f.).

Military officers are also attested epigraphically in both major and minor towns: *beneficiarii* at Winchester, Wroxeter, Dorchester and Catterick; a *singularis* at Catterick; and *stratores* at Irchester and Dover (Burnham and Wacher 1990, 33f.). The governor and legates both had a considerable *officium* of civil servants, drawn from army units, as did procurators (Jones 1973, 563). One thousand *singulares* were attached to the governor's retinue, for example, half *pedites* and half *equites*; interestingly, one of the Vindolanda documents records that 46 were on detached duty with Ferox, possibly the legate of the Ninth Legion at York (Bowman and Thomas 1994, 96). Whilst their primary role was to act as bodyguards, it is clear that they could undertake other duties as well (Davies 1976; Speidel 1978). Likewise, *beneficiarii* (60 of whom were attached to the staff of a legionary legate) and *stratores* (equerries) might undertake a variety of responsibilities. *Beneficiarii* in particular seem to have acted as general administrators, police officers and tax collectors, and also carried out surveillance work (Salway 1981, 521f.).

Whether any of these classes of soldier played a part in the creation and administration of the site at Stonea Grange is entirely a matter of conjecture without written evidence. Here the still undeciphered writing tablets (themselves an indication that written records of some sort were kept) may one day provide a clue. However, one is reminded of the highly complex variations in the way that Imperial estates were administered in different parts of the Empire (Crawford 1976), whether by a junior procurator, *conductor* or *vilicus*. But we also hear of *tractatores* and *exactores*, who collected the rents (Jones 1973, 417). The use of *conductores*, who acted as head lessees, was particularly common, and they figure prominently in second-century inscriptions from the African provinces. They were generally in Crawford's phrase, 'substantial citizens'; but they might also be slaves, and were often soldiers, including centurions (Richmond 1945, 25; Jones 1973, 791).

Centurions might also be appointed to administer a *regio*, a geographical area that contained an assortment of communities and political organisations. This was the case in the flat-lands of the Fylde, around the fort at Ribchester, where Sarmatian veterans were settled in the late second century. Two inscriptions (*RIB* 583, 587) show that in the third century it was in the charge of a *centurio legionarius*, who was *prae(positus) n(umeri)* (i.e. commander of the fort garrison), *et regionis* (Richmond 1945, 21). A *centurio regionarius* based at *Luguvalium* (Carlisle) is also known from one of the Vindolanda tablets, and others are attested in Gaul, Noricum, Pannonia and at Antioch in Pisidia (Bowman and Thomas 1983, 110). Neither the duties of such officers, nor the status of the region that they administered, are clearly understood; but the possibility that such an officer, based at Stonea, was responsible for some or all of the Fenland cannot be ignored.

An appointment of this sort would certainly be consistent with the relatively unromanised nature of the area, where indigenous government of what was clearly a large population can at best have been at a rudimentary level.

The economy in Phase III

The wealth of environmental data shows that the settlement was surrounded by damp meadows, with patches of woodland and some hedgerows. There were some areas of bare ground, but the cumulative effect of studies of the seeds, pollen, animal bones and molluscs is to rule out a cultivated landscape. There will, however, have been no shortage of grazing, albeit somewhat ill-drained, and a picture of fields divided up by ditches and hedges is probably not far from the truth. This is consistent with earlier conclusions (Salway 1970, 13f.; Potter 1981, 127f.), which interpreted the evidence of the droveroads and paddocks, so conspicuous on the aerial photographs, as evidence of large-scale stock-breeding.

Cereal cultivation did take place in the environs of the site at some periods in its history, notably in Phases I and II, when quite large quantities of grain and chaff found their way into pits. However, the densities of wheat (mainly spelt) and barley in the deposits of Phase III are such as to imply very little production, and comparatively little import of these crops. Agricultural tools are similarly rare amongst the ironwork (although some wooden tools were found, including a hayrake and a pitchfork). Even millstones, with a total of only 23 for all phases, seem extraordinarily rare for a Fenland site, especially given the size of the excavation. However, a sufficient number of flax seeds (for oil or linen) were found to suggest that this may have been of some importance, while Celtic beans, peas, lentils and figs are also attested. The lentils and figs are of particular interest since they normally occur in urban or military contexts, another component in the many strands of evidence pointing to the presence of some individuals of higher (and perhaps military) status.

If the testimony of the seeds is decisive in rejecting the notion that Stonea might have been a centre for the production, or collection, of grain, then the animal bones tell a rather different story. As on virtually every Fenland site (Estover – see pp. 49–60 – is an exception), sheep are numerically predominant amongst the three main domesticated species, amounting to between 48 and 51% in Phase III. Cattle total between 34% and 40%, while pig comprise some 12–15%. Stallibrass (pp. 591–4), following King (1984), argues for a relatively unromanised diet, although her figures would allow for a higher-status element amongst the population. Pork and beef were very much favoured dishes in the Roman diet, as both the literary sources and the archaeological assemblages clearly demonstrate (e.g. Davies 1971; Grant 1989, 142). Certainly there are

sufficient bones of both to provide for those who lived in the stone-built complex, although there is no spatial justification for this possibility. Similarly, there are the bones of some horses, which might relate to such individuals as much as for transport or traction; yet, at only 1% of the sample, the implication must be that very few people were mounted, as indeed the dearth of harness equipment also implies.

However, the most telling statistic is that the great majority of the sheep were slaughtered as lambs and, on the evidence of the bones left at the site (particularly the heads and feet), exported as carcasses or joints. In the absence of significant pointers towards arable cultivation, or other artisan activity, this would seem to emerge as the principal economic role of the settlement. Some leather-working is attested by offcuts in the sump, and a single crucible is a slight sign that metal objects may have been made, or repaired: but the scale of these industries appears to have been minor.

The export of meat (and presumably fleeces and perhaps hides) makes some sense. The region is after all especially noted for the scale of the salt-production, not least on the margins of the 'island' of Stonea itself (Hall 1992, 71), and it was of course the main food preservative used in antiquity. Indeed, its importance is such that it features three or four times on the Vindolanda tablets (Bowman and Thomas 1994, 147), and two sites in Britain, probably Droitwich and Middlewich, were named *Salinae* (Rivet and Smith 1979, 451). The significance of the Fens as a production centre for salt is well brought out by the maps of Jones and Mattingly (1990, 226, 227), and thoroughly confirmed by the results of the Fenland survey (Hall and Coles 1994, 115f.).

It has to be said that no briquetage salt containers were found at Stonea Grange, so that it must have been transported in some different way. Moreover, no area of the site could be identified as specifically for butchery or processing the meat. Some of the pits did have a somewhat tank-like appearance, especially in the south part of block 9; but the probability is that these activities all took place above ground, and have left no trace in the archaeological record.

This picture of a centre exporting joints of lamb is very contrary to models of the Fenland economy developed previously (Potter 1981). These tended to envisage the region as primarily a wool-producing area, although this inference was really one based on animal-bone studies from Grandford (Stallibrass 1982), Hockwold (Cram 1967) and the Golden Lion Inn, Stonea (Barker 1975–6). Wool may indeed have been processed at Stonea Grange (and here we should note Greep's comment, p. 525, that the bone work contains an above average element of weaving equipment); but sheep-rearing was not geared to it. Local environments may here have been a significant factor. Stallibrass, p. 591, makes the interesting point that liver fluke, while generally detrimental to sheep, can help to fatten young lambs. The study of the molluscs (French, p. 653) does indeed show that liver fluke was present in the environs of Stonea Grange, a correlation which may be significant. Halstead (1985) has likewise concluded that sheep were slaughtered early at the Fen-edge site of Maxey. He suggests that a shortage of winter pasture may have been a factor; but the export of carcas-ses would also be a possibility, and would help to account for the few 'luxury' items on an otherwise very low-status settlement.

One can only speculate as to the destination of these carcasses. They were presumably sent over a reasonably long distance, since it was normally more expedient to drive animals on the hoof to market. However, they would not appear to have been destined for military sites, if the supposed dietary preferences of soldiers is any guide. Lamb or mutton do not figure at all in the Vindolanda accounts, although sheep bones are represented in the archaeological deposits there (Bowman and Thomas 1994, 160). Yet one should probably not be dogmatic about this. The figures set out by King (1984, 203, 206) for the occurrence of sheep/goat on both British and Continental military sites do show a consistent presence, and long-distance supply cannot be entirely excluded. Indeed, Jones (1973, 845) is categorical on the point: 'salt meat was conveyed considerable distances by the government for the use of the troops'.

Sites where there is osteological evidence for the trading of meat remain, however, few. An exception is Baldock where Chaplin and McCormick (1986, 412) conclude that there was quite substantial export, not least of lamb carcasses. Like Stonea, Baldock is a somewhat curious site, where one or more temples appear to provide the focus for a series of ditched enclosures, covering some 30 ha. The domestic buildings, where they survive, are generally modest, and 'luxury' items such as amphorae conspicuously rare in post-Conquest contexts (Stead and Rigby 1986, 235). The burials attest a not unwealthy element in the population, as do some of the finds; but the presence of a good many artisans, perhaps *coloni*, would not be an inconsistent reading of the evidence.

The nature of the second-century settlement

That the settlement was rather grandly conceived seems not in doubt. The intention was apparently to provide it with a lavish piece of 'display architecture' as its centre-piece, quite possibly modelled on buildings in or around Rome itself. As such, the whole venture smacks of officialdom rather than a private initiative, and leads quite naturally to its identification as an administrative and market centre on Imperially-owned land.

Some are sceptical that the Fens were, at any rate in part, Crown property (Millett 1990, 120ff.). The doubts largely hinge upon the absence of any centuriation of the landscape. Yet, as was stressed earlier, centuriation is nowhere

properly attested as late as the second century AD, and in any case would hardly have been appropriate in a region seamed with myriad watercourses (Frederiksen 1959; Salway 1970, 11), and largely devoted to stock-rearing. This was a very different terrain from the flat-lands of the Tavoliere of Apulia, or the rolling countryside of Tunisia, where the requirement was for neatly laid-out olive groves and vineyards. Indeed, the canals and straight-line roads seem more than sufficient evidence for State intervention in the region. Land surveying of this sort was a highly skilled business, (Dilke 1971), and emphatically Roman in design and purpose. Moreover, *mensores* were in short supply, as a letter of Pliny the Younger (x, 17B) shows. The straight-line roads in the Fens could well mark the beginnings of a system of *limitatio*, which was then allowed to develop in a piecemeal way, with tenants providing a percentage of their produce: this, as Salway (1970, 11) has underlined, was very much a feature of the period.

Salt was often, as has been frequently pointed out, a state monopoly (as it was in Ptolemaic Egypt, although usually farmed out to contractors: Jones 1973, 158). According to Livy (1, 33, 9), the salt beds of Ostia were the reason for founding the colony there, and major resources like this are likely always to have been closely regulated. Thus the salt pans of the Dalmatian coast were under the control of *tribuni maritimi*, even in Gothic times (Cassiodorus, *Variae* 12, 24), while two Vespasianic inscriptions (*CIL* xi, 390, 391) from Rimini were erected by the *salinatores civitatis Menapiorum* and *Morinorum*. These civic salt-workers of the Belgian coast were making dedications to the legionary centurion L. Lepidius Proculus, who presumably supervised their work. We also hear of a *conductor pascui et salinarum* in Dacia, who was probably operating as an Imperial lessee (Rostovtzeff 1957, 689). While business men might also own salt-works (*CIL* iii, 1209), the level of state involvement is significant.

In Britain, as we have seen two places were known as *Salinae*, probably Middlewich and Droitwich. There was also production in many other areas (Jones and Mattingly 1990, 224f.), but most intensively in Essex and the Fens. Birley (1953, 88–90, 94–6) has adduced evidence to show that there were state-owned salt-works in the province, and it is entirely reasonable to number the Fenland industry amongst them (*pace* Millett 1990, 121). It is now quite apparent that the scale was very considerable (Hall and Coles 1994, 115f.). The salterns at Norwood, March, for example, covered an area of about 75 m square (Potter 1981, 104f.), with densely intercutting pits filled with enormous quantities of briquetage. It is more than likely that peat was used as fuel, as it was in medieval Lincolnshire (Hallam 1970, 87), and Silvester (1991, 104) has provided a dramatic illustration of Roman silt-filled turbaries, bordering the Fen Causeway in the Upwell area. Hallam (1970, 85) had also tentatively identified the same phenomenon in Lincolnshire. Here is surely evidence of a level of production on an industrial scale, a further hint of state ownership.

One further point should be added. Part of the Fens, especially in the Stonea–March area, clearly fell into Icenian territory, as the coins make clear. We should not therefore forget that Prasutagus in his will made Nero a co-heir. 'The Icenian chiefs were deprived of their hereditary estates as if the Romans had been given the whole country' observes Tacitus (*Annals* xiv, 30). We might legitimately speculate whether Stonea, where there are virtually no finds of the period between the reigns of Nero and Hadrian, might have been amongst the estates added to the *res privata*. At the very least, it provides a plausible context for Imperial acquisition.

The status of the settlement at Stonea Grange is naturally important to this debate. In an earlier paper (Potter 1989b, 168), it was suggested that the original intention may have been to create a settlement of the type known as a *forum*. Common foundations in Republican Italy (Ruoff-Väänänen 1978), they were intended as market and administrative centres, as is recorded on an inscription (*CIL* x, 6950) from *Forum Popillii*, on the road from Capua to Reggio Calabria; 'I made the road…set up bridges…here I made a market-place and public buildings'. Sherwin-White (1973, 75), describes them as a 'rudimentary' form of municipality, 'although they might have *magistri* and even a local council'. Interestingly, a foundation of this sort lay in the Fenland of Holland, at Arentsburg (Bogaers 1964, 1972). Formerly the capital of the *civitas Cananefatum*, it was granted the *ius nundinarum* by Hadrian, and became known as *Forum Hadriani*. The plan of the settlement was however most unusual, with a fort-like shape, buildings that resemble barracks and no conventional civic centre; the army may well have been involved in its layout.

The contemporaneity of the Hadrianic development of both Arentsburg and Stonea is rather striking, as is their origin as tribal centres. Likewise, the suspected military involvement at both sites sounds a further chord in common. In Britain, indeed, there is some reason to suppose that *Venta* foundations (like *Venta Icenorum*) were the counterpart to *Forum* settlements elsewhere, both probably meaning 'market-place' (Rivet and Smith 1979, 263–4). Might, we must ask, the original intention have been to create a *Venta* settlement at Stonea? Civic centres certainly existed on Imperial estates in North Africa (Kehoe 1988, 202f.), and fulfilled a role both as foci for civic loyalty of the *coloni* and as places for commerce. In the plains around Sétif (*Sitifis* in Numidia), for example, existing agricultural communities were combined into Imperial estates under Hadrian. There grew up 'quasi-municipal institutions' (Kehoe 1988, 207), with both functional buildings such as *tabernae*, and also structures like arches and colonnades (often paid for by the *coloni*: e.g. *CIL* viii 587, 588, 11731). Such places could also develop on private estates, as at

Casae, in Africa, whose inhabitants sought permission from the Senate to establish a market for the *saltus Beguensis* (*CIL* viii, 11451 = 23246). But they were founded mainly on Imperially-owned land, under the administration of the procurator's staff.

To seek analogies from other provinces is a process requiring very great care; but the comparison between our archaeological reconstruction of the nature of the site at Stonea Grange and, in particular, the North African evidence is too striking to ignore. If we have interpreted matters aright, Stonea was under the supervision of military staff, producing goods, especially salt-meat, perhaps for the army and other state personnel. There was a market in front of a prestigious stone building (where a hall might have served as a place, amongst other things, to settle legal disputes); and a temple of Minerva, designed in a way that reflects Classical traditions – especially a *pronaos* and an elevated position – but constructed over an earlier shrine. Here was a religious centre intended to promote a sense of *Romanitas*, as was clearly the case with the temples at Ribchester, likewise the centre of an unromanised region (Richmond 1945). However bungled in practice, the concept behind the foundation of the settlement at Stonea was in essence a familiar one, attested in other provinces, not least in Hadrianic times. That it was ultimately unsuccessful is a comment upon a blueprint that was at best ambitious, an equally familiar feature of the age.

The demise of the second-century settlement

The evidence is explicit that in the early third century, *c.* AD 220, the stone complex R1 was thoroughly demolished, as was the temple. It is probable that this was preceded by a phase of disuse, since it is the overall impression from study of the finds that there was a fall-away in quantity in the later second century. Moreover, some buildings such as R10 may have been abandoned prior to this date. However, all the pointers are that the decision to pull down the 'official' buildings was taken in the Severan period. Interestingly, it would appear that the stores were systematically emptied, since some 40 whole but slightly damaged or worn pots were thrown away, mainly into the boundary ditch, 9, along the east side of the principal block 1. This very much echoes military practice.

We can, of course, only conjecture about the reasons behind this. It is quite clear that there were problems with the water-table, and there was increasing resort to the use of drainage ditches during the second century. Likewise, some of the pits contained flood silts, up to 10 cm in thickness, and the molluscan evidence is for increasing dampness. However, there were no signs of a general flood horizon across the site, and we are in no position to infer a single catastrophic event, of the sort experienced in 1947 and 1953 (cf. Phillips 1970, Pls XVIII, XX).

The Severan era was of course a time of significant organisational changes (Salway 1970, 16), not least on Imperial estates (Crawford 1976, 53). These could well provide a context for the shutting down of the 'official' component of a place which was very far from being a success. By contrast, Durobrivae on the western Fen edge was by way of being something of a boom town, and around AD 250, an enormous complex was built at nearby Castor, which has all the appearance of officialdom (Mackreth 1984). Similarly, at Godmanchester, a basilica constructed in the early third century may have been connected with tax-collection or the like (Green 1975; Burnham and Wacher 1990, 127). There are hints here that whatever role had originally been envisaged for the site at Stonea may have devolved upon these much more flourishing Fen-edge towns. When taken in conjunction with Stonea's location, remote from lines of communications and set in a melancholy landscape, especially in winter, then the reasons for abandoning the administrative centre and 'official' temple become much more understandable.

They are coupled, indeed, with what appears to be a general fall in the scale of settlement in the Fens, very likely connected with problems of flooding (Hallam 1970, 58; Salway 1970, 14). About one fifth of the sites founded on the silts in the Hadrianic period were abandoned by the end of the century, as was the enormous complex at Hockwold, where waterlogging became severe (Salway 1967). Inadequate maintenance of drainage systems was surely a major factor. As with Stonea itself, one has the feeling that, after heavy initial investment in the region in the form of roads, canals and possibly some attempt at *limitatio*, then interest lapsed. Perhaps it was expected that individual or corporate munificence, of the sort attested, as we have seen, on Imperial estates in Africa, would provide for these tasks of upkeep: this after all was the prevalent ethos of the time. If so, such expectations were optimistic. Excavated second-century Fenland sites have yielded few signs of prosperity, especially coins, and a sense of *Romanitas* must have been wafer-thin. At the end of the day, a grand scheme, perhaps even envisaged by Hadrian himself, did not really work. The demolition gangs who were employed at Stonea around AD 220 are a sure proof of this.

The later Roman period

There is no third century 'gap' of a sort much discussed in the context of the Fens (e.g. Salway 1970, 15), at Stonea Grange. While a significant number of the buildings appear to have been abandoned, the pottery and coins leave no doubt that a proportion of the population remained after the destruction of the 'official' complex. Moreover, the study of the animal bones indicates that the preparation of joints of salt-meat, especially lamb, continued to be an important industry throughout the third and fourth centuries. This, as

will be seen, probably remained under official control. Nevertheless, there was a considerable drop in the quality of life. None of the amphorae postdate the Severan period, nor do any of the glass vessels. Likewise, there is very little East Gaulish samian. All the indications are that, once the 'official' complex had been demolished (and turned into what must have been a stagnant pool), the status of the settlement dwindled into relative insignificance.

This would appear to have been the case throughout the third century. There are ill-recorded hoards of the period, notably about 2000 bronze coins, from Gallienus to the Tetrici, perhaps found near the railway; and also one or more hoards of coins, again of Gallienus, discovered with a silver vase (Phillips 1970, 218–19, with references). There is in addition a small hoard of 25 bronze coins, similarly of Gallienus–Tetricus II, which may have been found at Stonea Camp (Shotter, pp. 35–6). In the same period, the site at the Golden Lion Inn, which lies at about 2.5 m AOD on the east side of the Stonea 'island', was evacuated: flood-silts in the ditches, overlain by peat, point to the probable cause (Potter 1975–6). Likewise, there were deposits of silt over buildings R11 and R12 in block 9 at Stonea Grange; perhaps of late third century date, they too may indicate an episode of alluviation.

This is entirely consistent with a wealth of evidence from the central and southern Fenland which shows that the region suffered severely from flooding in the course of the third century. The silt-filled turbaries along the Fen Causeway east of March are but one, albeit dramatic, affirmation of this, even though close dating evidence for this is lacking (Silvester 1991, 114). These may have been deposits of marine origin, whereas elsewhere the flooding was probably freshwater (Salway 1970, 14f.; Potter 1981, 132). But the causes, mechanics and chronology of what seems to have been an environmental calamity remain little understood. Failure to maintain drainage systems has already been alluded to as a likely factor in the flooding of the later second century; but other elements such as a climatic deterioration may have come into play in the course of the third century.

Whatever the truth of that, the early fourth century would appear to mark an upturn in the fortunes of the settlement at Stonea Grange (and in the central Fens generally). The molluscs in particular suggest that the environment became drier, and there are signs that major building work was initiated. The great hole left by the gangs who demolished the tower was systematically filled in (including much building rubble), and a stone structure laid out over it. Modern ploughing had alas obliterated most traces of it, and we can say nothing of the plan; but its very existence is important. Iron T-shaped clamps suggest that, if they are not residual, the building could have been provided with a hypocaust, and there was also window glass. To the south were mortar floors, which may have been part of the same structure. Here was evidently an edifice of some pretensions in a

Fenland context, and one is reminded that at Grandford, too, there were stone structures, window glass and box-tile in the late Roman period (Potter and Potter 1982). Similarly, the large settlement at Flaggrass has yielded surface finds of ragstone, and at Honey Hill excavation in 1924 suggested the presence of relatively substantial buildings (Phillips 1970, 216). Most recently, an aisled barn-like structure with stone footings, and also of later Roman date, has been uncovered at the large site at Langwood Hill, Chatteris (Taylor and Evans 1993, 169). A generally more prosperous period for the larger settlements may perhaps be inferred, matching that so well attested for Romano-British villas.

That 40% of the coins in the surface collection from Stonea Grange are fourth-century issues certainly supports this view. However, coins of this date from the excavated area amount to only 8% of the sample (although this is a figure surely distorted by the raids of metal-detectorists), and there are other indications that settlement was not on the scale of before. Parts of the former piazza were undoubtedly built over with timber enclosures, and at least one wooden structure. There was also activity in block 2, preceded by a levelling of some pits and wells with yellow clay. But the overall distribution of features is relatively sparse. Very few pits were dug, and the traces of other buildings were at best exiguous. Likewise, the quantity of finds shows a sharp fall. The total weight of pottery, for example, is in Phase IV just one third of that found in Phase III contexts. This may in part reflect the destructive impact of modern ploughing, which has erased virtually all of the stratigraphy; by contrast, the site at Grandford, which was excavated before any modern agricultural intervention, revealed deposits up to 1.5 m in depth. Given that ploughing began there in 1967, one fancies that, nearly thirty years on, many of the later Roman features will have been obliterated. It is a question that needs to be examined by renewed investigation.

This aspect apart, Grandford and Stonea Grange afford other interesting comparisons. At both sites, pits were in fact conspicuously rare in the third and fourth centuries, perhaps supporting the inference that deductions about the size of the late-Roman settlement at Stonea Grange may be misleading. Although pits and wells were levelled up with refuse at this time, the implication is that refuse may have been disposed of in an alternative way. Likewise, a notable feature of the two settlements is the appearance of baked-clay ovens, located around the buildings. While of somewhat different design (cf. Potter and Potter 1982, 21), and of undetermined purpose, they must reflect some significant reorientation of activity. This may have been to do with the processing of crops, for one is reminded that the so-called corn-drying ovens are predominantly a late-Roman phenomenon, perhaps linked to other changes in agricultural strategies (Jones 1989). Indeed, the study of the seeds from Stonea (van der Veen, pp. 613–39) suggests there was now some growing of crops, especially spelt wheat and barley,

albeit at a subsistence level. When taken together with some indications of iron-working, there may be evidence here that the economic basis of the settlement was somewhat expanded from that of the second century. Nevertheless, the contrast between Grandford, always a wool-producing place, and Stonea Grange, where the sheep continued to be slaughtered young to produce joints for export, should not be forgotten. Moreover, the virtual absence of bread wheat (*Triticum aestivum*) at Stonea, a sign of intensive cereal farming (Jones 1989, 132), is a valuable indicator that the main thrust of the agricultural regime remained.

This in turn raises the question of the status of the settlement at Stonea Grange in the third and fourth centuries. The demise of the 'official' buildings might be taken as testimony that it had no longer a part to play in the broader economic affairs of the province. Some of the artifacts leave a contrary impression. One of the most notable 'small finds' from the excavation was an early silver-gilt crossbow brooch (no. 17), dating *c*. AD 200–50. It acquires real significance however when compared with the surface collection. This includes no fewer than seven brooches of the 'divided bow/crossbow' type, ranging in date from the earlier part of the third century to the late fourth century. Two are of gilt-bronze, and were likely to have been owned by individuals of higher rank (Clarke 1979, 263).

Crossbow brooches are not particularly common finds (Hull 1968: 76; Hattatt 1989, 202), lending some significance to the relatively large size of the collection from Stonea (although they do represent a chronological spread over the third and fourth centuries). Moreover, it is clear from the evidence of reliefs, mosaics and the like that they were worn by military and official personnel, although to dub them as insignia exclusive to these classes would be to go too far (Clarke 1979, 262–3). Nevertheless, given the inferred presence of military staff at the site in the second century, it is reasonable to suggest that the crossbow brooches are an indication of a continued official element in the population of the later Roman period. This is supported by the presence of two bronzes from a *cingulum*, a belt fitting and a belt buckle plate (cat. 125, 126). Datable to the mid-late fourth century, these also commonly have military associations, the type IIA buckle, to which class our example belongs, being a British form (Clarke 1979, 289–91).

The overall conclusion must be, therefore, that in its essentials the role of the settlement at Stonea Grange did not greatly change in the post-second century period. The scale of the operation may have dropped (and the building work of *c*. AD 300 could have been an attempt to reverse this), and there was unquestionably a fall in the quality of life. But the archaeological evidence is best read as demonstrating an unbroken sequence of activity down to the last years of the Roman administration of Britain, the 'official' element in the population apparently remaining throughout this time. This is supported by the coins which, while not post-dating the period AD 364–78 in the excavated assemblage, include in the surface collection seven of the period AD 378–88 and six which are post AD 388. The worn state of these issues is a clear indicator that they are unlikely to have been lost before the first decade of the fifth century.

THE ANGLO-SAXON PERIOD AT STONEA GRANGE

Given the apparent paucity of early Anglo-Saxon occupation in the Fens, especially in the southern part, the discovery in 1981 of buildings and pottery of this period at Stonea Grange came as something of a surprise. Although only broadly datable to between *c.* AD 400 and 650, they represent the first excavated evidence for an early Anglo-Saxon community within the region. Indeed, with the marked exception of the silt-lands of southern Lincolnshire (Lane 1992), the recent programme of field survey supports this impression of a scarcity of habitation (Hall and Coles 1994, 122f). Silvester (1988, 156f.), for example, located just one early Anglo-Saxon site in the Norfolk marshlands, although Middle Saxon pottery was abundant. Some casual finds are known (summarised by Welch, pp. 235–8), and a sixth-century cemetery has recently been excavated at Haddenham (Robinson and Duhig 1992); but the archaeological testimony is for a thinly settled landscape in the fens of Cambridgeshire and Norfolk at this time.

It should, nevertheless, be emphasised that many early Anglo-Saxon sites yield little in the way of pottery, especially if there are no *Grubenhäuser*. Stonea itself is a case in point, the assemblage being of very modest size, and the same is true of the clearly important and extensive settlement at Cowdery's Down, Hampshire (Millett 1983). That Mucking (Essex), occupied from the first half of the fifth century, should by contrast yield prolific quantities of finds is almost entirely due to the presence of more than 200 *Grubenhäuser*, many of them filled with refuse (Hamerow 1993). We must be careful therefore not to assume that an apparent dearth of early Anglo-Saxon pottery from the southern Fens means an absence of habitation sites.

Indeed, there is no real evidence to show that there was any significant environmental deterioration either at Stonea or in the southern Fens in the fifth and sixth centuries. Rather the pointers are towards the contrary. Both the molluscs and the pollen from Stonea can be interpreted as indicating a somewhat drier phase in this period, a conclusion that is endorsed by the complete lack of new drainage ditches. This is a remarkable feature in a Fenland context, although advantage was taken of the higher elevation afforded by the main Roman road, on which three of the four buildings were sited.

The structures add little to our understanding of early Anglo-Saxon architecture. This is principally because the post-holes, where they could be identified, did not readily lend themselves to a clear interpretation of the ground plan, a matter compounded by a significant degree of post replacement. The linear arrangement of the buildings is nevertheless consistent with Anglo-Saxon practice, and all were evidently rectangular, with maximum dimensions of *c.* 10.5 × 4.5 m. Numerically, buildings with a ground plan of less than 50 m² predominate on many sites (James *et al* 1984, 188) and, while larger structures are to be expected, with so small a sample from Stonea, it is not surprising that they were not found. The successive fences around S1 are, however, of interest, and could indicate the residence of a family of higher status.

The four pits that are likely to belong to this period – three of them containing more or less complete animal skeletons, two of pigs (Pl. XX) and one of a dog – all lie at some distance from the buildings. There is likewise a scatter of pottery across large parts of the main excavated area, mainly deriving from the top fills of Romano-British features. The import of this is wholly lost, unless there were ephemeral structures in this area which have been totally erased. One of the pits (3) was however extremely substantial, measuring 5.3 × 2.95 m. and with a depth of 0.95 m. It had been dug into the elevated ground where the former stone building, R1, had stood, and its dimensions and sub-rectangular shape are suggestive of a *Grubenhaus*. If so, no post-holes were identified, and no proper floor was found, making the identification tentative, if not dubious.

The plant remains, although numerically small, indicate some cultivation, especially of spelt wheat and barley, as in the Romano-British period. The use of spelt is interesting in that it is paralleled at other early Anglo-Saxon sites in East Anglia, especially West Stow and Mucking (Murphy 1985; van der Veen 1993, 81); the change over to bread wheat in this region would seem to have taken place after about AD 700. Similarly, the animal bones indicate that the raising of sheep for meat (rather than wool) continued to be the principal activity. No longer, however, was a surplus being generated for export; this was essentially a subsistence economy. Two bone pin-beaters and a comb may be pointers that there was some weaving of sheep wool, but this too must have been on a small scale, if the animal bones are any guide.

We must now address the problematic questions of the character and chronology of the site. Whether the buildings were constructed and occupied at the same time is a matter on which the archaeological evidence is largely mute. The variable degree of post-replacement might be an argument for the existence of sub-phases within the early Anglo-Saxon period, with some buildings being reconstructed (especially S1) and others going out of use; but the preservation of the structures is such as to exclude any certainty. It is moreover more than likely that other buildings lie outside the excavated area, making any inferences concerning the nature of the settlement a matter of guesswork. In assessing this, we must recall Russel's conclusion (p. 657) that the scarcity of pottery must reflect a low level of activity. Yet this should not go unchallenged. His demonstration that the clays used for the vessels are unlikely to be local is here of relevance: the implication, that they were imported, may indicate that access to wider markets was sporadic, and that resort may have been made to utensils fashioned of wood or leather. The geographical isolation of Stonea, where even the main Roman road was put out of commission, could well be a significant factor.

This in turn raises the currently topical question (e.g. Higham 1992) of the ethnicity of the people who lived at Stonea Grange in the early Anglo-Saxon period. It is an extremely striking feature of the top fills of some of the Romano-British pits, ditches and wells that they incorporated Anglo-Saxon sherds, but showed no stratigraphical interruption (peats and silts) with the late-Roman deposits beneath. Given that the Fenland is a region of rapid sedimentation, the implication is that there was no significant chronological gap – indeed, any gap – between the two. It would seem to follow that this was not a replacement but a continuity of population, presumably the direct descendants of the former Romano-Britons, now existing somewhat marginally within a new culture. Certainly, the buildings do not appear very different from the wooden structures of before (cf. James et al 1984), and it is easy to envisage how S2 could have been the successor to R4, and S3 to R5b. With the breakdown of Roman authority, evoked by the crossbow brooches and *cingulum* fittings, a new order came into being: the buildings constructed on the main Roman road, effectively putting it out of use, are a tangible sign of this. Gradually, there was some integration into the developing Anglo-Saxon markets; but the people at Stonea, and doubtless at some other Fen 'islands' too, would seem to have been essentially indigenous, a point reinforced by the continuity of the agricultural regime (the lack of a surplus apart). Eventually, we might surmise, they emerge in history as the *Gyrwe*, 'fen-people' of Bede's *Historia Ecclesiastica* (cf. Welch, pp. 235–8), to be absorbed in the seventh century into an Anglo-Saxon Kingdom, whether East Anglian or Mercian.

Whatever the truth of this speculative sketch, a complete absence of Ipswich ware (otherwise common in many parts of the Fens: e.g. Silvester 1988, 158) indicates that occupation at the Grange site had come to an end by the mid seventh century. However, there must have been some settlement in the middle and later Saxon periods at Stonea. The excavation yielded a bronze pin of mid seventh–ninth century date, and the surface collection a ninth century strap-end. There are also reports (T. Gregory, personal communication) of the discovery of a coin of the obscure mid eighth century East Anglian king, Beonna, and of a late-Saxon silver casket mount, with interlace decoration. Most significantly, the excavations revealed that a low mound, some 8–9 m in diameter, had been constructed partly over the

Anglo-Saxon building S1. Cut into it were three post holes, one still retaining part of the wooden post. This yielded a radiocarbon date of 1005 ± 40 BP, which calibrates to between AD 955 and 1045. Whilst the structure remains enigmatic, and there was no associated refuse, this is palpable proof of late-Saxon activity.

The main thrust of these observations is to suggest that Stonea illustrates the phenomenon which has come to be known as the 'Middle Saxon shift' (Hamerow 1993, 96–7). This is a process whereby, for a variety of reasons, the nucleus of a settlement was moved over the course of time. It is a pattern now brilliantly demonstrated at the site of Mucking (Hamerow 1993), and provides an entirely plausible explanation for the sporadic mid–late Anglo-Saxon finds from Stonea. One might indeed offer the conjecture that the centre of this period lay beneath the Grange itself, reflecting a gradual northwards shift over time. Thus the early Anglo-Saxon site lay to the north of the Roman settlement, which itself represents a move in a northerly direction from the main focus of Iron Age activity at Stonea Camp. It is an intriguing aspect of this long-occupied part of the island.

THE MEDIEVAL AND POST-MEDIEVAL PERIODS

Archaeological and historical evidence combine to show that there was no occupation at Stonea Grange in the Middle Ages. It reverted instead to cow pasture, bringing to an end what had been millennia of settlement. However, the testimony of both the documents (Hall, pp. 238–40) which first refer to the Grange in 1600, and the finds, show that it was subsequently reinhabited, probably around the later sixteenth century. The small objects – horse equipment, dress fittings, domestic metal vessels and the like – evoke the beginning of a small Fen community founded a generation or two before the start of the modern age: the era of the draining of the Fens. Occupation was thereafter to be maintained down into the middle years of the present century, focused around a fine farmhouse, alas demolished without proper record in the early 1970s. The contents of a ha-ha, demarcating the farmhouse grounds, lay within the northern part of the main excavation, and yielded a remarkable collection of refuse, mainly eighteenth-century pottery and glass. Interestingly, the animal bones indicate little significant reorientation of earlier agricultural strategies, with sheep remaining predominant: it was probably only in the last 250 years that the landscape began to assume the arable mantle that is so conspicuously its feature of the present day. Studied only in a preliminary way in this volume, the post-medieval finds from Stonea Grange will in time have much to tell us about the life of a pioneering farming community facing, like their myriad predecessors, a world of adversity.

CONCLUSION

It is hard in assembling this interpretative essay to escape the influence of Braudel's *longue durée* (Braudel 1949). Confronted with artefacts which range from the Lower Palaeolithic to post-medieval times, and with a record of settlement that begins with the Neolithic and has hardly ended, it is indeed the longevity of occupation that is so very striking. Whilst we cannot substantiate the idea of continuous settlement in the environs of Stonea Grange and Stonea Camp from Neolithic times (the medieval abandonment is but one proof of this), it was a place that was repeatedly returned to. Moreover, it seems clear that, almost from the first, Stonea was singled out as a centre of especial significance within the landscape. Why this should be so is beyond modern comprehension; but the creation of a cursus, very possibly a henge, Bronze Age barrows, a substantial Late Bronze Age settlement, a large Iron Age enclosure and the most impressive Roman building complex known from the Fens, combine to underline its high status within the region, notwithstanding increasing signs that many Fen 'islands' also had their major foci. Even in the 1950s, monuments like Stonea Camp and the adjacent barrow remained as eloquent statements of a proud past and, prior to the onset of modern agriculture, there will have been so very much more that was visibly striking. The importance of the place must have become cumulatively more obvious as time went on, at any rate down to the late-Roman period.

Whether we should interpret this as manifesting 'the long life of a ritual folk centre', as has been argued for Sutton Hoo (Carver 1986), or as 'attempts by a social elite to legitimise their position through reference to the past', as has been postulated for Yeavering (Bradley 1987b, 1), is a matter of stance. But we should not forget the innate conservatism of the Fenlander, a mentality inculcated, one suspects, by a hostile and isolated environment; nor the visual impact of such monuments, erected in the flattest of settings, but one with the most singular power to fire the imagination (as any Fen person knows). Whatever the vicissitudes brought about by the passage of time, a collective memory surely survived of the ritual and political importance of a relatively small area of land, with an extraordinary palimpsest of features; and this rendered all the more remarkable by the sheer barrenness of the terrain today.

Something of this will have emerged from the pages of this volume; but much more, we can be certain, is still to be found. Not the least will be the cemeteries which could so significantly illuminate the overall picture of the long succession of communities. But that is a challenge of the future. Here, we can only recognise that, however extensive the present work, the interim nature of our conclusions cannot be avoided. The ground of Stonea has already given us much; but many secrets still remain.

BIBLIOGRAPHY

Alderton, A. 1983–4, 'Environmental report', *Fenland Res.* 1, 19–22.

Allason-Jones, L. 1985, 'Bell-shaped studs?' in Bishop, M. C. (ed.), *The Production and Distribution of Roman Military Equipment*, BAR Int. Ser. no. 275, 95–105. Oxford.

Allason-Jones, L. and McKay, B. 1985, *Coventina's Well, a Shrine on Hadrian's Wall*, Chesters.

Allason-Jones, L. and Miket, R. 1984, *The Catalogue of Small Finds from South Shields Roman Fort*, Soc. Antiq. Newcastle upon Tyne Monogr. no. 2.

Allason-Jones, L. and Page, H. 1988, 'New discoveries on Roman brooches', *Archaeol. Aeliana*, 5th ser., 16, 245–9.

Allen, D. 1986, 'The glass vessels', in Zienkiewicz 1986, vol. II, 98–116.

Allen, D. F. 1963, *Sylloge of Coins of the British Isles. The Coins of the Coritani*. London.

Allen, D. F. 1970, 'The coins of the Iceni', *Britannia*, 1, 1–33.

Anderson, A. 1981, 'Some Continental beakers of the 1st and 2nd centuries AD', in Anderson and Anderson 1981, 321–47.

Anderson, A. C. and Anderson, A. S. (eds) 1981, *Roman Pottery Research in Britain and North-West Europe*, BAR Int. Ser. no. 123. Oxford.

Anderson, K. J. and Barrett, J. C. 1992, 'A preliminary examination of the pottery from the Fengate (Power Station) site and the Flag Fen platform', *Antiquity* 66, 502–3.

Apted, M. R., Gilyard-Beer, R. and Saunders, A. D. (eds) 1977, *Ancient Monuments and Their Interpretation, Essays Presented to A. J. Taylor*. Chichester.

Arsdell, R. D. Van *see* Van Arsdell, R. D.

Arthur, P. and Williams, D. F. 1992, 'Campanian wine, Roman Britain and the third century AD', *J. Roman Archaeol.*, 5, 250–60.

Atkins, F. B. 1971, 'Egyptian Blue', in Brodribb, A. C. C., Hands, A. R. and Walker D. R., *Excavations at Shakenoak Farm, near Wilcote, Oxfordshire. Part II*, 56–8. Oxford.

Atkinson, D. 1916, *The Romano-British Site on Lowbury Hill, in Berkshire*. Reading.

Atkinson, D. 1932, 'Three Caistor pottery kilns', *J. Roman Stud.*, 32, 33–46.

Atkinson, D. 1942, *Report on Excavations at Wroxeter (The Roman City of Viroconium) in the County of Salop, 1923–1927*. Oxford.

Austen, P. S. 1991, *Bewcastle and Old Penrith. A Roman Outpost Fort and a Frontier Vicus*, Cumb. & Westmorland Antiq. & Archaeol. Soc. Res. Ser. no. 6. Kendal.

Bailey, J. B. 1915, 'Catalogue of Roman inscribed and sculptured stones, coins, earthenware, etc., discovered in and near the Roman fort at Maryport, and preserved at Netherhall', *Trans. Cumb. & Westmorland Antiq. & Archaeol. Soc.*, new ser. 15, 135–72.

Bamford, H. M. 1982, *Beaker Domestic Sites in the Fen Edge and East Anglia*, East Anglian Archaeol. Rep. no. 16. Gressenhall.

Bang, P. and Dahlstrom, P. 1972, *Animal Tracks and Signs*. London.

Barclay, G. J. and Fairweather, A. D. 1984, 'Rye and ergot in the Scottish later Bronze Age', *Antiquity*, 58, 126.

Barker, G. W. W. 1975–6, 'The animal bones', in Potter 1975–6, 46–8.

Barrett, J. C. 1980, 'The pottery of the later Bronze Age in lowland England', *Proc. Prehist. Soc.* 46, 297–319.

Barrett, J. C. and Bond, D. 1988, 'The pottery' in Bond 1988, 25–37.

Barrett, J. and Bradley, R. (eds) 1980, *Settlement and Society in the British Later Bronze Age*, BAR Br. Ser. no. 83. Oxford.

Bass, W. M. 1987, *Human Osteology. A Laboratory and Field Manual*, Missouri Archaeol. Soc. Spec. Publ. no. 2. Missouri.

Bassett, S. (ed.) 1989, *The Origins of Anglo-Saxon Kingdoms*. Leicester.

Baudoux, J. 1990, *Les Amphores d'Alsace et de Lorraine: Contribution à l'Histoire de l'Économie Provinciales sous l'Empire Romain*, PhD thesis, University of Strasbourg.

Baxter, M. and Cool, H. 1991, 'An approach to quantifying window glass', in C. Lockyear and S. Rahtz (eds), *Computer Applications in Archaeology*, BAR Int. Ser. no. 565, 127–31. Oxford.

Bayley, J. 1988, 'Non-ferrous metal working: continuity and change', in E. A. Slater and J. O. Tate (eds), *Science and Archaeology. Glasgow 1987*, BAR Br. Ser. no. 196, 193–208. Oxford.

Beedham, G. E. 1972, *Identification of the British Mollusca*. Amersham.

Behre, K. E. 1984, 'Zur Geschichte der Bierwuerzen nach Fruchtfunden und schriftlichen Quellen', in van Zeist and Casparie 1984, 115–22.

Beijerinck, W. 1947, *Zadenatlas der Nederlandsche Flora*. Wageningen.

Bell, M. 1977, 'Excavations at Bishopstone', *Sussex Archaeol. Coll.*, 115, 1–299.

Belo, A. R. 1970, 'Algumas palavras sobre a Torre Centum Cellae de Belmonte', *Actas e Memórias do I Congresso Nacional de Arqueologia*, Vol. II, 35–55. Instituto de alta Cultura, Lisboa.

Berggren, G. 1969, *Atlas of Seeds, Part 2: Cyperaceae*. Lund.

Berggren, G. 1981, *Atlas of Seeds, Part 3: Salicaceae – Cruciferae*. Arlov.

Beveridge, E. 1931, 'Excavations of an earth-house at Foshigarry and a fort, Dun Thomaidh in North Uist', *Proc. Soc. Antiq. Scot.*, 65 (1930–1) [1931], 299–356.

Bidwell, P. T. 1985, *The Roman Fort of Vindolanda at Chesterholm, Northumberland*, HBMCE Archaeol. Rep. no. 1. London.

Birch, W. de Gray 1892, *Liber Vitae: Register and Martyrology of New Minster and Hyde Abbey, Winchester*, Hampshire Record Soc. London and Winchester.

Birley, E. 1953, *Roman Britain and the Roman Army*. Kendal.

Birley, E. B. and Charlton, J. 1934, 'Third report on excavations at Housesteads', *Archaeol. Aeliana*, 4th ser., 11, 185–205.

Birley, R. E. 1963, 'Excavation of the Roman fortress at Carpow, Perthshire', *Proc. Soc. Antiq. Scot.*, 96 (1962–3) [1963], 184–207.

Bishop, M. C. 1985, 'The military *fabrica* and the production of arms in the early Principate', in M. C. Bishop (ed.), *The Production and Distribution of Roman Military Equipment*, Proc. Second Roman Military Equipment Research Seminar, BAR Int. Ser. no. 275, 1–42. Oxford.

Bishop, M. C. 1991, 'Soldiers and military equipment in the towns of Roman Britain', in V. A. Maxfield and M. J. Dobson, *Roman Frontier Studies 1989*, 21–7. University of Exeter.

Blake, E. O. 1962, *Liber Eliensis*. London.

Blockley, K. 1985, *Marshfield, Ironmongers Piece, Excavations 1982–3, An Iron Age and Romano-British Settlement in the South Cotswolds*, BAR Br. Ser. no. 141. Oxford.

Blockley, K. 1989, *Prestatyn 1984–5, An Iron Age Farmstead and Romano-British Industrial Settlement in North Wales*, BAR Brit. Ser. no. 210. Oxford.

Boekel, G. van 1987, *Roman Terracotta Figurines and Masks from the Netherlands*. Groningen.

Boesterd, M. H. P. den 1956, *Rijksmuseum G. M. Kam 5, The Bronze Vessels*. Nijmegen.

Bogaers, J. E. 1964, 'Forum Hadriani', *Bonner Jahrbücher*, 164, 45–52.

Böhme, A. 1972, 'Die Fibeln der Kastelle Saalburg und Zugmantel', *Saalburg Jahrbuch*, 29, 5–112.

Bond, D. 1988, *Excavation at the North Ring, Mucking, Essex: A Late Bronze Age Enclosure*, East Anglian Archaeol. Rep. no. 43. Chelmsford.

Boon, G. C. 1966, 'Roman window glass from Wales', *J. Glass Stud.*, 8, 41–5.

Boon, G. C. 1969, 'Belgic and Roman Silchester: the excavations of 1954–8, with an excursus on the early history of Calleva', *Archaeologia*, 102, 1–81.

Boon, G. C. 1974, *Silchester: the Roman Town of Calleva*. Newton Abbot.

Boon, G. C. 1991, '*Tonsor humanus*: razor and toilet-knife in antiquity', *Britannia*, 22, 21–32.

Bordes, F. 1979, *Typologie du Paléolithique Ancien et Moyen*. Paris.

Bourdillon, J. and Coy, J. 1980, 'The animal bones', in P. Holdsworth (ed.), *Excavations at Melbourne Street, Southampton, 1971–76*, CBA Res. Rep. no. 33, 79–121. London.

Bowman, A. K. 1994, *Life and Letters on the Roman Frontier*. London.

Bowman, A. K. and Thomas, J. D. 1983, *Vindolanda: The Latin Writing-Tablets*, Britannia Monogr. Ser. no. 4. London.

Bowman, A. K. and Thomas, J. D. 1994, *The Vindolanda Writing-Tablets*. London.

Boycott, A. E. 1934, 'The habitats of land mollusca in Britain', *J. Ecol.*, 22, 1–38.

Boycott, A. E. 1936, 'The freshwater mollusca in Britain', *J. Anim. Ecol.*, 5, 116–87.

Bradley, R. 1984, *The Social Foundations of Prehistoric Britain*. Harlow.

Bradley, R. 1987a, 'Radiocarbon and the cursus problem', in J. Gowlett and R. Hedges (eds), *Archaeological Results of Accelerator Dating*, Oxf. Univ. Comm. Archaeol. Monogr. 11, 139–41.

Bradley, R. 1987b, 'Time regained: the creation of continuity', *J. Br. Archaeol. Assoc.*, 140, 1–17.

Bradley, R. and Fulford, M. G. 1980, 'Sherd size in the analysis of occupation debris', *Bull. Univ. Lond. Inst. Archaeol.*, 17, 85–94.

Bradley, R., Lobb, S., Richards, J. and Robinson, M. 1980, 'Two Late Bronze Age settlements on the Kennet Gravels: excavations at Aldermaston Wharf and Knight's Farm, Burghfield, Berkshire', *Proc. Prehist. Soc.*, 46, 217–95.

Brailsford, J. W. 1958, *Guide to the Antiquities of Roman Britain*. London.

Brailsford, J. W. 1962, *Hod Hill, Vol. 1, Antiquities from Hod Hill in the Durden Collection*. London.

Branigan, K. 1977, *Gatcombe Roman Villa*, BAR Br. Ser. no. 44. Oxford.

Braudel, F. 1949, *La Méditerranée et le monde méditerranéen à l'époque de Philippe II*. Paris.

Brewer, R. J. 1986, 'The bronze brooches', in Zienkiewicz 1986, 168–72.

Brewster, T. C. M. 1963, *The Excavation of Staple Howe*. Malton.

British Museum 1958, *Guide to the Antiquities of Roman Britain*. London.

Britton, D. 1968, 'The bronzes', in M. Cotton and S. S. Frere (eds), 'Ivinghoe Beacon excavations 1963–5', *Records of Buckinghamshire*, 18, 187–260.

Brodribb, A. C. C., Hands, A. R. and Walker, D. R. 1968, *Excavations at Shakenoak Farm, near Wilcote, Oxfordshire. Part I*. Oxford.

Brodribb, A. C. C., Hands, A. R. and Walker, D. R. 1971, *Excavations at Shakenoak Farm, near Wilcote, Oxfordshire. Part II*. Oxford.

Brodribb, A. C. C., Hands, A. R. and Walker, D. R. 1972, *Excavations at Shakenoak Farm, near Wilcote, Oxfordshire. Part III*. Oxford.

Brodribb, A. C. C., Hands, A. R. and Walker, D. R. 1973, *Excavations at Shakenoak Farm, near Wilcote, Oxfordshire. Part IV*. Oxford.

Brodribb, G. and Cleere, H. 1988, 'The *Classis Britannica* bath-house at Beauport Park, East Sussex', *Britannia*, 19, 217–74.

Brooks, N. 1989, 'The formation of the Mercian kingdom', in Bassett 1989, 159–70.

Brown, N. 1988, 'A Late Bronze Age enclosure at Lofts Farm, Essex', *Proc. Prehist. Soc.*, 54, 249–302.

Brown, N. and Adkins, P. 1988, 'Heybridge, Blackwater Sailing Club', in D. Priddy (ed.), 'The work of the Essex County Council Archaeology Section, 1987', *Essex Archaeol. & Hist.*, 19, 240–59.

Brown, R. A. 1986, 'The Iron Age and Romano-British settlement at Woodcock Hall, Saham Toney, Norfolk', *Britannia*, 17, 1–58.

Brunt, P. A. 1975, 'Did imperial Rome disarm her subjects?', *Phoenix*, 29, 260–70.

Bryant, S., Morris, M. and Walker, J. S. F. 1986, *Roman Manchester, A Frontier Settlement*, The Archaeology of Greater Manchester, Vol. 3. Manchester.

Buchem, H. J. H. van 1941, *De Fibulae van Nijmegen*, Bouwsteenen voor een Geschiedenis van Nijmegen 3. Nijmegen.

Buckland, P. C. and Magilton, J. R. 1986, *The Archaeology of Doncaster, 1, The Roman Civil Settlement*, BAR Br. Ser. no. 148. Oxford.

Bulleid, A. and Gray, H. St G. 1911, *The Glastonbury Lake Village, Vol. I*. Glastonbury.

Bulleid, A. and Gray, H. St G. 1917, *The Glastonbury Lake Village, Vol. II*. Taunton.

Bullinger, H., 1969, *Spätantike Gurtelbeschläge*, Dissertationes Archaeologicae Gandenses, 12. Bruges.

Bullock, P., Murphy, C. P. and Waller, P. J. 1981, *The Preparation of Thin Sections of Soils and Unconsolidated Sediments*. Harpenden.

Bullock, P., Federoff, N., Jongerius, A., Stoops, G. and Tursina, T. 1985, *Handbook for Soil Thin Section Description*. Wolverhampton.

Bunch, B. and Corder, P. 1954, 'A Romano-British pottery kiln at Weston Favell, near Northampton', *Antiq. J.*, 34, 218–24.

Burgess, C. B. 1968, 'The later Bronze Age in the British Isles and North-western France', *Archaeol. J.*, 125, 1–45.

Burnett, A. M. 1986a, 'II: Chatteris, Cambs.: 9 ancient British coins and 14 Roman denarii to AD 61', in Burnett and Bland, 1986, 5–7.

Burnett, A. M. 1986b, III: Scole, Norfolk: 202 Icenian silver and 87 Roman denarii to AD 61', in Burnett and Bland 1986, 7–13.

Burnett, A. M. and Bland, R. F. 1986, *Coin Hoards from Roman Britain. Volume VI*, Br. Mus. Occas. Pap. no. 58. London.

Burnham, B. C. and Wacher, J. 1990, *The 'Small Towns' of Roman Britain*. London.

Bushe-Fox, J. P. 1913, *Excavations on the Site of the Roman Town at Wroxeter, Shropshire, in 1912*. Oxford.

Bushe-Fox, J. P. 1914, *Second Report on the Excavations on the Site of the Roman Town of Wroxeter, Shropshire, 1913*. Oxford.

Bushe-Fox, J. P. 1916, *Third Report on the Excavations on the Site of the Roman Town at Wroxeter, Shropshire, 1914*. Oxford.

Bushe-Fox, J. P. 1926, *First Report on the Excavation of the Roman Fort at Richborough, Kent*. Oxford.

Bushe-Fox, J. P. 1928, *Second Report on the Excavation of the Roman Fort at Richborough, Kent*. Oxford.

Bushe-Fox, J. P. 1932, *Third Report on the Excavations of the Roman Fort at Richborough, Kent*. Oxford.

Bushe-Fox, J. P. 1949, *Fourth Report on the Excavations of the Roman Fort at Richborough, Kent*. Oxford.

Butcher, S. A. 1977, 'Enamels in Roman Britain', in Apted *et al* 1977, 41–70.

Butcher, S. A. 1978, 'A note on two brooches from Chichester', in Down 1978, 288–9.

Calkin, J. B. 1966, *Discovering Prehistoric Bournemouth and Christchurch*. Christchurch.

Cameron, F. 1987, 'Appendix III: The Roman Pottery', in Hall 1987, 68–9.

Carreras, C. 1991, *Transport in Roman Britain: Two Simulation Models in SPANS and PASCAL*, MSc thesis, Southampton University. (In press, Barcelona UP.)

Carreras, C. (forthcoming) *A Spatial and Economic Analysis of Long-Distance Exchange: the Roman Amphora Evidence from Britain*.

Carson, R. A. G. 1971, 'The Willersey, Glos. treasure trove of 4th century Imperial silver coins', *Numismatic Chronicle*, 7th ser., XI, 203–6.

Carson, R. A. G., Hill, P. V. and Kent, J. P. C. (eds) 1960, *Late Roman Bronze Coinage*. London.

Carver, M. 1986, 'Research potential and feasibility', *Bull. Sutton Hoo Res. Comm.*, 4, 33–50.

Casey, P. J. 1974, 'The interpretation of Romano-British site-finds', in P. J. Casey, and R. Reece (eds), *Coins and the Archaeologist*, BAR Br. Ser. no. 4, 37–51. Oxford.

Castagnoli, F. 1958 *Le ricerche sui resti della centuriazione*. Rome.

Chadburn, A. D. B. 1990, 'A hoard of Iron Age silver coins from Fring, Norfolk, and some observations on the Icenian coin series', *Br. Numismatic J.*, 60, 1–12.

Chadburn, A. D. B. 1991a, 'New links between the Icenian coins of Aesv and Saenv', *Celtic Coin Bull.*, 1, 9–14.

Chadburn, A. D. B. 1991b, 'Some observations on the Icenian uninscribed gold series', *Celtic Coin Bull.*, 1, 14–19.

Chadburn, A. D. B. 1992, 'A preliminary analysis of the hoard of Icenian coins from Field Baulk, March, Cambridgeshire', in Mays 1992, 73–83.

Chadburn, A. D. B. and Gurney, D. 1991, 'The Fring coin hoard', *Norfolk Archaeol.*, 41 (2), 218–25.

Chambers, F. M. and Jones, M. K. 1984, 'Antiquity of rye in Britain', *Antiquity*, 58, 219–24.

Champion, T. 1975, 'Britain in the European Iron Age', *Archaeol. Atlantica*, 1, 127–45.

Chaplin, R. E. and McCormick, F. 1986, 'The animal bones', in Stead and Rigby 1986, 396–415.

Charlesworth, D. 1959a, 'Roman glass in Northern Britain', *Archaeol. Aeliana*, 4th ser., 37, 33–58.

Charlesworth, D. 1959b, 'The glass', in C. M. Daniels, 'The Roman bath house at Red House, Beaufront, near Corbridge', *Archaeol. Aeliana*, 4th ser., 37, 164–6.

Charlesworth, D. 1966, 'Roman square bottles', *J. Glass Stud.*, 8, 26–40.

Charlesworth, D. 1972, 'The glass', in Frere 1972, 203–7.

Charlesworth, D. 1974–6, 'The glass', in D. S. Neal, 'Northchurch, Boxmoor and Hemel Hempstead Station: the excavation of three Roman buildings in the Bulborne Valley', *Herts. Archaeol.*, 4, 1–135.

Charlesworth, D. 1976, 'Glass vessels', in A. MacGregor, *Finds from a Roman Sewer System and an Adjacent Building in Church Street*, The Archaeology of York. The Small Finds 17/1, 15–18. York.

Charlesworth, D. 1979, 'Glass (including material from all other Exeter sites excavated between 1971 and 1976', in P. T. Bidwell, *The Legionary Bath-house and Basilica and Forum at Exeter*, Exeter Archaeol. Rep. I, 222–31.

Charlesworth, D. 1981, 'The glass' and 'Glass from the burials', in Partridge 1981, 119 and 268–71.

Charlesworth, D. 1984, 'The glass', in Frere 1984, 145–73.

Charlesworth, D. and Thornton, J. H. 1973, 'Leather found in Mediobogdum, the Roman fort of Hardknott', *Britannia*, 4, 141–52.

Chatwin, C. P. 1961, *East Anglia and Adjoining Areas*, British Regional Geology. London.

Childe, V. G. 1952, 'Bone dart head from Carlisle', 158–9 in R. Hogg, 'The historic crossing of the River Eden at Stanwix...', *Trans. Cumb. & Westmorland Antiq. & Archaeol. Soc.*, 52, 131–59.

Chowne, P., Girling, M. and Greig, J. 1986, 'Excavations of an Iron Age defended enclosure at Tattershall Thorpe, Lincolnshire', *Proc. Prehist. Soc.*, 52, 159–88.

Christison, D. 1901, 'Account of the excavation of the Roman station of Camelon, near Falkirk, Stirlingshire...', *Proc. Soc. Antiq. Scot.*, 35 (1900–1901) [1901], 329–41.

Churchill, D. M. 1970, 'Post-Neolithic to Romano-British sedimentation in the southern Fenlands of Cambridgeshire and Norfolk', in Phillips 1970, 136–46.

Clapham, A. R., Tutin, T. G. and Warburg, E. F. 1962, *Flora of the British Isles*. Cambridge.

Clark, J. G. D. 1938, 'Early man', *Victoria County History: Cambridgeshire*, Vol. 1, 247–303. Oxford.

Clark, J. G. D. and Fell, C. I. 1953, 'The Early Iron Age site at Micklemoor Hill, West Harling, Norfolk, and its pottery', *Proc. Prehist. Soc.*, 19, 1–40.

Clarke, D. L. 1970, *Beaker Pottery of Great Britain and Ireland*. Cambridge.

Clarke, G. 1979, *The Roman Cemetery at Lankhills*. Oxford.

Clarke, R. Rainbird, 1956, 'A hoard of silver coins of the Iceni from Honingham, Norfolk', *Br. Numismatic J.*, 28, 1–10.

Clifford, E. M. 1961, *Bagendon: A Belgic Oppidum, A Record of the Excavations of 1954–56*. Cambridge.

Clough, T. H. McK and Green, B. 1973, 'Gazetteer of Anglo-Saxon cemeteries and burials in East Anglia', in *The Anglo-Saxon Cemeteries of Caistor-by-Norwich and Markshall, Norfolk*, 258–62, map 3. London.

Clutton-Brock, J. 1976, 'The animal resources', in D. M. Wilson (ed.), *The Archaeology of Anglo-Saxon England*, 373–92. London.

Colgrave, B. 1956, *Felix's Life of Saint Guthlac*. Cambridge.

Condamin, J., Formenti, F., Metais, M. O., Michel, M. and Blond, P. 1976, 'The application of gas chromatography to the tracing of oil in the ancient amphora', *Archaeometry*, 18, 195–202.

Cool, H. E. M. 1979, 'A newly found inscription on a pair of silver bracelets from Castlethorpe, Buckinghamshire', *Britannia*, 10, 165–8.

Cool, H. E. M. 1990a, 'Roman metal hair pins from Southern Britain', *Archaeol. J.*, 147, 148–82.

Cool, H. E. M. 1990b, 'The problem of 3rd century drinking vessels in Britain', *Annales du 11ᵉ Congrés de l'Association pour l'Histoire de Verre, 1988*, 167–75.

Cool, H. E. M. and Price, J. 1991, 'The Roman vessel and window glass', in McCarthy 1991, fasc. 2, 165–76.

Cool, H. E. M and Price, J. 1995, *Roman Vessel Glass from Excavations in Colchester 1971–85*, Colchester Archaeol. Rep. 8.

Coombs, D. 1979, 'A Late Bronze Age hoard from Cassiobridge Farm, Watford, Hertfordshire', in C. Burgess and D. Coombs (eds), *Bronze Age Hoards: Some Finds Old and New*, BAR Br. Ser. no. 67, 197–220. Oxford.

Coombs, D. 1991, 'Bronze objects', in C. R. Musson, *The Breiddin Hillfort: A Later Prehistoric Settlement in the Welsh Marches*, CBA Res. Rep. no. 76, 132–41. London.

Corcoran, J. X. W. P. 1952, 'Tankards and tankard handles of the British Iron Age', *Proc. Prehist. Soc.*, 18, 85–102.

Cotton, M. A. 1947, 'Excavations at Silchester 1938–9', *Archaeologia*, 92, 121–67.

Courtney, P. 1981, 'The Early Saxon Fenland: a reconsideration', *Anglo-Saxon Studies in Archaeology and History 2*, BAR Brit. Ser. no. 92, 91–102. Oxford.

Cowell, M. 1992, 'An analytical survey of the British Celtic gold coinage', in Mays 1992, 207–34.

Crabtree, P. J. 1989, *West Stow, Suffolk: Early Anglo-Saxon Animal Husbandry*, East Anglian Archaeol. Rep. no. 47. Ipswich.

Craddock, P. T. 1994, *Roman Non-ferrous Metallurgy*, Brit. Mus. Occas. Pap. no. 100. London.

Cram, C. L. 1967, 'Report on the animal bones from Hockwold', in Salway 1967, 75–80.

Cram, L. and Fulford, M. 1979, 'Silchester tile marking: the faunal environment', in A. McWhirr (ed.), *Roman Brick and Tile*, BAR Int. Ser. no. 68, 201–9. Oxford.

Crawford, D. 1976, 'Imperial estates', in M. I. Finley (ed.), *Studies in Roman Property*, 35–70. Cambridge.

Crawford, M. H. 1974, *Roman Republican Coinage*. Cambridge.

Crouch, K. R. and Shanks, S. A. 1984, *Excavations in Staines, 1975–76: The Friends Burial Ground Site*. London.

Crowfoot, G. M. 1945, 'The bone "gouges" of Maiden Castle and other sites', *Antiquity*, 19, 157–8.

Crummy, N. 1983, *The Roman Small Finds from Excavations in Colchester 1971–9*, Colchester Archaeol. Rep. 2.

Crummy, N. 1985, 'The brooches', in Pryor *et al* 1985, 164–6.

Cunliffe, B. 1968a, 'Early pre-Roman Iron Age communities in Eastern England', *Antiq. J.*, 48, 175–91.

Cunliffe, B. W. (ed.) 1968b, *Fifth Report on the Excavations of the Roman Fort at Richborough, Kent*. Oxford.

Cunliffe, B. 1971, *Excavations at Fishbourne 1961–1969. Vol. II: The Finds*. London.

Cunliffe, B. 1975a, 'The origins of urbanisation in Britain', in B. Cunliffe and T. Rowley (eds), *Oppida in Barbarian Europe*, BAR Supp. Ser. no. 11, 135–62. Oxford.

Cunliffe, B. 1975b, *Excavations at Portchester Castle, Vol. 1: Roman*. London.

Cunliffe, B. 1978, *Iron Age Communities in Britain*, 2nd edn. London.

Cunliffe, B. 1984, *Danebury: An Iron Age Hill-fort in Hampshire. Vol. 2. The Excavations 1969–78: The Finds*. London. 1984.

Cunliffe, B. 1988, *Mount Batten, Plymouth, A Prehistoric and Roman Port*, Oxf. Univ. Comm. Archaeol. Monogr. 26.

Cunliffe, B. W. 1991, *Iron Age Communities in Britain*, 3rd edn. London.

Cunliffe, B. W. 1992, 'Pits, preconceptions and propiation in the British Iron Age', *Oxf. J. Archaeol.*, 11, 69–84.

Cuncliffe, B. W. and Poole, C. 1991, *Danebury: an Iron Age Hillfort in Hampshire. Volume 5: The Excavations 1979–88: the Finds*, CBA Res. Rep. no. 73. London.

Cunnington, M. E. and B. H. 1923, *The Early Iron Age Inhabited Site at All Cannings Cross Farm, Wiltshire*. Devizes.

Curle, J. 1911, *A Roman Frontier Post and its People: The Fort of Newstead in the Parish of Melrose*. Glasgow.

Dannell, G. B. and Wild, J. P. 1987, *Longthorpe II, the Military Works-Depot: An Episode in Landscape History*, Britannia Monogr. no. 8. London.

Darby, H. C. 1974, *The Medieval Fenland*. Reprint of 1940 edn. Newton Abbot.

Darling, M. J. 1989, 'A figured colour-coated beaker from excavations of the East Gate at Lincoln, by D. F. Petch in 1959–62', *J. Roman Pottery Stud.*, 2, 29ff.

Davey, N. and Ling, R. 1982, *Wall-painting in Roman Britain*, Britannia Monogr. no. 3. London.

Davies, J. A., Gregory, T., Lawson, A. J., Rickett, R. and Rogerson, A. 1991, *The Iron Age Forts of Norfolk*, East Anglian Archaeol. Rep. no. 54. Gressenhall.

Davies, R. W. 1971, 'The Roman military diet', *Britannia*, 2, 122–42.

Davies, R. W. 1976, '*Singulares* and Roman Britain', *Britannia*, 7, 134–44.

Davies, W. and Vierck, H. 1974, 'The contexts of Tribal Hidage: social aggregates and settlement patterns', *Frühmittelalterliche Studien*, 8, 223–93.

Dawson, M. 1990, 'Roman military equipment on civil sites in Roman Dacia', *J. Roman Milit. Equip. Stud.*, 1, 7–16.

Déchelette, J. 1904, *Les Vases Céramiques Ornés de la Gaule Romaine*. Paris.

De Franceschini, M. 1991, *Villa Adriana. Mosaici-pavimenti-edifici*. Rome.

Dickinson, T. M. 1979, 'The origin and chronology of the early Anglo-Saxon disc brooch', in Hawkes *et al* 1979, 39–80.

Dilke, O. A. W. 1971, *The Roman Land Surveyors*. Newton Abbot.

Dix, B. 1987, 'The Roman settlement at Kettering, Northants: Excavations at Kipling Road, 1968 and 1971', *Northants Archaeol.*, 21 (1986–7) [1987], 95–108.

Dix, B. and Taylor, S. 1988, 'Excavations at Bannaventa (Whilton Lodge, Northants), 1970–71', *Britannia*, 19, 299–339.

Donaldson, A. M. and Rackham, D. J. 1984, 'Environmental work in Northern Britain', in Keeley 1984, 134–51.

Dool, J., Wheeler, H. *et al* 1985, 'Roman Derby: Excavations 1968–1983', *Derbyshire Archaeol. J.*, 105, 7–345.

Down, A. 1974, *Chichester Excavations II*. Chichester.

Down, A. 1978, *Chichester Excavations III*. Chichester.

Down, A. 1981, *Chichester Excavations V*. Chichester.

Down, A. 1989, *Chichester Excavations VI*. Chichester.

Down, A. and Rule, M. 1971, *Chichester Excavations I*. Chichester.

Dragendorff, H. 1895, 'Terra Sigillata', *Bonner Jahrbücher*, 96, 18ff.

Dressel, H. 1899, *Corpus Inscriptionum Latinarum* XV, Pars 1. Berlin.

Driesch, A. von den 1976, *A Guide to the Measurement of Animal Bones from Archaeological Sites*, Peabody Mus. Bull. no. 1. Harvard.

Driesch, A. von den and Boessneck, J. 1974, 'Kritische Anmerkungen zur Widderist-höhenberechnung aus Längenmassen vor- und frühgeschichtlicher Tierknochen', *Säugetierkundliche Mitteilungen*, 22, 325–48.

Drury, P. 1980, 'Non-Classical religious buildings in Iron Age and Roman Britain: a review', in Rodwell 1980, 45–78.

Drury, P. J. 1988, *The Mansio and Other Sites in the South-eastern Sector of Caesaromagus*, Chelmsford Archaeol. Trust Rep. 3.1. London.

Dudley, D. 1967, 'Excavations on Nor 'nour in the Isles of Scilly, 1962–6', *Archaeol. J.*, 124, 1–64.

Dudley, H. E. 1949, *Early Days in North-west Lincolnshire, A Regional Archaeology*. Scunthorpe.

Dumville, D. 1989a, 'The Tribal Hidage: an introduction to its text and their history', in Bassett 1989, 225–30.

Dumville, D. 1989b, 'Essex, Middle Anglia, and the expansion of Mercia in the South-East Midlands', in Bassett 1989, 123–40.

Duval, P.-M. and Quoniam, P. 1963, 'Relevés inédits des monuments antiques d'Autun', *Gallia*, 21, 155–89.

Dyer, J. 1972, 'Earthworks of the Danelaw frontier', in P. J. Fowler (ed.), *Archaeology of the Landscape*, 222–36. London.

Eggers, H. J. 1951, *Der Römische Import im Freien Germanien*. Hamburg.

Ellenberg, H. 1979, 'Zeigerwerte der Gefaesspflanzen Mitteleuropas', *Scripta Botanica*, 9(2). Gottingen.

Ellis, A. E. 1969, *British Snails*. Oxford.

Ellison, A. 1980, 'Deverel–Rimbury urn cemeteries: the evidence for social organisation', in Barrett and Bradley 1980, 115–26.

Ennion, E. A. R. and Tinbergen, N. 1967, *Tracks*. Oxford.

Erith, F. H. and Longworth, I. H. 1960, 'A Bronze Age urnfield on Vince's Farm, Ardleigh, Essex', *Proc. Prehist. Soc.*, 26, 178–92.

Es, W. A. van 1967, *Wijster, a Native Village Beyond the Imperial Frontier, 150–425 AD*, Palaeohistoria, 11. Groningen.

Es, W. A. van and Verlinde, A. D. 1977, 'Overijssel in Roman and early Medieval times', *Berichten van de Rijksdienst voor het Oudheidkundig Bodemonderzoek*, 27, 7–89.

Etté, J. P. A. 1993, 'The late Bronze Age', in A. Clarke, *Excavations at Mucking. Volume 1: The Site Atlas*, 18–19. London.

Ettlinger, E. 1977, 'Aspects of amphora-typology, seen from the North', in G. Vallet (ed.), *Méthodes Classiques et Méthodes Formelles dans l'Étude des Amphores*, Mélanges de l'École française de Rome Antiquité 32, 9–16.

Evans, C. 1984, 'A shrine provenance for the Willingham Fen hoard', *Antiquity*, 58, 212–14.

Evans, C. 1991, *Archaeological Investigations at Arbury Camp, Cambridgeshire, 1990*. Cambridge.

Evans, C. 1992, 'Commanding gestures in lowlands: the investigation of two Iron Age ringworks', *Fenland Res.*, 7, 16–26.

Evans, C. and Hodder, I. 1983–4, 'Excavations at Haddenham', *Fenland Res.*, 1, 32–5.

Evans, C. and Serjeantson, D. 1988, 'The backwater economy of a fen-edge community in the Iron Age: the Upper Delphs, Haddenham', *Antiquity*, 62, 360–70.

Evans, J. 1864, *The Coins of the Ancient Britons*. London.

Evans, J. 1890, *The Coins of the Ancient Britons: Supplement*. London.

Evans, J. and Millett, M. 1992, 'Residuality revisited', *Oxf. J. Archaeol.*, 11(2), 225–40.

Evans, J. G. 1972, *Land Snails in Archaeology*. London.

Evans, J. G. and Jones, H. 1973, 'Sub-fossil and modern land snail faunas from rock rubble habitats', *J. Conchol.*, 28, 103–29.

Evison, V. I. 1982, 'Anglo-Saxon glass claw-beakers', *Archaeologia*, 107, 43–76.

Exner, K. 1939, 'Die provinzialrömischen Emailfibeln der Rheinlande', *Ber. Römisch-Germanischen Komm.*, 29, 33–121.

Fant, J. C. 1989, *Cavum Antrum Phrygiae: The Organization and Operations of the Roman Imperial Marble Quarries in Phrygia*, BAR Int. Ser. no. 482. Oxford.

Feugère, M. 1985, *Les Fibules en Gaule Méridionale de la Conquête à la Fin du Ve Siècle après J.-C.*, Rev. Archéol. Narbonnaise Suppl. 12. Paris.

Fifield, P. W. 1988, 'The faunal remains', in Potter and Trow 1988, 148–53.

Fingerlin, G. 1972, 'Dangstetten, ein augusteisches Legionslager am Hochrhein', *Ber. Römisch-Germanischen Komm.*, 51–2(1970–1) [1972], 212–32.

Fleischer, R. 1967, *Die Römischen Bronzen aus Österreich*. Mainz.

Floca, O. 1969, *Le Musée Archéologique de Sarmizegethusa*. Bucharest.

Forster, R. H. and Knowles, W. H. 1911, 'Corstopitum: Report on the excavations in 1910', *Archaeol. Aeliana*, 3rd ser., 7, 143–267.

Fossey, J. M. 1979, 'The cities of the Kopais in the Roman period', in H. Temporini (ed.), *Aufstieg und Niedergang der Römischen Welt*, Principat 8, 549–91.

Foster, J. 1986, 'Bronze/brass-working debris', in Stead and Rigby 1986, 143–4.

Foster, J. A. 1980, *The Iron Age Moulds from Gussage All Saints*, Br. Mus. Occas. Pap. no. 12. London.

Foster, P. J., Harper, R. and Watkins, S. 1977, 'An Iron Age and Romano-British settlement at Hardwick Park, Wellingborough, Northamptonshire', *Northants Archaeol.*, 12, 55–96.

Fowler, G. 1934, 'Fenland waterways, past and present. South Level District, Part II', *Proc. Camb. Antiq. Soc.*, 34, 17–33.

Fowler, G. 1950, 'A Romano-British village near Littleport, Cambs.', *Proc. Camb. Antiq. Soc.*, 43, 7–20.

Fox, C. 1923, *The Archaeology of the Cambridge Region*. Cambridge.

France, N. E. and Gobel, B. M. 1985, *The Romano-British Temple at Harlow*. Gloucester.

Freestone, I. C. 1991, 'Extending ceramic petrology', in A. Middleton and I. Freestone (eds), *Recent Developments in Ceramic Petrology*, Br. Mus. Occas. Pap. no. 81, 399–410. London.

Frederiksen, M. W. 1959, Review of Castagnoli 1958, *J. Roman Stud.*, 49, 167–8.

Freke, D. J. 1976, 'Further excavations in Lewes, 1975', *Sussex Archaeol. Coll.*, 114, 176–93.

French, C. A. I. 1992, 'Fengate to Flag Fen: summary of the soil and sediment analysis', *Antiquity*, 66, 458–61.

French, C. A. I. and Pryor, F. M. M. 1993, *The South-West Fen Dyke Survey Project 1982–86*, East Anglian Archaeol. Rep. no. 59.

Frere, S. S. 1941, 'A Claudian site at Needham, Norfolk', *Antiq. J.*, 21, 40–55.

Frere, S. S. 1962, 'Excavations at Dorchester-on-Thames, 1962', *Archaeol. J.*, 119, 114–49.

Frere, S. S. 1967, *Britannia. A History of Roman Britain*. London.

Frere, S. S. 1972, *Verulamium Excavations, Vol. I.* Oxford.

Frere, S. S. 1982, 'The Bignor villa', *Britannia*, 13, 135–95.

Frere, S. S. 1984, *Verulamium Excavations, Vol. III.* Oxford.

Frere, S. S. and St Joseph, J. K. S. 1974, 'The Roman fortress at Longthorpe', *Britannia*, 5, 1–129.

Frere, S. S. and St Joseph, J. K. S. 1983, *Roman Britain from the Air.* Cambridge.

Frere, S. S., Stow, S. and Bennett, P. 1982, *Excavations on the Roman and Medieval Defences of Canterbury*, The Archaeology of Canterbury, Vol. II. Maidstone.

Frere, S. S. and Wilkes, J. J. 1989, *Strageath, Excavations within the Roman Fort, 1973–86*, Britannia Monogr. no. 9. London.

Friendship-Taylor, R. M. 1979, 'The excavation of the Belgic and Romano-British settlement at Quinton, Northamptonshire, Site 'B', 1973–7', *J. Northampton Mus. & Art Gall.*, 13, 2–176.

Frisch, T. G. and Toll, N. P. 1949, *The Excavations at Dura-Europos, Final Report IV.4.1.* Yale.

Fulford, M. 1989a, *The Silchester Amphitheatre, Excavations of 1979–85*, Britannia Monogr. no. 10. London.

Fulford, M. 1989b, 'A Roman shipwreck off Nor 'nour, Isles of Scilly?', *Britannia*, 20, 245–9.

Gaitzsch, W. 1984, 'Der Wachsauftrag antiker Schreibtafeln', *Bonner Jahrbücher*, 184, 198–207.

Gechter, M. 1980, 'Die Fibeln des Kastells Niederbieber', *Bonner Jahrbücher*, 180, 589–610.

Gelling, P. S. 1958, 'Close ny Chollagh: an Iron Age fort at Scarlett, Isle of Man', *Proc. Prehist. Soc.*, 24, 85–100.

Gelling, M. 1988, 'Towards a chronology for English place-names', in Hooke 1988, 59–76.

Gerharz, R. R. 1987, 'Fibeln aus Afrika', *Saalburg Jahrbuch*, 43, 77–107.

Gibson, A. 1980, 'Pot beakers in Britain?', *Antiquity*, 54, 219–21.

Gillam, J. P. 1957, 'Types of Roman coarse pottery vessels in Northern Britain', *Archaeol. Aeliana*, 4th ser., 35, 180–251.

Gillam, J. P. 1970, *Types of Roman Coarse Pottery Vessels in Northern Britain.* Newcastle upon Tyne.

Gingell, C. 1992, *The Marlborough Downs: A Later Bronze Age Landscape and Its Origins*, Wilts Archaeol. & Nat. Hist. Soc. Monogr. 1. Devizes.

Goddard, J. P. (forthcoming) 'Roman brockages: a preliminary survey of their frequency and type', in M. M. Archibald and M. R. Cowell (eds), *Metallurgy in Numismatics III.*

Godwin, H. 1936, 'Studies in the ecology of Wicken Fen. III. The establishment and development of fen scrub (carr)', *J. Ecol.*, 24, 82–116.

Godwin, H. 1975, *The History of the British Flora*, 2nd edn. Cambridge.

Godwin, H. 1978, *Fenland: Its Ancient Past and Uncertain Future.* Cambridge.

Godwin, H., Clowes, D. R. and Huntley, B. 1974, 'Studies in the ecology of Wicken Fen. V. Development of fen carr', *J. Ecol.*, 62, 197–214.

Going, C. 1981, 'Some Nene Valley folded beakers with anthropomorphic decoration', in Anderson and Anderson 1981, 313–19.

Going, C. J. 1987, *The Mansio and Other Sites in the South-eastern Sector of Caesaromagus: The Roman Pottery*, Chelmsford Archaeol. Trust Rep. 3.2. London.

Goodchild, R. G. 1941, 'Romano-British disc-brooches derived from Hadrianic coin-types', *Antiq. J.*, 21, 1–8.

Gould, J. 1964, 'Excavations at Wall (Staffordshire), 1961–3, on the site of the early Roman forts and of the late Roman defences', *Trans. Lichfield & South Staffs. Archaeol. & Hist. Soc.*, 5, 1–50.

Gould, J. 1967, 'Excavations at Wall, Staffs., 1964–6, on the site of the Roman forts', *Trans. Lichfield & South Staffs. Archaeol. & Hist. Soc.*, 8 (1966–7) [1967], 1–40.

Gower, J. L. 1984 'Three pellets of Egyptian Blue from the Ashtead Roman villa', *Surrey Archaeol. Coll.*, 75, 303–4.

Graham-Campbell, J. 1990, 'Three copper alloy pins', in McCarthy 1990, 181–3.

Grant, A. 1982, 'The use of tooth wear as a guide to the age of domestic ungulates', in B. Wilson, C. Grigson and S. Payne (eds), *Ageing and Sexing Animal Bones from Archaeological Sites*, 91–108. Oxford.

Grant, A. 1989, 'Animals in Roman Britain', in Todd 1989, 135–64.

Green, F. 1979, 'Phosphatic mineralization of seeds from archaeological sites', *J. Archaeol. Sci.*, 6, 279–84.

Green, F. J. 1985, 'Evidence for domestic cereal use at Maxey', in Pryor, French *et al* 1985, 224–32.

Green, H. J. M. 1975, 'Roman Godmanchester', in W. Rodwell and T. Rowley (eds), *The 'Small Towns' of Roman Britain*, BAR Brit. Ser. no. 15, 183–210. Oxford.

Green, H. J. M. 1986, 'Religious cults at Roman Godmanchester', in M. Henig and A. C. King (eds), *Pagan Gods and Shrines of the Roman Empire*, Oxf. Univ. Comm. Archaeol. Monogr. 8, 29–56.

Green, H. S. 1980, *The Flint Arrowheads of the British Isles*, BAR Brit. Ser., no. 75. Oxford.

Green, M. J. 1976, *A Corpus of Religious Material from the Civilian Areas of Roman Britain*, BAR Br. Ser. no. 24. Oxford.

Green, M. J. 1978, *A Corpus of Small Cult-objects from the Military Areas of Roman Britain*, BAR Br. Ser. no. 52. Oxford.

Green, M. J. 1986, *The Gods of the Celts*. Gloucester.

Greep, S. J. 1990, 'Objects of worked bone', in Wrathmell and Nicholson 1990, 126–8.

Greep, S. J. 1995, 'Objects of worked bone, antler and ivory from C.A.T. sites', in K., M. and P. Blockley, S. Frere and S. Stow (eds), *Excavations in the Marlowe Car Park and Surrounding Areas*, The Archaeology of Canterbury, Vol. V, 1112–69. Canterbury.

Greep, S. J. (forthcoming) 'Objects of bone and antler', in R. Brewer, *Excavations at Caerwent.*

Gregory, T. 1991, *Excavations in Thetford, 1980–1982*, East Anglian Archaeol. Rep. no. 53. Gressenhall.

Gregory, T. 1992, 'Snettisham and Bury; some new light on the earliest Icenian coinage', in Mays 1992, 47–68.

Greifenhagen, A. 1975, *Schmuckarbeiten in Edelmetall*. Berlin.

Greig, J. 1988, 'Traditional cornfield weeds – where are they now?', *Plants Today* 1 (6), 183–91.

Greig, J. 1990, 'Practical ecology; experiments in growing traditional cornfield weeds and a comment on their archaeological records in Britain', in D. E. Robinson (ed.), 'Experimentation and reconstruction in environmental archaeology', *Symp. Assoc. Environ. Archaeol.* 9, 41–62.

Grew, F. and Griffiths, N. 1991, 'The pre-Flavian military belt: the evidence from Britain', *Archaeologia*, 110, 47–84.

Guido, M. 1978, *The Glass Beads of the Prehistoric and Roman Periods in Britain and Ireland*, Soc. Antiq. Lond. Res. Rep., 35. London.

Guildhall Museum, 1908, *Catalogue of the Collection of London Antiquities in the Guildhall Museum*, 2nd edn.

Guiraud, H. 1989, 'Bagues et anneaux à l'époque romaine en Gaule', *Gallia*, 46, 173ff.

Gurney, D. A. 1985a, 'Phosphate and magnetic susceptibility survey', in Pryor, French *et al* 1985, 38–41.

Gurney, D. A. 1985b, 'Soil phosphate analysis of subsoil features', in Pryor, French *et al* 1985, 197–205.

Gurney, D. 1986, *Settlement, Religion and Industry on the Roman Fen-Edge, Norfolk*, East Anglian Archaeol. Rep. no. 31. Gressenhall.

Gurney, D. 1991, 'The Roman pottery', in R. J. Silvester, *The Wissey Embayment and the Fen Causeway, Norfolk*, Fenland Project Number 4, East Anglian Archaeol. Rep. no. 52, 143–5. Norwich.

Hall, D. 1987, *Fenland Landscapes and Settlement between Peterborough and March*, Fenland Project Number 2, East Anglian Archaeol. Rep. no. 35. Cambridge.

Hall, D. N. 1992, *The South-western Cambridgeshire Fenlands*, Fenland Project Number 6, East Anglian Archaeol. Rep. no. 56. Cambridge.

Hall, D. and Coles, J. 1994, *Fenland Survey. An Essay in Landscape and Persistence*. London.

Hall, D. and Switsur, R. 1981, 'A buried peat band at Manea', *Proc. Camb. Antiq. Soc.*, 71, 75–80.

Hallam, S. J. 1970, 'Settlement round the Wash', in Phillips 1970, 22–113.

Halstead, P. 1985, 'A study of mandibular teeth from Romano-British contexts at Maxey', in Pryor, French *et al* 1985, 219–24.

Hamerow, H. 1993, *Excavations at Mucking 2: The Anglo-Saxon Settlement*, English Heritage Archaeol. Rep. no. 21. London.

Hamshaw-Thomas, J. F. and Bermingham, N. 1993, 'Analysis of faunal remains', in A. R. Hands, *The Romano-British Roadside Settlement at Wilcote, Oxfordshire. 1. Excavations 1990–92*, BAR Br. Ser. no. 232, 167–210. Oxford.

Hanworth, R. 1968, 'The Roman villa at Rapsley, Ewhurst', *Surrey Archaeol. Coll.*, 65, 1–70.

Harcourt, R. A. 1974, 'The dog in prehistoric and early historic Britain', *J. Archaeol. Sci.*, 1, 151–75.

Harden, D. B. 1947, 'The glass', in Hawkes and Hull 1947, 287–306.

Harden, D. B. 1958, 'Four Roman glasses from Hauxton Mill, Cambridge, 1870', in J. Liversidge, 'Roman discoveries from Hauxton', *Proc. Camb. Antiq. Soc.*, 51, Appendix 1, 12–16.

Harden, D. B. 1961, 'Domestic window glass: Roman, Saxon and medieval', in E. M. Jope (ed.), *Studies in Building History: Essays in Recognition of the Work of B. H. St J. O'Neil*, 39–63. London.

Harden, D. B. 1968, 'Roman glass from Huntingdon and Rapsley, Surrey', *Antiq. J.*, 48, 308.

Harden, D. B. 1974, 'Window glass from the Romano-British bathhouse at Garden Hill, Hartfield, Sussex', *Antiq. J.*, 54, 280–1.

Harden, D. B. 1977, 'Report on the glass bowl', in C. Partridge, 'Excavations and fieldwork at Braughing 1968–73', *Herts. Archaeol.*, 5, 102.

Harden, D. B., Hellenkemper, H., Painter, K. and Whitehouse, D. 1987, *Glass of the Caesars*. Milan.

Harden, D. B. and Price, J. 1971, 'The glass', in Cunliffe 1971, 317–68.

Harding, D. W. 1972, *The Iron Age in the Upper Thames Basin*. Oxford.

Harker, S. R. 1970, 'Springhead – the Well, F19', *Archaeol. Cantiana*, 85, 139–48.

Hart, C. 1971, 'The Tribal Hidage', *Trans. R. Hist. Soc.*, 5th ser., 21, 133–57.

Hartley, B. R. 1960, 'Notes on pottery from some Romano-British kilns in the Cambridge area', *Proc. Camb. Antiq. Soc.*, 53, 23–8.

Hartley, B. R. 1972, 'The Roman occupation of Scotland: the evidence of samian ware', *Britannia*, 3, 1–55.

Hartley, K. F. and B. R. 1970, 'Pottery in the Romano-British Fenland', in Phillips 1970, 165–9.

Haselgrove, C. C. 1987, *Iron Age Coinage in South-East England. The Archaeological Context*, BAR Br. Ser. no. 174. Oxford.

Haselgrove, C. C. 1988, 'Iron Age coins', in Potter and Trow 1988, 21–30.

Hattatt, R. 1982, *Ancient and Romano-British Brooches*. Milborne Port.

Hattatt, R. 1985, *Iron Age and Roman Brooches, A Second Selection of Brooches from the Author's Collection*. Oxford.

Hattatt, R. 1987, *Brooches of Antiquity, A Third Selection of Brooches from the Author's Collection*. Oxford.

Haverfield, F. 1911, 'The Corbridge excavations of 1910', *Proc. Soc. Antiq. Lond.*, 2nd ser., 23, pt 2, 478–90.

Haverfield, F. 1916, 'Modius Claytonensis: the Roman bronze measure from Carvoran', *Archaeol. Aeliana* (3), 13, 84–102.

Hawkes, C. 1927, 'Excavations at Alchester, 1926', *Antiq. J.*, 7, 147–84.

Hawkes, C. F. C. and Fell, C. I. 1943, 'The Early Iron Age settlement at Fengate, Peterborough', *Archaeol. J.*, 100 [1945], 188–223.

Hawkes, C. F. C. and Hull, M. R. 1947, *Camulodunum*. Oxford.

Hawkes, S. C. 1974, 'Some recent finds of late Roman buckles', *Britannia*, 5, 386–93.

Hawkes, S. C., Brown, D. and Campbell, J. (eds) 1979, *Anglo-Saxon Studies in Archaeology and History 1*, BAR Br. Ser. no. 72. Oxford.

Hawkes, S. C. and Dunning, G. C. 1961, 'Soldiers and settlers in Britain, fourth to fifth century; with a catalogue of animal ornamented buckles and related belt fittings', *Medieval Archaeol.* 5, 1–70.

Hayes, P. P. 1988, 'Roman to Saxon in the South Lincolnshire Fens', *Antiquity*, 62, 321–6.

Hayes, P. P. and Lane, T. W. 1992, *Lincolnshire Survey, the South-west Fens*, Fenland Project Number 5, East Anglian Archaeol. Rep. no. 55.

Hedges, J. D. and Buckley, D. G. 1981, *Springfield Cursus and the Cursus Problem*, Essex County Council Occas. Pap. no. 1. Chelmsford.

Helbaek, H. 1952, 'Early crops in southern England', *Proc. Prehist. Soc.* 18, 194–233.

Helbaek, H. 1964, 'The Isca grain, a Roman plant introduction into Britain', *New Phytologist*, 63, 158–64.

Henig, M. 1978, *A Corpus of Roman Engraved Gemstones from British Sites*, BAR Brit. Ser. no. 8. Oxford.

Henig, M. 1984, 'A bronze stamp found near Brough-on-Humber', *Yorks. Archaeol. J.*, 56, 167.

Henig, M. 1989, 'Religion in Roman Britain', in Todd 1989, 219–34.

Henig, M. and King, A. (eds) 1986, *Pagan Gods and Shrines of the Roman Empire*, Oxf. Univ. Comm. Archaeol. Monogr. no. 8. Oxford.

Henkel, F. 1913, *Die Römischen Fingerringe der Rheinlande und der Benachbarten Gebiete*. Berlin.

Higham, N. 1992, *Rome, Britain and the Anglo-Saxons*. London.

Hill, D. 1981, *An Atlas of Anglo-Saxon England*. Oxford.

Hillman, G. 1981a, 'Crop husbandry: evidence from microscopic remains', in I. G. Simmons and M. J. Tooley (eds), *The Environment in British Prehistory*, 183–91. London.

Hillman, G. 1981b, 'Reconstructing crop husbandry practices from charred remains of crops', in R. Mercer (ed.), *Farming Practice in British Prehistory*, 123–62. Edinburgh.

Hinchliffe, J. and Green, C. S. 1985, *Excavations at Brancaster, 1974 and 1977*, East Anglian Archaeol. Rep. no. 23. Gressenhall.

Hobley, B. 1969, 'A Neronian-Vespasianic military site at "The Lunt", Baginton, Warwickshire', *Trans. & Proc. Birmingham Archaeol. Soc.*, 83 (1966–7) [1969], 65–129.

Hobley, B. 1973, 'Excavations at "The Lunt" Roman military site, Baginton, Warwickshire, 1968–71, second interim report', *Trans. Birmingham & Warks Archaeol. Soc.*, 85 (1971–73), 7–92.

Hobley, B. 1975, '"The Lunt" Roman fort and training school for Roman cavalry, Baginton, Warwickshire, final report, excavations (1972–73) with conclusions', *Trans. Birmingham & Warks Archaeol. Soc.*, 87, 1–56.

Hodder, I. 1977, 'Some new directions in the spatial analysis of archaeological data at the regional scale', in D. L. Clarke (ed.), *Spatial Archaeology*, 223–351. London.

Hodges, H. 1954, 'Studies in the Late Bronze Age: 1. Stone and clay moulds and wooden models for bronze implements', *Ulster J. Archaeol.*, 17, 62–80.

Holbrook, N. and Bidwell, P. T. 1991, *Roman Finds from Exeter*. Exeter.

Hooke, D. (ed.) 1988, *Anglo-Saxon Settlements*. Oxford.

Horne, P. D. 1981, 'Romano-Celtic temples in the third century', in A. C. King and M. Henig (eds), *The Roman West in the Third Century*, BAR Int. Ser. no. 109, 21–6. Oxford.

Horne, P. D. 1986, 'Roman or Celtic temples? A case study', in Henig and King 1986, 15–24.

Horne, P. D. and King, A. C. 1980, 'Romano-Celtic temples in Continental Europe: a gazetteer of those with known plans', in Rodwell 1980, 369–556.

Houlder, C. 1968, 'The henge monuments at Llandegai', *Antiquity*, 42, 216–21.

Howard, M. M. 1962, 'The early domestication of cattle and the determination of their remains', *Zeitschrift Tierzüchtung und Züchtungsbiologie*, 76, 252–64.

Howe, M. D., Perrin, J. R. and Mackreth, D. F. 1980, *Roman Pottery from the Nene Valley: A Guide*, Peterborough Mus. Occas. Pap. no. 2.

Hull, M. R. 1942, 'An early Claudian burial found at Colchester', *Antiq. J.*, 22, 59–65.

Hull, M. R. 1963, *The Roman Potters' Kilns of Colchester*. Oxford.

Hull, M. R. 1967, 'The Nor 'nour brooches', in Dudley 1967, 28–64.

Hull, M. R. 1968, 'Brooches', in Cunliffe 1968b, 74–93.

Hull, M. R. and Hawkes, C. F. C. 1987, *Pre-Roman Bow Brooches*, BAR Br. Ser. no. 168. Oxford.

Hume, A. 1863, *Ancient Meols; Or, Some Account of the Antiquities found Near Dove Point, on the Sea-Coast of Cheshire*. London.

Hume, I. N. 1980, *Artifacts of Colonial America*. New York.

Hundt, H.-J. 1960, 'Eiserne römische Schwertriemenhalter', *Saalburg Jahrbuch*, 18, 52–66.

Hunter, R. and Mynard, D. 1977, 'Excavations at Thorplands near Northampton, 1970 and 1974', *Northants Archaeol.*, 12, 97–154.

Hurk, L. J. A. M. van den 1976, 'The tumuli from the Roman period of Esch, Province of North Brabant, I', *Berichten van de Rijksdienst voor het Oudheidkundig Bodemonderzoek*, 23, 189–236.

Hurk, L. J. A. M. van den 1977, 'The tumuli from the Roman period of Esch, Province of North Brabant, III', *Berichten van de Rijksdienst voor het Oudheidkundig Bodemonderzoek*, 27, 91–138.

Hurst, H. R. 1985, *Kingsholm, Excavations at Kingsholm Close and Other Sites, with a Discussion of the Archaeology of the Area*, Gloucester Archaeol. Rep., vol. 1. Gloucester.

Hurst, H. R. 1986, *Gloucester, the Roman and Later Defences, Excavations on the E. Defences and a Reassessment of the Defensive sequence*, Gloucester Archaeol. Rep., Vol. 2. Gloucester.

Isings, C. 1957, *Roman Glass from Dated Finds*. Groningen.

Isings, C. 1971, *Roman Glass in Limburg*. Groningen.

Jackson, D. A. and Ambrose, T. M. 1978, 'Excavations at Wakerley, Northants, 1972–75', *Britannia*, 9, 1985, 115–242.

Jackson, D. and Dix, B. 1987, 'Late Iron Age and Roman settlement at Weekley, Northants.', *Northants Archaeol.*, 21 (1986–7) [1987], 41–93.

Jackson, D. and Knight, D. 1985, 'An Early Iron Age and Beaker site near Gretton, Northamptonshire', *Northants Archaeol.*, 20, 67–86.

Jackson, R. P. J. 1985, 'Cosmetic sets from Late Iron Age and Roman Britain', *Britannia*, 16, 165–92.

Jackson, R. P. J. 1986, 'A set of Roman medical instruments from Italy', *Britannia*, 17, 119–67.

Jackson, R. P. J. 1990a, 'Roman doctors and their instruments: recent research into ancient practice', *J. Roman Archaeol.*, 3, 5–27.

Jackson, R. P. J. 1990b, *Camerton: The Late Iron Age and Early Roman Metalwork*. London.

Jackson, R. P. J. 1992, 'The iron objects', in J. Hinchliffe and J. H. Williams, *Roman Warrington: Excavations at Wilderspool 1966–9 and 1976*, 78–86. Manchester.

Jacobi, G. 1974, *Werkzeug und Gerät aus dem Oppidum von Manching*. Wiesbaden.

Jacobi, L. 1897, *Das Römerkastell Saalburg bei Homburg vor der Höhe*. Homburg.

James, S. T. 1985–6, 'The Fen Causeway and an earthwork enclosure at Estover, March, Cambs.', *Fenland Res.*, 3, 29–30.

James, S., Millett, M. and Marshall, A. 1984, 'An early Medieval building tradition', *Archaeol. J.*, 141, 182–215.

Jarrett, M. G. and Wrathmell, S. 1981, *Whitton, An Iron Age and Roman Farmstead in South Glamorgan*. Cardiff.

Jenkins, F. 1957, 'The cult of the *dea nutrix* in Kent', *Archaeol. Cantiana*, 71, 38ff.

Jenkins, F. 1962, 'The horse deity of Roman Canterbury', *Archaeol. Cantiana*, 77, 142ff.

Jessup, R. F. 1939, 'Further excavations at Jullieberrie's Grave, Chilham', *Antiq. J.*, 19, 260–81.

Jockenhövel, A. 1980, *Die Rasiermesser in Westeuropa*, Prähistorische Bronzefunde Abt. VIII, 3. Munich.

Johns, C. M. 1976, 'A Roman gold and emerald necklace from Cannon Street, London', *Antiq. J.*, 56, 247.

Johns, C. 1981, 'Colour-coated sherds with barbotine decoration from Grandford', in Potter 1981, 90–3.

Johns, C. 1982, *Sex or Symbol: Erotic Images of Greece and Rome*. Reprinted 1990. London.

Johns, C. 1991, 'Some unpublished jewellery from Roman Britain', *Jewellery Stud.*, 5, 55–64.

Johns, C. and Potter, T. 1983, *The Thetford Treasure: Roman Jewellery and Silver*. London.

Johns, C., Thompson, H. and Wagstaff, P. 1980, 'The Wincle, Cheshire, Hoard of Roman gold jewellery', *Antiq. J.*, 60, 48–58.

Johnston, F. E. 1962, 'Growth of the long bones of infant and young children at Indian Knoll', *Human Biol.*, 23, 66–81.

Jones, A. H. M. 1973, *The Later Roman Empire AD 284–602: A Social, Economic and Administrative Survey*. Oxford.

Jones, A. K. G. 1982, 'Human parasite remains: prospects for a quantitative approach', in A. R. Hall and K. H. Kenward (eds), *Environmental Archaeology in the Urban Context*, CBA Res. Rep. no. 43, 66–70. London.

Jones, A. K. G. 1984, 'Some effects of the mammalian digestive system on fish bones', in *Deuxième Rencontre d'Archéo-Ichthyologie*, Notes et Monographies Techniques no. 16. Valbonne.

Jones, A. K. G. 1985, 'Trichurid ova in archaeological deposits: their value as indicators of ancient faeces', in N. R. J. Fieller, D. D. Gilbertson and N. G. A. Ralph (eds), *Palaeobiological Investigations*, BAR Int. Ser. no. 266, 105–14. Oxford.

Jones, G. D. B. and Mattingly, D. J. 1990, *An Atlas of Roman Britain*. Oxford.

Jones, M. 1981, 'The development of crop husbandry', in M. Jones and G. Dimbleby (eds), *The Environment of Man: The Iron Age to the Anglo-Saxon Period*, BAR Br. Ser. no. 87, 95–127. Oxford.

Jones, M. 1985, 'Archaeobotany beyond subsistence reconstruction', in G. W. W. Barker and C. Gamble (eds), *Beyond Domestication in Prehistoric Europe*, 107–28. London.

Jones, M. 1989, 'Agriculture in Roman Britain: the dynamics of change', in Todd 1989, 127–36.

Keay, S. J. 1984, *Late Roman Amphorae in the Western Mediterranean. A Typology and Economic Study: The Catalan Evidence*, BAR Int. Ser. no. 136. Oxford.

Keeley, H. C. M. (ed.), 1984, *Environmental Archaeology, A Regional Review*. London.

Kehoe, D. P. 1988, *The Economics of Agriculture on Roman Imperial Estates*, Hypomnemata 89. Göttingen.

Keller, E. 1971, *Die Spätrömischen Grabfunde in Südbayern*, Münchener Beiträge zur Vor- und Frühgeschichte 14. Munich.

Kempisty, A. and Okulicz, J. 1965, *Période Romaine Tardive et Période des Migrations des Peuples en Marzovie*, Inventaria Archaeologica, Corpus des Ensembles Archéologique, Pologne, Fascicule XV. Warsaw.

Kennedy, D. A. *et al* (forthcoming) 'Investigations of the Roman fort at Scaftworth, near Bawtry'.

Kent, J. and Burnett, A. 1984, 'Eriswell, Suffolk', in A. M. Burnett (ed.), *Coin Hoards from Roman Britain. Volume IV*, Br. Mus. Occas. Pap. no. 43, 6–14. London.

Kenward, H.K. and Williams, D. 1979, *Biological Evidence from the Roman Warehouses in Coney Street*. The Archaeology of York. The Past Environment of York 14/2. York.

Kenyon, K. M. 1935, 'The Roman theatre at Verulamium, St Albans', *Archaeologia*, 84, 213–61.

Kenyon, K. M. 1938, 'Excavations at Viroconium 1936–7', *Archaeologia*, 88, 175–227.

Kenyon, K. M. 1948, *Excavations at the Jewry Wall Site, Leicester*. Oxford.

King, A. 1988, 'Villas and animal bones', in K. Branigan and D. Miles (eds), *The Economies of Romano-British Villas*, 51–9. Sheffield.

King, A. C. 1984, 'Animal bones and the dietary identity of military and civilian groups in Roman Britain, Germany and Gaul', in T. F. C. Blagg and A. C. King (eds), *Military and Civilian in Roman Britain*, BAR Br. Ser. no. 136, 187–218. Oxford.

Kirby, D. P. 1991, *The Earliest English Kings*. London.

Kirk, J. R. 1951, 'Bronzes from Woodeaton, Oxon.', *Oxoniensia*, 14 (1949) [1951], 1–45.

Knight, D. 1984, *Late Bronze Age and Iron Age Settlement in the Nene and Great Ouse Basins*, BAR Br. Ser. no. 130. Oxford.

Kovrig, I. 1937, *Die Haupttypen der Kaiserzeitlichen Fibeln in Pannonien*, Dissertationes Pannonicae, 2nd ser., 4.

Kuchenbach, F. 1954, 'Die Fibel mit umgeschlagenem Fuss', *Saalburg Jahrbuch*, 13, 5–52.

Kunow, J. 1980, 'Der Leithorizont der Augenfibel und die Stufe Eggers B', *Archäologisches Korrespondenzblatt*, 10, 157–61.

Lambrick, G. 1980, 'Excavations in Park Street, Towcester', *Northants Archaeol.*, 15, 35–118.

Landy, R. 1984–5, 'Colour-coated slip and firing tests', *Bull. Exper. Firing Gp*, 3, 11ff.

Lane, T. 1988, 'Pre-Roman settlement on the Fens of South Lincolnshire', *Antiquity*, 62, 314–21.

Laubenheimer, F. 1985, *La Production des Amphores au Gaule Narbonnaise*. Paris.

Lawson, A. J. 1980a, 'A Late Bronze Age hoard from Beeston Regis, Norfolk', *Antiquity*, 54, 217–19.

Lawson, A. J. 1980b, 'The evidence for later Bronze Age settlement and burial in Norfolk', in Barrett and Bradley 1980, 271–94.

Lawson, A. J. 1983, *The Archaeology of Witton, near North Walsham, Norfolk*, East Anglian Archaeol. Rep. no. 18. Gressenhall.

Lawson, A. J., Martin, E. A. and Priddy, D. 1981, *The Barrows of East Anglia*, East Anglian Archaeol. Rep. no. 12. Gressenhall.

Leach, P. 1982, *Ilchester, Vol. 1, Excavations 1974–1975*. Bristol.

Leah, M. 1992, 'A Roman saltern mound at Blackborough End and a section across the Fen Causeway', *Fenland Res.*, 7, 49–54.

Leech, R. 1986, 'The excavation of a Romano-Celtic temple and a later cemetery on Lamyatt Beacon, Somerset, *Britannia*, 17, 259–328.

Leese, M. N. 1982, 'The statistical treatment of grain size data from pottery', in A. Aspinall and S. E. Warren (eds), *Proc. 22nd Archaeometry Symp.*, 47–55. Bradford.

Legge, A. J. and Dorrington, E. 1985, 'Animal bones', in France and Gobel 1985, 122–35.

Lehmann, L. Th. 1965, 'Placing the pot beaker', *Helinium*, 5, 3–31.

Lehmann, L. Th. 1967, 'Pot beaker news', *Helinium*, 7, 65–9.

Levitan, B. 1989, 'The vertebrate remains from Chichester Cattle-market', in Down 1989, 242–76.

Lewis, M. J. T. 1966, *Temples in Roman Britain*. Cambridge.

Ling, R. 1991, *Roman Painting*. Cambridge.

Longley, D. 1991, 'The Late Bronze Age pottery', in Needham 1991, 162–70.

Longworth, I. H. 1984, *Collared Urns of the Bronze Age in Great Britain and Ireland*. Cambridge.

Ludowici, W. 1901–5, *Stempel-Bilder römischer Töpfer aus meinen Ausgrabungen in Rheinzabern*. Rheinzabern.

Luff, R.-M. 1982, *A Zooarchaeological Study of the Roman North-west Provinces*, BAR Int. Ser. no. 137. Oxford.

Lyttleton, M. and Sear, F. 1977, 'A Roman villa near Anguillara Sabazia', *Pap. Br. School Rome*, 45, 227–51.

Macaulay, S. and Reynolds, T. 1993, 'Excavation and site management at Cambridgeshire Car Dyke, Waterbeach', *Fenland Res.*, 8 63–9.

MacGregor, A. 1975, 'Problems in the interpretation of microscopic wear patterns: the evidence from bone skates', *J. Archaeol. Sci.*, 2, 385–90.

MacGregor, A. 1985, *Bone, Antler, Ivory and Horn*. London.

MacGregor, A. 1994, 'A pair of late Saxon strap-ends from Ipsden Heath, Oxfordshire', *J. Br. Archaeol. Ass.*, CXLII. 122–7.

Mack, R. P. 1975, *The Coinage of Ancient Britain*, 3rd edn. London.

Mackreth, D. F. 1969, 'Report on the brooches', in Hobley 1969, 107–11.

Mackreth, D. F. 1973a, 'The brooches', in Hobley 1973, 65–9.

Mackreth, D. F. 1973b, *Roman Brooches*. Salisbury.

Mackreth, D. F. 1974, 'The brooches', in Down 1974, 143–4.

Mackreth, D. F. 1978, 'The Roman brooches', in Down 1978, 277–87.

Mackreth, D. F. 1979, 'Brooches', in Partridge 1979, 34–40.

Mackreth, D. F. 1981, 'The brooches', in Partridge 1981, 130–51.

Mackreth, D. F. 1982a, 'Two brooches from Stonea, Cambs. and Bicester, Oxon., and the origins of the Aesica brooch', *Britannia*, 13, 310–15.

Mackreth, D. F. 1982b, 'The brooches', in Leach 1982, 241–8.

Mackreth, D. F. 1984, 'Castor', *Durobrivae*, 9, 22–5.

Mackreth, D. F. 1985a, 'Brooches from Roman Derby', in Dool *et al* 1985, 218–29.

Mackreth, D. F. 1985b, 'The Roman brooches', in Taylor 1985, 13–29.

Mackreth, D. F. 1986, 'Brooches', in Gurney 1986, 61–7.

Mackreth, D. F. 1988, 'Excavation of an Iron Age and Roman enclosure at Werrington, Cambridgeshire', *Britannia*, 19, 59–151.

Mackreth, D. F. 1989a, 'Brooches', in Blockley 1989, 87–99.

Mackreth, D. F. 1989b, 'The Roman brooches from Chichester', in Down 1989, 181–94.

Mackreth, D. F. 1990, 'Brooches', in McCarthy 1990, 105–13.

Mackreth, D. F. 1991, 'Brooches of copper-alloy and iron', in Gregory 1991, 120–8.

Mackreth, D. F. and Butcher, S. A. 1981, 'The Roman brooches', in Down 1981, 254–61.

Macmullen, R. 1970, 'Market days in the Roman Empire', *Phoenix*, 24, 333–41.

Macpherson-Grant, N. 1980, 'Archaeological work along the A2: 1966–1974; Part 1: the Late Bronze and Early Iron Age sites', *Archaeol. Cantiana*, 96, 133–83.

Malim, T. 1992, 'Excavations and site management at Stonea Camp', *Fenland Res.*, 7, 27–34.

Maltby, M. 1981, 'Iron Age, Romano-British and Anglo-Saxon husbandry – a review', in M. Jones and G. Dimbleby (eds), *The Environment of Man: The Iron Age to the Anglo-Saxon Period*, BAR Brit. Ser. no. 87, 155–203. Oxford.

Manning, W. H. 1985, *Catalogue of the Romano-British Iron Tools, Fittings and Weapons in the British Museum*. London.

Marney, P. T. and Mackreth, D. F. 1987, 'Brooches', in Mynard 1987, 128–33.

Marshall, F. H. 1911, *Catalogue of the Jewellery, Greek, Etruscan and Roman in the Department of Antiquities, British Museum*. London.

Martin, E. 1988, *Burgh: The Iron Age and Roman Enclosure*, East Anglian Archaeol. Rep. no. 40. Ipswich.

Martin, E. 1993, *Settlements on Hilltops: Seven Prehistoric Sites in Suffolk*, East Anglian Archaeol. Rep. no. 65. Ipswich.

Martin-Kilcher, S. 1983, 'Les amphores romaines à huile de Bétique (Dressel 20 et 23) d'Augst (Colonia Augusta Rauricorum) et Kaiseraugst (Castrum Rauracense). Un rapport préliminaire', in J. M. Blázquez and J. Remesal (eds) *Producción y Comercio del Aceite en la Antigüedad. Il Congreso*. Madrid.

Matthews, C. L. 1976, *Occupation Sites on a Chiltern Ridge: Excavations at Puddlehill and Sites near Dunstable, Bedfordshire*, BAR Brit. Ser. no. 29. Oxford.

Mattingly, H., Sydenham, E. A. and Sutherland, C. H. V. (eds), 1923–, *The Roman Imperial Coinage*. London.

May, T. 1930, *Catalogue of the Roman Pottery in the Colchester and Essex Museum*. Cambridge.

Mays, M. (ed.), 1992, *Celtic Coinage: Britain and Beyond*, BAR Brit. Ser. no. 222. Oxford.

McCarthy, M. R. 1990, *A Roman, Anglian and Medieval Site at Blackfriars Street, Carlisle: Excavations 1977–9*, Cumb. & Westmorland Antiq. & Archaeol. Soc. Res. Ser. no. 4. Kendal.

McCarthy, M. 1991, *Roman Waterlogged Remains at Castle Street, Carlisle: Excavations 1981–2*, Cumb. & Westmorland Antiq. & Archaeol. Soc. Res. Ser. no. 5. Kendal.

McKinley, J. 1989, 'Cremations: expectations, methodologies and realities', in C. Roberts *et al* (eds), *Burial Archaeology. Current Research, Methods and Developments*, BAR Brit. Ser. no. 211. Oxford.

McWhirr, A. D. (ed.) 1979, *Roman Brick and Tile. Studies in Manufacture, Distribution and Use in the Western Empire*, BAR Int. Ser. no. 68. Oxford.

Meaney, A. 1964, *A Gazetteer of Early Anglo-Saxon Burial Sites*. London.

Meates, G. W. 1987, *The Roman Villa at Lullingstone, Kent, Volume II: The Wall Paintings and Finds*. Maidstone.

Meeks, N. D. 1993, 'Surface characterisation of tinned bronze, high-tin bronze, tinned iron and arsenical bronze', in S. La Niece and P. Craddock (eds), *Metal Plating and Patination. Cultural, Technical and Historical Developments*, 247–75. Oxford.

Menzel, H. 1966, *Die Römischen Bronzen aus Deutschland II: Trier*. Mainz.

Middleton, A. P., Freestone, I. C. and Leese, M. N. 1985, 'Textural analysis of ceramic thin sections: evaluation of grain sampling procedures', *Archaeometry*, 27, 64–74.

Middleton, R. 1990, 'The Walker Collection: a quantitative analysis of lithic material from the March/Manea area of the Cambridgeshire Fens', *Proc. Camb. Antiq. Soc.*, 79, 13–38.

Mielsch, H. 1985, *Buntmarmore aus Rom im Antikenmuseum Berlin.* Berlin.

Miket, R. 1983, *The Roman Fort at South Shields: Excavation of the Defences, 1977–1981.* Gateshead.

Miles, D (ed.) 1986, *Archaeology at Barton Court Farm, Abingdon, Oxon.* Oxford and London.

Miller, S. H. and Skertchly, S. B. J. 1878, *The Fenland Past and Present.* Wisbech.

Millett, M. 1990, *The Romanisation of Britain.* Cambridge.

Millett, M. and Graham, D. 1986, *Excavations on the Romano-British Small Town at Neatham, Hampshire 1969–1979*, Hampshire Field Club Monogr. 3. Gloucester.

Millett, M. with James, S. 1983, 'Excavations at Cowdery's Down, Basingstoke, Hampshire, 1978–81', *Archaeol. J.* 140, 151–279.

Milne, J. S. 1907, *Surgical Instruments in Greek and Roman Times.* Oxford; reprinted Chicago 1976.

Monkton, A. 1979, 'Romano-British site at Lower Runhams, Lenham', *Kent Archaeol. Rev.*, 55, 118–21.

Morris, C. A. 1990, 'Wooden finds', in Wrathmell and Nicholson 1990, 206–30.

Morris, S. and Buckley, D. G. 1978, 'Excavations at Danbury Camp, Essex, 1974 and 1977', *Essex Archaeol. & Hist.*, 10, 1–28.

Murphy, J. and Riley, J. P. 1962, 'A modified single solution method for the determination of phosphate in natural waters', *Analytica Chimica Acta*, 27, 31–6.

Murphy, P, 1984, 'Environmental Archaeology in East Anglia', in Keeley 1984, 13–42.

Murphy, P. 1985, 'The cereals and crop weeds', in West 1985, 100–8.

Murphy, P. 1991, 'Early crop production and wild resources in the coastal area of Essex, England', in Renfrew 1991, 329–48.

Mynard, D. C. (ed.) 1987, *Roman Milton Keynes, Excavations and Fieldwork, 1971–1982*, Bucks Archaeol. Soc. Monogr. Ser. no. 1. Aylesbury.

Myres, J. N. L. 1977, *A Corpus of Anglo-Saxon Pottery of the Pagan Period.* Cambridge.

Nash-Williams, V. E. 1932, 'The Roman legionary fortress at Caerleon in Monmouthshire. Report on the excavations carried out in the Prysg Field, 1927–9. Part 2: the finds', *Archaeol. Cambrensis*, 87, 48–104.

NBI: National Bronze Implements Index, British Museum.

Neal, D. S. 1974, *The Excavation of the Roman Villa in Gadebridge Park, Hemel Hempstead, 1963–8.* London.

Neal, D. S. 1984, 'A sanctuary at Wood Lane End, Hemel Hempstead', *Britannia*, 15, 193–215.

Neal, D. S. 1989, 'The Stanwick villa, Northants: an interim report on the excavations of 1984–88', *Britannia*, 20, 149–68.

Neal, D. S., Wardle, A. and Hunn, J. 1990, *Excavation of the Iron Age, Roman and Medieval Settlement at Gorhambury, St. Albans*, English Heritage Archaeol. Rep. no. 14. London.

Needham, S. P. 1980, 'An assemblage of Late Bronze Age metalworking debris from Dainton, Devon', *Proc. Prehist. Soc.*, 46, 177–215.

Needham, S. P. 1990, *The Petters Late Bronze Age Metalwork: An Analytical Study of Thames Valley Metalworking in Its Settlement Context*, Br. Mus. Occas. Pap. no. 70. London.

Needham, S. P. 1991, *Excavation and Salvage at Runnymede Bridge, 1978: The Late Bronze Age Waterfront Site.* London.

Needham, S. P. (forthcoming) 'Chronology and periodisation in the British Bronze Age', in K. R. Randsborg (ed.), Proc. Verona Conf. European Bronze Age Chronology, *Acta Archaeol.*

Niblett, R. 1985, *Sheepen: An Early Roman Industrial Site at Camulodunum*, CBA Res. Rep. no. 57. London.

Nieto, J., Jover, A., Izquierdo, P., Puig, A., Alaminos, A., Martin, A., Pujol, M., Palou, H. and Colomer, S. 1989, *Excavacions Arqueològiques Subaquàtiques a Cala Culip*, Vol. 1. Girona.

Norfolk Museums Service, 1977, *Bronze Age Metalwork in Norwich Castle Museum*, 2nd edn. Norwich.

O'Connell, M. 1986, *Petters Sports Field, Egham: Excavations of a Late Bronze Age/Early Iron Age Site*, Surrey Archaeol. Soc. Res. Vol., no. 10. Guildford.

O'Connor, B. 1980, *Cross-channel Relations in the Later Bronze Age*, BAR Int. Ser. no. 91. Oxford.

O'Connor, T. P. 1986, 'The Roman animal bones', in Zienkiewicz 1986, Vol. II, 226–41.

Oldenstein, J. 1977, 'Zur Ausrüstung römischer Auxiliareinheiten', *Ber. Römisch-Germanischen Komm.*, 57 (1976–7), 49–284.

Olivier, A. 1988, 'The brooches', in Potter and Trow 1988, 35–53.

Ordnance Survey, 1966, *Map of Britain in the Dark Ages*, 2nd edn. Chessington.

Orton, C. 1982, 'Computer simulation experiments to assess the performance of measures of quantity of pottery', *World Archaeol.*, 14 (1), 1–20.

Orton, C. 1989, 'An introduction to the quantification of assemblages of pottery', *J. Roman Pottery Stud.*, 2, 94–7.

Oswald, F. 1936–7, *Index of Figure-Types on Terra Sigillata, 'Samian Ware'.* Liverpool 1937; reprinted London 1964.

Oswald, F. and Pryce, T. D. 1920, *Introduction to the Study of Terra Sigillata.* Reprinted 1964. London.

Padley, T. G. 1991, *The Metalwork, Glass and Stone Objects from Castle Street, Carlisle: Excavations 1981–2*, Cumb. & Westmorland Antiq. & Archaeol. Soc. Res. Ser. no. 5, fasc. 2. Kendal.

Padley, T. G. and Winterbottom, S. 1991, *The Wooden, Leather and Bone Objects from Castle Street, Carlisle: Excavations 1981–2*, Cumb. & Westmorland Antiq. & Archaeol. Soc. Res. Ser. no. 5, fasc. 3. Kendal.

Parker, A. J. 1988, 'The birds of Roman Britain', *Oxf. J. Archaeol.*, 7, 197–226.

Parker Pearson, M. 1993, *Bronze Age Britain.* London.

Partridge, C. 1979, 'Excavations at Puckeridge and Braughing, 1975–79', *Hertfordshire Archaeol.*, 7, 28–132.

Partridge, C. 1981, *Skeleton Green: A Late Iron Age and Romano-British Site*, Britannia Monogr. no. 2. London.

Passmore, A. D. 1922, 'Roman Wanborough', *Wilts. Archaeol. & Nat. Hist. Mag.*, 41, 272–80.

Peacock, D. P. S. 1978, 'The Rhine and the problem of Gaulish wine in Roman Britain', in J. du Plat Taylor and H. Cleere (eds), *Roman Shipping and Trade: Britain and the Rhine Provinces*, 49–51. London.

Peacock, D. P. S. and Williams, D. F. 1986, *Amphorae and the Roman Economy.* London.

Pearson, G. W. and Stuiver, M. 1986, 'High precision calibration of the radiocarbon time scale, 500–2500 BC', *Radiocarbon*, 28(28), 839–62.

Peers, C. R. and Radford, C. A. R. 1943, 'The Saxon monastery at Whitby', *Archaeologia*, 89, 27–88.

Pendleton, C. F. 1985, 'A gold "hair-ring" from Wimblington parish, Cambridgeshire', *Proc. Camb. Antiq. Soc.*, 74, 85–6.

Penn, W. S. 1957, 'The Romano-British settlement at Springhead: excavation of the bakery, Site A', *Archaeol. Cantiana*, 71, 53–102.

Penn, W. S. 1959, 'The Romano-British settlement at Springhead: excavation of Temple I, Site C1', *Archaeol. Cantiana*, 73, 1–61.

Penn, W. S. 1964, 'Springhead: the temple ditch site', *Archaeol. Cantiana*, 79, 170–89.

Perring, F. H., Sell, P. D. and Walters, S. M. 1964, *A Flora of Cambridgeshire*. Cambridge.

Peterken, G. F. 1981, *Woodland Conservation and Management*. London.

Pfeiler, B. 1970, *Römischer Goldschmuck*. Mainz.

Phillips, C. W. 1948, 'Ancient earthworks', in *The Victoria County History of Cambridgeshire, Vol. II*, 1–47. Oxford.

Phillips, C. W. 1951, 'The Fenland Research Committee, its past achievements and future prospects', in W. F. Grimes (ed.), *Aspects of Archaeology in Britain and Beyond: Essays Presented to O. G. S. Crawford*, 258–71. London.

Phillips, C. W. (ed.) 1970, *The Fenland in Roman Times*. London.

Philp, B. 1981, *The Excavation of the Roman Forts of the Classis Britannica at Dover, 1970–1977*, Kent Monogr. Ser., Third Res. Rep. Dover.

Pitt-Rivers, A. H. L. F. 1887, *Excavations in Cranborne Chase, Vol. I*. Privately printed.

Pitt-Rivers, A. H. L. F. 1888, *Excavations in Cranborne Chase, Vol. II*. Privately printed.

Pitts, L. F. 1979, *Roman Bronze Figurines from the Civitates of the Catuvellauni and Trinovantes*, BAR Brit. Ser. no. 60. Oxford.

Pitts, L. F. and St Joseph, J. K. 1985, *Inchtuthil. The Roman Legionary Fortress Excavations 1952–65*, Britannia Monogr. no. 6. London.

Polunin, O. 1976, *Trees and Bushes of Britain and Europe*. St Albans.

Ponsich, M. 1970, 1974, 1991, *Implantation Rurale Antique dans le Bas-Guadalquivir*. Vol. I, Madrid 1970; Vol. II, Paris 1974; Vol. IV, Paris 1991.

Potter, T. W. 1965, 'The Roman pottery from Coldham Clamp and its affinities', *Proc. Camb. Antiq. Soc.*, 58, 12–37.

Potter, T. W. 1975–6, 'Excavations at Stonea, Cambs.', *Proc. Camb. Aniq. Soc.*, 66 (1975–6) [1976], 23–54.

Potter, T. W. 1979, *Romans in North-west England. Excavations at the Roman Forts of Ravenglass, Watercrook and Bowness-on-Solway*, Cumb. & Westmorland Antiq. & Archaeol. Soc. Res. Ser. no. 1. Kendal.

Potter, T. W. 1981, 'The Roman occupation of the central Fenland', *Britannia*, 12, 79–133.

Potter, T. W. 1989a, 'Recent work on the Roman Fens of Eastern England and the question of Imperial Estates', *J. Roman Archaeol.*, 2, 267–75.

Potter, T. W. 1989b, 'The Roman Fenland: a review of recent work', in Todd 1989, 147–73.

Potter, T. W. and Hall, D. 1981, 'The Iron Age in the Central Fenland', in Potter 1981, 81–5.

Potter, T. W. and Jackson, R. P. J. 1982, 'The Roman site of Stonea, Cambridgeshire', *Antiquity*, 56, 111–20.

Potter, T. W. and Potter, C. F. 1982, *A Romano-British Village at Grandford, March, Cambs.*, Br. Mus. Occas. Pap. no. 35. London.

Potter, T. W. and Trow, S. D. 1988, *Puckeridge-Braughing, Herts.: The Ermine Street Excavations, 1971–1972, The Late Iron Age and Roman Settlement*, Hertfordshire Archaeol., 10.

Potter, T. W. and Whitehouse, D. B. 1982, 'A Roman building in the Cambridgeshire Fens and some parallels near Rome', *World Archaeol.*, 14, 218–23.

Powlesland, D., Haughton, C. and Hanson, J. 1986, 'Excavations at Heslerton, North Yorkshire 1978–82', *Archaeol. J.*, 143, 53–173.

Price, J. 1980, 'The Roman glass', in G. Lambrick, 'Excavations in Park Street, Towcester', *Northants Archaeol.*, 15, 63–8.

Price, J. 1985, 'The glass', in Bidwell 1985, 206–14.

Price, J. 1987, 'Glass from Felmongers, Harlow in Essex. A dated deposit of vessel glass found in an Antonine pit', *Annales du 10e Congrés de l'Association Internationale pour l'Histoire de Verre*, 185–206.

Price, J. 1989a, 'The glass', in T. J. O'Leary, *Pentre Farm, Flint, 1976–81*, BAR Brit. Ser. no. 207, 77–86. Oxford.

Price, J. 1989b, 'Glass', in Stead and Rigby 1989, 40–50.

Price, J. and Cool, H. E. M. 1985, 'Glass', in Hurst 1985, 41–54.

Price, J. and Cool, H. E. M. 1993, 'The vessel glass', in M. J. Darling and D. Gurney, *Caister-on-Sea Excavations by Charles Green, 1951–55*, East Anglian Archaeol. Rep. no. 60. Gressenhall.

Price, J. and Cottam, S. 1994, 'Glass', in S. Cracknell and C. Mahaney (eds), *Roman Alcester: Southern Extramural Area. 1964–1966 Excavations, Part 2: Finds and Discussion*, CBA Res. Rep. 97, 224–9. London.

Price, J. and Cottam, S. (forthcoming) 'The Roman glass', in T. G. Padley (ed.) *Roman and Medieval Carlisle, The Lanes, Vol. 1: The Roman and Medieval Finds*, Cumb. & Westmorland Antiq. & Archaeol. Soc. Res. Ser.

Pritchard, F. A. 1986, 'Ornamental stonework from Roman London', *Britannia*, 17, 169–89.

Prummel, W. 1989, 'Appendix to atlas for identification of foetal skeletal elements of cattle, horse, sheep and pig', *Archaeozoologia*, III (1, 2), 71–8.

Pryor, F. M. M. 1980, *Excavation at Fengate, Peterborough, England: the Third Report*, Northants Archaeol. Soc. Monogr. 1/Royal Ontario Mus. Archaeol. Monogr. 6. Northampton.

Pryor, F. M. M. 1984, *Excavation at Fengate, Peterborough, England: the Fourth Report*, Northants Archaeol. Soc. Monogr. 2. Northampton.

Pryor, F. M. M. 1987, 'Etton 1986: Neolithic metamorphoses', *Antiquity*, 61, 78–80.

Pryor, F. M.M. 1991, *Flag Fen. Prehistoric Fenland Centre*. London.

Pryor, F. M. M. 1992, 'Discussion: the Fengate/Northey landscape', *Antiquity*, 66, 518–31.

Pryor, F., French, C., Crowther, D., Gurney, D., Simpson, G. and Taylor, M. 1985, *Archaeology and Environment in the Lower Welland Valley*, Fenland Project Number 1, East Anglian Archaeol. Rep. no. 27. Cambridge.

Pugh, R. B. 1953, *The Victoria County History of Cambridgeshire and the Isle of Ely*, Vol. 4. London.

Rackham, O. 1980, *Ancient Woodland*. London.

Radnoti, A. 1938, *Die Römischen Bronze-gefässe von Pannonien*. Budapest.

Rae, A. and V. 1974, 'The Roman fort at Cramond, Edinburgh. Excavations 1954–1966', *Britannia*, 5, 163–224.

R-B Guide, 1964, *Guide to the Antiquities of Roman Britain*, 3rd edn. London.

Reaney, P. H. 1943, *The Place-names of Cambridgeshire and the Isle of Ely*, Eng. Place-name Soc. 19. Cambridge.

Reece, R. 1973, 'Roman coinage in the Western Empire', *Britannia*, 4, 227–51.

Rees, S. E. 1979, *Agricultural Implements in Prehistoric and Roman Britain*, BAR Brit. Ser. no. 69. Oxford.

Reid-Henry, D. and Harrison, C. 1988, *The History of the Birds of Britain*. London.

Remesal, J. 1986, *La Annona Militaris y la Exportación de Aceite Bético a Germania*. Madrid.

Renfrew, J. (ed.) 1991, *New Light on Early Farming. Recent Developments in Palaeoethnobotany*. Edinburgh.

Reynolds, J., Beard, M. and Roueché, C. 1986, 'Roman inscriptions 1981–5', *J. Roman Stud.*, 76, 124–46.

Rhodes, M. 1980, 'Leather footwear', in D. Jones with M. Rhodes, *Excavations at Billingsgate Buildings, Lower Thames Street, London, 1974*, London & Middlesex Archaeol. Soc. Spec. Pap. 4, 99–128. London.

Rhodes, M. 1991, 'The shoe', 194–6 in R. C. Turner, M. Rhodes and J. P. Wild, 'The Roman body found on Grewelthorpe Moor in 1850: a reappraisal', *Britannia*, 22, 191–201.

RIB II, 1 1991, S. S. Frere *et al* (eds), *The Roman Inscriptions of Britain Volume II: Instrumentum Domesticum*, fasc. 1. Oxford.

Richards, J. D. 1991, *The Viking Age in Britain*. London.

Richardson, K. M. 1944, 'Report on excavations at Verulamium: Insula 17, 1938', *Archaeologia*, 90, 81–126.

Richardson, K. M. 1960, 'A Roman brooch from the Outer Hebrides, with notes on others of its type', *Antiq. J.*, 40, 200–13.

Richmond, I. A. 1925, *Huddersfield in Roman Times*. Huddersfield.

Richmond, I. A. 1931, 'Excavations on Hadrian's Wall in the Birdoswald-Pike Hill sector, 1930', *Trans. Cumb. & Westmorland Antiq. & Archaeol. Soc.*, new ser., 31, 122–56.

Richmond, I. A. 1945, 'The Sarmatae, *Bremetennacum Veteranorum* and the *Regio Bremetennacensis*', *J. Roman Stud.*, 35, 15–29.

Richmond, I. A. 1968, *Hod Hill, Vol. 2. Excavations Carried Out Between 1951 and 1958...* London.

Ricken, H. 1942, *Die Bilderschüsseln der römischen Töpfer von Rheinzabern: Tafeln.* Speyer 1942 and 1948.

Ricken, H. and Fischer, C. 1963, *Die Bilderschüsseln der römischen Töpfer von Rheinzabern: Textband*. Bonn.

Rigby, V. 1988, 'The late prehistoric, Roman and later wares', in I. H. Longworth, A. Ellison and V. Rigby, *Excavations at Grimes Graves, Norfolk, 1972–1976. Fascicule 2: The Neolithic, Bronze Age and Later Pottery*, 100–10. London.

Riha, E. 1979, *Die Römischen Fibeln aus Augst und Kaiseraugst*, Forschungen in Augst 3. Augst.

Riha, E. 1986, *Römisches Toilettgerät und Medizinische Instrumente aus Augst und Kaiseraugst*, Forschungen in Augst 6. Augst.

Rivet, A. L. F. 1983, 'The first Icenian revolt', in B. R. Hartley and J. S. Wacher (eds), *Rome and Her Northern Provinces*, 202–9. Gloucester.

Rivet, A. L. F. and Smith C. 1979, *The Place-names of Roman Britain*. London.

Roach Smith, C. 1857, 'Romano-British pottery', 80–94 in *Collectanea Antiqua* 4. Privately printed.

Robinson, B. and Duhig, C. 1992, 'Anglo-Saxon burials at the "Three Kings", Haddenham 1990', *Proc. Camb. Antiq. Soc.*, 81, 15–38.

Robinson, B. and Gregory, T. 1987, *Norfolk Origins 3: Celtic Fire and Roman Rule*. North Walsham.

Robinson, H. Russell 1975, *The Armour of Imperial Rome*. London.

Robinson, M. and Hubbard, R. N. L. B. 1977, 'The transport of pollen in the bracts of hulled cereals', *J. Archaeol. Sci.*, 4, 197–9.

Rodríguez Almeida, E. 1989, *Los Tituli Picti de las Anforas Olearias de la Bética*. Madrid.

Rodwell, J. S. (ed.) 1991, *British Plant Communities: Woodlands and Scrub*, Vol. 1. Cambridge.

Rodwell, K. A. 1988, *The Prehistoric and Roman Settlement at Kelvedon, Essex*, Chelmsford Archaeol. Trust Rep. 6, CBA Res. Rep. no. 63. London.

Rodwell, W. (ed.) 1980, *Temples, Churches and Religion in Roman Britain*, BAR Br. Ser., no. 77. Oxford.

Roes, A. 1963, *Bone and Antler Objects from the Frisian Terp Mounds*. Haarlem.

Rogers, G. B. 1974, *Poteries Sigillées de la Gaule Centrale, I, les Motifs Non Figurés*. Paris.

Rogerson, A. 1977, 'Excavations in Scole, 1973', *East Anglian Archaeol.* 5, 97–224.

Rook, A. G. 1973, 'Excavations at the Grange Romano-British Cemetry, Welwyn, 1967', *Hertfordshire Archaeol.*, 3, 1–30.

Rostovtzeff, M. 1957, *The Social and Economic History of the Roman Empire*, 2nd edn. Oxford.

Rouvier-Jeanlin, M. 1972, *Les Figurines Gallo-romaines en Terre Cuite au Musée des Antiquités Nationales, Gallia*, Suppl. XXIV. Paris.

Rowlands, M. J. 1976, *The Organisation of Middle Bronze Age Metalworking* BAR Br. Ser. no. 31. Oxford.

Rumble, A. 1981, *Domesday Book*. Chichester.

Ruoff-Väänänen, E. 1978, *Studies on the Italian Fora*. Wiesbaden.

Ruprechtsberger, E. M. 1978, *Die Römischen Bein- und Bronzenadeln aus den Museen Enns und Linz*. Linz.

Russel, A. D. 1984, *Early Anglo-Saxon Ceramics from East Anglia: A Microprovenience Study*, PhD thesis, University of Southampton.

Russell, M. J. G. 1989, 'Excavation of a multi-period site in Weston Wood, Albury: the pottery', *Surrey Archaeol. Coll.*, 79, 3–51.

Sági, K. 1981, *Das Römische Gräberfeld von Keszthely-Dobogó*. Budapest.

Salway, P. 1967, 'Excavations at Hockwold-cum-Wilton, Norfolk, 1960–1962', *Proc. Camb. Antiq. Soc.*, 60, 39–80.

Salway, P. 1970, 'The Roman Fenland', in Phillips 1970, 1–21.

Salway, P. 1981, *Roman Britain*. Oxford.

Sawyer, P. H. 1968, *Anglo-Saxon Charters*. London.

Scarth, H. M. 1864, *Aquae Sulis, or Notices of Roman Bath*. London and Bath.

Schmidt, P. K. and Burgess, C. B. 1981, *The Axes of Scotland and Northern England*, Prähistorische Bronzefunde Abt. IX, 7. Munich.

Sellwood, L. 1984a, 'Objects of bone and antler', in Cunliffe 1984, 371–95.

Sellwood, L. 1984b, 'Tribal boundaries viewed from the perspective of numismatic evidence', in B. Cunliffe and D. Miles (eds), *Aspects of the Iron Age in Central Southern Britain*, Oxf. Univ. Comm. Archaeol. Monogr. no. 2.

Semenov, S. A. 1964, *Prehistoric Technology*. London.

Sherwin-White, A. N. 1973, *The Roman Citizenship*. Oxford.

Shiel, N. 1977, *The Episode of Carausius and Allectus*, BAR Br. Ser. no. 40. Oxford.

Shotter, D. C. A. 1978, 'Unpublished Roman hoards in the Wisbech and Fenland Museum', *Coin Hoards* IV, 47–50.

Shotter, D. C. A. 1979, 'Coin evidence and the Roman occupation of North-west England', in N. J. Higham (ed.), *The Changing Past*, 1–13. Manchester.

Shotter, D. C. A. 1981, 'Roman coins from the Central Fenland', in Potter 1981, 120–7.

Silver, I. A. 1969, 'The ageing of domestic animals', in D. Brothwell and E. Higgs (eds), *Science in Archaeology*, 283–302. London.

Silvester, R. J. 1988, *Marshland and the Nar Valley, Norfolk*, Fenland Project Number 3, East Anglian Archaeol. Rep. no. 45. Cambridge.

Silvester, R. J. 1991, *The Wissey Embayment and the Fen Causeway, Norfolk*, Fenland Project Number 4, East Anglian Archaeol. Rep. no. 52. Norwich.

Sparks, B. W. 1961, 'The ecological interpretation of Quaternary non-marine mollusca', *Proc. Linnaean Soc. Lond.*, 172, 71–80.

Sparks, B. W. 1964, 'Non-marine mollusca and Quaternary ecology', *J. Animal Ecol.* 33, 87–98.

Sparks, B. W. and West, R. G. 1959, 'The palaeoecology of the interglacial deposits at Histon Road, Cambridge', *Eiszeitalter Gegenw.*, 10, 123–43.

Sparks, B. W. and West, R. G. 1970, 'Late Pleistocene deposits at Wretton, Norfolk', *Phil. Trans. R. Soc.* (B), 258, 1–30.

Speidel, M.P. 1978, *Guards of the Roman Armies*, Antiquitas, Reihe 1.28. Bonn.

Sprague, R. 1968, 'A suggested terminology and classification for burial description', *Am. Antiq.*, 33(4), 479–85.

Spratling, M. G. 1972, *Southern British Decorated Bronzes of the Late Pre-Roman Iron Age*. Unpublished PhD thesis, University of London.

Stafford, P. 1985, *The East Midlands in the Early Middle Ages*. Leicester.

Stallibrass, S. 1982, 'The faunal remains', in Potter and Potter 1982, 98–122.

Stallibrass, S. M. 1991, 'Animal bones from excavations at Annetwell Street, Carlisle, 1982–4. Period 3: the earlier timber fort', *Ancient Monuments Laboratory Report* 132/91.

Stanfield, J. A. and Simpson, G. 1958, *Central Gaulish Potters*. London.

Stanford, S. C. 1974, *Croft Ambrey*. Hereford.

Stead, I. M. 1968, 'An Iron Age hill-fort at Grimthorpe, Yorkshire, England', *Proc. Prehist. Soc.*, 34, 148–90.

Stead, I. M. 1976, *Excavations at Winterton Roman Villa, and Other Roman Sites in North Lincolnshire, 1958–1969*, DoE Archaeol. Rep. 9. London.

Stead, I. M. 1980, *Rudston Roman Villa*. Leeds.

Stead, I. M. 1991, *Iron Age Cemeteries in East Yorkshire*, Eng. Heritage Archaeol. Rep. no. 22. London.

Stead, I. M. and Rigby, V. 1986, *Baldock*, Britannia Monogr. no. 7. London.

Stead, I. M. and Rigby, V. 1989, *Verulamium: The King Harry Lane Site*, Eng. Heritage Archaeol. Rep. no. 12. London.

Straker, V. 1984, 'First and Second century carbonised cereal grain from Roman London', in van Zeist and Casparie 1984, 323–9.

Stukeley, W. 1766, 'Letter from the late Dr. Stukely, to Mr Peter Collinson, F.R.S. giving an Account of several British Antiquities lately found near Chateris, in the isle of Ely', *Gentleman's Mag.*, 36, 118–21.

Sunter, N. and Woodward, P. J. 1987, *Romano-British Industries in Purbeck*, Dorset Nat. Hist. & Archaeol. Soc. Monogr. Ser. no. 6. Dorchester.

Taylor, A. 1985, 'Prehistoric, Roman, Saxon and Medieval artefacts from the southern fen edge, Cambridgeshire', *Proc. Camb. Antiq. Soc.*, 74, 1–52.

Taylor, A. 1993, 'A Roman lead coffin with pipeclay figurines from Arrington, Cambridgeshire', *Britannia*, 24, 191–225.

Taylor, A. and Evans, C. 1993, 'Field-work in Cambridgeshire, January–September 1993', *Proc. Camb. Antiq. Soc.*, 82, 163–71.

Taylor, R. J. and Brailsford, J. W. 1985, 'British Iron Age strap-unions', *Proc. Prehist. Soc.*, 51, 247–72.

Thomas, R., Robinson, M., Barrett, J. and Wilson, B. 1986, 'A Late Bronze Age riverside settlement at Wallingford, Oxfordshire', *Archaeol. J.*, 143 (1986) [1987], 174–200.

Thompson, F. H. 1965, *Roman Cheshire*. Chester.

Thornton, J. 1973, 'A glossary of shoe terms', *Trans. Mus. Assistants' Gp*, 44–8.

Thorpe, W. A. 1935, *English Glass*. London.

Tilson, P. 1973, 'A Belgic and Romano-British site at Bromham', *Bedfordshire Archaeol. J.*, 8, 23–66.

Todd, M. 1969, 'Margidunum: Excavations 1966–8', *Trans. Thoroton Soc. Notts.*, 73, 5–104.

Todd, M. 1973, *The Coritani*. London.

Todd, M. (ed.) 1989, *Research on Roman Britain, 1960–89*, Britannia Monogr. no. 11. London.

Tomber, R. 1988, *Pottery in a Long-Distance Economic Inference: An Investigation of Methodology with Reference to Roman Carthage*. PhD thesis, University of Southampton.

Tomlin, R. S. O. 1979, 'Graffiti on Roman bricks and tiles found in Britain', in A. D. McWhirr (ed.), *Roman Brick and Tile*, BAR Int. Ser. no. 68, 231–52. Oxford.

Tomlin, R. S. O. 1983, 'Non Coritani sed Corieltauvi', *Antiq. J.*, 63, 353–5.

Topping, P. 1982, 'Excavation at the cursus at Scorton, N. Yorkshire', *Yorkshire Archaeol. J.*, 54, 7–22.

Townend, P. and Hinton, P. 1978, 'Glass', in G. Dennis, '1–7 St Thomas Street', *Southwark Excavations 1972–4*, Lond. & Middlesex Archaeol. Soc. and Surrey Archaeol. Soc. Joint Publ. 1, 387–9. London.

Toynbee, J. M. C. 1964, *Art in Britain under the Romans*. Oxford.

Trow, S. D. 1988, 'Excavations at Ditches hillfort, North Cerney, Gloucestershire, 1982–3', *Trans. Bristol & Gloucs. Archaeol. Soc.*, 106, 19–85.

Turnbull, P. 1978, 'The phallus in the art of Roman Britain', *Bull. Inst. Archaeol.*, 15, 199–206.

Turner, R. C. and Rhodes, M. 1992, 'A bog body and its shoes from Amcotts, Lincolnshire', *Antiq. J.*, 72, 76–90.

Tyers, P. 1993, 'The plain samian', in W. H. Manning (ed.), *Report on the excavations at Usk 1965–1976. The Roman pottery*, 127–43. Cardiff.

Ubelaker, D. H. 1989, *Human Skeletal Remains. Excavation, Analysis, Interpretation*, Smithsonian Institution Manuals on Archaeology 2, 2nd edn. Washington, DC.

Van Arsdell, R. D. 1987, 'The coinage of Queen Boudicca', *Numismatic Circ.*, 95(5), 150–1.

Van Arsdell, R. D. 1989, *Celtic Coinage of Britain*. London.

Van Arsdell, R. D. 1992, 'Three new Celtic staters', *Numismatic Circ.*, 100(3), 80.

Veen, M. van der 1991, 'Consumption or production? Agriculture in the Cambridgeshire Fens?', in Renfrew 1991, 349–61.

Veen, M. van der 1993, 'Grain impressions in early Anglo-Saxon pottery from Mucking', in Hamerow 1993, 80–1.

Verzàr, M. 1978, *Aventicum II: un temple du Culte Impérial*. Lausanne.

Vuorela, I. 1973, 'Relative pollen rain around cultivated fields', *Acta Botanica Fennica*, 102, 1–27.

Wacher, J. S. and McWhirr, A. D. 1982, *Early Roman Occupation at Cirencester*, Cirencester Excavations I. Cirencester.

Wainwright, G. J. 1979, *Gussage All Saints: An Iron Age Settlement in Dorset*. London.

Wait, G. A. 1985, *Ritual and Religion in Iron Age Britain*, BAR Br. Ser. no. 149. Oxford.

Walker, D. R. 1976, *The Metrology of Roman Silver Coinage, Part I: From Augustus to Domitian*, BAR Supp. Ser. no. 5. Oxford.

Walker, F. G. 1912, 'Roman pottery kilns at Horningsea, Cambs.', *Proc. Camb. Antiq. Soc.*, 17, 14–69.

Waller, M. 1988, 'The Fenland Project's environmental programme', *Antiquity*, 62, 336–43.

Walsham, J. R. 1996, *Identification of Post-medieval Sheep Management at Stonea, Cambridgeshire*. Unpublished BSc dissertation, Dept of Archaeology, University of Durham.

Walters, H. B. 1908, *Catalogue of Roman Pottery in the Departments of Antiquities, British Museum*. London.

Ward-Perkins, J. B. 1938, 'The Roman villa at Lockleys, Welwyn', *Antiq. J.*, 18, 339–76.

Ward-Perkins, J. B. 1962, 'Etruscan engineering: road-building, water-supply and drainage', in M. Renard (ed.), *Hommages à Albert Grenier*, Collection Latomus 58, 1636–43.

Ward-Perkins, J. B. 1981, *Roman Imperial Architecture*. Harmondsworth.

Warner, P. 1988, 'Pre-conquest territorial and administrative organization in East Suffolk', in Hooke 1988, 9–34.

Watling, R. and Seaward, M. R. D. 1976, 'Some observations on puff-balls from British archaeological sites', *J. Archaeol. Sci.*, 3, 165–72.

Webster, G. 1957, 'Further excavations at the Roman fort, Kinvaston, Staffordshire', *Trans. & Proc. Birmingham Archaeol. Soc.*, 73 (1955) [1957], 100–8.

Webster, G. 1981, 'Final report on the excavations of the Roman fort at Waddon Hill, Stoke Abbot, 1963–69', *Proc. Dorset Nat. Hist. & Archaeol. Soc.*, 101, 51–90.

Webster, G. 1986, *The British Celts and their Gods under Rome*. London.

Webster, G. 1989, 'Deities and religious scenes on Romano-British pottery', *J. Roman Pottery Stud.*, 2, 1ff.

Webster, G. 1991, 'Romano-British scenes and figures on pottery', in *Archaeologist at Large*, 129ff. London.

Webster, J. 1990, 'An unusual brooch from Caerleon', *Britannia*, 21, 297–9.

Webster, L. and Backhouse, J. 1991, *The Making of England: Anglo-Saxon Art and Culture AD 600–900*. London.

Wedlake, W. J. 1958, *Excavations at Camerton, Somerset*. Camerton.

Wedlake, W. J. 1982, *The Excavation of the Shrine of Apollo at Nettleton, Wiltshire 1956–1971*. London.

Welch, M. G. 1985, 'Rural settlement patterns in the Early and Middle Anglo-Saxon periods', *Landscape Hist.*, 7, 13–25.

West, S. 1985, *West Stow: The Anglo-Saxon Village*, East Anglian Archaeol. Rep. no. 24. Ipswich.

Wheeler, R. E. M. 1930, *London in Roman Times*. London.

Wheeler, R. E. M. 1943, *Maiden Castle, Dorset*. Oxford.

Wheeler, [R. E.] M. 1954, *The Stanwick Fortifications, North Riding of Yorkshire*. Oxford.

Wheeler, R. E. M. and Wheeler, T. V. 1928, 'The Roman amphitheatre at Caerleon, Monmouthshire', *Archaeologia*, 78, 111–218.

Wheeler, R. E. M. and Wheeler, T. V. 1936, *Verulamium: a Belgic and Two Roman Cities*. Oxford.

Whitelock, D. 1972, 'The pre-Viking age church in East Anglia', *Anglo-Saxon England*, 1, 1–22.

Whiting, W. 1923, 'A Roman cemetery discovered at Ospringe in 1920', *Archaeol. Cantiana*, 36, 65–80.

Whiting, W., Hawley, W. and May, T. 1931, *Report on the Excavation of the Roman Cemetery at Ospringe, Kent*. Res. Rep. Soc. Antiq. Lond. 8.

Whitwell, J. B. 1982, *The Coritani. Some Aspects of the Iron Age Tribe and the Roman Civitas*, BAR Br. Ser. no. 99. Oxford.

Wild, J. P. 1970, *Textile Manufacture in the Northern Roman Provinces*. Cambridge.

Willcox, G. H. 1977, 'Exotic plants from Roman waterlogged sites in London', *J. Archaeol. Sci.*, 4, 269–82.

Williams, A. 1947, 'Canterbury excavations in 1945', *Archaeol. Cantiana*, 60, 68–00.

Williams, D. E. 1973, 'Flotation at Siraf', *Antiquity*, 47, 198–202.

Williams, J. 1976, 'Excavations on a Roman site at Overstone near Northampton', *Northants Archaeol.*, 11, 100–33.

Wilson, D. R. 1975, 'Romano-Celtic temple architecture', *J. Brit. Archaeol. Assoc.*, 38, 3–27.

Wilson, D. R. 1980, 'Romano-Celtic temple architecture: how much do we actually know?' in Rodwell 1980, 5–30.

Wilson, G. 1980, 'Prehistoric finds from the central Fenland', *Proc. Camb. Antiq. Soc.*, 70, 9–12.

Woodward, A. 1992, *Shrines and Sacrifice*. London.

Woodward, P. J. 1987, 'The excavation of a Late Iron Age settlement and Romano-British industrial site at Ower, Dorset', in Sunter and Woodward 1987, 45–124.

Worsfold, F. H. 1943, 'A report on the Late Bronze Age site excavated at Minnis Bay, Birchington, Kent, 1938–40', *Proc. Prehist. Soc.*, 9, 28–47.

Wrathmell, S. and Nicholson, A. 1990, *Dalton Parlours Iron Age Settlement and Roman Villa*. Wakefield.

Wymer, J. 1968, *Lower Palaeolithic Archaeology in Britain as Represented by the Thames Valley*. London.

Yorke, B. 1990, *Kings and Kingdoms of Early Anglo-Saxon England*. London.

Young, A. and Richardson, K. M. 1959–60, 'A Cheardach Mhor Drimore, South Uist', *Proc. Soc. Antiq. Scot.*, 93 (1959–60) [1962], 135–74.

Zadoks-Josephus Jitta, A. N. *et al*, 1969, *Roman Bronze Statuettes from the Netherlands II: Statuettes Found South of the Limes*. Groningen.

Zadoks-Josephus Jitta, A. N. *et al*, 1973, *Description of the Collections in the Rijksmuseum G. M. Kam at Nijmegen, VII: the Figural Bronzes*. Nijmegen.

Zalkin, V. I. 1960, 'Die Variation der Metapodien und ihre Bedeutung für die Erforschung des Rindes in der Frühgeschichte; *Bull. Moskauer Ges. Naturforscher Abt. Biol., Moskau*, 66, 115–32. [In Russian with an English summary.]

Zeepvat, R. J., Roberts, J. S. and King, N. A. 1994, *Caldecotte: Excavation and Fieldwork 1966–91*, Bucks Archaeol. Soc. Monogr. Ser. no. 9.

Zeist, W. van and Casparie, W. A. (eds) 1984, *Plants and Ancient Man, Studies in Palaeoethnobotany*. Rotterdam.

Zienkiewicz, J. D. 1986, *The Legionary Fortress Baths at Caerleon, Vol. I: The Buildings. Vol. II: The Finds*. Cardiff.

STONEA GRANGE:
INDEX OF SITE CONTEXTS

This index is designed to localise every context, though it does not give individual page references. To locate contexts in the text, first check the Primary Feature Phase column. If the context is phased III, IIIa or IV, its block location, given in the adjacent column, corresponds to the section of the text in Chapter 5, Phases III–IV, where the blocks are described in numerical sequence (p. 106ff). If the context is phased 0, I, II, V or VI, it will be found in the corresponding text section for those phases. For ditch/block concordance, see Table 4, p. 86.

Unit number	Group code	Description	Location	Primary feature phase
1980				
2	AB	Walling, bldg R2(?)	Block 1	IV
3	AC	Layer, pit 3	Block 1	V
4	AD	Robbed wall footing, bldg R1, E wing	Block 1	IIIa
5	AE	Sub-floor surface, bldg R1, E wing	Block 1	IIIa
6	AF	Robbed floor footing, bldg R1, N range	Block 1	IIIa
8	AH	Robbed wall footing, bldg R1, E wing	Block 1	IIIa
9	AJ	?Robbed wall, bldg R2(?)	Block 1	IV
11	AL	Layer, gully 49	Block 1	III
12	AM	Robbed wall footing, bldg R1, NE quadrant	Block 1	III
13	AN	Layer, pit 3	Block 1	V
14	AP	Robbing debris/levelling, bldg R1, NE quadrant	Block 1	III
15	AQ	Robbing debris, bldg R1, NE quadrant	Block 1	III
16	AR	Robbing debris, bldg R1, NE quadrant	Block 1	III
17	AS	Robbed wall/footing, bldg R1, N range	Block 1	IIIa
18	AT	Robbing debris, bldg R1, W range	Block 1	IIIa
19	AV	Burnt spread, W of bldg R1	Block 1	III
20	AW	Burnt spread, W of bldg R1	Block 1	III
21	AX	Layer, gully 48	Block 1	III
22	AY	Cobble surface, W of bldg R1	Block 1	III
23	AZ	Ashy spread S and W of bldg R1, small hypocausted room	Block 1a	III–V
24	BA	Layer, bldg R1, small hypocausted room	Block 1a	IIIa
26	BC	Layer, bldg R1, S room	Block 1a	III
27	BD	Robbing debris/levelling bldg R1, SW quadrant	Block 1	III
28	BE	Furnace structure and debris, bldg R1, small hypocausted room	Block 1a	IIIa
29	BF	Robbed wall footing, bldg R1, E wing	Block 1	IIIa
31	BH	Layer, pit 3	Block 1	V
32	BJ	Robbing debris, bldg R1, SE quadrant	Block 1	III
33	BK	Robbing debris, bldg R1, SE quadrant	Block 1	III
34	BL	Robbed wall footing, bldg R1, E wing	Block 1	IIIa
35	BM	Wall footing, bldg R1, SW quadrant	Block 1	III
36	BN	Silted robbing void below 35	Block 1	III
37	BP	Robbing debris, bldg R1, SE quadrant	Block 1	III
38	BQ	Robbing debris, bldg R1, SE quadrant	Block 1	III
39	BR	Wall footing, bldg R1, E wing	Block 1	IIIa
40	BS	Layer, gully 49	Block 1	III
41	BT	Wall footing, bldg R1, S room	Block 1a	III
42	BV	Layer, bldg R1, S room	Block 1a	III
43	BW	Layer, bldg R1, S room	Block 1a	III
44	BX	Robbing debris, bldg R1, W range	Block 1	IIIa
45	BY	Robbing debris, bldg R1, SW quadrant	Block 1	III
46	BZ	Debris on mortar surface beyond SE corner bldg R1, E wing	Block 1	III
47	CA	Wall footing, bldg R1, NE quadrant	Block 1	III
48	CB	Mortar floor, bldg R1, N range	Block 1	IIIa

Unit number	Group code	Description	Location	Primary feature phase
49	CC	Clay surface below 48	Block 1	III
50	CD	Wall footing, bldg R1, SW quadrant	Block 1	III
51	CE	Robbing debris, bldg R1, W range	Block 1	IIIa
52	CF	Robbing debris, bldg R1, SW quadrant	Block 1	III
53	CG	Layer, gully 48	Block 1	III
54	CH	Robbing debris, bldg R1, SW quadrant	Block 1	III
55	CJ	Robbing debris, bldg R1, SE quadrant	Block 1	III
56	CK	Robbing debris, bldg R1, SE quadrant	Block 1	III
57	CL	Wall footing, bldg R1, SE quadrant	Block 1	III
58	CM	Layer, gully 48	Block 1	III
59	CN	Burnt deposit below 46	Block 1	III
60	CP	Layer, gully 48	Block 1	III
61	CQ	Robbed wall footing, bldg R1, W range	Block 1	IIIa
62	CR	Clay slump, bldg R1, SW quadrant	Block 1	III
63	CS	Layer, bldg R1, small hypocausted room	Block 1a	IIIa
64	CT	Robbing debris, bldg R1, SE quadrant	Block 1	III
65	CV	Robbing debris, bldg R1, NW quadrant	Block 1	III
67	CX	Foundation, bldg R1, SW quadrant	Block 1	III
68	CY	Robbing debris, bldg R1, SE quadrant	Block 1	III
69	CZ	Occupation debris SW of bldg R1	Block 1	III
70	DA	Robbed wall footing, bldg R1, E wing	Block 1	IIIa
71	DB	Wall footing, bldg R1, NW quadrant	Block 1	III
72	DC	Robbed footings, bldg R1, W range	Block 1	IIIa
73	DD	Sub-floor surface, bldg R1, N range	Block 1	IIIa
74	DE	Robbing debris, bldg R1, W range	Block 1	IIIa
75	DF	Robbing debris, bldg R1, W range	Block 1	IIIa
76	DG	Robbing debris, bldg R1, W range, SE quadrant	Block 1	III
77	DH	Robbing debris, bldg R1, W range, SE quadrant	Block 1	III
78	DJ	Robbing debris, bldg R1, W range, NE quadrant	Block 1	III
79	DK	Robbing debris, bldg R1, W range, NE quadrant	Block 1	III
80	DL	Clay natural, bldg R1, SW quadrant	Block 1	–
81	DM	Clay natural, bldg R1, SE quadrant	Block 1	–
82	DN	Clay natural, bldg R1, SE quadrant	Block 1	–
83	DP	Wall footing, bldg R1, NE quadrant	Block 1	III
84	DQ	Cobble surface, bldg R1, S and W of small hypocausted room	Block 1a	III
85	DR	Layer, gully 44	Block 1a	III
86	DS	Layer, bldg R1, small hypocausted room	Block 1a	IIIa
87	DT	Silty clay below 69	Block 1	III
88	DV	Wall footing, bldg R1, S room	Block 1a	III
89	DW	Robbing debris, bldg R1, W range	Block 1	IIIa
90	DX	Post-hole or part of beam slot 92/431	Block 1a	II
91	DY	Layer, beneath 84	Block 1a	III
92	DZ	?Beam slot (=431) beneath bldg R1, small hypocausted room	Block 1a	II
93	EA	Footing, bldg R1, W range	Block 1	IIIa
94	EB	Wall footing, bldg R1, E wing	Block 1	IIIa
95	EC	Wall footing, bldg R1, SE quadrant	Block 1	III
96	ED	Foundation, bldg R1, SE quadrant	Block 1	III
97	EE	Foundation, bldg R1, SE quadrant	Block 1	III
98	EF	Foundation, bldg R1, SE quadrant	Block 1	III
99	EG	Footing, bldg R1, W range	Block 1	IIIa
100	EH	Wall footing, bldg R1, E wing	Block 1	IIIa
101	EJ	Clay natural, below 100	Block 1	–
102	EK	Clay natural, below 61	Block 1	–
103	EL	Pila bases, bldg R1, small hypocausted room	Block 1a	IIIa

Unit number	Group code	Description	Location	Primary feature phase
104	EM	Ashy deposit, bldg R1, W of small hypocausted room	Block 1a	III→
105	EN	Robbing debris, bldg R1, NE quadrant	Block 1	III
106	EP	Foundation, bldg R1, SE quadrant	Block 1	III
107	EQ	Silted robbing void below 71	Block 1	III
1981				
117	FB	As 23	Block 1a	III–V
118	FC	Robbing debris, bldg R1, NW quadrant	Block 1	III
119	FD	Robbing debris, bldg R1, SE quadrant	Block 1	III
120	FE	Robbing debris, bldg R1, SW quadrant	Block 1	III
121	FF	Topsoil/cleaning	Block 1a	–
122	FG	Robbing/dereliction debris, bldg R1, S room	Block 1a	III
123	FH	Topsoil/cleaning	Block 1, SE	–
124	FJ	Topsoil/cleaning above bldg R1, N	Block 1	–
127	FM	Upper layer, NW quadrant, low rubbly mound sealing bldg S1	Block 1, NW	Va
128	FN	Cobbled surface N of bldg R1	Block 1	III→
129	FP	Silt layer, N of 128	Block 1, N	III→
130	FQ	Surface of Street 1 E/W	Block 11, W	III→
131	FR	Layer, pit 132	Block 1	IV
132	FS	Layer, pit 132	Block 1	IV
133	FT	Sub-floor foundation, bldg R1, NE and SE quadrants	Block 1	III
134	FV	Layer, NW corner block 1	Block 1	IV–V
135	FW	Layer, well 135	Block 1	III
136	FX	Robbing debris/levelling, bldg R1, NW and NE quadrants	Block 1	III
137	FY	Lower layer, NW quadrant, low rubbly mound sealing bldg S1	Block 1	V
138	FZ	Metalled surface, W of bldg R2 (=459)	Block 1a	III
139	GA	Mortar floor, bldg R2	Block 1a	IV
140	GB	Layer, gully 60	Block 11	V
141	GC	Layer, gully 59	Block 11	V
142	GD	Layer, gully 58	Block 11	V
143	GE	Post-hole, bldg S1 (=341)	Block 11	V
144	GF	Post-hole, bldg S1 (=340)	Block 11	V
145	GG	Post-hole, bldg S1	Block 11	V
146	GH	Post-hole, bldg S1	Block 11	V
147	GJ	Post-hole, bldg S1	Block 11	V
148	GK	Post-hole, bldg S1	Block 11	V
149	GL	Post-hole, bldg S1	Block 11	V
150	GM	Post-hole, bldg S1	Block 11	V
151	GN	Robbing debris, bldg R1, NW quadrant	Block 1	III
152	GP	Rubbly spread, N of gully 48	Block 1	III
153	GQ	Robbing debris, bldg R1, NW quadrant	Block 1	III
154	GR	Robbing debris, bldg R1, NW quadrant	Block 1	III
155	GS	Silty spread, below 59	Block 1	III
156	GT	Layer, well 135	Block 1	III
158	GW	Layer, well 135	Block 1	III
159	GX	Layer, well 135	Block 1	III
160	GY	Robbing debris, bldg R1, NW quadrant	Block 1	III
163	HB	Plinth/floor, bldg R2	Block 1a	IV
164	HC	Layer, gully 48	Block 1	III
165	HD	Layer, gully 49	Block 1	IIIa
166	HE	Layer, gully 49	Block 1	IIIa
167	HF	Clay surface, W of bldg R1	Block 1	III
168	HG	Metalled surface, W of bldg R1	Block 1	III
169	HH	Layer, gully 49	Block 1	IIIa

Unit number	Group code	Description	Location	Primary feature phase
170	HJ	Layer, pit 170	Block 1	III
171	HK	Layer, well 171/558	Block 1	IV
172	HL	Sub-floor natural, bldg R1, E wing	Block 1	–
174	HN	Robbing debris, bldg R1, NW quadrant	Block 1	III
175	HP	Clay and mortar spread, S of bldg S1	Block 1	III–V
176	HQ	Robbing debris, bldg R1, NW quadrant	Block 1	III
177	HR	Robbing debris, bldg R1, NE quadrant	Block 1	III
178	HS	Soil spread, bldg R2	Block 1a	III
179	HT	Layer, gully 44	Block 1a	III
180	HV	'Platform clay', S of bldg R1	Block 1a	III→
181	HW	'Platform clay', N of bldg R1	Block 1	III→
182	HX	Robbing debris, bldg R1, NE quadrant	Block 1	III
184	HZ	Upper layer, SW quadrant, low rubbly mound sealing bldg S1	Block 1	Va
185	JA	Robbing debris, bldg R1, NE quadrant	Block 1	III
186	JB	Layer, gully 43	Block 1a	III
189	JE	Mortar spread below 178	Block 1a	III
190	JF	Layer, pit 132	Block 1	IV
191	JG	Layer, pit 132	Block 1	IV
192	JH	Layer, pit 132	Block 1	IV
193	JJ	Layer, pit 132	Block 1	IV
194	JK	Layer, pit 132	Blcok 1	IV
195	JL	Robbing debris, bldg R1, NE quadrant	Block 1	III
196	JM	Layer, ditch 71	Block 1	VI
197	JN	Mortar surface S of bldg R1	Block 1a	III/IV
198	JP	'Platform clay', S of bldg R1	Block 1a	III
199	JQ	Upper layer, SE quadrant, low rubbly mound sealing bldg S1	Block 1	V
200	JR	Part of silt layer 129	Block 1	III→
201	JS	Upper layer, NE quadrant, low rubbly mound sealing bldg S1	Block 1	V
202	JT	Layer, gully 54	Block 1	IV
203	JV	Dereliction debris, SE of bldg R1	Block 1	IV
204	JW	Robbing debris, bldg R1, NE quadrant	Block 1	III
205	JX	Layer, well 135	Block 1	III
206	JY	Cobbled surface SW of bldg R1, small hypocausted room	Block 1	III
207	JZ	?Hearth, S of bldg R1, small hypocausted room	Block 1a	III/IV
208	KA	Layer, gully 44	Block 1a	III
209	KB	Layer, gully 44	Block 1a	III
210	KC	Layer, well 171/558	Block 1	IV–V
211	KD	Layer, gully 41	Block 1b	III
212	KE	Layer, gully 54	Block 1	IV
213	KF	Layer, well 135	Block 1	III
214	KG	Layer, well 135	Block 1	III
215	KH	Robbing debris, bldg R1, SE quadrant	Block 1	III
216	KJ	Robbing debris, bldg R1, SE quadrant	Block 1	III
217	KK	Layer, gully 44	Block 1a	III
218	KL	Layer, ditch 9	Block 1	III–IV
219	KM	Layer, gully 44	Block 1a	III
220	KN	Layer, pit 170	Block 1	III
221	KP	Layer, pit 3	Block 1	V
222	KQ	Layer, well 171/558	Block 1	IV–V
223	KR	Layer, ditch 9	Block 1	III–IV
224	KS	Layer, beneath 134	Block 1	IV/V
225	KT	Robbing/footing debris, bldg R1, SE quadrant	Block 1	III
226	KV	Layer, well 135	Block 1	III
227	KW	Layer, well 135	Block 1	III

Unit number	Group code	Description	Location	Primary feature phase
228	KX	Layer, gully 54	Block 1	IV
229	KY	Layer, well 171/558	Block 1	IV–V
230	KZ	Layer, well 171/558	Block 1	IV–V
231	LA	Layer, well 171/558	Block 1	IV–V
232	LB	Layer, ditch 9	Block 1	III–IV
233	LC	Silted robbing void, same as 36, bldg R1, SW quadrant	Block 1	III
235	LE	?Portico footing trench, bldg R1	Block 1	III
236	LF	Burnt clay spread, bldg R2	Block 1a	IV
238	LH	Metalled surface, SW part of 138	Block 1a	III
239	LJ	Cobbled surface, part of 206	Block 1a	III
240	LK	Limestone chipping surface, below 206	Block 1a	III
241	LL	Layer, gully 45	Block 1a	III
242	LM	Layer, ditch 9	Block 1	III–IV
243	LN	N wall footing, bldg R1, NW quadrant	Block 1	III
245	LQ	Denuded surface of street 1 E/W, E of bldg S1	Block 11	III→
246	LR	Layer, pit 170	Block 1	III
247	LS	Burnt spread, bldg R2	Block 1a	IV
248	LT	Layer, ditch 9	Block 1	III–IV
250	LW	Layer, gully 49	Block 1	IIIa
251	LX	Layer, gully 61	Block 1	V
252	LY	Layer, gully 57	Block 11	V
253	LZ	Layer, gully 64	Block 1	IV
254	MA	Layer, pit 170	Block 1	III
255	MB	Layer, pit 170	Block 1	III
256	MC	Layer, gully 64	Block 1	IV
257	MD	Layer, gully 62	Block 1	V
258	ME	Layer, gully 49	Block 1	IIIa
259	MF	Layer, well 135	Block 1	III
260	MG	Occupation debris, S of bldg R1	Block 1a	IV
262	MJ	Layer, pit 170	Block 1	III
263	MK	Layer, pit 170	Block 1	III
264	ML	Layer, oven 1	Block 1	IV
265	MM	Post-hole, S of bldg S1	Block 1	Va
266	MN	Part of 265	Block 1	Va
267	MP	Post-hole, S of bldg S1	Block 1	Va
268	MQ	Silt layer	Block 1, N	IV
269	MR	Silt layer	Block 1, N	IV/V
270	MS	Layer, pit 270	Block 1	III/IV
271	MT	Layer, pit 170	Block 1	III
272	MV	Layer, pit 272	Block 1	III
273	MW	Layer, low rubbly mound sealing bldg S1	Block 1	Va
274	MX	Layer, gully 49	Block 1	IIIa
275	MY	Gravel/mortar surface, S of bldg R1	Block 1a	IV
276	MZ	Layer, gully 49	Block 1	IIIa
277	NA	Layer, pit 277	Block 1	?
278	NB	Layer, gully 64	Block 1	IV
279	NC	Lower layer, SW quadrant, low rubbly mound sealing bldg S1	Block 1	V
280	ND	Gravel/silt layer	Block 1, N	IV/V
281	NE	Silt layer, below 269	Block 1, N	III/IV
282	NF	Cobbled surface, below 281	Block 1, N	III
283	NG	Layer, gully 54	Block 1	IV
284	NH	Layer, gully 63	Block 1	IV(?)
285	NJ	Layer, pit 170	Block 1	III
286	NK	Foundation of floor 139, bldg R2	Block 1a	IV

Unit number	Group code	Description	Location	Primary feature phase
287	NL	Layer, pit 170	Block 1	III
288	NM	Part of 235	Block 1	III
289	NN	Robbed wall-footing, bldg R1, E wing	Block 1	IIIa
290	NP	Robbed wall-footing, bldg R1, E wing	Block 1	IIIa
291	NQ	Stake-hole in gully 63	Block 1	IV/V
292	NR	Silt spread, E of 265	Block 1, N	IV
293	NS	Layer, pit 270	Block 1	III/IV
294	NT	Part of cobble spread 128	Block 1	III→
295	NV	Layer, pit 295	Block 1	?
296	NW	'Platform clay', N of bldg R1	Block 1	III/IV
297	NX	Layer, gully 44	Block 1a	III
298	NY	Layer, gully 64	Block 1	IV
299	NZ	Robbed wall-footing, bldg R1, E wing	Block 1	IIIa
300	PA	Part of cobble spread 128	Block 1	III→
302	PC	Robbed wall-footing, bldg R1, E wing	Block 1	IIIa
303	PD	Post-hole, bldg S1	Block 11	V
304	PE	Post-hole, bldg S1	Block 11	V
305	PF	Post-hole, bldg S1	Block 11	V
306	PG	Post-hole, bldg S1	Block 11	V
307	PH	Post-hole, bldg S1	Block 11	V
308	PJ	Post-hole, bldg S1	Block 11	V
309	PK	Post-hole, bldg S1	Block 11	V
310	PL	Post-hole, bldg S1	Block 11	V
311	PM	Layer, pit 170	Block 1	III
312	PN	Part of cobble spread 128	Block 1	III→
313	PP	Part of cobble spread 128	Block 1	III→
314	PQ	Silt layer, NW of bldg R1	Block 1	III→
315	PR	Silt layer, NW of bldg R1	Block 1	III→
316	PS	Stake-hole, bldg S1	Block 11	V
318	PV	Layer, low rubbly mound sealing bldg S1	Block 1	V
319	PW	Burnt spread, W of bldg R2	Block 1a	IV
320	PX	Wall-footing, bldg R1, E wing	Block 1	IIIa
321	PY	Layer, oven 1	Block 1	IV
322	PZ	Wall-footing, bldg R1, E wing	Block 1	IIIa
323	QA	Layer, pit 323	Block 1	?
324	QB	Post-hole, N of pit 170	Block 1	IV/V
325	QC	Layer, oven 2	Block 1	IV
326	QD	Post-hole, N of pit 170	Block 1	IV/V
327	QE	Layer, pit 327	Block 1	?
328	QF	Layer, bldg R2 (=461)	Block 1a	IV
329	QG	Post-hole, bldg S1	Block 11	V
330	QH	Post-hole, bldg S1	Block 11	V
331	Q J	Post-hole, bldg S1	Block 11	V
332	QK	Post-hole, bldg S1	Block 11	V
333	QL	Post-hole, bldg S1	Block 11	V
336	QP	Layer, well 336	Block 1	III
337	QQ	'Platform clay', N of bldg R1, E of 296	Block 1	III/IV
339	QS	Post-hole, SW of well 336	Block 1	V
340	QT	Post-hole, bldg S1 (=144)	Block 11	V
341	QV	Post-hole, bldg S1 (=143)	Block 11	V
343	QX	Layer, pit 270	Block 1	III/IV
344	QY	Wall-footing, bldg R1, S room	Block 1a	III
345	QZ	Post-hole, SW of well 336	Block 1	IV/V
346	SA	Post-hole, E of well 336	Block 1	IV/V

Unit number	Group code	Description	Location	Primary feature phase
347	SB	Post-hole, bldg S1	Block 11	V
348	SC	Clay spread, W of bldg R2	Block 1a	III/IV
349	SD	Layer, pit 349	Block 1	III
350	SE	Post-hole, bldg S1	Block 11	V
351	SF	Post-hole, bldg S1	Block 11	V
352	SG	Post-hole, bldg S1	Block 11	V
353	SH	Stake-hole, bldg S1	Block 11	V
354	SJ	Post-hole, bldg S1	Block 11	V
355	SK	Post-hole, bldg S1	Block 11	V
356	SL	Post-hole, bldg S1	Block 11	V
357	SM	Post-hole, bldg S1	Block 11	V
358	SN	Layer, oven 2	Block 1	IV
359	SP	Layer, well 336	Block 1	III
361	SR	Layer, pit 513/361	Block 1	III
362	SS	Layer, bldg R1, small hypocausted room	Block 1a	IIIa
363	ST	Layer, pit 363	Block 1	?
364	SV	Silt layer, E of bldg S1	Block 1	V
365	SW	Post-hole, bldg S1	Block 11	V
366	SX	Post-hole, bldg S1	Block 11	V
367	SY	Layer, well 336	Block 1	III
368	SZ	Post-hole, bldg S1	Block 11	V
369	TA	Post-hole, bldg S1	Block 11	V
370	TB	Post-hole, bldg S1	Block 11	V
371	TC	Layer, well 336	Block 1	III
372	TD	Post-hole, cut into well 336	Block 1	Va
373	TE	Post-hole, bldg S1	Block 11	V
374	TF	Post-hole, bldg S1	Block 11	V
375	TG	Cobbled surface, part of 128	Block 1	III/IV
376	TH	Clay and pebble surface, SE of bldg R1	Block 1	III
377	TJ	Layer, gully 47	Block 1	III
378	TK	Mortar surface, below 376	Block 1	III
379	TL	Cobble/rubble surface, W of bldg R1, small hypocausted room	Block 1a	III
380	TM	Post-hole, bldg S1	Block 11	V
381	TN	Lower layer, SE quadrant, low rubbly mound sealing bldg S1	Block 1	V
382	TP	Robbing debris, bldg R1, S room	Block 1a	III
385	TS	Post-hole, bldg S1	Block 11	V
386	TV	Post-hole, bldg S1	Block 11	V
387	TW	Post-hole, bldg S1	Block 11	V
388	TX	Stake-hole, bldg S1	Block 11	V
389	TY	Stake-hole, bldg S1	Block 11	V
390	TZ	Stake-hole, bldg S1	Block 11	V
391	VA	Stake-hole, bldg S1	Block 11	V
392	VB	Stake-hole, bldg S1	Block 11	V
393	VC	Stake-hole, bldg S1	Block 11	V
394	VD	Stake-hole, bldg S1	Block 11	V
395	VE	Stake-hole, bldg S1	Block 11	V
396	VF	Stake-hole, bldg S1	Block 11	V
397	VG	Stake-hole, bldg S1	Block 11	V
398	VH	Stake-hole, bldg S1	Block 11	V
399	VJ	Post-hole, bldg S1	Block 11	V
400	VK	Stake-hole, S of bldg S1	Block 1	IV/V
401	VL	Layer, post-hole 265	Block 1	Va
402	VM	Post-hole, E of bldg S1	Block 11	V
403	VN	Post-hole, E of bldg S1	Block 11	V

Unit number	Group code	Description	Location	Primary feature phase
404	VP	Layer, post-hole 265	Block 1	Va
405	VQ	Dark soil spread around well 336	Block 1	III
406	VR	Post-hole, N of oven 1	Block 1	IV/V
407	VS	Post-hole, N of oven 1	Block 1	IV/V
408	VT	Part of 405	Block 1	III
409	VV	Post-hole, bldg S1	Block 11	V
410	VW	Silt-layer, below 268	Block 1, N	III/IV
411	VX	Same as 279	Block 1	V
412	VY	Layer, well 336	Block 1	III
413	VZ	Pot in small pit, NW of well 336	Block 1	IV
414	WA	Layer, post-hole 267	Block 1	Va
415	WB	Layer, well 336	Block 1	III
418	WE	Post-hole, bldg S1	Block 11	V
419	WF	Layer, post-hole 267	Block 1	Va
420	WG	Post-hole, bldg S1	Block 11	V
421	WH	Post-hole, bldg S1	Block 11	V
422	WJ	Small hearth	Block 1	II(?)
423	WK	Stake-hole, W of well 336	Block 1	IV/V
424	WL	Layer, pit 424	Block 1	?
426	WN	Stake-hole, W of well 336	Block 1	IV/V
427	WP	Post-hole, W of well 336	Block 1	IV/V
428	WQ	Stake-hole, N of well 336	Block 1	IV/V
429	WR	Post-hole, bldg S1	Block 11	V
430	WS	Post-hole, bldg S1	Block 11	V
431	WT	?Beam slot (=92), beneath bldg R1, small hypocausted room	Block 1a	II
432	WV	Post-hole, bldg S1	Block 11	V
433	WW	Post-hole, bldg S1	Block 11	V
434	WX	Cobbled surface, same as 282	Block 1, N	III
435	WY	Post-hole, bldg S1	Block 11	V
440	XD	Post-hole, E of bldg S1	Block 11	V
441	XE	Post-hole, N of bldg S1	Block 11	V
1982				
442	AAA	Topsoil/cleaning	Block 1b	–
443	AAB	Layer, well 446	Block 1a	III
444	AAC	Hearth, bldg R7	Block 4	III
445	AAD	Layer, above 449	Block 1	III→
446	AAE	Layer, well 446	Block 1a	III
447	AAF	Topsoil/cleaning	Block 5a	–
448	AAG	Topsoil/cleaning	Block 5	–
449	AAH	Mortar surface, E of bldg R1, E wing	Block 1	IIIa
450	AAI	Layer, gully 41	Block 1b	III
451	AAK	Layer, sump	Block 6	III
452	AAL	Layer, below 449	Block 1	III
453	AAM	Layer, below 452	Block 1	III
454	AAN	Layer, gully 41	Block 1b	III
455	AAO	Layer, gully 41	Block 1b	III
456	AAP	Layer, gully 41	Block 1b	III
457	AAQ	Layer, gully 41	Block 1b	III
458	AAR	Layer, gully 41	Block 1b	III
459	AAS	Metalled surface W of bldg R2 (=138)	Block 1a	III
460	AAT	Mortar surface, bldg R2	Block 1a	IV
461	AAV	Layer, bldg R2 (=328)	Block 1a	IV
462	AAW	Layer, sump	Block 6	III

Unit number	Group code	Description	Location	Primary feature phase
463	AAX	Layer, gully 42	Block 1b	III
464	AAY	Layer, sump	Block 6	III
465	AAZ	Layer, bldg R3	Block 1b	III
466	ABA	Layer, bldg R3, (=468)	Block 1b	III
467	ABB	Layer, gully 41	Block 1b	III
468	ABC	Layer, bldg R3, (=466)	Block 1b	III
469	ABD	Layer, bldg R3	Block 1b	III
470	ABE	Layer, gully 50	Block 1	IV
471	ABF	Topsoil/cleaning	Block 1	–
472	ABG	Layer, ditch 9	Block 1	III–IV
473	ABH	Layer, ditch 71	Block 1	VI
474	ABI	Layer, ditch 9	Block 1	III–IV
475	ABK	Layer, N of sump	Block 1	IV–V
476	ABL	Layer, beneath 475	Block 1	III
477	ABM	Mortar surface, beyond SE corner bldg R1	Block 1	III/IV
478	ABN	Foundation of 477	Block 1	III/IV
479	ABO	Clay natural	Block 6, NW	–
480	ABP	Layer, ditch 71	Block 1	VI
481	ABQ	Topsoil/cleaning	Blocks 2–4	–
482	ABR	Layer (=955) in region of ovens 6–8 and bldg R5	Block 2	IV
483	ABS	Layer, pit 483/918	Block 2	III/IV
484	ABT	Layer, sump	Block 6	III
485	ABV	Layer, pit 485	Block 5a	III
486	ABW	Post-hole, bldg R3	Block 1b	III
487	ABX	Layer, ditch 9	Block 1	III–IV
488	ABY	Layer, ditch 71	Block 1	VI
489	ABZ	Layer, ditch 6	Block 1	III
490	ACA	Post-hole, bldg R3	Block 1b	III
491	ACB	Layer, ditch 7	Block 1	III
492	ACC	Layer, well 446	Block 1a	III
493	ACD	Layer, gully 41	Block 1b	III
494	ACE	Layer, ditch 9	Block 1	III–IV
495	ACF	Post-hole, S of gully 41	Block 1b	?
496	ACG	Layer, ditch 71	Block 1	VI
497	ACH	Fence slot, E side of 489	Block 1	III
498	ACI	Layer, gully 41	Block 1b	III
499	ACK	Layer, well 446	Block 1a	III
500	ACL	Layer, ditch 9	Block 1	III–IV
501	ACM	Layer, gully 50	Block 1	IV
502	ACN	Small gully, bldg R2	Block 1a	IV
503	ACO	Layer, bldg R2	Block 1a	IV
504	ACP	Layer, pit 504	Block 1	V
505	ACQ	Layer, pit 505	Block 1	IV?
506	ACR	Layer, gully 50	Block 1	IV
507	ACS	Layer, ditch 9	Block 1	III–IV
508	ACT	Cobbled surface, part of 128	Block 1	III→
509	ACV	Layer, ditch 74	Block 1	?0–IV
510	ACW	Layer, gully 51	Block 1	IV
511	ACX	Layer, pit 511	Block 1	IV?
512	ACY	Layer, pit 512	Block 1	IV
513	ACZ	Layer, pit 513/361	Block 1	III
514	ADA	Layer, sump	Block 6	III
515	ADB	Layer, well 446	Block 1a	III
516	ADC	Layer, ditch 71	Block 1	VI

Unit number	Group code	Description	Location	Primary feature phase
517	ADD	Layer, ditch 71	Block 1	VI
518	ADE	Layer, sump	Block 6	III
519	ADF	Layer, gully 53	Block 1	IV/V
520	ADG	Layer, pit 520	Block 1	III
521	ADH	Layer, gully 51	Block 1	IV
522	ADI	Silt layer	Block 1, NE	–
523	ADK	Layer, sump	Block 6	III
524	ADL	Layer, well 446	Block 1a	III
525	ADM	Layer, ditch 9	Block 1	III–IV
526	ADN	Layer, pit 604	Block 5a	III
527	ADO	Oyster midden deposit, bldg R4	Block 1	IV
528	ADP	Layer, pit 528	Block 1	III/IV
529	ADQ	Layer, gully 42	Block 1b	III
530	ADR	Post-hole, below 527	Block 1	III/IV
531	ADS	Layer, ditch 9	Block 1	III–IV
532	ADT	Layer, ditch 9	Block 1	III–IV
533	ADV	Silt layer, part of 522	Block 1, NE	–
534	ADW	Layer, ditch 74	Block 1	?0–IV
535	ADX	Layer, gully 50	Block 1	IV
536	ADY	Layer, ditch 9	Block 1	III–IV
537	ADZ	Layer, sump	Block 6	III
539	AEB	Layer, pit 539	Block 1	III
541	AED	Layer, gully 67	Block 1	III?
542	AEE	Layer, ditch 9	Block 1	III–IV
543	AEF	Layer, pit 543	Block 1	III/IV
544	AEG	Layer, ditch 6	Block 1	III
545	AEH	Layer, pit 545	Block 1	IV
546	AEI	Layer, well 446	Block 1a	III
549	AEM	Mortar floor fragment, bldg R2	Block 1a	IV
550	AEN	Layer, ditch 74	Block 1	?0–IV
551	AEO	Layer, gully 50	Block 1	IV
552	AEP	Layer, ditch 9	Block 1	III–IV
553	AEQ	Layer, sump	Block 6	III
554	AER	Layer, well 446	Block 1a	III
555	AES	Layer, ditch 74	Block 1	?0–IV
556	AET	Layer, ditch 9	Block 1	III–IV
557	AEV	Layer, ditch 71	Block 1	VI
558	AEW	Layer, well 171/558	Block 1	IV
559	AEX	Layer, oven 3	Block 1	IV
560	AEY	Post-hole, S of oven 3	Block 1	?
561	AEZ	Post-hole, bldg R3	Block 1b	III
562	AFA	Layer, pit 562	Block 5a	III/IV
563	AFB	Layer, pit 563	Block 5a	III/IV
564	AFC	Layer, ditch 9	Block 1	III–IV
565	AFD	Layer, ditch 9	Block 1	III–IV
566	AFE	Layer, ditch 9	Block 1	III–IV
567	AFF	Post-hole, bldg R3	Block 1b	III
568	AFG	Post-hole, E of gully 53	Block 1, NE	?
569	AFH	Layer, ditch 74	Block 1	?0–IV
570	AFI	Layer, ditch 74	Block 1	?0–IV
571	AFK	Layer, ditch 74	Block 1	?0–IV
572	AFL	Layer, ditch 9	Block 1	III–IV
573	AFM	Layer, oven 4	Block 1	IV
574	AFN	Layer, ditch 9	Block 1	III–IV

Unit number	Group code	Description	Location	Primary feature phase
575	AFO	Post-hole, bldg R3	Block 1b	III
577	AFQ	Post-hole, bldg R3	Block 1b	III
578	AFR	Layer, ditch 9	Block 1	III–IV
579	AFS	Layer, well 446	Block 1a	III
580	AFT	Post-hole, bldg R3	Block 1b	III
581	AFV	Layer, ditches 6 and 71	Block 1	III and VI
582	AFW	Post-hole, bldg R2	Block 1a	III
583	AFX	Layer, well 171/558	Block 1	IV
584	AFY	Layer, ditch 9	Block 1	III–IV
585	AFZ	Layer, ditch 9	Block 1	III–IV
586	AGA	Post-hole, bldg R3	Block 1b	III
587	AGB	Layer, pit 587	Block 1	III/IV
588	AGC	Layer, ditch 6	Block 1	III
589	AGD	Post-hole, N of gully 50	Block 1	?
590	AGE	Post-hole, N of gully 50	Block 1	?
591	AGF	Silt spread NE of bldg R1	Block 1	?
592	AGG	Post-hole, N of gully 50	Block 1	?
593	AGH	Layer, ditch 9	Block 1	III–IV
594	AGI	Layer, pit 610	Block 5a	III
595	AGK	Layer, ditch 9	Block 1	III–IV
596	AGL	Layer, ditch 9	Block 1	III–IV
597	AGM	Layer, well 446	Block 1a	III
598	AGN	Layer, bldg R2	Block 1a	III/IV
599	AGO	Layer, ditch 9	Block 1	III–IV
600	AGP	Layer, pit 600	Block 1	III
601	AGQ	Layer, gully 42	Block 1b	III
602	AGR	Layer, ditch 74	Block 1	?0–IV
603	AGS	Layer, well 446	Block 1a	III
604	AGT	Layer, pit 604	Block 5a	III
605	AGV	Layer, well 171/558	Block 1	IV
606	AGW	Layer, pit 606	Block 5a	III
607	AGX	Layer, pit 607	Block 5a	III
608	AGY	Layer, pit 608	Block 5a	III
609	AGZ	Layer, bldg R2	Block 1a	III
610	AHA	Layer, pit 610	Block 5a	III
611	AHB	Post-hole, bldg R3	Block 1b	III
612	AHC	Post-hole, bldg R3	Block 1b	III
613	AHD	Layer, pit 613	Block 5a	IV
614	AHE	Post-hole, bldg R2	Block 1a	III
615	AHF	Layer, ditch 74	Block 1	?0–IV
616	AHG	Layer, S of bldg R1 (cf. 609)	Block 1a	III
617	AHH	Post-hole, bldg R2	Block 1a	III
618	AHI	Layer, bldg R2	Block 1a	III
619	AHK	Post-hole, bldg R2	Block 1a	III
620	AHL	Gully/slot, bldg R2	Block 1a	III
621	AHM	Post-hole, bldg R2	Block 1a	III
622	AHN	Post-hole, bldg R2	Block 1a	III
623	AHO	Layer, pit 623	Block 5a	III/IV
624	AHP	Post-hole, bldg R2	Block 1a	III
625	AHQ	Well-head post-hole, well 446	Block 1a	III
626	AHR	Decking slot, well 446	Block 1a	III
627	AHS	Post-hole, bldg R2	Block 1a	III/IV
628	AHT	Layer, bldg R2	Block 1a	III
700	AZT	Layer, gully 40	Block 5	IV

Unit number	Group code	Description	Location	Primary feature phase
701	AZV	Layer, pit 701	Block 5	III/IV
702	AZW	Layer, gully 36	Block 4	III
703	AZX	Layer, gully 35	Block 3	III
704	AZY	Layer, well 704/1663	Block 3	III
705	AZZ	Layer, well 705	Block 2	III
706	BAA	Layer, oven 5	Block 3	IV
707	BAB	Layer, oven 6	Block 2	IV
708	BAC	Layer, gully 35	Block 3	III
709	BAD	Layer, oven 7	Block 2	IV
710	BAE	Layer, well 705	Block 2	III
711	BAF	Layer, pit 711	Block 5	III/IV
712	BAG	Layer, oven 5	Block 3	IV
713	BAH	Layer, well 704/1663	Block 3	III
714	BAI	Layer, well 808	Block 2	III
715	BAK	Layer, gully 36	Block 4	III
716	BAL	Layer, well 808	Block 2	III
717	BAM	Layer, well 705	Block 2	III
718	BAN	Post-hole, bldg S3	Block 2	V
719	BAO	Post-hole, bldg S3	Block 2	V
720	BAP	Post-hole, bldg S3	Block 2	V
721	BAQ	Post-hole, bldg S3	Block 2	V
722	BAR	Layer, well 905	Block 2	III
723	BAS	Post-hole, bldg S3	Block 2	V
724	BAT	Post-hole, bldg S3	Block 2	V
725	BAV	Layer, pit 725	Block 2	IV
726	BAW	Layer, ditch 71	Block 1	VI
727	BAX	Layer, well 705	Block 2	III
728	BAY	Layer, well 704/1663	Block 3	III
729	BAZ	Layer, pit 725	Block 2	IV
730	BBA	Layer, well 730	Block 2	III
731	BBB	Layer, ditch 71	Block 1	VI
732	BBC	Layer, pit 736/737	Block 3	III
733	BBD	Layer, oven 5	Block 3	IV
734	BBE	Layer, well 704/1663	Block 3	III
735	BBF	Layer, oven 5	Block 3	IV
736	BBG	Layer, pit 736/737	Block 3	III
737	BBH	Layer, pit 736/737	Block 3	III
738	BBI	Layer, well 730	Block 2	III
739	BBK	Layer, well 905	Block 2	III
740	BBL	Layer, oven 7	Block 2	IV
741	BBM	Layer, pits 760, 822, 830	Block 5	III
742	BBN	Layer, pits 761/1545, 826, 841	Block 5	III/IV
744	BBP	Layer, pit 744	Block 4	III/IV
745	BBQ	Layer, well 705	Block 2	III
746	BBR	Post-hole, bldg S3	Block 2	V
747	BBS	Post-hole, bldg S3	Block 2	V
748	BBT	Layer, well 730	Block 2	III
749	BBV	Layer, well 730	Block 2	III
750	BBW	Layer, well 808	Block 2	III
751	BBX	Layer, gully 65, bldg S4	Block 2	V
752	BBY	Layer, ditch 71	Block 1	VI
753	BBZ	Flue, oven 7	Block 2	IV
754	BCA	Layer, gully 35	Block 3	III
755	BCB	Layer, oven 5	Block 3	IV

Unit number	Group code	Description	Location	Primary feature phase
756	BCC	Layer, oven 5	Block 3	IV
757	BCD	Layer, pit 757	Block 5	?
758	BCE	Post-hole, bldg S3	Block 2	V
759	BCF	Post-hole, bldg S3	Block 2	V
760	BCG	Layer, pit 760	Block 5	III
761	BCH	Layer, pit 761/1545	Block 5	IV
762	BCI	Layer, well 730	Block 2	III
763	BCK	Layer, well 808	Block 2	III
764	BCL	Post-hole, bldg S3	Block 2	V
765	BCM	Layer, ditch 9	Block 1	III–IV
766	BCN	Layer, ditch 9	Block 1	III–IV
767	BCO	Layer, ditch 9	Block 1	III–IV
768	BCP	Layer, oven 7	Block 2	IV
769	BCQ	Layer, pits 826, 841	Block 5	III/IV
770	BCR	Post-hole, bldg S3	Block 2	V
771	BCS	Layer, well 705	Block 2	III
772	BCT	Layer, well 808	Block 2	III
773	BCV	Post-hole, bldg S3	Block 2	V
774	BCW	Layer, pit 774	Block 3	III/IV
775	BCX	Layer, well 905	Block 2	III
776	BCY	Post-hole, bldg S3	Block 2	V
777	BCZ	Post-hole, bldg S3	Block 2	V
778	BDA	Post-hole, bldg S3	Block 2	V
779	BDB	Post-hole, bldg S3	Block 2	V
780	BDC	Post-hole, bldg S3	Block 2	V
781	BDD	Layer, well 705	Block 2	III
782	BDE	Layer, ditches 6 and 71	Block 1	III & VI
783	BDF	Layer, pit 783	Block 4	III
784	BDG	Post-hole, bldg R7	Block 4	III
785	BDH	Post-hole, bldg R7	Block 4	III
786	BDI	Layer, well 705	Block 2	III
787	BDK	Layer, oven 7	Block 2	IV
788	BDL	Layer, well 808	Block 2	III
789	BDM	Post-hole, bldg R7	Block 4	III
790	BDN	Post-hole, bldg R7	Block 4	III
791	BDO	Post-hole, bldg R7	Block 4	III
792	BDP	Post-hole, bldg R7	Block 4	III
793	BDQ	Post-hole, bldg R7	Block 4	III
794	BDR	Layer, pit 794	Block 2	III
795	BDS	Layer, pit 795	Block 2	III
796	BDT	Post-hole, bldg R7	Block 4	III
797	BDV	Layer, pits 797 and 826	Block 5	III/IV
798	BDW	Layer, gully 36	Block 4	III
799	BDX	Layer, well 905	Block 2	III
800	BDY	Layer, well 905	Block 2	III
801	BDZ	Layer, ditch 9	Block 1	III–IV
802	BEA	Post-hole, bldg R7	Block 4	III
803	BEB	Post-hole, bldg R7	Block 4	III
804	BEC	Post-hole, bldg R7	Block 4	III
805	BED	Post-hole, bldg S3	Block 2	V
806	BEE	Layer, oven 6	Block 2	IV
807	BEF	Layer, pit 774	Block 3	III/IV
808	BEG	Layer, well 808	Block 2	III
809	BEH	Post-hole, bldg R7	Block 4	III

Unit number	Group code	Description	Location	Primary feature phase
810	BEI	Layer, gully 35	Block 3	III
811	BEK	Layer, gully 36	Block 4	III
812	BEL	Post-hole, bldg R7	Block 4	III
813	BEM	Post-hole, bldg S3	Block 2	V
814	BEN	Post-hole, bldg S3	Block 2	V
815	BEO	Layer, pit 795	Block 2	III
816	BEP	Rake-out, oven 6	Block 2	IV
817	BEQ	Layer, well 730	Block 2	III
818	BER	Layer, pit 818	Block 4	III
819	BES	Post-hole, bldg R7	Block 4	III
820	BET	Post-hole, bldg R7	Block 4	III
821	BEV	Post-hole, bldg R7	Block 4	III
822	BEW	Layer, pit 822	Block 5	III
823	BEX	Post-hole, bldg R7	Block 4	III
824	BEY	Layer, pit 794	Block 2	III
825	BEZ	Layer, pit 795	Block 2	III
826	BFA	Layer, pit 826	Block 5	III/IV
827	BFB	Layer, oven 6	Block 2	IV
828	BFC	Layer, ditch 9	Block 1	III–IV
829	BFD	Layer, pit 829	Block 3	III
830	BFE	Layer, pit 830	Block 5	III
831	BFF	Layer, pit 826	Block 5	III/IV
832	BFG	Post-hole, bldg S4	Block 11	V
833	BFH	Post-hole, bldg S4	Block 11	V
834	BFI	Post-hole, bldg S4	Block 11	V
835	BFK	Layer, ditch 6	Block 1	III
836	BFL	Post-hole, bldg S4	Block 11	V
837	BFM	Layer, pit 837	Block 11	?
838	BFN	Post-hole, bldg S4	Block 11	V
839	BFO	Post-hole, bldg S4	Block 11	V
840	BFP	Layer, pit 794	Block 2	III
841	BFQ	Layer, pit 841	Block 5	III/IV
842	BFR	Layer, pit 842	Block 3	III
843	BFS	Layer, well 730	Block 2	III
844	BFT	Post-hole, bldg S4	Block 11	V
845	BFV	Post-hole, bldg S3	Block 2	V
846	BFW	Post-hole, bldg S4	Block 11	V
847	BFX	Layer, pit 847	Block 3	?
848	BFY	Post-hole, bldg S4	Block 11	V
850	BGA	Layer, pit 850	Block 3	?
851	BGB	Post-hole, bldg R5b	Block 2	III/IV
852	BGC	Post-hole, bldg S4	Block 11	V
853	BGD	Post-hole, bldg S4	Block 11	V
854	BGE	Post-hole, bldg S4	Block 11	V
856	BGF	Post-hole, bldg R7	Block 4	III
857	BGG	Post-hole, bldg R7	Block 4	III
858	BGH	Layer, pit 818	Block 4	III
859	BGI	Layer, pit 859	Block 3	III/IV
860	BGK	Layer, pit 860	Block 3	III
861	BGL	Post-hole, bldg S4	Block 11	V
862	BGM	Sondage into 'flood' silt	Block 11, E	–
863	BGN	Layer, well 808	Block 2	III
864	BGO	Layer, pit 483/918	Block 2	III/IV
865	BGP	Layer, gully 35	Block 3	III

Unit number	Group code	Description	Location	Primary feature phase
866	BGQ	Post-hole, bldg R7	Block 4	III
867	BGR	Post-hole, bldg R7	Block 4	III
868	BGS	Layer, well 905	Block 2	III
869	BGT	Post-hole, bldg S3	Block 2	V
870	BGV	Post-hole, bldg S3	Block 2	V
871	BGW	Layer, pit 871	Block 11, E	IV
872	BGX	Layer, gully 35	Block 3	III
874	BGZ	Layer, pit 874	Block 5	III/IV
875	BHA	Post-hole, bldg R7	Block 4	III
876	BHB	Layer, pit 860	Block 3	III
877	BHC	Layer, pit 483/918	Block 2	III/IV
878	BHD	Layer, well 905	Block 2	III
879	BHE	Layer, ditch 14	Block 11	VI
880	BHF	Post-hole, bldg S4	Block 11	V
881	BHG	Layer, pit 483/918	Block 2	III/IV
882	BHH	Post-hole, bldg R7	Block 4	III
883	BHI	Post-hole, bldg R7	Block 4	III
884	BHK	Slot bldg R7	Block 4	III
885	BHL	Layer, pit 885	Block 5	III/IV
886	BHM	Layer, ditch 9	Block 1	III–IV
887	BHN	Post-hole, bldg S4	Block 11	V
888	BHO	Layer, pit 483/918	Block 2	III/IV
889	BHP	Layer, pit 483/918	Block 2	III/IV
890	BHQ	Layer, ditch 9	Block 1	III–IV
891	BHR	Post-hole, bldg S4	Block 11	V
892	BHS	Layer, pit 483/918	Block 2	III/IV
893	BHT	Beam slot, bldg R5a	Block 2	III
894	BHV	Post-hole, bldg S4	Block 11	V
895	BHW	Layer, pit 895	Block 11, E	?
896	BHX	Post-hole, bldg S4	Block 11	V
897	BHY	Layer, well 905	Block 2	III
899	BIA	Layer, pit 899	Block 3	III
900	BIB	Layer, pit 900	Block 4	III
901	BIC	Layer, well 808	Block 2	III
902	BID	Layer, pit 899	Block 3	III
903	BIE	Layer, pit 899	Block 3	III
904	BIF	Layer, pit 860	Block 3	III
905	BIG	Layer, well 905	Block 2	III
907	BII	Layer, ditch 9	Block 1	III–IV
908	BIK	Layer, ditch 9	Block 1	III–IV
909	BIL	Layer, ditch 9	Block 1	III–IV
910	BIM	Layer, pit 885	Block 5	III/IV
911	BIN	Layer, pit 483/918	Block 2	III/IV
912	BIO	Layer, ditch 9	Block 1	III–IV
913	BIP	Layer, ditch 9	Block 1	III–IV
914	BIQ	Layer, well 808	Block 2	III
915	BIR	Layer, gully 39	Block 5	II?
916	BIS	Layer, pit 818	Block 4	III
917	BIT	Layer, well 808	Block 2	III
918	BIV	Layer, pit 483/918	Block 2	III/IV
919	BIW	Layer, gully 38	Block 5	II
920	BIX	Layer, pit 920	Block 2	I
921	BIY	Layer, pit 483/918	Block 2	III/IV
922	BIZ	Layer, pit 483/918	Block 2	III/IV

Unit number	Group code	Description	Location	Primary feature phase
923	BKA	Rake-out, oven 7	Block 2	IV
924	BKB	Layer, ditch 9	Block 1	III–IV
925	BKC	Layer, pit 925	Block 4	III
926	BKD	Layer, well 905	Block 2	III
927	BKE	Layer, pit 927	Block 2	I/II
928	BKF	Layer, pit 920	Block 2	I
929	BKG	Post-hole, bldg R5b	Block 2	III/IV
930	BKH	Post-hole, bldg R5b	Block 2	III/IV
931	BKI	Post-hole, bldg R5b	Block 2	III/IV
932	BKK	Post-hole, bldg R5b	Block 2	III/IV
933	BKL	Layer, ditch 9	Block 1	III–IV
934	BKM	Layer, above 937	Block 1	VI
936	BKO	Layer, ditch 9	Block 1	III–IV
937	BKP	Layer, ditch 9	Block 1	III–IV
938	BKQ	Post-hole, bldg R5b	Block 2	III/IV
939	BKR	Post-hole, bldg R5b	Block 2	III/IV
940	BKS	Post-hole, bldg R5b	Block 2	III/IV
941	BKT	Layer, well 905	Block 2	III
943	BKW	Layer, well 944	Block 3	III
944	BKX	Layer, well 944	Block 3	III
945	BKY	Layer, ditch 9	Block 1	III–IV
946	BKZ	Post-hole, bldg R6	Block 3	III
947	BLA	Post-hole, bldg R6	Block 3	III
948	BLB	Post-hole, bldg R6	Block 3	III
949	BLC	Post-hole, bldg R6	Block 3	III
950	BLD	Post-hole, bldg R6	Block 3	III
951	BLE	Post-hole, bldg R6	Block 3	III
952	BLF	Layer, ditch 9	Block 1	III–IV
953	BLG	Post-hole, bldg R6	Block 3	III
954	BLH	Layer, ditch 9	Block 1	III–IV
955	BLI	Silt spread, within bldgs R5a & S3	Block 2	I–V
956	BLK	Layer, pits 958, 966	Block 2	III/IV
957	BLL	Layer, pit 920	Block 2	I
958	BLM	Layer, pits 958, 966	Block 2	III/IV
959	BLN	Post-hole, bldg R6	Block 3	III
960	BLO	Layer, well 905	Block 2	III
961	BLP	Post-hole, bldg R6	Block 3	III
962	BLQ	Layer, well 808	Block 2	III
963	BLR	Layer, ditch 9	Block 1	III–IV
964	BLS	(?)Hearth, bldg R5a (=1330)	Block 2	III?
965	BLT	(?)Hearth, bldg R5a (=1330)	Block 2	III?
966	BLV	Layer, pit 966	Block 2	III
967	BLW	Post-hole, bldg R6	Block 3	III
968	BLX	Post-hole, bldg R6	Block 3	III
969	BLY	Post-hole, bldg R6	Block 3	III
970	BLZ	Post-hole, bldg R6	Block 3	III
971	BMA	Post-hole, bldg R6	Block 3	III
972	BMB	Stake-hole, bldg R5b	Block 2	III/IV
973	BMC	Post-hole, bldg R5b	Block 2	III/IV
974	BMD	Post-hole, bldg R5b	Block 2	III/IV
975	BME	Post-hole, bldg R5b	Block 2	III/IV
976	BMF	Beam slot, bldg R5a	Block 2	III
977	BMG	Layer, oven 8	Block 2	IV
978	BMH	Layer, ditch 9	Block 1	III–IV

Unit number	Group code	Description	Location	Primary feature phase
979	BMI	Post-hole, bldg R5b	Block 2	III/IV
980	BMK	Silt spread, beyond NE corner of bldgs R5a and S3	Block 2	I–V
981	BML	Layer, pit 920	Block 2	I
982	BMM	Metalled surface, street 1 E/W	Block 11, E	III→
983	BMN	Layer, ditch 3	Block 11	III
984	BMO	Post-hole, bldg R6	Block 3	III
986	BMQ	Post-hole, bldg S3	Block 2	V
987	BMR	Beam slot, bldg R5a	Block 2	III
988	BMS	Post-hole, bldg S3	Block 2	V
989	BMT	Beam slot, bldg R5a	Block 2	III
990	BMV	Layer, pit 990	Block 2	III/IV
991	BMW	Post-hole, bldg R6	Block 3	III
992	BMX	Post-hole, bldg R6	Block 3	III
993	BMY	Layer, ditch 9	Block 1	III–IV
994	BMZ	Post-hole, below 980	Block 2	I
995	BNA	Post-hole, below 980 (=1185)	Block 2	I
996	BNB	Layer, pit 1184	Block 2	III
997	BNC	Layer, pit 997	Block 1	?
998	BND	Layer, ditch 9	Block 1	III–IV
1983				
1000	CAA	Topsoil/cleaning	Block 11, E	–
1001	CAB	Topsoil/cleaning	Block 11, E	–
1002	CAC	Silt layer	Block 2, NW	–
1003	CAD	Layer, ditch 71	Block 1	VI
1004	CAE	Layer, gully 66	Block 1	IV
1006	CAG	Post-hole	Block 1, NE	VI
1007	CAH	Post-hole	Block 1, NE	VI
1010	CAL	Clay spread	Block 1, NE	?
1012	CAN	Layer, ditch 13	Block 11	VI
1013	CAO	Layer, gully 66	Block 1	IV
1014	CAP	Post-hole	Block 1, NE	VI
1015	CAQ	Post-hole	Block 1, NE	VI
1016	CAR	Layer, ditch 13	Block 11	VI
1017	CAS	Layer, ditch 14	Block 11	VI
1018	CAT	Layer, ditch 11	Block 11	IV?
1020	CAW	Layer, pit 1020	Block 1	IV→
1021	CAX	?Post-hole	Block 1, NE	V?
1022	CAY	?Post-hole	Block 1, NE	V?
1023	CAZ	?Post-hole	Block 1, NE	V?
1024	CBA	Post-hole	Block 1, NE	V?
1025	CBB	?Post-hole	Block 1, NE	V?
1026	CBC	?Post-hole	Block 1, NE	V?
1027	CBD	?Post-hole	Block 1, NE	V?
1028	CBE	?Post-hole	Block 1, NE	V?
1029	CBF	?Post-hole	Block 1, NE	V?
1030	CBG	Post-hole	Block 1, NE	V?
1031	CBH	Post-hole	Block 1, NE	V?
1032	CBI	Post-hole	Block 1, NE	V?
1033	CBK	?Post-hole	Block 1, NE	V?
1034	CBL	?Post-hole	Block 1, NE	V?
1035	CBM	?Post-hole	Block 1, NE	V?
1036	CBN	?Post-hole	Block 1, NE	V?
1037	CBO	?Post-hole	Block 1, NE	V?

Unit number	Group code	Description	Location	Primary feature phase
1038	CBP	?Post-hole	Block 1, NE	V?
1039	CBQ	?Post-hole	Block 1, NE	V?
1040	CBR	?Post-hole	Block 1, NE	V?
1041	CBS	Layer, gully 54	Block 1	IV
1042	CBT	Post-hole	Block 1, NE	VI
1043	CBV	Layer, ditch 11	Block 11	IV?
1044	CBW	Post-hole	Block 1, NE	VI
1046	CBY	Layer, ditch 13	Block 11	VI
1047	CBZ	Layer, gully 54	Block 1	IV
1049	CCB	Layer, ditch 9	Block 1	III–IV
1051	CCD	Layer, ditch 13	Block 11	VI
1052	CCE	Layer, ditch 9	Block 1	III–IV
1053	CCF	Layer, ditch 12	Block 11	VI
1054	CCG	Layer, ditch 13	Block 11	VI
1055	CCH	Layer, ditch 13	Block 11	VI
1056	CCI	Layer, ditch 12	Block 11	VI
1057	CCK	Layer, ditch 11	Block 11	IV?
1058	CCL	Layer, ditch 9	Block 1	III–IV
1059	CCM	Layer, ditch 3	Block 11	III
1062	CCP	Layer, E of bldg S3	Block 2	I→
1063	CCQ	?Post-hole	Block 1, NE	V?
1064	CCR	?Post-hole	Block 1, NE	V?
1065	CCS	Post-hole	Block 1, NE	V?
1066	CCT	Post-hole	Block 1, NE	V?
1067	CCV	Layer, ditch 9	Block 1	III–IV
1068	CCW	Layer, gully 66	Block 1	IV
1069	CCX	Layer, ditch 13	Block 11	VI
1070	CCY	Topsoil/cleaning, block 1, N and block 11, centre		–
1071	CCZ	Layer, ditch 14	Block 11	VI
1072	CDA	Layer, ditch 3	Block 11	III
1073	CDB	Layer, ditch 9	Block 1	III–IV
1074	CDC	Layer, ditch 9	Block 1	III–IV
1076	CDE	?Post-hole	Block 1, NE	V?
1077	CDF	Layer, ditch 9	Block 1	III–IV
1078	CDG	Layer, ditch 3	Block 11	III
1079	CDH	Layer, ditch 9	Block 1	III–IV
1080	CDI	Layer, ditch 2	Block 11	II(?)
1081	CDK	Layer, ditch 3	Block 11	III
1082	CDL	Topsoil/cleaning	Block 11, W	–
1083	CDM	Denuded surface of street 1 E/W, E of bldg S2	Block 11	III→
1084	CDN	Layer, ditch 9	Block 1	III–IV
1085	CDO	Layer, ditch 11	Block 11	IV(?)
1086	CDP	Layer, ditch 71	Block 1	VI
1087	CDQ	Layer, ditch 12	Block 11	VI
1088	CDR	Layer, ditch 4	Block 11	III
1089	CDS	Layer, ditch 12	Block 11	VI
1090	CDT	Layer, pit 1090	Block 11	IV
1091	CDV	Layer, ditch 9	Block 1	III–IV
1092	CDW	Layer, ditch 9	Block 1	III–IV
1095	CDZ	Layer, gully 1	Block 11	I
1096	CEA	Layer, ditch 6	Block 1	III
1097	CEB	Layer, ditch 12	Block 11	VI
1098	CEC	Layer, ditch 12	Block 11	VI
1099	CED	Layer, ditch 6	Block 1	III

Unit number	Group code	Description	Location	Primary feature phase
1100	CEE	Layer, ditch 9	Block 1	III–IV
1101	CEF	Layer, ditch 2	Block 11	II(?)
1103	CEH	Post-hole, E of gully 1	Block 11	I
1104	CEI	Layer, gully 1	Block 11	I
1105	CEK	Layer, ditch 14	Block 11	VI
1106	CEL	Post-hole, E of gully 1	Block 11	I
1108	CEN	Post-hole, bldg S2	Block 11	V
1109	CEO	Post-hole, bldg S2	Block 11	V
1110	CEP	Post-hole, bldg S2	Block 11	V
1111	CEQ	Post-hole, bldg S2	Block 11	V
1112	CER	Post-hole, bldg S2	Block 11	V
1113	CES	Several post-holes, bldg S2	Block 11	V
1114	CET	Layer, gully 56	Block 11	V
1115	CEV	Post-hole, bldg S2	Block 11	V
1116	CEW	Shallow scoop, bldg S2	Block 11	V
1117	CEX	Post-hole, E of gully 1	Block 11	I
1119	CEZ	Post-hole, E of gully 1	Block 11	I
1120	CFA	Layer, ditch 9	Block 1	III–IV
1121	CFB	Green-yellow silts	Block 2, NE	II→
1122	CFC	Grey silt, below 1121	Block 2, NE	I→
1123	CFD	Layer, ditch 9	Block 1	III–IV
1124	CFE	Layer, ditch 3	Block 11	III
1125	CFF	Layer, gully 1	Block 11	I
1126	CFG	Layer, ditch 2	Block 11	II(?)
1127	CFH	Layer, ditch 2	Block 11	II(?)
1128	CFI	Post-hole, bldg S3	Block 2	V
1129	CFK	Post-hole, E of gully 1	Block 11	I
1130	CFL	Layer, ditch 3	Block 11	III
1131	CFM	Layer, ditch 3	Block 11	III
1132	CFN	Layer, ditch 13	Block 11	VI
1133	CFO	Layer, ditch 13	Block 11	VI
1134	CFP	Layer, ditch 13	Block 11	VI
1135	CFQ	Layer, ditch 13	Block 11	VI
1136	CFR	Layer, ditch 2	Block 11	II(?)
1137	CFS	Layer, ditch 2	Block 11	II(?)
1138	CFT	Layer, ditch 3	Block 11	III
1139	CFV	Layer, gully 1	Block 11	I
1140	CFW	Layer, gully 1	Block 11	I
1141	CFX	Layer, ditch 4	Block 11	III
1142	CFY	Layer, ditch 3	Block 11	III
1143	CFZ	Layer, ditch 13	Block 11	VI
1145	CGB	Layer, ditch 12	Block 11	VI
1146	CGC	Layer, ditch 13	Block 11	VI
1147	CGD	Layer, ditch 3	Block 11	III
1148	CGE	Layer, ditch 3	Block 11	III
1149	CGF	Post-hole, bldg S1, gully 57	Block 11	V
1150	CGG	Layer, ditch 12	Block 11	VI
1151	CGH	Layer, ditch 4	Block 11	III
1152	CGI	Post-hole, bldg S1, gully 57	Block 11	V
1153	CGK	Layer, ditch 4	Block 11	III
1156	CGN	Layer, ditch 4	Block 11	III
1157	CGO	Post-hole, bldg S1, gully 57	Block 11	V
1158	CGP	Layer, gully 55	Block 11	V
1159	CGQ	Layer, gully 54	Block 1	IV

Unit number	Group code	Description	Location	Primary feature phase
1160	CGR	Layer, ditch 4	Block 11	III
1161	CGS	Layer, gully 54	Block 1	IV
1162	CGT	Post-hole	Block 1, NE	VI
1163	CGV	Layer, ditch 4	Block 11	III
1164	CGW	Layer, ditch 12	Block 11	VI
1165	CGX	Layer, ditch 12	Block 11	VI
1167	CGZ	Layer, ditch 12	Block 11	VI
1169	CHB	Layer, ditch 12	Block 11	VI
1170	CHC	Layer, ditch 12	Block 11	VI
1171	CHD	Layer, ditch 4	Block 11	III
1172	CHE	Layer, ditch 12	Block 11	VI
1173	CHF	Layer, pit 1173	Block 11	VI
1174	CHG	Layer, gully 66	Block 1	IV
1175	CHH	Layer, gully 66	Block 1	IV
1176	CHI	Layer, ditch 14	Block 11	VI
1177	CHK	Layer, ditch 4	Block 11	III
1178	CHL	Layer, ditch 4	Block 11	III
1179	CHM	Layer, ditch 4	Block 11	III
1180	CHN	Layer, ditch 12	Block 11	VI
1181	CHO	Layer, ditch 14	Block 11	VI
1182	CHP	Layer, ditch 13	Block 11	VI
1184	CHR	Layer, pit 1184	Block 2	III
1185	CHS	Post-hole (=995)	Block 2	I
1186	CHT	Post-hole (=994)	Block 2	I
1187	CHV	Post-hole	Block 11, E	V?
1188	CHW	Post-hole	Block 11, E	V?
1189	CHX	Layer, ditch 2	Block 11	II(?)
1191	CHZ	Layer, pit 1191	Block 2	III
1193	CIB	Layer, pit 1184	Block 2	III
1194	CIC	Metalling, street 1 E/W	Block 11, E	III→
1195	CID	Layer, ditch 12	Block 11	VI
1196	CIE	Layer, ditch 12	Block 11	VI
1198	CIG	Post-hole	Block 2	I
1199	CIH	Post-hole, E of gully 1	Block 11	I
1200	CII	Layer, ditch 12	Block 11	VI
1201	CIK	Layer, ditch 14	Block 11	VI
1202	CIL	Layer, ditches 6 and 14	Block 11	VI
1203	CIM	Layer, ditch 13	Block 11	VI
1205	CIO	Layer, ditch 5	Block 11	III
1208	CIR	Layer, ditch 4	Block 11	III
1209	CIS	Layer, ditch 4	Block 11	III
1210	CIT	Layer, ditch 4	Block 11	III
1212	CIW	Layer, ditch 4	Block 11	III
1213	CIX	Layer, ditch 12	Block 11	VI
1214	CIY	Layer, ditch 12	Block 11	VI
1215	CIZ	Layer, ditch 4	Block 11	III
1216	CKA	Layer, ditch 4	Block 11	III
1217	CKB	Layer, ditch 4	Block 11	III
1218	CKC	Layer, ditch 4	Block 11	III
1220	CKE	Layer, ditch 4	Block 11	III
1221	CKF	Layer, ditch 12	Block 11	VI
1222	CKG	Layer, ditch 6	Block 1	III
1224	CKI	Layer, ditch 5	Block 11	III
1226	CKL	Layer, ditch 14	Block 11	VI

Unit number	Group code	Description	Location	Primary feature phase
1227	CKM	Layer, ditch 12	Block 11	VI
1230	CKP	Post-hole	Block 11, E	I
1241	CLB	Layer, ditch 4	Block 11	III
1242	CLC	Layer, ditch 4	Block 11	III
1243	CLD	Layer, ditch 4	Block 11	III
1244	CLE	Layer, ditch 4	Block 11	III
1245	CLF	Layer, ditch 4	Block 11	III
1246	CLG	Layer, ditch 4	Block 11	III
1248	CLI	Layer, ditch 3	Block 11	III
1249	CLK	Layer, pit 1249	Block 11	?
1251	CLM	Layer, ditch 12	Block 11	VI
1252	CLN	Post-hole, bldg S2	Block 11	V
1253	CLO	Post-hole, bldg S2	Block 11	V
1254	CLP	Stake-hole, bldg S1 (=1411)	Block 11	V
1255	CLQ	Scoop, bldg S2	Block 11	V
1256	CLR	Layer, ditch 12	Block 11	VI
1257	CLS	Post-hole, bldg S1	Block 11	V
1258	CLT	Post-hole, bldg S1	Block 11	V
1259	CLV	Layer, ditch 6	Block 1	III
1260	CLW	Layer, gully 52	Block 1	IV(?)
1264	CMA	Layer, ditch 12	Block 11	VI
1265	CMB	Layer, ditch 3	Block 11	III
1266	CMC	Small pit, bldg S3	Block 2	V
1267	CMD	Layer, pit 1267	Block 11	VI
1268	CME	Layer, ditch 12	Block 11	VI
1269	CMF	Layer, ditch 12	Block 11	VI
1272	CMI	Layer, ditch 2	Block 11	II(?)
1274	CML	Layer, ditch 3	Block 11	III
1275	CMM	Post-hole	Block 11, E	I
1278	CMP	Post-hole	Block 11, E	I
1281	CMS	Layer, gully 53	Block 1	IV/V
1282	CMT	Layer, gully 53	Block 1	IV/V
1283	CMV	Silt spread near bldg R4	Block 1, NE	?III/IV
1285	CMX	Layer, pit 1285	Block 11, W	VI
1288	CNA	Clayspread (=1400), bldg R4	Block 1, NE	III/IV
1289	CNB	Layer, gully 55	Block 11	V
1291	CND	Layer, ditch 4	Block 11	III
1292	CNE	Post-hole, bldg S1	Block 11	V
1293	CNF	Post-hole, bldg S1	Block 11	V
1295	CNH	Metalling, street 1 E/W, above 1136	Block 11	III→
1296	CNI	Layer, ditch 2	Block 11	II(?)
1297	CNK	Layer, ditch 10	Block 11	IV(?)
1298	CNL	Layer, ditch 10	Block 11	IV(?)
1299	CNM	Layer, ditch 12	Block 11	VI
1300	CNN	Layer, ditch 5	Block 11	III
1301	CNO	Layer, ditch 6	Block 1	III
1302	CNP	Layer, ditch 12	Block 11	VI
1303	CNQ	Layer, gully 1	Block 11	I
1304	CNR	Layer, ditch 6	Block 1	III
1305	CNS	Layer, ditch 6	Block 1	III
1307	CNV	Post-hole, bldg S3	Block 2	V
1308	CNW	Post-hole	Block 2, NE	I
1309	CNX	Post-hole	Block 2, NE	I
1310	CNY	Post-hole	Block 2, NE	I

Unit number	Group code	Description	Location	Primary feature phase
1312	COA	Post-hole, bldg S3	Block 2	V
1315	COD	Post-hole	Block 2, NE	I
1316	COE	Post-hole	Block 2, NE	I
1317	COF	Post-hole	Block 2, NE	I
1318	COG	Post-hole	Block 2, NE	I
1319	COH	Post-hole	Block 2, NE	I
1320	COI	Post-hole	Block 2, NE	I
1321	COK	Layer, gully 1	Block 11	I
1323	COM	Post-hole	Block 2, NE	I
1324	CON	Post-hole	Block 2, NE	I
1325	COO	Post-hole	Block 2, NE	I
1326	COP	Layer, ditch 2	Block 11	II(?)
1327	COQ	Post-hole	Block 2, NE	I
1328	COR	Post-hole	Block 2, NE	I
1329	COS	Layer, gully 1	Block 11	I
1330	COT	?Hearth, bldg R5a (=964)	Block 2	III?
1334	COY	?Hearth 964	Block 2	III?
1335	COZ	Post-hole, bldg S2	Block 11	V
1336	CPA	Layer, ditch 2	Block 11	II(?)
1337	CPB	Layer, ditch 10	Block 11	IV(?)
1338	CPC	Layer, ditch 10	Block 11	IV(?)
1339	CPD	Layer, ditch 4	Block 11	III
1340	CPE	Layer, ditch 10	Block 11	IV(?)
1342	CPG	Post-hole, SW of bldg R4	Block 1	IV?
1343	CPH	Layer, ditch 2	Block 11	II(?)
1344	CPI	Layer, pit 1344	Block 11	IV?
1345	CPK	Post-hole, within gully 1	Block 11	I
1348	CPN	Layer, gully 1	Block 11	I
1349	CPO	Post-hole, cuts ditch 5	Block 11	IV→
1350	CPP	Layer, ditch 2	Block 11	II(?)
1351	CPQ	Post-hole, bldg S3	Block 2	V
1352	CPR	Post-hole, bldg S3	Block 2	V
1353	CPS	Layer, ditch 2	Block 11	II(?)
1354	CPT	Layer, ditch 3	Block 11	III
1355	CPV	Post-hole, bldg S3	Block 2	V
1356	CPW	Post-hole, bldg S3	Block 2	V
1357	CPX	Layer, ditch 12	Block 11	VI
1359	CPZ	Post-hole	Block 2, NE	I
1360	CQA	Pit containing human cremation	Block 2, NE	I
1363	CQD	Layer, gully 57	Block 11	V
1364	CQE	Post-hole, bldg S2	Block 11	V
1365	CQF	Post-hole, bldg S2	Block 11	V
1366	CQG	Layer, ditch 2	Block 11	II(?)
1368	CQI	Post-hole	Block 2, NE	I
1369	CQK	Post-hole	Block 2, NE	I
1370	CQL	Post-hole	Block 2, NE	I
1371	CQM	Layer, ditch 2	Block 11	II(?)
1373	CQO	Layer, ditch 12	Block 11	VI
1374	CQP	Layer, gully 1	Block 11	I
1375	CQQ	Post-hole, bldg S2	Block 11	V
1379	CQV	Layer, gully 57	Block 11	V
1380	CQW	Post-hole	Block 2, NE	I
1381	CQX	Post-hole	Block 2, NE	I
1382	CQY	Post-hole, within gully 1	Block 11	I

Unit number	Group code	Description	Location	Primary feature phase
1383	CQZ	Post-hole, within gully 1	Block 11	I
1384	CRA	Layer, gully 1	Block 11	I
1385	CRB	Layer, ditch 10	Block 11	IV(?)
1386	CRC	Layer, ditch 5	Block 11	III
1387	CRD	Silt spread, W of gully 53	Block 1, NE	–
1388	CRE	Layer, ditch 2	Block 11	II(?)
1389	CRF	Silts beneath street 1 E/W	Block 11, E	I/II
1390	CRG	Silts beneath 1389	Block 11, E	I
1391	CRH	Post-hole	Block 2, NE	I
1392	CRI	Post-hole	Block 2, NE	I
1393	CRK	Post-hole	Block 2, NE	I
1394	CRL	Post-hole	Block 2, NE	I
1395	CRM	Post-hole	Block 2, NE	I
1396	CRN	Post-hole	Block 2, NE	I
1397	CRO	Post-hole	Block 2, NE	I
1398	CRP	Post-hole	Block 2, NE	I
1399	CRQ	Post-hole, bldg S3	Block 2	V
1400	CRR	Layer, ditch 69	Block 1	II
1401	CRS	Post-hole, bldg R4	Block 1	IV
1402	CRT	Silt spread, below 1283	Block 1	?III/IV
1403	CRV	Post-hole, bldg R4	Block 1	IV
1404	CRW	Post-hole, bldg R4	Block 1	IV
1405	CRX	Layer, ditch 10	Block 11	IV(?)
1406	CRY	Layer, ditch 10	Block 11	IV(?)
1407	CRZ	Post-hole, bldg R4	Block 1	IV
1408	CSA	Post-hole, bldg R4	Block 1	IV
1409	CSB	Post-hole, bldg R4	Block 1	IV
1410	CSC	Post-hole, bldg R4	Block 1	IV
1411	CSD	Stake-hole, bldg S1 (=1254)	Block 11	V
1412	CSE	Post-hole, bldg S1	Block 11	V
1413	CSF	Post-hole, bldg S1	Block 11	V
1414	CSG	Post-hole, bldg S1	Block 11	V
1415	CSH	Post-hole, bldg S2	Block 11	V
1416	CSI	Post-hole, bldg R4	Block 1	IV
1417	CSK	Layer, ditch 10	Block 11	IV(?)
1418	CSL	Post-hole, bldg S2	Block 11	V
1419	CSM	Post-hole, bldg S2	Block 11	V
1421	CSO	Layer, ditch 69	Block 1	II
1422	CSP	Layer, ditch 69	Block 1	II
1431	CSZ	Post-hole	Block 2, NE	I
1433	CTB	Post-hole	Block 2, NE	I
1434	CTC	Post-hole	Block 2, NE	I
1435	CTD	Post-hole	Block 2, NE	I
1436	CTE	Post-hole	Block 2, NE	I
1437	CTF	Post-hole, bldg S3	Block 2	V
1438	CTG	Post-hole	Block 2, NE	I
1439	CTH	Post-hole	Block 2, NE	I
1440	CTI	Post-hole	Block 2, NE	I
1984				
1501	DAA	Topsoil (cleaning), block 6 and block 5, S		–
1502	DAB	Topsoil/cleaning, blocks 7 and 8		–
1503	DAC	Layer, pit 1503	Block 5	III/IV
1506	DAF	Post-hole	Block 6, NW	?

Unit number	Group code	Description	Location	Primary feature phase
1508	DAH	Layer, pit 1508	Block 5	III
1511	DAL	Layer, pit 1511	Block 5	?
1512	DAM	Layer, pits 1512 and 1595	Block 5	III/IV
1513	DAN	Layer, pit 1513	Block 5	III/IV
1514	DAO	Layer, pit 1514	Block 5	III
1515	DAP	Layer, pit 1585/1515	Block 5	III
1516	DAQ	Layer, pits 1516 and 1604	Block 5	III
1517	DAR	Layer, pit 1612/1517	Block 5	III/IV
1518	DAS	Layer, pits 1586 and 1600	Block 5	III
1519	DAT	Layer, pit 1519	Block 5	?
1520	DAV	Layer, pit 1815/1520	Block 5	III/IV
1521	DAW	Layer, pits 1592 and 1611	Block 5	III/IV
1522	DAX	Post-hole	Block 6, NW	?
1523	DAY	Post-hole	Block 6, NW	?
1524	DAZ	Layer, pits 1567 and 1588	Block 5	III/IV
1525	DBA	Layer, pit 1525	Block 5	III/IV
1528	DBD	Post-hole	Block 6, N	?
1529	DBE	Post-hole	Block 6, N	?
1530	DBF	Post-hole	Block 6, N	?
1531	DBG	?Hearth	Block 6, N	III/IV
1532	DBH	Layer, gully 21	Block 6	III
1533	DBI	Layer, ditches 7 and 71	Block 1	III & VI
1534	DBK	Layer, pit 1534	Block 6	III
1535	DBL	Layer, pit 1535 (?latrine)	Block 6	III/IV
1536	DBM	Layer, pit 1536 (?latrine)	Block 6	III
1537	DBN	Layer, gully 22	Block 6	III
1538	DBO	Layer, pit 1538	Block 6	III
1539	DBP	Layer, pit 1539	Block 6	III
1540	DBQ	Layer, pit 1540	Block 6	?
1541	DBR	Layer, pit 1541	Block 6	III
1542	DBS	Layer, pit 1542 (?latrine)	Block 6	III/IV
1543	DBT	Layer, pit 1543	Block 6	III
1544	DBV	Layer, ditch 15	Block 6	III
1545	DBW	Layer, pit 761/1545	Block 5	IV
1549	DCA	Layer, pits 1567 and 1588	Block 5	III/IV
1550	DCB	Layer, ditch 8	Block 6	III
1551	DCC	Layer, pit 1542 (?latrine)	Block 6	III/IV
1552	DCD	Layer, pit 1552	Block 6	?
1554	DCF	Layer, pit 1554	Block 6	III
1555	DCG	Layer, pit 1555	Block 6	III
1556	DCH	Post-hole	Block 6, SE	?
1557	DCI	Post-hole	Block 6, SE	?
1558	DCK	Layer, pit 1558	Block 6, SE	?
1559	DCL	Layer, pit 1559	Block 6, SE	?
1560	DCM	Layer, pit 1560	Block 6, SE	?
1562	DCO	Layer, ditch 15	Block 6	III
1563	DCP	Layer, pit 1563 (?latrine)	Block 6	III/IV
1564	DCQ	Layer, gully 22	Block 6	III
1565	DCR	Post-hole	Block 6, N	II/III
1566	DCS	Layer, ditch 8	Block 6	III
1567	DCT	Layer, pit 1567	Block 5	III/IV
1568	DCV	Layer, ditch 15	Block 6	III
1569	DCW	Post-hole	Block 6, SE	?
1570	DCX	Post-hole	Block 6, NE	?

Unit number	Group code	Description	Location	Primary feature phase
1571	DCY	Layer, gully 22	Block 6	III
1572	DCZ	Layer, ditch 20	Block 6	III
1573	DDA	Layer, ditch 7	Block 1	III
1574	DDB	Layer, ditch 20	Block 6	III
1575	DDC	Pit layer, same as 1521	Block 5	III/IV
1576	DDD	Layer, pit 1503	Block 5	III/IV
1577	DDE	Layer, pit 1577	Block 6	III
1578	DDF	Hearth	Block 6	III
1579	DDG	Layer, pit 1579	Block 6	III
1580	DDH	Post-hole	Block 6, S	?
1581	DDI	Post-hole	Block 6, S	?
1582	DDK	Post-hole	Block 6, S	?
1583	DDL	Post-hole	Block 6, S	?
1584	DDM	Layer, pit 1541	Block 6	III
1585	DDN	Layer, pit 1585/1515	Block 5	III
1586	DDO	Layer, pit 1586	Block 5	III
1587	DDP	Layer, pit 1567	Block 5	III/IV
1588	DDQ	Layer, pit 1588	Block 5	III/IV
1589	DDR	Post-hole	Block 6, SW	?
1590	DDS	Post-hole	Block 6, SW	?
1591	DDT	Layer, pit 1591	Block 6	?
1592	DDV	Layer, pit 1592	Block 5	III/IV
1593	DDW	Layer, ditch 15	Block 6	III
1594	DDX	Layer, ditch 8	Block 6	III
1595	DDY	Layer, pit 1595	Block 5	III/IV
1596	DDZ	Layer, ditch 15	Block 6	III
1597	DEA	Topsoil/cleaning, blocks 8 and 9, and blocks 3 and 4, E		–
1598	DEB	Layer, pit 1541	Block 6	III
1599	DEC	Layer, pit 1595	Block 5	III/IV
1600	DED	Layer, pit 1600	Block 5	III
1601	DEE	Layer, ditch 8	Block 6	III
1602	DEF	Layer, well 1602	Block 7	III
1603	DEG	Post-hole	Block 6, N	?
1604	DEH	Layer, pit 1604	Block 5	III
1605	DEI	Layer, ditch 15	Block 6	III
1606	DEK	Layer, pit 1536 (?latrine)	Block 6	III
1607	DEL	Layer, ditch 8 (fence-line)	Block 6	III
1609	DEN	Layer, ditch 8 (fence-line)	Block 6	III
1610	DEO	Layer, ditches 6 and 71	Block 1	III & VI
1611	DEP	Layer, pit 1611	Block 5	III/IV
1612	DEQ	Layer, pit 1612/1517	Block 5	III/IV
1613	DER	Layer, ditch 8	Block 6	III
1615	DET	Layer, ditch 8	Block 6	III
1620	DEZ	Post-hole, bldg R11	Block 9	III
1621	DFA	Post-hole, bldg R11	Block 9	III
1624	DFD	Layer, gully 33	Block 9	III
1625	DFE	Layer, well 1625	Block 9	III
1629	DFI	?Hearth or post-hole, bldg R12	Block 9	III/IV
1631	DFL	Post-hole, bldg R11	Block 9	III
1633	DFN	Layer, pit 1633	Block 9	III
1635	DFP	Layer, pit 1635	Block 9	III
1636	DFQ	Layer, gully 32	Block 9	III
1637	DFR	Layer, gully 32	Block 9	III
1638	DFS	Layer, pit 1638 (?latrine)	Block 9	III

Unit number	Group code	Description	Location	Primary feature phase
1639	DFT	Layer, gully 28	Block 9	III/IV
1640	DFV	Layer, gully 24	Block 9	III
1649	DGE	Layer, gully 34	Block 9	III
1650	DGF	Layer, gully 27	Block 9	III
1654	DGK	Layer, gully 73	Block 9	IV?
1655	DGL	Layer, gully 27	Block 9	III
1656	DGM	Post-hole, bldg R12	Block 9	III/IV
1657	DGN	Layer, gully 29	Block 9	III
1659	DGP	Layer, part of 1965	Block 9	III/IV
1660	DGQ	Layer, gully 30	Block 9	III
1661	DGR	Layer, gully 31	Block 9	III
1663	DGT	Layer, well 704/1663	Block 3	III
1665	DGW	Layer, gully 35	Block 3	III
1667	DGY	Layer, well 1667	Block 9	III/IV
1668	DGZ	Layer, over pit cluster, 1834, 1835/2007, 1850, (=2054)	Block 9	III/IV
1669	DHA	Layer, well 1669	Block 9	III/IV
1673	DHE	?Drip-gully, bldg R14	Block 9	III/IV
1675	DHG	Post-hole, bldg R11	Block 9	III
1678	DHK	Layer, well 1678	Block 9	III
1680	DHM	Post-hole, bldg R14	Block 9	III/IV
1681	DHN	Post-hole, bldg R14	Block 9	III/IV
1685	DHR	Disturbed silt layer, bldg R13	Block 9	III
1686	DHS	Disturbed silt layer, bldg R13	Block 9	III
1689	DHW	Silt spread	Block 9, NW	III/IV
1690	DHX	Silt spread	Block 9, NW	III/IV
1692	DHZ	Layer, gully 33	Block 9	III
1693	DIA	Layer over pit cluster 1960, 1982 etc.	Block 9	III/IV
1694	DIB	Layer, gully 31	Block 9	III
1695	DIC	Layer, pit 1695 (?latrine)	Block 9	III
1697	DIE	Layer, gully 18	Block 8	III
1698	DIF	Layer, pit 1698	Block 8	III/IV
1699	DIG	Layer, gully 18	Block 8	III
1700	DIH	Layer, gully 21	Block 6	III
1701	DII	Layer, gully 30	Block 9	III
1702	DIK	Layer, gully 24	Block 9	III
1703	DIL	Layer, gully 24	Block 9	III
1704	DIM	Layer, above 1705 and 1706	Block 9	III/IV
1705	DIN	Layer, gully 33	Block 9	III
1706	DIO	Layer, gully 32	Block 9	III
1707	DIP	Layer, above 1708 and 1637	Block 9	III/IV
1708	DIQ	Layer, gully 33	Block 9	III
1709	DIR	Layer, gully 29	Block 9	III
1712	DIV	Layer, gully 29	Block 9	III
1713	DIW	Layer, gully 29	Block 9	III
1716	DIZ	Layer, gully 70	Block 9	III
1717	DKA	Layer, gully 32	Block 9	III
1718	DKB	Layer, gully 70	Block 9	III
1719	DKC	Layer, pit 1635	Block 9	III
1721	DKE	Layer, well 704/1663	Block 3	III
1722	DKF	Layer, well 704/1663	Block 3	III
1723	DKG	Layer, gully 29	Block 9	III
1724	DKH	Layer, well 1625	Block 9	III
1725	DKI	Layer, pit 1725	Block 9	III/IV
1726	DKK	Post-hole, bldg R11	Block 9	III

Unit number	Group code	Description	Location	Primary feature phase
1727	DKL	Post-hole, bldg R11	Block 9	III
1728	DKM	Post-hole, bldg R11	Block 9	III
1729	DKN	Post-hole, bldg R11	Block 9	III
1730	DKO	Layer, gully 33	Block 9	III
1731	DKP	Layer, gully 32	Block 9	III
1732	DKQ	Layer, well 704/1663	Block 3	III
1733	DKR	Layer, well 1625	Block 9	III
1734	DKS	Layer, gully 30	Block 9	III
1736	DKV	Layer, gully 18	Block 8	III
1737	DKW	Layer, well 704/1663	Block 3	III
1738	DKX	Layer, pit 1638 (?latrine)	Block 9	III
1739	DKY	Layer, pit 1638 (?latrine)	Block 9	III
1740	DKZ	Layer above 1836, 1855 etc	Block 4	III/IV
1741	DLA	Layer, gully 18	Block 8	III
1742	DLB	Layer, well 1602	Block 7	III
1743	DLC	Layer, well 1602	Block 7	III
1744	DLD	Layer, pit 1536 (?latrine)	Block 6	III
1745	DLE	Layer, ditch 68	Block 6	III
1746	DLF	Layer, ditch 8 (fence-line)	Block 6	III
1747	DLG	Layer, ditch 8 (fence-line)	Block 6	III
1748	DLH	Layer, pit 1536 (?latrine)	Block 6	III
1749	DLI	Layer, pit 1749	Block 5	III
1750	DLK	Layer, gully 36	Block 4	III
1751	DLL	Layer, pit 1776	Block 5	III/IV
1752	DLM	Layer, pit 1752	Block 6	III
1753	DLN	Layer, ditch 15	Block 6	III
1754	DLO	Layer, gully 46	Block 5	III
1755	DLP	Layer, gully 46	Block 5	III
1756	DLQ	Layer, gully 23	Block 6	III
1757	DLR	Layer, gully 23	Block 6	III
1758	DLS	Layer, gully 23	Block 6	III
1759	DLT	Post-hole	Block 6, S	?
1760	DLV	Post-hole	Block 6, S	?
1761	DLW	Post-hole	Block 6, S	?
1762	DLX	Post-hole	Block 6, S	?
1763	DLY	Post-hole	Block 6, S	?
1764	DLZ	Post-hole	Block 6, S	?
1765	DMA	Layer, pit 1765	Block 6	?
1766	DMB	Layer, ditch 68	Block 6	III
1767	DMC	Layer, pit 1767	Block 6	?
1768	DMD	Post-hole	Block 6	?
1769	DME	Post-hole	Block 6	?
1770	DMF	Post-hole	Block 6	?
1771	DMG	Post-hole	Block 6	?
1773	DMI	Post-hole	Block 6	?
1774	DMK	Layer, pit 1538	Block 6	III
1776	DMM	Layer, pit 1776	Block 5	III/IV
1778	DMO	Layer, ditch 15	Block 6	III
1779	DMP	Layer in gully, cut by 1778	Block 6	I/II?
1780	DMQ	Layer, ditch 8	Block 6	III
1781	DMR	Layer, gully 19	Block 7	III
1782	DMS	Layer, gully 22	Block 6	III
1783	DMT	Layer, pit 1752	Block 6	III
1784	DMV	Layer, pit 1784	Block 5	III

Unit number	Group code	Description	Location	Primary feature phase
1785	DMW	Layer, gully 22	Block 6	III
1786	DMX	Layer, pit 1786	Block 4	III
1787	DMY	Layer, pit 1787	Block 5	III/IV
1788	DMZ	Layer, gully 36	Block 4	III
1789	DNA	Layer, pit 1789	Block 6	III
1791	DNC	Wood lining, pit 1536 (?latrine)	Block 6	III
1792	DND	Layer, gully 46	Block 5	III
1793	DNE	Layer, gully 37	Block 5	0?
1794	DNF	Layer, pit 1749	Block 5	III
1795	DNG	Layer, pit 1795	Block 5	III/IV
1796	DNH	Layer, ditch 8 (fence-line)	Block 6	III
1797	DNI	Layer, gully 18	Block 8	III
1798	DNK	Layer, ditch 15	Block 8	III
1799	DNL	Layer, gully 18	Block 8	III
1800	DNM	Layer, gully 19	Block 7	III
1801	DNN	Layer, ditch 15	Block 8	III
1802	DNO	Layer, gully 19	Block 7	III
1803	DNP	Layer, pit 1803	Block 7	III/IV
1806	DNS	Layer, well 1602	Block 7	III
1807	DNT	Topsoil/cleaning	Blocks 7, 8	–
1808	DNV	Layer, pit 1577	Block 6	III
1809	DNW	Layer, pit 1786	Block 4	III
1810	DNX	Layer, gully 18	Block 8	III
1811	DNY	Layer, gully 24	Block 8	III
1812	DNZ	Layer, gully 17	Block 8	III
1813	DOA	Layer, pit 1825	Block 8	III/IV
1814	DOB	Layer, pit 1814	Block 8	III/IV
1815	DOC	Layer, pit 1815/1520	Block 5	III/IV
1816	DOD	Layer, pit 1536 (?latrine)	Block 6	III
1817	DOE	Layer, pit 1577	Block 6	III
1818	DOF	Layer, pit 1818	Block 5	III/IV
1819	DOG	Layer, well 1602	Block 7	III
1820	DOH	Layer, well 1602	Block 7	III
1821	DOI	Layer, well 1602	Block 7	III
1822	DOK	Layer, gully 19	Block 7	III
1823	DOL	Layer, pit 1577	Block 6	III
1824	DOM	Layer, pit 1577	Block 6	III
1825	DON	Layer, pit 1825	Block 8	III/IV
1826	DOO	Layer, well 1625	Block 9	III
1827	DOP	Layer, gully 27	Block 9	III
1828	DOQ	Layer, gully 27	Block 9	III
1829	DOR	Layer, gully 27	Block 9	III
1830	DOS	Layer, gully 29	Block 9	III
1832	DOV	Layer, gully 18	Block 8	III
1833	DOW	Layer, well 1625	Block 9	III
1834	DOX	Layer, well 1834	Block 9	III
1835	DOY	Layer, pit 1835/2007	Block 9	III/IV
1836	DOZ	Layer, well 1836	Block 4	III
1837	DPA	Layer, gully 24	Block 8	III
1838	DPB	Layer, pit 1698	Block 8	III/IV
1839	DPC	Layer, pit 1814	Block 8	III/IV
1840	DPD	Layer, gully 18	Block 8	III
1841	DPE	Layer, gully 18	Block 8	III
1842	DPF	Layer, gully 36	Block 4	III

Unit number	Group code	Description	Location	Primary feature phase
1843	DPG	Layer, gully 36	Block 4	III
1844	DPH	Layer, pit 1844	Block 5	III
1845	DPI	Layer, pit 1994 and gully 30	Block 9	III/IV
1846	DPK	Layer, gully 31	Block 9	III
1847	DPL	Layer, pit 1847	Block 4	?
1848	DPM	Layer, well 1667	Block 9	III/IV
1849	DPN	Layer, well 1669	Block 9	III/IV
1850	DPO	Layer, pit 1850	Block 9	III
1851	DPP	Layer, well 1836	Block 4	III
1852	DPQ	Layer, pit 1814	Block 8	III/IV
1853	DPR	Layer, well 1853	Block 8	III
1854	DPS	Layer, pit 1695 (?latrine)	Block 9	III
1855	DPT	Layer, gully 35	Block 3	III
1856	DPV	Layer, well 1836	Block 4	III
1857	DPW	Layer, gully 18	Block 8	III
1858	DPX	Layer, pit 1695 (?latrine)	Block 9	III
1859	DPY	Layer, gully 17	Block 8	III
1860	DPZ	Layer, well 1667	Block 9	III/IV
1861	DQA	Layer, gully 35	Block 3	III
1862	DQB	Post-hole, bldg R8	Block 8	III
1863	DQC	Layer, well 1834	Block 9	III
1864	DQD	Layer, pit 1695 (?latrine)	Block 9	III
1865	DQE	Layer, well 1853	Block 8	III
1866	DQF	Layer, pit 1814	Block 8	III/IV
1867	DQG	Disturbed silt layer, bldg R13	Block 9	III
1868	DQH	Layer, gully 36	Block 4	III
1869	DQI	Layer, gully 30	Block 9	III
1870	DQK	Layer, gully 30	Block 9	III
1871	DQL	Layer, gully 31	Block 9	III
1872	DQM	Layer, gully 31	Block 9	III
1873	DQN	Layer above pits 1973, 1974, 1975, 1972/1976	Block 9	III
1874	DQO	Layer, as 1873	Block 9	III
1875	DQP	Layer, pit 1960	Block 9	III
1876	DQQ	Layer, pit 1835/2007	Block 9	III/IV
1877	DQR	Layer, pit 1695 (?latrine)	Block 9	III
1878	DQS	Layer, well 1667	Block 9	III/IV
1879	DQT	Layer, well 1678	Block 9	III
1880	DQV	Layer, well 1669	Block 9	III/IV
1881	DQW	Layer, pit 1960	Block 9	III
1882	DQX	Layer above pits 1887, 2087	Block 9	III/IV
1883	DQY	Layer above pits 1906, 1907 and gully 30	Block 9	III/IV
1884	DQZ	Layer, gully 18	Block 8	III
1885	DRA	Layer, well 1885	Block 7	III
1886	DRB	Layer, well 1667	Block 9	III/IV
1887	DRC	Layer, pit 1887	Block 9	III
1888	DRD	Layer, well 1678	Block 9	III
1889	DRE	Layer, gully 30	Block 9	III
1890	DRF	Layer, well 1834	Block 9	III
1891	DRG	Layer, well 1678	Block 9	III
1892	DRH	Layer, well 1669	Block 9	III/IV
1893	DRI	Layer, gully 30	Block 9	III
1894	DRK	Layer, gully 29	Block 9	III
1895	DRL	Layer, pit 1887	Block 9	III
1896	DRM	Layer, gully 18	Block 8	III

Unit number	Group code	Description	Location	Primary feature phase
1897	DRN	Layer, well 1834	Block 9	III
1898	DRO	Layer, gully 29	Block 9	III
1899	DRP	Layer, well 1678	Block 9	III
1900	DRQ	Surface of street 2 N/S	Block 9	III→
1901	DRR	Layer, well 1678	Block 9	III
1902	DRS	Layer, well 1914	Block 7	III
1903	DRT	Layer, well 1669	Block 9	III/IV
1904	DRV	Layer in pits 1973, 1974, 1975, 1972/1976	Block 9	III
1905	DRW	Layer, gully 31	Block 9	III
1906	DRX	Layer, pit 1906	Block 9	III
1907	DRY	Layer, pit 1907	Block 9	III
1908	DRZ	Layer, pit 1960	Block 9	III
1909	DSA	Layer, pit 1909/1968	Block 9	III
1910	DSB	Layer, pit 1909/1968	Block 9	III
1911	DSC	Layer, gully 34	Block 9	III
1912	DSD	Layer, well 1667	Block 9	III/IV
1913	DSE	Layer, gully 18	Block 8	III
1914	DSF	Layer, well 1914	Block 7	III
1915	DSG	Layer, pit 1915	Block 7	III
1916	DSH	Layer, pit 1916	Block 7	?
1917	DSI	Layer, pit 1917	Block 7	?
1918	DSK	Layer, pit 1918	Block 8	?
1919	DSL	Post-hole, bldg R9	Block 8	III
1920	DSM	Layer, ditch 15	Block 8	III
1921	DSN	Post-hole, bldg R9	Block 8	III
1922	DSO	Post-hole, bldg R9	Block 8	III
1923	DSP	Layer, pit 1923	Block 7	?
1924	DSQ	Layer, pit 1535 (?latrine)	Block 6	III/IV
1925	DSR	Layer, pit 1925	Block 7	?
1926	DSS	Layer, well 1885	Block 7	III
1927	DST	Layer, gully 18	Block 8	III
1928	DSV	Layer, pit 1928	Block 8	?
1929	DSW	Layer, gully 17	Block 8	III
1930	DSX	Layer, oven 9	Block 8	IV
1931	DSY	Layer, pit 1931/2091	Block 8	III
1933	DTA	Layer, pit 1933	Block 8	V
1934	DTB	Layer, well 1914	Block 7	III
1937	DTE	Layer, pit 1937	Block 7	?
1938	DTF	Layer, pit 1938	Block 7	?
1939	DTG	Layer, pit 1939	Block 7	?
1941	DTI	Post-hole	Block 7, S	?
1942	DTK	Post-hole	Block 7, S	?
1943	DTL	Layer, pit 1943	Block 7	III
1944	DTM	Layer, gully 16	Block 7	III
1945	DTN	Layer, well 1914	Block 7	III
1946	DTO	Layer, pit 1915	Block 7	III
1947	DTP	Layer, gully 16	Block 7	III
1948	DTQ	Layer, pit 1915	Block 7	III
1949	DTR	Layer, well 1885	Block 7	III
1950	DTS	Layer, well 1885	Block 7	III
1951	DTT	Layer, pit 1951	Block 7	III
1952	DTV	Layer, gully 18	Block 8	III
1953	DTW	Layer, gully 18	Block 8	III
1954	DTX	Layer, well 1885	Block 7	III

Unit number	Group code	Description	Location	Primary feature phase
1955	DTY	Layer, pit 1915	Block 7	III
1956	DTZ	Layer, gully 18	Block 8	III
1957	DVA	Layer, gully 18	Block 8	III
1958	DVB	Layer, pit 1915	Block 7	III
1959	DVC	Layer, pit 1951	Block 7	III
1960	DVD	Layer, pit 1960	Block 9	III
1961	DVE	Layer, gully 31	Block 9	III
1962	DVF	Layer, pit 1962	Block 9	III
1963	DVG	Layer above pits 1989, 1996	Block 9	III/IV
1964	DVH	Layer above pits 1986, 1987	Block 9	III/IV
1965	DVI	Layer above well 2020 and pits 2021/2110, 2022	Block 9	III/IV
1966	DVK	Layer, pit 1960	Block 9	III
1967	DVL	Layer, pit 1967	Block 8	III/IV
1968	DVM	Layer, pit 1909/1968	Block 9	I
1969	DVN	Layer, pit 1909/1968	Block 9	I
1971	DVP	Layer, well 1836	Block 4	III
1972	DVQ	Layer, pit 1972/1976	Block 9	III
1973	DVR	Layer, pit 1973	Block 9	III
1974	DVS	Layer, pit 1974	Block 9	III
1975	DVT	Layer, pit 1975	Block 9	III
1976	DVV	Layer, pit 1972/1976	Block 9	III
1977	DVW	Layer above well 2020 and pits 2021/2110, 2022	Block 9	III/IV
1978	DVX	Layer, well 1678	Block 9	III
1979	DVY	Layer, pit 2022	Block 9	III/IV
1980	DVZ	Layer, well 2020, pits 2021/2110, 2022	Block 9	III/IV
1981	DWA	Layer, gully 29	Block 9	III
1982	DWB	Layer, pit 1982	Block 9	III/IV
1983	DWC	Layer, pit 1984	Block 8	III/IV
1984	DWD	Layer, pit 1984	Block 8	III/IV
1985	DWE	Layer, well 1678	Block 9	III
1986	DWF	Layer, pit 1986	Block 9	?
1987	DWG	Layer, pit 1987	Block 9	III/IV
1988	DWH	Layer, gully 29	Block 9	III
1989	DWI	Layer, pit 1989	Block 9	III
1990	DWK	Layer, pits 1989, 1996	Block 9	III/IV
1991	DWL	Layer, gully 30	Block 9	III
1992	DWM	Layer, gully 30	Block 9	III
1993	DWN	Layer, gully 30	Block 9	III
1994	DWO	Layer, pit 1994	Block 9	III/IV
1995	DWP	Layer, gully 29	Block 9	III
1996	DWQ	Layer, pit 1996	Block 9	III/IV
1997	DWR	Post-hole, bldg R12	Block 9	III/IV
1998	DWS	Post-hole, bldg R12	Block 9	III/IV
1999	DWT	Layer above pits 1835/2007, 2021/2110	Block 9	III/IV
2000	DWV	Layer, pit 1984	Block 8	III/IV
2001	DWW	Layer, well 1885	Block 7	III
2002	DWX	Layer, pit 1996	Block 9	III/IV
2003	DWY	Layer, pit 2003	Block 9	III
2004	DWZ	Layer, pit 2003	Block 9	III
2005	DXA	Layer, bldgs R10 and R12	Block 9	III
2006	DXB	Layer, well 2020 and pit 2021/2110	Block 9	III/IV
2007	DXC	Layer, pit 1835/2007	Block 9	III/IV
2008	DXD	Layer, pit 1951	Block 7	III
2009	DXE	Layer, pit 1962	Block 9	III

Unit number	Group code	Description	Location	Primary feature phase
2010	DXF	Layer, pit 1962	Block 9	III
2011	DXG	Layer, pit 1633	Block 9	III
2012	DXH	Layer, pit 1982	Block 9	III/IV
2013	DXI	Layer, pit 1982	Block 9	III/IV
2014	DXK	Layer, pit 2014	Block 9	III
2015	DXL	Post-hole, bldg R12	Block 9	III/IV
2016	DXM	Post-hole, bldg R12	Block 9	III/IV
2017	DXN	Post-hole, bldg R12	Block 9	III/IV
2018	DXO	Post-hole, bldg R12	Block 9	III/IV
2019	DXP	Layer, well 1914	Block 7	III
2020	DXQ	Layer, well 2020	Block 9	III
2021	DXR	Layer, pit 2021/2110	Block 9	III/IV
2022	DXS	Layer, pit 2022	Block 9	III/IV
2023	DXT	Layer, pit 2023	Block 8	III/IV
2024	DXV	Layer, well 1914	Block 7	III
2025	DXW	Layer, ditch 15	Block 8	III
2026	DXX	Layer, gully 18	Block 8	III
2027	DXY	Layer, gully 18	Block 8	III
2028	DXZ	Layer, pit 2021/2110	Block 9	III/IV
2029	DYA	Layer, gully 18	Block 8	III
2030	DYB	Layer, gully 18	Block 8	III
2031	DYC	Layer, gully 19	Block 7	III
2032	DYD	Layer, gully 19	Block 7	III
2033	DYE	Layer, bldg R10	Block 9	III
2034	DYF	Post-hole, bldg R12	Block 9	III/IV
2035	DYG	Post-hole, bldg R12	Block 9	III/IV
2036	DYH	Post-hole, bldg R12	Block 9	III/IV
2037	DYI	Post-hole, bldg R12	Block 9	III/IV
2038	DYK	Post-hole bldg R12	Block 9	III/IV
2039	DYL	Layer, pit 1989	Block 9	III
2040	DYM	Post-hole, bldg R12	Block 9	III/IV
2041	DYN	Post-hole, bldg R12	Block 9	III/IV
2042	DYO	Post-hole, bldg R12	Block 9	III/IV
2043	DYP	Post-hole, bldg R12	Block 9	III/IV
2044	DYQ	Post-hole, bldg R12	Block 9	III/IV
2045	DYR	Layer, pit 2045	Block 5	?
2046	DYS	Post-hole, bldg R12	Block 9	III/IV
2047	DYT	Layer, pit 2021/2110	Block 9	III/IV
2048	DYV	Layer, pit 2021/2110	Block 9	III/IV
2049	DYW	Post-hole, bldg R12	Block 9	III/IV
2050	DYX	Post-hole, bldg R12	Block 9	III/IV
2051	DYY	Layer, gully 17	Block 8	III
2052	DYZ	Layer, pit 2052	Block 8	III
2053	DZA	Layer, pit 2052	Block 8	III
2054	DZB	Layer over pit cluster 1834, 1835/2007, 1850 (=1668)	Block 9	III/IV
2057	DZE	Post-hole, bldg R12	Block 9	III/IV
2058	DZF	Post-hole, bldg R12	Block 9	III/IV
2059	DZG	Layer, gully 18	Block 8	III
2060	DZH	Post-hole, bldg R12	Block 9	III/IV
2061	DZI	Layer, pit 2061	Block 8	III
2062	DZK	Layer, pit 2061	Block 8	III
2063	DZL	Post-hole, bldg R12	Block 9	III/IV
2064	DZM	Post-hole, bldg R12	Block 9	III/IV
2065	DZN	Post-hole, bldg R12	Block 9	III/IV

Unit number	Group code	Description	Location	Primary feature phase
2066	DZO	Layer, pit 2061	Block 8	III
2067	DZP	Layer, pit 2067	Block 8	III
2068	DZQ	Layer, well 1914	Block 7	III
2069	DZR	Layer, gully 72	Block 9	?
2070	DZS	Layer, gully 29	Block 9	III
2071	DZT	Layer over pits 2094, 2097	Block 9	III/IV
2072	DZV	Layer, pit 1943	Block 7	III
2073	DZW	Layer, pit 1943	Block 7	III
2074	DZX	Layer, pit 1943	Block 7	III
2075	DZY	Layer, pit 1943	Block 7	III
2076	DZZ	Disturbed silt layer, bldg R13	Block 9	III
2077	EAA	Layer, pit 2061	Block 8	III
2078	EAB	Layer, pit 1943	Block 7	III
2079	EAC	Layer, pit 1943	Block 7	III
2080	EAD	Layer, pit 2080	Block 7	III
2081	EAE	Layer, well 1853	Block 8	III
2082	EAF	Layer, pit 2023	Block 8	III/IV
2083	EAG	Post-hole, bldg R12	Block 9	III/IV
2084	EAH	Post-hole, bldg R12	Block 9	III/IV
2085	EAI	Post-hole, bldg R7	Block 4	III
2086	EAK	Layer, pit 2061	Block 8	III
2087	EAL	Layer, pit 2087	Block 9	III
2088	EAM	Layer, well 2020	Block 9	III
2089	EAN	Layer, well 2020	Block 9	III
2090	EAO	Layer, well 2020	Block 9	III
2091	EAP	Layer, pit 1931/2091	Block 8	III
2092	EAQ	Post-hole, bldg R11	Block 9	III
2093	EAR	Layer, gully 18	Block 8	III
2094	EAS	Layer, pit 2094	Block 9	III/IV
2095	EAT	Post-hole, bldg R11	Block 9	III
2096	EAV	Layer, gully 24	Block 8	III
2097	EAW	Layer, pit 2097	Block 9	III/IV
2098	EAX	Layer, ditch 15	Block 7	III
2099	EAY	Layer, gully 16	Block 7	III
2102	EBB	Layer, well 2020	Block 9	III
2103	EBC	Layer, pit 2103	Block 8	III/IV
2104	EBD	Layer above pits 2121, 2124	Block 7	III/IV
2105	EBE	Layer above pits 2106 and 1937–9	Block 7	III/IV
2106	EBF	Layer, pit 2106	Block 7	III
2107	EBG	Layer, pit 2106	Block 7	III
2108	EBH	Layer, gully 18	Block 8	III
2109	EBI	Post-hole, bldg R12	Block 9	III/IV
2110	EBK	Layer, pit 2021/2110	Block 9	III/IV
2111	EBL	Post-hole, bldg R12	Block 9	III/IV
2112	EBM	Post-hole, bldg R12	Block 9	III/IV
2113	EBN	Post-hole, bldg R12	Block 9	III/IV
2114	EBO	Post-hole, bldg R12	Block 9	III/IV
2115	EBP	Layer, gully 24	Block 9	III
2116	EBQ	Layer, pit 1835/2007	Block 9	III/IV
2117	EBR	Layer, pit 2021/2110	Block 9	III/IV
2118	EBS	'Flood' silt, bldgs R11, R12	Block 9	III/IV
2119	EBT	Layer, gully 24	Block 9	III
2120	EBV	Disturbed silt layer, bldg R13	Block 9	III
2121	EBW	Layer, pit 2121	Block 7	III/IV

Unit number	Group code	Description	Location	Primary feature phase
2122	EBX	Layer, pit 2121	Block 7	III/IV
2123	EBY	Layer, pit 2106	Block 7	III
2124	EBZ	Layer, pit 2124	Block 7	?
2125	ECA	Layer, pit 2106	Block 7	III
2126	ECB	Layer, pit 2106	Block 7	III
2127	ECC	Layer pit 2106	Block 7	III
2128	ECD	Layer, gully 16	Block 7	III
2129	ECE	Layer, pit 2129	Block 8	III
2130	ECF	Layer, pit 2130	Block 7	?
2131	ECG	Layer, pit 2106	Block 7	III
2133	ECI	Layer, gully 16	Block 7	III
2134	ECK	Layer, pit 2106	Block 7	III
2135	ECL	Layer, ditch 8	Block 6	III
2136	ECM	Layer, ditch 15 and gully 19	Block 7	III
2137	ECN	Layer, gully 26	Block 8	III
2138	ECO	Layer, gully 25	Block 8	III
2139	ECP	Layer, pit 2139	Block 7	?
2140	ECQ	Post-hole	Block 7, E	?
2142	ECS	Post-hole, bldg R9	Block 8	III
2144	ECV	Layer, gully 25	Block 8	III
2145	ECW	Layer, pit 2145	Block 8	III
2147	ECY	Post-hole, bldg R9	Block 8	III
2148	ECZ	Post-hole, bldg R9	Block 8	III
2149	EDA	Post-hole, bldg R9	Block 8	III
2150	EDB	Post-hole, bldg R8	Block 8	III
2151	EDC	Post-hole, bldg R8	Block 8	III
2156	EDH	Post-hole, bldg R8	Block 8	III
2161	EDN	Layer, pit 2021/2110	Block 9	III/IV
2162	EDO	?Floor foundation, bldg R11	Block 9	III
2163	EDP	Layer, pit 2021/2110	Block 9	III/IV
2164	EDQ	Layer, pit 2021/2110	Block 9	III/IV
2165	EDR	Layer, gullies 24 and 29	Block 9	III
2166	EDS	Layer, gully 30	Block 9	III
2167	EDT	Layer, gullies 24 and 29	Block 9	III
2168	EDV	Layer, bldg R11	Block 9	III
2169	EDW	Layer, pit 2087	Block 9	III
2170	EDX	Part of 2162	Block 9	III
2171	EDY	Post-hole, bldg R10	Block 9	III
2172	EDZ	Post-hole, bldg R10	Block 9	III
2173	EEA	Post-hole and infant burial, bldg R10	Block 9	III
2174	EEB	Post-hole, bldg R10	Block 9	III
2175	EEC	Post-hole, bldg R10	Block 9	III
2176	EED	Post-hole, bldg R10	Block 9	III
2177	EEE	Post-hole and infant burial, bldg R10	Block 9	III
2178	EEF	Post-hole and infant burial, bldg R10	Block 9	III
2179	EEG	Post-hole, bldg R10	Block 9	III
2180	EEH	Post-hole, bldg R10	Block 9	III
2181	EEI	Post-hole, bldg R10	Block 9	III
2182	EEK	Post-hole, bldg R10	Block 9	III
2183	EEL	Post-hole, bldg R10	Block 9	III
2184	EEM	Post-hole, bldg R10	Block 9	III
2186	EEO	Post-hole, bldg R11	Block 9	III
2190	EES	Post-hole, bldg R12	Block 9	III/IV
2192	EEV	Post-hole, bldg R12	Block 9	III/IV

Unit number	Group code	Description	Location	Primary feature phase
2193	EEW	Post-hole, bldg R12	Block 9	III/IV
2194	EEX	Post-hole, bldg R12	Block 9	III/IV
2195	EEY	Post-hole, bldg R12	Block 9	III/IV
2196	EEZ	Post-hole, bldg R12	Block 9	III/IV
2200	EFD	Post-hole, bldg R12	Block 9	III/IV
2201	EFE	Post-hole, bldg R13	Block 9	III
2202	EFF	Post-hole, bldg R13	Block 9	III
2203	EFG	Post-hole, bldg R13	Block 9	III
2204	EFH	Post-hole, bldg R13	Block 9	III
2206	EFK	Post-hole, bldg R12	Block 9	III/IV
2207	EFL	Post-hole, bldg R12	Block 9	III/IV
2210	EFO	Post-hole, bldg R12	Block 9	III/IV
2211	EFP	Post-hole, bldg R12	Block 9	III/IV
2212	EFQ	Post-hole, bldg R13	Block 9	III
2213	EFR	Post-hole, bldg R13	Block 9	III
2214	EFS	Post-hole, bldg R13	Block 9	III
2215	EFT	Post-hole, bldg R13	Block 9	III
2216	EFV	Post-hole, bldg R13	Block 9	III
2217	EFW	Post-hole, bldg R13	Block 9	III
2218	EFX	Post-hole, bldg R13	Block 9	III
2219	EFY	Post-hole, bldg R13	Block 9	III
2220	EFZ	Post-hole, bldg R13	Block 9	III
2221	EGA	Post-hole, bldg R13	Block 9	III
2222	EGB	Post-hole, bldg R13	Block 9	III
2223	EGC	Post-hole, bldg R13	Block 9	III
2224	EGD	Post-hole, bldg R13	Block 9	III
2225	EGE	Post-hole, bldg R13	Block 9	III
2226	EGF	Post-hole, bldg R13	Block 9	III
2227	EGG	Post-hole, bldg R13	Block 9	III
2228	EGH	Post-hole, bldg R13	Block 9	III
2230	EGK	Post-hole, bldg R13	Block 9	III
2231	EGL	Post-hole, bldg R13	Block 9	III
2232	EGM	Post-hole, bldg R13	Block 9	III
2233	EGN	Post-hole, bldg R12	Block 9	III/IV
2234	EGO	Post-hole, bldg R12	Block 9	III/IV
2235	EGP	Post-hole, bldg R12	Block 9	III/IV
2236	EGQ	Post-hole, bldg R13	Block 9	III
2237	EGR	Post-hole, bldg R13	Block 9	III
2239	EGT	Post-hole, bldg R11	Block 9	III
2240	EGV	Post-hole, bldg R11	Block 9	III
2241	EGW	Post-hole, bldg R11	Block 9	III
2242	EGX	Post-hole, bldg R11	Block 9	III
2243	EGY	Post-hole, bldg R12	Block 9	III/IV
2244	EGZ	Post-hole, bldg R12	Block 9	III/IV
2245	EHA	Post-hole, bldg R12	Block 9	III/IV
2246	EHB	Post-hole, bldg R12	Block 9	III/IV
2248	EHD	Post-hole, bldg R13	Block 9	III
2249	EHE	Post-hole, bldg R13	Block 9	III
2250	EHF	Post-hole, bldg R13	Block 9	III
2251	EHG	Post-hole, bldg R13	Block 9	III
2252	EHH	Post-hole, bldg R13	Block 9	III
2253	EHI	Post-hole, bldg R13	Block 9	III
2254	EHK	Post-hole, bldg R13	Block 9	III
2255	EHL	Post-hole, bldg R13	Block 9	III

Unit number	Group code	Description	Location	Primary feature phase
2256	EHM	Post-hole, bldg R13	Block 9	III
2257	EHN	Post-hole, bldg R13	Block 9	III
2258	EHO	Post-hole, bldg R13	Block 9	III
2259	EHP	Post-hole, bldg R13	Block 9	III
2260	EHQ	Post-hole, bldg R14	Block 9	III/IV
2261	EHR	Post-hole, bldg R14	Block 9	III/IV
2262	EHS	Post-hole, bldg R14	Block 9	III/IV
2263	EHT	Post-hole, bldg R14	Block 9	III/IV
2264	EHV	Post-hole, bldg R14	Block 9	III/IV
2265	EHW	Post-hole, bldg R14	Block 9	III/IV
2266	EHX	Post-hole, bldg R14	Block 9	III/IV
2267	EHY	Post-hole, bldg R14	Block 9	III/IV
2268	EHZ	Post-hole, bldg R14	Block 9	III/IV
2269	EIA	Post-hole, bldg R14	Block 9	III/IV
2270	EIB	Post-hole, bldg R14	Block 9	III/IV
2271	EIC	Post-hole, bldg R14	Block 9	III/IV
2272	EID	Post-hole, bldg R14	Block 9	III/IV
2275	EIG	Post-hole, bldg R14	Block 9	III/IV
2276	EIH	Post-hole, bldg R14	Block 9	III/IV
2277	EII	Post-hole, bldg R14	Block 9	III/IV
2278	EIK	Post-hole, bldg R12	Block 9	III/IV
2279	EIL	Post-hole, bldg R12	Block 9	III/IV
2280	EIM	Post-hole, bldg R12	Block 9	III/IV
2281	EIN	Post-hole, bldg R14	Block 9	III/IV
2282	EIO	Post-hole, bldg R14	Block 9	III/IV

Trench code	Feature number	Description	Primary feature phase
1983			
A	–	For all contexts with the prefix A (Trench A, the sump), see pp. 93–4	
B	1	Layer, gully 48	III
B	4	Gully	III?
B	5	Gully	III?
B	6	?Ditch	?
D	4	South ditch, street 1 E/W	III?
D	9	North ditch, street 1 E/W (ditch 4)	III
D	11	Surface, street 1 E/W	III→
E	2	North ditch, street 1 E/W (ditch 4)	III
E	3	Surface, street 1 E/W	III→
F	1	South ditch, street 1 E/W	III?
F	4	Surface, street 1 E/W	III→
F	8	North ditch, street 1 E/W (ditch 4)	III
G	2	Layer, ditch 20 (=1574)	III
G	4	Well, block 6, NE	III
G	6	Layer, ditch 15, block 8	III
G	7	Layer, ditch 15, block 8	III
G	8	Layer, gully 18	III
G	9	Layer, gully 18 (=1896)	III
G	10	Layer, gully 18 (=2059)	III
G	11	Post-hole, block 8, N	?
G	12	Post-hole, street 2 E/W	?
G	13	Layer, gully 24, block 9	III
G	14, 1	Layer, gully 27 (=1655)	III
G	14, 2	Surface, street 2 N/S, block 9, SE	III→
H	7	Gully	IV?
H	8	Large pit or ditch	IV?
J	1	Two intercutting pits, block 10, SW	IV
J	3	Pit, block 10, SW	III/IV
J	4	Well, block 10, SW	III
J	5	Gully, block 10, SW	?
J	6	Gully, block 10, SW	?
J	7	Post-hole, block 10, SE	?
J	8	Pit, block 10, SE	?
J	9	Gully (as gully 24), block 10, E	III
J	10	Surface, street 2 N/S, block 10, E	III→
J	11	Layer, gully 27, block 10, E	III
K	7	Surface, street 1 E/W	III→
K	8	Surface, street 1 E/W	III→
K	9	Surface, street 1 E/W	III→
L	11	Surface, street 1 E/W	III→
1984			
M	1	Layer, gully 30, block 9, NW	III
M	2	Layer, gully 70, block 9, NW	III
M	3	Gully, block 10, SW	?
M	4	Gully, block 10, SW	?
M	5	Layer, gully 30, block 10, SW	III
M	6	?Pit cluster, block 10, W	?
M	7	Layer, gully 31, block 10, W	III
M	8	?Pit cluster, block 10, W	?
M	9	Layer, gully 31, block 10, W	III
M	11	?Pit, block 10, W	?

Trench code	Feature number		Primary feature phase
M	18	Surface, junction of streets 1 E/W and 1 N/S, block 10, NW	III→
N	2, 1–2	Gully 78, block 10, S	III
N	2, 3	Layer, cf.2005, block 10, S	III
N	2, 4	Pit, block 10, S	III
N	3	Gully 77, block 10, S	III
N	4	?Pit, block 10	?
N	6	?Pit, block 10	?
N	7	?Pit, block 10	?
N	9	?Pit, block 10	?
N	10	Oven 10, block 10	IV
N	29	Surface, street 1 E/W, block 10, N	III→
O	9	Pit	Ia
O	11	Gully 79	Ia
O	12	Gully 80	Ia
O	14	Gully 81	Ia
O	15	Gully 82	Ia
O	17	?Post-hole	I?
O	26	?Pit	I?
O	33	Pit	Ia
O	36	Pit	Ia
O	49	Layer, ditch 83, bldg R15	II–III
O	57	Hard-standing, bldg R15	III
O	58	Hard-standing, bldg R15	III
O	59	Post-hole, portico, bldg R15	III
O	60	Hard-standing, bldg R15	III
O	61	Cella wall, robbed, bldg R15	III
O	62	Layer, ditch 84, bldg R15	IV
O	63	Gully/footing trench, bldg R15	IV
O	65	Hard-standing, bldg R15	III
O	72	Pit	Ia
O	77	Cella wall, robbed, bldg R15	III
O	79	Black silt layer, below O65	II/III
O	80	Post-hole, ambulatory, bldg R15	III
O	81	Cella floor, bldg R15	III
O	82	Cella wall, robbed, bldg R15	III
O	83	Central pit/post-hole, bldg R15	III
O	86	Layer, ditch 83, bldg R15	II–III
O	87	Ambulatory floor, bldg R15	III
O	88	Layer, ditch 84, bldg R15	IV
O	89	Ambulatory floor, bldg R15	III
P	2	Approach road, bldg R15	III
P	5	Layer, ditch 85, bldg R15	II/III
P	10	(?Votive) pit/shaft	III
P	15	Approach road, bldg R15	III
P	16	Approach road, bldg R15	III
P	21	Pit	I(?)
Q	5	Hard-standing, bldg R15	III
Q	7	Hard-standing, bldg R15	III
Q	10	Hard-standing, bldg R15	III
Q	11	Forecourt debris, bldg R15	III/IV
Q	13	Layer, ditch 84, bldg R15	IV
Q	14	Layer, ditch 84, bldg R15	IV
Q	15	Post-hole, ambulatory, bldg R15	III
Q	16	Forecourt flooring, bldg R15	III

Trench code	Feature number		Primary feature phase
Q	17	Post-hole, portico, bldg R15	III
Q	18	Post-hole, portico, bldg R15	III
Q	19	Post-hole, portico, bldg R15	III
Q	22	?Sill beam slot, bldg R15	II/III
Q	23	Silt make-up, bldg R15	II(?)
Q	26	Post-hole, bldg R15	II(?)
Q	27	Post-hole, bldg R15	II(?)
Q	28	Post-hole, bldg R15	II(?)
Q	29	Post-hole, bldg R15	II(?)
Q	30	Post-hole, bldg R15	II(?)
R	8	?Surface of street 1 E/W	?III→
R	10	?South ditch of street 1 E/W (ditch 86)	III?
R	24	?North ditch of street 1 E/W (ditch 87)	III?
T	10	Approach road, bldg R15	III
W	9	Ditch 76, possibly southern continuation of ditches 6 and 7	III?
X	1	North ditch, street 1 E/W	III?
X	2	Surface, street 1 E/W	III→
X	7	?South ditch, street 1 E/W	III?
Y	1	Ditch 75	0
BB	11	Surface, street 1 E/W	III→
CC	2	Layer, gully 19, south of block 7	III
FF	3	As W9	III?

THE PLATES

Plate I

Plate I Stonea Camp before ploughing, looking west. Arrowed: the Neolithic site and Bronze Age barrow (1961–2).
(Cambridge University Collection: copyright reserved)

PLATE II

Plate II Stonea Camp after ploughing, looking north–east. (Cambridge University Collection: copyright reserved)

PLATE III

Plate III Stonea Camp (foreground) and Stonea Grange, looking north-east. (Cambridge University Collection: copyright reserved)

PLATE IV

Plate IVa Stonea Camp: the interior and inner rampart, looking west, 1980.

Plate IVb Stonea Camp: the ditch, with turves lying in the bottom, 1980.

PLATE V

Plate V Estover: a view looking west across trenches J (foreground), H and C. The droveway is in the foreground, and is seen meeting with the Fen Causeway.

PLATE VI

Plate VI Estover: a view looking north–east across trenches C (foreground) and H. The *agger* of the Fen Causeway shows prominently to the right, as does its north ditch.

PLATE VII

Plate VII Estover: trench L, looking east, with trench B beyond. There is a complex series of ditch intersections between enclosures E5, E7 and E8.

PLATE VIII

Plate VIII Stonea: infra-red vertical photograph, showing traces of a large enclosure and the Roman road.
(ADAS Aerial Photography: Crown copyright)

PLATE IX

Plate IX Stonea: the Grange site, 1984, showing the sump excavation, the possible cursus and the Neolithic site and Bronze Age barrow, 1961–2.

PLATE X

Plate Xa Stonea Grange, 1981, showing the stone-built complex (building R1).

Plate Xb As Plate Xa, looking east.

PLATE XI

Plate XIa Stonea Grange: the raft-like foundations of the central block of building R1, 1981.

Plate XIb As Plate XIa, looking north, 1981.

PLATE XII

Plate XIIa Stonea Grange: base of *opus signinum* drain, over earlier soakaway, draining westwards from building R1.

Plate XIIb Stonea Grange: view south-eastwards across the hypocausted room and probable *praefurnium* of building R1.

PLATE XIII

Plate XIIIa Stonea Grange: wall trench of the east wing of building R1; south wall near the east corner.

Plate XIIIb Stonea Grange: second century AD makeup in the open space ('piazza') to the north of building R1. Looking west, 1981.

PLATE XIV

Plate XIVa Stonea Grange: second-century AD wooden building (R10) in block 9, looking east, 1984.

Plate XIVb Stonea Grange: post-hole 2178 of building R10, with adjacent infant skeleton, cat no. 2.

PLATE XV

Plate XVa Stonea Grange: view southwards down street 1 N/S. Note the conspicuous modern agricultural damage, 1984.

Plate XVb Stonea Grange: complex of pits and a well (1853) in block 8. Second century AD. Looking north, 1984.

PLATE XVI

Plate XVIa Stonea Grange: the sump under excavation.

Plate XVIb Stonea Grange: the sump after excavation, looking south, 1984.

PLATE XVII

Plate XVII Stonea Grange: the south-west corner of the central block of building R1, looking south. Note the robbed masonry, the slumped silts in the robber pit and (arrowed) the old ground surface, 1980.

PLATE XVIII

Plate XVIII Stonea Grange: late Roman oven (oven 5), block 3, 1982.

PLATE XIX

Plate XIXa Stonea Grange: Anglo–Saxon building S1.

Plate XIXb Stonea Grange: Anglo–Saxon building S3.

PLATE XX

Plate XX Stonea Grange: skeleton of pig in Anglo–Saxon pit 1933, block 8.

PLATE XXI

Plate XXI Stonea Grange: part of the assemblage from pit P10 adjacent to the temple (building R15), including samian vessels, pipeclay horse figurine fragments, limestone tesserae and bone point.

PLATE XXII

Plate XXIIa Stonea Grange: artist's impression of building R1, north front, as conceived at the end of the 1982 excavation season. (*By Robert Pengelly*)

Plate XXIIb Stonea Grange: faced limestone block from building R1, apse (unit 27), and tufa voussoir found with other building debris in the sump.

PLATE XXIII

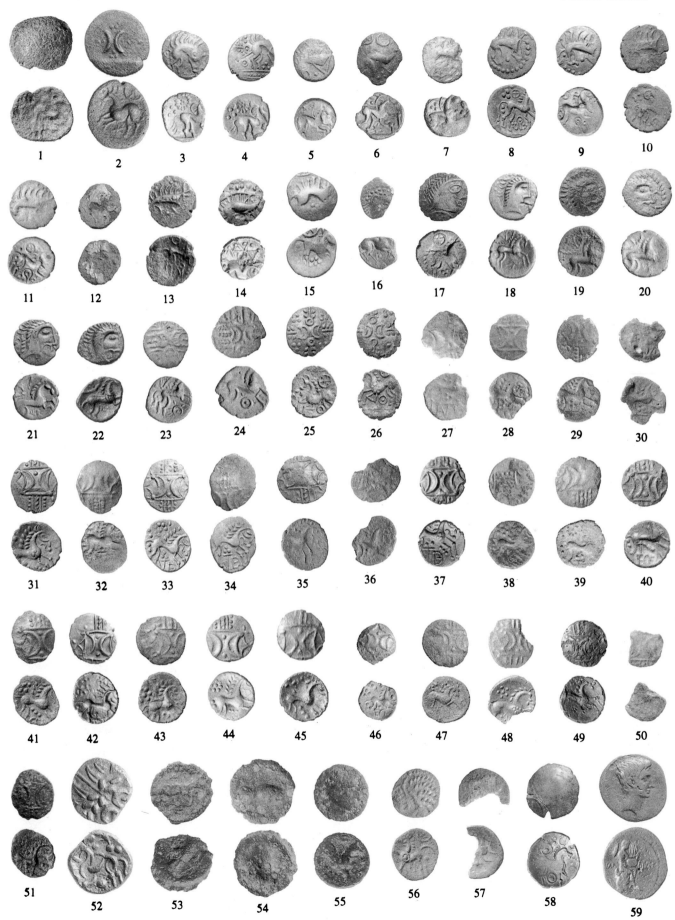

Plate XXIII Iron Age coins from the Stonea Grange Surface Collection. Scale 1:1.

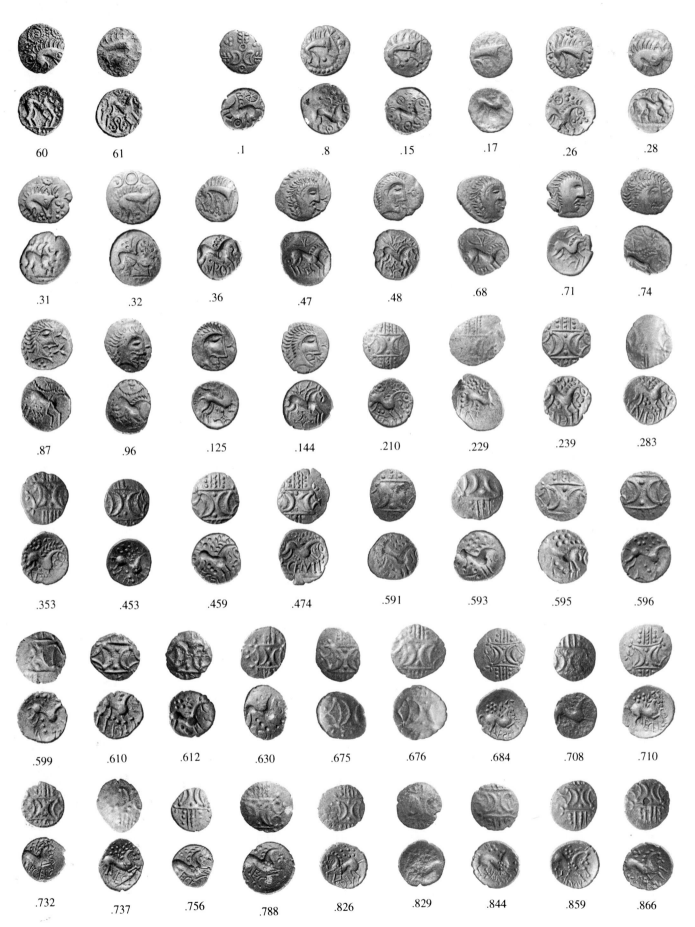

60   61   .1   .8   .15   .17   .26   .28

.31   .32   .36   .47   .48   .68   .71   .74

.87   .96   .125   .144   .210   .229   .239   .283

.353   .453   .459   .474   .591   .593   .595   .596

.599   .610   .612   .630   .675   .676   .684   .708   .710

.732   .737   .756   .788   .826   .829   .844   .859   .866

Plate XXIV Iron Age coins from the Stonea Grange excavations (60, 61), and
a selection from the Field Baulk hoard (1983.3–30.1–.866). Scale 1:1.

PLATE XXV

Plate XXVa Stonea:
Roman gold necklace links.

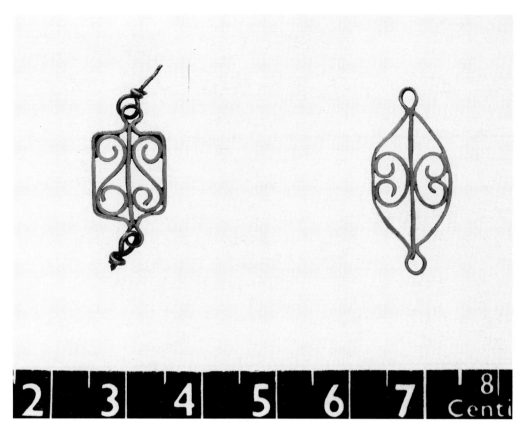

Plate XXVb Stonea
Grange: military metalwork
from the excavations and
Surface Collection (Iron
Objects cat. no. 1, and
Other Copper-Alloy
Objects cat. nos 65–9 and
119–26).

PLATE XXVI

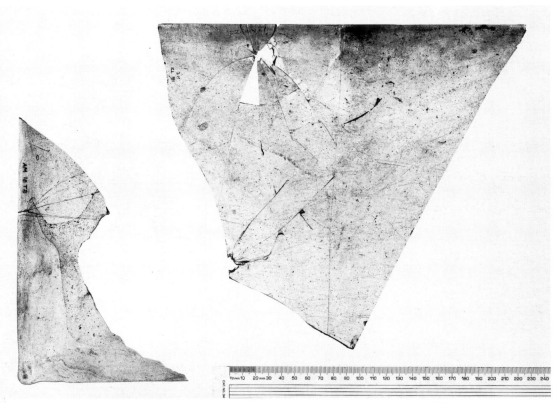

Plate XXVIa Stonea Grange: window glass from pit 170, units 254 and 285.

Plate XXVIb Stonea Grange: decorated colour-coated ware, human-figured scenes, cat. nos 1-4.

PLATE XXVII

Plate XXVIIa Stonea Grange: decorated colour-coated ware, phallic motifs
on complete and semi-complete beakers, cat. nos 6, 11, 5.

Plate XXVIIb Stonea Grange: decorated colour-coated ware, animal scenes
on complete and semi-complete beakers, cat. nos 12–14.

PLATE XXVIII

Plate XXVIIIa Stonea Grange: a selection of some of the complete and semi-complete pots from the 'boundary ditch' (ditch 9).

Plate XXVIIIb Stonea Grange: tiles with animal imprints. Top row, dog; middle row, cat; bottom row, caprine. Cat.nos 2, 8, 9; 35, 37, 38; 45, 46.

PLATE XXIX

Plate XXIX Stonea Grange: wooden writing tablet (cat. no. 1) from the sump.

PLATE XXX

Plate XXX Stonea Grange: the wooden spade (cat. no. 5) from the sump, immediately after excavation.

PLATE XXXI

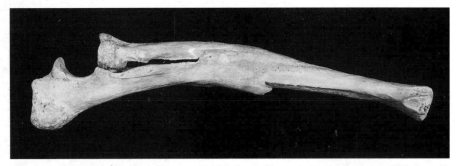

Plate XXXIa Stonea Grange: Romano–British dog radius and ulna from context 1733, in well 1625. Both bones have been broken through the midshaft, and the proximal ulna has healed onto the distal radius. Scale 1:1.

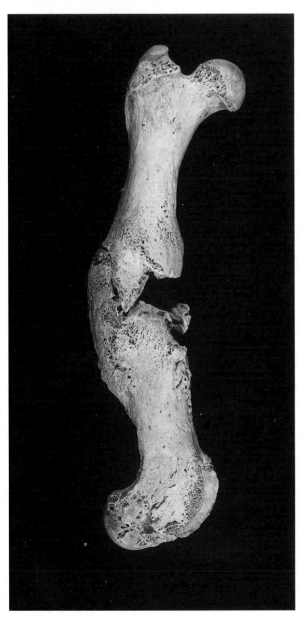

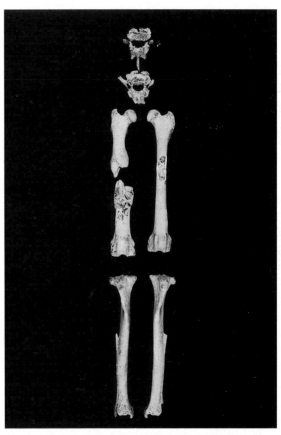

Plate XXXIc Stonea Grange: Romano–British dog bones from context 1756, in gully 23. The broken femur has become shortened and has not fully healed. An infection has spread to the lower vertebrae of the spine and to both knee joints. Scale 1:4.

Plate XXXIb Stonea Grange: Romano–British dog femur from context 1756, in gully 23. This thigh bone was broken through the midshaft but never fully healed, leaving a false joint. Scale 1:1.

PLATE XXXII

Plate XXXII Stonea Grange: macrobotanical group from the sump, comprising moss, bracket fungus, (?)gall, acorn, acorn caps, hazel nut, cherry stones, hawthorn, thorn, briarthorn, puffballs and pine cones.